EDWARD HEATH

A Biography

EDWARD HEATH

A Biography

John Campbell

JONATHAN CAPE

LONDON

First published 1993

1 3 5 7 9 10 8 6 4 2

© John Campbell 1993

John Campbell has asserted his right under
the Copyright, Designs and Patents Act, 1988
to be identified as the author of this work

First published in the United Kingdom in 1993 by
Jonathan Cape
Random House, 20 Vauxhall Bridge Road, London SW1V 2SA

Random House Australia (Pty) Limited
20 Alfred Street, Milsons Point, Sydney,
New South Wales 2061, Australia

Random House New Zealand Limited
18 Poland Road, Glenfield
Auckland 10, New Zealand

Random House South Africa (Pty) Limited
PO Box 337, Bergvlei, South Africa

Random House UK Limited Reg. No. 954009

A CIP catalogue record for this book
is available from the British Library

ISBN 0-224-02482-5

Set in Bembo by SX Composing Limited, Rayleigh, Essex
Printed and bound in Great Britain by
Mackays of Chatham PLC, Chatham, Kent

For Alison, again

Contents

Acknowledgments   xi
Introduction   xiv

PART ONE: *Scholarship Boy*
1   Broadstairs   3
2   Balliol and the Union   15
3   'A Good War'   40
4   Some False Starts   51

PART TWO: *Rising through the Ranks*
5   The Class of 1950   71
6   Chief Whip   90
7   'Mr Europe'   108
8   After Blackpool   139
9   'A New Kind of Tory Leader'   166

PART THREE: *Preparing for Power*
10 Establishing Authority   189
11 Pressures of Opposition   212
12 'Selsdon Man'   239
13 Victory from the Jaws of Defeat   268

PART FOUR: *Power*
14 'A New Style of Government'   289
15 'The Quiet Revolution'   307
16 Special Relationships   334
17 Reversing the Veto   352
18 'Kill the Bill'   364
19 Heathmen on the Home Front   376
20 The Vote for Europe   396

· Contents ·

21	First Blood to the Miners	406
22	The Abolition of Stormont	423
23	U-Turn: Industry	436
24	The Collapse of the Industrial Relations Act	457
25	U-Turn: Inflation	468
26	The Prime Minister and His Office	484
27	The Prime Minister and His Party	509
28	The Barber Boom	522
29	Whitelaw in Ulster	542
30	Oil and Coal	555
31	The Three-Day Week	574
32	'Who Governs?'	598

PART FIVE: *Rejection*

33	'National Unity'	623
34	'The Peasants' Revolt'	654

PART SIX: *Spectre at the Feast*

35	Unreconciled	679
36	Internal Exile	716
37	The Nemesis of Thatcherism	754
38	Grandfather of the House	793

Epilogue	808

Notes and References	813
Bibliography	860
Index	865

Illustrations

between pages 204 and 205
1. Aged three, with his mother, Edith
2. With Edith and his younger brother, John
3. With his father, William, in 1967
4. Prospective Tory candidate, Bexley, 1948
5. Returned to Westminster, 1951
6. With Patricia Hornsby-Smith and Margaret Roberts
7. With Harold Macmillan
8. First party conference as leader, Brighton, 1965

between pages 236 and 237
9. Campaigning in Orpington at the 1970 General Election
10. The new Conservative Cabinet in the garden at Number 10
11. With Liam Cosgrave and Brian Faulkner
12. With French President, Georges Pompidou
13. Outside Number 10 with Kenneth Kaunda
14. At the helm of the third *Morning Cloud*
15. Rehearsing with the London Symphony Orchestra
16. At Chequers in 1970 with the Queen and President and Mrs Nixon

between pages 716 and 717
17. With Margaret Thatcher at the party conference, 1972
18. Into Europe: Heath signs the Accession Treaty
19. Students demonstrate at Birmingham University, 1973
20. The battle of Saltley gate: the 1972 miners' strike

· Illustrations ·

21 Canvassing in Bexley in the February 1974 General Election
22 Enoch Powell at the 1973 party conference in Blackpool
23 With Jeremy Thorpe and Harold Wilson
24 The new leader carries off the old

between pages 748 and 749
25 Heath and William Whitelaw on the platform at the 1976 party conference
26 Heath speaking from the floor at the 1978 party conference
27 The 1975 referendum: leading the 'Yes' campaign with Roy Jenkins
28 With Deng Xiaoping in Peking, 1987
29 Launching the North–South Commission's second report in 1983 with Willy Brandt
30 Negotiating with Saddam Hussein for British hostages in Baghdad, 1990
31 Margaret Thatcher and her three predecessors
32 At home in Salisbury

CARTOONS

	page
'Into Europe', Vicky	196
'Grocer Heath', John Kent	304
'Thatcher's First Defeat', Garland	771

CREDITS

The author and publishers are grateful to the following sources for permission to reproduce illustrations: Birmingham Post & Mail Ltd, pl. 19; Camera Press, pls 1–3, 9, 13, 17, 24–5, 29, 31; Hulton Deutsch, pls 8, 10–12, 16, 21, 26–7; Popperfoto, pls 4, 28, 30; Press Association, pl. 7; Rex Features, pls 15, 23; Syndication International, pls 22, 32; Times Newspapers Ltd, pls 14, 18; Topham Picture Source, pls 5, 6, 20.

Acknowledgments

Tʜɪꜱ is not an 'authorised' biography, but neither is it exactly unauthorised. Sir Edward Heath has known about it since its inception, and while he has not been willing to help me directly with papers or interviews – giving priority, understandably, to his own long-promised memoirs – he has placed no obstacles in my way. He has made no attempt to stop his friends and former colleagues talking to me. I know that several checked with him before they agreed to see me: those few who refused did so, I believe, on their own initiative. His office has on a number of occasions sent me the full transcript of speeches only partially reported in the press. I should like to record my appreciation of his attitude, which in my view is probably the ideal relationship between a biographer and a living subject.

Next, I should like to thank the large number of Sir Edward's friends, associates and former colleagues and others who have worked, played or sailed with him – he has no relations – who have talked to me, often at length, in formal interviews and informal conversations over the past six years. The following list excludes, at their own request, a number who prefer not to be mentioned. To all of them I am most grateful for helping me get closer to a subject they all agree is exceptionally difficult to know well: Robin Aisher, Lord Aldington, Sir Ashley Bramall, Sir Paul Bryan, Richard Burn, Sir Alistair Burnet, Lord Carr of Hadley, Colonel George Chadd, Sir Robin Chichester-Clark, Lord Croham, Sir Edward Du Cann, Lord Ezra, Lord Forte, Lord Fraser of Kilmorack, Lord Gilmour, Jane Glaser, Lord Goodman, Clare Hollingworth, Lord Home of the Hirsel, Barbara Hosking, David Howell MP, Lord Hunt of Tanworth, Lord Jenkins of Hillhead, Tom Jolly, Lord Joseph, Sir Timothy Kitson, Moura Lympany, Michael McGahey, Lady Macleod of Borve,

Sir Donald Maitland, Simon May, Mrs Sara Morrison, Lord Murray of Epping Forest, Owen Parker, Mrs Jo Pattrick, Sir Leo Pliatzky, Enoch Powell, Lord Prior, Reginald Pye, Lord Pym, Lord Roll, the late Lord Rothschild, Andrew Rowe MP, Anthony Sampson, Madron Seligman MEP and Mrs Nancy-Joan Seligman, Brendon Sewill, Dr Thomas Stuttaford, Jeremy Thorpe, Michael Trend MP, Lord Walker, Sir Brian Warren, Lord Whitelaw, Mrs Rosemary Wolff.

I am also grateful to a large number of fellow historians and journalists who have helped me in one way or another, by giving me information or ideas, or starting me on a fruitful train of thought. The following list is far from complete; but I would particularly like to thank John Barnes, John Grigg, Professor Peter Hennessy, Dr Martin Holmes, Dr Rodney Lowe, Professor Keith Middlemas, Dr Frank Prochaska, Dr John Ramsden, Andrew Roth, Robert Silver and Jeremy Treglowne. I beg that those whom I have not specifically mentioned will forgive me.

I am grateful to the following for allowing me to quote material for which they hold the copyright: Aurum Press for quotations from *The Whitelaw Memoirs*; *Contemporary Record* for quotations from the transcripts of Institute of Contemporary British History witness seminars; The Economist Newspaper Ltd for quotations from *The Economist*; Faber & Faber Ltd for quotations from Eric Roll, *Crowded Hours*; Nicholas Garland for one of his cartoons from the *Independent*; John Kent for one of his 'Grocer Heath' strips from *Private Eye*; Dominic Lawson for quotations from the *Spectator*; Longman Group UK for a quotation from George Hutchinson, *Edward Heath*; Pan Macmillan Ltd for quotations from Edward Heath, *Sailing, Music* and *Travels*, published by Sidgwick & Jackson; Professor Lord Skidelsky for an extract from a letter to Lord Boyle; Solo Syndication & Literary Agency for a Vicky cartoon from the *Evening Standard*; Times Newspapers Ltd for quotations from *The Times* and the *Sunday Times*; Weidenfeld & Nicolson Ltd for quotations from Marcia Falkender, *Downing Street in Perspective*, Brian Faulkner, *Memoirs of a Statesman*, and Nigel Fisher, *The Tory Leaders: Their Struggle for Power*. In respect of a number of other authors and publishers I sought permission to quote but received no reply: in these cases I have taken silence for consent. Where I have been unable to trace a copyright holder I can only ask to be forgiven.

I am also grateful to Mrs Ann Gold for permission to see Lord Boyle's papers at Leeds University; to Robin Harris for allowing me to use the library at Conservative Central Office; to the Labour Party Library for their excellent collection of press cuttings; and to the

London Library for being one of the last places where one can still read bound volumes of *The Times* instead of fiddling around with microfilm. At a time of lamentable cuts in public libraries, I should also like to record my debt to Kensington and Chelsea Central Library.

The contribution of picture researchers is too rarely recognised, so I should like to make a point of thanking Cathie Arrington of Jonathan Cape for tracking down such an excellent collection of photographs to illustrate the book.

I should like to thank Graham C. Greene for commissioning the book in the first place; there are four people without whom it would never have been finished. For twenty years now Dr Paul Addison has been an unfailing source of wisdom, encouragement and understanding when I have flagged or doubted: never has his help been more appreciated. For almost as long Bruce Hunter of David Higham Associates, my agent, has sustained me and believed in me from book to book; while it has been a great pleasure to be re-united on this book with Tony Colwell of Jonathan Cape, who has been a most patient and supportive publisher. All of these read chapters and commented constructively. But the person who has had the greatest hand in shaping and sharpening this book has been Liz Cowen. With infinite skill and tact she reduced an excessively long typescript to manageable proportions: no author ever had a more sensitive or sympathetic editor. I wish every book published could be submitted to her scrutiny. Needless to say the responsibility for any errors that may remain is solely mine; likewise the judgments and interpretations in the book are all my own.

Finally, as ever, I must thank my wife Alison for her love, patience and support – emotional and financial – through another long biographical haul. Without her, it goes without saying, the book could not have been written. This time, however, I should also mention my children, Robin and Paddy, who have lived with Ted Heath for almost as long as they can remember. They have often questioned what I have been doing all this time: they too will be pleased that at last I am moving on to something new. I am only sorry that neither my father nor my mother-in-law lived to see the book completed.

JOHN CAMPBELL
London, March 1993

Introduction

TED Heath was Prime Minister for only three and a half years. His premiership, which started out with such high hopes in June 1970, collapsed in chaos and humiliation in February 1974. Within twelve months he had lost the Conservative leadership as well. For the next sixteen years he was consigned to the political doghouse, condemned to a sort of internal exile while everything he stood for was disowned, reviled and reversed by his all-conquering successor. It is a truism that most political careers, excepting only those whose promise is cut short by early death, end in rejection and/or failure; but Heath's appeared to end in more complete isolation, obloquy and embarrassment than any other in modern times. During the years of Margaret Thatcher's long hegemony, Conservative Central Office effectively wrote him out of the party's history, as though his leadership had been an unfortunate mistake that was best forgotten. Yet at the age of seventy-seven he remains defiantly unbowed. He has never given an inch to his critics, never retired, never accepted a peerage, never even written his memoirs, but has stayed on to become Father of the House of Commons while men and women fifteen years his junior, some of whom were not even in the House when he was Prime Minister, have come and gone. A whole generation has grown up for whom his baleful presence – slumped impassively on his seat below the gangway, or choleric on television, furiously denouncing his successor – has been a permanent feature of political life. Not only can this generation not remember his premiership: they cannot imagine how such a crusty old curmudgeon could ever have been Prime Minister in the first place.

The question is not a new one. He was always an unusual politician. In the 1960s, as his poll ratings dropped to record levels, Tory MPs asked themselves how they could ever have chosen as their leader a man so lacking in electoral appeal. In 1975 they got rid of him not for the most part because they rejected his policies, nor even because he had lost two General Elections, but principally because so many of them had been personally repelled by his rudeness that they were ready to vote for almost anyone, even an inexperienced woman, who would stand against him. Yet here is the central paradox of Heath's career. For he first made his name in the party as an exceptionally sensitive and popular Chief Whip, widely lauded for his 'skill in human relationships'. (The myth that he was a famous disciplinarian grew up later.) He was elected leader in 1965 because he was seen as the Tories' answer to the supreme politician, Harold Wilson; he was thought to be particularly good on television. In 1970 he confounded the polls to achieve the biggest swing of seats at a General Election since 1945 – the only time that a clear majority for one party has been converted at a single election into a clear majority for the other. Once elected, he was in many ways the best-equipped Prime Minister of modern times: cool headed, clear sighted, courageous and conscientious, thoroughly professional, immensely well informed, with a high sense of his responsibility and a clear vision of what he wanted to achieve. Yet in the end all these qualities went for nothing because he lacked the essential quality of political leadership: the ability to communicate his vision and inspire loyalty beyond the narrow circle of his closest colleagues.

As a result, all his good intentions were cruelly misunderstood. He set out to be a Prime Minister above party who would set Britain on a new course of modernisation, regeneration and national pride. But he was portrayed by his opponents as the most reactionary Tory leader since Neville Chamberlain, bent on putting the clock back thirty years. Faced with simultaneously mounting inflation and unemployment, he reversed many of his original policies, with the almost unanimous approval of the press; yet he was still regarded as stubborn and inflexible. The more strenuously he sought consensus, the more he was denounced as extremist and 'confrontational'. He wanted above everything to unite the country: he finished up presiding over a country more bitterly divided than at any time since the immediate aftermath of the First World War.

The British public has never understood Ted Heath. As a good amateur musician and successful international yachtsman he is without question the most multi-talented Prime Minister this century: by comparison with his principal rivals, Harold Wilson and Margaret Thatcher, he is a veritable Renaissance Man. Yet in office he came across as a one-dimensional political robot: his interests were remote from ordinary people, and his occasional attempts to convey his enthusiasm for them astonishingly banal. The one thing everyone knows about him is that he is passionately committed to a united Europe. Yet the springs of that commitment remain a mystery: no one could be more quintessentially English. Not only does he speak no European language: he speaks English like a man who is tone deaf. How can a musician have no ear for the music of words? The paradoxes multiply. As a bachelor, he is widely supposed to dislike women; but many of his most loyal friends are women. Stories abound of his rudeness, lack of conversation and long, disconcerting silences: Douglas Hurd has memorably written of his 'Easter Island' face. But on the right occasion, in the right company, he can be charming, relaxed and witty. He is often frankly selfish; but he can also be immensely thoughtful. He is as consistent as a block of granite; yet he is also moody and unpredictable. Friends and colleagues who claim to know him as well as anyone will confess in the same breath that they do not really know him at all. He remains impenetrable, self-sufficient, self-contained: as Churchill famously described the Soviet Union: 'A riddle wrapped in a mystery inside an enigma'.

Yet history will surely judge him less harshly than his contemporaries. For as the tide of Thatcherism ebbs it is becoming possible to take a more balanced view of his achievement. Notwithstanding the disappointments of 1970–4 and all the vitriol and condescension levelled at him since, Heath can now be seen – in at least three respects – as the pivotal figure around whom the history of the modern Tory party has turned.

First, his rise to the leadership both reflected and accelerated the social transformation of the party. It was Heath who broke the hitherto patrician mould of Tory leaders. In 1965 the four previous leaders had been successively a duke's nephew, the son of a seventh baronet, the son-in-law of another duke and a fourteenth earl. Ten years later the carpenter's son from Broadstairs was succeeded by a grocer's daughter from Grantham, who was followed in her turn by the son of a sometime trapeze artist and manufacturer of garden ornaments. It is easy today to forget the social revolution which that shift represented. It was in fact a painful process in which Heath as the pioneer suffered years of snobbish mockery. The party knew it needed to broaden its appeal, but thirty years ago many traditional Tories found it hard to accept a leader with no 'background', no private wealth and a ghastly accent. He won through only at great personal cost: it was at this time that the popular Chief Whip withdrew into his shell. Others have widened the breach he made, to the extent that he in his turn now seems a grandee from a vanished world, blaming Mrs Thatcher for bringing 'football hooligans' into the party. But it was Heath, by his personal example as much as by his policies, who first set the Tories on the way to becoming the party of individual opportunity and social mobility, leaving Labour still struggling to shake off the image of a backward-looking class-based anachronism.

Second, Heath more than anyone else committed the Conservatives to Europe. Harold Macmillan made the first move to try to join the EEC in 1961; but following General de Gaulle's veto in 1963 the party could easily have retreated from that objective had it elected any leader but Heath in 1965. Europe was central to Heath's political vision. He succeeded in 1971, where possibly no other British Prime Minister could have succeeded, in negotiating British entry to the Community. In doing so he identified the Tories so firmly as the pro-Europe party – while Labour still veered between reluctant acquiescence and outright opposition – that even Mrs Thatcher was unable to do more than slow the pace of integration. Twenty years after Heath signed the Treaty of Accession, Britain's relations with Europe remain a matter of intense controversy; the Tory party is divided on the subject as never before. As the leading champion of Britain-in-Europe over the past thirty years, Heath must shoulder much of the blame for the public's persistent suspicion of the European enterprise: here again he has failed to communicate his vision. Yet the fact that the future of the Community is today the central issue of British politics is above all Heath's achievement.

Third, Heath's Government was the precursor, for better or worse, of the Conservative governments of the 1980s. Here the legacy is ambiguous; but the fact is that the so-called 'Thatcher revolution' was in part the fulfilment of an agenda initially set by Heath and partly an exaggerated reaction to his retreat from that agenda. On the one hand – as Heath's critics never ceased to remind him – it was his 1970 manifesto which first proclaimed many of the goals which formed the core of 'Thatcherism': lower taxes, less public spending, Government disengagement from industry, legal curbs on trade unions and more selective targeting of welfare. On the other, the scale and consequences of his Government's enforced abandonment of the 1970 agenda – the unsustainable inflationary boom of 1973, the complex straitjacket of prices and incomes policy and the 1974 miners' strike which encompassed the Government's defeat – came to furnish the negative precedent against which his successor set her face: though unemployment rose in 1981 to three times the level that had compelled Heath to change course, Mrs Thatcher staked her reputation on her determination not to do the same. When all the talk at the 1981 party conference was of when she would be forced to emulate his famous 'U-Turn', she vowed emphatically: 'The lady's not for turning.' It was explicitly by contrast with Heath that she defined herself. When she first attained the Tory leadership in 1975 cynics had jeered that she was merely 'Heath with tits'. Now her admirers retorted that, on the contrary, she was 'Heath with balls'.

So long as she seemed to carry all before her, the best case that could be made for Heath was that he had tried prematurely to anticipate some of her reforms, in unfavourable circumstances, before the public or the party was ready to accept them. On this argument the 1970–4 Government was part of a painful but necessary learning experience which prepared the ground for Thatcherism: the darkest hour before the glorious dawn. Loyal Thatcherites, however, jeered that he had simply lacked the courage of her convictions. All through the 1980s his famous 'U-turn' was ruthlessly derided in order to highlight Mrs Thatcher's contrasting 'resolution'. Heath's refusal to recognise her achievement was ascribed to bitter jealousy of the woman who had supplanted him.

Of course he was bitter. But at the same time he genuinely and fundamentally disapproved of the whole thrust of her policies, which soon went far beyond anything he had ever dreamed of in 1970. Heath was a member of the generation whose values had been shaped by the Second World War. He had come into politics as a convinced supporter of the postwar settlement, founded on the mixed economy and the Welfare State, which had delivered full employment, social stability and ever-rising living standards since 1945. By 1965 he recognised that this settlement was under increasing strain: his purpose in 1970 had been to modernise and reform it, injecting more enterprise and efficiency into the economy to enable it to continue to deliver the standards the country had come to expect. But he never doubted that this could be achieved within the existing institutional and conceptual framework. The 1970 manifesto makes it quite clear that he never dreamed of abdicating the Government's fundamental responsibility for maintaining full employment and decent social provision, as Mrs Thatcher quite deliberately proceeded to do after 1979. 'Selsdon Man' was a myth largely created by Harold Wilson. Heath was genuinely angered by Mrs Thatcher's contemptuous jettisoning of the 'One Nation' tradition of Toryism which had been the party's mainstream since 1940. On the one hand he denounced her exclusive reliance on market forces and neglect of infrastructural investment as short-sighted and destructive; on the other he damned her social philosophy as morally repugnant and socially divisive. So long as she and her successive chancellors could maintain that they had discovered the key to unlock the long-delayed 'economic miracle' which had eluded all her predecessors, he was isolated and ignored: the party and a sufficient minority of the country were persuaded that the price in permanent unemployment and visible poverty was worth paying. Now that the 'economic miracle' has evaporated, however, and the country finds itself in the early 1990s plunged back into an even deeper recession than in the early 1980s – but now with a weaker economy than ever with which to try to spark recovery – Heath's lonely doom-mongering looks more prescient than he was given credit for in the heady boom years.

Of course the fact that Thatcherism too has ended in painful disillusion does not make Heath's Government a success, even in hindsight: the dismal record of the British economy merely continues to unfold, from one aborted miracle to another. But it does put his tribulations in perspective, and demolishes the right of the Thatcherites to disparage his record as uniquely bad. In truth he was exceptionally unlucky. International and domestic factors in the fevered 1970s conspired to derail his Government. He was confronted by the collapse of the international financial system and massive global inflation, culminating in the 1973 'oil shock'; an irresponsible trade union movement at the height of its power, backed by an unscrupulously opportunist Opposition; Northern Ireland on the edge of civil war; plus a social climate disturbed by a whole range of fears and dislocations, from terrorism and rising crime through student revolt and violent demonstrations to coloured immigration, sexual permissiveness and decimalisation of the currency, which coincided with and seemed to exacerbate galloping inflation. Five years earlier or ten years later, with all his shortcomings, Heath might have been a great Prime Minister. But he was caught at a moment of transition between two traditions, when the earth moved under his feet. Arguably he was the true Tory who set out in 1970 to find a middle way between the exhausted tradition of interventionism which he inherited from Macmillan and the emerging free market doctrines seized on and carried to extremes by Mrs Thatcher. Had he been able to strike and hold this balance the country might have been spared much of the wasteful agony of the Thatcher years.

But the irony is that it was Heath himself who inflicted Mrs Thatcher on the party. His fate was not entirely the result of irresistible historic forces and the swing of intellectual fashion. His own awkward personality played a crucial part. Heath was in three critical respects the author of his own misfortune. First, making every allowance for the difficulties it faced, his Government fell because he was unable to persuade the country to support what he was trying to do: he should have won the February 1974 election. Then his pride and stubbornness in refusing to stand down when he had lost the support of Tory MPs enabled Mrs Thatcher to seize the reins and set off on her dizzy joyride through British politics. With a little modesty Heath could easily have secured the leadership for Whitelaw, Prior or some other leader more congenial to his own brand of Toryism: Mrs Thatcher was not remotely a contender until he gave her the opening. Finally, by refusing to accept his defeat but appearing instead to conduct a sour personal vendetta against his successor, he made it easy for her to sideline him. Had he only played the part of the loyal but worried elder statesman, he still had a sufficient following in the party to have made it difficult for her to kick over the traces as thoroughly as she did. Alternatively he could have provided a focus of constructive opposition for the discarded 'wets'. But he was too proud and solitary to co-operate with any faction. On the contrary, by simply sounding off indiscriminately against all her policies without exception, giving credit for nothing, he embarrassed his old friends and frightened off younger supporters who could not afford to jeopardise their careers by association with him. As a result Mrs Thatcher positively thrived on his tirades. If, as Oscar Wilde wrote, 'each man kills the thing he loves', Heath unwittingly did more than anyone to sustain the thing he loathed.

For the past twenty years Heath has been a political Cassandra – very largely right, but not believed. It is his own fault; but a tragedy, too – certainly for himself and maybe for Britain. Over a long lifetime he has been a politician of remarkable qualities; well intentioned, high minded, honourable, patriotic in the best sense and in many respects far-sighted, but cursed with a sort of blight which has turned to ashes practically everything he has sought to achieve. He aimed high, promised much, but ultimately was denied the place in history his ambition craved. His is the Shakespearean tragedy of a nearly great man brought down by his own flaws.

PART ONE

Scholarship Boy

1

Broadstairs

GEOGRAPHY, class and family made Ted Heath what he is. He was born in the extreme south-eastern corner of England, in the small seaside resort of Broadstairs on the easternmost tip of Kent, just twenty miles up the coast from Dover – within sight, on a very clear day, of the coast of France. He was born into the upwardly mobile, socially aspiring skilled working class just where it merges into the lower middle class, in a socially homogeneous small-town community far removed from the sharper social differentials and antagonisms of the great cities or the hunting shires. And he was born the bright elder son of ambitious parents who were ready to incur immense sacrifices to push him up the educational and social ladder. The combination of these three circumstances shaped his personality and his ideas, forging both the formidable strength of character which took him all the way to Downing Street but also, ultimately, the limitations which led to his defeat.

The Isle of Thanet – 'this sea-girt isle where I was born', as Heath somewhat romantically described it to the 1953 Conservative party conference at Margate[1] – is no more a real island than the Isle of Ely or the Isle of Dogs, merely a knobby promontory on the north-eastern extremity of Kent. But it has a symbolic significance in English history as the point where, for centuries before 1066, successive waves of Anglo-Saxon and Viking invaders from the continent traditionally landed. It is, at the least, historically satisfying that the man who, more than any other, made it his life's work to rejoin Britain's destiny finally to Europe – ending what Hugh Gaitskell called 'a thousand years of history' – should have drawn his first breath in Thanet. Clearly it is possible to be an equally dedicated European though born in, for example, Pontypool; nevertheless it

3

is difficult to overestimate the importance of his birthplace in setting the major theme of Edward Heath's subsequent career.

Fancifully, 'The Boyhood of Heath', with the youthful Teddy casting his eyes prophetically across the Channel, might make a painting to rival Millais's 'The Boyhood of Raleigh'. More prosaically, Europe was, for the young Heath, simply *there*. As a boy of ten or twelve he used to cycle the twenty miles down to Dover to sit on a mound by the castle and watch the ferries leaving and entering the harbour. At the age of fourteen he made his first visit to France with a school party in the Easter holiday. Later, as a student, he spent his summers travelling cheaply around the continent – not, in the 1930s, so normal an activity as it became in the 1960s. He was aware of Europe at an unusually early age.

The obverse of the proximity of Europe, however, was the relative isolation of Thanet from the rest of Britain. Physically, east Kent was even then very effectively cut off by the spreading mass of London from the rest of England, while Wales and Scotland were both geographically and psychologically still more remote. Broadstairs in the 1930s was not untouched by the Depression: dependent on the holiday trade, it suffered some seasonal unemployment, and the Kent coalfield was only twenty miles away. Yet it was a long way from the real blackspots of mass industrial unemployment. Secure in its own modest prosperity, respectably Conservative in the particular manner of the English seaside, Broadstairs was a sheltered backwater on the margin of the political map of interwar Britain.

Not only was his own upbringing thoroughly and exclusively southern English, but Ted Heath's whole ancestry is unusually uncomplicated by any trace of Scottish, Welsh or Irish. Nor – unusually again at that period – had he any family connection with the Empire: he is English through and through. His father's forebears came originally from south Devon; but both sides of his family had been settled in Thanet for several generations before he was born. There was in addition a strong nautical inheritance, though this remained submerged until the Leader of the Opposition suddenly rediscovered an affinity with the sea in his fifties. It was Ted Heath's great-great-grandfather, Richard Heath, a coastguard, who moved around the south coast from Cockington, near Torquay, initially to Ramsgate. His son, George, born in 1830, was a merchant seaman who ended as keeper of Ramsgate pier. Stephen, born in 1865, the Prime Minister's grandfather, broke from the sea but never settled to much else: he was variously a dairyman, railway porter and vanman. He married the daughter of a Ramsgate greengrocer but moved in 1889 to Broadstairs, where for a time he ran a fruit stall on the beach. Perhaps in reaction to this, the eldest of his four sons, William, born in 1888, quickly apprenticed himself to a steady trade and became a carpenter. This was Ted Heath's father.

William Heath was both in personality and physique extraordinarily unlike his son. He was in his youth a slight, wiry, dark-haired man, easy-going, good with the girls, fond of a drink with the boys, a bit of a lad, even a bit of a dandy: his wedding photograph shows him with a centre parting and something very near to a handlebar moustache. Yet at the same time he was hard-working, a good craftsman, and ambitious to get on. He had a streak of stubbornness, as was demonstrated in the determination with which, from the age of seventeen, he courted Edith Pantony, the pretty daughter of a farm worker from the village of St Peter's, just outside Broadstairs. It took him three years to persuade her, against the opposition of her family, to become engaged to him. Her parents, it seems, thought she could do better for herself. Slim, fair, gentle mannered but strong willed, she was considered the belle of the village. What set her apart was that she had stayed at school till she was fourteen – two years longer than William. She had then gone into service with a Hampstead family named Taylor who spent their summers in Broadstairs; she became Mrs Taylor's personal maid and several times travelled with her on the continent. (Another source, one must imagine, of her son's early awareness of 'abroad'.) Despite the refinement she had thus acquired, she nevertheless agreed – in 1908, when they were both twenty and William had just completed his apprenticeship – to marry the young carpenter. They were in no position to make good the engagement for another five years, but were finally married in the summer of 1913.

By this time William was earning a good wage of £2 a week and had managed to save £100; Edith too must have been able to save something. For 6s 6d a week they could afford to rent the ground floor of 2 Holmwood Villas, a small semi-detached house in Albion Road, St Peter's. Barely a year later, the First World War broke out. As a newly married man, William was fortunate in being able legitimately to resist the call to join Kitchener's volunteers. Presumably he soon benefited from the growing shortage of skilled craftsmen. But Kent was not unscathed by the war. On 9 July 1916 Ramsgate was shelled from the sea. The same alarming night, five miles away in Broadstairs, Edith at last gave birth to her first child – a boy, christened Edward Richard George. Edward was after Edith's brother, killed in the war; Richard and George were old Heath names. He was known in the family from the start as Teddy.

Soon after Teddy was born William was sent, under the wartime direction-of-labour scheme, to work in a Vickers aircraft factory at Crayford, on the south-east edge of London (the next-door suburb, as it happens, to Bexley). There the family – enlarged in 1920 by the birth of a second son, John – stayed for seven years. William's independent spirit jibbed at the factory conditions and the unionisation; but in the economic uncertainty of the immediate postwar years the money was too good to throw up. So Teddy did not spend his earliest years in Broadstairs after all, though he went back regularly to see his grandparents. He first went to school in a tin hut in Crayford. The family returned to Broadstairs, however, in 1923; and it is to that homecoming, when he was seven, that Ted Heath later dated the real beginning of his life.

From this point he enjoyed a secure and happy childhood, of steadily expanding horizons. When they first came back to Broadstairs William and Edith moved back to Albion Road, though to a different house from that in which Teddy had been born. They shared it initially with Edith's widowed sister-in-law, and Edith took in summer visitors. Then, after three years, they were able to buy a semi-detached, bow-windowed house of their own in Broadstairs proper, 4 King Edward Avenue – at the top of the town, a short walk up from the esplanade with a glimpse of the sea from the upper windows. A further four years on, in 1930, the local builder for whom William had been working since their return, first as a carpenter, then as outside manager, died. William bought the business and set up on his own as 'W. G. Heath, Builder and Decorator'. From now on, though never remotely wealthy, the family prospered in a quiet way. Employing craftsmen of his own, William built up a reputation for reliability and good quality work for some of the 'best' people in Broadstairs. In realising his ambition to become his own man, he had crossed the narrow line that divides the skilled working class from the middle class. His political views evolved accordingly. From having been mildly Liberal, he became increasingly Conservative. As an employer he had still less time for unions than in his days as an employee. 'I was never Labour,' he told Anthony Sampson many years later. 'I had too much to do with labour to vote Labour.'[2] Like Margaret Thatcher in her father's small-town grocer's shop a decade later, Ted Heath grew up in the ethos and the ethic of proudly independent small business.

Yet the influence of his mother went deeper. William worked long hours and was often out, while Edith devoted herself wholly to her children – particularly to Teddy. Traditionally it is the youngest child who becomes the mother's favourite, and Teddy was already four when John was born. But Teddy was from the first an exceptionally intelligent and rewarding child, whereas John was by comparison very ordinary. There is no question that Teddy was the favoured brother, whose promise Edith set herself to nurture and to mould, instilling into him her own values and her ambitions for him. If William was always the independent craftsman, she was ever the lady's maid: prim, strait-laced, serious minded, responsible – endowed, as one family friend put it, with all the copybook virtues to excess: 'cleanliness, Godliness, good manners – the lot'.[3] She had learned in service to be deferential to her social betters, but at the same time she aspired to the same standards for her family and was determined to see her own clever boy rise to be their equal. She accordingly impressed on Teddy – who was in turn a willing pupil – the importance of hard work, clean living, responsibility, service to others and honourable ambition. She furnished the moral framework by which he has lived his life. He described her in 1966 – one of the few times he has ever been induced to speak publicly of her – as

a fine character with a strong personality, a high sense of morality and public responsibility . . . She had the spiritual sense of her Christian faith. Not that she was at all ethereal about it – she kept our feet on the ground . . . She had high standards and strong views and yet she was wonderfully forbearing towards her children.[4]

The last phrase suggests one way in which perhaps her influence was not all for good. She was possibly too forbearing. Not that Teddy was in any conventional sense of the term spoilt. High standards were certainly demanded of him. But if he met them he was well rewarded. His talents were encouraged as far as lay within the family's power. As it became clear to his parents that he was something special, he was increasingly made to feel the centre of the household. The best armchair was reserved for him and he was spared the washing up; nothing must interfere with his homework or his piano practice. At some sacrifice a piano was bought for him: nothing that could be afforded was denied him. From an early age Teddy grew accustomed to thinking of himself as a high flyer and of his family – not only his parents but his brother too – as a support system dedicated to easing his path. Arguably this did spoil him, developing – contrary to the ethic of service – a streak of selfishness. In later life, as Leader of the Opposition and Prime Minister, he often seemed to take it for granted that everyone around him was there to do things for him; he was extraordinarily bad at offering the simple word of thanks or appreciation that would have made colleagues and subordinates happy to go on serving him. Some who knew him well

– and very often admired him despite his gracelessness – marvelled that a boy brought up in such a home by such a mother could grow up so lacking in elementary good manners. In one sense Ted Heath was, and remained, a spoiled child.

He was also a mother's boy. He enjoyed from a very early age an exceptionally close relationship with Edith; at the same time he was temperamentally and in every other way utterly unlike his father – introverted where William was extrovert, inhibited where William was sociable, formal where William was genial. William and Edith were complementary but opposite; whether there was any friction in their marriage between his easy-going conviviality and her sense of propriety there is now no knowing. But it is difficult to avoid the speculation that Edith brought up their elder son in some way in re-action against his father: in particular that she, whether explicitly or implicitly, consciously or unconsciously, warned him off the company of girls. This might be simple puritanism: there is a story of her forbidding young Teddy to go swimming with an attractively well-developed young cousin. Or it might derive from disapproval of her husband's roving eye. More likely, perhaps, rather than an active prohibition, it was what might be called the *Sons and Lovers* syndrome – an adoring mother's determination not to lose her son to any other woman – combined with his exceptionally close emotional dependence upon her. Looking at Ted Heath's life as a whole, it would seem that he never escaped emotionally from her. She was his one great source of love and support. While she was alive he did not need any other; when she died he did not want any other, but rather shut off that side of his nature entirely. He was thirty-five when she died; he had just got into Parliament and already had his foot several rungs up the ladder on which she had started him. He should have been old enough to bear the loss; but he took it very hard. He has rarely been able to talk about her to this day; friends have noted that he will shut up like a clam if asked anything about her. It is a plaus-ible and perhaps sufficient explanation of his having never married that he could not imagine anyone replacing her. Instead he retreated into himself, choosing to become more than ever solitary and self-sufficient. On this reading, Edith Heath's over-protective mother love resulted in Teddy growing up emotionally stunted.

However this may be, Teddy was a precociously mature small boy, almost unnaturally clean and tidy, and well behaved. Another boy who grew up in the same street retained, many years later, a vivid picture of his 'going down the road with his parents, im-maculately dressed – his hair smacked down. He was never a member of any gang, he never played marbles or went about with

8

the other boys, he was always very much to himself.'[5] While John by contrast was a normal, scruffy, noisy urchin, Teddy even at that age held himself aloof and spotless – the responsible elder brother. 'He was bigger than the other boys of his age,' remembered an assistant master at St Peter's Primary School, which he attended for his first three years back in Broadstairs, 'and his bones were well-covered. This and the fact that his mother always sent him to school impeccably dressed, a condition he managed to maintain all day, made him a model pupil.'[6] Academically too, his final report noted, he was 'in advance of his age . . . easily ahead of any other in his group'.[7] He was especially good at maths and history. Despite being the son of a craftsman, however, he was – perhaps significantly and with one important exception – hopeless with his hands.

The exception was his talent for music. William and Edith were not particularly musical, but the whole extended family, Heaths and Pantonys, used to come together quite regularly – like many other families at the time – for sing-songs round the piano on Saturday or Sunday evenings: 'Roses of Picardy' and 'Love's Old Sweet Song' were 'firm favourites', with Sullivan's 'The Lost Chord' to finish off.[8] Teddy joined in happily with the rest. But it was the aunt who played the piano on these occasions who first detected his aptitude to play himself. She lived in Margate and Teddy used to beg her to play for him when he visited her house – popular pieces of the day like Grieg's 'Wedding Day' and Paderewski's Minuet, which gave her the opportunity to explain how Paderewski had been not only a brilliant pianist but also (briefly) Prime Minister of Poland. He was so keen that she persuaded his parents that they should get a piano themselves so he could learn. This was a tall order, but they agreed: for £42, the payments spread over twenty-four instalments, they bought a new upright for his ninth birthday. They also engaged a local girl, aged only seventeen, to give him weekly lessons. Miss Locke found him 'a serious unsmiling little boy who never had to be reprimanded for not knowing his lessons'. He was 'full of questions' ('one would have had to be an encyclopaedia to answer them all') and practised hard: he was impatient of the scales and exercises she made him play, and she was soon astonished to find that he had learnt Grieg's 'Wedding Day' all by himself.[9] Soon he was making rapid progress. Characteristically, his mother 'would sit in the same room with him and knit while he practised so that he wouldn't feel shut away from the family'.[10]

He also sang as a treble in the church choir – Matins and Evensong every Sunday, with practices on Tuesdays and Fridays. The organist at St Peter's took the choir seriously and they sang an ambitious repertoire of modern English as well as classical composers. Many years later, in his book *Music: A Joy for Life*, Heath made a point of noting that 'practically every leading composer, conductor, organist or music administrator [in English musical life] received his basic grounding in church music'.[11] It was certainly a major influence in forming his own taste. In due course, when his voice broke, he moved on naturally to playing the organ and conducting the choir himself. Music, as he first experienced and learned to perform it, was essentially bound up with the life of the church. Equally his lifelong though unpublicised fidelity to the Christian faith in which he was brought up has reflected and expressed itself principally through his love of music.

His music, however, was another factor which inevitably put a distance between Teddy and his less talented contemporaries at school. While they played football and cricket, he played the piano and the organ; while they hung around on the street together, he was practising at home with his mother, or discussing musical arrangements with the organist or the vicar. In so far as it was not a purely solitary activity, music encouraged his preference, already noticeable, for the company of adults from whom he could learn rather than that of boys of his own age. To them he must have appeared more than ever priggish and aloof; in his own eyes too it can only have underlined the sense of separateness which was always with him.

There is in all the descriptions of Ted Heath as a boy so much that uncannily prefigures the adult he became. Most people develop as they grow older, shedding for the better or worse many of the characteristics of their youth. Heath's personality appears to have set at an unusually early age. In his case, to an exceptional degree, the child was father to the man. Already as a boy he was extraordinarily self-sufficient, spending long hours up in his room reading, sometimes to the point of rudeness when visitors came to the house, to the extent that even his mother worried that he was working too hard. ('Mother, sometimes I don't think you *want* me to get on,' he is said to have told her once.)[12] He had little need of the company of other boys. Team sports held no interest for him; for exercise he preferred solitary pursuits like cycling and swimming. But self-sufficiency carried the danger of self-centredness, the expectation that others would always accommodate themselves to him – as his father most revealingly recalled. 'Suddenly he would stop what he was doing and say, "Let's go for a walk, Mummy." And the rest of us would have to stop what we were doing and go out with him.'[13] Sixty years later he still expects his friends to be there when he wants them. There is, too, a startling egotism in a boy calling his dog 'Erg' after his own initials.

At the age of ten, St Peter's 'model pupil' won a scholarship to Chatham House, a fee-paying county grammar school at Ramsgate, three miles down the coast. The fees were only £12 a year, but Teddy's scholarship gained him a free place. It may not be strictly true that he could not have gone there without a scholarship, remembering that his parents had already managed to find twice that for the piano (which was now half paid for). Four years later they were able to send John to Chatham House without a scholarship. Nevertheless William's entire earnings in 1926 – he was not yet in business on his own – were declared to be only £120, so it must have been a substantial help. At his interview, Teddy told the headmaster that he wanted to be an architect – that is to say the professional equivalent of his father's trade. Getting into Chatham House was Ted Heath's first step up the social ladder, out of his parents' class.

Chatham House was a first-rate school with high academic standards and a range of extra-curricular activities that would have done credit to a public school. Like a public school it was organised on a house system, explicitly intended to 'teach the individual to subordinate himself and his own interests to that of the community'.[14] In time Teddy throve in this atmosphere. Just at first, however, he seemed to do less well. The reason, paradoxically, was his precocity: he was consistently placed in classes with boys one or even two years older than himself. This had the consequence that though he was ahead of his age group, he never really had the chance to excel: it was always a struggle to keep up. By dint of hard work he did keep up; but in his first four years at Chatham House, his place in classes of thirty ranged between fifth and sixteenth. He was never top. The continual pressure did not encourage in him that relaxation which comes from effortless superiority. Thus the school underestimated him. Towards the end of his fourth year, when his classmates were preparing to sit their School Certificate, the headmaster would not allow Teddy to take it at the same time, declaring him to be 'most promising' but still 'too immature for an examination of this standard'. Teddy persuaded his father to appeal. William told Dr Norman that his son was 'very depressed' and urged that he be allowed to carry on. The boy's weakness was stated to be in French and Latin. Very well: he had already arranged for him to have extra tuition during the Easter holidays.[15] Faced with such determination, Dr Norman relented. Teddy sat the exam that summer – a month before his fourteenth birthday – and passed.

In his later years at Chatham House, with School Certificate out of the way so early, he began to come into his own. Seniority gave him the chance to follow his own interests – music, but also increasingly current affairs and politics – and to take on positions of responsibility. He won prizes for his piano playing and conducted the school orchestra. He became secretary of the debating society. He also became a prefect and – anticipating the Chief Whip of twenty years later – a stickler for discipline. 'He was very down on kids who had their hands in their trouser pockets, or weren't behaving well in the street in their school cap and blazer,' one of the masters remembered. 'He thought that breaking a school rule amounted to disloyalty to the school.'[16] As a result, a contemporary recalled, he was 'anything but popular'. But then 'he never tried for popularity. He wasn't actively liked or actively disliked. He was respected and accepted, though a little bit intolerant.'[17] Precisely the same was repeatedly said of him throughout his life. In proof of his acceptance, he was elected scorer to the cricket eleven – considered a great honour for a non-games player; and he won a special prize, voted for by the fifth and sixth forms, for 'character'. Appropriately, he played the Archangel Gabriel in the school play. He was the very model of 'school spirit'.

His contributions to the debating society offer the first glimpse of his emerging political views. As might have been expected, he took a firmly puritanical line on social questions – he spoke against sweepstakes, Sunday cinemas and co-educational schools – and a conventionally patriotic one when the school staged its own rerun of the Oxford Union's famous 'King and Country' debate of 1933; on the other hand he also revealed an early interest in international affairs, an awareness of the nature of fascism and even, prophetically – in 1935 (his final year) – in European unity as the only means of averting future wars. Though narrow party questions were generally discouraged, there seems no doubt that he would already have called himself a Conservative: that summer he was the 'National' candidate in the school's mock election. (He won.) Though politics as such were rarely discussed within the family – in this respect Heath's background was quite unlike the much more explicit political education of Margaret Thatcher at the feet of Alderman Roberts – the early certainty of his allegiance nevertheless clearly reflected the influence and example of both of his parents. In a newspaper interview in 1966 Heath told Kenneth Harris that 'I am what I am politically because of a combination of home background and the times in which I lived as a boy, and a certain amount of thinking about both.' 'Home background' meant primarily the moral teaching of his mother. 'The times in which I lived' meant partly his consciousness of fascism and the need for Britain to oppose it in the name of freedom; but also the domestic economic climate of Depression and William's successful struggle to rise above it. Even though there was no mass unemployment in Broadstairs, he insisted, 'conditions were tough for nearly everybody nearly everywhere and I saw my father working hard, showing enterprise, taking risks, and gradually developing to his capacity in spite of very difficult circumstances.'[18]

He was also beginning, with the support of his teachers, to form the ambition to go on to Oxford – especially to Balliol, with its reputation for being readier than other colleges to admit clever boys from lower-class backgrounds. But it seemed out of the question that he could go without a scholarship. He therefore set about working for an open scholarship to read PPE (philosophy, politics and economics). He became particularly interested in economics. One teacher devoted half his time to taking a small group of boys in the subject; years later he recalled tremendous arguments with young Heath, who disagreed with Marshall's view of the behaviour of monopolies and adamantly refused to accept it. Unfortunately he remained very much less gripped by Latin and French: his French teacher recalled that he would only 'bite' on the subjects that interested him.[19] The result was that when he sat the scholarship exam in the summer of 1934, he failed to reach the necessary all-round level: while his economics papers were 'on the borderline of . . . Exhibition standard, his general work was not quite so good and his French [was] really rather weak'. Balliol would have given him a place as a commoner, but that, as his form master regretfully wrote to the admissions tutor, was financially 'quite impossible'.[20] The headmaster agreed, however, to allow him to stay on another year at school to try again.

He was nearly nineteen by the time he sat the exam a second time in 1935. (At that age, it is no wonder he was a prominent figure in the school.) But the result was a second disappointment, more serious than the first in that while his economics was still good (α– and β+?+) and his French marginally better than the year before, his literature was 'definitely worse' and his general paper only γ+; 'on balance', the admissions tutor wrote, 'he does not appear to have made any marked advance'.[21] Perhaps the extra year at school had bored him; perhaps he had reached his level. Nevertheless the offer of an ordinary place still stood if he could afford to take it up. Rather less than half the sum required was offered by Kent County Council in the form of a loan for £90 a year, repayable when he came down. But the rest – £120–£130 a year – would have to come from William and Edith. It appears that William – apprenticed at thirteen – was not easy to persuade that it was possible. But Teddy had set his heart on going to Oxford: 'It would have broken his heart if we had refused.'[22] His teachers supported him, Dr Norman even suggesting that he might be Prime Minister if he was given the chance; and Edith backed her boy, offering her own savings. So it was decided. Teddy would go to Balliol that autumn as a commoner.

His final report from Chatham House was a remarkable document – an unstinting encomium not so much of his class work as of his character, his leadership qualities and his service to the school. The music master set the tone, noticeably praising his playing less than his conducting:

> I cannot speak too highly of the tremendous amount of work he has done. He has been a help to me and an inspiration to the boys. As a conductor of choirs, both here and elsewhere, he has been outstanding; as a performer he has been successful; in orchestral work he has had splendid opportunities of widening his experience . . .

The headmaster wrote a eulogy that would have made most boys squirm:

> The purity of his ideals, his loyalty to them and his sense of duty have made him outstanding among the boys who have helped to build the school. That his mental and moral worth may have the reward they deserve is my wish for him.[23]

Going on to Oxford with such a valediction in his pocket, the carpenter's son was well on his way to becoming head prefect to the nation.

2

Balliol and the Union

GOING up to Oxford in October 1935 was Heath's second immense step up the ladder of the British class system. Not only that, it also gave him entry to the junior ranks of the ruling élite. Since at least the time of Gladstone in the 1820s, Oxford, far more than Cambridge, had been established as the political university. The Oxford Union was acknowledged – not only in its own estimation – as the principal nursery of aspiring politicians: only two years before, the famous 'King and Country' debate had been widely taken as a serious expression of British youth's unwillingness to fight Hitler. Simply by winning a place at Oxford, Heath had got his foot several rungs up the political ladder.

Still more important was the fact that he was going to Balliol. For within Oxford Balliol had achieved an extraordinary pre-eminence as the staff college of the Establishment, turning out year after year far more than its share of future Cabinet ministers, ambassadors, editors, permanent secretaries and bishops. In the previous ten years Balliol had provided no less than nine presidents of the Union, including Dingle and John Foot, John Boyd-Carpenter and Anthony Greenwood. (In the next five it was to provide another seven, including Heath himself and Hugh Fraser, who many years later challenged him for the Tory leadership.) This remarkable dominance had originally been established under the legendary mastership of Benjamin Jowett in the 1860s: Jowett's star pupil was H. H. Asquith, the epitome of 'effortless superiority' who had proceeded with smooth inevitability to the premiership in 1908. Since 1924 the Jowett tradition had been carried on by another exceptional Master, A. D. Lindsay, a Labour-voting Scot and leading champion of adult education who was Professor of Philosophy at Glasgow University for two years before coming back to Balliol at the age of forty-five.

Amid the upper-class frivolity which still largely characterised Oxford between the wars, Lindsay's Balliol was self-consciously a serious college. Its distinctiveness consisted, first, in a respect for brains over money or social connections, reflected in an unusually democratic and cosmopolitan admissions policy (by 1939 no more than half of Balliol entrants came from public schools and fourteen came from overseas); and, second, in a powerful ethos of public service. Brains, it was clearly understood, were to be directed outward towards the world of affairs, not inward to the service of scholarship.

This mixture of idealism and practicality suited Teddy Heath down to the ground. It was not merely that only Balliol's relatively egalitarian admissions policy gave him the chance to go to Oxford at all. Unlike other future prime ministers from lower-middle-class backgrounds – Harold Wilson a year before him, Margaret Roberts a dozen years behind him – who went up to Oxford primarily to work for their degrees, took no part in the Union and did not become involved in politics until much later, Heath went to Oxford with his mind already set on becoming a politician. With characteristic directness he told the admissions tutor so at his interview. Years later the tutor, Charles Morris, could not recall any other applicant ever having stated this so baldly as his ambition.[1] But if he had not yet learned the reticence of the Establishment he had come to the right place. Balliol, as he himself later expressed it, 'opened all the doors to me. And more important than the doors, the windows. Such a variety of people, of types and classes and character, not only from this country but from all over the world, the Commonwealth, the United States, Europe, Asia, everywhere.' At Balliol, with its tradition of 'high thinking and easy mixing',[2] neither his Broadstairs background nor his rather earnest approach to public service were a handicap, as they might have been at another, more 'hearty' college. On the contrary, he was the almost perfect embodiment of Lindsay's ideal: a new Asquith, as it were, to Lindsay's Jowett. After his mother, 'Sandy' Lindsay was certainly the greatest influence in Heath's life. He had found another community, like Chatham House, in which his particular talents and application almost guaranteed that he would thrive.

He had another stroke of good fortune in his first term. Having gone up as a commoner, with only a loan from the Kent Education Committee, money was going to be a serious problem for him, even at Balliol – unless he could win the college organ scholarship, which he knew was about to fall vacant. The previous year he had already tried, 'admittedly rather half-heartedly',[3] for organ scholarships at Keble and at St Catherine's, Cambridge; so he knew what was required and worked hard to bring his playing up to standard. 'I feel you may think it strange that I, already up here, should compete for an award which would allow someone else to come up,' he wrote a little guiltily to his old headmaster; 'but I feel from the financial point of view I must.'[4] The scholarship was worth £100 a year. By winning it, Heath lifted much of the burden of supporting him from his parents and at the same time relieved himself, for the rest of his Oxford career, from the money worries that would otherwise have pressed on him. Though he was not by nature extravagant and did not live expensively, he was now for the first time in his life able to buy books: in his second year he bought his first gramophone records – the beginnings of what became an immense collection. The possession of enough money to indulge his interests – whether music, collecting pictures or sailing – has always meant a lot to Heath throughout his life: his organ scholarship was in this respect a crucial emancipation.

It had other important effects on his Oxford career. First of all it ran for three years from the following October. This meant that he enjoyed the opportunity of four years altogether at Balliol instead of the usual three: already nineteen when he went up, he was nearly twenty-three by the time he went down in 1939. As at Chatham House, he had by the time he left the advantage of age over his con-temporaries. Second, his responsibilities as organ scholar gave him both a role and a standing in the college which he would not have had as a commoner but which helped him overcome whatever social embarrassment he may have felt. He was not just another under-graduate, but the organ scholar. He was required to play the organ in chapel every morning at eight o'clock and again on Sundays and had opportunities for conducting, direction and even composition which he eagerly embraced. He was effectively in charge of the musical life of the college. Above all, by an extraordinary chance, he was almost immediately called upon to advise on the design and then supervise the installation of a new college organ. As well as giving him an exceptional opportunity to steep himself in the merits of alternative designs, this threw him into closer daily contact than he could other-wise have expected with Lindsay and other senior Fellows. The Balliol organ to this day is the instrument whose building Heath supervised. He is justly proud of it and still makes a point of playing it when he is in Oxford.

Finally his scholarship affected the whole course of Heath's life by ensuring that music remained a major part of it. Without the duties it imposed on him, music might easily have slipped down the order of his priorities at Oxford to the extent that it became, as with so many others, merely an occasional diversion when time allowed. Instead it was confirmed as a central and continuing strand of his life; indeed for a while he thought seriously of making it his career.

Even in the relatively democratic atmosphere of Balliol, however, and even with the help of his scholarship, Heath had problems of adaptation to his new surroundings. A trace of them is audible to this day in his curious accent, which suggests that his speech must have undergone fairly drastic and rapid change on encountering Oxford: the result, with its tortured and artificial vowel sounds which later attracted such mockery, was an accent markedly different from the soft Kentish burr of his father or – more significantly – of his brother John, who went to the same school but not to Oxford. It is one of the mysteries of Heath's life, which applies not simply to his accent but to the woodenness of his public speaking, how someone with such a highly developed ear for music should be apparently deaf to the rhythms and intonation of speech; but it has to be said that the oddity of his accent excited no satirical comment until he became Leader of the Opposition.

Heath was evidently reasonably successful in putting his back-ground behind him. Lord Fulton, who tutored him in politics, did not remember him as one of those – a familiar type at Balliol – self-consciously struggling to retain their working-class authenticity.[5] He belonged already, in his own view, to the middle class, but he was still sufficiently sensitive on the subject when he began to be active in the Union to want to sue *Isis* for describing his father as a jobbing builder: he consulted Arnold Goodman, then a young solicitor in Oxford, whom he had met at the house near Broadstairs of a wealthy solicitor called Royalton Kisch for whom his father had once done some work. (Kisch took a close interest in his builder's promising son and prophesied to Goodman that he would be Prime Minister – further indication that Heath's adolescent ambition already lay that way.)[6] Goodman wisely dissuaded Heath, but the slight clearly hurt him. The letter, already quoted, which Heath wrote to his old head-master in his first term, offers another hint of social insecurity: in college, he wrote, 'everyone mixes very well, unfortunately not always the case'.[7] Whatever agonies he suffered at this time surfaced only once more in a remarkable article which he wrote in April 1940, after coming down from Oxford, in the *Spectator* in reply to one by Mark Bonham Carter (then still at Winchester) proposing the open-ing up of the public schools by admitting a higher proportion of poor boys on state scholarships. Heath argued forcefully that this would merely be to use a few individuals as pawns to help preserve the public schools. The secondary schoolboy, he contended, did not want to be lifted out of his class and offered a special privilege, but only the opportunity to compete on equal terms with all his contemporaries. 'For he knows that when it is a question of academic ability he has nothing to fear from his public school rival, as is rapidly becoming more and more evident.' Bonham Carter's well-intentioned proposal gave no thought for the unfortunates selected for this experiment:

> Of course the secondary schoolboy recognises with regret that he is sometimes not blessed with many social graces; he is so busy specialising in order to make his own way against privilege that he lacks breadth and culture; he gets little from his home and too little of both time and money is spent on it at school. So even the best diamond may remain unpolished.

Heath went on to give some vivid examples, evidently based on personal experience, of the sort of casual hurts to which the public-school guinea-pig would be exposed. There is surely more naked autobiography in this paragraph than in anything else he has ever written or allowed himself to admit in any interview.

> To have to answer that one's father is a busdriver or a carpenter, perhaps; to know that one's parents cannot afford to travel to school functions, or to see them there, unhappy and ill at ease and feel oneself shudder at a rough accent or a 'we was'; to be asked to stay with a school friend and to have to refuse for fear of asking him back to a humble villa; to have no answer to others' stories of travel in the holidays; worst of all to see one's parents, who have made such sacrifices, grieve because they know one cannot have all the things one's associates have; that is what it will mean for a state scholar.

He had doubtless felt some of this as a scholar even at Chatham House; but it was only at Oxford that he had encountered the massed class-consciousness of Etonians, Harrovians and Wykehamists. It was clearly the painful memory of this experience which prompted him to write to the *Spectator*. 'At Oxford I've seen public and secondary schoolboys together; and even in that home of tolerance there is the unhappiness which I'm sure would exist, many times multiplied, were this scheme to be adopted in our schools.' The aim, he concluded boldly, instead of merely tinkering with the problem, should be to 'establish equality of opportunity . . . by abolishing inequality of education'.[8]

Part of the protective colouring that Heath quickly adopted, at least in his early years at Balliol, was to avoid appearing overtly pushy or ambitious. He treated his time at Oxford much as he had at Chatham House: seriously, as part of his apprenticeship, an opportunity to learn from his elders and prepare himself for the responsibilities he intended to take on in life, not as most undergraduates do as a chance to shine precociously before settling for obscurity. There was about him, as one of his more privileged contemporaries, Hugh Fraser, recalled, 'no great ebullience of youth'.[9] In his first-term letter to his headmaster he reported that 'settling down and work . . . have left no time for doing great things, and I am now sceptical of biographies in which it is related how great men "hit" Oxford in their first week'. The implication is unmistakable that he intended to be a great man in due course but was content to bide his time. 'I have joined the Union where I have spent the term sitting at the feet of the great men of the day, so that next term perhaps I may speak the better.'[10] Even when he did speak he was in no hurry to make a splash. To his slightly older, non-Balliol contemporaries at the Union like Ashley Bramall, later to be his opponent in his first parliamentary election, or Philip Toynbee, he appeared in his first two years serious, diligent, energetic but in no way remarkable. Toynbee remembered 'a gentle, amiable, kindly, competent man, but not one with a very striking personality': the very last person he would have predicted would become Prime Minister. Interviewed in 1969, he had difficulty reconciling the Teddy Heath he had known thirty years before with the thrusting image Heath now projected.

> His physical appearance has changed enormously . . . His whole face has become very much more definite. It was a soft, unformed, very unformed face at that time . . . He's got a much more jutting and forceful face, almost as if he'd given himself a forceful face, which he certainly didn't have at that time . . . I do feel, when I see him talking on the television, that there is a tremendous effort being made to turn him into something which he wasn't originally.[11]

There are two ways of taking this testimony. Either Heath's personality changed radically some time after Oxford, as he made his way up the political ladder to the top; or else he successfully suppressed his more abrasive side while at Oxford in the interest of getting on with people while he laid the foundations for his later career. Clearly a man's personality can change, harden and toughen as he grows older, and perhaps most do; on the other hand, Heath at school – solitary, single minded, self-sufficient – was much more like the mature Heath than the pleasantly competent undergraduate Toynbee describes. He still made few close friends. Probably only Madron Seligman, a Harrovian who came up to Balliol in Heath's second year, merits that description: he and Heath discovered a shared interest in politics, paintings and music which has lasted to this day. But it does appear, from Toynbee's and other recollections, that Heath was more genial and more widely liked while at Oxford than at any other period in his life. *Isis* refers several times to his 'charm'. If he could only have recovered a little of that human warmth between 1965 and 1975 how much more successful he might have been. But it is the Oxford years that seem to present the aberration. The best explanation would appear to be that he was simply more relaxed while at Oxford than at any other period: not making such a violent effort to get on, but pursuing his political ambition modestly under cover of his musical and other college activities.

Another contemporary interviewed for a 'Panorama' profile in 1962 did not think of Heath as being particularly interested in politics as such at all, but remembered rather his 'friendly sympathetic interest in his fellow men'.

> I think he came to politics through people rather than ideas . . .
> A lot of my contemporaries were interested in politics at that time, but Ted Heath seemed to be mostly interested in – oh, running things like the Balliol concerts and the choir, and looking after freshmen, and generally taking over . . . I don't recall he had any sort of strong ideas about how to set the world right . . . which the others had.[12]

'Running things' and 'generally taking over' might not have seemed what politics was about to young men excited about the Spanish Civil War and unemployment; but it was exactly the sort of practical apprenticeship Heath was looking for, and typical of his approach.

By this means, however, he achieved, by his later years, a position of prominence both in college – he was President of the Junior Common Room – and in the Union, so that by the time Roy Jenkins, for instance, came up to Balliol in 1938 – another politically ambitious grammar-school boy from a provincial background – he was 'a thoroughly successful, well-established Balliol figure'. Jenkins found him 'grave, courteous, perfectly agreeable, not sparkling . . . old for his years . . . He didn't show any feelings of insecurity, considering his background at Broadstairs, and although he was never arrogant, he was perfectly self-assured.' Indeed, Jenkins considered, 'He seemed to me more self-confident then than he is now [1969].'[13] By his final year Heath had unquestionably become a 'great man' in the university, pointed out to freshmen in the street as 'a person of consequence'.[14] Julian Amery, yet another future colleague, thought him 'clearly somebody one noticed'; he was to be found 'in all kinds of groups and parties'. And yet, Amery noted, 'he was in a way rather detached from any of them'.[15] Philip Kaiser, an American Rhodes scholar, picked up this detachment behind the geniality:

> He was serious, but with a good sense of fun when you were in a party with him. Retrospectively, perhaps . . . there was a little bit of a quality which comes out more prominently in the person presented today – essentially self-protective, a certain obliqueness about him which came through in a rather charming way in those days.[16]

How, then, from his cautious start, did Heath achieve this transformation of the way people saw him in his latter years? He certainly did not shine conspicuously in his academic work. One has the sense of him very deliberately picking up what he needed to know – and only what he needed to know – of politics and economics, rather than of any great intellectual excitement or discovery. Lord Fulton found him 'well-organised . . . with no spectacular intellectual vice . . . His essays . . . were full of detail, very conscientiously worked out, and he was very good at standing up for his thesis.'[17] He was most strongly influenced intellectually by A. D. Lindsay, who lectured on morals every week – interpreting the subject very broadly to embrace the nature of the state and the whole culture of democracy. In addition to his formal teaching Lindsay held open house in the Master's Lodge once a week to any members of the Junior Common Room who cared to come along: Heath attended regularly. Though Lindsay was a socialist, Heath has stated that his high-minded approach to public life 'strengthened my own Conservatism. He was a completely non-dogmatic and non-doctrinaire thinker and doer.'[18] Essentially he taught democracy to a generation of undergraduates alarmed by the march of fascism and subject to the contrary temptation to respond by embracing communism. He taught democracy both in theory and by practical example. There was first of all, as Heath recalled,

> always this emphasis on discussion, on getting the other point of view, all sides as the key function of a democratic society. Not only . . . with a view to the best course of action being adopted,

but discussion as the right of the individual in a free society, making continual expression of everybody's views so habitual that repression was impossible.[19]

Reverence for the ideal of democracy, linked to a rooted disgust of ideology of any kind, was the major intellectual legacy Heath took away from his time at Oxford. Second, Lindsay's educational philosophy was founded on the encouragement of individuals, whatever their background, to achieve their full potential: this too not only struck an obvious chord with Heath as a gauche undergraduate but became the central principle of his mature formulation of his own political philosophy in later life. Lindsay did not convert Heath to Labour, but he did teach him a social democratic outlook which deeply coloured his Conservatism.

It was through music, however, that Heath first made his mark at Balliol. In his first term he joined the college musical society; by his third he had got himself elected secretary and immediately proposed the formation of a choir to be composed of Balliol men with sopranos and altos from the women's colleges. They performed, with Heath conducting, at the regular Sunday evening Balliol concerts, established in 1885 in Jowett's day. In November 1937, at the beginning of Heath's third year, they sang at the thousandth concert – accompanied by the composition scholar, George Malcolm, at the piano. Other past and present Balliol musicians played other pieces with the Oxford Chamber Orchestra, E. R. G. Heath conducting. Bach and Handel were elected honorary Fellows for the evening. It was a memorable occasion, which his parents drove up from Broadstairs to attend.

The following summer, extending his musical activity beyond Balliol, Heath directed the incidental music for a university production of *The Taming of the Shrew*; but, more boldly, he also composed music for the Balliol Players' English language performance of Aristophanes's *The Acharnians*, and then accompanied them as they toured it around southern England. The programme actually attributed the music jointly to E. R. G. Heath and W. W. Rostow, but Walt Rostow – then a Rhodes Scholar at Balliol – is clear that the credit was properly Heath's.[20] 'I remember Teddy being in charge of a strange and rather weird Greek chorus,' another member of the group (later a bishop) has recalled,

and getting remarkable music from them . . . We performed in the open in places like Corfe Castle and then retired to the pub for bacon and eggs and beer afterwards and then slept out under the

Castle or in the ruins of Old Sarum and such places before we moved on the next day . . . Teddy . . . was completely a part of this typical Balliol scene.[21]

In addition he took the opportunity to play the organs of Salisbury cathedral and Bath abbey, and to conduct a silver band.

Through his varied musical activity at Balliol Heath got to know many of the leading figures in English musical life of the day: Ernest Walker, who examined him for his scholarship and subsequently enthralled him with his recollections of Brahms; Sir Donald Tovey, whom he met only once but whose influential writings helped to arouse his enthusiasm for Mahler; Sir Hugh Allen, Professor of Music, whose annual town-and-gown carol concerts inspired Heath to attempt the same sort of thing in Broadstairs; and Dr Thomas Armstrong, then organist at Christ Church and conductor of the Oxford Bach Choir in which Heath sang as a bass throughout his time at Balliol. Armstrong in particular – later Principal of the Royal Academy of Music – became a lifelong friend; his son Robert, a good amateur musician himself, was Heath's Principal Private Secretary when he was Prime Minister and later Margaret Thatcher's Cabinet Secretary – while managing, remarkably, to remain on good terms with Heath.

In the days before long-playing records, music lovers were heavily dependent on live performances to develop their knowledge of the repertoire. Heath had already, as a schoolboy, discovered the Proms and, by staying with friends in London, managed to experience many of the major works of the great composers which Sir Henry Wood in those days believed it the Proms' purpose to parade; he even contrived to get in during the mornings to watch rehearsals. Oxford offered further opportunity to hear some memorable performances which helped to shape his musical taste. Toscanini came to conduct Brahms's First Symphony in the New Theatre, and Sir Thomas Beecham brought the RPO to play Sibelius's Seventh in the Sheldonian. With the Bach Choir he was able to sing several of the great choral masterworks, including Beethoven's Missa Solemnis: while the Balliol concerts introduced him to a wide range of chamber music and lieder. But as a young man, conventionally enough, he tended to respond most deeply to 'big' symphonic music: Beethoven, Brahms, Sibelius and, when he could get to hear it, Bruckner and Mahler. It has often been remarked that for a man so outwardly inhibited and apparently suspicious of emotion, Heath's taste in music is surprisingly romantic: it seems that only through the abstract and ordered medium of music will he allow his carefully guarded emotions to be released. He derives great solace at the end of the day from quietly playing the piano by himself. But he also clearly relishes – or used to when he was younger – the power of the organ: the great swelling sound filling a church or an empty cathedral, or leading a congregation of voices. There is something intrinsically commanding about playing the organ. Conducting is somewhat similar. Instead of making the sound all by himself, the conductor has to draw it from a dozen or a hundred other people. But it is still an exercise of power, as Heath recognised in his 1976 book, *Music*: 'It seemed to me [as a schoolboy] that having control over a choir and orchestra, shaping them to produce the sound one wanted, having soloists singing out of one's hand, so to speak, was really something worthwhile.'[22]

There can be no doubt that these two forms of power, the solitary power of the organist and the conductor's power of leadership, represent complementary expressions of the will to domination that was already latent in the undergraduate Ted Heath and a large part of the appeal for him of performing music.

It was already apparent to him at Oxford, however, that music alone was not going to be enough to satisfy that urge.

The arena in which Heath was most determined to succeed at Oxford was the Union. Of course the historian must beware of taking the Union too seriously. It is, after all, merely a student debating society – the playground of a tiny clique of privileged adolescents whose juvenile posturings should be of no interest to anyone but themselves. The international fuss about the 'King and Country' debate was absurdly exaggerated. Yet the fact remains that it is the forum in which a disproportionate number of subsequently prominent British – and Commonwealth – politicians cut their political teeth. One can see there played out, as it were in rehearsal, some of the roles and rivalries which are later re-enacted on the national stage. For this reason it does have undeniable biographical fascination. This is especially so in the case of someone like Ted Heath, who took it very seriously himself and consciously used it as an apprenticeship for real life. For many others it is true that their Union career represents no more than a juvenile aberration: John Biggs-Davison, for example, a fierce left-winger in the Union debates of the 1930s, metamorphosed into a staunchly right-wing Tory MP. The political stance of the undergraduate Teddy Heath, on the contrary, was almost indistinguishable from that of the Prime Minister thirty-five years later: the brand of liberal Toryism, and the view of international relations, for which he argued in his Union speeches remained essentially unchanged all his life. What is more, both the methodical determination of his climb to the presidency, and his purposeful use of the position once he had attained it, very clearly anticipate his adult assault first on the Tory leadership and then on Downing Street – while undoubtedly furnishing in his own mind a model of success. Heath's approach to student politics was very far from playground posturing.

There is a wider national significance, too, in Heath's success. The Union was at a low ebb in 1935. The 'King and Country' debate had dented both its reputation and its finances: outraged benefactors had withdrawn their support and fathers declined to subsidise their sons' subscriptions. Politically it was more than ever dominated by the Labour Club, which boasted somewhere between 800 and 1,500 members in the university, most of them strongly under the influence of G. D. H. Cole and younger left-wing dons like Richard Crossman and Patrick Gordon Walker. The trend of debates ran steadily in the left's favour: the National Government was regularly condemned, calls for collective security and rearmament as regularly defeated, and solidarity with the downtrodden workers stirringly affirmed. Another calculatedly provocative motion 'That this House recognizes no flag but the Red flag', carried in May 1936, aroused disappointingly little public outcry. But ordinary undergraduates were increasingly turned away by this attitudinising. *Isis* complained that the Union was being 'strangled by politics'.[23] Attendance at debates was lower in 1936 than at any period before or since. It was against this unpromising background that Heath made his Union career. Gradually, between 1935 and 1939, the Labour tide was turned. The trend of debates was reversed, from majority support for disarmament, appeasement and every form of utopian escapism to a grim acceptance of the necessity of resistance. The young men of the 1930s knew that if ultimately it came again to war they would be the ones who would have to do the fighting. By 1938 Union debates had attained a new level of seriousness, responsibility and realism, lifted by the eloquence of a generation now ready after all, if necessary, to die for 'King and Country'. Moreover, the accident of the Oxford by-election, four weeks after Munich, briefly lifted undergraduate politics out of the introverted hothouse of the Union and into the forefront of the national debate. Heath's Oxford generation, exceptionally, found themselves playing out their Union charades for real and earnest in the full glare of national attention. This was a formative influence in Heath's political career. Once again, the memory of his part in helping to secure this turnaround in Oxford's – and indirectly the nation's – attitude towards the approach of war, served as a model for the sort of transformation he later aspired to achieve for Britain as a whole.

He spent his first term, in his own words, 'sitting at the feet of the great men of the day',[24] although the generation immediately before his was not particularly distinguished. On the socialist side the rising stars were Christopher Mayhew, who was a junior Foreign Office minister as early as 1946, but whose career foundered after he resigned from the Wilson Government in 1966 on his way to joining the Liberals; Max Beloff, considered the wittiest speaker of his day but too much of a maverick to win the presidency, later a distinguished historian and a trenchant Conservative; Ashley Bramall, who was MP for Bexley from 1945 to 1950 (until defeated by Heath) and subsequently Labour Leader of the Greater London Council; and Philip Toynbee, the writer, then a flamboyant Communist. On the Conservative side the 'great men' were Ian Harvey and Ronald Bell, who had already begun to revive the University Conservative Association to meet the Labour challenge. Both became MPs after the war. Harvey's promising career was ended by a homosexual scandal in 1958; Bell remained a backbencher and became one of the leading Tory opponents of Britain joining the EEC. These were the most conspicuous of the undergraduate politicians whose example Heath set himself to emulate and surpass.

He also had the opportunity, in his first terms, of hearing a large number of distinguished guest speakers. The visitor who made the strongest impression on him, by speaking and answering his opponents' points without a note, was Sir John Simon, who came in his second term. Heath determined then and there that he must learn to do the same – and did so, very successfully.[25] The result, unfortunately, was that although throughout his career he could always amaze audiences with his fluency and grasp of detail when speaking off the cuff, he was always desperately stilted when speaking – as he had to do on big occasions – from a script.

He nerved himself to make his début in the fourth debate of his second term, against the hoary motion 'That this House considers that England is fast following in the footsteps of Imperial Rome'. *Isis* praised 'an extremely forcible and able maiden speech'.[26] For what it is worth he helped to defeat the motion by 83 votes to 77. Thus encouraged, he spoke again three weeks later, surprisingly *against* the motion 'That the present education system is unsuited to a democratic state'. He argued, according to *Isis*, that 'equality of education means equality of wealth, and equality of wealth meant communism'. Was he trying to assure the serried public schoolboys that a grammar-school boy could be a sound Conservative? The President (Ian Harvey) noted approvingly that 'Mr Heath has plenty of confidence: he must be careful not to appear too aggressive.'[27]

The next term he spoke four times, and appears to have taken Harvey's warning to heart. He was commended by the new President for speaking 'as one having authority – a technique that might profitably be followed by others'.[28] In another debate opposing the admission of women to the Union – he 'took the laudable course of answering the three main arguments' used by his opponent: evidently an unusual practice, but typical of Heath's serious approach. This was 'an exceedingly good speech'.[29] Having won his spurs, he was – 'to my great joy'[30] – invited at the beginning of his fourth term to make his first speech 'on the paper' (that is, opening the debate), against the return to Germany of her former colonies. Again he impressed by having done his homework:

> E. R. G. Heath (Balliol), who opened, anticipated all his opponent's arguments and dealt methodically with each . . . This was just what was needed early in the evening – a thorough and informed speech, enlivened by an occasional rather good story. Mr Heath should, however, try to find some means of connecting his paragraphs other than the words, 'Now, sir'.[31]

Hansard shows that he never did find an answer to this problem. (His characteristic link in later life was 'I now turn to . . . ' or 'I will now say a word about . . .'). But he won the debate – an important milestone in the gradual turning of Union sentiment against Germany. Christopher Mayhew, reviewing 'Union Prospects' in *Isis*, noted that among the rising Tories, Heath 'can always be relied upon for a sound speech'.[32]

All his solid speeches, however, failed to get him anywhere near election to one of the Union's coveted offices: in his fifth term he came bottom of the poll for Librarian, and in his sixth he was fourth out of six candidates for Secretary. His breakthrough came at the beginning of his third year – November 1937 – when he led for the Tories against a motion approving the Labour Party's Immediate Programme: the formidable guest speaker was Hugh Dalton. With characteristic thoroughness, but also humour, Heath rose superbly to his opportunity:

> *E. R. G. Heath (Balliol)* was greeted with enthusiastic applause by the Conservatives. He did not disappoint them. Welcoming Dr Dalton as one whose intimate knowledge of the working classes was no doubt gained on the playing fields of Eton, he recalled that at a Labour Party Conference Dr Dalton had said, 'Comrades, let

us be logical.' So original was this remark, and such a striking impression did it make on the delegates that he was at once elected chairman for the next conference. Mr Heath then went through the programme, analysing its defects. Point by point he dissected it, its cost, its mistaken principles, and its nebulous proposals about the Special Areas [of high unemployment] such as 'Measures will be taken to increase employment' – but no hint of what these measures would be. In conclusion Mr Heath contrasted this programme with the constructive work done by the Government in the past, and the further measures now being undertaken.

'This', enthused the President (Alan Fyfe, of Balliol, later killed in the war), 'was one of the best speeches by an Oxford Conservative that I have ever heard.'[33] What is more it won the day. In a well-filled House, against the trend of recent years and despite the convention that visiting celebrities usually carried the day, the Labour motion was heavily defeated by 162 to 125. Fifteen months later *Isis* could still refer to Heath's 'great speech last winter which helped to defeat Dr Dalton'.[34] Less than two weeks after this triumph, Heath was elected Secretary, comfortably defeating Ashley Bramall. He had now very definitely arrived. The new President, Raymond Walton (yet another Balliol man, subsequently a judge), remarked significantly on the revelation that 'Mr Teddy Heath is more than an ineffectual young man with a charming smile.' He proved an exceptionally efficient Secretary. Toynbee, when his turn came to write 'Union Prospects', judged him not only 'a very good speaker indeed: reasonable, sincere and lucid', but added that 'by a particularly brilliant tenure of the Secretaryship' he had shown that he 'has real administrative ability'.[35] His possession of this evidently rare commodity was now sufficiently widely recognised to ensure his election as Librarian by an overwhelming vote.

But his goal was of course the President's chair. To win it, he had to demonstrate that he was not just a good serious debater but could make at least a stab at a lighter style. Accordingly he took part in an Eights Week debate, proposing – incongruously – the motion 'That this House deplores the decline of Frivolity'. *Isis* recognised that this was something akin to a dog walking on its hind legs ('Mr Heath is first and foremost a politician, and was delivering, so to speak, his maiden funny speech') but judged that he did pretty well: 'Reasons of space (and in one instance decorum) forbid repetition of the string of jokes and stories of which it was composed. He ended up, surprisingly enough, by discussing the motion, and appealed for a spirit of *joie de vivre*' – advocating 'the importance of not being earnest'.[36]

This did not deceive anyone, however, that he was not in deadly earnest. Two weeks later he debated against the same opponent – an Australian Rhodes scholar named Alan Wood – for the Presidency. Unluckily at that time, 1938 – the summer before Munich – though increasingly unhappy, Heath was still loyally supporting the National Government. As a result, *Isis* noted, he spoke from 'very full transcript notes, which caused a lack of spontaneity'.[37] He lost the debate by 154 votes to 113, and with it the presidency, by 197 to 165.

But for his organ scholarship, that would have been the end of Heath's Union career. As it was, he still had his fourth year to come in which to reach the prize – a momentous year, as it turned out, which began with the Munich crisis and ended with Europe once again, but this time inescapably, on the brink of war. It was his opposition to Munich that was to lift Heath to the presidency. His clear understanding of the folly of appeasement had been signalled very early in his Union career. In October 1936 Churchill paid a rare visit to Oxford and addressed a packed meeting of the Conservative Association, pressing his sombre warning of the urgency of rearmament. Heath had been one of those who had gone on afterwards to 'Prof' Lindemann's rooms in Christ Church to listen to him talking into the small hours ('far past the time when we ought to have been back in college')[38] The experience made a deep impression on him. It was two weeks after this that he made his maiden 'paper' speech opposing the return of German colonies. Against an opponent (J. R. J. Kerruish, subsequently a clergyman) who took the pacifist/defeatist line that Britain could never hope to defeat Germany and therefore must conciliate her, Heath asserted uncompromisingly that 'Paying Danegeld never did pay and never will', and carried the debate by a majority of nearly a hundred (191–94).[39] His victory marked the beginning of the Union's shift against appeasement. Heath in the meantime never wavered from the position he took up in this debate. When he eventually won the presidency, it was – appropriately – against the same opponent.

His understanding of the threat of Nazism was further deepened by a visit to Germany in the summer of 1937. Characteristically undeterred by the fact that he spoke no German, he determined to see for himself the nature of the régime which others in England either abhorred at second hand or underestimated. By means of an exchange with a German student who came to stay in Broadstairs for a short time at the beginning of the vacation, he went first to Düsseldorf for a few days, then travelled on alone – uncomfortably, by train, in extreme heat – to Frankfurt, Munich and the Bavarian Alps, with a one-day musical pilgrimage to Salzburg. In Bavaria he had the good fortune to make the acquaintance of a recently retired, liberally inclined Professor of English at Berlin, Professor Winckler, and stayed a month with him and his wife, walking in the mountains and talking 'continuously' of Hitler and fascism. He then quite unexpectedly received an invitation – arranged for him through the German Embassy in London by a Broadstairs solicitor whose brother was a Tory MP – to attend the Nazi rally in Nuremberg.

This was an extraordinary opportunity for a 21-year-old English student. At the party conference which preceded the rally, attended by the whole Nazi leadership, he found himself in a gangway seat as Hitler marched alone up the centre aisle, 'almost brushing my shoulder . . . He looked much smaller than I had imagined and very ordinary. His face had little colour and the uniform seemed more important than the man.' Next day, at the rally, Heath witnessed the full panoply of Nazi power – the processions, the banners, the tanks and the aeroplanes, the massed ranks of disciplined Brownshirts and eager Hitler Youth, and a rapturously received harangue from the Führer, transformed from the ordinary little man of the previous day. 'Here was the mob orator, the demagogue, playing on every evil emotion in his audience . . . This man was obviously capable of carrying the German people with him into any folly.' For Heath, this was a 'traumatic experience'. He knew now, if he had not before, that war was unavoidable. After the rally, he was invited to a party given by Himmler, who 'received us all, peering rather short-sightedly through his pince-nez. I remember him for his soft, wet, flabby handshake.' Goebbels was there, too, 'his pinched face white and sweating – evil personified'.[40] If Heath's account of these meetings, forty years later, is somewhat hackneyed it is impossible to overestimate the effect on him, at the time, of having met the Nazi leaders face to face and experienced Nazism for himself at the height of its grubby arrogance. He went back to Oxford that October older, wiser and surely stiffened by what he had seen.

The experience can only have enhanced his prestige among his contemporaries; it must have contributed to the increased authority which enabled him to demolish Dalton in November. Already the previous June his growing reputation as an anti-fascist had helped to win him the presidency of the Conservative Association (OUCA); the candidate he narrowly defeated was an avowed supporter of Franco, John Stokes (later a very right-wing Tory MP). As President, Heath carried on the revival of the OUCA begun by Ian Harvey and Ronald Bell. But the association was deeply split. The hero of the anti-appeasement young Tories at this time was not so much Churchill as Anthony Eden. Appointed Foreign Secretary at the age of only thirty-eight, handsome, glamorous and gallant (he had won the Military Cross in 1917), Eden was a figure whom young men could identify with; he also seemed to stand for a firmer line with the dictators than the 'old gang' – Chamberlain, Halifax, Simon and Hoare. Eden's resignation in February 1938, the culmination of a series of disagreements with Chamberlain, therefore came as a tremendous blow. Heath heard the news in Philip Kaiser's rooms in Balliol. 'Ted said very little that night,' Kaiser recalled. 'It affected him. Eden was important to him . . . A great thoughtfulness settled on him . . . He thanked me and then walked out.'[41] Having resigned, however, Eden did not follow up his resignation by developing his criticism of Chamberlain's policy. It was a difficult time for his young admirers in the universities who would have liked to rally to him. In his presidential debate against Alan Wood in June, Heath could not do more than make the best case he could for Chamberlain's understanding with Mussolini ('Whatever one thought of the Pact, no-one could deny that the situation in the Mediterranean had been eased'), while loyally asserting that Chamberlain had made Britain's position in the event of a German invasion of Czechoslovakia 'perfectly clear': 'To have given Czechoslovakia written guarantees of our assistance would only have made her overconfident and unwilling to solve her problems.'[42] He maintained, somewhat unconvincingly, his outward faith in the National Government by pouring scorn on the cohesiveness of any popular front alternative; even though it cost him the presidency, he cannot have been altogether unhappy to lose the vote.

That summer – immediately following his gentle ramble round southern England with the Balliol Players – he made a second European journey to see for himself the effects of fascism in action. As President of the Federation of University Conservative Associations he travelled as one of a five-man, all-party student delegation invited by the Spanish Republican Government to experience the civil war in Catalonia. From Paris the party took the sleeper to Perpignan, from where they were driven to Barcelona and then to the Ebro front to talk to British volunteers of the International Brigade. Back in Barcelona they were received by the Prime Minister, Juan Negrin, and had some two hours of talks with the Foreign Minister, Alvarez del Vayo: both urged them to use whatever influence they had to persuade the British Government to reverse its policy of non-intervention and come to the aid of the Spanish Republic before it was too late. They spent several days in and around Barcelona, meeting Spanish students, inspecting schools and refugee camps;

they also visited the monastery at Montserrat, where the treasures from the Prado and other galleries – priceless Goyas and El Grecos – were stored, stacked loosely in the cellars. Finally they tried to fly to Madrid – still partly in Government hands – but their plane came under fire from fascist guns and they were forced to turn back. This was not their only narrow escape. Once their car was machine-gunned by a plane while they dived for the nearest ditch; and in Barcelona their hotel was bombed. Heath and his companions spurned the basement shelter and stayed in their rooms: the bomb fell straight down the lift shaft and killed all those in the shelter. By the time they returned to England, Heath had experienced something of war as well as of the situation in Spain.[43]

Munich finally broke his loyalty to Chamberlain. In the first debate of the autumn term he teamed up across party lines with Christopher Mayhew (an ex-President, but still up at Christ Church) to propose the motion 'That this House deplores the Government's policy of Peace without Honour', against his old antagonist Kerruish. Before the biggest attendance seen at the Union for years, Heath condemned the settlement root and branch – not only the settlement itself, but 'the muddled policy of the Government, which had been largely responsible for bringing us to the verge of this disaster', the indecisiveness of Chamberlain's whole approach to Germany, and the failure to re-arm adequately in time. He had no faith in a lasting peace, but foresaw further trouble 'in Switzerland, Holland and elsewhere'. It was now 'clear to everyone, save Mr Chamberlain' that Hitler could not be trusted. His latest speech showed that Munich had not won his 'good will'. Finally – his cardinal point – there could be justice but no sympathy for Nazi Germany, 'for Nazism was essentially incompatible with Democracy'.[44]

It was, considered as a speech, not one of his best. Alan Wood in *Isis* thought it no more than 'competent' and 'a little too long'. Roy Jenkins, attending his first Union debate, remembered it as 'highly polished and very effective', but thought that Mayhew's, calling directly for Chamberlain to go, was better.[45] The sensation was that Heath, as the leading young Tory in the university and hitherto regarded as a steady loyalist, should have made such a speech at all. 'Mr Heath', *Isis* commented, 'must have astonished some of his confrères by his bitter attack.'[46] Heath and Mayhew carried the debate, however, by 320 votes to 266.

The extraordinary Oxford by-election followed almost immediately. The prospective Labour candidate, Patrick Gordon Walker, was reluctantly persuaded by his colleagues on the Oxford

City Council, Richard Crossman and Frank Pakenham, to stand down – the Liberal did the same – in favour of an anti-Munich Popular Front candidate who could attract the maximum anti-Government vote from all parties, including dissident Conservatives. The candidate who agreed to stand on this anti-appeasement ticket was none other than A. D. Lindsay. It was unheard of for the Master of an Oxford college to stand for Parliament, particularly such a remote and lofty figure as Lindsay and at such a moment of high political tension. But at least in the university – less so in the town, where he was not well chosen for appealing to Cowley car workers – he was the perfect disinterested, idealistic candidate to make a stand for democracy against surrender to dictatorship – which was how the campaign was fought. For Ted Heath there was no question of not supporting him. He could not have openly backed Gordon Walker – though he could not easily have worked for Quintin Hogg, the Chamberlainite candidate, either. But Lindsay, the Master of his own college, who personified the democratic values he most earnestly revered in politics, was an entirely different matter. He was one of the first to commit himself whole-heartedly to Lindsay's side, and his example – as a prominent Conservative – helped to bring in a lot of others who might have hesitated to take the plunge. The next two weeks' frenetic activity – speaking, canvassing and organising – still rank among the high points of his life, as they do also for his Balliol contemporaries, Roy Jenkins, Dennis Healey, Julian Amery and many others caught up in the excitement of the cause. A whole Oxford generation had its first taste of real politics in the Oxford City by-election.

The Conservative Association was more split than ever. Hugh Fraser, who the previous term had combined with Amery to carry an important vote at the Union in favour of conscription, was one Balliol Tory who nevertheless disliked Lindsay even more than he did Chamberlain and stuck with the Hogg camp.[47] The two sides maintained friendly relations throughout, lunching each day at the Carlton Club opposite Balliol, Lindsay's supporters on one side of the room, Hogg's on the other, exchanging good-humoured abuse across the gap between. Harold Macmillan came to speak to a Lindsay rally, hugely attended; but Eden, though invited, did not feel able so directly to oppose the Government, nor did Churchill. Some ill-feeling was caused on polling day by the Lindsay camp's use of the slogan (of which Lindsay himself disapproved) 'A Vote for Hogg is a Vote for Hitler'. The result looked as though it could go either way. In the end the Conservative majority was nearly halved, from 6,645 to 3,434, but the Government was spared a serious embarrassment –

though only temporarily, since four weeks later a Popular Front candidate, Vernon Bartlett, did capture Bridgwater.

Having thus conspicuously burned his boats, Heath returned to the Union on 17 November to propose the motion for the presidential debate, 'That this House has no confidence in the National Government as at present constituted'. In almost reckless mood, quite unlike the weighty style of his earlier condemnation, he assailed the Government with unusual savagery.

It was nothing more nor less than an organised hypocrisy, composed of Conservatives with nothing to conserve and Liberals with a hatred of liberty. As for Mr Chamberlain's foreign policy, it could only be described in the maxim 'If at first you don't concede, fly, fly, fly again'. He quoted an American journalist's opinion that in the next crisis Mr Chamberlain would again turn all four cheeks at once.[48]

This was a very different Teddy Heath. Opposing the motion, Ian Harvey twitted him by comparing him to the red, red robin whose breast gets redder and redder as Christmas approaches. But the anti-Chamberlain motion was carried by 203 to 163. The next day Heath was elected President by the overwhelming margin of 280 to 155 over Kerruish.

Recognising the achievement and what it meant to him, *Isis* made him its '*Isis* Idol' at the beginning of the Hilary term with a witty but perceptive portrait which conveys a good impression of how much his Oxford contemporaries liked as well as admired him.

Teddy Heath was born in the summer of 1916, some two months before the Tank. Lacking the thickness of skin of this early rival, he soon outstripped it in charm of manner, and has since proved its equal in force of utterance and ability to surmount obstacles.

The writer claimed that 'his election to the Presidency . . . was due, not to his politics, but to his ability and character'.[49] This was undoubtedly true in the sense that he would not have won on a simple party vote; he was a popular figure in his own right. Nevertheless his victory was, at least in part, a reward for his political courage; it offered the anti-Chamberlain forces in the Union some compensation for Lindsay's defeat in the by-election.

Having achieved the prize, Heath characteristically set himself to be a President out of the ordinary, recognising that he had only eight weeks to make his mark.

Predictably, he arranged a meaty programme of predominantly political subjects – beginning with a straight party motion of no confidence in the home policy of the National Government (which was carried) – but he lightened it with an imaginative choice of guest speakers which ensured the best attended series of debates for years. First he pitted the notorious 'Red Dean' of St Paul's, the Very Reverend W. R. Matthews, against the poet Stephen Spender (then a Communist) on the motion 'That a return to religion is the only solution to our present discontents'. This drew a huge attendance and was surprisingly carried by 276 to 94.[50] Then he invited Lady Astor to maintain, provocatively, against the young Labour MP John Parker, that 'the future of the working classes lies with progressive Conservatism'; her inimitable advocacy failed only narrowly (164 to 169) to carry the House. The following week Leo Amery, a senior anti-Munich Tory, debated the immediate introduction of conscription against the Popular Front victor of the Bridgwater by-election, Vernon Bartlett, who opposed it on the ground that it would divide the nation just when it needed to be united; Bartlett won by 192 to 173. (Amery, incidentally, noted in his diary that the President was 'a very nice youth'.)[51] The week after this one of Heath's few debates without a star speaker was notable, at least in retrospect, for the teaming of John Biggs-Davison with Anthony Crosland as firebrands of the left in denouncing the Government's recognition of Franco, defended by Julian Amery.

Heath set himself to tackle the Union's perennial financial crisis by encouraging members to make more use of the social facilities of the building; here again he showed both administrative ability and flair. The quality and service offered in the bars and dining room were greatly improved and members were allowed £5 a term credit. He also staged the first Oxford Union Ball ('a wild success').[52] Not until Michael Heseltine in 1954 did the Union see another President who made such a constructive impact. *Isis*, which had welcomed his election, was moved at the end of his term of office to offer a remarkable encomium to his success:

> We would for a moment break with tradition, and here pay tribute to Teddy Heath and the work he has done this term for the Society. No President for many years has provided a more interesting series of debates and visitors; no President has done more to re-establish the prestige of the Union not only as a debating society . . . but also as a club. He was *Isis* idol six weeks ago and we need say nothing further of his varied talents and his charm. But he will not be soon forgotten . . . when he joins the ranks of

the elder Oxford statesmen. The *Isis* offers him its sincere congratulations and best wishes.[53]

The third aspect of Heath's presidency was his continued political activity outside the Union. Although no longer President of the OUCA, and despite his rebellion over Munich, he clearly still saw himself as a leader of university Conservatism and was determined to use his position to advance his personal vision of a modern, progressive, self-consciously *young* Toryism. In an obviously cheer-leading article in *Isis* in January he admitted that the party was divided over Munich, but insisted that dissent was healthy; after a period of apathy, the OUCA was growing again and 'very much alive'. During the vacation he had attended the annual conference of University Conservative Associations in London, which he found to be no longer a negatively anti-socialist body but 'a progressive force with ideals of its own'. It had rejected Chamberlain's foreign policy, and endorsed a call for candidates to be selected on grounds of talent, not wealth. 'All of which goes to show that young Conservatives here and elsewhere have positive ideas of their own which they are not afraid to uphold.'*[54] Three weeks later, in a second article mainly about the need for Tories to match the modern propaganda methods of the socialists (he instanced newsletters, book clubs and Penguin paperbacks), he quoted press criticism suggesting that some of the opinions expressed at the London conference 'might more appropriately have come from the Federation of University Socialists'. This, he wrote tantalisingly, was 'very interesting because it revives the problem of what is a Conservative'. At no stage of his political career, however, was this a problem which Heath chose to address. In 1939 he dismissed it with the same impatience with which he would brush aside questions of ideology thirty and forty years later: 'This is not very urgent, however, (a) because the Party as such is not so keen on heresy hunts as another I have heard of, and (b) because the Party is broad enough and strong enough to contain diversity within that unity which is constituted by Party loyalty.'[56]

This is a very characteristic sentence. Fifty years later he was still objecting in identical terms to heresy hunts and insisting on the right to diversity – though as Leader himself he was rather more inclined to stress the need for unity and loyalty. The striking thing

---

* During this conference Heath declared that 'Appeasement is a perfectly loathsome word'. Robert Silver, who has made a special study of the subject, believes that this is the first recorded use of the word 'appeasement' as a pejorative expression.[55]

throughout is the consistency of his lack of interest in defining long-term goals or answering the 'very interesting' question 'What is a Conservative?'

Politics left Heath little time to spare for his academic work, for which he had naturally less inclination. After the end of his presidential term he had barely three months left before his final 'Schools'. In the circumstances it was not surprising, indeed rather creditable, that he got a solid second. 'He was probably disappointed,' Lord Fulton reckoned, 'but then he had done a lot of other things. There was a solid virtue and steadiness about him, industry applied to the right points, sensible and self-controlled use of his time.'[57] One way and another, with the presidency of the Union, the Balliol JCR, the OUCA and the Federation of University Conservative Associations, not forgetting his conducting of the Balliol Choir and his composing for the Balliol Players, he could not have made much fuller use of his time, nor been much more successful at everything to which he turned his hand. He now had to decide what to do next.

He seriously considered the possibility of making a career in music. Sir Hugh Allen, however, steered him away from this option. Teaching music was a tedious life, and there was no point setting out to be a conductor unless he was going to aim right for the top: the clear implication was that Heath was not of this quality, though he softened it by suggesting that he was not enough of a 'four-letter man'. 'On the other hand, if you go into politics, you will always have music as an amateur to enjoy for its own sake.'[58] This good advice was probably what Heath wanted to hear. His whole Oxford career had committed him too deeply to politics to draw back now. He had already, before 'Schools', won a scholarship to Gray's Inn to read for the Bar – a traditional route into politics – and that was presumably the direction he would have taken if the war had not intervened. At the same time, the law itself held very little attraction, and it may well have been that the prospect of immersing himself in it tempted him to wonder whether music might not be more rewarding. In later life, however, he had no doubt that he had made the right choice. As Prime Minister and ex-Prime Minister he conducted more and better orchestras than he would probably have done as a professional musician.

Meanwhile he had one more long vacation in which to travel in Europe. This time, having been refused a visa to return to Spain, he went with Madron Seligman through Germany to Danzig – the very eye of the coming storm – and Warsaw. This was an extraordinarily foolhardy journey in August 1939, particularly for Seligman, who was half-Jewish. In Warsaw British Embassy officials warned them to get out of Poland as quickly as they could. By a mixture of crowded trains and hitch-hiking they got to the border. At Dresden they met Heath's friend from his previous visit, Professor Winckler; Heath never saw him again. They were at Leipzig on 26 August when the news broke of the Nazi-Soviet Pact; they escaped into France only just in time to avoid being caught in Germany at the outbreak of hostilities. Paris, when they reached it, was already blacked out. Seligman stayed in France to join his family in Brittany. Heath got safely back to England on 1 September – the day that Hitler invaded Poland and only two days before Britain declared war on Germany.[59]

3

'A Good War'

HEATH reached England just in time for the declaration of war.
His relieved parents met him at Dover in the family's newly
acquired Hillman Minx and drove him back to Broadstairs, where he
listened to Chamberlain's reluctant announcement with relief. War
solved the problem of what to do next with his life. He immediately
enlisted and, expressing no particular preference himself, was
assigned to the Royal Artillery. But the army, overwhelmed with
conscripts, had no use for him at once, so he was left kicking his
heels until he was called up. For the first ten months of hostilities,
during the 'Phoney War' and right up to July 1940 – by which time
the Germans were daily expected along the south coast and the Battle
of Britain was raging overhead – he endured a frustrating 'phoney
war' of his own.

Fortunately he had one piece of unfinished business from his
Oxford life which he was allowed to discharge before he disappeared
into uniform. He had been invited, with Hugh Fraser, to represent
British universities on a debating tour of the United States. He consulted both the War Office, which confirmed that he could be
spared, and the Foreign Office, which saw no objection – indeed saw
positive benefit in the tour going ahead. Fraser had already been
called up, so his place was taken by another Oxford man, Peter
Street, and he and Heath sailed from Liverpool in mid-October.

They were away for three months, covered 8,000 miles and spoke
at twenty-six universities on the eastern seaboard, in the mid-West
and the deep South. They ran into a problem right at the outset when
they discovered that the only subject American students wanted to
debate with the British was the one subject they had been strictly
warned by the Foreign Office to keep off – the war and America's
possible participation in it. Scrapping the dozen anodyne subjects

40

Heath and Street had come prepared to debate, the University of Pittsburgh had set down for their first engagement the resolution 'That the United States should immediately enter the war on the side of the Allies'. The two Britons were expected to propose, the Pittsburgh team would oppose: the debate was to be broadcast over all the eastern states. Heath and Street thought they would have to pack up and go home. The British Ambassador, Lord Lothian, however, saved the day, shrewdly proposing that one of them should argue for the motion and one against, taking it in turns on alternate evenings to speak for or against American participation. On the basis of this judgment of Solomon the tour went ahead. The visitors met an enthusiastic reception wherever they went: they debated in front of audiences of up to 1,500 people, and contrived not to provoke a diplomatic incident.

Heath has described the tour in his book *Travels*. He also recorded his impressions in a BBC broadcast immediately on his return. They were any visitor's first impressions – the immense size of the United States, the dynamism of American society and the hospitality of the people. But travelling by Greyhound bus and shown around by their student hosts at every stop, he and Street managed to see a good deal of American life. They experienced an American football match, a traditional Thanksgiving dinner of turkey and cranberries in Atlanta, and a variety of music: open-air jazz in Alabama, Gene Krupa at a New Year's Eve ball in Cleveland, Barbirolli conducting at the Carnegie Hall. One thing Heath was very struck by was the seriousness with which the Americans took debating. 'It's treated like an athletic sport. There's a debate coach, you train with him, you are awarded colours for it'[1] – quite unlike the individualism and studied flippancy of the Oxford Union style. So far as the war was concerned, however, he found the Americans warmly sympathetic, very willing to supply the Allies but determined not to get involved: most disappointingly from his particular perspective, he found the students more isolationist than the older people.

He was impressed by many things in America. He responded to the lack of class distinction, the natural egalitarianism of American society. He admired its energy, the sense of get up and go, the lack of crusted tradition standing in the way of individual advancement. All this, translated into British terms, became a part of his own political creed. At the same time his first visit to the United States did not supplant the deeper impact already made on him by Germany and Spain or diminish the primary commitment he instinctively felt to Europe. The memory of his visit may possibly have helped counteract the latent anti-Americanism to which in later life he was increasingly prone: it certainly did not leave him with that sense of close cousinship and common destiny with America which marks so many British politicians who are captivated by America at an impressionable age. Heath did not come back with an American wife.

His US trip was, however, another valuable exercise in junior statesmanship in which he acquitted himself, as usual, impeccably. Heath and Street returned, through mine-infested seas, on an almost empty ship, from the bright lights of New York to blacked-out Liverpool in the middle of January 1940. For the next six months Heath had nothing to do but sit at home in Broadstairs, reading desultorily while waiting to be called up. (His brother John was already in action in France.) In February he made a return visit to the Oxford Union in support of the exiled Prime Minister of ravaged Czechoslovakia, Eduard Beneš, who was rapturously received in belated expiation of the guilt of Munich. Three months later Chamberlain fell at last, when two-thirds of the tame majority on which he had been able to rely during the appeasement years evaporated following the Norwegian fiasco. Now with the Germans overrunning the Low Countries and the rapid collapse of France, the preliminaries were over. At the end of July Heath was finally called up. He was sent first to a training camp on the Sussex Downs, where he was recommended for a commission; then to Shrivenham in Wiltshire to be turned into an officer. Eventually, in March 1941, 179215 Second Lieutenant E. R. G. Heath was assigned to the 107th Heavy Anti-Aircraft Regiment and posted to Liverpool to help defend the Mersey docks against German long-range bombers.

Heath was in the army for just over six years, until he was demobbed in August 1946. By far the greater part of that time was spent in England, guarding installations, undergoing combat training, learning gunnery tactics, constantly on the move from one part of the country to another, but above all waiting for the moment when his unit would be sent to France. A lot of the training – notably a strenuous month on the Northumberland moors – was very tough; but the closest he came to physical danger was having his appendix out in Newcastle. For much of the rest of this long period of preparation the 107th HAA led a relatively comfortable existence, and the only enemy it faced was boredom.

At last, three weeks after D-Day on 3 July 1944, they went to war. They sailed from Tilbury, landed under enemy fire at Arromanches, took part in the bombardment of Caen and the battle of the Falaise gap, and then pushed east and north with the rest of the Allied armies, through Amiens, Arras, Lens and Tournai to Antwerp, where the 107th liberated the suburb of Wilryck. All the way they were greeted ecstatically by adoring crowds anxious to shower them with presents, touch them, and welcome them uninhibitedly in every way. In September they saw their most serious action, keeping open the vital bridge at Nijmegen in the face of fierce German air attack. Early in the New Year they were pulled back to a practice firing camp near Ostend, then sent back to the defence of Antwerp against Hitler's last throw, the Doodlebugs. In April 1945 they crossed into Germany and moved on to Kleve – less in a combat role now than clearing up behind the Allied advance. VE-Day found them in the small Rhineland market town of Kalkar, after which they returned again to Antwerp to hand over their guns before being sent forward to Hanover as part of the army of occupation. They remained in or around Hanover until the regiment was disbanded in 1946.

Such was Heath's war – an eternity of preparation and training, followed by the exhilaration of being in at the finish. In both phases he did conspicuously well; both experiences made their mark on him. In later life he denied having enjoyed the war. 'You don't enjoy giving up a number of years of your life, do you?'[2] Nevertheless it is clear that army life suited his abilities and temperament down to the ground. Even more than at Balliol, he felt himself in his element in a relatively small social unit – 107 HAA's fighting strength in Europe was only 35 officers and 830 men – with a clear command structure, highly disciplined, entirely male and uncomplicatedly directed to the accomplishment of certain set goals.

As soon as Heath was posted to Liverpool his commanding officers were delighted with him. Major George Chadd, then commanding 335 Battery, swears that he sent him on to a site commander near Frodsham with the recommendation 'I am sending you a future Prime Minister of England.'[3] His efficiency and stamina were exceptional. 'We had one or two fellows who were charming but utterly incompetent,' the site commander, Tony Race, recalled. 'He was the opposite. We were firing most nights, and exhaustion set in, but he was resilient.'[4] Very soon Race was promoted elsewhere and Chadd appointed Heath in his place. 'We had four guns, heavy ack ack, plus a hundred and twenty men – it was a bit of a responsibility for a chap of twenty-four and I had a sleepless night wondering whether Heath would make a site commander. Then I found out that he had sat up all night writing orders for the site.'[5]

In March 1942 his administrative zeal was given full rein. He was appointed Adjutant, responsible for the smooth functioning – the feeding, accommodation and movement – of the whole regiment. By this time the German attacks on Liverpool had ceased and 107

HAA had moved further south – initially to the Birmingham area, then to Chichester, Beaconsfield, up to Northamptonshire, down to Portsmouth ... 'Throughout this period', the regimental history records, 'the Regt. must have covered practically the entire length and breadth of the country', trailing its guns and equipment wherever it went.[6] In his new role, for the next two and a half years, Heath's dedication and super-efficiency found their perfect outlet. Only a year after gaining his commission, he was still very raw. 'He didn't know much at first,' the Quartermaster, Major Harrington, remembered, 'but if he didn't understand something he would ask how to do it, rather than make a mess of it. When he had been told once he never needed to ask again.'[7] This is characteristic: at each successive stage of his career – and in his private pursuits too – Heath has set himself quickly and thoroughly to learn the ropes. He has always been a formidably quick learner. Once on top of the job, he displayed, in Harrington's own words, 'a genius for organisation':[8] 'deciding about food, petrol, where to stay – he made the moves as if they were on a chess board'.[9] Sometimes, perhaps, his perfectionism was excessive. What even Harrington called 'a fetish for documentation'[10] was remembered less kindly by another officer: 'He churned out reams and reams of paper to make sure everything was done by the book. Sometimes I thought he overdid it – after all, there was a war on.'[11] But 107 Regiment was an exceptionally well-prepared unit when the time came finally to go into action.

Off duty, Heath kept himself very largely to himself, not letting on too much about either his background or his ambitions (though he did take part in ABCA discussions on current affairs). Reserved and respectful towards his seniors, never forgetting his junior rank despite his important responsibilities, he was seen by his brother officers as 'a loner';[12] he nevertheless made a lifelong friend of George Chadd and formed a relationship of close trust with Major Harrington, a regular soldier fifteen years older than himself. With the other ranks, drawn mainly from the London area, he was not chummy but quite adequately sociable. 'I've never seen him put a foot wrong,' Chadd recalled. 'He was always meticulous in his conduct and behaviour. The men liked him. He was never impatient with dullards or arrogant to people not as bright as himself. He drank a glass of beer in the mess and he read a lot; he was always reading in bed, but he didn't go out much except with his band.'[13]

The exception was very important. Even during the war music remained Heath's principal source of relaxation; he was happy to play a piano wherever he could find one, and in the early days on Merseyside formed a five-piece battery band which played at dances and in the mess. (Their signature tune was 'When you're smiling'.) Three years later they were still together to provide the music at victory celebrations in liberated Europe. The band occasioned Heath's one fall from grace, when they borrowed an ambulance to take them to a date in Chester, and were overheard by the commanding officer rehearsing in the back. Heath got a 'rocket' over this incident;[14] but at least his music – rather as it had done in his early days at Balliol – gave him a distinctive role within the battery, aside from his military efficiency, which must have helped to humanise him in the eyes of his fellows.

Above all, though, Heath won the respect of his men because he was fair, hard-working and shared with them all the hardships that were going. As an administrative officer, he could have skipped some of the arduous battle training. 'Not so Teddy Heath,' Harrington recalled. 'He was out all day with the men, returning to his office desk in the evening when everyone else was relaxing. He was a glutton for work.'[15] In fact he has always been good at relating to people in a functional role, where there is a job to be done and a clear chain of command, and every member of the team knows what he has to do. Whatever his difficulties of communicating on a wider scale, Heath has great capacity to inspire small groups by his example – a capacity he first developed in the army. He created around him in these years a camaraderie of loyalty and mutual trust which was reflected in the annual reunions which he organised and initially hosted at the House of Commons, and later in his former comrades' pride that George Chadd's prediction should have so improbably come true.

Heath was still Adjutant when the regiment went to France in July 1944. Now he had new responsibilities, organising as before the regiment's movement and supply, but on foreign soil, as part of a huge Allied military operation and very often under enemy fire. He discharged them as efficiently as he had in England. In the most strained situations, one fellow officer recalled, he 'never flapped . . . He was much too big a man to flap . . . He was always under control.'[16] But he was not confined to his administrative function. He led one of the two reconnaissance columns – the other was led by the commanding officer, Colonel Slater – which on 3-5 September preceded the British forces into Antwerp. Heath officially described the advance for the regiment's 'War Diary':

The column received a tremendous welcome all along the route, being the first tps [troops] to pass along the road after the tanks of 11 Arm Div. [11th Armoured Division]. The route recce parties were in several cases the first British tps to enter villages – which they captured! There were many instances of DRs [Dispatch Riders] being pressed to take prisoners giving themselves up. And so the regt moved into harbour that night decorated with flags and flowers and laden with fruit, before moving into Antwerp the next day, the first British tps to enter the city after the tanks and some 48 hs ahead of the infantry.[17]

This, even more than VE-Day, was the high point of the war for 107 HAA. The suburb of Wilryck adopted the regiment as its own. 'The inhabitants' wonderment at our arrival', the regimental history recorded, 'was most touching to see. They just could not believe that the British soldiers had really arrived – that for them the war was over.'

They showered on the men everything they could find – bottles of rare stuff were brought up from the cellars or dug up from hiding places in the gardens. Garden produce was provided, cigars were proffered, baths were offered, the women undertook the washing and voluntarily assisted at the Camp with the preparing of meals and the washing-up. The whole population, in fact, rarely left us at all.[18]

'In addition,' the history happily goes on, 'quantities of wine and cigars and so on were captured and shared around. It was an enjoyable spell.' The 'liberation' of several cases of Wehrmacht champagne, however, prompted a memorable display of priggishness on the part of Captain Heath, who strongly disapproved of what he regarded as stealing and virtuously refused to touch a drop. Even in the moment of victory he believed that officers should give moral leadership to their men.

One year later the regiment returned to Wilryck for a special victory celebration; and thirty years later, in September 1974, sixty-six former members, including Heath – now ex-Prime Minister – attended a ceremony of remembrance. Although in September 1944 there were still eight arduous months of war to go and another year with the army of occupation after that, the entry into Wilryck was the climax of Heath's war.

Soon afterwards – shortly before Christmas 1944, which the regiment 'observed rather than celebrated'[19] in frozen dug-outs near Venlo, while heavy fighting continued in the Ardennes to the south of them – Heath was promoted to command 334 battery, with the

rank of Major. Some doubts were felt about his suitability for a command of his own. The battery's orderly room sergeant, James Hyde,
admitted that 'we were none too happy. Up to then he had been an
administrator. He hadn't done any fighting worth speaking of. I was
suspicious of him.'

> But I think it's right to say that within a fortnight or three weeks
> he exercised such a persuading influence that one found – much as
> one had loved one's previous CO, who'd undergone all the priv-
> ations – that Heath was first class. So far as administration was
> concerned, he was perfect. The other reason why he was first-class
> – and this was to my surprise – was that he rapidly understood
> men and their reactions. He made no changes that were apparent
> on the surface, but underneath the surface he'd made them. Within
> a month or two it was Heath's battery. The men liked him because
> they thought he was a fair man.[20]

In the last months of the war, Major Heath was able to develop his
leadership qualities in the field, taking his battery across the Rhine
and into Germany and eventually all the way to Hanover. On top of
his former stamina and efficiency in a subordinate role was now
grafted a new authority in command. 'He was a tough skipper,'
Hyde recalled. 'If he said the battery was going to do it this way,
that was it.'[21] He clearly relished the new challenge, and made a success of it. Yet it was still a very junior command. He was still
carrying out orders more than he was giving them. That, arguably,
in the context of his whole career, was always his best role. The ultimate test would not come for twenty-five years when he was really
in command of his own operation and had to set his own direction
for himself.

For the last phase of Heath's war service, 107 HAA Regiment
formed part of the Allied army of occupation stationed initially in
Hanover and subsequently in Hanelm. Comfortably housed in a
large modern sanatorium with excellent recreation facilities, with the
surviving amenities of Hanover at the disposal of the occupying
forces and the use of a leave centre magnificently situated in the
Hartz mountains, it was – in the words of the regimental history –
'by no means an arduous life'.[22] Their responsibilities included running a large prisoner-of-war camp as well as rounding up displaced
persons, maintaining curfew and generally enforcing law and order.
More distressingly, some of the men were involved in clearing up
the horror of Belsen. But they enjoyed a good deal of leave, which

enabled Heath to revisit some of the places he had last seen before the war in 1937 and 1939. He returned to Düsseldorf and found it devastated. 'The centre was nothing but a mass of rubble. It proved impossible for me to find my way to the street, let alone the house, where I had stayed as a student.'[23] He also revisited Frankfurt, similarly destroyed, and Nuremberg, where nine years earlier he had seen the Nazi leaders strutting in their pomp. Now he attended the War Crimes Tribunal and saw Goering, Hess, Ribbentrop and the other survivors brought to retribution.

On all the men of the Allied armies what they had seen as they made their way across a shattered Europe in 1944–5 made an unforgettable impact: first, the carnage and the terrible destruction wreaked by modern war – much of it, in the case of 107 HAA, by their own guns; second, the wonderful outpouring of gratitude and relief their arrival had brought to liberated Frenchmen, Belgians and Dutch; and, third, the even greater destruction and more mixed emotions they found in occupied, defeated Germany. On Ted Heath, however – possibly because of his pre-war travels and his early opposition to fascism, possibly because his love of music inoculated him against crude anti-Germanism – the experience of the liberation and occupation had an especially profound effect. Having known the ruined German cities as they were before the war, he felt an obligation to European culture to try to restore them. In his book *Travels: People and Places in My Life*, he recalls taking the German commander round the remains of Hanover:

> At the end of the tour I said to him, 'This is going to be a very long job. It will take a quarter of a century to clear up this town.' 'If you British will only get off our backs,' he replied, 'we'll have this city in good shape in ten years,' He proved to be right.[24]

There can be no doubt that the Second World War confirmed and deepened in Ted Heath, even more than in most of his generation, the idea that the great task of the future was European reconstruction and unity. *Travels* was written thirty years later, in 1977. But there is no reason to doubt that what he wrote then, at the end of the chapter describing his wartime experience and the Nuremberg trials, truly represents what he felt in 1946.

> As I left the court I knew that those evil things had been beaten back and their perpetrators brought to justice. But at what a cost. Europe had once more destroyed itself. This must never be

·allowed to happen again. My generation could not live in the past; we had to work for the future. We were surrounded by destruction, homelessness, hunger and despair. Only by working together had we any hope of creating a society which would uphold the true values of European civilisation. Reconciliation and reconstruction must be our tasks. I did not realize then that it would be my preoccupation for the next thirty years.[25]

In September 1945 Heath was posted as second-in-command to another heavy anti-aircraft regiment, 86 (HAC) HAA – the Honourable Artillery Company, the oldest regiment in the British army and one of the most socially exclusive. For three months, in the absence of a commanding officer, he was acting CO with the temporary rank of Lieutenant-Colonel, based at Osnabruck, halfway between Hanover and the Dutch border. Whether or not it was a transfer he had deliberately sought, or one that was granted him with an eye to a future political career, it was a connection which he assiduously cultivated, steeping himself in the history of the regiment, applying successfully to become a member of the Honourable Company and maintaining the connection as a territorial after the war. In 1947 he was appointed commanding officer of the 2nd Regiment of the HAC and for three years from 1951 he held the position of Master Gunner within the Tower of London – responsible for firing salutes on the King's birthday and similar occasions. His reluctance to let go of the army is indicative of how much it had meant to him. He always retained from his army experience a distinctly military outlook and style, carrying with him into civilian life a brisk, problem-solving approach to the tasks that confronted him and an expectation – evident in his conduct as Eden's and then Macmillan's Chief Whip (a job not unlike being Adjutant to a regiment) and later as Prime Minister himself – that orders will be followed and no questions asked. His military experience was a factor whose importance cannot be exaggerated in shaping Heath's understanding of political leadership.

He was allowed home on leave in June 1946 and was finally demobbed in August. He had had a successful war – not spectacular, but very definitely meeting that essential requirement for an aspiring politician in the postwar world, a 'good' war. (He was mentioned in dispatches and had been awarded the MBE.) On his way home, by chance, he ran into his Oxford Union contemporary, Ashley Bramall, in the officers' bar at Tournai. Bramall had already stood unsuccessfully as a Labour candidate in the 1945 General Election; within a few months he was to enter the House of Commons at a by-election as Member for Bexley. But the Oxford Union was now a distant memory. Several of his contemporaries were already ahead of him on the political ladder. Gray's Inn no longer attracted, if it ever had. He was thirty. The question posed itself with some urgency for Lieutenant-Colonel Heath as he returned to Mr Attlee's Labour Britain. What next?

4

Some False Starts

THE next three and a half years, from the summer of 1946 to the beginning of 1950, were the most unsettled of Heath's life. He had the problem, if he was to pursue his political ambition, first of finding a winnable seat in time for the next Election and then of finding some way of earning his living that would allow him to nurse it. Briefly he embarked on what might have been a successful career in the Civil Service; but this could not be combined with politics and he had to give it up when he was adopted for a constituency – even though it was not one which he had any certainty of winning. Eventually the cards fell fortunately for him: within five years of the end of the war he was successfully launched on the career he cherished with a constituency which, as it happened, would last him the rest of his life. In August 1946, however, the future looked very uncertain.

During the war William and Edith had been evacuated from Broadstairs to Sutton, where William had worked for the local council. Now they were back at 4 King Edward Avenue and William was starting up his business again: the end of the war was a good time to be a builder. John, like Teddy, had survived the war unscathed, finishing up as a craftsman in the REME (Royal Electrical and Mechanical Engineers), but he declined to join his father: he worked for a time in a radio shop in Broadstairs High Street, then qualified as a local authority building inspector. At the same time he was 'walking out' with Marian Easton, a bright girl several years younger than himself – she was only seventeen – whose parents had just moved to Broadstairs. They were married in October 1947. Introduced into the close-knit family at just this period of greatest uncertainty in Teddy's life, Marian had an unrivalled opportunity to observe her fiancé's strange and enigmatic older brother. Twenty years later she wrote down her recollections.[1]

As a nomadic newcomer to Broadstairs, she liked the stability of the Heaths, rooted in Thanet for generations. She found 'Helmdon', as 4 King Edward Avenue was called, almost excessively neat and tidy – 'the most uncomfortable three-piece suite I've ever sat upon', the 'special china' brought out only on very rare occasions, the bedrooms upstairs 'neat and austere'; but she evidently got on well with her prospective mother-in-law, despite noting – something she might have been expected to resent on John's behalf – that the household was disproportionately centred on Teddy, even though he was there only at weekends. His piano still took up one wall of the sitting-room, and was covered with photographs – 'mainly of Teddy at various stages of development'. In the kitchen was a radiogram ('I never saw any records in the house, but the radio was much used, especially by Teddy, who likes his music turned on full blast') and two comfortable chairs. ('Teddy usually commandeered one and Mummy would sit for hours in the other knitting socks. She was always knitting socks.') Both John and his father helped with the washing up, 'but Teddy was never expected to'. Teddy's bedroom, in contrast to the neatness of every other room in the house, 'was so full of books you had to clamber over them to make the bed'.

Teddy himself was aloof and preoccupied. 'He spent hours without speaking, had no time for visitors at home and would either disappear behind a book or retire to his room if anyone called.' Marian's father once came to lunch 'and was astounded to find Teddy walking in and out of the rooms without seemingly seeing anyone. He was so wrapped up in his thoughts and plans for the future.' She and John would see him 'striding along the seafront or cliffs, immersed in thought, never pausing for more than a brief nod'. He was so much the elder brother – and had in addition put on so much weight – that Marian, when she first saw him, mistook him for his own uncle, aged nearer forty-five than thirty. 'He preferred the company of mature people and except for an occasional game of tennis didn't seek out younger ones.'

And yet, when she did get to know him, 'I felt he had a sense of fun, a sense of humour that would always be boyish, every ounce of him quivering with laughter if something appealed as funny.' Also, curiously, he was 'very clannish and expected us all to do things as a family'. When he suddenly came out of himself and wanted his family, he expected them to be there; and that now included Marian. 'The only quarrel we ever had was when John and I had made arrangements to go on the river with some cousins and Teddy thought we should go on a family picnic . . . We did go on the river and hated every minute of it, knowing that Mummy was shedding silent tears on a picnic for three because Teddy had been upset.'

When John and Marian were married, Edith insisted that Teddy should be best man – though John would have preferred a friend of his own age. In his speech he made a joke of saying that as there were no bridesmaids he felt he had in no way committed himself. Marian also noted that he was 'the only one not to kiss the bride'. The unspoken question was clearly when – if at all – Teddy himself would marry.

He had never shown much interest in girls. He had lived his life – at school, at Oxford, in the army – in predominantly male institutions in which women played little part. His ambition was fixed on the overwhelmingly male world of politics; his recreations were music and the church, where women's role was firmly secondary. At Oxford he had needed soprano and alto voices for his choirs, but had been strongly opposed to admitting women undergraduates to the Union. In the army he had as little to do with ATS girls as possible and did not misbehave himself with liberated Belgians. He gave the impression of regarding women as by definition frivolous; others might waste their time with them, but they had no place in the serious business of his life.

Yet many men like this, with no very high view of the purpose or abilities of women, nevertheless acquire wives at the appropriate stage of their careers. It is a recognisable English pattern which calls for no great romance, and one which Ted Heath could easily have followed. Though he seems to have made no women friends at Oxford, Madron Seligman's mother ran a sort of young people's *salon* in London in the vacations at which he met several well-connected girls, any of whom might have been a political asset to him; and there were at least two nice girls in Broadstairs whom he might have married – girls whom his mother would have been happy to have seen him marry.

The more important of these was Kay Raven, a local doctor's daughter whom he had first met as a boy when still at school. They had remained good friends while he was at Oxford: they played tennis together and shared a love of music. She became secretary of the Broadstairs carol concerts which he organised in emulation of Sir Hugh Allen's in Oxford. After the war, Kay taught in a boys' prep school but she was back in Broadstairs in the holidays and was still, according to Marian Easton, 'looked on by all as Teddy's girlfriend'. In reality it was more a brother–sister relationship than anything deeper. She was treated – and appears to have been happy to regard herself – as part of the family. 'Teddy never seemed very attentive, yet she didn't seem to mind, often dropping in to bring Mummy small presents.' When Marian married John, Kay wrote to her that she was marrying into 'the nicest family in Broadstairs'. There seems to have been an expectation that she would eventually do the same. She and Teddy went to concerts and even dances together. George Chadd for one believes that she wanted to marry him. But in the end she got tired of waiting for him and married someone else. Marian remembers that Edith was very upset at the news, and so perhaps in his own way was Teddy, though he would not show it. He probably knew that if he was ever going to marry anyone it would be Kay.

So why did he not? One possibility, which cannot be dismissed out of hand – if only because it is whispered today of any bachelor – is that he was homosexual. There is no positive evidence for this at all, except for the faintest unsubstantiated rumour of an incident at the beginning of the war.[2] All that can be said is that he had an exceptionally close relationship with his mother, and a somewhat wary relationship with his father, which is consistent with one common pattern of homosexuality: he reacted – under his mother's influence – primly and pointedly against his father's easy relations with women. It is not impossible that he is a latent or repressed homosexual. The alternatives are that he is a repressed heterosexual or that he is simply asexual.

He does not dislike women. He is contemptuous of many women, and he has always disliked a certain type of strident, bossy woman familiar in the Conservative Party. He does not, generally speaking, like working with women. But he has had, in the course of his life, and particularly as he has got older, a number of close women friends: from these it is possible to generalise that he likes clever women who stand up to him, but do so humorously – who do not take him quite seriously, but tease him and allow him to tease them without taking offence; he likes to banter with women. This suggests not an indifference to women – he is surprisingly observant of dresses and hairstyles, for instance, though his comment will often be derisively unflattering – so much as a need to keep them at a distance. Not hostility to women, but a nervousness which can best be disguised by mocking humour. This would be consistent with repressed heterosexuality: a man not used to women, by no means unaware of their attraction but unable to handle it.

The third, frequently asserted, alternative is that he is asexual – lacking sexual instincts of any sort, normal or abnormal, perfectly untroubled by the needs and temptations which other men find so unsettling. Clearly sexual drive varies greatly from individual to individual. Many men have very little; for others sex is an occasional necessity to be satisfied quickly and without fuss. Ted Heath might well be one of these. It is a delusion of our time, promoted by the popular media, that sex is a matter of dominating importance to everyone. For many it is not important at all. And yet Heath does not quite fit this pattern. He conveys too strongly the sense of repression. He is too puritanical. He has a powerful fear of scandal, knowing well how it can ruin a career. It is almost as if he did have some fleeting episode to hide, or could not wholly trust himself. In 1958 he saw his Oxford contemporary Ian Harvey brought down by an incident in Kensington Gardens; and it is said that as Chief Whip he took a close interest in the skeletons in other Tories' cupboards. Whenever the press has tried to link his name with a woman friend he has dropped her abruptly and ruthlessly. He is exceptionally unrelaxed about the whole subject. What all this suggests is not that he lacks a sexual side to his nature but that he has suppressed it. Whether what he has suppressed might have been homosexual or heterosexual is then beside the point. It has been thoroughly sublimated in politics.

From the beginning of his life Heath was an exceptionally serious-minded, well-behaved and ambitious boy, determined to do well. He was also unusually self-motivated and self-sufficient. As a result, by the time he was thirty and trying to break into politics, he neither wanted nor needed a partner. He was too single-mindedly pre-occupied with pursuing his career to have the time to spare for much social recreation, let alone the encumbrances of a wife and possible family; and unlike most men, whose equally urgent ambitions do not seem to preclude finding time to marry, he did not appear to need the support of a wife to partner him on his journey. He travels fastest who travels alone; Ted Heath also travels most happily alone.

Yet he still might have married Kay Raven if she had been prepared to wait a little longer, or perhaps had pressed him. Marriage was the conventional thing for a young man to do around the age of thirty, and he was a very conventional young man. He liked her, she shared his love of music and – most important – he was used to her being there. There are indications that he did expect to marry some time. Questioned at his adoption meeting at Bexley in 1947, he replied that he had 'no prejudice against matrimony. I just think that it is not a matter that should be rushed.'[3] This might have been simply politic, but it may equally have expressed exactly what he felt. The same year he remarked to Madron Seligman, who had mentioned how 'extremely capable' his own wife was, 'That's one thing a wife must be – capable.'[4] Kay would have fitted the description admirably. Then in 1950 George Chadd married: Heath was best man, and Chadd asked him directly when he was going to follow suit. He replied guardedly, 'We can see daylight.'[5]

This was three months after his election to Parliament. It may be that now he felt for the first time that he could afford to marry. What prevented him asking Kay earlier may simply have been that he had no home of his own to offer her and was too responsible, too honourable or too old-fashioned to think of marrying until he had. Meanwhile he was too shy, too proper or too self-absorbed to behave in any way like a suitor – George Chadd tells of Heath characteristically not thinking to escort Kay home after an HAC ball, leaving her to walk to her door up an unmade road in high-heeled shoes and long dress[6] – but took it for granted that she would always be there when he was ready; until one day she was not. In 1951 she married a young former airman, Wing-Commander Richard Buckwell. Heath was temporarily upset, but the story that he still kept her photograph beside his bed ten years later is disputed by those who knew his rooms in Albany in the 1960s and are sure they would have seen it. Heath probably knew then that he would not marry anyone else; but he is unlikely to have been greatly bothered.

In the late 1940s, by contrast with today – when wives are routinely interviewed with their husbands and a presentable spouse is an essential requirement for a would-be Conservative candidate – being unmarried was not a handicap to him in seeking a seat: if anything, Bexley felt it an advantage. Once in the House, it was an undoubted benefit to him over the next fourteen years, as a Whip and later as a Minister, to be unencumbered. When he became Leader of the Opposition the question was persistently raised whether the British public would elect a bachelor Prime Minister, assumed to be out of touch with family life and unable to appeal to women. But this doubt was laid to rest in 1970; there is no evidence that his lack of a wife was an electoral factor working against the Conservatives, and a good deal that he actually appealed more to women than to men. Only in Downing Street did his bachelorhood finally tell against him, and then not with the electorate but rather because it deprived him of any source of human companionship and disinterested advice when the going got rough: unlike other harassed prime ministers Heath had no one with whom he could let his hair down in the evening, no one to prop up his morale when things went badly or puncture his pride when they went well – in short to maintain his sense of perspective. In February 1974 for the first time he may have felt lonely. But that was twenty-five years in the future. There is no evidence that on his way to the top his remarkable self-sufficiency was anything but a source of strength.

On coming out of the army in the summer of 1946, Heath's first move was to sit the Civil Service entrance examination. He passed equal top, with another Balliol man, Ashley Raeburn. The contrast with his second class degree exemplifies the particular quality of his mind: not an abstract intellectual, he was exactly the sort of clear, practical, well-organised thinker the administrative grade of the Civil Service is always looking for. Several officials who served him as a Minister in the years to come reckoned that he would have made an outstanding Permanent Secretary: he was in many ways much better suited to administration than to politics. It was not merely a question of shyness and lack of personal projection: the instinctively unideological – almost apolitical – cast of his mind seemed made for the Whitehall backroom rather than the public platform. In the end it was his lack of political sensitivity that let him down. The puzzle is why he was so determined to choose politics, when he appeared to have the Civil Service at his feet. One reason was ambition, the deep compulsion not only to get to the top but to be seen to get to the top which the Civil Service could never satisfy. But he was also disappointed that, instead of the Treasury, as he might reasonably have expected, he was allocated to the Ministry of Civil Aviation.

Heath himself is said to have once confided that had he been assigned to the Treasury in 1946 he might have stayed there and risen to become, perhaps, Permanent Secretary or Secretary to the Cabinet instead of going for a political career.[7] It is a fascinating thought; but in fact the choice may not have arisen in quite this form. The reason he was not offered the Treasury was probably that he had already, in applying to the Civil Service, made clear his political ambitions: his purpose, as recorded at the time by Peter Masefield, the head of the long-term planning and projects directorate within the Ministry to which he was actually assigned, was frankly 'to gain experience of the workings of the Civil Service machine from the inside'. 'Whether an odd quirk decided that this objective was "not quite cricket" in a budding politician, I know not. But Ted was immediately despatched to what was clearly a somewhat unorthodox and untypical department – my newly-formed directorate. From there, however, he was able to range widely throughout the Ministry's tasks.'[8] It turned out to be an excellent and stimulating appointment.

Masefield was a temporary Civil Servant, a leading aviation correspondent seconded by Lord Beaverbrook during the war to advise on the future of civil aviation; he headed the long-term planning directorate for only two years before moving on to become chief executive of BEA, followed by a string of other jobs in the airline industry. Heath was one of a team of three helping him, and in turn had three assistants of his own, all housed on the second floor of Aerial House in the Strand. For a small unit they had wide responsibilities, covering the development of British civil aircraft, the structure of the airline industry, airports, air safety and light aviation. They poked their noses into everything. In the terminology of twenty years later, they acted as a sort of 'think tank' within the ministry: Heath almost certainly had his own brief Whitehall experience very much in mind when he set up the Central Policy Review Staff in 1970. One of his particular duties in 1946–7 was to represent Masefield on the London Airport Planning Committee, concerned with the long-term development and expansion of Heathrow: terminals, covered walk-ways, car parks, planning for future growth. 'Ted Heath put in a lot of time and work,' Masefield recalled. 'He used to go and fight on the committee and come back and cry on my shoulder about all the spokes put in the wheel by bumbledom.'[9] One tangible achievement concerned the ill-fated Comet, then being developed. Heath and another member of the unit did some research on runway strengths around the world and showed that most of the airports in the Far East could not have taken the plane with its proposed single-wheel undercarriage. As a direct result of their work it was modified to a multiple-wheel bogey. 'They fought quite a battle to get the change,' Masefield remembers. 'Without it, the Comets would not have been able to use the Kangaroo route and the Spring-bok route, and BOAC would not have been able to buy them.'[10]

Masefield wrote a contemporary report on Heath which testifies to the excellent impression he made. As well as admiring his efficiency, Masefield also evidently liked him:

Ted Heath has a direct logic which is both stimulating and helpful. And, with all, when you get to know him (which isn't easy) he is a sensitive and warm-hearted chap who has a direct approach and an endearing sense of the ridiculous – which we so often encounter.

But I fear that I shall not have him here for long because, outside the office, he lives and dreams politics and, with the Civil Service machine the way it is, as soon as he is adopted for a parliamentary seat he will have to resign.[11]

So it was. After only twelve months, Heath did win adoption for a seat. Masefield tried to intercede to keep him. 'I sent him off to see Armstrong, in Establishments' – this was the future Sir William Armstrong, twenty-three years later Heath's most trusted adviser – 'but there was no way around it . . . he had to leave, and leave immediately . . . He was really quite bothered about it. He was suddenly pitchforked out of a job which he thoroughly enjoyed and he was very sad about it.'[12] He might well have had regrets about leaving a sphere in which he was so clearly in his element. But his year in Whitehall had served its purpose. He had seen the working of the machine from the inside: another stage in his learning process. Despite his impatience with some of the 'bumbledom' he had encountered, he was impressed. At his adoption meeting at Bexley he went out of his way to defend the integrity of Civil Servants against allegations that they were obstructing the Labour Government.[13] As a Minister in years to come he always appreciated and understood the Civil Service and lost no opportunity to show his high regard for it. No other modern Prime Minister – not even Harold Wilson, who spent the war as a temporary Civil Servant with the Board of Trade – has taken a closer or more sympathetic interest in the machinery of government.

Heath's political prospects in 1946 were for some time not so rosy. The war had pushed his Oxford triumphs into a distant past. There was no shortage of idealistic young Tories coming out of the forces as keen as he to help remake the postwar world, while a good many former Members unseated by the Labour landslide were equally anxious to get back into the House to resume their interrupted careers. The Labour tide was at its flood, and the way back for the Conservatives looked long and hard. Among Heath's Oxford contemporaries it was those on the Labour side who were getting ahead. Christopher Mayhew was already in office. (So too was the dark horse Harold Wilson, whom no one had noticed at Oxford.) There were two trends, however, from which Heath could take encouragement. There was a clear disposition in the constituency associations, reinforced by the shock of 1945, to go for youth in the selection of new candidates; in addition Conservative Central Office, recognising the need to broaden the social base of the party, was at last beginning to put pressure on the constituencies to drop their expectation that candidates should pay most of their own expenses. Lord Woolton's overdue reforms were designed specifically to encourage the selection of poor but able candidates like Ted Heath.

Even so, there was a crowd of hopefuls in this category. Three of the ablest – Iain Macleod, Reginald Maudling and Enoch Powell, already picked out as high flyers – had been recruited to working with Rab Butler in the Conservative Research Department, reformulating Tory policy to meet the vastly increased expectations of the postwar world. They were already on the inside track in a way that Heath in the Ministry of Civil Aviation was not. But Heath knew Michael Fraser, then on the staff and soon to be Director of the Research Department, who had briefly instructed him in anti-aircraft gunnery during the war. He got himself placed on the approved

Central Office list of prospective candidates. Then he set about applying for constituencies – concentrating in his own south-eastern area.

He was shortlisted for three before he was successful: Ashford (where he lost out to William Deedes – locally well connected with the Military Cross to boot); East Fulham (a Labour seat where he was probably fortunate to come second to Vyvyan Adams, one of the pre-war brigade trying unsuccessfully to make a comeback); and Sevenoaks (where he came no better than fourth behind John Rodgers). In all three cases – Woolton notwithstanding – he was beaten by candidates of traditional public school background. His luck changed only when his name came to the attention of a constituency chairman who was consciously looking for something different.

Though only a dozen miles from Sevenoaks, Bexley was another world – not rural but suburban Kent, a south London dormitory whose population had suddenly mushroomed since the electrification of the commuter line in the 1930s. Where formerly had been the separate villages of Old Bexley, Bexleyheath and Welling, there was now a sprawl of indistinguishable neat semi-detacheds and new council estates, densely populated with white-collar workers, 'artisans' and technicians, a large homogeneous population of the lower-middle class and upwardly mobile skilled working class. A new sort of constituency called for a new sort of Tory. In 1945 it had been won comfortably by Labour with a majority of over 11,000. At a by-election the following year, however, Ashley Bramall had held it with a majority reduced to just 1,851. (The Labour Government was proud of its record of losing not a single by-election in the six years after 1945; but it came quite close to losing Bexley.) Following his second defeat, however, the Tory candidate, Colonel Lockwood (another pre-war Member seeking a comeback) went off to claim a winnable seat in Romford. In July 1947 Bexley adopted a self-made businessman named Lewis May. But only six weeks later May resigned, following 'differences of understanding as to your candidate's prerogative'.[14] (This probably meant that he could not spare the time from his business that the constituency felt entitled to demand.) So the local Tories needed yet another new candidate. This time the chairman, Edward Dines, knew what he wanted: neither another pre-war toff nor another rough diamond but a 'local boy made good', a scholarship boy from an 'ordinary' background similar to that of the constituents he hoped to represent, willing to work hard to win the seat.[15] It could have been an identikit picture of Ted Heath.

From Heath's point of view, too, Bexley was nearly perfect – not a safe seat, but a winnable one and moreover neatly situated on the way from London to Broadstairs: the A2 ran through Bexleyheath and Welling. Even the name Bexleyheath was curiously apt. Yet Heath did not put his own name forward. Dines heard of him, perhaps from Sevenoaks, and asked the agent to find out more about him. He was impressed by what he heard, and still more by the fact that Heath was away in camp with his regiment of the HAC. A telegram was sent inviting him to attend a selection meeting in Bexley on 18 October 1947. He was one of three candidates interviewed – the others were a *Times* journalist and the wife of the Member for Hove – but he carried the day easily; the selection committee of two men and five women recommended him to the full executive, which endorsed him overwhelmingly. 'To me', Dines congratulated himself, 'he personified the best sort of young British ex-serviceman. He was modest. He was very enthusiastic about it all. He'd got a grasp of the political situation. He'd travelled about a bit, too.'[16] The ladies on the committee did not mind in the least that he was not married; they were charmed. 'That half-smile of his is what I will always remember,' one recalled in 1970. 'It was not the broad grin which we are used to from him now, but a shy kind of half-smile.'[17]

He was formally adopted at an enthusiastic meeting on 7 November. The Tories had just gained four seats on the district council and they felt confident that they were on the way back. Heath's speech met this mood, asserting that the country was beginning to tire of the Labour Government:

> The people are tired of its specious policy . . . their lack of leadership, their maladministration, their lack of foresight and their crises. Above all they are tired of the dogma of nationalisation . . . the centralisation of power which is putting the ordinary citizen in a straitjacket.

He attacked socialist controls which led only to rationing and shortages. But he also asked his own party to face up to the legacy of distrust it still carried from the 1930s. What they must get across, he urged – echoing Anthony Eden's phrase to the previous year's Tory conference – was the party's 'fundamental belief in a property-owning democracy', an idea which was 'particularly applicable to the electors of this area'. In addition he wanted to associate the Conservatives with a commitment to ensuring 'a minimum standard of life' for all, with incentives to encourage hard work and enterprise; and a tripartite approach by Government, employers and unions together to promote good relations in industry.[18] This was all conventional stuff for a young self-consciously progressive Tory, fully in line with the overhaul of party attitudes being undertaken by Butler's young men in Central Office.

Over the following weeks and months the new candidate spent all the time he could in Bexley, touring the streets with a loudspeaker, canvassing the council estates and getting to know the party activists. The local paper is full of pictures of him grinning nervously at the Women's Conservative Luncheon Club, animatedly indicating the size of 'one that got away' at the Bexleyheath Angling Society dinner (held in the Conservative Club), posing awkwardly alone amid the bright young things at the Conservative Association Ball and guest of honour at the Association's Christmas lunch – putting down roots that have assured him unwavering support now for more than forty years. He spoke regularly to the different branches of the association, helping to increase the membership spectacularly, held several public debates on issues of the day with Ashley Bramall (drawing audiences – in the infancy of television – of several hundred), and exerted himself in every way to get himself known. Fortunately, in accordance with new Tory practice he was not expected to finance the association. Nevertheless, having resigned from the Civil Service, he had to get a job that would allow him time for all this single-minded politicking.

On the recommendation of the Oxford University Appointments Board he found what must have seemed a suitable one as news editor of the *Church Times*. Apart from the odd article in *Isis* he had no experience of journalism, nor had he any gift for it. But he was a loyal member of the Church of England, the job must have seemed likely to be undemanding, it paid pretty well (£650 a year, £200 more than he was getting in the Civil Service) and it would sound eminently respectable in Bexley. He quickly found that he had made a mistake. He did not get on with the editor, who did not really want a news editor at all, was unsympathetic to Heath's political ambitions and took delight in wasting his time in uncongenial theological arguments when he wanted to get away to Bexley. The work was largely office administration and sub-editing: it has been said that he did very little writing himself. In fact, he may have done more than he let on. The paper had a weekly summary of world and domestic news which was both political and opinionated. It would have been difficult for the news editor not to contribute to such a column; moreover many of the views expressed – on the nationalisation of steel, on the 1949 devaluation, on the Labour party – are strikingly close to Heath's as he was simultaneously voicing them in Bexley. It is hard to believe that he did not write much of this political comment. Nevertheless he was reputedly 'bored stiff',[19] describing

62

himself ironically to friends as 'a political fish in holy water'. Even in these surroundings, however, his capacity to lead a small team shone through. 'After a couple of months', one of the other two members of the tiny staff recalled, 'he had us eating out of his hands. He did it by force of personality, mainly by making it obvious how hard he worked himself.'[20] It was another task to be done and he did it conscientiously. But it had no place in his preparation for a life in politics. He was not learning anything. He stayed in Portugal Street from January 1948 to October 1949, by which time the General Election on which his hopes were pinned was drawing very near. Then he threw it in, thinking he could get more relevant experience from a spell in the City. The local papers in Bexley never even knew that he had worked on the *Church Times*. It was an interlude which he himself chose to forget: he has always omitted it from his entry in *Who's Who*. He did finally come clean to the House of Commons in 1967, however, claiming most unconvincingly that 'every time I go into a newspaper office today I have only to get the smell of ink for the same tingle to be in the blood again'.[21]

Through an acquaintance, he managed to get himself an introduction to the managing director of the merchant bankers Brown, Shipley, and persuaded them to take him on as a trainee. Although at thirty-three he was old for a trainee, and made no pretence of intending to make Brown, Shipley his career, the directors were impressed with his straightforwardness and eagerness to learn. They agreed to take him for one year, at a nominal salary of £200 plus lunches, during which time he was given a crash introduction to the various branches of the banking business – handling cheques, credit, securities and investments, foreign exchange. 'We realized very early his mental ability,' one of the directors remembered. 'He was outstanding, extremely quick and worked very hard. He made the fullest possible use of the training. He was shy and reserved at first . . . but once he had established a personal relationship he was a wonderful friend.' Unlike the editor of the *Church Times*, his superiors at Brown, Shipley were sympathetic to his political aspirations. 'Large numbers of people here went to help him in his election campaign. People don't do that unless they like a man.'[22]

In fact Heath's connection with Brown, Shipley lasted longer than originally envisaged. He stayed with them for eighteen months after his election to Parliament, resigning only when he became a Government Whip in 1951; he briefly rejoined in a more senior capacity on losing office in October 1964, resigning again when he became Leader of the Opposition the following summer. This too, however, he chose to leave unrecorded in *Who's Who*.

During 1948 and 1949, while enduring his chores on the *Church Times*, he had continued to spend all the time he could in Bexley. Before he was adopted he had been lodging during the week with a Balliol friend, Timothy Bligh (later to be Harold Macmillan's private secretary in Downing Street) at Old Swanley, just a few miles down the road; and this remained his base for the next few years. Even when, after he was elected, he got a flat of his own in London, his life continued to be lived for the next thirty years along the same London–Bexley–Broadstairs axis. In 1949 his salary enabled him to afford his first car, 'a second-hand MG sports with red wheels',[23] which facilitated his continuous dashing back and forth along the clogged A2. ('He loved to drive fast,' his former sister-in-law Marian Evans recalled, 'with every nerve concentrated on the road,' sarcastically impatient of slower drivers, adept at making 'quickly thought out diversions to avoid jams or hold-ups').[24] When he joined Brown, Shipley, however, he took a salary cut of more than two-thirds; money for the next few months was very tight – an extra incentive, if he needed one, to make sure of securing an MP's salary (then £1,000) as soon as possible.

As the 1950 General Election approached, the Bexley Conservative Association which he had been nursing so strenuously suddenly faced a crisis which threatened the reward of all his effort. Towards the end of 1949 the agent left at a day's notice, leaving the Association all but bankrupt: he had seriously overspent on the local elections, leaving nothing for the parliamentary test to come. The crisis was surmounted, partly by vigorous action by Heath himself – he persuaded five wealthy supporters to put up £50 each, which the president more than matched, giving an election fighting fund of £750 – but mainly by the arrival of a new agent, Reg Pye, who was to run the constituency with immense success for the next twenty-five years. Eight years older than Heath, a rubber planter in Sumatra before the war, Pye immediately formed with Heath an exceptionally close agent/candidate relationship. Heath came to rely absolutely on Pye to take care of the organisational side of his constituency when he was fully taken up with parliamentary and ministerial duties; over the years he transformed it from a Labour marginal into a Tory stronghold. During elections and whenever he needed to stay overnight in the constituency Heath stayed with the Pyes, treating their flat above the Association office as his temporary home. In December 1949, however, Pye was the new boy with very little time to learn. Then it was Heath who showed him the constituency, driving him round every street, demonstrating the intimate knowledge of it he had gained in the previous two years. From that moment Pye had no doubt that Heath meant to go right to the top.

The election was called two months later. It was clear that Bexley was likely to be very close. Labour's large majority in 1945 had been an aberration, due to the run-down state of the Conservative organisation, now greatly improved. But the closing of the gap in 1946 had also been due very considerably to the absence of a Liberal candidate; in 1945 the Liberal had won nearly 6,000 votes, most of which had evidently gone to the Conservative in 1946. Now the Liberals were back in the field with an energetic new candidate who clearly threatened Heath's chances. On the other hand, the size of the electorate had increased by 11,000 since 1945, so all predictions were uncertain. In addition, there was a fourth candidate, a Communist, who could only take votes from Bramall.

At his formal adoption meeting Heath was introduced as a local man★ and an economist, a former Civil Servant, now a banker who understood the country's problems (no mention of the *Church Times*) and a 'future statesman'.[26] He also demonstrated his versatility by playing the national anthem on the piano! Unlike some ex-servicemen, he refused absolutely to be known as Colonel Heath; but his publicity gave prominence to his MBE. The local paper described him as having special knowledge of economics and foreign affairs. This reflected his speeches in the constituency over the previous two years: in addition to continuing to berate the Government for crippling the economy with doctrinaire controls, he had not hesitated to range more widely – condemning the Soviet absorption of Czechoslovakia in March 1948, praising the 'amazing clarity and truth' of Churchill's 'iron curtain' speech,[27] responding defiantly to the announcement of the Soviet nuclear bomb in September 1949 ('Come what may we shall not yield to Russian tyranny, or Russia with the atom bomb')[28] and warning, in January 1948, of the 'dangerous psychological condition' of the Germans who, he thought, had not accepted the blame for the war. From his knowledge of German mentality gained before the war he believed that they still looked back on the Hitler years as a good time: the challenge facing the Allies was to bring them to democracy, but this was difficult so long as the country was starving. It was necessary, he concluded, to give Germany the hope of recovery, while at the same time preventing it from ever again becoming 'a fighting unit'.[29] This was an interestingly double-edged view in 1948, surprisingly unforgiving yet constructive: it underlines what was always to be in Heath's view the primary purpose of European integration, to contain Germany and prevent the possibility of another German war.

★ He was 'born in Kent, went to school in Kent, lived in Kent and understood Kentish people'; to which a heckler cheerfully added, 'And for all we care he can die in Kent!'[25]

His domestic line was more conventional – heaping scorn on Labour's mismanagement of the economy, nationalisation, rationing, shortages and all the ills of socialism, culminating in devaluation, strangling the initiative and enterprise which alone could stimulate production and maintain full employment when Marshall Aid ran out. Full employment was the principal battleground, in Bexley as elsewhere. Bramall made it the cornerstone of Labour's record, alleging that the Tories positively wanted to return to an unemployment level of around a million, to 'teach the workers a lesson'.[30] Heath indignantly denied it, denying that full employment owed anything to Labour and pledging the Tories to maintain it. But, as he had predicted in 1947, he had to fight at least in part on the defensive, to dispel the suspicion that the old Tory party had not really changed. When Bramall charged that the Tories were a class party, he tacitly admitted that in the past they had been but insisted that now they represented 'a cross-section of the community'.[31] It was the same when the election campaign proper started: he spent much of his time refuting 'Labour lies'.[32] The high point of the campaign was a debate on unemployment in the Scouts' Hall, Bexleyheath, before an audience of over 800, with hundreds more locked out. Bramall repeated his claim that the Tories would deliberately increase unemployment as an instrument of policy, quoting a number of somewhat obscure industrialists in support; Heath vigorously denied it, describing mass long-term unemployment as 'the worst social affliction except tyranny'.[33] The *Bexleyheath Observer* was even-handed in its praise of both candidates, but its report shows Heath to have had the better of the argument.

In other speeches Heath condemned nationalisation and pledged the Conservatives to denationalisation where possible: he had previously indicated, however, that he did not think that it would be possible in many cases. Gas and electricity might possibly be returned to the local authorities; road transport might be denationalised, but not the railways, nor coal, though he thought that the organisation of the coal industry might somehow be 'humanised'.[34] Repeatedly what he objected to in nationalisation was not so much its economic inefficiency as the centralisation of power in the state; he made a running theme of the liberty of the citizen against the overmighty state – echoing Churchill's slogan 'Set the people free'. Identifying Conservatism with the extension of individual opportunity, he advocated co-operation and incentives in place of socialist restrictions; at the same time he promised that a Tory Government would build more houses (encouraging home ownership with 5 per cent deposits) and more schools under the 1944 Act and also maintain support for the National Health Service, making it more efficient by cutting waste.★ In all this, though it accorded with his own conceptions, he was doing no more than following the calculatedly moderate and progressive line laid down by Butler's backroom boys in Central Office. The Tories had determined to come to terms with the Welfare State; they could not hope to return to power by proposing to dismantle it. Internationally, Heath like other candidates put his faith in Churchill, advocating on the one hand the closest possible alliance with the United States and on the other – a radical idea which Churchill in opposition had appeared to favour – 'a united Europe'.[36] When questioned about his attitude to the Empire, however, he replied with an unconvincing bromide that did not suggest enthusiasm. All in all, allowing for the passage of twenty years, the prospectus on which he fought his first election in 1950 differs remarkably little from that which he himself put before the electorate as Leader of the Opposition in 1970.

It was a hard-fought but clean and serious contest: all four candidates were much the same age and treated each other with respect. Bramall brought in the bigger guns to speak for him: Edith Summerskill and Ernest Bevin; Heath – surprisingly in a marginal constituency – had the help of only one sitting Tory MP, Derek Walker-Smith. But he made up for the lack of star speakers by his own energy – anything between two and nine meetings every day – and almost military efficiency. As well as banking colleagues from Brown, Shipley he organised an invasion of territorials from the HAC, rallying to support their Colonel. With Pye's help he began to develop the technique of intensive canvassing, with party workers going ahead of the candidate to bring out voters to meet him, which in years to come became a feature of Conservative electioneering. Faced with such professionalism, Bramall could feel the seat slipping away from him. At his final crowded meeting – the audience was reported to be as high as a thousand – Heath publicly predicted that he would win; Reg Pye thinks he was genuinely confident that he would. But the count was desperately tense. Pye was alarmed to find him absolutely shattered. Even the returning officer collapsed and had to be given first aid. The first count gave Heath a majority of 166. Bramall asked for a recount. At 1.45 am came the final result:

★ He made one blunder, charging that the housing shortage might have been solved more quickly if Nye Bevan (the Minister responsible) and Jennie Lee had had to live with their in-laws, only to be corrected by a well-informed heckler: 'They do!'[35]

Edward Heath (Conservative)	25,854
Ashley Bramall (Labour)	25,721
Mary Hart (Liberal)	4,186
Charles Job (Communist)	481
Conservative majority	133[37]

Heath had won, but only by a whisker and thanks to the intervention of the Communist, whose vote was more than three times his majority. The Liberal vote had held up astonishingly well. No matter: he was in. Moreover Bexley was one of eighty Tory gains around the country which had reduced the Government's overall majority from 142 to only five. (Kent had done particularly well, with several narrow wins in seats adjoining Bexley: only in neighbouring Dartford had a 24-year-old research chemist named Margaret Roberts failed to make much impression on a massive Labour majority.) Labour was left barely clinging on to power. The future for the Conservatives looked bright: the opportunities for a hard-working and ambitious young MP abounded. At the age of thirty-three, after a few false starts, Ted Heath was on his way.

PART TWO

Rising through the Ranks

5

The Class of 1950

THE new Conservative intake at the 1950 General Election was unusually able, reflecting the substantial clear-out of older members by defeat or retirement in and after 1945. Most of the eighty seats which the Tories regained in 1950 were won by new, younger candidates, almost all of whom had fought in the war, welcomed the revolution in expectations which it had wrought, and were keen to help the Conservative party recover the political initiative in the postwar world. Their election in such numbers transformed the party in the House of Commons. It would be an exaggeration to call them classless. Some, certainly – Aubrey Jones, Reginald Bevins, Gerald Nabarro, Bernard Braine – came from quite lowly backgrounds. On the other hand just as many still sprang from the traditional Tory nurseries of Eton or Harrow – Julian Amery, Christopher Soames, Nigel Fisher, William Deedes – or other great public schools: Robert Carr (Westminster), Angus Maude (Rugby), Cuthbert Alport (Haileybury). But perhaps the most significant group came from less famous schools: Reginald Maudling from Merchant Taylors', Iain Macleod and Ian Harvey from Fettes, Enoch Powell from King Edward's, Birmingham, Harold Watkinson from Queen's College, Taunton. These were the sons of the professional middle class – the middle-middle class – coming of age in the Tory party, not before time.

It was as part of this talented intake that Ted Heath arrived, green and eager, at Westminster in February 1950. The 'class of 1950' furnished the competition whom Heath set himself to outstrip in the years ahead. Almost without exception his principal colleagues and rivals on the road to Downing Street were drawn from this outstanding group of parliamentary contemporaries. (When he was deposed it was by the standard-bearer of a later generation, the smaller and less distinguished 'class of 1959'.) Socially he came from the lower end of the spectrum represented in the 'class of 1950'. Nevertheless he had a useful pedigree as a former President of the Oxford Union: he had known Amery, Harvey and others at Oxford and was visibly anxious from the start to identify upwards, with the university group, drawing attention from his poor beginnings. He was unquestionably wise to do so: men like Bevins and Ernest Marples could get so far in the new democratic Tory party, but it was not yet ready to think of them as leadership material. Heath was concerned to assimilate himself thoroughly with the officer class. He was noted as an *habitué* of the Smoking Room, not the tea room.[1]

Yet part of him always remained the small-town boy: he was good at living his life in separate compartments. He never forgot how much he owed to his parents; he still needed their approval and he made sure that they shared in his success. Immediately after his election he took William and Edith and John and Marian out to dinner, their favourite dishes thoughtfully and secretly ordered in advance, which set the pattern for family celebrations at every subsequent step in his career. He showed them round the House of Commons, where Marian embarrassed him by commenting in a loud voice on the outsize Labour MP, Bessie Braddock. And he liked to buy them presents, increasingly lavish as he grew more successful. He still regarded Broadstairs as home, and tried to get back there for at least part of each weekend.

For the first time, however, he had to find a place to live in London. Very briefly he took a flat in the HAC headquarters in the City. This was convenient for Brown, Shipley, where he continued to work in the mornings, but a long way to get back in the evening when the Commons rose. So he moved to a tiny service flat in Artillery Mansions, Victoria Street. He furnished it, with Marian's help, from Harrods. (To her amusement, he had 'discovered' Harrods, opened an account there and 'began to use it as the rest of us did Woolworth's'.)[2] Later he moved again to an equally tiny flat – described by the few friends who saw it as 'a cupboard' – in Petty France. None of these were in any true sense homes; he rarely invited anyone back – they were simply places to sleep. Not until he moved to Albany in 1961 did he begin to entertain in a home he was proud of and happy to show off. These first flats were little more than digs.

His life as a new MP was centred on the House of Commons. He was shown round on his first day by Derek Walker-Smith. He was naïvely excited to have arrived: he dutifully described his first impressions to his constituents with the wide-eyed wonder of a schoolboy: the election of the Speaker, the splendour of the state opening, the thrill of seeing Churchill deal with interruptions. He was impressed that the policeman on the door knew who he was. The basic rules of procedure were familiar from the Union; but he characteristically set himself to learn everything there was to know, steeping himself in the history and practice of Parliament. 'Anyone in the House for the first time has much to learn,' he noted humbly, 'but everyone, friend and foe alike, tries to make it easy for him.'[3] He was determined to be a good House of Commons man.

At the same time, sitting on a majority of 133, he made a point of keeping in close touch with Bexley. In addition to going round all the local groups, attending luncheons and dinners and following up individual grievances – at which he was, and has remained for forty years, assiduous – he held monthly public meetings at which he reported on the month's events in Parliament. He invited groups of supporters from his local party up to the House of Commons and in every way let them share the advantages of having elected a Tory MP. At the same time he maintained his social distance, making it a rule – this was at Reg Pye's shrewd insistence – that he never dined in constituents' houses but only on neutral territory at a local hotel. Pye also kept him away from ladies' coffee mornings, a form of social chat at which he did not shine. Above all, however, he encouraged the Association to raise the money to buy a fine new party headquarters – a whole house, 22 Crook Log, with a garden at the back big enough for garden parties and a flat above for the Pyes. The 1950 election had been fought from a single room: the acquisition of Crook Log gave space for a wide range of social and political activities, from Heath's weekly 'surgery' on Friday evenings to whist drives, luncheon clubs, discussion groups, Young Conservative activities and bazaars. Soon there was some event every day of the week. Having narrowly achieved his bridgehead in Bexley, Heath was digging in in his most efficient military manner for a long occupation.

He asked his first questions in the House in May, asking the Chancellor, Stafford Cripps, about the foreign currency earnings of British civil aviation, with a supplementary specifically about dollar earnings – the first time his voice was heard in the chamber.[4] He followed this up with a number of written questions – about student grants and loans, teacher training and housing allocation.[5] Then during the Whitsun recess he visited Germany to gather material for his maiden speech.

It so happened that this maiden speech assumed an importance in Heath's career which could not have been anticipated at the time he made it. Soon afterwards he became a Whip, and as a result did not speak again in the chamber for more than nine years. His maiden speech therefore became his only significant parliamentary utterance before he became a Cabinet Minister. In addition – whether by design, by accident or by fate – his subject was European unity and specifically the importance of Britain not being left behind by the beginnings of what became the EEC. It could not have been a more appropriate maiden speech for the eventual architect of Britain's belated entry to have on his record to demonstrate the consistency of his European vision.

The occasion was the Labour Government's negative response to the Franco–German Schuman Plan (named after the French Foreign Minister) to create a single European market in coal and steel. The Conservative Shadow Cabinet, moved by a mixture of routine opposition opportunism, genuine backbench pressure and Churchill's somewhat volatile enthusiasm, put forward a critical motion which was actually proposed by Eden with patent lack of conviction: as the sequel was to show, Eden fully shared Bevin's hostility to pooling any jot of British sovereignty in Europe. The two-day debate provided an opportunity, however, for Tory Europeans to show their colours. They could feel they had their leaders with them, for Churchill wound up with a stirring hymn to the principle of supranationalism.

Heath's speech lasted only fourteen minutes, but in that time he laid down the main themes that would preoccupy him for the rest of his career. He began by describing his Whitsun visit to Germany, where he had toured the industrial regions of the Rhineland and the Ruhr and talked with politicians, both Christian Democrat and Socialist, in Bonn. What he had seen had convinced him that the Schuman Plan offered the only way to reconcile Germany peacefully within Western Europe. He rebutted Cripps, who had declared that joining would put the whole economy at risk:

> We on this side of the House feel that, by standing aside from the discussions, we may be taking a very great risk with our economy – a very great risk indeed. He said it would also be a very great risk if we went in and then withdrew. We regard it as a greater risk to stand aside altogether at this stage.

Heath ridiculed Labour's doctrinaire suspicion of a capitalist Community, pointing out – as so often in the years to come – that the German socialists were baffled and disappointed by Britain's attitude. The Germans' reasons for welcoming Schuman, he asserted, were entirely political. They wanted, first, reconciliation with France and, second, the unity of Western Europe against the Soviet Union. For these political ends they were willing to sacrifice a degree of economic sovereignty. Of course within the plan there would still be the possibility of conflict between Germany and France over coal and steel production. But this offered an opening for British influence. 'I submit', Heath argued, 'that that is a very strong reason why we should take part in these discussions, in order that we may balance out the difficulties between France and Germany which are bound to arise.' Above all, he insisted, was the problem of containing Germany: 'Anyone going to Germany today is bound to be impressed by the fact that the German dynamic has returned; that Germany is once again working hard and producing hard, and that therefore Germany will become a major force in Europe.'

There were only two ways of dealing with this resurgence. One was to prolong indefinitely the control of Germany by the Allies; this was both impractical and undesirable. 'The only other way is to lead Germany into the one way we want her to go, and I believe that these discussions would give us a chance of leading Germany into the way we want her to go.'

Heath ended characteristically with an appeal to the Government to raise the level of their aspiration:

What I think worries many of us on this side of the House is that, even if the arguments put forward by the Government are correct, we do not feel that behind those arguments is really the will to succeed, and it is that will which we most want to see. It was said long ago in this House that magnanimity in politics is not seldom the truest wisdom. I appeal tonight to the Government to follow that dictum and to go into the Schuman Plan to develop Europe and to co-ordinate it in the way suggested.[6]

The essential arguments of the British pro-Europeans for next ten, twenty, forty years are contained in his maiden speech: the belief that Britain should go into Europe to *lead* Europe; the worry that staying outside an integrated Europe would be an increasingly chilly option; and the fear that the terms of entry would only get more onerous if the opportunity was missed at the outset. As a matter of fact Heath expressed this last fear much less strongly in the Commons than he had done a few days earlier in Bexley, when he had rehearsed much of his speech in the form of one of his monthly reports to his constituents. Then, untrammelled by the convention that maiden speakers be uncontroversial, he had roundly declared that the Government 'stood condemned' for its failure to show any interest in the stability and co-operation of Europe. 'It is a great chance, perhaps the greatest in twenty years, and it may well be that this Government has thrown that chance away.' Questioned from the audience, he did not deny that there were implications in joining which would need to be studied. But, he insisted,

> we should have done better to be in at the formative stages so that our influence could be brought to bear, rather than wait and be presented with a detailed plan. If inside the Plan we could to some extent influence the details. Now we may be left with the choice of taking or leaving a prepared Plan.[7]

No one could say in 1970 that Heath had not foreseen in 1950 the difficulties Britain would encounter twenty years later.

Heath's début was 'a definite success',[8] duly noted by the party leadership. Harold Macmillan clearly remembered it when he came to appoint a negotiator to lead his attempt to join the EEC in 1961. In the meantime, however, the Tory party as a whole was no readier than Labour to embrace the European idea. Heath was deluding himself when he spoke confidently of 'we on this side of the House' and insisted that the Tories were not 'play-acting' about Europe but were serious. In 1950 he was one of a small band – Duncan Sandys, Christopher Soames and a dozen or two more. Churchill's enthusiasm faded once he got back into office. The Conservative Government returned in 1951 was content to look on from the sidelines – benevolent but aloof – as the Coal and Steel Community evolved into the EEC: Churchill, Eden, Butler and Macmillan all equally took it for granted that Britain had wider interests, with the United States and with the Commonwealth, that precluded any closer involvement with the continent of Europe. It was ten years before Macmillan acknowledged his mistake.

Heath's other early claim on the attention of his party, rather surprisingly, was as a member of a backbench dining club. As it happened, the 'One Nation' group both contained the cream and embodied the essential spirit of the 'class of 1950'; so it is appropriate that he should have been, at least briefly, a part of it. His membership was by most accounts, however, somewhat accidental. The precise beginnings of any such group are impossible to pinpoint with certainty, but it seems that the moving spirits were initially Angus Maude and Cuthbert ('Cub') Alport. Their starting point was a shared dismay at the weakness of the Tory Front Bench on social matters, highlighted by Nye Bevan's contemptuous demolition of

Walter Elliot in a housing debate on 13 March. Maude and Alport
then quickly recruited Gilbert Longden, Robert Carr, Richard Fort
and John Rodgers; it was Rodgers who brought in Heath.* These
seven decided to invite Iain Macleod to join them. Macleod had been
asked to write a pamphlet on social services for the Conservative
Political Centre (CPC). He now proposed that it should become a
joint production, each of them contributing a chapter. He also proposed bringing in his former colleague in the Research Department,
Enoch Powell. Both suggestions were agreed. The group now had
nine members and a project, but no name.

Over the summer they met together to read each other their draft
chapters. Heath did not take a prominent part in the discussions. 'He
listened', Rodgers recalled, 'while intellectuals like Macleod, Maude
or Powell pontificated. Then he would surface with something like
"Well, what are we going to do about it?" '[10] Social policy was not
really his subject. It is not even clear whether he wrote a chapter, or if
so, which it was: Robert Carr does not believe he did. Indeed Carr
thinks that Heath had left the group before the book appeared; this is
not so, but the fact that Carr can think it confirms that his contribution was not great.[11]

Nevertheless Heath valued his membership of the group, which
expressed the sort of modern Conservatism in which he believed.
When *One Nation* was published – in time for the party conference in
October 1950 – it was prominently advertised on the front of the
Bexleyheath Observer, and Heath was thenceforth always credited in
the constituency as one of its authors. The name *One Nation* was
coined by Maude and Macleod when they were putting together the
thirteen chapters ready for publication. Recalling Disraeli's condemnation of the 'two nations' of Victorian Britain – rich and poor – it
neatly reconciled their self-consciously progressive stance with Tory
tradition. At the same time the idealism of the notion, and the mere
fact of the group's concern with welfare policy, led to the misconception that their ideas were more to the left of the party than they
really were. In fact, a reading of *One Nation* today reveals a more
radical approach to the social services than anything attempted by
any Conservative Government before 1979.

One Nation took pride in the Welfare State, but regarded it as

---

* This was not how Heath remembered it in 1960. He believed that he had been in
at the beginning 'one night in May 1950' when he, Alport, Maude and Rodgers,
'dining together', decided to develop a coherent approach to social services and 'invited some of our colleagues to join us'.[9] But no one else's recollections give Heath
such a central role.

essentially complete. The task now was to administer it better. The social services could expect no general increase in resources. On the contrary the share of the nation's wealth going on public spending was already too high and would need to be reduced. The priorities, after defence – frankly termed 'the war against communism' – were housing and education. If the present standards of the Health Service were to be maintained and improved it would have to raise more of its own resources by means of prescription charges and hospital charges. On grounds equally of morality and economy, private provision for housing, education and health should be encouraged.

In three other respects *One Nation* put down important markers for the future. First, while it accepted that 'full employment is a first responsibility of government', it emphasised that 'in the long run . . . full employment depends on the competitive power of British industry in the world markets'. Second, the chapter on industrial relations (written by Robert Carr) insisted that a future Conservative Government would 'feel compelled to take some action' on trade union reform. Third, the nine signatories committed themselves to the reform and revival of local government, in order to resist the centralising tendency of socialism.[12]

One Nation reflected the ideas primarily of three men: Iain Macleod, Angus Maude and Enoch Powell. They were, in the context of 1950, radical ideas and they remained in most respects too advanced for the Conservative governments of the 1950s. Neither Macleod nor Powell as Minister of Health attempted to dent the universality of the social services which by then had become a political sacred cow; nor did either Macleod or Heath as Minister of Labour attempt to tackle the trade unions. There was no need of hard choices in the affluent 1950s, when the economy seemed able to support the continuous expansion of the social services without serious difficulty. Nevertheless *One Nation* represented a pool of ideas whose relevance returned in the 1960s when the assumption of affluence came under increasing strain. Merged with the very similar ideas developed during the later 1950s by the Bow Group, they resurfaced in the proposals which the Tory party formulated in opposition under Heath's leadership after 1965, which in turn formed the basis of the programme on which he won the General Election in 1970.

There is a clear line of descent linking *One Nation* with some of the central tenets of 'Thatcherism' after 1975. Yet Heath consistently denounced Mrs Thatcher for betraying the *One Nation* tradition. To Heath in the 1980s, *One Nation* implied a humane, consensual Toryism opposed to the hard-faced capitalist doctrines of the new radical right. The confusion is between the spirit and the actual proposals of *One Nation*. Macleod, Maude, Powell and Heath in 1950

were advocating a loosening of some of the rigidities of the Welfare
State in reaction against the still dominant philosophy of socialism;
but at the same time they were sincerely anxious to be seen as socially
progressive and concerned, in the best Disraelian tradition, with the
condition of the people. To Heath at least, and probably to Iain
Macleod – though not to Powell – the idea of social unity remained
more fundamental than the means which they had proposed in 1950
of promoting it. It was to that ideal that Heath still held in the 1980s.
Faced with the mean-spirited social divisiveness of Mrs Thatcher's
Government, his forty-year-old association with *One Nation* was a
defiant assertion of the decency, compassion and social concern
which had characterised his generation of Conservatives. His membership of 'One Nation' in 1950 allowed him to claim continuity and
legitimacy for his consensual approach as representing the 'true'
Tory tradition.

But Heath was not a member of 'One Nation' for very long. In
February 1951 he was invited to become a Whip. He was in some respects an unusual choice. Tory Whips were traditionally somewhat
dim figures – well-born younger sons or military men; loyal party
hacks rather than aspiring statesmen. The Whips' office did not offer
many prospects to the ambitious. The fact that Heath was invited
may have been a compliment to 'One Nation', indicating that the
Whips felt the need to open a line of communication to the group.
On the other hand it suggests that they did not see him as a leading
member of it. What recommended him was not his pedigree as a
former President of the Union, but rather his background, representing the new intake, and his army record. He was recognised as an
extremely efficient, single-minded but self-effacing staff officer. His
friends in 'One Nation' thought it was the end of him. He himself
hesitated. He undoubtedly knew he could do the job well. It would
be a good way to get known and an unrivalled way to get to know
the party. He may well have calculated that he could make more of
the job of Whip than anyone had done before. But he was worried
that it might block him off for ever from conventional promotion.
He accepted only on condition that he might be allowed an escape
clause after eighteen months. The Chief Whip, Patrick Buchan-
Hepburn, a debonair charmer of the old school who was anxious to
broaden the social basis of the Whips' office, agreed. So Heath became an unpaid assistant Opposition Whip. Appointing him,
Churchill characteristically told him, 'This will mean much hard
work and it is unremunerated; but as long as I am your leader it will
never remain unthanked.'[13]

He did not have to resign from the 'One Nation' group immediately. But his duties inevitably gave his energies a new focus,

leaving him less time for group discussions. He was obliged to resign only in October, after the General Election, when he became a Government Whip and thus a (very junior) member of the Government – to this extent stealing a march on his rivals. (His place was filled by Reginald Maudling.) Nor did becoming an Opposition Whip entirely stop him speaking. In March he spoke in support of the Territorials, and in June he proposed a new clause in the Finance Bill.[14] It was only after October that he disappeared totally into purdah.

In the summer of 1951 Heath persuaded Brown, Shipley to send him to America for six weeks, where he was able usefully to extend both his business and his political contacts. He was still in Ottawa when he heard – as a result of finding himself in a hotel lift with the Foreign Secretary, Herbert Morrison – that Attlee had called a General Election for 25 October. He flew at once to New York and sailed home on the *Queen Mary*. Another Cabinet Minister, Manny Shinwell, Minister of Defence, was on board. Shinwell told Heath that he expected Labour to lose the election by a small majority.[15]

But if he came home eager for the fray he ran into a terrible shock. His mother was dying of cancer. She had been suffering stomach pains for some time, but had kept them to herself and refused to see the doctor. In August she finally went into hospital in Ramsgate and William was told that she had only two or three months to live. Marian Evans has described the painful scene when he broke the news to John and Teddy.[16] A few days later they brought her home. But there was nothing to be done for her. She was characteristically insistent that Teddy should go on with his Election campaign. It was lucky now that Bexley was so close to Broadstairs. He commuted backwards and forwards every day, to spend as much time as possible with her, playing the piano for her, without his personal grief ever becoming known in Bexley. She died on 15 October, ten days before polling day.

It was a dreadful loss, and cruelly timed just as he had his foot on the ladder which she, more than anyone, had encouraged him to climb. At thirty-five he was still closer to his mother than to anyone else, and he felt her death exceptionally deeply. It was a blow which helped to shape his personality, making him more lonely, single-minded, self-contained and buttoned up than ever. She had been the emotional focus of his life. Without her, he had no one. It became more unlikely that he would ever marry: idealised now by death, no other woman could replace her. Rather he seemed to close off that side of his personality entirely and dedicate himself more completely than ever to fulfilling her ambition for him. Though he never spoke of her, his mother's death redoubled his determination to vindicate her faith and sacrifice.

He was still punctilious in spending time with his family, bringing them presents from his foreign trips, marking the steps in his career with family celebrations. But he had never been so close to his father; and he was upset when, two years after Edith's death, William remarried. Doris Lewis, a divorcée, was a fussy, talkative woman of the type Teddy most disliked. He signalled his disapproval by arriving an hour and a half late for the wedding; he was bringing John and Marian with him from Woodford, so they were all late. Marian thought it 'the saddest wedding I've ever been to': there were no congratulations and none of the three of them even kissed the bride.[17] Thereafter Teddy's relations with his stepmother were correct but never warm; she did not understand him and could not easily accept that her new home should continue to be arranged, as it had been in Edith's time, around his convenience. William was proud of his son's progress but was still bewildered by a personality so different from his own.

In this election Heath had a straight fight in Bexley. Ashley Bramall stood again for Labour, but both the Liberal and the Communist stood down. In the local elections of both 1950 and 1951 the Conservatives had strengthened their grip on the borough council, so his prospects of increasing his tiny majority looked good. Publicly he was confident that this time Attlee's exhausted and discredited Labour Government would be defeated. At his meetings he concentrated on four issues: peace, housing, the cost of living and nationalisation – with particular emphasis on the first. Angrily he denied the lie that the Tories were warmongers – this was the election of the *Daily Mirror*'s famous headline 'Whose Finger on the Trigger?' – alleging that the real danger to peace was Morrison's 'fumbling'. He compared the Government's humiliating climbdown over Dr Moussadeq's nationalisation of Anglo-Iranian Oil with the betrayal of Czechoslovakia in 1938 and actually charged Morrison with having turned down a final offer without even reading it: 'He was on the *Queen Mary* and I was on the same ship. The offer was turned down by a Foreign Office official.'[18] This was uncharacteristically wild. But he continued throughout the campaign to press the Tories' commitment to strong defence – his chairmen never failed to mention his own service with the Territorials – by contrast with Labour's weakness.

At home he attacked the Government's economic management and the high cost of living, claimed that nationalisation was now an acknowledged failure and promised that a Conservative Government would make housing – after rearmament – its first priority. He also made a strong pitch for the Liberal vote, stressing the older parties' common anti-socialism. To judge from the *Bexleyheath Observer* it was not a very positive campaign; but then his heart was in Broadstairs with his mother. It must have taken exceptional self-control to carry on at all, though he was touched by the fact that Labour suspended campaigning for a day out of respect for his mother's funeral. He had more support this time from visiting speakers – mainly neighbouring MPs, but also the 25-year-old Margaret Roberts, once more the candidate for Dartford: regrettably that meeting was not reported. Bramall again had the bigger stars, including Herbert Morrison. The candidates debated together twice (something which Heath, less generous than Bramall in 1947–50, had hitherto declined). The outcome, in line with the national result, was a modest increase in Heath's majority:

Edward Heath	29,069
Ashley Bramall	27,430
Conservative majority	1,639[19]

On a slightly higher poll, both candidates had increased their 1950 vote. But assuming that all the Communist's 481 votes switched to Bramall, Heath took the bulk of the Liberal votes by a margin of nearly three to one. The seat was still marginal, but a majority of 1,639 was a lot more comfortable than 133. Elsewhere the Conservatives picked up another 23 seats, enough – even though Labour had still won more votes in the country – to give them a majority at Westminster of 17. Churchill was Prime Minister again; but the Government Whips were going to have their work cut out.

The Tory Whips are a closed order. They never talk to the press; they never write their memoirs. They are the keepers of the party's secrets; they never reveal their methods or their information. A self-selecting, self-reinforcing group, they work in absolute confidence with one another, bound together by the special *esprit de corps* of shared knowledge and shared responsibility. They are not loved, but need to be respected, even a little feared.

The Whips' office in November 1951 comprised Patrick Buchan-Hepburn and his deputy, Brigadier Sir Harry Mackeson, plus five Junior Lords of the Treasury (paid) and three assistant Whips (unpaid). (As a full Whip, Heath now received a salary of £500, on top of his basic parliamentary salary of £1,000.) There is little indication that his colleagues recognised the future Prime Minister in their midst; more probably they saw him only as an exceptionally thorough organisation man, like themselves only more so. In a sense they were right. As part of a small team with a clearly defined command structure and an important job to do, Heath was once more in his element.

He was personally as shy as ever, kept his private interests to himself and never discussed in the office what he did at the weekends; but he was cheerful, businesslike and absolutely reliable and quickly made himself indispensable. After only six months Brigadier Mackeson was squeezed out and Heath was promoted Deputy Chief Whip with a further salary increase to £750. Immediately he wrought 'a sea change in the Office'.[20] He introduced a new system of index cards for keeping closer tabs than ever before on the movements and proclivities of each MP, and very soon was effectively running the whole whipping operation, taking over large areas of Buchan-Hepburn's job. Being so junior, however – thirty-five and only two years in the House – he had to work through tact and understanding rather than authority. At this period of his career, by all accounts – in complete contrast with his later manner – he could still deploy the charm which had been a feature of his character at Oxford. 'A Chief Whip', Buchan-Hepburn recalled, 'has to take the responsibility and be jolly rude at times, then the Deputy has to pick up the pieces. He became very good at that. He could be very nice to people.'[21] Ned Carson, the Member for the Isle of Thanet (and thus Heath's own MP in Broadstairs), confirmed the contrast between Heath's style and Buchan-Hepburn's:

> Ted Heath would use more of a 'soft sell' to get his way. If I had shown signs of not voting with the party, he would walk up casually and say something on the lines of 'Now be a good chap. It's not really a matter of your conscience this time, is it? Do come into the lobby with us. There's no point in abstaining.' I remember, however, one occasion when he was very stern in a tactful way and I was so surprised at this I went into the lobby at his bidding.[22]

Looking back in 1960 on his eight years as a Whip, Heath was at pains to stress that the job was not, as people imagined, primarily about discipline, but organisation: the organisation of the legislative timetable, the co-ordination of tactics and ensuring the physical presence of Members in the House when they were needed. 'The Whips' real problems', he told the Conservative Political Centre, 'are only seldom the compulsion of principle and conscience; they are more usually the competing demands of business and constituency activities, of family and social life': what kept Members away was not so much 'the prick of principle' as 'the attractions of Ascot and the lure of Lord's'.[23] His own immunity from most of these temptations gave Heath a strong moral advantage over truants: having no family and little social life he had no wish to be anywhere but in the House of Commons. Once in exasperation Carson asked him, 'Why don't you get married and go home and let me get to bed?' 'He looked up slowly, with a very blank face, and answered simply: "I don't want to get married." '[24] He was, as his father told the press in 1965, 'married to politics'.[25]

Paradoxically, Heath ran the Whips' office more like a military operation, though in a less crudely military manner, than previous Whips. He saw the job explicitly, as he told his constituents, as comparable to his wartime role as adjutant:[26] not giving orders, but conveying them down the line from the commanders – the Cabinet – to the troops whose support was required to carry them out and reporting back on any discontent or grievance in the ranks. The intermediary function suited his particular talent admirably. He was a good listener but not much of a talker; he was still quite deliberately studying the politician's trade and eager to learn all he could by listening, observing, remembering but saying little. As a Whip he was the recipient of the confidences, the hopes and doubts and fears of the whole party, building up an immense store of knowledge of the ambitions, weaknesses and peccadilloes of all his colleagues – all carefully docketed on his index cards. Exceptionally, though, Heath was a Whip with ambitions himself who would be able in the years to come to put all this privy information to good use. Unobserved and unsuspected in the engine room of the Whips' office – rather like Stalin building his position as General Secretary of the Soviet Communist party – while rivals like Macleod and Maudling progressed rapidly to the Cabinet, he was building up between 1952 and 1959 a deep knowledge of the Tory party which would be a powerful source of strength when he eventually emerged to make his own run for the leadership in 1965. His years as Deputy and later Chief Whip were the making of Ted Heath. In turn he transformed the office, opening up a new route to the top.

The Tory Whips in the 1951–5 Parliament were not so hard pressed as at first seemed likely. For the first year or so, with a majority of only seventeen, a Labour Opposition keen to repay some of the harassment the Tories had delighted in inflicting on them in 1950–1, and by-elections showing a steady swing against the Conservatives, there was no certainty that the Government would long survive. But a small majority actually makes it easier to coax MPs to toe the line; and Labour had its own problems with the Bevanites. Tory back-benchers made their views felt on a number of specific issues but there was only one organised group to cause the Whips any serious headaches. This was the so-called 'Suez group' of 30–40 imperialists (including two members of 'One Nation', Enoch Powell and Angus Maude) who objected to the Government's military withdrawal in 1953 from Sudan and Egypt. In July 1954 twenty-seven rebels voted against the decision to evacuate the Suez Canal base; but Eden faced them down without serious difficulty. Only one, Sir Harry Legge-Bourke, went so far as to resign the Whip.

A more delicate problem with which the Whips had to deal was the position of the Prime Minister. Churchill was seventy-seven in 1951. He was hardly back in Downing Street before murmurs began to be heard that he was no longer up to the job and ought to go. In June 1952 it fell to Buchan-Hepburn to suggest to the great man that he ought to name a date for his departure. Churchill gave him short shrift; but Tory backbenchers could not be stopped from talking and the Whips themselves – Buchan-Hepburn in particular – came in for a good deal of criticism. It was distressing for Heath, who had revered Churchill since 1935, to be the conduit for this mounting disquiet: the situation became still more delicate in the summer of 1953 when Churchill suffered a stroke, the severity of which was kept secret not only from the public and the press but from the party. The old man hung on stubbornly, however, until he was finally per-suaded to step down in 1955. Uncertainty about his intentions was probably the trickiest problem the Whips had to handle in these years.

Meanwhile Heath was careful not to neglect Bexley. He compensated for his enforced silence in the House of Commons by using his access to ministers to take up constituency cases more diligently than ever, and Reg Pye made sure the local paper got the story: the problem of cement dust from a local factory, noise disturbing residents near Bexley station, the future of Woolwich Arsenal (where many of his constituents worked); pensions, disability allowances, building licences and housing allocation. He was available to con-stituents at Crook Log every Friday evening from 6.30 to 8 pm. He brought Cabinet ministers to speak in the constituency: Buchan-Hepburn, Derek Heathcoat Amory, David Maxwell Fyfe . . . What he could not do, even in Bexley, was to speak much for himself. All ministers are bound by collective responsibility, but a Whip cannot afford to let his own views be known at all. Heath no longer held his monthly report meetings, and when he did speak at luncheon clubs and society dinners – mainly in the recess – he rarely ventured beyond the most conventional praise of the Government's record: justifying tax cuts in 1953, applauding Monckton's settlement of a threatened rail dispute, hailing Macmillan's achievement in building 300,000 houses in a year, supporting commercial television with the argument that it was dangerous to liberty to leave the BBC a monopoly of such a powerful medium.[27] In March 1954, perhaps prompted by the appearance of a new Labour opponent, he gave a rare press conference in which he went a little further: most significantly he supported the rearmament of Germany in the context of the proposed European Defence Community; and he defended the Anglo-Egyptian agreement, while stressing the need still to maintain troops in the Middle East, primarily 'to look after the oil installations and the canal' but also 'to have men fit for worldwide fighting . . . in the event of a world war'.[28] For what they are worth, such meagre scraps form the only record of Heath's views in these years of unnatural public silence.

He had only one opportunity to be noticed by the wider party. At the 1953 party conference, held in Margate, he was chosen to move the vote of thanks to Churchill following his address on the final afternoon. This was Churchill's comeback after his stroke. Welcoming him to Thanet, and recalling his last visit at the height of the Battle of Britain in 1940, Heath voiced the party's thanks for his recovery and paid tribute to 'his vision . . . his inspiration and . . . his leadership throughout the past two years'. Then, after a quick plug for the importance to the Government of holding marginal seats like Bexley ('I never wish to sit on one hundred and thirty-three again if I can help it') he picked up the theme of Tory democracy – which Churchill had traced back to his father, Lord Randolph, in the 1880s – and neatly placed himself in the same tradition: 'It is still the challenge today, it is the challenge to our generation to go forth and to convert our democracy to the principles of Toryism, so that we can purge ourselves of the weakening influence of Socialism.'[29] He used his two minutes well.

In addition, away from the limelight, he was making himself known by attending regional and sectional party conferences – Tory women, Tory trade unionists, Young Conservatives – and policy weekends at Swinton College in Yorkshire, spreading himself indefatigably through the organs of the party, getting to know its workings from top to bottom. Once again, the fact of having no family to go home to except his now remarried father back in Broadstairs freed him to devote six and sometimes seven days a week totally to politics. At the same time he was shrewdly cultivating some of the lobby correspondents – men like Derek Marks (*Daily Express*), Robert Carvel (London *Evening Standard*) and Ian Trethowan (*Yorkshire Post*). At this stage of his career – by contrast with his later suspicious and embattled relations with the press – he seems to have mixed remarkably easily with journalists. He could still relax with them, more easily than with his party colleagues – partly, perhaps, because, as Andrew Roth has suggested, journalists tend to be relatively 'classless',[30] partly because he was not yet 'copy' and could talk to them without finding himself quoted and distorted. 'In private', Ian Trethowan has written, 'he was excellent company, with a sharp, rather mordant sense of humour and an unusually wide range of interests. He was, and has always remained, one of the most amusing companions I have ever known.' At the time, Trethowan noted in his memoirs, 'those of us who were becoming his friends attached no great importance to [the] awkward dichotomy between the rather uncomfortable public persona and the lively amusing private man.' But Trethowan and his colleagues did not then imagine that it would ever matter. By contrast with the obvious brilliance of Maudling, Macleod and Powell, 'in those early years Heath seemed a conscientious but rather plodding man, admirable for the whips' office but unlikely to rise much further ... I had not the smallest premonition of greatness, then or for some years.'[31]

Heath used his years as Deputy Chief Whip in one further way to advance his political education. He still took every opportunity to travel abroad. In 1953 he paid his first visit to Africa and found Victoria Falls splendid – 'not spoiled by commercialism like Niagara with honeymoon couples drooling over it'.[32] Formally he was in Africa to attend the Commonwealth Parliamentary Association conference in Nairobi, as part of a British delegation including Heathcoat Amory and Jim Griffiths. But rather than go only to Nairobi Heath determined to see the whole length of the continent from Cairo to the Cape.

In Cairo, in addition to the treasures of Tutankhamun, he visited the Suez Canal, talked with members of the British forces guarding it (including a number of his constituents), and became convinced that their withdrawal was inevitable. He also contrived a late-night meeting with the architect of the Egyptian revolution, Colonel Nasser. Improbably, Nasser was keen to talk about democracy. 'What he now wanted was an elected parliament, but he wondered how he could be sure that this would provide a stable system of support for Egypt's interests instead of fragmenting into numerous small groups.'[33] Evidently he thought a British Whip could give him some tips. Less than two years later Nasser overthrew President Neguib and seized the canal, provoking a showdown with Britain. It can have done Heath no harm as Government Chief Whip during the Suez Crisis that he was one of the few British politicians to have talked with Nasser. The next time they met, fifteen years later, Heath was himself within a few months of becoming Prime Minister.

From Cairo Heath flew on to Kenya, Uganda, Rhodesia, Tanganyika and finally South Africa. Apart from having himself photographed, for the benefit of the *Bexleyheath Observer*, with the Prime Minister of the Central African Federation, Sir Godfrey Huggins, who was born in Bexley, he met no African leaders of the significance of Nasser. His experiences, as he described them in *Travels* twenty years later, were the conventional ones of any tourist. Of greater interest are two contemporary accounts which he gave to his constituents. It was routine to condemn apartheid in 1977; to be shocked, as Heath evidently was, by the inequality of pay in the Northern Rhodesian copper mines – whites earning £100 a month, blacks no more than £6 for the same work – was in 1954 more unusual. At the same time he had only praise for the enterprise and spirit of the Kenyan settlers, and appreciated the complexity of the racial problem: the tension in East Africa was not simply between black and white, but between Africans and Asians too.[34] He did not know then that the consequences of this tension would land on his own plate in 1972.

Six months later, Churchill finally retired. Eden came at last into his long-delayed inheritance, and immediately called a General Election. This time Heath faced a new opponent in Bexley, the journalist, author and film producer R. J. Minney; but he was fortunate once again to have a straight fight. For the first time he had to fight positively on the Government's record, instead of attacking Labour's. At his adoption meeting he set out the issues with his usual thoroughness, covering three fronts: peace, prosperity and freedom. 'The Conservatives', he concluded, perfectly encapsulating the philosophy of 'One Nation', 'govern for the good of the nation as a whole.'[35]

It was a rowdier campaign than Bexley had seen previously. At one meeting both candidates were shouted down by rival claques of supporters. Heath's new status was marked by two Cabinet ministers – Harold Macmillan as well as Iain Macleod – coming to speak for him: in addition he was invited to Leamington to speak for Eden. With Eden's personal popularity high and Labour distracted and divided, there was never much fear that Bexley would be lost. Reg

Pye's electoral machine was now finely tuned, with teams of canvassers methodically knocking up the whole constituency, while Labour still relied much more on loudspeaker vans. With a 2·8 per cent swing in his favour, Heath increased his majority to a comfortable margin:

Edward Heath	28,610
R. J. Minney	24,111
Conservative majority	4,499[36]

   Overall the Conservatives increased their majority to 58 – the first time in more than a century that a sitting Government had strengthened its position at the polls. Despite this mandate, however, Eden did not immediately reconstruct his Government – an omission widely interpreted as his first sign of weakness in the top job. Not until the end of the year, seven months later, did he grasp the nettle, removing Butler from the Treasury and Macmillan from the Foreign Office to the Exchequer, with other consequential changes lower down. After seven years as Chief Whip, Buchan-Hepburn was rewarded with the Ministry of Works. (A year later Macmillan gave him his regulation peerage and sent him to govern the West Indies.) His successor was not in doubt. As Eden put it, 'Ted Heath took over as Chief Whip by what seemed a natural process.'[37] He had already for some time been doing most of the organisational side of the Chief Whip's job. He now took over in addition the more sensitive political role of principal parliamentary adviser to the Prime Minister. He was not a member of the Cabinet, and was totally unknown to the country; but after less than six years in the House he now occupied a position of greater potential influence than most ministers. He was not yet forty.

6

Chief Whip

HEATH was Government Chief Whip for a little under four years – one year under Eden and three under Harold Macmillan. In this time he was responsible for guiding the Conservative party through some of the roughest political weather faced by any British Government this century. The eye of the storm was Suez, which divided the country and the party and raised the temperature of party politics more sharply than any other crisis since 1911. But Eden's difficulties did not begin with Suez, nor did Macmillan's succession end them. Though in December 1955 Eden had only been Prime Minister for eight months and should still have been buoyed up by his General Election triumph in May, his grip on his administration was already being called in question. There were mutterings on the back benches and in the press that he should step down, which became so persistent that in January 1956 he was driven to the indignity of denying that he intended to do so. Then in the summer came Nasser's nationalisation of the Suez Canal and in the autumn Britain's bungled and hastily aborted invasion of Egypt, culminating in Eden's resignation under cover of illness in January 1957. But even after Macmillan had unexpectedly and controversially taken over from Eden, he still faced a formidable task restoring the party's shattered morale and standing in the country in time to stand a chance of winning a further election victory in 1959. The extent of that victory, when Macmillan pulled it off, has tended in retrospect to obscure the magnitude of the task confronting him in 1957–8. When he kissed hands he told the Queen he might not last more than a few weeks. Ted Heath was Tory Chief Whip both during the Suez crisis itself and during the post-Suez period of Macmillan's early leadership. No one has ever held the position in more difficult times. His success, in these exceptionally testing circumstances, was the making of his career. To him – rather than to Eden, Macmillan or Butler – was widely awarded the credit that the Tory party did not tear itself apart during Suez; while Macmillan's achievement in restoring the party's self-confidence and credibility after Suez was generally recognised to rest heavily upon the partnership he formed with his Chief Whip. The years 1956–9 transformed the way the political world regarded Heath: no longer merely an efficient party functionary, he emerged as a man with a future.

He was Chief Whip for nine months before the Suez Crisis broke. With Eden he had a good relationship, though not nearly so close as he was later to enjoy with Macmillan. He had had a high regard for Eden ever since his anti-appeasement days at Oxford; even today he still speaks of Eden's 'great capacity to inspire hero-worship' and will hear no criticism of him. Eden, he recalled in 1988, had no 'side' at all – one of his very rare admissions that he did suffer from class condescension at the hands of some other senior members of the party.[1] Eden, for his part, wrote in his memoirs that he had 'never known a better-equipped Chief Whip',[2] and paid tribute to Heath's 'especial qualities of patience, adroitness and dependability. His instinctive reserve could sometimes conceal these, but the rougher the weather the steadier was his advice.'[3] Heath's access to him was sufficiently intimate that 'while I was shaving, bathing and dressing . . . [he] would arrive with some suggestion or point for decision'.[4] Yet he was never a confidant, as he was to become with Macmillan.

Eden showed his regard for Heath by having him present as a matter of course at Cabinet meetings, not called in – as Buchan-Hepburn and all previous Chief Whips had been – only when matters of parliamentary management were under discussion. This is a precedent which subsequent prime ministers have followed. Having no department, he played no substantive part in Cabinet debate; but simply being there gave him further valuable experience. It also meant that he was present at the critical meetings that gave the green light to Suez.

His primary responsibility, however, remained the management of the Government's majority. In partnership with Rab Butler, now Leader of the House, he quickly achieved a marked improvement in the mood of the back benches. 'Both', *The Economist* noted, 'are relatively young "new Tories" able to talk to their exceptionally young party in contemporary terms, and not in the language of the Edwardian era.'[5] (A somewhat curious comment this, since Butler was then fifty-four; but it underlines how elderly the party had seemed before.) Between them they successfully defused a number of threatened revolts. Britain's relations with Europe threw up a particularly piquant test of Heath's loyalty. With Eden still adamant against any involvement with the nascent EEC, no fewer than eighty-four Tory backbenchers (led by Geoffrey Rippon) signed a resolution in favour of Britain exploring the possibility of joining. "I had several up-and-downs with Ted on this,' John Rodgers recalled.[6] But Heath succeeded in persuading the pro-Marketeers to drop their motion.

The Government's only serious political embarrassment in this period occurred when it ignored Heath's advice. In a free vote on 26 February on the ever-sensitive issue of capital punishment, an abolitionist amendment was carried, against the Government's declared wishes, by thirty-one votes. Heath had warned the Cabinet of this likely outcome, but Eden had preferred to believe the assurances of his two predecessors, Buchan-Hepburn and James Stuart, whose sense of the party's changing feeling was out of date.[7] Still determined to retain the rope, the Cabinet now set the Lord Chancellor, Lord Kilmuir, to find a compromise formula which might win back enough Tory abolitionists to forestall Sidney Silverman's abolition Bill. Since the whole point of the exercise was a political calculation, Heath was co-opted to the committee to try to ensure that this time they got it right. It was his first experience of drafting legislation. The essence of Kilmuir's proposals was to distinguish between different types of murder, retaining the death penalty for the killing of police and prison officers and for killing in pursuit of theft, by firearms or by explosives, while exempting 'domestic' murders committed within the family or without premeditation. On 26 July, however, Heath advised the Cabinet that it was still 'open to some doubt whether a Bill on the lines envisaged would be acceptable to a sufficient number of Government supporters to ensure that it would be carried'.[8] Two months later – as a result perhaps of wavering abolitionists being exposed to their constituents over the recess – he was able to be more encouraging: a Homicide Bill was accordingly included in the Queen's Speech in November and was duly carried into law as a Government measure in 1957. But it was regarded on all sides as an unconvincing and temporary compromise, a halfway house to the eventual abolition of hanging in 1965.

It was on 26 July that Egypt suddenly nationalised the Suez Canal. Thereafter the crisis developed in three phases. The first, which lasted until the end of October, was a period of rising tension, shadow boxing and backstairs diplomacy during which the Americans tried earnestly but ambiguously to dissuade Eden from contemplating the use of force to recapture the canal, while the British and French cooked up with Israel a secret plan for a joint simultaneous invasion. This phase ended on 29 October when Israel moved into Sinai. Two days later British planes started bombing Egyptian airfields; on 5 November British and French troops landed at Port Said, ostensibly to separate the Egyptian and Israeli combatants, and began to take over the canal. Scarcely had they landed, however, before American pressure – particularly financial pressure – forced the British to call a halt, accept a ceasefire and a few weeks later to withdraw, leaving the canal in the hands of the United Nations and British prestige in tatters. Even before this final humiliation Eden, exhausted by the strain, had been obliged by his doctor to withdraw to the West Indies to recuperate.

From the Whips' point of view each of the three phases was quite different. The first presented no particular problem, except the logistical one of recalling 344 Tory MPs from their holidays all around the world at a few days' notice when Parliament was recalled for two days on 12-13 September. The House divided on straight party lines. Eden won a rapturous reception from his own supporters for his tough line with Nasser, and the Government had a majority, boosted by some Labour abstentions, of seventy. At this stage the party was anxious but united. There was talk of forcing the canal if necessary, but as yet no serious idea of an invasion. The second and third phases faced the Whips with opposite but complementary challenges. On the one hand the resort to military action outraged a small but significant number of liberal Tories – most prominently two junior ministers, Anthony Nutting and Sir Edward Boyle, who resigned from the Government in protest. On the other hand the halting of the action equally infuriated a much larger and better organised right-wing group – predominantly the 'Suez Group' of two years before. In the middle, throughout, was the mass of ordinary Tory members, anxious to be loyal but alarmed and bewildered by the unfolding of events.

Heath was present at the critical Cabinets on 25 and 30 October which decided on military intervention, but as Chief Whip he had no voice. He never expressed a view of his own on either the morality or the practicality of the enterprise. (In Bexley, at the beginning of October, he declared impenetrably that 'considerable moral issues were involved ... but he volunteered no opinion'.)[9] There has always been a strong suspicion among his friends that he was personally unhappy about the invasion; but he has never said a word to confirm it, remaining publicly as loyal to Eden's memory as he was at the time. The suspicion of his private doubts makes his achievement in keeping the party more or less united throughout the crisis all the more remarkable. It was essential that he suppress them if he was to retain the confidence of all sections of the party, and suppress them he did. More than ever he saw his job as analogous to his wartime role as Adjutant. It was not for him to reason why: his task was simply to keep up the Government's majority in the lobbies with as few losses – to either left or right – as possible.

The secret of Heath's whipping was that he listened sympathetically to all sides while remaining, in the words of one distinguished journalist, 'calm, courteous and confident amid the smell of disaster'.[10] He encouraged members of every shade of opinion to confide in him, collected and faithfully reported all their doubts and fears, but appealed to them in return, for the sake of the party, not to carry their dissent into the voting lobby. By his evident fairness and integrity he won the party's trust, respect and gratitude – even its affection. They trusted him to represent their feelings accurately. They were grateful to him for what he was trying to do, recognising – as a profile in the *Sunday Times* suggested some years later – that 'if the Chief Whip did not look after the party, no one else would'. But above all it was because they *liked* him that they did not want to make his job any more difficult than it was already. 'Conservatives are much governed by affection and friendship – like schoolboys they do not like to be beastly to men they know and like well.' Heath at this time, the writer affirmed, 'enjoyed . . . the personal affection of a large majority of the Conservative Party'.[11]

Of course there are differing views about precisely how he operated. Robert Carvel wrote in the middle of the crisis that Heath 'has handled turbulent groups of MPs with a remarkably successful mixture of toughness and charm'.[12] Naturally some saw more of the toughness while others were subjected to the charm. But the preponderant view is that he handled the party with exemplary tact. 'He was very seldom a "tough" whip,' one of his juniors recalled, adding revealingly: 'and that was not an effective role for him anyway'.[13] Lord Kilmuir was not in the Commons in 1956, but his account expresses the general view:

> Had it not been for the quiet skill with which Edward Heath and his colleagues in the Whips' office handled the parliamentary party throughout the crisis, the situation might well have become desperate. It was the sort of situation where only the most tender handling was possible; any attempt to dictate to Members, as some Chief Whips of my acquaintance would have done, would have been absolutely disastrous. While never showing weakness or forgetting his responsibilities to the Government, Heath calmly and gently shepherded the party throughout a crisis which might have broken it.[14]

Nevertheless he was noticeably gentler with the 'wets' on the left than with the fire-eaters on the right. Nigel Nicolson was one of only six opponents of the invasion to abstain from supporting the Government in the critical censure debate on 8 November. His opposition landed him in trouble with his Bournemouth constituents and eventually cost him his seat. But he found Heath unfailingly understanding and helpful. Nicolson was one who thought he sensed Heath's tacit sympathy. Once when pressed to say if the Government was telling the House of Commons the whole truth, Heath 'silently and eloquently turned away', as though he knew more than he could say.[15] With the left at least, showing a hint of sympathy was a way to persuade them that they did not need to carry their protest into the division lobby. After all, the invasion had already been halted and Heath was able to divulge privately that the Government was about to bow to American pressure to withdraw in favour of the United Nations.[16] One of the most influential critics of the invasion, Sir Alexander Spearman, whose house had been the meeting place of the dissenters over previous days, was persuaded not to rock the boat by the argument that jeopardising not only the Government but his seat and his career by withholding his support would merely leave the right in control of the party – a view which the fate of Nicolson, Nutting and one or two others tended to bear out. Keith Joseph succumbed to similar arguments; two more of the younger intending rebels, Peter Kirk and David Price, were won round on the floor of the House just before the vote. It was a considerable achievement on Heath's part to limit the 8 November rebellion to just six abstentions.

It is clear that he took a harder line with at least some of the right-wing rebels who threatened to vote against the abandonment of the invasion. Certainly all the stories that have surfaced of the Whips attempting a 'tough' approach relate to members of the Suez group. The most persistent has Heath calling one right-winger a 'bloody fascist'. A refinement of this story is that he told the man, 'You were a Communist at university and now you're nothing but a bloody fascist.' This, if true, could only have been Heath's Oxford Union contemporary John Biggs-Davison; but Biggs-Davison denied it.[17] Nevertheless such stories could not have circulated without some incidents to lend them colour; along with the golden opinions he won from most of the party during Suez, Heath undoubtedly made some enemies on the right. The one unquestionable case of him having threatened anyone was Patrick Maitland: despite denials that the Whips ever tried to influence dissidents through their constituencies, Heath did telephone the chairman of Maitland's local party in

Lanarkshire, who told him robustly where to get off. In an article in
the *Daily Express* Maitland complained publicly of 'extraordinary
and unexampled pressures – some of them altogether underhand –
which have been used to force Tories into line'.[18] So it was not all
'gentle shepherding'.

The critical vote for the Suez group took place on 6 December.
Initially eighty-six rebels had signed a letter threatening to abstain if
the Government tamely withdrew from Egypt. This would have
been more than enough to bring the Government down, so Heath
got to work. The *Observer* described his persuasive method in detail:

> One by one the weaker brethren were summoned to Mr Heath's
> room. Some who could not be charmed off their perch were given
> a shove. Some were reminded of their past services to the party;
> others were abruptly told that every abstention would mean a
> drop of £10m in the gold and dollar reserves.[19]

Heath bargained with the leading rebels to limit their protest to a
number sufficient to make their point, but not to threaten the
Government or the pound. In the end only fifteen abstained; the
Government had a majority of fifty-two.

The retreat from Suez was conducted in the absence of the Prime
Minister. Eden left for Jamaica on 23 November and did not return
until 14 December. While he was away, it was not so much Butler
and Macmillan – rivals for the succession and both saddled by different sections of the party with the blame for the disaster – as Heath
who filled the leadership vacuum and held the demoralised party together. It was then, even more than during the crisis itself, that it
might easily have fallen apart. Like a good junior officer stepping up
to take command when the commanding officer is killed, Heath
made himself the focus of party unity. *The Economist* on 1 December
commented sarcastically that the stop-gap triumvirate (Butler–
Macmillan–Heath) had 'raised the art of being all things to all men to
new and undreamt-of heights', but admitted that the leadership had
'commanded admiration for its dexterity, if not necessarily for its
political honesty' at a difficult time.[20] 'Ted had immense influence
then,' one of his junior Whips recalled. 'He was the one very tangible
link between the party and the Government.'[21] Others have suggested that in those few weeks Heath virtually ran the Government,
giving a glimpse of his future potential for those who witnessed it.

Even at the time his achievement was widely recognised as the one
plus for the Tories from the whole miserable tale. James Margach in

the *Sunday Times* wrote that his 'generalship . . . was superb. He never for a second lost command of the situation.'[22] 'Generalship' was not a quality which anyone had ever previously looked for in a Chief Whip. *The Economist* on 8 December summed up the general view of his performance: 'Mr Heath will surely have earned a niche in the Tory pantheon as the man who gave the party a second chance; at a time when the spotting of Tories who may some day move to a much higher office has become the most popular Westminster occupation, here is a name to enter on the list.'[23] The implication is clear that he had not been on anybody's list before. Suez made Ted Heath.

The only other Conservative to do well out of Suez was Harold Macmillan – ironically and undeservedly, since he bore a share of the responsibility for the fiasco second only to Eden himself. Just before Christmas Eden returned home fully intending to continue in office, but a combination of renewed ill health and reduced authority persuaded him to announce on 9 January that he was standing down. The immediate almost universal assumption was that Butler would succeed him. Macmillan's emergence was a surprise, yet reflected the clear judgment of the party that he was the better equipped of the two to lead it out of the mess he had played a large part in leading it into. Butler had had doubts about the Suez adventure, but had hesitated to press them: his weakness won him no friends in either camp. The party was determined not to be ashamed of Suez: Macmillan could better brazen it out, while restoring relations with the Americans at the same time. Heath was not directly involved in the choice, except in so far as it was his job as Chief Whip to sound opinion. His decisive finding – that there was a lot of strong feeling against Butler, but not much against Macmillan – mirrored the overwhelming view of the Cabinet, polled by Lords Salisbury and Kilmuir. The head count was not complete: Enoch Powell, a Butler supporter, maintains that he was never polled.[24] But no one has ever doubted that it was essentially accurate.

Heath himself shared the general preference for Macmillan – despite the fact that Macmillan was at that time seen as a right-winger while Butler was the 'One Nation' liberal. He remembered Macmillan coming to speak for Lindsay in the Oxford by-election, while Butler was a loyal apologist for Munich. Pre-war attitudes still cast a long shadow in the postwar Tory party. There is no ground for believing that Heath in any way abused his position to influence or misrepresent the party's decision in Macmillan's favour. But the suspicion was sown when Macmillan was caught by press photographers celebrating his appointment as Prime Minister with oysters and champagne at the Turf Club, *à deux* with his Chief Whip. It

looked as though he was paying a debt. In truth he was simply getting down to the job of reshuffling the Government, a task in which
the Chief Whip is always closely consulted. Asked what they had
discussed, Heath replied tersely, 'Form, of course.'[25] Macmillan,
taking over a shattered party, also needed more than most prime
ministers his Chief Whip's advice on how to heal wounds and how
fast he could afford to go in educating it to the geo-political realities
which Suez had exposed.

From this point on Heath established an unusually close relationship with Macmillan. He was with him behind the platform at the
Central Hall, Westminster, calming his nerves with a stiff drink
before he went on to be formally elected party leader. (A few days
earlier he had drawn the short straw of being the one to tell Rab that
he had been rejected.) Thereafter he was never far from Macmillan's
side. He saw him at 10 Downing Street 'pretty well every morning'
at ten o'clock, and very often again throughout the day, dropping
in as required from his own office at Number 12.*[27] Though not
strictly a member of the Cabinet, he was from the start a member of
the inner Cabinet: for instance he was one of six – the others were
Butler, Selwyn Lloyd, Lord Salisbury, Peter Thorneycroft and Duncan Sandys – present at a weekend conclave at Chequers on 23–4
February 1957; and throughout the next three years he was a frequent
guest both there and at Macmillan's Sussex home, Birch Grove. As a
bachelor he had no family ties to keep him from attending the Prime
Minister whenever he was wanted. He played a key role in containing the 'little local difficulty' in January 1958 when Thorneycroft,
Nigel Birch and Enoch Powell resigned and Macmillan had to find a
whole new Treasury team over a weekend before he flew off on a
Commonwealth tour. Macmillan wrote in his diary that Heath's performance in this crisis was 'superb'.[28] Once again it was Heath and
Butler who kept the Government running during the six weeks Macmillan was away; and Heath was there at Chequers to brief the Prime
Minister on his return. 'I do not suppose', Lady Dorothy Macmillan
declared a few years later, 'anyone realizes the overwhelming regard
and affection my husband has for Mr Heath.'[29] In fact it was a com-
monplace in Fleet Street by 1958 that 'Ted Heath is probably the
most influential man around the Prime Minister today. The PM con-
sults him about practically everything – not just his work as Chief

---

* 'Unrecognised by the thousands bustling around St James's Park station, a
pleasant-faced and plumpish figure makes off for Downing Street from his bachelor
quarters near the Passport Office in Petty France. Well turned-out, in bowler hat,
this man has risen from small beginnings to become – at forty-two – one of the most
influential in the country.'[26]

Whip.'[30] In April 1959 he was again at Chequers when Macmillan decided against a spring election.

It was in some ways a surprising relationship. At one level Macmillan simply appreciated Heath's thorough professionalism. The survival of his Government depended to an exceptional degree on re-uniting the party behind his leadership, and Heath's intelligence system was the key to that. But their *rapport* went deeper than the nuts and bolts of party management. Macmillan liked to talk, and Heath was a good listener. Macmillan liked to take a broad strategic view of politics, drawing sweeping parallels from Herodotus or Trollope; Heath was a good foil, the man of detail who could bring him back to practical reality. John Wyndham, Macmillan's private secretary, thought that Heath was 'tremendously loyal to the Prime Minister and also tremendously frank with him . . . [with] no messing about',[31] Heath's directness nicely complemented Macmillan's studied ambiguity. It was also important that he posed no threat. A whole generation younger than Macmillan, Heath was not yet spoken of among the pretenders (Maudling, Macleod) who would soon be snapping at his heels. As Chief Whip he was the Prime Minister's man: he could not be a rival. As a matter of fact Heath soon began to worry that he would fall behind his contemporaries by remaining Chief Whip too long: there were even suggestions that he would have liked a move to a department of his own as early as January 1957.[32] But Macmillan needed him where he was; and in fact Heath gained an infinitely more valuable education in the whole business of government than he could have got in any normal job on the ministerial ladder. He was more than Chief Whip: he was more like Macmillan's chief of staff.

But what lessons did Heath learn from his apprenticeship with Macmillan? Clearly he learned a great deal about the mechanics of running a Government. Both literally and politically he got used to the view from Number 10. When he came back as Prime Minister himself eleven years later he knew his way around. Though he still went home every night to his cupboard flat in Petty France, these years with Macmillan accustomed him to the life of Downing Street and Chequers, the sweets and the status of high office. He surely began to believe that in due course he could enjoy them in his own right. Of the subtler arts of politics he did not perhaps learn enough from Macmillan: he picked up all too little of Supermac's understanding of the importance of theatrical effect in politics and the value of camouflage. These were contrary to his character and he never tried to imitate them. What he did pick up – perhaps he was inclined that way already – was Macmillan's approach to the task of running the economy: the philosophy of the 'Middle Way', which involved a degree of planning, conciliating the trade unions, rating the maintenance of high employment above the prevention of inflation and the spread of material prosperity as the highest political good. Even when, as Leader of the Opposition and initially as Prime Minister, he came to propose more abrasive methods, and was critical of some of the lazy economic attitudes that were the legacy of the Macmillan years, he did not cease to avow his admiration for the achievement of those years or fundamentally depart from the values he had imbibed at Macmillan's knee – as became clear after 1972. Several of his later critics who were dismayed by his abandonment of the more hard-nosed approach he had apparently embraced in 1965–71 felt in retrospect that the influence of Macmillan at the critical period of his political education went too deep. Heath today is happy to acknowledge his debt. He still declines to concede any prescience to Thorneycroft for anticipating the inflationary effects of high government spending in 1958; he sees that episode purely as a political challenge to Macmillan's leadership inspired by the malevolent Powell, but easily brushed off.[33] There may have been times during the latter stages of Macmillan's government when he became impatient with the perversely backward-looking image Macmillan cultivated, and anxious to press on faster with the modernisation which he increasingly recognised to be overdue. But his difference from Macmillan, even during what may be called his 'Selsdon' period, was essentially one of style, not of ultimate goals or values. He remains proud to trace his political descent from what he regards as the true Conservative tradition represented by the four prime ministers he served between 1951 and 1964 – Churchill, Eden, Macmillan and Douglas-Home. Of these the critical formative influence on him was unquestionably Macmillan.

The job of Chief Whip itself had a powerful influence too. Heath continued to be universally regarded as an outstandingly good one. Perhaps in one respect he had it relatively easy. The Conservative party in its confused state following Suez, consistently behind in the opinion polls and suffering in 1957–8 a string of appalling by-election results, was in no mood to be difficult. There were few sustained or serious rebellions. The party put its trust in Macmillan, and he repaid it. But Heath too deserved credit for the gradual recovery of confidence, which could not have been achieved by discipline alone. The legend has grown up, fathered by the hostility he aroused in the 1970s and then projected back on to the 1950s, that Heath was an exceptionally tough Chief Whip. For example Lucille Iremonger (whose husband was a Tory MP at the time) wrote in 1978 that

Heath was 'an implacable Chief Whip, notoriously unforgiving to those who crossed him';[34] since then the Thatcherite orthodoxy, routinely trotted out – as for instance by Professor John Vincent in 1983 – has been that 'a generation of Tories learned the virtues of mute obedience at his knee'.[35] To those who know only the stiff unsmiling iceberg of the 1980s this can seem all too plausible. And of course there are plenty of stories to bear it out, stories of bullying, insensitivity and tactlessness. He made a lifelong enemy of Airey Neave, for example, who returned to Westminster after suffering a coronary, expecting to be welcomed back with congratulations on his recovery, only to be told bluntly by Heath that he was 'finished'. Neave never forgave him, but took his revenge in 1975.

Undoubtedly he made some enemies. He could be tough when necessary; he could be rude when it was not necessary. Yet there is at least as much contemporary comment on the sensitivity of his handling of individuals. 'With his amazing instinct for detaching the varying degrees of vanity, ambition and public spirit which motivate politicians, Teddy Heath knew exactly whom to be rude to and who to pat on the back,' one MP remembered.[36] He himself believed, as he told Kenneth Harris in 1966, that 'If I had any above-average influence as Chief Whip it was not because I was more autocratic but because I was more democratic than some Chief Whips had been before me. I acted on the principle that the more you know about the people you are speaking for, and having to give the leader's instructions to, and the more they know about you, and what you are being asked to do, the better.'[37] Some saw a sinister side to this uncanny knowledge, alleging that he kept a 'black book' of Members' weaknesses, so that he had a hold over them akin to blackmail. But most saw him as a much simpler and nicer character than this. 'How has he done it?' asked the *Observer* in a profile on his promotion to the Cabinet in October 1959. 'The answer is partly that he is a very likeable man. He is not a snob. He is always natural except for his rather embarrassing habit of shaking his shoulders up and down when he laughs – and he laughs a great deal.'[38]

His *bonhomie* might be a bit forced, but he could be quite normally convivial. It was part of his job to frequent the bars and tea rooms of the House, and he did it in those days easily and with apparent enjoyment. It was only later, when he became Leader and came under increasing criticism, that he began to wrap himself in the protective mantle of impenetrable silence. As Chief Whip, the man now remembered by his party as prickly and authoritarian was actually astonishingly popular.

Those who were most exposed to the tough side of his character were not in fact the ordinary MPs but his fellow Whips. He drove them as hard as he drove himself, sometimes unreasonably, tending to forget that they had wives and families whom they would have liked to see occasionally. He ran the Whips' office like a military operation, keeping the main threads firmly in his own hands. He delegated to his deputy, Martin Redmayne, much less responsibility than Buchan-Hepburn had delegated to him. On the other hand he was concerned that everyone knew exactly what they had to do and liked his whole team to feel fully involved. 'We used to meet at least once a day,' he recalled in 1965, 'and for a long period at least once a week, to put me in the picture and so that we should know the basis on which we were all doing our jobs.'[39] One of his hard-pressed juniors, Michael Hughes-Young, remembered rather differently: 'We had these interminable Whips' meetings, two or three a week. Ted would chew a subject over and over again, not saying much himself. I would guess he loathed having to make up his mind on his own. He took the most extraordinary amount of trouble over things.'[40] His characteristic method, which was to become very familiar to his colleagues and subordinates in the years to come, was to consult by means of provocation. He would say something outrageous, just to see if the person he was talking to was foolish enough to agree: his juniors soon learned that if they stood up to him and argued with him, then he would listen. Alternatively he would remain silent, forcing the other man to speak. It was precisely such techniques that could easily be mistaken for bullying or rudeness by those who did not know him. Most of those who did came, in spite of everything, to be devoted to him. His Whips' office in these years included Anthony Barber (1955–7) and Willie Whitelaw, who joined in 1958 and eventually succeeded Redmayne as Chief Whip in 1964. Both were among his closest colleagues in government in the 1970s. Yet even Barber and Whitelaw were not exactly friends. 'There can be few things more rewarding in friendship', he claimed in 1960, 'than working in a Whips' office with colleagues among whom there are no political secrets and with opponents who take an equal pride in ensuring that usual channels remain open.'[41] But in fact it was noticeable that even in the intimacy of the Whips' office Heath did not make real friends as other men understand the term. Sir Paul Bryan, who served the full four years with Heath between 1955 and 1959, found himself in later years ignored as if that period had never been. Heath's attitude to working relationships can be chillingly functional.

He gained a great deal from his experience as Chief Whip. The job – inside and outside the House – made him more widely known throughout the party than any of his future rivals and gave him the chance to build a network of contacts and protégés for the future. He paid particular attention to the youth organisations of the party. From 1957 he was Vice-President of the Young Conservatives (Eden was President). In 1959 he became President of the Federation of University Conservative and Unionist Associations. His standing with the Prime Minister gave him the chance actively to advance the careers of those younger Members who impressed him: Macmillan, like all prime ministers, relied heavily on his Chief Whip for junior appointments. Keith Joseph was only one aspirant to office in these years who believes that it was Heath who picked him from the crowd. By 1964 there were few below the highest levels of the Government who did not owe their start in office to Heath. Conversely, of course, those who had not got the nod held him to blame.

Yet at the same time it was an unprecedented route to the top which carried some serious disadvantages. First, it was a sergeant's route which prevented some members of the party ever taking him quite seriously as a leader: they could never shake off the view of him as an efficient functionary promoted out of his sphere. Having been the party's valet, he could not easily become its hero. Second, being a Whip prevented him opening his mouth in the House of Commons for eight years, except formally to move the closure. He thus never got the chance to develop, as a backbencher or even as a junior minister, the easy speaking style that mastery of the House demands. At Oxford he had been a good debater. By 1959, when he came to address the House for the first time as a Cabinet minister, breaking his eight-year silence, he was unpractised and stiff with the responsibility of his new position. He did not begin to shed that stiffness until after he had lost office, after 1975. Reputations in British politics are still made essentially in the House of Commons. Heath was at an intangible disadvantage in that his was made primarily in the lobbies.

Third, the experience of having been Chief Whip – whatever it did for the party's view of him – distorted his view of the Tory party. It gave him an essentially disciplinary view of party management. It is on the face of it one of the central paradoxes of his career that a leader who had been Chief Whip should lose the leadership in 1975 precisely because he had lost the support of the party in Parliament. The explanation would seem to be that just because he had been Chief Whip – at a period when the party was chastened and relatively biddable – he took it for granted that backbenchers would always ultimately do what the Whips told them, as they had in his day. He assumed that his own Chief Whips, Francis Pym and Humphrey Atkins, should be able to keep the troops loyal to him as he had done for Macmillan.

But there were crucial differences. The new generation of Tory MPs in the 1970s was less amenable to the idea of discipline than the generation who had been through the war. In addition, Heath as Chief Whip had enjoyed the advantage of a Prime Minister who could be produced in the Smoking Room when necessary to charm and disarm potential malcontents by the wit and worldly wisdom of his conversation. Pym, though a very good Chief Whip, had no such secret weapon: by 1973 Heath's appearance in the Smoking Room was more likely to alienate support than win it. Heath as Prime Minister did not make the effort to retain the party's personal loyalty – either by flattering Members' vanity by listening to what they had to say or by soothing their disappointment by the judicious use of honours, with which he was notoriously mean. Yet both techniques had been the staple of his successful whipping in the 1950s. The truth is that every Chief Whip is liable to develop a jaundiced view of human nature, and that Heath – with his own high-minded and somewhat puritanical approach to politics – came to despise the political arts he had practised in Macmillan's service and ultimately to despise the Tory party itself for requiring that it be led by such methods. No former Chief Whip had ever risen to the leadership of either major party before, and none has done so since (though Whitelaw came close in 1975 and John Major served briefly in the Whips' office before his meteoric rise in the 1980s). It is a serious question whether his success as Chief Whip – the very success which gave his career its vital lift-off – did not in the end crucially disable Heath for the successful exercise of leadership.

At the beginning of 1959, for practically the first time in his life, Heath became ill with a bad attack of jaundice, which kept him away from work for six weeks. Never previously having needed a doctor, he was recommended to Brian Warren, who thus became one of the few people to see inside his tiny flat. Warren has attended him ever since, becoming a close friend and, since 1975, the companion of much of his globe-trotting. Heath took his illness as a warning that he was working too hard and was in danger of burning himself out. In the years to come he tried deliberately to take more exercise – he even took up golf – and make more time for music, which had been pushed into the background by his long hours as Chief Whip. At this time he had no piano to go home to except when he could get away to Broadstairs; and with calls to Chequers and other weekend engagements that was less often than it used to be. It was not until 1965 that he discovered sailing.

He made two important additions to the small number of his close friends in these years. Toby Low, later Lord Aldington, was the Member for Blackpool North, but he and his wife Araminta had a country house near Ashford in Kent, where Heath became a regular visitor. Low was a junior minister from 1951 to 1957, became Deputy Chairman of the Conservative Party organisation in 1959, but left politics with a peerage in 1962. He remained, however, very close to Heath and is one of his most trusted confidants to this day. Sir Edward Boyle, seven years younger than Heath, but the Member for Handsworth, Birmingham from November 1950, was one of the few political colleagues with whom he could share his love of music: normally he kept the two worlds strictly separate. Patrician, intellectual and unmarried, Boyle was really too sensitive for politics, yet he was rising rapidly up the ministerial ladder: two months after resigning over Suez he was back in the Government, and by 1962 he was in the Cabinet. It was a personal as well as a political loss to Heath when Boyle chose to leave politics in 1969 (to be replaced as Shadow Education Secretary by Margaret Thatcher).

His closest friends in these years, however, were still the Seligmans, Madron and Nancy-Joan: Heath was by now godfather to several of their children, who became a sort of substitute family to him. In 1958 he spent a strenuous holiday with them in Venice, methodically exploring all the churches. More often he took his holidays alone. In August 1959 he went to Malaga, the first time he had been back to Spain since 1937; in previous years he had returned several times to the Mediterranean village of Miramar, near Cannes, where 'undisturbed, I could swim and sunbathe all day, occasionally walking in the woods behind or going to one of the nearby restaurants for a meal'.[42] Off duty his lifestyle was still modest. When he was ill in 1959 Aristotle Onassis – whom he had met at Chartwell when staying the weekend with Churchill – offered him his yacht to speed his convalescence. Heath declined.

During the previous four years he had continued to devote as much time as he could spare from his duties in the House to securing his constituency base in Bexley. In the nervous aftermath of Suez Bexley once more looked a vulnerable marginal: Heath was one of a number of prominent Tories who stood to lose their seats if an election had been held in 1957 or the first half of 1958. By-election losses like Rochdale and Torrington in the spring of 1958 were not at that date to be brushed off as normal mid-term phenomena. To bolster his position Heath used his influence to bring more than a dozen Cabinet ministers to speak in Bexley, including in May 1957 Macmillan himself (whose own seat was just down the road at Bromley). In addition to his Friday evening surgeries, he spent a full three weeks every autumn meeting all the local professional and trade associations; and every year he and Reg Pye toured the pubs and clubs on New Year's Eve. As Chief Whip he still made speeches only rarely; but when he did he was always optimistic – at first defiant, then as the tide began to turn in 1958 increasingly confident, following Macmillan's lead by unashamedly measuring the Government's success in terms of rising personal consumption – lower taxes, more cars, more televisions – as well as more schools, new modern hospitals and higher pensions.[43] Despite Suez, he was also bullish about Britain's place in the world. Though dwarfed economically by the United States and USSR, he declared in 1957, Britain still led the world in scientific inventiveness and specifically nuclear power.[44] He invariably promoted the Tory party as forward-looking and progressive, by contrast with the tired and backward-looking Labour party.

By the time Macmillan went to the country in October 1959 the Government's prospects looked better than anyone would have believed possible eighteen months before. But still the result was expected to be very close. Labour had real hopes of winning; and Bexley was on paper just the sort of seat they would have to recapture if Gaitskell was to come to power. 'As Bexley goes,' Heath's constituency chairman declared, 'so goes the rest of the country.'[45] In the event he was quite right. Heath – opposed once again by his old antagonist, Ashley Bramall, but no Liberal – nearly doubled his majority yet again to 8,633* while nationally the Government increased its majority to a round 100. The highlight of a 'quiet but serious' campaign in Bexley was Macmillan's visit. Eight hundred people crowded into the Girls' Technical School in Bexleyheath to hear the Prime Minister praise his faithful adjutant:

He represents everything that is best in the new progressive modern Tory party. He is one of the creators of the new policies which are brought up to date with modern life . . . He stands for the new philosophy and modern thought in the party. You send him back, for he is a good man.[46]

His promotion to the Cabinet in the event of a Tory victory was taken for granted. He had served a long stint in the Whips' office.

---

* The figures were:

Edward Heath (Conservative)	32,025
Ashley Bramall (Labour)	23,392
Conservative majority	8,633

Now he had earned his reward. As soon as his count was over in Bexley he hurried to Macmillan's side to advise for the last time on the restructuring of the Government. There was some expectation that he himself might be offered a post on the foreign side. Instead, when the new appointments were released a few days later it was announced that he was to succeed Iain Macleod as Minister of Labour.

7

'Mr Europe'

HEATH'S promotion straight into the Cabinet was widely regarded as an excellent appointment. It was something of a
risk, in view of the failure of previous Chief Whips to shine subsequently in office. But the Ministry of Labour was thought to be a
peculiarly suitable position for a former Chief Whip, requiring just
that sensitive handling of men, wielding the alternating disciplines of
stick and carrot, by which over the past eight years Heath had made
his reputation. Ever since the return of the Conservative Government in 1951, when Churchill had given Walter Monckton the task of
keeping the trade unions sweet, it had been seen essentially as a
ministry of conciliation, the agency by which successive governments had bought off the risk of damaging strikes. Since 1955 Iain
Macleod, though a sharper personality, had followed broadly in the
Monckton tradition. The *Observer* summed up the emollient ethos of
the Department, noting that Heath had been dealt a difficult assignment to follow two 'born conciliators'.

> Monckton was a lawyer; Macleod was not, but he inherited from
> his forerunner a tradition that – in industrial disputes – the men are
> as good as their masters, that justice must prevail and that no poli-
> tical consideration must influence an industrial settlement.
>
> This high principle, and the judicial technique that goes with it,
> demands of any Minister of Labour, Tory or Socialist, a rare
> degree of impartiality and patience.

'No-one yet knows', the paper concluded, 'whether Ted Heath has
it.'[1] But the predominant opinion was that these were just the qualities he did abundantly possess.

There were some, however, on the Tory back benches and in parts of the press, who thought it was time for a change from the softly-softly Monckton-Macleod approach and hoped Heath would be the man to project a new toughness towards the unions. 'Mr Heath is unlikely to be a popularity-seeker,' *The Economist* predicted, 'but whether he will at last bring in his ministry as an active participant in the battle against inflation remains to be seen.'[2]

As it happened, Heath's tenure at the Ministry of Labour was too short to show clearly how he might have played it if he had been allowed to grow into it. When Macmillan moved him on the following July he was still only feeling his way. He had no time to put his own stamp on the Department. The only Bills he introduced were minor measures, already prepared before he arrived. He faced the threat of only one major strike, and averted it in the time-honoured way. Yet there are hints that he might have taken a tougher attitude had he stayed in the job longer. In view of the central place industrial relations were to occupy in the history of his own Government a decade later, Heath's nine months at St James's Square are a tantalising first brush with the problem. But it is difficult to be sure what lessons he drew from his first experience.

The one episode that thrust him into prominence was the threat of a major rail strike by the NUR. It was in fact a bit of a try-on by the union, since a committee on railway pay was within a few weeks of reporting. In these circumstances the Government was more than usually anxious not to have a crippling stoppage. Under pressure from the Cabinet to find a settlement, Heath summoned both sides for talks at St James's Square on 12 February. He succeeded in persuading the employers to increase their offer from 4 per cent to 5 per cent; and on this basis got the strike called off. The settlement represented, as *The Times* admitted, 'an almost complete victory for the NUR'; nevertheless the prevention of the strike was 'a first success of note' for the untried Minister.[3] Such was the sense of national relief that Heath – to his surprise – awoke to find himself a hero. The *Sunday Times* hailed his 'conspicuous personal success with the eleventh-hour settlement . . . when all the odds seemed weighted heavily against him'.

His diplomacy and powers of gentle persuasion in the past few days, and his fair-minded anxiety to find a formula to bridge the gap between unions have impressed the trade union leaders to a remarkable extent. His achievement should reinforce his influence with the TUC in any future labour crisis.[4]

Some disquiet was voiced on the Tory benches that the Government had surrendered to the threat of industrial action. But *The Economist* reported on 20 February that there was 'no question of a "revolt" against Mr Heath's way of settling the threatened strike'.[5]

The committee on railway pay recommended rises of between 8 per cent and 20 per cent; and Heath pressed successfully in Cabinet for these to be paid at once. On 12 March, however, *The Economist* took the argument an important stage further, suggesting that well-meaning committees which tried to fix 'fair' wages on social grounds in an economic vacuum were 'a gigantic red herring'. The real question was how to make the railways pay for themselves.[6] This was a prescient warning that would be heard again, much amplified, thirteen years later. In 1960, however, it was a small voice crying in the wilderness against the whole thrust of Macmillan's running of the economy, with which to all appearances his new Minister of Labour went along quite happily. Whatever initial doubts Heath may have felt about giving the NUR all they asked in February, he had found himself acclaimed as a popular saviour for getting the Government off the hook. It was a political lesson he was unlikely to forget.

On the wider problem of industrial relations Heath seemed in 1959–60 equally ready to accept the traditional view of his Department against any attempt to impose a legislative framework. For some time, as the incidence of unofficial stoppages, 'wildcat' strikes and petty demarcation disputes increased, there had been growing demands on the Tory benches for the Government to take steps to enforce some form of discipline on the unions. As long ago as 1950 *One Nation* had advocated outlawing the closed shop. Since the accession of Frank Cousins to the leadership of the TGWU in 1956 union militancy had been on the increase; and inflation, attributed to unrealistic pay settlements, was a growing worry. But Macleod had repeatedly rejected calls to tame the unions by legislation, preferring to try to improve industrial relations by implementing the Industrial Charter instead – more consultation, greater job security and the like; and now Heath took the same line. In April *The Economist*, in a sharply critical editorial entitled 'Macmillan Pink', explicitly condemned 'Mr Heath's policy of avoiding any annoyance to the trade unions'.[7]

There is no doubt that the Government was still in 1960 nervous of upsetting the unions; from a purely political point of view they had some reason, as the events of the next fifteen years were to show. Successive Ministers of Labour did hope – with more reason in 1960 than could readily be sustained in later years – that the unions would be willing and able to reform themselves. Heath had established excellent relations with George Woodcock, the new General Secretary of the TUC, who was certainly sympathetic to the need for greater discipline (they used to be seen dining together behind a screen at the Carlton Club); and also with Vic Feather, then Woodcock's deputy, ten years later his successor and Heath's principal antagonist when, as Prime Minister, he did try to impose legislation. He was almost bound to give them the chance to tackle the problem in their own way. Nevertheless there are grounds for thinking that he would have been prepared to consider Government action if they showed no serious evidence of doing so. The *Daily Express* reported that as his intention as early as November: 'Mr Heath is likely to be tougher than any Labour Minister since the war.'[8] His reply to the back-benchers in January clearly carried the threat of legislation held in reserve. Likewise the lecture which he gave to the Conservative Political Centre in March 1960 – his closest approach to a statement of his broad political philosophy before 1965 – is open to more than one interpretation. Mainly it was an impeccable statement of 'One Nation' ideals, invoking the Industrial Charter and emphasising conciliation, consultation and good will on both sides of industry. Yet speculating on why some firms and industries were more 'strike prone' than others, and warning that the present infinite variety of voluntary bargaining procedures tended to produce inflationary settlements, he seemed to be tempted by the possibility of some sort of Government-imposed solution – until he remembered the Tories' philosophic preference for voluntarism. 'It would be unlike us as Conservatives', he declared, 'to wish to impose some tidy plan on what has been a natural growth.' But then he added: 'But neither would we claim that the present methods of handling these affairs have reached finality.'[9]

These were precisely the arguments – between freedom and control – which convulsed the Tory party and destroyed his Government in the 1970s. Anticipated in 1960, they point to the conclusion that Heath might well have been tempted to bring forward some sort of Industrial Relations Act in 1961 or 1962 if he had still been Minister of Labour and the TUC had come up with no proposals of its own in the meantime. He was certainly not prepared to rule out the possibility. The origins of the gradual shift within the Ministry of Labour towards accepting the eventual necessity of trade union legislation are a matter of historical dispute; but at least one distinguished industrial relations historian has pointed to 1959–60: 'Perhaps it began with Edward Heath, the future Prime Minister with the laughing shoulders and the cold eyes.'[10]

He was certainly persuaded of the need for legislation by the time he became party leader in 1965; and it is unlikely that his own experience five years before was not a factor in making up his mind.

Between 1970 and 1974 the memory of his time at the Ministry of Labour influenced his thinking and his actions in two ways. First, although his responsibility for industrial relations had been short-lived, he retained from that time the conviction that he understood the problems and knew the principal union leaders. He believed also that they knew him and knew him privately to be fair-minded and reasonable, not (as they liked publicly to portray him) hell-bent on class confrontation. His speeches in the 1970s are full of this theme. Second, however, he also believed that they knew that he and sub-sequent Ministers of Labour, including Barbara Castle in 1968–9, had given them the chance to put their own house in order and that they had failed to take it. The fact that he himself had been round the course before in 1960 made him less willing to leave it to the unions ten years later. He did not believe that with his record he could seriously be accused of 'union-bashing'. When in 1972 he turned around and entered into unprecedentedly close co-operation with the unions in pursuit of a workable voluntary incomes policy, he saw no inconsistency with his previous attitude. In his own view he had always enjoyed good relations with the unions. In this way his brief service at the Ministry of Labour coloured both his tough initial approach to the unions in 1970 and his later 'consensual' approach to industrial problems after 1972.

After only nine months, however, he was translated to a very different sphere, of even greater significance for his future. He was on a tour of North Wales, in June 1960, when he was suddenly recalled to London to see the Prime Minister. In the Government reshuffle necessitated by Derek Heathcoat Amory's wish to retire from the Treasury, Macmillan had decided to make Lord Home Foreign Secretary, with a second Cabinet Minister to answer for foreign affairs in the House of Commons. This was the somewhat unusual proposal he now put to Heath. Heath may have felt some doubt about giving up so soon his own Department; but he accepted, on the assurance that he was to be not merely Home's number two, but Lord Privy Seal, with special responsibility for relations with Europe. The controversial double-headed arrangement was announced on 27 July.

With this appointment Heath found his life's cause. By choosing him the following year to lead the negotiations to try to secure Britain's belated entry into the EEC Macmillan reawakened in Heath a voca-tion that had lain dormant since 1950, binding him irrevocably and indissolubly to the historic mission of Britain in Europe. In the public eye he now emerged for the first time as a major national, and international, figure; the almost universal praise which he won for his conduct of the negotiations – even from those who were by no means sure they wanted him to succeed – helped to project him two years later to the Tory leadership. Even when the negotiations failed he remained indelibly established in the public mind as 'Mr Europe', the undisputed leader of the growing movement in British public life that was determined to take Britain into the Common Market sooner or later. His identification went much further than a minister's normal responsibility for a particular area of policy: Europe unlocked in Ted Heath a level of emotional commitment which his coolly efficient performance hitherto in the Whips' office and the Ministry of Labour had lacked. In the cause of getting Britain into Europe the loyal technocrat discovered a transforming vision which he could pursue with unexpected passion.

The Cabinet reshuffle which took him to the Foreign Office as Alec Home's number two was widely criticised, however, on all sorts of grounds: first, that it was improper in the second half of the twentieth century to have a Foreign Secretary in the House of Lords (Eden had thought it impossible to appoint Lord Salisbury in 1955); second, that Home was an amiable nonentity who would simply allow the Prime Minister to continue to run his own foreign policy unchecked; and third, that divided control in the Foreign Office was a recipe for confusion (as when Eden had been Minister responsible for League of Nations affairs under Sir Samuel Hoare in 1935). The significance of Heath's appointment to be 'specially concerned with European affairs in all their aspects' was not generally picked up. *The Times* considered that 'to remove one of the ablest of the younger members of the Government from the charge of an important department after so short a time to be a spokesman in the Commons – on a subject where he will have two masters when Mr Selwyn Lloyd had only one – is an extravagant use of the highest talent.'[11] Though a paper demotion for Heath in the short term, however, the appointment was widely regarded as Macmillan's way of giving him some necessary experience on the overseas side – leading perhaps to the Foreign Office itself in a couple of years' time – to complete his grooming as the Prime Minister's favoured eventual heir.

But was this all? Why did Macmillan choose Heath for this – as it turned out – critical appointment? There was as yet, in the summer of 1960, no question of Britain applying to join the EEC, though clearly Macmillan's mind was moving towards considering it a possibility. Heath's initial brief was simply to explore the options of closer association between Britain and EFTA (the European Free Trade Association) on the one hand and the EEC on the other. There was no certainty that if Britain applied Heath would be the man to lead the negotiations. Yet in practice the one job led naturally to the other. Macmillan knew better than the press in July 1960 that he was positioning Heath for a role that might make or break the Government. Was he then merely picking a trusted functionary who would efficiently and uncomplainingly carry out his policy, whatever that might turn out to be? Or did he choose Heath because he knew him to be a convinced European? The evidence is curiously ambiguous. Despite his maiden speech in favour of joining the Schuman Plan ten years before, Heath was *not* at this date known at Westminster as a committed European. 'His views in this vital aspect of UK policy', the *Financial Times* could write on his appointment, 'are unknown, and he has never had a chance to show in public whether he has any.'[12] Nora Beloff, writing in 1963, did not think that Heath was chosen for his known convictions; rather the contrary, he was chosen for his record as Chief Whip in keeping the party united around a contentious policy. Had Macmillan been ready to commit himself, and the Government, in advance of the soundings that began in July 1960, he would have chosen one of the Government's established advocates of closer links with Europe – Peter Thorneycroft, Christopher Soames or Duncan Sandys. As it was, he shrewdly switched Sandys and Soames to the key departments of Commonwealth Relations and Agriculture (though once again the significance of the shuffle was largely missed at the time); but for the critical European portfolio itself he carefully picked a relatively junior protégé who would be seen to approach the subject with an open mind. Did Macmillan know from private conversations that Heath was more favourably disposed than he admitted in public? Nora Beloff cites Heath himself denying that he had been committed to Europe before taking up his new job in 1960.[13]

On the evidence, then, Heath would appear to have owed the decisive appointment of his life less to his previous convictions than to his lack of them. It was the job that consolidated his European faith, rather than his faith that recommended him for the job. Once appointed, he quickly became enthusiastic – even possessive – about the European cause. Negotiating a closer relationship with Europe was the latest task he had been called upon to discharge, and he threw himself into it with total dedication, knowing that his career might be made or marred by his success or failure. Honourable ambition coincided with opportunity: it was not in his character to have questioned what he was asked to do. Thus it is arguable that Heath's European vision – the vision which sustained and fired the rest of his career – was an extraneous implant, formed by Macmillan's disposition of offices in 1960, rather than a spontaneous growth springing from his own thought processes. This would explain the paradox that several close colleagues, sympathetic to his belief in Britain's European destiny, have noted in his commitment, which strikes them as oddly rootless. For an ardent European he seems to lack any instinctive feel for the culture or languages of Europe: his French is an embarrassment, his German non-existent. Unlike Soames or Sandys, for instance, devoted francophiles both, he remains stubbornly, quintessentially English. On the other hand, he seemed at this period equally to lack Macmillan's broad historical sweep, the grand strategic imagination to seize on the necessity and opportunity of Britain realigning herself on the world stage with the recovering continent of Europe. Good judges who worked with Heath at close quarters during the 1961–3 negotiations could not at that date see quite what it was, apart from personal opportunism, that drove his European conviction.

Yet this is surely unfair. Seen over the span of his life as a whole, the consistency and the springs of his Europeanism are quite clear. His physical closeness to Europe as a boy in Broadstairs and his unusual interest in travelling around Europe as an undergraduate; the early awareness which this gave him of fascism, of the menace of war in 1937–9 and the importance of promoting Franco-German unity after 1945 to prevent its recurrence; his love of music, originally nurtured in English church music but very quickly spreading to embrace German and Austrian music – he may not have spoken the languages of Europe but he is deeply imbued with the pan-European language of music; for all his undented Englishness, all this predisposed him far more than most Britons of his generation to a recognition of the importance of Europe and of Britain's natural place within it. Little though it seems to have been remembered in 1960, his maiden speech does show that he was prepared to make a political commitment to Europe right at the outset of his career. Finally, though less lofty in his expression, he surely had as much grasp as Macmillan of the strategic dimension of Britain going into Europe. Admittedly he tended to see it very much in terms of finding a new outlet for British greatness, a new forum for British leadership, in a way that a pure European federalist might find less than fully *communautaire*; but then so did Macmillan and so have almost all British pro-Europeans. Heath's Europeanism certainly springs from an extended patriotism, an extension of his Englishness: but it is no less genuine for that. There is really no good reason to doubt the depth and sincerity of his European faith. The fact that so many people who knew him well continued to feel that there was some sort of mystery about it is only the most striking testimony to the exceptional difficulty he has in communicating his deepest beliefs.

The first thing he did after his appointment was to go on holiday to Venice (this time with his successor at the Ministry of Labour, John Hare, and his family). He returned to London on 13 August to take temporary charge of the Foreign Office while Home went off to the grouse moors. He threw himself straight into his first round of exploratory talks, visiting Rome in late August and Paris in early October to follow up the successful meeting which Macmillan and Home had had in early August with Adenauer in Bonn – the break-through which is generally reckoned the starting point of the slow process which led a year later to Britain's decision to apply formally to join the Common Market. A combination of many factors had driven Macmillan to consider the benefits of closer association with Europe. On the international level the humiliation of Suez and the failure of Blue Streak – Britain's last attempt at a genuinely independent nuclear deterrent – had painfully exposed Britain's isolation and dependence upon America, while the collapse of the 1960 super-power summit had increased the sense of Europe's military vulnerability. Both politically and economically it seemed that the Six had made a striking success of their joint venture since coming together – in the face of British scepticism – in 1957. British economic growth was beginning to lag perceptibly behind the dynamic pace being set by the community, which was increasingly Britain's key market; while the self-confident leadership of Adenauer and de Gaulle exuded a powerful, if intangible, sense that something important was happening on the continent from which Britain could not afford to be excluded. Informed opinion, expressed in such journals as *The Economist* and the *Financial Times*, but critically co-ordinated in Whitehall by the conversion of Sir Frank Lee, newly appointed Joint Permanent Secretary at the Treasury in 1960, was coming to the conclusion that Britain had somehow to come to terms with the new Europe before she was permanently locked out. The problem – or one of them – was that in 1957, following the failure of Reginald Maudling's attempt to negotiate a halfway house arrangement to secure British access to the Community without all the burdens of membership, Britain had joined with six smaller countries – Denmark, Norway, Sweden, Switzerland, Austria and Portugal – to form a looser rival trading bloc, the European Free Trade Association, to which the British Government now had obligations. When Heath first took up his European portfolio in August 1960 the emphasis of his task was still very much on not abandoning EFTA, but finding some way of reconciling EFTA with the EEC, healing what Britain tried to present as the damaging division of Europe between the Six and the Seven.

Britain's second and more serious set of obligations was to the Commonwealth. In 1960 it was still axiomatic right across the political spectrum that Britain could not join the EEC at the expense of traditional trading links with the Commonwealth, old and new. As Heath himself promised the Tory party conference in October: 'If it ever came to a choice between Europe and the Commonwealth, of course, there could be absolutely no doubt whatever about our answer . . . But', he insisted, 'that is not the question.'[14] The British hope at this stage was still that they could somehow gain access to the benefits of the European market without losing the right to import cheap food from the Commonwealth. At Strasbourg in September Heath told the Council of Europe bluntly that 'for Britain to sign the Treaty of Rome in its present form would be impossible'.[15] His expectation was that the Six would be prepared to relax their exclusivity to accommodate Britain. He started from the assumption that they wanted Britain to join them as much as Britain wanted to join.

Over the following months, however, it was made very plain to him that Britain would have to adapt itself to the Community and not vice versa. At this early stage Heath was only doubtful whether British public opinion was ready to make the leap of imagination necessary to join with Europe. Characteristically he expressed the choice less in terms of tariffs and trading patterns than as an almost spiritual opportunity:

> But Europe, I find, says this to us: 'We accept that the unity of Europe is not complete without the UK with all that it has stood for and stands for today. But we ask you this question. In an association are you prepared to share with us this new dynamic outlook which we believe we are creating in Europe? Are you prepared to take part with us in all these other activities which we are developing, expanding and leading to a fuller life for so many people?' That is the question which Europe is putting to us. I do not know how long it is going to take the people of this country to think over the answer to that question. I do not know to which answer they will finally come. What I do know is the importance which will depend on it.

In this speech Heath showed himself well aware of the difficulties of reconciling the British and European trading systems, but he anticipated more problems from British conservatism than with the Six. He saw the need to find some accommodation between EFTA and the EEC overwhelmingly in political terms; typically he saw the matter of overcoming technical difficulties merely as a question of political will. 'We have the will,' he concluded. 'We hope that Europe will respond and that together we can make an arrangement.'[16]

For the present, however, he stressed that Britain was trying only 'to find a position from which we can move into a negotiation'. Over the next several months the soundings continued. The pro-Market commentators applauded the Government's shift of attitude – 'Mr Heath has even got on civil terms with Professor Hallstein [the President of the Commission]' *The Economist* remarked, 'a startling change from what may be called the Maudling era'[17] – but thought its approach still much too slow. The *Guardian* condemned as 'feeble' Heath's announcement to the Commons in November that formal negotiations would not begin until there was absolute certainty of their success.[18] In fact by the end of the year he was getting an unprecedentedly critical press all round: nothing seemed to be coming of his European discussions, while he was cutting a poor figure speaking on other Foreign Office matters in the lower House. From the Labour side Richard Crossman wrote him down as 'a most bromidic kind of junior Foreign Secretary, who burbled along'.[19] From the gallery Peregrine Worsthorne offered some sympathy for him but echoed the same judgment: 'Pitched into foreign affairs, about which he knows little, with his tongue tied because of Lord Home's seniority, he has made a sadly poor impression on the House.'[20] Those who had always said that ex-Chief Whips never did well in other offices seemed to be vindicated.

Yet this was a low point from which his reputation recovered steadily during the spring and summer as Macmillan inched his Cabinet and public opinion towards the point of a formal application for entry. A key moment came in February, when Heath announced, in a carefully worded statement to the Western European Union in Paris, that provided the Six could meet Britain's difficulties over agriculture and the Commonwealth, Britain would 'consider' accepting a common external tariff on raw materials and manufactures from countries other than EFTA and the Commonwealth, and reducing preferences to the Commonwealth.[21] Though a pathetically small one as it turned out, this was Britain's first tentative step towards acceptance of the common obligations of the Common Market. Even supposing that Macmillan himself understood how much more ground Britain would yet have to give, he still felt that he could only break it very gradually to the party and the public. In retrospect it is clear that this period of minimising the adjustments that membership of the Community would involve only helped to convince the French that Britain was not yet ready for Europe.

On 17 May, however, in the House of Commons, though he still did not announce a decision, Heath gave the Government's clearest indication yet that it saw no alternatives to going in. He rehearsed the reasons as usual in frankly political terms, stressing 'the dangers which face us of decline in political influence' if Britain remained outside; he ended with his personal conviction that Europe was the great challenge for 'our generation', submerging the technicalities in the grand perspective of unity and freedom.[22] Though his major rhetorical effort to date, the speech was still a disappointing parliamentary occasion. *The Economist* thought it 'anti-climactic', partly because Heath failed to draw the conclusion from his own arguments, partly because he was now 'vying with Mr Watkinson to establish his claim to be the Government's most pedestrian speaker'. Despite his peroration, 'Mr Heath's Peelite plea of national expediency did not warm the hearts of the handful of fervent Europeans sitting behind him.' Nevertheless it was well tailored to persuade the uncommitted. Heath went further towards committing the Government than Macmillan had yet dared to do, and was heard 'in respectful and attentive silence' which indicated that the bulk of the party would follow when the Government gave a lead.[23]

Two weeks later, overriding the persisting doubts of Butler, Maudling and one or two more, the Cabinet took its decision to apply. Before it was announced, a flurry of ministers was dispatched to different parts of the Commonwealth to allay fears and try to forestall the premature expression of opposition: Heath visited Cyprus, and also Vienna for further talks with EFTA. Then he went on holiday with the Seligmans to Brittany, so as to be out of the country when the news was announced on 18 August that he had been appointed to lead the negotiations. The next day he collected the English papers from the village shop and found himself hailed on every front page as 'Mr Europe'.[24] *The Times* judged him the right choice for his 'negotiating abilities and his skill in human relationships'.[25] *The Economist* also approved and added, 'If he is successful, he will find himself well in the running for the leadership of the party.'[26]

The official team which was now assembled, under Heath's leadership, to conduct the British side of the negotiations was by general consent a group of exceptional quality. It was headed, formally, by the Ambassador to France, Sir Pierson Dixon, with Sir Eric Roll from the Ministry of Agriculture as his deputy and Sir Frank Lee co-ordinating the work of the departments back in London. Dixon's appointment reflected the decisive importance of winning French support for Britain's application. (As *The Times* commented prophetically on 31 July, 'No-one, except perhaps

General de Gaulle, can know the final outcome.'[27] Dixon had established exceptionally good relations with de Gaulle, which it was hoped he could exploit to keep the General favourable. In the event it was widely felt that Dixon's influence was compromised by involving him directly in the negotiations; with hindsight it would have been better to have kept him in Paris, concentrating all his attention on de Gaulle, undistracted by responsibilities in Brussels. The appointment of Roll, however, could not have been bettered. Educated in Germany, deputy head of the British Food Mission to North America during the war, he was effortlessly trilingual – he was said to be able to lip-read in three languages, an invaluable asset to Heath at tense moments in the negotiations – and experienced in international haggling. Roll was not only one of the most subtle but one of the most cosmopolitan minds in Whitehall. He was assisted by an almost equally top-flight team from the Foreign Office, the Commonwealth Relations Office, the Colonial Office, the Board of Trade, the Ministry of Agriculture and the Treasury. Despite the disappointing outcome of the negotiation, over the sixteen months it lasted the negotiators of the Six were immensely impressed by the calibre of their British counterparts.

Nor is there any doubt that they were superbly led. Heath, in the words of Eric Roll,

> proved to be an outstanding leader. He combined in a unique way the qualities of a first-rate official having complete mastery of complex technical details with the necessary political touch in his contacts with Ministers and officials of other countries . . . with the press and with London. He was the sort of Minister British senior Civil Servants particularly admire and like to work with, always ready to listen to advice yet quite clear in the end as to what ought to be said and done . . .
>
> There is no doubt that he [was] highly respected by our negotiating partners despite many sharp and sometimes even disagreeable passages. Heath was equally good in these encounters, often over lunch or dinner, with one or two of the other delegations, as he was in larger, more formal meetings, including the plenary ones.[28]

Once again, as in the war, as in the Whips' office, Heath was in his element leading a small team with a clear job to do, taking his orders ultimately from Macmillan in London but firmly in command of his own operation. There are a number of criticisms that can be made of the strategy and politics of the British approach to the negotiations;

but at the technical level of detail and teamwork Heath's conduct of them was beyond reproach. In this context of professional respect and mutual trust he had no difficulty with personal relations. In Brussels respect and trust extended even to the specialist press corps attached to the negotiations, whom Heath learned to take into his confidence as he never could the press at home. Roll has recalled the regular press briefings held in the basement of the British delegation hotel:

> These meetings . . . should have proved to anyone present that the widely supposed coldness and unapproachability of Heath was and is a complete myth. He is, to be sure, a reserved man, but he is entirely capable of the warmest and friendliest feelings and of great personal kindnesses. He is also quite capable of losing his temper, though in my experience this was more likely to happen with his own ministerial colleagues than with officials. After one particularly stormy midnight session with one of them I tried to argue with him that he would more effectively carry out his task as 'conductor' of the orchestra by allowing some of his colleagues an occasional 'solo'. He listened patiently enough, but it made little difference in practice.[29]

This was an example of Heath's possessiveness. Politically, Europe was his show and he was jealous of any of his colleagues who tried to get in on the act. On one occasion, Roll remembers, he was furious when he thought that Soames, as Minister of Agriculture, had been talking with the Italian Agriculture Minister behind his back. As he got nearer the top of the greasy pole and was increasingly spoken of as a possible future leader, he began to view his contemporaries as rivals who must be kept from stealing any of the glory which should be his alone. An important result of this period of close working intimacy with first-rate officials in Brussels – and not only in Brussels but shuttling continuously back and forth between Brussels and London, Paris, Bonn and Rome – was to confirm Heath's preference, very marked during his premiership, for working with his senior officials rather than with his fellow politicians.

The negotiations finally opened with Heath's formal presentation of Britain's application in Paris on 10 October 1961. His statement has been criticised for still hedging Britain's bets, still seeming to want some form of association rather than full membership. Yet the expression of intent was clear enough:

> We recognise it as a great decision, a turning point in our history,

and we take it in all seriousness. In saying that we wish to join the EEC, we mean that we desire to become full, whole-hearted and active members of the European Community in its widest sense and to go forward with you in the building of a new Europe . . .

We accept without qualification the objectives laid down in Articles 2 and 3 of the Treaty of Rome, including the elimination of internal tariffs, a common customs tariff, a common commercial policy, and a common agricultural policy.[30]

The statement went on to set out the three major areas of difficulty which it would be the task of negotiations to overcome: the problem of the Commonwealth; the problem of reconciling the British system of agricultural support by means of deficiency payments with the European system of import levies; and the problem of EFTA. (In fact EFTA proved not to be a great problem: the third area of difficulty actually turned out to be the 'financial regulation' – the level of Britain's contribution to the Community budget.) On all these Britain naturally pitched its opening position high: having affirmed clear acceptance of the broad principles of the Community the British negotiators felt entitled to bargain hard on the detailed terms. But there was a tricky course to steer between, on the one hand, alarming domestic and Commonwealth opinion by giving away too much too soon and, on the other, confirming Community doubts of the seriousness of Britain's commitment by demanding too much special treatment. Within the closed world of the negotiators the British statement was well received. But when it leaked, it seemed better calculated to reassure the Commonwealth than to impress the Six.

In Brussels everything leaked. This was one of the technical problems of the negotiation: with so many separate multilateral and bilateral conversations going on outside the plenary sessions between ministers, officials and journalists of seven countries (plus all the Commonwealth and EFTA representatives anxious to be heard) nothing could be kept secret. Rumour and misinformation abounded, creating what Roll has called 'a sort of quagmire of information'.[31] A deeper structural problem arose from the format of the negotiations. Britain did not negotiate with the EEC Commission but with the six existing countries of the Community 'acting as far as possible together'. Before they could talk to Britain, the Six had to have long talks among themselves to formulate their common position. Once this had been achieved, they were naturally reluctant to reopen matters which had been agreed in order to accommodate Britain. Yet this was just what Heath had time and again to ask them to do. Britain was thus always placed in the uncomfortable position of the *demandeur*, seeking concessions and having to risk appearing *non-communautaire* by insisting that arrangements already painfully arrived must be unpicked. The neutral staff of the Commission were on hand to help clear obstacles when they arose; but there was no fixed chairmanship, which might have helped to drive agreements through. The chairmanship rotated among the Six, making matters settled at one session liable to be reopened at a later stage. The whole process could not have been more wearisome for the British team. As Nora Beloff commented: 'A less resilient personality than the Lord Privy Seal would have been driven to distraction by the long hours he was to spend pacing in ante-rooms.'[32]

A more substantive problem was that in the autumn of 1961 the Six were still in the process of settling between themselves the principles of the common agricultural policy (CAP). It would have been helpful to Britain if this could have been left over until Britain was inside the Community and able to take part in shaping the CAP as a member. But the French were determined that the CAP negotiations must be concluded first – very much to French advantage – before there was any consideration of how it might be modified to accommodate Britain. Until January 1962 the Six were still locked in agricultural/financial wrangling of their own which would settle the outlines of the CAP for thirty years to come. Britain initially hoped for a quick negotiation – for the very reason that they wanted to get in before the shape of the Community was set in concrete. As *The Economist* wrote in July, at the time of the final decision to apply: '1961 may well be the last year in which Britain can enter with a fair hope of helping to shape it.'[33] This was precisely why the French had no intention of letting Britain in until the last major element of the structure envisaged in 1957 was in place. There was a good deal of criticism, after the British application had failed, that the negotiation had been too slow, that Britain had dragged it out by insisting on haggling in painstaking detail over every item of agricultural produce (kangaroo meat was always cited), instead of plunging in with a whole-hearted acceptance of the principle of entry, leaving the details to be worked out later. There are several answers to this criticism, but not the least important is that it was the French who, for reasons of their own, were determined to impose delay.

The main reason on the British side why it was not possible to plunge in without regard to the detailed terms was the political need to educate public opinion gradually to the idea of entry. Heath himself, Roll and several other of the participants looking back after January 1963 asked themselves whether de Gaulle's veto might have been avoided by a quick acceptance of the principle of membership, followed by a period of adjustment once inside. The father figure of the Community, Jean Monnet, believed that this should have been the British course.[34] But they practically all concluded that, whereas such an early commitment might have disarmed de Gaulle it was simply not politically possible at home. Certainly Macmillan believed that he could not rush it. In fact the Tory party took the Government's conversion astonishingly easily. At the 1961 conference ministers had been fully prepared to see an anti-Common Market motion moved by Sir Derek Walker-Smith carried; in the event Walker-Smith found very little support and Heath and Duncan Sandys between them got it overwhelmingly rejected. The anti-Marketeers at this time lacked effective leadership: the strident opposition of the *Daily* and *Sunday Express* found no heavyweight champion in the upper levels of the party. Beaverbrook was a maverick old man: Eden declined to lend his name. By the time of the 1962 conference the party was swept up in a mood of optimistic enthusiasm for Britain's imminent entry. The fact that Labour was painfully split on the question and that Gaitskell eventually came down – against his own closest supporters – against entry only made the Tories keener to trumpet their commitment to Britain's European future. Public opinion was much less excited, but during the first half of 1962 the polls showed increasing acquiescence to the idea of going in: at any rate little violent opposition.

Generally speaking, the Government's line was to play down the extent of the new departure which going into Europe would represent. In his important speech to the 1961 conference – just two days after delivering Britain's opening bid in Paris – Heath was careful to place EEC membership in the context of other international organisations to which Britain already belonged: NATO, the OECD, EFTA, the Council of Europe.[35] On television, while always firm and positive in his determination to go in, he was repeatedly at pains to allay fears that the British way of life would be undermined. The long-term implications of the Treaty of Rome were far in the future and, once in, Britain would have a veto on developments she did not like. In particular he stressed that Britain would not be turning her back on the Commonwealth. 'Ultimately', he insisted in the House of Commons and to a hundred other audiences over the next year, British membership of the Community would be '– and I fundamentally believe this – for the benefit of our partners in the Commonwealth.'[36]

If this line was to be accepted, however, it was necessary to secure the best possible deal for the Commonwealth; and this was the second reason why Britain could not simply sign the Treaty of Rome and go in. Britain had originally hoped to secure favourable terms of access to the European market for the Commonwealth as a whole. It was a major shock to British illusions, in the spring of 1962, when the Six, having finally settled the CAP among themselves, rejected this proposition out of hand. After that there was no alternative to an exhausting series of bilateral deals, country by country and product by product, to win the best possible transitional terms. It was in these that the negotiations became bogged down, but Britain had to be seen to be fighting to safeguard the interests of every one of her former colonies and traditional trading partners. Progress might have been quicker if the negotiators could have delegated more of the hammering out of individual deals to specialist groups chaired by the Commission, as was eventually done with temperate foodstuffs (cereals and dairy produce) at the end of 1962; but essentially there was no short cut. By the end, when the negotiations were suspended in January 1963, terms for some 2,500 separate products had been agreed, with less than thirty still outstanding.★

Yet a third reason why the negotiations took so long comes back to the French, who deliberately dragged them out as part of their diplomatic strategy. It is impossible to know whether de Gaulle intended to veto the British application all along. Sir Pierson Dixon, who knew him better than anyone else on the British side, always feared so. He minuted his apprehensions to Macmillan in May 1962: Macmillan, with typical insouciance, wrote in the margin 'Interesting, but not convincing.'[37] More likely – this was the fear Heath expressed to Macmillan about the same time – de Gaulle hoped that he would not need to veto, believing either that the talks would break down or that any terms agreed would prove unacceptable to the House of Commons.[38] But he wanted to keep open the option of veto, and for this he needed to ensure that the negotiations were not concluded too soon. He had to secure his own domestic position, by means of a referendum in June and Assembly elections in the autumn, before he felt strongly enough to risk such an imperious act of will. Accordingly the French negotiators persistently slowed down the pace through the spring and summer and then quite calculatedly – to the exasperation of the Five – presented an entirely new set of proposals on temperate foodstuffs at the end of July to prevent any possibility of agreement being reached before the summer break

★ It was during these negotiations – not as is often thought at the time of his battle to abolish retail price maintenance in 1964 – that *Private Eye* took to calling Heath 'Grocer'.

on 4 August. This was a bad moment, which in retrospect clearly foreshadowed the eventual outcome and even at the time seemed to put the prospects of success suddenly in jeopardy. Heath and Dixon reported back to Macmillan at Chequers. According to Dixon's account, 30 July was 'crunch day' when the Cabinet had to decide either to settle for what had been offered so far or hold out for further concessions without which it would be difficult to maintain that the interests of the Commonwealth had been protected.[39] In the Commons, Heath had a rough ride from the defenders of the Commonwealth, both Conservative and Labour. The Cabinet resolved to hold out. Over the next few days, back in Brussels, Heath and the Belgian Foreign Minister, Paul-Henri Spaak, managed to narrow the differences to three points, which would have enabled broad agreement to be concluded before the summer. But the French, in the austere person of the Foreign Minister, Maurice Couve de Murville, still procrastinated, demanding an impossibly steep financial settlement which Heath (backed by the Germans and the Dutch) was bound to refuse. At 7 am on the morning of 5 August, after a final session lasting fifteen hours, the talks broke up in exhaustion. Heath was despondent, anxious to reconvene in September; Couve, his object achieved, was in no hurry to resume before October.

As they absorbed this setback the British persuaded themselves that there might after all be some advantage in not having the whole deal tied up before the summer. The next domestic hurdle they faced was the Commonwealth conference in mid-September, followed by the Tory party conference. In the event the Commonwealth conference, skilfully massaged by Macmillan and Sandys, went off reasonably well: the assembled prime ministers voiced their anxieties but did not in the end seek to dictate to Britain. 'The blunt truth', *The Economist* asserted, 'is that the terms offered in Brussels so far are slightly better for the white Commonwealth, and very much better for the black Commonwealth, than anybody dared to expect a year ago.'[40] With the risk of a Commonwealth veto averted, the party conference presented no problem. For the second year running Walker-Smith's anti-Market amendment was massively defeated, and Heath was the hero of the hour. Though *The Economist* wrote unkindly of his 'dully technocratic dissertation which ground on above his audience's head, desperately eager though the conference was to cheer him',[41] the BBC report accorded him a 'great personal triumph'.[42] Rhetorically at least he had an easy target, Gaitskell having now come out emotionally against the Market, taking up a position more protective of the Commonwealth than the Commonwealth leaders themselves. Heath dealt with him robustly:

Mr Gaitskell said at Brighton, 'Is it inevitable that if we go in we shall become stronger and more prosperous?' I understand he gave the answer, a resounding 'No!' Of course not. Nothing is inevitable. Unless you are a determinist in general, and a dialectical materialist in particular, nothing is inevitable. What he did was to ask himself the wrong question, and he really must not be surprised if he gives himself the wrong answer. What he should have asked is, 'Will the opportunities, if we go in, enable us to become stronger, and would we become, comparatively speaking, weaker if we stayed out?' And the answer to that is, of course, 'Yes!' The opportunities, if we seize them, would enable us to become stronger. The Government itself has never disguised the challenge which we shall face and the need to seize the opportunities if we are to succeed economically in the Common Market.[43]

He ended by winning the conference's overwhelming approval to go back and conduct the negotiations to a successful conclusion. Despite the warning which the August breakdown should have sounded, the attention of the British Government and the British press was still too exclusively concentrated on their own difficulties, believing that once they had overcome these the way would be clear, not enough on developments across the Channel. The British team returned to Brussels in October confident that though some hard bargaining still lay ahead an acceptable deal would eventually be concluded. The *Sunday Times* cheerfully predicted that British entry was now certain.[44] The reality was that the failure to achieve a deal before the summer proved fatal to Britain's cause. Not only did de Gaulle comfortably win his elections in October, but at least two new factors now emerged to stiffen his inclination to keep Britain out.

First, the Labour party's decision to oppose entry contradicted the Government's claim that Britain was whole-heartedly ready and determined to take the European plunge. A Labour Government might want to take the country out again or try to renegotiate whatever terms might be accepted by Macmillan and Heath; and in the autumn of 1962 Labour looked very likely to be the next British Government. The Conservatives were trailing in the polls. Moreover public opinion, as it began for the first time to focus seriously on the question of Europe, seemed to be turning *against* going in. Here was one good justification for de Gaulle's veto.

Second, events that autumn conspired to exacerbate his deep suspicion of the Americans and of the British for being too much in their pocket. The Cuban missile crisis proved to de Gaulle's mind that the Americans would consult only their own interest in deciding whether or not to use nuclear weapons. Then Macmillan's meeting with President Kennedy at Nassau in December, at which Macmillan desperately sought a replacement for the abandoned Skybolt rocket and Kennedy agreed to let him have Polaris on favourable terms, further convinced de Gaulle that Britain's primary international relationship was still with the United States. Kennedy's subsequent offer of Polaris to France as well he regarded as an insult. What, it appears, de Gaulle had really wanted all along from Britain was a promise of nuclear co-operation, sharing Britain's more advanced nuclear technology. This was the key which might have persuaded the General to allow Britain into Europe. But in the course of the several meetings they had during 1961–2 – at Birch Grove in November 1961, at Château des Champs in June 1962 (on both of which occasions de Gaulle had seemed to be prepared to look favourably on British membership) and finally at Rambouillet in December 1962, just before Macmillan flew off to Nassau – Macmillan had not offered it and de Gaulle had been too proud to ask. The Rambouillet meeting was a chilly one, from which Macmillan guessed the worst. When the veto came he at least was forewarned.

But Heath was not. At first, hopes that the negotiations would go more easily after the summer were disappointed. Progress was still sticky on the harmonisation of British domestic agriculture and on the 'financial regulation'. Nevertheless by the end of the year agreement appeared to be in sight. On 14 December the problem of the British farmers was handed over to a special commission headed by Dr Sicco Mansholt, which undertook to come up with a solution in mid-January. On 19 December Heath was turning his mind confidently to practical aspects of British membership, such as the appointment of two British members of the enlarged Commission.[45] The first public hint of de Gaulle's intention came in his New Year message on French television, when he wondered aloud whether Britain was really 'European' enough to join the Community. Yet five days later Macmillan found Heath 'still hopeful of a successful outcome.'[46] On 11 January Dixon, Heath and Roll had Couve de Murville and the principal French negotiator, Olivier Wormser, to lunch at the British Embassy in Paris. In view of alarming rumours coming from the Elysée, Heath asked Couve directly if he thought the President was going to veto Britain's entry. Couve said he did not expect it. Heath then asked if political objections would prevent Britain's entry if the economic difficulties were solved. Couve replied that if the technical difficulties could be solved 'no power on earth could prevent you from coming in'.[47] Was he being disingenuous? It was Dixon's view that Couve genuinely did not know

what was in the General's mind. At any rate Heath was reassured. At
dinner that evening the American Under-Secretary of State, George
Ball, found him 'in ebullient good spirits'.[48]

The following Monday, 14 January, at one of his quasi-regal press
conferences in the Elysée, de Gaulle dropped his bombshell. He
announced quite bluntly that Britain was different from the countries
of continental Europe. 'In her daily life, her habits and traditions are
very special and very original.' Britain had declined to join the Community at the outset and actually had done her best to prevent it
being formed. Her trading system was 'obviously incompatible'
with that which the Six had established to suit themselves. Was
Britain, he demanded, really ready to abandon her system and con-
form to the European one – renouncing *all* preferences for the
Commonwealth, abandoning *any* special privileges for her own
farmers? By expressing the choice in such absolute terms, de Gaulle
abruptly swept aside the months of effort to work out acceptable
transitional arrangements to ease Britain gradually into conformity
with Community rules. These efforts were on the brink of success:
Dr Mansholt's commission presented its proposals the very next day.
But de Gaulle himself gave the answer to his own question: 'It cannot
be said that at the present time Britain is ready to do these things.'

So far de Gaulle was asserting that the technical problems had not
been solved: that assessment could be, and was, disputed. But then
he broadened his indictment, revealing his deeper, unanswerable
reason for wishing to keep Britain out. If Britain came in, he said, a
lot of other countries would have to come in too; and the present
close-knit Europe of the Six would be overwhelmed. 'A colossal
Atlantic Community would emerge under American dependence
and control, which would soon swallow up the European Community.'[49] Britain, on this view, was merely a Trojan horse for the
American domination of Europe.

What so outraged the British and indeed the other five members of
the Community who wanted Britain in was that everything de
Gaulle alleged about the historic differences between Britain and the
Six, and Britain's special relationship with the United States, had
been known before the negotiations started. The sixteen months of
arduous negotiations had been undertaken on the basis that the political will was there to overcome and reconcile those differences; and
on that assumption they had virtually succeeded. Now de Gaulle was
saying that it was all a waste of effort and the differences were after
all unbridgeable. Eric Roll afterwards recalled an ominous (and very
French) story which Olivier Wormser had told him at the outset of
the negotiations of a suitor who insisted that he must see the girl

naked before he would agree to marry her and then finally, when she stood stripped before him, objected to the shape of her nose![50] That was – humiliatingly – what de Gaulle had done with Britain. Why could he not have rejected Britain's application at the beginning, when it was first made? The bitterness for Heath and his team was that de Gaulle had felt compelled to use his veto to abort the negotiations precisely because they had come so unexpectedly close to success. He had not expected Britain to be prepared to strip so far.

The French, in the person of the unfortunate Couve, stoutly maintained the opposite, asserting that all they had done was to face the fact that the negotiations had been getting nowhere since October and were now deadlocked. This was not the view of the other participants. Their initial response was to carry on as if nothing had happened, as though the French negotiators in Brussels were not bound by the Olympian pronouncements of their President, hoping perhaps that the chorus of outrage from the Five at de Gaulle's high-handedness would force him after all to back down, having delivered the salutory shock that would bring the negotiations to a quick conclusion. On 15 January the Mansholt compromise was ready. On 16 January Heath coolly presented new British proposals on tariffs, but Couve insisted on a fortnight's adjournment. During the interval it became clear that the General meant what he said and was immovable. So the last scene was enacted in Brussels on 29 January, in an atmosphere of high emotion and recrimination. In turn, round the table, the Foreign Ministers of the Five condemned and deplored the General's action. Again Couve defiantly denied French responsibility for the collapse. Then Heath, with Soames and Sandys sitting beside him, gave his response to the unilateral sabotage of all his efforts.

Observers in Brussels had already been amazed at the 'astonishing *sang-froid*' with which he had taken the blow.[51] Now he won renewed admiration for the dignity with which he delivered Britain's reply to the General's action. He was determined that Britain should treat the French veto not as a reason for turning her back on Europe, but merely as a petty-minded temporary setback. He delivered 'a long, moving and forthright statement which put the blame for the breakdown squarely on the French, but did so without vindictiveness'.[52] He reiterated the view of Britain, the Five and the Commission that 'all remaining problems of the negotiations were capable of solution'. Britain, he insisted, had shown herself fully willing to satisfy all the conditions of membership.

He refuted the suggestion that Britain was 'not European enough' by recalling the common experience of the two World Wars: 'There are many millions in Europe who know perfectly well how European Britain has been in the past and are grateful for it.' This, he admitted, was 'a sad moment for European unity'. 'The events of the past few weeks have placed in jeopardy progress towards that true European unity which, I believe, many millions of people desire.' But Britain was not going to retract her commitment now. The words of her application 'were very carefully weighed. They remain true today.' Britain had been greatly encouraged 'by the upsurge of support . . . which has been demonstrated in so many quarters in these recent weeks'.

And so I would say to my colleagues: they should have no fear. We in Britain are not going to turn our backs on the mainland of Europe or on the countries of the Community. We are a part of Europe: by geography, tradition, history, culture and civilisation. We shall continue to work with all our friends in Europe for the true unity and strength of this continent.[53]

'The eyes of at least three distinguished listeners', according to Nora Beloff, 'were seen to glisten, and the simultaneous-interpreter girls discreetly took hankies out of their bags. For the first time in history, an international economic negotiation was literally ending in tears.'[54] The ministers and officials of the Five all lined up to shake Heath's hand, while Couve stood awkwardly aside. Whatever else the negotiations had failed to achieve, they had at least, in the summing up of their first historian Miriam Camps, 'gone far to wipe out the feeling that had persisted since 1955 that the British were at worst hostile and, at best, unsympathetic to the unity of Europe. And Mr Heath had earned more genuine respect and affection from his European colleagues than had any British minister concerned with European questions since the end of the war.'[55]

Thus although the 1961–3 Common Market negotiations ended for Britain in historic failure, Heath emerged from the débâcle with his own reputation not diminished but enhanced. Whatever criticisms may be made of the British approach to the negotiations – too slow a build up, an unrealistic negotiating posture early on – no one ever suggested that his conduct of the tedious and complex talks had been other than superb. Moreover, while the French in particular retained doubts about the true depth of Britain's commitment to Europe, no one could have done more than Heath to persuade them that Britain was serious. He won two notable tributes from the Europeans. Publicly, in recognition of his outstanding efforts in the cause of European unity, he was awarded the Charlemagne Prize in April 1963. Previous winners included Churchill, Adenauer, Monnet and Schuman. Its award to Heath, less than three months after de

Gaulle's veto, was a pointed rebuff to the General. At the presentation ceremony at Aachen in May, the fulsome speech of the German Finance Minister, Ludwig Erhard (shortly to succeed Adenauer as Chancellor) in praise of Heath 'almost assumed the nature of a public repudiation of General de Gaulle's charges'. Erhard looked forward confidently to Europe's recovery from the present setback: 'If not today, tomorrow.'[56] Privately de Gaulle himself appeared to accept that it was only a matter of time before his veto was overborne. To Maurice Schuman in 1965 he predicted not only that Britain would eventually join the Community but that Heath, after an interval of Labour government, would be the man to lead her in.[57]

De Gaulle's readiness to accept that Britain might join the Community in due course makes possible a more favourable judgment on his 1963 veto. It is arguable that – through no fault of Heath or his dedicated team – the preceding negotiations, and in particular the British Government's evident anxiety about securing Commonwealth and public approval, had demonstrated that Britain was not yet, as a nation, wholly ready to commit her destiny to Europe. In so far as de Gaulle simply wished to maintain French hegemony in a cosy European club of Six – the single cock in a farmyard with five hens, unwilling to admit a second cock – then he was acting selfishly in the interest of France. He had no compunction about talking candidly in these terms to Macmillan at Rambouillet in December 1962.[58] There was also the danger that his veto might have had the effect of turning Britain permanently against Europe: to some extent perhaps it did. In many respects it would have been better, from Britain's point of view and Europe's, if Britain had been able to join the Community in 1963. When she did finally join – as de Gaulle predicted, under Heath's leadership – in 1973 it turned out to be at the worst possible moment. Yet the passage of another ten years, though it allowed the development of much more passionate opposition than existed in 1961–3, also led to a much wider and more settled understanding of the necessity and rightness of Britain joining than had existed at the time of the Macmillan–Heath attempt. Given all the doubt and anguish in 1971–5 it is difficult to maintain that Britain was readier for membership in 1963. There is a case for arguing that in the broad perspective de Gaulle was right to use his veto to delay Britain's entry in 1963.

Heath had impressed not only the Europeans. Both his conduct of the negotiations and his reporting back – to the Cabinet, to the Tory backbenchers' 1922 Committee, above all to the House of Commons – on the progress of the negotiations had revealed a lucidity of exposition, a power of analysis and an encyclopaedic grasp of detail which greatly enhanced his position within the party. At a time when the Government as a whole was losing its way, *The Economist* commented in December 1961, 'only Mr Heath has gained notably in stature and in confidence in addressing the House'.[59] The *Sunday Times*, noting the 'layer of tungsten beneath the affable exterior', saw him as more than just a skilled negotiator:

> If he does succeed it will quite largely be because he has thoroughly understood what he is trying to do . . . Far more than most politicians, he thinks in a concentrated way about what he is trying to do before he does it . . .
>
> He is the man who knows most about the European negotiations, and he expounds them with a confidence and vigour, without notes and often at considerable speed. He has increasingly mastered the House of Commons, where he is now one of the real strengths of the Government Front Bench.[60]

His new authority at the dispatch box even survived the breakdown of the negotiations. Having to admit the collapse of a central plank of Government policy is normally a humiliating ordeal for a minister; but Heath, giving the House the considered British view of the breakdown on 12 February, met only sympathy and admiration, as T. F. Lindsay recorded in the *Daily Telegraph*:

> Mr Heath's complete dominance of the House arose naturally from the fact that he is the only man in the country who has the whole facts at his fingertips. But there was more to it than that.
>
> Ministers with facts at their fingertips too often play cat's cradle. Mr Heath has learned during the past 18 months, how to be patient with the ignorant and persuasive with the bemused.[61]

It was a remarkable transformation from the dull Minister of Labour and the under-briefed junior Foreign Office spokesman of only two years earlier.

In the months following de Gaulle's veto Heath's task was damage limitation. He had to go on repeating that there would be no retreat from Europe, that Britain's application was still on the table and would stay there, and try to prevent any anti-European reaction arising from wounded national pride, so that some time in the future a renewed application could begin where the 1963 attempt had left off, without having to go back over all the same ground again. This was in his own interest, as much as anything else: Europe was now above

all his issue, and he had to keep it alive if his career was not to falter.
He was angry when Harold Wilson, the new Labour leader, tried to
exploit the setback by alleging that the Government's relations with
the Community, the Commonwealth and EFTA were alike in
ruins.[62] He missed no opportunity to assert that de Gaulle's high-
handedness only made the British more determined to stand their
ground.('If there is one thing an Englishman cannot stand', he told
the *Sunday Express*, 'it is being diddled.')[63] Meanwhile he drew the
lesson that, inside or outside the Community, Britain must urgently
set about modernising her economy to compete effectively with the
new Europe.

This was his new theme. Just three weeks after the confirmation of
de Gaulle's veto, Heath made a speech to a Young Conservative conference in London which might have served as his personal manifesto
for the next seven years, right up to his election as Prime Minister in
1970. In it he set out bluntly all the principal objectives with which he
would seek to identify himself and the Tory party in the last year of
Conservative government and in the years of opposition which lay
ahead:

We need to be just as ready to face change, to adapt ourselves,
now that we are not in the Community, as we were when we
were prepared to go into it.
Indeed we need to be more ready to face change.
We cannot afford to shelter industries which cannot stand on
their own feet with efficiency and justify themselves on economic
grounds.
We cannot allow ourselves the luxury of bad industrial relations.
We cannot allow ourselves the cosy reassurance of various restrictive practices.
We have to keep costs to a minimum, accept new techniques
and innovations and set high standards of business management
and industrial training. The nation's livelihood depends more than
ever before on finding new paths for our trade throughout the
world.[64]

His close exposure to the more dynamic economies of the Six over
the past two and a half years had convinced him of the relative back-
wardness and inefficiency of the British economy. Seized with this
revelation, he was impatient to take personal charge of doing something about it. Now that his European assignment was completed,

honourably even though unsuccessfully, he tried to persuade Macmillan to switch him back to the home front to tackle the unemployment blackspots of the declining industrial regions of the north. But Lord Hailsham, as part of a ragbag of functions as Lord President, was already supposed to be doing that in the north-east. Moreover having already sacked a third of his Cabinet the previous July Macmillan could not face another reshuffle. So Heath stayed where he was, no longer the Prime Minister's favourite political son. There was a widespread impression that Macmillan was trying to make Heath the scapegoat for the failure of the Government's central policy, or at any rate that he thought that a minister associated with a failed policy must expect to be sidelined for a while. Either way he miscalculated, since the collapse of its European venture was in reality much more damaging to the Government as a whole, and to Macmillan personally, than it was to Heath, whose increased stature was the Tory party's principal gain from the débâcle.* The fact remained that during the spring and summer of 1963, until the situation was unexpectedly transformed in the autumn, Heath's career was stalled. Now he really was in the supernumerary position he had appeared to be in when first appointed to the Foreign Office in 1960, spokesman for the Foreign Secretary in the House of Commons with no distinct responsibilities of his own. Even as deputy Foreign Secretary he was passed over when Macmillan chose to send Hailsham to Moscow in June to carry out the preliminary discussions which led to the signing of the nuclear test ban treaty. Heath accompanied Home to the signing ceremony in August, but only in his subordinate capacity. He suffered other embarrassments, too, first in March when he had to hold the fort for the Government on the Katanga crisis and, contrary to his own instincts, was obliged to give ground to the baying of the Tory right;[66] and, second, in July when he had to tell the House that Kim Philby was the 'Third Man' who had helped the spies Burgess and Maclean to escape to Moscow in 1951, and try to explain why the Government had subsequently recommended him to the *Observer* as a correspondent in Beirut.[67] The Philby disclosure followed on a string of security scandals in 1961–2 involving the Krogers, Gordon Lonsdale, George Blake and William Vassall and culminating in the sensational revelations of the

---

* The cartoonist Vicky, in the *Evening Standard*, commented ironically on the suggestion that Heath should have been promoted, not punished, following the collapse of the Common Market negotiations. His drawing on 7 March 1963 showed Heath as a boxer, flat on his back, while the crowd shouts 'Heath for Premier' and 'Ted for FO', with the caption 'Bravo! The boy's ready to tackle a bigger job.'[65]

Profumo affair, which found Heath palpably and painfully out of his depth. In July Dick Crossman went to see him privately about something else and found that 'Heath, poor man, was absolutely overwhelmed by the latest part of the security scandal.'[68] It was not a happy time to be Foreign Office spokesman in the Commons, even if Heath had not already been depressed by the failure of his great exertion of the previous two years and the refusal of Macmillan to move him. Friends reported that he was 'close to the end of his tether' at this time. 'He was more irritable with his colleagues, but he never broke out: they often wished he had.'[69]

In the career of every major politician, however, there are periods of adversity and temporary eclipse from which they re-emerge the stronger; bitter though it was at the time, Heath probably needed this interlude to recruit and redirect his energies. He was lucky it was no longer than nine months. Had Macmillan not fallen ill in October he would probably not have had the opportunity to reclaim a leading position in the party before the election; then, assuming the Tories lost, he would have been in no position to challenge for the succession. As it was, in that febrile summer of 1963, when Macmillan's survival looked most uncertain, he was not seriously in the running. Of his own generation Maudling was now Chancellor of the Exchequer, Macleod was Leader of the House and Chairman of the party, and even Enoch Powell was back with a department of his own as Minister of Health: Heath's bid to overtake them all with a triumphant Common Market negotiation had backfired. When Tory MPs were polled by the *Daily Telegraph* in June and again in July, Maudling had pulled far ahead of Butler, with Hailsham the new dark horse and Heath nowhere.[70]

Nevertheless 1963 was an important year in his private life, when he finally emerged from his 'cupboard' flat in Petty France and began to fashion for himself a grander style more appropriate to a senior minister of the Crown. By chance the lease on his flat, which had suited him very well as a *pied-à-terre* when he was shuttling continuously around the capitals of Europe, ran out at almost exactly the moment of de Gaulle's veto. He sought the help of women friends – Nancy-Joan Seligman and Jo Pattrick – to help him find another, but they found him hard to please: he was now looking for something a bit 'special'. He found it when a set of chambers fortuitously came up in Albany, a superior haven of cloistered peace off Piccadilly. He had put his name down for a set some years earlier, but he was lucky that a vacancy arose when it did. The rooms were perfect for him for at least three reasons apart from their style, seclusion and relative cheapness (£670 per annum). The previous tenant whose death had created the vacancy had been a musician – the composer, Arnold Bax. Among the other tenants were both Eric Roll and Sir Pierson Dixon. And the lease was for seven years. Though no one could have guessed the appropriateness of this in 1963, it so happened that it expired just a few weeks after the General Election of 1970, when Heath moved across St James's Park to an even better address.

The rooms – set F2 – were in a poor state of repair and decoration when Heath took them over; there was no bathroom (bathrooms were upstairs) and no proper kitchen. Heath hired Jo Pattrick, an interior designer whom he had met a couple of years earlier, to help him convert it into a comfortable duplex apartment, with a separate flat for a housekeeper. Then, with great thoroughness and guided by her advice, he set about furnishing and decorating it to his own taste. He had first to discover what his taste was. He knew he wanted to find a distinctively modern style – the whole self-image he was now developing was to be thrustingly modern – but he knew very little about contemporary design. With characteristic application he set himself to learn. Mrs Pattrick brought him samples of material, catalogues, pieces of cutlery to look at. He learned quickly, but was willing to take infinite trouble to get everything just right. They bought everything together. She found him 'a wonderful client'.[71]

Having – at the age of forty-seven – a proper home of his own for the first time, Heath was like a child with a new toy. He was 'tickled pink'[72] and showed it off to friends with irresistibly naïve pride. The eventual décor was modern but restrained – cream walls, orange curtains, chocolate carpet, black leather Scandinavian armchairs, Finnish glass – offset by an eclectic mixture of prints and paintings on the walls: 'a Picasso lithograph next to a Gillray cartoon, an Augustus John drawing beside Pugin House of Commons prints'; a number of military prints which he had had in Petty France, two Churchills which the great man had given him – his proudest possessions – and some of the water-colours which he was now beginning quite seriously to collect. In the study the blue velvet chair on which he had sat at the Coronation and subsequently bought contrasted with a modern stainless steel desk. The showpiece was his new Steinway piano, which he bought with the £450 he received for the Charlemagne Prize – the first he had owned since the old upright his parents had bought for him as a boy. (The prize could not have come at a better moment.) In addition he installed the most modern hi-fi equipment, with huge speakers, to play his now enormous collection of records. On a special shelf he mounted a discreetly self-congratulatory display of photographs – signed portraits of the three prime ministers he had served, Churchill, Eden and Macmillan, and news pictures showing himself with the Queen, Khrushchev and the Pope.[73]

This was the bachelor flat of an ambitious man who had come a long way but meant to go further. The acquisition of Albany marked Heath's arrival close to the very top of the political tree. Although at that precise moment he had met the first check in his career, within two years he was Leader of the Opposition. Albany was a statement that he had made it at least into contention for the top. For the first time he had a home and a presentable setting appropriate to a potential leader. Here he could entertain friends and play the expansive host to colleagues, younger supporters – and journalists. For the first twelve years of his political career he had lived virtually out of a suitcase, which emphasised his lack of 'background', still an immense if unmentionable handicap in the Conservative party of the early 1960s. Now, with an impeccable address, where Byron, Gladstone and Macaulay among others had lived before him, surrounded by the trophies that proclaimed his rites of passage and his right of membership, he had practically completed – in so far as he ever would – his absorption into the protective colouring of the Establishment.

And then came Blackpool.

8

After Blackpool

O N 8 October 1963 the Conservative party gathered in Blackpool for its annual conference, hoping to put behind it the setbacks and scandals of the previous nine months in readiness for the election which was generally expected in the spring. After a summer of mounting speculation that he might retire, Macmillan was expected to announce his intention of leading the party into the election. The reality was very different. Macmillan was taken ill and was forced to retire at short notice. The consequent contest for the succession between four well-supported candidates under the full glare of conference publicity, and the emergence of Lord Home as the unexpected winner amid bitter allegations of intrigue and manipulation, scarred the soul of the Tory party for a generation. The events of October 1963 are still recalled – with a shudder – by many Tories as the critical watershed in the history of the party since the war. It was not simply that one Prime Minister was replaced by another, with the inevitable disappointment of the hopes of the defeated rivals. The undemocratic manner of Home's 'emergence' aroused such recriminations, and exposed the party to such public ridicule, that it turned out to be a pyrrhic victory for the old order. Although the 1963 contest produced in the short term a startling throwback with the elevation to the leadership of a little-known Scottish aristocrat, it actually ensured that Home's successor, less than two years later, must be a leader of a very different stamp.

Specifically, the 1963 fiasco led directly to the leadership of Ted Heath. In October 1963 Heath was not a serious contender; in August 1965 he was elected leader. The effect of the earlier contest was to remove from his path, virtually at a stroke, practically all of those who would in normal circumstances have been his rivals. Rab Butler and Lord Hailsham, Reggie Maudling, Iain Macleod and Enoch Powell were all, in one way or another, damaged: either by their failure to win in 1963, by the manner of their candidacy or by their reactions to the result. The first two could not expect another chance on grounds of age alone; Macleod and Powell lost credit by their refusal to accept the result; while Maudling, though still ostensibly the front runner of the coming generation, was subtly diminished by having failed to take the prize at his first attempt. Heath, by contrast, gained both from not having been expected to win in 1963 (and therefore not disappointing anyone's hopes) and also, paradoxically, from Home's victory. For Home, too, was damaged by the controversy surrounding his succession and could clearly be no more than a stop-gap leader, keeping the seat warm until the party was ready for one of the class of 1950.

Heath in 1963 was like a horse safely back in fifth or sixth place when the leaders were involved in a multiple fall at Becher's. Fortunate to escape unscathed, he had suddenly only a single rival left to beat, on ground moreover that favoured his particular qualities: for the next leader would have to be as unlike a fourteenth earl as possible, and he was more unlike a fourteenth earl than Maudling. Of course he might have come into the leadership anyway, if Macmillan had hung on till 1965 or if either Butler or Hailsham had won and then gone on, like Home, to lose the election. The choice in 1963 of any leader from the older generation would have kept Heath in the running for the next time round. Where he was so fortunate was in the bizarre sequence of events at Blackpool that not only held back the front runner of his own generation, Maudling, giving him a chance to catch up, but then hobbled his other two principal contemporaries, Macleod and Powell, while producing a result which ensured that a new leader would have to be chosen before very long from within this group. The Blackpool circus could not have been plotted more perfectly to serve Heath's career if he had planned it all along.

There was a down side to Heath's good fortune, however. In clearing his path to the top through the fallen bodies of his rivals, Blackpool also ensured that the leadership, when he attained it, was something of a poisoned cup. The turmoil and bad blood generated at Blackpool left the Tory party demoralised, divided and ripe for defeat in 1964. The habit of semi-mystical loyalty, which in 1957 had enabled Macmillan to take over remarkably smoothly despite the circumstances of his succession, was destroyed by the undignified public contest in October 1963 and its unexpected outcome, bitterly denounced by Iain Macleod in the *Spectator* and subsequently chronicled in unedifying detail by Randolph Churchill and others. The divinity that had hitherto hedged a Tory leader was diminished even for Home; by the time Heath succeeded, as a result of a rational but prosaic new method of election, it had all but disappeared. Of course by 1965 the unwelcome fact of finding itself in opposition, after thirteen years in office, added to the strain; but the events of Blackpool undoubtedly destabilised the party for years to come. Heath was the lucky beneficiary; but he inherited a disturbed and unhappy party, which is one reason why the party was never entirely happy with him.

The possibility of Macmillan's retirement in the summer of 1963 placed Heath in something of a dilemma. He was no longer in the Prime Minister's confidence. He had some reason to feel aggrieved at Macmillan's treatment of him, and he could see that the supreme political operator he had served between 1957 and 1959 had lost much of his touch. He was increasingly impatient that the Government should strike out a new course of social and economic modernisation. Yet at the same time he knew that his own personal interest would best be served by Macmillan staying on for another year or two. From soundings discreetly undertaken by his PPS, John Howard, it was clear that the parliamentary party was not yet ready to see him as a potential successor. Earlier in the year there had been a brief flutter of support for him around the lobbies; but by the summer, in addition to his identification with the European setback, there was a perceptible – though quite irrational – backing off from the idea of a bachelor leader: after the Profumo scandal the party wanted an unimpeachably normal, happy, family man. (Maudling fitted the required image admirably.) In another year or two, in a less jumpy political atmosphere, that consideration should have diminished and his chances would have improved – so long as the succession was still unresolved. As the pressure on Macmillan mounted and the rival supporters of Maudling and Butler began organising around their candidates, Heath was bound to hope that the Prime Minister would hold on. He could not have been expected to relish the possibility of Maudling, eight months younger than himself, taking over. Nor had he ever had much to do with Butler. Neither Maudling nor Butler had ever been more than lukewarm over the European adventure. He was still – if only from self-interest – Macmillan's man.

Thus the news of the Prime Minister's illness on 8 October came to him as an unpleasant shock. That very morning he had seen Macmillan before Cabinet and had thought he was not looking well: he was already in pain from an enlarged prostate and had spent a sleepless night. But he had appeared 'much better' by the time the meeting had started and had given the Cabinet the clear impression that he had made up his mind to carry on.[1] Immediately afterwards Heath, Macleod, and a number of other ministers left by train for Blackpool where Macleod (as party chairman) briefed the press that Macmillan would announce his decision in his speech to the conference at the end of the week. Barely two hours later both men were attending the Conservative agents' annual dinner when Macleod was called to the phone; he then called out Heath and the other Cabinet ministers present to tell them that Macmillan had been rushed to hospital for urgent surgery: he would not be able to come to Blackpool and would be out of action for several weeks. It was clearly unlikely that his retirement could be long delayed.

While still absorbing the impact of this bombshell, but before the public announcement, Heath had to make a speech. It was a measure of his eclipse, compared with his triumph of the previous year, that this after-dinner speech was his only scheduled utterance during the week: he had no chance, when the news of Macmillan's illness broke, to thrust himself into the running by a brilliant performance on the conference floor. He had very little time to change what he had intended to say to the agents, though by the time it was reported in the next day's papers the news would be out. Was his call for the party to face the coming election with a 'clear eye and a fresh mind, uninhibited by the achievements and unencumbered by the legacies of the past', as though it would be seeking office for the first time, not the fourth, already drafted to emphasise Heath's claim as an apostle of modernisation within the Cabinet – a coded criticism of Macmillan? Or was it, in the suddenly changed circumstances, intended to be read as his bid to be considered a candidate if the leadership were regrettably to become vacant? Either way it carried the danger that it might equally be interpreted as an endorsement of Maudling.[2]

As soon as the dinner was over, Heath had to go on television to fend off the questioning of Robin Day. (Macleod, whose job it should have been, was angry that his earlier briefing had been made to look ridiculous, and refused to appear.)* Naturally, he gave little away, declined to accept that Macmillan would necessarily resign, emphasised the affection in which he was still held by the whole party and studiously denied any significance in his own speech to the agents. When Day suggested that a first step towards his declared goal of 'making Britain a true democracy' might be to elect the next

---

* Macleod's position in the leadership stakes was similar to Heath's. Seen by many as a future leader, he was temporarily under a cloud, partly as a result of having antagonised the right by the speed with which he had pursued decolonisation when at the Colonial Office (1959–61), partly because as party chairman he was blamed for the by-election losses of 1962–3. An early contest forced by Macmillan's illness was no more in his interest than it appeared to be in Heath's.

Tory leader by ballot he would not be drawn, falling back on the bromide that it was the Queen's prerogative.[3]

The next day the normally staid conference was transformed into something resembling an American party convention. Instead of the leadership being determined by the customary processes of consultation at Westminster, it seemed that it was going to be decided by the length and volume of ovations given to the prospective candidates in the conference hall. The likely effect of this appeared to favour the chances of the ebullient bell-ringing former party chairman, Lord Hailsham. By an extraordinary coincidence Tony Benn's long struggle to enable reluctant hereditary peers to disclaim their titles had finally been concluded just two months earlier, with a late amendment carried in the House of Lords to allow the new provision to take effect immediately. It was quickly realised that the possibility of returning to the House of Commons made Hailsham a new potential challenger to succeed Macmillan. On 9 October, the first full day of the conference, the Tory faithful went wild for Hailsham. If Butler was reckoned to be the choice of most of the Cabinet, and Maudling the majority choice of Tory MPs, Hailsham seemed to be the party's choice. He was also, as was quickly made known, Macmillan's favoured candidate.

This was not altogether welcome to Heath, who did not greatly admire Hailsham's personality or judgment. Hailsham, after all, had been the Chamberlainite candidate in the Oxford by-election twenty-five years before. But he overreached himself, announcing his intention to disclaim his peerage in an opportunistic manner which offended the party's sense of propriety; the enthusiasm of the Young Conservatives, distributing American-style 'Q' (for Quintin) lapel buttons, likewise alienated older Tories. This was not the way the Conservative party chose its leader. Sensing this antagonism, but still determined, for different reasons, to exclude both Butler and Maudling, Macmillan, directing operations from his hospital bed, dropped Hailsham and brought forward as his second runner Lord Home. This was much more to Heath's liking. He had worked closely and, in the circumstances, amicably with Home as his superior at the Foreign Office: he much preferred Home's quiet style to Hailsham's noisy showmanship. In addition Home clearly represented less of a threat than any other candidate to his own long-term ambitions: while in the short term he might reasonably hope to inherit the Foreign Office. So as the contest moved from the overheated atmosphere of Blackpool back to London, Heath allied himself whole-heartedly with the sick Prime Minister's valedictory manoeuvre to secure the succession for Home.

At first sight, Heath should have been the last person to have supported Home. As the epitome of the self-consciously modern, classless Tory, he should have been as appalled as were Iain Macleod and Enoch Powell by Macmillan's shameless manipulation of the wheels of party patronage to elevate a little-known hereditary aristocrat – a foreign affairs specialist ignorant equally of economics and of the rough world of domestic party politics – over the heads of obviously better-qualified candidates. There were three or four reasons why he was not appalled. First, he had been closer than either of them to Macmillan, and was more likely to respect his judgment. Second, he knew Home better than they did. Third, much more than either Macleod or Powell, he was at least an associate member of what Macleod derisively called 'the magic circle'. (Part of Macleod's anger was that, though party chairman, he felt himself bypassed by the workings of the 'magic circle'.) Heath had been Chief Whip; he knew very well the levers which Macmillan was now so expertly pulling; he had been a close observer and a minor participant in Macmillan's own unexpected emergence as leader over Butler in 1957. For all his commitment to the modernisation of British society, he retained a highly conventional streak of reverence for the ancient institutions of the country – including the Tory party and the monarchy. Finally, he cannot have failed to calculate that Home's succession would give him the opportunity to emerge, by contrast, as the party's modern face.

There were one or two voices raised to suggest that the party should take its courage in its hands and go for Heath at once. The most prominent was the editor of *The Times*, Sir William Haley, who wrote a remarkable editorial on 10 October reviewing the candidates, rejecting Hailsham and Maudling but giving only qualified support to Butler:

> If Mr Heath is too young – after all he is a mere year older than President Kennedy – then Mr Butler is the best choice. But that 'if' needs to be questioned. Sooner or later the reins of Conservatism will have to be placed in the hands of a new generation. There is much to be said for doing that now.★[4]

But no other newspaper took up Haley's lead. *The Economist* two

---

★ Haley wrote off Maudling, the other Kennedy generation candidate, with faint praise: 'He is able and likeable . . . [But] he has yet to show that there is in him that last vital ounce of fibre' – a widely shared judgment that was to lose Maudling the contest with Heath in 1965.

days later judged that 'despite the enthusiasm with which he is undoubtedly regarded by many of the younger members of the party' Heath was 'thought of more as the next Tory leader but one rather than being in line for the immediate succession'.[5] Yet he remained on the fringe of the contest. A Gallup poll published in the *Daily Telegraph* placed him fourth in the preference of both Tory voters and the wider public, not far behind Maudling and ahead of Macleod, Selwyn Lloyd and Home;[6] the cartoonists regularly included Heath (and often Macleod, but never Home) among the contenders scrabbling for the crown.[7] It is a serious question whether Heath might not have emerged as an alternative compromise candidate if Home had refused the party's call. David Wood wrote in the *Spectator* on 11 October that on a recent tour of constituencies he had found 'astonishingly many' local party chairmen ready to support Heath; a week later he repeated that Heath would 'without doubt' be the constituencies' choice among the younger candidates.[8]

If there was any possibility of Heath making a late bid, however, it was closed off the moment Home was persuaded to throw his coronet into the ring. Had Home disappointed him, Heath would surely have been Macmillan's third choice, ahead of Maudling. But once Home was in the race Macmillan exerted all his influence to ensure that the party should rally to him. In these circumstances Heath's course was clear. Back in London, on 15 October, he was one of the first ministers to visit Macmillan in hospital; he stayed for forty minutes. He was effectively back in his old role as Chief Whip: just as in 1957–9, it was his task to rally the party to Macmillan's policy – in this case his choice of successor. It was his last service to his old chief, once again carried out with impeccable efficiency.

Initially Home had only two other identifiable supporters in the higher reaches of the party: Selwyn Lloyd (who probably also foresaw his return to a front-rank role in a Home government) and the influential chairman of the 1922 Committee, John Morrison.* In the space of a very few days, however, widespread incredulity at the seriousness of Home's candidature was overcome by a realisation that – in a situation where there was no majority for any of the other candidates and strong opposition to each of them – Home might, after all, be the type of uncontentious, universally respected figure

---

* Heath had already taken trouble to cultivate Morrison on his own account. In August he had even been to stay for a few days at Morrison's Scottish home on the island of Islay – not at all his usual holiday stamping ground. It was here that he first met Sara Morrison, then married to John Morrison's son Charles, later MP for Devizes, who was to become over the years one of his closest and most trusted women friends.

who alone could unite the party. By comparison with the urgency of restoring unity, the question of whether he was the leader most likely to defeat Wilson was reduced to secondary importance. Heath's role in assisting the process cannot be precisely measured. After the excesses of Blackpool there was a strong desire in the party to close ranks around an obviously decent man. Yet Heath's active endorsement – not only by the exercise of his old whipping skills but also as a potential leader himself with an important following among the modern-minded younger Tories who were most likely to be upset by the choice of Home – undoubtedly played a significant part in smoothing Home's succession. At the same time there was an awareness that Home might be a stalking horse for Heath himself. There has never been any suggestion of an overt deal; but years later Jim Prior wrote that he had always found Heath 'very reticent about the way in which the "Magic Circle" was able to secure the Premiership for Alec': 'It does reveal Ted in a more scheming guise than I was to associate with him on virtually any other occasion.'[9]

On 17 October Powell and Macleod made a late-night, last-minute attempt to stop Home by persuading Butler to refuse to serve under him; but Butler, famously, would not use the 'loaded revolver' that Powell handed to him.[10] Events had moved too fast for them and Rab was not the man to split the party he had served for thirty years by insisting on his own right of precedence. Maudling and Hailsham likewise swallowed their sense of outrage and accepted Macmillan's sick-bed *coup* with an outward grace. When the Queen, on Macmillan's recommendation, invited Home to try to form a Government, he found only Macleod and Powell among senior ministers determined to be unreconciled. (Another minor dissident was Toby Aldington, who resigned from his post as a special assistant at Central Office. 'I thought you were a friend of mine,' Heath remonstrated with him, revealing a growing tendency to see politics in personal terms.)[11] It was Heath, however, who went on television to commend the new Prime Minister to the nation. He praised Home's integrity, his gift of expounding policy simply, his judgment, his perseverance and (dismissing doubts about his health) his toughness. He rejected criticism of the choice of a fourteenth earl, pointing out that it was Labour which had been keen to let peers move from the House of Lords to the House of Commons, and insisted that Home was chosen as the best man for the job, following much wider consultation with the party than in 1957. He earnestly hoped that all present Cabinet ministers would agree to serve him.

He then went on to pay warm tribute to Macmillan, singling out in particular his 'extraordinary constructive imagination', his power of conciliation, his 'recognition of interdependence as being the most important feature of this part of the century' and his sense of history.[12] It was Macmillan's inheritance which Heath saw himself carrying on as he aspired to lead, first the Tory party and then the country, over the next eleven years.

Heath cannot in truth have been greatly upset at the refusal of Macleod and Powell to serve under Home. Their action, ill received in a party which has never liked public displays of pique, only completed the satisfactory outcome of the leadership struggle, from his point of view, by underlining his own enhanced importance in the new Government. Macleod, in particular, with more fire in his belly than Maudling, might have been a formidable rival in 1965 had he not placed himself in baulk by staying out of Home's Cabinet in 1963. As it was, Heath was allowed to establish himself almost without challenge as the champion of modern progressive Toryism in the new Cabinet. Maudling still ranked ahead of him: but as Chancellor of the Exchequer at a time of mounting balance-of-payments problems he had the most difficult and, as time would show, politically unrewarding job in the year running up to the election. Heath would really have liked to become Foreign Secretary. But Home was obliged to offer Butler whatever job he wanted, and the Foreign Office was the one great office Rab had never held. Instead Home offered Heath the job he had sought unsuccessfully from Macmillan earlier in the year – an expanded Board of Trade, with responsibility for regional policy and a brief to promote economic modernisation and competition. This served his career, at this moment, very much better than the Foreign Office would have done. It was the key symbolic job within the Government if in the twelve months left to him before the election Home was to snatch the initiative from Labour and put the Conservatives back on a winning path. Home himself, with his grouse-moor image and his disarmingly confessed reliance on matchsticks to work out economic problems, was under an enormous handicap in trying to present his Government as the agent of the dynamic change which it was widely agreed Britain urgently needed. Heath, on the contrary, was perfectly cast as the energetic new broom charged with giving fresh vigour to a tired old Tory Government entering its thirteenth year. He grasped the opportunity with relish.

With his appointment as President of the Board of Trade Heath's career took another major step forward. He was now for the first time a front-rank minister of independent political standing. With

Rab Butler at the Foreign Office and Reggie Maudling at the Treasury, he was one of the three or four key ministers on whom Home's Government was dependent. (The fourth was Hailsham, now returned to the Commons as Quintin Hogg; but while Hogg's adherence to the Government was essential he was not, as Lord President, a major departmental minister.) Heath was in a sense *the* key minister. The day after his appointment, he was interviewed on the BBC's 'Gallery' programme. After some dismissive words from William Rees-Mogg on Home's incapacity to lead the sort of modernisation drive that Britain needed, Heath was asked why he had not, like Macleod and Powell, refused to serve. In reply he strongly rejected the suggestion that the choice of Home meant that the Tory party had moved to the right, insisting that a Government that still contained not only Butler but younger Cabinet ministers like Keith Joseph, Edward Boyle, Anthony Barber and Joseph Godber (the two latter newly promoted by Home) was still a progressive Government which would adhere to the 'One Nation' principles of its predecessor. He deeply regretted Macleod's attitude, but denied that there were any grounds of policy or principle to justify his standing out. (He did not mention Powell.)[13]

Home not only needed Heath's endorsement; he needed to be seen to give him a leading role in the new Government. Accordingly Heath was appointed not simply to the old Board of Trade, but to an enlarged and beefed-up department taking over functions from several other ministries with the grandiloquent catch-all title of Secretary of State for Industry, Trade and Regional Development and President of the Board of Trade. The cartoonist Cummings drew Heath carrying an enormous briefcase marked SOSFITARDA-POBOT, compared with Rab's small one modestly marked FO. Even *The Economist* was satirical: 'This ugly mouthful seems at first sight to be a novel example of sticking part of the Conservative election manifesto into a ministerial title, a free vehicle of publicity that the party's public relations advisers had not thought of before.'

In fact Heath's new department was exactly what *The Economist* had long been demanding that the Board of Trade needed to become – 'a much more powerfully-directed economic department of state' responsible not only for overseas trade but for the modernisation of the economy (by 'instilling a lot more competition') and regional development.[14] It was principally in the third area that Heath was given new powers, taking over functions from the Ministry of Housing and Local Government as well as Hailsham's former special responsibility for the north-east. In retrospect the office Home created for Heath can be seen as a precursor of the Department of Economic

Affairs created a year later by Harold Wilson for George Brown, and of the giant Department of Trade and Industry which Heath himself put together under John Davies in 1970. In recent years the Board of Trade had rated only as a middle-ranking ministry. With Heath's appointment it rose several places in the Cabinet pecking order. Moreover Home's frankly confessed unfamiliarity with economics gave his two principal economic ministers, Maudling and Heath, exceptional influence.

Home gave Heath two new Ministers of State, Lord Drumalbyn and an ambitious young high-flyer, Edward Du Cann – then thirty-nine – who moved from the Treasury, where he had been Economic Secretary. The team was completed by David Price as Parliamentary Secretary. Heath immediately got on bad terms with Du Cann – the beginning of an antagonism that was to dog him for the next dozen years. He was temperamentally resistant to Du Cann's silkily insinuating *bonhomie* and became more than usually silent in his company. During an EFTA conference in Edinburgh they were thrown unexpectedly together because Du Cann's wife was ill: while Du Cann tried politely to make conversation Heath barely spoke a word to him. More seriously Du Cann found Heath reluctant to delegate him any real responsibility. Questioned about this two years later by the *Sunday Times*, Heath strongly denied it. 'At the Board of Trade', he claimed, 'I think they would agree that it was the hardest working time of their lives. So it's not a question of my doing all the work.'[15] But 'they' clearly meant his officials, headed by the Permanent Secretary Sir Richard Powell, a donnish grammar-school-educated bachelor with whom he got on well. Du Cann bore a good deal of the burden of pushing the Resale Price Maintenance Bill through the House of Commons; but Heath kept all the major provinces of his new empire under his personal control. He had no intention of sharing his opportunity with ambitious juniors.

His immediate target with regard to trade was to help the Chancellor close the widening balance-of-payments gap by boosting exports. The main problem he faced stemmed directly from de Gaulle's veto on Britain's entering the EEC the previous January. Even outside the Community, Britain's fastest growing markets were already with the Six. Heath's inclination, and the Government's policy, was to go on encouraging that trend in preparation for eventual membership of the EEC whenever de Gaulle's veto should be lifted. But meanwhile, in terms of existing trade preferences, Britain was stuck with EFTA and the Commonwealth. In the Commons Harold Wilson blamed Heath's European bias for the fact that trade with the Commonwealth and the Soviet bloc was *not* growing.[16] Wilson had been President of the Board of Trade himself in the

Attlee Government, and liked to parade his knowledge of trade matters: these months saw the first sharp exchanges in what was to be a twelve-year rivalry across the dispatch box.★

The second problem he faced was how to increase exports by improving competitiveness and raising the sales effort of British companies abroad. At present, Heath told the House of Commons in his first speech in his new job on 14 November, half of Britain's export trade was carried on by only 200 firms. His remedy, significantly, was not so much to encourage more small firms to try exporting as to merge them into bigger firms. 'If amalgamations are necessary,' he declared, 'we should not be afraid of them.'[18]

Heath put a lot of effort into another aspect of overseas trade: the United Nations Conference on Trade and Development (UNCTAD) held in Geneva in June. Here he was back in his Brussels milieu of complex and detailed multilateral negotiations. Carrying on from the arrangements he had tried to secure for the developing Commonwealth within the EEC, he was energetic in promoting schemes of aid and investment and favourable terms of credit from the developed to the undeveloped world. As he had in Brussels, he drove his officials at Geneva hard: he was determined to achieve a success, but he was equally concerned to be seen to be successful.

The major goal which Heath set himself when he went to the Board of Trade was 'a determined drive for the modernisation of Britain'.[19] But it was not clear how this was to be pursued in practice. The Queen's Speech spoke of encouraging the development of a modern transport system and port development and promised an Industrial Training Bill. Heath in his speech on 14 November promised a Hire Purchase Amendment Bill (which was duly brought forward, unopposed, in February) and talked of encouraging investment in research and development and technical and business education. All these were worthy, if uncontroversial, objectives. He also asserted once again that 'in many modern industries an increase in the size of firms is an essential condition of advance in this technological age'.[20]

But neither he nor the Queen's Speech made any mention of what turned out to be the major modernisation measure introduced by the Government in the forthcoming session: the abolition of Resale Price Maintenance.

This was a political hot potato which had been picked up and

★ On occasion Heath could mock Wilson more effectively than later – for instance in June 1964 when Wilson had been harking back as usual to 1949: 'Those, of course, were the days. What bliss it was to be politically alive, but to be young and at the Board of Trade was very heaven. There was that exciting meeting with Mr Mikoyan of which we never ceased to hear . . .'[17]

dropped by successive governments since 1947. The reason it was such a sensitive issue was that it exposed the historic tension at the heart of the Tory party – going back to Peel and Disraeli – between protectionism and free trade. In the 1950s younger Tories tended to see the system of price maintenance as an outdated obstacle to free competition which featherbedded the manufacturer by keeping prices high at the expense of the consumer. Traditionalists, on the other hand, saw it as an essential safeguard to protect the small shop-keeper from being undercut and put out of business by the new supermarkets – as was already happening in respect of groceries, where RPM was breaking down of its own accord. It was a classic argument between the demands of economic efficiency and the instinct to protect the interest of an important section of society which often contained prominent local Tories. While the view within Whitehall had long been clear that RPM should go, it was never going to be easy to persuade Conservative backbenchers to vote for its abolition.[21]

When he first arrived at the Board of Trade, Heath's political instinct was to put RPM back on the shelf, at least until after the election. But a Private Member's Bill introduced by the Labour MP, John Stonehouse, obliged the Government to take a stance. Moreover, another development which was already making nonsense of RPM was the introduction of Green Shield and other trading stamps; and the MP who had come second in the Private Members' ballot was threatening a Bill to abolish stamps. Under this double pressure Heath had no option but to grasp the nettle. Once persuaded, he quickly and characteristically made the issue his own. He was determined to put his name to some major piece of legislation before the election. If it had to be the abolition of RPM, so be it. It was pre-eminently his sort of subject – not only an admirable symbol of the drive to sweep away restrictive commercial practices but technically highly complex; and if it was a challenge which previous ministers had ducked, so much the better for his 'tough' image. He embraced abolition with the same missionary fervour he had brought to negotiating Britain into Europe, with the difference that this time there was no de Gaulle to snatch away the prize. Tory MPs could be whipped into line if the Government's survival depended on it. Yet just as it was Macmillan who had appointed him 'Mr Europe' so this new cause too was thrust on him by circumstances rather than by his own spontaneous convictions.

Having once decided to take it up, his major battle was in Cabinet. But his key position in the new Government made him hard to resist. Of the principal opponents, Rab Butler now wielded diminished influence and Iain Macleod had left the Government; while Home was not in a position easily to deny his right-hand man and principal moderniser any measure he had set his heart on. The Cabinet was almost evenly divided; but the only argument against abolition was one of timing – that it was an unnecessarily divisive measure to bring forward a few months before the General Election. Home, however, was persuaded that it was right in principle, so – 'with many mis-givings' – he gave his backing.[22] In Cabinet on 14 January 1964 Butler, Hogg, Selwyn Lloyd, the Chief Whip Martin Redmayne and the party chairman Lord Blakenham fought for three hours to per-suade Heath to postpone his Bill; but Heath – 'eyeball to eyeball', in the words of one witness – refused to back down.[23] 'I didn't feel I could overrule Ted Heath', Home remembered in 1985, 'because he was essentially right.'[24] Nevertheless, Heath did concede one major modification in the content of the Bill which he announced the next day and published the following month. Instead of the simple aboli-tion of RPM, he was persuaded to allow the right of judicial appeal in respect of each and every item of merchandise. This made for a Bill of immense complexity; but Heath now set his face against any further compromise.

The outcry on the Tory benches was not slow in coming. Im-mediately following his statement Dame Irene Ward character-istically declared that she had 'no intention of supporting throwing a lot of people to the wolves for pie in the sky';[25] and over the next few days anger mounted – directed as much against the sudden and high-handed way many Members felt the Bill was being sprung on them as against the principle itself. At crowded meetings of the back-bench Trade and Industry Committee, and a few days later at the full 1922 Committee, Heath was given a rough time by his critics, but he gave no ground. When the Bill was published on 16 February, a number of Tories took the unprecedented step of tabling a motion calling for the rejection of a major item of legislation brought for-ward by their own Government.

The Second Reading was on 10 March. Heath spoke for nearly an hour. He sought to place the Bill in perspective not as an isolated measure against shopkeepers but as 'one element . . . in a compre-hensive policy . . . to promote more competition in the economy'. The Government's accompanying proposals, he promised, would 'cover the whole field of monopolies, mergers and restrictive prac-tices in addition to resale price maintenance'.[26] This, in the view of many of his Tory critics, was all very well but why did he have to begin by picking on the small trader? An amendment put down by Tom Iremonger regretted that he had not directed his first efforts to reforming the trade unions. In this way he would have united the party against its natural enemies instead of dividing it against its friends. In reply to an interjection from Barbara Castle, however, Heath had to confess that none of the other proposed measures would be ready before the election.

His pedestrian, didactic and uncompromising manner did not mollify his opponents. Douglas Jay, leading for Labour, naturally did his best to fan the 'rather savage controversy' within the Government ranks, warning Heath that he was 'sometimes rather obstinate in the House . . . sure that he is right and everyone else is wrong'.[27] But it was Major Sir Frank Markham, the Member for Buckinghamshire, who most vehemently expressed the strength of feeling of the knights of the shires not only against the Bill but against the President of the Board of Trade personally for initiating and persisting with it. He had introduced a complete volte-face in party policy, Markham alleged, with no consultation whatever. 'In consequence, the Secretary of State must bear the charge of rocking the Conservative boat pretty badly at a very delicate time.' The Bill, he complained, 'strikes at the little man . . . The little man . . . is redundant to the Secretary of State's pattern of what the future should be'; and he appealed for concessions from Heath to Maudling, who was to reply to the debate, 'because I am certain that he knows far more about economics than the Secretary of State'.[28]

Twenty Tories (plus two tellers) voted against the Bill and another twenty-five abstained. It was the biggest Conservative revolt since 1940, helped by Labour shrewdly standing aside and by the fact that the Chief Whip was himself known to have been one of the strongest opponents of the Bill in Cabinet. Feeling against Heath ran very high. 'I have never . . . heard a Cabinet Minister so much abused by his colleagues, so badly spoken of and so widely condemned in the party, as Heath was then,' George Hutchinson (then the party's director of publicity) wrote a few years later.[29] He was accused of 'arrogance' and 'intolerance', of 'steamrollering' and 'bludgeoning' the Bill through. Members muttered that they could now see why Britain had failed to get into the Common Market: there was only room for one de Gaulle in Europe.[30] There was serious talk of Heath being forced to resign. To defuse the situation a steering committee was set up to negotiate between Heath and the rebels. When the Bill began its progress through Committee on 23 March Labour was disappointed to find that a number of amendments had been agreed behind the scenes. Yet still the Government came within an inch of defeat on 24 March on an amendment to exempt medicines, surgical

appliances and pharmaceutical products, as a general category, from
the operation of the Bill. The 'Chemists' Amendment', which Heath
strongly opposed in a fifty-minute speech, was only defeated by a
single vote, 204 votes to 203. While Heath predictably quoted
Churchill – 'one is enough' – and insisted that the issue was now
settled, Markham claimed that the Bill was now 'dead' and
demanded that the Government should recognise the fact. Labour
had a field day, hailing the vote as another nail in the coffin of a
Government that had lost all authority.[31] Michael Foot paid ironic
tribute to Heath's single-mindedness:

> In his remarkable speeches today we could detect why he has got
> the Government into so much trouble. The trouble with the Right
> Hon. Gentleman is that he looks at the world through rose-
> coloured spectacles. He has an extraordinary faculty for excluding
> from his vision all disagreeable factors. He tried to get us into
> Europe without noticing that General de Gaulle was there. Having
> failed in that enterprise, he went along to the Government and said
> that he had a bright new scheme for rescuing their fortunes – the
> resale price maintenance Bill.[32]

The criticism of blinkered wishful thinking was one that would be
heard again.

Heath later admitted that if the vote on the 'Chemists' Amendment' had gone against him he might have had to resign.[33] At the
same time he would for ever after (notably with reference to the
knife-edge votes on the European Communities Bill in 1972) cite this
episode to recall that he had been in tight corners before but had won
through. In fact this was the last time the RPM Bill was in danger.
The party could not afford a major Government crisis a few months
before the General Election, and Heath was persuaded to make just
enough minor concessions to save the rebels' face. The agreed
amendments were 'essentially meaningless'[34] – but they did the trick.
The remaining clauses of the Bill went through Committee quite
easily in five days amid mutual congratulations that good sense had
prevailed. On Third Reading, on 13 May, the chairman of the steering committee, Sir John Vaughan-Morgan, commented that 'Once
we accept that the object of the Bill is not, as was originally thought
by some, to abolish resale price maintenance but rather to restrain it –
once that step was taken, compromise was inevitable.'[35] This was
probably true, but the critical compromise had in fact been made in
Cabinet, before the Bill was ever published; it was the steering com-

mittee's achievement to bring the rebels to a realisation of this fact. The only Member knowledgeable enough to point out that the Bill as passed did not represent Heath's original intentions was John Stonehouse, whose own Bill had been superseded. Stonehouse criticised the 'cumbersome, clumsy and tedious' judicial procedure with which Heath had been forced to load his Bill in place of simple abolition. The function of Parliament was to make law; 'but . . . we are not making law, we are making a heyday for the lawyers'. RPM had been abolished in most of Europe, the United States and Canada, but 'none of these countries has constructed a fantastic, bureaucratic, legal machinery of the Restrictive Practices Court, which is the brainchild of the Right Hon. Gentleman'.[36]

This was an acute criticism which – once again – raised fundamental questions about Heath's approach to government which would recur a decade later. Whether or not such a complex regulatory structure was what he originally envisaged, and whether or not it is fair to father its complexities on Heath himself, rather than on the Cabinet opposition which had forced him to modify his original intention, the fact is that the judicial machinery of the RPM Act, with its elaborate system of 'gateways' under which manufacturers could claim exemption for individual products, closely resembled the sort of detailed attempt to legislate for every eventuality which overloaded and eventually sank both the 1971 Industrial Relations Act and the 1973 counter-inflation policy. The difference was that despite the controversy attending its passage the RPM Act was quickly accepted: a few leading cases established the principles on which it would operate, a number of key exemptions were confirmed (notably books) and major manufacturers were soon competing with one another to be seen to let their prices fall.

This success probably misled Heath into imagining that the same paradoxical formula – attempting to promote competition by means of regulation, using judges to invest government policy with the authority of law – could be applied equally successfully to other problems. Stonehouse called Heath, in relation to RPM, 'a good man fallen among bureaucrats'.[37] It is an enduring criticism of much wider application: many colleagues and critics consider that Heath was really a bureaucrat at heart, rather than a politician. Both administratively and politically – both in the nature of the solution which he adopted and in his single-minded determination to force it through – the RPM episode offers an instructive anticipation of his premiership.

Heath undoubtedly made lasting enemies by his handling of RPM. He displayed a stubbornness and an intolerance of opposition which in his previous offices had been largely veiled, but which now rang alarm bells with a good many Tories who feared him as a divisive force within the party. Yet on balance the episode probably did him more good than harm. First, the Bill itself was a success. Most of the fears expressed on behalf of the small shopkeeper turned out to be exaggerated (or, where not exaggerated, were recognised as unavoidable), and within an astonishingly short space of time it seemed inconceivable that so gross an anachronism could so recently have been in operation. Its abolition was a good trophy for a modernising Tory to wear on his belt. Second, the qualities he had displayed – viewed positively as conviction, resolution and steadfastness under fire – were seen by many, in the dying days of the Home Government and still more when the Tories found themselves out of office and desperate to find a quick way back, as precisely those of which the party stood in need. Little more than a year before the next leadership contest the battle over RPM persuaded many Tories that Heath, with all his faults, was the sort of leader they wanted. Certainly no Member of the 1963–4 Parliament who voted for Heath in 1965 had any excuse for not realising what kind of leadership he was likely to offer.

Nevertheless there remains the view that abolition, although right in principle, represented at that moment an error of timing which cast doubt on the political judgment of the Minister who had insisted on pushing it through. An important section of Conservative support in the country was gratuitously antagonised in the run up to a crucial election. Several marginal constituencies were said to have been put unnecessarily at risk. When the election was lost by a margin of four seats there were inevitably those who deduced that the abolition of RPM had been the decisive factor. Lord Home himself has since reflected that 'it probably cost us seats at the general election . . . It certainly lost us quite a lot of Conservative votes.'[38] But in an election so narrow as that of October 1964 any number of factors can plausibly be said to have been decisive. A subtler variation of the same criticism was offered in 1970 by Paul Johnson, who suggested that the struggle over RPM had been 'a waste of the party's emotional energy, at a time when it was badly needed'.[39] This can certainly be argued; on the other hand it was essential for the Home Government to be seen to be doing something purposeful to counteract the tired grouse-moor image, and in many respects RPM abolition was ideal – especially since Stonehouse had forced the Government's hand. It is equally arguable that the Tories would have lost more heavily in 1964 if at least one minister had not been seen to be pursuing an active policy. Moreover the shopkeeper vote has almost certainly been overstated. A measure that had the effect of lowering prices was thoroughly popular with everyone except the shopkeepers. After thirteen years in office RPM cannot really be made the scapegoat for the Tories' defeat.

Much less contentious at the time, though more controversial in the long run, were Heath's efforts to promote regional development. Since the 1930s governments of all colours had tried to direct new investment towards the old industrial regions of Scotland, south Wales and the north of England, to counteract the steady drift of industry and population to the south and east. But still unemployment remained disproportionately high in the north. In 1963 Macmillan, with his pre-war attachment to Stockton, had appointed Hailsham to lead a special effort to regenerate the north-east. Now Heath's enlarged responsibilities at the Board of Trade signalled a wider purpose to do the same for all the depressed regions. Only three weeks after taking office he was able to announce, in the debate on the Address, the publication of two White Papers, on the north-east and Scotland, with the promise of more to come. 'An expanding economy', he explained, 'requires a more even distribution of economic activity throughout the country. This is the only way to obtain consistent expansion without congestion, without shortages, without inflation and without the waste of unused resources.'[40] This was the unquestioned wisdom of the day; there was complete cross-party agreement between the two front benches. 'It has dawned on them at last,' jeered the Shadow Scottish Secretary, Willie Ross;[41] while Douglas Jay more graciously welcomed the Government's conversion 'to so many truths which we have been preaching for the last ten years'.[42] The idea that a Conservative Government should trust the market to create prosperity, leaving industry to site itself wherever its own economic advantage dictated, was not one that Heath felt he needed to bother with. 'Some people', he conceded, 'may still argue that these forces should be left to operate unchecked. We may hear that point of view expressed, but I feel that few would argue it.'[43] In 1963, outside the little-read pamphlets of the Institute of Economic Affairs, few did.

The White Papers on Scotland and the north-east proposed four themes: first, the creation of economic 'growth points' based on new towns on Tyneside and Teesside (Ayton, Peterlee) and in the Scottish central belt (Cumbernauld, Livingstone, East Kilbride, Glenrothes); second, improvement of the physical and social infrastructure (new roads, bridges, airports, housing estates and shopping centres); third, the importance of partnership between central and local government, employers and trade unions; and fourth, a promise of continued high investment in the future. Heath was very clear that the benefits of regional regeneration were not wholly or even primarily economic, but rather social and cultural. The *means* of regeneration, he explained on television a few days after his appointment, was the stimulation of the local economy, which was why the regional programme must be co-ordinated by the Board of Trade; but the *end* was 'something much greater in conception'. What was new, he claimed, about the Government's programme, was the emphasis on developing the whole life of a region, not simply offering inducements to industry to create jobs with no corresponding public investment in the social infrastructure. 'Our task is . . . to create plans for the different regions of the country which will . . . lead to the sort of country [in] which we all want to live.'[44]

This policy was not of course in origin Heath's own. The initiative for the White Papers which he now proudly published had been taken by Macmillan and most of the work already carried out under the direction of Hailsham and the Scottish Secretary, Michael Noble. Regional development was yet another case of Heath being presented with a ready-made opportunity and quickly, by the commitment he brought to it, making the cause his own. Nevertheless it was a cause which immediately chimed with his instincts and his ambition. The vision of regional regeneration which he invoked in November 1963 was the domestic complement to his great external cause of getting Britain into Europe. Together they formed the two central themes of his mature political philosophy which endured through the rest of his career – in opposition, in Downing Street and beyond. It became his personal interpretation of the ideal of 'One Nation'.

It was a typically grandiose vision, which expressed a greater faith in the capacity of government to plan prosperity than subsequent experience has shown to be justified, and allotted a greater role to the state than most Conservatives since 1974 have come to think effective or desirable. Yet it was a vision very much of its time, from which only a handful of derided ideologues in the Tory party – notably the already maverick figure of Enoch Powell – yet dreamed of dissenting. When, out of office over the next six years, Heath began to overlay it with newly fashionable and essentially incompatible ideas of disengagement of the state from industry, these were superficial accretions to his basic philosophy, not a revision of it. He was both temperamentally and by conviction an interventionist who believed in the duty and capacity of government to manage the resources of the country and thereby make life better for all its citizens. If the battle over Resale Price Maintenance had seemed to stamp him as a champion of the free market, the other side of his responsibility at the Board of Trade more truly expressed his deepest political beliefs. When, in 1972, market solutions failed to produce the quick results he needed, he was able to jettison them without compunction in favour of the sort of Government intervention he had first attempted to operate in 1963–4.

Travelling the country, meeting local leaders, devising blueprints, planning the future, gave Heath a powerful sense of *possibility*, of national potential just waiting to be tapped and of his own ability to tap it. When he visited Newcastle to launch the plan for the north-east, he met a warm welcome. 'I feel Mr Heath is the man who is going to get things done,' enthused the Director of the North-East Development Council. 'He has a massive Government department behind him and he is the sort of man who makes things happen.'[45] (The implied contrast with Hailsham was unmistakable.) Within a year, however, he no longer had a department behind him: Labour took over, in the shape of George Brown with his National Plan. Despite the enforced cutbacks in Government expenditure after 1966, Labour managed to keep up the projected level of regional investment surprisingly well – though the results remained disappointing. Naturally Heath could not see the continuity between his policies and Labour's. He considered Labour by definition incompetent. He liked to contrast the alleged rigidity of socialism with the Tory way of liberating the energies of the people by means of partnership with local government and local industry.[46] The difference was more rhetorical than real. But the principle of trying to even up the economic performance of the regions was emphatically not one he was willing to concede to Labour. As he continued to criss-cross the country over the six years between 1964 and 1970, the knowledge he had gained of what needed to be done in so many areas intensified his conviction that when he returned to office, with the whole resources of the next Conservative administration behind him, he could be the man of energy and vision who might do it. The regional development brief at the Board of Trade in 1963–4 made a lasting impression on Heath's conception of what he was in politics to achieve.

But he only held it for a year. It might have been still less; but in April 1964 Home announced that the election would not be held before October. At that time the Government's prospects of being returned looked dim – the county council elections, including those for the newly created Greater London Council, showed heavy swings to Labour and the Tories continued to trail badly in the polls. Over the summer, however, the Government's standing steadily improved. By September the parties were practically neck and neck: NOP even showed the Conservatives marginally ahead. Suddenly, despite all the scandals and rows of the past two years, it seemed that the Government was still in with a fighting chance of winning a fourth term.

In these circumstances it mattered very much how the Conservatives pitched their campaign and deployed their team. It was clear that Heath was bound to play a prominent role. Since Home's succession to the leadership the previous autumn he had been a member of the seven-strong steering committee charged with drawing up the party's manifesto. But more than that, the overriding issue of the campaign was going to be modernisation. Wilson, responding acutely to the mood of the moment, had cleverly sidestepped Labour's old doctrinal disputes about nationalisation and unilateral disarmament, identifying the party for the first time with scientific progress and 'the white heat of the technological revolution', stressing Labour's appeal to youth and classless professionalism by contrast with the Tories' obsolete ethos of gentlemanly amateurism, perfectly typified by their choice of leader. Home, though increasingly respected for his integrity, could not hope to compete with Wilson as a flag-waver for modernisation. While Home offered the reassurance of continuity, the Government's best answer to Wilson was plainly Heath. The trouble was that Heath's rapid advancement since the previous October and his overbearing conduct in relation to RPM had aroused the jealousy of some of his senior colleagues.

In June it was reported that he was going to act as link man of the Tory campaign, staying in London to handle the daily press conferences while Home travelled the country getting himself better known. The choice of Heath for this key role was interpreted as part of a deliberate decision to build him up as Home's eventual successor.[47] As such, however, it was seen as a slap in the face for Maudling which his supporters were not prepared to tolerate. By September the decision had been reversed: it was now understood that the campaign would be headed by a triumvirate of Home, Maudling and the party chairman, Lord Blakenham. 'This', *The Economist* considered, 'is a major mistake, since Mr Heath's cutting edge and identification with the modernisation programme would have made him an ideal campaign director.'[48] Right up to the beginning of the campaign it was still expected that Heath would take the morning press conferences. But in a late switch of plan it was decided instead that Maudling should handle the press – still considered the most important medium – while Heath took charge of television. Heath was then thought to be particularly good on television: during the summer he had been involved in a rowdy argument with George Brown about nationalisation which he was reckoned to have won. Choosing him to front the television campaign made his one of the most visible faces of modern Toryism: he appeared in four of the party's five television broadcasts, linking the contributions of a team of other (mainly younger) spokesmen: Maudling, Hogg, Thorneycroft, Joseph, Boyle, Du Cann and (the token woman) Mervyn Pike. (Home alone was featured, direct to camera, in the final broadcast.) It turned out to be a mistake. The authors of the Nuffield study of the election commented:

> Mr Heath became 'presenter' partly for internal party reasons, and partly because of his able television showing during the Brussels negotiations. But the command of fact and argument which served him then proved less appropriate in this more homely and intimate format where he was too stilted and ill-at-ease. The relaxed and colloquial Mr Maudling would surely have been a better choice. But by the time this was realised, change was politically impossible.[49]

Heath was desperately bad on television. Brendon Sewill, then a junior member of the Conservative Research Department, had helped several leading party figures prepare their television appearances. With Maudling and Macleod it was relatively quick and painless. With Heath it was agony. They would spend all day at the BBC studios in Lime Grove while he chewed the end of his pencil and rejected draft after draft that Sewill put up to him. Then the actual recording would drive the technicians to despair. Whereas talking off the cuff to small groups he could be very good, speaking to camera to a set script he immediately became wooden and unconvincing. However, it did not seem to matter very much. Though 90 per cent of British homes now had television, no party had yet learned how to use it effectively: Labour's broadcasts were no better than the Conservatives'. If television made a distinctive contribution to the result it was the satirical programme 'That Was the Week that Was' over the previous three years which undermined the Government's prestige, not the drawn battle of the party broadcasts in the final weeks.

When not chewing his pencil at Lime Grove Heath was obliged to devote most of his energy during the campaign to defending his home patch in Bexley. His majority had climbed to over 8,000 in 1959, but it could still be marginal if Labour did well, particularly with a Liberal intervening again (Orpington, scene of a sensational by-election victory in 1962, was very near by), as well as an anti-

Common Market independent. Over the past five years he had not been able to give the constituency nearly as much time as formerly. When he paid a curiously timed flying visit during the EFTA Conference in Edinburgh in April (perhaps trying to get away from Edward Du Cann!) it was noted that he had originally been invited in September. Reg Pye had to put out a placatory statement apologising for his long absences as 'the price of Ministerial duties'.[50] But Pye had built up a formidable machine to fill in for him, and in the weeks before polling day he made up for lost time. As a secret weapon he recruited the 24-year-old Winston Churchill, Sir Winston's grandson, to earn his spurs by accompanying Heath round the doorsteps.

Heath made his most interesting contribution to the election when the *Daily Mirror* invited him to put 'My Case for the Tories' in a huge centre-page spread on 9 October. (It was the *Mirror*'s one gesture towards balance in the whole campaign, but they did him proud, trailing him as 'the next Tory leader'.) Behind all Harold Wilson's American-style hullabaloo, Heath asserted, the issue was which party could *really* build a modern Britain. His answer was forthright: 'The Conservative Party is the party of change. While we have been in power we have transformed the face of Britain.' 'Look at the record,' he demanded, citing the number of houses, schools, hospitals and motorways built over the past thirteen years; the development of atomic power; new universities; and – his particular responsibility – regional development. 'I want to see the guts torn out of our older industrial cities and new civic centres and shopping areas built there, the older houses torn down and new ones in their place.' This was the very stuff of progress in 1964.

The next Tory Government, Heath promised, would carry on the constructive programmes he had set in hand at the Board of Trade, and would grasp the nettle of trade union restrictive practices. Yet in this area he was still cautious:

> We shall tackle these problems with the trade unions. [In other words in partnership with the trade unions.]
> And we shall have an enquiry into trade union law – it has not been looked at for nearly sixty years. [That is, no commitment to early legislation.]
> Above all, in Britain, we need a change in *attitudes* about industry and by industry.

This article is a most important and characteristic statement of

Heath's political philosophy nine months before he became Conservative leader. It was a philosophy in which 'modernisation' had
become the supreme goal of politics, the means by which it was to be
achieved of almost incidental importance: what was required was a
change of *national attitude*. After a few words about the improvement
in East–West relations under the Conservatives, the transformation
of the Commonwealth and the Tories' recognition of the need to join
the EEC as soon as it should become possible – plus a promise that
the one thing that would *not* change under the Tories was maintenance of the British nuclear deterrent – he returned to his central
theme of not letting Labour pose as the party of modernisation.
Harold Wilson, he noted, 'loads his speeches with scientific jargon'.
But no other Labour leader did even that. It was all words. 'In practice they don't mean a thing.' In hock to every backward-looking
interest group in the country, he insisted, Labour was institutionally
incapable of being the engine of Britain's modernisation.[51]

1964 was the first General Election at which modernisation was the
central issue. The notion of Britain's relative decline – the realisation
that in terms of economic prosperity, social services and the 'quality
of life' Britain was falling behind other industrialised countries – had
struck the previously complacent public consciousness quite suddenly within the previous five years. It was to be the staple
assumption of every subsequent election over the next three decades.
But in 1964 it was new. It was Harold Wilson's good luck, as much
as his achievement, to be able to harness this new alarm to Labour's
benefit. Having been in power for the last thirteen years the Conservatives, even had they not saddled themselves with the
incongruous handicap of Sir Alec Douglas-Home, had an obviously
paradoxical task in trying to present themselves as the better-
equipped party to reverse the decline over which they themselves
had presided. Heath tried heroically to do so, with unquestionable
conviction. He was right to be sceptical of Wilson's technological
jargon, which was quite as superficial as he alleged. Wilson was
thoroughly conservative in his personal tastes and habits and a
devout Little Englander at heart. If modernisation was to be the issue
of the 1960s, then Heath was a better embodiment of it than Wilson:
and despite the old knights of the shires, the new managerial generation within the Tory party was more forward-looking and less
class-bound than most of the Labour party. Over the next twenty
years the Conservatives succeeded in taking the modernisation issue
away from Labour, becoming incontrovertibly the party of radical
institutional reform and forcing Labour into the unrewarding role of
defender of the *status quo*. But this paradoxical transformation was

fully achieved only under Heath's successor. In 1964 the initiative lay with Labour. Heath's bold effort to proclaim the Tories the true 'party of change' was premature and doomed to frustration.

And yet the Tories came astonishingly close to winning. At the end of the first week of the campaign NOP put them narrowly ahead; but from then on Labour regained the lead. In Bexley, Heath confidently predicted a reduced but still comfortable Government majority of 30-50.[52] But Rab Butler notoriously voiced – to the *Daily Express* – the fatally self-fulfilling fear that 'things might start slipping in the last few days . . . They won't slip towards us.' In the same interview he was also quoted as saying that 'Alec . . . is a bit bored with Ted.'[53] He afterwards explained that he had only meant that Home was fed up with RPM; but the unflattering implication lingered. Much more serious was the fear – which Labour recklessly encouraged – of a balance-of-payments crisis. But more important than any issue was the sense of a tired Government. Unimpressed equally by the Tory old guard and by Labour's bright new slogans, *The Times* concluded unenthusiastically that the future promise of Heath, Maudling, Boyle and Joseph just tipped the scale the Tories' way. 'If Mr Heath were leading the Conservative party . . . the answer could be more confident.' As it was, 'whichever party is returned, there should be the largest possible Liberal vote'.[54]

In the end Labour won an overall majority of just 4 seats. (Labour 317, Conservatives 304, Liberals 9.) A significant number of voters followed *The Times*'s advice. Just as in 1951 the withdrawal of the Liberals from most seats had helped to put the Tories back, in 1964 the near doubling of the Liberal vote (from less than 6 per cent to over 11 per cent) was decisive in turning the Government out. Labour's vote actually fell slightly compared with 1959, while its share of the poll increased only marginally to 44 per cent: the Tory vote fell from 49 per cent in 1959 to 43 per cent. On this analysis it was the Orpington vote which did for Home. Liberal intervention helped Labour to capture 11 seats, including 2 in Kent – Rochester and Chatham, and Gravesend.[55] In Bexley the Liberal polled just about exactly the national average (11·4 per cent, or just over 6,000 votes), and Heath's vote fell by almost precisely the same amount; but the Labour vote also fell by 2,000, so Heath survived reasonably comfortably with his 1959 majority roughly halved. The Anti-Common Market candidate did well for an independent, but not well enough to affect the result.

E. R. G. Heath (Conservative)	25,716
L. L. Reeves (Labour)	21,127
P. L. McArthur (Liberal)	6,161
J. Paul (Anti-Common Market)	1,263
Conservative majority	4,589[56]

The national result, however, meant that the Conservatives' thirteen-year rule, spanning four prime ministers, had come to an end. Undeterred by his tiny majority, Harold Wilson entered 10 Downing Street, promising characteristically to make it 'a power house, not a monastery', beginning with 'a hundred days of dynamic action', while the rejected Tories were left to reconcile themselves as best they could to the unfamiliar indignity of opposition.

9

'A New Kind of Tory Leader'

Wɪᴛʜɪɴ a year of the Conservatives' defeat in the 1964 General Election, Heath was Tory leader. Less than two years earlier, when Macmillan resigned, he had not been even a serious contender. But the extraordinary run of events which since October 1963 had so unexpectedly advanced his prospects while retarding those of all his rivals continued to work steadily in his favour until on 27 July 1965 he emerged – narrowly but to general acclamation – at the top of the tree. His election represented a revolution in the history of the Tory party, the essential moment of rift between the paternalist patrician party of Churchill and Macmillan and the radical meritocratic party of Margaret Thatcher. There were many in the party who still had deep reservations about his lowly background, his political judgment and aspects of his personality. Yet his succession was astonishingly smooth. If he was never in subsequent years so lucky again, fortune seemed in these critical months to play into his hands.

First, the loss of the General Election not only effectively disabled Alec Douglas-Home as a long-term leader, confirming him as a stop-gap who was bound to give way sooner rather than later; it also damaged Reginald Maudling, who as outgoing Chancellor of the Exchequer bore the heaviest blame not only with the party for having failed to deliver victory – as chancellors are expected to do – but also with the public for the balance-of-payments deficit which the incoming Labour Government inherited. Heath, though responsible for overseas trade, was curiously unaffected. Second, the shock of being out of office, and the Tory party's need to be seen to be responding energetically to the unfamiliar challenge of opposition and specifically to the needling provocation of Harold Wilson, favoured Heath's harsher political style over the more relaxed approach of Maudling. Third, Home too seemed to favour him, giving Heath more opportunity than Maudling to shine in opposition. Finally the adoption in February 1965 of a new procedure for electing the next leader had the inevitable effect of hastening the moment when the party would want to put it to the test. As a result the nine months between October 1964 and Home's sudden resignation in July 1965 took on irresistibly the character of an undeclared electoral contest, at a time when all the momentum was with Heath.

Heath adjusted to opposition much better than most of his colleagues. He spent the weekend after the election with the Seligmans, who had been afraid that he would be very depressed: instead they found him relaxed and happy – at least briefly – to enjoy his freedom. He had been on a diet over the summer and had lost the 20 lb he had put on during the Brussels negotiations. He was fit and hungry for the new challenge. While Maudling and others looked on opposition as a chance to get back into the City and make good the financial sacrifice of thirteen years of office by piling up lucrative directorships – Maudling collected thirteen – Heath took on only one. He went back to Brown, Shipley, accepting a seat on the board where fourteen years before he had been a green trainee. Now, as well as putting in capital of £7,000, which he had saved from his nine years as a senior minister, he brought them his encyclopaedic knowledge of European and Commonwealth trade gained while conducting the Common Market negotiations and his unrivalled contacts in the capitals of the Six. In the next nine months he made several European trips for them. He took his work for Brown, Shipley seriously, quickly displayed his usual impressive grasp and energy and gave full value for his salary. But that was his only diversion from politics. He declined all other invitations, including an offer of £25,000 a year to join the board of Viyella. His first advantage in the race for Home's succession was his professionalism.

In his initial disposition of the tasks of opposition after the election Home took care to spread the jobs around so that none of the contenders should seem to be the heir apparent. Maudling was to deputise for him in the House when he was absent; but Rab Butler was given the Deputy Leader's room, while Selwyn Lloyd was to handle business questions. Heath was put in charge of the rapid reformulation of policy in time for a second General Election which might be called at any time, taking over the chairmanship of the Advisory Committee on Policy which Butler had held since 1945. (At the same time Butler surrendered the chairmanship of the Conservative Research Department which he had also held since 1945.) Finally, both Iain Macleod and Enoch Powell returned to the Shadow Cabinet. But there was at first no settled allocation of spokesmanships.

Three months later, however, when Parliament reassembled after Christmas, Home named Maudling Shadow Foreign Secretary and Heath Shadow Chancellor. (Macleod took on Steel, and Powell Transport.) Although at the same time Home affirmed his own intention to carry on as leader, this shuffle gave a critical boost to Heath at the expense of Maudling. The economy was the central issue of politics: it was on Labour's Budget and subsequent Finance Bill that the Tories would concentrate their attack in the months to come. Choosing Heath rather than the former Chancellor to lead this attack was both a recognition of Heath's greater aggression and an opportunity for him to show his paces. Conversely Maudling would be taken out of the political front line and subordinated – very much as Heath had been at the Foreign Office in 1963 – to Home in Home's own area of expertise. Foreign affairs could plausibly be represented as the senior portfolio needed to complete Maudling's all-round qualification for the leadership; but the way it worked out was that Maudling was left in a backwater while Heath led the attack on the Government.

He declared his aggressive intentions from the moment Labour took office, neither allowing ministers a honeymoon period to find their feet nor himself a rest. In a speech at Sussex University on 23 October – just eight days after the election – he was already mocking Wilson's dynamic new administration as 'old, fat and immensely disappointing from all points of view': it was both the largest and the oldest Cabinet of modern times.[1] Far from ushering in the technological revolution, he charged two weeks later at Winchester, 'The measures so far announced – surcharges on equipment for modernisation, the slowing down of the Beeching plan and the muddle over the Concorde – have all been blows to modernisation.'[2] When Parliament met at the beginning of November Heath immediately created a furious row by remarking – inaccurately – that it was 'most appropriate that an expert on tadpoles should be an adviser to the present administration'.[3] Sir Solly Zuckerman – the Government's chief scientific adviser – was actually an expert on apes; but tadpoles better suited Heath's satirical purpose. Always a quick learner, he seemed to have lost no time in mastering the less scrupulous techniques of effective opposition.

The press gallery was ecstatic. Norman Shrapnel in the *Guardian* was typical:

Mr Heath emerged last night as the hatchet man of the Opposition. In a jaunty but ruthlessly aggressive speech at the end of the debate on the address, he slashed at the Government, goaded

Labour backbenchers to sustained anger and moved Mr George Brown in particular to positive fury.

It was an astonishing performance – except perhaps to those Conservatives who may have got on the wrong side of Mr Heath in his Chief Whip days. His Commons reputation is that of a mild man, sunk in the deep freeze of economic horsetrading. This was a new Heath with a vengeance – a blasting Heath and (as Mr Brown and others were no doubt thinking) a blasted Heath.[4]

A few weeks later Heath made an astonishingly personal attack on his Balliol contemporary and fellow pro-Marketeer, Roy Jenkins, now Minister of Aviation. He criticised Jenkins's 'petulant and arrogant speech which is becoming all too characteristic of you. It has taken only four months of power to work its effect. The once promising and persuasive backbencher has become the intolerant and mentally obtuse Minister.'[5] Four months of opposition had worked a somewhat similar effect on Heath.

Labour blamed the financial crisis into which it was immediately plunged on taking office on the desperate economic legacy it had inherited – in particular a balance-of-payments deficit of £800 million, much larger than anticipated. Heath would have none of it. At Manchester on 27 November he accused Wilson of 'playing politics with economics' by deliberately exaggerating the crisis. His 'disreputable chicanery' only made the position worse.[6] The Tory line was that Maudling had had the situation perfectly in hand; it was the election of an incompetent Labour Government which had frightened the markets and created a crisis of confidence. 'The plain fact is', Heath charged the new Chancellor, Jim Callaghan, on television in February, 'that when they took over they lost their nerve, they panicked.' He specifically condemned the hasty imposition, the very first weekend after the election, of a 10 per cent import surcharge, in defiance of EFTA, which had 'angered our friends and damaged our exports'.[7] The Government was 'thoroughly discredited long before the end of its vaunted "hundred days"':

Who would have thought that within 30 days they would have broken 9 international agreements this country had put its name to?

After 50 days there was the greatest rescue act the pound had ever seen.

After 80 days a march by 10,000 trade unionists on Whitehall; and after 98 days the Foreign Secretary has been rejected, humiliated, and a safe seat lost. [On 21 January Patrick Gordon Walker had lost a by-election in a seat specially vacated for him in Leyton.]

The most astonishing thing, Heath charged, was Labour's lack of preparation. 'How Mr Wilson must be regretting those thirteen wasted years!'[8]

This was a theme to which Heath returned repeatedly: it made a deep impression on him. 'They have come into power completely unprepared,' he marvelled; and he vowed, 'We shall never be in that position.'[9] His determination that the next Conservative Government should come into office more thoroughly prepared than any in history was to be the central purpose of his leadership over the next five years. Immediately, in October 1964, it lent a sense of urgency to the task of recasting the party's policies before the next election.

There was a half-recognition in the political world that in giving this responsibility to Heath, Sir Alec had handed him a major opportunity. 'It has struck one or two of the top Conservative thinkers', the *Birmingham Post* noted in January 1965, 'that Mr Heath has been given the job of rewriting his party's long-term policy because he may be the man who will ultimately have to present it as leader.'[10] More immediately Heath was clearly the right man for the job partly because he was prepared – unlike Maudling – to give it all his energy, partly because he was particularly identified with 'modernisation'. Whether anything more was intended, by Home or by Heath, than a rapid sharpening and polishing of the party's image before Wilson was forced to go back to the country is a moot point. Heath has always maintained that he accepted the job on the understanding that he was to undertake a total rethink of Tory policy, with nothing excluded. Moreover he would claim that that is what he carried out. On the other hand, all who took part in the policy exercise between 1964 and 1966 are agreed that it was undertaken under severe political pressure in the knowledge that a second General Election might be held at any time. There was simply no time for a radical re-examination of fundamental philosophy, even if that had been to Heath's taste. But quite clearly it was not. There were those on the right of the party – most prominently Enoch Powell – who would have liked to use the breathing space of opposition to reflect on how far the exigencies of office had led the Government away from capitalist principles. But this was not Heath's view. His regional policies at the Board of Trade were precisely the sort of socialistic heresy that Powell wished the party to recant; but Heath had no thought of doing so. The party had lost an election. It had a tired and old-fashioned image. It needed some bright new policies to put in the shop window before the next election: in interviews and speeches he cited pensions, mortgages, the price of land, and the sort of practical proposals on restrictive practices and mergers that he had promised before losing office.[11] The last thing the party needed was an academic debate on Tory doctrine.

Yet there was a sense in which Heath, simply by seeming to be 'modern' and businesslike, was seen to represent a new political idea. In his weekly column in the *Spectator* in December 1964 Alan Watkins identified Heath and Macleod as the standard bearers of a new sort of Toryism dedicated to promoting efficiency through competition:

> They and their supporters have a distinctive basis to their Conservatism. The Conservative Party has long ceased being the party of the land. It is ceasing to be the party of big business (for big business dislikes competition). It is in the process of becoming, or trying to become, the party of the consumer. In other words, ceasing to represent any interest whatever. For, as Sir William Harcourt might have remarked, we are all consumers now.[12]

The point about this new classless orientation of Toryism around the consumer, however, was that while it was couched in the language of competition and efficiency, and therefore could appear to embody at least a partial acceptance of the sort of fundamental return to first principles advocated by Powell and the Institute of Economic Affairs, it was not in fact founded on any sort of theoretical rediscovery of the virtues of the free market, still less a reassessment of the practice of the outgoing Government. Heath took it for granted, as he wrote privately, that 'our basic principles are well known and easily distinguished from the Statist emphasis even of moderate Socialism'. The task was simply 'to find new practical ways to apply our principles to current problems'.[13]

His characteristic approach was to set up a lot of small groups to study specific problems and policy areas and make recommendations. By early 1965 there were over thirty such groups at work on subjects ranging from agriculture to immigration and overseas aid to law reform. The usual pattern was that each group was chaired by a member of the Shadow Cabinet or Front Bench spokesman and comprised four or five MPs, with perhaps a peer or two, and an equal number of outside experts – farmers, employers, academics, journalists, representatives of women's organisations – some of whom were not even members of the Tory party but were prepared to lend their advice. The results were then collated and channelled through the Advisory Committee on Policy for the approval of the Shadow Cabinet. The essential feature of this procedure was that every piece of paper the study groups produced went first to Heath in his capacity as chairman of the ACP.

The group's resolutely functional brief firmly precluded consideration of whether certain areas of policy should not be excluded from government activity altogether. Even within the Research Department itself doubts soon arose as to whether this was the most useful way of going about things. The deputy director James Douglas warned Sir Michael Fraser in March that 'too many people are doing too many things too superficially', working out instant reactions to problems instead of thinking out long-term ideas.[14]

A wider doubt arose from the sense that all these groups were beavering away separately in the dark, each unaware of what the others were doing. The atmosphere of secrecy aroused resentment and suspicion. More than 100 Tory MPs took part in one or more group. This was an impressive and unprecedented attempt to involve backbenchers in the formulation of party policy. But it was vitiated by the uncertainty caused by no one knowing who was on which group, by the fact that another 200 MPs were not involved and by the feeling of many that by participating in one group they were excluded from contributing to policy on other areas in which they might be equally interested. As an educational exercise, therefore, its value was limited. Moreover there were soon mutterings that the whole thing had an unspoken purpose, namely to advance Heath's challenge for the leadership.

'Mr Heath', the *Birmingham Post* reported in January, 'is known as "The Man with Sealed Lips", the oracle who has nothing to say about the hive of policy committees which have sprung up almost overnight. They meet like secret cabals in all sorts of places in London in addition to . . . Central Office.'[15] The following month the charge of 'secret cabals' was raised at the backbench 1922 Committee by a number of alarmed Maudling supporters, led by Harmar Nicholls. Heath was able to satisfy the majority of the meeting that he was doing a good job for the party.[16] But some suspicion of his 'wholly excessive passion for secrecy' remained.[17]

There is no doubt that Heath realised the opportunity his position gave him to gather all the threads of party thinking into his own hands, and he exploited it to the full. He even went so far as to forbid the Research Department to supply the papers coming out of the policy groups to Maudling – not that Maudling took much interest anyway.[18] At the same time Home's supporters, who were desperately anxious for Sir Alec to carry on as leader – among them the

Chief Whip, Willie Whitelaw – became alarmed that Heath by his energy and application was effectively usurping one of the central functions of leadership under Home's nose. They could not say that the policy review was a bad thing; yet the more Heath projected himself as the dynamic face of a modern party the more impossible Home's position steadily became.

Heath carried the same methods of hard work and attention to detail into the immediate political task of opposing the Government in the House of Commons. The major item of contentious legislation on which the Government's parliamentary timetable depended and its whole reputation would stand or fall was the Finance Bill following Callaghan's Budget, introduced on 6 April. As Shadow Chancellor, it fell to Heath to lead the Tory attack. This was another tremendous opportunity to seize the effective lead, and he grasped it: more than anything else it was his performance in fighting the Finance Bill – clause by clause over the spring and early summer – that consolidated his reputation and won him the succession in August. He approached the task like a military operation. He recruited a first-class team of economic spokesmen, split them up into small groups to specialise on particular aspects and clauses, drove them extremely hard and welded them into a political fighting unit unprecedented in parliamentary practice up to that date and rarely equalled since.

It was the longest and one of the most complicated Finance Bills since 1910. ('Nasty, brutish and long,' Heath called it. 'It soaks the rich. It also soaks the poor.')[19] The major provisions were the introduction of a new capital gains tax and the wholesale reform of company taxation, centred on a new corporation tax. Inevitably such a complex measure, introduced only a few months after the Government had taken office, was poorly prepared. There was rich scope for an Opposition that was ready to buckle down to serious criticism, both destructive and constructive. Taking advantage of the Government's tiny majority, Heath systematically refused the sort of comfortable give-and-take by which the 'usual channels' normally ease the passage of business in the interest of letting everyone get to bed. Between April and July the Bill occupied 211 hours of debate spread over 22 parliamentary days, with 6 all-night sittings. More than 1,200 amendments were tabled, 440 of them by the Government itself, while nearly 100 Tory amendments were accepted by the Government without a division. There were 108 divisions, resulting in three defeats for the Government and one tied vote.[20] The defeats were the first on a Finance Bill since 1924: inflicting them gave particular pleasure to Heath as a former Chief Whip. The successful dragging out of the Finance Bill also helped to deny the Government time for other legislation.

The five key members of the team which Heath recruited for this battle were Anthony Barber (who had four years' experience as a Treasury Minister), John Hall, Peter Walker, Peter Emery and William Clark. All, it was noted, were self-made businessmen from grammar-school backgrounds like Heath's own: quintessential 'new' Tories or, as they came to be called, 'Heathmen'. All but Clark were to become keen supporters of Heath in the years ahead. Having picked his team he ran it, like the Whips' office, on a tight rein. They met practically every day at noon with other experts as required – legal, industrial or commercial specialists – to co-ordinate tactics for the day ahead, and very often over working breakfasts in Albany as well. 'No less important', *The Times* suggested, 'he persuaded the backbench company directors to fall in with his general plan by saying little or nothing.'[21] This is perhaps unfair. In fact some 170 Tories took part in the debates on the Bill. Heath's real success was in training practically the whole parliamentary choir to sing the same tune. By doing so he went a long way to restoring the battered morale of the party, keeping the Government on the defensive, while impressing his powers of leadership, delegation and teamwork on a wider section of the party than had recognised them hitherto.

Two qualities particularly impressed Peter Walker, who had entered the House in 1961 as an admirer of Iain Macleod and an anti-Marketeer. It was Home who had appointed him an economic spokesman, and he initially viewed Heath with suspicion. He was converted into an ardent admirer by Heath's rare combination of political ruthlessness with absolute integrity. 'He had a strong grip on parliamentary tactics. There was a good debate when the notable press was there, and divisions when the Conservatives needed them – that was his Whip's training . . . He knew when to have a major row, and when not.'[22] At the same time he was furious when a backbencher made what he regarded as a dishonest speech and told the offender bluntly not to do it again. Walker still remembers his passionate desire to argue the case against the Bill and to win the argument.[23]

Meanwhile the question of how long Sir Alec could or should carry on as leader remained in the background, never openly stated – except by mischievous pollsters – but ever present. Immediately after the election 49 per cent of the public thought that he should go, 40 per cent that he should stay; but 56 per cent of Tory voters wanted him to stay.[24] A survey of Tory MPs in February found that less than a quarter thought they would do better under another leader, and even those did not want to see Home forced out before he was ready.[25] The next month, however, Home suffered a damaging setback when the Liberals (in the person of the 27-year-old David Steel) won the Roxburgh, Selkirk and Peebles by-election: if the Tories under Home could not win seats in his own Scottish Borders, it was asked, where could they win them? The *Daily Telegraph* ran a front-page story suggesting that the result 'could lead to the election of a new leader before Easter'.[26]

If Home did go, Maudling and Heath were now seen as neck and neck to succeed; but the likelihood of a close contest was in many minds a powerful reason for Home to stay on. Heath's alarming energy aroused as much apprehension as support. As early as January there were rumours of moves to 'stop Heath' at any cost. The *Sunday Express* reported that Maudling and Macleod were ready to back one another against Heath;[27] and the *Guardian* predicted that Home would appoint Selwyn Lloyd party chairman to counter Heath's growing influence.[28] (In fact he appointed Edward Du Cann.) By April Ian Aitken in the *Guardian* was writing that a number of Tories were fearful 'that Mr Heath may be stealthily recreating the Conservative Party in his own image. They have persistent nightmares that they may wake up one morning to find that Mr Heath has silently taken over everything but the title of party leader.'[29] Even Lady Douglas-Home chipped in with a barely coded warning to the same effect. Speaking at a Conservative women's conference at the Royal Festival Hall from the same platform as Heath – who told the ladies that the Tory party was embarked on 'the biggest policy reform in our history' which would make them 'the party of enterprise and opportunity, of discipline and compassion' – she won the biggest cheer of the day for warning that they might become 'such a shiny bright new party [that] no-one will recognize the true Conservatives in it'.[30] For all his limitations Sir Alec was a unifying figure, while a divisive leadership contest might tempt Wilson to catch the Opposition in disarray by calling a snap election.

The impression of Home's impermanency, however, was strengthened in February by the adoption of a new procedure for the election of the leader. This was the party hierarchy's concession to the view that the manner of Home's 'emergence' in 1963 was inappropriate in modern conditions and must not be repeated. Within weeks of the 1964 election Home himself had set up a committee to propose a more defensible method of selecting his successor when the time should come; the method recommended and approved by the 1922 Committee placed the decision clearly in the hands of Conservative MPs. To be elected on the first ballot a candidate was required to win an absolute majority of the votes cast plus a margin of 15 per cent over his or her nearest rival; on a second ballot an absolute majority would be enough. The adoption of these rules inevitably led to a growing impatience to try them out. In a concerted attempt to quell the uncertainty, Maudling, Macleod and other senior figures pledged the party's unswerving loyalty to Home; and on 26 June Sir Alec himself announced that there would be no leadership contest in 1965 – only to be wrongfooted by Wilson announcing that there would be no General Election in 1965 either. This removed the Tories' fear of being caught between leaders and offered a window of opportunity to get a new leader elected and played in before the election which must surely come in 1966. From this moment the pressure on Home mounted.

That weekend the *Sunday Express* ran a sensational story claiming that 100 Tory MPs were involved in a 'bid to oust Sir Alec'.[31] The plot, if plot there was, quickly collapsed in a rash of denials. But the impression lingered that Heath's supporters had overreached themselves and damaged their candidate in the process. Though Home characteristically accepted Heath's assurance that he had had nothing to do with it – joking that an empty chair at a private lunch they both attended was 'For one of your hundred men, I suppose?' – others were less charitable. As one 'Front Bencher' told the *Sunday Telegraph*: 'Ted must have known about it: he did not stop it.'[32] Naturally Heath did not want to be seen to be actively caballing against Home: at the same time there is no doubt that he was making his dispositions in preparation for the contest when it came. Several of those who would form his campaign team were already meeting discreetly at his flat in Albany. 'Supporters of Mr Heath,' the *Guardian* reported on 28 June, 'who until recently were hoping time would whittle away Mr Maudling's followers, and were therefore anxious to delay Sir Alec's departure, now see their opportunity. Sir Alec's defenders noted indignantly yesterday that it is Mr Heath's men who are making the running for a change.'[33] This is undeniable, but it was not exclusively so. On 5 July a resolution calling for a debate on the leadership was put up to the Executive of the 1922 Committee: it was supported by some twenty-five backbenchers, among them Sir John Eden, Peter Emery and Anthony Kershaw, all known Heath supporters, but also Neil Marten, a prominent Maudling man. In so far as Heath had been damaged by his supporters' over-eagerness an early contest might be expected to show a loyalist reaction in favour of Maudling. From both camps sufficient feeling was expressed that Home ought now to go that the chairman, Sir William Anstruther-Gray, a strong Home supporter, was able to avoid a vote only by undertaking to report the sense of the meeting to Sir Alec.[34]

On 9 July and again on 13 July Home repeated that he was not standing down. On 18 July James Margach reported in the *Sunday*

Times that he was in 'a tough, uncompromising mood' and was 'determined' to lead the party into the next election.[35] In fact he was determined not to hang on unless it was the overwhelming wish of the party that he should do so. That same day another article in the same paper by the deputy editor William Rees-Mogg – entitled 'The Right Moment for a Change' – convinced him that he should go. Whitelaw and Du Cann, Chief Whip and party chairman, could not deny that substantial sections of the party agreed with Rees-Mogg: he was no longer a unifying force. So, honourably, Home announced to a shocked meeting of the 1922 Committee on 22 July that he was resigning; and the first Tory leadership election under the new rules was on.

There were clearly going to be two candidates: there might be more. The front runners were so closely matched that there might be an opportunity for a third candidate to come through on the second or third ballot as an acceptable compromise (as Bonar Law had done in 1911 when there was a stand-off between Austen Chamberlain and Walter Long). Peter Thorneycroft and Christopher Soames were the names most frequently mentioned; but Quintin Hogg, Selwyn Lloyd or even Lord Blakenham were canvassed as long shots, especially if the party when it came to it could not face either Heath or Maudling and wished to fall back as in 1963 on a more reassuring figure from a traditional Tory background.[36] In the event Maudling was sufficiently reassuring for the traditionalists: neither Soames nor Thorneycroft entered the lists, at least for the first ballot. Nor did Iain Macleod: to many the 'lost leader' of the 1950 generation, he simply had too many enemies to be a serious candidate. But a third candidate did come forward – to the annoyance of both the Heath and Maudling camps – in the person of Enoch Powell, who stood not with any hope of winning but to put down a quixotic marker for his esoteric free-market ideas.

Maudling was generally assumed to be the favourite. *The Economist* judged that the surge in Heath's standing had peaked a few weeks earlier. Sir Alec's going had released a sentimental reaction in his favour which was likely to rebound against Heath for having seemed in too much of a hurry to push him out.[37] Many commentators doubted that the Tory party was yet ready to make the leap to a leader of Heath's style and background. Although, as Anthony Sampson wrote, Heath had 'the advantage of typifying a thriving, ambitious New Britain without snobbery or amateurism . . . in the Tory party he was still apt to be regarded as a creepy technocrat with too much zeal and not enough ballast'. More specifically 'he was still identified with the humiliation of Brussels, which his party were trying hard to forget'; while some still blamed his single-mindedness over Resale Price Maintenance for the loss of the election.[38] A good many Tory MPs had felt the roughness of his tongue; moreover there was a question mark over the electoral appeal of a bachelor. An NOP poll in the *Daily Mail* confirmed that Maudling would be the more popular choice by the wide margin of 44 per cent to 28 per cent (48 per cent to 31 per cent among Tory voters).[39] Nevertheless the press assessments of the two candidates showed a clear preference for Heath.

The television programme 'Panorama' exemplified the way the two rivals were presented: 'Thrustful, pugnacious, aggressive, Heath is admired for his skill as Chief Whip, brilliance as the Common Market negotiator and toughness in opposition. Ted is the man for those Conservatives who think the party needs "a tiger in its tank".' Maudling, on the other hand,

> is backed by those who value brain-power above energy, and judgement above drive. Supporters point to his lack of enemies, the appeal of his family life, his long experience of ministerial office, and the superiority of his intellect. Reggie is the man for those Conservatives who want the driver at the wheel to be steady, sound and shrewd.[40]

Elsewhere Maudling was repeatedly damned with faint praise as the safe – but by implication timid – choice. Heath's very faults, his unpredictability, were written up to count in his favour – for instance by *The Economist*:

> Mr Heath's powers of judgement have still to be put to the test. It is perfectly possible to doubt them. What he has shown is that he has nerve and will: once pointed in the right direction the cannon will batter down the walls. For that very reason he seems to possess, however marginally, the greater potential. Perhaps he is the riskier choice. But what the next firmly-based British government will need at its head is a man who will take decisions on the side of efficiency, however unpopular they may be. In those terms the better choice is Heath.[41]

The contrast in personalities was sharply reflected in the way the two candidates set about seeking support. Whereas Heath's campaign was characteristically energetic, tightly organised and thoroughly professional, Maudling's was loose, easy-going and amateurish. The moment Home resigned Heath asked Peter Walker to take charge of his operation. Walker agreed, on the understanding that he should have complete control. Heath was as good as his word and was content to be guided by Walker as to how much direct canvassing he should do, how much he should speak to the press and how often he should go into the Smoking Room. Walker quickly assembled a team of lieutenants including Geoffrey Lloyd, Charles Morrison and Ian Gilmour. Walker's method was to contact all Tory MPs individually over the next two or three days, with each member of the team deputed to speak to those colleagues whom he knew best, going back to them again where necessary and using the arguments best calculated to persuade each individual, ticking or crossing them off until they had an accurate picture of how every Member was likely to vote. In the event Walker's prediction of the result was very nearly spot on: his reckoning gave Powell two votes too many and Maudling two too few, but he got Heath's own figure exactly right.[42]

Maudling's campaign, by contrast, was haphazard. On the evening of the day that Home resigned, Maudling met a group of his supporters at William Clark's house in Barton Street.* His strategy as front runner was to refrain from any sort of high-pressure canvassing which, he believed, would merely irritate experienced politicians who were quite capable of making up their own minds. This was an adult and civilised attitude, but it was the wrong approach to a contest in which his whole task was to overcome an image of amiable indolence: the leadership was his if he could just convince his fellow Tory MPs that he wanted it badly enough and, if elected, would then have the energy and commitment to harry Wilson out of Downing Street. This he singularly failed to do. Maudling's very name suggested a combination of 'dawdling' and 'muddle'; the curious thing was that he seemed determined to live up to it. Maybe he was right not to try to act out of character: when his supporters did get him to come to the House early on Monday morning to meet the Scottish MPs coming off the overnight train it was most unconvincing. But the real fault of Maudling's campaign was complacency: Maudling expected to win and as a result his backers made only half-hearted efforts to beat up his support. Peter Walker felt that William Clark and Anthony Lambton, his two main lieutenants, simply had no idea how to go about it. They were too ready to accept at face value assurances of support from Members who were only being polite.[43] The contrast with the Heath team –

---

* Heath, with his campaign already up and running, spent the evening at Glyndebourne. The opera, appropriately, was *Macbeth*.

'openly energetic in scooping waverers into the Heath camp', as Gerald Kaufman described them in the *New Statesman*[44] – was visible, and decisive.

The contest was all about image. The two candidates' age and background were pretty similar. Maudling was marginally younger, and had been to a minor public school – Merchant Taylors – as against Heath's grammar school; but he was essentially another scholarship boy, not a traditional Tory. Yet Maudling was unshakeably cast as the 'old school' candidate against the brash outsider. Had the leadership fallen vacant in 1962, Edward Boyle wrote many years later – when the party was still in office, before Home was in a position to disclaim his coronet and before Wilson replaced Gaitskell – 'Maudling would have been better placed to "emerge" under the old system than any rival.'[45] By 1965, under the new system, and facing a Labour Government, he had missed his moment. The Tories were now electing a leader for opposition, a leader to beat Harold Wilson; they took it for granted that Wilson could be beaten only by someone as aggressive, professional and 'modern' as himself; and in a contest to be as like Harold Wilson as possible, Heath was indisputably more like Wilson than Maudling was.

'Those who thought of long-term Conservative Government', wrote Harry Boyne in the *Daily Telegraph*, 'preferred Maudling; those who just wanted to bundle Labour out quickly were all for Heath.'[46] It is ironic that Heath should have been elected – in part at least – because he was expected to be a good Leader of the Opposition, since he quickly turned out to be terrible in opposition and only really interested in government. But Boyne's was not the only view. A good many Tories saw Heath as a more dynamic executive than Maudling and looked forward positively to a Heath Government: John Grigg, for instance, writing in the *Guardian*, praised his 'originality, daring and stamina, the vision to see what needs to be done and the single-minded ruthlessness to carry it out'.[47] This was a much more perceptive view than that of those who saw Heath simply as the man to 'bundle out' Wilson.

But if Heath scored by being seen as more 'dynamic' than Maudling, this was largely because there was no ideological content to the contest at all, except the parrot cry of 'modernisation' which Heath had made his own. Only Enoch Powell – 'the Piltdown Man of the Conservative Party' as the *Guardian* described him – 'did his best to inject a conflict of issues into the contest. He was told, in effect, to take his principles elsewhere.'[48]

Speculation as to whether Powell's intervention would take votes from Heath or Maudling reflected ambiguity about whether Heath should be placed on the left or right of the party. Nora Beloff in the *Observer* saw him as a supporter of planning and incomes policy;[49] both *The Times* and *The Economist*, on the contrary, detected a growing interest in 'the gospel according to St Enoch' among Heath's study groups and judged Heath himself to be at least half-converted. ('Will Mr Heath find it convenient to wear Mr Powell's anti-planning trousers,' *The Economist* wondered, 'or are some other ideas filtering into what sometimes looks like an economic vacuum in that forceful mind?'[50] At least Heath appeared open to ideas, while Maudling appeared to have no interest in them, or any driving political purpose at all.

In the event, Powell's token vote probably made no difference to the result. Much more important was the vote that might have gone to Iain Macleod, had he chosen to stand. It is widely believed that this critical block of perhaps forty-five votes went, with Macleod's blessing, almost wholly to Heath. Contradicting rumours that he might combine with Maudling to stop Heath, Macleod actually came to the view that Heath was the more dynamic leader the party needed and advised his friends accordingly. His biographer Nigel Fisher believes that Macleod was the crucial kingmaker, whose advice helped to sway such different characters as Duncan Sandys and Ian Gilmour into the Heath camp; even though Fisher himself and at least two other of Macleod's supporters – Norman St John Stevas and Humphrey Berkeley – voted for Maudling.[51]

The same reasoning swung most – probably three-quarters – of the Shadow Cabinet. Alec Douglas-Home himself made known his tacit support for Heath, and most of those who were to come to the top of the Tory party over the next twenty years seem to have followed his lead. Margaret Thatcher was a significant waverer. On personal grounds she was drawn to Maudling, whose Barnet constituency adjoined hers in Finchley; but Keith Joseph, a keen Heathite, persuaded her to vote for Heath. (Peter Walker specifically remembers Joseph ringing to say that he had got her vote – a good individual example of the way the Heath network operated.)[52] There is an impression that Maudling was largely supported by the double-barrelled knights of the shires. But even they were not solid: Sir Arthur Vere-Harvey, Sir Walter Bromley-Davenport, Sir Tufton Beamish and Sir Godfrey Nicholson were all said to have supported Heath.[53] Such claims must of course be treated with care: after any such contest the number of people claiming to have backed the winner always exceeds the number of votes he or she actually received: the fact is that Maudling won a substantial vote which must have come from somewhere. Nevertheless the impression remains that the younger, abler and most ambitious Tory MPs supported Heath.

Beyond the 303 MPs who constituted the electorate, soundings among the Tory peers were said to show a 2-1 majority for Heath; while most constituency chairmen and local activists were likewise reported to prefer the underdog. Despite Maudling's multiple directorships, even the City was said to prefer Heath. The press was practically unanimous. From *The Times* ('Britain needs a tough man to lead her') through the *Daily Mail* (which wanted 'a leader who is a man of action') to the *Daily Sketch* (which thought Heath had 'fire in his belly') they echoed the same refrain. Only the *Sunday Telegraph* and the *News of the World* came out for Maudling.[54] Yet strangely the press still expected Maudling to win. Opinion polls showed that the public clearly preferred the more cuddly Maudling (by 44 per cent to 28 per cent), and it was expected that this would weigh more heavily with MPs than purely party opinion. Labour was said to respect Heath in the House of Commons, but to regard Maudling as the more dangerous electoral opponent.[55] In fact the evidence of subsequent contests in 1975 and 1990 shows that MPs make up their minds on the basis of their own observation of the candidates in the House, not on the basis of opinion polls. The public might well have voted for Maudling in 1965; but the public did not have a vote.

Heath spent the Sunday before the poll at Broadstairs. He attended church in the morning, then for the benefit of the cameras went for a family picnic with his father and stepmother, Teddy and Joy Denman and their children, and Toby Aldington, until they were driven off the beach by rain. (Maudling was likewise photographed with his wife and children in his garden.) Next day voting took place in Committee Room 14 at the House of Commons. Robin Chichester-Clark (Heath), Robert Carr (Maudling) and Nicholas Ridley (Powell) acted as polling agents for the three candidates. After voting, Heath went to await the result at Peter Walker's office in the old St Stephen's building on the Embankment, where for nearly two hours he talked to Walker more freely than ever before of his hopes and ambitions for himself and the country in the years ahead: of the great social change of which he felt himself to be at once the product, a symbol and a catalyst, and the unprecedented opportunities opening up for young people in Britain and for Britain itself in Europe. Walker has never forgotten the passion and optimism of this conversation, at a moment when Heath's hopes of leading the country into this rosy future hung in the balance.[56] Maudling characteristically spent this nervous interval lunching in the City.

The result was close, yet decisive: Heath 150, Maudling 133, Powell 15. Heath had a narrow absolute majority of votes cast, though not of those entitled to vote; and he was a long way short of the 15 per cent margin required for a first ballot victory. Yet it was plain that he had won. Maudling was reported to be 'shattered' when Carr rang him at Kleinwort's to give him the figures: his supporters had assured him of at least 154 votes, with no more than 100 for Heath. 'I will not deny that it was a bitter blow,' he wrote in his memoirs. 'I had been working for success for many years. I was looking forward to success and had reasonable grounds for expecting it.'*[57] But there was no way he could hope to overtake Heath's lead by forcing a second ballot. So he wasted no time consulting his friends, but immediately telephoned Heath to concede.

The outcome was seen, first of all, as a triumph for the new system of choosing the leader. Heath's 'bloodless victory', James Margach enthused in the *Sunday Times*, had been achieved with no blood-letting, horse-trading or recriminations; there had been no ideological split, just honest rivalry cleanly settled.[59] At last, after three years of debilitating uncertainty, the party could look confidently to the future, with no leadership crisis dragging it down. Heath's election – defeating two other candidates of his own generation – represented the coming of age of the Class of 1950: the culmination of the modernisation of the Tory party initiated after the war by Butler and Woolton. As so often in the past, the Tories had defied public opinion in choosing their leader, making the bold rather than the easy choice, preferring a good administrator to the more obviously popular politician. Heath's election unleashed a tremendous outpouring of gushing hype, concentrating heavily on his modest origins. For the *Daily Mirror* he was 'a new kind of Tory leader – a classless professional politician who has fought his way to the top by guts, ability and political skill'.[60] Atticus in the *Sunday Times* more precisely defined him as the first Tory leader to have wall-to-wall carpeting, and the first to look thoroughly at home on a beach.[61] (That rainy picnic was not wasted.) Only the Communist *Daily Worker* derided the 'fantastic snobbery' by which the capitalist press made such a fuss of Heath's 'humble' background, just because he went to grammar school and had collected only one directorship. They need not worry, the paper predicted. 'As a representative of the ruling class, he will be as ruthless as they come.'[62]

Heath was universally expected to open a new chapter in Tory

---

* 'Mr Maudling's campaign managers', the *Guardian* reported, 'confessed . . . with their usual engaging naivety, that they were still utterly unable to understand how their candidate had been defeated. Crumpled lists of collected promises were still in their pockets, and the totals came to a comfortable majority for Mr Maudling.'[58]

politics. Under the typical headline 'Formidable: This Man of Incisive Action', the *Daily Sketch* thought Wilson had made the
mistake of hitting Home for six once too often. 'Now he will have to
face a bowler who has been chosen for one purpose – to get him
out.'[63] The *Guardian* was only one of many papers to quote an unnamed Conservative MP: 'We have elected a rough rider and it is
time to fasten our seat belts.'[64] More considered comment in the
weeklies dwelt on the political radicalism that was assumed to go
with his social background. 'The party battle lines', Macleod's *Spectator* believed, 'will never be the same again.' Heath's leadership was
expected to emphasise 'the need for a radical, non-socialist, liberating
approach to our cobwebbed industrial set-up'. From now on the
political argument would be about 'which party can unlock the shut
doors and closed minds of Britain'.[65]

The Economist was more sceptical. Its new editor, Alastair Burnet,
believed that the Tories had picked the right man, but remained unconvinced that the party had changed overnight.

> Mr Heath certainly carries radical hopes in his baggage. But in
> electing him the Tories have primarily shown their instinct for
> power. They picked, by a narrow majority, the man they
> reckoned most likely to bullock their way back into power. They
> will remain united behind him just as long as his pursuit of power
> looks promising.[66]

While the Tory papers all portrayed Heath as a clear-sighted and
single-minded battering ram, the *Guardian* saw him as more pragmatic: 'opportunist and to some extent unpredictable . . . capable of a
sudden and complete change of course if he thinks it will pay . . . also
capable of ill-tempered misjudgements'.[67] With hindsight, however,
The Economist's appraisal was the most penetrating; it put its finger
unerringly on the missing factor in Heath's political make-up. Life
with Heath might be 'very uncomfortable'. The question was
whether he had the charisma to command devotion beyond the ranks
of his immediate staff:

> It may sound odd about a man who is always being photographed
> looking jolly, but the Tory party is littered with people still nurs-
> ing bruises from some Heath brusquerie . . .
> He likes to plan an operation in depth, to build up a team, in
> which each member has a clear role and gets the chance to carry it
> out, provided he is up to the job. If he is not, he gets the chop.
> The true Heath style . . . is based on mastery of detail backed by

formidable stamina. He will not fail through indolence; he has the will and the adrenalin to outwork anyone in politics.

The doubt was whether he had the necessary originality of mind. Did he too often miss the wood for the trees? It was to his credit that he saw the need for abolishing RPM and joining the EEC. But he had coined no memorable phrases. He could be witty in private and effective in the House of Commons; but he was uninspiring on the platform and on television. 'There is every chance that he will produce the right policies for the nation; what he has to find is his own new language to explain them.'[68]

This was a doubt which was to be echoed repeatedly up to 1970, and ever more insistently in the four years that followed. The failure to find a language to explain and inspire was to be, in the end, the central, crippling failure of Heath's career. Yet in August 1965, when he assumed the Conservative leadership, it was too easily believed – by most of Fleet Street and by Heath himself – that energy, will-power and determination were all that mattered.

PART THREE

Preparing for Power

10

Establishing Authority

HEATH's election as Tory leader was a triumph which quickly became a protracted nightmare. Exaggerated promise soon turned to cruel disappointment, both for Heath himself and for those who had placed their faith in him. The Leadership of Her Majesty's Opposition is a thankless job for which, it rapidly became clear, Heath was not after all so well cut out as his aggressive performance since the previous October had briefly suggested. He was elected at a difficult moment, when a second General Election could not be long delayed and a second and heavier defeat for the Conservatives was on the cards; it was scarcely his fault that he failed to stave it off, but nevertheless he was damaged by the result. He then had to face four or five years in opposition, lacking the authority of an ex-Prime Minister, lacking also the natural authority which still counted in a party heavily impregnated with respect for class and rank, a party moreover angrily unreconciled to the loss of office. Heath worked harder at the job than any Leader of the Opposition had ever worked before. Yet for five years he suffered relentless criticism, from the party and the press alike, for failing to get his message across, for failing to get his personality across. His public personality – stiff, cold, tense and humourless – became the issue of his leadership. His failure to project an attractive 'image' hung about him like an incubus, blighting his hopes of ever being Prime Minister, despite the Labour Government's extreme unpopularity. The more hurtfully he was criticised, the more defensive, tense and withdrawn he naturally became. By 1970, when he astonishingly snatched victory from apparently inevitable defeat, he had been all but written off as an embarrassing aberration. For his few loyal friends and those colleagues who admired his positive qualities, 1965-70 was a painful period.

Initially, however, Heath's election as the new Tory leader un-leashed a torrent of fawning press interviews and flattering profiles bearing very little relation to reality. As Christopher Booker pene-tratingly pointed out in his 1969 book *The Neophiliacs*, the fantasy merchants of the Swinging Sixties were quick to recruit him to their dream world as a dynamic British Kennedy figure.[1] Only two years earlier it had been Harold Wilson who had played successfully on this longing. But Wilson's glamour had already lost its sheen and the colour supplements needed a new hero. 'With his remarkable ability, his grasp of detail and his capacity for hard work,' gushed the *Week-end Telegraph*, 'he is probably the nearest thing British politics has to the whizz kids President Kennedy brought into his administration.'[2] The *Observer* Colour Magazine was wide-eyed with admiration:

> Ted Heath likes to gather people, younger people, around him. He summons them on the telephone. They come to breakfast with him at his chambers in the Albany.
>
> Like Kennedy he is very intelligent, but no intellectual. But he ruthlessly uses intellectuals and experts to advise him, to feed him with facts . . . it is . . . the computer mind at work.[3]

Much was made of the brilliant young 'whizz kids' who sur-rounded this maestro. (Wilson deftly mocked them as 'cub tycoons'.) The three who attracted most attention were Peter Walker, then aged thirty-three, who had masterminded Heath's victory in the leader-ship campaign – another grammar-school bachelor and self-made millionaire; John MacGregor, twenty-eight, a keen Scot who had helped him during the General Election in Bexley and was now head of his Private Office; and David Howell, twenty-nine, a thoroughly modern Old Etonian who was head of the Conservative Political Centre. The schools they had attended were an important feature of all these profiles. It was thought to typify the 'classlessness' of Heath's Tory party that he could bring together grammar-school boys and Old Etonians in a single dynamic team. Likewise both Willie Whitelaw, the Chief Whip, and Edward Du Cann, the party chairman, inherited from Douglas-Home, were said to fit smoothly into the new régime. 'The keynotes of the new leadership', the *Observer* assured its readers, were 'efficiency, success, public ease.'[4] Anne Scott-James in the *Daily Mail* interviewed Heath for the woman's angle. Calling at Albany at 9 am, she found that Heath 'looked as bronze and fit and blue-eyed as a swimming instructor', having supposedly been up and working since 6 am. She duly admired the 'thick dark carpets, enormous comfortable sofas, black leather chairs, and walls lined with paintings, drawings, 18th c. political cartoons and good prints . . . the style I call "House and Garden Bachelor"'. (Not for nothing was she married to Osbert Lancaster.) Heath talked to her of incentives, opportunity, affluence and a better quality of life, but also of books and music (on which she found him 'strangely unopinionated'). She felt that he was too bound by White Papers and should give his imagination freer rein; but concluded 'Incidentally, he has an awful lot of charm.'[5]

The supreme importance of style, and the illusion that success could be conjured up simply by talking about it: these were the characteristic fantasies of what now looks a very shallow period. The attempt to lavish on a staid 49-year-old politician the sort of adulation more usually given to pop stars, photographers and models was a symptom of unreality certain to end in disillusion. It was particularly inappropriate to apply it to Heath, who was not 'swinging' at all and – unlike Harold Wilson, who loved to be photographed with the Beatles – did not wish to be; though he did want to be thought modern and dynamic. He had no choice anyway but to go along with it. But political reality, or rather the political theatre of the House of Commons, broke in very quickly. The very day he was formally confirmed as leader by the party meeting at Church House he had to face Wilson for the first time in his new role in a much-heralded censure debate in which he was expected to live up to his publicity by wiping the floor with his opponent. Instead Wilson wiped the floor with him.

Heath's speech failed altogether to rise to the occasion. He was dull, evidently nervous and leadenly predictable as point by point he condemned the Labour Government's dismal record and contrasted it once again with the thirteen years of steadily increased social provision and widening opportunity under the Tories. The first essential of a new Tory Government, he promised, would be to 'stop trying to kid the people that everything can be done easily by gimmicks, by new Ministries, or merely by new and meaningless phrases'. But striving for a meaningless phrase himself, he could only mock the appointment of Frank Cousins as Minister of Technology. Instead of a tiger, he jeered, 'the Prime Minister has put a tortoise in the tank'. He expounded an unexceptionable vision of a high-wage, high-efficiency, low-cost economy to be achieved by productivity agreements, by encouraging investment, by co-operating with industry instead of antagonising it, by 'a real drive for regional development' and by working with Britain's European partners in EFTA.[6] But he failed to drive home his attack on the Government. In trying to appear properly statesmanlike by contrast with Wilson's gimmickry, he sacrificed the aggression which had carried him to the leadership. From the opposite side of the House Richard Crossman commented unkindly in his diary: 'There can't have been many Tories who didn't whisper under their breath, "My God, I see the point of Maudling now."'[7]

Wilson characteristically took full advantage. Winding up a debate which 'we were told would transform the political scene and electrify the Conservative party', he mischievously derided Heath's speech by praising Maudling's admittedly much punchier one. It was 'a great pity', he suggested, 'that he did not make it a fortnight earlier'. (But Maudling now had nothing to lose, whereas the pressure of expectation on Heath was terrific.) He had deadly fun with Heath's 'one memorable phrase', his 'tortoise in the tank' joke. 'I must say I liked that. I liked it the first time I saw it in a *Sunday Citizen* cartoon on 27 June. I am sure that the House will always be ready to hear the Right Hon. Gentleman again, especially if he keeps reminding us of that phrase.'[8]

Then, at the very end of his speech, amid mounting uproar, Wilson deflected Heath's criticism of the import surcharge imposed immediately after the election by revealing that the Tories themselves had plans to do exactly the same had they been returned. 'At this,' *The Times* reported, 'white-faced and goaded beyond endurance, Mr Heath sprang to his feet and clutched the despatch box.'[9] 'This is absolutely typical', he fumed, 'of everything which has characterised . . . [Interruption]. To raise a point at two minutes to ten [Interruption] when there is no time to discuss it . . . [Interruption].' He tried to counter that of course the Conservative Government had prepared contingency plans for all sorts of eventualities, but that did not mean they would have imposed the surcharge. 'The Prime Minister knows full well . . .' he spluttered; but Wilson got the last mocking word – 'The Right Hon. Gentleman is afraid. We treat his censure motion with contempt' – and carried the day (the Liberals abstaining) by a majority of thirteen.[10]

The vote, *The Times* concluded, was 'less important than the drubbing Mr Wilson handed out to his new rival . . . Amid scenes of fantastic uproar . . . he pulled the rug from under Mr Heath and left him gasping on the floor.' His last blow, admittedly, was a low one; but Heath's poor speech had left him open to it. Politics were not conducted under the Queensberry Rules. The Tories' new champion had 'a lot to learn'.[11]

This humiliating début was typical both of Wilson's parliamentary skill and of Heath's difficulty in dealing with him. The Prime Minister, still in the first confidence of his office and revelling in his tiny majority, was like a quick-witted matador teasing a bull. It had been supposed that Heath would be able to needle Wilson, but it was quite the other way round. This first exchange set the pattern for their contests at the dispatch box over the next five years. Time and again Heath, trying doggedly to make a serious point on some important issue would be tripped up by Wilson's lightning agility and clever use of ridicule. Heath had been chosen Tory leader above all because he was thought to be the candidate most like Wilson, and therefore best able to beat him at his own game. In fact, except in age and educational background he was not like Wilson at all. He was good at marshalling and expounding huge amounts of information, but he was not a ready phrasemaker and he was embarrassingly bad at parliamentary repartee. His jokes were laboured and invariably fell flat.* His doggedly serious-minded purpose was to show up Wilson's shallow opportunism by unanswerable weight of argument; but Wilson better understood the reality of Parliament as a cockpit for scoring political points. While Heath circled, looking for the knock-out punch, Wilson repeatedly shifted his ground and wrongfooted him, teasing him with low jabs and quick, stinging gibes, patronising him: 'If he can't do better than that . . .', Wilson would jeer;[13] or 'the Right Honourable Gentleman really must improve'.[14] Heath despised Wilson's tactics as cheap and unworthy of the dignity of his office. According to Jim Prior, his PPS, he 'really hated' Wilson at this time.[15] But the more angry and pompous he became, the more helplessly he delivered himself into Wilson's hands.

Heath and Wilson were utterly different in personality and temperament. Yet part of Heath's problem was that he was in one respect more like Wilson than he would have cared to admit, in that he too was – as Dick Crossman for one quickly recognised[16] – essentially a pragmatic politician. He had a clear vision of the sort of country he wanted Britain to become – much clearer than Wilson's. He had immense idealism and sincerity. But his political purposes were so broadly benevolent that they were in a curious way unpolitical. He simply wanted people to have the opportunity of leading richer and fuller lives. He had very little idea of how they were to be enabled to do so, except that British industry needed to become more efficient and the economy more competitive: that was the Tory way. But he had no interest in political philosophy or economic theory: that, he

---

* When Iain Macleod, cleverly inverting President Kennedy's description of himself ('an idealist without illusions') called Wilson 'an illusionist without ideals' the barb stung because of the way Macleod delivered it. Had Heath used the same phrase it would merely have seemed contrived.[12]

believed, was what the Labour party suffered from. He thought essentially that making Britain prosperous and successful was a matter of practical common sense and political will, vigorously applied. Despite the best of intentions and all their differences of personality, this intellectual vacuum at the heart of Heath's politics was in the last analysis little different from the opportunist trickiness he so despised in Wilson. It was to lead him, despite himself, into inconsistency in trying to oppose the Labour Government over the next five years, and to damaging reversals of policy when he eventually achieved power himself in 1970.

A particularly vivid impression of the limitations but also strengths of Heath's style was given by *The Economist*, reporting a press conference he gave in early October, just before the Tory party conference:

> His prepared opening statement was flatulent, for he is no public orator; his unprepared answers to the most detailed questions were overpoweringly impressive, perhaps almost too much so . . .
>
> Somebody fired off an extremely arcane question about some Nigerian tariff negotiations, about which few people at the press conference could have heard; but Mr Heath had heard of them, and he left his audience gasping when he started referring to some Sierra Leone tariff negotiations as well.
>
> The man's memory is Wilsonian, and it is a fair tribute that he did not seem to trim his every answer in a way that would look politically most favourable, as Mr Wilson does. He gave the impression of a man immensely and personally interested in every last detail of every policy that he regards as politically practical. Where he does not regard a policy as politically practical, he ignores it with equal verve . . . This was a push-button computer bidding for office at Number Ten. Whether people vote for computers remains to be seen.[17]

That autumn Heath gave a series of major interviews in which he set out his vision of the Britain he hoped to lead. Two themes recurred: his concern to raise the *quality* of British life and a wish to create a more classless society – both highly personal ambitions rooted in his own experience. He expounded them both to James Margach of the *Sunday Times*:

> I think that I would like to be associated with leading a Government which really gave ordinary people the opportunity of

leading fuller lives. This means giving them better material circumstances, better housing and the ability to enjoy better holidays, listen to music on long-playing records or whatever they want to do . . .

The second thing I'd like to be associated with is in helping to create a society in which barriers are broken down, a society in which one treats people, not so much on their merits – because that has a strange association that clever people should only meet clever people, and so on – but in which people respect the inner man or woman in each other.

But this, he insisted, 'can only be done if we have got a really vital economic life'.[18]

This really was the sum of Heath's purpose in politics. It was an altogether admirable ambition, but it lacked precision as to how it was to be achieved. He was inclined to think, as he told Andrew Alexander in the *Weekend Telegraph*, that it was simply a matter of getting 'rid of certain nonsenses'.[19] In yet another interview, with Kenneth Harris in the *Observer*, he struggled to describe his reason for going into politics in the first place, rather than the Civil Service or the law. It was, he suggested, 'the sense of achievement. Or of trying to achieve. Creating something, something useful, worthwhile, necessary. Leaving life different from what you found it.'[20] Such a temperament was always going to find opposition intensely uncongenial.

As soon as Parliament rose, following his disappointing parliamentary début, Heath escaped with relief for a much-needed holiday in the south of France, staying with the Seligmans in the fishing village of Villefranche, just along the coast from Nice. But he was too new a leader to escape the attentions of the world's press. He was photographed swimming, sightseeing, sunbathing and – tentatively – sailing a small dinghy; reporters noted his daily routine and logged his visitors, so that the image of Heath on holiday became an extension of the sort of wide-eyed hype penned about him at home: Villefranche became Camelot-sur-mer. ('Anything the Scillies can do', he told reporters, 'we can do better.')[21] At eight o'clock every morning he was said to take a call from John MacGregor in London, and at one o'clock another from Central Office. On 14 August David Howell arrived to work on some statements, followed by Edward Du Cann. Iain Macleod and even Selwyn Lloyd were reported to be on hand near by.

On his return from France Heath went north (still accompanied by Howell and Peter Walker) to spend a few days with Lord Margadale

Vicky, *Evening Standard* (18 October 1965)

(the former John Morrison) on Islay, then got back to politics proper with a mid-September tour of the Highlands and Orkney. His perfectly sensible purpose was to try to regain some of the thirteen Scottish Tory seats lost – several of them to the Liberals – in 1959 and 1964. But the spectacle of the great technocrat 'energetically travelling around the Scottish highlands telling the sheep not to vote Liberal'[22] was an easy target for metropolitan commentators who did not believe that this was where the next election was going to be decided. Already Heath's brief honeymoon was over. Having ludicrously overpraised him in August, the press was now beginning to decide that he was not after all the dream leader they had taken him for.

The first big test of his leadership was the Tory party conference at Brighton in mid-October.* In order to demonstrate that he was going to be a different sort of leader, Heath made a point of attending the whole conference. The Tory tradition had always been that the

---

* Wilson, typically, tried to 'bitch' Heath's conference début by flying quite spuriously to Balmoral to see the Queen, arousing rumours of a General Election.[23] Heath was furious, yet was still able to remark wryly to Jim Prior: 'Good Lord, no one's done this kind of thing since Harold Macmillan!'[24]

leader came down only on the final Saturday morning to deliver his annual address to the faithful. By contrast, Heath gave a keynote speech on the first morning, replying to a debate on the policy document *Putting Britain Right Ahead* which was the first fruit of the policy rethink, and then sat on the platform for the next three days listening to the debates before making his closing speech on the Saturday. He thus gave himself two chances to impress his new style on the party: in the end he was reckoned to have just about succeeded. His first speech – despite the fact that it was supposed to be all about creating dynamism and excitement – was for the most part heavy going, though *The Times* claimed to detect 'a new light and shade in delivery which held his audience through the dull patches'.[25] (*The Economist* thought he spoke for thirty minutes 'as if in his sleep'.)[26] But then 'he fought his way out with his finale',[27] an effective peroration based on his personal experience of attending the Last Night of the Proms a few weeks earlier. For once he managed to link the youthful patriotism of the occasion successfully to his vision of Britain's future in Europe. As always he was most eloquent when he allowed his love of music to breathe warmth into his politics.

> Perhaps as a musical occasion it is not one of the highest intelligence, but it is a magnificent occasion. As I looked at that crowded hall, with thousands of people there, the promenade filled with young people, but looking around also at those who were cheering with them, I heard them singing the great songs of our country. They stamped 'Rule, Britannia' and they sang 'Wider still and wider, shall thy bounds be set'. They sang it not only for the sake of singing at a Prom. They sang it with passion because they believed it.

They knew quite well, he went on, that the world had moved on from the days of Empire. But they were crying out for a new advance down a different path.

> How can we satisfy the inner urge of those who were that night with such passion singing the old words and wanting new meanings? I believe that we can do it, because we have so much to give to the world . . . The way will be hard, and it will take time . . . The way will be hard, but we can do it.

It was the Conservatives' mission, he concluded, 'to give the leadership to our nation which it rightly deserves'.[28]

This conclusion, because it was so frankly personal and heartfelt, transformed the speech, enabling the *Daily Telegraph* to declare his conference début 'a triumph . . . Members of the Shadow Cabinet are now convinced that Mr Heath, having once broken the emotional "sound barrier", can develop into an orator of great distinction.'[29]

The second speech was more combative, laden with contemptuous jokes about Labour ministers and notable for an explicit attempt to expose Labour's claim to be the party of technological revolution. On the contrary, Heath insisted, Labour were the true conservatives:

> They are evolutionary pessimists finding every conceivable argument why day to day change should not take place. They are rooted in vested interest. They are avid for the *status quo*. It is no paradox, strange as it may seem, that in a period of rapid change like this what the nation needs is leadership from a modern and progressive Conservative Party, for it is only we Conservatives who will get moving and seize the opportunities which exist for us as a country.[30]

With this speech, the London *Evening Standard* reported, Heath 'took the Tories by storm'. It was a 'personal triumph' which evoked 'a rapturous response . . . It was without doubt the best mass audience speech of Mr Heath's career . . . It marked his own real leadership breakthrough.'[31]

But it did not really. The faithful cheered because they wanted to believe in Heath, and they wanted the press to believe that they believed in him. But privately the doubts which had begun to arise almost from the moment they had elected him were by no means stilled. 'In their less guarded moments', Alan Watkins wrote in the *Spectator* in the middle of the conference, 'Conservative MPs . . . can be heard asking "Have we all made a terrible mistake?"' It was, Watkins conceded, desperately unfair. 'The fact that his performance is being criticised so soon after his accession is perhaps a commentary not on Mr Heath but on the expectations that were placed in him. He was, in short, oversold.' He never had been a great debater or an inspiring speaker and it was unreasonable to expect him suddenly to change. Nevertheless 'Leadership demands some kind of theme, and it is this which has so far been lacking in Mr Heath's speeches. His problem . . . is one of communication.'[32]

A problem there certainly was. The opinion polls differed widely in detail, yet all told the same story. Gallup, which had shown the Tories ahead in the early summer under Home and then surged into a

9-point lead in August when Heath first took over, plunged dramatically to give Labour a 5-point lead by November. NOP, consistently more favourable to Labour, briefly gave the Tories a 4-point lead in August before showing an even steeper slide to put Labour 18 points ahead in November. Labour ministers were gleeful and privately relieved. 'We agreed that Heath was not as formidable as we had feared,' wrote Tony Benn after dinner with members of Wilson's kitchen cabinet,[33] while Crossman in his diary reflected on why this should be so:

> The general impression from the Conference is that Heath has not proved as immediately successful as we feared he might. He is dry, and too cold, and the policy he is putting across seems to me to be attractive only to young and thrusting businessmen. Certainly, for the whole of what you might call the traditional, hierarchical, deferential Right, Maudling would have been far more attractive. One can't feel deferential to Heath; one is aware of him as a professional politician – cold, tough, efficient. In the public eye he is much colder than Harold Wilson, who has something rather warm and cosy about him compared to this calculating, driving politician. So though I am sure he is going to win tremendous enthusiasm among the business community and his own Party workers, I am more doubtful whether he will be able to pull out of their mood of abstention a number of Tory voters whose support he desperately needs and who are still out of sympathy with the kind of policy for which he stands.[34]

In fact Heath was never able to win the whole-hearted enthusiasm even of his own party that Crossman expected. The relationship remained guarded – on both sides. There was in this coolness an undoubted streak of snobbery, never of course stated in public or to his face but expressed in snide remarks behind his back which, inevitably, came to his ears. The party had chosen him because it was told it needed someone like him to lead it in the modern world. But in their hearts most Tories did not like his modern world. The social base and outlook of the party was changing, slowly, but the instincts of most members of most local associations in the 1960s still reflected the traditional predominance of the wealthy and the landed. After a succession of grand patrician leaders from Churchill to Home they were not yet fully ready for the abrupt leap to one of Heath's common background, strange accent and insistently commercial priorities. They might recognise, as a matter of political realism, that Home was an anachronism, but they still loved him – all the more to compensate for their sense of guilt at having got rid of him. (*The Times* noted that the loudest applause during Heath's first conference speech came every time he mentioned his predecessor.)[35] Conversely, though they had elected Heath precisely for his Wilsonian 'classlessness', they nevertheless resented the necessity for him; they blamed him more or less consciously for having pushed Sir Alec out and subtly punished him for not being Sir Alec. It was unfair, but it was palpable. At the very least Heath had to earn their love by being successful. And this was precisely what, for five years, he was unable to do.

Every political party loves a winner; but the Tory party, more than any other, demands victory as its right. Heath could not seriously be blamed for failing to win the March 1966 election – though the scale of the defeat was disappointing. From 1967, however, when the Labour Government plumbed unprecedented depths of unpopularity and the Tory party piled up enormous leads in the polls, Heath's personal rating continued to trail far behind the party's, and was often even lower than Wilson's. Every year until 1970 there was the same agony at conference time, with press speculation that this year he must finally assert his authority and assurances afterwards that he had succeeded. But the next year the same stories would be written all over again. Having chosen him the party knew that it was stuck with him. It wanted to be loyal: it desperately wanted him to succeed. But it worried that his failure to project a winning personality might yet drag the party to defeat when the election came in 1970 or 1971. In the spring of 1970 it appeared that this was exactly what was going to happen.

As a result of his initial difficulty in establishing himself either with the party or with the public, Heath himself became more withdrawn, prickly and aloof, thus setting up a vicious circle. He was a proud man, proud of having become leader and genuinely anxious to use his leadership to better the lot of his countrymen. He wanted, if not to be loved, then at least to be understood and appreciated. He was unquestionably hurt by the carping and sniping behind his back by those who were supposed to be his followers and whose loyalty he believed he was entitled to expect. It was noticeable that after he became leader he became more defensive and even more difficult to know. In part this may have been deliberate. Even as a schoolboy, Heath had taken himself very seriously; now as leader of the Conservative party, Leader of the Opposition and Prime Minister-in-waiting his tendency to self-importance was compounded. It was a part of his somewhat military view of leadership that a leader should maintain a proper distance from his troops. The geniality, the ready laughter which had contributed so much to his popularity as Chief Whip was accordingly suppressed as incompatible with the dignity of his position. In addition, however, as increasingly personal criticism mounted of his inability to defeat the Government, his wooden personality and his strangulated vowels, he became correspondingly more insecure, self-conscious and self-protective – at once more buttoned up than ever and more liable to snap – so that his social relations with members of the party, both at Westminster and in the constituencies, became more strained and awkward. Scorning social graces, he concentrated on what he was good at, formulating policy and preparing for government, while keeping himself as much as possible to himself, with just a handful of trusted advisers.

Immediately on becoming leader, Heath set up a far larger private office than any previous Leader of the Opposition had maintained. Home had only had a couple of girls, and even Wilson not much more. Heath's office was headed by John MacGregor, with three assistants and four secretaries – all paid for by the party, though Heath himself continued to pay his faithful personal secretary, Rosemary Bushe. In addition he had two PPSs, Anthony Kershaw and Jim Prior, chosen by Willie Whitelaw to keep him as far as possible in touch with Tory MPs. Prior has described how he was summoned to the leader's dingy room in the House of Commons:

> 'Willie says you have to be my Parliamentary Private Secretary. He says I know nothing about farming or the rural constituencies, and your experience at Central Office will help. You've got to help me keep in touch with grass roots feeling and get me into the Smoking Room as much as you can.'
>
> That was my introduction and my invitation. It was a style I was to grow accustomed to over the years – at times brusqueness amounting to rudeness, yet also the shyness of an introvert; and sometimes a reaction of great frustration that he could not always get through to people.[36]

Heath was not easy to work for. He was very demanding; he still tended, as a bachelor, to forget that others had families to whom they might wish to get home; his staff had to learn to recognise his moods, to know when not to cross him and to respect his long silences. But at the same time all those who worked closely with

him over the next few years found the experience exceptionally rewarding. 'I've never had such a stimulating three-and-a-half years,'
MacGregor told Margaret Laing. 'He changed the *scale* of my thinking.'[37] 'There was nothing that those of us who came to work closely
with Ted would not do for him,' Prior has written. 'He had quality
and vision and, even if he never dared to show it, he had a softer side
which we understood.'[38] As always, from his army days through the
Whips' office to the Brussels negotiations and the 1965 Finance Bill,
he was seen at his best leading a small team with a clear chain of command. The girls in the office worked mainly to Prior and Kershaw
rather than directly to 'EH'; his dealings with them were formal but
meticulous and they generally found him a considerate and even
generous boss. When any member of his staff was in some personal
difficulty there was nothing he would not try to do to help; to this
day he still remembers the birthdays of people who worked for him
in quite junior capacities years ago. Such touches explain the intense
loyalty of those few who have penetrated the thick defensive cara-
pace of his public personality.

Although elected explicitly as a vigorous new broom in August
1965, Heath could not afford to be too sweeping at first. An election
might still be called at any moment. The leadership contest had not
in the event been too divisive: Maudling had taken his defeat well.
But the margin had been narrow, and Heath's first task was to unite
the party. Hence in the short run he was obliged to retain the whole
of Sir Alec's Shadow Cabinet; he also appointed an unusually large
team of 72 Front Bench spokesmen, representing all wings of the
party. He promoted a number of younger faces (Peter Walker, Paul
Channon, Michael Heseltine), but he did not yet dispense with any
of the older ones. Though he switched some of them to new portfolios he was still stuck with Peter Thorneycroft, Selwyn Lloyd and
Duncan Sandys among others. Not until after March 1966 was he in
a position to dispense with most of those whom Enoch Powell has
called a 'lost generation',[39] and stamp his own image on the Shadow
Cabinet. Nor could he decently remove Edward Du Cann from the
party chairmanship.

His priority was the quick conclusion of the policy exercise. The
recommendations of all the study groups were first collated in *Putting
Britain Right Ahead*, published in time for the party conference in
October. (It was originally *Putting Britain Right*, a typically no-
nonsense title, until Maudling pointed out that this invited the obvious
question 'Who had put Britain wrong?' So the word 'Ahead' was
added at the last minute, giving a singularly clumsy and unmemor-
able result.)[40] *Putting Britain Right Ahead*, subtitled 'A Statement of

Conservative Aims', set out three main themes which were to remain essentially unchanged through the next five years: first, the encouragement of a more competitive economy by means of tax incentives, a shift of emphasis from direct to indirect taxation and the reform of trade union law; second, a shift from universality towards greater selectivity in the provision of social services; and third, a renewed commitment to try to join the EEC at the earliest opportunity.

In all these areas what is striking today, after more than a decade of Thatcherism, is the emphasis which Heath placed on promoting change *within* the existing social framework, building on the achievements of 1951–64 – specifically on the politically sensitive questions of trade union and welfare reform. In all his speeches expounding the new policies at the conference and elsewhere he made a point of denying any crudely partisan intention and rebuking the hankering of the right for a more robustly anti-socialist approach. For instance he insisted at Brighton that greater selectivity involved only the modernisation, not the abolition, of the Welfare State. 'There are some', he told the delegates, 'who think that if we are to have a more efficient economy this means a hardness of approach to the Welfare State. Nothing could be further from the truth.'

> After twenty years the Welfare State, by its very success, has made itself in part obsolete. People with higher incomes, with new horizons, with more time and money and more opportunity to develop their family life are seeking a new approach to so many of the services which are provided by the State. The old struggle to maintain the minimum standards is now receding into the past. So that there is an opportunity . . . for a wider choice, and that is what we are determined to give.[41]

Likewise he was insistent that the reform of trade union law should be seen not as an attack on the unions but simply as putting them on a proper footing to operate effectively in a modern competitive economy. His warnings to the party on these two points were a clear signal of the limits of his intended radicalism: for all the tax incentives he promised to those he called the 'pacemakers' – those, as he described them, 'blessed with particular skills, with greater imagination, with foresight, with inventiveness and with administrative ability, who can give the lead and can keep us to the fore in world affairs'[42] – he did not intend to abandon the 'One Nation' principles he had inherited from Macmillan.

On two key points *Putting Britain Right Ahead* was silent as compared with the manifesto on which Home's Conservative Government had fought in 1964. There was no mention of incomes policy, which had occupied a central place in 1964, nor of economic planning – though there was a section on regional development. These omissions prompted speculation that the new leader had embraced a *laissez-faire* approach to the economy. *The Economist* was alarmed by rumours that Heath 'thinks incomes policy is all tosh, that he is a right-wing advocate of keeping a curb on the money supply and all else will be solved, that he is almost an old-fashioned Powellite in this respect'.[43] Such rumours had no foundation. The truth was that the Shadow Cabinet was split, with Powell and Keith Joseph opposed to incomes policy and Maudling still unrepentantly in favour. This division was to persist for the next five years. Heath had no strong views on the matter. His prime concern was to avoid open disunity, so for the present he preferred to evade the issue, making no clear commitment either way. But the problem would not go away.

Incomes policy, however, was the least of his embarrassments in the autumn of 1965. Far worse was the disarray in the Tory party over Rhodesia, which Wilson exploited mercilessly. 'In those first months of his leadership', Heath's friend Ian Trethowan was to write in 1968, 'Rhodesia was the cross on which Mr Wilson nailed him.'[44] It was a horribly awkward problem for a new and untried leader, one which aroused atavistic sentiments in just that section of the party – the old imperialist right – which most distrusted him. The action of the white Rhodesian Government in unilaterally declaring its independence of Britain on 11 November, abrogating the 'five principles' for transition to eventual black majority rule which the Conservative Government had laid down in 1964, in fact put Wilson on the spot; but he – while blustering impotently about putting an end to the rebellion in 'weeks rather than months' without the use of force – skilfully managed to put Heath on the defensive by alleging repeatedly that the Tory party sympathised more or less openly with the rebels. Heath actually had a considerably more clear-sighted view of the situation than Wilson, pointing out that Ian Smith and his colleagues were not, as Wilson boasted, 'frightened men' who would easily be brought to heel, but on the contrary 'somewhat determined men' whom sanctions would only drive deeper into intransigence.[45] While Wilson refused to talk to Smith until he renounced his rebellion, Heath predicted correctly that he would have to talk sooner or later, urged him to stop looking for a quick solution – 'There may not be a quick solution to this problem'[46] – and begged him to

1   Aged three, with his mother, Edith

2   With Edith and his younger brother, John

3   With his father, William, in 1967

4–5   Prospective Tory candidate, Bexley, 1948; returned to Westminster, 1951

6   Young Conservatives: with Patricia Hornsby-Smith and Margaret Roberts

7 With Harold Macmillan in 1961 on their way to Rome for talks on Britain's EEC application

8 First party conference as leader, Brighton, 1965; with (*from left*) Iain Macleod, Peter Thorneycroft, Reginald Maudling, Sir Alec Douglas-Home, Sir Michael Fraser and Edward Du Cann

keep the door open to steady constitutional progress: the way forward was to seek to negotiate a new constitution that would provide for a staged transition to majority rule, not to insist on Smith backing down completely. All he got for his pains were sneers and jeers that he was pandering to racism.

The question of sanctions was the wedge that broke apart Heath's efforts to keep his party together. The right totally opposed them: a smaller number on the left supported them. Heath tried to take a middle line of supporting limited but not 'punitive' sanctions. The Tories, wrote Tony Benn gleefully, were 'splitting up and splintering before our eyes. Heath is a pathetic figure, kicked this way and that, and is incapable of giving firm leadership. Home and Selwyn Lloyd are really running the Tory party now.'[47] Just before Christmas, the party split three ways over the Government's imposition of an oil embargo on Rhodesia. The Shadow Cabinet decided ingloriously to abstain. But fifty Tories voted against the order while another thirty voted with the Government. Most galling for Heath was that it was not an issue about which he himself greatly cared one way or the other. Having no personal or family connection with Africa he was indifferent to the 'kith and kin' argument of the old imperialists. His natural sympathies were more with the liberal left, but he was enraged by the posturing cant by which Wilson milked the issue for credit with his own left wing, piously claiming that it was 'a moral issue' and demanding Opposition backing for the Government while deliberately exacerbating Heath's troubles with his right. Wilson's cynical exploitation of Rhodesia gave Heath every reason to loathe him.

The Rhodesian problem was to remain a thorn in Heath's side right up to 1970, and beyond. Every November he suffered the embarrassment of a revolt by thirty-odd right-wingers voting against the renewal of sanctions. He continued to urge Wilson to keep talking to Smith and honourably supported the abortive negotiations on HMS *Tiger* (December 1966) and HMS *Fearless* (March 1968), only to be accused of advocating appeasement when, if anything, it was Wilson who was desperate to secure a settlement which much of his own party would certainly have rejected.

Despite all the difficulties already pressing on the Government, the short 1965-6 session was a miserable one for Heath. Following his disappointing début in August, he badly needed to come back strongly at the start of the new political year. Instead, he gave another unconvincing performance in the debate on the Queen's Speech, which Wilson once again derisively brushed aside. ('However shrill and strident his tone, his words . . . are drowned by

thirteen years of history . . . Back to the drawing board, Ted.')[48]
Only five months into his leadership, Ian Trethowan wrote in *The
Times*, 1965 ended with 'his party in disarray, confidence in his
own capacity dented and more trouble in the pipeline'.[49] On 14
January, as the polls continued to show Labour poised to win a
solid majority whenever Wilson chose to call the election, an outspoken article by Angus Maude in the *Spectator* gave voice to
discontent on the right that went much wider and deeper than
Rhodesia. Maude was a Front Bench spokesman on colonial affairs,
but he did not let that inhibit him. 'The Conservative Party', he
wrote, 'has completely lost effective political initiative. Its own
supporters in the country are divided and deeply worried by this
failure, while to the electorate at large the opposition has become a
meaningless irrelevance.' The Tory party in the past, under Baldwin,
Churchill and Macmillan, had a feel for what the people wanted
which it now completely lacked. 'For the Tories simply to talk like
technocrats', he warned, 'will get them nowhere.' The party should
come out clearly and strongly in opposition to everything the
Government was doing that was *wrong*. They should stop pussyfooting on the trade unions. They should condemn high personal
taxation. And they should specify radical changes in the welfare
services.[50]

Yet these three things were precisely what Heath thought he was
doing! His proposals were unspecific as yet, but these were the very
themes that *Putting Britain Right Ahead* had been supposed to embody. What Maude was criticising, therefore, was Heath's inability
to project them; or perhaps – the 'technocrat' gibe – his lack of an instinctive Tory faith to lend them the force of conviction. His
'pussyfooting' at conference on trade unions and the Welfare State
was too pink for those in the party who wanted to see a clear break
from the socialistic consensus of the later Macmillan years. Some
saw the hand of Enoch Powell behind Maude's article. If so, Heath's
response was uncompromising: Maude was abruptly sacked from his
Front Bench position.

The next week the *Spectator* sprang to Heath's defence. He had
become leader at a peculiarly difficult time. In the circumstances he
had 'done remarkably well; and given time, will do better still'. The
'present Tory malaise' had nothing to do with Heath, but went back
long before 1965.

> The true cause is that the party no longer has an *idée force* in which
> it can believe and on which it can crusade. The Empire has gone,
> and the Commonwealth is no substitute. Old-fashioned liberalism

. . . needs too many qualifications today to pass as an *idée force* for anyone except Mr Powell. Europe, perhaps alone, could still be an *idée force* for the Conservatives, as Mr Heath well recognizes; but the time for that is yet to come.

In the meantime it was no use inveighing against socialism, since that was so discredited that even Labour had abandoned it. The only course open to the Opposition was the one which Heath and his colleagues were pursuing. 'It means getting down to brass tacks and attacking the real mistakes that this pragmatic and often conservative Government is actually making.'[51] This, from the pen of the *Spectator*'s new editor, Nigel Lawson, was Heath's answer to the ideologues.

The next week, however, the result of the Hull by-election dealt him a further blow. This was a marginal seat which Labour had won narrowly in 1964. The Conservatives had hopes of winning it back, which would have cut the Government's majority to just one. Instead – with the aid of the most notorious election bribe in recent memory, the Humber road bridge – Labour increased their majority to over 5,000 with a swing of 4.5 per cent. This was enough, if repeated at a General Election, to ensure a massive Labour majority in the House of Commons. It was now clear that Wilson would not wait long before seizing his moment. Heath watched the result in Albany with Jim and Jane Prior. It was so much worse than expected that for some days he was visibly depressed.

Yet he fought back. On 5 February he started trying to put some detail on the party's plans to modernise the Welfare State. In a major policy speech at Birmingham he called for 'a new Beveridge' based on quality and choice rather than universal state provision. He was promptly denounced by Labour, in a concerted attack led at Wilson's instigation by Dick Crossman, for planning to 'dismantle' the Welfare State – a charge he angrily dismissed as 'a pack of lies'.[52] Two weeks later in the House of Commons he made his best speech since becoming leader, posing a series of alternatives. Free prescriptions for all – or better hospitals? Subsidies for all council tenants – or real help for those who really needed it? The British people, he insisted, did not appreciate the quality of life that was available under less rigid systems in other countries. Universal provision prevented the targeting of assistance where it was really needed – large families on low pay, the elderly poor, the chronic sick and disabled. Cheekily adapting Nye Bevan, he laid Tory claim to 'the language of priorities' – Labour speakers were forever quoting Bevan's gnomic dictum that 'the language of priorities is the religion of socialism' –

holding out a glowing vision of a diverse and flexible system of mixed private and state provision leading to a fuller life for all.[53]

This was more like the Heath of a year before, as the *Daily Telegraph* enthusiastically reported:

> Mr Heath was in complete command, both of his own talents and of the House . . . The Labour benches were howling with rage. The louder they howled, the harder Mr Heath slapped their faces . . . Here was an achievement which triumphantly rallied the whole Conservative Opposition.[54]

Nevertheless the General Election which Wilson announced a few days later was lost before it had begun. The opinion polls gave Labour a steady lead in the range 9–12 per cent, which was not entirely due to Heath's failings. Whatever might have been the quality of their new leader or their new policies, the Tories in March 1966 were up against overwhelming sentiment on the part of the electorate that Labour had only been in office eighteen months, on a tiny majority which had given them no chance to show what they could do. Labour's confident slogan 'You *Know* Labour Government Works' claimed a good deal too much. Already, as Heath never tired of pointing out, the Government was struggling with rising prices, balance-of-payments difficulties, credit restrictions and cutbacks in promised spending programmes. Yet it could still plausibly be argued that the electorate did not yet know whether Labour Government worked or not. Most fair-minded floating voters felt that Labour should be given a further chance. The Tories, conversely, had hardly yet begun to get used to opposition and could reasonably be said to need more time before they would be ready to return to government. Nothing that Heath could have done or said would have altered that basic position.

In fact he fought a pretty good campaign. The emphasis throughout was firmly on Heath himself. The manifesto, bluntly titled *Action Not Words*, quintessentially expressed his impatient, unreflective style. (It was Alec Douglas-Home, ironically, who wondered 'if "Ideas" ought not to be brought into it'.)[55] It was based closely on *Putting Britain Right Ahead*, with the same themes of competition, enterprise and incentives, the same pledges to tackle trade union law and 'seize the first favourable opportunity' to join the EEC, a promise to create 'an entirely new social security strategy' and a stronger emphasis on housing ('We intend to see that this entire nation is decently housed'). The work of the policy groups yielded no less than 131 specific promises covering everything from beating crime to protecting the countryside.

Heath took most of the election broadcasts himself, on both radio and television, as well as the morning press conferences, though not without terrible anguish. He was coached intensively for each television appearance, and needed a half-bottle of champagne before every press conference. The strain on his staff was appalling. Yet his broadcasts – particularly the last, a characteristically unvarnished statement delivered straight to camera three days before polling – were widely judged to have been effective: he was dull, but he came over as honest and adult. Crossman noted in his diary on 27 March that 'Heath, who began terribly stiff and starchy, is beginning to catch up somewhat, and is getting something of the admiration Gaitskell got for his gallant 1959 campaign.'[56] More than any previous British General Election it was a presidential contest: 'Parson Heath v. Harold Hot Gospeller' as a *Sunday Telegraph* headline vividly put it.[57] Wilson made a point of being accompanied by his wife wherever he went, to play up the supposed handicap of Heath's lack of a family: but it did not appear to be an issue. *The Times* somewhat improbably described Heath canvassing housewives in Chatham 'with the knowing air of a bachelor who does his own shopping'.[58] The only real issue was which party should be blamed for the country's mounting problems. 'Heath desperately tried to warn people . . . that we were going bankrupt,' wrote Crossman with his usual disarming candour, 'but of course this was completely ineffective with an electorate who felt that on this score – the responsibility for our difficulties – honours were pretty even, if not tipped against the Tories.'[59] Wilson simply refused to debate the relative merits of Labour and Tory policies. 'Try as he did, most strenuously,' *The Times Guide to the House of Commons* summed up, 'Mr Heath could not get Mr Wilson away from his winning line: "If their policies are so good, why did they not implement them when they were in power?"'[60]

The result was as crushing as the polls predicted. Labour made 47 gains to pile up an absolute majority of 96. The Tory vote fell by 600,000 to their lowest level since 1945, their share of the poll to just under 42 per cent compared with Labour's 48 per cent. (The Liberals fell to 8 per cent, but gained 2 seats.) The national swing to Labour was 2·7 per cent, exceptionally uniform over the whole country. In Bexley, Heath's national prominence helped to increase his vote, but with Labour squeezing the Liberals his majority was cut to an uncomfortably narrow 2,333.*

* E. R. G. Heath (Conservative)	26,377
R. L. Butler (Labour)	24,044
R. F. Lloyd (Liberal)	4,405
Conservative majority	2,333[61]

The scale of the defeat was a disappointment to Heath, but he took it well. He had never expected to win and he knew that he had put up a better performance than many of his critics over the past few months had predicted. He could not reasonably be blamed for the result but had gained a good deal of grudging credit. 'The general feeling', the *Daily Mirror* magnate Cecil King recorded, 'is that Ted Heath has increased his stature in the last three weeks, while Wilson has lost some of his.'[62] 'His appearance on the day after the election', wrote Ian Trethowan, 'was one of the most impressive he has made. He had nothing to play for, he was dog-tired and so, for once, he appeared in public as the reasonably relaxed character that people are often surprised to find when they first meet him in private.'[63] Though five frustrating years of opposition stretched ahead, he had at least the opportunity now to set his stamp on his party more firmly than he had been able to do in the feverish conditions of the past eight months.

It can be argued, in view of the 1966 defeat, that it was a mistake for the Tories to have changed their leader when they did, between the 1964 and 1966 elections. If the 1966 election was going to be lost anyway, it is suggested, Home's greatest service to his party would have been to soldier on, taking on himself the odium of the second defeat before handing over to a fresh leader. By this means Heath would not have been saddled immediately with the label of a loser, which was undeservedly hung around his neck from 1966 to 1970.

This argument is rejected, however, by those close to Heath, like Peter Walker, who insist that the Tories were not at all defeatist in 1965–6 but hoped and firmly expected to win in 1966. It is true that the opinion polls in the summer of 1965 gave them grounds for optimism (though retrospectively this might be interpreted as a reason for sticking with Home, while their steep decline after Heath took over argues that the change was a mistake). No doubt senior Tories did hope to win in 1966: no party or individual can fight elections at any level without believing in the possibility of victory, however delusive. Nevertheless analysis of the election strongly upholds the view that the Conservatives could never have won it, and on that basis it is difficult to deny that it would have been better for both Heath and the party if he could have taken over untarnished in April 1966. Sir Alec could hardly have lost in March more heavily than Heath did.

Yet Heath did go on to win in 1970, despite the loser's tag from 1966. So perhaps after all it did not do him lasting harm. Perhaps in 1970 it was, to the electorate's sense of fair play, his turn to win as 1966 had been Wilson's. On this view, so far from damaging him, 1966 was a useful dry run for Heath personally and for the party organisation fighting under him. Sir Michael Fraser certainly believed that 1966 was a positive experience which enabled the party to put down some important markers for the future. 'No one likes to lose. But at least, in losing, we said the right things, we forced Labour onto a number of hooks which were to prove extremely embarrassing to them in the years ahead, and we went a long way towards establishing our credibility for the next battle.'[64]

But that battle was a long way off: and with Labour sitting on a majority of nearly 100 and boasting of having become 'the natural party of government', Heath had a steep mountain to climb.

11

Pressures of Opposition

WITH the 1966 Election out of the way and Labour confirmed in office for at least a full Parliament, the political world could at last settle down – for the first time since 1962 – to an anticipated period of normality and relative stability. Heath and his party had no choice now but to dig in for the long haul of opposition. Hitherto Heath had been a new leader, facing an election at any moment with at least the possibility of an early return to office. Now the horizon had lifted. He had lost his electoral virginity. He would no longer be under quite such intense pressure for instant success and should be able to settle down to reorganise, re-equip and redirect the party at relative leisure over four or five years before its next test. On the other hand his next chance, should he fail again, would almost certainly be his last.

Now if ever was the moment, freed from the pressure to produce instant policies for an imminent election, to have put in hand that real and fundamental rethink of the party's purpose and philosophy for which there was no time after October 1964. In fact this was not done, partly because Heath had no interest in fundamental rethinking – no more, it must be said, had most of his senior colleagues, certainly not Iain Macleod – and partly because any such exercise had already been pre-empted by the rapid policy review initiated under Home. The main lines of policy and the principal commitments on which the party would fight the next election had already been laid down: lower taxation, tax reform, trade union law reform. These were not going to be altered now. As Heath proudly told the 1966 conference: 'Never in our Party's history have we been so well equipped with constructive policies.'[1] When Enoch Powell tried to question some of the assumptions of the proposed trade union reform Heath got angry, insisting that the package was all sewn up and he was 'not just going to, at this stage, have it picked to pieces and examined and fought over' all over again.[2] The effort of the next four years – still co-ordinated by the Conservative Research Department headed by Brendon Sewill – would go into deepening the principal existing policies and adding detail.

What Heath could do now was to carry out the thorough re-structuring of the Shadow Cabinet from which he had refrained the year before. Six of the older faces were stood down. Selwyn Lloyd offered his resignation before it was demanded. Lord Dilhorne and Martin Redmayne could have no complaint. But Ernest Marples, Duncan Sandys and John Boyd-Carpenter were all still under sixty and entitled to feel disappointed that the future held no further advancement for them. A 49-year-old leader, however, was bound to feel that too many older colleagues would both diminish his personal authority and dull the youthful image of the party he was trying to project. He was practically obliged to retain both Home and Quintin Hogg. The former he was more than happy to keep on, though not as Shadow Foreign Secretary: Home was a model of loyalty and discretion in serving his successor both in opposition and in office for the next eight years. The latter Heath would as happily have done without, but that was not an option only three years after he had disclaimed his coronet in the party's cause, so Hogg was offered and accepted the home affairs portfolio. For the rest Maudling continued as deputy leader and Macleod as Shadow Chancellor, while Powell (defence), Boyle (education), Joseph (labour), Godber (agriculture), Noble (Scotland) and Lord Carrington (leader in the Lords) retained their positions. Most of these were colleagues with whom Heath could work reasonably comfortably, and all but Powell, Boyle and Noble survived into government in 1970.

Into the places left by the retiring warhorses came some new men – Anthony Barber, Geoffrey Rippon and Peter Walker – plus Willie Whitelaw as Chief Whip, and briefly Lord Harlech as deputy leader in the Lords and Mervyn Pike as the token woman. In 1967 Harlech was replaced by Lord Jellicoe and Pike by Margaret Thatcher. Robert Carr and Lord Balniel were added to bring the total back to nineteen, and in 1969 Gordon Campbell replaced Noble. This was a smaller and younger Shadow Cabinet than normal: after four years their average age was still only 52 (compared with 59 for Wilson's Shadow Cabinet in 1964). In accordance with Heath's view that the serious business of opposition was preparing for government most of them kept the same responsibility for relatively long spells, though in fact only Godber held the same portfolio throughout.[3]

One exception, who was given a new job every session between

1965 and 1970, was Margaret Thatcher. Outside the Shadow Cabinet up to 1967, she was spokeswoman successively for pensions, housing and Treasury matters. Both Peter Walker and Jim Prior have claimed the credit for recommending Heath to promote her. Prior says that he first suggested her in 1965. 'Heath replied, after a long silence: "Yes, Willie agrees that she's much the most able, but he says once she's there we'll never be able to get rid of her. So we both think it's got to be Mervyn Pike." '[4] Heath's hesitation was prescient. But by 1967 Mrs Thatcher was too obviously able and industrious to be excluded: she became Shadow Minister successively of power, transport and finally – when Edward Boyle withdrew – education. To political observers Mrs Thatcher, with her grammar-school background and formidable professional qualifications, seemed the perfect female prototype of Heath's new Tories. But Heath never had much time for her. She was in manner precisely the type of prissy, cut-glass Tory woman he most disliked. She irritated him by talking too much in Shadow Cabinet. 'She certainly talked,' Peter Rawlinson (then a Shadow law officer) has recalled. 'How she talked! And she certainly irked the Leader. Instinctively he seemed to bridle at her over-emphasis.'[5] Prior remembers only that 'There was little *rapport* between Ted and Margaret, and I was often used as a go-between. But at least they did not quarrel.'[6]

Outside the Shadow Cabinet, Heath cut his Front Bench down to just ten additional spokesmen in April 1966, getting rid of most of those he had reappointed the year before in the interest of unity. Among those most pointedly dropped were Enoch Powell's two most prominent younger disciples, Nicholas Ridley and John Biffen. Gradually over the next four years he made fresh appointments and reappointments – including Ridley – to bring the number back to 45 by 1970. His intention was to create as far as possible an alternative Government in his own image, not inherited from Home but loyal to himself. In 1970 the majority of these junior spokesmen got the jobs which they had been shadowing.

Second, Heath continued the process of overhauling the party organisation and shaping the party machine to his own purposes. He boasted of taking a closer interest in matters of organisation than any previous leader. The obstacle in his path, however, was Edward Du Cann, the party chairman only appointed the previous year by Home. Heath and Du Cann had learned to dislike one another at the Board of Trade in 1963–4. According to Prior they now 'could not stand each other'.[7] Du Cann had backed Maudling for the leadership in July 1965. On Heath's victory he had formally offered his resignation, but Heath could not decently accept it. Even after the 1966 election he could not immediately sack Du Cann: to have done so would have appeared to make him the scapegoat for the party's defeat. More than once during the next year he was prevented from removing him by press leaks that he was about to do so. Just before the 1967 conference he angrily dismissed such reports as 'damned lies'.[8] In fact Du Cann was now ready to go, so long as it was made clear that he was resigning of his own accord in order to return to his increasingly absorbing interests in the City. He insists that Heath also promised him office when the party returned to power.[9] Heath's first choice to replace him was Peter Carrington, but in fact he appointed another of his closest lieutenants, Tony Barber.

It was Barber, assisted by the discreet but omnipresent deputy chairman, Sir Michael Fraser, who got the party into fighting trim before the 1970 election. The key decision was to concentrate resources in seventy Labour marginals. The measure of the success of this strategy is that sixty-four of these constituencies were won in 1970. In addition the party made much more sophisticated use of opinion polling that any Opposition had done before. It commissioned a lot of specialised 'deep polls' to probe the underlying loyalties and attitudes of the electorate. These encouraged it to believe that opinion in the country on a range of broad political issues was moving significantly the Tories' way. As a result it was much less worried than it might otherwise have been by the sudden swing of the Gallup and NOP polls back towards the Government in 1970. (It is likely that what these 'deep polls' were beginning to pick up was the first stirrings of the shift among working and lower-middle-class voters away from collectivism which ten years later was to provide the popular climate for 'Thatcherism'. This turning tide helped Heath to power in June 1970; but it was not yet strong enough to sustain a seriously anti-collectivist Government in 1971–2.)

Once fully in the saddle, Heath ran his shadow government in a characteristically businesslike manner. The Shadow Cabinet met twice a week at 5 pm, on Mondays to deal with policy, on Wednesdays to arrange House of Commons business for the coming week. But even at the Monday meetings there was little general discussion: policy was effectively settled in the specialist committees, in the Research Department and in small brain-storming sessions in Albany, then taken to Shadow Cabinet merely to be rubber stamped. Heath's relations with his senior colleagues were correct but formal. Maudling he still kept firmly at arm's length, still seeming to fear him as a defeated rival; in fact Maudling had largely lost interest in politics since his defeat and devoted most of his time to his City interests. He was as loyal as Home, but had ceased to box his weight, even when he disagreed substantially with the party's emerging policy. Relations between Heath and Iain Macleod were closer politically, but still impersonal: Macleod stuck to his Treasury brief – a considerable loss to the effectiveness of the Opposition on wider issues – and worked hard on tax reform, where he and Heath saw eye to eye. 'As time went on', his biographer Nigel Fisher has written, he came increasingly to appreciate Heath's qualities and 'referred to him privately with growing admiration'.[10] For his part Heath came to recognise that Macleod – in constant physical pain from his back – had no higher ambition than to be a reforming Chancellor of the Exchequer, and so represented no challenge to him; but they were never intimate.

The only colleagues with whom Heath felt fully at ease were younger subordinates whom he had appointed himself or who otherwise posed no threat to him: Tony Barber, Peter Carrington and Willie Whitelaw. These three, with the members of his private office – Jim Prior and Tony Kershaw, John MacGregor (replaced in 1967 by Douglas Hurd), his personal policy adviser and principal speechwriter Michael Wolff and the economist Brian Reading – plus Sir Michael Fraser (well described in these years as the Conservative party's 'Permanent Secretary') formed the Leader of the Opposition's confidential entourage against a hostile world. The rest of the Tory party was kept firmly at a distance. Despite his instructions to Prior, Heath went into the Smoking Room very little. He regularly attended the backbench Business Committee on Wednesdays at 6.15, following the 5 pm Shadow Cabinet, but rather to tell the troops what the officers had decided than to listen to what they themselves might have to say. Various attempts to bridge the social gap between the leader and his party produced more embarrassment than success. At one never-repeated dinner with the Executive of the 1922 Committee Heath simply lost his temper. Many MPs formed the view that Heath actually despised the Tory party, and made little attempt to disguise the fact. When he bothered to exert himself, he could still be persuasive; but too often he did not seem to see the need. 'Ted's difficulty', Jim Prior has written, 'was that he would win one group round . . . but then it was as if he said to himself, "Well, thank goodness that's over, I won't have to worry about them again for a while." So six months later he would be back to square one, and he would have to make a special effort with them all over again.'[11] It was only due to the brilliantly emollient whipping of Willie Whitelaw and the continuous diplomacy of Prior and Kershaw, smoothing the ruffled feathers of slighted Members, that the style of Heath's leadership was tolerated and his authority with the parliamentary party gradually established without open revolt.

His lowest time was the winter of 1966–7. Despite the traumatic deflationary package of the 'July measures' the previous summer, Labour was still ahead in the polls and Heath's personal rating sank to 25 per cent. He was regularly blamed for the Tories' failure to exploit the Government's difficulties, and there was actually talk of his leadership being challenged, though there was no obvious challenger. The pressure was relieved in March, however, when the Conservative candidate won a by-election at Glasgow, Pollok, followed in May by sweeping victories in the local elections. In London the Tories won 82 of the 100 seats on the GLC. They also gained control, among other cities, of Bradford, Leeds, Liverpool, Manchester and Newcastle. From this point the improvement was maintained. Further by-elections were won in Walthamstow and Cambridge in September, and Leicester in November. The party built up increasingly massive leads over the Government during 1968 and 1969, with 'safe' Labour seats like Oldham West and Dudley falling to the Tory tide. Heath's personal failure remained worrying – in October 1967 Robin Day asked him bluntly on 'Panorama', 'How low does your personal rating among your own supporters have to go before you consider yourself a liability to the party you lead?'[12] – but it could be borne so long as the party was winning. Harold Wilson had been a dazzling Leader of the Opposition but was a disappointment as Prime Minister. Tories told themselves that Heath would be the other way round: he would be a great Prime Minister as soon as Labour's unpopularity had carried him over the threshold of Downing Street.

The Tories' confidence throughout most of the period 1966–70 that they would be returned to office just as soon as the electorate got the chance to throw Labour out lent an unusual seriousness to Heath's preparations for government. In part this simply reflected his naturally methodical approach, reinforced by his deep contempt for Labour's unreadiness, after thirteen years in waiting. It was also a way of concentrating on what he was good at, instead of trying unsuccessfully to please the party, press and television by doing what he was not good at, aping Wilson. For all these reasons, the main emphasis of the party's effort in these opposition years went on preparing for the future responsibilities of office, more thoroughly and seriously than any Opposition had ever prepared before. Heath was determined that his administration should come into office knowing exactly what it wanted to do and how it was going to do it, with a clearly planned programme from which it would not – he firmly intended – run away at the first sign of trouble. Yet for all his high intentions and some considerable achievements the policy exercise was not in reality quite so impressive – neither so thorough nor so well directed – as was claimed.

The process was still co-ordinated by Michael Fraser largely through the Conservative Research Department, but after 1966 it proceeded on less frenetic and more patchy lines. Many of the policy groups were no longer chaired by the relevant Shadow Minister and several chairmen were not even Front Bench spokesmen. So a good deal of the effort that still went on was not so closely directed to future responsibilities as at first appeared. Views of the usefulness of the whole exercise varied widely. While some of those involved felt themselves a part of a radical rethinking of policy, others considered it no more than a harmless way of occupying the energies of the party in opposition which looked impressive but ducked the real choices that would face the incoming Government after 1970.[13] Several of the senior figures – Maudling certainly, but also to a great extent Macleod – as well as some of the younger ones like Walker, made no secret of their belief that detailed policy making in opposition was at best a waste of time, at worst gave hostages to the Government. A great deal of policy was therefore made, as usual, opportunistically on the hoof by the leader, in response to events or the actions of the Government. But three areas of policy were prepared with particular care. These were *taxation*; the reform of *trade union law*; and plans to improve the *machinery of government* itself.

Tax reform was the primary concern of the largest and most important of the policy committees, the Economic Policy group, usually chaired by Heath himself or, in his absence, by Macleod as Shadow Chancellor. This group did a lot of detailed technical work, much of which was eventually implemented in the small print of Anthony Barber's Budgets between 1970 and 1973. On the broader political questions of fiscal policy, however, the group got sidetracked into a number of blind alleys from which it never escaped. First of all it wasted some months – beginning back in the period before the 1966 election – on a so-called 'Wealth Tax', which was really a graduated capital tax but proved unacceptable to the party. Then it wasted more time by committing itself over hastily to abolishing Labour's Selective Employment Tax (SET), only to find that doing so left a large revenue gap to be made up. Long before 1970 reducing taxation was looking much more difficult to achieve in practice than it was to promise.

The one unambiguous policy commitment which the Conservatives made early on, in 1965, worked out in precise detail over the next five years and finally carried into law in 1971 was the promise to tackle the reform of trade union law. It might be said that this was the test issue by which the whole principle of preparing legislation thoroughly in opposition can be judged. In that case, in the light of the outcome in 1971–2, it can only be judged a failure. Nevertheless the determination to place the unions within a framework of law was one policy which the Conservatives were convinced was both over-due and popular: they kept it in the front of their programme from 1965 to 1970 and the polls suggested it was a positive factor in their electoral success. The fault lay neither in the broad commitment, nor in the principle of careful preparation, but somewhere in between – in a failure of communication and of political intelligence to foresee how specific proposals would operate in practice.

The reform of industrial relations was something to which Heath personally was deeply committed. He was passionately convinced that wishing to bring the unions within a modern framework of law could not reasonably be seen as 'anti-union'. As he told Andrew Alexander in an interview in 1965 and went on repeating for the next five years, 'You cannot go on treating them as the old-style friendly societies. They are one of the great estates of the realm, to be catered for as companies are by the Companies Acts.'[14] He wanted to draw the unions out of their outdated posture of obstructiveness and per-suade them to become partners in industry on the German or American model. He tried constantly to assure the unions that his in-tentions – and hence the intentions of the Tory party – towards them were friendly.

The trouble was that a substantial element of the Tory party was and always would be militantly anti-union and did indeed want to curb rather than simply modernise them. The unions' legal immunity from prosecution for the consequences of industrial action; the politi-cal levy; intimidatory picketing and the closed shop – all had been burning grievances to more hawkish Tories right back to the Liberal Government's Trade Disputes Act of 1906. So long as the party was in Government and usually seeking union co-operation in some form of incomes policy, successive Tory Ministers of Labour since 1951 had judged it politically inopportune to antagonise the unions. But no sooner was the Conservative Government out of office in October 1964 than the demand within the party for a tougher policy became irresistible. Even before Heath became leader, trade union reform was one of the first policies to be inscribed on the new Tory banner, and he lost no time in endorsing it. The difference between Heath and the backbench hawks was made clear, however, in a policy paper written for the CRD by James Douglas in April 1965, which placed the emphasis firmly on dealing with the *economic* power of unions.

It is this power to strike and put up prices against the consumer that most people mean when they talk about the need to check the power of the unions. There seems a danger that we may talk big about taking a strong line on the unions but only deal with some of the minor tangential problems (such as the closed shop, trade union laws etc.) and miss the main abuse of union power.

'An excellent paper,' Heath minuted in the margin. 'I agree with almost all of it – I had no idea that-anyone held the same views as myself.'[15] In other words he was not interested in pandering to party feeling against the political levy and the closed shop. From the very beginning the central purpose of the proposals which eventually became the 1971 Industrial Relations Act was to legislate for legally enforceable contracts which should be binding, once negotiated, on unions as well as management, thereby ending the power of small groups of workers to blackmail employers by means of unofficial 'wildcat' strikes. High labour costs, he came to believe, due to restrictive practices and overmanning, were the central problem of the British economy. Tackling them by legislative means, he asserted in December 1966, was 'the most fundamental structural change of all, for which opinion abroad . . . is really watching'.[16]

Labour had shelved the problem by appointing a Royal Commission under Lord Donovan, which was not expected to report until 1968. The outline of the Tory proposals, by contrast, was settled very quickly. *Action Not Words* at the 1966 election called for legally enforceable agreements plus the registration of trade unions and a system of industrial courts to enforce a code of good industrial relations practice. The one major addition in the final policy statement *Fair Deal at Work*, published in April 1968 (just before Donovan produced an exceptionally cautious report recommending a minimum of legislation), was provision for a compulsory cooling-off period and a secret ballot before a strike could go ahead. Otherwise this framework remained essentially unaltered over the next four years, despite sporadic objections in Shadow Cabinet from Powell – who suspected a disguised incomes policy – and Quintin Hogg who always wanted to reopen the question of legal immunity which his father had tried to tackle in 1927.

The prime criticism of the policy as it finally emerged was that its approach to industrial relations was too concerned with the mechanics of establishing a new legal structure to consider the problems of application on the shop floor. Robert Carr, as Shadow Employment Secretary, did an immense amount of talking with employers' organisations and informally with trade unionists to try to get the details right. He still believes that all the work was thoroughly worthwhile, so that they really understood the subject when they came into office in 1970. But it was ominous that the party was unable to find any leading industrial relations academic willing to serve on the group. Moreover the policy was worked out entirely without the benefit of Ministry of Labour advice. That indeed was the whole point of it. Yet the Department's evidence to Donovan in 1965 predicted with uncanny accuracy the difficulties of attempting to force the unions to co-operate.[17] The experience of 1971–2 suggests that policies determined inflexibly in opposition, in defiance of official advice, may lack realism when they come to be implemented in office.

The third area where Heath's Young Turks did a lot of work in opposition was on the machinery of government itself. Ever since his brief experience as a Civil Servant after the war, Heath had been convinced that Whitehall was poorly managed, and increasingly he had come to believe that the poor performance of the British economy could be attributed in large part to inefficiency in government. His determination that it was possible to improve the quality of government was reinforced by two political considerations. First, the inefficiency of government was a good stick with which to attack Harold Wilson's gimmicky style of administration. Second, the contention that there were substantial economies to be made by better government was a useful means of squaring promised tax cuts with increased spending on defence, education and other desirable objects.

Plans for bringing modern management techniques to Whitehall were a key element in Heath's preparation for government. But they were only one element in a vision which also involved further rearrangement of the departments themselves, already shaken up by Wilson. Heath made it clear that he intended to wind up the Department of Economic Affairs and the Ministry of Technology, which he regarded as mere public relations stunts, absorbing them back into the Treasury and the Board of Trade respectively. But as *The Times* noted in February 1966, Wilson's innovations had demonstrated that 'the Civil Service and the departmental structure can be made to respond almost overnight to political needs as they rarely did before October 1964'.[18] Heath intended more serious restructuring. Already in 1966 he planned to bring together the Departments of Health and Pensions and National Insurance to form what in the characteristic language of the time he called 'a social services strategic command'[19] – only Wilson beat him to it in 1968. The same year Heath announced his intention to create more 'federal' departments, in order to 'reduce interdepartmental friction and streamline administration'; to establish a smaller Cabinet as a more efficient decision-making body; and to 'prune drastically the number of Civil Servants'. All this, he

assured the Tory party conference, would 'purge the body politic of
the toxins of waste, extravagance and procrastination'.[20] To reduce
the problem of 'overload' he also proposed to devolve increased
powers to local government and selected functions of central government from Whitehall to special agencies to be run by businessmen
seconded from industry.

As early as October 1965 he was speculating in an interview with
James Margach about creating 'small spearhead groups inside Whitehall' to look at specified problems quickly and come up with
solutions.[21] Once again he thought originally in terms of businessmen, until advised by Lord Plowden and Sir Robert Hall that
temporary irregulars floating between departments never did much
good: they proposed instead a permanent body based in the Cabinet
Office – the germ of the idea that was to become in 1971 the Central
Policy Review Staff, or 'Think Tank'.[22] In the same *Sunday Times*
interview Heath spoke of his wish to make Parliament more businesslike, but recognised the difficulty of persuading the House of
Commons to reform itself.[23] Four years later, however, Crossman
recorded an insight into the way his mind was working when Heath
let drop a hint that he was thinking of appointing ministers from outside Parliament who should be able to speak in either House.[24] This
was a suggestion he never in fact acted on, but it is one which vividly
illustrates his executive-minded impatience with the limitations of
Commons procedure and the restricted pool of talent available for
appointment to Government office – a point echoed in the 1980s by
Sir John Hoskyns, Mrs Thatcher's adviser on the machinery of
government.

All this was very well, characteristically serious minded, and in
some ways ahead of its time: many of the new management methods
being advocated, like the cost-cutting techniques, did not begin to be
fully accepted in Whitehall until the 1980s. On the other hand the
idea of huge 'super-ministries' was very much a fashion of the 1960s
which the subsequent decades have reversed. Typical of the age, too,
was Heath's belief – which he shared with Wilson, different as their
styles were – that institutional tinkering was a solution to deep-
seated economic problems. Likewise tightening up Whitehall
management might permit minor economies, but was no substitute
for a radical reassessment of the functions of government which
alone would yield major cuts in public spending. There was an element of wishful thinking which runs, paradoxically, as deep in
Heath's seemingly hard-nosed approach as in Wilson's more obviously self-deluding fantasies. Ultimately Heath trusted too much
to the belief that everything could be achieved simply by a positive

attitude and greater efficiency, avoiding the need for really hard decisions. It was a form of wishful thinking which was to end in painful disillusion.

But preparing for government was the easy part of opposition, the part which Heath was best at and which, despite the frustration of powerlessness, he most enjoyed, believing that it was effort well invested which would be rewarded in four or five years' time. The difficult and much more aggravating part was the political circus of opposing the Government, day in, day out, in Parliament, in speeches all round the country, and in instant reactions on television and the radio. Here, although the Government's mounting troubles offered an easy target, the Opposition too was put in real difficulty by Labour's pragmatism.

The trouble was that Wilson's Government attempted so little that could plausibly be attacked as socialist. Though the Conservatives from force of habit continued to condemn Labour as 'doctrinaire', the Government was in fact – as the bitter disillusion of its own left wing testified – pursuing quite moderate, bi-partisan policies that were not doctrinaire at all. There was embarrassingly little that a Tory of Heath's beliefs could honestly condemn on principle. He was thus left with two contradictory stances – on the one hand to attack Labour's incompetence, welcoming the Government's belated conversion to Tory views across a whole range of issues from Rhodesia through Common Market entry to trade union reform, while claiming that he would pursue essentially the same policies, only more effectively; and on the other to exaggerate the ideological gulf between the parties by furiously denouncing Labour's approach, allowing himself to be pushed into a more doctrinaire right-wing rhetoric than truly reflected his views. Neither stance was wholly convincing.

On the one hand, Heath kept up unceasingly the theme of Labour's incompetence, extravagance, cynicism, gimmickry and dishonour, amounting to unfitness to govern. By contrast he took it for granted that Tory government would be sensible, honest, open and efficient – not only functionally but morally superior. Repeatedly he accused the Government of downright trickery, sometimes in language that was astonishingly blunt, as when in August 1966 he claimed that the Government was now run by a triumvirate of Wilson, Crossman and George Wigg – 'just about the slickest three political tricksters in the whole business';[25] or when in November 1969 he denounced Jim Callaghan's decision to delay the implementation of revised constituency boundaries which would have cost Labour several seats. The postponement was 'absolutely typical: brazenly cynical and utterly indefensible', he raged, applying to

Callaghan and his 'shabby Government' Walpole's epitaph on the eighteenth-century Duke of Newcastle: 'His name is perfidy.'[26] Examples could be multiplied indefinitely. Heath genuinely believed that Wilson and his colleagues had degraded the standards of British politics to the point where he could allege that democratic government could not survive another Labour Government. He persuaded himself that – the content of policy apart – he offered the British electorate a 'real alternative, a Government as different in men and methods as it is in thought and action from what they have endured in these past four years' – a simple choice 'between bad Government and good'. 'Our task', he told the 1968 party conference, 'is to restore integrity to politics, honesty to Government and respect to Britain.'[27]

On the other hand, the pressure to be seen to oppose the Government vigorously at every turn dictated a good deal of reflex opposition to whatever Labour did which was itself not always honest. In a powerful 1968 polemic – *Left or Right? The Bogus Dilemma* – the distinguished financial journalist Samuel Brittan saw nothing to choose between Heath and Wilson: in a phoney contest of 'pseudo-toughness', each blindly denounced the other's policies without seeing that they were essentially no different from his own. Heath in particular, Brittan wrote, 'never seemed to appreciate that the small print of the National Plan – and indeed many of the other policies of the DEA – were identical with what he had previously been promoting himself at the Board of Trade'.[28] On several other major issues of the mid- and late 1960s – the devaluation of sterling, Britain's post-imperial military role, the control of inflation and Labour's attempted industrial relations legislation – Heath worked himself into passionate condemnation of policies which he would have done better to have broadly supported.

The Labour Government's failure to devalue the pound immediately on taking office in October 1964, or, failing that, in 1966, was the decisive mistake from which flowed all the other disappointments of the next six years. The Government's radical energies, such as they were, were diverted into an all-consuming and ultimately futile attempt to protect the fixed parity of sterling. It was a fatal decision taken primarily by Wilson personally, with Callaghan's acquiescence, for a mixture of political and patriotic reasons, and subsequently maintained against the mounting doubts of most of the rest of the Cabinet, led by George Brown. Wilson – who as President of the Board of Trade had been closely involved in Britain's previous devaluation in 1949 – felt that Labour could not afford to be labelled the party of devaluation: he also believed it would be an international humiliation and a breach of trust for Britain to devalue. In addition he was under strong pressure from Washington. In the end, of course, after three years' fruitless struggle, he was forced to devalue anyway – too late, in unfavourable circumstances, after much of Britain's gold reserves had been lost in trying to prevent it, when indeed it *was* a national humiliation.

Heath instinctively took the same patriotic view of sterling as Wilson. He was not interested in technical arguments that the pound was overvalued, still less in Powell's monetarist argument that its value should be set, like any other commodity, by the level of demand. He became angry when anyone even suggested the idea of variable exchange rates or floating the pound; and in a perfect mirror image of Wilson's ban on any discussion of the subject among ministers, he imposed his own *ukase* against consideration of it by the Shadow Cabinet. Both Macleod and Maudling were privately converted to the necessity for devaluation by the summer of 1967; while an economic policy seminar at Church House in July revealed near unanimity among the party's economic advisers that it was inevitable. 'Mr Heath's passionate personal opposition to the whole idea of exchange-rate changes', according to Samuel Brittan, 'made it advisable for dissenters to lie low.'[29] To him as to Wilson the pound was a symbol of Britain's standing in the world; accordingly Labour's failure to protect it was a symbol of its incompetence and international shame. He thus made great play, when devaluation came in November 1967, of condemning it as dishonourable and wrong in principle; when what he should have done was to welcome it as the right policy adopted far too late.

Heath's condemnation in this instance was perfectly sincere. Tony Barber told Crossman that his television broadcast – in response to Wilson's famous assurance the previous evening that 'the pound in your pocket or purse or in your bank' had not been devalued – was written 'in the white heat of anger'.[30] His anger made it unusually effective: he seemed to throw off the inhibitions that normally constrained him, insisting passionately in the face of Wilson's affected insouciance that it *was* a moral issue: the country *was* humiliated. Wilson's broadcast, he predicted, 'will be remembered as the most dishonest statement ever made . . . even by the Prime Minister'.[31] But *The Times* noted that he made a mistake by seeming 'to be coming forward in posthumous defence of the old parity'.[32] Over the following days he began to put more emphasis on the way the timing of the decision had been bungled and the need now to make the most of the opportunities offered by devaluation. To many observers, however, his initially furious response to what Brittan called 'the

first big correct decision' the Government had taken was the revelatory moment of his leadership. It was not only economic liberals
of the Powell/Brittan school who were dismayed. The historian
Robert Skidelsky was then a young Research Fellow at Nuffield College. In December 1967 he wrote to Edward Boyle:

> To a number of us in Oxford who have been on the verge of leav-
> ing the Labour party for a number of months now, the biggest
> single obstacle has been Mr Heath's appallingly negative reaction
> to the events of the last few weeks: talk about snatching defeat
> from the jaws of victory![33]

The devaluation crisis exposed the rigidity and blinkered conventionality of Heath's economic understanding, the limitations of
his simple patriotic approach to the economy, his lack of intellectual
curiosity and his intolerance of contrary views. By the irrational
vehemence of his opposition to the possibility of allowing sterling to
find its own value, he committed himself to defend the new parity at
which it was set in 1967 – only to find his own Government in its
turn forced off it in 1972 and obliged against all his assurances to let
the pound 'float' after all. Thus he put a rod in pickle for his own
back.

It was a similar story with defence. Here again Heath fell into the
trap of furiously attacking the Government for dishonouring
Britain's international obligations by cutting back on its military
commitments east of Suez, when he would have done better to mock
Wilson's reluctance to let go of Britain's world role. The central ideal
of Heath's political life was taking Britain into Europe; a recognition
of the need to withdraw from the last outposts of empire would have
seemed to be a natural part of his European vision. Yet one of his
arguments in favour of joining the EEC was that it was the only way
to sustain Britain's global obligations.[34] There are indications that
initially he was prepared to take a more radical view, especially when
he appointed Enoch Powell Shadow Defence Secretary. 'Mr Heath',
The Economist commented, 'must know that Mr Powell has harshly
realistic views about Britain's role overseas . . . This may be a sign
that the Government could find itself outflanked in the defence cuts
business.'[35] Heath, the writer believed, had been elected 'to be tough
with national illusions'.[36] Powell asked for the defence job in the
belief that it was the one major issue on which Heath shared his
thinking. If so, the patriotic conventionality of Heath's instinctive
outlook, the solemn responsibility of being Leader of the Opposition
and next Prime Minister, perhaps also a prudent reluctance to offend

the imperialist sentiments of the Tory right – fortified by a visit to Singapore in 1967, where he was exposed to the urgings of Lee Kuan Yew – quickly led him to think again.

When in July 1967 the Government was forced by economic necessity to announce the withdrawal of British forces from Singapore, Malaysia and the Gulf from the end of 1971, Heath immediately promised to restore them. Accusing Labour of 'deliberately, openly and frankly opting out of their responsibilities', he asserted that 'never before has a British Government exerted less influence on overseas affairs'.[37] From November he explicitly linked this latest humiliation with devaluation: Labour, he charged, had now failed in the two essential duties of government, defending the currency and defending the realm. He did not see that it was in part the unavailing struggle to defend the pound that had made far-flung military commitments finally unsustainable. He always insisted that sending the troops back to the Far East was not imperialist nostalgia, but simply keeping Britain's word to her Asian allies. 'Just as our friends have helped us in the past,' he told the 1968 conference, 'so are we determined that we shall never let them down in the future.'[38] He did not propose that Britain should continue to bear the defence burden east of Suez alone: his idea, following preliminary talks with the countries concerned, was to negotiate a five-power defence pact (Britain, Australia, New Zealand, Malaysia and Singapore) for south-east Asia, and a similar arrangement for the Gulf. On television he was at pains to minimise the extent of the commitment he was proposing: it was

> quite specifically having a presence in the Gulf and a presence in Singapore, Malaysia, which would be part of a joint operation with the other four Commonwealth countries . . . Now this isn't a world-wide role, there's no searching after imperial grandeur, no languishing for the past; this is a specific job of work in the present.[39]

Nevertheless it was bound to be expensive, at a time when the Tories were promising to cut public spending. Moreover it turned out in the event to be impractical to reverse the process of withdrawal once it had been begun. So the commitment to try to do so was merely another piece of excess baggage with which Heath saddled himself, to no avail, in his anxiety to dissociate the Opposition from even the most sensible and inevitable of the Labour Government's actions.

Similarly conventional thinking in another part of the defence field led Heath to lend uncritical support to the United States in Vietnam. He visited Vietnam during a tour of the Far East at the end of 1965, and came back convinced not only that it was a vital interest of the West that the Americans should win, but that it was certain that in the end they would win. In the Commons he repeatedly criticised Wilson for not supporting them whole-heartedly enough.[40] He justified the bombing of Hanoi and Haiphong on the grounds that the war would not end until the Vietcong realised that they could never win. Beyond his overriding commitment to Europe, Heath's world view at this date was still that of an unreconstructed cold warrior.

Defence and devaluation were two areas where Heath's strenuous opposition was misjudged but heartfelt. He responded to the pressure to oppose by attacking the Government predictably but wrongly, from within the same closed mindset as Wilson's own, when he should have mounted a much more subtle, independent and radical critique. In these instances, however, if he was wrong he was at least honest. There were two or three other major areas of Government policy where the pressure to oppose led him to attack immoderately when it would have been both more honest and in the long term politically more advantageous to have given the Government his qualified support.

The first was the Government's conversion, in late 1968, to the necessity of trying to regulate the conduct of industrial relations. As the number of strikes and unofficial stoppages continued to multiply, Wilson and his new Employment Secretary, Barbara Castle, judged that they had no choice but to disarm the Conservatives' insistent calls for legislation with some pre-emptive proposals of their own. Mrs Castle's White Paper, *In Place of Strife* (cheekily adapting the title of Nye Bevan's book *In Place of Fear*), was published in January 1969. Borrowing directly from the Tories' *Fair Deal at Work*, it gave the Secretary of State power to require a 28-day cooling-off period and a ballot before a strike could be called, with legal sanctions to ensure union compliance. It was a perilous course for a Labour Government, already discredited with many of its bedrock supporters, to try to impose legislative curbs on the party's trade union paymasters. The clever policy for the Tories would have been to welcome Labour's conversion and give the Government's proposals wholehearted backing. This, as Jim Prior subsequently wrote, 'would have done wonders for the country and still left the Labour Party seething with discontent. I believe that Ted and Iain Macleod should have spotted our opportunity . . . Once more, however, we sought to maximise our own short-term political advantage.'[41] The temptation to rubbish Labour's proposals was too strong. Trade union reform was such a central plank of their own platform – and expected to be such a vote-winner – that they could not allow Labour to steal it. So Heath and Robert Carr denounced *In Place of Strife* testily as misconceived and ineffective – 'hastily contrived and obviously inadequate', 'a ragbag of odds and ends' – while maintaining that only a Tory Government could be expected to deal with the problem properly: 'They have thrown away the opportunity for a comprehensive measure.'[42]

Certainly *In Place of Strife* was less comprehensive than *Fair Deal at Work*. The Tories were fully entitled to argue that it neglected the critical question of legally binding contracts, that it gave arbitrary and merely discretionary powers to the Employment Secretary instead of establishing a fully worked out system of union registration and industrial courts. Nevertheless they missed a heaven-sent opportunity, and once again stored up trouble for themselves in the future. Had they promised full parliamentary support for Mrs Castle's measures as a valuable step in the right direction, they would simultaneously have made it harder for the Government to back down, while embroiling them deeper than ever in conflict with their own supporters. As it was they were able to make great short-term capital out of the Government's humiliating surrender to union and party pressure; but at the cost of ensuring equally unscrupulous Labour opposition to their own legislation in 1971, which ultimately crippled it, leaving industrial relations unreformed for another decade.

The dramatic demonstration of what the Tories had always alleged – Labour's powerlessness in the face of the unions – gave Heath a new stick with which to beat the Government in the run up to the General Election, which he wielded to damaging effect. Not only had Labour for the first time acknowledged the seriousness of the union problem – Wilson had gone on record with repeated grave warnings of the menace of 'wildcat' strikes which were gleefully quoted from Tory platforms up and down the country – but they had shown themselves wholly incapable of dealing with it. In the House of Commons Heath for once floored Wilson with a single deadly question following his announcement of the TUC's 'solemn and binding' undertaking to use its influence to discourage strikes. 'What will happen', he asked, 'should unofficial strikers ignore the trade union leaders, and go on striking?' Wilson had no answer.[43] The Government's climbdown in the face of an admitted major problem furnished the clearest proof yet of Labour's unfitness to govern, and Heath made the most of it. 'Have no fear,' he told the Tory party conference that autumn. 'We have given our pledge. We do not withdraw, no matter where the pressure comes from or what it is.'[44]

He dismissed the suggestion that determined union opposition might force a Tory Government too to back down, or even that the unions would seriously resist a Tory Government's measures. The difference was that the Tories, unlike Labour, would have placed union reform at the centre of their programme and would therefore have an unquestionable mandate. 'When it is implemented,' he said on 'Panorama' in February 1970, 'I do not believe for one moment that the trade union leaders, let alone the trade union members, are going to challenge the verdict of the electorate in this democracy with a democratically elected Parliament in which the Government is carrying out the policy with which it went to the electorate.'[45] Robert Carr too believed that he had private assurances from the unions, whatever their public rhetoric, that they would not defy an elected Government. Others saw more clearly that such assurances were worthless. 'It just isn't true,' Cecil King wrote in his diary after watching Heath on television. 'The whole idea of a "mandate" is a politician's idea and has no meaning to the man in the street.'[46] Subsequent events were to prove King's scepticism better founded than Heath's confidence.

The second major area in which Heath and his principal colleagues committed themselves firmly but unwisely to reverse Labour's approach was the critical question of prices and incomes policy – critical for all postwar governments since 1947 but particularly so in the 1960s when inflation was coming to be seen as the central insidious disease at the heart of the British economy. Selwyn Lloyd had imposed his famous 'pay pause' in 1961–2. Even the expansionist Maudling had needed some restraint in 1963–4. Now Labour had a succession of policies, at first voluntary under George Brown in 1964–6, then a statutory freeze imposed by Callaghan as part of the crisis measures of July 1966. Following devaluation in November 1967 Roy Jenkins struggled to maintain a statutory ceiling on pay increases, then let it lapse in exchange for the Government's proposed trade union legislation, only to be left helpless to prevent a wage explosion in 1969–70 when *In Place of Strife* too was abandoned.

Labour's policy was unpopular, so it was an irresistible target for Tory denunciation. Nevertheless the question of pay restraint remained a serious problem for the Opposition. There had opened up in the party a clear doctrinal gulf between pragmatic Keynesian interventionists like Maudling, who believed that the next Tory Government would inevitably need an incomes policy, just as the last had done, and the first stirrings of monetarism, which believed the control of earnings by government to be economically irrelevant and practically self-defeating, and wanted to rely on the working of the free market to regulate the price of labour by means, if necessary, of unemployment. Within the Shadow Cabinet not only Powell, but also Keith Joseph, were already voicing this line. This was the central choice that would confront the Heath Government and split the Tory party in the next decade. But it was one which Heath, in opposition between 1965 and 1970, chose to fudge.

His natural disposition was to side with Maudling – as became clear when the choice became unavoidable in 1972. His 'problem-solving' approach to government was instinctively interventionist. But the irresistible pressure to attack Labour's policy led very easily to a tendency to condemn interference in the wages market on principle. The whole thrust of his modernising Toryism was free competition and the reduction of Government regulation. Moreover his Shadow Chancellor, Iain Macleod, was strongly attracted to the rhetoric of economic freedom. Macleod never pretended to understand economics, or even to be interested in the subject. (His friend Enoch Powell used to tell him he should learn some economics, but he would have none of it. 'It was a subject in which he was determined not to take an interest.')[47] Macleod was a politician to his fingertips who judged economic management purely by political criteria. His only concern was to oppose Labour's incomes policy uncompromisingly with whatever arguments lay to hand. Between Maudling and Macleod – his defeated rival and his Shadow Chancellor who had helped crucially to make him leader – there was no question whom Heath would back, even had the same political pressures not impelled him as influenced Macleod. Recognising, however, that he could not afford an open split between his two senior economic colleagues, he allowed the party's position on incomes policy to remain ambiguous and superficial.

At first he simply ducked the question, deflecting Wilson's mockery of the obvious division in the party by opaque formulations that incomes policy would have its place as one part of an overall policy geared to increased competition. *Action Not Words* promised to 'make a prices and incomes policy really effective' but gave no idea of how that might be done.[48] There were two ways of approaching inflation, he told the Young Conservatives in February 1966. 'The first is by exhortation and then, when that fails, by compulsion.' That, he predicted, would be Labour's way. 'The other way is through competition and through every modern way of cutting the costs of production.'[49] Six months later, when Labour had indeed been driven to compulsion, he let himself go in unrestrained denunciation. By voting itself 'dictatorial powers', creating 'the most strictly controlled economy which any democratic country has ever had', the

231

Government had laid bare 'the great divide' between freedom and state control. But then he retreated into woolly bathos. 'We believe that it is possible to reconcile a free economy with stable progress and individual liberty under a Government prepared to take the right action and follow the right policies with fairness and skill.'[50]

So it continued through the next three years – ringing condemnation of compulsory controls qualified by meaningless reservations. 'These powers are becoming a permanent feature of the Socialist Government of Britain,' he charged in March 1968. 'We are convinced that it is wrong in principle . . . and we now see its failure in practice.' Yet a moment later: 'I am quite prepared for a tough incomes policy to ensure that costs do not outrun productivity, but it must be achieved by using all the aspects of economic policy in a complete economic context.'[51] These contradictions betrayed the party's failure authoritatively to resolve its thinking. Powell told Crossman in December 1966 that it was only Maudling who was holding Heath and Macleod back from renouncing incomes policy 'and he is hardly ever with us'.[52] The following July Heath made a speech at Carshalton which was billed as a major statement of economic policy. Powell believed and still believes that it constituted an unequivocal repudiation of prices and incomes policy. Members of the Research Department, however, are incredulous at this interpretation of what they considered just another fudged compromise between Maudling and Macleod – a view supported by the fact that *The Times*'s report of the speech never even mentioned incomes policy.[53] So long as Maudling remained deputy leader and could be seen 'hankering after the old gods', Ian Trethowan wrote in July 1968, Heath was 'doggedly non-committal and . . . likely to remain so'.[54]

As the election drew near, however, Heath was naturally pulled – by political opportunism and rhetorical momentum, rather than economic conviction – to Macleod's way of thinking. For all his language of outraged libertarianism it is plain that he had no intellectual objection to incomes policy – rather the reverse. But he was under too much political pressure as leader of the party of economic freedom to be able to resist opposing it. He may not have been as cynical as Macleod, who simply considered it advantageous to take up the clearest possible anti-socialist cry before the election and frankly did not mind if he had to reverse himself in government. He was not consciously dishonest. He genuinely believed, at the time, the uncompromising declaration of principle which he allowed to be included in the 1970 manifesto, *A Better Tomorrow*: 'We utterly reject the philosophy of compulsory wage control.'[55] But he did not believe it deeply. A casuist might argue, in the light of subsequent events, that rejecting the *philosophy* of compulsion did not say any-thing about rejecting the *practice*, if in the Government's judgment it should become necessary. And in fact this comes to the heart of Heath's approach to politics. If he rejected the philosophy of com-pulsion, he equally rejected the philosophy of freedom: he took no interest in philosophy of any sort. He was as much a pragmatist as Harold Wilson. The point is not that the firm commitment against compulsory wage control in 1970 was wrong, but that Heath and Macleod did not understand its implicit consequences, or what con-viction would be required to hold to it under the pressure of office. Alternatively there was a case for acknowledging the likely inevit-ability of incomes policy and preparing the party and public, while still in opposition, for what it would involve – securing, for what-ever it was worth, a mandate for it at the election. The great failure of the Tories between 1965 and 1970 was that they did neither.

This was not the fault of Brendon Sewill or the Research Depart-ment, who saw quite clearly the yawning gap at the heart of the party's preparations for government and tried for four years with in-creasing desperation to get the leadership to address it. Typical was the famous Shadow Cabinet weekend conference at Selsdon Park in January 1970. Sewill had prepared a discussion paper on the control of inflation. But it was put down as the last item on the agenda and the gathering broke up on the Sunday afternoon before it was reached. The problem of incomes policy was always at the bottom of the agenda. As a result, as Sewill has recalled, 'We went into the 1970 election totally unprepared on what was going to be the crucial issue.' Ironically it was very largely on this issue that they won: 'I was very unhappy . . . with the enormous advertising campaign about the shopping basket and how the party was going to bring down the cost of living without any clue about how we were actually going to do it. In fact most of our policies were designed to put it up.'[56]

This was the fatal flaw at the heart of the ambitious exercise in pre-paring for government. For all Heath's high intentions and hard work in many fields, his alternative Government in waiting failed to prepare for what turned out to be *the* central issue, economic management. Douglas Hurd, who replaced John MacGregor as head of Heath's private office in 1967, wrote in 1979 that the policy exer-cise had been 'a sustained attempt to go beyond the coining of phrases and attitudes and to probe the real causes of Britain's poor performance'.[57] But this simply was not so. In order to avoid ex-posing disagreements that might have been politically embarrassing, the party leadership shrank from any serious thought about the causes of inflation and how to control it. They concentrated instead on micro-economic matters – tax reform and supply-side tinkering – vaguely hoping that trade union legislation would serve as a substitute for incomes policy, relying above all on exhortation and the hope that *talking* continually about competition, modernisation and efficiency would transform the economy. It was not enough. They neglected the major macro-economic question which confronted them in office. After years of hedging, the eventual firm commitment against incomes policy was a shallow political cry, not rooted in monetary theory as it was a decade later. The Tory party in the late 1960s was not intellectually armed to uphold, in the face of mounting inflation and unemployment, the pure doctrine it had so lightly taken up; yet it was fatally discredited by having neither moral nor electoral authority for the statutory policy – more comprehensive than anything Labour had attempted – to which it reverted in 1972–4. The débâcle of February 1974 had its roots in the fudge of 1965–70. With this central failure it has to be concluded that the whole policy exercise, for all its substantial marginal achievements, essentially failed.

Industrial policy was a third area in which Heath allowed himself, as the General Election approached, to be led increasingly into voicing a shallow rhetoric which conflicted with his real political beliefs. Partly stimulated by Keith Joseph, partly extrapolating from his theme of enterprise and competition, he began in 1968–9 to talk a lot about setting industry free from Government interference. Yet his definite policy commitments in this area were vague or marginal, while he never ceased to reaffirm – with much more conviction – his longstanding belief in a vigorous regional policy. Andrew Alexander in the *Weekend Telegraph* spotted the contradiction in Heath's simultaneous advocacy of competition and regional policy – 'the whole paraphernalia of sticks and carrots' – as far back as 1965 and thought he knew which went deeper: 'One feels that he would use the "man in Whitehall knows best" premise all too readily.'[58] Heath continued to feel strongly possessive about regional development as one of his particular policies: he repeatedly accused George Brown's DEA of abandoning the 'growth point' approach which he claimed to have pioneered at the Board of Trade in 1963–4, and promised to restore it. 'There is no stronger supporter of regional policies than myself,' he asserted in November 1967. 'I am convinced that the growth point is the key to regional development, using the resources which are available to provide the infrastructure for the development of industry, rather than hand out larger and larger subsidies to individual firms.'[59] The 1970 manifesto, while promising on the one hand to scrap most of Labour's paraphernalia of regional subsidies and inducements – the Industrial Expansion Act, the Industrial Re-organisation Commission, Regional Employment Premiums – also left a Tory Government ample latitude for reintroducing induce-ments of its own. Regional policies would be aimed at increasing 'the basic economic attraction of the areas concerned'. Government in-vestment would be directed at creating new jobs 'in industries with growth potential'. 'We will maintain financial incentives for invest-ment in the development areas . . . Special assistance for particular industries like shipping will be continued.'[60] In such affirmations Heath was true to himself and gave clear notice of how he was likely to act in government.

His nods towards disengagement from industry were by contrast very modest. In particular he stamped firmly on a proposal put up by the nationalised industries policy committee, chaired by Nicholas Ridley, to announce a radical programme of denationalisation. This was the only way the state was really going to be 'rolled back' from the economy. But in the mid-1960s privatisation was a crackpot fan-tasy of the far right, not to Heath's practical mind a serious policy. In 1965 he committed himself to reversing Labour's renationalisation of steel – as Churchill had done in 1951; and he told Andrew Alexander: 'We might get to the point where internal airlines were denational-ised.'[61] But that was all he would contemplate. Ridley's report was suppressed as politically unrealistic and electoral suicide if word of it were ever to leak out. The possibility of the Government divesting itself of whole industries was simply not on the agenda. Heath was keen to promote increased efficiency, but strictly within the estab-lished framework of the mixed economy as accepted by the Conservatives since 1951.

It was much the same story in the end with the Welfare State, despite Heath's bold pronouncements in 1966. As *The Times* noted after the Selsdon conference in early 1970, the National Health Ser-vice 'still resists a neat electioneering solution'.[62] Here again Heath was not prepared to do more than tinker with the structure of com-prehensive provision as developed since 1948. Apart from the retention of prescription charges, there were to be no further en-croachments on the principle of a free and universal service. A Conservative Government would encourage more people to make private provision for their own families; but most of the under-takings in *A Better Tomorrow* implied *more* spending on health and social services – pensions, family allowances, provision for the dis-abled and the chronic sick – rather than less.

Of all the social services, education aroused by far the strongest feelings among the party rank and file. Specifically Labour's policy of promoting comprehensive schools to abolish the 1944 divide between grammar schools and secondary modern schools was one of the few areas where Tory activists felt there was a clear difference between the parties which they wanted their leaders to highlight. Edward Boyle, however – Secretary of State for Education from 1962 to 1964, reappointed education spokesman by Heath in 1965 – broadly supported comprehensivisation. To the fury of the Tory shires, there was no perceptible difference between his views and those of Labour's successive Education Secretaries – Michael Stewart, Tony Crosland, Patrick Gordon Walker and Edward Short. Every autumn at the party conference Boyle faced angry demands that he commit the next Tory Government unambiguously to halt the spread of comprehensives and save the grammar schools. In 1967 his right-wing critics forced the first conference ballot since 1950 and the leadership's even-handed motion was only carried by 1,302 votes to 816. At Westminster the chairman of the backbench education committee was unseated and the right-winger Ronald Bell elected in his place.

Heath was placed in a dilemma. Boyle was one of his closest political friends; more precisely, Boyle was one of the very few political colleagues with whom he had a relationship outside politics, based on their common love of music. Unmarried, with a record collection to match his own, Boyle was the ideal companion for concert and opera going or late-night sampling of the latest Solti or Karajan recordings. One side of Heath's personality responded warmly to Boyle's civilised patrician Toryism: Boyle had a lot to do with converting him to the abolition of hanging, that other symbolic shibboleth of the Tory right. At the same time, however, the abrasive, impatiently modern side of Heath often found the gentle baronet *too* civilised. As Shadow Education Secretary Boyle was increasingly a liability to a leader who needed to give his restless supporters as much red meat as possible. Heath himself was pulled both ways: while sympathetic to the 'classless' appeal of comprehensives, he was, as a grammar-school boy himself, equally loath to see the grammar schools swept away. Tory policy, therefore, was a balancing act. The party did not oppose comprehensivisation in principle, but it made a virtue of diversity, charged Labour with the doctrinaire imposition of a single system and stood up for the right of local education authorities to decide the pattern and pace of transition appropriate for their own areas. 'We strongly oppose hasty and makeshift plans ... for turning good grammar and secondary modern schools into comprehensive schools.'[63]

Within this formula, however, Heath began to strike a more

9   Campaigning in Orpington at the 1970 General Election

10   The new Conservative Cabinet in the garden at Number 10: (*from left*)
Lord Carrington, Sir Keith Joseph, William Whitelaw, Margaret
Thatcher, Edward Heath, Anthony Barber, Robert Carr, Sir Alec
Douglas-Home, Peter Thomas, Gordon Campbell and James Prior

11   *Above left* With Liam Cosgrave, Irish Taoiseach, and the Northern Ireland Prime Minister, Brian Faulkner, at the Sunningdale conference in 1973

12   *Above right* With French President, Georges Pompidou

13   Outside Number 10 with Zambian President, Kenneth Kaunda

14   At the helm of the third *Morning Cloud*

15   Rehearsing with the London Symphony Orchestra

16   At Chequers in 1970 with the Queen and President and Mrs Nixon

conservative note than Boyle, responding to party concern about standards. In a major policy speech in June 1967 he stressed his personal commitment to state education and his 'passionate desire' to expand and improve it; but went on to sound a warning against 'what I consider to be an undesirable trend towards egalitarianism . . . threatening the erosion of accepted standards and values'.[64] 'Of course it is right to broaden the opportunity for the less able', he told the 1969 party conference, 'but also let us not deprive the very able of the opportunities they ought to have.'[65] Two weeks later, sensing that he was not going to be Education Secretary in the next Government, Boyle decided to leave politics to become Vice-Chancellor of Leeds University. Heath was not so sorry to lose him as might have been expected. He demurred at giving Boyle another job, but took the chance to replace him with someone who more faithfully reflected the views of the rank and file – Margaret Thatcher.* Heath regarded her simply as a competent all-rounder whose sex recommended her for one of the departments regarded as suitable for a woman. The change represented a shift of tone more than of actual policy – as Mrs Thatcher's record in approving comprehensive schemes after 1970 was to show. Yet taken in conjunction with other pronouncements in 1969–70 on immigration and law and order questions it seemed to confirm a significant hardening of the party's face. In the longer evolution of the Tory party over the twenty years from the 1960s to the 1980s, the symbolism of the change – the 'pink' intellectual Old Etonian giving way to the authentic voice of the true blue suburbs – could hardly be more striking.

The other social question which stirred even deeper passions in the Tory breast was Commonwealth immigration. But on this emotive subject, recognised by both parties as an unexploded bomb to be handled with extreme discretion, Heath and his home affairs spokesman, Quintin Hogg, had to strike a delicate balance. Their overriding concern was to prevent race relations becoming a matter of political controversy. To do this they had to make the necessary commitments to satisfy those on the right of the party who demanded an end to coloured immigration – if possible, indeed, a reduction in the numbers of Asians and West Indians already in Britain – without making it a live issue. Race had surfaced as an ugly factor

---

* Heath has always maintained, as he wrote in the *Dictionary of National Biography* in 1990, that he 'made a number of attempts . . . to persuade Boyle to move to other Front Bench positions to enable him to widen his experience in preparation for the highest offices in government', but that Boyle 'repeatedly refused'.[66] Reviewing the volume in *The Times*, however, John Grigg wrote that it was his impression at the time that there were 'at least three positions' which Boyle would have accepted, and so remained in politics instead of going to Leeds.[67]

in a handful of Midlands constituencies in 1964, but Heath wanted nothing to do with it. The formula adopted in *Action Not Words* in 1966 was to promise 'stricter control of entry', a register of dependents and financial assistance for any immigrants who wanted to go back, combined with the assurance of equal treatment for those who chose to stay and special help for areas with a high concentration of immigrants.[68] This package did the trick so long as no one tried to spell out too precisely what it should mean. In April 1968, however, Enoch Powell – calculating with maximum effect his *grand démarche* against Heath's leadership – blew it apart. After that, with immigration thrust into the full glare of public attention, Heath was forced to be more explicit. He was bound to resist Powell's challenge: but in doing so he could not help but give some ground.

12

'Selsdon Man'

THE immigration issue precipitated the final rift in a titanic quarrel between Heath and Powell which had been building for years. While they had first known each other as colleagues in 'One Nation' in 1950, their mutual hostility went back at least as far as Powell's resignation from the Treasury with Thorneycroft in 1958, when Heath was Chief Whip. Disregarding the resigning ministers' monetarist arguments, Heath treated that episode purely as an attempted *coup* against Macmillan and never ceased to regard Powell from then on as congenitally disloyal. For his part Powell regarded Heath simply as Macmillan's stooge who had slyly advanced his own prospects by helping to rig the succession for Home in 1963. From the moment Heath became Tory leader in 1965, an open breach was only a matter of time. The deep ideological divide between their opposite schools of Conservatism was exacerbated by temperamental incompatibility, mutual incomprehension and political rivalry.

Powell was continually exasperated by Heath's impatience with ideas ('If you showed him an idea he immediately became angry and would go red in the face')[1] and resented his way of running the Opposition. He was deeply sceptical of the problem-solving approach to policy making – the belief that if you only assembled enough experts and got all the facts right then you would be sure to come up with the right answer; and as a member of the Shadow Cabinet he objected to being confined to speaking only on his own designated subject. He disapproved on constitutional principle of Heath's attempt to enforce collective responsibility on the Shadow Cabinet as though it were a real Cabinet.

For his part Heath found Powell's insistent intellectualism intensely irritating and thought his economic theories anachronistic and irrelevant. Powell was a colleague he was obliged to put up with for party reasons, but not one whom he either trusted or respected. In 1965 he probably thought defence – where Powell would come under the restraining influence of the service chiefs – the safest portfolio he could find for him: at least it should keep him away from economic and welfare policy. But that autumn Powell gave warning of his growing oratorical power at the party conference. He made a speech questioning the continuation of Britain's world role, yet couched in such compelling language that the representatives applauded ecstatically. 'At the moment, admittedly, Mr Powell is no more than a stimulating theoretician,' Alan Watkins wrote in the *Spectator*. 'But the reaction he evoked will not have escaped Mr Heath. He remains a potential threat to Tory party unity.'[2] Powell had cleared his speech in advance with Home and Soames, but not with Heath, who afterwards disowned it, saying that Powell was 'posing questions, not formulating policy'.[3] Powell had believed, when he took the defence job, that he would have Heath's support in advocating the radical reassessment of military commitments. He was quickly disillusioned.

Heath could quite legitimately have dropped Powell from the Shadow Cabinet after the 1966 election. Powell had already outraged other senior colleagues, including both Maudling and Macleod, by his public contradictions of the party line over a whole range of issues. At that point he still had little support in the parliamentary party, probably no more than the handful who had voted for him in the leadership election. But Heath judged that he would be more dangerous outside than in. In April 1966 the two men came to a concordat which, characteristically, each interpreted entirely differently: Heath believed that Powell had agreed to accept collective responsibility, Powell that Heath would allow him a degree of licence so long as he cleared anything controversial with the relevant official spokesman. Each subsequently thought that the other broke his word. Even on his own subject, Powell continued to expound views contemptuously discordant with Heath's. On the one hand he openly called Britain's continuing role east of Suez, which Heath was pledging the party to maintain, 'a piece of humbug';[4] on the other he began to question the usefulness of Britain's nuclear deterrent and the whole 'nuclear hypothesis'.[5] Nor did his heresies stop at defence: from his advocacy of floating exchange rates to his ridicule of overseas aid he espoused provocatively unorthodox views on practically everything. Even his admiring biographer Patrick Cosgrave admits that between 1966 and 1968 'in no ordinary sense of the word . . . could Powell be called a good colleague. His interpretation of his duty, exact and honourable as it was, was at least gnomic, if not even Jesuitical.'[6]

Two incidents illustrate the incomprehension and mistrust that existed between Powell and Heath. First, Heath, in his modernising zeal, proposed to make no objection to a Labour move to abolish the ceremonial interruption of parliamentary proceedings by Black Rod. Powell – among his other interests a historian of the mediaeval House of Lords – was horrified:

> I remember bursting out and saying, 'But, Ted, we can't do this
> . . . Do you realise that the formula which is used . . . is that which
> was used in 1306 when Edward I was ill at the time of a parliament
> of Carlisle, and it was probably two hundred years old at that
> time. You simply cannot destroy a thing like that.' And Ted
> flushed with anger. He said, 'This is exactly the sort of thing that
> does us so much harm. People simply do not understand that
> mumbo-jumbo.[7]

A more serious incident arose over the Vietnam War. Again Powell's version is that he was specifically asked by Central Office, in his capacity as defence spokesman, to trail a rumour that Britain was being pressed to send troops to fight alongside the Americans and invite Wilson to deny it. He duly did so, only to find himself publicly disowned by Heath. This, on one occasion when he was speaking dutifully to order, convinced Powell that he had few obligations of loyalty to Heath.[8]

The row over immigration which resulted in Powell's dismissal from the Shadow Cabinet in April 1968 was thus only the last straw which precipitated the breakdown of an already poisoned relationship. Consciously or unconsciously, Powell was looking for a cause around which to widen and develop his opposition to everything that Heath stood for; and Heath was not sorry to be presented with the opportunity to be rid of him.

Powell had been taking an interest in immigration for some time. His theoretical interest in the subject went back to his opposition to the 1948 British Nationality Act and the 1952 Royal Titles Bill: his objection to the citizens of Commonwealth countries being allowed to retain the privileges of British subjects even when they repudiated allegiance to the Crown was dismissed at the time as mere constitutional pedantry. But the privileges of British subjects included the right to come and live in Britain, and during the next decade many hundreds of thousands of West Indians, Indians and Pakistanis – encouraged by labour shortages in Britain and active recruitment by the British Government, not least the Ministry of Health under Enoch Powell himself in 1962–3 – took advantage of the right, until mounting concern at the build up of immigrant populations in certain areas drove the Conservative Government to impose the first restrictions on Commonwealth immigration in 1962 – against the opposition both of the Labour party and of many old imperialist Tories who still honoured the Commonwealth link. In the mid-1960s, however, new arrivals were still coming at the rate of 50,000–60,000 a year, and the number of Tory MPs calling for tighter controls continued to swell. It was now that Powell became alarmed at the possibilities of racial conflict in his own Wolverhampton constituency and began to lend his distinctive voice to the campaign.

He came very close to provoking Heath to sack him in February 1968, with a speech at Walsall demanding a halt to the sudden influx of Kenyan Asians who had been given British passports at the time of Kenyan independence and were now being expelled by the Africanisation policy of the Kenyan Government. The Labour Government reluctantly rushed through an emergency Bill to stagger their entry over several years. The Shadow Cabinet, balancing Britain's undoubted obligation against what Heath called 'serious social consequences' if they were to come 'at a rate which could not be satisfactorily absorbed', took the middle course and decided to back the Bill.[9] Fifteen Tories, however, joined thirty-five Labour Members in voting against it as a dishonourable betrayal of a solemn undertaking. Among these Tory rebels was Iain Macleod. In the circumstances Heath could hardly dismiss Powell.

The break came only a few weeks later, however, over the Government's Race Relations Bill, a measure brought forward – as a positive counterweight to the Kenyan Asians Bill – to outlaw racial discrimination against immigrants already resident in Britain. Once again the Opposition had a delicate path to tread between the Tory right, which strongly opposed the Bill, and liberals who were anxious to support it. At least four members of the Shadow Cabinet – Macleod, Boyle, Carr and Joseph – would have preferred not to oppose the Bill. But at a meeting on 11 April it was decided to put forward a reasoned amendment declining to support the Bill but expressing support for the principle of equal treatment: Powell specifically supported this compromise and actually helped to frame it. By securing his agreement to this formula, his colleagues congratulated themselves that they had turned a tricky corner. As a result they were enraged when a few days later Powell delivered at Birmingham his notorious 'rivers of blood' speech predicting large-scale racial conflict unless the tide of immigration was not merely halted but reversed.

It was the apocalyptic language of Powell's speech, rather than its specific content, that outraged his colleagues. Innocently, Powell professed himself bewildered by the outcry. He claimed, and still to this day insists, that he had no idea that he was saying anything controversial. He believed the decision to oppose the Race Relations Bill was an important turning point in party policy, and claims that he made his Birmingham speech to explain it. [10] Because he was merely expounding party policy he saw no need to distribute it in advance through Central Office: he cleared it instead with the Midlands regional agent who – he maintains – thought it would be very helpful. He pointed back to *Action Not Words* to argue that not only stricter controls but also assisted repatriation were already party policy. As always with Powell there is a certain formal plausibility in his defence, but also a transparent disingenuousness. The point was that the Shadow Cabinet's amendment, which he had helped to draft, was carefully designed to defuse the issue, by opposing Labour's Bill but *not* the principle of promoting good race relations. *Action Not Words* had indeed spoken of help for immigrants who wished *voluntarily* to return home, but it was never envisaged as a means of seriously reducing the immigrant population. Powell was deliberately putting a weight on the party's words which he knew very well his colleagues had not intended them to bear: moreover he deliberately used the heightened language of racial conflict. An orator of his precision does not use such language without intending his words to make an impact. Finally, to maximise that impact, someone made sure the television cameras were there to record the speech. Powell could not be surprised that his colleagues felt he knew exactly what he was doing.

It was the betrayal of trust that was the last straw as much as the wilful stirring up of racial hatred. Willie Whitelaw, as Chief Whip, was 'totally outraged'. 'Frankly,' he wrote in his memoirs twenty years later, 'I knew then that I could never fully trust him again.'[11] Quintin Hogg felt his position thoroughly undermined and immediately told Heath that he could not remain home affairs spokesman unless Powell was sacked. Edward Boyle and also, according to some accounts, Iain Macleod told Heath that they too would resign if Powell was not dismissed. Heath therefore had no choice, even had he wanted to try to keep Powell. In fact he was if possible even more angry himself and had already made up his mind. Realising that the combination of Powell and immigration was going to spell trouble, he was careful to ring all his colleagues, to be sure that he would have their support, and also got Whitelaw to carry out wider consultations in the party. But these precautions only confirmed his purpose. He sent a message to Powell – who extraordinarily had no telephone in his Wolverhampton house – to ring him the next day. He then summarily dismissed him.

Within the political world, where it was recognised that Powell's conduct had long been intolerable, Heath's firm and prompt response was generally admired. He was seen to have acted decisively and courageously. Public reaction to Powell's speech and sacking, however, was more divided. Large spontaneous demonstrations took to the streets in his support: most famously and symbolically, the Smithfield meat porters marched to the House of Commons. Powell received an enormous, largely favourable, postbag. By contrast Heath was flooded with hostile letters, often obscene. Opinion polls found that something like 74 per cent of the public thought that on the issue of immigration Powell was right, and Heath wrong to sack him for daring to voice at last what ordinary people felt. Overnight Powell was transformed from a donnish maverick known only to a few *cognoscenti* into a popular tribune with a large, devoted and vocal following: some alarmed observers – misjudging Powell – feared the beginnings of a fascist movement. Powell had struck a chord which no British politician had touched for decades.

No doubt Heath was right to dismiss Powell in April 1968. In practice he had no option. Nevertheless the effect was immensely to increase Powell's influence. Constrained within the Shadow Cabinet, he was an irritant of little political importance. Now, free of all constraints but hugely promoted by the press, the object of violent student demonstrations wherever he spoke (which only increased his wider popularity), the hero alike of the patriotic white working class represented by the marching dockers and of the new suburban middle class grumbling at the golf club – Powell seemed suddenly the central figure on the national stage, almost the arbiter of politics. More than one cartoonist drew him as a sinister genie escaped from the bottle.

For Heath, Powell's transformation represented a direct personal challenge – both to his authority within the Tory party and to his already poor rating with the electorate. Though it was immigration which initially gained him press attention and popular support, Powell's sudden notoriety and the hypnotic oddity of his personality created new interest in his economic thinking too. For many frustrated Conservatives Powell seemed to embody the clear and distinctively anti-socialist vision that was lacking in Heath's technocratic pragmatism, as well as the power to communicate excitement which Heath so painfully lacked. As David Watt wrote in the *Financial Times* in 1969, 'One reason why constituency workers are besotted with Mr Enoch Powell is that he gives the strongest impression of any leading figure in the party of believing that there is more to politics than simply "getting the economy right".'[12] Thus Powell could be represented as both a more popular leader than Heath and a better Tory.

In some ways, perhaps, Powell's challenge strengthened Heath. The great majority of Tory MPs rallied to him: in July 1969 Whitelaw estimated Powell's supporters in Parliament at only twenty-eight.[13] Moreover in the Shadow Cabinet 'life without Enoch [was] considerably more relaxed'.[14] At conference in 1968 and 1969 the fact of a declared rival ensured longer and louder applause to demonstrate that the party was overwhelmingly behind its leader. Yet Powell now offered a focus of opposition within the party, a repository for all the muttering and discontent with Heath's leadership. Powell effectively put Heath on probation. Powell's emergence made it practically certain that Heath would not be given a third chance if he lost again in 1970–1.

At the same time, paradoxically, Heath needed Powell. Even though he was no longer a member of the Shadow Cabinet, Powell was now the best-known and most-admired figure in the Tory party, with enormous appeal to precisely that section of the electorate – the patriotic working and lower-middle class – which the Tories needed if they were to win the election. Polls continued to show Powell's popularity running ahead of Heath's, while the party's huge leads over Labour could be plausibly attributed at least in part to Powell's influence. Reluctantly, therefore, and without appearing to embrace his views, Heath was bound to trim his sails over the next two years to catch the Powellite wind.

There is no question that under pressure from Powell he toughened the party's stance on immigration. His principal proposal, unveiled in September 1968 in a speech at York, was to take away the remaining special privileges of Commonwealth citizens wishing to settle in Britain: henceforth they should be classified simply as aliens. In addition there would be further restrictions on the right of dependents to join heads of family already arrived; and Heath confirmed that a Conservative Government would indeed offer assisted repatriation to those who wanted it.[15] At the same time he was adamant that there was no question of compulsory repatriation. 'If there are any', he warned the 1968 conference, 'who believe that immigrants to this country, most of whom have already become British citizens, could be forcibly deported because they are coloured people . . . then that I must repudiate, absolutely and completely.'[16]

Heath's clarification was welcomed by most Tories, but his

attempts to distance himself from Powell's language failed to satisfy the race relations lobby. Following a speech in Walsall in January 1969 – when Powell, with other Midland MPs, was present on the platform, sitting grimly behind Heath as he spoke – Sir Learie Constantine of the Race Relations Board accused Heath of jumping on Powell's bandwagon, while other spokesmen of the immigrant communities denounced the speech as 'vicious and dangerous'.[17] What Heath was doing, essentially, was bringing the content of Tory policy into line with what Powell had claimed it was already, while rejecting Powell's menacing implication that the blacks should somehow be persuaded to go home, insisting all the time on the right to equal treatment for those immigrants already settled. A year later, when Powell made a speech attacking the policy of giving extra Government help to areas of high immigration, Heath denounced it with unforced anger as 'unChristian' and 'an intolerable example of man's inhumanity to man', which in turn infuriated Powell.[18] Whitelaw tried to effect a reconciliation, but Heath refused to withdraw. In truth he handled the immigration issue after 1968 with considerable skill and honour, taking his stand on a firm but even-handed policy which *The Economist* acknowledged in 1970 as 'consistent, humane and even courageous'.[19]

The Powellite wind did not blow only on immigration. On a wide range of other issues – from comprehensive schools and Rhodesian sanctions to law and order and the economy – Heath faced rising pressure during 1969 to toughen his policy stance. To an extent he acceded, at least at the level of rhetoric: the language of his speeches became harsher, more overtly capitalistic, less socially conciliatory. Yet, as David Watt recognised, this was largely window dressing. 'With the exception of one or two tactical lapses . . . the Shadow Cabinet has made almost no concessions to the more illiberal and vindictive side of the Conservative temperament, and considering the pressures involved this in itself has been a remarkable achievement.'[20] But Heath found it prudent to backpedal on his deepest conviction of all – Europe.

For some years after de Gaulle's veto in 1963 the question of Britain joining the Common Market had been effectively shelved. Heath, of course, remained firmly committed to entry as soon as it should become feasible. By choosing him as its leader in 1965 the Tory party implicitly endorsed that commitment, explicitly renewed at the 1966 election. But so long as de Gaulle retained power in France the door remained shut. In the meantime, however, Labour executed a characteristically Wilsonian somersault to come out, in November 1966, in favour of making a second application, de Gaulle or no de Gaulle. Heath was rightly sceptical, both of the sincerity of Labour's conversion and of the prospects of success. From the party point of view there was danger in Labour stealing yet another of the Tories' most distinctive policies; while from the national perspective he was apprehensive that inviting a second veto would only turn public opinion against Europe. Nevertheless he could only welcome the Government's change of heart, with only the mildest satire at the expense of Wilson's new enthusiasm. Labour's new tune, he purred, was 'music to my ears . . . "Abject surrender" has become at least a "merchant adventure" . . . How much sweeter the words would have been five years ago, but I am grateful for them now.' He could not resist puncturing Wilson's boast that he was entering 'uncharted seas': 'In fact these seas are just about the best charted . . . in the post-war world. What we have to know is how to read the chart.'[21] Possessively he jibbed at Wilson calling his Government's application in May 1967 'historic'; but he tried not to carp – personally galling though it would have been if Wilson had succeeded in carrying off the prize. 'Having gone through these negotiations myself, I do not wish to see our present negotiations subjected to the sort of things we were subjected to. I know what it means.'[22]

Honourably he kept the Tories lined up in support of Labour's application, which was approved by 488 votes to 62. Both Government and Opposition applied a three-line whip. Not only Tony Benn, Peter Shore and Barbara Castle, but also Powell (still in the Shadow Cabinet) and John Biffen voted in favour: only 34 Labour Members and 21 Tories, with 6 Ulster Unionists and the sole newly elected Welsh Nationalist, voted against. The result, of course, was another French veto. But Labour's conversion led a growing number of Tories to question their own commitment to Europe. Still more was this the case when de Gaulle abruptly resigned in 1969 after losing a minor constitutional referendum. His successor, Georges Pompidou, was much less hostile to British entry. Suddenly the door, if not open, was at least unlocked. Immediately the Tories' unity began to crack. At just this moment Enoch Powell was looking for another popular patriotic platform from which to broaden his attack on Heath. With all three parties now officially in favour, it was irresistible for Powell to come out against. 'Within weeks of Enoch's sacking,' Jim Prior wrote in his memoirs, 'Alec Home was betting that it would not be long . . . before Enoch came out against British entry into the Common Market.'[23] Henceforward Europe was another issue on which Heath had to guard his right flank.

Although it was perfectly clear that it was the keenest ambition of

his political life to take Britain into the EEC, he had to avoid giving
the impression – of which Wilson was always quick to accuse him –
that he was willing to go in on any terms. At the 1969 party conference, therefore, Home promised that a Tory Government would be
committed only to negotiate with the Six; and that remained the
party's public stance going into the election. The 1970 manifesto
stated, 'Obviously there is a price we would not be prepared to pay
. . . Our sole commitment is to negotiate: no more, no less.'[24] The
Shadow Cabinet actually came very close to promising a referendum
on the terms.[25]

Thus Powell's challenge reached to the heart of Heath's political
belief. Europe quickly became the supreme political issue which
divided them, and through the reversals of fortune of the next two
decades it remained the supreme issue for both men. Powell railed
furiously against Heath's success in taking Britain at last into the
Community, even to the point of resigning his seat and advising the
electorate to vote Labour in 1974. He may have helped to bring
Heath down; but he did not succeed in getting Britain out of the
Community. Nor, though she learned so much from Powell, and
latterly tried to put a brake on the Community's development, did
Mrs Thatcher ever seek to take Britain out of the EEC. Heath's historic *fait accompli* stands. In the end, therefore, despite his personal
disappointments, on the question that mattered most to both of
them, Heath can be said to have won his duel with Powell.

Politics remained more than ever in these years the all-absorbing
purpose of Heath's life, filling even the hours which another man
might have given to his family. Being Leader of the Opposition gave
him a substitute for a family. Members of his private office, aides and
advisers were at his beck and call at all times of day. He made no distinction between home and office. He used his shabby room at the
House of Commons very little. John MacGregor (or from 1967
Douglas Hurd) was based there, with half a dozen assistants and
secretaries, dealing with correspondence and other business. Heath
himself worked mainly from Albany, where his political family
would come to him as required: Willie Whitelaw, Jim Prior and
Anthony Kershaw to deal with parliamentary matters, Tony Barber
and Michael Fraser reflecting wider party concerns; Brendon Sewill,
David Howell, Brian Reading and others for intensive policy sessions; Michael Wolff, his chief speechwriter, and Geoffrey Tucker,
the party's publicity director, charged with trying to improve his
television performance. All were expected to be there when he
wanted them, and equally to disappear when he did not. There was

no sitting around gossiping. Although in some respects quite informal, with Heath himself often casually dressed, they were business, not social occasions. Though he could be a lavish host when he set himself to be so, he did not as a rule provide much in the way of food or even drink. Stories are told of his having a single cup of tea or coffee brought in by his housekeeper for himself, without thinking of offering one to his guest. Sometimes he seemed unaware that anyone was there until he was ready to give them his attention. Those who were used to him accepted his self-absorption; others, exposed to it for the first time, thought him insufferably rude.

Likewise he would play the piano when he felt like it, when someone was waiting to see him or even in the middle of a meeting. Music remained his great relaxation, a source of spiritual refreshment which engaged parts of his personality which the daily life of politics did not. Those who overheard these soul-cleansing performances at the end of a hard day have testified that they could never again imagine Heath to be a cold man lacking in deep feeling. But he played for himself, to get Wilson or Powell out of his system, not for others. He continued to go to concerts and the opera whenever he could find the time (and he made it a priority to make time). His political eminence increasingly opened doors for him to meet and talk with the conductors and performers. Yet he still kept his political and musical lives strictly separate. Except with Edward Boyle, he never talked music with political colleagues; and he never talked politics with musical friends like Moura Lympany. He made scrupulously little attempt to capitalise on his music for political purposes, as many other politicians would have done, perhaps because classical music was not a popular hobby, more likely because he regarded it as private. A rare exception was that he used regularly to cite Beethoven's *Fidelio*, with its message of human freedom, as his favourite opera and the highest expression of his political philosophy. (Curiously, Samuel Brittan, arguing in 1968 that Heath belonged to the authoritarian not the liberal Tory tradition, defined the test of a liberal as 'one who responds . . . to the trumpet call in the Second Act of *Fidelio* announcing the liberation of the prisoners'.[26] By this definition Brittan disproved his own contention.) Heath's only public performance was the Christmas carol concert which he still conducted every year in Broadstairs, which now annually drew the press and sometimes television cameras to his home town and became an established part of his public image.

A quite new element in his life, and in his image, was sailing. Unlike music, which had been his passion from boyhood, Heath only took up sailing in middle age, a few weeks before his fiftieth birthday, when he was already in the full glare of media attention as Leader of the Opposition. The fact that, with the limited time at his disposal, he turned himself within five years into an international-class yachtsman and captain – on merit – of Britain's Admiral's Cup team is one of the most extraordinary achievements of his career, possibly unparalleled in any sport. He began in the smallest possible way, taking lessons from an instructor whose kiosk happened to catch his attention on Broadstairs jetty in the summer of 1966.[27] Up to that time he had done no more than mess around in a dinghy on holiday with the Seligmans in Brittany in the 1950s and at Ville-franche the previous summer. In his book *Sailing* Heath claims that as a boy he had always been fascinated by boats and the sea, but could never afford to do anything about it. Salt water must have been in his blood, but he took a very long time to recognise it. When he decided to try sailing it was only because he felt he needed some physical recreation, for the sake of his health, to get him away from politics. He had tried golf but found it insufficiently absorbing: he was not good at it, and his playing partners would insist on talking politics down the fairways. He needed an activity that was mentally as well as physically strenuous: sailing fitted the bill admirably.

For Heath, as soon as he had learned the rudiments, sailing was emphatically not a gentle relaxation but intensely competitive. He was never interested in cruising but only in *racing* – and, naturally, in winning. Though one part of the attraction was that it took him away from politics, another was that captaining a racing yacht called for very similar qualities of careful preparation, judgment, nerve and leadership, simply transferred to a different context. He proved so successful because he brought to sailing the same absolute dedication, the same determination to master the subject and the same unflinching professionalism that in the political context carried him to Downing Street. From 1966 onwards he made a point of getting down to Broadstairs on either Saturday or Sunday most weekends during the summer, and he spent the whole of every August sailing. In commissioning his successive boats, each designed down to the last detail to his particular requirements; in assembling the best possible master and crew, in winning their devotion and delegating responsibility to them when he could not be there; in setting the strategy for each race and taking the helm, he displayed leadership of the highest order and demonstrated again his ability to weld a small group into a happy and cohesive team. His remarkable sailing success in the late 1960s offered a perfect metaphor for what he hoped would be comparable political success in the 1970s.

The first boat he bought, rather oddly, while he was learning to sail in the summer of 1966, was a small speedboat which he named *White Heather*. ('I used her for fishing, for towing water-skiers and for going off to picnics around the coast. When we were racing, others took her out as an additional safety boat for the club.') Later she used to carry his police detective at a discreet distance while he sailed.[28] The next year he bought his first dinghy, a two-year-old, sixteen-foot fibreglass Snipe for £200. He renamed her *Blue Heather*; witty picture editors used to cut off the last two letters, so that it read *Blue Heath*. At the end of that summer he sold her (for £175 – 'It seemed to me that I had had a very good summer's enjoyment for about £30') and commissioned a new Fireball, *Blue Heather* II, the same size as the Snipe but more challenging and more exciting to sail. 'The sailing that we got that summer [1968]', he recalled, 'was in many ways the most enjoyable I ever had in a small boat.'[29]

But he was already being introduced by some of his parliamentary colleagues to bigger boats and ocean racing. He first acted as crew for the MP for Winchester, Rear-Admiral Morgan Giles, in the 'Round the Island' race at Cowes. (The rest of the crew were all admirals.) Then the Member for Sutton, Richard Sharples, took him sailing off Portsmouth, before he had his first taste of ocean racing with Sir Maurice Laing (of the construction company), who invited him to take part in the Cowes–Dinard race in late July. His rhapsodic description of finishing this race in St Malo suggests that this is when the bug of ocean racing really bit him: it is one of his great regrets that in several subsequent attempts he never managed to win the Cowes–Dinard event. Though parting with *Blue Heather* II 'almost broke my heart', he quickly decided to get an ocean racer of his own. In January 1969 he paid a highly publicised visit to the Boat Show, where he was impressed by a 34-foot fibreglass design by the American Olin Stephens. He commissioned it to be built for him at Upnor on the Medway, and the first *Morning Cloud* was launched by his stepmother – breaking the champagne at the third attempt – just three months later on 12 April. The name – originally spelled as one word, *Morningcloud* – was not his own but the designer's, one of a series of variations on the 'morning' theme: all Heath did was to split it into two words. But the name became so much associated with him – despite much mockery that his curious vowels rendered it as *Morning Cleoud* – that he kept it for four subsequent boats over the next ten years.

One of the best things Heath ever did was to ask Owen Parker to be his master. Parker was a shipwright from Southampton, reputedly the best in the whole country at 'tuning' a new boat: Heath initially engaged him to tune *Morning Cloud*, then after some teething problems invited him to manage the organisational side of getting her ready for each race, assembling a crew and moving her around the coast between races. *Morning Cloud* was such a good boat, Parker had such a high reputation and Heath himself soon proved such a good skipper that Parker was able to recruit and retain a first-class crew from season to season. The best crews naturally want to sail in the best boats. There was of course prestige in crewing with the Leader of the Opposition and later the Prime Minister; but the intensive media attention was distracting, and yachtsmen of the calibre of Anthony Churchill, Sammy Sampson and Jean Berger, who all joined him at the end of 1969, would not have stayed with Heath for his celebrity status alone if they had not admired his dedication and his professionalism. They were a mixed bunch – Churchill was a journalist, Sampson an East Anglian farmer who had been a mine-sweeper captain in the war, Berger (a Swiss) ran a machine tools business, and Duncan Kay (the fifth member of the team) was managing director of a Kingston dressmaking firm – but on *Morning Cloud* they were all equal: they were all hand-picked specialists and Heath treated them with the respect he always showed to experts. He himself was unquestionably the skipper, never exactly one of the boys; but as always he was at his most relaxed with a completely trusted group concentrated single-mindedly on the same end.

It might be imagined that the ocean racing fraternity would have resented this highly publicised beginner breaking so successfully into their world, but not at all. There were some sneers from those – mainly in the snobbish Royal Yacht Squadron – whose interest in sailing was primarily social, but the serious yachtsmen welcomed him unreservedly: they appreciated the publicity he brought to the sport and respected the advances his professional approach stimulated in boat design, crew quality and strategy. In fact Heath played a major role in raising standards. In 1969 *Morning Cloud* had the edge over most of her rivals; by 1975 others had caught up. Here again Heath's sailing career was a paradigm of his political ambition for Britain. He showed what could be achieved. He found ocean racing still a predominantly amateur and amateurish sport: he left it a decade later so thoroughly professionalised that he, a part-time amateur without great wealth, could no longer compete.[30]

In 1969, his first season of competitive racing, *Morning Cloud* performed creditably in the Cowes–Dinard race (finishing in thick fog) and won the Ramsgate Gold Cup; but Heath's first experience of the Fastnet race (from Cowes to the southern tip of Ireland and back to Plymouth) taught him a lesson he never forgot. The race coincided with the outbreak of trouble in Northern Ireland and the Labour Government's decision to send in troops. On the first day out from Cowes, Heath was obliged to hold two long conversations with Reggie Maudling by radio telephone; when they tried to start the engine to recharge the battery, it would not spark – and the starting handle could not be used without removing the mast! They were left to sail without instruments or lights: fortunately conditions that year were light, but Heath made sure that in future double batteries were fitted on all his boats, and the engine could be started by hand without difficulty.

Late that summer Heath was persuaded by his crew to have a go at the 640-mile Sydney–Hobart race, one of the world's three classic ocean races, which began on Boxing Day. It was an ambitious objective, but Heath approached it with typical thoroughness, holding intensive team discussions in his Albany flat over the autumn, making a number of carefully judged alterations to *Morning Cloud* to improve her performance within the handicapping rules and arranging subsidised transport to Australia and accommodation for both boat and crew. Heath himself took the chance of a visit to New Zealand in October to slip over to Sydney to see for himself and talk to some previous winners. The idea of entering the race quickly acquired semi-political overtones for him. 'My admiration both for Australia and Australians was unbounded,' he wrote in *Sailing*:

> On the other hand, many of the Australians to whom I had spoken had not bothered to conceal their view that Britain was pretty well down and out, unable to meet her obligations economically, politically or militarily, and largely populated by long-haired lay-abouts and ne'er-do-wells . . . It seemed to me that if we could take out a boat and a crew who could beat them in their own waters, we might do something to change that depressing view of Britain. But it was quite an undertaking.[31]

In fact the Royal Ocean Racing Club decided independently to send a three-boat team – including *Morning Cloud*'s sister ship, *Morning After* – to compete for Britain in the Southern Cross series, of which the Sydney–Hobart race was the climax; *Morning Cloud* was named reserve boat. Heath could not get to Australia for the whole series, which began before Parliament rose on 17 December, but he arrived in time to take the helm for two short races before the big one, the second of which they won. He was characteristically determined that everything on *Morning Cloud* should be ready and stores stowed by Christmas Eve: he was amazed to find others still making last-minute preparations and major alterations on Christmas Day. That was not his way.

The race was started by the Australian Prime Minister, John Gorton, with some 4,000 small boats to see the contestants off and tens of thousands of spectators massed along the shore. *Morning Cloud* was one of the smallest of seventy-nine competitors. The critical strategic decision was whether to go right out to sea to try to find the southerly 'set', or current, or take the direct route, hugging the coast. Heath decided to gamble on the longer route, relying on astro-navigation to keep track of their position. (Churchill, Sampson and Berger could all use a sextant.) It worked. They found the 'set' some sixty miles offshore, and for three days a brisk northerly wind hurried them south in warm sunshine. Then the wind died, and a gale blew up from the south-east. This was just the wind they needed to bring *Morning Cloud* in towards Tasmania; but it was frighteningly strong, 35–40 knots gusting to more than 50. It was now bitterly cold, with hailstones stinging their faces, and water started coming in through the bilges, flooding the cabin floor. They had to bale furiously by hand, with buckets, to keep it out. Instead of four-hour watches, they cut to just one hour at a stretch: 'Even an hour in those conditions was almost unbearable.' But as dawn came up on the fourth day the storm subsided and they could see the Tasmanian coast. Eventually they inched up the Derwent River to the finishing line at six o'clock that evening with almost no wind at all. *Morning Cloud* was not the first home. Three of the bigger boats which had chosen the inshore route – including one of the official British entries, Sir Max Aitken's *Crusade*, and Alan Bond's *Apollo* for Australia – were already in; but adjusted for handicap, and despite having covered some 700 miles, *Morning Cloud* came out first, 51 minutes ahead of another British boat, Arthur Slater's *Prospect of Whitby*.[32]

In the moment of victory Heath's first concern seems to have been to get the crew looking respectable. ('I had told them that as we were in a winning position we had better freshen ourselves up after more than four days at sea and make ourselves look as seaman-like as possible.')[33] The politician had his eye on the pictures in the press back home. It was indeed a fairytale victory for the Leader of Her Majesty's Opposition, just months before he hoped to become Prime Minister. No British boat had won the Sydney–Hobart race since the very first event in 1945: now, with British boats first and second, Heath had shown the Australians, as he had hoped, that the British were 'not quite such a decadent people after all'.[34] If only *Morning Cloud* had been a member of the British team and not just the reserve, he could not help reflecting, Britain would have won the

Southern Cross series. That evening he left his crew for a time to
have dinner with the Governor, but rejoined the celebrations later.
Next day he flew up to Canberra to spend the day with Gorton, returning to Britain just in time for the 1970 Boat Show. There, sitting
in the cockpit of *Morning Cloud*'s sister ship, surrounded by members
of his winning crew, he gave a triumphant television interview on
'Sportsnight with Coleman'. Harold Wilson was furious.[35]

It was a tremendous achievement which briefly captured the headlines and raised his image. Yet over the years Heath never got the
credit from the British public that his sailing exploits deserved. Sailing was portrayed by the press as a rich man's sport, of no interest to
ordinary people. Like his passion for classical music at a time when
pop music was at its fashionable zenith, sailing was another élitist
pursuit which emphasised his remoteness from common experience.
Wilson's carefully cultivated philistinism – Gannex raincoat, Hud-
dersfield Town FC and HP Sauce – had wider public appeal than
Heath's highbrow interests. Heath continued to be seen as a narrow
technocrat, single-mindedly devoted to politics. Yet his commitments to politics still left him time and energy to spare. With
international sailing success now added to his near-professional
accomplishment as a musician, he was actually a phenomenally well-
rounded politician. By comparison Wilson was truly one-dimensional,
seriously interested in nothing outside politics; while a decade later
Margaret Thatcher's 'hinterland' (to use Denis Healey's word) was
narrower still. It is greatly to Heath's credit that he understood the
importance of maintaining other interests: it is still more remarkable
that he kept up both his sailing and his music to such a high standard
while Leader of the Opposition and Prime Minister. There is no
parallel to such versatility among British prime ministers since Gladstone. Yet it cut extraordinarily little ice with the electorate.

The newspapers' main interest in his sailing was to wonder how he
was able to afford it. The first *Morning Cloud*, it was widely reported,
cost £7,450 (equivalent to perhaps £60,000 today) and each subsequent boat was progressively more expensive. In the 1960s a builder's
son from Broadstairs was not expected to have this sort of money,
unless of course he were a pop singer or a film star. Ocean racing was
assumed to be the preserve of millionaires like Max Aitken or Owen
Aisher (founder of Marley Tiles). Yet there was no great mystery.
Heath was not rich, but he had earned a Cabinet Minister's salary,
(£5,000) from 1955 to 1964, and not much less (£4,500) as Leader of
the Opposition since 1965. He had no wife or children to support, no
school fees to meet and only one home. Albany, though select, was
not expensive; he had no need of a house in Bexley; and in Broadstairs he stayed with his father and stepmother. Though he was

beginning to acquire some expensive tastes – notably champagne – and he could be generous with presents to his staff, his small army of godchildren and others, he was nevertheless careful with his money. As a single man he was able to enjoy a good deal more hospitality at others' expense than he was called upon to repay. He is also distinctly good at securing sponsorship or subsidy to ease his expenditure. He persuaded Qantas to fly the crew of *Morning Cloud* to Australia for the Sydney–Hobart race at a substantial discount; on another visit to Australia the year before he was given a set of sails for *Blue Heather* II. In addition it seems that when he became leader in 1965 – the first Tory leader since Churchill without independent means – his personal finances were discreetly managed for him and his money well invested. The Tory party has ways of ensuring that its leader is not financially embarrassed.

But unquestionably the main reason that he could afford to sail was that he was unmarried. His bachelor status attracted a certain amount of coded comment in the press. The spectacle of a leading politician without the usual complement of elegant wife and smiling children ready to let slip homely details of the great man's love of gardening or hopelessness at washing up was a novelty in 1965. It added to his image as a strange, aloof, solitary man.★ But it was not in itself a political handicap. Contrary to a lot of psephological speculation, there is no evidence that the lack of a wife reduced his appeal to women voters. If anything the reverse: the popular papers made some mileage out of presenting him as an eligible bachelor, and kept trying to link his name romantically to any woman he was seen with, notably the pianist Moura Lympany. Another time they fell for a Central Office photo opportunity and snapped him with a pretty girl on his boat. There was nothing in such stories. Heath had absolutely no intention of encumbering his life with a wife – he was, as his father put it, 'married to politics'[37] – and he had an extreme fear (perhaps derived from his days as Chief Whip) of allowing himself to be touched by any whiff of gossip or scandal. The only result of reports linking him with Moura Lympany was that he dropped her for a long time like a hot brick. In public he coped rather well with the question of why he was not married. Quite early on he gave the

★ He made one clumsy effort at suggesting that he knew all about family life, in his New Year message at the end of 1966, when he drew an unusually saccharine picture of excited children at Christmas, 'knee deep in wrapping paper', and went on to talk of the 'vitality and colour . . . frankness and vigour' of the young.[36] Heath has always liked to see himself as having a special understanding of 'young people today'. His first-hand knowledge of the young is based largely on his numerous godchildren (Seligmans and others) to whom he takes his avuncular responsibility very seriously.

definitive answer to one interviewer who suggested that a wife might help him to become Prime Minister, saying that anyone who married for that reason would make neither a good Prime Minister nor a good husband. That remained his answer whenever the question was raised, and it effectively closed it.[38]

The suggestion that he might be homosexual was never raised in public, though it was certainly discussed in pubs. There were whispers of goings on in Albany, but these were prurient fantasy with no basis in fact. Heath was far too terrified of scandal to risk giving it any foothold, whatever his inclinations. The only plausibility in such rumours derived from the fact that he was not married and was said to dislike the company of women. This, however, was not so. He could certainly be shy with women, having had throughout his life relatively little to do with them; he could also be appallingly rude to them. But he was very often just as rude to men. The only difference was that women – some women – minded it more. Those Tory ladies, in particular, who expected to be complemented on their appearance and flattered with gallant courtesies were disappointed. Heath paid women the back-handed compliment of treating them exactly as he treated men.

The sort of woman Heath likes is the one who is not afraid of him, but will stand up to him, pull his leg and tease him – and whom he in turn can tease without her taking offence. Shy of paying conventional compliments, he likes a woman to whom he can be as rude as he wishes. His idea of a joke is to tell a woman that she is looking frightful. Those who can take it will pass his test and be granted a reciprocal licence to say what they like to him. Probably the chief of these strong-minded ladies is Sara Morrison – the former wife of the Member for Devizes, Charles Morrison, and a Wiltshire County Councillor in the 1960s whom Heath brought into Central Office as a Vice-Chairman of the party in 1970. As such, she was one of the few people who could tell him when he was behaving intolerably. Since 1980 she has been a Director of GEC, the Abbey National and a number of other large companies; but she remained a close and candid friend of Heath throughout the Thatcher years, often acting as an unofficial housekeeper or hostess when required.

Other women friends with this degree of intimacy are Jo Pattrick, the interior designer who helped him with the decoration of his flat in Albany, the redecoration of Downing Street in 1970 and finally his house in Wilton Street; and Clare Hollingworth, the redoubtable *Telegraph* journalist and foreign correspondent, whom he met on his first visit to China in 1974 and who has several times accompanied him on subsequent visits.

Heath's relationship with all these women represents a sort of sub-limated sexuality. By establishing at the outset a characteristic language of mutual insult he is able to exorcise the danger which a more conventional relationship with a woman might pose. By strip-ping the relationship of any sexual threat, he endows his women friends with the honorary status of a male colleague – but without the danger, which too close a relationship with a man would carry, of whispers of homosexuality.

Heath's sense of humour is an important part of the mechanism by which he keeps the world at arm's length while admitting a select few inside his defences. Calculated rudeness is one weapon: it is only the few who know that he is joking. Another characteristic technique is to make some outrageous statement with a perfectly straight face: if the person he is talking to is fool enough to take it literally he has failed the test. A good many Tory MPs have been shown up in this way: it was not a good way to make the party love him. His sense of humour is in fact distinctly cruel: he gets inordinate delight from others' discomfiture, and has a disturbing taste for practical jokes. (He once rang Moura Lympany pretending to be Sir Thomas Beech-am wanting to book her for a series of concerts: she fell for it, though one wonders how she failed to recognise his voice!)[39] He rarely tells anything that could be called a joke, which is why his efforts at injecting humour into his speeches were usually so painful. But his private conversation can be very funny in a defensive/offensive style that is entirely his own: mocking, sly, allusive, frequently bizarre and almost always ironic. The reason people so often think he has no sense of humour is that his humour is strictly not for general consumption.

In the difficult years of opposition Heath learned to distrust all but his few real friends. The easy openness which had appeared to characterise him as Chief Whip disappeared. His once-broad smile became a tense grin; his shoulder-heaving laugh became forced and awkward. In private he became prickly, irritable, quick to take offence or alternatively to retreat into brooding silence; his public persona increasingly wooden, pompous and strained. Cecil King found him in September 1967 'tense, serious and extremely difficult . . . He was obviously deeply hurt by newspaper criticisms and the opinion polls, but battling on nonetheless.'[40] Three things kept him going. The first, not to be underestimated, was his religion. 'It's not a thing that one talks about very much,' he told James Margach in 1965, 'but it has a secure hold.'[41] In fact he kept his Christian faith almost entirely hidden: he was photographed going to church far less often than Wilson, whose supposed Methodism was an important element of his Yorkshire nonconformist image. Nevertheless in his deeply private way his belief remained one of the fixed decencies of Heath's life: a lasting inheritance from his mother.

Second, there is a strong element of sheer stubbornness in Heath's character which meant not only that he was not likely to give up – there was no question of that – but that the more he was criticised the less ground he would give to his critics. He would conduct the Opposition in his own way and if the critics did not like it that only reinforced his belief that he was right. He was in a strong position, after all, with the Tories consistently far ahead in the polls and the Government surely too discredited to recover. His own low ratings were personally hurtful, but not ultimately what mattered. He came positively to despise the political arts which everyone said he lacked, and it became a matter of perverse pride that he would win without them. So he did; but he paid dearly in the long run for neglecting them.

Finally, Heath's confidence that he would win in the end was sustained by his immediate circle of loyal supporters – the inner few who saw him at his best; who shared his vision of a more affluent, leisured, classless and tolerant Britain, admired his courage and integrity and looked forward as ardently as himself to seeing him Prime Minister. Jim Prior, Douglas Hurd, Willie Whitelaw have all written of the sense of shared excitement they felt in working for Heath in these years, a comradeship intensified by the knowledge that the world at large did not appreciate his qualities. Whitelaw expressed this devotion most unreservedly in an interview with the London *Evening Standard* in October 1970, four months after Heath's General Election triumph:

> If he told me that tomorrow I should become Ambassador to Iceland I should go straight off to Iceland . . . I trust his judgement absolutely. It's not because he has charm, because he hasn't any charm. It's not because he's easy to work for, because he isn't easy to work for. I don't know what it is – it's a mystery to me. I only know I trust him more than I've ever trusted anybody.[42]

Heath's extraordinary ability to inspire this degree of loyalty in his immediate colleagues, even after he had lost the support of most of the rest of the Tory party, was to have immense and paradoxical consequences for the party and the country five years later.

To the electorate at large, however, or perhaps more accurately to the journalists whose job it was to explain him to the electorate, he remained a puzzle, even after five years as leader. Even the well-disposed *Economist* was driven to wonder in May 1970 why he was in politics at all when by all the normal canons of the trade he was so bad at it?

> Too many people still do not know what this music-loving bachelor whose hobby is yachting is doing in politics, and because he can be so obviously uncomfortable performing the public rites of politics they have come to expect him to make them feel uncomfortable too.
>
> He does not inspire awe, as an aristocrat might, and he does not seek affection or approval; he does not even try to con his way to political power. The British electorate does not expect its public men to be shy, as Mr Heath is. Strength is a virtue to many voters, especially Tory working class voters. Unadorned simplicity is not.
>
> It is a serious charge against Mr Heath that he does not appear to have learned this side of the politician's craft.[43]

His speaking style remained for the most part desperately dull – deliberately so, for he exasperated his aides by carefully cutting out all the frills and clever phrases they tried to insert into his drafts. 'Eloquence', Hugo Young reported in the *Sunday Times*, 'is artifice and trickery, and therefore deeply offends his sense of priorities.'[44] He was admirably determined to be himself. But the results were dire. His typical speech in the House of Commons was a flat catalogue, one self-contained paragraph following another, with no flow of ideas from one to the next and no unifying theme to bind them together: 'I come to the incomes policy . . . I should like now to say a word about parliamentary reform . . . I will make a few remarks about Europe . . .'[45]

Every autumn his opening speech in the debate on the Queen's Speech was virtually the same as the previous year: the same sincere but stale condemnation of the Government, the same recital of the Tory alternative. Crossman commented after his 1967 effort that his speech read well enough, but 'it was delivered with a tension and nervous tautness which made it very unconvincing. At no point did he relax, or wave an arm, or do anything to make you feel he was a live person.'[46] He annually berated the Government's programme as dreary, repetitive, unimaginative and unexciting: but the same criticism lay far more damagingly against himself, undoing in an hour the partial rehabilitation he had usually managed to achieve a few weeks previously at the party conference. Labour backbenchers, taking their cue from Wilson, jeered at Heath's inability to enthuse his own side, interrupting his attempts with cries of 'You poor fish'[47] or referring to him derisively as 'The Right Honourable Gentleman the temporary Leader of the Opposition'.[48] Like Neil Kinnock in the 1980s, he was criticised by his own backbenchers for taking up too much of Prime Minister's Question Time, instead of leaving it to others more skilled at tripping Wilson up. Perhaps as a result, for several months in 1968 he barely spoke in the House of Commons at all.

He usually did better with his annual closing address to the Tory conference, the most intensively prepared speech of the leader's year. Intensively prepared by Michael Wolff and Jim Prior, that is: for, as Prior has related, Heath himself took a strangely distant interest:

> Ted's approach was extraordinary. He was struggling to retain his control of the Party all through his years as Leader of the Opposition, yet he would hardly look at our final draft for this, his crucial annual address to the party faithful till around breakfast time on the day of his speech.
>
> I used to put our last attempt under his bedroom door at about 4 a.m. so that he could start working on it first thing in the morning. Quite often when I turned up a little after seven o'clock to see if his final version was ready for typing, he was still dressing. I found the whole business hair-raising. On one occasion I went to his room in my slippers, saying to Jane that I would only be away for a few minutes and would be back for breakfast. I ended up going to the Conference in my slippers, as I hadn't a moment to go back and change. I was having to give the speech to the typists as Ted cleared each page. With the Press we had to keep up the appearance of being calm and in control. The only person who wasn't flustered was Ted: he was very much a last-minute man.[49]

This is very curious in such a methodical man, and contrasts with his meticulous preparation of *Morning Cloud*. Was it his counter-suggestive perversity that refused to acknowledge the importance of what the press invariably built up as a major test of his position? If so, the results suggest that he should have left the preparation of more of his big speeches to his staff. For the annual conference speech was normally somewhat more high-flown, less shorn of rhetorical contrivance, than other Heath speeches. The bulk of it might be the usual catalogue of policy proposals. But his 1968 speech at Blackpool, for instance – the year of anti-Vietnam demonstrations in America, *les événements* in Paris, the Soviet invasion of Czechoslovakia – ended with a neo-Churchillian peroration invoking Britain's special responsibility to 'a world in turmoil'.

> It is in such a world of shifting currents and contrasting tides that Britain stands out as a rock, a rock of political stability throughout our history, and on that rock is a lighthouse that proclaims fairness and tolerance, democracy and freedom. Sometimes it has been shrouded in mist; sometimes its light has grown dim; but never yet has it been extinguished.
>
> It falls to us here in the Conservative Party to keep that light ablaze so that in all the turmoils and upheavals through which the world is passing men will still be able to point to Britain and say, 'There – there stands the rock to give us faith. There stands the light to guide us.'[50]

This won Heath his longest standing ovation to date, timed at seven and a half minutes.

Yet despite the occasional flight of rhetoric Heath never succeeded in shaking the public perception of him as a dry technocrat. His earnest exhortations to the British people were far too often couched in language of the deepest banality, like his December 1967 New Year message: 'This is the moment to adopt this new approach to our problems, to put first things first, to rely on individual effort, to take our destiny in our own hands.'[51] Having – despite his musical ear – no gift for language, such tired clichés came naturally to him: they had meaning to him, but they struck sparks off no one else. His attempts to sound radical and energetic were smothered by such flannel. In June 1969 David Watt in the *Financial Times* put his finger on the lack of any middle ground in Heath's speeches between detailed means and visionary ends: 'a cautious, rather uninspiring portrayal of political means (Government efficiency, businesslike methods, hard-headed realism) overlaid with extremely vague layers of rhetoric about ends (opportunity, self-respect and so forth)'.

Watt warned that there was an electoral danger in the failure to project a clear vision, for without it the Tory prescription could easily be presented by Labour as a narrow class policy with nothing to offer the skilled workers whose votes the Tories would need to win. The Opposition was still far ahead in the opinion polls. Yet, Watt predicted:

> There seems a strong chance that these voters will flock back to Labour when the economic cost for them of Tory policy becomes

plain . . . The fact is that you cannot get people of any class or age to give much of themselves to the idea of business efficiency.[52]

It is the central paradox of Heath's career that he was unable to get his vision of Britain's future across to commentators or the electorate, since very few British politicians of recent times have been driven by a loftier view of high national purposes. Business efficiency was only meant to be a means to higher goals. His vision was indeed vague – a Britain at once classless, competitive and compassionate, and above all European: a forward-looking, progressive Britain that should still conserve the best of its inheritance from the past. Perhaps it was contradictory. But it was no vaguer or more contradictory than most political programmes – or than any successful political programme probably has to be. Nor was it the vagueness or the contradictions which stopped the message getting through. It was Heath's cold and unappealing public personality which was unable to project it. He wanted to be the leader of Britain's national regeneration – a sort of British Roosevelt or de Gaulle. But he lacked the power to communicate his vision. He could only project business efficiency. So even when he won, he won largely by default and without the public understanding of his purpose which was needed to accomplish it.

Nevertheless things started to look up sharply for Heath towards the end of 1969. If one incident more than any other marked a shift of mood it was the Government's humiliation by the trade unions over *In Place of Strife*, which for many destroyed the last vestiges of Labour's authority and credibility. In the House of Commons, *The Times* reported, Heath 'showed a new and impressive confidence as he thrashed Mr Wilson unmercifully'.[53] *The Economist* too was struck by his 'growing self-confidence': 'In all his recent public appearances he has given the impression that he is convinced that he will be the next Prime Minister and that he is reconciled to his standing in the opinion polls remaining low until he has proved himself in that office.'[54]

His sailing triumph at the turn of the year gave a fresh boost to his belief that he was on the way at last, as Crossman in the privacy of his diary acknowledged:

I suppose there is one other thing that, as a party, we have to admit – the new enthusiasm, courage and drive of Ted Heath, who rather gallantly went out to Australia and won the first prize in the great Sydney–Hobart yacht race. He's back again with his cup, and now this week he showed real courage in standing up to an even more provocative racial speech by Enoch Powell. Ted dismissed him as inhuman and made it clear that he'll have nothing to do with Powell. I would say Heath has reached his nadir and is now on the way up.[55]

The climax of this recovery was the Selsdon Park conference at the end of January. After five frustrating years of opposition, enjoying huge leads in the opinion polls yet failing to excite any positive enthusiasm for the alternative they offered, the Tories finally made a breakthrough in public recognition. Yet it came about almost by accident. Ironically the success of Selsdon owed more to the derided gimmickry of Harold Wilson – backfiring, for once, against himself – than to the deliberate efforts of Conservative Central Office. 'Selsdon' was a public relations windfall which became a potent – but doubled-edged – myth.

It was planned merely as a weekend gathering of the Shadow Cabinet to pull together the strands of the policy exercise in readiness for a General Election some time in the coming year and make sure that they all knew the details – a recognition that some of the policy-making had been less than collective. The Research Department was desperate to get them all under one roof and keep them there until they had gone through the whole prospective programme. (Willie Whitelaw yearned for the golf course, but it was strictly a working weekend.) It was not intended as a public relations event at all until the press found out about it and turned up at lunchtime on Saturday, with television crews, wanting pictures and statements. Something had to be thrown together hurriedly for them. Iain Macleod with his usual cynicism suggested that law and order always went down well. In fact, as Robert Carr has recalled, 'It hadn't been discussed during the weekend at all and it had nothing to do with what we had been talking about.'[56] As it happened, however, both Quintin Hogg, the Shadow Home Secretary, and Peter Rawlinson, Shadow Attorney-General, had recently made speeches calling for a stronger emphasis on law and order – in particular a change in the law of trespass to cover demonstrations. The press put two and two together and assumed a concerted offensive. As a result the Sunday papers on 1 February were full of stories that the Tories were going to come out with a tough new attack on crime.

Monday's papers broadened the picture but still presented the conference as having consolidated a swing to the right. *The Times* reported that the Tories' five legislative priorities on coming into office would be tax cuts, trade union reform, higher pensions for the over-eighties, law and order and immigration control.[57] Of these, three could be regarded as aggressively right wing. Some papers applauded the new thrust, others were disturbed by it. *The Economist* was worried by the exploitation of social problems which it believed should not be party issues. Titling its cover story 'The Stainless Steel Tories', with a picture of the Shadow Cabinet captioned 'The hard men', it warned: 'Mr Heath and his friends emerged from their Croydon weekend looking like the next Government all right – but not a visibly compassionate one.'[58]

The impression that the Tories had adopted a hardline policy on immigration and policing was quickly seized on by Wilson and skilfully combined with the allegation that the Tories were planning to dismantle the Welfare State and return to the capitalist jungle. He invented a composite model of the new breed of hard-faced Tory – economically liberal but socially authoritarian – which he christened 'Selsdon Man': 'Selsdon Man is not just a lurch to the right, it is an atavistic desire to reverse the course of 25 years of social revolution. What they are planning is a wanton, calculated and deliberate return to greater inequality.'[59]

'Selsdon Man' was a brilliant phrase, but it rebounded on Wilson, first because it lent the Opposition's earnest catalogue of humdrum policies precisely the cloak of philosophic unity and political impact that they had hitherto lacked, and second because it turned out that the electorate was at least as much attracted as repelled by them. At a stroke Wilson had succeeded, as Heath and all his advisers had consistently failed to do, in sharpening the Tories' image and opening up the appearance of a clear political choice between Labour and Conservative.

The spotlight that was suddenly turned on Tory policies, and the pictures all over the papers of the Shadow Cabinet chatting in the grounds of Selsdon Park, brought into every home the reality of an alternative Government in waiting. 'It was', the *Spectator* commented, 'a good week for Mr Heath, who returned from the Tory weekend council of war ... to celebrate his jubilation on "Panorama", "News At Ten" and "Woman's Hour".'[60] Dick Crossman watched 'the new confident Heath' on 'Panorama' and 'found him extremely unconvincing'.

He was jumping down the throats of the two people who were examining him, being rude and domineering, interrupting them. I don't think he made a particularly attractive impression, but I suppose from the point of view of proving that he was on top of his form, even this appearance was a good follow-up to the Selsdon Conference.[61]

'Has Ted Heath broken through at last?' asked Alan Watkins in the *New Statesman*, recalling other moments in recent history when a party leader had suddenly gripped the public imagination: Macmillan in 1958, Hugh Gaitskell in 1961, Wilson in 1963.

Is early 1970, the time of winning the great yacht race and answering back Mr Robin Day on television . . . the time of Mr Heath's emergence? Enough people have been saying so . . . to make last weekend's conference at least a highly successful exercise in public relations. And if enough people keep saying so, then I suppose Mr Heath really has emerged. Yet he remains exactly the same person as he was six months ago.

The difference was that 'For the first time since 1966 Conservative politicians have convinced themselves that they can win.' As a result they were all belatedly jumping on Heath's bandwagon.[62]

But Wilson's phrase, though in the short run it may have helped Heath into Downing Street, rebounded against Heath too. For in 1970 he *was* 'Selsdon Man'. As with the glamorously dynamic image that was briefly foisted on him in 1965 he went along with it, smiling nervously, content after all his trials to ride the wave wherever it took him. He allowed himself to be identified with ideas and attitudes which were not really his own. He thus encouraged expectations among right-wing Conservatives (including a new generation who entered Parliament for the first time on his coat-tails in 1970, typified by Norman Tebbit) which he was bound to disappoint. Conversely, by allowing himself to appear hard-faced, reactionary and doctrinaire, he antagonised a swathe of centre, progressive and trade union opinion whose support – or at least assent – he was going to need in the years ahead. It took Heath a long time to shake off 'Selsdon Man'. And even when he did, it remained a skeleton in his cupboard which his critics could rattle gleefully in the years after 1975 whenever he criticised Mrs Thatcher for departures from Tory tradition.

The philosophy of 'Selsdon Man', as formulated in certain phrases of the 1970 manifesto *A Better Tomorrow* and in a number of other dogmatic-sounding statements by Heath himself and others during and after the election, was widely perceived as signalling a decisive break with the postwar 'Butskellite' consensus and the 'One Nation' Toryism in which Heath's career had started. From the perspective of the 1980s it could be represented as proto-Thatcherite. It was claimed by Mrs Thatcher's admirers that he had fought the 1970 election on essentially the same prospectus that she offered in 1979, with the difference that she had the courage to stick to her convictions whereas he, a decade earlier, had not. There is a limited degree of truth in this analysis, notably with regard to trade union reform and the intention to create an economic climate conducive to enterprise. But to a much greater degree it reflects the misunderstanding which Heath allowed to arise – indeed positively encouraged – by going along with an aggressively free-market rhetoric which he did not in his heart accept. Behind this superficial rhetoric there was abundant confirmation scattered throughout *A Better Tomorrow* that Heath's essential views – his belief in regional policy, for instance – had not changed. He never intended to break the postwar social settlement accepted by Churchill, Eden, Macmillan and Home. His proposed 'revolution' was all about trying to change attitudes and remove obstacles to growth within the existing economic and social structure. His purpose was to persuade the country to perform better by means of relatively minor tinkering with incentives and restraints; it was not fundamentally to change the Government's role in relation to the economy.

It was a fatal error for Heath to allow himself to be thought to have more radical intentions than in fact he had. He ended up between two stools, convincingly neither one thing nor the other: a fierce bark, with no real intention to bite – but the bark was enough to antagonise those he sincerely wanted to make 'social partners' in his new competitive/co-operative Britain. The result of his 'Selsdon' aberration effectively ensured that neither the initial policies with which he started out in Government in 1970–1 nor those to which he turned in 1972–4 when he repudiated 'Selsdon' carried sufficient moral or political conviction to succeed. Heath's failure in government stemmed from this confusion.

13

Victory from the Jaws of Defeat

THE welcome boost which the Selsdon conference and his triumph in Australia gave to Heath's self-confidence, however, served only temporarily to disguise a more disturbing trend in the direction of the opinion polls since the previous autumn. Though the results of the different polling organisations (Gallup, NOP, ORC) were inconsistent from month to month, all three had shown a narrowing of the Tory lead to single figures in the last quarter of 1969. By March the Selsdon effort had come and gone and the trend was resumed, giving the Opposition a still useful but no longer overwhelming lead of between 5·5 per cent and 7·5 per cent. In April Gallup showed the gap closing further to only 3·5 per cent. Several reasons may have contributed to the Government's remarkable recovery. First, there is a well-established tendency for voters to move back towards the Government as an election approaches: the huge leads piled up by oppositions in mid-term are generally somewhat unreal. Second, that process was helped in this case by the Government's apparent success in at last getting on top of the balance-of-payments problem. Devaluation and successive bites of deflation finally had their effect: the trade figures inched into surplus in September and continued to improve. Third, the abandonment of pay restraint in 1969 had produced a wages explosion, while prices had not yet had time to catch up. All these factors were already operating to reduce the Tories' lead before the end of 1969. They were reinforced in mid-April by Roy Jenkins's studiously responsible Budget, which disappointed Labour MPs by eschewing pre-election bribes (and was subsequently blamed by some for the loss of the election) but which seems to have impressed a majority of the electorate by its restraint.

In May Labour's revival continued. In the local council elections the party recaptured several hundred seats which it had lost over the previous three years with a swing large enough to see the Government re-elected with a majority of 50, and the polls showed Labour moving into the lead: on 13 May Gallup gave Labour a lead of 7·5 per cent. With everything suddenly coming up roses, Wilson could not resist seizing the moment for an opportunist election. As well as the obvious political benefit of going to the country before prices began to catch up with pay, Wilson was swayed by the supposed advantage to the Government of a summer election, the shrewd calculation that a June poll would be likely to catch more Tory than Labour voters away on holiday, and the gamble that England successfully defending the World Cup in Mexico would somehow reflect vicarious glory on Labour. For all these reasons, Wilson took the plunge while the going seemed good and, on 18 May, called a General Election for 18 June.

Suddenly, after all his dogged efforts, Heath was facing defeat – or even the humiliation of being thrown over on the starting line. Only weeks after the party had finally seemed to be rallying to him with new enthusiasm, rumours sprang up once again that it was after all ready to ditch him. 'I have never seen a party plunged more suddenly . . . into such black despair,' James Margach wrote in the *Sunday Times*.[1] There was wild talk among the backbenchers of bringing back Sir Alec, who had so nearly salvaged victory in 1964. Just for a moment Heath himself seemed ready to throw in the towel. 'Ted was very depressed and dejected,' Jim Prior has written, 'and it showed through in his every word and action.' On 17 May, when election fever was already in the air, he made a terrible speech to the conference of the Industrial Society in London. His staff were alarmed. Michael Wolff sent Prior to tell Heath that he must 'snap out of it. Another performance like that and we are all lost.' With some trepidation Prior delivered his message, but found that Heath's wobble had passed. 'He had great reserves of inner strength. Not much had come easy to him in life. He had fought hard for most things and because he was a loner he was dependent on his own strength and no one else's.'[2] Whitelaw and Barber were sent off to rally the party in the House and in the country and Heath prepared to fight back, starting with a much more effective speech to the Scottish Tory conference in Perth that weekend.

When in the event, against all predictions, the Tories won the election, there was a rush among Heath's senior colleagues to claim that they had never doubted the result for a moment. If so they kept their confidence very much to themselves. It is often said that Iain Macleod was confident throughout; but Willie Whitelaw, who with rare honesty confesses that he never expected anything but defeat, has pointed out that Macleod was a gambler who liked betting on long odds. Though he went about predicting a Tory majority of 35, Whitelaw does not believe that he believed it: a view confirmed by Macleod's biographer Nigel Fisher, who quotes Macleod confiding grimly, 'We'll go out and have a bloody good fight, but I am worried about Ted.'[3] Among themselves the concern of Whitelaw, Carrington and most of Heath's close colleagues had frankly switched to damage limitation and how to stop Powell seizing the leadership following a Tory defeat.[4]

'From the apparent certainty of overwhelming victory,' reflected *The Economist*, 'the Conservative party has now slumped to the almost equally apparent certainty of humiliating defeat . . . The sudden turnaround in public opinion is the biggest test of character that could have been devised for Mr Wilson and Mr Heath alike.'[5] The anonymous writer was absolutely right; moreover both leaders reacted perfectly in character. Wilson, from the moment he announced the election puffing genially on his pipe in the sunny garden of 10 Downing Street, ran a complacent, relaxed and superficial campaign, moving for the benefit of the television cameras from one presidential-style walkabout to another, shrugging off his opponent with well-practised jokes but rarely making a speech and saying almost nothing about what a re-elected Labour Government would do. Heath, conversely, after his brief wobble, drew strength from adversity and plugged on doggedly with a full programme of set speeches, hammering away relentlessly at Labour's abysmal record and the Tories' plans. Despite all the doubts about his appeal, the Tory campaign concentrated as heavily on Heath as Labour's did on Wilson. Heath took the press conferences in London every morning before flying off around the country in a chartered plane. He was featured in the party's opening and closing television broadcasts. Gradually, although he appeared to be making no impression whatever on the polls and his defeat was still taken for granted, the political commentators began to recognise that he was fighting the more professional and effective campaign.

The tone was set by the manifesto, *A Better Tomorrow*, which was unusually well produced and well written compared with Labour's much more hastily produced and clumsily titled *Now Britain's Strong – Let's Make Her Great To Live In*. Like *Action Not Words* in 1966 it opened with a personal foreword by Heath (the first draft was actually written by David Howell) which emphasised his belief that the central issue of the election was the quality of government. There followed a damning indictment of Wilson's style of political management:

During the last six years we have suffered not only from bad policies, but from a cheap and trivial style of government. Decisions have been dictated simply by the desire to catch tomorrow's headlines. The short-term gain has counted for everything: the long-term objective has gone out of the window.

In place of this opportunist shambles Heath promised, in the key phrase of his campaign, to introduce 'a new style of government' which should 're-establish our sound and honest British traditions in this field':

I want to see a fresh approach to the taking of decisions. The Government should seek the best advice and listen carefully to it. It should not rush into decisions, it should use up-to-date techniques for assessing the situation, it should be deliberate and thorough.

So far, so good. But then came the categoric pledge which would come back to haunt Heath after 1972:

Finally, once a decision is made, once a policy is established, the Prime Minister and his colleagues should have the courage to stick to it. Nothing has done Britain more harm in the world than the endless backing and filling which we have seen in recent years . . . courage and intellectual honesty are essential qualities in politics, and in the interest of our country it is high time that we saw them again.[6]

Defining 'courage' and 'intellectual honesty' so bluntly as sticking to predetermined policies through thick and thin, no matter how circumstances might change, was the most imprudent of several hostages to fortune with which *A Better Tomorrow* was studded.

'Coming from a lesser man', Douglas Hurd has written, the foreword 'might have been claptrap, but from him it was not':

There runs through it a note of genuine puritan protest, which is familiar in British history, sometimes in one party, sometimes in the other. It is the note struck by Pym against the court of Charles I, by Pitt against the Fox–North coalition, by Gladstone against Disraeli, by the Conservatives in 1922 against Lloyd George. It is the outraged assertion of a strict view of what public life is about, after a period in which its rules have been perverted and its atmosphere corrupted.[7]

The manifesto itself contained few surprises. So clearly had the priorities been set at the very beginning of Heath's leadership, and then merely filled out by the policy exercise of the following five years, that it was remarkably little changed from the programme on which the party had fought and lost in 1966. Despite the decoy flown at Selsdon, there was no particular emphasis on law and order. What was new was the uncompromising language in which a number of promises were couched. As a result *A Better Tomorrow* offered at least four more specific hostages to fortune in addition to Heath's generalised rejection of 'backing and filling'. For anyone who wished to read them, however, there were plenty of let-out clauses for the U-turns to come.

The first hostage was the absolute repudiation of statutory incomes policy, apparently on principle: 'Labour's compulsory wage control was a failure and we will not repeat it.' And again, more categoric still: 'We utterly reject the philosophy of compulsory wage control.'[8] But this unequivocal assertion was followed by a much weaker statement of the alternative: 'We want instead to get production up and encourage everyone to give of their best.' Moreover it was preceded by a broad caveat which could later be used to justify any form of incomes policy that might become necessary: 'In implementing all our policies, the need to curb inflation will come first.'[9]

Second, the section entitled 'Industrial Progress' began by stating boldly: 'We reject the detailed intervention of Socialism which usurps the functions of management and seeks to dictate prices and earnings in industry.' It went on to reaffirm not only that 'We are totally opposed to further nationalisation of British industry' (which must have seemed a pretty safe assertion for a Conservative Opposition) but also that 'We will progressively reduce the involvement of the State in the nationalised industries ... so as to improve their competitiveness.' However these firm declarations of intent were again followed by curiously tentative alternatives: 'We much prefer a system of general pressures, creating an economic climate which favours, and rewards, enterprise and efficiency. Our aim is to identify and remove obstacles that prevent effective competition and initiative.' Conversely there were clear undertakings to increase investment in roads, railways and ports, to continue 'special assistance for particular industries like shipping' and to pursue 'an effective regional development policy'. Most unambiguously, and significantly at a time when unemployment was already rising following Labour's post-devaluation deflation: 'We are not prepared to tolerate the human waste and suffering that accompany persistent unemployment, dereliction and decline.'[10]

Away from economic policy, the section on immigration and race relations contained the clear undertaking 'There will be no further large-scale permanent immigration.' But again the words 'large-scale' and 'permanent' were open to some interpretation, while the previous sentence reserved a loophole that might have been expressly designed to make an exception of the Ugandan Asians: 'These policies mean that future immigration will be allowed only in strictly-defined special cases.'[11]

Finally, on the question of Europe the manifesto did *not*, as is often alleged, promise not to take Britain into the Common Market without 'the full-hearted consent' of the British people. (That hostage was offered later.) It did, however, lay surprising emphasis on the possibility that the cost of entry might be too high: 'Obviously there is a price we would not be prepared to pay . . . Our sole commitment is to negotiate; no more, no less.' It would then be for Parliament to decide. 'Ministers and Members will listen to the views of their constituents and have in mind, as is natural and legitimate, primarily the effect of entry upon the standard of living of the individual citizens whom they represent.'[12]

These assurances attracted little notice during the election, since all three parties were now in favour of entry and Europe was therefore not a campaign issue. The Tories had to cover themselves against the charge that they were so committed that they would join on any terms; on the other hand Labour were so confident that it would be they who would be conducting the negotiations that they did not bother to pay the close attention to the Tory manifesto that they might have done. Only after 1971 did opponents of British entry, both Conservative and Labour, exhume the careful wording of *A Better Tomorrow* to allege that Heath was driving the European legislation through Parliament in defiance of his mandate.

For four years the Tories had expected that the election when it came would be a crisis election, fought amid the incontestable evidence of Labour's failure. 'High unemployment, record taxation, enormous overseas debts,' Heath had told the Tory conference at Brighton the previous October. 'Fight on that record? You bet we will. We will wrap that record round them, time and again, night after night, day after day, and they will sink like a stone.'[13] Yet now that the election was here, it was not like that at all. Houdini-like, Wilson had somehow contrived to go to the country in warm summer sunshine, with the balance of payments at last in healthy surplus and Labour apparently coasting to victory on a warm tide of national well-being. 'For Mr Heath of all politicians', wrote Peter Paterson in the *Spectator*, 'this is an unhappy plight. Stern as Gladstone, stubborn as Attlee, the Tory leader detests opposition and its attendant humiliations. Now, after years of careful preparation and planning, he is faced with a vacuum election in terms of issues. What is he to do?'[14]

He tried to bang on at Labour's record and the Tories' alternative plans, but the electorate was not interested and – as in 1966 – Wilson declined to respond. Instead Heath increasingly concentrated on the themes of his foreword, the alleged lowering of political standards and Britain's international prestige under Labour and his personal mission to restore them. The danger was that by choosing to fight on style Heath was paradoxically fighting on Wilson's strengths. Despite or because of all his trickiness, Wilson remained astonishingly popular, admired for his quick-wittedness and cheeky humour; conversely Heath, despite or because of his earnestness, was widely regarded as a priggish bore. (Transport House actually considered using a picture of Heath as a Labour poster, but rejected it as below the belt.)[15] The most galling thing for Heath, believing passionately that he offered the country the moral and political antithesis of Wilson, must have been the difficulty many commentators had in seeing any difference between them. A Liberal poster portrayed the two leaders as identical, asking, 'Which twin is the Tory?'

Even *The Times*, though it commended Heath for telling the country the truth and endorsed him as likely to make a better Prime Minister than Wilson, did so with remarkably little enthusiasm and a clear impression that the difference was fairly marginal.[16] Most observers of the campaign – influenced by their assumption that Wilson was going to win – stressed the difference between Wilson's easy, confident, boastful style of electioneering, always apparently surrounded by eager crowds, and Heath's remote formality. Heath, an *Economist* reporter wrote, was 'never less than the commanding officer, flying from one mass meeting to the next' in his 50-seat Dart Herald, flanked by aides in blue suits, blue shirts and blue ties, but scorning to talk to the journalists who filled the plane, who all took it for granted he was going to lose. At each venue he lectured the troops with the 'stiff, crisp manner' and 'military bark' of a staff officer, 'using a basic vocabulary, hammering home some well-tried jokes with elephantine subtlety'. Unlike Wilson, Heath always seemed to be alone. 'If it goes on like this, people are going to believe that no other Tory leader wishes to be seen dead with Ted Heath.' When Heath claimed that he had actually met more voters than any other leader, the writer commented cruelly: 'No journalist had the heart to ask him if that was why he was so unpopular.'[17]

The contest seemed so one-sided that commentators began to feel sorry for Heath. 'There is a streak of cruelty in Wilson's performance,' wrote George Gale in the *Spectator*. 'Wilson has begun to flaunt his own superiority. The performance . . . is . . . somewhat gruesome, like bullfighting, cock-baiting [or] fish-teasing.'[18] Wilson had a lot of fun with Heath's portable stage set, which was carted around with him from meeting to meeting: a pale blue background with concentric circles against which Heath was seen every night on television repeating his starchy exhortations. The circles, Wilson jeered, 'represent a vortex, up into the middle of which Heath will disappear, shortly before polling day'.[19]

Nevertheless it was Heath who got in the best joke of the campaign, when someone threw an egg at Wilson:

> The implications of this are really very serious . . . because this was a secret meeting on a secret tour which nobody was supposed to know about, and what it shows is that there are men walking the streets today, also women, with eggs in their pockets just on the offchance that they'll meet the leader of the Labour party.[20]

Slowly, but almost unnoticed by the commentators, Heath's dogged insistence that all was not suddenly rosy in Labour's garden began to drip through. Valuable corroboration was provided by the former Governor of the Bank of England, Lord Cromer, who asserted on 'Panorama' on 1 June that there was 'no question that any government that comes into power is going to find a very much more difficult financial situation than the new government found in 1964'.[21] Heath was initially slow to exploit Cromer's gift, fearing to be seen unpatriotically talking up a crisis as he had accused Labour of doing in 1964. Increasingly, however, as the polls failed to respond, such scruples were forgotten and Cromer's words were featured regularly in Tory speeches and broadcasts. The latter – masterminded by Geoffrey Tucker – were particularly effective. In place of the tired format of politicians talking to camera, they used two smoothly accomplished presenters, Christopher Chataway and Geoffrey Johnson-Smith, in a set built to resemble ITV's 'News at Ten', introducing a quickfire montage of anti-Government grievances with spurious impartiality, interspersed with even shorter mock 'commercials', showing a wastepaper basket full of Labour promises, a frozen wage packet and – most vivid of all – a pound note being steadily snipped away with scissors. Private polls showed that the theme of rising prices was the one which most worried the voters. Having stumbled at last on a potentially winning issue the Tories concentrated on it, as the campaign developed, with increasing ruthlessness and skill.

At the end of the first week the Tory leaders gathered in Albany for a council of war. It was by all accounts a gloomy meeting, but it was early days yet and Heath was not discouraged. In view of the fine weather and the absence of the sort of noisy demonstrations that had originally persuaded the Tory strategists to restrict Heath's appearances to all-ticket rallies, it was decided that Heath should copy Wilson by getting out more to meet the voters. This he did in the second week, with considerable success, notably at Exeter, Edinburgh and Manchester. (Less so at Norwich, where the streets were deserted: it turned out, embarrassingly, to be early-closing day.)[22] Heath was surprisingly good at personal electioneering. 'The well-worn argument about his lack of the common touch', Hurd noted, 'applied to a different part of his life. I quickly learned that Mr Heath felt far more at home in a crowded street than at a dull lunch party, or a difficult press interview.'[23] Yet the polls failed to reflect the good response Heath felt he was getting on the ground. His worst moment came as he left the platform following a good meeting at Manchester on 12 June, to be told by a journalist that the NOP poll in the next day's *Daily Mail* gave Labour a 12·4 per cent lead. 'I can remember that blank look on his face,' Hurd wrote later. The same evening they received the advance text of a speech Enoch Powell was to deliver the next day. 'He seemed determined that we should lose, and lose badly. It was a dramatic and unsettling moment.'[24] When Jim Prior rang him the next morning to discuss his response, Heath fleetingly allowed himself to admit the possibility of defeat. 'If we are to go down,' he told Prior, 'we will at least go down honourably and with our flags flying.'[25]

In South Croydon later that morning he tried once more to prick the bubble of Labour's complacency. The country, he declared, had never looked more beautiful. There was only one thing wrong.

> As a people we are in danger of falling asleep. As a people we have been flattered and lulled for too long by a trivial Government. The real problems, the real issues have been kept from us as if we were children. We have been fed on a fare of gimmick and instant government . . .

Other European countries already enjoyed higher standards of life and leisure, arts, sport and travel. Other countries took more risks and reaped the rewards. Others made better provision for the old and helpless. Britain already lagged behind.

> My warning, which is given with all the force at my command, is this: As things stand, we are contracting out of the 20th century.

As things stand, we are throwing away our opportunities through sheer inertia and trivial government.

My message is this: Unless Britain wakes up, Britain will lose the future.[26]

As the vultures gathered around the Heath campaign, Enoch Powell chose his moment to deliver what looked like the *coup de grâce*. In four explosive speeches, skilfully delayed to detonate in the last week of a dull campaign, he returned unrepentantly to the subject of immigration, insisting that he had hitherto underestimated the figures and alleging a conspiracy within the Foreign Office to suppress the truth; he denounced the all-party agreement to 'smuggle' Britain into the EEC by stealth; and he accused the 'enemy within' of brainwashing the British people to accept the subversion of their historic institutions.[27] He did not directly attack Heath, but everything he said seemed designed to emphasise his contempt for him – stealing the headlines, showing up Heath's oratorical inadequacy and ensuring that Heath's morning press conferences were taken up with nothing but questions about Powell. It seemed evident that Powell had decided that Heath was going to lose and was positioning himself to capture the party. On 16 June, while making bitterly clear his own exclusion from any possibility of office, Powell made a final, outwardly loyal but carefully double-edged appeal to the electorate to vote nevertheless for a Conservative Government.[28] When, two days later, the country did exactly that, this speech enabled Powell's supporters to claim that it was his last-minute advice that had turned the scales.

But several factors helped to turn the scales in the last few days. Monday 15 June was, with hindsight, the day the tide turned. First, the Heath camp decided that the only way to stop his press conferences being entirely taken up with questions about Powell – Would he repudiate Powell as a Conservative candidate? Would he expel him from the party? – was to state firmly at the outset that he would not accept any more. Amazingly it worked, and that morning Heath gave his most positive performance of the campaign. Then, as he toured West London marginals, the May trade figures were announced, showing – after nine months in the black – a sudden dip back into the red. Labour tried to explain it as an aberration due to the exceptional purchase of four jumbo jets. But the balance-of-payments surplus was the one clear success the Government had to boast of; and now it was suddenly called into question. Heath's warnings of a fresh crisis looming seemed to have been vindicated. Third, the previous evening Wilson's gamble on England repeating their 1966 victory in the World Cup came unstuck when West Germany came back from 2–0 down with twenty minutes left to win 3–2. Wilson quickly tried to distance the Government from this traumatic national defeat. But the psychological jolt was considerable. A short letter to *The Times* on polling day made the connection with uncanny prescience.

> Sir,
>
> Thinking of strange reversals of fortune: Could it be that Harold Wilson is 2-nil up with 20 minutes to play?
>
> Yours faithfully
> Peter Grosvenor[29]

Finally, on 15 June Heath made a notably successful final television broadcast. It began with a sequence of film showing him campaigning over the previous few days, mingling with people, signing autographs, drinking beer and apparently enjoying himself, while Christopher Chataway's voice explained that this was the real Ted Heath: 'not an easy man to know, but a man to trust'. He would be 'the best-equipped Prime Minister ever'. Then, following pictures of his victory in the Sydney–Hobart race, Heath himself came on to draw an explicit parallel between his ambitions for Britain and that achievement, explaining that the phrase 'a better tomorrow' came from a man in Australia who had told him 'everyone knows that tomorrow will be better than today'.

> Nobody in this country would say that. Not these days. And yet, why not? . . . We may be a small island. We're not a small people . . . For the last six years the Government of this country . . . have let us be treated as second rate. They even plan for us to stay second rate. Because that's what Labour policies mean . . . Now I don't intend to stand by and see this happen . . . Do you want a better tomorrow? . . . That's what I will work for with all my strength and with all my heart. I give you my word and I will keep my word.[30]

The Tories' private polls showed that this broadcast made an unusually good impression; also that the warning of another economic crisis was beginning to be believed and that more people now trusted the Tories than Labour to deal with it if it came.[31] Even the sunny weather clouded over. Quite suddenly Heath seemed to get a whiff of victory. 'We are winning this election,' he insisted, and he sounded as if he believed it. 'Our canvasses show excellent results. Everything shows we are going to win. Some people are going to be in for an awful lot of shocks.'[32] *The Economist* noted the new confidence with which he brushed aside Powell, pounced on the trade figures ('He punched home the half truth. He was doing a Wilson with a vengeance'), took off his coat and plunged into the shopping centres. 'He looked so good at all this that some strong men among his colleagues nearly wept that he had not started in this mood three weeks before . . . As a sheer slugging political infighter, Mr Heath at last came good in the last week of the campaign.'[33]

The polls did not have time to catch up with the change, however, and the papers' summing up of the campaign, even as they paid tribute to his improved performance, still took it for granted that he had fought bravely in a losing cause. The *Spectator*'s political correspondent, George Gale, described the attitude of the journalists who had followed Heath's campaign as one of 'sorrowing admiration'. 'Witnessing Heath's electoral ordeal has been painful.' Yet his 'wounded dignity . . . in the last week of the campaign may persist longer in the recollection than the false heartiness of his laughter, the blueness of his suits and shirts and ties, the awful knotted ganglion of his nervous tension'.[34]

Yet the press should have known what was going on. A number of Labour figures had private doubts. Wilson's political secretary Marcia Williams became worried by the contrast coming over on the television between Wilson's rumpled appearance and joky backchat in half-empty committee rooms and Heath, fit, tanned and silver-haired, punching out his message night after night to packed halls against the same cool blue background.[35] As early as the last Saturday – that is *before* Heath's late improvement – Barbara Castle was confiding to her diary:

> I wish there weren't another five days before the election! I don't believe those poll figures, and although Heath is making such a pathetic showing personally and is getting such a bad press, I have a haunting feeling that there is a silent majority sitting behind its lace curtains, waiting to come out and vote Tory.[36]

That was certainly the impression of most Tory workers in the constituencies. Heath was right: the local canvass returns *were* good. But the nationwide opinion polls were so uniformly bad, and the polls were regarded with such complete veneration – they had never been more than 1–2 per cent out since 1945 – that most candidates and local associations on the ground drew the (personally flattering) conclusion that their own constituency was untypical. Canvassing a Lowestoft housing estate the day after the devastating NOP poll giving Labour a 12 per cent lead, Jim Prior 'was never more depressed and simply discounted the good response I was getting as being no more than politeness. It was very positive, yet I simply didn't believe it.'[37] Those not fighting seats themselves had broader grounds for confidence. After the election Ted Leather, a deputy chairman of the party, wrote to *The Economist* that in nineteen marginals he had visited he had spoken to only one candidate who was not confident of winning (and he was right). There was even one little-noticed opinion poll which spotted the trend: as early as 1 June ORC picked up a small anti-Labour swing in key marginals.

The puzzling question is why the journalists covering the election around the country failed to register this Tory optimism on the ground or – if any did – why they failed to grasp what it might mean. The answer would seem to be that like everyone else, but with less excuse, they allowed themselves to be blinded by the polls. Instead of setting out with an open mind to report what was happening in the constituencies, the press took the result as given and set themselves only to explain why, despite the record of the last six years, Harold Houdini was nevertheless winning and poor old boring Ted was once more doomed to defeat. The leading commentators attached themselves too closely to the travelling entourages of the party leaders – who were themselves mesmerised by the polls – and paid too little attention to the rank-and-file party workers who were taking the pulse of the nation on the doorsteps. As Douglas Hurd wryly observed, 'Two of them were already writing a book during the campaign to explain how we had lost. Their starting point was the evidence of the opinion polls, and they sought diligently for incidents and anecdotes to reinforce that evidence, discarding other information which pointed to the direction in which they were not looking.'*[38]

It has never been fully explained why the polls were so wrong. There is evidence of a late swing in the final days of the campaign. The very last ORC poll published in the *Evening Standard* on polling day gave the Tories a 1 per cent lead. This was based on a late re-interview of just 257 voters, of whom 14 had changed their intention from Labour to Conservative since their previous interview.[39] The

---

* The book, hastily rewritten after 18 June, was Andrew Alexander and Alan Watkins, *The Making of the Prime Minister* (Macdonald, 1970).

bad trade figures, Heath's final broadcast, Powell's advice and the loss of the World Cup have all been adduced as possible reasons for such a swing. At the same time both the Tories' 'deep' polls over the previous five years and their canvassing returns during the campaign suggest that a Tory victory was always on the cards. The only safe conclusion would seem to be that Labour's lead in May represented no more than the tentative beginnings of a recovery from the depths of the previous few years; it had not yet put down deep enough roots to sustain the Government through a three-week campaign when the electorate was systematically reminded of the gap between its promise and its achievement. Wilson's haste to seize the favourable moment left him vulnerable to the suspicion that renewed difficulties might indeed be around the corner; Heath might be dull, but his evident sincerity, the Tories' superior broadcasts and better organisation on the ground, and their effective exploitation of worry about rising prices steadily exposed Labour's lack of any new proposals. Crossman's post-mortem was pretty accurate:

> In the last three days of the campaign Heath's warnings had begun to count, particularly his final warning on the trade figures and . . . the threat of a further devaluation . . . Harold's comfy, complacent, good-humoured mixing with the crowds hadn't been able to sustain itself for more than a fortnight and by the end of the second week the voice of doom, the endless repetitive reminders of rising prices, broken promises, unfavourable trade figures, all took their toll.[40]

It was not in fact true that the Tories predicted a second devaluation. The charge arose from a detailed economic briefing which was made available to the press as background material on 16 June, in the course of which it was stated that Labour policies might lead to another devaluation if continued for some years. Heath and Macleod did not make an issue of it. Rather it was Wilson who impetuously rushed in to attack the Opposition for unpatriotically launching a run on the pound – the charge which Heath was most anxious to avoid, but which in the event backfired against Labour by raising yet further doubts about Britain's supposed recovery.

The same background briefing contained another notorious phrase, little noticed at the time, which was subsequently disinterred and hung around Heath's neck for ever after. This was a proposal to 'break into the price/wage spiral' by cutting SET and holding down prices in the nationalised industries. 'This would, at a stroke, reduce

the rise in prices, increase productivity and reduce unemployment.'[41] Like Wilson's 'the pound in your pocket', the phrase 'at a
stroke' passed into political mythology: after the election Heath was
widely but wrongly believed to have promised to reduce not
merely the *rise* in prices but prices themselves. This was a damaging
charge when inflation continued to rise under a Tory Government.
It was strictly unfair. Yet there was poetic justice in it, since it has
to be said that the Tories' exploitation of the prices issue in the 1970
election was unscrupulous. They had no clear idea themselves how
they were going to get inflation down; it was not a question to
which, despite Brendon Sewill's best efforts over the previous four
years, they had devoted any serious attention. On the contrary, in
Sewill's words, 'Most of our policies were designed to put it up.'[42]
They simply identified, late in the day, a major worry among the
electorate and went for it. The tactic worked. The prices issue
above all was the Tories' winning card. But in retrospect their use
of it tarnished a famous victory. 'I think it was an extremely clever
campaign,' Willie Whitelaw has admitted, 'but I was always
anxious that it wasn't based on any clear grounds.'[43] It was ironic,
following all his high-minded condemnation of Wilson's shallow
promises and his sincere aspiration to a higher level of political
rectitude, that Heath should after all enter Downing Street on the
basis of a false prospectus.

The result of the election was the greatest upset in British politics
since Attlee's victory in 1945. Only with hindsight did the straws in
the wind which should have enabled commentators to predict it suddenly become obvious. On election night virtually no one in politics
imagined anything other than a Labour Government – probably not
even Heath himself. It has often been asserted that he alone never had
any doubt that he would win, but this is almost certainly part of the
mythology of victory. His immediate concern was to hold his own
seat, which was by no means secure. In 1966 his majority in Bexley
had fallen to a bare 2,333. There had been speculation that he might
seek a safer constituency: in 1969 he had been offered the Cities of
London and Westminster, but he declined to move.[44] It would have
looked defeatist and, anyway, he was genuinely attached to Bexley.
But more than ever the local campaign had to be run for him by the
faithful Reg Pye, with an army of helpers from within and beyond
the constituency. Heath benefited from his national exposure, but he
was also in a curious way threatened by it; for he had to contend not
only with a disgruntled Independent Conservative candidate, but
also with the bizarre intervention of another anti-Common Market
candidate who had changed his name by deed poll to Edward Heath.

The real Ted Heath got down to Bexley only on the last day of the campaign, following his final rally on the Tuesday night in Bradford. He was among friends at the last, going round the committee rooms and polling stations as he had done at every election for the previous twenty years. But this time his whole future hung on the national result. He might achieve at last the summit of his life's ambition, the hard-earned reward for all his efforts; it seemed more likely that he would be rejected a second time and cast aside by the Conservative party, with few thanks, as an embarrassment to be quickly forgotten. His closest colleagues admired his courage but gave him little comfort. Peter Carrington and Madron Seligman were with him in Bexley that evening. Neither privately expected him to win, nor does either believe to this day that Heath himself really expected it. 'I doubt if he was confident of the result,' Carrington has written, 'but he showed no worries – he is a particularly brave man.'[45]

The journalist Terry Coleman, on the other hand, has written vividly of Heath sitting exhausted and alone over a tumbler of whisky in a Bexley school when it was all over, answering his questions – understandably – with monosyllabic grunts until suddenly roused to a last passionate affirmation of the importance of achieving economic growth as the key to giving people freedom – the freedom to buy books and records, the freedom to travel. 'If you've ever been poor,' he said, 'you will know that.' Not that he had ever been really poor, he hastened to add, but young people now had 'an immeasurably freer life than I ever had'. He spoke 'with a direct strength I hadn't seen in the two days I had been following him' of the 'joy' it gave him to see this new freedom: 'There's an old saying of the Salvation Army: "You can't cast out the devil on an empty belly." And they're right.' Facing defeat at this crisis of his career, Heath was looking back over his life, realising how far he had travelled; yet thinking, remarkably at such a moment, not of himself but of the public good he was in politics to advance.[46]

The first declaration, around eleven o'clock, was David Howell's result from Guildford. It showed a 6 per cent swing to the Conservatives, which was confirmed or exceeded by the next half dozen seats to be announced, both Labour and Conservative. Instantly it was clear that the Conservatives had won: the first projections gave a majority as high as 70, though it soon came down to nearer 30. In Bexley, Heath's own majority soared to 8,058, despite the two mavericks, who took 1,700 votes between them. (Heath's own vote went up by only 1,400, while Labour's fell by 5,000 and the Liberal candidate's by 1,200.)★ Heath decided to return immediately to London. On the way, Douglas Hurd recalled, 'the car radio persisted in telling us extraordinary good news . . . Extraordinary news to me, but not to Mr Heath. To him it was simply the logical result of the long years of preparation, and of the fact that the people of Britain, like the people of Bexley, were at bottom a sensible lot.'[48] It was easy, when the nightmare was suddenly lifted, to forget that he had ever doubted it.

From a triumphant reception in Smith Square – where a disgusted Labour supporter stubbed a cigarette painfully on the back of his neck – Heath and Hurd returned to Albany. At three o'clock Willie Whitelaw came on the phone. It was the only time, Whitelaw revealed later, that he had ever known Heath give way to emotion. 'I rang him up. He couldn't speak. I couldn't speak.'[49] Wilson had not yet conceded, but by the time counting stopped for the night Labour had lost 42 seats. Heath went to bed at five o'clock, leaving a note for his housekeeper to wake him before noon. When she did so, she told him that a Mr Nixon had telephoned. In the morning Westminster and Fleet Street came to terms with a world turned upside down. The Queen, royally unmoved, was attending Royal Ascot. Wilson conceded at midday, as the removal vans descended on Downing Street, but could not go to the Palace to resign until Her Majesty returned at half past six. Heath was waiting in Albany, watching the television. At ten to seven he was driven to the Palace to kiss hands and then to Downing Street shortly after seven. This was the supreme moment that he had been preparing for ever since he was a schoolboy. Against the odds, written off by all, he was Prime Minister.

It was not only the most unexpected General Election victory of recent times. It was also the biggest: the only time since 1945 that a working majority for one party – a majority of nearly a hundred – has been turned at a single election into a working majority for the other. The final figures gave the Conservatives 330 seats (a net gain of 77 over 1966) to Labour's 287, while the Liberals were reduced from 12 seats to only 6. The Tories polled just over 13 million votes (46 per cent) to Labour's 12 million (43 per cent) and the Liberals'

★ Edward Heath (Conservative)	27,075
John Cartwright (Labour)	19,017
E. Harrison (Liberal)	3,222
E. J. R. L. Heath (Conservative/ Consult the People)	938
M. P. Coney (Independent Conservative)	833
Conservative majority	8,058[47]

2 million (7·5 per cent). The swing (average 4·8 per cent) was exceptionally uniform throughout the country. Despite above-average swings in Wolverhampton and some neighbouring seats the evidence for a significant Powell effect, even in the West Midlands, is inconclusive.[50] The victory was to an unusual degree Heath's own. Had he lost, there is no question that defeat would have been laid at his door, so in simple justice he deserved the credit for victory. But more positively than that, he deserved it for his courage, determination and dignity in the face of the derision of the press and widespread defeatism in his own party. Whether or not, deep down, he really believed that he would win, the result vindicated him in the end. It also powerfully reinforced his sense of destiny.

The unexpectedness of his victory put him in an exceptionally strong position. Had he won easily in 1968, while trailing his party in the polls, it would have been seen as the party's victory, achieved despite his leadership, and he would have remained a leader on probation. As it was, the press was unanimous that without his sheer stubbornness the party would have stumbled to defeat. 'Let there be no mistake,' cheered the *Daily Express*, 'the Tory victory was won by the Prime Minister's own guts and leadership.'[51]

David Wood agreed in *The Times*:

He will go to Downing Street full of authority and command as the leader who was doubted and who conquered against the most daunting psychological odds.

He is now the master of his own fate inside the Conservative party, perhaps for the first time, as well as master of Britain's fate in the immediate future.[52]

At the same time the manner of his victory, and the universal acclaim which suddenly engulfed him after five years of carping, was not entirely good for him. Victory achieved in defiance of the pundits was doubly sweet. Douglas Hurd has written that at the moment of victory his strongest feeling was not pleasure for Heath or triumph over the Labour party, but 'satisfaction that the experts, the know-alls, and the trend-setters had been confounded'.[53] Heath was fully entitled to feel the same. Upsetting the conventional wisdom appealed to his sense of humour. But it also encouraged him to believe that he could henceforth go his own way, paying no more regard to polls and critics who told him he could not communicate. To him the result proved that he *could* communicate, or that 'communication' in the way the newspapers went on about it did not matter. He had his own direct line to the electorate, who understood what he was saying better than the blinkered metropolitan press. The *Daily Mail*, performing a quick U-turn, now perfectly expressed his mood: 'The pundits said his plain speaking would never win. They said that honesty was not enough. They said he needed a gimmick or a wife. Where are those pundits now? Their reputations are buried under the tattered waste of the opinion polls.'[54]

Understandably, but dangerously, the result of the 1970 election confirmed Heath's low view of journalists – and a good many of his colleagues too. He had won by his own efforts, in his own way, despite them all, and he was now inclined to think that he could do no wrong. The years of nagging criticism had made him more than ever solitary, defensive, distrustful of advice and stubbornly self-sufficient, a curious mixture of self-confidence and insecurity. Now victory in such heady circumstances restored his self-belief, freed him to follow his own instincts without obligation to the party faint-hearts who had never believed he would win and released in him a powerful streak of arrogance. This too would bring its nemesis in the years ahead.

PART FOUR

Power

14

'A New Style of Government'

WINNING the General Election against all expectations enormously boosted Heath's self-confidence. Suddenly he was the Man of Destiny who had pulled victory out of the fire by his undaunted efforts. There was general agreement in the press and in the political world that it was to a unique degree his victory. Not only was he Prime Minister but he was Prime Minister with no debts to anyone and a clear personal mandate to impose his new authority on those who had sniped at him for so long. It is not entirely clear why it should have been seen to be so peculiarly Heath's own rather than the party's victory; perhaps in wry recognition that it would undoubtedly have been his defeat. But unquestionably it was seen as such; and Heath himself had no inclination to disclaim the credit. 'They've been telling me all week I was going to lose,' he remarked as he watched the results coming in. 'Now they're picking my bloody Cabinet for me.'[1] He felt no humility in victory, rather a massive sense of relief that the ultimate prize which he had worked for and which he thought his due, which had looked agonisingly as if it might be wrenched away from him at the last, was his after all. ('You won't forget to say who won, will you?' he teased David Butler, writing the Nuffield study of the election.) Now he would show them. His personal authority was actually greater than it would have been had he entered Downing Street a year or two earlier on the back of a sweeping and predicted Tory landslide.

But there were dangers, too, in this very personal triumph. To an extent, after the years of frustration and the final months of anxiety, victory was good for Heath. With victory he could at least afford to relax, let his guard down a bit, let his hair grow longer, be himself; for a time at least he was less embattled. But at the same time some of his friends felt that victory had another effect: it increased his lonely sense of self-sufficiency and encouraged him to believe that he could henceforth ignore unwelcome advice and steer his own course regardless, confident in the belief that he had after all been shown to have a better understanding of the British electorate than his critics. 'Bugger them all – I won' crudely expressed this side of his reaction; some colleagues had found him more attractive in adversity. June 1970 dangerously confirmed his disinclination to regard questions of image and communication as important.

Yet he entered Downing Street with the most high-minded intentions in this respect, as in others. The words he spoke on the steps of Number 10 – 'To govern is to serve . . . Our purpose is not to divide but to unite and, where there are differences, to bring reconciliation' – were the conventional pieties uttered by all incoming prime ministers.[2] But Heath was the least cynical of premiers, and he meant them. He believed passionately that his first mission was to restore the standards of public life which had been lowered by Harold Wilson. 'My first responsibility', he told Kenneth Harris two days after taking office, 'is to maintain the freedom of discussion in the country, which is, and has been, its life-blood, and to keep its exchange of views confident, candid, lucid and direct.'[3] In practice these high ideals were to be quickly neutralised by his suspicion of anything that smacked of media manipulation.

To an exaggerated degree, Heath appeared determined in his first days in office to be as unlike Wilson as possible – in little things, so as to symbolise the change he intended in big things. He immediately discontinued Wilson's television rental, for instance, and replaced the housekeeper at Chequers; he set in hand the complete redecoration of both Downing Street and Chequers. Contrary to the normal conventions of Civil Service continuity, he declined to take on the principal private secretary, David ('Sandy') Isserlis, whom Wilson had appointed only weeks before, but appointed instead Robert Armstrong, the son of his old musical mentor at Oxford, Sir Thomas Armstrong, and an excellent musician in his own right.[4] On the other hand – very much to her surprise – he did keep on an assistant press officer, Barbara Hosking, who had joined the Government Information Service a few years before from Transport House. Wilson would not have dreamed of allowing anyone near him who had worked at Conservative Central Office; but paradoxically this was just another way of marking his difference from Wilson.[5]

The clearest signal of the new tone in Downing Street was Heath's choice of a chief press officer in succession to Wilson's mouthpiece, Joe Haines. Rather than appoint a similarly sympathetic Tory journalist, he chose a career Civil Servant, Donald Maitland –

formerly head of the news department at the Foreign Office and principal private secretary to George Brown and then Michael Stewart, before being appointed in 1969 Ambassador to Libya, whence Heath unexpectedly recalled him. The choice of a Foreign Office man reflected in part the priority Heath intended his Government to give to Europe. But nothing could have better symbolised the change of government between Wilson and Heath than the contrast between Haines's *Daily Mirror* style of news management and Maitland's dapper Foreign Office style. Where Haines had manipulated the presentation of government information with the creative resourcefulness of one sort of old pro, Maitland deployed the skills of a very different school of professionalism to give very little away. Maitland's punctilious straight bat suited Heath's personal style; but it contributed little to the promotion of open government.

The replacement of Marcia Williams by Douglas Hurd as the Prime Minister's political secretary made another piquant contrast. Though the son of a Tory MP with political ambitions of his own, Hurd had been until he joined Heath's private office in 1967 another Foreign Office man with the smooth and formal manner of his kind. His relationship to Heath was much more that of a trusted Civil Servant to his Minister than the confidential friend – sounding board, nanny and fiercely loyal protectress – that Mrs Williams was to Wilson. Heath was from the beginning determined not to surround himself with a Wilsonian kitchen cabinet of cronies. He never did: alongside Hurd he retained Michael Wolff as his chief political aide, while Timothy Kitson – another bluff hunting squire specifically picked to keep him in touch with the shires – replaced Jim Prior as his PPS. But to an unusual extent Heath was content to be advised by officials. His scrupulousness in this respect left him with no source of candid political advice or moral support when problems mounted up.

When Heath and Hurd arrived at Downing Street from the Palace the entire permanent staff was lined up on each side of the hall to clap him through the door – a scene of triumph reminiscent of the presentation of the rose in the second act of *Der Rosenkavalier*, spoiled only (as Heath's moments of triumph have so often been spoiled) by a woman throwing paint over him as he went in.[6] Marcia Williams was still upstairs packing up Wilson's private office; she could not move out until Heath had vacated the Leader of the Opposition's room at the House of Commons. But Heath was in no hurry to move in. In fact he spent less than an hour at Downing Street before driving to Windsor – as if he had not more important things to do – for the Queen Mother's seventieth birthday party, leaving Hurd,

Wolff and Prior to make the first sketches of the shape of the new Government. That night, and every night for the next week, he went back to Albany to sleep.

More than most prime ministers he determined to make Downing Street his home. By chance his lease on Albany was just expiring; he did not renew it. He did not expect to need another home for many years. To emphasise his confidence he set out to make Downing Street his own, moving in not only his piano but his furniture and all his personal belongings, pictures, glass and china. Overcoming the resistance of the Ministry of Works, he called in his designer friend Jo Pattrick, who had helped him with the Albany flat, to advise him on a total redecoration of the house. Though last redecorated only seven years before at the very end of Macmillan's premiership, the general impression was dingy and drab, lacking any sort of style or character. Apart from enlarging the Prime Minister's first-floor study, dividing an unnecessarily large washroom and switching around the sitting-room and bedroom in the second-floor flat, Heath and Mrs Pattrick made no major structural alterations. But they replaced the chintzy furnishings favoured by Dorothy Macmillan and Elizabeth Home with strong 'masculine' colours that reflected both Heath's personal taste and his view of what a modern Prime Minister's residence should look like. Unlike the Wilsons, who had lived in the flat upstairs and used the state rooms only for formal occasions, Heath installed his piano in the White Drawing Room on the first floor (it would not have fitted upstairs) and made that his personal sitting-room – though he had his stereo equipment and his newest toy, a clavichord specially built for him, in the flat. As a further personal touch he kept the whole house filled with flowers – at Government expense. He also totally refurbished the Cabinet Room, as Marcia Williams found when Labour returned to office in 1974:

> Gone was the dark red carpet on the hall and corridor floors leading to the Cabinet Room: this was replaced by a rich gold. Gone were the dark greens and reds of the room itself – the green felt on the long, coffin-shaped Cabinet table, the old, dark green leather blotters, the even more worn leather of the chair seats. Now there was a symphony of muted browns ranging from palest to deep tobacco: the table top was covered with fawn baize, even the blotters were new light brown leather. It all looked elegant and co-ordinated, but I felt a touch of nostalgia for those dark and serious colours, shabby though the room had become, that seemed to underline the weightiness of office.[7]

Barbara Castle by contrast loathed the new look unreservedly. 'Gone was the familiar functional shabbiness,' she wrote in 1974. 'Instead someone with appalling taste had tarted it up. New old-gold carpeting everywhere; white and silver patterned wallpaper; gold moiré curtains of distressing vulgarity; "nice" sideboards with bowls of flowers on top. It looked like a boudoir.'[8]

This typical Labour nostalgia for the old and shabby was just what Heath thought he had been elected to sweep away. In the same spirit he replaced most of the heavy portraits of long-dead statesmen with light French pastoral paintings: even the portrait of Churchill that had hung outside the Cabinet Room was banished to Timothy Kitson's office. Wilson on his return in 1974 immediately had the familiar portraits restored. Most of Heath's other changes, however, he recognised as improvements.[9] What really irked Wilson, Marcia Williams and Barbara Castle was the fact that Heath had dared to spend so much public money without incurring a word of criticism. 'Heath must have spent a bomb,' Mrs Castle tutted to her diary; and a few weeks later, on first seeing his similar refurbishment of Chequers, '*We* would never have dreamed of such extravagance.'[10] They knew that the Labour party and the Tory press between them would never have let them get away with it.

If Downing Street was to be his town house, Heath also intended to make full use of Chequers as his country house, giving it the same treatment to bring it up to his standards of modern comfort combined with appropriate grandeur. He was the first Tory Prime Minister since Bonar Law without a country house of his own. Macmillan had preferred Birch Grove and had lent Chequers for most of his premiership to Selwyn Lloyd. Wilson made use of Chequers, but had been content to take it as he found it. Heath had no such inhibitions. He was not allowed to use Jo Pattrick here – Colefax and Fowler already had the contract – but once again his purpose was to make the whole house lighter and airier. The dark oak panelling was stripped throughout: 'it now looked warm and glowing', Marcia Williams discovered, 'rather than dark and forbidding'. Carpets and curtains were replaced, the pictures cleaned. Upstairs the number of bathrooms was increased: previously there had been so few that visiting heads of state had been obliged to share.

Most important of all, Edward Heath also had the contents of the house catalogued. Some of the treasures there had been stored away in attics and more or less forgotten; Heath had them all looked at, repaired where necessary, and brought out and put on display or where possible used. He had everything inventoried, from the collections of porcelain and glass to the rare books on the shelves, whose cataloguing was a long and difficult task. By instituting these changes, Edward Heath has made a great and lasting contribution to the history of Chequers.[11]

He installed another stereo system with enormous speakers and had a swimming pool built – but this he managed to get donated by the American Ambassador, Walter Annenberg, in commemoration of President Nixon's visit in October 1970.

This time even Barbara Castle approved: 'I liked the light wood, the careful display of china treasures and the urns of flowers in every corner of hall and landings, but it made everything look so much more *feminine* – another clue to Heath's character?'[12]

Surrounding himself with the trappings and rewards of power was important to Heath at two levels. It was important to show himself that he had really made it, to dispel the haunting sense of insecurity that had nagged him not only over the last few weeks in Opposition but over the whole six years since he had become Tory leader, when he was always conscious of the snobbish sneers of the well-born behind his back. Simply to have achieved the premiership at last was a source of immense pride and personal satisfaction and he intended to enjoy it. At the same time, however, he also believed that he owed it to the country to restore some of the dignity and grandeur to the office of Prime Minister which he thought had been cheapened by Wilson's middle-class homeliness. He believed as a matter of national pride that Britain's Prime Minister should live and be able to entertain his counterparts from other countries in a style that properly reflected Britain's standing as a major European power. It was a political statement that this style should be modern, stylish and appropriately lavish – not old-fashioned and apologetic as it had been under Macmillan and Wilson.

The second consideration, of course, conveniently justified the indulgence of the first. This was particularly so when it came to Government entertaining, which Heath used in two ways to flatter his own self-esteem. First, he liked to use Downing Street and Chequers to host parties and receptions not only for visiting heads of government but also for heroes of his own whom he wished to honour – both political grandees, like Macmillan, Eden and Rab Butler ('He likes to see himself', Anthony Sampson noted in 1971, 'as part of the great Tory pageant'),[13] and eminent musicians, like Yehudi Menuhin and William Walton, whose seventieth birthday he marked with a dinner and a special concert, attended by the Queen Mother and practically the whole British musical establishment, in

March 1972. He held parties for his ex-secretaries, for his old regiment, for his Bexley constituency association – these of course were not all Government occasions, but he was nevertheless pleased to be able to hold them in Downing Street. On one occasion he satisfied a romantic fantasy by inviting the American actress Olivia de Havilland, for whom he nursed a particular admiration, to lunch at Chequers: she arrived by helicopter and Heath was on the lawn to meet her, dressed in a white suit. He loved the power his position gave him to set the stage, pick the cast and – not least – choose the music.*

Music was the second and most specific way Heath indulged himself in Downing Street. More than any other Prime Minister before or since he made Government functions into musical occasions, and used music to celebrate political events such as entry into the EEC. With the help of Robert Armstrong – this was why he needed a musician for a private secretary – he would lay on madrigals (sung by the choir of St Margaret's, Westminster), a piano recital or perhaps a string quartet to play after dinner. His very first such concert in September 1970, with Isaac Stern, was ruined by the Palestinian hostage crisis: Heath himself could not be present and Stern almost declined to play out of respect for the hostages. Stern also performed, by chance, at what turned out to be the last concert of Heath's premiership at Chequers three years later. This time it was the outbreak of the Yom Kippur war which overshadowed the occasion, and Pinchas Zuckerman who felt unable to perform; but the Amadeus Quartet played instead. Another time the Amadeus played at Downing Street to mark the first publication of the annual statistical survey *Social Trends*. Heath has explained in his book *Music* how this curious occasion came about:

> As Mrs Muriel Nissel, the editor of *Social Trends*, is the wife of the second violin in the Amadeus Quartet, the connection was not as tenuous as it appears at first sight. The audience was made up in part of those concerned with social developments whom we thought might be interested in music, and those known to us as musicians whom we considered might become involved in these social matters.[15]

---

* Heath once disclosed, in a rare moment of self-revelation, that he had always had 'a hidden wish, a frustrated desire to run a hotel'. To the Labour MP and amateur psychoanalyst Leo Abse this surprising fantasy fitted perfectly with his forced smile and inability to form deep friendships. 'Not for Heath the dream of a home, wife and children; only the impersonal hotel over which he presides and where undemanding transitory acquaintances but not relationships are formed.'[14]

Though it was not what the profile writers had in mind, back in 1965, when they compared him enthusiastically to President Kennedy, Heath's ambition to harness music to reflect glory on his administration and at the same time to use his office to honour musicians in particular and the arts in general was one of the few things he had in common with Kennedy: for three and a half years, from a mixture of private and public motives, he tried to create in Downing Street and Chequers his own 'Camelot', a small island of culture at the heart of British government. Not one of his predecessors or successors has attempted anything remotely similar.

The first task of his premiership was to appoint his Cabinet. In one sense it was true that he had no obligations to anybody. At the same time, like any incoming Prime Minister, Heath was in practice constrained to give the jobs they expected to his senior colleagues. Moreover, more explicitly than anyone before him, he had conducted the Opposition for five years as preparation for government, thereby increasing the presumption that most Shadow Ministers would get the portfolios they had been covering. Thus his room for manœuvre was in reality limited. In his interview with Kenneth Harris published three days after the election he had expressed the hope that he could keep the size of the Cabinet down to sixteen. 'Otherwise there is bound to be too much talk.'[16] In fact he could not immediately get it below eighteen – though this was still a significant reduction from Wilson's outgoing twenty-one.

Most of the principal appointments were made very quickly. If there was a difficulty it revolved around two of the most senior figures, Alec Douglas-Home and Reginald Maudling. Iain Macleod was no problem: he had been Shadow Chancellor for five years and his appointment to the Treasury was automatic. But Home and Maudling both had a claim to the Foreign Office. Maudling had been Shadow Foreign Secretary in Opposition. On the other hand Sir Alec had been Foreign Secretary before he became Prime Minister in 1963; there was no other job he could appropriately fill and if he wanted another turn at it before he retired he could not be denied. The general expectation was that he would not stay in the Government more than twelve or eighteen months, after which he would hand over to Maudling. In the meantime, with the critical Common Market negotiations coming up, it suited Heath much better to have Home – his boss during the previous negotiations in 1961–3 – at the Foreign Office rather than Maudling, whose commitment to Europe had always been cool. Maudling, therefore, went to the Home

Office. But this in turn displaced Quintin Hogg from his legitimate expectation. Hogg's ultimate ambition, however, had always been to follow his father on the Woolsack; so he was persuaded to resume once again his former title (though only on a life basis this time) and return to the Lords as Lord Chancellor. Only later, when Macleod's death and Maudling's resignation left the Government seriously depleted in the Commons, did Hailsham regret that he had not stayed in the Lower House.[17]

These four senior figures – Macleod, Maudling, Home and Hailsham – gave the new Cabinet an apparent weight of experience which turned out for different reasons – death, resignation and elevation – to be somewhat illusory. Maudling in particular, in the two years that he was in the Government, did not pull his weight. His appointment was widely welcomed: but he was too easy-going for the Home Office in the new climate of violent demonstrations, besides having to devote much of his attention to Northern Ireland. He was further distracted by personal difficulties arising out of the Poulson affair. Finally, though nominally deputy Prime Minister, he was not in Heath's confidence and never attempted to play the sort of co-ordinating role behind the scenes that every Government needs. In so far as it was filled at all, this role fell to Willie Whitelaw, as Lord President. But Whitelaw had never sat in a Cabinet before: though he had been a superb Chief Whip, he lacked in 1970 the seniority and wisdom he would later bring to Mrs Thatcher's Cabinet. Moreover in April 1972 he was appointed Secretary of State for Northern Ireland. The other trusted colleague in whom Heath placed special confidence was Lord Carrington, who became Defence Secretary but also in practice the Government's diplomatic troubleshooter over a wide range of defence-related problems from Washington to Belfast. Heath/Whitelaw/Carrington quickly formed the central triumvirate of the Government; but with Whitelaw so often absent after 1972 Carrington increasingly became Heath's effective deputy.

Heath initially appointed another of his special protégés, Tony Barber, Chancellor of the Duchy of Lancaster to handle the EEC negotiations. This was the job nearest to his own heart, for which he needed – or thought he did – someone with whom he could work particularly closely. Most other members of the Shadow Cabinet went to the jobs they had been shadowing: Robert Carr to Employment to bring in the Industrial Relations Bill; Peter Walker to Housing and Local Government; Margaret Thatcher, the token woman in the Cabinet, to Education; Gordon Campbell to Scotland. But Keith Joseph was unexpectedly switched from industry to Health and Social Security, while Geoffrey Rippon (regarded as the only right-winger in the Cabinet) went to the Ministry of Technology, with Michael Noble at the Board of Trade. Lord Balniel, Health and Social Security spokesman in Opposition, was one of two Shadow Ministers who did not find a place in the Cabinet. The other was Joseph Godber who, after five years shadowing agriculture, was denied to make room for Jim Prior. Prior had never held even junior office before, but as Heath's PPS for five years he was in a strong position to demand a senior job, and did so. (Godber and Balniel became Ministers of State, at the Foreign Office and Defence respectively; Godber eventually went to Agriculture in 1972.) The Cabinet was completed by Peter Thomas, who had been out of Parliament since 1966, who became Welsh Secretary and also chairman of the Conservative Party; and Lord Jellicoe, who became Lord Privy Seal and Leader in the House of Lords.

These dispositions were of course tragically upset within four weeks. Heath also carried out some rearrangement of ministries in the autumn, one effect of which was to put an end to the Board of Trade and with it Noble's brief membership of the Cabinet. Subsequent events forced further innovations – notably the Northern Ireland Office – in the years ahead. By 1974 the size of the Cabinet had crept back to twenty. Seven new members had been added. With the exception of Maudling and Jellicoe, however, who resigned for personal reasons, no Cabinet Minister either left the Government or was sacked over the next four years – though only six served throughout in the same office. This, so far as he could make it, was Heath's team. He stuck to it, and they stuck to him.

Of those left out, the one with most cause for grievance – though perhaps least for surprise – was Edward Du Cann, who claims that he was categorically promised office in 1967 when he surrendered the party chairmanship.[18] Promise or not, Heath did not want him in his Cabinet; and Du Cann would scarcely have accepted a lesser post. Generally Heath used his opportunity to promote to positions outside the Cabinet a new generation of younger ministers – people like Terence Higgins and Patrick Jenkin (respectively Minister of State and Financial Secretary at the Treasury); Peter Kirk and Ian Gilmour (Under-Secretaries at Defence); Paul Channon and Michael Heseltine (Parliamentary Secretaries respectively at Housing and Transport); Geoffrey Howe (Solicitor-General, charged with drawing up the legal framework of the Industrial Relations Bill); and David Howell (given the chance to introduce his shiny new management reforms under Heath's eye in the newly established Civil Service Department). There was nothing for John Biffen, or initially for John Nott; though Powell's most outspoken supporter, Nicholas Ridley, went (for a time) to the DTI.

Douglas Hurd found the process of filling the junior jobs 'amazingly haphazard'. 'There's a sort of casualness about the way it's done,' he told Terry Coleman some years later, 'which I must say I did find surprising. Particularly [in] someone like Ted, who prided himself on having everything organised in his mind.'[19] In fact there was a pattern: 41 out of 45 Opposition spokesmen received jobs, and 30 of these got jobs they had previously shadowed. There was thus a far greater carry over of specialisation than had been the case when Labour took office in 1964. It was also a much younger Government than Wilson's had been, with an average age of 47 as against 57; and a substantially smaller one, with a total complement of 71 ministers as against 88.[20] In all these respects Heath's appointments were in line with his repeated criticism of Labour's administration as elderly, inflated and unprepared.

While the Cabinet was announced very quickly, on Saturday afternoon, it took another four days to complete the whole Government. In the meantime the new Cabinet held its first meeting on Tuesday 23 June. As a foretaste of things to come it was confronted immediately with a threatened dock strike. It was also plunged quickly into controversy by Home's precipitate announcement that Britain would resume the sale of arms to South Africa – as if that was the Conservatives' first priority on getting back into government. Heath had promised to resume sales when Wilson backed down in response to backbench pressure in 1967, claiming that Britain was in breach of the Simonstown Agreement – an opinion now endorsed by the Law Officers, Peter Rawlinson and Geoffrey Howe. There was a good deal of hypocrisy in the heated condemnation of the Government by Labour ex-ministers like Denis Healey who had wanted to do the same themselves. Nevertheless the unnecessary haste of the announcement antagonised liberal opinion and got the Government's relations with the Commonwealth off to the worst possible start.

Though Heath had foresworn 'instant government' in deliberate reaction against the frenetic first 'hundred days' of his predecessor in 1964, there were two other problems which required an immediate response even before Parliament had met. First, the new Government was greeted with fresh fighting in the Falls Road, Belfast, and the Cabinet agreed on 29 June to send extra troops to Northern Ireland to reinforce those sent in by Wilson and Callaghan in 1969. Trouble continued, and as early as 10 August Maudling was obliged to warn that the Government might be driven to impose direct rule. Second, on 30 June Home and Barber went to Brussels to reopen discussions with the EEC and arrange the timetable for renewed negotiations for British entry. No time was to be lost on this central plank of the Government's programme. After three weeks of pre-liminary soundings, the serious talking was set to start in mid-October. In addition two ministers anticipated the Queen's Speech by making pre-emptive announcements of their own. Peter Walker declared the Government's intention to reject Sir John Maud's report on local government in favour of his own scheme of reform, and announced that local authorities would be encouraged to sell their stock of council houses; while Margaret Thatcher wasted no time in cancelling Labour's circular requiring education authorities to draw up plans for comprehensive schools. All three announcements contributed to a sense of a Government determined to make a radical break with the recent past.

The Government's programme was formally unveiled in the Queen's Speech for the new session of Parliament on 2 July. Apart from the Industrial Relations Bill, however, and the promised Bill to tighten immigration control, there were few clear legislative com-mitments (abolition of the Land Commission, the establishment of commercial radio, pensions for the over-eighties). The heart of the Government's radicalism lay in declarations of intent to 'strengthen the economy and curb the inflation' by means of tax incentives and reduced Government intervention – though once again the Speech repeated the Government's commitment to full employment and regional policy, and stressed that the purpose of faster growth was to provide better social services.[21] Wilson, instantly back on biting form as Leader of the Opposition, cleverly mocked its emptiness while hoping, interestingly, that Heath would continue to distance himself from 'the themes of Selsdon'.[22] Heath in reply, making his first sub-stantial speech as Prime Minister, had fun chaffing Wilson on his evident pleasure 'in resuming the place which he once occupied with such distinction and will now continue to enjoy. Happiness', he gibed, 'came through every sentence. Words no longer carry respon-sibility. What a happy position. Verbal activity instead of action.' By contrast he offered quiet, responsible, competent government – not instant politics but the steady pursuit of economic success and a coherent modern assessment of Britain's interests in the world. He ended with a stumbling restatement of the Disraelian ideal which in his own eyes still underlay his 'abrasive' manner:

> Perhaps at this moment, speaking for the first time in this House as Prime Minister, I look back to the first work I undertook as a new backbencher, when we then put forward once again a concept which was an old one: that of one nation. It goes far wider than social and economic spheres. It covers our industrial relations,

education, the young people and those who have now retired. It covers both the spheres of race and religion.

I firmly believe . . . that the great task which lies before us, humbly, as an Administration . . . is to work to create unity in our country . . . to create within freedom in Britain one nation.[23]

Ironically, in the light of the bitter conflicts of the next four years, he meant it.

Five days later Iain Macleod made his only statement to the House as Chancellor. He was already ill when he made it, and as soon as he sat down he was rushed to hospital for an appendix operation. It was a disappointing occasion for Macleod's admirers who had hoped that he would make an early 'dash for freedom', taking advantage of the strong balance of payments to relax Roy Jenkins's tight monetary squeeze and cut corporation tax to stimulate investment. Instead he was cautious, giving rise to suggestions that he had already been 'turned round' by the Treasury view that there was enough demand in the economy as it was. 'As he did not know what to do about wage inflation,' commented *The Economist*, 'he had accepted the advice of his Civil Servants that he had better not do anything yet about stagnant production either.'[24] Thus from the very first the new Government's ambitions were bedevilled by the problem of inflation. The most positive announcement Macleod made on 7 July was that price increases in the nationalised industries would be subjected to 'searching investigation' and where possible disallowed, in accordance with the Government's election promises. This was a short-term expedient dictated by the need to be seen to be doing something about inflation without recourse to any form of incomes policy. But acceptance of the idea that the Treasury should absorb these costs to shield the public from price rises that would otherwise fuel wage claims was an early step away from the market principles on which the Government was supposed to have come to power – the first step from which, in the view of the Government's critics, all else inevitably flowed.[25]

Meanwhile the Government's response to its first major industrial dispute – a dock strike – likewise set a pattern which was to become familiar. While talking toughly of the need to resist inflationary demands, the Employment Secretary Robert Carr declared a State of Emergency to ensure supplies to the shops on 16 July but simultaneously appointed a judge experienced in such disputes, Lord Justice Pearson, to conduct an enquiry: two weeks later he accepted Pearson's difference-splitting recommendation that the strikers be offered an average rise of 7 per cent. The impression was given that the

Government did not want to plunge straight into a bruising show-down with the TGWU.[26]

By then the Government had already been rocked back on its heels by the death of Iain Macleod. His health had never been good. He had been in constant pain throughout the opposition years from spinal injuries sustained in the war, complicated by arthritis. But he had apparently recovered from his appendicitis and was back in 11 Downing Street when he suffered a heart attack on the evening of 20 July and died, less than five weeks after taking office. It was a devastating blow to the Government and, not least, to Heath person-ally. Since 1965 he had learned to place great trust in Macleod's political judgment. The Chancellor, indeed, was the only one of his contemporaries – one might say the only colleague in his entire career – with whom he enjoyed anything like a partnership of equals. (Maudling and Powell were always rivals, while Carr, Carrington, Barber and Whitelaw were never his equals.) He was deeply affected by the tragic irony of Macleod dying just as he was taking the measure of the office he had been preparing to fill for the previous six years. In the midst of the political emergency into which the loss of his Chancellor plunged him, his first thought was for Eve Macleod and her children. He devoted the whole of that evening to consoling her; and remarkably, for a man normally so shy of emotion, his sen-sitivity to her grief was greatly appreciated.[27]

Politically, Macleod's death was a blow from which, in the view of many of its members, Heath's Government never fully recovered. The immediate shock necessitated an early reshuffle which upset much of the careful preparation of the past five years; but at a deeper level Macleod's loss was felt ever more seriously as time went on. The first consequence was an extension of the personal one: Macleod was the one senior colleague with a mind of his own and the in-dependence to stand up to the Prime Minister when necessary, to whose advice he would always have listened. It was increasingly a weakness of the Government that Heath was almost entirely sur-rounded by ministers who owed their position solely to himself. Second, with Hailsham sidelined on the Woolsack, Macleod was the one charismatic personality the Government possessed. 'Politically', as Robert Carr put it, 'he was our trumpeter.'[28] Desperately turgid himself, Heath imperatively needed a trumpeter to proclaim his mes-sage; and this his Government now lacked. In this respect Macleod was irreplaceable. Whether his death made any difference to the direction in which the Government developed, however, is much more doubtful. His admirers claim that the 1972 reversal of the policies with which the Government started out would not have hap-pened if Macleod had lived. But the fact is that Macleod had no more deeply held economic principles than did Heath. He was attracted, for political reasons, by the clear repudiation of incomes policy: but he had no other idea of how to deal with inflation and he would certainly not have been indifferent to the political pressure of mounting unemployment. There is every reason to think that Macleod would have been ready to modify his policies, in pursuit of rapid growth, for the same pragmatic reasons that Heath did: only with Macleod at the Treasury the new policies would have been better defended and explained – and perhaps in the final crisis applied with greater imagination and flexibility.

Heath's immediate problem was to find a new Chancellor, with as little displacement of other ministers as possible. One possible solution would have been to go back to Reggie Maudling; but there was never any likelihood that Heath would have looked seriously at that. Had he still been available Edward Boyle might have been a candidate. Alternatively Keith Joseph and Geoffrey Rippon were mentioned – even Edward Du Cann.[29] In fact Heath quite quickly settled on Tony Barber. He wanted someone above all with whom he could work closely and with confidence. He has been criticised for appointing a political lightweight who would do his bidding. But – Maudling apart – there was no heavyweight on offer and Barber had good qualifications for the job. He had served four years at the Treasury in the early 1960s under Heathcoat Amory, Selwyn Lloyd and Maudling – three years as Economic Secretary and one year as Financial Secretary – followed by a year in the Cabinet as Minister of Health. *The Times* thought him the 'most logical' appointment.[30] Nevertheless he *was* a lightweight: an unimpressive speaker with a high voice who never really grew into the job and was never able to stand up to Heath. (The cartoonist John Kent in *Private Eye* always portrayed him addressing Heath nervously as 'Sir'.) Over the next three and a half years – though he carried through Macleod's planned tax reforms with quiet skill, impressed his officials with his aptitude for international diplomacy, and won for a time golden opinions in the press – Barber signally failed to develop a political personality independent of his master. Heath had already a poor opinion of the Treasury, which he suspected of a lack of enthusiasm for Europe. Lacking the powerful voice which Macleod would have given it, it was increasingly marginalised, as Heath sought more congenial economic advice elsewhere.

A second important consequence flowed from the reshuffle. To take over the handling of the Common Market negotiations from Barber, Heath moved Geoffrey Rippon from the Ministry of Technology and replaced him with John Davies, the former

John Kent, *Private Eye* (10 March 1972)

Director-General of the CBI, who had just been returned to Parliament for the first time five weeks before. This was on paper a bold and imaginative appointment, consistent with the idea of trying to inject businessmen and businesslike attitudes into Whitehall. Nevertheless the experiment of throwing non-politicians straight into high office with little or no apprenticeship in the House of Commons has rarely proved successful: the experience of Frank Cousins in 1964–6 was only the most recent example. Within three months of his appointment, Davies's job was immensely enlarged by Heath's restructuring of ministries which merged Technology with the Board of Trade to create the new super-department of Trade and Industry. It was too much for an inexperienced minister, lacking sensitive political antennae and unused to dealing with the House of Commons. Moreover Davies was not only politically inept, he was also an instinctive interventionist, out of sympathy with the idea of Government disengagement from industry which was supposed to be the new administration's watchword. In making his original appointments Heath had put together an assertively free-market team at Technology: Rippon was buttressed by Sir John Eden as Minister of State and Nicholas

Ridley as Parliamentary Secretary. Both Eden and Ridley remained in the new DTI, but the appointment of Davies to head it signalled – as Alan Watkins astutely noted at the time – that behind the conference rhetoric a retreat to more orthodox policies was on the cards.[31]

One of the most striking expressions of Heath's 'new style' was that the Government had barely taken possession of the seats of power before the Prime Minister and all his senior colleagues virtually shut up shop and simultaneously went off on holiday. This was another calculated declaration of difference from Wilson's restless headline-seeking. Heath was determined not to miss his summer's sailing. He had already lost no time in escaping to *Morning Cloud* on only his second weekend in office, causing mischievous questions to be asked in Parliament by Labour members wanting to know the cost to public funds of guarding him and maintaining communications while he was at sea – questions he brushed aside with contempt.[32] He had a very clear conviction of the importance of getting right away from Downing Street at frequent intervals to keep himself mentally fresh. As he told Kenneth Harris, he had seen too many prime ministers 'broken on the wheel of their obsession', and he did not intend to be another.[33] The novelty of the Government's summer vacation was further intended to give the impression of an administration quietly in control of events, preparing itself unhurriedly for the tasks ahead before getting down to business in the autumn. The idea was admirable. Nevertheless it was strongly criticised in sections of the press unused to the sight of ministers taking holidays. Heath's response was one of the best deadpan jokes he ever made, a perfectly timed dig at the difference between himself and the sedentary Wilson which convulsed the Tory party conference in October: 'A holiday!' he mocked. 'What an extraordinary idea!'

> People's hands were lifted in horror and some of those who had already been away were loudest in their shrill shrieks. Of course, if I had gone and sat on an island somewhere, out of the way, and just watched the boats pass by, that would have been unexceptional, perhaps even commendable; but because I got on a boat and sailed past the islands . . . *(Laughter and applause.)*[34]

For practically the whole of August, however, there was no political news. By the time ministers returned to their desks at the beginning of September even *The Economist* was suggesting that a good principle had been carried too far. There was, it claimed, a sense of drift in the air, an unease that the Government had not yet begun to tackle the problems the country faced. Despite all the policy work in opposition and the fine talk at the election, the Tories gave the impression – the Industrial Relations Bill excepted – that they had no more idea of what to do than Labour had in 1964. It was time for Heath to assert himself.[35]

15

'The Quiet Revolution'

HEATH returned to Downing Street on 1 September rested and ready to launch the Government's autumn offensive. Instead, however, he was confronted almost immediately by his first international crisis, involving the brutal blackmail of modern terrorism. On 6 September the Popular Front for the Liberation of Palestine hijacked four airliners (two American, one Swiss and one Israeli). Two were flown to Jordan and one to Cairo, where it was blown up the next day. The hijackers of the Israeli plane, however, were overpowered and the plane landed at Heathrow, where the surviving terrorist, a young woman named Leila Khaled, was arrested and held at Ealing Police Station. The PFLP then announced that it would blow up the two planes at Amman, with their passengers, unless Britain released Khaled and Switzerland and West Germany freed six other Palestinian terrorists held in their prisons.

Hostage taking was a relatively new barbarity in 1970, and the response of the international community was uncertain. The Swiss and Germans were inclined to accede to the terrorists' demands. Heath, however, with the support of his senior colleagues and most of the British press, took the clear view that hijacking should not be allowed to succeed. While the five threatened Western governments held emergency talks in Washington, the International Red Cross secured the release of eighty women, children and elderly passengers. Then, to step up the pressure on Britain, hijackers seized a fifth plane, this time a British VC-10 flying from Bombay to London, which was also diverted to Jordan. On 12 September the remaining hostages – over 200 of them – were taken off the planes and all three aircraft were blown up. Heath merely repeated that Leila Khaled would be released only when all the hostages were safe.

For two weeks stalemate ensued, with the eyes of the world on the untested British Prime Minister. In offering to swap Khaled for the hostages Heath was already conceding more than many commentators thought he should; but he held a weaker hand than was generally appreciated. The decision whether to prosecute Khaled was, under British constitutional convention, entirely a matter for the Attorney-General, Peter Rawlinson. The problem was that unless the attempted hijacking of the Israeli plane could be shown to have been committed over British soil there would be no case against Khaled under British law. Since the captain had reported that the incident had happened 'south of Clacton' the likelihood was that any attempted prosecution would have failed.[1] The Palestinians, however, did not know this. Heath, advised by Rawlinson, was thus enabled to play a delicate game of bluff.

Eventually, partly through the mediation of President Nasser, with whom Heath had established good relations on a visit to Egypt the previous year, a deal was struck.[2] On 29 September all the hostages were released, and the next day Khaled was driven from Ealing to Heathrow and from there flown in an RAF plane to Cairo, stopping off in Munich and Zurich to pick up the other six imprisoned terrorists. Public relief was tempered by strong criticism from the Tory right. Enoch Powell condemned the Government for setting aside the rule of law in order to secure the hostages' release – an unconstitutional act 'not only wrong in itself but fraught with grave consequences for the future'.[3] Eighteen years later, in his memoirs, Norman Tebbit still recalled the Khaled affair as having 'cast a doubt over the Government's determination not to compromise vital principles to avoid short-term problems'.[4] Yet in fact there was no interference in the course of law – at least in Britain – and no vital principle was compromised. Hard though it was to understand, there was no case against Khaled. All that Britain could have done was to deport her. In exchange for her release, however, Heath managed to secure the safety of the hostages. By those who knew the true situation his cool diplomacy was much admired. It was characteristic, too, that his private request to Nasser remained secret until the crisis was over. Altogether the affair was a nasty baptism, skilfully and honourably surmounted.

While the hostage crisis was still going on, on 24 September, Heath gave his first television interview since becoming Prime Minister. Questioned by Alastair Burnet for ITV, he looked 'infinitely more confident and relaxed' after his holiday, despite being put somewhat on the defensive over the Government's apparent inactivity.[5] The main thrust of the interview was the Government's determination to resist 'wildly inflationary' wage demands. He unequivocally rejected direct control of wages or prices, but admitted that there were more price rises in the pipeline than they had known about before the election and affirmed the Government's right to use its position as an employer to hold down public sector claims. Asked if he was therefore ready to stand up to strikes over the winter, he replied firmly, 'Yes indeed.'

'Would you face a general strike?'
'Yes. I have always made it plain. I have said we are going to carry through reform of industrial relations.'[6]

The Government, Heath insisted, would not be deflected from its purpose by either the TUC or the CBI. Trade union leaders immediately attacked his broadcast as provocative. Already the projected Industrial Relations Bill was becoming confused with the battle against inflation. Before it had even introduced the Bill the Government found itself in confrontation with the unions, obliged despite its pre-election promises to operate a sort of unofficial wages policy against the public sector while debarred by the level of inflation already in the economy from going boldly for faster growth as Macleod had planned. Within the Cabinet Maudling – supported by *The Economist* – still argued that only a proper incomes policy would create room for expansion. Heath and Barber would come round to that view in another two years, but they were not ready for it yet. Less than three months after coming into office, the Government's years of diligent preparation were already irrelevant to the situation it faced. Heath's response was to press on regardless with his programme in an attempt to transform the country's economic performance by tough talking, shock tactics and exhortation alone.

The Tory party conference at the beginning of October was the platform for probably the best speech of Heath's life. The whole conference was both a week-long victory celebration and an opportunity for one minister after another, now settled into their jobs, to tell the adoring faithful what they had already done and what they planned to do. After years of whispered reservations, Heath was at last the party's undisputed hero. The vivid personalities who had dominated previous conferences – Macleod, Hogg, Powell – were absent, their places filled by Heath's men – Jim Prior, John Davies, Willie White-law and Francis Pym.[7] The most remarkable speech, apart from Heath's own, was made by Davies, replying to the industry debate. The established memory is that it was in this speech that he promised that the Tory Government would not intervene to support 'lame ducks' but would let market forces take their course. In fact he did not mention 'lame ducks' until the following month in the House of

Commons; and his pledge not to support them was more qualified than is usually remembered: 'To abandon great sectors of our productive community at their moment of maximum weakness would be folly, but I will not bolster up or bail out companies where I can see no end to the process of propping them up.'[8] Like *A Better Tomorrow*, Davies's Blackpool declaration of unfettered capitalism was a good deal less robust than was generally noticed.

Heath's own speech, however, which closed the conference, was a rhetorical *tour de force* of unqualified – if imprecise – radicalism. He allowed himself a brief gloat, at the outset, at the discomfiture of the pundits who had been so sure that the Tories were losing the election. 'To the satisfaction of winning, which we all feel, must be added the additional satisfaction of proving so many people wrong – outside our own party, of course,' he slyly added. Quickly, however, he turned to the ambitious agenda which he believed the new Government had come to office to carry through: 'We were returned to office to change the course of history of this nation – nothing less. It is this course, the new course, which the Government – your Government – is now shaping.'

He dealt broadly with foreign affairs – defence, the EEC, the Commonwealth – claiming boldly that the Government's successful handling of the hostage crisis had opened 'a new era of British diplomacy': 'We are leaving behind the years of retreat.' Then, foreshadowing his imminent announcement of the restructuring of Whitehall departments, he promised an unprecedented review of the functions of government and the withdrawal of the Government from some functions altogether. This would be 'something entirely different from the previous exercise in making sudden and arbitrary cuts in Government expenditure . . . This is the redirection of Government expenditure.'

> You will see that our strategy is clear. It is to reorganise the functions of Government, to leave more to individual or to corporate effort, to make savings in Government expenditure, to provide room for greater incentives to men and women and to firms and businesses. Our strategy is to encourage them more and more to take their own decisions, to stand on their own feet, to accept responsibility for themselves and for their families.

This strategy, he affirmed, would lead to an expanding economy, giving higher living standards for all and better social services, plus secure defence and aid for the developing world. It would also, he hoped, help to defeat inflation. But here his tough talking exposed not only the Government's lack of a clear policy but also, critics would argue, a basic failure to understand the nature of inflation:

> No one can deny that today the major cause of the inflation from which we are suffering is the excessive wage demands, not only those which have been made but those which have been met. We have said that in the public sector we have a particular responsibility. It is the responsibility of an employer, direct or indirect . . . We do not expect any discrimination between the public and the private sectors. We shall act as responsible employers and we expect others, the private employers, to do the same. But this we have also made clear: if they go their own way and accede to irresponsible wage demands which damage their own firms and create a loss of jobs for those who work in them, then the Government are certainly not going to step in and rescue them from the consequences of their own actions.

It sounded magnificent in the conference hall: but it was to prove an increasingly difficult line to hold in the months and years that lay ahead.

The fundamental task which Heath set the Government and the Tory party was a perilously cloudy one: to 'change the attitude of the people of Britain', as the Conservatives had failed to do between 1951 and 1964. This time they must win 'the hearts and minds of our people, and we shall permanently change the outlook of the British nation'. There was, he warned solemnly, 'no alternative. To stand still today is to go backwards. To cling desperately to the present will be to find ourselves embracing only the past.'

Finally, the phrase that defined the whole ambitious enterprise:

> If we are to achieve this task we will have to embark on a change so radical, a revolution so quiet and yet so total, that it will go far beyond the programme for a Parliament to which we are committed and on which we have already embarked: far beyond this decade and way into the 1980s . . . We can only hope to begin now what future Conservative Governments will continue and complete. We are laying the foundations, but they are the foundations for a generation.[9]

This speech was a great propaganda success. For once in his life Heath had coined – or at any rate used – a phrase, the 'quiet revolution', which seemed to give philosophical coherence to what his Government was setting out to do. He had talked ambitiously in opposition about 'putting Britain right' and 'making a fresh start'. But all oppositions do that. This was now the Prime Minister speaking, four months into his job, and for the first time a sceptical press and public began to believe that the country really had elected a Government that was seriously different from previous governments over the past twenty-five years – that 1970 was to be, like 1945, a watershed year in British politics, from which future historians would date the ending of the collectivist era and the beginning of a new age of diversity and unrestricted competition. The representatives in Blackpool loved it. The American reporter Jean Campbell, writing in the London *Evening Standard*, caught the revivalist mood:

It was aggressive Toryism at last. A far cry from the defensive Toryism of Rab Butler which had shared room and board with Socialism for the last 22 years.

Heath was pulling down the Butler boarding house . . . Instead he plans to build a skyscraper with self-operating lifts. When the speech ended the crowd went wild, and being accustomed to American conventions, I know a happy crowd when I see one.[10]

Some commentators – for instance Alan Watkins in his *New Statesman* column – were still sceptical that anything would really change. But others, like Paul Johnson in the same paper, thought Heath was indeed a different sort of Prime Minister who would not be diverted from his purpose. Compared with Wilson, 'we have swapped an india-rubber ball for a spanner'. Heath was 'the toughest operator since Neville Chamberlain. He knows what he has gone there to do; and nothing will stop him. Nothing.'[11] 'There is no alternative,' Heath had declared and he appeared to believe it. Harold Wilson charged him with trying to 'turn the clock back' to 'mid-Victorian values'. But in an interview with the American magazine *Fortune*, he was robustly unrepentant:

We are . . . a controversial government because we are a radical reforming government. That's what we need to be. Nothing is more difficult than to persuade people to cast off their chains. If you can't persuade them, you have to break the chains.[12]

Of course, as a chastened Douglas Hurd reflected some years later, every new Government thinks that it opens a fresh chapter in the nation's history. Nevertheless Hurd still believed in 1979 that there had been a special air of destiny around Heath's enterprise in 1970:

Without, therefore, any wild hopes of being credited, I would simply put on record that I, and I believe others, thought there was a real chance in 1970 that Mr Heath and his colleagues would break out of inherited attitudes and make possible a sharply higher level of achievement by the British people. In short, there was a chance that they could do for Britain what Adenauer and Erhard had done for Germany and de Gaulle for France. We saw that this was Mr Heath's passionate determination. Knowing his character and his record, we thought it might work.[13]

What was wrong with the 'quiet revolution' was that determination alone was not enough. Behind the lofty rhetoric the programme was neither sufficiently precise nor, in practice, all that radical. Heath talked of changing attitudes – only marginally of changing structures. His purpose, essentially, was not to dismantle the existing framework of the postwar political settlement – the mixed economy and the Welfare State – but simply, by reforming it at the edges, to make it function better. This modesty sharply distinguished Heath's Government from that of Margaret Thatcher a decade later, which really did set out to tilt the balance decisively from state ownership and public provision of services to private enterprise and self-reliance. Heath hinted at some of the same solutions, based on a similar diagnosis of the failure of the British economy. But he hoped to achieve a transformation of economic behaviour primarily by exhortation. As *Fortune* correctly commented, 'What he is asking of Britain is something that can be achieved only by arousing the nation's will. It will not be easy to reverse the thrust that has been built up for a quarter of a century.'[14] It was not easy. The nation had elected him, but not because it was ready to be jolted out of its established ways. It was not in the least keen to be aroused. Heath came to office at a moment when it was simply not possible to create that sense of excitement and opportunity which might have created public acceptance of his promised revolution. As well as inflation and strikes at home, his Government faced the threat of international recession and steeply rising world commodity prices. Heath spoke at Blackpool of creating 'room for manœuvre' which should enable the Government to transcend these difficulties; but this was easier said than done. The 1970 Government enjoyed no room for manœuvre. It was plunged immediately into a series of industrial disputes which quickly dissipated whatever public good will it had possessed. The preconditions for a 'quiet revolution' were never present. Yet Heath's speech set an agenda for the Tory party which gained in relevance, urgency and – most important – public acceptability over the next ten, fifteen, twenty years. The difference was that Mrs Thatcher, after the experience of 1970–2, realised that her revolution could not be quiet.

The easy part of Heath's 'quiet revolution' was the institutional side. A Prime Minister has the untrammelled power to reshape the machinery of government as he sees fit. Heath had long been fascinated by Whitehall, ever since his own brief experience as a Civil Servant in 1946–7, and he now had the chance to put his ideas into effect. His reforms, taken together, added up to the most ambitious attempt to reshape the structure of government since 1918; yet such is the desire of all prime ministers to tinker with their predecessors' legacy that, twenty years later, little remains of Heath's innovations.

The most obvious changes to the Whitehall landscape were announced in a White Paper published on 15 October. Two new 'super-ministries' were to be established (in addition to the Department of Health and Social Security, already created by Wilson in 1968): the Department of Trade and Industry (DTI), made up of the old Board of Trade and Wilson's Ministry of Technology, which itself had already swallowed the Ministry of Aviation and the Ministry of Power; and the trendily titled Department of the Environment (DoE), which brought together the Ministries of Housing and Local Government, Public Building and Works, and Transport. The former was to be headed by John Davies; to lead the latter Heath appointed the 38-year-old Peter Walker. The idea was to encourage more co-ordinated consideration of related problems and to resolve conflicts within the enlarged departments, reducing the need to bring them to Cabinet. The DTI was also the latest in a series of attempts, going back to Heath's own enlarged responsibilities at the Board of Trade in 1963–4 and George Brown's Department of Economic Affairs, to create a second powerful economic department to rival the Treasury. Divided counsels between Davies and his subordinates prevented this experiment receiving a fair trial before November 1972; thereafter, with Walker switched to the DTI at the head of an entirely new team, it probably did carry greater weight than the Treasury, whose advice Heath was by then disinclined to hear.

The success of the super-ministries depended on the ability of the Secretary of State to manage a large team of six or seven colleagues, delegating responsibility while retaining strong overall control. Despite his lack of previous ministerial experience, Peter Walker did well at both Environment and the DTI; Michael Heseltine displayed similar managerial flair at the DoE in the first Thatcher administration. Generally speaking, however, the super-ministries were simply too big to be run effectively by a single Cabinet Minister and subsequent prime ministers have split them up again.

Within the departments, Heath – with the help of Lord Jellicoe (Lord Privy Seal) and David Howell, now installed as a junior minister in the Civil Service Department, working out of Number 10 – tried to introduce the system of Programme Analysis and Review (PAR) derived from American business practice and designed to eliminate unnecessary bureaucracy and cut waste. In the first enthusiasm of the 'quiet revolution'. this was one of the ways the Government hoped to create 'room for manœuvre'. Heath explained the principle to the Blackpool conference:

> I have . . . asked each Minister to organise an examination of every function carried out in his department, to examine personally the consequences and then to recommend whether it is essential for each of these functions to continue. The purpose of my request is to ensure that Government withdraws from all those activities no longer necessary either because of the passage of time or because they are better done outside government, or because they should rightly be carried on, if wanted at all, by individual or voluntary effort.[15]

The trouble with PAR was that it fell between two stools. On the one hand, the initial review of existing programmes predictably failed to produce savings on the scale anticipated, partly due to official suspicion – the Treasury made no secret of its dislike of the system – but partly also for lack of political will to scrap any major functions of government beyond those agencies (the Land Commission, the Prices and Incomes Board) that had already been earmarked for abolition before the election. Like other aspects of the Blackpool programme, PAR was not really as radical as it sounded: behind the ambitious rhetoric of rolling back the state it was essentially just another search for small economies. On the other hand even that useful exercise was not maintained with any vigour after the first setbacks. Heath might insist in June 1972 that officials found it 'rather exciting'.[16] In fact the Civil Service smothered it, in best 'Sir Humphrey' style, as the historian of Whitehall, Peter Hennessy, has described:

> Their first step . . . was to remove it from the grasp of Heath's businessmen in the CSD and to draw it into their own citadel in Great George Street from which it never emerged alive . . . To be brutal and brief about it, PAR became slow, top heavy and the victim of the relentless interdepartmental grind, complete with its

own steering committee, PARC, a classic example of what Derek Rayner . . . would later call a 'stifling committee'.[17]

More fundamental even than this, however, was the fact that the Government itself, from 1972 onwards, abandoned its attempt to keep a firm control on spending. On the contrary, as part of the 1973 'dash for growth', public spending was expanded to unprecedented levels, and the number of Civil Servants – which it had been one of the original purposes of PAR to cut – actually increased during the four years of Heath's Government by 400,000. In this climate PAR was itself just another bureaucratic programme cluttering the ground. It actually increased the workload on ministers and officials alike. It withered under Wilson and Callaghan after 1974, and was finally scrapped by Mrs Thatcher. Yet Heath and Howell had planted a seed which, though it did not thrive immediately, eventually bore fruit after 1979 in the form of Sir Derek Rayner's Efficiency Unit and Sir Robin Ibbs's 'Next Steps' programme of devolving functions from Whitehall to private agencies. At the second attempt, and building on the earlier experience of PAR, Mrs Thatcher's Government did succeed in injecting more businesslike methods of decision making and programme management into Whitehall. Once again, among ministers, it was Michael Heseltine at the Department of the Environment and the Ministry of Defence who most enthusiastically introduced these innovations. By the mid-1980s all departments used one or other management system, known by such acronyms as MINIS, MAXIS and ARM. In 1970 PAR was an idea whose time had not yet come.

Much the same could be said of the experiment of importing businessmen into the departments. Several of the team put together in 1969 by Richard Meyjes of Shell to advise the Opposition on ways of shaking up Whitehall found places as temporary Civil Servants, seconded from their companies for two years. Like most free-floating outsiders transplanted without adequate support into the established bureaucracy, however, they were able to make little perceptible impact – with one exception. This was Derek Rayner from Marks & Spencer, who set up and ran a new Defence Procurement Executive, hived off from the Ministry of Defence, which did succeed in introducing some financial discipline into the notoriously wasteful area of weapons development. Rayner went back to Marks & Spencer in 1972, but seven years later he was called back into government by Mrs Thatcher to lead a renewed drive for greater efficiency in Whitehall. Here again the 1970–4 experience taught lessons which were only fully acted upon a decade later.

The most successful of Heath's Whitehall innovations was the Central Policy Review Staff – the so-called 'Think Tank'. Its origins lay in the same impulse to bring in outsiders that prompted the introduction of businessmen and special advisers. The greater success of the CPRS, however, derived from its being properly constituted as a permanent entity within the official machine, set up with the support and blessing of the Cabinet Secretary. Sir Burke Trend himself recognised the potential usefulness of a high-powered, multi-disciplinary group of non-departmental thinkers at the heart of government and spoke later of a 'remarkable coincidence of diagnosis' with Heath's ideas.[18] In opposition, David Howell and Mark Schreiber had in fact thought more in terms of a strengthened policy unit in Number 10 to serve the Prime Minister personally. But Heath's concern was with widening the range of advice available to the Cabinet as a whole. He had been struck, he told the members of the Think Tank at their first meeting, by the fact that in opposition it was possible for the Shadow Cabinet to take a long-term view which became impossible as soon as they got into government. 'What I wanted to do was to change things so that the Cabinet could do that.'[19]

A minor but telling difference between Heath and Trend arose over the new unit's name. Heath – with characteristic directness – wanted to call it simply the Think Tank. It was Trend who stuffily insisted that this would not look right on the cover of a White Paper and came up with the suitably bureaucratic formulation 'Central Policy Review Staff'.[20] On the other hand it was also Trend who made the most critical contribution to the Tank's success by suggesting Lord Rothschild to head it – an inspired choice generally considered one of the best appointments Heath ever made. Like many inspired appointments there was a touch of luck about it, since the job had previously been offered to two other less glamorous figures – a banker and a professor of mechanical engineering – before Rothschild accepted it. Yet Victor Rothschild answered perfectly the description of a powerful, original, independent, roaming intellect. A maverick member of the famous banking family, he had been a brilliant biologist, wartime bomb-disposal expert and sometime MI5 agent, then for ten years chairman of the Agricultural Research Council. He was now about to retire (at sixty) after five years as research co-ordinator of Shell. The Think Tank was the ideal new challenge for his restless energies. Nevertheless it was a bold stroke which speaks volumes for Heath's self-confidence in the autumn of 1970. Rothschild made no secret that his political sympathies tended to the left. Not many prime ministers before or since would have been willing to invite such a powerful rogue elephant to wander at large through their governments. Despite a somewhat sticky first interview, however, Heath had no hesitation in giving Rothschild his head.

Rothschild recorded his recollection of that difficult first conversation in his memoirs.

Mr Heath. 'It's funny we have never met before.' Then there was a sort of row of dots. I could not think of what to say; after a while I said rather desperately: 'Prime Minister, do you think it would be better to have an economist in charge of this Unit?'

Mr Heath. 'I did economics at Oxford.' Another row of dots. Again, after a while, I said rather desperately: 'Prime Minister, could you give me an example of the type of problem you want the Unit to tackle?'

Mr Heath. 'Concorde.' At that moment I thought, perhaps wrongly, that I detected some anguished vibrations emanating from Sir Burke Trend and Sir William Armstrong . . . who were hovering in the background. There was some justification for their anguish, if I did not imagine it, because an hour beforehand they had told me it was precisely things like Concorde that the Government Think Tank would *not* be expected to study.

While I was still feeling the vibes, a Secretary came in and handed the Prime Minister a piece of paper which he read with some signs of displeasure, and said, 'Oh well, I had better see him.' Turning to me he concluded the interview by saying, 'Let me know if there are any other points.'[21]

Once appointed, Rothschild was left to recruit most of his own team and to determine for himself his own job description. It was Rothschild who gave the Think Tank its initial character, infusing it with his own informality, irreverence and glamour – and lubricating it with his independent wealth. With his wide contacts in the universities, the City and the oil industry he was able to put together a talented team of bright young 'boys and girls', mostly on secondment for spells of anything between six months and three years. There were normally about sixteen of them – just enough to fit around Rothschild's office table on a Monday morning – divided roughly half and half between high-flying Civil Servants and outsiders, with an average age of thirty-five. Perhaps the archetype of them all was the 25-year-old William Waldegrave, recruited fresh from Harvard, who later served in Heath's private office before going into politics himself. In addition Rothschild was able to draw on an exceptionally wide network of outside expertise – usually as a personal favour to himself, without payment.

Rothschild always made it clear that he was working as a licensed independent operator within the Government machine, not as a part of it. He insisted successfully that he and his deputy should have the right of direct access to the Prime Minister at all times, and the right to attend and speak at ministerial meetings, with no doors barred to him. He presented his recommendation in short, pithy, sometimes provocative memos, shorn of conventional Whitehall circumlocution, and arranged for them to be printed and bound in distinctive red covers to set them instantly apart from normal departmental briefs. He also pioneered the use of oral presentations to ministers, complete with graphics and other visual aids. Such methods helped to give the Think Tank, despite its tiny size, a special sense of intellectual excitement quite different from the rest of Whitehall. If this was Rothschild's achievement, it was only possible with Heath's support. They enjoyed, after that first interview and with the exception of one spectacular row in 1973, a good relationship which reflects great credit on Heath. He is often described as an autocratic Prime Minister, intolerant of dissenting advice and rigid in his ways. Yet he both appointed and backed Rothschild, than whom no one could have been less deferential or less conventional. Rothschild never established the same relationship with Wilson and resigned after the October 1974 election. Under his successors the Tank became steadily greyer and less exciting as it was gradually absorbed into the bureaucracy. The Heath–Rothschild Think Tank was a unique episode, a brief heady moment of creative energy and one of the most notable achievements of Heath's premiership.

It functioned, in Heath's time, in three distinct ways. First, and most originally, it made regular presentations to the whole Cabinet gathered at Chequers, setting out the broad picture of how the Government's strategy was faring in relation to worldwide trends and upcoming problems. The sessions were repeated in London a few days later, with Heath again present, for the benefit of second-rank ministers and a third time for parliamentary secretaries. They were originally supposed to be held every six months. In fact only three were held, in August 1971, May 1972 and June 1973. A fourth, arranged for November 1973, was cancelled. Nevertheless they were a remarkable innovation – testimony once again to Heath's surprising willingness to be told unwelcome things, as Douglas Hurd has described:

These were extraordinary occasions. Ministers would gather

upstairs at Chequers round a long table. At one end sat Lord Rothschild, flanked by the more articulate members of his team. Taking subjects in turn, they would expound, with charts and graphs, the likely consequences of government policy. Their analysis was elegant but ruthless. They made no allowances for political pressures. They assumed the highest standards of intellectual consistency. They rubbed Ministers' noses in the future. It is a tribute to Mr Heath that he instituted these reviews, and to his colleagues that they endured them. They were at once abolished by Mr Wilson.[22]

The last sentence is not strictly true. Wilson did hold one such session, in November 1974, devastatingly recorded in her diary by Barbara Castle.[23] Nevertheless Hurd's point holds. Neither James Callaghan nor Margaret Thatcher ever repeated the exercise. The Think Tank strategy seminars in Heath's time therefore raise two important questions. First, how was it that the Government which of all modern governments made most effort to monitor its own progress was in practice the one which most dramatically departed from its original declared strategy? And second – perhaps not unrelated – how far is an elected Government politically wise or indeed constitutionally entitled to abdicate its central political judgment to a non-elected body headed by a known political opponent? Some critics of the Heath Government would claim that it was exactly because it allowed its central strategy to be swayed by Rothschild and his irresponsible young colleagues that it abandoned the party policy on which it was elected. On this argument, the CPRS was not at all the custodian of the 'quiet revolution', but its enemy.

A secondary aspect of this strategic function was the Tank's attempt to set up within Whitehall a form of early warning system to alert the Government to tricky issues and hard decisions that might be coming up in six or twelve months' time – 'to give Ministers the chance to think about problems before they became problems'.[24] (This function was irreverently referred to within the Tank as 'Mr Whitelaw's bath'.) To have worked properly, however, such an exercise would have required more co-operation than was forthcoming from the departments, which were unwilling to divulge the necessary classified information or admit to hypothetical crises which might never happen. In 1972 the attempt at systematic early warning had to be abandoned, in favour of Rothschild's own hunches, of the sort remembered by Trend's successor, Sir John Hunt:

I remember Victor Rothschild sort of ambling into my room from time to time and saying 'How much time have you spent in the last month thinking about X?' And he would go out again because, as you know, he had a rather Delphic approach. But a few months later I would realise that X was a very important subject.[25]

Rothschild's private antennae were to be most spectacularly vindicated in 1973 in relation to the price of oil.

The Tank's other two characteristic modes of operation were concerned less with strategic thinking than with direct policy advice. This took the form, first, of 'collective briefs' to the whole Cabinet on short-term decisions coming before it, and, second, of full-scale enquiries into major problems, lasting several months. The former – about fifty a year, on subjects ranging from the retail price index to nuclear reactors – were designed to cut through the special pleading of the competing Whitehall departments to offer ministers a synoptic digest, in layman's language, of the various policy options and their implications. But the Tank did not have the manpower to contribute anything useful on more than a few selected topics; and even then it tended to get wind of items on the Cabinet agenda too late to be able to affect decisions already effectively taken. For these reasons they probably created more irritation than illumination. 'For a while', Rothschild recalled in 1974, 'Departments were quite allergic to our Collective Briefs because they provided an independent analysis by a group of people uncontaminated by years of Whitehall experience, of the subject under consideration.' They were accused of 'naïveté' and 'superficiality' – sometimes, Rothschild admitted, justifiably (but sometimes the apparent naïveté was deliberate). Later the regulars learned to nobble the Tank for their own purposes.[26]

The major enquiries, into a number of deep-seated long-term problems which spanned several departments, were more successful. Even though the eventual reports were not always acted on, they raised the level of Whitehall thinking in some important areas, with ultimate benefit in the future. The only CPRS report to be published in the Heath years – not under its own imprimatur, but as a White Paper – was on the Government sponsorship of scientific research and development, a particular concern of Rothschild's. His recommendation, though denounced by the universities as a threat to academic freedom, was accepted and resulted in the reorganisation of Government research contracts on a more businesslike basis, recognising the Government's interest as customer. Another unpublished but widely leaked enquiry looked – despite Burke Trend – at Concorde, which it roundly declared 'a commercial disaster', before concluding that the project must nevertheless be continued for political reasons. ('And, if it's of any interest to you,' Rothschild later told Peter Hennessy, 'it also said, "And for God's sake stop bellyaching about it, just get on with it."')[27] Other enquiries investigated the computer industry; lessons to be learned from Japanese industrial success; the future of London as an international financial centre; and energy policy. It was the last, begun in early 1972, when the price of oil was $1.90 a barrel, which really made the Think Tank's reputation. Drawing valuably on Rothschild's contacts in the oil industry, it presented disbelieving ministers in the summer of 1973 with a shocking scenario in which it predicted a steep rise in the price of oil by 1985, probably to $6 and possibly as much as $9 a barrel.[28] It failed only to predict the Arab-Israeli war, which precipitated the immediate quadrupling of the price (to $11) only a few months later. Nevertheless the Think Tank gained great kudos in Whitehall for having warned before it happened that the age of cheap fuel was coming to an end. Informed foresight on this global scale, leaving the rest of Whitehall gasping, did more than anything else to vindicate the Tank's existence. Even after Rothschild had left, it continued to cultivate a special expertise in the energy field.

One or two of the Think Tank's reports on economic policy, however, encroached very closely on highly controversial political questions of the Government's central strategy. For instance a 1972 study of Government support to industry tried to lay down some clear criteria for distinguishing declining industries ('lame ducks') which should not be propped up – the Tank advised against the rescue of Upper Clyde Shipbuilders – from potential 'growth points' where Government investment would be justified. Another report the same year tried to find ways of distancing the Government from the detailed running of the nationalised industries. Both these reports were in line with the Think Tank's remit to help the Government hold to the course of disengagement on which it had embarked in 1970. Both, however, were delivered to a Government which had changed its collective mind and was now rushing headlong in the opposite direction, finding pressing political reasons for pouring money into industry in the hope of stimulating rapid growth and intervening more closely than ever in the nationalised industries. In these circumstances the Tank's recommendations fell on deaf ears.[29]

If the Think Tank tried to resist one element of the Government's U-turn, however, it actively encouraged others. It played a significant part, for instance, in persuading Heath to abandon his earlier rooted opposition to variable exchange rates and to agree to float the pound in June 1972. Still more important, Rothschild and his team strongly supported the introduction of a statutory prices and incomes policy in the autumn of 1972. It is most likely that Heath and the Cabinet would eventually have been driven to the same resort by the pressure of events and the weight of advice they were receiving both from within the Government machine and from the press. While some who were present felt that the Chequers seminar in May 1972 marked a decisive turning point, there is other evidence that the critical shift in Government thinking had already taken place.[30] Whatever the truth, this was a key area of policy on which the Think Tank did not contradict, but strongly reinforced the official advice.

Despite Burke Trend's initial attempts to keep it away from economic policy, therefore, the Think Tank was a central player in the 1970–4 Government, overstepping the line which notionally confined it to safeguarding the Government's strategy by taking an active part in helping to reverse it. For most of the period Rothschild was a powerfully influential voice in Downing Street, second only to Sir William Armstrong. His and the Tank's influence was only reduced in the final months of 1973 when, as it happened, it might have played a critical role in saving the Government from the disaster which ultimately overtook it. This was the result of the one spectacular row which spoiled the otherwise excellent relations between Heath and Rothschild, when Rothschild made an unguardedly alarmist speech which embarrassingly contradicted an upbeat one by Heath the same day. Addressing a gathering of research scientists in Wiltshire, Rothschild warned, in words that he thought so unexceptionable that he did not bother to clear them with Downing Street, that if Britain did not dramatically improve its economic performance it would face continuing inexorable decline.[31]

Speaking the same day in Hertfordshire, Heath painted an optimistic picture of rising living standards produced by the success of Government policies.[32] His speech, however, was eclipsed by huge headlines reporting Rothschild's message of impending doom. Heath was understandably furious. Rothschild was summoned to Number 10, as he later recalled:

He gave me a rather unpleasant dressing down. I apologised. And in a very typical Heath-like way there came a moment in the interview when he said, 'Well, now, let's discuss nuclear reactors.' And that was the end of it. The matter was never raised again and our relationships were perfectly OK afterwards.[33]

That may have seemed the case to Rothschild, but in fact Heath's confidence in him was damaged. This was ironic, since their views of the country's position were in reality very similar. Heath had been trying to persuade the country of the need to 'take a very strong pull' at itself before it was too late for as long as he had been Tory leader, or even longer. (Witness his speech in the 1970 election urging the country to 'Wake up'.) Rothschild's strong support for a statutory incomes policy, and his even more alarmist letter of resignation to Harold Wilson in October 1974, appealing for a wartime spirit of national unity to defeat 'that neo-Hitler, that arch-enemy, inflation', revealed an apocalyptic mood of patriotic urgency very close to Heath's own at the same time.[34] In September 1973, however, when Heath was trying to convince himself and the country that the Government was winning the battle for sustainable growth, warnings of continued decline were not what he wanted to hear, certainly not in public. By speaking out pessimistically at such a moment, Rothschild had blotted his copybook; the result was that the Think Tank fell from prime ministerial favour at just the moment when its oil-price forecast was about to be vindicated and the Government entered on its final crisis. The Chequers strategy seminar planned for the autumn of 1973 was cancelled; a Think Tank report which attempted to shape the spending cuts which finally brought the 'Barber boom' to an end in December in accordance with a rational view of social priorities was rejected; and in the same month it was announced that Rothschild himself was to 'rest'.[35] There was at least one quite specific consequence of the Think Tank's eclipse. During the miners' strike in January 1974 Rothschild proposed that the increase in the price of oil gave legitimate ground for the Government to sanction a higher pay award to the NUM than could be justified under the strict terms of its incomes policy. Heath took the view that this was politically impossible, with results disastrous for his Government. [36] In this crisis he paid dearly for rejecting the sort of lateral thinking – seeing a domestic problem in its wider international context – which the Think Tank specialised in and which might in this instance have helped to get the Government out of the corner it had painted itself into.

The Think Tank outlived its creator by a further nine years, serving three subsequent prime ministers under three more heads – Kenneth Berrill, Robin Ibbs and John Sparrow – before Mrs Thatcher abolished it in 1983. By then it had long become a much less distinctive addition to the Whitehall scene than it had been at its zenith under Rothschild; moreover a part of its function had been usurped by the Downing Street Policy Unit in Number 10, set up by Wilson in 1974, initially under Bernard Donoughue. This, though still very small, was something much more like the sort of Prime

Minister's Department originally envisaged by Howell and Schreiber in 1970. Mrs Thatcher expanded the Policy Unit, bringing in more personal advisers of her own. The CPRS was confined much more than previously to long-term reports on specific problems: its licence to roam – as Douglas Hurd described Rothschild – 'like a condottiere through Whitehall, laying an ambush here, there breaching some crumbling fortress which had long outlived its usefulness'[37] had long since lapsed. Mrs Thatcher had her own ways of shaking up the Government machine: she had no wish to be told what to think. Nevertheless the Think Tank was mourned in Whitehall. It was a bold experiment in its heyday which, even when absorbed into the bureaucracy, still remained useful. The glow of romance that still surrounds its memory practically ensures that some future Prime Minister will want to recreate a new unit on similar lines. For all its shortcomings the Think Tank was unquestionably one of Heath's successes.

Rothschild always vigorously resisted attempts to attribute party political allegiance to the members of the Think Tank, claiming (in 1976) that 'one who professed himself to be a Conservative was more radical than most and clearly more so than another . . . who described himself as a Socialist; and one who claimed to be a Conservative when he came to us said later that he had joined the Labour Party.'[38] The members of the Tank were temporary Civil Servants who were supposed to leave their politics outside when they joined.

There was yet one more group of outsiders whom Heath brought into government in 1970, however, who were specifically expected to be political. These were the so-called 'special advisers' from Tory Central Office and the Conservative Research Department, where they had helped to run the policy-making exercise in opposition, who were now carried over from opposition into government in far greater numbers than had ever occurred before. These appointments gave rise to criticism that the Civil Service was being politicised, especially when a second wave of advisers was appointed in 1972. Lord Rothschild commented tartly: 'On the whole, all that seems to me special about these new advisers is that their position combines the functions of lesser politicians with the salaries of higher Civil Servants, and I must admit that that is rather special.'[39] The threat they posed to the impartiality of Whitehall was minimal, however, and as a group they quickly sank without trace. They were too few and too isolated to fulfil either the hopes or the exaggerated fears entertained of them.

Their introduction was consistent with Heath's desire – manifested in a number of ways – to blur the line between politicians and officials. It is often said that he was a Permanent Secretary *manqué*, who was more at ease dealing with officials than with his political colleagues. This was true up to a point; but he was also a politician and the officials he liked were those with a well-developed political sense. 'Heath wished his officials had more about them of the French Civil Service method of strong political advocacy,' Peter Hennessy has written. 'Trend would sometimes infuriate him by sticking to the traditional British style of displaying the options, the pros and cons of each, and insisting it was the Prime Minister's job to do the choosing.'[40] He much preferred Sir William Armstrong, an unusually political Civil Servant with pronounced views of his own which he was not afraid to argue. It was no accident that Heath came increasingly to regard Armstrong as his most trusted confidant. In the same way Heath tried to break the conventional Whitehall pattern of ministers and officials meeting separately and experimented with 'mixed' committees at which officials were encouraged to take part equally in the exchange of views. The experiment was not successful, largely because most Civil Servants are by temperament and training reluctant to argue openly with their political masters.

It was, in the end, one of Heath's faults, as his Government ploughed into ever-deepening crises, that he tended to look to officials, rather than to his colleagues, for advice which they were not trained or qualified to give. Observing helplessly from his privileged but junior position as the Prime Minister's political secretary, Douglas Hurd became sharply aware of the inadequacy of the Civil Service at moments of political crisis. Three times in 1972–3 – once over Northern Ireland, twice in relation to inflation and incomes policy – Hurd felt that the Civil Service let Heath down when he needed clear guidance. He tried, belatedly, in the autumn of 1973, to organise the special advisers to meet regularly as a group to try to offer the Government the frankly political advice it lacked. But it was too late.[41] The lesson of 1970–4 was that governments do need political advisers to prevent ministers becoming entirely smothered by the pressures of administration and to keep them in touch with their party. Subsequent governments have carried the idea further, so that special advisers are now an accepted species within Whitehall. In this respect, as in so many others, Heath's innovation, seen as bold at the time, was in fact too cautious to be immediately effective and was only fully developed a decade later.

Of course Heath did not solve the problems of what Harold Wilson termed 'the governance of Britain', any more than he solved the problems of the British economy. But he made a brave try. His diagnosis was sound and his attempted solutions well directed. Peter Hennessy's authoritative verdict gives him his due:

The Heath reforms, the most ambitious deliberate attempt at re-shaping the machinery of government since Lloyd George, were hugely unlucky in the circumstances of their crucial formative years. When launched in 1970 there was no crisis atmosphere to 'speed up the historical process' and enable a determined premier to sweep away the slow bureaucratic accretion of decades. When crisis did come it struck a system far from fully run-in, and, in-evitably, diverted ministerial – and, particularly, prime ministerial – eyes and attention elsewhere. In combination with the failed ex-periments of the Wilson years, it resulted, too, in a fashionable dismissal of all structural solutions to any governmental problems which was still apparent in the late 1980s . . . Thanks to the con-tinuing animosity within Tory ranks about the legacy of the 1970–74 government, Heath as PM has still to receive his histor-ical due. When he does, the potential importance of his administrative reforms, and the care with which they were pre-pared in Opposition, will be a substantial element in the 'revisionist' literature.[42]

There was a sense of impatience and expectation by the time the Government finally opened its autumn offensive. On 27 October Tony Barber presented to a packed House what was effectively an autumn Budget. A summer of inaction had been followed by Heath's ambitious declarations of intent at Blackpool. This at last was the moment when the Government stopped talking and un-veiled the first steps of its programme. Tory hopes were high, and Barber did not disappoint them. For five years Heath and Macleod had promised to reduce taxation and cut public expenditure. Barber's package combined substantial cuts in both personal and company taxes with some highly controversial economies in the fields of both industrial policy and the social services. On one side of the ledger, the standard rate of income tax was cut by 6d from 8s 3d to 7s 9d in the £ – bringing it back to the level at which the Tories had left it in 1964 – and corporation tax was reduced by 2·5 per cent to 42·5 per cent. On the other, Barber announced several measures intended to signal the Government's disengagement from detailed intervention in industry. Meanwhile a trawl around the spending departments had produced a diverse crop of savings on health, housing, education and public transport, designed to fulfil all those opposition promises to concentrate social provision on the most needy. These included steep rises in prescription charges (from 2s 6d to 4s) and charges for false teeth and spectacles; increased charges for school meals and the withdrawal of free milk from older primary school children (eight-to eleven-year-olds); the ending of universal subsidies for council house tenants, to be legislated in an early Housing Finance Bill; the withdrawal of subsidy from the London rail commuter service; and the introduction of admission charges for national museums and art galleries. The overall effect was to save around £300 million in the first year, rising to £1,600 million in 1974–5.

The genuinely poor, the old and the chronically sick were to be exempted, and Barber simultaneously announced a new Family Income Supplement (FIS) to bring extra assistance to poor families. Nevertheless the burden of the cuts fell squarely on ordinary people, who faced higher costs right across the board – rents and fares as well as increased charges for school meals and prescriptions – which would in the short term more than cancel out the benefits of any tax advantage. Labour attacked them vigorously as mean-spirited, inequitable and socially divisive. The withdrawal of school milk was a particularly emotive issue which thrust Margaret Thatcher into public prominence for the first time. Unforgettably dubbed 'Thatcher, Milk Snatcher' and 'The Most Unpopular Woman in Britain' by the popular press, she was henceforth identified as the female embodiment of Heath's hard-faced new Toryism.*

Labour accused the Government of deliberately attacking the living standards of the poor and of trying to reverse thirty years of social progress by planning to dismantle the Welfare State. Labour's outrage was predictable and exaggerated and might have been discounted had it not been that the new charges came on top of a rate of inflation that was already rising. By adding to the cost of living, at a time when the Government was already struggling to keep pay rises down, Barber's mini-budget inevitably provoked the unions to put in still higher claims, which the Government was bound to resist. The result was to create a climate of class confrontation between Government and unions, which was the last thing Heath and Robert Carr had wanted.

In opposition the Tories had condemned Labour's incomes policy and promised to restore free collective bargaining. The abolition of the Prices and Incomes Board, duly announced by Carr on 2 November, had been envisaged as a sweetener to ease the unions' acceptance of other parts of the Government's programme, the withdrawal of benefits and the reform of industrial relations. In

---

* She had in fact fought hard for her Department and done pretty well for it. In particular she saved the nascent Open University, which Macleod had marked down for the axe. She tried to ensure that the cuts fell on non-educational expenditure like milk and meals, rather than on teachers and buildings, and was unprepared for the outcry that the withdrawal of free milk caused.[43]

contrasting Tory freedom with socialist controls, however, they had not foreseen that Labour would itself have abandoned incomes policy in 1969, letting wages rip before the election, so that the new Government was faced immediately with the need to try to restrain them. Carr appealed repeatedly to both unions and employers to show restraint: wages, he told the TUC in August, had risen 12 per cent over the past year, twice the rate of inflation, while production had risen by less than 2 per cent.[44] But the TUC, urged on by Jack Jones and Hugh Scanlon, rejected his pleas. Following the settlement of the dock strike in July, the first major dispute of the autumn involved local authority dustmen and sewage workers. After five weeks Sir Jack Scamp, called in as arbitrator, awarded the men an extra £2 10s a week (NUPE had asked for £2 15s) specifically to keep up with inflation. The Government was dismayed by the award. Heath condemned Scamp's arguments on television as 'completely nonsensical', but continued to set his face firmly against a return to incomes policy:

> People must face up to their own responsibilities . . . Employers have responsibilities, so do trades union leaders and trade unionists . . . The alternative to accepting responsibilities is for the Government to compel the people . . . What I am trying to do, what this Government is trying to do, is to solve the country's problems in a free society.[45]

The press and public, however, were not impressed. It seemed that a Prime Minister who had repeatedly promised 'action not words', had after all only words to offer. Opinion polls showed overwhelming public support for some sort of incomes policy – statutory or voluntary – while Fleet Street expressed a near-unanimous view that the Government's hands-off position would prove unsustainable. *The Times* thought it ' a great pity that Mr Heath and Mr Barber have committed themselves so strongly'. Without an incomes policy, Government economic policy was 'a mint with a hole'.[46] The Government's response was, first, to recognise that it did, as employer, have the responsibility for resisting excessive pay claims in the public sector, hoping that the example it set would be followed by the private sector; and, second, to propose as a sort of 'norm' for the coming pay round that each settlement should be, not higher, but slightly lower than the one before, thus putting the inflationary spiral into reverse. This was known as the 'n-1' policy. It was only an indicative norm, with no statutory force. It could still be maintained that it was not, in the sense in which the term was normally used, an 'incomes policy': there was no specified permitted percentage rise. Nevertheless there was another sense in which, even by setting an indicative norm, the Government had already abandoned the position that pay should be determined by the market in each individual industry, without reference to social comparisons – thus intellectually opening the door to the setting of specific figures later on. Since Heath's abjuring of incomes policy had been determined by political opportunism rather than market theory in the first place, it was easily abandoned. Still, the adoption of 'n-1' marks a significant stage in the transformation of the Government's philosophy.

The first test of the Government's determination to resist unjustified demands in the public sector was posed by the power workers, who on 7 December started a work to rule in pursuit of an increase of 25 per cent. In mid-winter the effect on the public was severe, with large parts of the country suffering a nightly loss of heating and light: television sets and Christmas lights were blacked out. There was a run on candles – that enduring symbol of the early 1970s. On 12 December the Government declared a State of Emergency – already its second in six months – to spread the cuts evenly on a rota basis, but once again appointed a judge, Lord Wilberforce, to head a Court of Enquiry while normal working was resumed in time for Christmas. They took the precaution of specifying that the Court's terms of reference included 'consideration of the public interest'. Despite this broad hint, however, Wilberforce when he eventually reported on 10 February came up with a massive award generally calculated to be worth at least 15 per cent and possibly 19 per cent.[47] If this was 'n', it was a dangerously high norm from which to try beating other groups of workers down.

The next challenge was easier to defeat. On 18 January the postmen – led by the engagingly moustachioed but singularly unthreatening figure of Tom Jackson – began a seven-week strike in support of a claim for 15 per cent. The Government stood firm. The public was inconvenienced but suffered no hardship comparable to power cuts and the union was eventually forced to settle for 9 per cent. Ministers were said to be privately sorry that a small moderate union like the postmen had to be the one to bear the force of the Government's resolve – Labour alleged on the contrary that they had deliberately singled out the postmen as easy victims[48] – but it was nevertheless an important victory which helped to establish 'n-1' for the rest of 1971 as a rough-and-ready but viable policy, at least in the public sector.

Alongside these running battles with individual unions over pay, and the wider confrontation looming with the TUC as a whole over the Industrial Relations Bill, which was published on 3 December, the Government was further antagonising the public-sector unions by the first tentative applications of the philosophy of denationalisation and refusal to rescue 'lame ducks'. Lord Robens at the Coal Board and Lord Melchett at the British Steel Corporation successfully resisted the 'hiving-off' of their more profitable subsidiaries. But in November the state airlines BEA and BOAC were forced to concede some routes to the independents, British Caledonian and British United Airways; in January the Transport Minister John Peyton announced that British Rail's tame travel agent, Thomas Cook, would be sold off; and in June 1971 the Government finally divested itself of the anomaly of the Carlisle pubs, acquired as an experiment in liquor control during the First World War. All these were, as it were, small beer but they could be represented, both by Davies's more hawkish juniors at the DTI and by the Opposition, as the first straws in a wind of wholesale deregulation and privatisation. Likewise in November the Minister of Posts and Telecommunications, Christopher Chataway, abruptly sacked the chairman of the Post Office, Lord Hall, widely believed to be out of sympathy with the Government's wish to make the postal service more profit-oriented – a contributory factor to the postmen's strike two months later; John Davies allowed the Mersey Docks and Harbour Board to go into liquidation rather than rescue it with public money; and in December Frederick Corfield announced Britain's withdrawal from the European Airbus project. Taken together, all these actions appeared to affirm the Government's determination to enforce a tough competition policy. In the *New Statesman* Alan Watkins correctly sensed that Davies's heart was not wholly in the new policy, and – shrewdly again – even confessed himself still not sure of Heath's real views; but he was persuaded that the Government as a whole was serious. Sir John Eden and Nicholas Ridley at the DTI, he wrote on 25 November, were supported by

> the more aggressively Tory members of the Cabinet, such as Geoffrey Rippon and Sir Keith Joseph and, I assume (for the Prime Minister is still a mystery to me, a man of unplumbable shallows), Edward Heath . . . Enoch Powell may not actually be in the Government: but Powell is firmly installed at Power.[49]

The impression of undeviating doctrinaire rigour was badly dented, however, only two months later when the aircraft division of Rolls-Royce ran into serious trouble over the engines it was supposed to be supplying for the American Lockheed RB-211 airbus.

Rolls-Royce was one of the most prestigious names in British industry, internationally synonymous with quality and luxury. Admittedly the popular reputation derived more from the famous cars than from the aero engines; nevertheless the company was a symbolic talisman of British excellence. The Lockheed contract, however, had been badly miscalculated. Already under the Labour Government the company had needed £20 million from the Industrial Reorganisation Commission and in November 1970 Corfield had reluctantly put together a further £60 million package (£42 million from the Government, £18 million from the banks) to pay its debts. But even this was not enough. By January Rolls-Royce was again facing bankruptcy. This was something the Government simply could not allow to happen: prestige apart, Rolls-Royce was too important a supplier to the Ministry of Defence. On 4 February, to ironic Labour jeers, Corfield announced that the aircraft side of the company was to be nationalised.

This was intensely embarrassing for a Government committed to reducing the size of the public sector. There were good grounds for arguing that the Government genuinely had no choice: as well as defence, there were important diplomatic considerations. The American Government was deeply concerned, and Heath was obliged to give personal assurances by telephone to President Nixon that Lockheed would get its engines at the price contracted. Lord Carrington and Peter Rawlinson flew to Washington to negotiate the new terms. Though Enoch Powell bitingly asserted that the rescue cast doubt on the Government's belief in capitalism, he found little serious support: the keenest backbench privatisers – like Norman Tebbit – were prepared to swallow Rolls-Royce as a special case.[50] Though admitting that it was 'a bitter shock', Heath was able to present the company's collapse as proving his longstanding warnings that 'much of our apparent prosperity is based on illusions'.[51] Even so, the fact that within eight months of coming to power the tough new Tory Government had been driven to carry through the first new nationalisation of a privately owned industry since 1949 gave rise to a good deal of public amusement. As David Wood noted in *The Times*: 'Mr Heath has been robbed of something of great value to him.'[52]

At the same time the opinion polls confirmed that the Government's honeymoon, in so far as it had ever had one, was over. The election had dealt such a blow to the pollsters' credibility that for the first six months few commentators paid them much regard. It was striking, even so, how short lived was the boost the Tories and Heath personally derived from his unpredicted triumph. By the end of the year ORC – the one poll which had been right in June – showed Labour back in a five-point lead, with 40 per cent of the electorate thinking that Heath was doing 'a bad job' (against 36 per cent who thought he was doing well).[53] The Government's apparently firm handling of the power workers' dispute was reflected in an improvement in January. But the events of February – the Rolls-Royce rescue, the Wilberforce award, the protracted postal strike – saw Labour once more into a comfortable lead, with no more than 31 per cent now prepared to say the Government was doing well. Labour had not plumbed this depth of unpopularity until 1968, three and a half years after taking power: Heath had achieved it in nine months. His personal rating still lagged some ten points behind Wilson's. Though the margin fluctuated, in the whole of next three years – until January 1974 – the Tories were never to hold a lead again. There was one shred of consolation: despite or because of union opposition, the public still strongly supported the proposed Industrial Relations Bill. On the other hand, on another central plank of Heath's strategy the voters had swung sharply against the Government: by a margin of 3–1 they now declared themselves opposed to joining the EEC. Heath had designated 1971 'the Year of Europe'. Already embattled on the industrial and economic fronts, the Government faced a stiff uphill fight to realise his European dream.[54]

16

Special Relationships

MOST prime ministers take office primarily intent on achieving cherished projects in domestic policy, but become increasingly preoccupied with foreign affairs as they go on, finding a welcome escape from intractable economic difficulties in the chance to cut a figure on the world stage. Neville Chamberlain, Harold Macmillan, Harold Wilson and Margaret Thatcher all – with differing degrees of success – exemplify this familiar progression. Ted Heath was – with Eden and Home – one of the few who all his life had been more interested in foreign than in domestic affairs. From his early trips to Spain and Germany as a student, through his war experience and the earnest self-educating travels with which, as a young backbencher and Government Whip, he used to fill the parliamentary recess, he had always been unusually interested in 'abroad'. Specifically he was not so much interested in other countries and cultures for themselves – he never learned a second language – but rather in geopolitics – the management of relations between powers as a means of preventing the recurrence of war and promoting international prosperity. Above all, by the time he emerged from the Whips' office as a political figure in his own right, he was concerned with discovering and maintaining a worthwhile role for Britain in a world changing to her disadvantage. From the moment he came into office in June 1970 the domestic and economic policies of his Government – pre-eminently his determination to take Britain into the EEC – were dictated by his overriding ambition to recover what he believed to be Britain's proper place on the international stage.

Heath's lifelong devotion to making Britain part of a united Europe was founded on a paradox. For it derived, as much as the contrary commitment of the most determined little Englander, from sturdy English patriotism, pride in the uniqueness of Britain's history and an ardent desire to reassert British leadership in the world. He was never a European idealist, except secondarily in so far as he judged that British leadership could only be asserted through whole-hearted participation in an integrated Europe. He was unusual in his generation in that he came to that conclusion early and was then prepared to make it the central principle of his career, subordinating to it all other considerations of trade, sentiment and defence. But Europe was not, in his view, a substitute for a role in the wider world: it was rather a broader platform, a wider economic base, from which British influence could be exercised and amplified. Europe was absolutely not to be seen as a retreat – the end, as Gaitskell had put it, of 'a thousand years of history' – but as an opportunity for Britain to be 'great' again.

This corny but passionately held ambition was the constant theme of his rhetoric in opposition. So long as General de Gaulle was President of France the door to Europe remained closed. Nevertheless he was determined, as he had promised the Five in 1963, that Britain should not turn its back on the commitment represented by Macmillan's application but should keep banging on the door until admitted, while continuing to align its foreign policy increasingly towards the continent in preparation for that moment. Meanwhile he believed that Britain's reputation in the world had been dragged in the mud by Wilson's unprincipled and shifty posturing. The 15 per cent import surcharge imposed without consultation in October 1964 had cynically affronted EFTA, just as devaluation in 1967 was a betrayal of sterling holders around the world. Over Rhodesia Wilson's hollow threats and violent condemnation of the Smith régime for the benefit of his left wing had wrecked any chance of a settlement; while his attempts to play the peacemaker in Vietnam, toadying to President Johnson in Washington while failing to support the Americans where it mattered, had brought Britain only ridicule. Even Wilson's application to join the EEC, though he had been bound to support it, Heath considered frivolously ill-prepared and misconceived. Above all he regarded Labour's decision on grounds of cost to withdraw British forces from East of Suez as a shameful abdication of responsibility and a breach of obligation to allies. In all these areas Heath came into office promising to restore honesty and straight dealing to the conduct of foreign affairs and thereby to rebuild Britain's honour and influence in the world.

There was never any question about who would be Foreign Secretary. The job had to be Alec Douglas-Home's if he wanted it, and he did. There is no indication that Heath ever thought of anyone else. Though Heath as Prime Minister was now the senior, the division of responsibility between them was much the same as it had been in 1960–3; Heath concentrated on Europe (with Geoffrey Rippon handling the detailed negotiations), leaving Home to handle the rest of the world. Though Home was by background and experience more sensitive both to the Atlantic alliance and to the Commonwealth, there was no significant divergence of outlook between them: Home's old-world emollience balanced Heath's abrasiveness, while on the Soviet Union and on the Middle East they saw eye to eye. After his early mishandling of the South African arms issue there was speculation in the press that Home would retire after eighteen months or so; in fact he stayed throughout the life of the Government. There was no reason why Heath should have wished to replace him. Some eyebrows were raised when Heath appointed another peer, Lord Carrington, as Minister of Defence, but the fuss did not last. Carrington asked for and got Ian Gilmour as his deputy in the Commons; while Home's Minister of State, with the job of answering for the Foreign Office in the Commons, was Joseph Godber.

Heath's first priority was to negotiate Britain's entry to the EEC as quickly as possible and – within the constraint of political acceptability – at almost any price. His purpose was to realign the country's sense of identity irrevocably towards Europe. The long-cherished 'special relationship' with the United States was to be abruptly ended, and sentimental allegiance to the Commonwealth briskly shelved. This did not mean, however, that Heath saw himself as in any way anti-American, anti-Commonwealth or anti-Third World. On the contrary, he believed strongly that an enlarged Europe, including Britain, should shoulder a larger role within NATO, becoming a true partner of the United States instead of a resentful dependent, to the benefit of both parties. It was in America's interest – indeed it had long been American policy – that Britain should become a part of Europe. There could be nothing anti-American about that.

He believed that Britain owed it both to the United States and to the nations of the Far East and the Gulf to continue to accept at least a share of responsibility for the defence of those regions. It was neither fair nor healthy that the Americans should have to bear the whole burden of containing communism; nor did such a continuing world role in any way conflict with Britain's primary commitment to Europe. On the contrary, it was only the new economic strength to be expected from EEC membership that would enable Britain to continue to play such a role.

Likewise he maintained that Britain as a member of the EEC would be able to give more help to the countries of the developing world – including Commonwealth countries – both by development aid and by giving access to the wider market of the whole Community, than Britain could possibly do outside the Community. If not his first consideration, it was a consistent theme of Heath's case for a united Europe that it would benefit the whole world, not just Europe itself. He always talked of an outward-looking Europe, aware of its global responsibilities, not of an inward-looking protectionist Europe. Tony Benn, however, attending a Downing Street dinner for a Senegali delegation in 1972, took a jaundiced view of this vision. Heath, he wrote in his diary, made 'a mad impassioned speech' about Europe and Africa in the post-imperial age. 'It was nineteenth-century imperialism reborn in his mind through status within the Common Market.'[1]

Heath's overriding commitment to Europe did make him intolerant of the Commonwealth. So much of the anti-Common Market argument in the early 1960s had appealed to Commonwealth sentiment that he was bound to react against it. He thought it patent nonsense to pretend that the amorphous, diverse, loose-knit Commonwealth could offer Britain a practical alternative to the enlarged economic opportunities of the EEC. Having no personal or family ties with the Commonwealth himself he felt no sentiment for it at all; and feeling no guilt for the sins of empire he had no time for the pretensions of African and Asian leaders of doubtful democratic credentials who presumed to lecture Britain about racism and civil rights.

The running sore inflaming Commonwealth relations after 1965 was the Rhodesian rebellion, a sore gratuitously exacerbated by the row over arms sales to South Africa. On the major issue the new Government faced strong pressure from the Tory right to recognise the Smith régime and lift sanctions immediately. This Heath and Home were not prepared to do. Home hoped to achieve a settlement to bring Rhodesia back to legality on the basis of the Five Principles he had laid down before leaving office in 1964, the most important of which required 'unimpeded progress to majority rule'. (This was a much weaker condition than Wilson's famous Sixth Principle, 'NIBMAR – No Independence Before Majority Rule'.) But he was not willing to lift sanctions until the constitutional position had been restored. At the party conference in October he announced only a few minor humanitarian concessions, such as British courts recognising Rhodesian divorces. As a result the annual embarrassment of the right-wing vote against the renewal of sanctions continued, with twenty-three rebels voting against the Government on 9 November.

Meanwhile the Government had provoked the fury of the black Commonwealth by Home's inept announcement of its intention to resume selling defence equipment to South Africa. One after another

African leaders came to Britain to denounce the Government's support of apartheid. President Nyerere of Tanzania, visiting Heath at Chequers on 11 October, threatened to withdraw from the Commonwealth; in November the Nigerian Foreign Minister went one better and threatened that the other members would expel Britain. On 16 October a Downing Street dinner for Kenneth Kaunda of Zambia ended in an open row. Heath was furious that Kaunda had declared on arrival at Heathrow that he had come to appeal to the British people over the heads of their Government. He sat stony-faced for most of the evening while Carrington and Sir Denis Greenhill tried to make polite conversation, then burst out in angry denunciation of Kaunda's hypocrisy in condemning Britain while Zambia itself continued to trade with South Africa without scruple. Kaunda was so shocked at being spoken to in such a way by a British Prime Minister that he left early, shaking his head in disbelief.[2] Government sources tried to minimise the scene, saying the talks had been 'rational not emotional'. Kaunda, leaving London two days later, likewise denied that he had walked out; but he admitted that the evening 'did not have a happy ending'.[3]

This sort of double standard was just what Heath could not stomach. At the Tory party conference he declared uncompromisingly that Britain was independent too. The British Government, he said, valued the Commonwealth and listened gladly to its views. 'But the Commonwealth can only thrive . . . if all its members realize that Britain, like themselves, enjoys full independence of action . . . British policy is, and is going to remain, a matter for decision by the British Government.'[4]

Two weeks later, at a press conference in New York where he was attending the twenty-fifth anniversary of the founding of the United Nations, he declared again that the Commonwealth was 'a free association of individual member countries' and gave a blunt warning: 'Unless members are prepared to respect each other's positions then, of course, it is not an organisation that can continue for long.'[5]

The South African issued overshadowed the Commonwealth conference held in January 1971 in Singapore. 'The prospect of nine days in the dock', Douglas Hurd has written, 'was not attractive.'[6] As well as the Africans, Pierre Trudeau of Canada had publicly condemned the British Government's action. Heath did not in fact care strongly about arms sales for themselves; but he was determined not to be pushed around. He held a series of sticky meetings with all the African leaders in turn: Milton Obote of Uganda dubbed him 'Edward the Silent'.[7] (Heath was not sorry when Obote, while out of the country, was deposed by Idi Amin.) *The Times*'s Commonwealth editor contrasted Heath's ill-concealed irritation with Home's unruffled old-world courtesy: 'Mr Heath seems not to be secure enough for that.'[8]

Behind the scenes the issue was defused by a study group set up to fudge a compromise. As a result, as Hurd put it, 'The Government neither renounced its policy not sold any significant arms.'[9] Yet Heath nearly wrecked the delicate agreement by another angry performance at the press conference called to announce it. Normally a consummate diplomat, Heath allowed the posturing of African leaders to get under his skin in very much the same way that Margaret Thatcher some years later let herself by riled by European leaders. His attitude was not racist: but he had little respect for them and saw no reason for Britain to kowtow to their racial sensitivities.

By the end of 1971 Home thought he had solved the Rhodesian problem. Following secret soundings by Lord Goodman (who had previously acted in the same capacity for Wilson) and Max Aitken (an old friend of Ian Smith from RAF days) agreement was reached on the basis of Smith's 1969 white supremacy constitution, amended to allow the possibility of an eventual African majority in the very long run. The terms were widely condemned as a sell out, but Home and Heath only wanted to be rid of the problem. In the House of Lords Goodman virtually admitted as much, maintaining that the agreement could not be a sell out since Britain had nothing to sell.[10] That, essentially, was Heath's view. The proposed constitution was just about within the Five Principles so long as the Africans could be persuaded to accept it. Home flew to Salisbury to sign the agreement on 21 November 1971. Heath openly rejoiced that an issue that had plagued his leadership ever since 1965 had finally been resolved.[11] But he rejoiced too soon. Provision had been made for a Commission led by a High Court judge, Lord Pearce, to go to Rhodesia to test African consent before the agreement came into effect. To the surprise and chagrin of Smith and Home, Pearce reported in May 1972 that the majority population overwhelmingly rejected the settlement. In truth the Pearce Commission was a misconceived exercise which was always likely to backfire: the Africans simply did not trust Smith. So Home's solution went the same way as Wilson's various attempts: it was another ten years before Lord Carrington and Mrs Thatcher managed to extricate Britain from the Rhodesian imbroglio. For the remainder of Heath's Government the stalemate continued, but the pressure from both the Commonwealth and the Tory right was reduced. Sanctions were maintained in theory – though in practice they were widely evaded – with the ritual rebellion every November; but the heat was largely taken out of the issue.

Britain's credit with the Commonwealth was improved in 1972 when Idi Amin started expelling Asians from Uganda. The Government accepted that it had a legal and moral duty to allow a substantial number of refugees – ultimately 28,000 – to come to Britain. Enoch Powell, the right-wing Monday Club and a number of backbenchers threatened serious revolt on the issue; but Sir Alec and the new Home Secretary, Robert Carr, stood firm on Britain's obligation while managing to persuade Canada, India and a number of other countries to share the responsibility. Partly as a result of this episode, the next Commonwealth conference, held in Ottawa in August 1973, was – in Heath's own words – far less 'stormy' and 'painful' than Singapore in 1971. Heath was able to tell the party conference that autumn that other Commonwealth countries now respected Britain's right to determine her own policy. In particular they now accepted Britain's entry into the EEC as an accomplished fact and recognised the benefits Britain's membership could bring them. As a result, he believed, the Commonwealth was 'now established on a much more realistic basis'.[12]

One practical use the Commonwealth did have for Heath was to help him honour – at least in part – his pledge to reverse Labour's announced withdrawal of British forces from the Far East. Already in opposition he had laid the groundwork for a five-power defence pact between Britain, Australia, New Zealand, Malaysia and Singapore. (He had fitted in the necessary diplomacy around his victory in the Sydney–Hobart race at the end of 1969.) No sooner was the Government installed in office than Carrington was dispatched to finalise the details, which Heath was able to announce to the party conference in October, making a point of stressing that it was a Commonwealth agreement.[13] The pact represented only a very minor restoration of Labour's cuts, however: Britain undertook to keep only 4,500 men in the region, and there was to be no reprieve for the Singapore military base, the headquarters of Far East Command, due to close in 1971. Moreover, despite his assurances to the rulers of the Gulf states whom he had visited with Douglas Hurd in 1969, promising that Britain would not abandon them, once in office Heath was obliged reluctantly to accept that it was too late to reverse the withdrawal of British forces. The sheikhs were already making their own arrangements. Broadly speaking the reduction of overseas commitments which Heath had denounced so bitterly since 1968 proceeded without interruption after 1970. Recognition of reality had been too long delayed as it was. By the time Heath returned to power the absurdity of trying to put the clock back was clear to all. As Hurd characteristically expressed it in *An End to Promises*, 'Events had moved on. As so often happens, the old arguments seemed irrelevant.'[14]

Nuclear defence was a different matter. There was of course no question of a Conservative Government abandoning or seriously running down Britain's independent deterrent, but Heath had long aspired to the idea of pooling it with the French, as a practical step to European integration and at the same time as a means of reducing Europe's dependence on the United States. Nuclear technology was one positive contribution Britain could make to the building of Europe; the sharing of British expertise was something de Gaulle had been interested in back in 1962, if only Macmillan had then felt able to offer it. In a series of lectures which he delivered at Harvard in 1967 Heath had publicly committed himself to the vision of 'a nuclear force based on the existing British and French forces which could be held in trusteeship for Europe as a whole', forming the nucleus of 'an eventual European defence system'.[15] The proposal was not to be seen as a condition of British membership of the Community, but he claimed that it had 'recently begun to find favour among influential opinion on both sides of the English Channel'.[16] This was wishful thinking: French nuclear self-confidence had increased since 1962 and President Pompidou showed no interest in giving up national control of the *force de frappe*. Though Heath still asserted in 1990 that President Nixon 'was fully prepared to see us move in that direction',[17] Lord Carrington's memoirs confirm that the Ministry of Defence was strongly opposed to any suggestion of Anglo-French pooling which would have breached the 1958 agreement with the Americans.[18] In truth nuclear pooling was a pet notion of Heath's which was never seriously on the table. The only thing he could do in the nuclear field was modernise Britain's own arsenal. He and Carrington reopened the question of building a fifth Polaris submarine, scrapped by Labour, but decided against it; they also considered and rejected buying the Poseidon system. But in 1973 they did initiate the development of the Chevaline programme to update Polaris, a programme secretly continued by Labour after 1974.[19] There was virtually no public controversy about nuclear weapons between 1970 and 1974.

The most radical aspect of Heath's foreign policy – differentiating his Government sharply from every previous postwar administration, Conservative or Labour, and from all his successors over the next sixteen years as well – was his determination *not* to have a special relationship with the United States. On the contrary, he was determined to assert Britain's European identity. Remembering de Gaulle's reaction to Macmillan's nuclear deal with President Kennedy at Nassau in 1962, he was specifically determined to show

Pompidou that Britain was not an American Trojan Horse. He therefore quite deliberately made no early visit to Washington and made very little use of the transatlantic telephone. Instead, President Nixon had to come and see him, for a brief stopover at Chequers in October when the Queen's presence ensured that there was no time for serious talking. This was distressing to Nixon, who actively admired Heath, had been elated by his victory against the odds in June and desperately wanted to have a special relationship with him. They were in some respects, as Henry Kissinger noted, similar men – both loners whose struggles to reach the top from similar social backgrounds had left them introverted, self-reliant and suspicious.[20] But this was no reason to expect them to strike up a personal bond: neither was good at social relaxation. In fact, when they got down to hard discussion they did not get on badly – their views of international politics were broadly parallel; but the essential point was that Heath did not intend to have a personal relationship at all. The Americans found his determination to keep his distance bewildering. Used to Wilson fawning on Johnson and before that Macmillan's avuncular relationship with Kennedy, they could not understand a British Prime Minister deliberately wanting to keep relations cool, especially at a time when Pompidou and Willy Brandt were trying to get closer to Washington. Kissinger wrote in 1982:

> Paradoxically, while the other European leaders strove to improve their relations with us . . . Heath went in the opposite direction. His relations with us were always correct, but they rarely rose above a basic reserve that prevented – in the name of Europe – the close co-operation with us that was his for the taking.[21]

The intimate access to the President which previous prime ministers had enjoyed was reduced to formal diplomatic exchanges. Kissinger found Heath 'incisive, decisive and astute' in discussion of world affairs;[22] yet 'of all British political leaders, Heath was the most indifferent to the American connection and perhaps even to Americans individually'. He 'dealt with us with an unsentimentality totally at variance with the "special relationship"'. As a result, Nixon's relationship with Heath 'was like that of a jilted lover'.[23]

The first formal meeting between the two leaders – discounting Nixon's brief visit to Chequers in October – took place in Washington in December 1970. Heath 'left no doubt about the new priorities in British policy'. Kissinger immediately sensed 'a revolution in Britain's post-war foreign policy', and wrote in his memoirs of a 'painful' transformation.[24] Nevertheless there was no rift. Heath was as supportive of Nixon's gradual disengagement from Vietnam as he had been of the vigorous prosecution of the war when in opposition: 'he argued vigorously that an American withdrawal . . . under conditions interpreted as a collapse of American will might unleash a new round of Soviet aggression in Europe.'[25] Nixon for his part welcomed Heath's Five-Power Defence Pact in the Far East, though the Americans remained sceptical of his apprehension of a Soviet threat in the Indian Ocean and privately critical of the policy of selling arms to South Africa.

Differences multiplied in 1971, however, initially on the economic front. The United States had long supported British membership of the EEC on political grounds, but now that it was about to become reality the Americans suddenly felt themselves threatened by the enlarged Community. For some years the dollar had been coming under mounting pressure, and there were growing demands in Congress for protection against what was perceived as unfair European competition. On 15 August Nixon's combative Treasury Secretary, John Connally, abruptly imposed a 10 per cent import surcharge and suspended the convertibility of the dollar, thus ending the dollar-centred international financial system which had prevailed since the Bretton Woods agreement in 1944. His unilateral action evoked shock and outrage in Europe and Japan, where it was seen almost as an act of economic war. Heath, despite his deliberate refusal of a special relationship, was furious at what he regarded as an act of international irresponsibility on the part of Washington.* The world economy was thrown into a period of uncertainty which was not resolved for several years. A temporary realignment of currencies was achieved by the Smithsonian Agreement negotiated by the leading industrial nations in Washington in December. Heath met Nixon a few days later in Bermuda – a summit widely reported as marking the formal ending of the 'special relationship': the contrast was drawn with the Kennedy–Macmillan meeting on the same island ten years earlier.[27] The atmosphere was eased by Nixon's announcement of the lifting of the American import surcharge; but the suspension of convertibility remained. Six months later Britain was obliged, despite Heath's past assurances, to allow the pound to 'float'. The devaluation of the dollar continued to have serious repercussions for the British economy right through 1972–3.

---

* With typically black humour he blamed Connally, who had been wounded in the assassination of President Kennedy. 'I knew they killed the wrong man in Dallas,' he is said to have remarked.[26]

Further tension between London and Washington arose over the war between India and Pakistan which resulted in the creation of Bangladesh. Heath had established a good relationship with Mrs Gandhi, sympathised with India's support for Bengal and hoped to play a mediating role. To his annoyance Nixon and Kissinger – regarding India as a Soviet puppet and just at that moment preparing to reopen relations with Pakistan's protector, China – branded India the aggressor and vigorously supported Pakistan. Nixon regarded the war simplistically as another episode in the Soviet Union's continual testing of Western resolve.[28] Twenty years later, in an unbuttoned interview, Heath asserted that Kissinger tried to involve Britain in the conflict, as Kennedy and Johnson had earlier tried to involve Britain in Vietnam. Whatever the accuracy of his recollections, the contemptuous tone of his remarks vividly expressed his hostility to the 'special relationship':

> What they wanted from the special relationship was to land Britain in it as well. There was the question of the Indo–Pakistan war and what Henry wanted was to land us in that and I was determined not to be landed. We discussed this in Bermuda [in December 1971] . . . President Nixon . . . opened up the discussion and said, 'There seems to be some misunderstanding about this, Henry, try to explain why this was what you wanted', and so then we had a lecture about the conceptual nature of Kissinger policy. Well, we easily despatched that and Nixon said, 'Well, that's the end of that one, Henry, isn't it?' . . . Did we lose anything by it? No, of course not. We gained an enormous amount. I can quite see that it's rather difficult for some Americans, including Henry, to adjust themselves to this, but it's necessary for them to do it. Now, there are some people who always want to nestle on the shoulder of an American president. That's no future for Britain.[29]

In late 1972, following Nixon's historic opening to China and the conclusion of the first SALT agreement for nuclear parity with the Soviet Union, Kissinger tried to reassure the Europeans by declaring 1973 the 'Year of Europe'. Willy Brandt believed that 'the President had only a superficial knowledge of what Kissinger has set in motion'.[30] Heath, looking back, was equally scornful of this stillborn initiative:

> [Kissinger] created the Year of Europe, which never of course came about, without any discussions with us . . . or with anybody else. He just declared he was going to have a Year of Europe. I said

to him, 'Now you've done this, we must have a year of the United States. Who are you to propose that there should be a Year of Europe? You're not part of Europe.'[31]

At this time Heath, Brandt and Pompidou were pressing on hard with trying to create new structures and set ambitious timetables to advance the unity of the enlarged Community. Kissinger found their unresponsiveness to his pressure for a new Atlantic Charter intensely frustrating, Heath's especially so. Meeting Nixon again in the supposedly informal setting of Camp David in February 1973, he was more than ever on his guard:

> There was a nearly impenetrable opacity about Heath's formulations which, given his intelligence, had to be deliberate . . . [He] could not have been more helpful on diagnosis or more evasive on prescription . . . He wanted Europe *as a unit* to formulate answers to our queries: he was determined to avoid any whiff of Anglo-American collusion.[32]

In July Heath spelled out in a letter to Nixon that the Nine would henceforth hold all communication with the Americans on a common basis: there would be no more confidential bilateral relations such as Britain had enjoyed in the past. To this, Nixon returned a reply 'of unusual coolness'.[33] Since a united European foreign policy was as yet no more than an aspiration – as the Middle East crisis in the autumn was to demonstrate – the Americans were left feeling that they had no trusted ally in Europe they could confidently deal with. According to Kissinger, old hands in the Foreign Office were deeply unhappy at Heath's wanton breaking of traditional Anglo-American relations. Visiting Washington that summer, Burke Trend – 'my wise and gentle friend', with whom Kissinger had enjoyed close dealings in the past – 'came as close to showing his distress as the code of discipline of the British Civil Service and his high sense of honor permitted'.[34] Nevertheless another document from London in August sharply reiterated – with just a hint of regret? – Britain's new *communautaire* line:

> We are . . . in trouble already with some of the smaller members of the Nine for the delay with which they have learned of some of our discussions with the White House . . . We think wherever possible we should go for multilateral discussions from the outset . . . The nature of the Atlantic relationship is not something that can be agreed through purely bilateral discussion. Action,

as opposed to explanations, will have to be multilateral.[35]

In the event 1973 turned out to be for Nixon the year of Watergate. Their own concerns apart, one reason for the European leaders' coolness to the 'Year of Europe' was their unwillingness to be associated with a deeply tarnished President. But, more importantly, they were trying to build Europe in 1973, not rebuild the Atlantic alliance. This shared perspective dovetailed perfectly with Heath's overriding political purpose. Kissinger's overtures actually gave him the ideal opportunity to assert Britain's new European alignment by declining to be wooed. Watergate, coming on top of Washington's highhanded behaviour in 1971, only confirmed Heath's conviction that Europe should look to its own salvation and place no reliance on the United States.

The Americans may have found Heath a difficult partner, but they could have no complaints about his vigour as a Cold Warrior. As a good European, he loyally supported Willy Brandt's *Ostpolitik*; but he had no doubt about the need for the West – America and Europe in partnership – to keep its guard up, both in Europe (the invasion of Czechoslovakia was a very recent reminder of Soviet ruthlessness) and in Asia. (Nixon was sincerely grateful to Heath as the only European leader who defended the renewed bombing of North Vietnam in December 1972.)[36] He fully shared the view uncompromisingly expressed by Home in his memoirs, published in 1976:

> One must always force oneself to remember – odious and boring though it is – that all Communists are dedicated to a single end – victory over every other creed and every other way of life . . . The democratic peoples must . . . however regretfully and painfully, supply the sinews for defence; for unless they are ready to do so the Communist persistence will win.[37]

In keeping with this philosophy, Home quickly determined – with Heath's support – to make a stand against the Russians' increasingly flagrant abuse of their London Trade Mission for espionage. Following repeated warnings delivered directly to Gromyko, and acting on information supplied by a Soviet defector, the Foreign Office finally took the bull by the horns in September 1971 and expelled 105 named individuals (out of 550 accredited diplomats: Britain maintained only 83 in Moscow). The Russians protested furiously, but their retaliation was not more than token. An invitation for Home to visit Moscow was cancelled, and Heath in his term of office never did meet Kosygin or Brezhnev. After a couple of years of frozen relations, however, normal contacts were resumed in 1973. Home believed that the *démarche* – ecstatically described by Peter Wright in *Spycatcher* as 'a brilliant coup'[38] – was thoroughly justified and achieved its purpose. 'The Russian leaders learned that there was a limit to our tolerance; and thereafter there was a new respect in their dealings with us.'[39]

Meanwhile Britain closely followed the historic lead taken by the Americans in opening relations with China. Heath was initially inclined to resent Nixon's astonishing volte-face as another example of unilateral American action taken without consultation with the European allies. Ever since 1950, when Britain had been among the first powers to recognise Communist China, successive British Governments had been critical of the Americans' continued support for Taiwan and refusal to admit China to the United Nations. It took a little adjustment to get used to Washington's sudden conversion, but Nixon's visit to Peking in February 1972 set off a flurry of British contacts – cultural and commercial as well as diplomatic: the junior Foreign Office Minister Anthony Royle was followed by Home in October 1972, and Heath himself was due to visit in the first week of 1974. In the event he was unable to go until after he had ceased to be Prime Minister; but that trip, when he eventually made it in 1975, proved to be the first of many. In the years that followed he became increasingly convinced of the growing importance of China and cast himself as a major, if unofficial, intermediary in Sino-British relations.

At the other end of the diplomatic scale, some minor countries provided major headaches for the Heath government. In June 1971 the unpredictable Dom Mintoff came to power in Malta and immediately demanded a greatly increased rent for the naval facilities enjoyed by Britain and NATO. At Chequers in September Heath handled him skilfully and appeared to have amicably secured a new agreement, only for Mintoff to tear it up on Christmas Eve, giving British and allied forces a week to leave the island. Despite ties of tradition and sentiment, however, Malta was no longer so essential to Britain or NATO as it had been in the war: both France and Italy offered alternative facilities. So Heath coolly called Mintoff's bluff and ordered British forces to prepare to leave. To his irritation, his tough stance was undermined by the Secretary-General of NATO, Dr Luns: NATO commanders were afraid of the island's facilities falling into Soviet or Libyan hands. But Carrington – whose memoirs give a vivid account of the 'positively operatic experience of doing business with Mintoff'[40] – eventually succeeded in negotiating a settlement halfway between the £10 million a year Britain initially offered and the £18 million Mintoff demanded.*

Another disproportionate headache was the so-called 'Cod War' with Iceland, which began in February 1972 when the Icelandic Parliament unilaterally declared a fifty-mile exclusion zone for boats from other countries fishing around Iceland. Britain appealed to the International Court of Justice, but Iceland was unmoved. Feeling on both sides became dangerously heightened when Icelandic gunboats began to cut the gear of British trawlers. In May 1973 a trawler was holed; Britain responded by sending a frigate. Finally, in talks at 10 Downing Street in October 1973 Heath accepted a compromise whereby the British catch within the fifty-mile limit was reduced by 50,000 tons a year (about 27 per cent). But this was a long-running dispute which dragged on for years after Heath left office.

The major foreign policy crisis of the period occurred – as so often – in the Middle East. Once again it exposed a wide gulf between the Europeans and the United States, and once again Heath aligned Britain firmly on the side of Europe. On 6 October 1973, on the Jewish holy day of Yom Kippur, Egypt and Syria launched a massive two-pronged attack on Israel in an attempt to recover the territory lost in the Six-Day War of 1967. At that time, reflecting Labour's close and longstanding links with Zionism, the Wilson Government, behind the cover of formal neutrality, had unhesitatingly supported Israel. The position in 1973 was very different. From the moment they took office Heath and Home had been much less sympathetic to Israel. When the Israeli Prime Minister, Golda Meir, visited London in November 1970, they pressed her to relinquish the conquered territories, in accordance with United Nations Resolution 242, in exchange for guaranteed recognition by the Arabs and security within her pre-1967 boundaries. Home publicly endorsed the UN's assertion of 'the inadmissibility of the acquisition of territory by war': the British Government took the view that an exchange of land for recognition offered the only basis for a lasting settlement in the region.[42] Mrs Meir went home regretting that 'to my sorrow there has been no meeting of minds on this issue'.[43]

The other EEC countries, particularly France, took the same line – partly reflecting their critical dependence on Arab oil, but partly also (at least in France's case) reflecting longstanding colonial links with

---

* Carrington also tells an extraordinary story of Heath being called upon to help patch up the Maltese leader's marriage. While Mintoff was at Chequers in September 1971, his estranged wife – the daughter of an English admiral – suddenly turned up, insisting on talking things over with him over tea with Heath. 'I managed to get them off fairly soon,' Heath told Carrington. 'It was all very embarrassing. I persuaded her to sit in the car with him, anyway!'[41]

the Arab world. The Americans, however, under sustained pressure from the powerful Jewish lobby in the United States, continued to give virtually unquestioning support to Israel, putting little pressure on the Israelis to be more flexible. While both Americans and Europeans nominally accepted Resolution 242, and the latter no more than the former wished to see Israel extinguished, there was already a clear difference of emphasis between the Western allies well before 1973. When war broke out, those differences sharpened. The Europeans were inclined to blame the Americans for having encouraged Israeli intransigence while ignoring the vital interest of Europe in maintaining the flow of Arab oil. Though the Nine failed signally to speak with a united voice, their eventual common line was to call for a ceasefire on the basis of a return to the 1967 frontiers: their overriding concern was not to antagonise the Arabs. Hence they mostly stopped supplying arms or spares to either side, while Britain, France and Germany refused to allow the United States to use air bases in their countries or overfly their territory in order to supply Israel, arguing that the Middle East was outside the NATO area. Only the Dutch braved Arab retaliation by continuing to let the Americans use their facilities. (It made little difference: the Arabs cut the supply of oil and raised the price to all countries.) As a result the Americans were forced to make a 2,000-mile detour from their bases in Holland out over the Atlantic in order to enter the Mediterranean at Gibraltar. In the House of Commons Heath defended the Government's policy as even-handed: it would be absurd for Britain to call for a ceasefire while continuing to sell arms to both combatants. Labour, he charged, only wanted to supply Israel. He declined to condemn the Americans for putting their forces in the area on alert, publicly denying that he had not been consulted; but he told Willy Brandt that he was *not* consulted, and he pointedly failed to endorse the American action.[44]

The view from Washington was that the European allies – Heath regrettably included – had betrayed the obligations of the Atlantic alliance at a critical moment of common danger. Technically the Middle East might be outside the NATO area, but it was an overwhelming common interest that the region should not be dominated either by the Soviet Union or by radical Arab régimes bent on destroying Israel. Kissinger thought the Europeans' anxiety to appease the Arabs craven and short-sighted. Heath, conversely, thought American policy unduly dictated by subservience to Israel. He agreed with the strategic aim but believed that encouraging Israeli intransigence only fuelled Arab determination and played into the Russians' hands. At the same time Washington's expectation that the

European allies should tamely follow the American line aggravated yet again his conviction that Europe must – as a matter of principle – assert its independence. Speaking with unusual frankness to American journalists in late November, he specifically rejected American leadership and virtually blamed American policy for the recent war. His words were reported to Washington by the London Embassy: 'The tenor of Heath's comments made it clear that, in his view, Britain had disagreed with US policy since 1967 and British views have been given no consideration on the part of the US in formulating Mideast policy.'[45]

The Middle East war thus dramatically widened the gulf of misunderstanding already revealed by the 'Year of Europe' and vindicated Heath's view of the imbalance of the Atlantic relationship as then constituted. It confirmed, first, that American and European interests often diverged; second, that the Americans still took it for granted that their interest should prevail, with no more than cursory consultation; and, third, that the Europeans still had a long way to go to co-ordinate their common perspective into a united policy capable of being quickly and clearly enunciated and acted on. In more statesmanlike mode at the Lord Mayor's banquet in the Guildhall a week or two earlier he did not disguise that there had been strains within the alliance. But the lesson he drew publicly was that Europe must play a greater role in a multipolar world which could no longer be shaped by the two superpowers. Washington and Moscow, he warned, must recognise that Peking and Tokyo, Cairo and Tel Aviv, as well as Western Europe, were 'vitally important too'. 'The immensity of the nuclear threshold gives to others an influence in the course of history, which those who were not militarily speaking great powers have previously lacked . . . I believe this to be of great importance to the nations of Western Europe.'[46]

In other words, membership of a united Europe offered to Britain a means of recovering in partnership the leadership role in the world which she could no longer hope to play alone. This – in his last major foreign policy speech as Prime Minister before the energy crisis triggered by the war engulfed him – encapsulates the core of Heath's geo-political faith.

Heath was not in Downing Street long enough to accomplish the irreversible transformation of Britain's foreign policy that he dreamed of. But he made a fair start between 1970 and 1974 in achieving his major goals. Above all, of course, he succeeded in his historic purpose of taking Britain into the EEC – even though the opportunist somersaulting of the Labour party continued to cast doubt on the decision, which was not finally confirmed until the referendum held in 1975. In addition the 1971 dislocation of the international financial system, worldwide inflation and the impact of the 1973 oil shock aborted the rapid progress which he, Brandt and Pompidou had hoped to make towards closer political and economic integration. He failed to solve the Rhodesian problem, and was obliged to accept Labour's withdrawal from military commitments east of Suez as a *fait accompli*. Nevertheless he and Home did succeed in giving Britain a clearer and more consistent posture in the eyes of the world than had been the case in the previous six years. Sometimes painfully, Britain was set on a new course. Unfortunately it was not maintained by his successors between 1974 and 1990: Harold Wilson, Jim Callaghan and above all Margaret Thatcher were all instinctive Atlanticists bent on reviving and exploiting for all it was worth the old 'special relationship' with Washington which Heath had tried to end. Heath's brave attempt to wrench British foreign policy on to a new basis remained for another decade and a half an aberration in postwar history. Yet it was a forward-looking aberration: amid the dismal saga of missed national opportunities since 1945 his premiership shines out as a brief, honourable exception to the backward-looking norm.

17

Reversing the Veto

HEATH's highest political ambition was to lead Britain into the European Community. Seven years earlier de Gaulle had slammed the door in his face – the greatest personal reverse of his career so far. But the General himself had predicted that Britain would join eventually, under Heath's leadership. There was an enticing historical symmetry in the idea that he might fulfil de Gaulle's prophecy; but it is not often that history turns out so neatly. In the event, the opportunity did indeed fall to Heath, and he grasped it unhesitatingly: the one unquestionable success of his premiership. Yet the outcome was not achieved by any means so smoothly or so inevitably as may appear in retrospect. Heath was extraordinarily fortunate to come back into office just at the moment when British entry became a real possibility: the opportunity could so easily have fallen to Harold Wilson. But it was still not a foregone conclusion: it took enormous nerve, skill, courage and determination on Heath's part, first, to secure the lifting of the French veto and then to drive the agreement through an increasingly divided and fractious House of Commons. Between the rock of French scepticism on one side and the whirlpool of domestic politics on the other, it was a perilous voyage which he accomplished to realise his – and Britain's – European destiny.

The prospects for a successful application had been transformed by President de Gaulle's resignation in April 1969. His successor, Georges Pompidou, immediately began to make much more positive noises about the possible enlargement of the Community – though not before the primary French interest, the Common Agricultural Policy (CAP), was completed and fully operational in 1970. With the Five still pressing for UK admission, and all three British parties now apparently committed to entry, the omens looked very favourable. The Labour Government had already fixed a date for renewed negotiations to begin as soon as the General Election was out of the way. The Common Market was scarcely an issue in the campaign.

In the event, of course, it was not Labour's chief negotiator, George Thomson, but Anthony Barber who represented Britain at Luxemburg on 30 June 1970. The substitution undoubtedly increased the chances of a successful negotiation – not so much, as Wilson immediately and repeatedly alleged, because Heath would negotiate less toughly and accept less favourable terms than Labour, but rather because the Europeans respected the new Prime Minister's passionate commitment to the Community and were therefore more ready to smooth Britain's path. Seven years on from 1963, Heath approached the Community a second time in 1970 with his credit high and a tacit understanding in Paris and Brussels that he could not decently be rebuffed again. As before, there were still formidable practical difficulties to be overcome, but it was widely assumed that the political will now existed in both London and Paris to overcome them.

Heath's crucial contribution to the eventual success of the negotiation was his realisation that the fate of the third British application, like the first two, lay with the President of France. It seems obvious, yet Wilson and George Brown in 1967 had repeated Macmillan's mistake by thinking they could circumvent French opposition by mobilising the support of the Five; and this was still the Foreign Office approach. Douglas Hurd has described Heath's greater strategic grasp very clearly:

> It would be a great mistake to suppose that he was ready to give the French whatever they wanted. On the contrary he saw them as tough negotiators with whom we would need again to bargain toughly. But he understood what the Foreign Office appeared to ignore, namely the real structure of the European Community. The French had the veto, and on the question of British entry had already used it once. There was no question of them accepting British membership just because the Five wanted us in . . . Therefore if Britain wanted to enter it was to the French that we should pay attention. We must gain friends in France and outmanœuvre our enemies . . . We must not try to organise the Five against the French, for that was the best way to ensure that the French would again frustrate us.[1]

Heath always knew that it would ultimately be up to him to

convince Pompidou that de Gaulle's objections to British entry no longer applied. But first the tedious groundwork of detailed negotiation had to be gone over one more time.

The talks formally opened in Brussels on 29 October. By now Barber's place at the head of the British team had been taken by the convivial, expansive figure of Geoffrey Rippon. But the brief was still essentially that prepared for Thomson before the election. This time the procedure was less Byzantine than in 1961–3. Then, Heath had been obliged to deal with all of the Six simultaneously, leading to endless confusion and frustration: now the President of the Council of Ministers spoke for the Six – though they still had to agree among themselves beforehand – with the Commission as before on hand to resolve difficulties. As it happened, France held the chair in the crucial period January–June 1971. (Germany chaired the earlier sessions up to Christmas, Italy the final stages in July.) On balance, this was probably a good thing, since it involved the French centrally in trying to reach agreement. Below the ministerial level, the British delegation was led by Sir Con O'Neill, formerly British Ambassador to the Community, and John Robinson, who had been one of Heath's lieutenants in 1961–3. This time the British had much more understanding of how the Community worked than in 1961. In London Rippon reported back to a committee composed of Home, Hailsham, John Davies and Jim Prior, as well as directly to Heath, who took a close interest without interfering too much. Finally, Heath established a special EEC Unit in the Cabinet Office, headed by Sir William Nield, to brief Rippon and co-ordinate the Whitehall departments.[2]

With all the experience and good will that was brought to bear, the negotiations were still far from easy. The French were determined to strike a hard bargain, while the British – with public opinion increasingly suspicious and Wilson quick to pounce on any weakness – could not afford to be seen to be giving too much away. Even more than Heath in 1961–3, Rippon faced the problem of having to negotiate in public; televised press conferences after every session made it difficult to present a balanced overview of the emerging package. The least difficult problems this time around were those involving specific commodities. Provision had to be made for New Zealand dairy produce and West Indian sugar; but the Commonwealth was a much less emotive obstacle than in 1961. The problem of territorial fishing grounds proved intractable – involving as it did not only Britain but the other three applicants for membership, Denmark, Norway and Ireland – but it never seriously threatened the outcome. The question of the transitional period for British acceptance of the common Community tariff posed an early problem: Rippon initially sought a three-year transition for industry, six years for agriculture, but he quickly compromised on five years for both. The two issues which really gave trouble were financial: the level of the British contribution to the Community budget and the role of sterling as a world currency. On either or both of these rocks it looked as though the negotiations might once again founder.

Even ten years later, when Britain was inside the Community, it still took Mrs Thatcher several bruising summits to reduce the British budget contribution to a level which reflected her economic strength. Negotiating as an applicant, Rippon was in a much weaker position. While the Germans had for years been willing, for political reasons, to pay more than their share to subsidise French agriculture, there was no reason why Britain should do the same. But the French had made it a condition for considering British entry at all that the CAP was now fixed. This was the price of joining the Community late. When Rippon proposed an initial British contribution of just 3 per cent of the Community budget, Pompidou himself cuttingly dismissed it as an example of the famous British sense of humour.[3] France demanded 21 per cent immediately, with no transition period. This of course was posturing – by both sides – but it augured badly. Moreover, whatever sympathy the Five felt for Britain's disadvantage was offset by irritation that the British approach of calculating its 'net contribution' so precisely offended the fundamental ethos of the EEC.

By the beginning of February 1971 the negotiations were stalled. Rippon reported gloomily to the House of Commons on 4 February, and a few days later Heath, speaking to Members of the European Parliament in London, gave a warning – clearly aimed across the Channel – of the possibility of failure:

> We must find terms for our entry . . . which are tolerable in the short term and clearly and visibly beneficial in the long term. The British Government would not be able to present for the approval of Parliament terms which did not meet these tests.[4]

In March the French made another devastating *démarche* on the subject of sterling and the future of the London capital market, insisting that sterling's world role be ended immediately, as a precondition of progress towards European monetary union. The British – and Heath in particular – wanted nothing better than to reduce Britain's vulnerability to world capital movements, in order to become a European currency. But it had been tacitly accepted that it could not be done overnight. For this very reason the question of sterling had officially been excluded from the negotiations. The sudden French insistence on bringing it up was so unreasonable that it raised for the first time serious doubt as to whether they really wanted the negotiations to succeed. 'Barring a highly improbable French change of heart,' the experienced Brussels watcher Nora Beloff suggested in the *Observer* that Heath would soon have to decide 'whether to persevere or cut his losses'.[5]

The pessimistic apprehension in London was that the French, if not actually preparing to impose another outright veto, were once again working to achieve the same result by insisting on impossible terms. The alternative hope was that Pompidou did intend to let Britain in, but meanwhile had instructed his negotiators to keep bargaining hard as a test of Britain's resolve. The danger of this was that the talks would develop a negative momentum, while the impression of French obduracy risked hardening British opinion against joining at all. With polls now showing nearly 70 per cent of the public against entry, the Labour party was beginning ominously to shift its ground: in April 120 Labour MPs signed a Commons motion opposing entry (though another 100 signed a *Guardian* advertisement in support). Wilson was evidently preparing to cover his retreat by declaring that the terms – whatever they turned out to be – were unacceptable.[6] At the same time long-term Conservative anti-Marketeers were drawing encouragement from the deadlock in Brussels and beginning to find their voice. It was becoming imperative to complete the negotiations quickly if they were to succeed at all.

In fact, behind the scenes there was more progress than appeared before the television lights. From February onwards direct bilateral Anglo-French talks had been proceeding at the Quai d'Orsay between the British Ambassador, Christopher Soames, and Michel Jobert, then Secretary-General of the Elysée, Pompidou's right-hand man. Appointed by Wilson, Soames was the right man in the right job at the right time: a politician, not a career diplomat, he was as passionately committed as Heath himself to securing Britain's entry to the Community. He reported his discussions not through official channels but *via* Robert Armstrong direct to Heath. 'Very few of the senior men in the Foreign Office', Uwe Kitzinger has written, 'were told of what was afoot.'

So, while at Brussels the trench warfare was carried on without mercy on either side, in Paris from late February onwards the secret peace talks were beginning to gel. This tiny nucleus of half-a-dozen people . . . analysed the log-jam and began to unlock it.[7]

Part of the solution was to lift the negotiations out of the mire of detailed haggling by reminding both sides of the larger issues. To this end Heath paid a visit in early April to Willy Brandt in Bonn, where he spoke strongly of the 'utmost urgency' of reaching agreement, warning of the dangers not only in Britain but to Europe of a third and possibly final failure. 'If we miss this opportunity, it will not be there for us to pick up again in a year or two.' Not only would Britain turn its back on Europe:

> The world will not stand still. If Europe fails to seize this opportunity, our friends will be dismayed and our enemies heartened. Soviet ambitions of domination would be pursued more ruthlessly. Our friends, disillusioned by our disunity, would more and more be tempted to leave Europe to its own devices.[8]

Publicly and privately, Brandt assured him again of German hopes for a successful outcome of the talks: he could not put pressure on France, but it was his impression that Pompidou did not want them to fail. The two leaders' personal relationship was good, as Brandt – somewhat pedantically – described in his memoirs. 'I never felt Edward Heath's reputed lack of personal warmth,' he wrote in 1976. 'Uncomplicated and characterised by mutual trust, our talks might almost have been described, without triteness, as friendly.'[9] Though scarcely effusive, this is probably as much as can be said of Heath's relations with any foreign leader.

In May the log-jam broke. After three months the secret talks in Paris at last bore fruit in Brussels. An all-night session on 12–13 May yielded a French climbdown on sugar in return for a British compromise on farm prices plus, most crucially, outline agreement on the British budget contribution. (A starting figure of 8·6 per cent, rising to 19 per cent over five years.) Sterling was now the last major stumbling block, and there were indications that the French President – a former banker himself – might be persuaded to take a sympathetic view of British difficulties. The way was now clear for a direct personal approach by Heath to Pompidou. A summit meeting between the two men was fixed for 20–1 May in Paris.

Heath prepared himself with characteristic thoroughness, like a student – with access to all the resources of Whitehall – preparing himself for a vital examination, as Douglas Hurd described:

> For hours on end the Prime Minister sat under a tree, dunking biscuits in tea. Experts were produced individually and in groups . . . They all had their session under the tree, while ducks from the

park waddled amorously across the lawn and over the wall on the Horse Guards workmen banged together the stands for the Queen's Birthday Parade.[10]

In a sense all this detailed preparation was beside the point. What mattered was that he should make a good impression on Pompidou. (They had never met before, except briefly after de Gaulle's funeral.) Heath's task in Paris was to persuade de Gaulle's heir, not that he personally knew every detail of the negotiations – he had known those in 1963 – but that Britain was now truly ready to link her destiny with Europe. Pompidou had to be convinced that the British Government unreservedly accepted the Treaty of Rome and would not, as soon as she was inside the club, start trying to change the rules. As Pompidou himself told a BBC interviewer a few days before the summit, arguments over butter and sugar were not the problem. 'The crux of the matter is that there is a European conception or idea, and the question to be ascertained is whether the United Kingdom's conception is indeed European. That will be the aim of my meeting with Mr Heath.'

By 'Europe', Pompidou specifically assured British viewers, he did not mean federalism. He believed that France and Britain shared the same approach to European integration, 'because I can hardly imagine that the British nation as I know and admire it would wish suddenly to renounce its national identity'.[11] On the other hand he mischievously told the Paris newspaper *Le Soir* that the British, if they joined, should accept French as the main language of the Community, since English was the language of the United States!*[12] The probability is that after all the careful preparation of the ground by Soames and Jobert, Pompidou fully intended to lift the veto. Nevertheless the issue remained tantalisingly in doubt. Much would depend on the personal chemistry. 'We didn't want a good meeting,' a member of the British delegation told Kitzinger. 'We needed a very, very good meeting indeed between the two men.'[13] They also needed an unmistakable demonstration of political harmony to announce to the world that a new era of Franco-British friendship had dawned.

They got what they wanted. In more than twelve hours of face-to-

---

* Showing willing, Heath recorded a message in his dreadful French for French television, which was shown simultaneously with Pompidou's appearance on 'Panorama'. Meeting him at Orly the next day, Pompidou pretended to be so impressed by his fluency that he immediately launched into rapid French, leaving Heath gaping helplessly.

face talks over two days, with only interpreters present, Heath performed superbly and the two men, in Con O'Neill's word, 'clicked'. 'They liked each other and they trusted each other.'[14] At a splendid dinner at the Elysée Palace on the Thursday evening, Pompidou struck a lofty note which – while not quite clinching it – left a successful outcome in no real doubt:

> Through two men who are talking to each other, two peoples are trying to find each other again. To find each other to take part in a great joint endeavour – the construction of a European group of nations determined to reconcile the safeguarding of their national identities with the constraints of acting as a community . . .

'Our views are sufficiently close', he concluded, 'that we can go forward without pessimism.'[15] Heath in reply spoke somewhat mawkishly of a united Europe as 'a city . . . at unity in itself, that has peace within its walls and plenteousness within its palaces', and quoted his own words at Aachen in 1963 when receiving the Charlemagne Prize.

The next day the talks continued far longer than expected. The two leaders broke for lunch at the British Embassy – in diplomatic protocol it was a rare compliment for the President of France to lunch with a mere Prime Minister. The closing press conference was expected to follow immediately. Heath had planned to fly back to London and go straight to Cowes to sail *Morning Cloud* in a race that evening. At lunchtime, however – as Heath recalled in *Sailing* – 'we found we could make much greater progress than we had expected; we decided to carry on with the talks. My private secretary sent a message to *Morning Cloud* to sail on without me.'*[16] Not until late in the afternoon did the two men emerge, but when they appeared they were wreathed in smiles. Symbolically the press conference was held in the same room – the *Salon des Fêtes* – in which de Gaulle had pronounced his two vetoes. This time there were long handshakes for the cameras and a heady mood of mutual congratulation.

Once again Pompidou had the words for what had been achieved:

---

* Heath continues the story characteristically:

That evening, when all had been settled, President Pompidou said to me, 'Well, you have missed your race. A fortnight ago you won. What do you want to happen this time? Is it better for them to win without you, in which case it will show you don't matter, or not to win, in which case *Morning Cloud* has lost an important race just before your Admiral's Cup trials? Which is it to be?' There was nothing I could do either way. *Morning Cloud* settled it by coming second.[17]

Many people believed that Great Britain was not European and did not wish to become European and that Britain wanted to enter the Community only to destroy it. Many people also thought that France was ready to use all kinds of means and pretexts to impose a new veto on British entry . . . You see before you two men who are convinced to the contrary . . . It would be unreasonable now to believe that an agreement will not be reached in June . . . The spirit of our conversations yesterday and today allows me to think that the negotiations will be successful.[18]

Heath was banal as always, rolling out well-worn clichés. Yet to those journalists and others who remembered 1963 and knew how much it meant to him to lift the veto that had been slapped on his efforts seven years before, his triumph was a moving occasion. By convincing Pompidou, he appeared to have cleared at last the highest obstacle to British entry to the Community. The champagne flowed freely on his plane back to London that night. He was not to know at that stage how formidable some of the later domestic hurdles were to prove.

On Monday, Heath gave the House of Commons 'an almost aggressively optimistic report' of the outcome of the summit.[19] Though all the details still remained to be resolved, he was certain that agreement on acceptable terms was now assured and disposed of questions from Wilson and others with complete command. Indeed so bullish was he in his hour of victory that he gave considerable offence by slapping down too brusquely a query from the Chairman of the 1922 Committee, Sir Harry Legge-Bourke.[20] Pressed on the future evolution of the Community he looked forward confidently to the development of economic and monetary union, but was careful to stress the Luxemburg Compromise which reserved to each member country a veto on matters touching its vital national interest: 'Joining the Community does not entail a loss of national identity or an erosion of essential national sovereignty.'[21]

When the negotiations were resumed in early June the pieces duly fell into place. On instructions from the Elysée Palace, French obstruction miraculously ceased. Agreement was quickly reached on sugar and on New Zealand, to the declared satisfaction of both the New Zealanders and the Commonwealth sugar producers. Most dramatic of all, in a bewildering *coup de théâtre* Valéry Giscard d'Estaing, the French Finance Minister, suddenly accepted Rippon's proposals on sterling, hitherto declared to be quite out of the question. It was agreed – as Britain had always insisted was the only way – that overseas holdings of sterling should be run down gradually, with no explicit commitment as to how and when sterling's international role should finally be ended. This was clearly something that had been settled between Heath and Pompidou in Paris, a bilateral deal concluded without reference to the Five. Only the problem of the fishing grounds was left to be resolved at a later date.

After a final session in Luxemburg on 22–3 June Rippon returned in triumph with the terms, which were widely regarded as being better than could have been expected. Though there was still great uncertainty about the likely effect of entry on the balance of payments and on the price of food, the deal secured for the Commonwealth was hard to fault when the New Zealanders and the sugar producers themselves gave it their blessing. A White Paper outlining the terms was rushed out on 7 July. It was accompanied by a 16-page glossy brochure setting out the case for entry, and Heath went on television to tell the public that the moment of decision was at hand. This was the beginning of a 'great debate' which lasted over the summer. Heath's first instinct had been to go for a quick vote to get the terms accepted by Parliament before the recess. Both *The Economist* and, within his private office, Douglas Hurd warned that support for entry was fraying alarmingly: with Labour hardening against joining, it would be harder to win the crucial vote if he delayed until after the party conferences.[22] He was reluctantly persuaded, however, by the Chief Whip, Francis Pym, and a majority of the Cabinet that it would be better not to rush it. Instead, following a five-day debate at the end of July the Commons was merely invited to 'take note' of the terms. So the first stage ended, and a massive Government publicity campaign was launched to win the second stage in the autumn.

What then of the terms which Heath and Rippon negotiated? Largely because Labour was so badly split on the principle of membership, it was on 'the terms' that the debate on entry to the Community now focused. The only way Wilson could keep his party united was by insisting on the one hand – to satisfy the Pro-Europeans – that he still supported membership on the right terms, while claiming on the other – to please the anti-Marketeers – that the terms which Heath had accepted ('Tory terms') were ruinous and unacceptable. In fact the difference between 'good' and 'bad' terms never amounted to more than 1 per cent of GNP. The disproportionate emphasis on the terms was a purely political device to cover Labour's divisions. (Tory opponents of entry, by contrast, rarely based their opposition on the terms. Their objection was more fundamental, centring on the loss of sovereignty.) Nevertheless it coloured the whole debate about Britain and Europe for the next ten years. It has been argued that because Wilson and Callaghan successfully 'renegotiated' Heath's terms in 1974–5, and still more because Mrs Thatcher had to fight so hard to reduce Britain's budget contribution after 1979, the Heath–Rippon terms must necessarily have been bad. It is further argued – following Wilson's lead – that Heath was so determined on entry that he would have accepted virtually any terms, thus ensuring that he made a bad bargain.[23]

Yet both contentions are distorted by hindsight. So far as the negotiations are concerned, they were unquestionably tough. Rippon did not roll over and give away essential interests in his eagerness to get agreement at any price. Far from it: the negotiations were close to collapse until Heath's direct intervention with Pompidou unlocked them, after which it was the French who largely gave way. On this analysis, as Christopher Lord has written, Heath's personal commitment, so far from costing Britain more, 'may have been worth a few percentage points off Britain's financial contribution'.[24] Later difficulties do not alter the fact that Heath's terms were seen by most commentators at the time as pretty favourable, certainly better than many – including the Labour ministers who had initiated the application – had thought likely at the outset. All the leading Labour pro-Marketeers recorded their conviction that a Labour Government would have been happy to have achieved such a deal.[25] The point is that there was always going to be a steep admission fee for Britain, seeking to enter the Community sixteen years after it was founded, just at the moment when the Six had finally completed the financial arrangements that suited them. The fault was Churchill's and Attlee's and Eden's, as well as de Gaulle's, that the price was high. But that price seemed reasonable in 1971. It was based on the expectation, first, of continued economic growth and, second, of a fresh impetus towards closer integration in which Britain and the other new members would be fully involved and hence fully protected. Agriculture was expected to take progressively less of the Community budget, industrial and regional policy – from which Britain would have expected a greater return – progressively more. That the 1971 terms came to appear unreasonable by 1979 – the 1975 renegotiation was largely cosmetic – was due, first, to the 1973 oil shock and the international economic recession, which set back any new Community initiatives by several years, and, second, to Britain's exceptionally poor economic performance in the 1970s, which made her contribution to the Community Budget more burdensome than had been anticipated or intended in 1971. In sum, the fact that the 1971 terms required later adjustment was the result of subsequent events and unlucky timing rather than of weak bargaining.

What mattered in the long run was that Britain – at last, and still subject to the approval of Parliament – was in. De Gaulle's fateful 'Non' had been removed from the path. This was Heath's doing. Those closest to the negotiation were certain that it could not have been achieved without his single-minded commitment. 'The winning round of President Pompidou', Douglas Hurd has written, 'was probably the greatest single feat of Mr Heath's premiership. In these talks he repaired the errors of twenty years of faulty French and British policy. A few years more and the errors might have been irreparable.'[26] The outcome may have disappointed in the short run. But it was an historic achievement none the less.

18

'Kill the Bill'

Back on the home front, the new Government's first legislative priority was the Industrial Relations Bill, the one major measure unambiguously promised ever since 1965 and thoroughly prepared in opposition. With the incidence of strikes running at ever-higher levels – 1970 turned out to be the worst year for days lost in industrial disputes since 1926 – and overwhelming popular support in the opinion polls, it was the policy above all others that the Conservatives felt they had been elected to enact. If ever any Government had a mandate for anything, *The Economist* declared, this one had for trade union reform.[1] Delay was further ruled out by the memory of Labour's retreat the year before. The Government took office determined that its long-promised reform must be put through quickly and entire, with no messing around.

They did not anticipate serious opposition, partly because they had such an indisputable mandate which they thought the unions would be democratically bound to recognise; partly because they believed that in opposition they had established good relations with trade union leaders who had privately assured them that they would accept the Bill – and even tacitly welcomed it – even though they would not say so publicly; and partly because they honestly believed that the reform they intended was a fair and balanced package which was not 'anti-union' but would actually strengthen the unions and responsible union leaders in the proper exercise of their role.

As a result they did not see the need to go through the motions of consulting publicly with the TUC, who accordingly felt slighted. The whole ethos of trade unions is negotiation. If union leaders were to be won over to support the Bill they badly needed to be given at least the shadow of consultation. Denied the face-saver of a shadow fight, it was predictable that they would feel obliged to have a real fight; and so they did. It was right and proper that the Government should be determined to have its Bill; but it was a serious political misjudgment on Robert Carr's part to have slapped it so uncompromisingly on the table with what appeared to union leaders 'unblinking severity'.[2] Even *The Economist*, keen on the Bill as it was, urged the Government to remember that it was supposed to *improve* industrial relations: they should see it as 'a major public relations exercise as much as a parliamentary battle'.[3] Their exaggerated determination not to be seen to be pushed around by the unions, on the contrary, appeared to the TUC as the action of a politically motivated Government out to 'tame the unions, one way or another'.[4] When Carr met the General Council on 13 October 1970 he made it plain that the eight central 'pillars' of the proposed Bill were not negotiable. The TUC promptly issued a statement that on this basis it was not prepared to engage in further talks and committed itself to outright opposition. On 26 November in the House of Commons, before the Bill was even published, Barbara Castle likewise pledged the Labour party to fight it 'tooth and nail, line by line . . . We shall destroy this Bill.'[5] The Government had not bargained for this degree of hostility, or, if it had, took it to be merely rhetorical posturing.

The Bill was finally published on 3 December, and received its Second Reading on 14–15 December. Its central purpose was to reduce the number of strikes, particularly unofficial strikes, by making collective agreements, once negotiated, legally binding unless – and this was to be a crucial loophole – agreed otherwise by both parties. A range of specified 'unfair industrial practices' would forfeit legal immunity, making the unions liable to pay compensation. To regulate and enforce this new code of practice the Bill established a special branch of the High Court, the National Industrial Relations Court, with which recognised unions would be expected to register. In addition to its punitive role, however, the NIRC was also given a role in the prevention of strikes. The Tories' Bill borrowed from *In Place of Strife* provision for a sixty-day cooling-off period and the requirement to hold a secret ballot before strike action; but it gave the power to invoke them not to the Secretary of State, as Barbara Castle had proposed, but to the NIRC on application from the Secretary of State. Finally there were a number of provisions securing the statutory right to belong or not to belong to a union; restricting (though only marginally) the operation of the closed shop; and strengthening safeguards against unfair dismissal.

Heath and Carr believed that the Bill represented no more than an overdue modernisation of the law, which would put Britain's archaic industrial relations on an orderly and equitable footing, to the benefit of unions and employers equally. Opening the second day of the Second Reading debate on 15 December, Heath poured scorn on the idea that trade unions were not already governed by the law: the trouble was that the relevant laws were fifty years out of date. The demand for reform, he asserted, was now virtually universal and the Bill, once in operation, would be quickly accepted and widely welcomed.

> The rules and procedures will undoubtedly secure growing support from the majority of employers and trade unionists as they are seen to work to their advantage. It will exert a growing influence for good . . .
> I do not believe for one moment that the unions are likely to put themselves in breach of the law. They will not choose to act in such a way as to risk their funds . . . in ill-judged and unlawful actions.

('You hope!' interjected the Labour left-winger, Russell Kerr.)[6]
The weakness of the Bill was that it tried to do both too much and too little. It tried to do too much too quickly in setting up a whole new apparatus of law, with new institutions to enforce it, covering every aspect of industrial relations, workers' rights and the conduct of strikes all at once, in a like-it-or-lump-it manner certain to antagonise the proud and prickly organisations principally affected. There were warnings of this overloading at the time. *The Times* warned the Government on 3 July to use the gestation period of the Bill to 'ensure that it is not born overweight';[7] while the former Labour Minister of Labour, Ray Gunter, privately advised Carr to introduce his reform by gradual stages, beginning with the principle of registration.[8] Willie Whitelaw had long been apprehensive of the danger of alienating the unions. But Heath, with the confidence of his radical mandate, was determined on a once-and-for-all reform.

At the same time, however, there was a yawning gap between the Bill's ambitions and its practical reach. Peter Jenkins in the *Guardian* commented that Heath's Second Reading speech was impressive, persuasive, almost Baldwinesque, so long as he kept his head in the clouds, but less convincing when he came down to the factory floor. Did he really believe that the Bill would transform the conduct of industrial relations? 'Or is he simply trying to "change the climate", like a rainmaker, with incantations?'[9]

Faced with a massive Bill and no pretence of public consultation the unions were practically bound to oppose it. One or two moderate leaders of smaller unions, notably Tom Jackson of the Postal Workers and Jack Peel of the Dyers, Bleachers and Textile Workers, argued for collaboration, but the mood of the General Council was against them. It was unlucky for the Government that it was simultaneously having to fight the unions on pay. The original hope had been that the ending of Labour's incomes policy would be the quid pro quo for acceptance of the Industrial Relations Bill. It was in the expectation that the Conservatives would restore free collective bargaining that some union leaders had been willing to offer private assurances of co-operation. In the event, however, Labour had already abandoned pay restraint a year before, leading to a pay explosion: the Tories came into office obliged to try to hold settlements down. The resulting climate of 'confrontation' cut the ground from under the union moderates, as Jack Jones – with Hugh Scanlon joint leader of the militants – recalled:

> Union leaders whose policy was 'peace at any price' began to realise that they were faced with a policy of confrontation which had not been experienced since the 1930s . . .
> There was little room for manœuvre because the Government had told Vic Feather that under no circumstances would they change the main planks of their platform . . . The reason that Jackson and Peel got short shrift was that even the respectable old guard on the Council knew that it would not do the movement any good to crawl to the Government.[10]

By contrast with the 'respectable old guard', Jones and Scanlon were determined to exert again the political muscle that had humbled Wilson and Barbara Castle in order to inflict a similar defeat on Heath and Carr. Having helped to destroy the Labour Government the year before, the majority of the General Council felt guiltily bound to make amends by making life at least equally difficult for the Tories, mandate or no mandate. Wilson and Castle for their part felt no compunction in denouncing proposals similar in intention and to a substantial degree in detail to those they had tried but failed to introduce themselves. So a classic British political dogfight was joined, full of sound and fury and exaggerated claims on both sides wholly out of proportion to the likely impact of the Bill for good or bad.

The battle in Parliament was long and bitter, with the Committee stage taken on the floor of the House in an attempt – Whitelaw's idea – to expose Labour divisions. Between 18 January and 24 February the Bill occupied over a hundred hours of parliamentary time, the most devoted to any Bill (other than Finance Bills) since 1945; but such was Labour's obstruction, marked by several demonstrations and more than one suspended sitting, that there was no debate at all on more than half the Bill's 150 clauses – including the whole section setting up the NIRC – before the guillotine came down. At the end of the Report Stage Members had to vote continuously for 11½ hours on 63 successive divisions (breaking a record set in 1907) before the Government thwarted the Opposition's attempt to block the Third Reading by scrapping its last 42 amendments.[11] Passage through the Lords was more leisurely, before the Bill came back to the Commons in late July. The Act finally received the Royal Assent on 5 August 1971.

The opposition that mattered, however, was outside Parliament. On 12 January the TUC staged a 'day of protest', culminating in a rally at the Albert Hall addressed by Feather and Wilson. On Sunday 21 February something like 120,000 trade unionists carrying placards demanding 'Kill the Bill' marched from Hyde Park to Trafalgar Square in a column seven miles long, said to be the biggest union demonstration ever. Further one-day stoppages, organised by Scanlon's AUEW, took place on 1 and 18 March, while on the latter date a special TUC Congress was held at Croydon to endorse the General Council's stand. All this the Government could have ridden out. Protests could not stop the Bill becoming law. What really undermined its operation, however, was the unions lighting on the simple tactic of refusing to register under the Act. This – the idea, it is said, of Professor Bill Wedderburn of the LSE – was something the Government had never expected: Carr has called it, ruefully, 'a damnably effective tactic'.[12] It was a double-edged weapon, since non-registration excluded unions from the rights, immunities and tax advantages secured to them by the Act, while leaving them still liable to its penalties; and it met serious reluctance on the part of many unions unwilling to incur the risk. On the other hand non-registration had the beauty of being entirely legal, and offered a wonderful way of rendering the Act ineffective and making the Government look silly. Although it was approved only narrowly by the Croydon Congress – and still more narrowly endorsed at Blackpool in September (when it only needed the vote of one medium-sized union to swing the result the other way) – the tactic nevertheless gradually won general acquiescence. By March 1972 146 unions and other groups which had initially registered under the Act had deregistered: of major unions only the ever-independent electricians refused to toe the line and were temporarily suspended – with seventeen smaller fry – from the TUC.

The Act ultimately came into force by stages early in 1972. The NIRC opened its doors on 1 January, and the code of 'good' practice became law on 1 March. By this time, however, from having been the principal showpiece of the Government's programme, the Act was already beginning to be overtaken by wider economic problems. During 1972 it became effectively irrelevant, partly as a result of the unions' non-co-operation, partly due to flaws revealed in its own operation, partly as a consequence of the Government's changed approach to the management of the economy in response to rising unemployment and the miners' strike of January–February 1972. The long battle to put it on the Statute Book in 1971 turned out to be all in vain.

On the central economic front 1971 was a frustrating year for the Government. On the one hand, the 'n-1' counter-inflation strategy seemed to be working: the level of pay settlements was steadily reduced and after the defeat of the postmen there were no more major strikes (though still a lot of minor ones). Tony Barber delivered two further packages of tax cuts. Inflation peaked at 10 per cent in the autumn and then started to fall, while the balance of payments continued in healthy surplus. The other side of the picture, however, was not so rosy. In defiance of Treasury expectations, unemployment continued to mount inexorably every month towards politically alarming levels. Gradually, as the year went on, the reduction of unemployment by every means available displaced the control of inflation as the Government's most urgent priority. Even before the overt U-turns of the following year, the Government's declared readiness to trust the market was already more honoured in the breach than the observance. Moreover in September the National Union of Mineworkers put in a claim for a pay rise of 47 per cent.

Up to that point, no major group of public sector workers had seriously challenged 'n-1'. It was a different story in the private sector, where in April Ford workers secured a 33 per cent increase following a two-month stoppage, a figure promptly matched by similar awards in the rest of the motor industry. Nurses and other NHS workers, however, accepted 8–9 per cent. A short-lived work to rule by train drivers ended with a 9·5 per cent settlement and in June steel workers backed away from strike action and accepted a similar increase. Cautiously, behind the public posturing over the Industrial Relations Bill, Vic Feather and members of the Economic Committee of the TUC reopened a dialogue with ministers over pay. To help them, the Government did its best to hold down those prices it could control directly or indirectly: in April the British Steel Corporation was allowed to raise the price of steel by only half the 14 per cent it had wanted, while in July ministers succeeded in persuading the CBI to apply a voluntary ceiling of 5 per cent on price rises. And all the while Heath, Barber and Carr continued categorically to rule out any resort to a statutory policy. The voluntary approach, they insisted, was working very well. 'There is concrete and encouraging evidence', Carr was able to declare in April, 'that the rising tide of the general level of wage settlements in both private and public sectors has been checked and is beginning to recede.'[13] In a radio interview in June to mark the first anniversary of his election, Heath lucidly explained the Government's view that statutory restraint simply stored up trouble for the future:

> What we have been suffering from . . . has been the consequences first of all of guidelines, then of voluntary arrangements, then of compulsory arrangements and a freeze. The result has been that deep resentments have been bred among trade unionists. After the last government abandoned the compulsory policy, in fact abandoned all sorts of incomes policies, they said, 'Well, now is the time when we must make up the leeway' . . .
> When we get these wage increases under control, then of course the economy can expand and work will be provided by firms for people. What we have been seeing is wages increasing at a slower and slower rate.[14]

By the end of the year Heath was able to claim that 'n-1' had halved the going rate of wage rises over the previous twelve months to an average of 7–8 per cent.[15] In 1972 the Government hoped to bring them down further to around 5 per cent.

While holding down inflationary wage demands with one hand, however, the Government was simultaneously trying to 'reflate' the economy with the other. In his first proper Budget on 30 March, Barber cut taxes by nearly £550 million by means of a further reduction of corporation tax, the halving of selective employment tax (as a step towards its abolition in 1973), increased tax allowances in respect of children and a reduction of surtax. These measures delighted Tory backbenchers; but as unemployment continued to rise past the three-quarter million mark, it seemed that still more stimulus was needed. In July, therefore, Heath relaxed his former 'implacable opposition' to further action[16] and Barber introduced yet another package of measures including an 18 per cent cut in purchase tax, the lifting of hire purchase restrictions and increased capital allowances to encourage industry to invest in new plant and machinery. At the same time Peter Walker announced a £100 million programme of public investment in roads, railways and housing designed specifically to boost employment in the development areas. Though widely applauded as both necessary and overdue – *The Times* titled its editorial 'Some Welcome First Steps'[17] – these were the traditional instant remedies for a recession. The Government was beginning to try to spend its way to rapid growth.

There was nothing in this directly contrary to its election programme. Heath and Macleod had always laid great emphasis on cutting taxes to release resources for investment, and *A Better Tomorrow* had repeated Heath's longstanding commitment to well-directed regional policy, aimed particularly at improving the national road and rail network. The criticism was rather that the Government – relying on over-optimistic Treasury forecasts – had been too cautious in the beginning. Moreover John Davies had given notice in June that the Government's tough policy towards 'lame ducks' was still in force by announcing the ending of DTI support for Upper Clyde Shipbuilders, a loss-making consortium put together by Tony Benn's Ministry of Technology in 1968. On 16 June Heath repeated the Government's refusal to intervene to save the workers' jobs; and on 29 July Davies confirmed the liquidation of the company with the closure of two of the three yards. The men responded with a 'work in' brilliantly led by a highly articulate Communist, Jimmy Reid, eagerly backed by Benn. Between them they turned UCS into a potent symbol of working-class self-help in defiance of hard-faced capitalism, winning considerable sympathy and popular support. For the moment, however, the Government stood firm.

UCS posed a test of the Government's resolve which it passed initially with flying colours. The right-wing commentator T. E. Utley, reviewing the Government's first year in the *Daily Telegraph*, was impressed. 'What is different about Mr Heath', he wrote, 'is that he actually administers the medicine he advertises. Under him the people really do suffer.' The philosophy of self-reliance was being applied 'with relentless political courage'. Inheriting a country 'conditioned by decades of collectivism', the Government was 'trying, by a rigorous and even ruthless therapy, to remobilise the crippled patient, to give him back the self-assurance needed to enable him to live in a competitive world'. Utley went on, however, to wonder how much longer the Government's nerve would hold. Inflation and unemployment were both still rising, and he was worried by the interventionist potential of the new DTI.

Can the policy succeed without far more radical cuts in public spending . . . and without a stricter control of the money supply?

If the policy continues to fail, will not Mr Heath and his colleagues be exposed to an irresistible temptation to use the vast administrative apparatus which they have created for the purpose of trying to achieve quicker results? Might not even they drift, via a wages policy, into something like the kind of economic regime from which they set out to deliver us?[18]

This – in an article which had begun so admiringly – was a prediction of quite uncanny prescience.

At the Tory party conference in October, however, Heath was bullish. 'We have come a long way,' he assured the representatives, 'a lot further than many people dared to hope just twelve short months ago.' Unemployment was still 'far too high', but the Government was – quite properly – acting directly to bring it down. Ministers, he claimed, were carrying out their programme of modernisation of structures and practices that acted as an obstacle to growth. Tony Barber was removing the disincentive effect of the tax system by 'root and branch reform'. Robert Carr was sorting out 'the outmoded system of industrial relations'. (Indeed, Heath boasted, he had already done so: 'Thanks to the admirable work of Robert Carr and his colleagues, that field, too, has been put right.') Without referring explicitly to UCS, he reaffirmed the philosophy of not throwing money at declining industries.

Finally, following a quick resumé of the government's achievements in other fields, he emphasised once again in heightened language his determination not to be deflected from the course he had set. History had reserved a special place for Britain in the dangerous new world of the 1970s, he claimed, 'because we have a special kind of strength'.

Our strength is not just figures on a balance sheet, although we have those too, our strength is not just courage in adversity, although we have shown that time and time again. Our special strength lies in our sense of history, of knowing the right time to do the right thing.

Our special strength is our stamina in going on with what needs doing until it is done, in running a race as long as that race has to be run. We never know when we are beaten and that way we never are beaten. We know no other way than to win . . .

For too long we have walked in the shadows. It is time for us now to walk out into the light to find a new place, a new Britain in this new world . . . Let history record that when we were shown the way we took the way and walked out to meet our destiny.[19]

The fustian rhetoric is desperately banal and reads still more painfully with knowledge of what followed. But it was also, at the time, desperately sincere. Heath firmly believed that Britain under his leadership, poised at last to find its true place in Europe, was entering on a moral as well as an economic renaissance. Patrick Cosgrave in the *Spectator* did not doubt the strength of his resolve.

Mr Heath intends to save Britain, no more and no less; and he intends to save her in his own way . . . He has no doubt about the validity of his instinctive aims; nor has he ever suffered the remotest pang of uncertainty about his ability to pursue them. But he has an obsessive awareness of the temptations politicians suffer while in office to move away from the policies designed to implement their aims.

His greatest problem, Cosgrave recognised, was winning public support for what he was trying to do:

This is the difficulty that lies behind the banality of the Government's presentation of its policies. Neither Mr Heath nor his Ministers seem able to make an emotional as well as an intellectual connection between the detailed legislative programme and the aspirations of the people . . . he must still find another political dimension . . . to inhabit, if his self-appointed heroism is not to end in political tragedy.[*][20]

At Brighton, Heath and his speechwriters tried hard to find an exalted language appropriate to his heroic vision; and the conference at least was roused to wild enthusiasm. The wider public was a different matter. Cosgrave's criticism of Heath's inability to communicate is apposite in general, as applied to the whole period of his premiership: his 'self-appointed heroism' did indeed end in 'political tragedy'. Yet it was beside the point at this particular moment, since the seeds of his tragedy lay not in his failure to communicate his goals but in his own abandonment of them. For all his lofty talk of 'stamina' and 'destiny' and his determination still to insist that government subsidy was not the answer, the emphasis in his

* *Private Eye* perfectly captured the sheer tedium of Heath's wooden exhortations to the public in its regular column *Heathco*, which portrayed him as the petty-minded managing director of a small company always fussing about the staff's time-wasting and sloppy habits (particularly regarding the coffee machine) while trying to jolly them along with earnest pep talks. The trouble was that the column itself quickly became tedious.

Brighton speech on reducing unemployment signalled that the Government had already significantly changed tack. At the beginning of the year the emphasis had been on conquering inflation. Heath and Barber had then made it clear that rising unemployment was a consequence of high inflation and repeatedly warned the unions that the responsibility for pricing their members out of jobs would be on their own heads if they continued to press unrealistic wage demands.[21] In his March Budget, Barber specifically confirmed that controlling inflation remained the Government's 'first priority'.[22] The public works programme unveiled with his July budget, however, told a different story. As the unemployment figure continued to mount, passing 800,000 in June and 900,000 by October, the Government increasingly accepted the responsibility to take action itself to bring it down. The Queen's Speech opening the new session of Parliament on 2 November was explicit; the Government's 'first care will be to increase employment'.[23] Speaking in a party political broadcast two weeks later, both Prime Minister and Chancellor underlined the point. 'The Government is committed completely and absolutely to expanding the economy and bringing unemployment down,' Heath promised; while Barber positively boasted, 'No British Government has ever before taken so much action with the direct purpose of creating more employment.'[24] The same day Christopher Chataway announced the retention – contrary to previous indications – of the Post Office Giro Bank, saving 2,500 jobs on Merseyside; and a few days later Barber announced a further package of public-sector building projects, totalling £160 million, to be brought forward immediately.

There was still no widespread perception of a major U-turn. In adopting conventional Keynesian measures to prevent a politically unacceptable level of unemployment the Government was doing no more than was virtually accepted as its duty, pressed on it not least by nervous Tory backbenchers. When Sir John Eden had dared to suggest in September that the 'enormous obsession with unemployment' was exaggerated, the result was a flurry of demands that he and Ridley be sacked from the DTI as 'deficient in political flair'.[25] (Heath was accordingly obliged to keep them in place for another six months: but they were clearly sidelined.) Enoch Powell alone was openly critical, predicting after the Giro reprieve that 'From this egg a whole farmyard of lame ducks will speedily be hatched.'[26] There was as yet no widely understood monetarist analysis to suggest that Government spending would only fuel inflation and create greater unemployment in the long term. Nor was the Government yet taking on itself the whole responsibility for stimulating employment. Heath was impatient at the reluctance of industry to take advantage of the incentives offered by the Government's tax reductions to increase investment. On 3 December he invited eight leading industrialists to Chequers to urge them – between blasts of Bruckner – to seize their opportunity and do their bit to expand the economy.[27] But the key word was now 'partnership' between Government and industry and the unions, between the public and the private sectors. The Government had already by the end of 1971 moved a long way from its initial stance of standing back, lifting from industry the burdens of excessive taxation, regulation and restrictive practices and then leaving it to free enterprise to work its wealth-creating magic. If necessary, the Government had shown that it was as ready as any of its postwar predecessors to step in directly to speed the process. It only needed further shocks at the beginning of 1972 to induce it to throw off the last vestiges of non-interventionism.

19

Heathmen on the Home Front

THE 1970–4 Government was unmistakably Ted Heath's Government. It was generally seen as marking a radical departure – both socially and politically – from previous Tory Governments, reflecting at once Heath's dominance over his colleagues, his unprivileged background and his personification of a new hard-nosed ideology of efficiency, self-reliance and unfettered capitalism. The Government was routinely attacked by Labour as the most reactionary for decades, intent on reversing all the advances in social provision and economic management since the war, dismantling the Welfare State, bashing the unions and deliberately creating unemployment in order to grind the faces of the poor. This was nonsense, but it served Labour's need for a bogey against which to reunite after the disappointments of its own six years in office; and it gained credence from Heath's aloof manner and from a narrow interpretation of some of his rhetoric. So far as social policy went, however, it was contradicted not only by the record – spending on all the social services rose as fast and faster than under Labour – but by the 1970 manifesto: the high level of social spending was not the result of a policy U-turn, but was clearly signalled among the Government's aims from the beginning. The most that Heath had indicated in opposition was that a Tory Government would marginally redirect spending to where the need was greatest; at the same time he repeatedly talked of improving services, of abolishing poverty and squalor and raising standards of care for the old and sick. The best possible social services – equal to the standards now being set in Europe – were an essential part of his vision of a modern, competitive and socially mobile Britain. He was not personally interested in the details of welfare policy; but no one who knew him well doubted the social compassion that lay beneath his chilly public image.

He was unquestionably the dominating figure in his Government: not more so perhaps than Wilson had been in 1964, but certainly more commanding – even in 1973–4 – than Wilson had ever been after 1967, and more than Home or the later Macmillan. After the death of Iain Macleod the only independent figures in the Government who did not owe their positions to him were Maudling, Home and Hailsham. Home and Hailsham were distanced by their jobs from the central business of the Government, and Maudling was for personal reasons somewhat detached. Otherwise the leading figures in Heath's administration were widely seen as his creatures – 'new' men (and one woman) of predominantly lower-middle-class background whose managerial style and outlook seemed to mimic his own. They were all lumped together by Andrew Roth in 1972 as 'Heathmen'.[1] In fact in class terms the only true 'Heathmen' were Peter Walker and Margaret Thatcher; but wherever they had been to school Tony Barber, Geoffrey Rippon, Keith Joseph, Robert Carr and John Davies all embodied many of the same characteristics: they were all 'modern' Tories of the same stamp as their leader. Joseph, Barber and Rippon had sat in Cabinet before under Home and Macmillan; yet in 1970 they were all regarded as owing their positions essentially to Heath and as unlikely to oppose him. There was another group in the Cabinet who could not by any social categorisation be called 'Heathmen'; but these, the old-style landed patricians – Willie Whitelaw, Peter Carrington and Jim Prior (not forgetting the Leader of the House of Lords, Lord Jellicoe) – were if anything more devoted to Heath personally and more in his confidence over the next few years than the others. Still it was the classless 'Heathmen' who occupied the most visible positions: Barber, Carr, Davies and Rippon on the contentious economic, industrial and European fronts; Walker, Joseph and Mrs Thatcher in the welfare departments.

They were all assumed to have been appointed to do their master's bidding; and so very largely – in an exceptionally united Cabinet – they did. Nevertheless Heath's reputation as a dominating, even authoritarian, Prime Minister is misleading. He certainly set the tone and agenda of his Government; and in some areas of policy – the European negotiations, the economy, Northern Ireland at moments of crisis and later the prices and incomes policy – he took a close interest and ultimately took charge. In other areas, however, he let the ministers he had appointed get on with the job without interference. In particular this was true of the three social services departments: Housing and Local Government, subsumed in Peter Walker's Environment empire; Health and Social Security, unexpectedly entrusted to Keith Joseph; and Education, given to Margaret Thatcher. In these three fiefdoms the Heathmen were given free rein.

Peter Walker was the youngest minister in the Cabinet but was given one of the biggest jobs. He had been brought into the Shadow Cabinet in 1966 as a reward for masterminding Heath's successful leadership campaign the previous year. Still only thirty-eight in 1970, he was a financial whizz kid who had not been to university, a self-made millionaire with no previous ministerial experience; yet no one doubted his qualifications to run the new mega-Department of the Environment. In fact both there and subsequently at the DTI he was one of the undoubted successes of the Government: he was so conspicuously capable a minister, indeed, that Margaret Thatcher – despite the political chasm that by then divided them – could not leave him out in 1979 and retained him in office right up to 1990. At the DoE between 1970 and 1972 he was responsible for two major pieces of legislation: the Housing Finance Act and the reorganisation of local government.

The Housing Finance Act was one of those measures which Labour seized on to portray the Government as hard-faced, reactionary and divisive. Yet Walker – and Heath – regarded it as a major and progressive social reform aimed at tackling the problems of bad housing and homelessness. It was a clear manifesto commitment, whose rationale had frequently been spelled out by Heath in opposition. The idea was to redirect housing subsidies from all council tenants to those, whether public or private tenants, in greatest need. There were to be generous rent rebates and rent allowances, and the extension to private lettings of the system of 'fair rents', on the principle of subsidising tenants not buildings; but the price was that council house rents for those tenants deemed to be able to afford them should rise to something nearer an economic level. The principle was impeccable: Dick Crossman told Walker privately that his Bill was more socialist than he would have dared to propose![2] But of course it handed to Labour an irresistible opportunity to denounce the wicked Tories for putting up the rents of working people. At a time when the Government was also raising Health Service charges and the cost of school meals and trying to hold down wage increases it fuelled a tremendous political row. Some Labour authorities refused to implement the rises. Eventually eleven councillors in Clay Cross in Derbyshire were personally surcharged: their case became a *cause célèbre* which caused serious embarrassment to the returning Labour Government in 1974 when the left demanded that the penalty be retrospectively quashed. Most of the provisions of the Act were duly repealed by Anthony Crosland in 1975 – a casualty of adversary politics at their most clear cut; though council rents did not return to their previous levels.

Walker also tried hard to encourage local authorities to sell council houses to sitting tenants; but with only limited success. Not only Labour but Tory councils too were reluctant to relinquish their empires. By 1974 no more than 7 per cent of the housing stock had been sold, and those were mainly the best houses to the wealthiest tenants; while continuing council building more than made up for the loss. This was another idea whose time had not yet come in the early 1970s. Crosland immediately stopped it in 1974, and even in 1979, when Walker tried again, putting up to Mrs Thatcher a more radical scheme to sell off houses for a song, she still objected that 'our people' would not like it.[3] It was Michael Heseltine who eventually persuaded her to embrace (and take the credit for) a policy which Heath and Walker had pioneered a decade earlier. Other ideas to further the ideal of home ownership made no more headway. The raw statistics for house building in both private and public sectors showed a fall (from 307,000 completions in England and Wales in 1970 to 241,000 in 1974).[4] A Government scheme to encourage the building societies to favour first-time buyers had not got off the ground by February 1974, by which time mortgage rates had reached 13 per cent.

Walker's lasting legislative monument was the wholesale redrawing of the map of local government in England and Wales. Gordon Campbell carried through a simultaneous but less contentious restructuring in Scotland. This reform is one of the few innovations of the Heath Government which has lasted; it also remains among the most unpopular. Yet reform was long overdue – the traditional patchwork of counties, county boroughs, non-county boroughs, rural and urban district councils and parish councils involved immense duplication, confusion and waste: boundaries no longer reflected realities and some small counties were clearly unviable as deliverers of efficient services. The trouble was that any reform was bound to be unpopular: the ancient units were the focus of deep loyalties. The irony of Walker's solution is that it was actually the least radical on offer. It abolished fewer counties than was proposed by the Redcliffe-Maud Report, published in 1969, which the Labour Government had accepted, and created smaller and less remote authorities than the eight provinces which Redcliffe-Maud had envisaged. The Liberals' alternative too proposed an ambitious structure of regional devolution. Walker's scheme, which won him a standing ovation at the Tory party conference in 1971, opted for a two-tier system of counties and districts designed to achieve a balance between the claims of efficiency and local sentiment. Education, social services, transport, fire services, police and some planning were allotted to the upper tier; housing, local planning, refuse collection and environmental services to the lower. Some famous names like Rutland disappeared from the map; other proud counties found themselves merged, like Hereford with Walker's own Worcestershire; new administrative units like Avon and Teesside were created; while Wales was comprehensively carved up into new counties with unrecognisable names (Gwynedd, Clwyd, Dyfed, etc.). In addition six new metropolitan authorities were created in Birmingham, Manchester, Liverpool, Newcastle, Sheffield and Leeds. In the end a structure of 58 counties was reduced to 54, and a maze of some 1,300 lesser units reduced to around 400. (Scotland was recast into nine regions, with 49 local districts.)[5]

There was some localised unhappiness and a handful of parliamentary rebellions to preserve the autonomy of towns such as Bristol and Plymouth. (In Scotland Fife was saved to become a region on its own.) But generally the reform went through without serious controversy, receiving the Royal Assent in October 1972 and coming into effect in April 1974 (Scotland a year later). It only became widely unpopular once it was in force. Then it seemed part of a general disorientation, a loss of familiar landmarks that was disrupting people's lives in all sorts of ways in the 1970s: decimalisation, inflation, terrorism and an ever-rising level of civil violence. There was a general perception that reorganisation had simply resulted in more well-paid jobs for local government administrators. As inflation sent rates bills soaring, the new councils seemed more profligate, wasteful and unaccountable than the old. There was growing criticism that Walker had failed to address the key question of local government finance. The whole exercise quickly came to be seen as typical of its period – a monstrous bureaucratic abortion derived from a misplaced belief in institutional change for its own sake. This was in fact unfair to Walker's relatively modest scheme, which stopped far short of most expert advice of the day. It is a valid criticism none the less.

The Department of the Environment was also responsible for two major development projects, the Channel Tunnel and the proposed third London airport plus deep-water seaport at Maplin, to both of which – along with Concorde – Heath personally attached great importance as far-sighted investments in the national infrastructure. Walker was still at the Department in the early stages of both projects, but by the time they came before Parliament in 1973 he had been replaced by Geoffrey Rippon. Both attracted determined opposition, though mainly from constituency interests in Kent and Essex.

The Maplin Bill was very nearly defeated: after being forced embarrassingly to postpone the Second Reading from January to February, the Government lost a key division on Report Stage by 17 votes before it managed to secure the Third Reading by just 9 votes on 13 June.[6] By comparison the majority on the Second Reading of the Channel Tunnel Bill in December was a relatively comfortable 18. Heath staked a good deal of his authority on both. As always he saw them in a European context as tests of the country's determination to compete ambitiously. 'As a nation', he told the 1922 Committee in July 1973, 'we should not falter in major projects which other countries take in their stride.' The tunnel was to be a symbol of Britain's commitment to the continent; Maplin – a major international sea- and airport – was 'a necessity' if Britain was to compete with Rotterdam.[7] Such expensive projects, however, were hard to pursue at a time of mounting pressure on public expenditure. In September Rippon made a partial concession and postponed the planned opening of Maplin by two years from 1980 to 1982. Yet still all three 'prestige' projects – Heath strenuously denied the description – survived Barber's final spending cuts in December 1973. When Heath fell, however, Maplin and the Channel Tunnel fell with him. Concorde had Tony Benn to fight for it in the Labour Cabinet; but the others were seen as Heath's follies and were quickly scrapped.

Heath's appointment of Sir Keith Joseph to the huge new Department of Health and Social Security (created in 1968 for Dick Crossman) was a surprise, since in opposition Joseph had been shadowing industry. In 1968–9 he had been the leading voice in the Shadow Cabinet in setting a non-interventionist agenda for the next Government, tentatively exploring free-market ideas to which he only returned with the force of revelation in 1974. Nevertheless there was probably no significance in Heath's deciding to switch him. A rich Jewish liberal intellectual, tortured by social conscience, Joseph was a very rare Tory who had entered politics specifically to try to relieve poverty: the DHSS was the job he wanted, and he was the best possible choice for it. His appointment alone should have given assurance that the Government had no intention of dismantling the Welfare State – though his austerity of manner initially contributed to the ethos of hard-faced penny-pinching. He quickly turned out to be one of the most open-handed secretaries of state the social services have ever had: with Mrs Thatcher at Education he was one of the two biggest spenders in a Government that came into office promising to cut public expenditure. There is in fact no contradiction, since Heath in opposition had never suggested that a Tory Government would do other than extend and improve the social services, while attempting to cut administrative waste. The former goal Joseph in several areas unquestionably achieved: where he disastrously failed was in the latter.

As Prime Minister Heath did not often speak about the social services, but at the 1971 party conference he devoted a substantial section of his speech to setting out the Government's philosophy towards the Welfare State. He made it very clear that he was not looking to cut it, but the legacy which the Government had inherited was one of welfare policies 'which were not even maintaining the advances of the past, let alone moving forward to meet the needs of the future'; education policies 'which were simply not giving a fair start to many children'; and health policies 'which were denying decent care to so many of the old and the mentally sick'. Broadly speaking, then, he was promising the conference more of everything. At the same time he distinguished three specific approaches. First, there were gaps in the existing net: the persistence of homelessness and poverty could not be tolerated in the Britain of the 1970s. The Government had determined 'as a matter of urgency, to see that those who have been neglected get the extra help they need'. The second approach was to get the priorities right – as in housing, not to subsidise those who did not need subsidising, but concentrate available resources where they could do most good: he gave the example of increased prescription charges (with appropriate exemptions) to pay for better hospitals and care for the old and mentally ill. Third, the Government must shape future social policies 'which fit the long term needs of an increasingly prosperous and responsible society.' It was a question of developing a new, more discriminating attitude to the provision of welfare:

> Unless we are prepared to take on more of the responsibilities for the things we can do for ourselves, then the State itself will never be able to do properly the jobs which genuinely demand community action . . . This is the only way in which we can carry our social concern into effective action.[8]

In sum, Heath's social agenda envisaged some marginal adjustments within a continuously expanding health and welfare budget. This was a very long way from the wholesale, mean-spirited withdrawal of benefits and services from the poor which Labour liked to allege. On the contrary, from the perspective of the 1980s and 1990s it looks absurdly optimistic. The true criticism of Heath is not that he set out in some minor respects to trim the Welfare State to economic reality and real social need, but rather that he – in common, it must be said, with his critics and the whole political establishment – failed sufficiently to foresee the financial and demographic pressures which the social services would increasingly face. His tentative groping for greater selectivity within the norm of ever-improving universal provision created an immense political furore, but it was only a faint anticipation of the more radical solutions to the problem of the late 1980s. His policy remained predicated on the assumption of continuous economic growth. His social philosophy – at least up to the oil crisis of 1973 – was still firmly rooted in the 1960s.

Within these assumptions – which he later publicly recanted – Joseph was a successful Secretary of State. In his first year, as long promised, he righted the anomaly which denied pensions to those over 80 who had been too old to qualify for the National Insurance scheme when it started in 1948; extended pensions to younger widows (between 40 and 50); and introduced a new invalidity benefit for the severely disabled. He also raised the ordinary old age pension by substantially more than the rate of inflation; and introduced a new benefit designed to tackle family poverty, the Family Income Supplement (FIS). This – in effect a state-guaranteed minimum wage – was intended to give direct assistance to some 150,000 families with one or more children, where the breadwinner was in work but earned less than he would have got in benefit had he been unemployed. The idea was to concentrate help where it was needed, without a conventional means test or loss of incentive to work. The flaw – as Sir Brandon Rhys-Williams, the persistent Tory backbench champion of Family Allowance, warned in the debates on Joseph's Bill – was that take up was low: the benefit simply did not reach the people at whom it was aimed.[9] FIS survived until 1988, but it never fulfilled the ambitious hopes held out for it in 1970.

At the time it seemed both simple and imaginative. Joseph was rewarded by a standing ovation from the annual conference of the Child Poverty Action Group. FIS, increased pensions and the new disability benefit effectively balanced the raising of prescription charges (from 2s 6d to 4s) and higher charges for false teeth and glasses simultaneously announced in Barber's 1970 autumn statement. 'Sir Keith Joseph', wrote Jonathan Aitken, reviewing the Government's first year in the London *Evening Standard* in June 1971, 'has become the embodiment of the Liberal-Tory conscience, introducing measures which appear to have blunted early criticism that this is a government without a soul.'[10] His mixture of toughness and compassion, Aitken noted, was typical of the Heath Government and characteristic of Heath personally. But Joseph also brought concerns of his own to the DHSS. On the health side he made a conscious decision to switch resources to what he called 'the afflictions' – like rheumatism and senility – which the NHS could only relieve, not cure; while on the social security side he focused public attention and concentrated research on the 'cycle of deprivation' (his own term) as a cause of family poverty.[11] Joseph was an exceptionally thoughtful and well-intentioned Secretary of State: he also had the advantage that he stayed at the Elephant and Castle for the whole term of the Government's life. In the end, however, his record of steadily rising social spending was checked by the oil crisis, the collapse of the Government's economic miracle and Barber's swingeing public expenditure cuts at the end of 1973, which converted a projected 2 per cent rise in public sector spending for the following year into a 2 per cent cut.[12]

In September 1971, having scrapped Crossman's proposed universal earnings-related pensions scheme, Joseph introduced his own more modest plan for a two-tier system comprising a flat rate basic state pension with the option of either a private earnings-related pension on top or a significantly less attractive state scheme. Enacted in 1973, Joseph's scheme was due to come into effect in April 1975; but it in turn was largely scrapped by Barbara Castle in 1974. In formulating her own State Earnings-Related Pensions Scheme (SERPS), however, Mrs Castle went out of her way to carry the Tory Opposition with her, so that pensions ceased – for a decade, anyway – to be a political football between the parties. (Mrs Thatcher made a bid to privatise SERPS in 1985 but was forced to retreat.) Mrs Castle thus succeeded where both Crossman and Joseph had failed.[13]

Joseph's disaster, however, was his reorganisation of the NHS. This was another example of the characteristic folly of the period, the belief that improved efficiency could be achieved simply by rationalising management structure on paper. The intention was to establish, in place of the tripartite division between hospital, GP and local authority services created by Nye Bevan in 1948, a single comprehensive integrated service which should be both more efficient and more equitable between regions. The new structure was 'a national pyramid of heroic proportions',[14] composed of district management teams at the base, ninety area health authorities on top of them (parallel with Walker's new counties), these in turn responsible to fourteen regional health authorities, with the Secretary of State at the top charged with overall planning and resource allocation. Far from being simpler, as intended, centralisation actually produced an administrative labyrinth more complex and less efficient than before. The new structure – designed with the help of the management consultants McKinsey – was quite wrongly attacked as too 'managerial'. In fact, with at least one tier too many and too many fingers in the pie at every level, a clear chain of command was exactly what was lacking.[15] It was 'managerial' only in the sense that it created an army of new managers – between 1973 and 1977 the number of administrative and clerical staff rose by 28 per cent: by 1980 staff costs accounted for 70 per cent of total expenditure[16] – while the needs of patients seemed to have been forgotten. Joseph's reorganisation was an undoubted cause of poor performance, low morale and industrial disruption in the Health Service during the 1970s and 1980s.

Margaret Thatcher was in all but sex the archetypal 'Heathman'. Though nine years younger than Heath, her class and educational background were identical: while *Private Eye* had long ago nick-named Heath 'Grocer', she really was a grocer's daughter. Though she had served her apprenticeship at the Ministry of Pensions under Macmillan and Home, it was Heath who had promoted her in 1967 to the Shadow Cabinet. Once he had given her Edward Boyle's Education portfolio in 1969 there was no question but that she would be Secretary of State in 1970. She was brisk, efficient, clearly the most competent woman available for a job which had twice before been held by women (Ellen Wilkinson and Florence Horsburgh) and generally regarded as a woman after Heath's heart. In office she quickly proved herself as tough and unsentimental as him, skilfully sympathetic with the right-wing party activists who had abominated Boyle yet at the same time pragmatic: she was not seen as doctrinaire, a high flier or potentially disloyal, but as a conscientious and successful departmental Minister.

In fact Heath cordially disliked her, and she had no love for him. It is by no means the case that he dislikes all women; but she – with her perfect complexion, well-cut clothes and precious accent – was exactly the type of Tory woman he most abhorred and least knew how to handle. He likes mannish women who place little overt value on their femininity, who talk like men and do not expect to be complimented on their appearance: Mrs Thatcher may have been as tough and businesslike as any man, but throughout her career she also used her femininity ruthlessly to disarm her male colleagues. With Heath this was counterproductive; it only irritated him. Though he was obliged to have her in his Government and recognised her competence, her penetrating voice and tendency to talk too much raised his hackles. He tried quite deliberately to keep her out of sight and earshot by placing her down the far end of the Cabinet table on the same side as himself. Admittedly someone has to sit there, and she was a fairly junior member of the Cabinet, whose Department had relatively little input into other areas of Government policy. But stories emerged in the press (particularly after 1974) of him brusquely shutting her up whenever she tried to speak.[17] It was said that he never asked for her view, except right at the end of a discussion when he was already shuffling his papers to move on to the next item. Sometimes she used to get her neighbour, Joseph Godber, to raise a question for her.[18] Against this it can be argued that Heath treated her no differently from anyone else. Like Shaw's Henry Higgins cheerfully insulting his friend Pickering, Heath could be appallingly blunt with all his ministers: the difference was that Mrs Thatcher – like Eliza Doolittle – expected the courtesies due to a lady.

'When Margaret Thatcher was a member first of his Shadow and then of his real Cabinet', Peter Rawlinson has written, 'he did not treat her well. Or more exactly, he did not treat her right.' She was, in Rawlinson's perhaps surprising view, 'neither sensitive nor clever enough' for him. 'But then she was, probably, always quite impossible to handle.'[19] This would not have mattered, of course, had not circumstances most improbably made her his nemesis and his successor: as a result his treatment of his tiresome Education Secretary assumed retrospectively an importance no one could have predicted in 1970 or 1973. Rawlinson's 1989 recollection that Heath and Thatcher 'were enemies, naked and unashamed, and they had been from the start'[20] is in reality greatly overdramatised. Peter Walker was probably Mrs Thatcher's closest ally in the Heath Cabinet. They saw eye to eye on the issues affecting their respective departments and worked well together on the educational aspects of local government reform. But Walker had no impression of hostility to her on Heath's part, any more than of suppressed dissent from Government policies on hers. ★[21] Francis Pym judged her an excellent Minister and a good prospect for promotion.[22] That she did not get it within the lifetime of the Government has been held to indicate a determination on Heath's part to keep her corralled in a department removed from the central business of the Government.[23] But it equally reflected his reluctance to move his ministers around

---

★ A minor but telling indication of Heath's view of her, however – which must in turn have annoyed her – can perhaps be gleaned from the fact in all his party conference speeches as Prime Minister, when he made a habit of singling out his ministers by name to praise their respective achievements, he never once named her.

more than necessary if they were doing a good job – part of his deliberate reaction against Wilson's continual reshuffles. As a matter of fact he did consider offering her a move in 1972, to the new Department of Consumer Affairs within the DTI under Walker, but it would have been a bad moment to move her since she was just about to publish her major Education White Paper.

She had come through a tough baptism by then. Two policies in particular had put her right in the forefront of the Government's early controversies. First, she wasted no time in acting to slow the onward march of comprehensive schools. Tony Crosland, vowing to his wife in 1965 to 'destroy every fucking grammar school in England',[24] had issued a circular requesting all education authorities to submit plans for comprehensivisation. In February 1970 his successor Edward Short had introduced a Bill to compel them to end selection. Short's Bill fell with the Labour Government; within a few days of taking office Mrs Thatcher also withdrew Crosland's circular. This was consistent with the non-doctrinaire policy of leaving it to local authorities themselves to decide the appropriate organisation for their own areas which Heath and the Tory party had expounded at both the 1966 and 1970 elections. Nevertheless the speed with which she acted, without the customary round of consultations, gave the appearance of a determinedly doctrinaire *coup* against the educational orthodoxy of the day, which enraged the educational establishment. In the event it made remarkably little difference. By 1970 the process of comprehensivisation had its own momentum which no Secretary of State could do much to impede. Between June 1970 and February 1973 Mrs Thatcher rejected fewer than 150 of the 2,765 comprehensivisation schemes that were put up to her: she approved more, ironically, than any other Secretary of State before or since – more than either Crosland or Shirley Williams, with whose names the policy is enduringly linked.[25] Her tenure happened to coincide with the high tide of the comprehensive movement. Heath did not interfere. He shared her regard for the grammar schools which had given them both their stepping stone to Oxford; but as in so many other areas he went along with the governing ethos of the age.

The action that really put Margaret Thatcher at the eye of the political storm, however, was the announcement in Barber's autumn budget in October 1970 of the ending of free school milk for eight- to eleven-year-olds. This, with a simultaneous staged increase in the cost of school meals from 1s 9d to 2s 10d, was Education's modest share of the savings required to balance the tax cuts which were the essential motor of the Government's economic strategy. It is not obvious why the ending of free milk attracted so much more public outcry than, for instance, higher prescription charges. Labour seized on it with righteous outrage. Edward Short called it 'the meanest, most unworthy Bill' he had seen in his twenty years in the Commons: it was 'typical of the philosophy of this astounding, pre-Disraeli Government'. Mrs Thatcher was able to retort that Labour had itself stopped free milk for secondary schools: she was only lowering the cut-off age by another three years.[26] But there was something deeply emotive about a woman stopping the supply of milk: she was dubbed 'Milk Snatcher' by the tabloid press, and the then Labour-supporting *Sun* called her 'the most unpopular woman in Britain'.[27] She is said to have been badly shaken by the furore. She had in fact done notably well for her Department in the negotiations with the Treasury which preceded the autumn package. Her approach was consistent with the Government's philosophy of priorities, as Heath unapologetically expressed it at the 1971 party conference: 'We believe it is more important to see that every child goes to a decent primary school than to provide subsidies regardless of whether they are needed or not.'[28] School milk and meals had been marked down by Iain Macleod before the election as prime targets for savings: she therefore felt somewhat aggrieved to find herself personally vilified for the policy of the whole Government. At the same time she demonstrated independence of judgment as well as her ability to fight her corner by sparing the Open University – also marked down for extinction by Macleod – despite the fact that it was clearly identified in Tory minds as a Labour creation.[29]

Though the 'Milk Snatcher' label was hung around her neck ever after, Mrs Thatcher was in reality a notably expansionist Education Secretary. She had first of all to find the money for the raising of the school-leaving age to sixteen, a long-cherished reform postponed by Labour in 1968 which was eventually realised in 1973. In June 1971 she was able to announce extra spending on primary school buildings – making the point that it was paid for out of the savings on milk and meals.[30] She also doubled the grants to the direct grant schools, drawing criticism that she was only concerned with perpetuating privilege. But the following year she disarmed her critics with the scale of her projected provision for the state system for the rest of the decade. The White Paper *A Framework for Expansion*, published in December 1972, earmarked an extra £1,000 million a year for education by 1981. The main emphasis was on the opposite ends of the educational process: nursery schools and polytechnics. On the one hand, the Government set itself the target of providing free nursery education for all 3–4 year-olds within ten years: echoing Keith Joseph's thinking about how to break the 'cycle of deprivation', Mrs

Thatcher emphasised that a good start on the educational ladder would 'help redress the balance for those born unlucky'.[31] By the same token she channelled extra resources to the most deprived areas. In the schools system as a whole there was provision for 145,000 more teachers: pupil–teacher ratios were to fall from 22:1 to 18:1 by 1981. At the other end the White Paper projected a continuing expansion of the number of students in higher education from 463,000 to 750,000 (an increase in the proportion of 18-year-olds receiving higher education from 15 per cent to 22 per cent). Altogether there was to be a 5 per cent real increase in education spending over the next five years.[32]

Those who had hitherto regarded Mrs Thatcher as a penny-pinching élitist concerned only with preserving the grammar schools for the children of the middle class were 'agreeably surprised' by this White Paper.[33] From the perspective of the 1980s it appears even more astonishing. Yet it was entirely consistent with the social objectives of the Heath Government and the ambitions of the Prime Minister personally: Mrs Thatcher won her spurs as an effective Minister by her success in securing from the Treasury the sums needed to carry out a universally applauded policy. In the event, of course, the boom on which these optimistic projections had been dependent burst. Education suffered its share of the public spending cuts announced by Tony Barber in December 1973 following the oil crisis. Mrs Thatcher secured exemption in principle for her nursery schools programme; but in practice it foundered after she had left office. Nor was it ever heard of again when she returned as Prime Minister. Without explicitly repudiating her high-spending past as Keith Joseph did after 1974, she seemed simply to forget her time at the Department of Education as though it had never been. Yet it was a good record, which would have brought great national benefit if only it had been fully carried out.

One very unpopular policy which became Mrs Thatcher's responsibility, though it was not hers originally, was the attempt to oblige the leading national museums and galleries to impose admission charges. The proposal to raise money for the arts by charging the public to see the national collections originated with Lord Eccles, one of Heath's most imaginative appointments, brought back after some years out of politics as Minister for the Arts. Eccles was by no possible definition a 'Heathman'. Now aged sixty-five, he had been a distinguished Minister of Education under Macmillan. Museum charges made their appearance in Barber's first autumn budget: if not precisely a spending cut, that was very much the way they were presented. The announcement provoked an immediate outcry from the arts world: Sir John Betjeman, Osbert Lancaster and others joined the trustees of all the major galleries in protesting that charges would deter the public from visiting museums and represent a breach of faith with those who had given works of art to the nation in the expectation that they would be exhibited free of charge. Against this the Government argued that people only valued what they had to pay for. In a letter to Sir Robert Sainsbury, chairman of the trustees of the Tate Gallery, Heath firmly defended the policy, maintaining that it was right in principle that those visiting art galleries should be asked to contribute to their upkeep, just as music lovers and theatre-goers expected to pay.[34] His adoption of this narrowly materialist line – in many ways out of character in the most artistically minded Prime Minister for decades – was a bizarre product of the enthusiasm for market forces and businesslike accounting which temporarily gripped him around 1970.

There was no room in the parliamentary timetable for a Bill before 1972. Meanwhile opposition to the principle mounted, while the mechanics of collection and disbursement of the money raised looked less and less worth the disruption and public resistance that would be provoked. (On a smaller scale, the argument was not unlike that over the poll tax in 1989–91.) By the summer of 1972, as a result of inflation and VAT, the anticipated return from a 10p admission charge (20p in July and August) at 12 major galleries in London and 6 in Scotland and Wales was down from £1 million to just £800,000. Moreover there were legal problems with donors' bequests which had stipulated free exhibition. When the Government tried to alter the terms of benefactors' wills they were forced to back down. In October 1972, following the narrow defeat of amendments which would have allowed the galleries to open free of charge one day a week and retain for themselves half the money taken on other days (instead of surrendering it to the Treasury), the Third Reading was carried by only 5 votes, 3 Conservatives (including Jeffrey Archer) voting against and several more abstaining.[35] The Government now hesitated for a year, but then announced that charges would take effect on 1 January 1974.

On 20 November 1973 the Opposition tabled a motion declaring the imposition of charges to be 'inopportune and undesirable'. The Liberals (who had previously abstained) decided to support it, and ten Tories were said to be ready to join them. 'It is hard to see', *The Times* reported, 'how the Government can avoid defeat.'[36] It did so by means of some last-minute concessions. During the debate Mrs Thatcher announced that the galleries would be allowed to keep their own takings and some at least would be allowed free days. It was enough: only 2 Tories voted against – though another 8 abstained – and the Government survived by a majority of 6.[37] A week later, as part of the reshuffle caused by Willie Whitelaw's return from Northern Ireland, Eccles left the Government: Norman St John Stevas became Arts Minister within the Department of Education and immediately announced further concessions, including free admission for pensioners. ('A fitting gesture,' in *The Times*'s view.)[38] Charges did indeed come into operation on 1 January. But their impact on admissions was disastrous. Visitors to the National Gallery in February 1974 were a third of their level the previous year – and 40 per cent of those came on the free day. The cost of extra staff, ticket machines and turnstiles seemed likely to eat up most if not all of the money taken.[39] The moment Labour won the February 1974 election the new Arts Minister, Hugh Jenkins, announced that the charges would be scrapped. They ended on 29 March after just twelve weeks of operation. The galleries heaved a sigh of relief and disposed of their expensive new equipment.

The whole episode was futile and misguided. Of all the original aspirations of Heath's Government of which he did not like to be reminded in later years, this was perhaps the most purely and prematurely 'Thatcherite' (to use the later word). It was curious that he persisted with it even when he had abandoned so much else. In due course the case for admission charges came up again in the Thatcher years. The Government once again required museums and galleries to meet more of their own expenses; but this time they did it more insidiously, by starving them of funding and encouraging them to seek 'voluntary' contributions from the public, not so heavy-handedly by legislation. In this area as in others, the Conservative Government of the 1980s learned from the experience of the 1970s. Meanwhile the abortive fiasco to which Heath so perversely and stubbornly pinned his waning authority in January 1974 was one of the strangest aberrations of 'Selsdon Man'.

The fourth major department with responsibility for domestic policy was the Home Office. This senior but traditionally thankless job Heath gave in 1970 to his defeated rival for the leadership and nominal deputy leader, Reginald Maudling. Maudling was not of course a 'Heathman'. In terms of social origin, in fact, his background was not dissimilar. But he was his own man, Heath's equal in seniority; moreover his style was too relaxed and sceptical. He lacked Heath's missionary zeal. Nevertheless for two years – until obliged to resign as a result of his ill-judged association with the corrupt architect John Poulson – he gave loyal if somewhat semi-detached support to

Heath's Government. Though heavily preoccupied for most of this time by the troubles in Northern Ireland – then still a Home Office responsibility – he was by no means a bad Home Secretary.

It was a peculiarly difficult time for a liberal-minded Conservative Home Secretary, faced with what seemed to many Tories an alarming tide of anarchy and 'permissiveness' – drugs, pornography, demonstrations and terrorism. In his easy-going way Maudling trod a skilful path between the conflicting pressures on him to act on such matters as blue film clubs, indecent advertising and ambiguous pop songs without overreacting. He also had to cope with the beginning of the IRA bombing campaign on the British mainland – in October 1971 the Post Office tower, in February 1972 a bomb at Aldershot which killed seven civilians – as well as the 'Angry Brigade' attack on the home of the Employment Secretary, Robert Carr. He dismissed demands for the return of the death penalty. One law and order issue on which he took an uncompromising line, however, was the application of the German revolutionary student Rudi Dutschke, who had come to Britain for treatment in 1968 after being shot in Berlin, to prolong his stay. After hearing undisclosed police evidence that he had broken an undertaking to refrain from political activity, Maudling in January 1971 refused his permission and Dutschke was effectively deported.[40]

The principal manifesto commitment on Maudling's plate was a new Immigration Bill on the lines which Heath had been obliged to promise in response to Enoch Powell's unscrupulously alarmist campaign since 1968. The Bill which he introduced in February 1971 was frankly designed, in Maudling's own words, to 'draw Enoch's horns'.[41] It restricted the numbers of Commonwealth citizens entitled to settle in Britain by placing them essentially on the same footing as aliens, but with provision for 'patrials' – those with parents or grandparents born in the mother country (by definition largely white citizens of the 'Old' Commonwealth) – to enter freely. Immigrants were required to have a work permit applicable to a specific job for a fixed period and to register any change of job or home with the police: only after five years would they qualify for the right to settle permanently. Stronger powers were taken to expel those who had entered illegally, and the number of dependents admitted was more strictly limited. At the same time financial help was offered to immigrants already in Britain who wished to go back. This fell far short of the large-scale programme of repatriation demanded by Powell, who accordingly denounced the Bill as a feeble half-measure. Maudling's relaxed handling, however, succeeded skilfully in selling it to both wings of the party as a reasonable compromise and had pretty well defused the issue – until it was brutally reopened by Idi Amin, who in August 1972 followed the example of Kenya in 1968 and expelled large numbers of Asians from Uganda.

The year before, Maudling had provoked right-wing displeasure by speeding up the rate at which Kenyan Asians could be admitted – though only by slowing the numbers from other sources. The prospect of a new wave of possibly 60,000 Ugandans with British passports claiming sanctuary immediately sparked a campaign by the Monday Club, stridently supported by the National Front, to keep them out. Powell, furiously recalling the party's manifesto promise to allow 'no further large-scale permanent immigration', dismissed as 'twaddle' the argument that the Government had a legal obligation to honour the implied promise of the passports given at the time of Ugandan independence in 1962.[42] The Cabinet, however, stood firm and insisted that it did have a legal and a moral obligation and would honour it. By now Robert Carr was Home Secretary, but Heath took the lead in defending the Government's position. On 20 September he published a lengthy reply to Jonathan Guinness, the Chairman of the Monday Club, in which he vindicated the Immigration Act (emphasising that some assisted voluntary repatriation was taking place, but recalling also the manifesto promise that there should be no attempt to 'harass or compel' anyone against his or her will); insisted that the obligation to Kenyan and Ugandan British passport holders 'has its roots in our imperial history'; gave details of a 'major diplomatic effort' to persuade other countries to take some of the refugees (which they would not do if Britain shirked her responsibility); and acidly rejected the Monday Club's demand that the Government put British interests first: 'We hold that it is in the interest of the British people that the reputation of Britain for good faith and humanity should be preserved. I had assumed that this was also one of the purposes of the Monday Club.'[43]

At the party conference in October Powell attempted a showdown but was outmanœuvred. Though the subject of immigration had deliberately been kept off the agenda, he managed to introduce a critical motion, speaking in unfamiliar guise as spokesman of the Hackney South and Shoreditch Conservative Association. With the help of an uncharacteristically stinging speech by Carr, however, a loyal Young Conservative amendment congratulating the Government on its stance was carried by a majority of 2–1. If the vote reflected, as *The Times* suggested, 'the struggle between the two men [Heath and Powell] for the soul of the Conservative Party',[44] then the party was still with Heath. The next month, speaking to London

Tories, he once again vigorously justified the Government's action. What would have happened, he asked, if Britain had not taken the Asians in?

They would be rotting in concentration camps prepared by President Amin, and they would be there simply because of the colour of their skin and the fact that they held British passports. That would have been the sight presented to us on our television screens night after night this Christmas.[45]

In the event, some 28,000 Asians came to Britain from Uganda, and were absorbed without difficulty, being for the most part unusually highly skilled and motivated refugees. Nevertheless the row helped fuel a minor surge in support for the National Front over the next few years: at the West Bromwich by-election in May 1973 the Front's candidate won 16 per cent of the poll. As a result of the 1971 Act, however, the numbers of 'New Commonwealth' immigrants fell sharply in 1973 (to 32,000, compared with 44,000 in 1971); it crept up again steadily thereafter, but these were predominantly the dependents of heads of household already arrived.[46] The Act can reasonably be said to have achieved its purpose: race relations remained a major social problem, but immigration as such largely ceased to be a political issue.

It was a greater blow to Heath than might have been expected when Maudling was obliged to resign from the Government in July 1972. He had been tarred by his unwise business association with Poulson, from whom he had accepted donations to charities which his wife supported. His reputation had already been damaged by another dubious business venture, his chairmanship of Abe Hoffman's Real Estate Fund of America. What forced his resignation was not that he had himself in either case done anything strictly wrong, but simply that he could not properly remain Home Secretary, responsible for the Metropolitan Police, when the Director of Public Prosecutions opened investigations into Poulson's affairs. Heath offered him another position in the Government; but it was symptomatic of the strain he had been under that he preferred to withdraw altogether.[47] Even so it was widely expected that he would soon be back. Not only was he the last heavyweight of Heath's own generation left in the Government: there was a sense that with the Government now modifying most of the more abrasive policies which Heath had embodied since 1965, and specifically turning towards incomes policy which he had never ceased to advocate, the party was in the process of 'rejoining Reggie'. 'The loss of Mr Maudling', *The Times* lamented, 'removes the strongest counterpoise that existed to the defined activism of Mr Heath's own temperament.' He represented 'a large part of the Cabinet's ballast of judgement'.[48] The fact that Heath named Robert Carr to succeed him while remaining Lord President and Leader of the House as well encouraged speculation that he was merely keeping Maudling's seat warm for him. In the event Jim Prior soon took over the Lord Presidency and Maudling – at his own wish – stayed on the back benches for the remainder of the Parliament. 'Ted Heath acted like a true friend,' Maudling wrote in his *Memoirs*.[49] Back in opposition, Heath again invited him back into Shadow Cabinet in late 1974: Maudling accepted in principle, but not immediately. (He eventually returned – briefly – under Mrs Thatcher.) Meanwhile a Commons Select Committee investigated his behaviour towards the House and finally came up with a critical report which was debated in March 1977. On this occasion Heath came handsomely to his support, with a 'devastating' speech vindicating his integrity which was 'in effect decisive'.[50] His suspension from the House was overwhelmingly defeated and a supportive Tory amendment carried by acclamation. At a low period in his own fortunes, Heath won admiration for the way he stood by his old rival and saved him from political disgrace.

20

The Vote for Europe

THE one clear success of the Government's first year had been the satisfactory conclusion of the EEC negotiations, which had removed at last the external obstacle that had blocked Britain's entry into the Community. Now, however, the domestic obstacle – to which no one had given much thought in 1970 when all three parties were solidly in favour – loomed threateningly larger. The negotiations had been carried out against a background of public scepticism, not to say hostility; and Labour in opposition had quickly trimmed its sails to the wind. By the time Geoffrey Rippon brought home the terms the question of joining or not was well on the way back to being a straight party issue – though still one complicated by dissenters on both sides. Heath had been persuaded to delay the decisive vote over the summer while the Government endeavoured to revive public support for entry; but the moment of truth was now approaching. The critical date was fixed for 28 October 1971 at the very beginning of the new parliamentary session, following an unprecedented six-day debate. For weeks beforehand the vote was the focus of intensive speculation, calculation and nervous apprehension.

Over the years since Macmillan had first put it on the political agenda public opinion on the principle of joining the Common Market had fluctuated wildly. Broadly speaking, the electorate had favoured the idea so long as there was no imminent likelihood of it happening, but shied off whenever it began to seem a realistic possibility. During Heath's negotiations in 1961–3 support for joining fell steadily, though the majority never quite tipped into opposition. Following de Gaulle's first veto, however, the public perversely cried for what it could not have: in the period 1963–7 pro-Market majorities went as high as 70 per cent only to fall sharply again as soon as Wilson put in Labour's application. De Gaulle's second veto had the effect that was widely predicted for the first: British opinion now turned against an unwelcoming Europe, to the extent that by 1970 – despite the unanimous view of the political establishment and both front benches – no more than 20 per cent supported a third attempt, while around 60 per cent were opposed. The 1970–1 negotiations did nothing to improve these figures.[1] As a result by the spring of 1971 not only the Labour party but sections of the Tory party which had never been enthusiastic for Europe began to rediscover doubts about the political wisdom of pressing on.

Visiting Willy Brandt in April 1971, Heath admitted that public opinion was 'sceptical'. He believed, however, that it contained 'a substantial "grey area" in which pro-Market attitudes would gain the upper hand if it became evident that success was feasible'.[2] The next three months seemed to prove him right. Following his triumphant summit meeting with Pompidou in May, the conclusion of the negotiations in June and the publication of the terms in July support for entry leaped gratifyingly. By July all four major polls showed the pro and anti votes level pegging at around 40 per cent each, while ORC – Heath's favourite poll, the only one which had correctly predicted his 1970 victory – actually gave a 45–41 per cent lead to the pro-Marketeers. This sudden turnaround – at a time when the polls of voting intention showed the Government's popularity on other issues plummeting – gave great encouragement to the pro-Market camp, who confidently predicted 50 per cent by October. In fact support slipped back again over the following months: by October ORC once again showed the antis 12 per cent ahead.[3]

Meanwhile the 'great debate' was launched. While Labour attempted to cover its hasty volte-face by attacking the terms, and Tory heart-searching was largely concentrated on the question of sovereignty, the Government rested the case for entry squarely on the high ground of Britain's standing in the world. The White Paper published on 7 July was unusually forceful for an official document: it was still somewhat short on figures, particularly on the likely effect of entry on the balance of payments, but it stated the choice before the country in uncompromising terms:

> Either we choose to enter the Community and join in building a strong Europe on the foundations which the Six have laid; or we choose to stand aside from this great enterprise and seek to maintain our interests from the narrow – and narrowing – base we have known in recent years.[4]

On television the same evening Heath reiterated his familiar theme of

397

national greatness. 'This time', he stressed – by contrast with 1963 and 1967 – 'the choice is ours . . . For twenty-five years we've been looking for something to get us going again. Now here it is. We must recognise it for what it is. We have the chance of new greatness. Now we must take it.'[5]

The next night Wilson broadcast in utterly contrasting tones of niggling agnosticism. He did not yet absolutely condemn the Rippon terms, but as several of his senior colleagues came out against the Market he was clearly preparing to follow. By the time Labour held a special one-day conference to debate the terms just nine days later he astonished listeners by the strength of his hostility to the basic concept of the Community which he had himself so recently applied to join. But the conference served only to advertise the depth of Labour's split, as those former ministers who had had responsibility for Labour's application queued up to testify that they would have been happy to have negotiated the terms that Rippon had achieved and were confident that a Labour Cabinet would have accepted them.

The sense of their own consistency helped the Labour pro-Marketeers to stick to their principles in the weeks ahead: it was not they who had abandoned the party's previously clear policy in support of entry. The special conference took no vote; but a week later the TUC came out against entry and it was a foregone conclusion that the party conference in October would do the same. In fact, maintaining his careful balancing act to preserve his pretence of consistency, Wilson managed to ensure that a future Labour Government was not committed to withdraw from the Community – supposing Britain was by then a member – but only to 'renegotiate' more favourable terms (specifically on the Common Agricultural Policy, the Commonwealth, and regional policy). By this means Wilson contrived to keep open the option to reverse himself again in 1975; but in the meantime it was a severe blow to Heath, since it meant that even if he succeeded in taking Britain into the Community as planned in 1973 the achievement would remain provisional for some time to come.

Heath would clearly have preferred to lead a united nation into Europe with the support and applause of an admiring Opposition. On the other hand there was some political advantage to the Conservatives, both from Labour's public disarray and from its official change of line. For – just as it had done in 1962 – Labour's opposition helped to unite the Tory party in support of the Market. At the beginning of the year there were clear signs that the party was beginning to back away from its commitment to Europe. The constituency associations had gone distinctly cool on the issue. In May the local party in Macclesfield embarrassingly reflected the prevailing mood by selecting an anti-Marketeer, Nicholas Winterton, to fight an imminent by-election. (Among the rejected candidates was Douglas Hurd, whose close association with the Prime Minister had become a liability to him.) Yet the mood was quickly reversed as soon as the Brussels deadlock was broken. The positive outcome of the negotiations, the glimpse of a possible success at last for the embattled Government and the easy political target offered by Wilson's U-turn, assisted by an intensive propaganda campaign by Central Office and a barrage of ministerial speeches, all helped to recall the party to its former loyal enthusiasm.

On 14 July Heath addressed the Conservative Central Council – the party officers and activists – at the Central Hall, Westminster. Speaking for an hour and then taking questions from the floor he treated them to a virtuoso exposition of his European vision, contrasting the Tories' responsible support for Labour's application with Wilson's cynical manœuvring; he received a 'tumultuous reception' which signalled conclusively that the danger of a serious revolt against the Government's flagship policy was over.[6] The anti-Marketeers sourly dubbed this triumph Heath's 'Nuremberg Rally'. A week later he opened the four-day Commons debate to 'take note' of the terms with another 'powerful, almost messianic performance', quoting scornfully from Wilson's past effusions.[7] The debate clearly demonstrated the predominant return to party lines on the European issue. The Conservative Group for Europe now claimed the support of more than 200 Tory MPs, with new adherents every day as the momentum of the Government campaign gathered pace and the opinion polls appeared to respond. Only one junior Minister (Teddy Taylor) resigned from the Government; while several MPs previously reckoned as 'doubtful' on the issue announced that they would consult their constituencies over the recess before making up their minds.★ Pym's wisdom in urging Heath to postpone the crucial vote until the autumn was thoroughly vindicated. By the time of the party conference the Tory opponents of entry were reduced to an isolated rump of diehards. Enoch Powell made an impassioned plea to the party not to surrender the historic sovereignty of the Queen in Parliament. But he was effectively answered by Alec Douglas-Home

---

★ Nicholas Winterton was a symbolic representative of this process of conversion: selected as an anti-Marketeer in May, he was elected in September – still with the support of his local party – as a pro-Marketeer and duly voted for entry on 28 October.[8]

at his most disarming; and on a card vote – on which Heath unusually insisted, to put the issue beyond doubt – the pro-Market motion was carried by 2,474 votes to 324. The atmosphere was almost as emotional as at Llandudno nine years before.[9]

Yet the October vote was still a daunting hurdle. The parliamentary arithmetic was confused, the outcome alarmingly unpredictable. The Government's overall majority, allowing for the Speaker and his two deputies (all Conservatives) and one lost by-election (Bromsgrove in May), was down to 25. On the credit side the Government could rely on the support of 5 of the 6 Liberals; but the 6 assorted independents, nationalists and Democratic Unionists were all opposed to entry. If the Labour party could whip all its members into the No lobby, it would only need 21 Tory rebels for the government to be defeated; and all the open and covert pressures of the Whips could not bring the number of unreconcilables down as low as that. As Parliament reassembled and the critical debate finally got under way on 21 October, following weeks of canvassing, disinformation, bluff and counter-bluff – a period of what Uwe Kitzinger has called 'nose-counting, arm-twisting, weak knees and stiff upper lips'[10] – Pym and the unofficial Whip for the pro-Marketeers, Norman St John Stevas, still reckoned on at least 30 Tories (including most of the Ulster Unionists) determined to stick to their guns. To secure its majority the Government was going to have to depend upon a counterbalancing block of Labour pro-Marketeers sticking to theirs.

This was a situation Heath was very anxious to avoid. As a former Chief Whip, it was a matter of principle to him that the Government should be able to get its policy through by the votes of its own supporters. It was the job of MPs, in his view, to support the Government in carrying out its programme. To have to rely on Labour votes on such a major plank of its platform was uncertain and humiliating. Quite early in the summer the suggestion arose of allowing a free vote in the crucial division. It was argued that this would make it easier for the Labour pro-Marketeers to vote against their party line. William Rodgers wrote personally to Heath begging him to allow a free vote, urging that he would get a bigger majority that way, since the Labour pro-Europeans easily outnumbered the Tory antis.[11] But Heath was adamantly against it. Not only was the Government, he insisted on 12 July, 'absolutely entitled' to ask its supporters to back it in the lobby: he also maintained that the Governments of the Six expected the British Government to use its majority to approve the terms they had agreed. 'This, after all, is the only basis on which they are prepared to negotiate.' He thought it 'a strange approach' to suggest that the Government should whip its supporters on every other item of its business but leave them free to vote as they liked on the most important policy of all.[12] He was loudly applauded when he repeated this unbending line to the party faithful at Central Hall.[13] His senior colleagues – Home, Maudling and Carrington – supported him. As a matter of constitutional principle the whips should stay on.

The problem was that over the summer, while the bulk of the Tory party swung enthusiastically or uncertainly back into line, at least 30 determined anti-Marketeers remained unshakeable. They were not Powellites, since Powell – though by far the most compelling and outspoken orator against the Market – operated essentially as a lone voice. Most were longstanding opponents of joining the Community, mainly on the principle of sovereignty. They justified their defiance partly by the depth of their own convictions but also on the cautious words of the 1970 manifesto, which committed a Tory Government to 'negotiate, no more, no less', and still more on Heath's carefully worded statement in May 1970 that enlargement of the Community should not take place 'except with the full-hearted comment of parliaments and peoples in the new member countries'.[14] While the Government could quite properly assert that it had negotiated successfully and was now, in the normal course of Government business, recommending the result of its negotiation to Parliament, the rebels interpreted the latter condition as a promise not to proceed against the will of the British people, as reflected in the opinion polls; more, they could argue that a whipped vote in the House of Commons, producing only a narrow and conscripted majority, did not represent the 'full-hearted consent' even of Parliament. Their increasingly bitter contention was that Heath, in his arrogant determination to take Britain into Europe at any cost, had betrayed all the promises he had given in opposition and was embarked on a massive deception of the British public for which he had no mandate.

None of these arguments cut any ice with Heath. But the fact was, as October approached, that on a whipped vote Pym could not guarantee to deliver a majority. As late as 11 October, as the Tory conference opened in Brighton, Heath was still publicly insisting that a free vote was out of the question.[15] But Pym was now marshalling the calculations to convince him to change his mind. Contrary to the hopes of the anti-Marketeers, a free vote was unlikely to increase the number of Tory rebels by more than a handful – perhaps from 30 to 40. On the other hand while only 20–5 of the most determined Labour Europeans would bring themselves to defy their party by supporting the Tory Government – routinely vilified as the most divisive and reactionary for forty years – on a whipped vote, Pym knew that as many as 70 had promised to vote for entry on a free vote. On a whipped vote he would at most get a narrow majority of 10–15, and there was a real danger that he could lose. On a free vote, he would not only be sure of winning a respectable majority; such a majority could also more readily be described as embodying the 'full-hearted consent' of Parliament.

Heath still resisted the logic. Pym has described the battle to persuade him as the hardest he ever had.[16] But he won the support of his predecessor, Willie Whitelaw, and between them, on 18 October, at a meeting at the House of Commons with Rippon, Barber and Carrington, they finally convinced Heath. It was announced the same day that – on the Conservative side at least – the whips would be off. The assumption was that Labour would follow suit. Wilson, concerned above all to preserve party unity, would have been happy to go along with this. But he was prevented by Tony Benn, anxious both to commit Labour firmly against the Market and to keep the pressure on the Government: if Labour polled its full strength, he argued, the Government could be defeated.[17] The decision was left to the parliamentary party: the next day Labour MPs voted by 140 to 111 against allowing themselves a free vote.

This was a key moment. By conceding a free vote – even though he did so only grudgingly and out of weakness, from fear of defeat, not out of strength – Heath got the credit for seeking a true expression of the will of the House. He was rewarded with a much larger majority than he would have got on a whipped vote, which was to be of immense value in the months ahead when the whipped majorities on the consequential legislation sank to single figures. Labour, conversely, by imposing a three-line whip which a large number of its MPs nevertheless defied, was seen to be trying to curtail the expression of deeply held views and only exposed its own divisions the more deeply. It was the fact that the Government side was not whipped that allowed the Jenkinsites to defy their own Whips without feeling that they were supporting the Government. Subsequently Heath brought himself to acknowledge publicly that Pym and Whitelaw had been right.[18] He never, however, acknowledged it privately or thanked his Chief Whip for his foresight.[19] Nevertheless the three-figure majority for Europe which was triumphantly secured on 28 October was not Heath's achievement but Francis Pym's.

The six-day debate was opened by Alec Douglas-Home on 21 October. The motion was purely declaratory, without legal effect, since the detailed terms had not yet been finalised. Carefully framed in consultation with the Jenkinsites to draw the maximum possible support, it simply invited the House to approve the Government's decision to join the Community 'on the basis of the arrangements which have been negotiated'.[20] There was nothing new to be said on either side: all the arguments for and against entry had already been rehearsed endlessly for the previous ten years and with very few exceptions every speaker's position was known in advance. Even so, the debate was a great parliamentary occasion. The public galleries and the peers' and diplomatic galleries were crowded throughout. Among those present on the final day was Jean Monnet, the 'Father' of the Community, who had always hoped to see Britain finally take its place in Europe. In all, 176 MPs spoke, though the balance was somewhat skewed by the fact that the pro-Marketeers on the Labour Front Bench were debarred from speaking against the party line: Roy Jenkins, George Thomson and Harold Lever were all condemned to silence. Wilson opened on the last day (curiously leaving Callaghan to wind up for Labour). He was deliberately 'soporific . . . well below the level of events' (Douglas Hurd's description), fudging the issue in such a way as to leave Benn convinced that if he got back to office he would accept entry as a *fait accompli*.[21] If the Community refused to renegotiate the 'Tory terms', he declared bathetically, 'we would sit down amicably and discuss the situation with them'.[22] The House, crowded and tense, just laughed at him. Later Powell delivered one of his chilling philippics; but it fell to Heath, closing the debate, to try to match the historic nature of the occasion.

'I do not think', he began, 'that any Prime Minister has stood at this Box in time of peace and asked the House to take a positive decision of such importance.' He was able to announce a thumping result from the parallel debate in the Lords, just concluded: the peers had voted 451–58 for entry. He pitched his speech at the high level of world affairs, not deigning to bother with the terms. He urged his familiar theme of a rapidly changing, increasingly multi-polar world, with China emerging as a third superpower, in which Britain could no longer rely on a special partnership with the United States: a world in which Europe needed to speak with a united voice to protect its interests and assert its influence for good. The Community was 'a living, changing, developing organisation': if there were problems following British entry the machinery existed to resolve them. The point was to stop thinking in terms of 'Us' and 'Them'.

We are approaching the point where, if the House so decides tonight, it will become just as much *our* Community as their

Community. We shall be partners, we shall be co-operating, and we shall be trying to find common solutions to common problems of all the members of an enlarged Community.

Repeating that the decision would be taken by Parliament – 'the Parliament of all the people' – he ended by quoting the words of the Indian negotiator at the time of de Gaulle's 1963 veto, which had made a deep impression on him. 'When you left India, some people wept. And when you leave Europe tonight, some will weep. There is no other people in the world of whom these things could be said.' This was a significant tribute to recall at such a moment; it reveals a lot about the springs of Heath's post-imperial Europeanism. He concluded, with perhaps pardonable exaggeration: 'Tonight when this House endorses this Motion many millions of people right across the world will rejoice that we have taken our rightful place in a truly united Europe.'[23]

'Heath did not set the Thames on fire,' wrote David Spanier of *The Times*, 'but he did not need to. The vote was coming.'[24] There was no doubt that the Government would win: Roy Jenkins had firmly rebuffed a last personal appeal from 101 colleagues that he should reconsider, in the higher interest of the party, 'your declared intention of voting in the Prime Minister's lobby on Thursday evening'.[25] The only question was how many would follow him, and how many Tories would vote with the Opposition. The Whips and the press had got their calculations all but perfect: *The Times* that morning predicted the size of both rebellions within four votes.[26] And yet somehow no one predicted the size of the majority: the bookmakers were giving odds of 25–1 against a majority over 100.[27] The result, when Mr Speaker Lloyd read out the figures, was an unexpected triumph: Ayes 356, Noes 244, giving a majority of 112. Sixty-nine Labour pro-Marketeers had voted for entry, with 20 more abstaining. Thirty-nine Tories (a slightly higher figure than generally expected) had voted against, with just 2 abstaining. One Tory was absent ill.

Heath and all those who had worked and lobbied and negotiated for entry for twelve years were euphoric. This surely was the end of the argument – the moment of irreversible decision. Such an emphatic majority would put to flight the spectre of renegotiation or withdrawal. On the cliffs of Dover Harold Macmillan had been waiting to light a bonfire, symbolically answered by another on the Pas de Calais. Congratulations poured in from Brandt, Pompidou and other leaders – even Nixon. Heath spent another two hours at the House, celebrating with supporters in Annie's Bar, before going on to another party, attended by Jean Monnet, at Geoffrey Rippon's flat in Admiralty Arch.[28] When he finally got back to Downing Street he gave thanks not by thumping triumphantly on the piano, but quietly on the clavichord:

> With just a few friends, those who had been closest to me throughout all this time, I went quietly back to No. 10 and up to my sitting room. There, as they stood by, I played Bach's First Prelude and Fugue for the Well-Tempered Clavier. The clavichord had its effect: after ten years of struggle and setbacks, in success it gave us peace of mind.[29]

But the antis were not correspondingly cast down. They knew there was still a long way to go. They believed they could still defeat the consequential legislation that would be required to give effect to the purely declaratory motion of intent. From now on the Government was on its own. Having saved their consciences by voting for the principle of entry, the Jenkinsites had promised not to support the Government any further: ministers must henceforth take responsibility for carrying their own legislation through the House. There was indeed a hard road ahead. And yet 28 October *was* the decisive moment. More than any later vote it did express the real view of the House of Commons. And despite some narrow squeaks, Labour's charade of renegotiation and ultimate recourse to a referendum, the vote that night did stand as the moment when Britain cast in her lot with the continent. It was – with Pym's help, and thanks to the steadfastness of Roy Jenkins and his followers – Heath's finest hour.

21

First Blood to the Miners

1972 was a traumatic year for the Heath Government – a year of crises, humiliations and emergencies from which it emerged battered, unbowed and still determined, but facing in a very different direction from that in which it had set out so confidently in 1970. The pattern of the year was set in the first two months, which must rate as the most dreadful short period of concentrated stress ever endured by a British Government in peacetime – at any rate before the autumn of 1992. Two events in particular shook the Government to its core. On 9 January the miners began an unexpectedly determined six-week strike in pursuit of a wage increase of 47 per cent; and on 20 January the monthly figure for unemployment in the United Kingdom reached one million for the first time since 1947. The first was a direct challenge to the Government's authority whose full impact was not felt until February. The second was a moment of heavy symbolism no less devastating for being long predicted. It would be hard to say which was more instrumental in pushing the Government off its original course.

But these were not the only hammer blows. To understand the pressure that Heath and his colleagues were under at this critical moment of the Government's fortunes it is necessary to appreciate that they were simultaneously assailed by two further desperate crises which absorbed the Cabinet's time, drained its energy and stretched its nerve to the limit. First, Northern Ireland was erupting in a new wave of bombings and killings of unprecedented ferocity and the province was slipping closer to the abyss of all-out civil war. Second, the Government was embarked on a perilous parliamentary battle as the enabling legislation to take Britain into the EEC began its fiercely contested passage through the Commons: on 17 February it survived a confidence motion, which might have ended Heath's premiership, by a majority of only eight. Never has a Government been so desperately embattled on so many fronts at once. It is against this background that its reaction to ever-rising unemployment must be judged.

The Government was already on the defensive before the end of 1971, waiting for the total to break through the seven-figure barrier which had been arbitrarily accepted by both parties and the press as politically insupportable. The whole political world, as one junior Minister put it, was 'mesmerised' by this one statistic.[1] Already in November there had been uproar in the House of Commons, violent demonstrations in the lobby and grave editorials in the papers as the figure neared the dreaded mark. *The Times* set the tone: 'It is morally, economically, socially and politically intolerable', it thundered on 19 November, 'that unemployment should remain at its present level.'[2] Five days later, when Barber responded with a 'hastily assembled assortment' of measures whose 'effects this winter will be virtually nil', the paper nevertheless felt 'bound to welcome almost anything the Treasury can scratch together even if it gives only psychological comfort'.[3] It was clear in December that the next monthly figure would take the aggregate over the symbolic threshold. *The Economist* tried to point out that it was simply superstition to attach magical importance to the last 50,000.[4] But political theatre required a concentrated explosion of outrage, both genuine and fake. On 20 January it came.

Labour determined to make the most of the moment. At Prime Minister's Question Time Heath faced a concentrated barrage of booing, catcalls and chants of 'Resign' and 'Heath out'. The Member for Bolsover, Dennis Skinner, stood directly in front of him and shook his fist in his face; another Derbyshire MP, Tom Swain, slammed down on the dispatch box an evening newspaper headlining the infamous figure – 1,023,583. The Speaker was obliged to suspend the House for fifteen minutes.[5] The following day Heath flew to Brussels for the signing ceremony formally marking Britain's accession to the EEC. On his return he had to face an emergency debate on unemployment, opened by Wilson at his most opportunist, taunting him on his return to reality – 'the reality of the Government's attainment of one million unemployed'. With a typically clever unspoken comparison of Brussels with Munich, Wilson slyly dubbed Heath 'the first dole-queue millionaire since Neville Chamberlain' and went on to throw back at him his castigation of much lower levels of unemployment under Labour and the Tories' confident promises in opposition to bring the figure down, blaming the Government's 'obsession with the balance sheet and not human beings' for putting it up instead.[6] In reply, Heath made a speech of remarkable dignity. He did not seek to dispute the Government's responsibility, confessed his disappointment that the measures already taken had not so far proved effective, but expressed confidence that they soon would. Characteristically he tried to explain to the House the new phenomenon, bewildering to Keynesian orthodoxy, of simultaneous unemployment and inflation. What was happening was that high labour costs had forced industry to shed workers: the same level of production as two years earlier was now being achieved with 400,000 fewer men. If only, he begged again, firms would now seize the opportunity to invest in new plant and equipment and the unions kept their wage claims moderate, entry to the EEC in twelve months' time offered great prospects.[7] In the circumstances it was an impressive performance, described by *The Times* as a 'powerful and confident message' to British industry, 'affirming that the Government would not be diverted from its present policies in the hope of temporary popularity'.[8]

Nevertheless the million figure was a profound shock to the Government. Though Douglas Hurd has sought to deny that ministers lost their nerve, insisting that the Government had always been committed before anything else to promoting faster growth,[9] there is an abundance of contrary evidence – from former ministers, their advisers and senior officials – of something close to panic in the ranks. Robert Carr certainly cut a very poor figure at this time, wringing his hands helplessly and undercutting Heath by admitting on 23 January that the Government was still losing the battle.[10] Jim Prior thought that Heath himself was privately 'very shaken, and I think this had a marked effect on his wish to reflate the economy'.[11] Lord Rothschild felt that Heath was 'emotionally very upset' by unemployment and ready to take 'maximal steps' to reduce it.[12] Neither Willie Whitelaw nor Peter Carrington, nor Heath himself, has ever denied that they believed it imperative for the Government to be seen to react to the January announcement with conspicuous urgency.

A generation that has seen Conservative governments since 1979 repeatedly re-elected despite unemployment levels two and three times higher can only wonder why they were so sensitive. After all it was not difficult to demonstrate that the rise in unemployment in 1971 was not the Tory Government's fault but the delayed result of actions taken by the Labour Government two years earlier. Specifically it could be traced back to the combination of Roy Jenkins's severe squeezing of the economy in 1968 following devaluation and the pre-election wage explosion which followed the abandonment of Labour's pay policy. The former was necessary at the time, and successful in righting the balance of payments, but was arguably kept on for too long both by Jenkins himself in his 1970 Budget and by Macleod and Barber that autumn. To this extent the new Government did share the responsibility: misled by over-optimistic Treasury forecasts, it was slow initially to let the brakes off; but throughout 1971 it had been administering ever stronger doses of reflation in successive packages of increasing desperation. It really could not be argued that the Government had not done everything the Keynesian textbook prescribed to counter unemployment: still less – as Labour never ceased to allege – that it had deliberately willed high unemployment as an instrument of policy. The worrying irony of the January rumpus was that unemployment had reached the million mark despite the Government's best efforts.

Then again, it can be argued, the Government should have been able to reduce the impact of the supposed million, both by the sort of statistical massaging of the raw figure at which later governments have become adept but also, quite legitimately, by more sophisticated analysis of different types of unemployment, distinguishing the temporary and transitional from the long-term and the unemployable. They could have done more to remind the public that, demoralising as unemployment unquestionably was, it no longer involved the degree of physical privation that it had done in the 1930s: not only were social security benefits much higher, but the vast expansion of the 'black economy' offered opportunities which significantly blurred the hard line between regular employment and the dole. Ministers as much as the press and public allowed themselves to be too easily swayed by grim but outdated images of hopeless, hungry men in caps and mufflers.

Finally, it was widely agreed by critics of Britain's economic performance since the war that a substantial shake out of manpower from overmanned and unproductive occupations was necessary and overdue. In the time of the Labour Government, Wilson had coined the euphemism 'redeployment' to put an acceptable gloss on the process. (This, indeed, was what Selective Employment Tax was designed to achieve, except that SET stood economic progress on its head by trying to 'redeploy' labour from service into manufacturing industry instead of the other way round.) With hindsight it is easy to see that a truly radical Tory Government, more clear-sighted than Heath ever was in his determination to modernise the British economy, would have faced the necessity for a temporarily high level of unemployment and concentrated all its effort on explaining the facts to the electorate, while doing all it could to ease the impact of the transition on its short-term victims.

But this was the wisdom of a decade later. In 1972 very few commentators and even fewer politicians imagined such harsh medicine to be politically practicable or morally acceptable. The fact that the most prominent exception was the outcast Enoch Powell only reinforced the conventional view. The example of *The Times*, already quoted, graphically illustrates the emotional confusion even of commentators who recognised with one part of their mind that a shake out might be economically healthy. A further editorial following the Commons debate on 24 January first criticised Wilson's twelve-point catalogue of orthodox counter-cyclical measures which the Government should take, then warned that, with improved productivity, even achieving the Government's target of 4 per cent growth would not necessarily soak up the labour that industry had shed, before concluding weakly that Wilson's remedies had their attractions after all, merely to ameliorate the shocking figure.[13] The editor of *The Times* in 1972 was William Rees-Mogg; the economics editor was Peter Jay. Both were leading monetarists after 1974: in 1972 they were among the most articulate and influential Keynesians.

Unemployment was still the great taboo of British politics. Surpassed in public affection only by the National Health Service, full employment was the central rock upon which postwar and social harmony had been founded. For twenty-five years it had been taken for granted by both parties that serious unemployment was a ghost of the bad old days, now exorcised for ever. For Heath's generation of Tories, who had grown up in the 1930s, fought through the war, and survived and entered politics with the ambition to help build a fairer society, the possibility of presiding over a return to mass unemployment was morally insupportable. As Jim Prior has written, 'Ted ... utterly despised and detested the pre-war Conservative Governments, who had tolerated between two and three million unemployed.'[14] For Heath and Whitelaw, Carrington and Carr, the maintenance of full employment overrode all other domestic issues. Willie Whitelaw is still frankly and unrepentently emotional about it: Heath hides his emotions, but there is no question that he felt the same way. He had little direct experience of unemployment in his own boyhood; but he had not served as Harold Macmillan's Chief Whip for three years without hearing a good deal of the sufferings of Stockton between the wars. For all of them, the men in caps and mufflers were a real presence whom no amount of sophisticated rationalisation could explain away.*

---

* 'I am sometimes accused of being oversensitive about unemployment,' Heath told the House of Commons in 1978. 'I do not believe that is possible, certainly not for anyone who lived through the 1930s and saw the political consequences of high unemployment throughout western Europe and what happened in 1939.'[15]

In addition, of course, they also believed it to spell certain defeat for the Conservative party if it were ever again to allow itself to become identified as the party of unemployment. It was, they believed, the memory of the dole queues that had defeated Churchill in 1945; since 1950 the whole of their political lives had been spent in helping to rid the party of that incubus. The Tories' thirteen years in office up to 1964 had been a tribute to their success; the last thing they could afford in 1972 was to let Labour hang that tag around the party's neck once more – as Wilson had immediately done by invoking the name of Neville Chamberlain. It was quite simply taken for granted that the electorate would not tolerate a million unemployed: whether the Tory Government had caused it or not, if it did not quickly get the figures down below the level of public consciousness it would lose the next election – and deservedly so. It was a political as well as a moral imperative to take whatever remedial action was required.

Third, though the bare figure was probably enough to doom any Government that permitted it, behind that statistical calculation lay a deep-seated fear that the fragile social fabric could not support a return to high unemployment. The late 1960s and early 1970s had witnessed a surge of political violence such as had not been seen for decades – on the one hand, student demonstrations against the Vietnam War, against apartheid, in support of civil rights; on the other, indiscriminate acts of terrorism by the IRA, by Palestinian Arabs, by self-styled anarchist groups like the Angry Brigade, who only a few months earlier had tried to blow up Robert Carr. Recourse to violence of one sort or another was suddenly the natural – almost the accepted – weapon of alienated groups in society: in such a climate a million unemployed who felt that the Government was not doing all it could to help them might easily prove more than the police could handle. This fear was clearly present in the Cabinet Room on at least two occasions in the next few weeks.

There were two further particular circumstances which made it still more impossible for the Government to tolerate unemployment in January 1972. First, it was already too heavily embroiled with the trade unions over the Industrial Relations Act – just about to come into force – and over pay to be able to afford another battle with them over unemployment. After a bad beginning, Heath and Carr had been trying hard for some time to win the good will and cooperation of the TUC in moderating wage claims and averting strikes. If they were to have any chance of maintaining that cooperation into 1972 they needed to be able to show the unions that they were doing everything possible to deal with unemployment.

Second, Heath had finally achieved his central ambition by negotiating Britain's entry into the EEC. The country had just a year to
get itself into shape. It was vital to go in with the economy at full
stretch: to join with a million unemployed would have been to lose
out on the opportunities which the enlarged market offered and thus
to get off to the worst possible start. Getting fit for Europe was the
overriding reason why Heath was in a hurry to achieve rapid
growth. To this end he was prepared to jettison the 'quiet revolution'
policies of lower taxes, lower spending and reliance on the market to
pull the economy round. He had believed in them so long as he had
been persuaded that they would work. But he needed quick results.
With unemployment still rising and Europe just over the horizon,
there was no time to wait for such slow therapy to take effect. A
clinching moment in Heath's conversion was a visit he paid to the
Midlands in the late autumn of 1971. This was not a 'development
area' of traditionally high unemployment, but the very heart of
British manufacturing industry: it appeared to him to be in no state
to meet the challenge of European competition.[16] If industry would
not restructure and modernise itself, he concluded, then the Government must get off the sidelines and help. It was as simple and as
urgent as that.

Then came the second trauma which was to shake the Government's
authority. The miners, curiously, were the last union from whom
the Government expected a serious challenge to its pay guidelines.
Coal was a declining industry. Over the past decade, under the chairmanship of the former Labour Minister Lord Robens, more than 400
pits had been closed; the number of miners had been more than
halved from around 700,000 to less than 300,000. The National
Union of Mineworkers had acquiesced tamely in this steady rundown. Militancy in the coalfields seemed a thing of the past: while
dockers, railwaymen and others were always going on strike, there
had not been a national coal strike since 1926. From their traditional
place at the top of the earnings league the miners had slipped far
down the table. By 1971, however, the years of decline had created a
powerful conviction in what was left of the union that it was time to
recover lost ground. A new President, Joe Gormley – though
personally a moderate – was elected on a mandate to pursue a substantial pay increase, not merely to match the rate of inflation but to
restore the miners' proper position at the head of the league. The
National Coal Board, also under a new chairman, Derek Ezra, was
sympathetic and left to itself would have been ready to go a long way
to meet the union's aspiration. Unfortunately it was a bad moment

to seek such a major adjustment. Ezra's hands were tied by the Government's 'n-1' policy of trying to hold each pay settlement below the level of the last. The going rate was no more than 8 per cent.

To the union's claim for rises ranging from an extra £5 for coalface workers to £8 for surface workers and £9 for the most seriously underpaid underground support workers, the Board was only able to offer average increases of less than £2 – around 7 per cent. Gormley warned both Ezra and Peter Walker before the strike began that they would not get a settlement for less than £3.50. It is possible that it would not have taken an enormous improvement to have averted the strike: in December only 56 per cent of the membership of the NUM voted in favour of strike action. Ezra believed that the marginal improvement which the Board offered on 4 January might have been enough to make the difference, had it been put to a ballot. As it was the Executive decisively rejected it and the strike began on 8 January. The belief that the miners were unenthusiastic for action, however, underestimated their pent-up sense of grievance. Once the strike was under way their 100 per cent solidarity and determination surprised even Gormley.

Neither the Government nor commentators in the press initially took the miners' challenge seriously. In *The Times*, Bernard Levin pointed out complacently that what he called 'the doomed miners' strike has started almost exactly one year to the day after the no-less doomed post-workers' strike'. The miners, he believed, could not defy the inexorable decline of their industry.[17] A cartoon in the *New Statesman* showed a hatted Tory lady telling a grinning Heath: 'So silly of the miners not to realise that we've all gone over to oil-fired central heating.'[18] There was no conception, in the first weeks of the strike, of the damage the miners could inflict. Even after a ten-week overtime ban, coal stocks at the power stations were believed to be high: the Central Electricity Generating Board reckoned it had eight weeks' supply and thought that would be more than enough. If the CEGB was unprepared, so was the Department of Employment. With all its experience of mediating industrial disputes since 1945, it had never handled a miners' strike. 'There was no doubt about it,' Robert Carr later admitted, 'our intelligence about the strength of opinion within the miners' union generally was not as good as it should have been . . . We just didn't know the miners. They hadn't been to St James's Square . . . for nearly fifty years.'[19]

These twin misjudgments – of the miners' mood and the state of the coal stocks – came together in the Government's failure to anticipate the union's devastating use of a new industrial weapon –

'flying pickets'. The practice of strikers picketing their own work-
place to deter blacklegs was long established and protected by law –
even by the new Industrial Relations Act. The tactic of bussing men
rapidly from site to site to concentrate overwhelming persuasive
force at key points, however, had only been developed by Yorkshire
miners during an unofficial dispute in 1969. (Nevertheless the
Department of Employment should have known about it.) From the
beginning of the 1972 strike two of the leaders of those Yorkshire
miners, Arthur Scargill and Jock Kane, set out to employ flying
pickets on a much more ambitious scale to prevent coal reaching the
power stations. With elaborate military-style planning, pickets
sometimes up to 1,000-strong were dispatched all over the Yorkshire
area and as far away as Bedford, Great Yarmouth and Ipswich,
where they closed the port. By the end of January Scargill claimed to
have closed all the power stations in Yorkshire and East Anglia.[20]

For Scargill, flying pickets were a frankly revolutionary device:

> We took the view that we were in a class war. We were not play-
> ing cricket on the village green like they did in '26. We were out to
> defeat Heath and Heath's policies . . . We had to declare *war* on
> them and the only way you could declare war was to attack the
> vulnerable points . . . the power stations, the coke depots, the coal
> depots, the points of supply . . . We wished to paralyse the
> nation's economy.[21]

Joe Gormley's purpose was more pragmatic. He was not out to
bring down the Government, simply to win a big pay increase for his
members. But he was happy to claim credit for the pickets' success.
More quickly than even Scargill could have expected, his flying
pickets came close to paralysing the economy. The Government was
fatally slow to react. Had it moved more quickly, the NUM General
Secretary Lawrence Daly believed, 'it's possible we might have been
defeated. But they waited a few weeks.'[22] From a mixture of complacency, a desire not to overreact and a failure of co-ordination
between departments, the Government had taken no effective precautions and, for more than a month after the strike began, imposed
no serious restrictions on the use of coal. Robert Carr still hoped,
through the good offices of Vic Feather, to persuade the miners to
settle within the guidelines. The Cabinet's emergencies committee,
chaired by Reggie Maudling, was said to be watching coal stocks but
saw no cause for alarm: the Government had already declared two
States of Emergency in its first eighteen months, and Heath was
anxious not to have another. On top of everything else, Heath and

Maudling were distracted by what they regarded as the much more serious crisis in Northern Ireland.

Moreover the miners enjoyed substantial public support. It was the first time they had gone on strike since 1926. There was still a romance about the miners, a widespread sense of guilt about their dangerous and dirty work, admiration for their tight-knit, isolated communities and a recognition that they had fallen behind less deserving groups. Gallup found that 55 per cent of the public backed the miners, only 16 per cent the Coal Board, which was known to be only doing the Government's bidding.[23] Even many Tory MPs openly supported the miners' case – for instance the Member for Canterbury, David Crouch, who told the House on 18 January:

> This is not a time for economists to pontificate on what we can or cannot afford. Let us for once forget percentages and consider people instead. I believe it is time for management to decide what is a just payment for.men doing an essential and dangerous job in an industry providing an essential fuel for our economy.[24]

Despite Scargill's flying pickets, the dispute was generally conducted with a responsibility and good humour which did not alienate the public. The union remained scrupulously within the law. Where there was violence it was directed at lorry drivers who tried to break the lines, not at the police: in many places the police helped the strikers to maintain their pickets. On 3 February, however, tension was heightened when a picket was killed – accidentally – by the tail of a turning lorry. The next day Scargill's men began to picket the huge coke depot at Saltley Gate in Birmingham. In the Cabinet John Davies was now pressing for fuel rationing, but Heath and Maudling still resisted. For a few days a spell of warmer weather relieved the pressure, but eventually they were persuaded: on 9 February a Council of State – presided over (in the Queen's absence abroad) by the Queen Mother and Princess Margaret – declared the Government's third State of Emergency. The same day Carr made a last effort to achieve a face-saving settlement, empowering the Board to make an increased offer of around £3.50 to surface workers (about 15 per cent).[25] This would probably have been enough to avert the strike if made two months earlier; but it was too little now when the union had the Government on the run.

If there was any doubt about that it was dramatically dispelled by the outcome of the legendary 'Battle of Saltley Gate'. For six days Scargill had poured in men in a determined effort to close the biggest coke depot in the Midlands where, it was claimed, a mountain of

100,000 tons of coke was held. Before the picketing started, 600–700 lorries a day were going in and out; by 9 February the number was down to 43. Faced with a crowd of several hundred chanting pickets, the police helped to persuade many drivers to abandon the attempt, but they were obliged to force a passage for those who insisted. Considering the numbers, there was remarkably little violence: over the six days the 'battle' lasted, only 16 policemen and 14 pickets were injured and only 76 pickets were arrested.[26] The climax came on 10 February. Scargill assembled a crowd of 10,000–15,000 pickets with banners and bagpipes, baying for the police to close the gate. By mid-morning the police were entirely surrounded and heavily outnumbered. Then, in one of the more highly coloured accounts, 're-inforcements of Midlands trade unionists arrived . . . like Prussian columns at Waterloo'.[27] Bowing to sheer force of numbers, in order to prevent serious violence, the Chief Constable ordered that the gate be closed: the crowd then peacefully dispersed. Next day it needed only 24 men to keep the depot closed. Scargill hailed a great victory – 'living proof that the working class had only to flex its muscles and it could bring governments, employers, society, to a complete standstill'.[28]

It was certainly an impressive assertion of union power. In Downing Street that morning the Cabinet was meeting. Maudling assured his colleagues that the Chief Constable had enough men to keep the depot open and was determined to do so. But halfway through the meeting the Home Secretary was handed a note telling him that the Chief Constable had decided to close the gates after all. 'This unexpected turn of events', Jim Prior recalled, 'had a profound effect upon us.'[29] It was another powerfully symbolic moment. For some Tories it was the moment when the Heath Government surrendered to the unions. They maintain that the Government should have accepted the challenge and kept the gates open at any cost. 'If Heath had persisted with lorry convoys into the power stations guarded by the police,' one historian suggested in 1978, 'the strike could well have gone down to defeat.'[30] This overlooks, however, the fact that the decision to close it was a *police* decision, taken on grounds of public safety by the responsible Chief Constable on the ground. The Government had wanted and expected the depot to be kept open; but in 1972 – by contrast with the third and climactic miners' strike in 1984–5 – the policing of industrial action was determined locally, not dictated from Whitehall. In the view of the historian of political violence, Richard Clutterbuck, 'The police could, without question, have kept the road open, and strictly it was their duty to do so.' But they could have done it only by the deployment of far greater manpower than they had available plus water cannon, tear gas or other methods which public opinion in 1972 would not have tolerated. 'Any of these things . . . would have unleashed far greater violence and sacrificed public sympathy.'[31]

Saltley Gate was probably not a turning point anyway. The power situation was already desperate. The Government had been driven to declare a State of Emergency and was on the point of announcing drastic restrictions on the use of electricity. The NUM had rejected the Board's improved offer, and the Government had decided that it had no choice but to refer the dispute to independent arbitration. The stirring scenes at Saltley only made the Cabinet's helplessness more visible. The same afternoon Carr announced the appointment of a Court of Enquiry, and the next day named Lord Wilberforce to chair it. This was the same Lord Wilberforce whose extravagant award to the power workers had so dismayed ministers a year earlier. That they should now turn to him again was the clearest possible signal that they wanted only to see the strike ended as quickly as possible. No one could doubt that Wilberforce had been called in to give the miners as much as was needed to get them back to work. As Douglas Hurd – the Prime Minister's Private Secretary – cruelly noted in his diary, the Government was 'now wandering vainly over the battle-field looking for someone to surrender to – and being massacred all the time'.[32] Brendon Sewill at the Treasury likewise remembered the mood of panic in Whitehall, with apocalyptic talk of activating nuclear shelters and regional government – sewage flowing in the streets leading to epidemics and riots – if the miners were not somehow bought off.[33] The Government simply had to pay up. *The Times*, in language only marginally more sober, did not dissent. 'We have now reached a situation', it declared on 11 February, 'which is more dangerous than that of any industrial dispute since the war.' The union's rejection of the Board's last offer had 'left the Government no obvious option . . . If the Court of Enquiry cannot find acceptable terms the prospect is appalling.'[34]

Only now did the strike really begin to bite. Under the provisions of the State of Emergency, the use of electricity for heating shops, offices and places of entertainment was outlawed: householders were asked to heat only one room: and much of industry was put on a three-day week. Schools closed. Babies were born by candlelight. Some 800,000 workers were already laid off. On 14 February, as more power stations closed, Davies warned of the possibility of a total blackout in two weeks' time.[35] As the situation worsened, the Government offered the miners an interim down payment of an extra £3-4 a week – without prejudice to Wilberforce's ultimate recommendation – to return to work while the Court was sitting.

Breaking his silence on the strike in the ill-chosen setting of a Young Conservatives' conference at Liverpool, Heath angrily attacked the miners' 'unreasonable' attitude. Even the interim offer was more than the gas, water and power workers had settled for.[36] But his appeal to moderation cut no ice. With the Government at its mercy and the public – despite the power cuts – still behind it, the NUM was determined to hold out for its pound of flesh.

Meanwhile the Government's handling of the strike faced criticism from its own backbenchers. The complaint was not that ministers had been too weak but that they had tried to be too tough. 'They made a fetish of non-intervention, and hesitated too long before setting up the Wilberforce enquiry.' They had failed to recognise the special characteristics of the miners which demanded special treatment. Though Maudling and Davies did not escape, Carr came in for the heaviest criticism; it was widely predicted that he would soon be moved, possibly swapping jobs with Willie Whitelaw.[37]

Wilberforce completed his report in just three days, and it was published on the morning of 18 February. He leaned even further towards the miners than had been expected. His report, *The Times* unblinkingly recorded, 'concedes almost all the miners' case and most of the money they demanded. It reads like a printed version of the arguments used by NUM leaders over the past six weeks.'[38] The miners had 'a just case for special treatment'; they deserved 'a general and exceptional increase'. Surface workers should get an extra £5, taking them to a basic £23 a week; underground workers an extra £6 (£25) and coalface workers an extra £4.50 (£34.50). (The union had always sought less for the relatively highly paid face workers – a shrewd factor in retaining public sympathy.) Though not quite the full increases the union had claimed, this worked out at around 28 per cent, 31 per cent and 15 per cent respectively, or about 27 per cent overall. The new rates were to be backdated to 1 November 1971, and were to run for sixteen months to February 1973.[39]

But still a majority of the miners' executive thought they could do better. Joe Gormley's first reaction on being presented with the Wilberforce recommendations at the Department of Employment that morning was that they had won a famous victory: it was the Yorkshire Scot, Jock Kane, who argued that they should hold out for another £1 all round.[40] Gormley recognised that it was politically out of the question for the Government to go beyond Wilberforce; but behind the cover of that extra £1 they drew up a 'shopping list' ('It was as long as your arm,' Gormley wrote later) comprising all the minor claims and marginal adjustments the union had been seeking for years: longer holidays, full pay for eighteen-year-olds and the like.[41] The Coal Board, with Carr's support, would not offer another penny. The miners insisted, as a last throw, on seeing the Prime Minister. Up to this point, Heath had kept scrupulously in the background. Now, when it looked as though the miners might actually reject Wilberforce, he agreed to see both sides at Downing Street that evening.

The Cabinet met at 8.30 pm – by candlelight, appropriately. Carr reported that the two sides were still deadlocked. The Cabinet agreed that there could be no more money and prepared to dig in for a fight, discussing seriously for the first time the use of troops to reopen the power stations, the possibility of importing coal and other measures which they might have taken weeks ago. At 9.15 Heath saw Vic Feather and the Director-General of the CBI, Campbell Adamson. Then at 10.20, flanked by Carr and Barber, he met the five leaders of the NUM. He told them that the Government accepted Wilberforce and so should they. He was firm that there could be no further increase in the basic terms on offer; but on condition that the union called off its pickets and went back to work immediately he was prepared to concede the whole 'shopping list' of additional claims. 'We pushed him like hell,' Gormley claimed afterwards, 'but he wouldn't budge . . . In the end I realised that there was not a cat in hell's chance of getting the extra £1 we were demanding.'[42] In fact Gormley had never thought there was. It was the additional fringe benefits – worth another £10 million on top of Wilberforce – that he was demanding to satisfy the militants: and he got them. This was the true measure of the Government's humiliation. So long as the Government could be seen to have stood firm on the main issue Heath was ready to give away practically everything else, leaving the Coal Board to sort out the details. Still it was nearly 1 am before the NUM executives agreed – still by quite narrow majorities of less than 2–1 – to withdraw the pickets (14–11) and recommend the final package to a pithead ballot (16–9). 'That evening at Number Ten', according to Douglas Hurd, 'Mr Heath persuaded the miners that they had won enough. Throughout he had been remarkably calm and self-possessed.'[43] Gormley's recollection was a little different: 'It was not "Smiling Ted" by any means. We didn't see much of his teeth at all that night. I wouldn't say he was humiliated, but he was very subdued.'[44]

The press over the next few days had no doubt that the NUM had won a remarkable victory. But the predominant reaction was relief that the crisis was over. Sympathy for the miners was such that the Government was not much blamed for giving in, but only for its stubbornness in holding out so long. *The Times* went out of its way to praise the 'scrupulously constitutional' way the union had conducted the dispute, was thankful that 'the worst possible outcome has been avoided' and believed that the right result had been achieved in the end.[45] Gallup found that 81 per cent of the public, too, considered the settlement 'fair'.[46] *The Times* hoped that the Government had now learned its lesson. 'Such a confrontation in the mining industry is unlikely for another generation, unless the aspirations and pressures are so glaringly overlooked again.' Coal was a vital national resource which must not be run down any further. The more general moral to be drawn from the strike was that the Government could not go on any longer without a proper incomes policy to handle pay adjustments flexibly without putting the country through the ordeal of strikes. There were, the writer declared airily, 'plenty of models to choose from', and prospects of success would now be improved.[47]

It was the near-unanimous view of Fleet Street, endorsed by the relieved but still anxious majority of Tory MPs, that the Government must now be willing to soften its abrasive approach and set itself instead to carry the unions and the nation with it in a more conciliatory style. Specifically they must accept that the declaratory but toothless 'n-1' policy had been irrevocably smashed and lose no time in adopting a properly comprehensive incomes policy. Heath still resisted the second conclusion. But he accepted the first and attempted immediately to act on it. As soon as the miners had voted – by a 27–1 majority – to accept the package finally recommended to them he went on television to make a sombre broadcast to the nation.

He tried to stamp on the idea that it was the Government that had suffered a defeat.

When people said 'the miners won a great victory' or 'the Government lost that one', what did they mean? In the country we live in, there could not be any 'we' or 'they'. There was only 'us' – all of us. If the Government is defeated then the country is defeated.

The country now faced a 'double danger': not only inflation, which the Government had been getting under control before the strike and was still, with the co-operation of industry and the unions, determined to beat, but also the 'invisible danger' to democratic values and 'our traditional British way of doing things'. On the first, he offered a new approach. The Government was ready to sit down with the employers and unions together to look for a better way of resolving pay disputes. 'We must find a more sensible way to settle our differences . . . After all, it is the Government's job to see that the

interests of all sections of the community are properly looked after.'
This sentence, though Heath did not yet acknowledge it, opened the
door to the sort of thorough-going prices and incomes policy the
Government would embrace later in the year. The second challenge
thrown up by the recent strike raised fundamental questions about
the British way of life: 'If one group is so determined to get its own
way that it does not care what happens to the rest of us, then we are
not living in the kind of world we thought we were, and we had
better face up to it.'[48]

For several months Heath continued to hope that he could carry
the unions and employers with him in a concerted effort to hold
down pay increases by voluntary means. Nevertheless he was
already embarked on the road that would lead inexorably to a statutory policy. At Prime Minister's Question Time on 28 February he
told the Liberal John Pardoe that he had already held eight meetings
with the TUC in the past twelve months, but added that he did not
regard them as the only spokesman of ordinary people. If Pardoe had
been in closer touch with the unions 'he would know how strongly
they are opposed to an incomes policy'.[49] In all his utterances from
now on he emphasised the idea of the Government as the trustee of
the national interest, actively mediating between the two sides of industry as the representative of the consumer, the pensioners and the
non-unionised. On 9 March the sixteen members of the General
Council of the TUC, including Jack Jones and Hugh Scanlon, held
talks with Heath, Carr, Barber and Davies at Downing Street. It was
quite like old times under the Labour Government, beginning with
tea and ending up with whisky. Incomes policy was not mentioned;
the unions did not withdraw their opposition to the Industrial Relations Act. Nevertheless, *The Times* reported, 'there was every
indication that a promising new phase in industrial co-operation had
opened up'.[50]

The outcome of the miners' strike, coming on top of the January
unemployment figures, gave the Government a second powerful
push towards the reversal of its original policies. Ministers learned,
or tried to learn, the lesson that they could not govern by confrontation. Henceforth they would proceed by conciliation. But
there is a cruel irony here. For the one thing Heath and his senior colleagues vowed to themselves after their humiliation by the miners
was that it should never happen again. Their authority could not survive another such defeat. Therefore they should not again get into
such an exposed position where defeat was possible. This was the
chastened mood which led them towards incomes policy. Yet, as it
turned out, it was precisely by locking themselves into an over-rigid

incomes policy that they found themselves, less than two years later, once again on a collision course with the NUM from which, this time, they could not back down. Thus the traumatic miners' strike of 1972 led directly to the second strike of February 1974 and the Government's downfall.

Two and a half weeks after the end of the strike *The Times* published a major editorial considering the government's record hitherto and its future prospects, entitled 'A Turning Point for Mr Heath'. It listed five serious problems confronting the Government – unemployment; inflation and industrial relations; Northern Ireland; Rhodesia; and the EEC – of which it judged the second and third to be the most difficult and dangerous. (Unemployment was already beginning to respond to treatment.) It recognised that the last two months had been an exceptionally testing time for the Government, and concluded sagely:

> Whether this period turns out to be Mr Heath's low point or the first signs of a more extensive failure depends quite largely on whether this is a learning Government. Successful Governments are not those which do not make mistakes, but those which learn the extremely difficult business of managing society by accepting the lessons of their own experience. Unsuccessful Governments reject their own mistakes and because they will not recognise them redouble the energy they put into mistaken policies. The evidence is that the Prime Minister has learnt from the mistakes that were made in handling the miners' strike. He should take no notice of critics who despise conciliation. 'George, be a King' is bad advice to a Prime Minister – after all it cost Britain America.[51]

Heath followed *The Times*'s advice. His misfortune was to discover that unsuccessful conciliation led just as surely to losing Downing Street.

22

The Abolition of Stormont

AMID all the economic and industrial traumas which battered it, the Government was simultaneously wrestling with a mounting crisis in Northern Ireland. 1972 was the year in which Ulster came closer to anarchy and outright civil war than at any other time in the whole dismal saga of murder and destruction which has blighted the last three decades. The statistics of the dead tell the story. From just 13 in 1969 and 25 in 1970, the number of those killed in the province – soldiers and civilians – jumped to 174 in 1971 and 467 in 1972 before falling back to 250 in 1973 and 216 in 1974. Since a second peak of 297 in 1976 it has fallen sharply in subsequent years: throughout the 1980s, though still horrifying enough, the annual death toll remained well below three figures.[1] The Heath Government, with all its other misfortunes, caught the very worst of the savagery. Over their four years in office, Heath and his senior colleagues probably spent more time on Northern Ireland than on any other single subject. It was a problem different in kind from any other, because it touched the very integrity of the United Kingdom. 'More than that,' as Douglas Hurd has written, 'the subject had a very high emotional content.'[2] 'In terms of human misery', Heath told the 1972 Tory conference, Ulster was 'the most terrible problem that we as a Government . . . have had to face. It haunts us every day.'[3]

Though the problem has never gone away, later governments have become used to living with it. Except briefly in 1985, Mrs Thatcher never had to make it a priority. Northern Ireland has been shuffled off to successive secretaries of state to contain the violence as best they can, with occasional doomed attempts at new political 'initiatives'. Few today seriously expect to find a 'solution'. The most that can be hoped for is that time – and perhaps European integration – will eventually drain the poison of communal antagonism. In the

early 1970s it was different. The 'troubles' were quite a new phenomenon which found the vast majority of English politicians wholly
ignorant of the realities of Ulster life. Since the age-old Irish problem
which had defeated Gladstone had been 'solved' by partition in
1920–1, Westminster had thankfully left the devolved Government at
Stormont – 'a Protestant Parliament for a Protestant People' – to
exercise its ascendancy undisturbed. Until the Civil Rights marches
began in 1968 the disfranchisement of the Catholic minority had
scarcely impinged on the consciousness even of the Labour party.
When it did, British public opinion was unprepared for the fierce
determination of the Unionists to maintain their domination. When
Heath came to power in 1970 Ulster was still a fresh problem on the
British political agenda, one which had been neglected for too long
but which now, with good will on all sides, could surely be resolved.
Even as the situation deteriorated rapidly in 1971–2 there was still
widespread optimism that it must be possible to find a reasonable
solution. In 1973, with the formation of a new devolved Executive
on which Unionists for the first time agreed to share power with
Catholics, Heath and his first Northern Ireland Secretary, Willie
Whitelaw, briefly appeared to have achieved it. They certainly came
closer to pulling off a settlement than any subsequent initiative in
later years. They failed; but it was a brave and honourable attempt.

Heath was perhaps slow to grip the problem. He had, after all,
other concerns. It was possible to hope in 1970 that the spasm of
violence which had forced the Labour Government to send troops to
Northern Ireland – initially to protect the Catholics – in August 1969
might be over. At British insistence most of the fundamental
demands of the civil rights movement had been conceded: the principle of one person/one vote and the redrawing of local government
boundaries to end flagrant gerrymandering, especially in Londonderry; the disarming of the Royal Ulster Constabulary and the
disbanding of the hated 'B-Specials'; reform of the system of housing
allocation to stop all forms of discrimination against Catholics.
Arguably what was now required was a period of time, with the
British army holding the ring, to give these reforms a chance to
work. Two sentences in the 1970 manifesto promised merely that the
Government would 'support the Northern Ireland Government in its
programme of legislative and executive action to ensure equal opportunity for all', while providing 'the military and other aid necessary'
to support the RUC in keeping the peace.[4] Heath left Reggie Maudling, the Home Secretary – with all his other responsibilities,
including the Immigration Bill – to implement this policy of benign
supervision.

It did not work. For one thing, the return of a Conservative Government encouraged a mood of triumphalism among the Protestants. The links between the Tory Party and the Ulster Unionists were historic and still close. The dozen or so Ulster Unionist MPs at Westminster had always taken the Tory whip: and in 1970 they formed a significant slice of Heath's modest majority.* (Among them was the brother of the Northern Ireland Prime Minister, Major James Chichester-Clark.) With the defeat of Wilson and Callaghan the more militant Protestants confidently expected to be left to get on with governing the province once again in their own way. Second, the initial Catholic welcome for the British troops on the streets of Belfast and Londonderry had rapidly given way to hostility as the army – untrained for civil peace-keeping – reacted clumsily to deliberate IRA provocation: house-to-house arms searches, often at night, and the use of rubber bullets and CS gas to break up demonstrations crudely fulfilled the propaganda stereotype of an occupying army and drove the Catholic population into the arms of their alternative 'protectors'. The newly formed 'Provisional' wing of the IRA (which had split from the 'Official' wing in January) grew from less than 100 members to more than 800 between June and December 1970.[5] Far from drawing together, the Community was becoming ever more sharply polarised.

Then the appointment of Maudling as Home Secretary was – in the words of the Irish historian J. J. Lee – 'from a Northern Ireland point of view . . . probably an unfortunate choice'.

> He combined intelligence with indifference at a time when time was all-important. His reputed comment on the plane back to London after his first visit to the North, 'What a bloody awful country!' testified more to his intelligence than to his sense of responsibility.[6]

Willie Whitelaw, who took over the problem from him with more success in 1972, has his own explanation of Maudling's unsuitability:

> Of course, with his clear and logical brain, Reggie Maudling found the Irish mentality almost impossible to understand. He could not be bothered with their constant determination to be

---

* Due to the emergence of Ian Paisley's Democratic Unionist Party, which split the Unionist vote in some seats, the usual phalanx of 11 or 12 official Unionists was reduced to 8, plus Paisley and 3 Nationalists (Gerry Fitt of the SDLP, and 2 'Independent Unity' members including the young firebrand, Bernadette Devlin).

governed by their preoccupations of the past rather than face up to the problems of the present and the future. He was a very un-emotional man himself and simply could not stand emotional tantrums in others.[7]

John Kent in *Private Eye* habitually portrayed Maudling asleep, in a nightshirt and nightcap and holding a candle.

Maudling's failure to get a grip on Northern Ireland resulted in him losing the momentum which Callaghan had established. Brian Faulkner who succeeded Chichester-Clark as Prime Minister in March 1971, soon had the impression that 'Maudling was losing in-fluence and being left out of decisions'. Heath began to take a closer interest in Northern Ireland from the moment Faulkner took office. Faulkner represented the business community of Ulster – a major break with the old squirearchy which had dominated Protestant politics hitherto. He was by far the ablest politician in the Unionist camp: Heath responded immediately to his energy, decisiveness and professionalism. At their first meeting in April 1971, Faulkner felt that he had found in Heath 'an ally who clearly could be relied upon in the crises that would inevitably occur'. 'I liked Heath's action-oriented approach,' he wrote in his memoirs.[8] Heath initially felt the same about Faulkner. 'The closest links ever between a British and a Northern Ireland Prime Minister were established with the two men in constant touch on the telephone.'[9]

With Heath's encouragement, Faulkner made a conciliatory start, forming a relatively broad-based administration and offering the SDLP seats on Stormont committees. Heath made it clear in the House of Commons that he must follow British policy: he would not be permitted to rearm the RUC or restore the B-Specials.[10] But Faulkner's attempted bridge-building was quickly undercut by the IRA and by the army's heavy-handed response. In July two unarmed men were shot and killed in Derry. When Faulkner refused an enquiry, the SDLP walked out of Stormont. Under mounting pres-sure at both Stormont and Westminster for tougher measures to break the control the IRA had established of the Catholic streets and housing estates and to halt the toll of killings, Faulkner was per-suaded to reach for the last-resort policy – which he had opposed under Chichester-Clark – and introduce the internment of suspects without trial. Internment had been used with some success on the border in the 1950s; but it was a very different matter trying to apply it in the urban ghettos in the highly charged climate of 1971. Signifi-cantly, the army did not want it. Nevertheless on 5 August Faulkner came to London and persuaded Heath and Maudling to agree. In

Faulkner's words: 'Heath formally announced to me . . . that if I, as the responsible Minister, decided to invoke the power of internment, they would concur and ensure the necessary Army support.'[11] Whitelaw – having as yet no responsibility for Northern Ireland – was not present, but as a close confidant of the Prime Minister he knew that Heath was anxious about the decision. He was right to be. He should have put his foot down and disallowed it. But he was impressed by Faulkner. He wanted to support him, and he wanted to smash the IRA if it could be done.

The trouble was that the RUC's intelligence was out of date. The Provisionals, by contrast, had known for days what was coming and had plenty of time to disappear over the border. As a result, when the army swooped at 4 am on 9 August, and 'lifted' 342 men from their homes, they netted very few currently active figures, and those mainly Officials: no senior Provisionals at all were picked up in Belfast, and only a handful in Derry.[12] Of the 2,400 'suspects' arrested in the six months up to April 1972, two-thirds were subsequently released without being charged. Internment was 'a colossal blunder'.[13] Its only effect was to alienate the last shreds of support for the army within the Catholic population, uniting the whole community in angry solidarity with 'the men behind the wire'. Instead of reducing the level of violence it had the opposite effect. The next day, in the sober description of the *Annual Register*, there was 'open warfare on the streets of Belfast, Londonderry and Newry'. 'Palls of smoke hung over Belfast and the city echoed to gunfire as troops fought pitched battles with terrorists, armed with automatic rifles and gelignite bombs.'[14]

Twenty-one people were killed over the next three days, and another 120 in the next three months. Internment evoked outrage in the Irish Republic and the United States and 'brought a hitherto inconceivable surge of recruitment to the IRA'.[15] The search for a political solution was suspended, since the SDLP leaders, John Hume and Gerry Fitt, had no option but to refuse any co-operation with Faulkner so long as it continued.

Yet right-wing British commentators like T. E. Utley in the *Daily Telegraph* on 27 August strenuously denied that internment had been 'a grotesque failure'. On the contrary, Utley insisted, 'internment has struck a formidable blow at the IRA', by demoralising them and by gaining valuable intelligence.[16] Neither claim was true, least of all the first. Internment was a huge propaganda gift to the Provisionals. It was compounded by the brutal interrogation methods which were used to try to extract information from those held. These notorious 'five techniques' – sensory deprivation and disorientation by means of hoods, continuous high-pitched noise and lack of food, drink and sleep: techniques to which in Utley's view 'internees were quite properly exposed'[17] – were subsequently condemned by the European Court of Human Rights as 'inhuman and degrading treatment', stopping only barely short of torture. Following an investigation by the former Ombudsman Sir Edmund Compton, Maudling set up a three-man enquiry to review procedures. When it reported in March 1972, Lord Parker and Sir John Boyd-Carpenter found it possible to condone the contentious practices; but the former Labour Lord Chancellor, Lord Gardiner, strongly condemned them as 'secret, illegal, not morally justifiable and alien to the traditions' of British democracy.[18] Heath, to his credit, accepted Gardiner's minority report and promised that the use of 'intensive techniques' would cease.

Despite the blunder of internment, Heath's confidence in Faulkner was undiminished in the autumn of 1971. When Faulkner visited Chequers on 18 August he found Heath initially preoccupied with the dollar crisis but then, over dinner, 'more relaxed and expansive than I have ever found him before or since', talking about sailing and playing his stereo. 'He seemed to me a man at the height of his powers, confident, relaxed and happy.' The next day, sitting on the terrace in the sun with Maudling, Carrington and Home, Heath utterly ruled out the possibility of imposing direct rule on Ulster. No one disagreed.[19]

Heath further gratified Faulkner by reacting very sharply to an open telegram from the Irish Taoiseach, Jack Lynch, demanding reforms in the North and an end to British efforts to enforce a military solution. Heath fired back an angry reply condemning Lynch's telegram as 'unjustified in its contents [and] unacceptable in its attempt to interfere in the affairs of the United Kingdom'. It could 'in no way contribute to the solution of the problem of Northern Ireland'.[20] Lynch in turn called Heath's view 'quite unacceptable',[21] and for some time Anglo-Irish relations were frosty, with shooting incidents along the border. On 6 September, however, Lynch came to Chequers and three weeks later Heath hosted the first tripartite meeting between all three prime ministers – British, Irish and Northern Irish – since partition (though the two Irish premiers had met three times since 1965). Furiously denounced by the militant Unionists, this was the first acknowledgment by a British Government of an 'Irish dimension' to the Ulster problem. Lynch had to accept that the border was not at issue, and promised security co-operation to deny terrorists easy sanctuary in the Republic; but he won the right to discuss Northern affairs, while Heath publicly recognised unification –

if it could be brought about by peaceful means – as a legitimate political ambition. This was the delicate balancing act the Government struggled to sustain for the next two years.

On 'Panorama' on 11 October, in his speech to the Tory party conference a few days later and in the annual Prime Minister's speech at the Lord Mayor's Banquet on 15 November, Heath talked toughly but at the same time optimistically of the link between political initiatives to promote a prosperous, harmonious society on the one hand and measures to 'smash the gunmen' on the other. He paid tribute to both Faulkner and Lynch as 'men of proved resource, moderation and good will'. He insisted that were British troops to be withdrawn from Northern Ireland – as 59 per cent of the public wished – the whole of Ireland would be condemned to 'civil war and slaughter on a scale far beyond anything we have seen elsewhere in recent years'. 'We are going to see this thing through', he promised, 'because to do otherwise would be an abdication of everything for which we stand.'[22]

Heath was trying hard to maintain a bipartisan approach to Northern Ireland. In November, with his approval – including the loan of a senior member of the Cabinet secretariat – Harold Wilson visited Dublin and returned with an ambitious, not to say fantastic, 15-point plan for unification by consent to be achieved over fifteen years. To allay Unionist fears, the Republic was required to recognise the Queen, rejoin the Commonwealth and amend the 'theocratic' nature of its constitution. The proposal was naturally anathema to everyone. Nevertheless Heath welcomed it as a 'constructive' contribution and proposed all-party talks at Westminster as a first step.[23]

This gradualist approach to bringing the communities together was shattered at the beginning of 1972 by the events of what was instantly christened in Irish nationalist folklore 'Bloody Sunday'. Thirteen demonstrators – all later shown to have been unarmed – were shot dead by paratroopers at the end of a march against internment in Londonderry on 30 January. The march was illegal, since all marches had been banned in Northern Ireland; but the ban was very widely defied, and the marchers were actually dispersing when the shooting broke out. It was established by the subsequent enquiry that the soldiers did not fire first;* nevertheless their reaction was undisciplined and disproportionate, and raised passions on both sides of the border to new heights. Maudling immediately announced an enquiry to be conducted by the Lord Chief Justice, Lord Widgery, but was physically assaulted on the floor of the House of Commons

---

* In 1992, on the twentieth anniversary of the shooting, this finding was challenged amid strong demands for a fresh enquiry.

by Bernadette Devlin. In Dublin a mob burned down the British Embassy. In Ulster the level of bombing, assassination and retaliatory killing of soldiers escalated again; and on 22 February the IRA struck for the first time on the British mainland with a bomb placed outside the Parachute Regiment HQ in Aldershot which killed seven people – five cleaning women, a gardener and a Catholic padré.

Bad as the situation had been before, 'Bloody Sunday' was the shock which convinced Heath and his senior colleagues that they must take an urgent grip of Northern Ireland before it slid uncontrollably into civil war. 'It was the most awful two days of my life,' Carrington told a friend.[24] With the EEC Treaty safely signed, Heath now 'sent for all the papers on Ulster and made it a top personal priority'[25] – at any rate until the miners' strike diverted his attention. Whatever assurances he might have given Faulkner the previous August, he was now quickly persuaded that Westminster must take direct responsibility for security. In a sense this was unfair, since 'Bloody Sunday' was the army's fault, not Stormont's. But the General commanding the forces in Northern Ireland, Sir Harry Tuzo – whose advice against internment had earlier been ignored – now argued that the IRA could not be beaten while the responsibility for law and order in the province remained divided. At the same time Heath was convinced that only a dramatic new policy initiative could bring peace. Over the next few weeks he began to examine the options. Changing the border? Regular plebiscites? Power-sharing? Proportional representation? Had the Government had its plans ready before 'Bloody Sunday' it is just possible that there was a moment when a sweeping package might have won broad consent. But the moment passed. As the IRA stepped up its bloody campaign, Faulkner came under mounting pressure from William Craig's fascistic Vanguard movement – complete with black uniform and Nazi-style salutes – to stand firm. In return for a scaling down of internment he insisted that he must have authority to rearm the RUC and restore the B-Specials. Heath refused. He was himself under considerable right-wing backbench pressure to resist any hint of surrender to terrorism. But he was also keenly aware of the European dimension. Britain and Ireland were about to come together as partners in the EEC: he was deeply embarrassed by the images flashing around the world of apparent British military repression in Northern Ireland and determined somehow to end it.

Direct rule was still not the preferred solution – except perhaps by Maudling, who claims in his memoirs that it was he who pressed for the appointment of a Northern Ireland Secretary in order to lift the burden from the Home Office.[26] The hope was that Faulkner would accept the transfer of responsibility for security but agree to carry on as head of a diminished local administration. Most ministers were deeply reluctant to see Britain take direct responsibility for Northern Ireland; others saw in Faulkner the last hope of Unionist-led reform and were anxious not to undermine him. Yet ultimately they were all persuaded that there was no alternative. It was, Heath insisted in a 1976 interview, a Cabinet decision:

> Dealing with something as controversial as the suspension of Stormont, of course, very strong and differing views were held . . . I was not prepared to rush into an initiative without the Cabinet being, all of them, absolutely satisfied that we were doing the right thing. That particular one was one of the most difficult and painful decisions we ever had to take, but we took it unanimously.[27]

Douglas Hurd, in the Prime Minister's private office, thought the whole process from 'Bloody Sunday' to the imposition of direct rule 'absorbing': 'Ministers went back to first principles on Ireland. A completely new policy had to be devised, and new people found to run it. Watched from the sidelines, it was one of the most impressive things the Government did.'[28] Eventually the new policy was agreed on 14 March. Westminster would take over responsibility not just for security on the streets but the whole apparatus of law and order – the judicial system and the prisons as well as the police. Internment would be phased out, plebiscites held on the border and discussions initiated with the SDLP to establish 'community government'. None of this was negotiable: it would be presented to the Northern Ireland Government as a *fait accompli* which they must accept in total or else resign.

Willie Whitelaw later regretted that more trouble was not taken to carry Faulkner along with this policy, which came to him as a dreadful shock.[29] On the other hand Faulkner should have seen perfectly well what was in the wind. From the Unionist right, Paisley and Craig certainly warned him.[30] Robin Chichester-Clark, too, insists that he had no cause to be surprised.[31] Faulkner, however, simply did not read the signs. He still 'believed firmly that he had established a special relationship with the British Premier which would preserve the constitutional *status quo*'.[32] At the beginning of March Heath had sent him a public telegram of reassurance that rumours of Direct Rule were only 'speculation'.[33] 'I have the mind of Heath,' he boasted.[34] In fact, as his former Minister of Community Relations, David Bleakley, has written: 'Only Brian Faulkner seemed unaware that plans for a takeover were well-advanced'.[35] Perhaps Heath should have apprised him more sensitively on the way the British Government's mind was moving; but Faulkner was certainly naïve in closing his eyes to what he did not want to see. As it was, when he and his deputy Jack Andrews flew to London on 22 March (the day after the Budget) to meet Heath, Home, Maudling and Carrington – significantly joined for the first time by Whitelaw – they were, in Whitelaw's words, 'completely taken aback and really could not believe that Ted Heath was in earnest'.[36] It took Faulkner some time to grasp that Heath was not 'making an opening bid to soften us up, but . . . was presenting what amounted to an ultimatum'.[37] 'He felt betrayed,' his wife remembered later. 'Had it happened . . . with a Labour Government, they would not have been so surprised. But there was this intense shock and almost disbelief that a Conservative Government could act in this way, having given assurances to the contrary.'[38]

The talks at Downing Street lasted for 9½ hours and ended with no hint being given to the press of what had occurred. It was clear that matters had come to a head, but *The Times* thought agreement was still within reach.[39] In fact Faulkner had already signalled his Government's intention to resign. Border plebiscites, phasing out internment, talking to the SDLP they could accept; but the transfer of responsibility for law and order to Westminster, in his view, took away the *raison d'être* of Stormont's separate existence. 'Heath admitted, when pressed by us, that he saw government at Stormont as eventually something along the lines of a county council. To us that was insulting and completely unacceptable.' His Government would not have survived if he had accepted it.[40] The Unionist population of Ulster simply did not believe that London took their security fears sufficiently seriously. The British, on the other hand, had come to believe that divided responsibility for security was 'always likely to end in disaster',[41] while a transfer would offer the chance for a fresh political departure. Between these positions there was no compromise. At 9 pm Faulkner and Andrews left to fly back to Belfast to consult their colleagues. At the door Heath told them bluntly: 'You may assume that the Cabinet will reaffirm this decision tomorrow. They have made up their minds and there is no going back.'[42] Next morning Faulkner telephoned his Government's resignation, then returned to London for a strained farewell dinner at Downing Street. The news that the British Government would be taking over direct responsibility for Northern Ireland, ending fifty years of devolved rule, was not announced until the following day.

Meanwhile, late that night Heath asked Willie Whitelaw to go to

Belfast as Secretary of State. It is not clear when the idea was first mooted to him. Reggie Maudling claims that he had already sounded him out and that Whitelaw was 'enthusiastic'.[43] The fact that he was present to witness the final showdown with Faulkner suggests that Heath at least had him in mind. Whitelaw himself, however, says that Robert Armstrong only discussed the possibility with him the following day. Then Heath called him in 'some time after midnight'.

> I had not given it a great deal of thought, but I knew that if I was offered the job I could not refuse . . . I could never have believed in myself again if I had failed to accept a really daunting challenge . . . There was little to be said, for we both knew each other so well and appreciated the situation. I felt better when I left him, for on such occasions Ted was at his best in a mood of quiet imperturbability and courage.[44]

Whitelaw had been to Northern Ireland only twice before, for a twenty-first birthday party before the war and a brief golfing trip in the 1950s. Yet he was unquestionably the right man for the job, possessing a rare combination of human warmth, military experience, negotiating skill and toughness to overcome the bitterness of the Unionists and win the confidence of both communities. It was a signal of the priority he gave to Northern Ireland that Heath sent to the province one of his closest and most trusted colleagues. The situation undoubtedly called for a senior minister; nevertheless Whitelaw's absence for most of the week in Northern Ireland for the next nineteen months was a severe loss to the Government, and to Heath personally. Whitelaw more than anyone else was the colleague he needed at his side in the trials of the next two years. By the time he felt able to recall him to London it was too late.

In the Commons on 24 March, 'looking tense and strained',[45] Heath announced that the Government had regrettably been left with 'no alternative to assuming full and direct responsibility for the administration of Northern Ireland until a political solution for the problems of the Province can be worked out in consultation with all those concerned'.[46] A period of direct rule was needed, he said, partly to take the control of security out of Ulster's domestic politics, partly also to allay international concern. But he stressed that the suspension of Stormont was intended to be temporary. The purpose, as the *Financial Times* put it, was to 'change the political climate' of Ulster, giving the two communities a breathing space to forge a new political structure, no longer dominated by a single party, to which devolved responsibility could once again be safely restored.[47] The decision was bitterly denounced by the Ulster Unionists and their supporters on the Tory benches as a craven surrender to the IRA. But press support was almost universal, with a repeated note of admiration in the quality papers for the Government's courage. The *Financial Times* thought direct rule 'the greatest gamble of Mr Heath's political career . . . Mr Heath has pulled off a remarkable trick: he has brought about a situation which even has Irishmen baffled. Despite the months of speculation . . . the announcement . . . left a lot of people not knowing what to say.'[48]

There was equally warm endorsement of Whitelaw as the man to bring the warring communities together. The next day Heath named the rest of a carefully balanced ministerial team to support him: Lord Windlesham (already dealing with Northern Ireland as Minister of State at the Home Office), Paul Channon and David Howell. Windlesham was a Roman Catholic and Channon had Irish family connections through the Guinness dynasty. In addition Whitelaw was to be served by an advisory commission representing all strands of opinion in Northern Ireland. The Unionists, however, promptly declared that they would boycott it. The way of the peacemaker was to be hard.

At least in Great Britain he had all-party backing. The Northern Ireland (Temporary Provisions) Bill was rushed through both Houses of Parliament on 28–9 March and came into force the following day. With both Labour and Liberal support, the Government had a majority of 483–18 on Second Reading: 9 Tories (including Enoch Powell) joined the official Unionists and Paisley in voting against the Bill, while another 12 abstained. So far as Northern Ireland was concerned it was a massively sufficient margin. But the figures underlined the danger the alienation of the Ulster Unionists posed for the Government's majority on other issues – notably the EEC Bill, the critical centrepiece of the Government's programme, at that very moment making its way through the Commons by the narrowest – often single-figure – majorities. If direct rule was a brave policy in respect of Northern Ireland, it was particularly so in the context of Heath's central preoccupation with getting Britain into Europe. In fact the nightmare that Ulster would jeopardise the EEC did not materialise. The two Unionists who had previously supported entry continued to do so, and the rest voted against it only sporadically. The short-term damage was subsequently described by a relieved Francis Pym as 'terribly marginal'.[49] In the long run, however, it was a different story. The enmity of the Ulster Unionists cost Heath his majority in February 1974. On this analysis the suspension of Stormont led directly to the downfall of his Government.

Yet it was surely right. It can be argued that the fact that it did not turn out to be temporary, but is still in force more than twenty years later with no very hopeful prospect even now of an agreement which would allow the return of significant powers to a reconstituted Stormont, is a measure of the failure of direct rule. On the other hand the security situation, though it has not been solved, has got very much better since 1972. The level of violence fell off immediately, and has never regained the fearful heights of that year. Second, the entrenched and gerrymandered Protestant ascendancy was indefensible. Though some Unionists in 1972 recognised the fact and were ready to remedy it, their change of heart was too little and too late; the fate of Brian Faulkner in 1973–4 shows that the Protestant community as a whole was not yet ready for significant reform. Finally, the very fact that no alternative has been found argues that direct rule remains the least objectionable form of government to both communities and the only way of containing the intractable problem of divided allegiance until attitudes soften – perhaps some time in the next century. To his credit it was Heath who grasped this nettle.

23

U-Turn: Industry

HEATH had signed the Accession treaty marking Britain's entry into the EEC (with effect from the beginning of 1973) at a formal ceremony at the Egmont Palace in Brussels on 22 January. He was flanked by Alec Douglas-Home and Geoffrey Rippon and the signing was attended by Harold Macmillan, George Brown (representing the Labour party: Wilson pointedly spent the afternoon at a football match) and Jeremy Thorpe. But it was an anti-climactic occasion, its symbolism diluted from a British point of view by the fact that Ireland, Norway and Denmark were signing up at the same time, and spoiled for Heath personally by a young German woman throwing ink over him just as he arrived. (She was protesting not about Britain joining the Community, but about the redevelopment of Covent Garden.) 'Mr Heath reacted stoically to the actual incident,' *The Times* reported, 'but he was later said to have been upset during the cleaning up operation which delayed the opening of the ceremony by 55 minutes.'*[1] It was typical of the lack of interest the historic moment aroused at home – two weeks into the miners' strike and two days after the unemployment figure reached one million – that the ink-throwing episode attracted more coverage in the Sunday papers than the signing.

That evening, in the bar of the Metropole Hotel – his old headquarters in 1961–3 – Heath gave a joint interview to Michael Charlton of the BBC and the European correspondents of *Le Monde* and *Die Zeit*. He spoke confidently of Britain's future in the Community, looking forward to both 'a great improvement in the standard of living of our people' and 'an immense increase in the influence of

---

* Timothy Kitson later described him 'going up and down in the lift, looking like something from one of those minstrel shows', while frantic arrangements were made to wash him down and the leaders of Europe waited.[2]

Europe in the world'. The new united Europe, he anticipated, would soon rival the United States as a world economic power: 'I never felt they really understood what would happen when it was enlarged.'[3] This sort of talk was not only optimistic; it was also premature. For Britain was not in Europe yet. The approval of Parliament for the principle of joining had been secured the previous October, by a gratifyingly large majority. But that required just a single vote. It still remained to carry through a bitterly divided House of Commons the complex and detailed legislation to bring British law into conformity with Community law. That would be a long process fraught with danger for the European cause. The Government was already wrestling with appalling difficulties on several other fronts: the economy, industrial relations and Northern Ireland. Yet the backcloth to all the other crises of this desperate year was the European Communities Bill inching its way precariously through Parliament.

The special circumstances which had made possible the handsome majority of October had been replaced – on the Labour side – by a return to normal parliamentary warfare. Having cast their declaratory vote of principle, most of the Labour pro-Marketeers had undertaken, for the sake of party unity, to grit their teeth and vote against the consequential legislation, on the argument that it was the Government's responsibility to carry its own business, or else resign. On the Tory side, however, there was still a hard core of 10–20 anti-Marketeers who placed the blocking of British entry into the Community higher than the preservation of the Government. Their numbers had been crucially reduced since the autumn, but still the arithmetic was perilously uncertain. The Government could not be sure how many diehards the Powellites – as the hard core can legitimately be called – might attract into the lobby on any particular division. To be safe they still needed some Labour Members to stay away.

In his 'Panorama' interview from Brussels Heath brushed aside the likelihood of small majorities. The October vote, he insisted, was 'the decisive one . . . That is what Parliament really thinks about coming into the Community.' The majority of only twenty-one the previous week – when Labour had objected to the signing of the Treaty before it had been presented to the House (a procedure which the Government insisted was perfectly normal) – he dismissed as 'really a bogus thing, a phony thing'. On that occasion only four Tories had cross-voted, but another seventeen had abstained, which by no means – as *The Times* suggested – indicated that diehard resistance had collapsed but, on the contrary, showed that they could

still muster a serious challenge to the Government on more substantive votes to come. Heath recalled Churchill's dictum that 'one is
enough' and recalled that he himself had carried a crucial clause of his
Resale Price Maintenance Abolition Bill by just one vote – then
quickly added that 'we shall get much more than that'.[4]

The Government achieved a considerable strategic *coup* at the outset by contriving to condense the legislation into a short Bill of only
12 clauses and 4 schedules, occupying just 37 pages. Labour and the
Powellites had looked forward with relish to an enormous Bill of
perhaps 1,000 clauses. Even on the eve of publication on 26 January it
was still expected to run to 50–100 clauses; but the Solicitor-General,
Geoffrey Howe, and the parliamentary draftsmen excelled themselves in skilful compression. The Bill was in effect an Enabling Bill:
instead of a mass of detailed instances, Clause II simply proclaimed
comprehensively that EEC law should henceforth prevail over
British law and be 'enforced, allowed and followed accordingly'.[5]
Michael Foot furiously denounced the Bill as 'a kind of lawyer's con-
juring trick', charging that the Government had 'decided to treat the
House of Commons with contempt'.[6] But Labour had given fair
warning that it intended to do everything it could to obstruct the
passage of the Bill by fighting it line by line: the Government had
simply taken prudent pre-emptive steps to give the Opposition as
little as possible to work with. It also announced that since the Bill
had been carefully framed to comply with the Treaty of Rome it
could not accept any amendments: the Bill would be debated clause
by clause on the floor of the House – no Committee could have fairly
reflected the division of views – but it must be carried whole. The
Second Reading was set for 17 February.

This was a much more formidable hurdle for the Government
than the vote of principle had turned out to be. With the Jenkinsites
committed to vote with the Opposition Pym had to squeeze the
Powellites very hard indeed to achieve a majority. In the days before
the division the most intense pressure was put on the 41 rebels of
October to come to heel. Heath himself saw 9 of them – 2 refused to
see him, and others were clearly unshakeable: 5 of these 9 were persuaded to change their vote. Enoch Powell has spoken bitterly of 'a
more intensive brainwashing operation on the potential dissenters
than any Prime Minister, reverting to his previous character as Chief
Whip, has ever carried out. I'm told that those who went into Ted
Heath's room in the week before the second reading came out looking more like ghosts than men.'[7] Heath told them that the division
would be an explicit vote of confidence: if the Government was
defeated it would resign. In the middle of a miners' strike, with

much of the country blacked out and Northern Ireland in bloody turmoil, a General Election was an uninviting prospect: several of the
potential rebels stood to lose their seats. Yet enough still resisted all
the pressures that could be brought on them to make the result too
close to call. *The Times* predicted a majority of 15–20, but Pym knew
it would be closer than that.[8] The Government's nervousness was reflected by the fact that Alec Douglas-Home was recalled from a trip
to the Far East in order to vote.

At the end of the three-day debate Heath had to break off from
trying to settle with the miners to come to the House and try to save
his Government from extinction. He was desperately tired, but his
defiant speech was, in Douglas Hurd's view, 'adequate'.[9] He spelled
out that if the Government were to be defeated 'this Parliament cannot sensibly continue'.[10] Wilson, however, probably swayed more
votes than Heath: at least 3 Tories, 2 of whom had been intending to
abstain and one to vote against, were so enraged by his performance
that they made a last-minute decision to support the Government.[11]
There have not been many moments in British politics this century
when the split-second decisions of individual MPs have determined
the fate of a Government, but this was one of them. The result was
309 votes to 301. Fifteen Conservatives voted against the Government – the first time since 1945 that Tory MPs had refused their
support on a vote of confidence – and 5 more abstained. There were
violent scenes in the Chamber as Labour realised how close it had
come. Jeremy Thorpe, whose 5 pro-European Liberals had crucially
stuck to their guns, was jostled and physically assaulted: Bob Mellish, Labour's Chief Whip, bitterly denounced the Liberals as 'the
gutter party'. Wilson was quickly on his feet declaring that the
Government had no mandate for its policy and should resign. Heath
– 'pale, tense, but still resolute and impassive' – coolly replied that
the House had approved the policy so the Government would carry
on; he then gathered his papers and walked out, followed by the rest
of the Front Bench. 'But every politician in the crowded Commons
who heard him knew that he and the Government had suffered a
severe setback that stopped short only of defeat.'[12]

The Government, as *The Times* reported, had come 'within a
hair's breadth of falling'.[13] But when the figures were analysed it was
seen not only that the Liberals could have ensured its defeat by voting in the other lobby: the margin of its survival had also been helped
by 5 Labour abstentions. Four of these were old hands who had
already announced their intention to retire at the next election and
were therefore impervious to the pressures of the Whips and their
constituencies; the fifth was Christopher Mayhew, who left Labour

to join the Liberals in 1974. Over the next five months Mayhew organised an informal rota of pro-Market veterans ready to absent themselves quietly from key divisions: they were a crucial factor in ensuring that the Government's majority, though it fell frighteningly low on occasion, never quite disappeared.[14]

The strain on both sides of the House was terrific. The passage of the European Communities Bill was the longest parliamentary battle of its sort on record. Between March, when the Bill went into committee, and the Third Reading on 13 July there were 104 divisions: Enoch Powell, Neil Marten and John Biffen with a varying number of allies voted against the Government in 85 of them.[15] The continuous challenge to Pym and his Whips to maintain the Government's majority over such a period was unprecedented. For Labour loyalists there was anger and frustration at being repeatedly thwarted by Mayhew's handful of blacklegs; while David Owen has recalled these months as

> one of the most unpleasant periods of my whole political career . . . It was a most depressing thing to have to do, voting night after night against the EEC Bill, all on the rather absurd theory that it was up to Ted Heath, as Prime Minister, to get his own legislation through, while the Labour party was publicly aligning itself with Tory rebels like Enoch Powell who were creating hell.[16]

For Heath above all it was a nerve-racking time, and a disillusioning one, too, as the euphoria of October was dispelled in a rancorous protracted struggle for tiny majorities. However 'bogus' the parliamentary arithmetic, the process of whipping the Bill through by such narrow margins could not easily be represented as 'full-hearted consent'. The one consolation was that the opinion polls were beginning to suggest a grudging public acquiescence in British entry.[17]

The Second Reading was the worst moment, the one time when the Government would indisputably have fallen if it had lost. Later votes, on Opposition amendments, could presumably have been reversed if necessary on a vote of confidence, though the damage to the Government's prestige would have been severe if it had ever happened. There were several close shaves. The second most serious challenge came on 2 May, when the Government moved to apply a timetable to the debate: the guillotine was approved by 304 to 293, a majority of 11. This was hailed as a triumph of good whipping; but the next day the margin fell to 4, as a number of Tory pro-Marketeers failed to get back to the House in time from a party at Duncan Sandys's house. On 24 May the Government had a majority of only 5: but since on this occasion the Liberals voted with the Opposition this was really a pretty good majority – Mayhew's irregulars doing their stuff to compensate. The final really dangerous moment came on Clause II – the sovereignty clause – on 14 June. The usual 15 rebels voted against, plus 8 abstainers: the Government was saved by the 5 Liberals and 8 Labour absentees, giving a majority of 8. ('An agonisingly close call' – *The Times*.)[18] After this, the Third Reading was something of a walkover. With the ship so close to harbour, as many as 13 Labour Marketeers broke ranks to abstain, including George Thomson, Michael Stewart and Dick Taverne. Pym was still taking no chances: 7 sick Tories were brought to Westminster to be 'nodded through'. The result was a relatively comfortable majority of 17: 301–284. With that, the Bill was through. Passage through the Lords was a formality. Pym breathed a public sigh of relief. It had been 'a terrific battle, full of tension and drama', but he was glad it was over. 'The determination and patience of the Conservative Party has been remarkable.'[19] The Act received the Royal Assent on 17 October. Three months later the United Kingdom finally joined the EEC.

Even before Britain formally joined, Heath was invited – with the Danish and Irish prime ministers – to attend the Community summit in Paris on 19–20 October. A few days earlier, at the Tory party conference in Blackpool, he had looked forward impatiently to taking up Britain's place at the European table. With rare eloquence he traced the leading part which Britain had played in shaping the modern world; but also the problems – of conflict, instability and poverty – which now faced it. He laid notable stress on the relatively new concept of the environment, emphasising that environmental problems transcended frontiers:

This week's territorial waters in the Baltic are next week's waters off Aberdeen. The pesticides carried up the Rhine can be washed off down the Thames. The sulphurs and particles in Britain's air fall in dirty rain on the continent of Europe.

This today is the contemporary world of economic imbalance, of environmental insecurity, of national rivalry, and yet at the same time global involvement. It is the world which we have helped to create and which we now inherit. We have all been, as it were, part of these problems. Now we can be part of the solution.

This is the context of our entry into Europe . . . I see in these immense problems, not a block to British action and ambition, but a deep and satisfying challenge to carry on the work of world building in which Britain in the past has played so great a part . . .

It is to make a start upon that work that . . . I go to Paris as your Prime Minister next week.[20]

The parliamentary obstacle course was cleared; his dream achieved at last. He could scarcely wait to sit down with Pompidou and Brandt.

With the achievement of British entry into the European Community finally confirmed, the central plank of Heath's purpose was now in place. Everything else was and always had been secondary. The management of the economy was to be judged in that context. It was the knowledge that Britain was at last about to face the competition of the enlarged European market in a few months' time which gave the final push to Heath's growing conviction that the Government had no choice but to intervene directly to promote rapid growth – whatever ministers might have said previously about government getting off industry's back. The shock of the unemployment figure reaching one million in January made it politically and socially essential to be seen to take immediate action; the imminence of Britain's entry into Europe made it economically imperative. A shift of emphasis towards boosting employment had already become visible during 1971, but it had been accomplished discreetly, without an overt change of strategy. During the first half of 1972 the complete reversal of the 'hands off' philosophy on which the Government had been elected became plain and undeniable. The 'U-turn', as the volte-face was immediately dubbed, unfolded in four stages: the rescue of Upper Clyde Shipbuilders in February was followed by the Budget in March and the Industry Bill in April, and finally the floating of the pound in June. And there was still a final reversal to come before the end of the year.

The salvaging of UCS was the Government's first explicit retreat. The nationalisation of Rolls-Royce a year before could be justified as an exceptional expedient dictated by international obligations and defence considerations which in no way invalidated the principle of not propping up lame ducks. The UCS rescue, by contrast, embodied an entirely new approach. Repeatedly since Davies's liquidation of the consortium the previous July ministers, including Heath himself, had insisted that UCS was precisely the sort of company they were determined *not* to rescue, despite the political pressure exerted by Jimmy Reid's successful work-in. The steady worsening of unemployment brought a change of mind. During January the 'three wise men' appointed to examine the prospects of preserving shipbuilding on the Clyde came up with a £35 million scheme to save three of the four yards: the American company Marathon was interested – if the Government made it worth their while – in taking over the fourth to build oil rigs. On 28 February – ten days after the end of the miners' strike – Davies announced the Government's acceptance of the scheme. Unemployment in Glasgow and the west of Scotland, he explained, was already exceptionally high: the closure of UCS would put another 4,300 men out of work overnight, with more inevitably to follow.[21] In addition there was apprehension of serious civil disorder if the yards were closed. The Chief Constable of Glasgow, David McNee, had submitted an alarming report estimating that he would need another 5,000 police to handle the situation. It was this which tipped the scale. 'Of all the places where death was in the air it was Glasgow,' one senior Minister has recalled. 'It was the worst area to allow the death of a lame duck. And then came the report from the Chief Constable.'[22]

The Government frankly gave in to the threat of violence. UCS was saved purely to preserve jobs. *The Times* gamely insisted that 'there is no reason to suppose that shipbuilding is a declining industry'. Though admittedly it needed Government subsidy to survive, the social cost of letting it die was too high. 'In practice', the paper argued on 9 February, 'the Government have little option but to put up the necessary money for Upper Clyde' – as it already had for Harland & Wolff in Belfast.[23] Davies's announcement three weeks later was duly welcomed as 'a further example of ideological commitment being abandoned in the face of political and economic reality . . . The Government cannot be blamed for thinking again.'[24] In the Commons, Davies professed to hope that the reorganised company would be profitable within three years. Scottish MPs were jubilant. Teddy Taylor – no friend of Heath, having resigned from the Government the previous summer in opposition to EEC entry – called the rescue 'magnificent news'. Other Tories were grudging only in so far as they wanted similar help for their own areas.[25] Only *The Economist* was bluntly unconvinced: 'If the Government is going to spend £35m on modernising any industry one of the worst possible economic choices is shipbuilding, whose future probably lies in low wage countries and certainly does not lie so many miles up the Clyde.'[26]

Heath did not seek to deny that the decision had been taken primarily on social grounds, but he too persuaded himself that it could be justified economically – for instance in an *Evening Standard* interview with Robert Carvel and Charles Wintour that summer:

We always said where we thought a firm or industry could be viable, then it was worthy of support. And we set out in our manifesto that an effective regional policy was vital to our strategy.

At the same time in Scotland we have had to take account of the general employment situation there, but I would hope that Upper Clyde can become viable.[27]

The very scale of the Government's investment, he argued, was the critical factor, offering the new company not just a temporary rescue such as Labour had attempted but a new beginning.

Now, with good management and a proper modernisation scheme, the prospects should at last be brighter, provided the unions and management learn from the past . . .

These measures prove beyond any doubt our determination to bring unemployment down. But do not let anyone suppose that the prosperity of the country and the standard of living of its people can be assured just by multiplying subsidies to industry.[28]

Seen thus, the rescue of UCS, though it may have been contrary to the non-interventionist philosophy enunciated in 1970, was not in-consistent with Heath's longstanding belief in regional policy as he had practised it in 1963–4. The Government's whole economic policy from 1972 onwards, indeed, was a rerun of Maudling's dash for sustainable growth in 1963–4. It had come quite close to succeeding then, and might have done so had the Tories not lost the election, provoking a loss of international confidence in the new Labour Government and a consequent balance-of-payments crisis. Heath's hope was that a similar strategy of Government-led expansion could work this time round, if only wages and imports could be controlled. The crucial thing was to break out of the deadly cycle of 'stop–go' by not stopping; industry must have the confidence that the Government's commitment to expansion would not falter. This represented an undoubted switch of method from the Government's initial reliance on tax cuts, deregulation and competition to stimulate the economy. But the underlying purpose was still the same.

Success depended on creating a self-sustaining atmosphere of confidence, and in this respect the unions were crucial. The Government needed to persuade the TUC to restrain wage demands in return for action on jobs and prices. Ministers still resisted any sort of formal incomes policy, but if they were to achieve growth without inflation they needed to involve the unions as responsible partners in operating an informal policy. Heath had been very impressed, when visiting Germany, by Willy Brandt's regular round-table consultations with the unions and the German system of co-partnership: his mind began moving towards establishing a similar relationship in Britain by which the unions should be given an acknowledged role in the running of the economy. The rescue of UCS, like the Government's willingness to buy off the miners at almost any cost the week before, was necessary to establish the Government's commitment to growth: the Downing Street meeting with the General Council of the TUC on 9 March was intended to inaugurate a new era of co-operation to achieve it.

The first extended exposition of the new strategy was contained in Tony Barber's Budget on 21 March. Of course it was not in reality the Chancellor's Budget, but the Prime Minister's. Barber and the Treasury were deeply unhappy with it. The balance of payments was already deteriorating as a result of inflation, the previous year's relaxation of hire-purchase terms which was sucking in imported goods and the 1971 devaluation of the dollar. In these circumstances economic prudence dictated at best a neutral Budget. But Heath had no time for the Treasury's caution. He had always thought it lukewarm on Europe, and was now convinced that it systematically underestimated the benefits to be expected from joining the EEC. The 1972 Budget was framed in opposition to the Treasury, as a deliberately *European* policy to take Britain into the Community at full stretch. It was a gamble, but one which Heath was prepared to take in the belief that there was spare capacity in the economy which would be taken up by access to the wider European market, and the expectation that productivity would rise as industrial relations improved, while pay rises could be contained with the help of the unions. Barber was too loyal to pit his judgment against Heath's or rock the boat by threatening to resign.

The 1972 Budget had two aspects. First, on the personal side, Barber took £1 billion off income tax by increasing allowances; he made cuts in purchase tax worth another £1,380 million and increased pensions and social security benefits, thereby putting an estimated extra £1 a week into 21 million pay packets. Second – and more striking, because directly contrary to the manifesto commitments of 1970 – he unveiled a whole range of encouragements to industry to invest, including the reintroduction of regional investment grants and 'free depreciation' for the first year of all new investment in plant and machinery. The next day John Davies introduced to the House the White Paper *Industry and Regional Development*, which became the 1972 Industry Act.

Barber was explicit that the prime purpose of the Budget was to cut unemployment. 'I am not', he declared, 'one of those who look to unemployment as the cure for inflation . . . A further boost to demand is required.' The country was offered 'a rare opportunity to secure a substantial and faster rate of growth over a considerable period of years'. The Government's aim was a 10 per cent expansion of the economy between the first half of 1971 and the first half of 1973. This, Barber insisted, would not be 'inimical to the fight against inflation'. The gamble was that the unions would accept all that the Government was doing for their members in the way of both personal income and investment in jobs and refrain from pressing for unreasonable pay rises as well. 'The British people will now have no patience with any group whose actions endanger our hopes for prices and employment.'[29] As even *The Times* commented, this was 'a virtual admission that he was taking a chance with inflation'. Even so, while the Budget won a standing ovation from delighted Tory MPs – as well as warm praise from Harold Wilson for a repenting sinner – *The Times* still doubted whether Barber had yet done enough 'on either economic or social grounds'.[30]

Meanwhile, in secret over the past couple of months, the Industry Act had been in preparation – not in the DTI or the Treasury, but by a small hand-picked group in the Cabinet Office working closely to the Prime Minister himself. The key figure was Sir William Armstrong, a former Permanent Secretary of the Treasury, now sidelined as Head of the Home Civil Service, and 'itching for a renewed involvement in economic policy'.[31] His chance came with Heath's loss of confidence in the Treasury; compared with the more conventional Sir Douglas Allen, Armstrong was an unusually political Civil Servant with whom Heath established a close *rapport*. He was a convinced interventionist in economic management – he had been involved in the creation of the DTI – and shared Heath's impatience to promote a thorough transformation of the economy. Alongside Armstrong – until April when he was transferred to Belfast to set up the Northern Ireland Office – was Sir William Nield, previously the last Permanent Secretary of Labour's Department of Economic Affairs.

The third central member of the team was Leo Pliatzky, a Deputy Secretary at the Treasury where he had already been responsible during most of 1971 for discovering public spending projects which could be brought forward to create employment. Pliatzky had known Heath thirty years before at the Oxford Union. They had been thrown together again in 1963 when he accompanied Heath on a tour of EFTA capitals after the collapse of the Common Market negotiations. Pliatzky was another instinctively interventionist official: he had warned incoming Tory ministers in 1970 that they would regret abolishing the IRC.[32] It was now one of the tasks of the working group to construct a replacement.

It was an extraordinary undertaking, an exercise of prime ministerial power comparable to Neville Chamberlain's conduct of foreign policy in 1937-9 or Eden's handling of the Suez crisis, previously unparalleled in domestic policy except in respect of necessarily secret operations like devaluation. The reason for this secrecy was that too many people – both officials and ministers – in the Treasury and the DTI would have been opposed to what was being planned if they had known about it. Barber, reluctantly, and Davies, more enthusiastically, were actively involved; but their juniors were kept in the dark. By proceeding in this undercover way Heath contradicted not only the economic philosophy with which he had ostensibly come into office but, more fundamentally, his promises of better, more honest and more open government. 'When so few people know what is going on,' Pliatzky recalled, 'naturally misunderstandings and contretemps are liable to happen until the mystery can be cleared up.' It was, to put it mildly, perverse to attempt to construct an ambitious national industrial policy behind the back of the large Department specifically created for that purpose. 'It was rather difficult to prevent excessively large numbers being attached to each proposal through a sort of bidding-up process . . . The PAR approach, which was supposed to involve the costing of options and a comparison of inputs with outputs, had no place in this numbers game.'[33] The Think Tank, on the other hand, did have an input – in Pliatzky's view a thoroughly confusing and irresponsible one.

'The concept was that we must strengthen our industrial capacity so as to take advantage of membership of the Common Market,' Pliatzky told Phillip Whitehead in 1984. 'And those really were the terms of reference of the exercise. Of course when conclusions were reached, and the wraps came off, it was a very great shock to some of the other members of the Government, and some of those who were most committed to the market economy philosophy were really quite taken aback by the whole thing.'[34]

The Bill made provision for two types of assistance to industry – general and specific. On the one hand, as disclosed in the Budget, there was to be a nationwide scheme of free depreciation on new plant and machinery amounting to a 100 per cent capital allowance; and the restoration of regional investment grants to areas of high unemployment, graded in four tiers – Special Development Areas, Development Areas. Intermediate Areas and Derelict Land Clearance Areas. Between them these categories made available some special help for practically the whole country outside the south-east. In addition, the Regional Employment Premium, previously being phased out, was to continue until September 1974. Second, the Bill established new machinery for giving selective assistance to individual companies. Armstrong initially explored the possibility of raising private capital for this purpose in the City; but without success. Pliatzky favoured a new semi-autonomous agency on the lines of Labour's IRC. In the end, however, Heath was persuaded by Sir Anthony Part, Permanent Secretary of the DTI, that the job would best be done by a new special agency within his department, to be called the Industrial Development Executive. Finally, to strengthen the Department's powers to control price rises, there was to be a new Office of Fair Trading and a new Consumer Protection Advisory Committee – effectively reviving, as critics did not fail to point out, the Consumer Council which the Government had abolished in 1970.

All this was agreed, and approved by the Cabinet, just in time for Barber to announce the main outlines in his Budget; Davies gave more detail in introducing the White Paper to the House the following day. Despite the unusual secrecy of its genesis, the package caused no great drama when it came to Cabinet. *The Times* reported in May, when the Bill was published, that a number of Cabinet ministers 'frankly confess their uneasiness about the socialist implications of the Bill', and singled out Mrs Thatcher as having opposed it.[35] One minister was said to have dubbed it privately the Lame Ducks (Unlimited) Bill.[36] But others insist that there was no argument about it, no sign of serious opposition on the part of Mrs Thatcher, Keith Joseph or anyone else. There was far more trauma in Cabinet over the crisis in Northern Ireland, coming to a head at just the same moment, than over the Industry Bill.[37]

It was the junior ministers who were – in both senses of the word – upset. It is clear that Heath should have carried out a wholesale reshuffle at the DTI *before* the planning of the Bill began: then it need not have been undertaken so hugger-mugger. Rumours that John Eden and Nicholas Ridley were for the chop had leaked out, however, at the party conference in October, with the result that he had felt obliged to keep them on. Now it was obvious that they must go. In recent years Ridley has claimed that he was not sacked but resigned from the Government 'on a matter of principle'.[38] The truth is that he was indeed sacked from the DTI – Heath summoned him back from a visit to Portugal to tell him so – but then declined to be shuffled sideways to become Minister for the Arts. He left the Government very quietly at the Prime Minister's convenience. The reshuffle had to be delayed for a few days while Frederick Corfield too was summoned home from a foreign trip and was finally announced, two weeks after the Budget, on 7 April. The main feature was the appointment of Robert Carr to replace Willie White-law as Lord President and Leader of the House, with Maurice Macmillan promoted to the Cabinet to replace Carr at Employment. Corfield, Eden and Ridley were all removed from the DTI, though Eden remained in the Government as Minister of Posts and Tele-communications. John Davies stayed at the DTI for the moment to see his Bill through Parliament; but his new team comprised Tom Boardman, Peter Emery (both promoted from the back benches) and Michael Heseltine, plus Christopher Chataway with the new title of Minister for Industrial Development to run the new Development Executive.

In the prevailing atmosphere of crisis following the miners' strike and the imposition of Direct Rule in Northern Ireland, the an-nouncement of the Government's U-turn caused more embar-rassment than criticism on his own side. 'Mr Davies's presen-tation of his new measures', *The Times* reported, 'was studded with jeers and shouts of derision from the Labour benches as one after another of the old familiar phrases of Government intervention were rolled out from the Treasury bench.'[39] Labour might jeer – Tony Benn wrote that 'The House just roared with laughter'[40] – but most Conservatives were relieved that the Government was seen to be taking action. By the time the Bill came before the House some dissent was beginning to make itself heard. On 16 May Chataway faced criticism from the party's backbench trade and industry com-mittee. Some 30–40 free-market 'neo-liberals' were believed to be seriously unhappy. Nevertheless the Bill passed its Second Reading on 22 May without a division. Most Tories who spoke in the debate welcomed the Government's return to pragmatism: Teddy Taylor again gave 'strong support'. When Jock Bruce-Gardyne, warning that 'we are on a slippery slope once we start providing individual in-dustries with inflation subsidies', tried to force a vote, no one was prepared to second him. John Biffen begged him not to persist, hop-ing instead that Labour's gleeful enthusiasm for the Bill would encourage the Government to accept some backbench amendments in Committee.[41]

They did make some concessions. The critics concentrated their concern on Clause 8, which allowed the Government to spend almost unlimited sums – up to £550 million over five years – wher-ever they judged it to be 'in the national interest' or 'likely to benefit the economy', even outside the assisted areas. Two Tories, Biffen and Tom Normanton, voted against it in Committee. The Whips then contrived to hold the Report Stage on a Friday evening when they knew that both Biffen and Normanton had other engagements. They cancelled them, however, and both were present to vote for an amendment requiring assistance of more than £1 million to be laid before the House. They were joined in the lobby by Bruce-Gardyne, Trevor Skeet and one Liberal (John Pardoe). The amendment was overwhelmingly defeated. But during the debate the Chairman of the 1922 Committee, Sir Harry Legge-Bourke, solemnly warned the Government of the large number of distinguished and senior members of the party who were unhappy about the Bill. It was, he bluntly declared, 'a Socialist Bill by ethic and philosophy . . . obnoxious for many reasons': he himself supported it only because some areas were in such desperate need of help.[42] In the Tory party such an intervention from the chairman of the 1922 cannot be ignored. The Government was forced to give ground: on the following Monday Chataway came to the House with a handwritten amendment limiting the amount that could be given to any one recipient without the express approval of Parliament to £5 million. It was a small enough concession, of detail rather than principle, but the rebels declared themselves delighted. With a number of other safeguards, the Bill got its Third Reading without even a debate.[43]

The question is where were the other neo-liberals, the 30–40 Powellites and future Thatcherites who would look back on the 1972 Industry Bill as the great betrayal of the Heath Government? Where was Powell himself? Where was Ridley? Where was Edward Du Cann? Why was the opposition to a Bill so fundamentally at variance with free market principles left to two such junior figures as Biffen and Bruce-Gardyne? The trouble was that Labour's support for the Bill, while in theory making it easier for Tories to rebel without endangering the Government, in practice made it impossible to exert any pressure on the Government. Had there been a normal party division on Second or Third Reading a substantial number of dissidents might have abstained. But forcing a division against their own Government was something few Tories could contemplate. Thus it was left to Legge-Bourke to voice their unease – while significantly giving the Bill his own reluctant support. At the same time there can be no doubt that the great majority of Tory Members, though they had been happy to subscribe to the bracing rhetoric of disengagement in the heady days of 1970, were equally happy that the Government was now taking measures to counter the mood of economic crisis. Even the dissidents did not want to push their opposition too far. The ease with which the Government got the Industry

Bill through the House undoubtedly reinforced Heath's confidence that the great bulk of the party was still behind him.

Heath, of course, resolutely denied that he had executed any sort of U-turn. 'I would have thought', he protested to Robert Carvel and Charles Wintour, 'that more than any Government since 1945 this one has kept on course and adhered to its policies. If you take Europe, immigration, housing finance, Government expenditure, the reform of taxation, Rhodesia – all of these things – we have adhered to our course.'[44] Including Government expenditure in this list was a whopper, but in other respects it was true enough – but beside the point. Economic policy was central, and it was foolish to pretend that this had not changed. He would have done better to argue that his ultimate purpose had not altered but that circumstances had made a change of approach unavoidable. He was certainly not ashamed of his flexibility. Lord Carrington is emphatic that he acted in good faith as his view of his duty as Prime Minister dictated:

> I don't think Heath was false to any principles of his own in the matter, still less was he in bad faith . . . Both from an electoral and human point of view we believed at that time that unemployment above a certain level was intolerable. I don't think now [1988] that all our measures were perfectly judged; but nor do I think that they constituted some sort of betrayal.[45]

The Industry Act was a return, on a grander scale, to the sort of policies Heath had begun to introduce as Home's Secretary of State for Trade, Industry and Regional Development in 1963–4. By 1972, as he told Carvel and Wintour, he had become more convinced than ever that Britain needed desperately to modernise all its industrial plant and equipment – not only in the old declining heartlands of the north and Scotland but also in areas long believed to be prosperous like the West Midlands. Old factories should be torn down and rebuilt from scratch. Such drastic remedies did not come naturally to the British character – which was why the Government had to help. The Government's aim, he explained in his best 'Heathco' tone of patient exasperation, was to 'regenerate our entire industrial capacity. *That's what we are about.* I still don't think that people realise how big an enterprise this is. And we're doing it in a way which will put us in a very advantageous position when we are in the European Economic Community.'[46]

Briefly, between 1965 and 1970, he had been prepared to believe that industry needed only to get an inefficient Labour Government off its back and it would do the job itself. But, just as the unions had not reformed themselves when given the chance, so British business had failed to respond to the new climate of enterprise which the Government had striven to create after 1970. As a result, Heath now believed, the Government had no choice but to take an active hand itself. Two years as Prime Minister had quickly disillusioned him as to the energy and even the patriotism of British industrialists, who he felt had let him down. He had. in Peter Walker's words, 'an immense desire to restore the fortunes of his country. Much of his political motivation is in fact simple patriotism.'[47] He became very impatient of what he saw as the business community's failure to invest even when the Government was doing everything in its power to encourage it. In private conversation, some who heard his tirades against industry and the City felt that he had begun to sound more like a Labour politician than a Tory.[48] But he did not see himself as having betrayed his party's faith in private enterprise; rather it was private enterprise which had disappointed him.

In truth his approach was that of a Civil Servant, but with a politician's ambition to achieve visible results. The Industry Act, due largely to the secrecy of its conception and genesis, was a bureaucratic monster. It attempted to accomplish far too much in one big comprehensive measure – reducing temporary unemployment, tackling deep-seated regional imbalances, easing EEC entry and improving consumer protection all at once. A less ambitious series of specific measures aimed individually at each target and emphasising continuity with past policies would have been politically more sensitive and might have avoided the shock of such a blatant U-turn. Its scope reflected Heath's characteristic belief that the most complex problems could be solved by clear-sighted men sitting down, setting politics aside and coming up with answers. This was a seductive delusion reinforced by his close relationship with William Armstrong, as Douglas Hurd, from his viewpoint as political secretary, noticed:

> Because of his justified respect for his senior advisers Mr Heath tended to exaggerate what could be achieved by new official machinery. If he had been somewhat more sceptical he would . . . have been less ready to believe that the Department of Trade and Industry was competent, even with the outside advice provided, to use the sweeping new powers to spend money selectively which were given them in the Industry Act.[49]

But, as Norman Tebbit wryly concluded in his memoirs, 'perhaps Selsdon Man was always a Civil Servant at heart, even before his partnership with . . . Sir William Armstrong'.[50]

Heath's Industry Act was gleefully hailed by Tony Benn in the House of Commons as 'spadework for socialism'. 'The instruments of intervention', he chortled, were 'virtually unlimited in their impact'. Even after the restraints imposed at Report Stage, they gave the Secretary of State for Trade and Industry far more extensive powers over the economy than any Labour Government hitherto had dreamed of taking, and Benn promised to use them, 'when we inherit power again, more radically than the right hon. Gentleman himself will use them'.[51] When he came to the Department of Industry in March 1974, Benn was indeed able to use the 1972 Act to accomplish most of what he wanted in the way of planning agreements and investment in favoured projects. But Heath's Government itself made energetic use of the Act over its last eighteen months in a tremendous effort to engineer an economic boom. As soon as it was operational, Heath moved John Davies from the DTI and replaced him with the younger and more obviously dynamic Peter Walker. Walker's two biggest investments were in coal and steel. In December 1972 he announced that the long-term rundown of the coal industry was to be put into reverse, with an annual subsidy of £175 million: its accumulated £475 million deficit was written off.[52] This vote of confidence in the future of coal delighted Derek Ezra: it was intended also to prevent further trouble with the NUM. A few weeks later Walker unveiled a similarly massive modernisation programme for British Steel, costing £3,000 million over ten years.[53] At a lower level Chataway spent £5 million in a vain attempt to save the last hope of the British motorcycle industry at Meriden (a notorious lame duck subsequently championed as a workers' co-operative by Benn). In addition Walker and Chataway poured money – as Heath had promised – into new factory building; and further developed the system of grants and inducements to encourage the movement of jobs to assisted areas and grants towards the rent of premises in development and intermediate areas.

Walker offers a vivid snapshot of Heath's commitment to regional policy. While still Environment Secretary, Walker appointed a young Scot named Dennis Stevenson to head the Peterlee and Aycliffe New Towns. Heath invited him to Downing Street, asked him if he knew the north-east and then marched him upstairs to his flat to show him a painting of a Durham miner sitting bowed with his head in his hands. 'That's the north-east,' he told Stevenson. 'You've got to give his children and grandchildren a better life than he has had.'[54]

The Government's new regional policy was presented as the reequipment of British industry to compete successfully in the wider

European market, not as the propping up of inefficient firms. In practice, however, it was open to the objection that it offered open-ended subsidy on no clear principle but political hunch: ministers were trying to act as entrepreneurs, a role for which they were not qualified. The intention was admirable: British industry unquestionably needed modernisation in the early 1970s. But throwing Government money at favoured projects and bribing firms to set up where they would not otherwise have gone was not the way to do it. A severe report by the House of Commons Expenditure Committee in 1974 described the effect of regional policy over the previous two years as 'empiricism gone mad, a game of hit and miss, played with more enthusiasm than success'.[55] Over the following decade, Heath's Industry Act – and the use made of it by the succeeding Labour Government – came to be derided as the quintessential folly of a misguided age. The new orthodoxy dictated that only the free market could create a competitive economy: the role of government in providing the physical infrastructure for expansion was systematically denied. In the 1970s, however, the expectation that it was the Government's responsibility to stimulate the economy was overwhelming. Heath fully accepted that responsibility. He saw himself leading a great national regeneration, similar to General de Gaulle's regeneration of France. Far more than his brief flirtation with market slogans, it suited his temperament to believe that determined Government action would produce results. The ambition and the failure of the Industry Act epitomises the ambition and failure of his Government as a whole.

The final U-turn forced on the Government in the first half of 1972 was the suspension of the fixed parity of sterling, allowing the value of the pound to float downwards. This was something which a growing number of economists and a few politicians, most prominently Enoch Powell, had advocated for years, but which Heath had resisted strenuously in the belief that Britain's national prestige and honour depended upon maintaining the fixed parity. Eventually he was compelled to relax his opposition by the Nixon administration's suspension of the convertibility of the dollar in August 1971, which put intolerable pressure on the pound. As the Government strove to reflate the economy it became imperative to let sterling float in order to avert a balance-of-payments crisis which would have put a stop to any possibility of growth. In mid-June, with the balance of payments plunging, heavy selling of sterling began. Heath and Barber furiously denied Denis Healey's prediction that they would have to devalue. A week later, however, Barber was forced to raise the bank rate by 1 per cent; and the next day, 23 June, the pound was floated. It was declared to be a temporary expedient to relieve short-term pressure and allow the markets time to come to a settled judgment: Barber assured the Six that he hoped to restore a fixed parity before Britain joined the EEC in six months' time – but in fact the value of the currency fell immediately and continued to drop steadily from $2.60 to around $2.40 during 1973. While Powell caustically hailed 'a fitful gleam of the recovery of sanity',[56] *The Times* was – as usual – extravagant in praise of Heath's willingness to change his mind: 'The capacity to take such decisions is the mark of a great Prime Minister. He has acted with insight, with confidence, with courage and above all, he has acted early.'[57] It was still – particularly in the European context – a bitter pill for Heath to swallow.

Moreover, as is the way of devaluations, floating the pound gave no immediate help to British exports, while having an instant impact on import prices and the cost-of-living index. It thus made the Government's attempt to operate a voluntary counter-inflation policy harder than ever; while the abandonment of the fixed parity had the additional effect of muffling the normal warnings against rising inflation which would previously have set off an exchange crisis.

In a limited sense the policy of risking everything for growth worked. The Government's first priority was to reduce unemployment, and unemployment did indeed fall steadily from its January peak to below 600,000 by the middle of 1973 and 500,000 by the year's end. (Ironically the million figure which created such a political storm in January was the peak; by the time the further measures embodied by the Industry Act took effect unemployment was already falling.) But at what cost? With all the money the Government was throwing at industry with one hand in order to maintain growth, and at the social services with the other in order to persuade the unions to restrain wage demands, public expenditure was allowed to soar out of control. The result was that inflation soared as well – fuelled by the government's own policies. At the same time it was being further fuelled by other factors. One of these – the steep rise in raw material and commodity prices – was a worldwide phenomenon outside the Government's control. The other was of the Government's own making. Since the mid-1960s the liberalisation of credit control had been a touchstone of the strong competition policy to which the Tories were committed. Its introduction with a flourish of trumpets by the Bank of England in September 1971, however, led immediately to a rapid expansion in the amount of money in circulation, a credit explosion (bank lending to the private sector rose 48 per cent in 1972, another 43 per cent in 1973) and a property boom, giving yet a further stimulus to roaring inflation. This was a theoretically admirable reform implemented at the wrong moment – one 'Selsdon' policy which *should* have been postponed in the circumstances of late 1971. But the Government seriously underestimated the inflationary impact of allowing the money supply to rocket. The logic of liberalisation required a willingness to raise interest rates when necessary to control credit. But this, in his anxiety to encourage investment at all costs, Heath was reluctant to do. Instead he gambled on continuing to pump money into the economy while trusting to incomes policy – at first voluntary, later statutory – to prevent the loose money going straight into wages, personal consumption and imports. Thus incomes policy became the essential prerequisite of the Government's economic policy.

But the biggest obstacle in the way of achieving it was the Industrial Relations Act.

24

The Collapse of the Industrial Relations Act

THE Industrial Relations Act had been the jewel in the Government's crown. It was genuinely intended by Heath and Robert Carr to lead to better industrial relations and more responsible trade unions. It was not designed to be anti-union, but merely to put the conduct of industrial relations on a clear and consistent legal basis, to the benefit of all. It should, in the Government's view, have been perfectly compatible with the new relationship of co-operation it was trying to foster between Government and unions.

The principal unions, however, had already committed themselves implacably against it. By the simple device of refusing to register under its provisions, they had called in question the possibility of it ever operating successfully. As the Government changed its tune and began to seek the TUC's help in making its new economic policy work, they remained determined that the Act was a sticking point which must be abandoned as their price for co-operation. During 1972 several unions set out deliberately to render it unworkable – and succeeded. By August, after a summer of industrial chaos and legal farce, the Act was for all practical purposes a dead letter.

Contrary to popular memory, the miners' strike at the beginning of 1972 had nothing to do with the Act, which did not become fully operational until 1 March. The first test of the new code of 'good' industrial practice arose almost immediately, however, in connection with a long-festering dispute over the new technique of containerisation, which bypassed the docks and threatened the traditional livelihood of the dockers, who responded by 'blacking' the container lorries. On 23 March, in its first important judgment, the new National Industrial Relations Court (NIRC), chaired by Sir John Donaldson, declared this to be an 'unfair' industrial practice and ordered Liverpool dockers who had been stopping the lorries of a

457

transport firm named Heaton's to desist. The dockers' union, the TGWU, following TUC policy, refused to recognise the Court and was fined £5,000 for contempt. Three weeks later, when it refused to pay, it was fined a further £50,000 and threatened with the sequestration of its entire assets – some £22 million. At this, the TUC voted narrowly to allow unions to recognise the NIRC and the fine was eventually paid. Despite appeals from Jack Jones, leader of the TGWU, to the men on the ground that they should stop, however, the 'blacking' of container lorries continued and spread to other docks around the country – London, Preston, Tilbury and Hull. The counterproductive potential of the Act was already demonstrated. A small local dispute was blown up into a major national confrontation, while public attention focused on the legal question of contempt of court instead of on the cause of the original dispute.

Meanwhile the Government tried to use the Act to prevent a national rail strike. On 13 April the three rail unions – for once negotiating together – rejected an offer of 11 per cent and began operating a work to rule which seriously disrupted services. As commuters suffered cancellations and long delays, Anthony Barber condemned as 'intolerable' the rejection of a 'generous' offer already well above the going rate.[1] The former secretary of Labour's Prices and Incomes Board, Alex Jarratt, was called in as an unofficial arbitrator: he proposed an improved offer of 12·5 per cent, but this too the unions refused. On 20 April, with a full-scale stoppage threatened, the new Employment Secretary, Maurice Macmillan, applied to the NIRC under the provisions of the Industrial Relations Act to order a fourteen-day cooling-off period.

Macmillan had just succeeded Robert Carr as part of the reshuffle following Willie Whitelaw's move to Northern Ireland. His appointment seems to have been intended by Heath as a gesture of conciliation to the unions – not that Carr had ever intended to confront them. But Francis Pym, who had recommended him, felt subsequently that Macmillan was the wrong man for this critical job. A reformed alcoholic, now described by one commentator as 'A tense, shy, thoughtful man, who lived on nerves and black coffee',[2] he had been a good Chief Secretary to the Treasury, but he had no *rapport* with trade union leaders. In reality the focus of relations between the TUC and the Government had shifted from St James's Square to Downing Street and the personality of the Employment Secretary counted for little over the next two years. Henceforth Heath was effectively his own Employment Secretary.

Rather than risk the sort of fines imposed on the TGWU, the rail unions accepted the NIRC's statutory cooling-off period, though for several days unofficial disruption continued and normal services were not restored until 25 April. When the fourteen days were up, however, there was still no sign of a settlement and the work to rule recommenced. Undaunted, the Government fired its second barrel and applied to the Court for a compulsory ballot, while continuing to insist that there was no more money on offer. The result was predictable: the men declined to repudiate their leaders and voted by more than 5–1 in favour of further action. This was precisely the opposite to the result which cooling-off periods and ballots were intended to achieve. The embarrassment for the Government was not in this case that the Act had been defied, but that it had operated perfectly: the unions observed the law meticulously and thereby rendered it an ass. As one Tory backbencher was quoted as remarking: 'Ask a silly question and you get a silly answer.'[3] The resources of the Act being exhausted, the dispute was eventually settled on 12 June with an average pay rise of around 13 per cent. This was not in fact an enormous increase; Heath went on television to defend it as an honourable compromise, claiming that the Act had worked well, in that the cooling-off period had reduced the inconvenience to the public.[4] But nothing could disguise the reality that the Government had suffered another humiliation. The operation of its cherished Act had served only to prolong the dispute, harden attitudes and strengthen the unions' hand. Though Gallup showed that the public still supported it in principle,[5] the Act was in practice already seriously discredited.

The next two months saw its final descent into farce, with the dockers – and the lawyers – resuming centre stage. On 28 April Sir John Donaldson had ruled, with respect to the Merseyside containerisation dispute, that trade unions were responsible in law for the actions of their members. This ruling correctly expressed the central intention of the 1971 Act: to make the unions as institutions – *not* individual trade unionists – legally accountable. Sanctions against the abuse of union power were to fall solely on union coffers. In framing the penal clauses of the Act, Carr and Geoffrey Howe had specifically sought to avoid any possibility of workers being sent to gaol.

The TGWU, however, with its new policy of recognising the courts, appealed from the NIRC to the Appeal Court where, on 13 June, the Master of the Rolls, Lord Denning, sitting with two colleagues, quashed the £55,000 fine imposed by Donaldson, ruling that after all the TGWU was *not* responsible for the actions of its officials. Here was another slap in the face for the Government which no one had anticipated. Denning's ruling destroyed the whole rationale of the Act, blithely setting aside all the safeguards which Carr and

Howe had laboured to erect. 'I remember', Carr told Phillip White-head, 'we both felt we might as well jump off Westminster Bridge that morning.' Denning's judgment was 'a torpedo below the water-line'.[6] Not only was the liability of unions now under question, but the very authority and legal competence of the NIRC appeared to have been shot down. Of course, the Appeal Court regularly re-verses decisions of the High Court without in any way challenging its competence; but it was different with a court so new and politi-cally sensitive as the NIRC. The unions were cock-a-hoop. Next day Donaldson was obliged to warn three London dockers that they now personally faced fines or prison if they persisted in 'blacking' a cold store in Hackney. 'By their conduct', he declared, 'these men are say-ing that they are above the rule of law.' The NIRC had no choice but to assert its authority.[7] But of course – as Carr and Howe well knew – sending men to prison only played into the unions' hands by creat-ing martyrs. The three dockers made it clear that they could scarcely wait to be arrested.

By now 35,000 dockers were on strike all round the country. Once again the existence of the 1971 Act had served only to magnify a local problem. 'The labour situation is getting steadily more confused,' Cecil King wrote in his diary. 'We are facing a confrontation be-tween the dockers and the High Court, and the unions and the Government; but the Government does not seem to realise that, as has been shown in the case of the miners and the railwaymen, this is all a trial of strength and the unions are stronger than the Government.'[8] The Government was only saved by the unlikely combination of Jack Jones and Lord Denning. Jones was as embar-rassed as the Government by members of his union making the leadership look foolish. At the instigation of the TGWU's lawyers, and with Denning's prior approval, the Official Solicitor was in-duced to apply to the Appeal Court to stop the warrants for the three men's arrest, on the ground that the NIRC had acted with insuffi-cient evidence.* This timely intervention provoked great national hilarity; but the issue was only postponed.

In July another case arose, involving five dockers – including two of the same men, determined not to be cheated of their martyrdom – ordered by the NIRC to stop obstructing container lorries crossing a picket line in Hackney. They refused, and two weeks later they were arrested and detained in Pentonville. This time the Official Solicitor made no move. Now the opponents of the Act had got what they

---

* 'Well,' Denning explained to John Mortimer a decade later, 'we'd been told there was the danger of a general strike.'[9]

wanted. As well as large demonstrations outside the prison, there was well-orchestrated uproar in the House of Commons: Heath was howled down by cries of 'Heil Hitler', accompanied by fascist salutes. Angrily he accused the five of 'exploiting trade union solidarity for ends which have nothing to do with genuine trade union aims'.[10] From the Labour Front Bench, Reg Prentice courageously agreed; but Tony Benn put out a statement comparing the 'Pentonville Five' to the Tolpuddle Martyrs. The situation seemed to be spiralling out of control. In addition to a national dock strike, there were sympathy stoppages in several other industries, including Fleet Street: for five days there were no national newspapers. On 24 July Vic Feather had an emergency meeting with Heath to demand the suspension of the Act, but Heath refused. The next day the TUC voted for a one-day general strike and – most serious of all for the Government – broke off the tripartite talks on which the Government's whole economic strategy depended.

Rescue this time came from the House of Lords. The immediate cause of the crisis was Lord Denning's maverick judgment in the Court of Appeal. Sitting 'with almost unprecedented speed',[11] the Law Lords – led by none other than Lord Wilberforce – were persuaded to overturn Denning and restore the interpretation of the law originally expounded in the NIRC by Donaldson. Trade unions, they ruled on 26 July, *were* accountable for the conduct of their members. The NIRC immediately reconvened and Donaldson ordered that the 'Pentonville Five' should be released.

This second timely escape aroused a good deal of criticism. The legal propriety of the men's release was highly questionable, since they had been arrested not for the blacking of lorries, which might possibly be regarded as the union's responsibility, but for contempt, which was surely their own. They did not apologise for it, nor did they give any undertakings to obey the court in future. They were released against their will, for frankly political reasons, to avert a national confrontation which threatened the Government. As Professor J.A.G. Griffith has written, the whole episode seemed to confirm suspicions that the NIRC was not a normal court at all, but an instrument of the Government. 'It appeared very much as if the judicial system had bent itself to the needs of the politicians and that, in particular, the principles of the rule of law to which the NIRC earlier paid such respect had been sacrificed to the expediency of the political and economic situation.'[12]

Whether or not the Government actively interfered with the course of justice, there can be no doubt that the Law Lords understood the Government's predicament and knew what was expected of them. The speed of the judgment – their Lordships normally take at least eight weeks – as well as its content strongly supports the impression that Wilberforce and his colleagues were, to say the least, aware of the political dimension of the case. Ostensibly the House of Lords by its endorsement of Donaldson vindicated the NIRC. In reality the whiff of political convenience surrounding its intervention dealt a further blow to its credibility and to the whole concept of using the law to regulate industrial relations.

Meanwhile the dock strike continued. In an effort to resolve the containerisation issue Heath asked his friend Lord Aldington, chairman of the Port of London Authority, representing the employers, and Jack Jones, representing the dockers, to conduct an urgent *ad hoc* enquiry and come up with proposals to compensate the dockers for the loss of their traditional work. But on 27 July the dockers voted to reject the Jones–Aldington interim report. A few days later the Government was driven to declare a State of Emergency – the fourth since 1970. The dispute dragged on for another fortnight before the dockers finally accepted an improved package which effectively guaranteed them a job for life, whether or not there was any work left in the docks for them to do. This was a ludicrous settlement for a Government supposedly concerned to modernise British industry. Though defensible in the very short term as a way of protecting workers from the consequences of economic change, the only effect of trying to preserve obsolete work practices was to hasten the rundown of the historic ports as transport firms transferred their business to smaller docks like Felixstowe which remained outside the Jones–Aldington scheme. It was a measure of Heath's desperation to secure the co-operation of the TGWU at almost any cost that he was willing to underwrite such a transparently uneconomic pay-off.

The docks settlement was a by-product of the wider shift in the Government's attitude to the unions. In his memoirs Jack Jones recalled a critical meeting with Heath and Aldington at Chequers at which the deal was agreed:

> Although I had known that Heath was not unsympathetic to labour, from the days when I had met him as Minister of Labour, the exchange at Chequers strengthened my conviction that he genuinely wanted to get on with working people. There was a marked change in his attitude towards the unions following the early abrasive months of his Government.[13]

The primary purpose of the improved relations which Heath and Armstrong had been working hard to establish over the summer, even while the turmoil over the Industrial Relations Act had been filling the headlines, was to win the unions' help with moderating wage demands. But Feather and his colleagues persisted in demanding the scrapping of the Industrial Relations Act as a condition of co-operation. Initially Heath refused to consider it, insisting that the Act would win acceptance in time. 'The Act is fulfilling its main function,' he assured the Society of Conservative Lawyers on 20 June, at the height of the confusion over Denning's judgment, 'of creating the pressure for a different and more orderly system of handling industrial disputes . . . The application of every law benefits from being argued in the courts . . . What is important now is that the unions should play their part in this process.'[14] Increasingly, however, as the Act proved in practice more and more unworkable, creating more problems than it solved, he began to look more favourably on ways of settling disputes informally without recourse to the clumsy machinery of the Act. Back in June the TUC and CBI had bilaterally started exploring the idea of establishing an independent conciliation body. At the NEDC on 18 July Heath and Barber gave the scheme their blessing, and the next tripartite meeting at Downing Street two weeks later set the seal on a new concordat. While the Act would remain on the Statute Book – Jones and Feather recognised that it was too much to expect the Government to repeal it – Heath agreed to put it effectively 'on ice'. Next day, 3 August, the TUC and the CBI signed an agreement to create what eventually took legislative shape under the succeeding Labour Government as ACAS – the Advisory Conciliation and Arbitration Service. In its embryonic form the new body began work on 1 September.

This was not quite a U-turn, since the Act remained formally in force, and indeed continued to operate inconspicuously in certain areas like cases of unfair dismissal; but as an instrument for the prevention and regulation of major industrial disputes it was to all intents and purposes shelved. Its abandonment also reflected the reversal of the Government's economic strategy as a whole. The Act had been conceived as a substitute for incomes policy, providing a framework of law in which collective wage determination should operate without detailed Government interference. For reasons not directly connected with the Act, this approach had proved inadequate to control inflation and the Government, following various informal attempts to set guidelines, was now moving inexorably back towards the adoption of a statutory incomes policy. In the new economic order that was emerging there was no longer any role for the Industrial Relations Act.

During the negotiations with the TUC over the successive stages of its counter-inflation policy which occupied the rest of the Government's life, Heath and his colleagues were able to use the prospect of amending the Act as a bargaining chip in exchange for concessions on the part of the unions. There was by now virtually universal recognition that it needed amending – not least on the part of the CBI and other employers' organisations to whom the Act was a continual source of trouble. So long as it remained in force it offered a fertile field for maverick individuals like James Goad, who used it to pursue a dispute with the AUEW which refused to admit him as a member, thus effectively denying him a job. The NIRC duly fined the union and, when it refused to pay, sequestrated its assets, provoking a rash of strikes which once again spread the dispute far beyond its original starting point. In another highly publicised saga, also involving the AUEW, a dispute over union recognition at a small engineering firm called ConMech ended with anonymous donors – reputed to be the Newspaper Publishers Association – paying the union's fine (by then £100,000) in order to avert a threatened national engineering strike. By 1973 the employers' organisations were as disillusioned with the working of the Act as the trade unions. Major companies made as little use of it as possible, and were easily persuaded to evade it by adding a clause to collective agreements specifying 'This is not a legally enforceable agreement'. (This was known in the trade as a TINA LEA.) The legal actions which caused so much trouble were all brought by small firms and aggrieved individuals. Campbell Adamson's remark during the February 1974 Election that the Act had only embittered industrial relations and should be repealed accurately reflected the general view of the CBI.

Why, then, did the Industrial Relations Act fail? Essentially because it could have worked only with the consent of the trade unions; and that consent was not forthcoming. The Act was introduced in a political atmosphere already polarised by the unexpected election of a radical Conservative Government following hard on the humiliating abandonment of Labour's attempt to curb the abuse of union power, after which the unions felt bound to be equally obstructive to the Conservatives. It was originally conceived as a substitute for statutory wage control; but in fact by the time the Tories were returned Labour had already abandoned its incomes policy, so that the introduction of the Act coincided with a series of bruising pay disputes. High unemployment, rising to levels not seen in Britain since the 1930s, and cuts in some benefits further antagonised the unions, who believed themselves to be facing a hard-faced, anti-labour Government and easily fell into the rhetoric of class war.

Heath and Carr, both before the election and after, placed unquestioning reliance on the readiness of the British public – including the trade unions – to obey the law, properly passed in fulfilment of its manifesto by an elected Government. But they underestimated the unions' capacity to make the law an ass. In defying the Act, the unions did not actually break the law on any large scale (though some individual trade unionists did). The tactic of non-registration under the Act was perfectly legal: so was TINA LEA. Though the unions, by strikes and demonstrations, extracted maximum mileage from the Government's embarrassment, the TUC cannot be blamed for failing to respect the law when the law was intrinsically un-worthy of respect. It has been convincingly argued by Professor J.A.G. Griffith that the very concept of the NIRC was flawed in principle:

> Many people doubted whether the issues before the Restrictive Practices Court were justiciable. What the NIRC was required to do was to make binding decisions, and to see that they were en-forced, in the context of dispute between trade unions, individual workmen, employers, and employers' federations. This . . . was not a function which judges and courts could perform success-fully.[15]

In 1975, looking back on the NIRC's brief life, Sir John Donaldson described his understanding of its function as the investigation of dis-putes in order to tell the suffering public which of the parties to a dispute was 'right'. 'Those who suffered injustice would then be sup-ported by the courts.'[16] As Professor Griffith has written, however, 'industrial conflicts are not of this kind. They can be solved only by compromise and by the exercise of economic and political strength, not by the application of legal principles and guidelines. This may be unfortunate, but it is the reason why the NIRC was bound to fail.'[17]

Labour opponents of the Act had always maintained that industrial relations were not susceptible to regulation by the courts. The ex-perience of 1970–4 seemed to bear this out. The Labour Party returned to office pledged to repeal the Act, and did so. Paradox-ically, however, the Labour Government passed in its place two new Trade Unions and Labour Relations Acts (1974 and 1975) which, while they abolished the NIRC and all provision for compulsory bal-lots and cooling-off periods, retained and expanded the more positive features of the 1971 Act relating to union recognition and un-fair dismissal, and extended union privileges in respect of closed shop agreements. In this way, Heath and Carr having brought the law into industrial relations, Labour kept it there: Michael Foot did not seek to restore the *status quo ante*, but rather to tilt the balance of

Carr's legislation in the unions' favour, retaining what served the unions' interest and scrapping the rest. As a result, as Michael Moran concluded his study of the Industrial Relations Act in 1977, the conduct of industrial relations changed profoundly, becoming – for a few years – 'much more collectivist than ever before'.

> The sense of confidence created in the trade union movement by the defeat of the Industrial Relations Act . . . means that unions are now much more determined than ever to take a central part in the industrial life of the nation . . . The Government is keenly interested in wage bargaining, the unions in the management of the economy.[18]

Once again, this was the opposite of what Heath and Carr had originally intended. In the medium term, therefore, as well as the short term, the Act appeared in 1977 to have failed comprehensively. Moran's view of the long-term legacy of the Act, however, turned out itself to be short-sighted. In 1979 a Conservative Government returned to office and began to introduce, step by step, a series of new measures – less ambitious than the 1971 Act but more carefully targeted – which steadily reversed Labour's legislation and eventually achieved, by different means, most of what Heath and Carr had hoped to achieve in 1971. In one sense the Acts successively put in place by Jim Prior, Norman Tebbit and Tom King underline the folly of Carr's 'Big Bang' approach. But in another the earlier Act can be seen as a necessary precursor of the later ones. The 1971 Act, its failure, the subsequent entrenchment of union power by Labour and the squalid and anarchic consequences which ultimately followed in the winter of 1978–9, all helped to change public attitudes towards the abuse of union power, making possible for Prior and Margaret Thatcher what was not possible a decade earlier for Carr and Heath (nor for Barbara Castle and Harold Wilson in 1969). The experience of 1971–2 was – in the matter of industrial relations legislation as in several other areas – part of a painful learning curve for the Conservative Party and the country, from which Mrs Thatcher was to be the ultimate beneficiary.

The July opinion polls showed the Conservatives trailing between 8 per cent and 13 per cent behind Labour. With Ireland, Rhodesia, the miners' strike, unemployment, sterling, Maudling's resignation and the dockers it had been a dreadful session – comparable to 1947, which Hugh Dalton dubbed the Attlee Government's *annus horrendus*, or the royal family's *annus horribilis* in 1992. 'The Government', *The Economist* wrote on 12 August, 'has got through to the holidays visibly battered, and if not actually bowed (Mr Heath is not a bowing man), with an appropriately low profile.'[19] The Prime Minister's image of iron determination had been severely dented. Yet the Government had survived and it did seem possible that it had turned the corner. The tripartite talks between ministers, unions and employers were beginning to bear fruit. Interviewed on 'Panorama' on 31 July, Heath gave a performance of unruffled optimism, repudiating any possibility of a crisis election. He maintained this confidence in private, too. On 9 August the chairman of Reed International, Don Ryder, went to Downing Street with a group of industrialists and ended, as he told Cecil King, by 'having a whisky with Ted'.

> Attempting to commiserate with a man in a sea of trouble, he said Ted was no doubt glad the Parliamentary session was over – implying that Ted had had a very rough ride. Ted said that on the whole it had been a good session, as he expected the autumn one would be too. He seemed extremely confident with no worries of any kind![20]

This was indeed the yachtsman relishing the storm.

25

U-Turn: Inflation

T HE last U-turn in the Government's year of reversals was in one
sense the most blatant, in that it contradicted not merely the
spirit of the 1970 manifesto but the clearest possible promise not to
resort again to the statutory control of wages. Yet in another sense it
was the most gradual, merely the logical culmination of the tendency
of the Government's policy towards inflation from the moment it
took office. Heath and his colleagues spent most of 1972 heroically
resisting a statutory pay policy, against the near unanimous advocacy
of the press; yet when it finally came there was a sense of inevitability
about it.

The government had begun a series of regular meetings with the
TUC and, separately, the CBI soon after the settlement of the
miners' strike in March. The NUM's victory appeared to have
smashed beyond repair the informal 'n-1' policy of wage restraint
which up to that point had worked remarkably well. By January
1972 the going rate of pay rises had fallen from an average of around
14 per cent to nearer 9 per cent. Ministers insisted, in the wake of
their humiliation by the miners, that the 27 per cent achieved by the
NUM was a special case; but no one, in or out of the Government,
seriously believed that it would be, unless the Government could
find some better means to persuade the unions to moderate their
claims. Astonishingly, in the event, the miners' award did turn out
to be exceptional. Thirty-three public sector settlements in the following three months averaged only 9 per cent; even the railwaymen
settled for 13 per cent. The private sector average was under 12 per
cent.[1] Thus the impression, widely believed at the time and since,
that the miners precipitated an avalanche of pay claims which ultimately compelled the Government to take statutory powers to stem
it, is a myth. The level of pay rises did not suddenly increase. Nor

did inflation, which in the third quarter of 1972 actually fell to 6·5 per cent, compared with 10 per cent the previous year.[2] The drift to incomes policy was a response not so much to an actual pay explosion as to a threatened one brought on by the Government's industrial policy, specifically its pursuit of 5 per cent growth, of which pay restraint was a natural and necessary ingredient.

Pressure also came from the Government's urgent political need not simply to contain wage inflation but to prevent further bruising strikes which were undermining its authority. The miners' strike really signalled the end of the policy of attempting to control inflation by standing up to successive groups of workers in turn – though there was yet one further confrontation with the railwaymen. Even while the Government still refused to consider suspending or repealing the Industrial Relations Act, the fundamental purpose of the talks with the unions and the CBI was – as Heath made plain in a series of speeches in the spring and early summer – to replace the climate of confrontation with one of conciliation and cooperation. The Act by itself, he told the Scottish Conservative conference in the middle of the rail dispute on 13 May, was not enough: 'We still have to find sensible means by which sensible men can reach sensible agreements before there is any question of industrial action, of courts of law, of cooling-off periods or of ballots.'[3] Or again, in a lunchtime speech to the Press Association on 14 June: 'We are working to find ways of checking more effectively wage claims which go far beyond the rise in prices, far beyond the capacity of any industry to pay, and which are sustained only by the power of those concerned to inflict hardship.'[4]

Heath continued repeatedly and catagorically to deny any intention of taking statutory powers. 'I am frankly puzzled', he told the Press Association, 'by those who urge us to return to policies which clearly and disastrously failed in the past – and which have indeed contributed to many of our present difficulties.'[5] Yet he was already seized by the idea that the Government had a duty to act in some formal sense as the representative of the public in pay negotiations. 'A situation in which an employer and an employee, each armed with monopoly powers, go away and make a bargain at the expense of the ordinary man in the street or the housewife is not acceptable,' he told the Scottish Tories. 'It is certainly not acceptable to a Conservative Government.' 'No Government in its senses', he added, giving a dangerous hostage to fortune, 'wishes to intervene in the details of bargaining between employer and employee. But no Government worthy of the name can abdicate its responsibility to

make sure that the consumer and the community as a whole are protected.'[6] This was a view of the Government's 'responsibility' which
led inexorably to the very conclusion he denied.

For more than a year already the so-called 'Four Wise Men' –
Campbell Adamson of the CBI, Vic Feather of the TUC, Sir
Douglas Allen as head of the Treasury and Sir Frank Figgures of the
NEDC – had been meeting secretly under the auspices of the NEDC
to try to work out the basis of a common approach to the economy.
From early 1972 they were joined by William Armstrong as Heath's
direct representative. It was as a result of these informal soundings
that Feather was able to persuade the most suspicious members of the
TUC General Council to consent to talks with the Government.
'We've got to talk,' he told Jack Jones. 'Ted's coming our way.'[7] But
it was a condition of talking, as Heath admitted to the House of
Commons in July, that there should be no question of statutory
wage control.[8] On this the Government and the unions were in full
agreement. Heath's purpose was to bind the TUC to the Government in the joint operation of a voluntary policy. To achieve this he
was prepared to go well beyond the mere restraint of wages to offer
the unions a role in the whole management of the economy, on what
he believed to be the successful example of West Germany.

But the pressure from within Whitehall, from the Tory back
benches and from Fleet Street for a stronger policy was overwhelming. The Treasury, despite the mixed success of previous policies
under Selwyn Lloyd, Reggie Maudling and Roy Jenkins, had never
ceased to hanker for a restoration of a statutory system and returned
to the argument with renewed conviction after the miners' settlement. Maudling himself, after leaving the Government in July,
restated in *The Times* his longstanding belief in incomes policy.

> I have no doubt that as much as possible should be done by volun-
> tary agreement . . . but the lesson of experience seems to be that
> we must be vigilant to detect the practical limits of voluntary
> action and ready if necessary to extend them by the use of legisla-
> tion. One thing is certain: we cannot just go on as we are.[9]

Independent pundits like Aubrey Jones (the former Tory Minister
and chairman of Labour's Prices and Incomes Board) and Professor
Hugh Clegg urged the case from outside; while in the press the consensus that the Government would sooner or later – and the sooner
the better – be forced to adopt statutory powers stretched from *The
Times* through *The Economist* to the *New Statesman*. A *Times* editorial
on 16 June headlined 'How to Fight Inflation' eloquently embodied

the conventional orthodoxy. Inflation, it believed, was a worldwide consequence of democratic governments bidding for electoral support. The solution lay in educating the electorate to more realistic expectations. 'As inflation is a political problem it can only be solved by political means.' The 'n-1' policy of confrontation with successive groups had led only to humiliating defeats for the Government. 'A statutory incomes policy with powers to delay unreasonable settlements, and powers to impose temporary freezes or cooling-off periods when inflation becomes particularly severe, ought to be a normal part of national economic policy.'

The whole climate of pressure for incomes policy took for granted that the major impetus of inflation came from wages rather than from monetary and other wider economic factors. In fact, wages were only one factor in an inflationary spiral which towards the end of 1972 was being fuelled by new pressures – some outside the control of the unions and Government alike, some actually caused by the Government. On the one hand there was the effect of the floating of the pound in the summer, and the onset of rising world food and commodity prices. On the other, the Government's own massively increased spending in pursuit of growth with social justice – the very policies *The Times* advocated as the essential accompaniments of incomes policy – was far more inflationary than any number of high pay settlements. Heath believed that growth, if he could prevent it all going into wages, would prove 'the most potent of all weapons against inflation'.[10] In reality the policies he pursued to try to promote growth only served to increase the amount of money in circulation, and thus fuelled inflation. But very few commentators realised this at the time; and those few were generally ignored.

The more Heath insisted that he was seeking a voluntary agreement with the unions, the more the commentators doubted that he would get it, or if he did that it would stick. 'It is by legal compulsion that Mr Heath will have to tackle wage inflation in the end,' *The Economist* reiterated on 8 July. 'That end might be only a week or two off.'[11] Such predictions themselves added yet another inflationary pressure, since the anticipation of a possible freeze encouraged unions to put in large claims while the going was good: settlements in the second half of the year, before the axe came down, crept up to an average of 17 per cent.[12] Over the summer, while the Industrial Relations Act remained a stumbling block to close relations, the TUC continued to fight shy of committing itself too far to the Government's embrace. In secret late-night meetings with Heath and William Armstrong in Downing Street Feather tried – in his biographer's words – 'to guide the Prime Minister's hand as to what would be acceptable. Heath asked questions, Feather offered answers, Armstrong listened. Feather came away satisfied that Heath wanted to reach an agreement.'[13] Heath for his part was persuaded that Feather could deliver one. But Feather was ahead of his colleagues on the General Council. Jack Jones and Hugh Scanlon were still thoroughly suspicious. At the beginning of September the Trade Union Congress, meeting at Brighton, once again unanimously rejected the possibility of wage restraint. Nevertheless the unions were bound to keep talking. There was another long session at Chequers on 14 September. Finally, on 26 September, again at Chequers, Heath was ready to put to the TUC and CBI together what he called 'a clear, simple and straightforward basis for a voluntary agreement between the two sides of industry'.[14]

'It is not a freeze,' he insisted. 'It is a carefully worked-out plan for economic growth, for prices, for pay and for pensions in the next twelve months. It has been designed to establish what the country can afford in that period.'[15] The plan had three central elements and a number of negotiable ones. First, the Government renewed its commitment to 5 per cent growth for the next two years. Within that context, the CBI was to accept a 4 per cent limit on price increases of manufactured goods (making 5 per cent in the shops) and the TUC a £2 per week ceiling on pay rises, both to last for one year. In addition there was to be unspecified further help for pensioners – a special concern of Jack Jones – and the low paid, and possibly special 'threshold' pay increases to compensate for the expected one-off rise in the cost of living due to entry into the EEC.

Most of this – the result, as Heath put it, of 'intensive staff work' since July – was specifically designed to be acceptable to the TUC. *The Economist* thought the package astutely calculated to put the unions on the spot.[16] *The Times* likewise praised it as a last chance for democracy: 'We Should Be Mad Not To Do It'.[17] Nevertheless the TUC General Council voted the next day to reject the Government's proposals as 'unacceptable in their present form at this stage'. Though Feather admitted that 'they offer a good deal of fair play to a good many people', they still wanted the Government to come further to meet them on a whole shopping list of additional points: the repeal of the Industrial Relations Act; stricter price controls; controls on the self-employed and dividends; the effect of the Housing Finance Act on rents; and the impact of VAT. This was deeply disappointing to Heath; but he was prepared to keep talking. He was sure that public opinion would eventually force the unions to accept reasonable terms in the national interest. That evening he went on television to appeal above the unions' heads: 'Think nationally. Think of the nation as a whole. Think of these proposals as members of a society that can only beat rising prices if it acts together as one nation.'[18]

A worrying portent was that even so moderate a union leader as Frank Chappell was not willing to accept a limit of £2 a week for his own members. The EETPU had just put in a claim for 37 per cent. A voluntary policy, Chappell remarked, assumed some volunteers and he could not see any of his members offering to oblige. ('Buy Those Candles Now', *The Economist* advised.)[19] Nevertheless Heath remained hopeful that he could bring the TUC to do a deal before the CBI's existing voluntary price curb expired at the end of October. The tripartite discussions were set to resume at Chequers on 16 October. Two days earlier in his closing speech to the Tory party conference at Blackpool, he gave his fullest and frankest account of their progress so far and the great opportunity he still believed they offered.

It was a sombre speech, largely defensive and justificatory in tone, totally lacking in the usual laboured jokes or visionary peroration, but all about uniting the country with the twin virtues of 'firmness and fairness'. Strenuously he defended the Government's record.

> We were returned to office with a clear mandate from the electorate – a mandate to reform the law on industrial relations, to reform the system of housing finance, to reform the social services, to reform the tax system and to reduce taxation. That was a clear mandate to allow the weak to be protected, the poor to be helped and others to be encouraged to expand the wealth of the nation.

'All of this mandate', he insisted, 'has been carried out. Yes – and we were given a mandate to reduce inflation.' That meant bringing down inflationary wage settlements – as they had done. 'We have been given all too little credit for the success we have achieved.'

'Over a wide area of the economy', he recalled, 'there was co-operation. But in parts there was also confrontation.'

> And so it was that Government, management and unions first met to discuss conciliation. As a result new machinery has been created by the employers and the unions. But that is not enough.
>
> We have now, therefore, jointly embarked for the first time in Britain, on the path of working out together how to create and share the nation's wealth for the benefit of all the people. It is an offer to employers and unions to share fully with the Government

the benefits and the obligations involved in running the national economy.

'All the evidence', he believed, 'shows that this approach has the support of the vast majority of the people in Britain', and that included millions of ordinary trade unionists.[20]

In this way the conquest of inflation came to assume for Heath the character of a great national crusade – like getting into Europe but more popular, a potentially unifying cause almost like the war, with himself in the role of Churchill. With entry to the EEC achieved, all his powerful ambition to be the great moderniser and regenerator of his class-ridden, backward-looking, inefficient country came to be concentrated in these talks which he really believed offered a second chance at the new beginning which up to now, in the first two turbulent years since June 1970, had been undermined by the unreasoning antagonism of the trade unions. This time he was determined to win them to his side, and keep them with him, as indispensable partners – 'social partners' – in his great project. Having experienced the ruin they could make of his hopes by their hostility, he set himself to treat them, over long sessions at Downing Street and Chequers, with almost exaggerated deference and consideration.

The talks were accordingly conducted in an atmosphere of remarkable good will – at least on two sides of the triangle. Though formally three-sided, with the Government acting as mediator between the TUC and CBI, the essential business lay between the Government and the unions. Heath was normally flanked by Barber, Carr and sometimes Maurice Macmillan, plus Sir Douglas Allen of the Treasury and the inevitable William Armstrong. The six-man union team was led by Feather with three generally acquiescent 'moderates' – Sir Sidney Greene (NUR), Lord (Alf) Allen (USDAW) and Jack Cooper (GMW) and the two left-wingers, Jack Jones and Hugh Scanlon. Even the last two, though they remained intransigent, quickly attained a real respect for Heath's patience, sincerity and open-mindedness. By comparison the CBI team, led by Campbell Adamson and Michael Clapham, felt somewhat taken for granted. 'One got the growing feeling', Adamson told Phillip Whitehead, 'that [Heath] loved the trade unionists more than he loved the industrialists . . . Not only did he consider them by far the more important partner but . . . he even seemed at times to be able to agree with them more than with his own kind, as it were.'[21]

The warm *rapport* between Heath and Feather, however, probably led both men to misinterpret the other's position. Heath looked to Feather to bring his side along with him in the same way that he

could speak for the Government. But Feather could not in the last resort speak for Jones and Scanlon. For his part Feather was probably
misled by Heath's anxiety to get an agreement into believing that he
had no sticking point. Heath was ready to go a long way – too far,
some of his colleagues and officials sometimes felt – to win the
TUC's co-operation. But in the end he insisted that he was
discussing with the unions, not negotiating. 'Her Majesty's
Government', he once angrily made clear, 'negotiates with no one.'[22]
'We always emphasised', he explained later, 'that these talks were not
carried on as a bargaining session. They were carried on in an endeavour to find a rational way of handling these economic problems
and try to get people to agree upon the figures.'[23] But in the TUC's
language 'trying to get people to agree upon the figures' *meant* negotiating. In the view of the labour historian Eric Wigham, Heath and
Feather 'each probably gave the other the wrong impression'.[24] Jack
Jones was inclined to blame Feather, for 'misleading Heath and Armstrong into thinking the Government could get agreement on wages
and prices without commitment on the wider issues we had raised'.[25]
On the other hand Sir Denis Barnes of the Department of Employment 'never disguised from Heath his view that the gap between the
positions of the Government and the unions could not be closed by
any agreement which would be counter-inflationary'.[26] In these
talks, however, Barnes's advice was unwelcome and went unheeded;
his place was effectively taken by Armstrong, who shared Heath's
passionate belief that reason would eventually prevail if only the facts
were explained to the unions often enough. Essentially Heath
deceived himself by his characteristic conviction that if he wanted
something enough he could get it.

The sticking point was Jones's and Scanlon's unswerving insistence on statutory control of prices – without a parallel legal curb on
wages. Following the 16 October meeting at Chequers, Adamson
was so infuriated by this demand that he publicly denounced it as
falling outside the scope of the talks, which were supposed to be
about voluntary controls.[27] There was indeed such an obvious imbalance in what the TUC was proposing that Heath and his
colleagues found it hard to credit that they continued to insist upon
it. From the Government's point of view it was politically impossible, even if it had been technically practicable. As The Times bluntly
expressed it after the final breakdown: 'Statutory price controls and
voluntary wage controls do not make sense and would not have
passed the House of Commons.'[28] Yet when the talks moved into
their last protracted phase at Downing Street, beginning with a
marathon seventeen-hour session on 26 October, lasting right

through from nine in the morning to the small hours of the following day, the unions would not be budged, as Lord Croham (then Sir Douglas Allen) has described:

> The union leaders, particularly Jones and Scanlon, were determined that there should be no pay policy if there wasn't a freeze on prices . . . But at so many of the discussions the Government explained that it was impossible to control every price and then Jones and Scanlon would insist on every price being controlled.[29]

Another seven-hour session on 30 October, followed by eight hours on 1 November, failed to break the deadlock. Jones continued to raise other issues, notably pensions, and according to his account it was these other matters – pensions, rents, VAT, the Industrial Relations Act – that Heath suddenly ruled out of order, declaring that they were matters for Parliament, not the TUC. 'A rigid posture was suddenly adopted by the Government,' he wrote in 1986. 'Even to this day I am unable to understand why.'[30] Obviously it was because the talks were getting nowhere; someone had eventually to take the initiative in breaking them off. There is no doubt that the unions' intransigence on prices was the real stumbling block.

A measure of the one-sidedness of the discussions can be gained from the recollections of Jones and Scanlon ten years later. Heath, Jones conceded, was 'a very decent man, there's no question about that. He was prepared to be patient and listen to our point of view and our arguments, and, within his limits as a Conservative Prime Minister, I think he did try to respond.' 'I don't know anyone who listened more than he did,' Scanlon acknowledged. 'But I equally don't know anyone who ignored what he'd listened to more than he did.'[31] This adamantine confidence that it was not for them to shift their ground vividly illustrates what Heath was up against in these talks.

His colleagues were amazed at his patience and stamina in searching for agreement for as long as he did. On 1 November Douglas Hurd recorded what he calls a 'typical' entry in his diary:

> At Number Ten again till midnight while the endless tripartite talks go on – or rather don't go on, as it is almost all separate little huddles in every room and passage – including mine. EH hanging on still, against almost every calculation, to his hope of an agreement. Just a small chance he can wear them down.[32]

Outside observers canvassed three theories as to why Heath

dragged the talks out for so long. The first, offered by Cecil King's son – a member of the CBI team – to his father at quite an early stage, was that he was simply desperate for 'almost any agreement' with the TUC.[33] The second, entertained by King himself when the talks were obviously close to breakdown, assumed that Heath was keen to demonstrate how hard he had tried to get an agreement, so as to be able to pin the blame for failure on the unions, and then call an election to win a mandate for his package.[34] The third possibility is that he remained genuinely convinced right up to the end that the unions would eventually come round. Feather and the other TUC leaders were willing: it was only Jones and Scanlon who held out, and he could not believe that they could continue indefinitely to resist his appeal to reason, the pressure of public anxiety about inflation and the obvious best interests of their members. There is probably some truth in the first explanation, and almost certainly a good deal in the second, except that Heath had no intention of calling an election. But the reality is surely that he could not believe that the unions could refuse what he was offering them. In the debate on the Queen's Speech which opened the new session of Parliament on 31 October he spoke again of the 'great prize' of checking inflation which the talks held out; and went on to describe 'another prize which, in the long run, if secured, may prove to be of even greater worth: a more sane, rational and peaceful method of organising the whole of our national economy'.[35]

Robert Carr later maintained that Heath had offered the unions – and to a lesser extent the CBI – an opportunity such as they had never before been afforded even by a Labour Government.

> We really did bring the trade union movement and employers into ... the guts of macroeconomic policy and we really did open the books ... to look at the national income figures, the expected growth in national income over the coming year ... to get common agreement that that was the most growth we could expect and how best to distribute it.[36]

One of the very few organs of opinion consistently and contemptuously hostile to the new thrust of the Government's policies, the *Spectator*, virulently edited since 1970 by George Gale, called this process of trying to fix the economy by cosy agreement with unrepresentative union barons 'syndicalism'.[37] Subsequently it has more often been described as 'corporatism', with pejorative allusion to the fascist governments of Mussolini and Juan Perón. Heath's patient efforts to reach agreement with the two sides of industry eventually led to the so-called 'Social Contract' concluded – but only patchily observed – between the TUC and the Labour Government of Harold Wilson and Michael Foot after February 1974. The collapse of this one-sided experiment in 1975–6 served to discredit all such attempts for some time to come – and retrospectively as well. The fact remains that there was near universal support for Heath's approach in 1972, if only he could have pulled it off, and little confidence that the country could be saved from the abyss by any other means.

By the time the Downing Street talks were finally abandoned on 2 November it was generally accepted that the Government would have no choice but to impose a statutory prices and incomes policy in the short term, while continuing the search for a voluntary policy to succeed it. That was one positive benefit of the protracted discussions. In fact, as *The Economist* suggested on 28 October in an editorial sombrely entitled 'Five Minutes to Twelve', it no longer made much difference. The choice lay between 'a nominally voluntary incomes policy (which will have to be buttressed by statutory policy eventually), or an admittedly statutory policy (based on Mr Heath's intendedly voluntary package)'. Inflation posed a threat to the cohesion of society which must be defused at almost any cost.

> If Mr Heath enforces his package plan, the consequent checking of inflation will be abundantly worth the billion pounds or so a year of emollient economic sillinesses that look like being attached to it. If he does not enforce it, he will have led this inflation nation [sic] down another few steps of its fatal descent.[38]

Heath had gone into the tripartite talks genuinely determined to try to secure agreement to a voluntary policy; but the logic of the immensely detailed discussions led inevitably to the Government taking upon itself the responsibility for imposing a scheme if the unions baulked at sharing it. Whatever had been his hopes before, it now became a question in Heath's mind of a patriotic duty which he could not shirk. Following the near breakdown on 30 October he took the opportunity of an eve-of-session speech to the 1922 Committee to warn the party, and at the same time the unions, of what the Government's response would have to be if the search for a voluntary policy failed: the country, he was confident, 'will respond to firmness and resolution'.[39] Even at this late stage he still hoped that the realisation that the Government was bound to go ahead with a statutory policy if they persisted in refusing to join in a voluntary one would persuade

the TUC to come to terms. When the talks were finally abandoned –
over a cold buffet supper at Downing Street on 2 November – he
emerged to face the press disappointed but determined. 'I am immensely sorry it has not been possible to reach agreement,' he
declared, and no one doubted him. The Government now had 'a
unique responsibility' which it fully accepted. The Cabinet would
meet the next day to decide its course of action and he would make a
statement to the House of Commons after the weekend.[40]

On Monday 6 November, accordingly, he faced the House to put
the best gloss he could on another U-turn. 'The responsibility for
action now rests with the Government,' he repeated. 'We have come
to the conclusion that we have no alternative but to bring in statutory
measures to secure the agreed objectives of economic management in
the light of the proposals discussed in the tripartite talks.' The
Government would legislate immediately for a complete freeze, lasting ninety days (renewable for a possible further sixty), covering
wages and salaries, rents and dividends, and all goods and services
except imports and fresh foods. There would be fines of up to £400
for infringement. In addition, as a gesture to Jack Jones, there would
be a £10 Christmas bonus to pensioners. This would merely be Stage
One, however, of a long-term counter-inflationary policy, a temporary measure to buy time while discussions continued to work out
more permanent and flexible arrangements. The aim, he insisted,
was still to achieve a voluntary policy. Thus there was no reversal of
the Government's consistent purpose. The search for a better way
forward would go on.[41]

'It went well,' Douglas Hurd wrote later. 'Mr Wilson failed to
create an occasion, Mr Powell hissed balefully from behind, and the
Prime Minister easily survived.'[42] Powell's intervention was intended to be deadly:

Does he [the Prime Minister] not know that it is fatal for any
government, party or person to seek to govern in direct opposition to the principles on which they were entrusted with the
right to govern? In introducing a compulsory control on wages
and prices in contravention of the deepest commitments of this
party, has he taken leave of his senses?[43]

Heath simply replied that the Government was elected to act in the
national interest. 'Having disposed of Mr Powell,' *The Times* reported, 'the Prime Minister had a remarkably easy ride,' cheered on
by the great majority of his own side. The one question that momentarily discomfited him came from Roy Jenkins, who asked suavely if

he had abandoned his previously stated view that statutory policy could only make things worse, or was the situation now so bad that he could not think beyond the short term? Heath seemed to wince before countering that the position was quite different from Labour's incomes policy, since his was a policy not for restriction but for growth.[44] Patrick Cosgrave in the *Spectator* commented that Powell's and Jenkins's questions struck at the heart of Heath's two claims to be different from Wilson; first that he was a man of unbending principle, and second that he thought of the long term. Both, Cosgrave suggested, were now 'shattered'.[45] But that was a minority view. Most of the press and the Tory party gave the Government credit for its patient efforts to avoid compulsion, but now that it had become inevitable welcomed the smack of firm government with relief.

The Times as always was most supportive. Pointing out that Heath's ninety-day freeze precisely followed the successful example of President Nixon in the United States, it judged it a good base for controlled expansion on lines that had come very close to being generally agreed. Of course Heath, like Nixon, had changed his mind, but he was right to do so. As for Powell, the paper had no time for his academic theories: 'We can see no evidence that inflation can be controlled simply through the money supply without abandoning full employment as an objective. Nor is Mr Powell prepared to state the price in unemployment we would have to accept.'[46]

It is not quite true, as this rebuttal of Powell shows, that the monetarist analysis of the causes of inflation went entirely by default in 1972. It was just that its proponents were not taken seriously, either at Westminster or in Whitehall. Powell had long ago put himself out on a limb. The *Spectator* was a refuge of choleric fogeys. In the Cabinet Office Professor Alan Walters of the LSE found himself in a minority of one. 'My advice was rejected,' he wrote later, 'and I was relieved of my part-time job.'[47] On 21 October he went public, writing to *The Times* that printing money would not cure unemployment, while 'the attempt to repress the inflation through the imposition of a bureaucratically controlled and regulated rationing system' would only make things worse by reducing the rate of output and growth.[48] On 2 November a leading free-market MP, Richard Body, published a pamphlet entitled *Memorial to the Prime Minister*, arguing the same case.[49] So there were straws in the wind of a new understanding of inflation which would sweep the economic profession over the next decade. But Walters could be written off as an ivory-tower academic, and Body as an isolated maverick. Within the Treasury the orthodox Keynesian consensus remained overwhelmingly dominant. Sir Douglas Allen has confessed that he regarded the publications of the Institute of Economic Affairs as interesting intellectual exercises, not practical politics;[50] Tony Barber only reflected the views of his officials when, in his speech to the Tory conference, he brushed aside those he called 'latterday laissez-faire liberal theorists'.[51] It is of course the Government's responsibility to seek the best advice available, and to distinguish good advice from bad; but it was not wholly ministers' fault that Government thinking in the early 1970s remained largely untouched by concern about money supply.

As with the industrial policy U-turn, most ordinary Tories positively welcomed the Government's return to what they saw as pragmatism and common sense. As *The Economist* noted during the party conference, the party had never found the radical abrasive Heath congenial and much preferred the new consensual model: 'He looks much more like any other Conservative Prime Minister. To the mainstream Tories his new pragmatism on wages and prices is reassuring. The Conservatives are a party of government and they are used to pragmatism.'[52]

The conference came at a critical point in the tripartite talks, just after the TUC's initial rejection of the Government's proposals. Yet 'there were few signs of the promised right-wing revolt against Mr Heath's consensus turn-about'.[53] Powell made his attack not on economic policy but on immigration, and was heavily defeated after an ugly debate. Tony Barber was the hero of the week. As a result of what Ronald Butt in *The Times* called 'his personal achievement at the Treasury (which almost nobody now denies)', the Chancellor was widely reckoned to have moved up to second place in the Government, Heath's likeliest long-term heir.[54] Speaker after speaker was worried about inflation, but representatives appeared satisfied that the Government now had it in hand. Heath in his closing speech returned the compliment, congratulating the conference on its 'moderation . . . decency and . . . good sense' which 'matched the national mood'. 'In your debates and by your votes', he told them, 'you have decisively shown that moderation, clearly expounded and firmly pursued, meets the need of the nation.'[55] Considering what the Government had been through in the last twelve months the conference was indeed an extraordinary success.

The rapid passage of the legislation through Parliament was equally untroubled. Barber introduced the Counter Inflation (Temporary Provisions) Bill on Wednesday 8 November, just two days after Heath's announcement. It was given its Second Reading two days after that, its Third Reading on 20 November, was pushed through the Lords in a single day and received the Royal Assent on

30 November. Rebellion, such as it was, was confined to a tiny handful of principled critics. Powell alone voted against the Bill. John Biffen, Jock Bruce-Gardyne and (on Second Reading only) Neil Marten abstained. That was all. Nicholas Ridley spoke against, but went tamely into the Government lobby – though this, he wrote in his memoirs, was a deliberate 'ploy' to get himself made a member of the Standing Committee, where he and Biffen were able to make difficulties for the Government at the next stage.[56] So did Richard Body and Robin Maxwell-Hyslop, who had strongly denounced the reversal of policy at the 1922 Committee. The Government had a comfortable majority of 35 on Second Reading (307–272). Even a dozen more abstentions would still have posed no threat to the Government's majority. The lack of any significant revolt was due not merely to good whipping by Francis Pym but to strong pressure on potential rebels from their constituencies. The Cabinet had evidently felt some nervousness on this score. As soon as the tripartite talks broke down on 2 November Lord Carrington, who had replaced Peter Thomas as party chairman in April, circulated a strongly worded letter to all constituency chairmen and agents, rehearsing the reasons which had compelled the Government to introduce a statutory freeze and counting on their support. Over the next few days senior ministers made a series of speeches justifying the Government's action. But if there was muttering against the Government, it was more that they had gone on talking to the unions for too long before taking action, rather than ideological objection to the action they had now taken. In an atmosphere of national crisis, heightened by appeals for unity, the pressure on potential rebels not to rock the boat was overwhelming.

Evidence of disquiet did surface, however, in the results of the annual elections for the chairmanship of backbench party committees. On 7 November Nicholas Ridley was elected chairman of the Finance Committee (with Bruce-Gardyne one of two vice-chairmen) and John Biffen chairman of the Industry Committee. More significant still, Edward Du Cann was two weeks later elected chairman of the 1922 Committee. It is difficult to interpret these victories as anything other than a slap in the face for the Government. But they should probably be seen less as evidence that the majority of backbenchers secretly agreed with monetarist criticism of the prices and incomes Bill than as a more generalised protest at the Prime Minister's increasingly authoritarian style and personal remoteness from his supporters. Though the party did not for the most part oppose the Government's specific measures, it was becoming bewildered and dismayed by the perpetual sense of emergency surrounding it;

backbenchers felt themselves treated with scant respect by ministers who seemed to have closer relations with the leaders of the TUC. The election of Ridley and Biffen, and particularly of Du Cann – not himself a popular figure but well known as a *bête noire* of the Prime Minister – to be the principal channel of liaison between the parliamentary party and Number 10 – was more than anything else a signal that the Government's loyal lobby fodder wanted more notice taken of their anxieties.

On 7 December the Government suffered a further blow when the Liberals achieved a spectacular by-election victory in the safe Tory seat of Sutton and Cheam. This was widely interpreted, however, as a middle-class revolt against inflation, which only reinforced the case for strong Government action to control it. Six weeks earlier the Liberals (in the outsize person of Cyril Smith) had taken Rochdale from Labour – an equally remarkable result which seemed to confirm that the Tories had little to fear from the divided and squabbling Opposition. In fact the year ended encouragingly for the Government. Though the unions professed themselves outraged by the Government's unilateral imposition of a freeze and called a number of one-day token strikes to protest at its 'unfairness', the polls indicated strong public support for the policy which appeared, in the short run at least, to have achieved its purpose. (The EETPU settled for 10·5 per cent just before the £2 limit was announced.) Gallup showed Labour's lead falling steadily for four months in a row to only 4·5 per cent by January, while the other polling organisations gave even smaller Labour leads – NOP 1 per cent and ORC 2 per cent.[57] Unemployment had fallen to 745,000, Peter Walker had just announced his massive investment plans for coal and steel and the Government's target of 5 per cent growth was being held. Talks with the TUC and CBI were under way again to try to settle Stage Two of the counter-inflation policy. After all the traumas of 1972, the Government seemed at last to have a built a secure platform from which it could enter the EEC on 1 January 1973 with a real prospect of sustainable expansion.

26

The Prime Minister and His Office

HEATH hugely enjoyed being Prime Minister. Despite all the problems which beset his Government and eventually overwhelmed him, he filled the office – or at least those aspects of it which appealed to him – with relish and even style. Moreover, notwithstanding the failure of many of his policies and the wholesale repudiation of his record by the Tory party under Mrs Thatcher, he was in some important respects a very good Prime Minister. He was exceptional among prime ministers in that he was genuinely more interested in government than in politics. This led him, inevitably, into political difficulties which ultimately brought his downfall. He fatally neglected the skills of communication and presentation of Government policies which are an essential part of leadership. He was criticised for leaning too much on the advice of his officials rather than his colleagues. Yet his faults were only the down side of his very real virtues. In the technical sense, judged from the point of view of how he operated the government machine, Heath ran an exceptionally smooth and well-ordered administration. Whatever view is taken of the policies pursued, his Government handled most of the crises it faced – from the Leila Khaled incident to sensitive financial operations like floating the pound and major constitutional departures like the suspension of Stormont, even the famous U-turns – remarkably skilfully, decisively, without leaks and above all without significant dissent. The legend is now firmly established that Heath was an autocratic Prime Minister. But this picture derives almost entirely from backbench critics who objected – a few of them at the time, most of them only with hindsight – to what the Government had done.[1] His Cabinet colleagues with only one exception have paid tribute to the harmony and unity of the Heath Cabinet. Those who went on to serve under Mrs Thatcher a decade later looked back to 1970–4 as a model period of genuine Cabinet Government.[2]

Heath normally held two Cabinets a week, on Tuesdays and Thursdays. Moreover he made extensive use of properly constituted Cabinet committees to take as many decisions as possible below the level of the Cabinet. In theory this left the Cabinet to decide the broad questions of strategy and direction – assisted by 'collective briefs' from the Think Tank. 'It's the Cabinet all the time', he insisted in an interview with the *Evening Standard* in 1972, 'which is dealing with strategy.'[3] At the same time he was characteristically brisk and businesslike in getting through the agenda: Alec Douglas-Home, who had himself tried to speed up Cabinet procedure in 1963–4, thought him a welcome contrast with Macmillan in this respect;[4] but in practice the opportunity for strategic discussion was reduced. Heath was punctilious in ensuring that major decisions – including the reversals of policy on industrial intervention and inflation – were taken by the Cabinet as a whole. In the case of Peter Walker's massive investment in the steel industry, for example, he called in members of the British Steel board to be interrogated by the full Cabinet before the go ahead was given[5] Of course it very often happened that the essential decision had already been determined so that it would have been difficult in practice for the Cabinet to reverse it: most obviously this was the case with the 1972 Industry Bill. But everything of importance came to Cabinet. Neither Keith Joseph nor Margaret Thatcher – the principal subsequent critics of the U-turns – has ever suggested that they were not fully informed and acquiescent at the time. They blamed themselves for concentrating too exclusively on their own departments, not Heath for steamrollering them.[6]

This is not to say that Heath was not a strong Prime Minister. The British system practically requires a Prime Minister to dominate his Cabinet, and Heath certainly did. Much of his dominance derived from the fact that after Iain Macleod died he had no senior colleagues of equal experience or political weight to match his own: Maudling, Home and Hailsham were all for different reasons effectively marginalised, while on the central economic front Tony Barber simply did not carry the guns to resist Heath's policy even when he was privately unhappy with it. Whitelaw, Carrington, Prior and Carr – his closest colleagues – were all at that time relatively inexperienced at the highest level. But his dominance also derived, more positively, from his own formidable mastery of detail. 'There was never an item on the Cabinet agenda', Peter Walker has written, 'upon which he personally was not exceptionally well briefed, and he always had a barrage of questions to put to the Minister propounding the particular case.'[7] Yet, Willie Whitelaw insists, he did not 'lead from the front', in the sense of laying down at the outset what the conclusion of every discussion was to be, as Mrs Thatcher did. He always wanted to hear every side of the case argued out before he revealed his own hand.[8] He could be brutal in his cross-examination. 'Much of his reputation for obstinacy', in Walker's view, 'was due to this technique of combative questioning. If, however, you managed to sustain your argument in face of his hostile questions, he would accept your case and press it with enthusiasm himself.'[9]

He had a very clear idea of the right way to lead a Cabinet discussion, as he told David Dilks in an interview in 1977:

> The Cabinet is always grateful if the Prime Minister can give an analysis which sets out clearly first of all what has happened, secondly what the problems are, and thirdly what the options are for solutions. If a PM is able to do that and his colleagues respect that he's being fair . . . I think they are immensely grateful for it. I used to try to do that as often as I could.[10]

At his best, Heath could do this superbly. On other occasions, however, when tired or otherwise preoccupied, he could be forbiddingly uncommunicative, as an unnamed colleague told Peter Hennessy:

> In the Cabinet he would sit there glowering and saying practically nothing. The colleagues would watch him to see what impression their words were making. Then he would come down one way or another and that was it. He wasn't terribly interested in the politics of it. He would just do it if it was right and that, in the end, was what got him into trouble.[11]

But this is surely a recollection from the last traumatic months of the Government's life, when the problems were piling up. It should not be allowed to stand for the more confident earlier years.

The essential character of Heath's exercise of power was that he was unquestionably dominant – even autocratic – in certain key areas, but happy to delegate in others. He did not feel the need to interfere across the whole range of Government business, but respected the traditional view that ministers once appointed should be left alone to run their own departments in their own way. On the social side especially – with Keith Joseph at the DHSS, with Mrs Thatcher at Education and Peter Walker at the Department of the Environment – he interfered very little: perhaps in the case of Joseph's reorganisation of the NHS too little. 'The job of a Prime Minister', Heath told David Dilks in 1977, 'is to decide himself in which spheres he is going to concentrate . . . It's then up to him to limit those and so organise himself that he can deal with it.' The three issues on which he chose to concentrate were Europe, Northern Ireland, and prices and incomes policy. These, he believed, were matters on which only the Prime Minister had the authority to deal with the parties concerned.[12] Of course he actually intervened a good deal more than this. He was centrally involved in economic policy, dominating his Chancellor, and in the framing of the Industry Bill, for instance. Nevertheless the point stands, that he limited his direct involvement to certain key areas and left most of his ministers far more autonomy than Mrs Thatcher ever did.

They responded with complete loyalty to him. Not only were there no resignations over policy between 1970 and 1974, there were no leaks. Robert Carr remembers John Junor, the editor of the *Sunday Express*, pressing him over lunch about the Cabinet's unprecedented and, to Fleet Street, frustrating harmony: unlike every other Government Junor could remember, this one did not leak, did not gossip and provided no stories of plots against the Prime Minister.[13] Sir John Hunt, deputy Cabinet Secretary before succeeding Sir Burke Trend in 1973, confirms this picture of unusual comradeship.[14] The Heath Cabinet was to an unusual degree a Cabinet of friends. ('A super Cabinet', is Carr's description.)[15] Heath himself remained always enigmatic. None of his colleagues ever felt that they were personally close to him. Yet the fact is that they were all – almost all – devoted to him. 'Out of school', as Alec Home characteristically put it, he was awkward, but his working relations with his colleagues were excellent. He tried as far as possible to keep the hour 8–9 am free of official papers so that colleagues could ring him 'on an informal basis about every conceivable thing'.[16] Lord Carrington, like Carr, found him 'delightful to work with'. He was, to those who got behind the mask, 'a delightful and happy companion, and at Chequers as well as Downing Street a charming host'. (He could also, Carrington adds, be 'abrasive and sometimes contrived to seem both touchy and autocratic. But in my experience Prime Ministers tend to become autocratic. It is probably necessary.')[17] Francis Pym, who as Chief Whip occupied a particularly sensitive position for most of the Government's life, was another who found him a pleasure to work for: even at the darkest moments he had a sense of humour and the saving perspective of interests beyond politics.[18] Even Mrs Thatcher – retrospectively revealed as the single malcontent in the Cabinet – told the *Evening Standard* with characteristic emphasis in October 1970 that 'The Prime Minister gives you the feeling that he would never do anything behind your back. He would never, never let you down.'[19] It might be added that he never did.*

The same sense of comradeship enthused his personal staff. The number of people working in 10 Downing Street – sixty-four in 1972 – was the same as in Harold Wilson's day. But the atmosphere, warmly recalled by Douglas Hurd, 'was wholly different from the strange enclosed bitterness described by Lady Falkender and by Mr Haines in their books about Mr Wilson's premiership ... There were very few quarrels or intrigues within the house.' This was partly, Hurd writes, 'because of the Prime Minister's personality, but ... also, I think, because we believed that we were part of an enterprise which was attempting something unusual and worthwhile.' Heath's ability to inspire small groups of subordinates working closely with him has already been remarked at previous periods of his career: in the army, in the Whips' office, in the 1961–3 EEC negotiations. Unable though he was to inspire the country, in Downing Street he worked the same magic with his personal staff. More precisely than anyone else, Douglas Hurd has tried to capture the peculiar pleasure of working for Heath:

> Most elusive, and perhaps most difficult for others to believe, was the wit, which was carefully concealed from the rest of the world, but was an essential part of his method of working. It did not take the form of verbal fireworks, let alone a string of jokes. The outrageous statement in a deadpan voice, the sardonic question, the long quizzical silence – these were hard for a newcomer to handle. Some never managed it, usually because they reacted nervously with a torrent of their own words. Those who found that they could slip into this idiom found it rewarding. It was more than just a flavour required to make hard work palatable. It marked an approach to life – tough, humorous, impatient of empty phrases. It was not surprising that Mr Heath found it particularly congenial to discuss the world with French and with Chinese leaders.[21]

The key figure in Heath's private office was his Principal Private Secretary, Robert Armstrong. Heath himself picked Armstrong – the son of his old Oxford musical mentor – partly at least for his

---

* Heath's conduct in this respect contrasted sharply with Mrs Thatcher's practice of using her press secretary, Bernard Ingham, to denigrate her ministers off the record. 'There was never any occasion when I commented on the performance of any Member of the Cabinet,' Donald Maitland has recalled, 'for the very good reason that the Prime Minister never discussed his Cabinet colleagues with me.'[20]

musical ability. He was also of course a superb private secretary, skilful, sympathetic and famously discreet, who went on to become Secretary to the Cabinet in 1979. Unquestionably, however, the bonds of music and family friendship created an exceptionally close – almost paternal/filial – relationship which further contributed to the warmth and camaraderie of the team in Downing Street. Outside working hours Armstrong found time to conduct the Treasury Singers – Edward Boyle thought a performance of the Fauré Requiem which he conducted among the best he had ever heard.[22]

The other principal members of Heath's personal staff in Downing Street were Michael Wolff, nominally a special adviser to the Lord President of the Council (successively Whitelaw, Carr and Prior) but in fact still Heath's chief speechwriter and all-purpose political odd-job man; Timothy Kitson, his PPS, who acted as the Prime Minister's eyes and ears in the House of Commons; Donald Maitland, Press Secretary until May 1973 (when he was appointed British representative at the United Nations and replaced by another Foreign Office man, Robin Haydon, previously High Commissioner in Malawi); and Geoffrey Tucker, director of publicity at Conservative Central Office, who continued to handle his television appearances. These four, with Hurd and Robert Armstrong, each with their differing inputs – plus additional material from others including the playwright Ronald Millar, later used by Mrs Thatcher – formed his regular speechwriting team. His former aide in opposition, David Howell, on the other hand, (now MP for Guildford), was appointed a Parliamentary Secretary in the Cabinet Office but quickly found himself excluded from the inner circle; he was not at all the chief of staff at the heart of an embryo Prime Minister's Department that he had hoped to be. If there was a Prime Minister's Department it was the Think Tank, with Victor Rothschild as its Permanent Secretary enjoying direct access to Heath at all times.

An unsung member of his entourage with a role that went well beyond her official duties was the assistant Press Secretary, Barbara Hosking, whom Heath inherited from Wilson and surprisingly kept on. In addition to helping with less important speeches, she became one of that select group of women whom Heath allowed under his guard to tease, chide and even mother him. She too initially recommended herself to him by her love of music. Very soon he trusted her to handle the musical side of his life, his concert going and his conducting, as well as other more personal attentions: when he conducted the LSO in November 1971 she was able to bully him into buying a more presentable cardigan for the rehearsal photograph. She accompanied him on a number of foreign trips on which he hoped to be able to take in some music – for instance to Germany for the Munich Olympics in 1972. (He was present to see Mary Peters win the gold in the women's 400 metres hurdles, but was too shy to congratulate her. Barbara Hosking had to push him forward.) Like others who once penetrated Heath's reserve, Miss Hosking never found him in the least mysoginist or difficult with women.[23] With all his female staff – secretaries and others – he was meticulously attentive and considerate. He was the same with the wives of some – but not all – his colleagues, notably Jane Prior and Sally Kitson. Many women, like many men, are devoted to him. The truth was that it was only with those very few men and women whom he wholly trusted that he could relax.

This reserve was one reason why he came to lean increasingly, and in the end dangerously, on officials who could pose no threat to him. Although his political colleagues were outstandingly loyal, they all had careers and constituencies and interests of their own, whereas his officials were devoted exclusively to serving him. Heath's greatest satisfaction in Downing Street was the sense of having the Government machine at his command. He was, Peter Hennessy has written, 'the most managerially minded Prime Minister since Attlee', fascinated by the machinery of government for its own sake as much as for what could be done with it.[24] Senior Civil Servants felt that he was at heart one of them, a Permanent Secretary *manqué*. He in turn appreciated their intellectual calibre – unequalled by any of his close colleagues – and enjoyed working with them. As problems mounted up and political nostrums failed he turned increasingly to the Civil Service to come up with new policies and new mechanisms to carry them out. Officials had the further advantage in his eyes that he could command their time. As a bachelor Heath never stopped, except for music or sailing. He thought nothing of summoning Permanent Secretaries to Chequers at the weekend. Sir John Hunt likewise recalls 'endless' meetings in the upstairs flat at Number 10 with Armstrong, Rothschild, Sir Denis Barnes and others poring over detailed formulae for wage and price controls.[25] This is the true contrast with Wilson sitting in the same flat drinking brandy with Marcia Williams, Joe Haines and Gerald Kaufman while they plotted to thwart the disloyalty, real or imagined, of his colleagues. Heath's preferred late-night companions were his senior officials, and one in particular – William Armstrong.

Armstrong's pre-eminence had a good deal to do with the fact that Heath did not see altogether eye to eye with his Cabinet Secretary for the first three years of his Government. Sir Burke Trend, who had held the job since 1963, was the epitome of the smooth, correct, always discreet English mandarin. Heath thought him *too* correct – too objective, too detached, too non-committal. Paradoxically, while he greatly admired the British Civil Service, he also wanted to infuse it with more urgency and practical commitment on what he believed to be the French model. When Trend retired in September 1973 he took the chance to instruct his successor, Sir John Hunt, to introduce a new style of briefing – less Socratic, more functional, clearly setting out first the problem to be solved, then the options and finally a recommendation.[26] Heath's greatest interest was always in problem solving. William Armstrong (no relation of Robert) was a Civil Servant after his own heart. With all the virtues of the classic mandarin – speed of intellect, skill in drafting, the quick dispatch of complex business – he had also an unusual desire to get things done and a politician's tendency to identify emotionally with a particular policy. Already a legend in Whitehall as Joint Permanent Secretary of the Treasury from 1962, he had been moved by Wilson in 1968 to become Head of the Home Civil Service, which cut him off from policy formation and left him understretched. Heath's distrust of the Treasury gave Armstrong the opportunity to come forward as a source of alternative economic advice when it was needed. He was the prime influence on the shaping of the Industry Bill in the spring of 1972 and then, over the summer and autumn, the architect of the counter-inflation policy which dominated the remainder of the Government's life. Vic Feather dubbed him the 'deputy Prime Minister' – a gibe which stung both him and Heath but which stuck, nevertheless, because it was effectively true.[27] There have been other notable partnerships between prime ministers and a favoured Civil Servant – Neville Chamberlain and Sir Horace Wilson, Harold Macmillan and Sir Norman Brook; but that between Heath and Armstrong was particularly close – Eric Roll, who knew both men well, confessed he never understood the 'inwardness' of it.[28] They complemented each other so well – Heath the bureaucratic politician, Armstrong the highly political official – that it was almost as though they swapped roles. Armstrong, however, tended to an apocalyptic view of politics which reinforced the *Götterdämmerung* mentality which overtook much of the Cabinet at the end of 1973. He was not in the end the cool political head Heath needed.

But this was later. The point is that from the very beginning of his Government Heath relied too heavily not only on Armstrong but on the Civil Service as a whole. All prime ministers are inclined to get cut off from reality, overwhelmed by the ceaseless demands of the job and increasingly blinkered by a narrow view of the world as seen from Whitehall. But Heath by temperament was particularly prone to this danger, and in the end he paid for it. Douglas Hurd blames himself in part, diagnosing a lack of political advice at the heart of the Government at moments of crisis which the Civil Service could not – and could not have been expected to – fill. As head of Heath's private office, he tried in the final weeks to bring together the various political advisers attached to individual ministers to offer a co-ordinated political perspective. But by then it was too late: they were too few and Heath was virtually out of reach.[29] Willie Whitelaw was struck by the change in Heath on his return to Westminster after eighteen months in Northern Ireland at the beginning of December 1973. The 'Armstrong syndrome', he found, was a reality; prices and incomes policy had become an 'obsession' and Heath was hopelessly caught up in its labyrinthine complexity.[30] Heath's downfall is a lesson to prime ministers of the consequences of an over-administrative approach to government which paid too little attention to the political dimension of national leadership.

Aspiring to be a Prime Minister above politics, Heath paid perhaps disproportionate attention to the non-political functions of the premiership. In deliberate reversal of the style of his predecessor, he approached the constitutional area of appointments and patronage, his relations with the Queen and the Church and the BBC, his responsibility for national defence, nuclear weapons and the security services very seriously. Yet in his concern to be punctilious and non-partisan, he tended to the conservative and safe. He made no very bad appointments of permanent secretaries, ambassadors or bishops, but he made few strikingly imaginative ones either. There was – certainly compared with Mrs Thatcher's permanently embattled régime in the 1980s – relatively little antagonism between Heath's Downing Street and the Church, the judges or the Civil Service; but equally it can be said that on these powerful bastions of the Establishment he left no very enduring mark.

He was said to take a close interest in MI5 and MI6, but did nothing to open them up to political accountability or tackle the abuses that were already rampant within them. In the Commons debate after the exposure of Anthony Blunt in 1979 he revealed that he had been informed about Blunt's treachery when he took office in 1970, but was not told the details until 1973. He insisted that the security services had operated perfectly properly during his premiership: he particularly praised their work in collecting the evidence for Home's expulsion of Soviet diplomats in 1971.[31] But the reality is that he did not in truth enquire very closely but left the supervision of the undercover agencies to Victor Rothschild – a former MI6 agent himself who was still hand in glove with some of the key players in MI5, including Peter Wright. Rothschild was liable to be gravely embarrassed if the truth about Blunt came out and seems to have persuaded Heath that the Government might fall if he were publicly exposed. Remembering Profumo, Heath had a powerful fear of scandal and agreed to maintain the cover up.[32]

The appointment of Sir Michael ('Jumbo') Hanley as head of MI5, according to Peter Wright, led to 'a decisive shift inside MI5 towards domestic concerns' – that is towards spying on home-grown subversives: left-wing trade unionists, radical journalists, revolutionary students and the IRA. With the Government apparently facing an orchestrated challenge to its authority on several fronts, 'intelligence on domestic subversion became the overriding priority'.[33] To his credit, Heath was unimpressed by this sort of stuff. When he first became Tory leader in 1965 MI5 had solemnly circulated stories that he was a closet homosexual – he was supposed to have had an affair with a Third Secretary at the Swedish Embassy.[34] Now when Wright named the TGWU leader Jack Jones as a Communist, on the ground that he had fought with the International Brigade in the Spanish Civil War, Heath – who had been in Spain at the same time and had met Jones there – was robustly dismissive.[35] This did not deter Rothschild, however, who continued to encourage Wright to feed sensational allegations about Soviet penetration of the unions and the Labour party direct to the Prime Minister.

No doubt Heath genuinely believed that he had firm control of the security agencies between 1970 and 1974; but Peter Wright's account in *Spycatcher* – which Mrs Thatcher and Robert Armstrong went to such lengths to try to suppress in the 1980s – reveals that elements within MI5 were totally out of political control by 1974. Rothschild was a brilliant choice as head of the 'Think Tank', but he was too compromised to have been entrusted with oversight of MI5. In later years Heath came to recognise that he had known much less than he had imagined at the time. In a debate on the reform of the Official Secrets Act in 1988 he deplored the cult of secrecy which surrounded intelligence activity in the United Kingdom – by comparison with the greater openness of the United States – and added ironically: 'I am beginning to realise that there is a period of history in which I moved, about which I shall never know the truth. I find that disconcerting and, to say the least, worrying.'[36]

Heath's relations with the Queen were correct but cool. It is paradoxical that recent Labour prime ministers have enjoyed a much greater *rapport* with Her Majesty than Conservative ones: both Wilson and Callaghan got on with her much more easily than either

Heath or Mrs Thatcher. In part it was simply that Heath's normal reserve was increased by the formality with which he naturally approached his weekly audiences at the Palace. Her Majesty must often have been reminded of Queen Victoria's complaint that Gladstone spoke to her 'as if I were a public meeting'. Wilson, like Disraeli, was both more flattering and more amusing. But there was also a specific source of friction in their different attitudes to the Commonwealth, to which the Queen is famously devoted. She was deeply unhappy with Heath's undisguised disrespect for the institution in general and most African leaders in particular, and greatly upset by the rows which disfigured the 1971 Commonwealth conference in Singapore. While Heath treated them with contempt, she could not be expected to relish African threats to 'expel' Britain from the Commonwealth. Two years later she positively insisted, against Heath's wishes, on attending the next meeting in Ottawa.[37]

On a number of lesser matters too, she may have found Heath's modernising zeal alarming. He was impatient to do away with some survivals of royal flummery, like the wearing of morning dress for the State Opening of Parliament; and he was notably parsimonious in the award of honours. Without actually abolishing them, he maintained Wilson's embargo on creating new hereditary peerages. At the same time, however, beneath the radical instincts which Heath brought to some superficial aspects of national life, his attitude to the ancient institutions of the country, including the monarchy, was marked by a fundamental conservatism. He came into office to change attitudes within the existing political and economic structure; he neither posed the personal challenge which Mrs Thatcher's predominance latterly offered to the Queen's primacy nor threatened the social fabric as she did by her determined assault on established institutions. In many essential respects Heath was a thorough traditionalist.

The hallmark of his premiership was his determination to restore the dignity to the office of Prime Minister which he believed had been tarnished by Harold Wilson. Of course there was a good deal of self-gratification in this. It flattered his vanity to create at Number 10 and Chequers a suitably elegant stage for the sort of Prime Minister he wanted to be. He used official entertaining to glorify not only the office and the country but also, by association, himself. By holding dinners and receptions at Number 10 for distinguished artists and musicians as well as visiting heads of state, by inviting leading international musicians to play for him on state occasions, it could be said that he simply indulged his own taste at public expense. Yet he did genuinely believe that by making Number 10 a showcase for British excellence in the arts – where Wilson had filled it with pop singers and TV stars – he was setting a new standard and promoting an enhanced image of Britain. By opening his homes, as he believed, to a wide variety of people from every period of his life – members of his old regiment, his Bexley constituency workers, his former secretaries and members of his private office, even Tory MPs – he imagined that he was sharing his own good fortune and making himself a figurehead of national unity and interdependence. There was a convenient congruence of private and public ambition.

Like no other Prime Minister before or since, Heath tried to use the patronage of his office to promote the arts. In addition to his regular use of music on state occasions, and his private celebration of such events as William Walton's seventieth birthday in March 1972 (for which he organised a memorable concert in Downing Street, in the midst of the Government's accumulating crises), the biggest expression of this impulse was the nationwide 'Fanfare for Europe' intended to celebrate Britain's entry into the EC. For political reasons it was something of a damp squib, but it was the most characteristic expression of Heath's ambition for his premiership. Indeed its failure to arouse national rejoicing makes it an apt symbol of the failure of his premiership. Other grandiose aspirations fell by the wayside, too. Like the successive presidents of the Fifth Republic, from de Gaulle to Mitterrand, Heath wanted to leave behind him some visible monuments of lasting national benefit to stand as his memorial. He was bitterly disappointed that both the Channel Tunnel and the Maplin airport development were scrapped by Labour in 1974.

He also wanted to be remembered as the Prime Minister who cleaned up London, as de Gaulle had cleaned up Paris. This gave rise to an uncharacteristic eruption in November 1972 when his car was caught in a traffic jam in Parliament Square. He was forced to walk the short distance from the Commons to Downing Street, and arrived late for a reception in honour of his cleaning programme. To the great amusement of the press, which was delighted at the spectacle of the Prime Minister discovering for himself what Londoners experienced every day, he insisted on an embarrassed Robert Armstrong telephoning the Conservative leader of the GLC, Desmond Plummer, then and there, to ask what he was going to do about it. Plummer was on a visit to Japan at the time, where it was early morning, but Heath – purple with fury – would brook no delay.[38] This was a very rare occasion when he allowed a display of private feeling to break through his normally aloof manner. To his staff it was quite unexpected and inexplicable: at the most difficult moments he normally kept quite calm.[39] The episode attracted a lot of satirical comment at the time, but it probably did him no harm with the public: it might have done him good, indeed, if he had blown his top more often.

Heath as Prime Minister did not only command music to be played for him: he continued to perform it himself, both privately and – on one famous occasion – in public. Often he would play the piano late at night, to express either jubilation – as after the signing of the EC Treaty – or frustration at the way things had gone during the day. Lacking a wife to share his triumphs and condole with his disappointments, his piano filled some of the same need. Sometimes colleagues or secretaries would be kept waiting while he vented his feelings in music: then he would turn back abruptly to the business in hand.

He continued every Christmas to conduct his annual carol concert in Broadstairs, which had now become a national event. But he had never yet conducted a symphony orchestra in public, until in November 1971 he was invited to do so by André Previn as part of the centenary celebrations of the LSO. It was an unprecedented and quite daunting thing for a serving Prime Minister to do. But he seized the opportunity with alacrity. At one level it was, as he confessed in *Music*, the fulfilment of a longstanding private fantasy. But he also saw Previn's invitation as the chance to make a political statement. Just as he had wanted to win the Sydney–Hobart yacht race to prove to the Australians that the British were not so decadent as they imagined, so now he wanted to reach out to his own countrymen, as Prime Minister, through music. The piece he chose to play was Elgar's concert overture *Cockaigne* (subtitled 'In London Town'). It is a bravura piece, suitable for a gala occasion. But more than that, it is a quintessentially English piece which expressed his ambition for the British people. Some years before he had heard it brilliantly played at the Festival Hall by Leonard Bernstein and the New York Philharmonic. Their performance, as he remembered it, 'contrasted strikingly with the rather lifeless, ironed-out versions to which we had become accustomed'.

> That night I felt that we needed to have this kind of faith in ourselves that this vigorous, buoyant American interpretation seemed to embody. As Prime Minister I wanted the British to regain their former pride and ebullience, not through empty pomp and circumstance but through the knowledge that deep down they were capable of coping with whatever might come. Perhaps the right performance of *Cockaigne* could show the way.

It was a fanciful idea, perhaps, but in his own mind he made an explicit link between 'the sort of performance I wanted from the orchestra' and 'the performance I was trying to elicit from the nation'.[40]

He had very little time with the orchestra. He was allotted just an hour in the Festival Hall at 4.30 pm the day before the concert, plus another quarter of an hour at 10 am the next morning. For the rest of the day he went back to being Prime Minister: a two-hour Cabinet meeting at 11 am, Prime Minister's Questions, a debate on Northern Ireland and some more meetings at Number 10 before he could change into his white tie and go back to the Festival Hall. He admits to having been acutely nervous. Among other hazards to which ordinary conductors are not exposed, Heath had received several death threats: there were a dozen detectives scattered throughout the hall, but he still had to turn his back on the audience and put the risk out of his mind.[41] Both Previn, who was conducting the rest of the concert, and Isaac Stern, who was playing the Sibelius Violin Concerto in the second half, looked in to his dressing room to wish him luck. Then Previn introduced him with some witty remarks, and he was off. The performance went pretty well. His own account of it in *Music* is ecstatic: 'I realized how fully the orchestra, together and as individuals, were responding to me. I felt I could do almost anything I wanted with them. Behind me, the concentration of the audience was intense. They, too, would follow wherever we led . . . I found myself laughing with delight.'[42]

The critics liked it too, or at least were more than polite. His performance was relatively slow – at 16 minutes 20 seconds nearly 2 minutes longer than Barbirolli (he found the time-lag in conducting a big orchestra greater than he had expected) – but it was well phrased and, after a hesitant start, as vigorous as he had hoped. 'There were some impressive climaxes,' Joan Chissell wrote in *The Times*, pretending to be reviewing a young débutant. 'Response to small *tenuto* markings in second subject lyricism showed understanding of Edwardian style . . . We could well hear more of this Mr Edward Heath.'[43] At the champagne reception after the concert Heath could feel that he had pulled off a unique musical/political event with considerable success. The whole concert was recorded, and the record sold well all round the world – though Heath was miffed to find that Previn had re-recorded his parts of the programme the following week. Politically, perhaps, the spectacle of the Prime Minister conducting an orchestra did not have the impact he might have hoped; musically, however, it was a fruitful début. He did not have time over the next two years to repeat the performance as Prime Minister, but it established a precedent which he was able to exploit increasingly in the long years after he left office. It was undoubtedly one of the high points of his life.

At the same time he was determined not to be deflected from his other high-level relaxation, sailing. When he became Prime Minister, he recalled in *Sailing*, he was advised that he would have to give up ocean racing for security reasons. 'This I flatly refused to do.'[44] Having only so recently taken it up, having invested so much in *Morning Cloud* and having tasted international success in the Sydney–Hobart race, he was not going to suspend it for the duration of what he intended to be a long premiership. As Prime Minister even more than as Leader of the Opposition, he believed it was important to keep himself fresh by cultivating a strenuous hobby that took him right away from politics. Over the summer months he arranged his schedule, so far as possible, around the racing calendar: 'April till September I sail. We never do anything except race. If you are racing hard you can't be thinking about anything else. You come back quite different and refreshed.'[45]

He ruled out absolutely having security personnel on board *Morning Cloud*. 'Even if there were two available who were first-class sailors it would mean getting rid of two of my existing crew, which was not on.'[46] Neither would he agree to a frigate following behind creating a wash for other competitors, nor to a helicopter overhead. Eventually it was agreed that no close security was needed; he did, however, have to carry special radio equipment to keep him in touch with London in the event of political emergencies. He could then always be winched off by helicopter if the need arose. 'But what is happening to *Morning Cloud* while all this is going on?' asked Owen Parker. 'Oh, I suppose she drops all her sails and heaves to while we carry out our operation,' was the reply. 'What, and lose precious minutes of racing time while you take the skipper off? Not on your life! If you want the skipper we'll push him off in a rubber dinghy and you can pick him up from there while we go on racing.'[47] Fortunately the need never did arise, though on several occasions political exigencies prevented him joining the crew when he had planned to do so. The crucial summit with President Pompidou in May 1971 which cleared the way for British entry into the EEC overran its schedule, so that Heath was unable to get away. Later that summer the crisis at Upper Clyde Shipbuilders prevented him getting to the first race of Cowes Week. Labour kept the House sitting for an emergency debate, and Wilson gleefully demanded that Heath should be present throughout. ('Of course,' Heath wrote, 'the House of Commons took priority.')[48] More seriously, the 1973 Commonwealth conference in Ottawa seriously curtailed his participation in that year's Admiral Cup.

Two years earlier he had captained the British team to victory. This was the next big prize on which he set his sights after the Sydney–Hobart race. The original *Morning Cloud* was too small to be eligible, so Heath commissioned a new boat for the 1971 season, six feet longer and – following the advice of Uffa Fox – built in wood. Like her predecessor, the second *Morning Cloud* was designed by Olin Stephens but built (as was politically obligatory) in Britain. Once again Heath held intensive discussions over the previous autumn – on Sunday evenings at Chequers – working out with the crew their exact specifications. ('We decided that the new *Morning Cloud* must be a racing machine . . . Anything unnecessary must be sacrificed.')[49] They also designed a new type of winch, which Heath boasted in *Sailing* proved an export winner for Britain. The second *Morning Cloud* was launched (by his stepmother again) in April 1971. The whole enlarged crew of eight, Heath included, somehow managed a full week's sailing over Easter to get used to her; and in June they were selected for the three-boat British team. Heath, naturally, was invited to be captain. He took the job very seriously, inviting all four crews (including the reserve boat) down to Chequers in July to foster team spirit and work out tactics. The Cup – contested that year by sixteen nations – consists of a cross-Channel race (Southsea to Le Havre and back) and two shorter races during Cowes Week, culminating in the 600-mile Fastnet Race. After three races, with only the Fastnet to go, the British held a narrow lead over the Australians, with the Americans third. *Morning Cloud* had a difficult race: her spinnaker poles came away from the mast and she only limped back to Plymouth with an improvised rig. But she secured a place, while another British boat, *Cervantes*, won her class. Britain won the Cup, with 825 points to the Australians' 782 and the Americans' 719.

'It was a moving moment for me to have captained the British team which regained the foremost racing trophy in the world,' Heath wrote. 'It was a great triumph for Britain. I was glad to have played my part.'[50] In fact it was an unprecedented feat for a serving Prime Minister to have captained his national team in an international sporting event, let alone won it. In later years, whenever sport was under discussion in the Commons, he never missed an opportunity to remind the House of his unique credentials. Yet he has never received the recognition this exceptional achievement deserved.

At the end of that year *Morning Cloud* was chosen for the Southern Cross Cup in Australia; but Heath could not go. Skippered in his absence by Sammy Sampson, however, *Morning Cloud* nearly won the Sydney–Hobart race again: she won her class, and the crew came back to Number 10 to celebrate. Political crises notwithstanding, they enjoyed another successful season in 1972, winning among other things the 'Round the Island' race in Cowes Week for the second year running; but now Heath was looking to the 1973 Admiral's Cup and planning yet a third *Morning Cloud* to defend the trophy won in 1971. He was particularly anxious to win the Fastnet Race. Accordingly *Morning Cloud* III – bigger again than her predecessors at 45 feet and three times as expensive – was built specifically to withstand heavy weather, with 'three skins of mahogany, one on top of the other, at different angles, giving her great strength'. Unfortunately the Fastnet that year was sailed in exceptionally still conditions; it was, Heath wrote in 1975, 'the most frustrating ocean race in which I have so far taken part'.[51] Having been obliged to miss the first three races because of the Commonwealth conference – he was not captain this time – he flew straight back from Ottawa to take the helm. But *Morning Cloud* was continually becalmed, took twenty-four hours to cover the last fourteen miles in heavy fog and finished nowhere: by hugging the coast this time he chose the wrong tactics. The Germans took the Admiral's Cup for the first time. In compensation Heath won the 'Round the Island' race for an unprecedented third successive year. But that was the limit of his successes while Prime Minister. At the end of the year he could not bear to let *Morning Cloud* compete again in the Sydney–Hobart without him: and a few weeks later he was out of office.

Heath sailed primarily for the excitement and satisfaction of sailing. But at the same time he unquestionably saw his sailing, like his music, as a means of reinforcing his image as a national statesman. Alas, the British public did not see him in that way. Since 1964 they had grown used to a full-time Prime Minister interested only in politics. There is a strong puritanical streak in British voters which disapproves of politicians relaxing: they were singularly unimpressed by Heath's amazing versatility. Indeed, as Bernard Levin suggested, it was perhaps his very versatility which enraged his critics: they could not write him off as a mindless hearty when he also played the piano, nor could they sneer at him as a cerebral aesthete when he also sailed.[52] But both his leisure activities were routinely portrayed in the press as élitist pursuits of no interest to the ordinary man. When *Morning Cloud* was selected for the 1971 Admiral's Cup Dennis Skinner and Eric Heffer denounced him in the Commons for pursuing his 'rich man's sport' while cutting the living standards of the unemployed; Wilson joined in with gibes that he was a 'part-time Prime

Minister'.[53] The newspapers speculated avidly about how much each new *Morning Cloud* had cost.* As a result of such carping, he derived little or no political dividend from either music or sailing. The political message which he hoped to convey by his example never got across.

At the heart of the failure of Heath's Government was a failure of communication. Had the electorate been able to share his passion for music and admire his nautical achievements, had they understood that the goal of his political ambition was to open the same opportunities to more of his fellow countrymen, they might have been readier to respond to his warnings and lectures about inflation, investment and national unity. In fact he never succeeded in making the connection. He continued to be perceived – ironically – as a remote, one-dimensional technocrat, lacking ordinary human feelings. This view of him was most cruelly propagated by Auberon Waugh in *Private Eye*:

> Grocer, as anyone who has ever stood within ten yards of him will know perfectly well, is not human at all. He is a wax-work. Many are even beginning to suspect as much from watching his television appearances.
>
> This is the secret of the amazingly unattractive blue eyes, the awful, stretched waxy grin, the heaving shoulders and the appalling suntan. Even scientists admit that something has now gone wrong with the pigmentation . . .
>
> The stark truth now appears. Grocer the waxwork, like Frankenstein's monster before him, has run amok.[55]

The Labour party and progressive commentators – to say nothing of the vigorous student movement and all the proliferating pseudo-revolutionary parties – had no difficulty portraying Heath as the most reactionary Prime Minister in living memory, a hard-faced throwback to the 1930s deliberately using high unemployment to attack the living standards of the workers and grind the faces of the poor. This is Paul Johnson in the *New Statesman* in February 1972:

> His hatred of the poor, the unlucky, the lazy, the undeserving, is absolutely genuine. When he dilates on these categories of the nation, he cannot keep the contempt from his voice. To him

---

* *Morning Cloud* II cost £21,000. But since he sold *Morning Cloud* I for twice the £7,500 he had paid for her, he had only £6,000 to find.[54]

failure is not merely a sign of incompetence but of immorality, to be punished in the next world but especially in this.[56]

This caricature not only bore no resemblance to the reality of the Government's social policy; it was a travesty of Heath's attitude towards the poor and the unlucky. (He was certainly impatient of the lazy, but then it was more often managers, not the unemployed, that he had in his sights.) His colleagues knew that it was a travesty. But at the same time they understood why it gained currency. Even in private Heath could be desperately clumsy, insensitive and rude. Those who worked closely with him knew that behind his intimidating manner – a mixture of shyness and single-mindedness – the 'real' Ted Heath was passionate, humorous and eloquent. But they were driven to despair by his inability – or, as it seemed, his refusal – to show that softer side of himself to the public. Whether he spoke to the party, to Parliament, to the press or to the country he invariably put on his 'official' manner, which was impersonal, pompous and banal. Once in Downing Street he wilfully neglected, even spurned, the mediating channels which in a modern democracy connect the Government with the people – Parliament, the press and television. In a Prime Minister who above all wanted to change national attitudes this was perverse in the extreme. But it was a function of his administrative, Civil Service-centred view of government, coupled with his vision of himself as a national leader, above the party fray.

He paid too little attention, first of all, to Parliament. He had never, of course, been much of a parliamentarian. As a result of his long silence in the Whips' office, he had never learned to speak in the House until he was a Minister with a Civil Service brief to speak to. In Opposition he had endured a difficult time, being repeatedly worsted by Wilson even when Labour was trailing in the polls. As Prime Minister he enjoyed the boot being on the other foot. With the authority of office he quickly established mastery over his former tormentor: as the *Guardian* sketch writer Norman Shrapnel observed in April 1972, 'roles are reversed with a vengeance'. But Heath made no attempt to charm or flatter the House; rather he simply battered it with facts and dealt brusquely with interrupters, even from his own side, 'dropping his voice with an arrogance his victims find unbearable, and shattering them with his quiet throwaway lines'. 'That underweening manner', Shrapnel commented, conveyed 'the reverse of modesty'.[57] He frequently showed a discourtesy to the House which alienated Tory backbenchers as much as it did Labour. An early example was the Government's heavy-handed determination to have Selwyn Lloyd elected Speaker in December 1970 – a decision traditionally the prerogative of the House as a whole. Further offence was given by Heath's innovation of presidential-style press conferences to make major policy announcements, instead of giving the details first to Parliament. The truth was that Heath's view of Parliament – influenced by his years as Chief Whip – was starkly functional: its job was to support the elected Government and pass whatever legislation was put before it without demur. For four years he had delivered Eden's and Macmillan's majorities on the nail: now it was Pym's job to do the same for him, and the job of Tory MPs to vote as they were told. He never gave the House the sense that any view but the Government's mattered, thereby storing up a resentment that was not forgotten when his mastery had passed.

He equally antagonised Fleet Street by treating journalists from the start as predatory vultures to be kept at a distance. The humiliation he had suffered over the five years since 1965, when he was repeatedly written off as an embarrassing failure, had hardened his heart. His unexpected victory in 1970 convinced him that he did not need the press. He had in fact some steady support, notably from Alastair Burnet on *The Economist* and William Rees-Mogg at *The Times*. (Ian Trethowan, another loyal friend, was at that time out of the journalistic line as Managing Director of BBC Radio.) But he regarded most journalists as basically Labour supporters – 'Maoists' – even if they no longer fawned on Wilson.[58] Heath set his face deliberately against anything that smacked of 'image-building'. The facts, he honestly believed, would then speak for themselves. He gave Donald Maitland, his Press Secretary, all the information he asked for but no direction on how to use it.[59] He himself was at his best with the correspondents of the foreign press, especially the French and the Americans, whom he had got to know in 1960–3. They were intelligent, well-informed and serious and he could open his mind to them frankly in small groups on a high level, without fear of being misrepresented. But he had a low opinion of the Fleet Street lobby correspondents, and did not bother to hide it: there were too many of them, they were not so intelligent or serious, and he felt they were always looking to distort him. He disliked the system of unattributable briefing on which the lobby operated and tried to change it in favour of on-the-record briefing. The lobby refused, insisting that they must retain discretion as to what was on the record and what was off it. There followed a tussle of wills between Downing Street and the lobby, with Maitland at one point proposing to shift the weekly briefings from Number 10 to the Welsh Office, before a compromise was agreed – daily briefings from Pym at the House of

Commons and a weekly one in Downing Street – and the old system was resumed much as before. From Heath's point of view this episode was an honourable attempt to fulfil his promises of more open government: he would give the press the facts and they would report them. To the press, however, it was simply a recipe for Government control of information.[60]

In February 1972, following the public relations disaster of the miners' strike, a rumour surfaced in the *Observer* that in order to improve the presentation of Government policy Heath was considering appointing William Rees-Mogg a Cabinet Minister with a seat in the Lords. The idea was said to be that Rees-Mogg should play a role similar to that which William Deedes had played as Minister without Portfolio under Macmillan.[61] The story was immediately denied on both sides, and nothing came of it; but it is clear that feelers were put out, and that Rees-Mogg – a politician *manqué* – was seriously tempted.[62] In fact from Heath's point of view Rees-Mogg was surely of more use as editor of *The Times*, where until his startling conversion to monetarism in late 1973 he continued to give the Government enthusiastic support, than he could ever have been as a minister. But the recognition that the Government was failing to present its case effectively was correct. Unfortunately Heath reacted as he always did when an intended appointment leaked, and dropped the whole idea, with the result that responsibility for Government information continued to fall between departments, with no single minister charged with pulling it together.

The introduction of prime ministerial press conferences amid the marble and chandeliers of Lancaster House was, for Heath, another way of trying to get around the lobby system. Visibly modelled on General de Gaulle's famous audiences at the Elysée – the first significantly followed Heath's successful summit with President Pompidou in the summer of 1971 – they were criticised for bypassing Parliament and betraying quasi-presidential ambitions. In an interview with the *Evening Standard* in June 1972 Heath defended them, saying that he was expected to give press conferences whenever he travelled out of London: why not in London, when he could talk to the international and not just the parochial British press, which reported only what suited its line? He firmly believed that he was practising more open government by addressing the world's press at Lancaster House than he did by talking off the record to the lobby. When asked whether the House of Commons did not expect him to report to Parliament first, he replied, 'I'm not sure they do any longer.'[63]

He held three further press conferences to announce successive stages of the counter-inflation policy. These could scarcely be presented as occasions of huge international interest: but the grand surroundings lent a solemnity to the announcement which was intended to demonstrate that the defeat of inflation was a national goal transcending party politics. This of course was not something the Opposition accepted: so another of Heath's well-intentioned innovations was derided as an un-British and unconstitutional *folie de grandeur*. They have never been revived, not even by Margaret Thatcher.*

The same desire to speak directly to the public without the distorting mediation of journalists led to a parallel wariness of television. It was not, as Douglas Hurd lamented, that Heath could not communicate effectively on television when he tried. As Leader of the Opposition he had no alternative but to use television to put himself across: with hard work and the help of Michael Wolff and Geoffrey Tucker he became much better at it, so that by the 1970 election his broadcasts were surprisingly successful. Once in office, however, he seemed deliberately to turn his back on the skills which had helped to put him there. The advertising men and film makers like Bryan Forbes and Dick Clement who had helped give him a softer image were thanked with a party at Number 10 and then shown the door.[64] With the authority of a Prime Minister he no longer felt he needed such packaging. 'The facts' would suffice. As part of his conscious rejection of 'instant government' he did not appear on television at all for three months. Then he gave an interview to Alastair Burnet for 'This Week' in September, followed by 'Panorama' with Robin Day and Nicholas Harman in October. On both programmes he immediately adopted a peremptory style designed to get over what he wanted to say: he was not prepared to be pressed by interviewers to answer questions he did not want to answer, and reacted angrily when they persisted. 'What I find infinitely boring', he complained, 'is when a questioner keeps on and on about the same subject, when you have already told him "no" . . . That is incompetence by the interviewer.'[65] Whenever he allowed himself to be interviewed the pattern was the same.

He could still be very good on television when he respected his interviewer or took enough trouble to make his points well. He did a superb interview with Michael Charlton for 'Panorama', filmed in the bar of the Metropole hotel in Brussels following the signature of the EEC accession treaty. At his moment of triumph, back on ground familiar from his 1961–3 negotiations, he was relaxed and

* Mrs Thatcher took to staging *ad hoc* press conferences in the street outside 10 Downing Street instead: a still more presidential procedure – continued by John Major – which in practice gives the scrum of journalists still less chance to ask serious questions.

even inspirational. In different vein, he made a first-class ministerial broadcast to explain the introduction of direct rule in Ulster, serious and eloquent. His broadcasts on domestic crises, however, when he tried to appeal for national unity following the 1972 miners' strike or the introduction of the incomes policy, failed to carry the same conviction. As Douglas Hurd noted, he forgot all the lessons the advertising men had taught him. Under pressure he had no time to work on his presentation and too much that he wanted to say to say it clearly. As a result, the argument would be 'lost in a mass of detail . . . Mr Heath believed that people deserved the evidence, and, by God, they were going to get it.' Through lack of practice as much as anything else – he made no television broadcast at all between November 1972 and October 1973 – his voice reverted to the stiff, wooden quality of which Geoffrey Tucker had begun to cure him. His vocabulary became stilted and his tone defensive. 'Instead of speaking to people, Mr Heath would too often speak at them.'[66] By the last months of his Government his language had become so technical as to be virtually incomprehensible and Heath himself too exhausted to speak clearly.[67]

Like all other modern prime ministers, Heath became bitterly convinced that the media were biased against him, relentlessly determined to misrepresent and undermine everything he was trying to do. Most prime ministers, however, begin by seeking to woo the press and television and only end by trying to punish them; Heath evolved rather the other way. He was deliberately distant and formal with journalists from the beginning. To his credit he did not lavish knighthoods on friendly editors or even on their proprietors. He believed that by publishing White and Green Papers he was practising open government: much of the reason that Fleet Street thought his Government secretive was simply that – compared with its predecessor – it did not leak. There was misunderstanding of motives on both sides. But inevitably, as things began to go wrong and the Government's popularity plummeted, he began to blame the media for the public's failure to support what he was trying to do. As early as June 1971 Jonathan Aitken in the *Evening Standard* noted his tendency to blame 'the commentators' for his inability to change the nation's attitudes.[68] In an interview with the same paper a year later he condemned the press for blurring fact and comment, and wished there was still a 'paper of record' such as *The Times* used to be.[69] By October 1973 a typically lurid comment by Paul Johnson on his first television interview for nearly a year picked up the same frustration, now turning to anger. (Colour television was still a novelty in the early 1970s.)

His florid, Kodachrome features flushed with indignation, his voice oscillating between petulance and unconcealed rage, he bids a sceptical nation follow him down the twists and turns of his labyrinthine policies. The shoulders rarely heave with laughter these days . . . A great many things have gone wrong with Mr Heath's administration, and he holds a great many people responsible.[70]

Unlike both Wilson before him and some of Mrs Thatcher's ministers in the 1980s, however, Heath generally avoided getting drawn into direct conflict with the BBC. There was one confrontation in January 1972 when Reggie Maudling put pressure on the Governors to cancel a three-hour 'special' on the deteriorating Northern Ireland situation, which the Government believed would be 'unhelpful'. But the Governors stood firm, and Heath personally remained aloof. It was a part of his style as Prime Minister – one reason why he so resented being harried by impertinent interviewers – that he considered it beneath the dignity of his office to engage in public recriminations with the BBC, furiously though he often resented its programmes in private. Later that year he made a notably graceful speech on the occasion of the Corporation's fiftieth anniversary; then in December he appointed a first-class chairman in Sir Michael Swann, a distinguished biologist with no political affiliation. The contrast with Wilson's mischievously vengeful switch of Lord Hill from ITV five years before was pointed and deliberate.[71]

Only at the end, and very much out of character, did Heath suddenly make a desperate effort to take journalists into his confidence and persuade the BBC to be 'responsible'. He summoned editors to Downing Street to try to make them understand the vital national importance of upholding the Government's incomes policy. But editors who had felt themselves cold-shouldered hitherto were not so easily cajoled. 'To them it was clear that Heath was not interested in their views, only in the need for better understanding of his.'[72] Having belatedly made the effort to woo the press Heath now felt betrayed.

Heath blamed the media for failing to report the Government properly. Yet even on his own terms he did not make it easy for them. It was not only that he did not take journalists into his confidence, time his announcements to catch their deadlines or feed them titbits off the record. If he wanted them to report what he said, he needed to find words that were worth reporting. But one of the oddest things about Heath was his chronic inability to develop an efficient procedure for evolving speeches, which remained as chaotic in Government as it had been in Opposition. Douglas Hurd devotes several pages of his ringside 'sketch' of the 1970–4 Government to the agony of drafting speeches, which constituted the principal drawback counterbalancing the satisfactions of working for Heath. In all the domestic crises of his Government, when the Government's authority was challenged by the unions, over pay on the one hand and the Industrial Relations Act on the other, it should have been the highest priority to mobilise and retain public support. A good speech or broadcast at the vital moment could have been the most effective weapon in the Government's hands. Yet too often Heath wasted the opportunity of putting his case to the nation. 'We often puzzled over this,' Hurd reflected.

> It was not that Heath failed to understand the importance of speeches. He knew the magic of words, and often talked about it. In fact I believe this was the trouble. He was a perfectionist. We served up adequate drafts, which he saw were only adequate. It would take him hours to transform them – but the necessary hours were never there. They were swamped by meetings, and yet more meetings. So at the last minute the adequate draft was looked at, reluctantly approved, and unenthusiastically delivered. Next time, of course, would be different; but next time turned out much the same. It was a mystery and a tragedy that a man who possessed such a talent of exposition could not find a working method which turned it to good effect.[73]

27

The Prime Minister and His Party

HEATH'S ambition to be seen as a national leader inevitably made for strains within the Conservative party. Under the pressure of office, prime ministers of every party sooner or later lose touch with their supporters, however earnest their intentions at the outset. It happened to Wilson, for all his skill at party management, and it eventually happened to Mrs Thatcher, though not for some years. Heath had in fact little feeling for the Tory party as a living political organism. He had little sympathy with the passions and prejudices of the retired majors, small businessmen and hatted ladies who organised fêtes and stuffed envelopes in the constituencies and demanded tougher penalties for criminals every year at conference. To him the party was merely a necessary vehicle for the achievement of his political goals, a source of organisational manpower to beat Labour, the embodiment of a high political tradition to which he saw himself the heir, but not a mirror or microcosm of public attitudes of which he, in governing the country, should take serious account, any more than Churchill or Macmillan had ever done. Unlike Macmillan, however, he made little effort to disguise his disdain, as Jim Prior noted somewhat devastatingly in his memoirs:

> I am quite certain that the more Ted saw of the party establishment . . . the more he became convinced that he could beat them, as of course he did; and the more successful he became, the more he came to despise them as well . . . He never liked them, and this was reciprocated.[1]

He was in a strong position at first, following his unexpected victory in 1970. Despite all the sniping and sneering he had won the election after all, and the party was in his debt. The result was universally recognised as his personal triumph, and since what the Tory party demands above all is victory he had won himself a respite for the moment to do with the party as he liked. Setting out to govern in the national interest as he saw it, he felt he could afford to ignore the mutterings of the suburbs and the shires. In fact they remained remarkably loyal to him: there was very little outright opposition to any of his Government's policies up to 1974. But the party was increasingly alarmed and bewildered, not so much by the reversals of policy – there was on the contrary a good deal of relief when the Government finally grasped the nettle of incomes policy in 1972 – as by ministers' apparent loss of grip. Tories in the country were worried – by inflation, by strikes, by terrorism, by the loss of by-elections to the Liberals; in addition the party in Parliament felt increasingly rebuffed by Heath's personal remoteness. It is easy in retrospect to trace the parliamentary party's rejection of Heath back well before 1974–5. Yet it is important not to exaggerate the level of discontent. Heath was never loved, but his determination was re-spected and he was supported so long as he was Prime Minister. His cool relations with the party would not have mattered if he had not lost the 1974 election.

A measure of the low priority he gave to party management after the election was his appointment of the Welsh Secretary, Peter Thomas, as party chairman. Thomas probably had more time for the job than any other Cabinet Minister, but 'though a genial and helpful person [he] was notably uninspiring'.[2] The following year, to inject more energy into modernising the organisation, Heath appointed Sara Morrison as vice-chairman. Propelled (to her own surprise) into Central Office in 1971, she was widely seen as Heath's woman, appointed to bring the party organisation under closer central con-trol. The specific reform that attracted most criticism was that – following the recommendations of the Chelmer Report in 1972 – the 'approved list' of prospective candidates for parliamentary seats was pruned, while at least four selected candidates not on the 'approved list' were disowned.[3] In the context of allegations of improper pres-sure being applied to the constituencies of anti-Marketeers to dissuade them from voting against EEC entry, this tightening up of selection procedure was portrayed as a sinister infringement of local autonomy and the right of dissent.[4] In fact it was just another stage in the professionalisation of the party already begun by Du Cann and Barber as the amateur tradition was progressively weeded out be-tween the 1960s and the 1980s. Under Mrs Thatcher, local autonomy was formally restored, but the procedure for getting on the 'approved list' became ever harder.

In his reshuffle of April 1972, following the appointment of Willie Whitelaw to Northern Ireland, Heath replaced Thomas with Peter Carrington. This was an even worse appointment. While it was certainly the case that a more senior figure than Thomas was needed at Central Office to steady the party after the trauma of the miners' strike, Carrington was not the man for the job. For one thing he held a particularly onerous portfolio at the Department of Defence, which was concerned primarily with foreign affairs and entailed a lot of overseas travelling. Second, as a member of the House of Lords since the age of nineteen, he had never had a constituency or fought an election in his life: he had no first-hand experience of the democratic process or the party battle he was now expected to direct. Finally his patrician manner, at once gloomy and supercilious, was not calculated to inspire the faithful. Lacking the ability to communicate himself, Heath badly needed a party chairman who could inspire the troops, as Lord Hailsham had done in Macmillan's day and Cecil Parkinson and Norman Tebbit were able to do under Mrs Thatcher. Carrington was not such a man. Morale, he recalled in his memoirs, was 'pretty low' when he took over in the summer of 1972. Even within Central Office he encountered 'what seemed to me a wholly unacceptable degree of resistance and backbiting . . . often touching the Leader of the party . . . personally'. Yet he seemed to accept this situation with something close to resignation:

> The Chairman of the party can't do a great deal, but he can do his best to show a cheerfulness he may not feel, he can try to enthuse those about him, he can work to see that the Government's achievements are described as widely and convincingly as possible, and that the Opposition's promises and criticisms are deflated.

Carrington's languid manner fitted him for none of these tasks. Not surprisingly he concludes, lamely, 'I did not find this a period of my life which brought great happiness or any strong sensation of success.'[5]

It was the sense that the Government was running away from problems that most upset the party stalwarts. What most ordinary Conservatives longed for, far more than ideological purity, was *strong* government. They largely welcomed the fact that the Government was at last taking firm action to control inflation; but they had been disturbed by the Government's successive humiliations at the hands of union militants, and they were bewildered by the unchecked tide, even under a Tory Government, of crime, comprehensive schools, pornography and every sort of permissiveness and immorality. The right was already upset by the abandonment of the Tories' traditional allies in Ulster and Rhodesia: the last straw was the Government's insistence on its duty to admit 50,000 Ugandan Asians expelled by Idi Amin. 'If faced with a choice between its friends and principles on the one hand and the expediency of placating its opponents on the other,' Norman Tebbit recalled, 'the government seemed always to dump its friends in an effort to buy its enemies.'[6] There were pressing reasons in every case, but they added up to a cumulative sense of a Government that was disappointing Conservative expectations right across the political agenda. In addition, the party was consistently trailing in the polls and, for a time in 1973 – following the loss of the Sutton, Ely, Ripon and Berwick by-elections – actually fell into third place behind the Liberals.

Yet by the time of the 1973 conference there were signs that the party was rallying. Under the shadow of the coming election, expected in another year or eighteen months, the Tories' traditional instinct of loyalty came into play. Economically and industrially the worst seemed to be over. The economy was growing fast, the incomes policy was holding and the oil crisis had not yet struck. It helped the Government that the opposition to its policies in every sphere – immigration, Ulster, Rhodesia and the economy (as well as Europe) – was spearheaded by Enoch Powell, whose loathing for Heath seemed to most Tories more pathological than rational; he already gave the impression of wanting to see a Tory defeat. When Tony Barber went for Powell in the most personal terms at Blackpool he was loudly cheered. In their hearts many Tories sympathised with parts of Powell's critique, but they were repelled by the sardonic glee with which he pursued it. The representatives relieved their feelings by defeating the platform on capital punishment, and pressed Home hard to recognise Rhodesia; but on the central economic issue anxiety took the form of motions criticising the poor presentation of Government policy, not the policy itself. After the shocks of the past two years the party desperately wanted reassurance that the Government knew where it was going and was back in control: but from the Prime Minister down there seemed to be no one in the Cabinet who could provide it. They were all good chaps doing their best, but not one of them could speak to the party's soul. Though the ultimate responsibility lay at the top, it was a collective failure of communication.

The Government's dangerous detachment from the party was clearly visible to those in Downing Street and Whitehall whose job it was to try to bridge the gap. After all the careful preparation in opposition, several of the leading members of the Conservative Research Department were seconded into Whitehall as political advisers. But they were isolated in their respective departments and quickly became absorbed into the Government machine. After June 1970 coherent CRD input into the Government ceased virtually overnight. Sir Michael Fraser used to lunch with Victor Rothschild, but that was all: the CRD was not invited to the Think Tank presentations at Chequers. At work from 1971 on laying the groundwork for the next manifesto, whenever it should be needed, the CRD was constantly frustrated by 'the strange reluctance of Ministers to act like politicians'.[7] Heath in particular seemed deliberately to set himself against listening to party advice, preferring to rely on the Civil Service; and this set the tone for the whole administration. 'The real problem', Michael Wolff minuted in November 1971, 'is to get Ministers continuously to present their work within a political framework': ministerial broadcasts, he complained, were so lacking in political content they might have been written by Civil Servants. Douglas Hurd warned Heath of 'a general impression at all levels within the party that this administration is . . . less politically conscious than its Conservative predecessor'.[8] The problem was that Heath seemed to like it that way.

Still less did Heath encourage much input to the Government from the parliamentary party. He had been in his own day a much more skilful and sensitive Chief Whip than party legend remembered; but now, as Prime Minister, he felt that he was entitled to command loyalty. He forgot that times, and specifically the composition of the Tory party, had changed; and also perhaps that he had received a good deal more help from Macmillan, circulating in the Smoking Room, then he ever gave to Pym. (When Heath did try to show himself he tended to alienate more good will than he engendered: it became part of Pym's task to keep the Prime Minister away from the House as much as possible.) In fact Pym, too, was a sensitive and flexible Chief Whip whose emollient style did a lot to smooth ruffled feathers when the Government's changes of direction and Heath's remoteness put it under strain. He indignantly rejects suggestions that he ran a 'tough' disciplinary régime. On the contrary, he firmly believes that he held the party together through a difficult period and carried a lot of controversial legislation without major dissension precisely by operating on a fairly loose rein, letting the dissenters have their say and not trying to suppress them;[9] and both the statistical evidence and the testimony of a number of disaffected MPs support him.

Philip Norton has demonstrated that the 1970–4 Government saw an unprecedented level of dissent expressed in the form of votes cast (or not cast) against the Government by its own backbenchers. The proportion of divisions in which one or more Tory MPs voted against the Government was 18 per cent in 1970–4 as a whole (and 29 per cent for 1971–4), compared with 11 per cent in 1959–64 and insignificant numbers in other postwar parliaments, including 1966–70. This clearly argues a strong undertow of dissatisfaction in the party, reflecting a wide range of grievances which Professor Norton has dissected. On the other hand the great majority of those divisions each involved no more than a handful of rebels. Despite a relatively small majority – 30 in 1970, reduced to just 16 by 1974 – the Government suffered only 6 defeats on the floor of the House, all on relatively minor issues.[10] The conclusion is that, by allowing an unprecedented degree of licence, Pym contained the expression of dissent pretty successfully. Had he tried to crack the whip – as Heath on more than one occasion wanted – he would almost certainly have provoked a higher level of rebellion.

Virtually the only votes before which potential rebels were subjected to serious arm-twisting were those on Europe; and even then the degree of pressure was greatly exaggerated by Powell and the diehard anti-Marketeers for their own purposes. In fact Pym's relations with known dissidents, on Europe as on other issues, were perfectly cordial: when he knew that a Member's mind was made up he would leave him alone, so long as he was kept informed of his intentions. 'He does not bully,' Julian Critchley wrote in 1971, 'nor does he jolly people along. He has charm and persistence.'[11] Most tellingly, Norman Tebbit believes that 'Francis was one of the truly great Chief Whips, perhaps too good ... for Ted Heath's own good.'

> A few more rebellions from those of us who believed then in the policies which have since proved successful might have saved the Heath Government from at least some of its follies and the 1974 defeat ... In fact ... we did little more than grumble and worry in private.[12]

Perhaps there is something in the point that Pym was too good a Chief Whip for the Government's good; or rather that he was better than Heath deserved, for the fault was Heath's that he did not listen enough to what Pym was telling him. As Chief Whip himself between 1957 and 1959 he had seen Macmillan practically every day; Pym sometimes saw Heath no more than once a week. Several times

Pym had to stand up to Heath and insist that he be allowed to do the job his own way.[13] When Heath did listen – notably on the question of allowing a free vote on the crucial European vote – Pym was usually right. Pym kept in close contact with Timothy Kitson – they used to hunt together – and with Heath's private office. He kept in touch with Conservative Central Office, and up to November 1972 with the chairman of the 1922 Committee, Sir Harry Legge-Bourke – though not so closely thereafter with Edward Du Cann. He did his best to represent to Heath the views of the parliamentary party. But the impression came back very strongly to the party that Heath did not want to know.

Heath did not give his backbenchers the sense that they were part of a team engaged in a common enterprise. In the early days of the Government's life they were prepared to accept this as simply the man's style: the price, as David Wood wrote in *The Times* in January 1972, of his 'extraordinary inner strength. Conservative backbenchers praise him for his consistency . . . and directness . . . Some junior ministers see him as remote and presidential, but they do not argue that they would necessarily prefer him to be otherwise.'[14]

During 1972, however, it became harder to discern his consistency, and with the institution of his Lancaster House press conferences he became more presidential. The party wanted to be told what was going on, wanted to be consulted about legislation in advance, wanted to be listened to. By the end of the year, on the contrary, Patrick Cosgrave was describing in the *Spectator* 'the growing conviction of Tory backbenchers that they are in the hands of, and regarded as the servants of, a Leader who has little regard for their affection or their principles, and who considers them as cattle to be driven through the gates of the lobby'.[15] Older Members recalled the way Heath had driven the abolition of Resale Price Maintenance through the House in 1964: he once claimed to have learned from that episode, but if so he had forgotten again. In his own way, Heath did try to carry the party with him: he took immense pains over speeches to the 1922 Committee, but the effect was still of a general lecturing his troops rather than a political leader seeking to share his understanding of what, with their support, he was trying to achieve. Likewise he tried to make them feel involved by inviting them in groups to Downing Street. 'The backbenchers all complain that I've never kept in touch with them,' he told Jim Prior in 1974. 'But more of them came to Number Ten whilst I was Prime Minister than ever before.' 'I am certain that this was true,' Prior reflected. 'He was a very generous host, but being a good host is about more than choosing good wine and good food. It's also about enjoyment and talking, making people feel happy and at ease. He was never very good at that.'[16] He was quite unable to give the impression that he had invited them to Number 10 because he wanted to know what they thought about things. Those who tried to tell him found him unresponsive and testy, if not downright rude. He appeared stubborn, arrogant, increasingly intolerant of even constructive criticism or dissent, 'a little Napoleon' who treated critics as enemies to be trampled underfoot.[17] By 1973 he seemed to many of his own MPs as embattled, paranoid and isolated as Richard Nixon holed up in the White House.

They expressed their frustration by electing Nicholas Ridley and John Biffen to chair the backbench Finance and Industry Committees. The support for two such prominent neo-liberals gave warning of the form which discontent with Heath was liable to take if it developed. More immediately significant was the election of Edward Du Cann as chairman of the 1922 Committee. The chairman of the 1922 is normally a senior and lifelong backbencher, a worthy old knight of the shires without ministerial ambitions. Du Cann was not only a former minister, but at forty-eight was still ambitious, indeed seen by some as a potential leader. While it was by no means clear at any point in his career what Du Cann stood for – apart from abstaining on the critical European vote in 1971 he rarely voiced any specific criticism of the Government – the one thing that was well known to every backbencher was that he loathed Heath and Heath equally loathed him: as the most obvious candidate for Cabinet office excluded from the Government in 1970 he had become a symbol of opposition to the Prime Minister second only to Enoch Powell. 'The prospect that he will be conveying the sentiments of backbenchers to the party managers cannot be particularly welcome in Downing Street,' wrote David Watt in the *Financial Times*, with some understatement, 'but the fact that it is welcome in the lobbies says something interesting about the sentiments he will be expected to convey.'[18] The choice of Du Cann as the chosen mouthpiece of the back benches was just about as clear a warning shot across Heath's bows as it is possible to imagine.

Inevitably Heath took Du Cann's election as an unfriendly act which only reinforced his conviction that the Executive of the 1922 was dominated by his enemies, disappointed men excluded from the Government who for that reason wished him only ill. The members of the Executive did not in fact all start out as his enemies: Nigel Fisher, for instance, was no right-winger but a longstanding 'One Nation' man, at that moment writing the biography of Iain Macleod. But Heath's attitude antagonised them, as Fisher recalled: 'He treated most of his Parliamentary colleagues with ill-concealed contempt, especially the Executive, whose meetings with him appeared to us to be no more than a necessary nuisance so far as he was concerned.' Fisher described one meeting at which he tried to raise the party's concern about the poor presentation of Government policy. Heath brushed him aside, muttering that 'he understood the press officers in some Government departments were inadequate'.

I suggested that good public relations come from the top and that the criticism was not of the public relations officers but of senior ministers in Whitehall and of No 10 Downing Street itself. He looked askance, grunted crossly, 'That is a point of view', and turned abruptly in his chair to begin a discussion on a different subject.[19]

'Macmillan always listened, but Heath did not,' complained the diehard anti-Marketeer and persistent dissident, Richard Body. 'And if the Prime Minister did not listen to you, then the only alternative was to vote against the Government.'[20] Throughout the 1970 Parliament there were regular right-wing rebellions on such predictably emotive issues as Rhodesia, Northern Ireland and the admission of the Ugandan Asians. There was very little opposition in the voting lobby, however, to the central measures of the Government's economic policies: there was little positive enthusiasm, some grumbling, but only a handful of known mavericks voted against the Government, nor was there ever any apprehension of a serious revolt on the economic front. Tory MPs, wrote Ronald Butt in *The Times* in March 1973, 'content themselves with little jokes about voting for socialism as they tramp through the lobbies to vote for the Counter-inflation Bill, but they vote for it just the same . . . If Tory hearts seem more Powellite these days, the Tory feet march solidly for Mr Heath.'[21]

The Government's defeats occurred on lesser issues, when back-benchers felt free to express their frustration without endangering the Government's central strategy. The two most significant were on the revised immigration rules in November 1972, intended to take account of the obligations of EEC membership but seen by both the anti-Market and the pro-Commonwealth factions as favouring 'aliens' over Commonwealth citizens; and the Maplin Development Bill in June 1973. On immigration the Government refused to give ground to strong representations and was defeated by thirty-five votes; only seven hardline anti-Marketeers, led by Powell, actually voted against the Government, but at least another forty-nine abstained, despite Pym's best efforts on a three-line whip. The unexpected size of this revolt was widely seen as having less to do with the new rules themselves than with Heath's unresponsive style of leadership. 'There was considerable feeling at Westminster last night', *The Times* reported, 'that the Prime Minister must no longer seek to ride roughshod over his backbenchers.'[22] The Government, wrote David Watt, 'was presuming too easily on the loyalty of the lobby, and their willingness to march up and down hill at the shortest bark of command'.[23]

Aside from the EEC and Rhodesia, the scale of parliamentary dissent in 1972–3 had less to do with specific policies than with accumulating personal resentment of Heath. Once again, Norton has analysed the various grievances feeding this resentment. First, there was generalised resentment of his personal rudeness: his inability to give the time of day to Tory Members – some of long standing – when he passed them in the lobby; his failure to compliment them on a good speech or enquire about their health, their wives or their constituencies; his refusal to acknowledge them as anything but lobby fodder. The long-suffering Timothy Kitson was for ever following behind him with an oil can trying to pacify outraged Members, apologising for the boorish behaviour of his boss.[24] This human failure, more than any other factor – extraordinary in a former Chief Whip who had once been famed for his 'skill in human relationships' – left him with no reservoir of affection or personal loyalty to draw on when he needed it. On the contrary, as Humphrey Berkeley noted as early as 1972: 'His incapacity to show gratitude for services rendered is building up a stockpile of resentment.'[25]

On top of this personal insensitivity and the wider political neglect of the views of the party as a whole, there were two further specific grievances which his backbenchers held against Heath concerning his use of patronage. It was alleged, first, that he failed sufficiently to promote talent within the Government, and second, that he was parsimonious in the allocation of honours. These charges deserve examination. As regards the first, it is true that there was an unusually low turnover of ministers, compared with previous Tory Governments. Out of a total of 338 eligible MPs, only 96 held office at any time during the 4 years, with only 14 leaving the Government for any reason at all, including death and resignation, and only 28 joining it. Once in, you generally stayed in; and more important, once overlooked your chances of advancement were small. While it can be argued that this degree of stability actually made for better government than the restless game of musical chairs on which politicians thrive, it exacerbated the sense of frustration among ambitious Tory MPs. Moreover it was believed in the bars and tea rooms that no one who had ever voted against the Government received promotion. The result was that those who had done so once – this applied particularly to the anti-Marketeers – believed that they had nothing to lose by doing so again: there was thus a self-reinforcing pattern about some of the dissent in 1972–3. Those who were denied advancement tended to disparage their more fortunate colleagues as yes men or toadies. Norton quotes one unnamed MP, subsequently promoted by Mrs Thatcher, who 'felt a certain resentment at seeing men, whom he considered to be less able than himself, being given office'.[26] Clearly this is the perennial complaint of the disappointed office seeker: it is unavoidable, and there is no reason at all to think it is always justified. The trouble was that Heath's refusal to play musical chairs left a dangerously high proportion of his MPs disappointed.

At Cabinet level, the criticism that Heath deliberately surrounded himself with mediocrities was unfair: it was not his fault that he had lost several major figures (Macleod, Maudling, Powell, Boyle), nor that the available replacements (Barber, Whitelaw, Carrington, Prior) were relatively inexperienced. There was in truth only one neglected contender for whose inclusion a plausible case could be made out, and that was Edward Du Cann. His supporters once sent a petition to Heath urging that he be invited to join the Government;[27] but his claim rested more on his known antagonism to the Prime Minister than on his overwhelming merits. It would certainly have shown broad-mindedness for Heath to have included him, but he can scarcely be blamed for declining to do so. Below the Cabinet, however, it was a different story. There were plenty of able people – John Biffen was perhaps the most prominent – whom he would have been wise to give office. For one thing, office silences potential critics; at the same time the sense that the *possibility* of office was open to all would have made for a happier and more biddable parliamentary party. But these were low political calculations, which were foreign to Heath's high-minded view of his office. He had left his knowledge of human nature behind him when he left the Whips' office.

The same applied to honours, the traditional sweeteners by which Tory prime ministers compensate those they have not promoted. Between 1951 and 1964 Churchill, Eden, Macmillan and Home between them conferred on their grateful backbenchers no fewer than 53 peerages (most of them hereditary), 40 baronetcies and 84 knighthoods. Heath had seen this system at close hand and he set his face against it.

He did reverse Wilson's supposed embargo on awarding political honours at all. But between 1970 and 1974 only two Tory back-benchers received peerages – life peerages – and only a handful got knighthoods. This was in many ways admirable: he regarded titles as part of the anachronistic legacy of class-consciousness he was trying to sweep away and he despised those who craved them. It was admirable; but it was bad party management. Pym urged him re-peatedly to be more generous; so did Whitelaw, Carrington and others. The expectation that a career of public service will be crowned with an appropriate gong – peerage, knighthood or OBE, depending on the level reached – is part of what Tory politics is about: Heath's refusal to gratify these expectations set him in oppo-sition to some of the party's deepest instincts. Not many MPs, perhaps, would have gone so far as the 'confidential source' who told Philip Norton that he voted against Heath in 1975 specifically because of his failure to restore hereditary honours;[28] but the drought of patronage certainly contributed to the parliamentary party's discontent. Significantly, Mrs Thatcher took care not to make the same mistake: however far she sometimes strained the loyalty of her MPs, she kept them happy for fifteen years by outdoing even Mac-millan in the prodigality with which she doled out the knighthoods, at the rate of 6 or 8 a year, to practically every backbencher of more than ten years' standing.

For all these reasons, some serious, others petty, Heath forfeited the support of his parliamentary party. For four years he tried, almost wilfully, to govern as a national leader in proud detachment from his party. By so doing, he offended against the fundamental canon of British political life. For so long as he succeeded, so long as he was Prime Minister, so long as he looked like winning the next election, and so long as he had no obvious challenger, he could get away with it. But when he lost the February 1974 election, when he was ejected from Downing Street and found himself reduced to a party leader once again, his days were numbered. The party – the parliamentary party above all – had no cause to love him: and it should have come as no surprise when the parliamentary party threw him over. He tried to govern without them: they eventually decided they would do better without him.

A minor – almost comical – footnote to Heath's relations with his party occurred in 1972 with the disappearance of his constituency as result of the redrawing of boundaries. Heath had invested twenty-five years in Bexley and had become deeply identified with the place; both geographically and socially it suited him. Now, however, it was to be divided into two seats, Bexleyheath and Sidcup, of which the latter looked very much safer than the former. Despite the attractions of a seat whose name so perfectly incorporated his own, it was natural for him to opt for Sidcup; and natural, too, that the Prime Minister's preference should be accommodated. The party could not risk the possibility of its leader being defeated in Bexleyheath. Unfortunately, however, the new constituency of Bexley, Sidcup contained around 70 per cent of Dame Patricia Hornsby-Smith's old Chislehurst seat: strictly speaking, she had a better claim to the new seat than he did. It was an awkward situation, since Dame Patricia had her loyal partisans who did not see why she should be pushed aside, while there were plenty of mischief makers delighted to seize the opportunity to embarrass Heath. In January it was announced that he had declined the offer of a new, rock-solid seat in Hampshire (Christchurch and Lymington). He was also offered the Cities of London and Westminster. But his answer was always the same: he was determined to stay in Bexley. In the circumstances, as a serving Prime Minister, he could scarcely be denied the seat of his choice. In May 1972, after some discreet arm-twisting, he was 'unanimously' invited to be the candidate in Bexley, Sidcup. Dame Patricia was subsequently compensated with a peerage in Heath's 1974 resignation honours. The episode was memorable, however, for a brief letter written by the Labour MP, Andrew Faulds, to both *The Times* and the *Guardian*: 'Once upon a time in Bexley', Faulds wrote, 'a gentleman would have offered his seat to a lady who was standing.'[29] It was unfair, but it was a measure of Heath's personal unpopularity that it gave a lot of malicious pleasure.

28

The Barber Boom

1973 was make or break year for the Heath Government. It had achieved one major objective: on 1 January 1973 Britain finally took its place as a member of the European Economic Community. But the Government had squandered the first two years of its life attempting an approach to the economy and to the unions which had not worked. Now, following the crises and reversals of 1972, it had only two years left in which to conjure results on which it could hope to win re-election in the autumn of 1974 or the spring of 1975.

With the statutory counter-inflation policy in place and apparently holding – Stage Two was announced on 17 January and came into operation at the beginning of April – the Government's overriding aim was to use the breathing space so dearly bought to go all out for growth. Heath was determined not to let fears for the balance of payments call a halt, as had happened in 1961, 1964 – when Labour, he believed, had thrown away Maudling's pre-election boom by unnecessarily crying panic and talking up a crisis – and 1966. This time, with the pound floated, the Government could stop it falling too far by borrowing and if necessary borrowing again. If the cost-price spiral could be controlled in the short term by means of incomes policy, sustained reflation would stimulate a permanent improvement in the profitability, investment levels and output of the economy without simply fuelling long-term inflation. It was a gamble, admittedly: but Heath believed it was the only way to break the cycle of failure, and that success was only a matter of will and nerve. It was, he told the Institute of Directors in a rare, revealing analogy from ocean racing, like sailing through rough water with submerged rocks: you must either 'tack and go off, losing direction and the race; or you go through, and come out on the other side'.[1] After all the rebuffs of the past two years he was determined to ignore the rocks and go through. It was not a reckless gamble. It was supported by most of the quality press – particularly *The Times* and *The Economist* – by the semi-official forecasting body, the National Institute for Economic and Social Research, by the great majority of Tory backbenchers and broadly by the TUC, the Labour Opposition and the CBI. As Tony Barber's special adviser, Brendon Sewill, later wrote:

> There seemed to be a real chance to get the economy on the path of sustained growth that had eluded Britain through so many stop-go cycles. The Treasury forecasts showed the possibility, without strain on the economy, of 5% growth for some time, thereafter declining to a long-term rate of about 3½%.[2]

Five per cent growth was therefore the Government's proclaimed target, and for most of the year it was achieved.

Ironically, the person who was least happy with the policy was the Chancellor. The 1973 'dash for growth' is remembered as the 'Barber boom'. But in reality, as one of its leading critics, Samuel Brittan, acknowledged in 1977: 'Mr Barber . . . was less responsible than almost any other senior member of the Cabinet for the so-called "Barber boom".'[3] It was more accurately Heath's boom, imposed by the Prime Minister with the support of an acquiescent Cabinet on a reluctant Treasury. Barber went along with a policy in which he had no confidence out of loyalty to Heath personally and to the party. He had never been a strong Chancellor. He had carried through Iain Macleod's tax reforms skilfully, to general applause, but he was no economist and he carried too little weight in Cabinet to stand up to Heath's much stronger political will and impatience with Treasury caution. He was 'frustrated' over the level of public expenditure in 1972–3; but there was no breaking point on which he felt strongly enough to threaten resignation. 'If the Chancellor of the Exchequer resigns,' he has said in a rare interview, 'it can have a very bad effect on sterling.' Having reached – or exceeded – the summit of his political ambition, he had already decided to retire at the next election. 'I was going to go anyway, so I thought I ought to soldier on . . . I was not prepared to throw in the towel and let my colleagues down.'[4] Meanwhile he continued to win reassuringly golden opinions for subordinating his own judgment. *The Times* – which was by then beginning to hedge its bets – believed that the boldness of the 1973 Budget strategy reflected the Chancellor's personality – 'brave, daring and optimistic – altogether more valorous than prudent'.[5]

In the weeks before the Budget – exceptionally early on 6 March –

Barber came under significant pressure from the Tory right to cut back the massive expansion of public spending, particularly on the nationalised industries, projected for the next two years. In the House of Commons on 7 February Jock Bruce-Gardyne, Hugh Fraser, Peter Hordern and Edward Du Cann all warned that expenditure was rising too fast, taking too high a proportion of GDP. They wanted consumption restrained, and possibly even taxes raised. Two weeks later the Public Expenditure Select Committee repeated the same warning. *The Economist* was worried that the Chancellor would be persuaded to heed these fainthearts. On the contrary, it urged, he should still be looking to *cut* taxes.[6] In the event Barber introduced a Budget which was officially described as 'neutral'. Even so, it gave away £120 million, mainly in increased benefits designed to cushion Stage Two of the incomes policy. Value Added Tax (VAT) was introduced at 10 per cent (replacing SET and purchase tax), with food and children's clothes exempt. Pensions and sickness and unemployment benefit were raised, employees' National Insurance contributions reduced. Barber explicitly refused to cut back expenditure, but made some attempt to encourage private savings.

'Mr Barber . . . gambled everything . . . yesterday on headlong economic expansion to be buttressed by control of inflation,' Peter Jay wrote in *The Times*. The Budget was acknowledged to be politically adroit and skilful, particularly in the way it wrongfooted Labour. On the editorial page, however, Rees-Mogg was beginning to get cold feet: 'It is devoutly to be hoped that Mr Barber's gamble will pay off, that all-out expansion will secure the prize of a successful counter-inflation policy rooted in popular consent and that over-heating and demand pressures will not develop before the middle of 1974.'

It was all too likely, however, that with a deficit in the region of £4.4 million – and despite the courageous refusal to accede to European pressure to peg the pound – it would come before then to a painful stop. It would have been wiser to have pulled back to a less ambitious growth target of 3·5 per cent. The Government's strategy was not necessarily disastrous, Rees-Mogg believed. 'But it is certainly incautious; and we fear that it is ill-judged.'[7] The *Spectator* agreed. The massive deficit could only lead to 'radical and punishing deflation, probably later this year'.[8] Conversely *The Economist* still insisted that the Chancellor had been too cautious. The risk of being forced to 'stop' came from targeting too low a rate of growth.[9]

The argument continued for most of the year, with *The Times* arguing for a more moderate rate of growth and *The Economist* urging the Government to press full ahead. The February trade deficit, published in March, was £77 million; the March deficit was £197 million. The optimists attached importance to the growth of exports; the pessimists paid more attention to the soaring cost of imports. On 2 May Peter Jay warned of 'the boom that must go bust': 'We have got the most acute prospect of general overheating on the back of the weakest balance of payments in the post-war period.'[10] The April trade figures supported the optimists. Exports reached a record £954 million, giving the first monthly surplus since October 1972. Speaking to the CBI the day they appeared, Heath hailed them as 'a fine achievement by British industry', but emphasised that there was still room for further improvement:

> Some say the pace is too hot, and that we shall have to slam on the brakes again. But is it true that we have used up the margin of spare capacity? Unemployment is still high by past standards. Your recent survey showed nearly half of the reporting firms as still working below capacity. So what is the law which says that we cannot do what others have done and are doing?[11]

This was a very characteristic Heath refrain. The same day Reggie Maudling, reflecting in *The Times* on the close similarity between the present position and 1964, broadly supported the Government's determination to press on, but suggested a touch on the brake.[12] Even *The Economist*, however, without abandoning the central aim, now advocated some trimming of public spending; and the following week Barber duly announced a package of cuts amounting to £100 million in the current year and £500 million in 1974–5. Many of the projects which had been brought forward in 1971–2 when unemployment was rising were now pruned back or postponed. The Government, Barber explained, was not waiting for the boom to burst, but keeping it going by acting to prevent overheating. 'Such flexibility', *The Times* wrote approvingly, 'is a strength.'[13] Even the monetarists were satisfied: Nicholas Ridley praised the Chancellor's 'timely and proper counter-cyclical action',[14] while John Biffen commended his 'very prudent reassessment of forward public spending'.[15] The NIESR's June forecast declared the boom to be 'well under control'. On 5 July Barber assured the House of Commons that the economy was still on target for an average growth rate of 5 per cent over the next eighteen months.

Of course the 'Barber boom' did end up on the rocks, like so many of its predecessors. Heath and his reluctant Chancellor made a heroic effort to break the cycle. But by the end of the year they too were compelled to call a halt, with a massive overseas deficit, the pound not floating but sinking, and inflation soaring. Several factors contributed to this result – some foreseeable and intrinsic to the whole enterprise, others unforeseeable and unlucky. It is still possible to argue that Heath's 'dash for growth' was the right policy, which could have worked – and very nearly did work – had it not been for international factors outside the Government's control.

Even domestically, however, there was a lot wrong with the boom which Heath and Barber unleashed. It was, first of all, seriously unbalanced between the private and public sectors. Too much of the massive increase in government expenditure went not into productive industrial investment but into expanding the public services. During the four years of Heath's Government – contrary to the Conservatives' declared intentions in 1970 – the total number of public servants increased by some 400,000. Just over half of these (208,000) were in education – a measure of Margaret Thatcher's effectiveness as a high-spending departmental minister – with another 97,000 added to the pay-roll of Keith Joseph's NHS, and the rest divided between local government and the various arms of central government – including the new breed of VAT inspectors. In an influential book published in 1976, the Oxford economists Roger Bacon and Walter Eltis diagnosed the core problem of the British economy as 'too few producers'.[16] It was a problem which the lavish public expenditure of the Heath boom exacerbated rather than solved.

The relative slowness of private investment was not for want of urgent and repeated exhortation of industrialists by the Prime Minister. During 1972 and 1973 Heath became increasingly critical of what he saw as the unpatriotic caution of businessmen in the face of the opportunities which he believed the Government was creating for them. The state, he told Young Conservatives in February 1973, had a vital role in providing the infrastructural support for major enterprises like North Sea oil extraction; but there was still 'ample room for private investment'. There was, he complained with ill-concealed irritation, 'not much virtue in a private enterprise system if its practitioners are always trying to find clouds in the sky as an excuse for staying indoors'.[17] He used to lecture the banks on their national responsibility, urging them to invest directly in industry like German banks. But the bankers tended to hear him sceptically: this was not how British banking operated.[18] He held regular meetings with groups of businessmen and industrialists, including the heads of most of the largest companies in the land; but he was unsympathetic to their difficulties.

Heath's impatience naturally did not go down well with hard-pressed businessmen who felt that he was trying to offload the Government's responsibility for the state of the economy on to them. But if his relations with the barons of industry were soured by these occasions, Peter Walker believed that the fault was at least as much on their side as on his:

> Where he made enemies was at those dinner parties, frequently with businessmen and men of the City, where he argued fiercely. Such men do not expect the Prime Minister and leaders of parties to question the conduct of their activities. They expect them to be grateful recipients of advice. Nor do they expect advice to be tendered to them. Whereas Ted Heath considered that the objective of such dinners was to debate current problems, debating was neither their objective nor their skill, and the next day they would retail their resentment at the failure of the Prime Minister to listen, when an outside observer would perhaps recognise that it was he who had listened and it was they who had not.[19]

The trouble was that while prime ministers can take huge gambles with the national economy as an act of political faith, a test of nerve or an exercise of will, industrialists have to make investment decisions on the narrower basis of their commercial judgment. Despite the government's repeated promises that it would keep the economy at full stretch come what might, and despite the strong support of the CBI for that policy, individual industrialists remained sceptical. As Lord Plowden, then chairman of Tube Investments, told Cecil King in February 1973 'no serious amount of investment is to be looked for until industrialists have confidence that the new investment will earn an adequate profit over a period. They have no such confidence at the present time.'[20] The key phrase was 'over a period'. Another symptomatic exchange is contained in the story of Heath, at one of his meetings with businessmen, challenging Nigel Broakes of Trafalgar House why he didn't invest 'north of a line from Bristol to the Wash', only to be told, crushingly: 'As far as I'm concerned, Prime Minister, Trafalgar would not invest north of Oxford Street the way things look now.'[21]

One reason why those with money to invest were slow to put it into industry was that there were vastly higher returns to be made more easily elsewhere. The financial climate had been seriously distorted by the Bank of England's liberalisation of credit controls in 1971, which led to an explosion of bank lending and a hectic property boom, marked by the proliferation of often dodgy secondary banks.

While lending for property speculation doubled and quadrupled, the level of industrial investment lagged behind. It was a self-financing bubble, borrowing on the constantly rising value of assets, easy money while it lasted, but unproductive and inflationary. In the feverish atmosphere a number of banks and property companies overreached themselves and came unstuck – many with prominent politicians on the board: Edward Du Cann (Keyser Ullman), the Liberal leader Jeremy Thorpe (London & County Securities), and the former Labour Minister John Stonehouse (London Capital Group) were just three whose fingers were burned.[22]

Particular scandal attached to the Anglo-African trading group Lonrho, where in the course of an unsuccessful boardroom *coup* against the buccaneering 'Tiny' Rowland it emerged that the chairman, the former Tory Minister Duncan Sandys – a member of Heath's Shadow Cabinet in 1965 – had been paid $100,000 tax free via the Cayman Islands. The revelation of such undercover handouts in the City, at a time when the Government was trying to hold down the earnings of ordinary workers, was seriously embarrassing to the Tory party and deeply offensive to Heath personally. Speaking at the Scottish party conference on 12 May, and again three days later in the House of Commons, he made the Government's condemnation plain. Lonrho, he asserted, represented 'the unpleasant and unacceptable face of capitalism', adding hurriedly that 'one should not suggest that the whole of British industry consists of practices of this kind'.[23] Immediately the phrase became the most famous line Heath ever spoke – equal with 'at a stroke' (which he never said) but more resonant. It was taken, inaccurately, to imply that capitalism itself was 'unpleasant and unacceptable'. It is said that, had he read his script correctly, he should have said 'facet', rather than 'face'. It would be characteristic if he had forged a memorable phrase only by mistake. The difference is, strictly speaking, marginal. But 'facet' implies just one face among many, whereas 'face' was open to the interpretation that the real nature of capitalism had been revealed behind the smiling mask. That, naturally, was how Labour used it; and, at a time when he was habitually expressing, at least in private, disillusion with the failure of British capitalists to seize the opportunities the Government was offering them, and appeared to be gathering more and more power over the economy into the hands of the state, there was a measure of justice in that view. As the Conservative party turned back to full-blooded capitalism after 1975, the phrase was remembered by his Tory critics as proof of his essential neo-socialism. 'It was symbolic', Lucille Iremonger wrote in 1977, 'that the only memorable phrase Heath coined was . . . gratuitously kicking into his own goal.'[24]

The get-rich-quick bubble associated with the property boom, of which the Lonrho scandal was just one symptom, was deeply harmful to the Government's attempts to achieve sustainable economic growth. Brendon Sewill has written that ministers regarded the property boom as the 'froth on the top' of a pint of beer, 'undesirable . . . but perhaps inevitable' if they were going to get industrial output up.[25] But this was a mistake. The spiralling property market represented a serious diversion of investment from industry. It was also hugely inflationary, both in the visible sense that house prices soared by 70 per cent in two years, and in the technical sense that it enormously increased the amount of money in circulation. Since the liberalisation of credit controls in 1971, the only method of controlling credit left to the Government was by means of interest rates. But this was a tool which Barber was reluctant to use. On the one hand, high interest rates would deter the investment which the Government was striving to encourage. On the other, they raised the cost of mortgages and hence the cost of living. During 1972 the Bank of England's Minimum Lending Rate had risen steeply from 5 per cent to 9 per cent. Over the first half of 1973 Barber cut it back by degrees to 7·75 per cent; but in late July he was obliged to raise it again in two drastic hikes in the space of eight days to 11·5 per cent – the highest level since 1914.

Measuring the growth of money supply, as the Treasury did in 1973, by means of the narrow-based M1, these measures were effective: M1 had grown too fast, by 16·5 per cent, in 1971–2 but was cut back to a rate of only 7·8 per cent in 1972–3. Monetarist critics of the Government, however, were increasingly taking the broader-based M3 (which includes bank deposits) as a truer measure of money growth, and this yardstick told a different story. M3 continued to grow unchecked from 10·4 per cent in 1970–1 to 25·9 per cent in 1971–2 and on to 28·1 per cent in 1972–3.[26] This was not, as was often alleged – for instance by Harold Wilson in July 1973 – the result of the Government literally printing money to finance its boom.[27] It was rather an expression of the amount of quite notional money circulating in the City and financing the property merry-go-round. Its effect, nullifying all the Government's efforts to squeeze out wage inflation, was powerfully inflationary. But it was not caused, as critics claimed, simply by the Government's over-expansion of public expenditure – though that contributed.

Despite all these diversions, industrial investment did eventually pick up. 'Industry was desperately slow to get moving,' Brendon Sewill recalled, 'but by the end of 1973 investment intentions were at a record level.'[28] By then, however, it was too late: Heath's gamble had been overtaken by external factors, outside the Government's power to control. The first was an international financial crisis, precipitated by the 10 per cent devaluation of the US dollar in February. As a result the pound fell against other currencies by a further 5 per cent, making it impossible to peg its value again as the Government had promised at the time of the original decision to float in 1972. Over a period of eighteen months from the end of 1971 sterling lost one-fifth of its value, suffering an effective devaluation of 20 per cent. This helped exports, but further increased the price of imports at a time when they were already soaring. Here, finally, was the submerged rock which really wrecked Heath's policy. During 1973 world commodity prices went through the roof. The cause was partly simultaneous expansion in America, West Germany and Japan, as well as Britain; partly speculation in commodities as a hedge against worldwide inflation. The result was that in the year from September 1972 to September 1973 the cost of basic materials used in manufacturing, as measured by *The Economist*'s commodity index, nearly doubled. Between the beginning of 1972 and the end of 1973 (but mostly during 1973) the price of copper rose 115 per cent, cotton 127 per cent, cocoa 173 per cent and zinc 308 per cent. Foodstuffs were as seriously affected as textiles and metals. An importing nation like Britain – with the pound already buying less – was hit especially hard. The government's policy of rapid growth depended upon a high level of imported raw materials, but import prices rose by 26 per cent, costing an extra £2,000 million and resulting in a record annual deficit of £1,120 million, putting yet further pressure on the pound.[29] At the same time, the commodity prices explosion translated directly into higher prices in the shops, making the Government's attempts to impose an effective incomes policy ever more impossible to enforce.

Almost to the end of the year the Government and the champions of unfaltering expansion in the press still hoped to be able to navigate through the storm. In June, and still in August, the NIESR forecast that commodity prices would soon ease.[30] In July, despite the sinking pound and Barber's swingeing hike of interest rates, *The Times* in an editorial entitled 'No Time to Moan and Weep' declared that now was the decisive moment when the Government must hold its nerve and maintain its commitment to growth.[31] *The Economist* still proclaimed on 1 September that 'Britain is two-thirds of the way to an economic miracle'.[32] 'The general view', Brendon Sewill remembers, 'was . . . that it would be wrong to slam on the brakes.'

To this day Peter Walker believes that the Government was on the brink of achieving its breakthrough, despite the commodity price explosion, the alarming trade balance and the sinking pound.[33] The balance-of-payments deficit, on this view, was due to increased imports of raw materials and machinery, not consumer goods. These raw materials and new plant represented the investment the Government had been striving to encourage, and duly resulted in increased exports in 1974. The figures support this analysis. Despite everything, it can be argued that the counter-inflation policy was holding until the autumn of 1973, and that if it could just have held through the winter, prices would then have fallen and the Government would have won through to an easier climate with the boom still intact. But it was not to be. Two further body blows – one external, one domestic – struck the Government that autumn and winter: first the Middle East War, with the quadrupling of the most important commodity price of all, oil; and then the decision of the National Union of Mineworkers, drawing lethal encouragement from that opportunity, to take the lead in defying, and breaking, the incomes policy. Under the impact of the oil shock, in December Heath was finally compelled to allow Barber to make drastic cuts in public expenditure, thus bringing the dash for growth to an end; while the same month the miners dug in for a confrontation which eventually encompassed the destruction not only of Stage Three but of the Government itself.

So the 'Barber boom' followed others in Britain's dismal postwar history to the ultimate disappointment of all the high hopes vested in it. Yet it was a brave and determined try, which failed as much through an accumulation of bad luck and poor timing as through mismanagement or essential misconception. It would certainly have been a better outlook for Britain in the next decade if Heath could have pulled it off.

Running parallel with the dash for growth was the continuing refinement of the Government's counter-inflation policy. It was still a statutory policy but the intention was that it should gradually be relaxed so as to rectify anomalies and restore differentials lost in the crude standstill imposed at the end of 1972, while still keeping pay increases within strict limits. The ninety-day freeze which constituted Stage One of the policy was due to expire at the end of February 1973. On 17 January, at another of his grand press conferences amid the gilt and chandeliers of Lancaster House, flanked by Barber on one side and William Armstrong on the other, Heath announced the outlines of Stage Two, due to run from 1 April to the end of the year.

Pay rises were to be limited to a basic £1 a week plus 4 per cent (excluding overtime), with a maximum annual increase of £250. A new Pay Board (to be chaired by Sir Frank Figgures) would have to approve all pay settlements involving more than 1,000 employees. A parallel regulatory body, the Price Commission (chaired by Sir Arthur Cockfield) would likewise monitor price increases and disallow those it considered excessive. Rent and dividend controls would be maintained, with permitted company profits limited to the average of the best two of the last five years. Finally it would be an offence to strike or to threaten a strike in order to force an employer to break the Pay Code.

Once again the package won general praise, with *The Times* as usual leading the applause. 'Mr Heath has fully discharged [his] special responsibility,' Rees-Mogg declared in a leader entitled 'Fair, Workable and Necessary', 'and our endorsement is unqualified.'[34] *The Economist* was more critical, thinking the package 'not as tough as it should be against income rises' – which were expected to average 8–10 per cent (double any likely increase in productivity) – and 'too complicated in its price controls' – which were likely to prove unworkable. Nevertheless 'it may succeed in averting a major social crisis'.[35] The 'social partners' reacted predictably. The TUC objected that even under Stage One the price controls had not worked and declined to co-operate with Stage Two – refusing, for instance, to appoint union representatives to the Pay Board or the Price Commission; while the CBI pointed out that the curb on profits would only restrict investment.[36]

The new legislation ran into some slight difficulty in the Commons, mainly because Francis Pym was tricked into allowing the handful of critics to be over-represented on the Standing Committee – calculating presumably that this was the best way of muzzling them. The Counter Inflation Bill passed its Second Reading comfortably, with only Powell voting against it, and no abstentions. But when Pym put both John Biffen and Nicholas Ridley on the Standing Committee they promptly tabled amendments to limit the application of the policy from three years (annually renewed) to just one year, and succeeded in carrying two divisions against the Government by 20 votes to 18. When the Government insisted on reversing these votes on the floor of the House, 5 Tory Members voted against the Government and another 8 abstained; but with some Labour absentees the Government still secured a majority of 58. The same evening the Bill passed its Third Reading by 276 to 197, with just 5 abstentions.[37] Once again the potential rebels failed to muster consistent opposition even among themselves. Dismissing their carping, *The Economist* lumped the Tory right and the TUC together as 'an unholy alliance for all that is reactionary'.[38]

The TUC too, though it declared its rejection of the Government's policy, was decidedly half-hearted in pressing its opposition, leaving it to individual unions to stage unofficial stoppages in pursuit of their own claims. The most serious action came from the gasmen: by mid-February 6,700 were on strike with another 25,000 working to rule. They were backed sporadically by hospital workers, train drivers, teachers, Ford car workers and even Civil Servants, who staged their first-ever strike on 27 February. But the Government was uncompromising. Heath met the TUC General Council at Downing Street on 17 February and told them there could be no exceptions under Stage Two or the entire policy would disintegrate. Anomalies could be sorted out – 'in an organised and systematic way', as he told the Young Conservatives a few days earlier – at Stage Three.[39] Speaking on television after his Budget on 6 March, Barber hinted at a General Election if the unions continued to defy the norm. After so many previous retreats Heath was this time absolutely determined to hold the line. Tory MPs, Ronald Butt reported in *The Times*, were delighted: 'The Government has bound itself by its own law and it will either triumph with it or go down fighting for it. That is a message that the Conservative Party badly wanted to hear.'[40]

Heath repeatedly insisted that there was no reason for the unions to oppose Stage Two. It was not – like Labour's incomes policies – designed to depress living standards but, on the contrary, was a policy for increased real earnings, underwritten by sustained expansion.[41] In a speech to Tory students at Swinton the weekend before the Budget – the sort of young audience with which he was at his most relaxed and confidential – he reaffirmed his faith in an eventual return to voluntary restraint:

I have not believed in the past, and I do not believe today, that statutory powers are the right instruments for this purpose. In a free and rational society it should be possible for government, employers and trade unions to sit round a table and to work out voluntarily, under the authority of parliament, how the economy is to be managed in the interest of different sections of the community and of the nation as a whole.

Despite all the unions' huffing and puffing, he persisted in seeing in the last few months 'the beginning of a new sense of national unity in peacetime'. 'This may seem a paradox to some at the present moment, but my recent experience suggests strongly that it is true. For divisive arguments, divisive practices, and those who urge them are being increasingly exposed as barren and self-defeating.'[42]

It did seem to be true. The opposition to Stage Two dramatically subsided. On 23 March the gasmen settled within the guidelines. Car workers, train drivers and lorry drivers all abandoned projected protests. Even the miners decisively rebuffed their leaders when invited to vote for possible strike action. On May Day a TUC 'day of action' – called against the advice of the General Council – was a resounding failure. Only 1·5 million people stopped work while many more demonstrated their annoyance at being stopped. The number of working days lost in the first half of 1973 fell steeply by comparison with 1972 – even excluding the miners' strike. No union was prepared to take the lead in trying to bust the limit. By May more than a hundred settlements had been concluded under Stage Two, involving 290,000 workers.

Once again *The Times* and *The Economist* led the chorus of approval. *The Times*, hailing 'the striking success of the present policy', deplored Heath's wish to return to a voluntary approach.[43] Likewise *The Economist*, at the end of March, saw the Government, having successfully enforced Stage Two, on the way to a 'historic, if temporary, victory'. Whereas inflation in the twelve months up to November 1972 had been about 17 per cent (and rising towards 20 per cent), the same figure in the twelve months following should be around 8 per cent. Recalling the ultimately ill-fated 'n-1' policy, the paper reckoned that the present statutory policy was equivalent to 'n-10'. But it could only be made to stick with continued rapid growth. Stage Three should set a high norm, but once again with almost no exceptions. That would cut inflation to 3–4 per cent. 'A repetition of the stage three formula in stage four', the writer concluded triumphantly, 'could then cause inflation to stop almost altogether in the election year 1974–5.'[44]

Heath and his colleagues shared this optimism in the spring of 1973. On Sunday 18 March senior ministers and their advisers met at Chequers. The gasmen's strike was crumbling. Labour was in disarray, having just lost the Lincoln by-election to the renegade Dick Taverne, who had been disowned by his local party principally over his support for joining the EEC; and the Opposition's long lead in the opinion polls had practically disappeared. (In June ORC put the Tories ahead for the first time since 1971.) Douglas Hurd recorded in his diary:

PM v. genial and relaxed in yellow pullover, rest of us tweeds . . . Everyone calm and reasonably reflective over the two year prospect. Prices should come right slowly after mid-1973, and unemployment come right too fast. Balance of payments will get worse, then better. If no horrors occur, Autumn 1974 might be best.[45]

But it could not last, for a number of reasons both practical and philosophic. First, commodity prices continued to rise inexorably, making imports more expensive and mocking the efforts of the Price Commission to hold down prices in the shops. This external pressure, coming on top of the inflation already being unwittingly fuelled by the Government's high spending and the soaring credit boom, stoked expectations for the next wage round which no conceivable Stage Three was going to be able to satisfy. The unions were bound to try to keep up with inflation and were no longer going to be persuaded that it was they who caused it. The Government, however, had painted itself into a corner. It is possible to enforce a statutory incomes policy for a time when inflation is relatively moderate and appears to be coming down. It quickly becomes impossible if prices continue to rise regardless. But having invoked the law to hold down wages to a fixed limit the Government now found itself bound by its own law. Initially this seemed a source of strength. As Heath himself declared in February, the option of compromise was 'no longer open'.[46] Nine months later the closing of that option would leave the Government helpless in a trap of its own making.

Ultimately, however, the philosophic case against incomes policy is even stronger than the practical – though perhaps it comes to the same thing. The fact is that even in the best of economic conditions you cannot in a Western capitalist economy suppress the free market for long. (Even the socialist command economies of eastern Europe could not do it for ever.) Samuel Brittan in the *Financial Times* put his finger most elegantly on this truth. 'Leading Ministers', he alleged, 'do not regard the present wage and price controls as emergency measures designed to produce lower and more realistic expectations. Instead, they see them as but the beginning of a permanent system of regulation.' In doing this they were defying the facts of modern life: 'They have resurrected the medieval concept of a just price and a fair wage – concepts that are quite unworkable without the underlying theological agreement on status and hierarchy that made the medieval system possible.'[47] On this perspective, Heath's policy was doomed to end in confrontation sooner or later. The extreme external circumstances of rising commodity prices and the oil shock only ensured that the end came sooner.

Heath continued to insist that he did *not* want statutory control to be permanent. But as the time for settling Stage Three approached he reminded the country why the Government had been obliged to suspend free bargaining in the first place. 'No Government', he declared once again in a speech at Hatfield on 24 September, 'has taken unions and employers more fully into partnership than we have. We therefore have a right to ask for a positive contribution from our partners.'

> The more they can do, the less has to be done by statutory controls, and the greater the freedom and flexibility of the system.
>
> It is natural that both employers and unions should want freedom of action . . . but this is where we came in.
>
> The Government would like to leave them free. We did so for the first two years of this Government. The result was a rate of inflation which we could not sustain and from which we are still suffering.
>
> It is no good now to become so preoccupied by the difficulties of intervention that we forget the greater evil which made intervention necessary.[48]

The trouble was that controls developed an institutional momentum of their own. In addition to the Pay Board and the Price Commission, a new department of Consumer Affairs was created within the DTI, with Geoffrey Howe promoted to the Cabinet to head it. The job of trying to keep detailed control of every price, wage, rent and dividend in the economy spawned an enormous and complex apparatus which absorbed a disproportionate amount of Whitehall time and manpower. Moreover Heath himself, with William Armstrong at his side, sat at the centre of the web. He believed it was of fundamental importance to the country: he felt he had to keep the operation in his own hands – the union leaders would not deal with anyone less than the Prime Minister. But with his phenomenal grasp of detail he allowed himself to get drawn so deeply into the wood that he lost sight of the wider political picture. When Willie Whitelaw returned from Belfast at the end of the year he was struck by the extent to which, in his absence, the incomes policy had taken over the whole machinery of Government: despite his protestations, Heath seemed 'obsessed' by the detail and the vocabulary of control.[49]

And yet, whatever the theoretical objections and practical doubts, Stage Two was a considerable success. No group of workers successfully defied it. The problem was going to be winning continuing public acquiescence in Stage Three, at a time when prices were still rising. The Government, as *The Economist* noted, 'gets no credit for the fact that, but for controls, prices would have risen even faster'.[50]

By the summer, the unions were growing increasingly restless: at its annual Congress in September the TUC renewed its rejection of continued pay restraint, demanding at the same time rigid price controls backed by subsidies. Likewise the CBI pleaded for the raising of the profits ceiling. More seriously for the Government, *The Economist* found evidence of falling public support: whereas a year before 75 per cent had wanted the unions to moderate their pay claims, now 52 per cent thought them justified in seeking more money. 'For the first time, the opportunity for a postwar economic miracle lies within our national grasp.' Yet 'the present signs are . . . that the opportunity will be thrown away. Why do we do this? Because we really are the stupid country?'[51]

Heath remained determinedly optimistic. Two catastrophic by-election defeats at the hands of the Liberals at Ripon and the Isle of Ely, widely attributed to Tory voters registering a protest against rising prices, only reinforced the necessity of maintaining tight controls. The polls still showed Labour doing little better than the Government, and Heath himself – persuaded by Douglas Hurd to get out around the country in September – had a 'markedly friendly' reception at public meetings and walkabouts in Scotland, the Midlands, Hertfordshire and Essex. 'A hot sunny day electioneering in Walsall', for instance, Hurd thought 'v. successful'.

> A primary school – he conducts a calypso – knots of waving women in sunny streets – a hospital – walk down the main street in a big cheerful crowd – local editors and gin – party workers and back to tea – another clear quiet speech . . . As he becomes accustomed to electioneering again he gets better at it.[52]

Stage Three was finally unveiled on 8 October. Designed to deal with as many as possible of the anomalies and grievances thrown up by Stage Two, it was an immensely complicated package: 37 out of 54 pages of the accompanying Green Paper consisted of minor amendments to the existing pay and prices codes. The central provision was for basic pay rises of no more than £2.25 or 7 per cent per week, up to a maximum of £350 per year. But there was added leeway allowed for productivity agreements, 'unsocial hours' and progress towards equal pay, which was supposed to restore scope for bargaining. The Government admitted that this would give average increases nearer 10–11 per cent; most commentators reckoned it would be worth a good deal more. In addition, in a well-meant but desperately ill-advised attempt to win union acceptance, there was provision for 'threshold payments' – a device imported from Canada –

whereby employees would be entitled to an extra 40p if the rate of increase in the retail price index reached 7 per cent and a further 40p for every additional 1 per cent rise. On 'Panorama' that evening Heath laid great emphasis on these threshold payments as a major innovation giving assurance of protection against future inflation.[53] They were based, of course, on the expectation that commodity prices had peaked and would soon start to fall. In the *New Statesman*, however, Alan Watkins shrewdly warned that they 'could turn out to be catastrophically expensive'.[54] He was right: threshold payments were actually triggered eleven times in the next few months, giving a further £4.40 on top of the maximum rise the Government had intended.

The Economist, which had been arguing for a tougher policy with no exceptions, called Stage Three 'a complicated sieve': it was full of holes. It might work, if import prices fell; but even then it would be a missed opportunity: 'Mr Heath has used the considerable success of his first two stages as a base for advancing only into a "flexible" holding operation, and past experience of flexibility suggests gloomily that the hold may not be maintained.'[55]

From the other side of the political spectrum the *New Statesman* gleefully shared this analysis. 'Mr Heath', it jeered, 'flounders into Stage Three ... like a paid-off mariner staggering into a dockside bar, distributing pound notes in random fashion and promising that there's plenty more where that came from. All pretence at order and control has vanished ... Not only has the norm been raised, but multiple exceptions have been created to allow any number of coaches and horses to be driven through at will.'[56]

The faithful *Times*, however, remained true. By going to the limit of flexibility, it believed, Heath had 'given himself the best possible chance of winning the general public support he needs, although in doing so he has taken the risk that inflation will accelerate rather than slow down next year'. Flexibility in this situation was a sign of strength. Rees-Mogg hoped that Heath had conceded enough to avert a winter of strife. If the country failed to support him it would be voting for South American levels of inflation, leading to heavy unemployment.[57]

Stage Three was announced at the beginning of Tory conference week. The representatives were not in fact particularly restive: the week went off pretty well for the Government. Enoch Powell delivered his customary lecture on the monetary causes of inflation, but was devastatingly seen off by Barber, who accused him, to 'thunderous applause', of showing 'all the moral conceit and all the intellectual arrogance which are the hallmarks of the fanatic'.[58] *The*

Economist commented dismissively that 'he was back on the old honest money kick, and no-one takes that very seriously'.[59] Heath's closing speech on the Saturday – a characteristically serious declaration of purpose with 'no speechwriter's phrases' but a ring of passionate sincerity – was well received.[60] Since it was the last speech he made to the party as Prime Minister – indeed the last he was to make as leader, since there was no conference in 1974 – it is worth looking at the case he made for his premiership.

He made a point of recalling – quite accurately – the programme promulgated at Selsdon Park in 1970 and claimed that it had been fully implemented. Tax cuts had been introduced by Tony Barber. Industrial relations had been reformed by Robert Carr. Pensions for the over-eighties had been brought in by Keith Joseph. Action on crime and tighter control of immigration had been delivered by Reggie Maudling and Robert Carr. It is perfectly true – contrary to the myth of 'Selsdon Man' – that the Selsdon conference had said little or nothing about a less interventionist economic policy. There was rather more on those lines in the June manifesto – including the categoric pledge not to introduce an incomes policy. But Heath preferred to point to the pledge in *A Better Tomorrow* to introduce 'an advanced regional policy'. The Government, he declared, had set out in 1970 'on a course of expansion'. It had taken time to show results. But 'through the Industry Act, we are now achieving results such as have never been achieved before', just in time to take full advantage of joining the EEC. 'In 1973 industrial output in Britain has risen by a massive 9 per cent. The volume of our exports has risen even faster, by over 12 per cent.' In the process 'the tragedy and the deprivation of unemployment are being eliminated . . . We have dealt with this social evil.'

The problems the country still faced were 'problems of expansion', no longer of deflation and decline. 'Let us not forget that the real standard of living has risen twice as fast since we took office as it did in the six years of the Labour Government.' As a result the Government had been able to increase pensions, to launch a massive programme of primary school building, and increase spending on the social services, providing 'new help to some of the least fortunate people in Britain who never had any help before under any Government'. Then, without admitting any reversal of approach, without even mentioning incomes policy directly, he returned to his favourite theme that the last twelve months represented a new beginning for Britain:

This year has shown for the first time in a long time what we as a nation are capable of doing . . . As a nation we are beginning to remember how to work together as we do at all the great moments in our history. We did not remember a moment too soon . . . Today we are moving nearer to the kind of place we want in the kind of world that we want. If we throw away now what is in our hands we do not deserve to keep it.

He lapsed finally into sub-Churchillian fustian about the British as an 'island race' whose great achievements were 'the fruit of British character, of British determination, of British tolerance', ending with the desperate affirmation of faith that ultimate success would be 'the victory of the British people acting as one'.[61] This sort of stuff reads woodenly, and it sounded pretty wooden at the time. Yet it honestly embodied what Heath thought he was about and passionately believed he was achieving. Five months later he was out of office, with all his dreams in ruins, the country rent as never before by industrial chaos. But there should be no doubting the sincerity, nor the patriotism, of the vision of unity he had tried to set before his party and the country.

His tragedy was that it did not come across. His attempts at inspirational rhetoric were heard with scepticism, just as the counter-inflation policy itself was supported *faute de mieux*, as a practical necessity, rather than the positive opportunity Heath tried to present it as. Even those Tories who were uneasy with it were generally prepared to give it a trial. The *Daily Telegraph* found it hard to swallow his 'straightfaced insistence' that the Government's policy was quite consistent with the 1970 manifesto: 'it is as well for Mr Heath that the British electorate is not much concerned about ideology.' But the *Telegraph* itself was not worried on ideological grounds, so long as the policy worked. Anything, it declared, should be supported that would serve to keep out Labour. If it did not work, however, the fault would be the Prime Minister's for 'unleashing ravenous expectations. For Ministers now claim that it is possible for Government to apportion economic reward among contending groups according to some abstract principle of fairness.'[62]

Here the paper put its finger on the fundamental political weakness of Heath's policy which would have given trouble even if the oil crisis, the miners' strike and all the other factors that combined to wreck it had never been. It is inherently difficult for a Tory Government to operate a successful incomes policy because Labour can always outbid it. 'Fairness', as well as being subjective, is primarily a socialist value. For a Tory government to make it the touchstone of its policy is to play the political game on Labour's terms. Labour is almost bound to raise the stakes, demanding better treatment for this or that disadvantaged group. Wilson understood this quite well and exploited it skilfully through every stage of Heath's policy. There was no satisfactory answer the Government could give beyond creating ever more complex machinery in an effort to eliminate anomalies while repeating that it was doing everything possible to be fair. Another aspect of the same difficulty was that the unions, however earnestly Heath tried to woo them, always reckoned that they would get a better deal from a succeeding Labour Government and therefore – as Jack Jones virtually admitted at Blackpool – had no interest in collaborating wholeheartedly with the Tories.[63] If they had favours to give they would keep them for their own side. They would take whatever Heath offered, but could always see Wilson over his shoulder promising more. This was the Catch-22 of British politics in the 1970s which Heath could not resolve.

29

Whitelaw in Ulster

Even in Northern Ireland, 1973 was a much more encouraging year following the horrors of 1972. Willie Whitelaw had gone to Ulster in March 1972 with a brief to 'introduce a new era' in the politics of the province.[1] After a difficult first few months it began to seem possible that he might succeed. By the end of 1973 he had persuaded at least some representatives of both communities to sit down together in an unprecedented experiment in sharing power across the tribal divide. This of course was Whitelaw's achievement. But Heath was closely involved in the background, trying – in vain as it once again turned out – to resolve in his premiership the enduring conflict which had defeated Gladstone, Asquith and Lloyd George.

Initially Whitelaw faced enormous hostility from the Protestants, as the quarrelling elements of the old Unionist Party temporarily re-united in outrage at the suspension of Stormont. On 27–8 March 1972 William Craig's Protestant Vanguard movement brought some 200,000 workers out in a two-day protest strike; on the second afternoon a huge demonstration, estimated at 100,000, gathered in the grounds of Stormont and was addressed from the balcony by Faulkner, Craig, Paisley and the 84-year-old former Prime Minister, Lord Brookeborough. In his first bitterness at having been betrayed by Heath, Faulkner appeared to make common cause with Craig, contemptuously declaring his refusal to co-operate with Whitelaw or serve on the all-party commission that was supposed to advise him: 'Northern Ireland is not a coconut colony; and no coconut commission will be able to muster any vestige of credibility or standing.'[2] Yet the Unionists were not united. Faulkner was a practical politician who soon saw more advantage in working with Whitelaw than in fighting him. Narrowly he persuaded a majority of his party to trust him. Craig, on the other hand, would accept nothing less than the full restoration of Stormont and even hinted at declaring an independent Ulster. Ian Paisley, conversely, began to argue for the full integration of Northern Ireland with the rest of the UK; and this line was echoed by Enoch Powell, now beginning to take a close interest in Ulster as another emotive patriotic issue on which to assail the Government's integrity. Between them, however, in their different ways, the Unionist leaders articulated a mood of fierce resistance to direct rule and the policies that were expected to flow from it. Protestant violence against Catholics flared. A new Protestant paramilitary organisation, the Ulster Defence Association, held aggressive demonstrations in Belfast in May. There were sectarian gun battles in the streets, and the prospect of large-scale armed confrontation – virtual civil war – loomed ever nearer.

The Unionists were the more alarmed because Whitelaw made it his first business on arriving in Ulster to try to win the confidence of the Catholic community. To this end he immediately began releasing internees: 73 were freed in April and more than 500 by the end of June. He lifted the ban on marches and demonstrations and instructed the army to keep a 'low profile' – effectively leaving Catholic areas to the undisturbed control of the IRA. The result – as the Unionists had warned him – was that they simply stepped up their bombing campaign, killing dozens of civilians and two soldiers a week with impunity. What Whitelaw was trying to do, however, was to detach the Catholic population from the terrorists; and there were some signs that he was succeeding. He was warmly received in the streets, and on 22 May met a delegation of brave women from the Bogside who came to appeal to him to end the violence. Four days later the SDLP called off its boycott of public bodies and agreed to talk to him. In return – against the advice of his officials – he conceded a key terrorist demand and granted 'special category' status to paramilitary prisoners. He insisted that this was not the same as 'political status', but in effect it was. The men were allowed to wear their own clothes, to do no work, to associate freely and elect their own leaders who ran the prison without interference by the warders. It turned out, Whitelaw confessed later, to be 'a thoroughly mistaken decision', though it helped him with the SDLP at the time.[3] Intended as a gesture of good will – it applied to prisoners of both communities – it bestowed legitimacy on the IRA's claim to be conducting a political struggle. Whitelaw's concession was reversed by Merlyn Rees in 1976.

In the very short run it achieved something. The Provisionals called a ceasefire to begin on 26 June (characteristically preceded by a redoubled orgy of killing right up to the deadline). Whitelaw welcomed it and promised that the army would 'obviously reciprocate'.[4]

The further impression that he was recognising the IRA as a legitimate antagonist unleashed a further storm of Protestant fury. In a direct challenge to his authority the UDA threatened to erect barricades to establish 'no-go areas' of its own. But Whitelaw outfaced them, letting it be known that the army had his permission to fire on the UDA if necessary. The barricades were withdrawn. 'That awful moment', he wrote in his memoirs, 'assisted me greatly thereafter in my dealings with the militant Protestants. They realized that I was prepared to stand up to them.'[5]

Meanwhile he was not to be deflected from his parallel strategy of trying to win over the Catholic population by kindness. On 7 July he went to the dangerous length of arranging a face-to-face meeting with the IRA. This was not the first time that senior British politicians had met the IRA: Wilson and Merlyn Rees met David O'Connell and Joe Cahill in Dublin in March. But Wilson and Rees were in opposition; it was a different matter for the British Government to meet them. Whitelaw's first instinct, he has written, was against it; but after long discussions with his officials 'I was persuaded that a refusal to talk would leave the political initiative in the hands of the IRA. Finally I decided that I wanted to go ahead and asked Ted Heath if I could hold a secret meeting of an exploratory nature. He immediately gave me his agreement and support.'[6]

Six leading Provisionals were flown to London in a Royal Air Force plane. (Two were released from internment especially to take part.) Whitelaw and his junior minister Paul Channon met them at Channon's house in Chelsea. The meeting, according to Whitelaw, was 'a non-event. The IRA leaders simply made impossible demands which I told them the British Government would never concede.'[7] From the IRA side Martin McGuinness does not dissent: 'We basically agreed that the only purpose of the meeting with Whitelaw was to demand the declaration of intent to withdraw.'[8] In fact they made three demands: British withdrawal from Northern Ireland within three years; the future of Ulster to be decided by a vote of the whole of Ireland; and an amnesty for all 'political' prisoners. Since all three were out of the question there was nothing to discuss. The Provisionals were disappointed. 'They had bombed their way to the conference table only to find to their disgust that they were still expected to negotiate.'[9] Two days later they ended the ceasefire, saying that they had got nothing in return, and gravely embarrassed Whitelaw by making public the fact of their meeting. Since Whitelaw had always maintained that he would not talk to the gunmen he was badly compromised. His first instinct was that he must resign. But Heath was calm and supportive, and the House of Commons for the most part understanding, though Powell, Biggs-Davison and one or two more bitterly condemned him and he had to promise never to do it again.[10]

Looking back in his memoirs, Whitelaw felt that he had been very lucky.

> If, as a result of deciding in favour of a secret exploratory meeting, I had become involved in further discussions with the IRA leaders, I would eventually have landed myself in great difficulties. Clearly those ought to have been the IRA's tactics. As it turned out, by returning to violence almost at once, they presented me with a considerable advantage. They proved that they were intransigent and that it was the British Government who really wanted an end to violence.

From this moment, he believed, many Catholics began to turn against the IRA and towards the SDLP who, as a result, 'became stronger, more self-confident and thus more co-operative in their relations with me'.[11]

Certainly that July marked a watershed. Having gone to the limit of conciliation, Heath and Whitelaw were now in a much stronger position to revert to strong action. While Sean Macstiofan for the Provisionals called uncompromisingly for 'war of the utmost ferocity', Heath formally repeated the 'solemn assurance' that the status of Northern Ireland within the United Kingdom would not be altered except by consent, and appealed to the people of both communities to 'assert themselves against the men of violence'.[12] Two days later, on 21 July, the Provisionals plumbed new depths of random atrocity by exploding 22 bombs within an hour and a quarter in the centre of Belfast – in shopping centres, railway and bus stations: 11 people were killed, 130 seriously injured. The horror of 'Bloody Friday' lost the IRA sympathy within the Catholic community. It also gave Whitelaw the perfect opportunity to send the troops in to clear the 'no-go' areas of Derry.

'Operation Motorman' was such a success it was an anticlimax. In an effort to avoid bloodshed it was deliberately announced in advance, allowing the terrorists to escape over the border into Donegal. Instead of the pitched battle the army had feared, 1,250 troops with tanks, armoured cars and bulldozers were allowed to dismantle the barricades and reoccupy the IRA heartlands in the Bogside and Creggan estates without resistance, watched only by silent women and children. This was a major symbolic victory, reasserting British control over the whole territory of Northern Ireland. It was also the first visible result of Whitelaw's shrewd and sensitive way of proceeding, which went far to restore the trust of the Protestants following what Faulkner called the 'unmitigated disaster' of his first four months.[13]

The next stage was to get the representatives of the two communities to talk to one another. At the end of September Whitelaw convened a conference on neutral territory at Darlington in County Durham. Only Faulkner's official Unionists, the small non-sectarian Alliance party and the Northern Ireland Labour Party, however, agreed to attend; Paisley's Democratic Unionists, Craig's Vanguard and – most disappointingly to Whitelaw, after all he had done to woo them – the SDLP refused. Gerry Fitt and John Hume, the SDLP leaders, still insisted that they would not co-operate until internment was entirely ended. Whitelaw was working on this: by the end of the year he was ready to announce a new system of trying suspected terrorists before a judge alone, sitting without a jury. 'Diplock' courts came into operation in 1973. They were designed to get round the problem that juries would not convict nor witnesses give evidence for fear of intimidation. They were a clear improvement on the crude system of internment on the word of the security forces; nevertheless over the next two decades they too became a shaming symbol of the permanent suspension of normal judicial process in Northern Ireland. They are still operating today.

Meanwhile the SDLP still refused to co-operate, while the Unionists reacted violently to a Green Paper which Whitelaw published after Darlington proposing local government elections by proportional representation to be held by the end of the year. Vanguard and the UDA asserted that they would not accept any dilution of first-past-the-post majority rule nor any voting system different from the rest of the UK. The elections had to be postponed. At this Heath's patience began to crack. On 16–17 November he paid his first extended visit to Ulster since becoming Prime Minister – he had made a flying visit to the troops the previous Christmas – with the clear intention of knocking some heads together. At a lunch for community leaders in Belfast City Hall he warned Craig and his supporters bluntly that threats of UDI would only 'bring about a bloodbath' in Ireland, north and south, and an immediate end to British subsidies to Ulster worth £200 million a year. He explicitly reminded all parties of the 'considerable sacrifices' which the rest of Britain currently made for Ulster and demanded some movement in return.

It is no good the parties stating dogmatic views and refusing to move from them. That way lies chaos and despair. If we are to reach a fair and effective solution there must be understanding and realism on all sides. Our fellow citizens in the rest of the United Kingdom are being asked to make immense efforts and considerable sacrifices on behalf of Northern Ireland. It is natural that they should look closely day by day in their newspapers, night by night on their televisions, to see why and in what circumstances this effort and these sacrifices are required of them. They see throughout Northern Ireland steadfastness, determination and suffering nobly borne by so many people . . . What they do not as yet discern is a willingness to put on one side the violence and the passions derived from the past in favour of that decent co-operation between neighbours which alone can ensure the future.

He was particularly severe on those so-called 'loyalists' whose violence only strengthened the IRA and made 'a mockery of loyalty to the Crown'. So long as the people of Northern Ireland wished it, their right to remain British would be respected:

But with that right goes a clear and necessary obligation . . . to remain also within our traditional framework of law, of peaceful debate, of willingness to meet other points of view; that framework of which we in the United Kingdom are intensely proud and which I must tell you we are determined to preserve throughout our land.[14]

While Heath talked tough, Whitelaw kept on working patiently to win the trust of the reasonable elements in both communities and detach them from the diehards. In March 1973 he came forward with a White Paper, more specific than his previous Green Paper, containing definite proposals for a new Northern Ireland Assembly of 78 members, to be elected by proportional representation, and a new Executive, not dominated by a single community but as broadly based as possible, to which most of the former powers of Stormont (but not control of security, law and order and the conduct of elections) would be restored. In addition there were to be further anti-discrimination laws and the Irish Republic would be invited to discuss the creation of an All-Ireland Council. The plan was routinely denounced as a sell out by Craig and Paisley and as perpetuating British rule by the nationalists. But Unionist feeling had been somewhat assuaged by a plebiscite held earlier that month which gave 58 per cent of the population the chance to vote formally to remain in the United Kingdom. The result was a foregone conclusion – the SDLP instructed Catholics to abstain, so the 'No' vote was only

6 per cent. But the Protestants were sufficiently reassured by this demonstration of their strength for Faulkner to be able to persuade a majority of the Ulster Unionist Council to swallow their doubts and give the Assembly a chance – the vote was 381–231 after Craig and about a hundred Vanguard supporters had walked out – and the SDLP too now agreed to co-operate. With an unopposed Second Reading, the Bill was rushed through Parliament with such speed that the first elections for the Assembly were held on 28 June, just fourteen weeks after the publication of the White Paper.

The results were just about satisfactory in the short term, but ominous in the longer term. Of the 78 seats, Unionists pledged to Faulkner won 22 and the SDLP 19, with the Alliance Party taking 8 and the Northern Ireland Labour Party one. But Vanguard and Paisley's DUP, combined in a 'Loyalist Coalition', won 18 seats and 'unpledged' Independent Unionists won another 10. Thus while the pro-Assembly parties had taken two-thirds of the vote (and hence two-thirds of the seats), more Unionists had actually voted against Faulkner than for him. This was to prove a flimsy basis of consent on which to build a new constitution.

There was still no certainty that a power-sharing Executive could be formed at all out of such a result. The first meeting of the Assembly was bedlam. Both Faulker's Unionists and the SDLP were still more concerned to guard their backs against accusations of betrayal than to sit down together with Whitelaw. Over the summer there were signs that the level of violence was diminishing. The security forces achieved some notable successes on both sides of the border: among other leading figures Gerry Adams was arrested in the north and Seamus Twomey in the south. Heath was emboldened to declare at the beginning of September that the IRA bombing campaign had clearly failed.[15] But he remained impatient with the pace of political progress. Visiting the province again at the end of August he urged the party leaders publicly to 'thrash out their differences and get on with it'. An Executive must be in place by March 1974 or the enabling legislation would lapse. Despite the improved security position, 'Every day's delay . . . can only mean more lives lost, more maimed and more wounded.'[16] On 5 October Whitelaw finally managed to bring together the leaders of the 3 pro-Assembly parties – 6 Unionists, 6 SDLP and 3 Alliance – for talks at Stormont Castle. It was a long, slow, patient process, but gradually he managed to build sufficient trust not only in himself but, more important still, between the traditional antagonists so that they began to leave their rooted prejudices behind and find a common purpose. Still, the going was hard.

There were two main sticking points on which the talks nearly broke down, one practical – the precise party balance on the proposed 12-man Executive – and one symbolic – the powers and composition of the Council of Ireland (on which Heath and Whitelaw insisted as a condition of devolving powers to the Executive). After six weeks the talks were close to collapse. On 21 November, Whitelaw wrote, 'I woke up in a very depressed mood.'

> I rang Ted Heath early and told him that I would be coming back that afternoon and that I was convinced I would be reporting failure. He accepted my news with a note of resignation and depression in his voice, for he was facing many other problems at that moment. As always on such occasions he said little, but curiously he made me feel all the more determined not to fail him and my Cabinet colleagues.[17]

In fact, from the brink of breakdown Whitelaw managed to snatch agreement. To concentrate the minds of the negotiators he had his helicopter parked on the lawn outside the windows of the conference room, ready to whisk him back to London the moment he decided the will to agree did not exist. The second trick he held up his sleeve until the last minute was mathematical. Instead of an Executive of 12 on which the Unionists had demanded 7 seats, the SDLP 5 and the Alliance Party 2, he substituted an 11-strong body on which it was agreed the Unionists should have 6 representatives, the SDLP 4 and the Alliance one. In addition there were to be 4 non-voting members of whom 2 would be SDLP, one Alliance and only one a Unionist. Suddenly, as Faulkner wrote, 'It was all over bar the allocation of portfolios.'[18] Faulkner was to be Chief Executive, Gerry Fitt his deputy, the other responsibilities amicably shared. There was, as Whitelaw records, 'considerable euphoria as we went out onto the steps of Stormont Castle to announce our agreement to the waiting media'.[19]

It was a brilliant achievement, testimony to Whitelaw's 'geniality, patience, genius in personal relations and statesmanship'.[20] It was testimony also to the distance Faulkner had travelled since 1972; nor was it much less of a risk for Gerry Fitt. Unquestionably the formation of the power-sharing Executive was the most hopeful development in Northern Ireland for decades. But its prospects were doubtful from the start. It was immediately denounced alike by Craig and Paisley and by the IRA. Faulkner's support within the Protestant community was desperately narrow: two days before the final breakthrough he obtained the sanction of the Unionist Council to keep talking by just ten votes (379–369). The formation of the

Executive was also still dependent on the success of tripartite talks to be held between Britain, the Ulster parties and the Irish Republic to give substance to the 'Irish dimension' by means of a Council of Ireland. Finally it was dealt a severe blow by Heath's decision, at this delicate moment, to bring Whitelaw back to London as Employment Secretary to try to work the same miracle on the miners' dispute that he had apparently contrived in Northern Ireland. Francis Pym succeeded, presumably on the principle that Ulster called for the skills of a Chief Whip. It was understandable that Heath – in the ultimate crisis of his Government – should want Whitelaw back at his side. But his departure left the power-sharing Executive orphaned before it was even born.

The seal was set on Whitelaw's success at the tripartite conference held at the Sunningdale Civil Service College, just west of London, on 6–9 December. As a full-scale round-table summit between the British and Irish Governments and representatives of both communities in the North, Sunningdale was an unprecedented diplomatic venture – and one which was not to be repeated for another eighteen years. Briefly, in the cordial atmosphere there generated, it looked as if the age-old Irish bloodfeud might at last be laid to rest. Heath – when he could get away from the domestic problems besetting him – led the British delegation, supported by Alec Douglas-Home, Pym, David Howell and (for constitutional matters) Peter Rawlinson; plus Sir Frank Cooper of the Northern Ireland Office and some forty officials. Dublin was equally strongly represented by the Taoiseach, Liam Cosgrave (who had replaced Lynch earlier in the year at the head of a Fine Gael/Labour coalition) and seven Cabinet ministers including Garret Fitzgerald and Conor Cruise O'Brien, also backed by a battery of Civil Servants. By comparison the three Ulster parties – but particularly Faulkner's Unionists (since the SDLP had access to the Republic's officials) – felt outgunned.[21]

The optimistic tone was set by the dinner which Heath hosted, in his grandest style, at Downing Street on the first evening. It turned out, as Faulkner wrote later, 'to be a very convivial occasion'.

A choir had been brought along for our entertainment, and sang a wide range of modern and classical music from Ireland and Britain while we drank our coffee and relaxed after our seven-course dinner. Drink had been flowing freely throughout the evening and by the end of the choral performance some of those present were becoming more informal than I think Heath had intended. Loud calls of 'Give us a song, Paddy' were heard, but Heath skilfully diverted any possible embarrassment by leading us into another room for coffee and more sober conversation.[22]

The whole conference was a bit like that, a superficial success achieved only by dissolving the trickiest problems in a glow of good will. The trouble was that the main objective – to establish a Council of Ireland – meant different things to the different parties. Essentially it was a sop to nationalist opinion, a symbol of the ultimate unity of the island – and potentially a step towards achieving it. Yet at the same time it could be sold to the Unionists as a practical forum for cross-border co-operation, particularly on policing but also on less contentious matters like sport, agriculture and pollution, so long as it did not affect the fundamental integrity of Ulster and was accompanied by an explicit declaration by the Republic that it accepted the status of Northern Ireland as part of the United Kingdom for as long as a majority of its inhabitants so wished. This last was on paper a prize worth securing: for the first time since partition Dublin formally waived the claim enshrined in the Irish constitution that its territory embraced all thirty-two counties of Ireland. To secure this, Faulkner and his colleagues were willing to swallow a lot of what they regarded as 'mystical nonsense surrounding the SDLP approach to the Council of Ireland . . . If this nonsense was necessary to bring their supporters along I did not see why we should be difficult, provided we could ensure that it meant nothing in practice.' A Council was duly agreed, with 14 Ministers, 7 each from the Republic and the North, a consultative assembly and a secretariat. But 'all our efforts were directed towards ensuring that, however many tiers and secretaries the Council of Ireland might have, it remained essentially propaganda and in no way impinged on the powers of the Northern Ireland Assembly. I felt confident that Unionists, being basically practical people, would judge our final agreement on a practical rather than symbolic level.'[23]

The issue on which Faulkner – at least according to his own account – dug in his heels was a suggestion that the police on both sides of the border should in some shadowy way come under the control of the Council. It took an all-night session to convince Heath that this was something the Unionists would absolutely not accept. Faulkner's recollection may owe something to his need after the event to show what a hard fight he had put up to deny the Council any real powers; but it gives a graphic picture of how far his 'special relationship' with Heath had deteriorated since direct rule:

It was after 4 a.m. when a grim Ted Heath descended on our party room, clearly determined to sort us out . . . He announced that we had done very well indeed on the recognition issue and were therefore duty bound to agree to give ground on policing. He made it clear that if the talks broke down on this issue he would lay the blame on the Unionists in public. But we were not going to be blackmailed in that way and we said so, one by one . . . Heath argued with several of the speakers and grew quite irritated, raising his voice heatedly, but by the time we had all spoken our determination not to concede must have been unmistakable, for he lapsed into one of his famous silences. After sitting for perhaps several minutes looking over our heads he got up suddenly and walked out without a word.[24]

It was the evening of the next day before agreement was finally reached. Heath undertook, 'extremely reluctantly', that the control of security in Northern Ireland would be restored to the devolved assembly as soon as the emergency came to an end. 'Because of our row over security control in March 1972 he seemed to regard this concession as a personal admission of error. But it was clear that the talks would collapse otherwise, so he agreed.' In return, the Unionists accepted a 'tenuous and, in practice, totally meaningless link between the police forces north and south of the border and the Council of Ireland'.[25]

'That Sunday evening', wrote Faulkner, 'all of us in the Unionist deputation were convinced that we had come off best . . . One member of our delegation remarked that Sunningdale would go down in history as a Unionist victory.'[26] He could not have been more wrong. The tragedy of Sunningdale was that Faulkner and his colleagues allowed themselves to be bullied and cajoled into giving their adherence to a constitutional hypothesis which had no chance of being accepted in the real world of Ulster politics. They should not perhaps be blamed for their willingness to suspend their doubts in order to keep the tender shoots of a settlement in Northern Ireland precariously alive. They should have known, however – in their hearts they did know – that Unionist opinion back home would regard agreement even to the shadow of a Council of Ireland as a rank betrayal. Heath, schooled by Whitelaw, likewise should have realised that his determination to get the hypothetical Council agreed, though temporarily successful, was wasted effort, founded on unreality.

By no means for the only time in 1970–4 Heath deceived himself, believing that reason as he saw it must eventually prevail. But he was exhausted in December 1973. He was facing the crisis of his Government. He desperately wanted to clinch the Irish settlement that seemed to be within his grasp, and at Sunningdale he no longer had Whitelaw at his side to remind him of Irish realities. Nor was it only his insistence on securing the Council of Ireland that failed to stick. The other half of the equation also quickly came apart. Cosgrave's agreement to recognise the fact of partition provoked as much fury in Dublin as the proposed Council did in Belfast: it was immediately challenged in the courts as unconstitutional, and Cosgrave was obliged to qualify it, raising once again all the old fears in the North. What Heath was attempting at Sunningdale was the same trick which Lloyd George had pulled in 1921, selling the same idea to different groups with contradictory arguments, in the hope that they would not notice. Sunningdale had to seem to Unionists to rule out unity, while to nationalists it had to advance it. By such duplicity Lloyd George achieved partition and got Britain out of the south of Ireland, at the cost of a bitter civil war between the pro- and anti-Treaty forces in the new Republic. But Heath was not Lloyd George; and the anti-Sunningdale Unionists in the North won the argument to render Sunningdale a dead letter.

Criticism has focused on the attempt to impose the unacceptable Council of Ireland as the error which sank an otherwise promising initiative. In reality, however, while the anti-Faulkner Unionists made his acceptance of the Council the pretext for disowning Sunningdale, it is doubtful whether it could have succeeded anyway: the size of the anti-Faulkner vote in the Assembly elections back in June showed that Unionist feeling was already profoundly hostile to the idea of power-sharing, before the Council was ever thought of. Power-sharing was a much more serious threat to Protestant ascendancy in Ulster than the pretensions of a distant Council. The likelihood must be that power-sharing – for all Whitelaw's heroic diplomatic efforts and the brave response of Faulkner and Fitt – was a non-starter even before the reaction to Sunningdale gave it the *coup de grâce*.[27]

At a euphoric press conference at the conclusion of the conference, and in the House of Commons next day, Heath was optimistic.[28] The press hailed a new dawn in Ireland. Euphoria was quickly dispelled, however, not only by the denunciations of Craig and Paisley, but by renewed IRA activity both in Northern Ireland and in London over Christmas. On 31 December the new power-sharing Executive was sworn in at Stormont and the next day it formally took office. Devolved government was restored as promised – after rather more than twelve months, admittedly, but still in less than two years of direct rule. It worked, for as long as it was allowed, surprisingly well. Over the weeks of their negotiations with Whitelaw a real sense of comradeship had been built between Faulkner, Fitt and their colleagues. This, however, only underlined how far they had all moved beyond the irreconcilables in their respective communities who held the initiative on the streets. On 4 January Faulkner was repudiated by the Unionist Council by 454 votes to 374. He immediately resigned the leadership of the official Unionist party to Harry West, though he remained Chief Executive and still led twenty Unionists in the Assembly loyal to the power-sharing experiment. A still more serious blow to the Executive's survival was struck by Heath's decision to call a General Election at the end of February. The election was of course advanced for wholly British reasons. Both Pym and Whitelaw warned of the near certainty that it would spell the end of the power-sharing experiment, but in a national emergency Ulster was no more than a marginal concern. So it proved. Without proportional representation – which did not apply to Westminster elections – Faulkner's pro-Sunningdale Unionists could not win a single seat. The United Ulster Unionists – an electoral pact between the 3 anti-Assembly groupings led by West, Craig and Paisley – took 11 of the 12 by virtue of 51 per cent of the vote. ('The other 49 per cent', as Gerry Fitt wryly put it, 'got me.')[29] The Executive's days were clearly numbered. In May 1974 its helplessness was cruelly exposed by a Protestant workers' strike which Wilson and Merlyn Rees declined to try to put down. On 28 May Faulkner gave up the struggle and resigned. Direct rule from London was resumed. The attempt to establish power sharing between the communities was a brave experiment in 1973 which Whitelaw had managed to carry surprisingly far before it crashed. It would be eighteen years before another Northern Ireland Secretary tried again.

30

Oil and Coal

ON I January 1973 Britain had at last become a member of the
EEC. After decades of relative decline, Heath had looked forward confidently to Britain now sharing in the prosperity that the
Six had enjoyed for fifteen years. Sadly these high hopes were to be
quickly dashed. Britain joined the Community just as the era of
growth was coming to an end. The dislocation of the world
economy and global inflation, followed in the autumn by the oil
crisis arising from the Arab–Israeli war, threw all the countries of the
Nine back on their own domestic problems, stalling further integration of the enlarged Community for a decade and more. On the
European front, therefore, 1973 was a frustrating and bitterly disillusioning year for Heath. He entered the secret garden at last and
found it becoming choked with weeds.

In speeches, articles and interviews on and around New Year's
Day he tried hard to rouse a sceptical public to share his excitement at
this 'tremendous moment'.[1] Above all, in a characteristic assertion of
one of the aspects of the European adventure which meant most to
him, he determined to mark the moment of entry with a nationwide
festival dedicated to the idea of Britain's European heritage. 'Fanfare
for Europe' ran for eleven days from 3 January, with a crowded programme of events, by no means all musical and by no means
concentrated in London. Music was to the fore, with concerts by
leading European orchestras, but there were plays and exhibitions
and pop concerts too, as well as cookery demonstrations, tree-
planting, town-twinning ceremonies and firework displays. A
special 50p piece was also minted to mark the occasion, showing nine
interlocked hands representing the countries of the enlarged Community. The coins are still in circulation. But who remembers the
intended symbolism? Inevitably, however, the festival came across

as an élitist jamboree, exemplified by the opening events: on the one hand a contrived football match at Wembley between teams drawn from the original Six and the three new members, which was poorly attended; on the other a gala evening at Covent Garden, attended by the Queen, the Prime Minister, the diplomatic corps and most of the Establishment. Heath wanted to throw a national party, something like the 1951 Festival of Britain. In reality, with the public at best apathetic and the Opposition hostile, the Fanfare fell sadly flat. Wilson condemned the spending of £350,000 as 'an outrage', suggesting that the money would have been better given to the children damaged by thalidomide.[2] Herbert von Karajan told Heath that he had brought the Berlin Philharmonic to London 'to please you':[3] and in truth the whole event seemed too obviously designed for the same purpose.

There seemed in the short term no benefits from membership at all, but only costs. After all the argument about the higher cost of food inside the Community, Britain's entry unluckily coincided with soaring world commodity prices which dwarfed the increases due to the Common Agricultural Policy. While food prices rose by 11 per cent in the first nine months of 1973, less than a penny in the pound was attributable to the EEC.[4] But inevitably the 'Common Market' got the blame – exacerbated in April when it was revealed that the Commission was selling surplus butter to the Soviet Union at a subsidised price less than a third of its price in Britain. (The next month the Government hastily introduced a butter subsidy – 2p a pound – for British consumers.) There was apprehension and anger, too, over proposals to increase the size of 'juggernaut' lorries allowed on British roads. For all Heath's talk of Britain now having a voice in Brussels, the to-ing and fro-ing of ministers seemed to have little effect. Britain now had two commissioners in Brussels – Christopher Soames and George Thomson, both of whom had played notable parts in the long battle to achieve membership; and on 16 January just over half of Britain's complement of 36 members – 18 Tories, led by Peter Kirk, and 2 Liberals – took their seats in the European Parliament at Strasbourg. Labour, however, boycotted the Community and refused to take up its allocation of seats. British membership was thus at best half-hearted and still provisional.

Heath put the best face he could on the lack of public enthusiasm: 'I think, in their phlegmatic and pragmatic way,' he told a radio interviewer, 'the British are now waiting for action and, as we in the Community take action together, more and more they will respond to it.'[5] Little happened in the course of 1973, however, to excite such a response. The Paris summit of the heads of government of the

about-to-be-enlarged Community which Heath attended with such
eagerness in October 1972 had set an ambitious timetable for progress towards closer integration on all fronts. Heath predicted 'a
massive move forward' in the coming year.[6] Proposals were to be
worked out in time for the next meeting in Copenhagen at the end of
1973 on economic and monetary union (which it was hoped to
achieve by 1980); on developing a common industrial policy and co-
ordinated social and environmental policies; and on streamlining the
Community's own decision-making procedures and strengthening
the European Parliament. But in the prevailing political climate they
were too ambitious, indeed quite unrealistic: proposals were prepared – the Commission did its work well – but the nine member
Governments were in no position to begin to carry them out. First,
there was no possibility of monetary convergence. Britain, by floating the pound in 1972, had already failed to join the European
currency 'snake' and Italy too had been forced to drop out. In
February 1973 the American dollar was devalued by 10 per cent. In
response six Community countries agreed to float their currencies
jointly against the dollar; but Britain, Italy and Ireland continued to
float separately. There was no basis for talking seriously about
monetary union at Copenhagen.

There was less obvious division, but equally little progress in most
of the other areas of proposed advance. The wheels of the Commission revolved, but the leaders were not ready to take the political grip
needed to take decisions. Frustrated, Heath proposed in October that
there should be more frequent summits between the heads of
government, meeting on their own without large staffs, to maintain
the political momentum.[7] This at least was agreed, and regular six-
monthly summits were instituted from 1975. By then, however,
Heath was no longer in office to participate in them.

The Community's distance from the ideal of unity was embarrassingly exposed in October by the outbreak of the Middle East War
and particularly by the threat of an oil embargo. For a whole month,
while the Americans and the Russians strove through the United
Nations to achieve a ceasefire, the Europeans were marginalised by
their inability to agree a common position. The Arabs played skilfully on the concern of each country to safeguard its own oil supplies
by treating them differently. The Dutch, who had expressed the
greatest sympathy for Israel, and alone allowed the Americans to fly
military supplies to Israel from their airfields, were 'punished' by a
complete embargo. France and Britain, on the other hand, which
both denied the Americans facilities and even-handedly suspended
the supply of military equipment to both sides, were deemed to be

'friendly countries' and rewarded with uninterrupted supplies. The other six were subject to moderate reductions. The warning was clear, and it appeared to have achieved its purpose when the EEC finally came up with an agreed statement on 6 November, calling for a withdrawal to the ceasefire lines of 22 October and a settlement on the basis of Resolution 242, which was widely interpreted as pro-Arab.

Israel claimed bitterly to have been 'betrayed and deserted' by European nations concerned only to protect their own interest. Sir Alec Douglas-Home, on the contrary, insisted that the British position was unchanged:[8] since 1970 Britain had consistently called on Israel to give up the territories occupied in 1967. More serious for European unity was the anger felt – particularly by the Dutch – at the refusal of Britain and France to agree to share their oil with the Community, and the suspicion that they were negotiating separately with the producers to assure their own supplies. Speaking in Brussels in early December, Heath sternly rejected the suggestion that Britain had sold the Dutch down the river, claiming that close co-ordination was going on behind the scenes. The point was that Europe was learning to take its own course, independent of the Americans: 'The day when the voice of the United States automatically prevailed over each of its individual partners has passed.'[9] The Franco-British argument was that it was in the interest of the Community as a whole that those countries which retained the Arabs' good will should not needlessly jeopardise it. This unheroic view could be said to have been vindicated when OPEC withdrew its embargo on supplying the Dutch; but by then it had served its purpose. The Community did achieve a united front in the end; nevertheless the whole episode left a legacy of distrust between the larger and smaller countries of the Nine.

Heath strove desperately to play down the setback the war had dealt the European vision. In his speech to the Tory conference in October – a conference which, as *The Times* noted, had barely mentioned Europe in the previous three days[10] – he tried to revive the representatives' flagging enthusiasm by insisting that everything was going splendidly. The war in the Middle East actually showed how far European unity had come: less than thirty years before it had been Europe that was riven by war, a possibility now inconceivable. In September the foreign ministers of the Nine had achieved – 'on a British proposal as a result of a British initiative' – a common response to Kissinger's call for a new Atlantic Charter, or as he called it, 'a common European policy towards our principal ally, the United States'. This, he claimed, had only been made possible by British membership. As for the internal development of the Community: 'Progress this year is already considerable. By the end of the year major decisions will have to be taken over a very wide field including economic and monetary union, and social and regional policy.'[11] If he really believed this he was to be cruelly disappointed.

The nine leaders gathered in Copenhagen on 14 December at a bad moment for Europe, and an even worse one for Heath domestically. Since mid-November the Government had been once again embroiled with the miners, with yet another State of Emergency in force and severe restrictions on the use of power. Barber was about to announce the massive package of spending cuts which finally called a halt to the pursuit of growth. After all the rhetoric about growing together, it was a bitter pill for Heath to have to come to Copenhagen to beg his European colleagues' understanding for whatever emergency measures he might have to take to protect the British economy. They were not sympathetic. The conference was overshadowed by the oil crisis and implications for all the Western economies of the ending of the era of cheap energy. With North Sea oil due to come on stream in the next few years, Britain appeared to its partners better off than most. Willy Brandt took the lead in proposing the equal sharing of energy resources within the Community; but Heath stoutly insisted that North Sea oil was British. Much as he might have liked to pool it, it would have been political suicide to have gone home having given away Britain's one windfall prospect of economic regeneration. The summit did in fact manage to achieve a superficially united common position on energy policy – a statement that the Nine would stand together in future negotiations with the oil producers, rather than bargain separately.[12] But it was little more than a declaration of intent, and within a few days the front of unity was once again in tatters.

Copenhagen made none of the progress Heath had hoped for on internal matters. Above all he desperately needed progress on the promised establishment of the regional fund, the one Community aspiration which offered immediate and tangible benefit to Britain. This would be Britain's quid pro quo for the CAP. The Germans, however, who would be the major contributor to such a fund, were not yet ready to pay up – somewhat to Brandt's discomfiture, as he recorded in his memoirs:

> Thanks to the restrictive attitude of my financial experts . . . I found myself in a rather embarrassing position at Copenhagen. Deliberately addressing myself to our own government as well as

others, I set the 'ante' for admission to European regional policy so low that those present could not have taken me seriously.[13]

Whereas the Commission had proposed a fund of £1,000 million over three years, and Britain had pressed for £1,250 million, Brandt proposed no more than £250 million. As on other critical occasions in his career, Heath had totally convinced himself of what was right but neglected to ensure that the other party to the bargain agreed. On the plane back to London he was 'shattered' by the German attitude.[14] Three days later when the foreign ministers met in Brussels to try to resolve the deadlock, Walter Scheel was prepared to accept a Danish compromise of £330 million, but no more. At this point, under intolerable domestic pressure, Heath's European idealism cracked. 'Faced with the prospect of a puny return on all the political capital he had invested in a huge Community regional fund which would help Britain's backward areas,' *The Times* reported, 'Mr Heath evidently gave instructions to Sir Alec Douglas-Home to link two wholly dissociated topics.'[15] To the fury of his eight colleagues Home threatened to veto the fragile agreement on energy policy adopted at Copenhagen unless the Community also agreed to establish a substantial regional fund. The year ended in deadlock. In the end, as usually happens in the EEC, the crisis passed. The effort, such as it was, to construct a specifically European response to the oil crisis was overtaken in February by an American-led initiative to which all the Nine except France adhered; while the regional fund was eventually established at the next Community summit in Paris in September. By then, however – once again – Heath was no longer in office to claim the political dividend.

Thus, at the end of 1973, with everything else collapsing around him at home, even his proudest achievement seemed to have foundered in acrimony and mistrust. His ambitious vision of Britain leading the enlarged Community into new spheres of ever-closer co-operation had ended humiliatingly, within a year, with Britain using its veto to block co-operation on the single most urgent issue facing the Community. This was a sobering collision of high-flown Euro-rhetoric with economic and national reality, from which the European ideal emerged – at least in the short term – badly bruised. The Community had to go through a long period of retrenchment before a fresh attempt could be made to scale even the foothills of unity – let alone the economic and monetary union by 1980 which Heath, Brandt and Pompidou had so blithely charted in 1972. Within five months of Copenhagen, all three were out of office. Heath called a General Election in February and lost; Pompidou died in harness at the beginning of April; and Brandt resigned following the exposure of an East German spy in his private office at the beginning of May. The rest of the decade was dominated by the very different trio of Giscard d'Estaing, Helmut Schmidt and Jim Callaghan – all former finance ministers primarily concerned with weathering the impact of world recession.

At the beginning of October the Government's prospects had looked brighter than at any time in the previous two years. But two sub-merged rocks lay in wait. First, the miners, having digested the record increase they had won from Wilberforce in 1972, were once again girding themselves to demand a further substantial instalment. Ministers were confident, however, that in framing the labyrinthine provisions of Stage Three they had made allowance for the miners. Their confidence might have been justified had it not been for the international oil crisis. It was the 'oil shock' which wrecked Heath's Government. At a stroke the era of cheap energy on which the West had prospered so complacently over the previous half century was ended and the whole industrialised world plunged into recession. Britain was particularly hard hit, partly because it depended on im-ported oil for 50 per cent of its energy needs, the proportion having been deliberately increased over recent years as the coal industry was run down – North Sea oil had only recently been discovered and was not due to come on stream for some years yet – but more specifically because British inflation was already very high and the Government had staked its authority on a prices and incomes policy designed to bring it down. The threat to oil supplies crucially strengthened the very group of workers most determined to bust the policy. But for the boost the oil crisis gave the miners, the Government might have been able to ride it out. But the temporary shortage of oil, followed by the rapid quadrupling of its price, lent the miners the economic muscle to defy Stage Three. It was not in the end the miners nor the oil crisis alone but the lethal combination of the two which brought the Government to defeat.

The irony of the Government's second confrontation with the NUM was that it had tried desperately to avert it. As Douglas Hurd wrote: 'We had most of us dreaded, beyond anything else, a further engagement with the miners.'[16] Following the 1972 strike Peter Walker's Coal Industry Act had poured £1,100 million of new in-vestment into the pits, reversing the Robens policy of closing uneconomic pits. In March 1973 ministers felt they had got their re-ward when the miners voted in a pithead ballot – against the advice of their Executive – to accept the offer made to them under Stage

Two. Accepting this result, however, Joe Gormley gave warning that the NUM was still bent on making up the ground it felt it had lost: it would 'go into battle when the time is right'.[17] The miners, he vowed, 'must be at the head of the wages league'.[18] The annual NUM conference in July duly rejected the Government's wages policy and instructed the Executive to seek a 35 per cent increase for the coming year. This was not, Gormley insisted in his memoirs, a deliberate challenge to the Government: 'We simply wanted the right wages to keep young men coming into the Industry.'[19] Two weeks later Heath invited Gormley secretly to Downing Street to see how the miners' ambition could be met within the terms of the incomes policy. On a hot summer day, Heath, Gormley and William Armstrong – unknown to the press, their colleagues, the Coal Board or the Department of Employment – sat in the garden of Number 10 and examined the options. It was a friendly talk. Gormley found Heath 'neither stubborn nor unapproachable' but a good listener – unlike Harold Wilson. He told Heath he had no choice but to follow his conference's instruction to pursue the 35 per cent claim; but he hinted that a possible loophole might be found in the idea of a special payment for 'unsocial hours'. Gormley was convinced that Heath and Armstrong 'had both taken the hint, because they turned to each other and said: "We never thought of that. We never thought of that at all!"'[20]

The trouble was that this was only an informal understanding, reached by a nod and wink between the three men without reference to the parties involved and never clearly spelled out. There were two reasons why it failed to stick. First, Heath could override the Department of Employment and the Coal Board, but he overestimated Gormley's ability to carry his Executive – as did Gormley himself. Gormley was a genial fixer with an engaging confidence in his power to pull off a deal; but on this occasion he deceived himself and misled Heath at the same time. Second, the agreement itself was based on a misunderstanding. Heath and Armstrong gratefully accepted the 'unsocial hours' loophole and built it into Stage Three; but in doing so they extended it to all shift workers, totalling at least another million people. Gormley had not made it clear that he expected it to apply exclusively to the miners. 'I must say that I wasn't best pleased,' he recalled. 'I had gone there to try to solve our problem, not to give them help in running the country as a whole.'[21] Heath was willing to frame Stage Three to help the miners. But he was 'absolutely solid' that they should not be seen to receive special treatment.[22] This remained his position throughout the dispute.

Over the summer and early autumn Heath and Peter Walker were confident that the miners had been squared. When it turned out that they had not been, then the sense of having been let down stiffened Heath's refusal to give any more ground. Heath and his colleagues have often been blamed for poor intelligence in misjudging the mood of the coalfields: they reply that it was Gormley who got it wrong – their mistake was to put too much faith in Gormley.[23]

It was the oil crisis which both dealt the miners a winning hand and strengthened their willingness to play it. In fact the shortages were very much less serious than at first predicted: the real damage was done to Western economies by the massive price rise. But the shock of the Arabs' discovery of the oil weapon, and the revelation of the West's dependence on cheap oil, had a traumatic psychological effect. In Hurd's words: 'The earth began to move under the Government's feet.'[24] Practically the only person in Whitehall who had foreseen the danger was Lord Rothschild, who had predicted that as soon as OPEC resolved its divisions (as happened in 1972) the Arabs would be bound to try their luck,[25] and so they did: the price was raised twice over the spring and summer of 1973 by 6 per cent each time, and OPEC was discussing a further rise when the war broke out, adding a political pretext for punishing those Western countries which might be inclined to support Israel. In October, as well as cutting deliveries of oil to America and Europe by around 25 per cent, it announced a further thumping price rise of 70 per cent, which took the price to more than $5 a barrel (compared with $2.40 at the beginning of the year). As reward for Britain's refusal to supply spare parts to Israel or allow American planes to fly from British bases, deliveries to Britain were cut by only about 15 per cent; by February supplies were nearly back to normal. Still the cutback came at the worst possible moment for the Government. As part of their contingency planning against another coal strike ministers had built up coal stocks by burning more oil; they would normally have countered the miners' threatened action by switching yet more heavily to oil. As it was, they had to burn coal in order to save oil. In this situation Heath was desperate to secure Britain's oil supplies – even at the cost of a common European policy. He bullied the Foreign Office to do more on the diplomatic front and called in the directors of Shell and BP to insist that, as British-owned companies, they had an obligation to give their British customers priority. (They refused.) In fact the shortages were not in themselves very serious. Coupons issued in preparation for petrol rationing were never used. What mattered more was the competitive advantage the new high price of oil – doubled again at the end of the year to $11.65 a barrel – gave to coal, and the encouragement this gave to the miners.

The lines were drawn in the coal dispute just four days after the outbreak of war in the Middle East and two days after Heath's announcement of the terms of Stage Three. In making their offer for 1974–5 the National Coal Board went to the limit of what was available under the Government's policy. On top of the 7 per cent basic they threw in another 4 per cent for unsocial hours plus 1 per cent holiday pay, which added up to the biggest increase the NUM had ever achieved without a strike: it was surpassed only by the 21 per cent awarded by Wilberforce in 1972. There was even scope for a further 3·5 per cent in return for a productivity agreement, making a possible 16·5 per cent in all. Norman Siddall (deputising for Derek Ezra, who was in hospital) frankly explained that the Board had 'tried to see how best the union's claim can be accommodated within the constraints' of Government policy. Press reaction was mixed. *The Times* thought that the threat of a strike had been neutralised: 'the skilfully designed package is expected to prove acceptable in the coalfields'.[26] *The Economist*, on the other hand, condemned Ezra for offering 'a horrifying pay rise' which would only challenge the NUM to ask for more.[27] The latter view was quickly borne out when the miners' leaders turned the offer down flat. While it was clearly the case that the Board could not have offered less than the basic allowed by Stage Three, ministers were appalled that they had put everything they had to offer on the table straight away, leaving nothing for negotiation. The ritual of wage bargaining – a trade union's *raison d'être* – demands that concessions must be wrung from an unwilling management. Offered so much so soon, Gormley had no choice but to ask for more. With a sinking feeling ministers realised that the bulwark they thought they had erected against another miners' strike had been swept away. 'Here we were,' wrote Hurd, 'being manœuvred once again towards the same fatal field, still littered with relics of the last defeat.'[28] Robert Carr 'quite suddenly . . . felt a sense of doom, as though a Greek tragedy was about to be acted out'.[29]

The Coal Board's blunder destroyed what little confidence Heath had either in Ezra or in Maurice Macmillan at the Department of Employment. Henceforth he determined to handle negotiations with the miners himself, persuaded that only his own authority as Prime Minister would convince them of the Government's unshakeable commitment to Stage Three. The NCB found itself, as Ezra recalled, excluded from dealing with its own workforce.

> The NCB were not really involved at all and we were very unclear, right through this period . . . exactly what was going on

. . . Our relationship with the NUM . . . remained very good, and every time they had a meeting with the Government they immediately came round and told us about it.[30]

It was understandable – perhaps inevitable given the scale of the threat which another miners' strike posed to the Government's central policy – that Heath should want to take his destiny in his own hands. If Stage Three was sacrosanct then indeed the Coal Board had nothing left to offer. Yet the effect of his intervening directly so early in the game was simply to raise the stakes and close off options, thereby ensuring that the dispute could only develop into another confrontation between the Government and the NUM, which was exactly what the Government did not want.

On 23 October Heath met the NUM negotiating committee at Downing Street, but got no change out of them. With 600 men a week leaving mining, and now with the oil crisis, they felt they had a strong case. Gormley and his colleagues in turn found Heath 'polite but unbending'.[31] He emphasised how well the miners stood to do out of the 'unsocial hours' provisions of Stage Three, offered the prospect of a further look at miners' pay under the proposed relativities machinery of Stage Three, but refused to consider any immediate special treatment. The following day a special conference authorised the Executive to call an overtime ban. *The Times* remained confident that the membership would accept the Coal Board's offer if it were put to them;[32] but instead the question put was only whether the men supported the union in its efforts to win more, which of course they did. On 8 November, therefore, Gormley announced an overtime ban to begin on 12 November.

Because of shift work and safety procedure, a miners' overtime ban cuts coal production by a great deal more than the number of hours lost. Within a few days output was cut by 40 per cent. Compared with 1972, coal stocks were high. Nevertheless, partly because of the simultaneous threat to oil supplies, partly to signal the Government's determination not to be caught out again as they had been before, Peter Walker immediately announced a State of Emergency – the fifth since 1970 – involving a ban on the use of energy for advertising and display, restrictions on the heating of shops, offices and schools, and possible petrol rationing. On television two days later Heath tried to put across a double message: first, that the Government had no intention of giving way, but, second, that the miners were already being offered a very good deal, stressing the extra 3·5 per cent they could negotiate above the initial 13 per cent. 'There is', he insisted, 'absolutely no question of taking

on the miners.'[33] *The Economist* paraphrased his position a good deal
more pungently than he put it himself:

> Mr Heath intends constantly to remind the public that the reason
> why shop lights are dimmed, offices are chillier and people may
> soon be limited to 50 miles of motoring a week, is because men to
> whom high wages are already being paid, and even higher wages
> are being offered, are refusing to work normally at a time when a
> bloody little war is causing a temporary shortage of energy round
> the world.[34]

A week later, on a rare venture out of London to Lancashire,
Heath was again at pains to remind the miners – and the public – how
much his Government had done for them by way of reversing
Labour's rundown of the coal industry and assuring it had a settled
future: how unreasonable, therefore, even ungrateful, it was for the
NUM to be using the oil emergency to ask for more (and how mon-
strously opportunist it was of Labour to encourage them). The
Government was not taking on the miners, but the other way
around. The difference between this dispute and the previous one
was that since 1972 the Government had taken – or, as he preferred to
say, been given by Parliament – responsibility to control inflation by
controlling wages: hence this time the miners were confronting not
just the NCB but 'the expressed will of the elected representatives of
the people . . . That is the main difference . . . and I believe it will
prove decisive.'[35]

Heath's faith in the essential reasonableness of the British people
did not allow him to believe that the miners could persist in their
action in the face of appeals alike to their patriotism and their self-
interest. When they proved unresponsive he became suspicious that
the moderates on the Executive were being manipulated for political
ends by the hard left – personified by the sinister, saturnine figure of
the Scottish Communist Mick McGahey. This suspicion was reinforced at a long-remembered meeting at Number 10 on 28
November when the entire NUM Executive, nearly thirty strong,
confronted Heath, Barber, Maurice Macmillan, Tom Boardman
from the DTI and the ever present William Armstrong. (The Coal
Board was not represented.) Recollections differ as to precisely what
McGahey said. Barber's memory (supported by Boardman) is that
Heath asked him, 'What is it you want, Mr McGahey?' McGahey replied, 'something to the effect, "I want to see the end of your
Government!"' There was then 'a long silence and Ted, who was
genuinely trying to reach some understanding, didn't reply'.[36]

Gormley in his memoirs does not dispute the incident, but insists (somewhat improbably) that McGahey actually said something like 'Of course I want to change the Government, but I want to do it by democratic means.'[37] McGahey himself vehemently confirms this version; but really it makes little difference. The impression he left on ministers' minds was menacing; moreover he had previously called publicly (at the NUM conference in July) for 'agitation in the streets' to defeat the Government.[38] Heath may have coloured McGahey's words – in order to embarrass Gormley and the Labour Party – in asserting on television that McGahey had told him to his face that his purpose was to 'get your Government out'.[39] But he did not essentially misrepresent McGahey's position. What he and his colleagues did do, however, was to exaggerate McGahey's import-ance. By frightening themselves – and then trying to frighten the country – with the Communist bogey they lost sight of the real eco-nomic strength of the miners' case.

Another vivid exchange at the same meeting made the point and – had ministers only been willing to see it – offered the Government an acceptable way out. After Heath had lectured them for some time on the effect of the Middle East War on the economic position of the country, William Armstrong remembered an unnamed member of the Executive

a little man . . . at the very back, almost out of the window, sort of putting up his hand and eventually getting a hearing and saying: 'Prime Minister, what I can't understand is this: You have told us that we have no option but to pay the Arabs the price they're demanding for the oil. Now, as far as I know, the Arabs never helped us in World War I, and in World War II, and we flogged our guts out in all of that. Why can't you pay us for coal what you are willing to pay the Arabs for oil?'

And although it was put in that way, not put as an economist would put it, that in fact was bang on the economic nose. And the Prime Minister really had no answer.[40]

After three and a half hours the miners complained that all they got out of Heath was avocado mousse. Gormley was looking for some flexibility which would enable him to persuade the moderate major-ity of his Executive that they had won enough. But Heath, though he offered a wide-ranging enquiry into the coal industry and the pos-sibility of extra money from the Pay Board's relativities report (expected before Christmas) if they went back to work now, would still not make any exception for the NUM under Stage Three.

Gormley was helpless as the Executive voted 20–5 against holding a ballot on whether to end the overtime ban – in effect, to continue it indefinitely. Such an overwhelming vote only reinforced Heath's belief that the dispute was being prolonged for political motives. *The Times* agreed, calling on the miners to accept an impartial review in order to 'correct the impression that their leadership is . . . inspired by political spite'.[41] In fact the size of the majority demonstrated that it was *not* a political strike. Two days later the NUM placed half-page advertisements in the newspapers skilfully making their economic case:

600 MORE MEN HAVE LEFT THE PITS THIS WEEK

20,000 men were leaving every year. For years, the advertisement went on, the NUM had been predicting an energy crisis if coal was run down, but nobody had listened. Now that the crisis had struck, it could only be met by an *expanding* coal industry. The NCB's offer was not enough to stop the exodus. 'Our claim is not based on greed. It is not an attempt to run the country or kick out the Government. We are just recognising the facts of life.'[42]

This was a difficult claim for the Government to resist, if they had only felt able to listen to it. Though the 'Think Tank' was not formally involved, at least two members – Dick Ross and Adam Ridley – were urging the Government to play the 'Arab card' and recognise that the oil shortage had created a new situation which would legitimise making the miners a special case. Douglas Hurd later criticised the Civil Service for failing to brief ministers with a clear strategic perspective before the 28 November meeting.[43] It was really an option which Heath and his senior colleagues should have grasped for themselves, but they had boxed themselves into a corner by the conviction that their authority as a Government was on the line. They were convinced, first of all, that they must uphold Stage Three absolutely without exception: otherwise the counter-inflation policy would be in ruins and the flood gates opened to catastrophic hyper-inflation. A paper which Hurd and William Waldegrave wrote for Heath in early December put this point most clearly: 'A settlement in manifest breach of Stage 3', they argued, 'would not be possible for this Government, because it would destroy its authority and break the morale of the Conservative Party beyond hope of restoration in the lifetime of this Parliament.'[44] This was fair enough, except that the war in the Middle East had genuinely created a new situation which it would have been sensible to allow Stage Three to reflect. In addition, however, over and above the general principle, politics dictated that, of all groups, the Government could least afford to make an exception of the miners. The scars of its previous humiliation in 1972 were still raw. While the Cabinet had been anxious to avoid a second confrontation with the miners, much of the Tory party was positively straining for a return match which the Government would this time win. The clear message which Central Office was receiving from the constituencies and which Carrington duly passed on to Heath was that the Government must on no account give in to the NUM again: this time the Conservative party expected to see the miners smashed.

Ironically, therefore, it could be said that it was the Government which treated the miners' action as a political challenge while Gormley – marginalising the revolutionary rhetoric of McGahey and Arthur Scargill – managed very successfully to keep it strictly as an industrial dispute about pay. Heath was in fact boxed in both ways – bureaucratically by the rigidity which is the very nature of a statutory incomes policy; and politically by the imperative need not be beaten again by the miners. The Government was wrongfooted whatever it did. It was not sure whether to play the crisis up as a subversive threat to the elected government and the fabric of the nation or play it down as a minor management problem which could still be resolved by patient persuasion.

Heath's instinct was for the latter course, even though the logic of his refusal to admit any exceptions to Stage Three led remorselessly towards confrontation. On 2 December he signalled his preference by bringing back Willie Whitelaw from Northern Ireland to replace Maurice Macmillan at the Department of Employment, with special responsibility under the Chancellor for the counter-inflation policy. After his success in Ulster, Whitelaw was credited with near-magical powers as a conciliator: a man who could get the Unionists and the SDLP to sit down together could surely find a way to square the miners. Hopes were high that he would conjure a settlement. 'Mr Whitelaw's first task', wrote The Economist, 'is to bring some flexibility into the Government's relations with the miners.'[45] 'He Must Get His Own Way', affirmed The Times.[46]

There were two flaws in this optimistic scenario, however. First, Whitelaw himself was thoroughly exhausted and out of touch with the intricacies of the dispute. 'I was emotionally affected by all that I had been involved with in Ireland. I was not mentally conditioned for home politics.'[47] Second, he had come back at least a month too late. By December there was no room left for flexibility. The Government had already taken up a position which it could not compromise: it had either to make the miners a special case or be prepared to fight them. It was well known that Heath had wanted to bring Whitelaw back three weeks earlier, but he could not be spared until the power-sharing executive had been agreed on 21 November. As it was he was badly missed at the Sunningdale conference. When he did return, however, his appointment only muddied the waters since the miners naturally assumed that he had been appointed with a brief to get the Government off the hook. His negotiating position was undermined by his reputation as a conciliator. The miners, he wrote, 'tended to regard me as a soft touch'.[48] They were the more aggrieved when they discovered that he had nothing to offer.

There was a flurry of hope when Whitelaw met Gormley secretly at Brown's Hotel, and later Gormley, McGahey and Lawrence Daly at the Department of Employment, and appeared to nibble at Gormley's idea that 'waiting and bathing time' might offer a pretext for extra pay uniquely applicable to the miners. According to Gormley's account, this offered a real possibility of a breakthrough until Harold Wilson betrayed his confidence by putting it forward in the House of Commons as his own idea, after which the Government could not touch it. Wilson characteristically objected that Gormley was 'pulling the Tory Government's irons out of the fire for them' and promptly thrust them back again. In his memoirs Gormley still swore that he would 'never forgive Harold Wilson' for sabotaging the best hope of averting a full-scale strike.[49] Yet in fact the proposal continued to be examined over Christmas: it was found that it would add much less to the miners' day than Gormley implied. Finally, on 8 January, the Pay Board ruled that washing time was already taken into account and any further payment would breach Stage Three.

Whitelaw was not the only senior minister who was exhausted: they all were. Barber, almost overwhelmed by the international financial implications of the oil crisis and his public spending package of 17 December, was suffering 'acute fatigue';[50] Robert Carr was close to collapse; Victor Rothschild suffered a heart attack in mid-December; and Heath himself was under intolerable pressure. 'Under an immense workload', Hurd loyally recorded, 'the Prime Minister remained calm and unfussed. He was kept going by his own gifts of humour and courage.'[51] Other colleagues, however, felt that the burden was getting on top of him. It had been an exceptionally heavy autumn with the Sunningdale conference on Northern Ireland (including a critical all-night session), followed within a few days by the dispiriting Copenhagen summit, interspersed with visits from the Italian Prime Minister and the President of Zaire.

The fact that Heath was not able to give his whole attention to the domestic crisis confirmed the impression of a Government torn between contradictory responses. On the one hand Whitelaw still strove to negotiate a way out of the impasse either by discovering a loophole that would allow the miners to be paid more under Stage Three, or by persuading them to accept unspecified assurances for the future if they would only return to normal working now. Simultaneously, however, the Government was being driven to impose further emergency measures which sharpened the sense of an impending showdown. Behind the scenes the Civil Contingencies Unit set up in the Cabinet Office after the 1972 strike (chaired initially by Lord Jellicoe, then by Jim Prior) prepared a complete emergency structure of regional government in the event of a large-scale breakdown of energy supplies. Whitehall was rife with alarming predictions of sewage flowing in the streets, hospitals unable to cope with the resulting epidemics for lack of electricity, old people dying in their homes of cold and hunger: social breakdown, riots and anarchy.[52] Across the country a network of regional commissioners was ready to maintain basic services, as in a nuclear alert. Publicly the CEGB warned on 6 December of 'grave danger' to power supplies: coal deliveries to power stations were already down by 35 per cent. A few days later the train drivers' union ASLEF added to the pressure with an overtime ban of its own, restricting the movement of coal. As a result further restrictions were placed on the heating of shops and offices; street lighting was halved and all television channels had to close down at 10.30 pm. Most dramatic of all, on 13 December – the day before he flew to meet Brandt and Pompidou at Copenhagen – Heath announced to a shocked House of Commons that after Christmas industry would be put on a three-day week.

The decision was a response to party pressure for a strong signal that the Government was going to stand firm and was not going to be beaten again, as in 1972, by low coal stocks and lack of forward planning. It was precipitated by bad November trade figures – a monthly deficit of £270 million – and the continued refusal of the NUM to put the Stage Three offer to a ballot. Three days later Barber introduced a £1,200 million package of expenditure cuts, bringing down the curtain on the dash for growth which as late as mid-November ministers were still insisting would not be curtailed.[53] In these gloomy circumstances Heath gave in momentarily to the Cabinet hawks, led by Carrington and Prior, whose advice throughout was to play up the gravity of the crisis, assert the Government's duty to govern and prepare to put the issue to the country in an early election. Yet coal stocks were still more than adequate for a long time to come, and the threat to oil supplies was receding. At heart Heath resisted dramatising the crisis: almost alone he supported Peter Walker's reluctance to introduce petrol rationing. With hindsight both Hurd and Prior agree that Walker was right.[54] By the time he wrote his memoirs Prior had come to believe that introducing the three-day week before it was clearly unavoidable was a tactical blunder: it looked as if the Government was deliberately raising the stakes. 'Having taken such drastic action at the very outset, it was subsequently more difficult to convince people that the situation was really as serious as we had claimed.'[55] Intended to increase pressure on the TUC to persuade the NUM to settle, the three-day week only antagonised the TUC, who saw it as an unnecessary threat to jobs and earnings. Instead of turning against the miners, public opinion blamed the Government. Even *The Economist*, which strongly supported the Government in standing firm, considered that the announcement of the three-day week was 'psychologically mishandled': the public was inclined to think it would be cheaper to pay the miners off.[56]

Heath's broadcast to the nation on 13 December explaining the need for the shutdown reflected the divided counsels that had gone into it. 'There had been,' Hurd recalled, 'as usual, too many hands at work on the text', which was 'snatched from Michael Wolff and myself by Sir William Armstrong, and snatched back again by us a few hours before delivery. The hour that afternoon which the Prime Minister should have spent putting his personal imprint on what he was going to say was spent instead ironing out a last-minute difficulty which had cropped up over the creation of a new Department of Energy.'[57] Then when he came to deliver it 'he was so tired he could scarcely speak'. His face was 'grey with fatigue . . . the Prime Minister had never looked worse on television'.[58] Moreover he really had nothing new to say. He reiterated the vital importance of beating inflation. If it 'leapfrogged' out of control the old and the sick would suffer first: that was why the Government had introduced its prices and incomes policy, 'a more sensible and orderly way of settling these wages questions'. He repeated that the miners would do well out of Stage Three, but while he regretted that their action would give the country 'a harder Christmas than we have known since the war', he did not condemn them. Instead he spoke solemnly as though it were a natural disaster or an Act of God which Government and people must face together:

> The Government is determined to ensure the survival of this nation at as reasonable a level of life and industrial production

as it may for the months ahead . . .

At times like these there is deep in all of us an instinct which tells us we must abandon disputes among ourselves. We must close our ranks so that we can deal together with the difficulties which come to us whether from within or from beyond our own shores. That has been our way in the past, and it is a good way.[59]

This was weak stuff. While by its actions the Government appeared to be squaring up for a confrontation with the miners, Heath's words signalled that he did not have the stomach for a fight. Appealing for unity in the face of 'difficulties' was no way to rouse the nation. But he did not *want* to rouse the nation. He simply wanted the nation to demonstrate that it was ready to endure discomfort, in order to shame the miners into accepting the already generous settlement they had been offered so that everyone could get back to work. He was not looking for confrontation at all, still less to exploit the situation for an early election. He still wanted to believe that reason must eventually prevail. Yet the election bandwagon was rolling in Central Office. Sir Michael Fraser had got the party machine geared up. Nigel Lawson had been called in to draft a manifesto. Carrington was doing nothing to discourage press speculation that an election sooner rather than later would prove the only way out. Heath himself postponed a projected visit to China in the New Year. But he gave no lead. In this crisis of his Government he appeared inert – grim, calm, determined but passive, entirely lacking a strategy to regain control of a situation that was slipping away from him. He shrank from exploiting the crisis for political advantage. He was much more worried about the long-term international implications of the oil price rise than about the miners. As the year ended, therefore, he refused to encourage preparations for an election, yet did not positively rule it out. His honourable reluctance did him credit: but it represented a failure of political leadership for which he would pay dearly in 1974.

31

The Three-Day Week

THE three-day week is one of those unforgettable episodes in the national memory, like the Blitz or the General Strike or the 'winter of discontent' in 1978–9 which sealed the fate of the Callaghan Government as surely as the miners' emergency brought down Heath's. All have become part of the national folklore, and as such heavily encrusted with myth and even – as the memory recedes – a sort of masochistic nostalgia. If there is an image which recalls the whole Heath period to most people who lived through it, it would be a conflated recollection of power cuts and flickering candlelight, the hoarding of candles and the rediscovery of oil lamps, all of which tend to be lumped together in the pigeonhole labelled 'three-day week'. In fact, this is a misapprehension. Power cuts were indeed a feature of the earlier emergencies of 1970 and 1972, when the Government was caught unprepared. But the whole point of the three-day week which began on 1 January 1974 was that it was designed to prevent the total loss of supply which plunged homes into darkness. It involved restrictions in the use of electricity for advertising and street lighting, and the heating of shops and offices; television closed down at 10.30 pm and there was a 50 mph speed limit on the roads. The public was asked to save power wherever possible: Patrick Jenkin, junior minister in the new Department of Energy, attracted national ridicule by advising people to clean their teeth in the dark, while in the universities (and doubtless elsewhere) a ludicrous game of cat and mouse was played between senior staff who went round dutifully switching off unnecessary lights while Labour-supporting students, doing their bit for the miners, went round turning them on again. Above all, most of industry was on short time, with consequent reduced earnings for millions of workers. But generally speaking the country was dim and chilly, rather than actually dark or cold. The weather in January and February was exceptionally mild.

Nor was the impact of short working nearly so bad as was expected. When the three-day régime was first announced there were dire predictions of one, two, even ten million unemployed and a drastic fall in output leading to a balance-of-payments crisis.[1] In the event many firms got around the restriction by offering their workers longer hours on the three days for which they had power: as a result average take-home pay fell only slightly and industrial production was cut initially by only about a quarter. By mid-February the CBI reported that output was nearly back to normal – a fact which cast a revealing light on 'normal' productivity in British industry. Technically, the three-day week was a considerable success: the nation's consumption of coal and oil was substantially reduced without serious economic consequences and the public was spared the misery of random blackouts. The lesson of the previous miners' strike had been well learned: the Government was not beaten by shortage of coal stocks.

Politically, however, it was a different matter. Politically the very success of the three-day week backfired on the Government. By so managing the power restrictions that they were inconvenient but bearable the Government got the worst of both worlds: once the novelty wore off the public became merely irritated, while the sense of crisis which might have persuaded people to rally to the Government faded. Labour attacked the introduction of the three-day week from the start as a political stunt simply aimed at turning public opinion against the miners: Tony Benn accused the Government of deliberately using the miners' dispute to drive down the living standards of working people, while Denis Healey alleged that they were 'forcing British industry to commit suicide'.[2] In fact the longer the emergency went on without inflicting serious hardship the less necessary it seemed to be. In December NOP found the public evenly divided on the need for it: as time passed the proportion approving it fell.[3] But the Government's success in neutralising the effect of the miners' overtime ban, far from persuading them to drop their action, only convinced them of the need to intensify it: by the time they escalated the dispute to a full-scale strike, the Government had lost the political initiative it had possessed at the turn of the year. Politically the three-day week was either an overreaction to the miners' action or an underreaction.

This fatal ambiguity stemmed from Heath himself. Throughout the miners' dispute he adopted a contradictory stance, at once stubbornly committed to a course that in practice led inevitably to confrontation yet reluctant to act on the implications of confrontation. As so often, Douglas Hurd offers a perceptive close up of his conduct. A by-election was pending in South Worcestershire, caused by the death of Sir Gerald Nabarro. On New Year's Day Heath paid a flying visit to the constituency to talk to party workers. To Hurd's exasperated yet admiring eye it was 'a remarkable occasion'. Arriving late, Heath was nevertheless enthusiastically received: the faithful were looking to him for a lead.

> Any other politician I have known would have seized and used the emotion hanging in the air. The country was tense, a struggle had begun on which our future seemed to rest. Here in this small market town [Upton-on-Severn] the Prime Minister was talking to his supporters at the start of a crucial by-election. He had led them to unexpected victory in 1970, his courage and doggedness were immensely respected. He could have worked that audience to a pitch of fiery loyalty. He could have whipped them up against the miners. He could have sent them excited and enthusiastic into the streets. It did not occur to him to do so. What mattered to him was that they should understand the complexities of the issue, the objective facts and figures. He saw it as his duty to educate and inform, not to inflame one part of the country against another. So in one sense the meeting was a missed opportunity; but to those who wished to notice (a dwindling minority) it showed a Prime Minister who desperately wanted to tackle not the miners, but inflation, the balance of payments and the desperate consequences for Britain of the oil crisis.[4]

It subsequently emerged that Heath was not well at this time. Many people noticed that he had become very slow, overweight, physically and mentally ponderous: the famous silences were longer, he had lost much of his quickness of mind, the sometimes brutal incisiveness with which he had challenged officials. Brendon Sewill, who had not had much direct dealing with him since 1970, was shocked at the change.[5] It was not just that he was tired, though he was. The truth was that he was already suffering from a thyroid deficiency which was not diagnosed until 1975. An underactive thyroid causes precisely the symptoms that Heath increasingly displayed from late 1973 and through the whole of 1974. It was cruel luck that it afflicted him at just the moment when he needed all the swiftness and clarity of judgment he could normally command. Unquestionably, it can now be said, his health was a contributory factor to the uncharacteristic indecisiveness, lethargy, even paralysis of will, with which he met his nemesis in February. Admittedly there were many who saw him daily who did not realise that he was ill. Hurd does not mention it. Victor Rothschild – before his own illness – believed that Heath was not unwell but simply depressed and frustrated.[6] Peter Walker rejects the idea that he was ill and puts his condition down to too many chocolate biscuits![7] The symptoms were disguised by exhaustion – and by the fact that his staff and colleagues were all as exhausted as he was. 'They were all very tired men', the Cabinet Secretary Sir John Hunt recalled in 1988, 'and they were not taking decisions in the most sensible way . . . It struck me that the smell of death was around.'[8]

Heath's indecision centred on the question of whether to call an early General Election. It was not simply that against the advice of many of his senior colleagues he declined to do so. There were strong arguments both ways, and Heath's reluctance was supported – for differing reasons – by several of those whose advice he trusted most. The trouble was not his reluctance but his refusal seriously to discuss the matter or rule positively against it. Frustrated colleagues spoke later of his state of 'hooded ambiguity'.[9] Douglas Hurd has compared his mood to Elizabeth I's reluctance to execute Mary, Queen of Scots.[10] Two days after Christmas he summoned Jim Prior to Chequers – uncharacteristically for no substantive reason but just because he felt the press expected him to be having emergency meetings with colleagues. 'We did no serious work,' Prior recalled. Heath was 'rightly relaxed and . . . his hospitality was, as always, generous'. But he made it quite clear that he did not wish to discuss a possible election. 'Every time I got round to the need to prepare a manifesto the subject was changed. It was almost as if he wished to be incommunicado as far as decisions on election preparations were concerned, although both Peter Carrington and myself were becoming convinced that it was the only answer.' After lunch, rather than be seen to leave early, Prior was solemnly sat down on his own to watch a film for the afternoon.[11]

Carrington and Prior, as chairman and deputy chairman of the party, were the officers responsible both for reporting to Heath the rank and file's eagerness for a showdown and for ensuring that the party's electoral machinery was ready to go as soon as he gave the word. He was not bound to take their advice but he did need to keep them in step with his thinking. There is nothing more damaging to party morale – as Jim Callaghan discovered in 1978 – than disappointed expectation. There was undoubtedly a strong opportunist case for going to the country quickly on a 'Who Governs?' platform while the sense of crisis was still fresh. The papers – primed admittedly by Carrington – were full of speculation and rumour. At the turn of the year both Gallup and ORC put the Tories narrowly ahead: by 10 January NOP stretched the lead to 4 per cent.[12] Moreover the party's private polling confirmed that they should win an election held on 31 January or 7 February, but suggested that the result would become more doubtful the longer they waited. After years of uncertainty the Conservative party was suddenly reunited; Labour, on the other hand, was divided by the miners' action, while the Liberals had not only fallen back but had still to select candidates in many seats. In addition, a new electoral register was due to come into force on 15 February: it would benefit the Tories to fight an election on the old register.

An opportunist election, however, timed to catch the opposition off balance and exploit the national emergency for party ends, was exactly what Heath did not want. He believed it would be divisive; moreover it would not help to solve the problem. The advocates of an election believed vaguely that it would 'create a new situation – both because the miners would face a Government armed with a fresh mandate and because the Government would have a freer hand'.[13] In Heath's view, however, the Government already possessed a sufficient majority whose authority the miners should recognise: he did not want a freer hand. To try to snatch a quick victory on the basis of a few favourable polls and an outdated register was the sort of Wilsonian manœuvre to which he would not stoop. 'He believed it would have been quite wrong to have gone on the old register and disenfranchised a lot of people.'[14] As one member of his staff recalled, 'These were just the kind of arguments *not* to put to him.'[15] More than that, he regarded calls for an election as a distraction from the serious situation facing the country: the mere possibility of a Labour Government would not only undermine the broad consent that had been achieved for Stage Three but also jeopardise the Northern Ireland settlement and cast in doubt Britain's hard-won membership of the EEC. Above all he genuinely did not want to fight an election 'against' the miners. He wanted to work *with* the TUC, not to treat the unions as enemies. 'Whether or not that was the right way to win an election,' wrote Hurd, 'it was certainly no way to run a country.' Instead Heath clung stubbornly to the hope that what he called 'reason' – and his critics dubbed 'corporatism' – would prevail: 'One more meeting, one more initiative, one more exposition of the national interest – it must be right to persevere rather than despair.'[16]

His instinct to carry on was supported by his three closest associates: Whitelaw, now effectively number two in the Government, who believed that he had been recalled from Ireland to resolve the miners' problem and still believed that he could do so; Michael Wolff in his private office, whose advice Heath rated above Hurd's; and, most surprisingly, William Armstrong. Armstrong's reasoning was the opposite of Whitelaw's. He was 'the hawk of hawks'[17] who saw the NUM action in increasingly lurid terms as a left-wing challenge which must be crushed to ensure the survival of democracy. His emotional analysis influenced normally moderate figures like Prior, who wanted to put the issue to the country.[18] But Armstrong himself regarded the idea of an election as running away. Heath's position was an uncomfortable amalgam of Armstrong and Whitelaw; but on the specific question of an election their advice was the same. Whitelaw was additionally influenced by the belief that a General Election in Northern Ireland would torpedo the Sunningdale agreement before it was properly afloat; and in this he was supported by his successor in the Northern Ireland Office, Francis Pym. On the domestic issue too, Pym – Chief Whip until just a few weeks earlier – believed that the public was behind the Government already and would only be antagonised by an election. Robert Carr's instinct was the same.[19] Thus the picture often painted of Heath alone stubbornly defying the urging of his colleagues to go to the country is quite untrue. The truth is that in declining to call an election at the beginning of 1974 he was following the near-unanimous advice of those he trusted most.

But if he was not going to have an election he needed somehow to resolve the miners' dispute. Against all the evidence, he remained convinced that they could yet be induced to settle within Stage Three. On 8 January, to underline the promise of a new deal opening up for the coal industry, he hived off responsibility for both coal and oil from Peter Walker's DTI and put them under a new Department of Energy, headed by Lord Carrington, with a strong team of juniors (Patrick Jenkin, David Howell and Peter Emery).* Ian Gilmour stepped up to become Defence Secretary, and the whole reshuffle was interpreted as a tilt to the left.[21] The establishment of the new department was seen by *The Times* as 'tactically well timed to support Mr Whitelaw's persuasions that . . . the miners, if they agree to live for the present within the frame of Phase Three, can look forward to a Government-sponsored future as the aristocrats among manual workers'.[22] If that was the intention, however, the choice of

---

* Peter Walker had objected almost to the point of resignation to the separation of Energy from the DTI, which he regarded as pure public relations quite contrary to Heath's normal style. He was persuaded by Whitelaw not to resign and succeeded in delaying the creation of the new Department until 8 January. But his relations with Heath were never quite so close again.[20]

Carrington – combining the job with continuing as Tory Party chairman – was singularly misjudged. Since he was known to be pressing for an early election, his every announcement concerning coal stocks and oil imports was regarded as politically inspired. Carrington himself in his memoirs described the new department without enthusiasm as 'inevitably something of a crisis management organisation'.[23] It was treated by the miners – with some reason – as an arm of Conservative Central Office.

On 9 January the TUC came up with what has come to be regarded as the Government's second lost opportunity of the crisis, a formula designed to allow ministers to compromise without loss of face. It was first proposed at a regular meeting of the NEDC in Millbank Tower by the moderate and highly respected Sidney Greene of the NUR:

> The General Council accept that there is a distinctive and exceptional situation in the mining industry. If the Government are prepared to give an assurance that they will make possible a settlement between the miners and the National Coal Board, other unions will not use this as an argument in negotiations in their own settlements.[24]

This was an unprecedented offer by the TUC, which reflected their concern for the effects of the three-day week on their members and a real desire to promote a solution that might end it. If it was accepted, the Government could claim to have recognised the changed circumstances created by the oil crisis without abandoning its elaborate counter-inflation strategy. Assuming that it was sincerely meant, however, the question for the Government was still whether the TUC had suffcient authority over its member unions to deliver on such a promise. Tony Barber at the Millbank meeting thought not. He rejected the TUC offer out of hand. Controversy has raged ever since over how and why this opportunity was missed – whether it was sincerely meant, whether the TUC could have honoured it, and whether the Government should not have grasped it anyway.

One reason Barber rejected it so curtly was that it was sprung on him without warning. Normally an initiative of such importance would have been trailed in advance to give all parties time to prepare their response. The fact that it was not led Barber to think it was not a seriously worked-out offer but just 'something which wandered into the TUC mind' on the spur of the moment.[25] Len Murray subsequently gave two versions of why it was not trailed. One was that the TUC only agreed it themselves over lunch immediately before the NEDC meeting, so that there was no time to clear it in advance.[26] He told Phillip Whitehead, however, that they deliberately kept it secret because they were afraid of a leak: 'We wanted it to be face to face, men to men, a bang-bang kind of situation.'[27] If so it was a serious misjudgment. Several observers have blamed the failure of communication on Murray's inexperience. He had only succeeded Vic Feather as General Secretary the previous autumn. Campbell Adamson of the CBI felt certain that in the same circumstances Feather would have telephoned him in advance.[28]

Lord Croham (Sir Douglas Allen) confirms that the Treasury had no knowledge of the TUC proposal before the meeting, but he recalls Greene telling him on the way in: 'We've got something which I think will solve this problem.' When Greene came out with it, 'There was a discussion round the table which was very brief, but the proposal was criticised by quite a number of people. I wrote a note to Barber saying, "It's not good enough but keep talking." But before I could get it to him he had said, "It's not good enough," and that ended the discussion.'[29]

There is conflicting evidence on whether or not Barber consulted Heath before turning the offer down. Phillip Whitehead asserts that he 'slipped out to call Heath from a pay phone – his mistrust extended to the NEDC officials'.[30] Barber himself has testified: 'I phoned Ted, who agreed with the line I had taken.'[31] On the other hand *The Times* reported that Barber acted 'without reference to the Prime Minister or the Cabinet'[32] and Jack Jones – backed 'absolutely' by Ronald Macintosh, Director-General of the NEDC – insists that Barber acted off his own bat: 'When we pressed the idea to inform Heath . . . it was Barber who firmly rejected it. There was no going to the telephone.'[33] Jones believed that Barber was the hard man who wanted a showdown, while Heath would have wanted to keep talking. This is strongly denied by Brendon Sewill, who remembers Barber coming back to the Treasury after the NEDC meeting, 'obviously extremely worried' at having had to make a 'split-second reaction': 'It was most unfortunate that, if it was a genuine offer, it was sprung on him. He felt he should have had a warning of it.'[34] Yet another recollection, Lord Hunt's, is that Barber did respond on the spot, but with Heath's full approval:

He came straight round after the meeting to No. 10, where there was another meeting going on with the PM, and reported it. There was a very short discussion indeed and it was self-evident that what he'd done was accepted by those present.[35]

Does it matter? Probably not, in detail. The conflict of evidence merely reflects the confused signals coming out of Whitehall. In practice the TUC offer remained on the table and continued to be explored in meetings between Heath and the TUC over the next two weeks. Barber's immediate rejection could easily have been reversed had Heath become convinced that the plan was a serious proposition which the TUC could enforce. But he was not convinced. The real reason Barber was so quick to reject the offer was not that he was given no warning but rather that ministers did not trust the TUC. Whereas in the course of the long tripartite talks which had preceded the introduction of Stage One in 1972 Heath and his colleagues had formed a warm (and reciprocated) regard for Feather, they regarded Murray as a deracinated backroom intellectual whose first loyalty was to the Labour party: they suspected him of playing politics, not genuinely seeking to promote a settlement. Second, even if the offer was genuine, ministers did not believe that the TUC could deliver. As Barber told a press conference later that day, there was 'no assurance . . . that other groups, who might also consider themselves essential to the running of the nation, would not also demand settlements outside the Stage 3 limits'.[36] The 'other group' they had particularly in mind was the electricians, whose leader, Frank Chappell – though politically a leading 'moderate' – had made it plain in accepting a settlement for his men under Stage Three that he would tear it up if the miners or anyone else got a penny more.[37] Here again, argument persists over whether or not the TUC could have held the line. Sir Michael Clapham of the CBI thought it no more than 'an offer not to use certain words'.[38] Years later, however, Len Murray was still adamant that it was a genuine offer: 'I'm sure we could have made it stick. Absolutely sure.'[39] The miners' leaders, however, were frankly disbelieving: 'Why shouldn't the other unions use the NUM as an argument for their own claim?' Gormley told the *Sunday Times*. 'That's what negotiation is all about.'[40]

This was Heath's view, shared by all his senior colleagues with the exception of Whitelaw. With Chappell and others in mind, he reiterated to Parliament on 10 January the Government's responsibility to the four million workers who had already settled under Stage Three: to make an exception of the miners would be a betrayal of them which would destroy the whole counter-inflation policy.[41] In successive meetings with the TUC 'Big Six' over the next fortnight he shifted his position slightly: he was after all willing to consider the TUC offer – so much for Barber's instant rejection – but he challenged them repeatedly to convince him that they could make it stick. He recalled these exchanges in an interview with Shirley Williams in 1979:

But I said, does this mean that there'll be no other special cases? You see you can say the miners have special circumstances, therefore they are a special case – now suppose special circumstances of a different kind come along, will you . . . agree that that is not a special case? And they were perfectly frank and I made no criticism of them at all; they said: 'No, we couldn't give the undertaking that circumstances of a different kind should not be a special case.'[42]

Even so, with hindsight Jim Prior and others came to believe that they should have grasped the TUC's offer anyway, putting the onus on to the unions to keep their word. Murray believed the Government had the TUC 'over a barrel':

Heath had us where he wanted us. We were in his hands, and he could not lose. If he had taken the offer and it had failed to work, and other unions had broken through he would have been home and dry with all his anti-union policies – Industrial Relations Act and incomes policy. If it had worked, it would have been his great political triumph, showing he could bring the unions to heel.[43]

Unquestionably this would have been the smart political thing to do. 'It would have got us off the hook', Prior realised later, 'and put the unions on their best behaviour. Had their self-restraint failed, we would then have been in a much stronger position to take whatever steps might have been necessary.'[44] But this was too cynical for Heath. The idea of putting the unions on their best behaviour was too reminiscent of Harold Wilson's 'solemn and binding' agreement with the unions in 1969, when the Labour Government withdrew *In Place of Strife*. They had not kept that bargain and he did not believe they would or could keep this one. He thought he had made a similar bargain with Gormley in the summer, but what had become of that? It was ironic that Heath should have come to the point where he did not trust the unions. All the hours he had spent in talking with the union leaders since 1972, patiently trying to draw them in to share responsibility for running the economy, had been devoted to the idea that they could be treated as social partners: when it had come to the crunch in November 1972 they had refused. Now they were offering to take responsibility – Murray was offering more than Feather had ever done – but he did not trust them enough to let them try, even though they offered him an escape route from a confrontation he did not want. One who had been through the previous talks, Ronald Macintosh of NEDC, had no doubt that the Millbank offer represented a new departure:

Anybody who had had anything to do with the trade union leaders at all could have sensed that the offer being made by Sid Greene . . . was both very serious and very well-considered beforehand . . . It came over with great conviction – if you wanted to believe it. If you were in a frame of mind to want to reject those things because you were very cynical about the TUC, or because you thought that the right thing to do was to call an election, then you wouldn't hear, I suppose, what was said . . . I believe that Barber . . . didn't want that offer to be accepted.[45]

Macintosh thought the Government's rejection of the TUC offer a 'huge missed opportunity'.[46] So, ironically, did Mick McGahey. McGahey claims that the one thing the left on the NUM Executive feared was an agreement between the Government and the TUC to give the miners their money. In those circumstances, he believes, the centre-right majority on the Executive, which had no interest in widening the dispute to bring down the Government, 'would probably have settled'. But Heath was too inflexible to see his chance.[47] He was in reality too honest. Whatever Jones and Murray might promise, they failed to satisfy him that they could deliver; that being so, whatever the political advantages, he could not go on television and recommend to the nation a solution in which he himself did not believe.

The gulf between Heath and the TUC was summed up by two pregnant silences in the third meeting of the series on 21 January. The TUC leaders, characteristically, remembered only Heath's silences:

Heath sat for minutes on end, head sunk deep on chest, pondering gloomily but saying nothing. To one witness he seemed to *want* to say something, but could not manage to. With desperate urgency, Hugh Scanlon addressed one ultimate question to him. 'Is there anything, anything at all, that we can do or say which will satisfy you?' The question hung in the air for many seconds . . . Heath did not answer, but left the silence to be broken by the cavilling Barber.[48]

Conrad Heron of the Department of Employment confirms this account. But he also remembers a parallel silence from the union side.

At a slightly later stage in the discussion, when the PM himself had thrown a good deal of doubt upon the ability of the TUC, however well-intentioned, to deliver, the PM turned across the table to the TUC and said, in essence, 'But, if an exceptional settlement were conceded to the miners, you know you couldn't hold the line, could you?' Equally, that too was followed by silence. It seems to me that represented the distance between the two positions.[49]

So long as the TUC offer was under consideration, however, it served as an argument against an election. The critical day, if Heath was to go to the country on 7 February, was Thursday 17 January. All that week, the battle for the Prime Minister's mind was intense. Hurd was cast down when the talks with the TUC were adjourned to the following Monday, hopeful again when they still broke up in deadlock. On Friday 11th Heath formally authorised Central Office to start making election preparations. He also sent a tough message to the monthly bulletin of the Conservative Political Centre which seemed to set out the basis of an appeal to the country:

> We all know that there are forces working in our society to under-mine and destroy it . . . Our task as Conservatives is to frustrate these designs. We must learn how to mobilise these forces of mod-eration and reason which alone can unite the country.[50]

But then on Sunday 13 January he met party officials at Chequers and seized gratefully on a number of practical difficulties in the way of 7 February. That evening the inner group of senior ministers was divided: Carrington, Barber and Prior on one side, Whitelaw and Carr on the other. 'A non-decision was made not to have an election.'[51] The next morning Heath, Whitelaw and Barber were due to have another meeting with the TUC. *The Times* took the view that this represented the last chance: unless the Government could secure a solid agreement – 'it would have to be an agreement in substance, not merely in form' – there would be no alternative to an election.

All the signs were that the policy already enjoyed public approval. Nevertheless, as Rees-Mogg put it, 'the Government's policies have changed so much since 1970 that there is ample constitutional justifi-cation for an immediate election'.[52] In his adjoining column David Wood spelled out the tactical danger to the Government of missing the moment:

> If the delegation of senior TUC leaders at 10 Downing Street today is unable categorically to underwrite Phase Three of the Government's counter-inflationary policy, the Prime Minister has

no choice but to decide on an early election or make himself a hostage to fortune until spring.[53]

Five and a half hours of talks produced no breakthrough, but the next day in the Commons Heath 'patiently and unprovocatively held open the door for a further meeting'.[54] On Thursday 16th a special conference of 178 general secretaries and union presidents was convened to endorse the principle of the TUC offer. Tory hawks were suspicious that this was simply a device to delay an election; if so it worked. So long as he could see any glimmer of hope Heath would not close his options. Though Carrington and Hurd were hopeful up to the last moment – Carrington believed that Heath had actually made up his mind on the 16th before Whitelaw took him out to dinner and talked him out of it again[55] – Heath deliberately let the 17 January deadline pass. That evening at the House of Commons he had an angry scene with Prior, who told him that Labour MPs were throwing their hats in the air with relief. Heath blamed Prior for steaming Central Office up to create election fever: Prior in turn blamed Heath for dithering. 'We had already marched the Party's troops up the hill, ready for combat, and then had to march them down again; it would be much harder to march them up a second time.'[56]

The opinion poll evidence supports the view that the Government missed a favourable tide on 7 February. ORC on 19 January gave the Tories a 4-point lead over Labour; a week later the same poll gave the Government a 3-point deficit. It can be argued that this shows that Heath was right not to call an election: a more likely interpretation is that he lost support by failing to do so. There was widespread criticism both in the Tory party and in the press of his apparent irresolution in postponing an election which had seemed inevitable. His personal rating – those thinking he was 'doing a good job' – slumped sharply from 45 per cent to 39 per cent in the same week, while those who said he was 'doing a bad job' rose to 52 per cent.[57] Too much should not be made of the polls, however. For one thing, the 3–4 point margin between the main parties falls within the area of sampling error. In addition, the difference between the two ORC polls was largely accounted for by a drop in support for the Liberals (from 19 per cent to 15 per cent), whose likely effect in terms of seats was impossible to predict. Finally, following their poor performance in 1970 politicians of all parties were wary of placing too much faith in polls as a basis for decision making. It may be that Heath would have won an election held on 7 February, but it is by no means certain. A second criticism often made of his timing is that, having missed 7 February, the Government should have ruled an election firmly off the agenda and buckled down with renewed determination either to secure a settlement or to fight the dispute out. Their mistake – it was easy to see in retrospect – was to pass up the chance of an election when they might have won it and then to hold an election after all when the favourable moment had passed. Years later, Whitelaw endorsed this line of criticism, telling the *Sunday Times*: 'My mistake was not that I opposed February 7, but that I ever gave in to February 28.'[58] The trouble was that the Government had forfeited the initiative. They did try to put the option of an election behind them. For a few days between 17 January and 23 January they thought that they had weathered the crisis. But then the miners raised the stakes and they were back where they started.

On 18 January, in a speech at Eastbourne, Heath made a strong assertion of his intention to carry on. 'You have a strong government, a fair government, and we intend to see that you continue to have a government that is capable of seeing the nation through the difficult times ahead.' He invited the TUC to Downing Street again on Monday, not primarily to have another try at solving the miners' problem but rather to discuss the possibility of relaxing the energy restrictions to industry and getting back to at least a four-day week.[59] The next day Carrington gave an optimistic assessment of the energy situation: oil supplies, though more expensive, were nearly back to normal and coal stocks at the power stations were holding up. In the House of Commons on Tuesday 22nd Heath shed his uncertainty and gave 'probably his most powerful performance at the dispatch box since he became Prime Minister . . . He heartened the Tory benches very greatly,' *The Economist* reported, 'not only because he refused to budge an inch on the miners' pay claim but by the manner in which he did it.'[60] On television that evening he repeated the message that the Government intended to use its majority to take whatever measures were needed to surmount the crisis. 'All his instincts, personal and political', wrote David Wood, 'are impelling him not to give Mr Wilson and Labour the excuse to say that he ran for cover.'[61] 'The job of a Government', he declared, 'is to accept its responsibility to govern, and that is what we are doing.'[62] Implicitly he challenged the miners to give way.

The next day his bluff was called. The evidence that the overtime ban was not having enough impact to achieve their object only provoked the NUM to further action. 'With fuel stocks holding out', Gormley wrote in his memoirs, 'and spring around the corner, our final card had to be played now or never.'[63] On 23 January the Executive voted (by a majority of only 16 to 10) to hold a pithead ballot on the 31st to seek authority to call a complete stoppage. 'This',

Douglas Hurd wrote, 'transformed the situation. It was clear that reason was not going to prevail.'[64] The miners' decision was a personal slap in the face for Heath. Before they met he addressed to them, through Gormley, a final patriotic appeal to reflect on what they were doing to the country – 'this country of which we are all citizens' – already as a result of the oil crisis facing 'economic problems . . . as severe as any we have faced since 1945'. On the one hand, he accepted, the new situation called for greater investment in coal, as well as other forms of energy; but on the other it was more imperative than ever to preserve Stage Three: 'As a country we have been made quite suddenly poorer by recent developments abroad, and in our new situation the increases in earnings provided for in Stage Three . . . now appear, if anything, too great.' The Stage Three offer to the miners was already 'substantial and fair': in addition the Government had promised a thorough revaluation of miners' pay and conditions to reflect the new economics of energy. Finally he flattered the miners and almost pleaded with them to be reasonable: 'The country owes the miners much and expects much of them. But particularly in the very difficult economic situation which faces Britain, we cannot do everything at once.'[65]

Every member of the NUM Executive received a photocopy of this candid appeal. It was treated, however, 'with contempt'.[66] 'It was obviously designed for the public's ears, as much as for ours,' Gormley wrote, 'and we were having none of it.'[67] The NUM leadership felt they had the Government on the run and were not to be bought off by the promise of 'cake tomorrow'. Briefly Heath and Whitelaw still hoped that the miners would not vote for a strike. But reports from the coalfields soon dashed that hope: the question to be put did not ask whether the men supported a strike – only whether they backed the union. Leaflets circulated in Yorkshire and Scotland invited the miners to choose between their leaders and the Government. On that basis they were sure to win a massive endorsement. The country braced itself for a strike. Instead of moving to a four-day week, Carrington now warned that industry faced the prospect of a two-day week. In that event the Government might have no option but to go for an election after all. David Wood in *The Times* could see only three alternatives, all appalling:

> Surrender by the Government, in circumstances that would make further surrenders inevitable; a fight to the finish, in which the British economy would be devastated; or a general election decided in conditions of bitterness and perhaps violence that would make Conservative Government nearly impossible and

the return of a Labour Government the signal for runaway inflation.[68]

The ghost of a fourth option, however, had surfaced a few days earlier with the publication on 24 January of the Pay Board's long-awaited report on 'relativities' – the problem of adjusting relative pay between different groups under a statutory incomes policy. Here at last, it seemed, was a defensible procedure by which the Government could make an exception of the miners within the machinery of Stage Three. Had it been published six weeks earlier, as originally expected, it might have been the instrument to get the Government off the hook. As it was, it still offered the Government a lifeline. But initially, in their besieged mentality, ministers failed to grasp it. In the Commons, Whitelaw blandly welcomed it as 'a valuable basis for discussion'.[69] But he saw it as a mechanism for the long-term adjustment of anomalies, not as a device which could be used immediately – an oversight for which he subsequently reproached himself. 'Barbara Castle said on the day it came out that she couldn't understand why on earth I hadn't used it to settle with the miners. She was quite right. I had never really thought of it. It was short-sighted of me to let it be published and then not to use it.'[70]

It was over the following weekend, with the miners apparently irrevocably set to strike, that the strain became too much for Heath's closest adviser, the architect of Stage Three, Sir William Armstrong. More than anyone else, Armstrong had come to see the fight against inflation in apocalyptic terms as a battle for the survival of the state against Communist subversion, a struggle of good against evil. He still regarded an election as running away: he spoke increasingly in military terms – the miners must be 'smashed'. Douglas Hurd spent the weekend of 26–7 January with Armstrong at an Anglo-American conference at Ditchley Park. 'The atmosphere was Chekhovian. We sat on sofas in front of great log fires and discussed first principles while the rain lashed the windows. Sir William was full of notions, ordinary and extraordinary.'[71] Another witness describes him, less diplomatically, as 'really quite mad at the end . . . lying on the floor and talking about moving the Red Army from here and the Blue Army from there'.[72] A few days later he broke down completely and had to be shipped off to Victor Rothschild's villa in Barbados to recover.

The loss of Armstrong at such a moment was a blow to Heath: it is to his credit, however, that he not only retained his own sanity, but in the face of Armstrong's overheated advice steadily preserved his own moderation. Only once did he allow himself to use anything

approaching the language of confrontation, when Mick McGahey –
that same weekend – let slip some standard Communist rhetoric calling on troops who might be used to move coal during the strike to
disobey their orders. This sort of talk was a propaganda gift to the
Government. Gormley moved quickly to emphasise that the NUM
was interested only in pursuing its pay claim: Wilson and more than
a hundred Labour MPs likewise signed a Commons' motion repudiating McGahey. Interviewed by Robin Day for 'Panorama' on
Monday 28th, Heath naturally took the chance to exploit McGahey's
blunder, denouncing him by name for conducting a political strike to
bring down the elected Government. He also hinted that the
Government might stop social security benefits to strikers' families.
But still he insisted that they would only be driven to this reluctantly, in response to public outrage, not because the Government
had any wish to confront the miners. 'We have had this under consideration', he explained, 'and the reason we have taken no action so
far is because we have been endeavouring, striving for all we are
worth, to get a working relationship with the trade unions.'[73] He still
looked to the TUC, in their own interest, to bring the miners to see
reason. In particular, in this interview he picked up for the first time
the idea that the new relativities procedure might be accelerated to
form the basis of a deal.

The beauty of the relativities mechanism for the Government was
not only that it offered a means of paying the miners more, almost
immediately, within Stage Three. It also promised to do what the
TUC offer on its own did not – that is, to bind the TUC to abide by
and help police not only Stage Three but a subsequent Stage Four.
Pay rises above the norm would be permitted only with the approval
of the Pay Board, in response to a specific need of the labour market;
if the unions accepted this, they would have swallowed the whole
principle of statutory incomes policy. It took a little time for the implications to dawn on both parties. On 24 January Wilson and Reg
Prentice for Labour were castigating Heath and Whitelaw for their
stubbornness in refusing an immediate referral of the miners' case to
the proposed board. Within a few days, however, positions were reversed. With the miners apparently certain to vote for a full-scale
strike, ministers – urged on by *The Times* – began to see the promise
of extra money under the relativities procedure as a last legitimate
means of averting it before it began; while the unions suddenly
sensed a trap. As a result, when Heath showed new interest in the
proposal in the House on Tuesday 30th and offered after all to refer
the miners' claim to the new board immediately if they would resume normal working in the meantime, he found Wilson suddenly

cold on the idea. 'Mr Heath', *The Economist* reported, 'again put up a tough and convincing performance but, unlike the previous week, he failed to secure a knock-out against Mr Wilson. He repeatedly called on Mr Wilson to say that a miners' strike would be against the public interest. Mr Wilson had no intention of saying any such thing, and to loud Labour cheers insisted that the extremists in the present situation were Mr Heath and Mr McGahey.'[74]

Wilson's volte-face, however, only served to increase the attractions of the relativities solution for the Government. If the NUM accepted it, well and good: the threatened strike could be bought off without triggering an inflationary free-for-all and the Government could proceed to framing a tough Stage Four to reflect the dire economic outlook. If, however, the NUM refused to delay a strike long enough to allow a referral to the new board, if the TUC declined even to examine the new proposals and the Labour party felt bound to support it, then their combined intransigence offered the Tories a strong case to put before the country. Over the next few days Heath threw all his authority behind the relativities procedure as the Government's final offer. Addressing the Birmingham Chamber of Commerce on Wednesday 31st he formally declared the Government's acceptance of the report and appealed to the TUC and CBI to accept it too: 'If ever there was a moment when the British people look to their representatives to make a constructive act of leadership in the interest of industrial peace, that time is surely now.'[75]

The TUC's willingness to co-operate, however, was at an end. They agreed 'without commitment' to one last round of talks with the Prime Minister to be held on 4 February, but Murray made it clear that they supported the NUM's refusal to resume negotiations without a clear promise of more money on the table.[76] In fact the Government had all but given such a promise: the only issue now was whether the Government should be allowed to save face by channelling the extra money through the Pay Board or whether the miners would insist, once again, on rubbing its face in the dirt. Essentially the relativities procedure was a figleaf to cover the Government's willingness to give the miners more; yet politically it furnished the Government with a defensible ground on which to stand and fight. For weeks the Tory party had been in confusion, torn between determination that the Government must not at any price back down and fear of the consequences of a trial of strength. Heath was criticised on the one hand for obduracy, on the other for being too conciliatory, by both sides for poor presentation of the Government's case. In the days after 17 January a number of ministers were rumoured to be ready to resign if the Government weakened. At the same time there were contrary rumours that if some solution were not found the party's instinct for self-preservation would assert itself and Heath would be thrown over in favour of Willie Whitelaw.[77]

In these circumstances the relativities gambit was a lifeboat into which the whole party could pile, preserving the principle that there should be no exemption for the miners under Stage Three while at the same time placing them first in the queue for special consideration under Stage Four. The Government's whole counter-inflation strategy would be strengthened by the involvement of the TUC in the resolution of anomalies. If the NUM and the TUC refused it, the Government had a constructive and reasonable platform – 'firm and fair' – on which to go to the country. *The Economist* was justifiably sceptical that the proposal was more than another Wilberforce award, designed to buy the Government out of trouble; but that was not the point.[78] The point was that the Government had to put the onus of acceptance on to Labour and the unions, as it had failed to do with the TUC's self-denying offer in January. By setting out the detail of his proposed solution in the form of a letter to the Leader of the Opposition published on 4 February, David Wood in *The Times* believed that Heath had pulled off a brilliant political *coup*. 'Mr Heath's subtly considered letter to Mr Wilson over the weekend', he wrote on Monday morning, 'must be reckoned a political work of art, all the more remarkable for having been produced by a Prime Minister coming under the strains of the most dangerous crisis of his career.'[79]

On Monday 4 February the result of the NUM ballot was declared: an overwhelming 81 per cent 'Yes' vote giving the Executive *carte blanche* to call a strike whenever it wanted. That afternoon the TUC 'Big Six' came to Downing Street for the last time but left after three and a half hours complaining that the invitation had been 'a charade'.[80] Whitelaw made a last appeal to the miners' leaders to meet him at 9 next morning, but was curtly rebuffed. Gormley actually refused to see him; instead he announced that the NUM would stop work at midnight on 9 February. That afternoon in the House Heath did not disguise his anger: he had gone to the limit – in the eyes of many well beyond the limit – in trying to satisfy the miners and he had finally run out of patience with their blinkered obstinacy. His position was still that they could have everything they wanted if they would only go through proper procedures. He dealt harshly with Wilson for suggesting that he should anticipate the relativities award and give them the money anyway, and brushed aside Jeremy Thorpe's proposal that the Government could 'pay the money into court' pending the board's judgment. It was clear that he now saw no alternative to an election.[81]

That evening, after a gloomy Cabinet, he dined with Francis Pym and Timothy Kitson at Prunier's. Hurd 'joined them for a glass after dinner. Mr Heath explained more clearly than ever before his desperate worry about the size of the stake on the table. Everything which he had tried to do seemed at risk. No one pressed him that evening. Events had already taken over the argument.'[82]

Next day the hawks took over. Jim Prior dropped a broad hint to a Press Gallery lunch: 'The miners have had their ballot; perhaps we ought to have ours.'[83] Soon afterwards Tony Barber told a tense House of Commons that the country would soon have to choose between democracy on the one hand and 'chaos, anarchy and a totalitarian or Communist regime' on the other.[84] Sir Michael Fraser was summoned to Downing Street to brief Heath on the state of the party's preparations and public opinion. The polls were not such as would normally encourage a Prime Minister to risk his job: the last Harris poll in the *Daily Express* had put the Tories 4 per cent ahead, but Gallup in the *Daily Telegraph* the next day gave Labour a 3 per cent lead.[85] On the other hand background polls continued to show steady support for the Government's incomes policy, scant enthusiasm for Labour and strong hostility to the abuse of union power. It was a reasonable expectation that opinion would rally to the Government during a campaign. Yet Heath still did not want an election. He did not expect to lose, but his deepest political instinct revolted against an election fought against the miners, pitching the Tories against the trade unions in a contest that would arouse class antagonism on both sides. This was not the politics he had learned from Churchill and Macmillan; it was not for this that he had spent so many hours patiently trying to bring the TUC into government. But the miners left him, quite simply, no alternative. He had nothing left to offer the party or the country. 'There was no pretence', Hurd wrote, 'in public or in private, that an election victory would by itself solve the coal dispute . . . But at least after an election victory the Government would have strong cards in its hand. On 7 February it had none.'[86] That evening, ironically, Heath attended a reception at the Soviet Embassy to mark fifty years of Anglo–Soviet relations: Joe Gormley (though not Mick McGahey) was a fellow guest. The next morning – 7 February, the day on which he could have held the election if Prior and Carrington had had their way, and might now have been forming his second administration – he finally announced that the country would go to the polls on 28 February.

Reflecting some years later on why, after resisting so long, Heath had ultimately caved in to an election after all, Douglas Hurd suggested that it was not really the miners' strike but the need for a fresh mandate to deal with the consequences of the oil shock that tipped his decision. 'It was partly the deterioration of events, and in particular the lurch into a strike. It became almost impossible to see how a tolerable settlement could be reached without an election. But in my view . . . another argument was decisive.'

> The more he studied the prospects, the more it emerged that oil rather than coal was the key. He had strongly practised and defended a policy of economic growth; it was now in ruins because of the oil price rise. The public expenditure cuts of December 1973 were only the first of the adjustments which would be needed. We were entering a period of lean years, perhaps many years of really harsh scarcity and impoverishment. The lean years would need new policies and a new vocabulary. There would have to be an end to promises. People would have to understand, because only with that understanding could their Government do what was needed. This was impossible for a Government elected in 1970, with policies and a vocabulary which were now out of date. The world had changed for Britain. Only a Government which had explained the change and been re-elected after that explanation could succeed.

'I believe', Hurd went on, 'that Mr Heath would have liked this to be the main theme of the February 1974 election. In his own mind it *was* the main theme . . . He disliked the election . . . I suspect that he would never have agreed to hold it at all on grounds of the coal dispute alone. It was the coincidence of the coal dispute with the disastrous change in our economic prospects which in the end clinched the argument.'[87]

This is an important argument, which must be respected; but it was published in 1979 and there is at least an element of *post hoc* rationalisation in it. Undoubtedly Heath disliked the election – and naturally came to regret calling it. Certainly he would have preferred it to have been fought on the wider issue of adjusting to the oil shock. But the reason he disliked it was precisely because it was *not* fought on the oil shock: it was unavoidably fought on the triangle of issues which had forced him to hold it – the miners' pay claim, the control of inflation and the use of trade union power. These were the issues on which the Tory party and most of his colleagues were straining to fight – as witness Prior's and Barber's comments quoted above. And this was unanimously how the press saw the contest.

'This election', the *Daily Express* declared, 'is different. It is concerned with the primacy of Parliament.'[88] 'The Government', *The Times* asserted, 'are risking their whole future on one strike: it is worth risking the future of an administration on the prevention of inflation at 20 per cent or above. That is more than one strike: it is the future of the country.'[89] Both the *Sun* and the *Daily Mirror* tagged their front pages every day throughout the campaign 'The Crisis Election'. Whatever Heath might have wished, Fleet Street had no doubt that the single question before the electorate was 'Who Governs?'

Heath himself took much the same line when he went on television to explain why he had called the election. He did make some reference to the 'grave problems' facing the country 'at home and abroad' and the need for a co-ordinated international response to the challenge of the oil price rise. But his emphasis was all on the domestic challenge:

> The issue before you is a simple one ... Do you want a strong Government which has clear authority for the future to take the decisions which will be needed? Do you want Parliament and the elected Government to continue to fight strenuously against inflation? Or do you want them to abandon the struggle against rising prices under pressure from one particular group of workers?

He did not attack the miners. On the contrary, he insisted that they *were* a special case and rehearsed again how much the Government had done to recognise the fact, framing Stage Three deliberately to allow them a bigger increase than anyone else, pouring new investment into their industry and now offering them priority consideration by the relativities board. But he did condemn those he believed were exploiting the NUM dispute for political ends, and attempted – in his most exasperated managing director's manner – to appeal to the ordinary reasonable British voter to repudiate them: 'You have seen them on television, and I have seen them in action at first hand. The great majority of you are fed up to the teeth with them and the disruption that they cause.'

The miners' action was only the latest episode in the saga of industrial conflict which had plagued his Government since 1970, holding back the economic growth which was otherwise within the country's grasp.

> This time the strife has got to stop. Only you can stop it. It's time for you to speak with your vote. It's time for your voice to be

heard, the voice of the moderate and reasonable people of Britain, the voice of the majority. It is time for you to say to the extremists, the militants and the plain and simple misguided: 'We've had enough. There's a lot to be done. For heaven's sake let's get on with it.'

Passionately he defended the Government's counter-inflation policy, which was designed specifically to protect the pensioners, the low-paid and – he added pointedly – those in dangerous and disagreeable jobs. 'That is the fair way.' The alternative – free collective bargaining as advocated by the unions and the Labour party on the one hand and Enoch Powell on the other – was to let everyone fend for himself: 'and we have all seen what happens in that situation. The strongest wins, as he always does, and the weakest goes to the wall.' That was 'the unfair way', and he would have no part of it.

Finally he came back to the wider oil problem, but still with a message clearly drawn from the immediate crisis. Britain, he insisted – with 'a great coal industry, despite everything that is happening now', with nuclear energy and the prospect of North Sea oil – was better placed than most countries. 'So if we don't allow ourselves to be deluded, if we understand and accept the realities of our situation, if we tackle our problems with resolution, courage and moderation, and if we tackle our problems together, we have a bright future to look forward to.'[90]

What this broadcast shows is that, while the election was clearly precipitated by the NUM, Heath was still determined not to conduct it as a crusade against the miners. Hence he announced that the Government was even now ready to refer their claim to the relativities panel of the Pay Board and would accept its adjudication. The next day Whitelaw duly did so. This was widely criticised, both by dismayed Conservatives and by the Opposition, as undercutting the whole point of holding an election. 'For the first time in history', Wilson jeered, 'we have a general leading his troops into battle with the deliberate aim of giving in if they win.'[91] But this was an interpretation based on the assumption that the Government was out to beat the miners. By this stage this was not the case. All that Heath wanted to do – all that he had ever wanted to do, indeed, right back to his meeting with Gormley in the garden of Number 10 the previous July – was to ensure that the miners got the money their industrial muscle commanded within the terms and machinery of Stage Three. His sticking point throughout was the sanctity of Stage Three, more than ever the essential framework for the containment of inflation. That was still his position. He could not comprehend the obstinacy with which the miners insisted that they had to break Stage Three, when the Government was giving them every assurance that more money would be available if they would only follow the proper procedure. It was this obstinacy that convinced him in the end that the strike was political and only an election would compel the NUM Executive to respect the Government's authority. It might not even need a Tory victory, if it was clear that that was the likely outcome. The point was to end the dispute as quickly as possible and get back to the business of government. So he kept the door to a settlement open during the campaign. It was part of his appeal to the country to demonstrate that the Government was being reasonable, still open to compromise, not vindictive. Despite the polarised nature of much of the press reporting and the yearning of his party to avenge 1972, he was not out to smash the miners.

As a result, the General Election of February 1974 was one of the strangest of modern times.

32

'Who Governs?'

JUST as June 1970 was the election no one expected Heath to win, so February 1974 was the election no one expected him to lose. It is easy today, in the wake of all that has been written about the fall of the Heath Government, to imagine that its demise was inevitable or predictable. On the contrary, it was almost universally assumed at the start of the campaign that he would win by a landslide. Admittedly the polls gave scant ground for such an expectation, but the polls were discredited. Pundits and politicians of both parties confidently backed the conventional wisdom that in a 'crisis' election the electorate would rally to the Government – as it had done in 1931, the only comparable precedent.[1] The bookmakers duly made the Tories favourites at 2–1 on.[2] Even when the campaign failed to take off as anticipated, and the polls continued to suggest a closer result than Heath had hoped for, few commentators believed that he would lose.

The assumption that the result was a foregone conclusion contributed to an unexpectedly low-key campaign, and doubtless also to the surprise result. At the outset the *Guardian* – in common with most other papers – had predicted 'the most polarised and virulent General Election since the war'.[3] Had it been so, Heath would indeed probably have won. But it was precisely the apprehension of such a campaign, and such a victory, which had deterred him from going to the country in January; and still in February he was determined not to fight a socially divisive election. He fought instead a serious, self-consciously responsible and insistently 'moderate' campaign. As a result he failed to rouse the country. So far from being polarised, the electorate shrugged its shoulders and listened with increasing sympathy to the Liberals, who fought a skilful campaign on the theme 'a plague on both your houses' – with disastrous consequences for Heath.

A number of circumstances helped to dissipate the crisis atmosphere. First, the Government immediately lifted the 10.30 pm curfew on television. This was essential if the election was going to be adequately covered without wiping out more popular programmes; but it immediately relieved the sense of emergency. The three-day week remained in force, but most firms had found ways of minimising its impact. Restrictions on street lighting and on heating shops and offices remained as well, but the weather continued exceptionally mild, so once again the effect was minimal. Then the expectation had been that the election would be fought against the background of the miners' strike, with mass picketing and a repetition of the violent scenes vividly remembered from 1972. Heath appealed to the NUM to suspend the strike for the period of the campaign. Gormley was willing to do so, but was overruled by his Executive. The strike duly went ahead on 10 February; but the NUM shrewdly ensured that there was no large-scale picketing and no violence, thereby crucially maintaining public sympathy for the miners' case. The train drivers' union ASLEF also called off an overtime ban which had threatened a number of Labour marginals around London. Even Heath was moved to comment sarcastically on this explicitly political suspension of industrial action in the interests of the Opposition.[4] The effect was subtly to confirm the impression that Labour's closer links with the unions offered a better prospect of industrial peace than Tory 'confrontation'.

Finally Willie Whitelaw's referral of the miners' pay claim to the Pay Board while the election was on seemed to call in doubt the point of having an election at all – especially when the NUM abandoned its refusal to co-operate and agreed to give evidence to the Board, and Heath in turn undertook to implement whatever settlement the Board proposed. Why, it was asked, could he not have done this earlier? If the coal dispute was on the way to being resolved, why was the country being put to the inconvenience of an election? If, as Harold Wilson jeered, the answer to the question 'Who Governs?' turned out to be 'the Pay Board', then the election was – as Enoch Powell alleged – an opportunist fraud.[5] Heath's position was in fact consistent: it was the miners who had hitherto refused to recognise the Pay Board, and even now they declined to be bound in advance by its ruling. Still their willingness to submit their case was a major advance which went a long way to establish the new relativities procedure as a permanent part of the counter-inflation policy: on 17 February Heath hinted that the next group to benefit from it might be the teachers.[6] Nevertheless he had great difficulty in the early days of the campaign explaining why the election was necessary. The best he could manage at his first morning press conference was that following a Tory victory, 'we should be in a good position because the electorate would have shown that it supported a Government which is going to carry through an incomes policy'.[7] The next day, questioned on a walkabout in Hatfield, he tried again. The main issue, he now declared, was 'Whether this country is going to return a strong Government with a firm mandate for the next five years to deal with the counter-inflation policy . . . a firm incomes policy which Parliament will approve. The challenge is to the will of Parliament and a democratically elected Government.'[8]

This was a line, however, which he was generally at pains to play down. He wanted an endorsement of the Government's incomes policy (which poll evidence showed the electorate overwhelmingly supported). He did not want to stir up feeling against the miners. 'I know the miners themselves are democrats,' he announced on 8 February. 'It is therefore especially disappointing that the politically motivated arguments of some of their leaders should have prevailed.'[9] As Cecil King noted in his diary: 'Ted attacks the miners and the trade unions, but with no real edge to his remarks – perhaps because he thinks he will have to deal with them afterwards.'[10] King was right. But a Prime Minister who failed to give a lead on the issue which the press and public believed the election to be about was asking for trouble. If the election was not to backfire on him he needed, if not a landslide, then certainly a substantially increased majority. He had to face the electorate with an unmistakable choice. Instead, by fighting on the woolly slogan 'firm but fair', insisting that the existing incomes policy was simultaneously sacrosanct and flexible, he confused the issue. Instead of a life or death struggle for British democracy and the rule of law, it seemed, as one cynical observer put it, merely 'an election to decide which party is to sell out to the miners'.[11] With the exception of the *Daily Mirror* the press was almost wholly behind the Government – much of it stridently so. Yet even those papers which were most alarmed about inflation and the predicament facing the country found it hard to maintain the high level of their initial commitment. By 16 February even *The Economist* could only manage a back-handed endorsement: 'It may be difficult for many people to believe that the right solutions will be found by a second-term Conservative government with a very greatly increased majority. But it is even more difficult to see how any other result would not be more disastrous.'[12] Such tepid support from the faithful *Economist* spelled danger to the Tory cause.

The Conservative manifesto – entitled *Firm Action for a Fair Britain* and largely written by Nigel Lawson – embodied the ambivalence of the whole Tory campaign. The opening sentences sounded the note that was maintained throughout: tough-sounding analysis followed by a vague appeal to national unity, moderation and good will. Essentially the Government simply asked for a blank cheque – what in 1931 was called a 'doctor's mandate'.

> It is essential that the affairs of this country are in the hands of a strong government, able to take firm measures in defence of the national interest.
> This means a Conservative Government with a renewed mandate from the people and with a full five years in which to guide the nation safely through the difficult period that lies ahead.

In proposing just how it would deal first with 'The Danger from Outside' – the consequences of the oil shock and the steep rise in the cost of most other raw materials since 1972 – and then with 'The Danger from Within' – 'the inflation which comes as a result of excessive wage increases here at home', inflation which 'could destroy, not just our present standard of living but all our hopes for the future' – the manifesto was astonishingly unspecific. The diagnosis was blunt and eloquent. But far from suggesting 'strong government', the repeated invocation of the virtues of 'firmness' and 'fairness' represented not so much a policy as a substitute for one. The tone of the document spoke of a Government at the mercy of events and interests beyond its control, anxious to appear strong but desperate not to antagonise elements of the community which it had learned that it could not command.

There was no condemnation of the unions and scarcely even of the miners. The manifesto simply rehearsed the history of the Government's 'strenuous' efforts to achieve a voluntary incomes policy; claimed credit for Stages One and Two of the statutory policy, which had 'proved more successful than our critics thought possible'; and regretted that the miners alone should have rejected 'an offer, within Stage Three, of a size which few other groups of workers can hope to achieve'. The Government still hoped that the NUM would accept the Coal Board offer, augmented by the promised relativities adjudication, but did not say what it would do if the miners still held out. Meanwhile the Government would 'renew our offer to the TUC and the CBI to join us in working out an effective voluntary pay and prices policy, ultimately to replace the existing statutory policy'.

The Government proposed to amend the Industrial Relations Act 'in the light of experience, and after consultation with both sides of industry, in order' – a characteristic phrase – 'to meet any valid criticisms'. Ultimately, however, the Government now believed, it was up to trade union members themselves to reform the unions. 'The best way of curbing the minority of extremists in the trade unions is for the moderate majority of union members to stand up and be counted.' To encourage them to do so, the Government proposed the one provocative item in the whole manifesto, which attracted more press attention – and more public approval – than anything else in it: the withdrawal of welfare benefits from strikers's families.★ The principle was set out boldly: how it was to be done, however, was not disclosed. The section merely concluded with the customary vague referral to tripartite talks: 'and after discussions with trade unions and employers, we will amend the social security system accordingly'.

For the rest, *Firm Action for a Fair Britain* made as good a job as possible of defending the Government's record since 1970. For the future the major effort would be concentrated on four fronts: fighting inflation, overcoming the energy crisis, improving industrial relations and continuing an active industrial policy. Beyond these, there were very few new promises, though the manifesto did its best to make a virtue of this: 'at this critical time in our nation's affairs, we believe it to be right to err on the side of caution; to promise too little rather than too much'.

Only at the very end did the manifesto deign to notice Labour's alternative programme of high taxation, nationalisation and no incomes policy, which it dismissed as extreme, doctrinaire and irrelevant:

> The total effect of Labour's policies would be to wreck the economy, undermine the free society, and accelerate the present inflation beyond the point of no return . . . In short, the return of a Labour Government at the present time would be nothing short of a major national disaster.
>
> The choice before the nation today, as never before, is a clear choice between moderation and extremism.
>
> We therefore appeal, at this critical time in our country's affairs, for the support of the great moderate majority of the British people, men and women of all Parties and no Party, who reject extremism in any shape or form.
>
> For extremism divides, while moderation unites; and it is only on the basis of national unity that the present crisis can be

★ A Harris poll found 75 per cent support for the proposal.[13]

overcome and a better Britain built.[14]

It was an honourable appeal, but as a prospectus it was weak, un-convincing and – above all – tactically flawed. For if the voters wanted 'firmness' it was singularly lacking: practically everything that was to be done would only be done in consultation with the unions. If, on the other hand, they wanted 'fairness', they were more likely, on all past evidence, to look to Labour. The essential flaw of *Firm Action for a Fair Britain* was that it played to Labour's traditional strength.

Heath himself dominated the Tory campaign. He chaired all the party's morning press conferences, rarely allowing whichever col-league was with him – most often Carrington, Whitelaw or Prior – a look in, then flew off in a specially chartered plane (inappropriately named 'Halcyon Days') to meetings and walkabouts around the country. Curiously the early part of the campaign was an inverted image of 1970, with each party leader choosing to adopt the style the other had used in 1970; Heath made fewer big speeches but many more constituency visits, while Wilson this time concentrated on major speeches.[15] In fact Heath had discovered walkabouts with some success in the final days of 1970; this time, however, he found the same disadvantages in them that Wilson had in 1970. Surrounded by journalists, camera crews – foreign as well as British – and detec-tives (with the IRA beginning to pose a serious threat, security was necessarily much tighter than in 1970), he got to meet hardly any voters. Those he did meet were generally friendly, but there was a permanent fringe of demonstrators wherever he went, and some scuffles. He abandoned walkabouts – just as Wilson had done – in the final week.

Again, Wilson had been criticised in 1970 for hogging the lime-light. This time, a somewhat shopsoiled figure fighting what seemed likely to be his last campaign, he was careful to share it, presenting his senior colleagues – Callaghan, Healey, Jenkins, Barbara Castle – as an experienced team ready to return to office to clear up the Tory mess; while Heath came across as a one-man band, the solitary embattled leader seeking his country's endorsement to finish the job he had begun. Yet with characteristic perversity he disdained to ex-ploit his greatest asset, the news-making potential of his office. Though he was still carrying the full burden of government at the end of long campaigning days, he refused to make capital of the fact. Henry Kissinger did pay a flying visit to Downing Street on 26 February, but Heath resisted pleas from his party managers that he

should summon ministers for a well-publicised crisis Cabinet to discuss declining coal stocks: that was 'the sort of thing Wilson would
do'.[16]

Nevertheless in his own way he fought a good campaign. At his
morning press conferences he was a revelation: 'much more relaxed
and amusing than in 1970: he spoke eloquently, without notes and
displayed great versatility and grasp of detail'.[17] 'Assured, but pleasantly so, good-humoured and good-natured, he has never been more
successful in his exchanges with the press.'[18] On television, some
commentators still found him stiff and stilted. But *The Times*, in an
editorial midway through the campaign, believed that his qualities
were beginning to come across:

> As the years go by he seems to become gradually more popular, as
> can happen with a man who is hard to get to know. What is more
> important is that he has an energy and attack which demonstrate
> his will to overcome the great crisis in which all parties say we are
> involved. Not everyone watching him is going to like him, but
> hardly anyone watching him can doubt that he is formidable, and
> many have come to feel that he has a strength and integrity on
> which they can rely.

Wilson by contrast was 'rather tired and ineffective',[19] a view echoed
by Tony Benn, who thought Heath's first party election broadcast
on 11 February 'brilliant', compared with Wilson 'floundering away
about the price of petrol'.[20]

At his evening meetings, too, mainly to all-ticket audiences of
paid-up Tories, with a different sound bite inserted every night for
the 'Nine O'Clock News', he generally went down well. His brusque unsmiling manner, *The Economist* noted, suited the mood of
Tory audiences. Significantly they cheered most enthusiastically
when he was 'firm', less so when he was 'fair': at Cardiff on 13
February 'the delighted audience went into near-frenzy when he
came to strikers' social security benefits'.[21] This was what they
wanted to hear; and sometimes he gave it to them. 'On the hustings',
George Clark wrote in *The Times* on 23 February, 'Mr Heath has
projected himself as the iron man. He looks stern; there is a curl in his
upper lip as he castigates the extremists and the wreckers who, he
says, have challenged the prices and incomes policy, their unions
and even democracy itself.'[22] The Nuffield analysis of his speeches
shows, however, that he devoted much more emphasis overall to the
'fair' side of his appeal than to the 'firm'.[23] A characteristic cry in all
his speeches, repeated every night, underlined the lesson to be drawn

from the fact that industrial output had not been significantly affected by the three-day week: 'Why, why, why does it require a crisis of this kind for the British to be able to work together in order to get an answer to our problems in the production of more goods?'[24]

The high point of his campaign was in Manchester on 20 February, where he was given a 'rapturous' reception by 3,000 supporters in the Free Trade Hall singing 'All the Nice Girls Love a Sailor'. The key passage of his speech that night was a classic statement of 'One Nation' Toryism; the audience – perhaps surprisingly – loved it.

We have no single group to represent. We as a Conservative party and a Conservative Government represent all the people. We are the trades union for the pensioners, and for children. We are the union for the disabled, and for the sick. We are the union for those who live in slums or for those who want to buy homes.

We are the union for the unemployed and the low paid. We are the union for those in poverty and for the hard pressed. We are the union of the nation as a whole. We cannot just say 'Give us the money and be hanged the rest'. We must balance all the carefully conflicting claims and reach a just solution.[25]

The Tory campaign, and Heath's conduct of it, were much criticised afterwards, with the recrimination of hindsight. But there was little criticism at the time, when it was taken for granted on all sides that the campaign was going well and the Government was on its way to being safely, if not resoundingly, returned.

Labour's strategy was to try to widen the issue from the narrow question of the miners' strike, industrial relations and 'Who Governs?' to the broader problems of the economy and the Government's record of economic management. Those like Willie Whitelaw who had always opposed an early election had warned of the difficulty of keeping the electorate's attention fixed on a single issue for the duration even of a short three-week campaign. They were right. An NOP poll at the beginning of the campaign found that the Government would have a handsome lead of 9 per cent if the election were to be decided solely on the coal strike.[26] But further polls showed that, between the first and third weeks, the issue of strikes and union power declined in importance in voters' minds, while other issues more favourable to Labour – rising prices, the state of the economy, housing problems and membership of the EEC – rose proportionately.[27] A further problem – foreseen by those who had wanted the election to be held on 7 February – was that the campaign was punctuated by the publication of some damaging economic statistics. As it happened, the unemployment figures, despite the three-day week, were not as bad as had been feared; but the retail price index, published on 15 February, and the January trade figures, published on 25 February, hit the Government hard.

The former showed an increase in retail prices over the past year of 20 per cent – the fastest ever recorded. It was only too easy for Wilson to recall the Tories' 1970 promise to cut the rate of price rises 'at a stroke' and to assert that on the central issue of that campaign Heath had 'failed the nation'. In the Government's defence, Heath blamed world factors, pointing out that world food prices had risen 79 per cent since 1970 and claiming that Britain had actually fared relatively well, thanks to the counter-inflation policy which Labour proposed to scrap.[28] A Harris poll suggested that a majority of the electorate accepted this explanation: 54 per cent blamed world causes, only 20 per cent the Government.[29] Nevertheless inexorably rising prices remained a potent source of voter dissatisfaction with a Government which had for two years made fighting inflation its central policy. (While the Tories talked about 'inflation' and focused on wages, Labour always spoke of 'prices' and the rising cost of living.) The only response the Government could make was to promise to beef up the powers of the Price Commission.

The record balance-of-payments deficit for January was even more damaging. At £383 million it was the biggest ever recorded for a single month, dwarfing the £31 million deficit which had helped to tip the election away from Labour in 1970. The figure could only partly be accounted for by the higher price of oil, since it reflected the increase of the previous October, but not yet the further doubling in December. Nor was it seriously attributable to the three-day week. Optimistically the steep rise in the volume (as well as the cost) of imports was made up of raw materials which should ultimately feed through into increased production and exports. Nevertheless the bare figure – published just three days before polling day – could be brandished as a damning indictment of the Tories' economic management. Heath's response, in Bradford that evening, was to claim it as a further reason to return a Tory Government: 'The trade figures merely confirm what I have said all along . . . They emphasise the gravity of the situation. It is too serious for the irrelevance of the Liberal programme or the destructiveness of Labour's. We have got to get the problem right.'[30] His argument moved Roy Jenkins – the architect of Labour's hard-won turnaround of the balance of payments between 1967 and 1970 – to sarcastic incredulity: 'He presumably thinks a still worse result would have given him a still stronger claim.'[31]

If the economic indicators were foreseeable, three other incidents unhelpful to the Government which blew up during the campaign were not. The first booby-trap was detonated – in two stages – by Enoch Powell, who first announced on the day Heath called the election that he could not stand in an election he regarded as 'essentially fraudulent' and was therefore resigning his seat. 'I personally cannot ask electors to vote for policies which are directly opposite to those we all stood for in 1970 and which I have myself consistently condemned as being inherently impractical and bound to create the very difficulties in which the nation now finds itself.'[32]

This was quixotic but easily shrugged off. The most common interpretation was that by his increasingly violent attacks on the Government and on Heath personally since 1971 Powell had been positioning himself to strike for the succession following Heath's defeat: he was now assumed to be leaving politics because with Heath apparently certain to be confirmed in power for the rest of the decade his calculation had been negated.[33] His second bombshell was more serious. After two weeks of uncharacteristic silence he made two heavily trailed speeches at meetings of the 'Get Britain Out' movement, at which he declared that the overriding issue of the election was not the miners or inflation but the EEC, and hinted, without yet expressly urging, that patriots should vote Labour as the best hope of securing withdrawal: then, with maximum drama, he revealed, two days before polling, that he had himself already voted Labour, by post.[34] By skilful playing of the media Powell managed to dominate the news for five of the last seven days of the campaign. He succeeded only marginally in raising the profile of Europe as an issue; but the spectacle of a former Conservative minister advising the public to vote Labour was deeply embarrassing to the Government – Carrington successfully put pressure on the BBC to keep him off 'Panorama' on the last Monday – and probably helped to stiffen the Labour vote, particularly in the West Midlands. There was some plausibility in his admirers' claim that just as his last-minute support had helped put Heath into office in 1970 so his egregious advice in 1974 played a significant role in turning him out.

The second booby-trap which exploded under the Government on 21 February, a week before polling day, was the leaked revelation that the Pay Board, in considering the miners' pay claim, had discovered an apparent error in previous calculations. NCB figures, it was reported, had overstated miners' pay by 8 per cent by including holiday pay while the payment of other comparable groups did not. The story broke around 6.30 pm and dominated the television news and the next day's papers (The *Daily Mail* headlined it 'The Great Pit

Blunder') before the Government was able to reply. Wilson, typically, got wind of it at once and pounced gleefully in a speech in Hampstead that evening. Heath, on his way to Exeter, was out of contact with Downing Street and was not told for five hours! Next day he insisted angrily that there had been 'no error of any kind'. Miners' pay had been calculated on the same basis for at least twenty years: if the NUM wanted to propose a different basis they were welcome to do so. But the damage was done: deliberately or not – ministers suspected bitterly that the leak had been politically inspired – for a crucial twenty-four hours the public had been given to believe that the Government's quarrel with the miners had been based on a misunderstanding. Wilson was in his statistical element, charging the Government solemnly with 'grave incompetence': 'No Government should ever have put itself in a position where such severe economic disruption can be caused by a simple error in arithmetic.'[35] Even if there was no error, the confusion still made it appear as though the Government – after all these weeks – was not fully aware of the facts and had not tried as seriously as it pretended to achieve a settlement. Public sympathy for the miners was perceptibly strengthened.

Finally, five days later – just two days before polling and the day after the awful trade figures – the Secretary-General of the CBI, Campbell Adamson, kicked away another prop from under the Government's credibility. Speaking to a conference of the Industrial Society on 26 February he expressed the hope that 'the next Government' would not merely amend the Industrial Relations Act but repeal it, 'so that we can get proper agreement on what should replace it'.

> It is so surrounded by hatred that we must have a more honest try at another Act. I have a feeling that the trade unions, faced with this sort of situation, would be quite ready to talk about it. This would give us a chance to start from a position where every relationship at a national level was not sullied by this Act.[36]

Adamson had supposed that he was speaking off the record, and was unaware that he was being taped by the BBC. When his words were reported, he offered to resign; but it was too late. Heath commented icily that Adamson had never indicated that this was his view in all the hours of talks with the Government and the TUC over the previous year. Wilson meanwhile hailed Adamson's indiscretion as 'the final collapse of the platform on which the Conservatives launched this election'.[37] It came too close to polling day to affect the polls; but it was yet another instance of the Government being gravely embarrassed by its own side, which further undermined the image Heath was trying to present of a strong, united Government seeking to unite the nation. Adamson focused attention on to the Tories' most vulnerable flank, which was paradoxically Labour's strongest: the ability or inability to 'get on' with the unions. Polls showed that the public disliked strikes, was critical of overmighty unions and supported the principle of prices and incomes policy. But at the same time it tended to blame the Government for what seemed like a permanent state of industrial conflict over the past four years. Heath made much of his wish to co-operate with the unions, but he did not seem to have the trick of it. If good relations between Government and unions were the prerequisite of industrial peace, then Labour's closer links with the unions seemed to offer the likelier prospect of success. On 17 February – with little or no consultation – Wilson put forward Labour's proposed 'Social Contract'. Heath immediately derided it. Indeed it had no content at all at that stage; Hugh Scanlon embarrassingly denied any knowledge of it, and Len Murray and Jack Jones had to be hastily mobilised to endorse it.[38] Yet it was no different in principle and no more shadowy in practice than Heath's own hopes for a voluntary incomes policy. Here again Heath was pitching his tent on Labour's territory.

For all his strenuous efforts to be 'fair', 'moderate', 'reasonable' and the rest, Labour continued to portray the Prime Minister as pig-headed, dictatorial and divisive. Right at the beginning of the campaign Tony Crosland compared him to Anthony Eden – 'headstrong, wilful and incorrigibly resistant to compromise', allegedly disregarding the advice of steadier colleagues.[39] Later Denis Healey accused him of threatening the structure of society by leading a 'virulent attack' on the working class, treating ordinary trade unionists as enemies of the state like blacks in South Africa.[40] This was wild stuff, and probably counterproductive. Yet the idea that Heath himself, perhaps unwittingly – by his stubbornness, his coldness, his remoteness from the concerns of ordinary people – was the cause of the country's troubles was a potent one with enough plausibility to stick. Conversely – though the polls showed little support for Labour's policies – there was an undoubted appeal to Wilson's more homely family doctor image. He presented his team of experienced and well-regarded colleagues (certainly better regarded than anyone in the Tory Cabinet except Whitelaw and Home) as the wise old firm, non-extremist and non-doctrinaire, who could get on with the unions and get the country back to work.

The sense that the country was in an unprecedented mess – but that neither of the major parties had the answer – also benefited the

Liberals. The expectation at the beginning of the campaign was that the Liberals would be squeezed, as usual. Their support in the polls had already fallen right back from the heady levels they had achieved at the time of the Ely and Ripon by-elections the previous summer. At the turn of the year it stood at around 10–14 per cent. In a polarised 'crisis' election they were likely to be squeezed even more than usual. In fact it was a measure of the unexpected quietness of the election that their rating crept up steadily as the campaign went on, reaching 23.5 per cent in one poll on 23 February. The danger which a strong Liberal performance posed to the Government was not at first appreciated. Early analysis indicated that the Liberals were taking support roughly equally from both the other parties; if so, Richard Rose argued in *The Times*, they would damage Labour more.[41] Even the *Daily Mail* looked forward to 'a notable Liberal presence in the next Parliament'.[42] Only in the last week did it strike the Government's supporters in Fleet Street that the Liberals might rob it of the increased majority it needed if the election was to be justified. On 21 February George Hutchinson had believed that 'with just a week to polling, the sun seems to be shining on the Tories. Unless some deep and formidable force, not yet detected, is working against them, Mr Heath can surely look forward to an unbroken tenancy at 10 Downing Street'.[43] Two days later Hutchinson had sniffed the wind. The only thing that could deny the Tories now, he wrote, was 'the combination, rather widespread, of boredom and irritation which the campaign itself has induced'; plus 'the feeling, not to be pooh-poohed, that the election is really unnecessary and could have been avoided'.[44] But this was exactly the feeling that was gaining ground.

'Are you voting Liberal to get rid of Mr Heath or Mr Wilson?' the cartoonist Marc had Joanna Stringalong ask her husband on 26 February.[45] It was a good question which neatly expressed the dissatisfaction with both parties which fuelled the Liberal vote. Jeremy Thorpe came across as much the most vigorous and attractive of the three leaders. He was helped by the accident that he was so nervous about his own fragile majority in North Devon – just 396 – that he conducted his national campaign entirely by closed-circuit link from Barnstaple. This had the unexpected effect that he appeared loftily detached from the dogfight being waged across Smith Square.★

★ Thorpe's physical distance also made it difficult for journalists to interview him aggressively. Heath later complained that the programme makers should not have fallen for this. 'The press cross-examined us with questions, no matter how penetrating, and there was the Liberal leader just quietly having a cosy time down in Devonshire and he wasn't subject to this cross-examination at all.'[46]

The Liberals' growing support was in large part a protest against the 'mudslinging' and rhetorical exaggeration of 'adversary politics', a vote in favour of the sort of co-operation and national unity which both big parties, absurdly, claimed that they alone could deliver.

There is evidence that the Liberals derived a special boost from a seriously misjudged Tory broadcast on 19 February. The Tories' use of television was altogether much less polished and less successful than in 1970. They abandoned the 'News at Ten' format which had worked so well: Heath did not think he needed presentational gimmicks any more to get his message across. The one broadcast which the advertising men did get hold of was the third, in which Barber fronted a crude attack on Labour extremism. The faces of Wilson and Callaghan were shown dissolving into the bogey figures of Tony Benn and Michael Foot, while an anonymous voice suggested that Labour would nationalise 'your bank account, your mortgage and your pay packet . . . It wouldn't take much more of a move to the left and you could find yourself not even owning your own home.' This, the Nuffield study judged, was 'a sorry broadcast in its ethical blindness, the clumsy cascade of visual gimmicks, and its abysmal view of the electorate's intelligence. It confirmed the fears of what can happen when admen are given their head without adequate political control.'[47] In the face of Labour and Tory protests Carrington was obliged to apologise. The effect of the broadcast was to antagonise both press and public, losing the Government much of the high ground Heath had claimed to occupy; the tone of the campaign was lowered, the Labour vote consolidated, and the Liberals' poll rating leaped into the twenties.

In the last week of the campaign the Tories began to take the Liberal threat seriously. In the party's penultimate television broadcast on 22 February Robert Carr appealed directly to intending Liberal voters as fellow moderates who agreed with the Government on the key issues of Europe and incomes policy.[48] The next day Heath warned for the first time of the danger of fudging a decision by voting for the easy option.[49] The same evening Thorpe made what was generally rated the most effective party broadcast of the election. Over the weekend Tory managers were said to be 'on tenterhooks' about what the Liberal surge might mean. But Heath spent the final Sunday at Chequers at least outwardly 'in a mood of high confidence . . . about the magnitude of his victory'.[50] Next day Marplan gave the Liberals 28 per cent: Thorpe began to talk of going for 'the jackpot', even of 'a landslide' and forming a Liberal Government.[51] This Marplan poll showed the Liberals mainly taking votes from Labour, who trailed the Government by seven points (31·5 per cent to 38·5 per cent). But ORC on 27 February told a different story: the Tories led Labour by only 36·5 per cent to 35 per cent, with the Liberals on 25·5 per cent. Harris was only marginally better. This, *The Times* warned, was 'dangerously threatening to Mr Heath'.[52] He still insisted he would get a 'substantial' majority. But the fact that (at his press conference on the 26th) he recalled his Whips' office experience of Churchill's 1951-5 Government (with a majority of 17), when foreign embassies watched to see how long the Government could survive, betrayed his apprehension. He warned that an effective Government such as the country needed must have an adequate majority: 'If it has to look over its shoulder every time it goes into the division lobby to see whether it is going to be supported, it is not in a position to carry through policies firmly and authoritatively.'[53] As Butler and Kavanagh later wrote, however: 'If the polls were . . . broadly accurate, and the Liberal vote stayed at 20 per cent or more while Labour did not fall below 35 per cent or 37 per cent, then it was highly doubtful that Mr Heath was going to get his "strong" mandate.'[54]

On the last Tuesday, Heath made his final television broadcast of the campaign, a direct personal appeal to the electorate. 'It was a broadcast', wrote *The Times*, 'in which the Prime Minister and his party managers exploited what until now has been held to be his public relations weakness – his remoteness and his appearance of stubbornness – and then added his passionate love of country in a closing burst of emotion.'[55] Heath was first presented, by means of a montage of film clips and photographs – including a statue of Churchill – as the saviour of his country, while an unidentified voice-over extolled his sterling qualities: 'It takes an extraordinary man to be Prime Minister. But this is an extraordinary man. A private man. A solitary man. Perhaps single-minded sums it up . . . This is a man the world respects. A man who has done so much and yet a man who has so much left to do.'

Then Heath spoke direct to camera. His theme was, as ever, that the Government had to be firm in order to be fair. The Government must be strong, 'because only the strong can protect the weak. You have got to be strong to be moderate.' He specifically warned against the temptation to duck the clear choice by voting Liberal. Finally he tackled head on the public perception of himself as stubborn:

> People tell me I am stubborn. Is it stubborn to fight and fight hard to stop the country you love from tearing itself apart? Is it stubborn to insist that everyone in that country should have the choice

and the chance to take his life and make of it what he can? Is it stubborn to want to see this country take back the place that history means us to have?

If it is – then, yes, I most certainly am stubborn. But surely 'stubborn' means not giving up when the going gets rough. And is not 'stubborn' another way of saying 'determined'?

I love this country. I'll do all that I can for this country. And isn't that what you want too? We've started a job together. With your will, we shall go on and finish the job.[56]

It had, as Michael Cockerell has written, 'a certain wooden poignancy, but was not among the rare occasions when Heath came out sympathetically on television'.[57] It was deeply, desperately sincere; but sincerity, patriotism and an unspecified determination were not enough. This was the last time he addressed the country as Prime Minister.

The final polls on Thursday morning still predicted a clear Tory win. Gallup gave a margin of only 2 per cent, but NOP, Harris and OPC all showed between 4 per cent and 5 per cent. Remembering 1970, there was a general assumption that the figures probably underestimated Tory support; ORC reported signs of another late swing and predicted an increased Government majority of 60–80.[58] The *Daily Mail* confidently headlined the findings of its NOP poll: 'A Handsome Win for Heath'.[59] The true story was in the small print. First, the decline over the course of the campaign in the importance of 'Tory' issues and the rise of 'Labour' ones; second, a significant stiffening in the number of Labour supporters declaring themselves certain to vote. This was borne out on polling day by the highest turn out since 1959 – nearly 79 per cent (compared with 72 per cent in 1970), a full three million more votes cast than four years before. To that extent, at least, Heath's plea that the voters must decide had got through. But in so far as there was a late swing it was away from the Government.

Heath spent polling day quietly in Downing Street, then went to Bexley in the evening for his count, accompanied by Michael Wolff and William Waldegrave, still confidently expecting a majority between 40 and 50. But even before the first results, exit polls from selected seats suggested a swing to Labour. The first returns, from Tory seats like Guildford and Cheltenham, showed the Liberals nearly matching their poll predictions, taking enough Tory votes to push Labour into third place. Then, around midnight, Wolverhampton North-East – Powell country, where unusually there was no Liberal standing – showed a 10 per cent swing to Labour. At Bexley, and simultaneously all around the country, the confidence of Tory workers was suddenly deflated. The BBC computers were predicting a stalemate. Heath arrived at 12.40 am, making only 'curt, negative comments' in reply to journalists' questions. By the time his own result was declared, around 1.30 am, the national picture was still unclear. The Sidcup result was satisfactory, given the extent of the boundary changes and the fact that it was essentially a new seat he was fighting: his majority was nearly 10,000, his share of the vote just under 50 per cent.★ 'But Mr Heath was obviously very worried. His smile seemed forced and weak, and there was none of the usual clasping high of the hands. Unlike Mr Wilson's expansive speech of thanks at Huyton, Mr Heath's was pared to the minimum.'[61]

He did not stay long in Bexley, but was driven straight back to Downing Street, facing the shattering prospect that he would have to make way for Harold Wilson again the following day.

It was clear only that the overall result was inconclusive. Overnight it was certain that Heath had lost his majority, but touch and go whether Labour might narrowly achieve one. That prospect receded during Friday, but the final picture was not complete until the last Scottish results came in on Saturday. The eventual state of the parties was Labour 301 seats, Conservatives 297, Liberals 14 (from 19 per cent of the national vote), plus 7 Scottish and 2 Welsh nationalists, 2 ex-Labour independents (Dick Taverne and Eddie Milne) and 12 Ulstermen. The Tories won fractionally more votes than Labour – 11,868,906 against 11,639,243 (37.9 per cent to 37.1 per cent) – but 4 fewer seats. Because of redistribution, however, and the creation of 5 additional seats, it is impossible to make a simple tally of seats won and lost. Compared with the position at the dissolution, the Government appeared to have lost 26 seats, while Labour gained 14, the Liberals 3, the SNP 5 (winning 22 per cent of the vote in Scotland) and Plaid Cymru 2. But 8 of these 'lost' 26 were in the special circumstances of Ulster, and 4 were lost to the SNP. In England and Wales the Tories lost no more than 12 seats to Labour (7 of them with majorities below 1,000), while actually gaining one (Berwick and East Lothian). They took back 2 of the 4 seats lost to the Liberals at by-elections (Ripon and Sutton & Cheam), but lost 2 more (Bodmin

---

★ E.R.G. Heath (Conservative)	20,488
C.F. Hargrave (Labour)	10,750
O. Moxon (Liberal)	9,847
Air-Vice-Marshal D. Bennett (anti-EEC)	613
Conservative majority	9,738[60]

and the Isle of Wight). There were unusually complex cross-currents in the voting, so that it is not possible to say exactly what was the effect of the strong Liberal performance. None of Labour's gains can be directly attributed to the increased Liberal vote. *The Economist* subsequently estimated that of the 4·5 million extra Liberal votes compared with 1970 the largest proportion (1·5 million) came from electors who had previously abstained, with a million each from Labour and the Tories, and another 0·75 million from new voters.[62] The decisive factor was probably the high turn out. Most of the seats which changed hands did so by very small margins on an increased poll. The overall swing from Labour to Conservative was no more than 0·8 per cent.[63]

There were far higher than average swings to Labour (5–10 per cent) in the West Midlands – not only in the three Wolverhampton seats but in the whole of the surrounding Black Country. This was plainly attributable to the maverick advice of Enoch Powell – the largest swing of all (16 per cent) was against his own Tory successor in Wolverhampton South-West. Despite the heavy regional swing, however, not one of the seats which changed hands was in Powell country. Much as his supporters might wish to see his intervention as decisive, therefore, the case for his direct influence cannot be sustained.

Far more important was Northern Ireland. The consequences in Ulster of calling a British General Election before the power-sharing Executive had had time to settle down fulfilled the worst fears of Willie Whitelaw and Francis Pym. Brian Faulkner's pro-Sunningdale Unionists were simply swept away, to be replaced by eleven diehard opponents of power-sharing (plus a single nationalist, Gerry Fitt). The consequence in England was just as serious for Heath. Now he paid the political cost of the abolition of Stormont. Up until 1972 the Ulster Unionists at Westminster had been counted unquestioningly as Conservatives: they had formed an integral part of every Tory majority in the House of Commons since 1921, and they formed a vital part of Heath's small majority in 1970. The eleven led by William Craig and Ian Paisley elected in February 1974 were bitterly opposed to Heath's Government and could not be counted on at all as part of a Conservative majority. This defection crucially affected the parliamentary arithmetic and the possibility of Heath's survival.

The result was clearly a devastating rebuff for Heath. Nevertheless there was just a chance, as the last returns trickled in over the weekend, that if neither party could command an overall majority then he – as the Prime Minister in possession – might still be able to carry on. Indeed it could quite properly be argued that it was his duty to try to carry on. 'No party was in a position automatically to form a government,' he later explained. 'Therefore my responsibility as Prime Minister at the time was to see whether I could form an administration with a majority.'[64] He held a quick, gloomy Cabinet late on Friday afternoon, which authorised him to see what he could do, and then went to Buckingham Palace to report to the Queen, who had just returned hurriedly from Australia. The first recourse was to talk to the Liberals who, despite their poor return of seats, were the moral victors of the campaign. Despite his earlier scorn for the idea of a Government dependent on a parliamentary arrangement, he now persuaded himself that if it were unavoidable, an agreement with the Liberals would make political sense. On the central issue of maintaining a prices and incomes policy, as well as on Europe, the Liberals broadly supported the Government: their 19 per cent public support could be seen as forming part of a clear majority against Labour's policies. If inflation remained the overriding national danger then the Liberals should be willing to back the only possible Government with a strategy and a determination to fight it.

The first difficulty was getting hold of Jeremy Thorpe: he was conducting a triumphant torchlight procession around Barnstaple and unavailable. Meanwhile there was nothing to be done. Prior and Carrington managed to smuggle Heath out of Downing Street for a 'decidedly wakish' scratch dinner, out of sight of the press, at the Wolffs' flat in Holland Park. 'Ted was completely shell-shocked,' Prior wrote. 'We had ordered oysters from Prunier's, as these were his favourite, but he barely seemed to notice them as a couple of dozen slipped down his throat.'[65] Rosemary Wolff – who had only had a couple of hours' notice of the Prime Minister's descent on her home – thought he looked 'like a beanbag' – crumpled, punch-drunk and unresponsive, utterly transformed from the confident Prime Minister of twenty-four hours before.[66]

Eventually Thorpe was contacted and travelled up for a two-hour meeting in Downing Street the next morning, alone with Heath and Robert Armstrong. Heath was calm, businesslike as ever, not outwardly as worried as he must have felt, but visibly embarrassed at having to seek Liberal support. His proposal was not particularly generous. He offered Thorpe a coalition, with just one Cabinet place for himself – probably the Home Office, though no specific post was mentioned – plus a Speaker's Conference to examine the case for electoral reform. Thorpe replied that he must have time to consult his party.[67] For himself, he would have loved to have been able to accept. But Liberal activists in the constituencies were already up in arms at the suggestion that the party in its hour of triumph might lend itself to propping up a defeated Tory Government. The only terms which might possibly be acceptable would be a definite commitment to introduce proportional representation. Late that night David Steel drove Thorpe secretly to the side door of Downing Street for a second meeting with Heath to clarify what was on offer: the answer was nothing more than a Speaker's Conference, with no promise to accept its recommendations.[68] Even if the Cabinet had been willing, Heath knew that the party in Parliament would never have voted for PR. In Peter Walker's view, 'Ted's honesty stood in the way of a shifty deal.' He would not make a bargain he could not honour.[69] So the talks failed.

In truth there was never much chance of them succeeding. For one thing, the arithmetic of a Tory–Liberal coalition did not add up: the two parties together would still have been a few seats short of an overall majority. Heath tried to bridge the gap by offering seven of the eleven Ulster Unionists the Tory whip (attempting to draw a distinction between Paisley's Democratic Unionists, who remained beyond the pale, and the rest).[70] But their terms would have been fresh elections to the Northern Ireland Assembly and the effective scrapping of the whole Sunningdale process, which he could never have accepted. Above all, even if he had somehow been able to scrape together a precarious majority, a continuing Conservative Government dependent on Liberal and Ulster votes would have lacked legitimacy. As Thorpe bluntly told Heath, it might not be clear who had won the election but there was no doubt who had lost it.[71] Heath had gone to the country before he needed to, seeking a new mandate, and had been denied it. Another Tory leader – Whitelaw perhaps – might conceivably have been able to carry on, if he could muster a majority; but not Heath.

There was nothing constitutionally improper about Heath exploring the options, despite a tendentious letter to *The Times* on the Monday morning from Lord Crowther-Hunt alleging that there was.[72] There was a good deal of press support for an anti-Labour coalition: *The Times* was particularly keen to see Jo Grimond as Secretary of State for Scotland.[73] Had there been a viable prospect of such an outcome he would have been wrong not to have pursued it. The criticism of Heath, however, is that there was no such prospect: it was therefore politically inept – not to say personally humiliating – to give the impression of clinging on to office. It was tactically inept because it used up his option. Had he resigned immediately and allowed Wilson to form a minority government, he would have retained the right to try again if Wilson failed: the Queen would not automatically have had to grant Wilson a dissolution, but could have turned back to Heath. It was personally humiliating because – long before he lost the Tory leadership to Mrs Thatcher – it saddled him with the image of a bad loser. Many Tories found the spectacle of the Government hanging on over the weekend demeaning. Even close colleagues like Carrington and Whitelaw were thankful when the talks with Thorpe failed;[74] to his enemies in the party the attempt furnished further grounds to be rid of him. 'The squatter in No. 10 Downing Street', crowed the following week's *Spectator*, 'has at last departed. Nothing became his leadership of the nation so ill as the manner of his leaving it . . . ':

> Mr Edward Heath's monomania was never more clearly seen than in the days after the general election when, a ludicrous and broken figure, he clung with grubby fingers to the crumbling precipice of his power . . .
> The spectacle was ludicrous; it was pathetic; it was contemptible. And Mr Heath, having been over the weekend a squalid nuisance, remains as leader of the Tory party just that . . . Mr Heath must now depart the Tory leadership as quickly as possible.[75]

In fact, it took the weekend for Thorpe to complete his consultations with his party; not until Monday morning did the fourteen Liberal MPs meet and agree their final rejection of Heath's offer, calling instead for an all-party government of national unity. 'I do not believe', Thorpe wrote to Heath, 'that a Liberal presence in the Cabinet, designed to sustain your Government, would be acceptable.'[76] With that, Heath had to concede defeat. He held two short final Cabinets, one in the morning, another at 4.45 pm. They were subdued occasions, but there were no recriminations and no tears, no emotion of any sort. It was typical of Heath's way of doing business that he neither thanked his colleagues for their support, nor did they pay any tribute to him. The atmosphere combined 'lack of sentiment' with 'grim solidarity'.[77] This, he was determined, was not the end of his Government, but a temporary interruption. He put out a dignified statement pledging his support to the new Government 'in whatever realistic measures it takes in the interests of all the people'.[78] Then, at 6.30 pm, he drove with Timothy Kitson to the Palace to resign. He had been Prime Minister for just three years, eight months and fourteen days.

He was still in a state of shock at the cruel reversal of fortune which had overtaken him. He had always counted on a second term, and suddenly it had been snatched away. He felt that he had deserved better from the British people. All the poll evidence was that they supported his policies. They overwhelmingly approved the principle of an incomes policy; they had no confidence in Wilson or Labour. Yet they had not been prepared to stand up and be counted. When asked to declare themselves firmly for the elected Government against sectional intransigence, they had preferred the easy option and voted, too many of them, for a quiet life. He had counted on the British people to support him and they had let him down. He had not called the election for partisan or opportunist reasons. On the contrary, he never wanted an early election at all: he had resisted it – missing what was probably the most favourable moment – until he felt he had no choice. Then, when forced to fight, he had fought honourably, responsibly, with one hand tied behind his back. This was perhaps why he had lost. By emphasising reason, fairness and moderation he had seemed to call in question the need for an election at all. By invoking national unity he actually encouraged much of the public to vote Liberal. It was an ironic, messy and unsatisfactory way to lose. There were all sorts of unlucky incidents, not to mention un-helpful contributions from his own side, during the campaign to brood over. Yet in the end he had no one to blame but himself. He had gambled his job, and he had lost.

PART FIVE

Rejection

33

'National Unity'

1974 was a dreadful year for Heath. The unexpected loss of the February election was only the start of twelve months of public and private disasters. Before the year's end he had not only led his party to a second electoral defeat which virtually ended his prospect of retaining the leadership. He had also suffered the loss of *Morning Cloud* III, with two members of her crew, in a storm in the Channel; and just before Christmas he had narrowly missed being blown up in a bomb attack on his house. It was a year in which practically everything went wrong for him: a period which his staff remember as a time of unparalleled unpleasantness, recrimination and mistrust. Yet through it all – once he had recovered from the initial shock – Heath remained defiant, determined, even confident. He still believed that he could win through and come back, vindicated, if only he could hang on through a difficult time. He had come through difficult times before. His growing number of enemies thought his determination merely stubborn; yet his resilience was astonishing.

What hurt him most about losing office was the loss of Downing Street and Chequers. Though Government property, these were the first real homes he had ever had. For three and a half years he had made them his own, lived in them, decorated them and entertained in them more fully than any previous modern Prime Minister. Now, almost overnight, he was homeless. His lease on Albany had expired in 1970 and he had not thought to make contingency arrangements for what had now occurred. It was his own fault, of course, but he had not expected to lose office so soon, and he would not pay good rent to keep an empty house in readiness. So his first problem, as he was driven with Timothy Kitson away from Buckingham Palace – in a humble Austin Metro, the prime ministerial black Rover having immediately gone back to Lord North Street to fetch Harold Wilson

– was where to live. The faithful Kitson nobly offered his own small flat in a functional modern block overlooking Vauxhall Bridge, while he moved in uncomfortably with Spencer le Marchant, the MP for High Peak, in the equally small flat next door. There Heath stayed for four months, like Pooh Bear stuck in Rabbit's doorway, while a house was found and made ready for him in Wilton Street, near Victoria. Cut off from his piano, his stereo and all his cherished mementoes while he fought for his political life, he was a Pooh Bear with a very sore head: not an easy tenant. His personal discomfort aggravated the difficulty of his political predicament.[1]

The political situation was exceptionally difficult, on two levels. First, his personal position as leader was gravely weakened. The loss of an election which he had himself chosen – however reluctantly – to hold fifteen months before he needed to inevitably raised questions about his judgment as well as his electoral appeal, and brought into the open simmering dissatisfaction with aspects of his leadership which would have remained suppressed so long as he appeared to be a winner. In the first days after 28 February, around a hundred MPs were reported to have told the Whips privately that he should step down, sooner or later; and that was the expectation of most commentators. At the same time the narrowness of the result also made it practically impossible for the party to think of changing leaders immediately. It was taken for granted on all sides that there would be another election almost at once, probably in June, at which Wilson would endeavour to convert his toehold on power into a secure majority – just as he had done between 1964 and 1966, except that this time he would not wait so long. There would scarcely be time for the Tories to hold a contest, let alone run in a new leader. In these circumstances Heath would virtually have had to carry on even if he had wanted to resign.

In any case, he had neither a challenger – Enoch Powell having placed himself beyond the pale by urging his followers to vote Labour – nor an heir apparent. His former Cabinet colleagues all shared the responsibility for the Government's defeat and were without exception loyal to him. Critics muttered that this was because he had surrounded himself with yes men; but it is not clear whom – except Edward Du Cann – they felt he had excluded. The fact is that – since the death of Macleod and the resignation of Maudling – Heath had dominated his Cabinet, alike by experience, force of personality and political vision. He did offer to submit himself for re-election but was assured that there was no point. It might in fact have strengthened his position, at least in the short term, to have gone through the motions of demonstrating formally that he had no rival. But when he met the 1922 Committee on 5 March the one member who raised the question of the leadership found no support. There was some mild criticism of the timing of the election, which he rejected; but in general, he was 'loudly applauded'. 'To all outward appearance,' *The Times* reported, 'he clearly has the full backing of the parliamentary party.'[2] The two groups who had always opposed his leadership – the diehard anti-Marketeers and those the paper called 'supporters of Mr Powell's economic and monetary theories' – together amounted to no more than 20–5 Members, and even many of these did not want an immediate change.[3] Blame for the party's defeat was shifted on to Central Office and the party organisation instead.

Second, the party faced an almost impossible tactical situation. The parliamentary arithmetic gave every prospect that Wilson's minority Government could be voted down on the division at the end of the Queen's Speech on 19 March. Yet to do so would only allow Wilson to ask the Queen for an immediate dissolution which most constitutional opinion judged she would be bound to grant: at the subsequent election the Conservatives would almost certainly be smashed. The party's best hope seemed to be to play for time, hoping that Wilson's precarious administration would fall apart of its own contradictions as the economic crisis Heath had predicted intensified; then after a few months the country might turn back to the Tories. But Wilson made it quite clear that he would expect to be granted a dissolution if defeated, and there can be little doubt that he would have been. What then was the Opposition to do? Speaking at the beginning of the debate on 12 March, Heath was carefully unprovocative – 'more mellow than most of his supporters could ever remember him being in the Commons'[4] – satirically congratulating Wilson for discovering that there *was* worldwide inflation, but promising no 'factious opposition' so long as the Government governed in the 'national interest'.[5] Next day, however, he let himself be persuaded by backbench pressure to table an amendment condemning the Government's intention to abandon Stage Three without putting anything in its place. The Liberals promptly announced that they would vote for the amendment and suddenly it seemed that the Shadow Cabinet had delivered itself into Wilson's hands.

They were saved from the prospect of committing political suicide only by a deeper embarrassment. The Selsdon Group publicly voiced its 'dismay' that the party still adhered to the failed policy on which it had lost the recent election, and some forty MPs indicated that they would not support the amendment. This threatened revolt was far larger than the handful of free-market purists who had regularly dissented from Government policy in the last Parliament, and gave the first warning that there might be a serious ideological basis to moves against Heath's leadership. More immediately, however, a critical division on which the Opposition could not command the votes of forty of its own supporters made the party look ridiculous. Fortunately Michael Foot – the new Employment Secretary – let the Shadow Cabinet off the hook by announcing in the debate that the Government would keep Stage Three in place for the time being (while settling with the miners on the basis of the Pay Board report), giving Whitelaw a pretext to withdraw the amendment. But the whole episode was a humiliating shambles which raised a storm of fresh criticism of the leadership's ineptitude. The position got no easier over the following weeks.

Heath was pretty much back where he had started nine years before, leader of a party which did not love him yet was stuck with him; leader of an Opposition still traumatised and discredited by the recent loss of office, with little option but to fight a defensive action towards a General Election which few observers gave it any hope of winning. The best that most senior Tories looked for, as in 1965, was to limit the size of Labour's majority when Wilson picked the optimum moment to go back to the country. The difference this time was that a section of the party – small, perhaps, but significant – did not *want* to win the next election, but looked forward to a second defeat as the only means of ridding the party of a leader they had come to regard as a liability. By the same token Heath knew that in order to survive as leader he would have to win in June, October or whenever the election came. Characteristically, once he had come out of the 'rather catatonic state'[6] which had descended on him immediately after the February débâcle, he quickly convinced himself – whatever the polls and the pundits might say – that he *could* win. He could not conceive that the February result could be anything but an aberration which would be reversed when the British public had experienced for a few months the consequences of a weak Labour Government dependent on the unions and with no policy to control inflation. He fully expected to be vindicated by events, and to be returned to office strengthened to resume the battle. There was absolutely no reason, in his view, for him to stand down. He had been right in February, he was still right and the electorate would quickly come to see that he was right. Nevertheless, the fact remained that his authority was reduced. His dispositions over the next few months, as he strove to reassert himself, were necessarily defensive and self-protective. More than ever, in this situation, Heath strove to tighten his grip on the party, surrounding himself with people he could trust.

His first task was to reshuffle his Front Bench. His instinct was to make as few changes as possible; but one at least was forced on him by Tony Barber's confirmation of his decision to leave politics at the next election. Probably the most obvious replacement would have been Keith Joseph, generally regarded as a successful Social Services Secretary – though even then criticised for having concentrated too narrowly on his own Department at the expense of the wider problems of the Government. Heath had in fact taken Joseph to lunch in January – possibly with the idea of testing him out as a potential Chancellor – and found him exceedingly gloomy.[7] Moreover, within a few days of the election Joseph, under the powerful influence of Alfred Sherman and Alan Walters, was already beginning to question the fundamental policies of the defeated Government. With hindsight Heath might have done better to have invited Joseph to pursue his *post mortem* on the failure of the late Government as Shadow Chancellor. He preferred, however, the safer course of promoting Robert Carr to the job. Carr was thoroughly loyal and universally liked; but he was no economist and lacked either the intellectual thrust or the personality to take on Labour's new Chancellor, Denis Healey. Meanwhile Joseph declined to accept any other specific portfolio but took on instead a roving commission seeking reasons for the persistent failure of the British economy, with special reference to the role of the market. The political dynamite concealed by this innocent-seeming job description was not immediately perceived. *The Economist* reported merely that Joseph had accepted 'the new and difficult task of realising the potential of private enterprise for the public good'.[8] Within a few weeks, however, he had obtained Heath's permission to set up a new Centre for Policy Studies, independent of Central Office, with Sherman as its Director. Heath initially regarded the CPS with complacency. He was assured that it would not compete for funds with the party's own Research Department; and he thought it would be good for Joseph and Mrs Thatcher (who was to be the Centre's vice-president) to learn more about the problems of industry![9] He felt betrayed when the CPS turned out to be the intellectual springboard for a determined challenge to his leadership, articulated by his former Social Services Secretary in a series of devastating speeches.

To shadow Carr's former responsibility – home affairs – Heath turned to Jim Prior; while to take over Social Services he promoted the equally unthreatening figure of Geoffrey Howe, who had made a quiet mark since November 1972 as Secretary of State for Consumer Affairs, responsible for the prices side of the counter-inflation policy. Though plainly now the second man in the party, Willie Whitelaw retained responsibility for Employment, shadowing Michael Foot. Still more surprisingly, Alec Douglas-Home carried on for the present as Shadow Foreign Secretary; Geoffrey Rippon returned to covering Europe and Maurice Macmillan went back to seconding Carr in the Treasury team. These were unimaginative appointments. Margaret Thatcher alone was released from Education and given charge of Environment – including the key area of housing, the one field in which Heath was already determined to develop fresh policies. He probably reckoned that she would be both amenable and zealous – as indeed she was. The purpose was presumably to suggest that the late Government stood unapologetic, ready to resume office as soon as required. But the impression given was tired and uninspiring. *The Economist* thought it a comment on Heath's failure to refresh the second eleven when in government that he now had little talent available for promotion.[10] One ex-junior minister formerly tipped as a high-flyer, Christopher Chataway, was so disappointed not to be offered the job on which he had set his heart – Education – that he left politics altogether.

The Shadow Cabinet had an unenviable task, facing a Government shamelessly filling its shop window with popular goodies to secure its re-election in a few months' time – a rent freeze, higher pensions, stiffer price controls, food subsidies, the abolition of museum charges – yet unable to oppose too vigorously for fear of precipitating the election too soon. In their Nuffield election study, Butler and Kavanagh actually rate them 'the most politically hardworking [Front Bench] the Conservative party has ever had': they did not immediately take up lucrative directorships in the City.[11] Nevertheless they were tactically on the back foot and outgunned, man for man, by Wilson's team of Healey, Callaghan, Jenkins, Crosland, Foot, Barbara Castle and the rest. Discussing possible contenders for the succession, *The Economist* suggested that Heath had – intentionally or not – done the Tory party a service by giving his 'only two conceivable successors [Whitelaw and Carr] . . . equal and considerable opportunity to display their talents': Whitelaw since the trade union question was bound to remain high on the political agenda, Carr with the chance to shine on the Finance Bill as Heath himself had done in 1965.[12] In fact the parliamentary performance of both men – decent, honourable but lacking bite – only served to underline the absence of any convincing alternative to Heath.

His second task was to shake up the party organisation in the short time available before the next campaign. Organisation always declines when a party is in office and its leaders are preoccupied with government. Following the February defeat there was a flood of criticism from candidates and agents of the role of Central Office. Carrington accepted the blame for a disaster which he more than anyone had helped to bring about and immediately offered his resignation. But the same consideration applied to the chairmanship as to the leadership: it was no time to change chairmen with an election possible at any moment. So Carrington stayed on until June, when it was clear that the danger of a summer election was past; then Heath named Willie Whitelaw as his replacement. Once again this was the safe, defensive choice. Ever since inheriting Edward Du Cann from Home, Heath had been determined to have one of his closest and most reliable colleagues as chairman; in his embattled situation in the summer of 1974 it made sense to put the faithful Willie in charge of the party machine. He thereby harnessed Whitelaw's loyalty and popularity with the rank and file to his own cause. But Whitelaw was essentially a political appointment, the front man. To take on the real organisational job of sorting out Central Office Heath had already in April put in his most trusted personal adviser, speechwriter and all-purpose dogsbody, Michael Wolff, in the new position of Director-General – a sort of permanent secretary to the chairman. This was a controversial appointment, tactlessly imposed by Heath and Carrington and initially much resented by the area agents and chairmen as a snub to the long-serving party professionals, Sir Michael Fraser and Sir Richard Webster, whose influence was reduced: it reinforced the impression of an insecure leader acting to protect his own position. In fact Wolff did well, and the job was quickly seen to be a necessary one which contributed to a much better co-ordinated campaign in October. Wolff himself, however, was still perceived as Heath's creature and was abruptly sacked by his successor in 1975.

In addition, Heath's candid friend Sara Morrison, whom he had installed as vice-chairman of the party organisation in 1971, assumed a greater prominence: as one of the few people able to speak bluntly to him when required, she had a considerable influence in the months up to the October election – not least in persuading Heath himself to improve his presentation. On the policy front Heath had to give some ground by agreeing for the first time to appoint a chairman of the Research Department. (Since 1965 he had held the job himself.) The man he chose, however, was Ian Gilmour – a colleague, as John Ramsden has written, so 'close to the Leader's own way of thinking [that] the appointment did not do much to satisfy the critics'.[13] As Director, he appointed another young intellectual clearly on the left of the party, Chris Patten. There were more new faces in the leader's personal entourage. Just before the February election William Waldegrave had replaced Douglas Hurd as head of his private office (Hurd had become MP for Mid-Oxfordshire); and in April Kenneth Baker (an MP since 1970) joined Kitson as his second PPS.

At the beginning of April Heath used the publication of his resignation honours list to thank some of those who had served him over the previous nine years. He still did little, however, to meet the grumble that as Prime Minister he had been conspicuously stingy in doling out honours to long-serving backbenchers. Half a dozen former ministers of the Macmillan era, whom he had passed over since 1965, received life peerages. One retiring and one defeated ex-minister received knighthoods; but only three sitting MPs, and one of those was Timothy Kitson. Another knighthood went to Heath's personal physician, Brian Warren. Robert Armstrong got a CB; Douglas Hurd and Brendon Sewill CBEs; and Heath's faithful personal secretary Rosemary Bushe an MBE. At the bottom of the strictly calibrated social scale, three members of the Downing Street staff – the retiring senior messenger, a telephonist and a driver – received the British Empire Medal.[14]

The biggest problem facing Heath, his colleagues and their advisers in the spring of 1974, however, was developing a strategy and a fresh appeal with which to face the electorate again in three or six months' time. On the one hand it was clear that they could not simply stand pat on the same manifesto that the country had rejected in February. But at the same time there was no time to go through the process of developing a full range of new policies, and Heath certainly had no intention of conducting a fundamental philosophic rethink, such as Joseph proposed. He was not going to say that the Government had been wrong in trying to control inflation by statutory restraint, still less admit that the Government had itself fuelled inflation by its reckless pursuit of expansion: he did not believe it. On the contrary, the dash for growth had been on target until derailed by world inflation and the oil crisis, while the statutory counter-flation policy had been very successful until unilaterally sabotaged by the miners. The country had ended up with a Labour Government, but the voters had given no sort of endorsement to Labour policies. Opinion polls showed that the electorate overwhelmingly accepted the principle of statutory incomes policy. Central Office analysis of the February result showed that the Government, while it had lost around a million votes to the Liberals, had actually *gained* something like 100,000 votes from Labour.[15] There was thus no call for the Tories to scrap their central policies. The most the situation demanded was a quick facelift designed to recover the votes lost to the Liberals while the party continued to hammer home the same fundamental message on inflation and the economy.

Accordingly the Shadow Cabinet set in train a much more limited policy exercise than in 1965. Just four policy groups were set up covering only the most urgent questions to which the party must quickly come up with more convincing answers than in February: incomes policy; what to do about the Industrial Relations Act; devolution (inescapable following the surge in support for the Scottish and Welsh nationalists); and housing. This last was the most important: housing was both the policy area on which the Tories had been admittedly most vulnerable in February and the easiest on which to bring forward attractive new bribes to woo back the hard-pressed middle-income home owners who had defected to the Liberals. Margaret Thatcher chaired this group. In appointing her Heath told her exactly what was expected of her: he had already determined on a triple package to be composed of a reduction in the burden of domestic rates, leading to their eventual abolition; mortgage subsidies; and an acceleration of council house sales. She argued initially against all three; but she soon gave in, accepted the hand dealt her and set to work.[16]

There was no economic policy sub-group because the subject was both too central and too contentious. The backbench Finance Committee from which such a group would have had to be largely drawn was chaired by Nicholas Ridley and disproportionately dominated by Powellites, including John Biffen. Just as in 1965–70, when a clear approach to inflation was ruled out by fundamental differences between Macleod and Maudling, so again in 1974 the determination of economic policy had to be retained in the Shadow Cabinet, with Heath himself in the chair. Keith Joseph has claimed that he tried to get the Shadow Cabinet to discuss the monetarist critique of the late Government's record but was simply not allowed to raise it: as a result he was forced to do his thinking in public.[17] Others, notably Peter Walker, insist that Joseph did bring his heretical ideas to Shadow Cabinet where they were comprehensively demolished.[18] It makes little difference in practice. The fact is that Joseph's quasi-religious revelation, which led him to condemn the whole approach to economic management not only of the Heath Government but of all British Governments, Conservative and Labour, since the war, was fundamentally unacceptable to virtually all his senior colleagues. They regarded his ideas, on the one hand, as cranky, theoretical and intellectually unproven; and, on the other – even if they were theoretically correct – as politically impractical and morally wrong, involving intolerable unemployment and social division. 'It seemed to some of us,' Robert Carr told Phillip Whitehead, 'that Keith Joseph had allowed his brain activity to run ahead . . . of his political sense.'[19]

The Shadow Cabinet was not split: only Margaret Thatcher gave Joseph any support at all – and then not much, as Peter Walker recalled:

> Margaret did not side openly with Keith, except to say she thought we should pay careful attention to what he was saying. Geoffrey Howe said he thought there were two sides to the argument and we should consider both. They were not passionately endorsing Keith's view. And the rest of the Shadow Cabinet was convinced that there was no magic which, with the wave of a wand of a particular indicator of money supply, could make your problems disappear.[20]

No more than Heath himself were Whitelaw, Prior, Carrington or Carr ready to disown everything they had stood for all their political lives.

On the contrary, their instinct was to defend the record of 1970–4. In his first major speech after the election, to the Conservative Central Council on 30 March, Heath was positively bullish. The central policies which his Government had set itself in 1970 and consistently pursued – entry into Europe, economic expansion and improved industrial relations – had been the *right* policies. EEC entry had been achieved. Rapid growth had been attained until halted by world inflation. The Industrial Relations Act had admittedly run into difficulties, but only needed amendment in the light of experience. It was, he declared uncompromisingly, 'the most contentious but most necessary of reforms . . . Sooner or later, this nettle will have to be grasped again.'[21]

In the first weeks after February, then, Heath was resolutely unapologetic, ready to fight on the same ground over again. Along with his promise to come up with some more attractive policies on the housing front, this was what most of the party wanted to hear. But tough talk could not appease Tory MPs' frustration at the 'farcical' tactics they were still obliged to pursue in the House of Commons. Both Labour and the Liberals jeered mercilessly as the Opposition Front Bench thundered impotently against the new Government's policies, unable to risk pressing its opposition to a vote. Heath explained that the party had to keep a 'steady nerve': what mattered was to win the debates, not the divisions, giving Wilson no chance to go back to the country before the electorate had had time to realise the effect of Labour policies.[22] But Tory morale only slumped further – *The Economist* reported in late April that the party was 'so afraid of an early election that it is on the point of complete panic'[23] – while Labour's lead in the polls stretched to 10 per cent, 12 per cent, 14 per cent. By the early summer Heath had been persuaded to adopt a different tack.

It was the party professionals in Central Office analysing the February results and studying the opinion polls who concluded that what the Tories must do to win next time was to outflank the Liberals – not merely by fiddling about with help for mortgage holders, but by recognising the positive appeal to which a significant proportion of the public had responded in February, and making it their own. Humphrey Taylor of ORC and Geoffrey Tucker, the party's former publicity director, found, first, that a large number of voters had been turned off both main parties in February by what they saw as 'confrontation'; but, second, that the public associated 'confrontation' peculiarly with Heath. On this analysis it would be fatal for the Tories to try to fight again over the same ground: they would simply lose again. While Labour was easily preferred to the Tories in a straight party contest, however, there persisted a strong public hankering for some sort of 'government of national unity'. They therefore urged Heath to drop the image of 'confrontation', stop refighting lost battles and make a positive appeal on the need for compromise, conciliation and co-operation.[24]

This advice was at first bitterly unwelcome to Heath, not at all because he clung to confrontation, but because he vigorously repudiated the idea that he had ever espoused it. Continually forced, in public and private, to justify his decision to go to the country in February, he was almost obsessively concerned to refute the established myth that he had picked a fight with the miners or had ever wished to 'confront' anybody. It was peculiarly hard for him to accept, after his tireless efforts over nearly two years to appease the unions and bring them into government, that he was seen by the public as the architect of confrontation. Yet if he could once swallow his sense of grievance, the idea of campaigning on a platform of national unity appealed to him as much as ever. In the end, Ian Gilmour recalled, 'Ted came along quite well.'[25]

Characteristically, however, he worked out his new line not in the Shadow Cabinet or Central Office, but informally with a group of his own supporters. He first asked Douglas Hurd, John MacGregor, Nigel Lawson and Tony Newton (all newly elected MPs who had worked either directly for him or in Central Office) to look at the polling evidence and report back to him. Then the strategy was fleshed out by Gilmour and Patten in the Research Department. In three articles in *The Times* at the beginning of May, Gilmour had set out the case for a new approach, arguing that the country wanted a rest from the sort of abrasive radicalism that had characterised 1970–4. ('The Heath Government . . . tried to do too much.') As a result Labour had got back into office on a minority vote, committed – if re-elected – to a madcap programme of extreme socialism which the country certainly did not want. In this dangerous situation the right formula for the Tories was to offer a period of moderate, sensible, non-doctrinaire government in the national interest. In these articles Gilmour cleverly demonstrated how the Tories could bounce back from February by exploiting the ostensibly non-party appeal of 'national unity' for party benefit.[26]

A few days later Heath himself used the opportunity of a lecture in memory of Iain Macleod to announce, with unaccustomed humility, that the Tories had, after all, no monopoly of political virtue. He went on to propose what he called a 'Charter for the People', embodying a number of very broad citizens' rights which he hoped might be generally agreed, including the right to work, the right to a fair reward, the right to a home (and help to own it) and the right to a voice at work, in the unions and in education.[27] This was still a distinctively Tory programme. Essentially, indeed, it was a restatement of the aims of the 'quiet revolution' – but in more consensual clothing. The key word was 'Charter', a deliberate echo of the series of Charters – Industrial, Agricultural, Imperial – associated particularly with Rab Butler, by which the Conservatives after 1945 had signalled their acceptance of the world of welfare and full employment.* To Tories of Heath's generation the word carried an unmistakable overtone of social consensus. Two weeks later, in Ayr, he proposed a 'Charter for Scotland' as well.[28]

With this decision to espouse a new consensus, Heath seemed to rediscover his sense of direction. At the same time his self-confidence was greatly boosted in late May by his first visit to China. Originally planned to take place in January, to mark the opening of a new era in British relations with China, this trip had had to be postponed as a result of the miners' strike. Now the Chinese might reasonably have cancelled it and invited Wilson instead. In fact they not only insisted that Heath should still come, but received him with extraordinary signs of favour. He was met at the airport by 2,000 girls waving Union Jacks. He had three days of talks with Deng Xiaoping, Chou Enlai and even the 82-year-old Mao Zedong, who normally met no one but heads of government. (Mao, Heath reported, was very well

---

* The word resurfaced seventeen years later with John Major's 'Citizen's Charter', and sundry other charters, in 1991. It is unlikely that Chris Patten – by then party chairman – had forgotten the earlier document produced when he was Director of the Research Department.

informed, 'and he has a delightful sense of humour'.) He presented Mao with a copy of Darwin's *The Descent of Man*, and next day was given in return two eighteenth-century vases. He visited the Great Wall (of course) and was told that he had got further up it than President Nixon on his historic visit the previous year; he attended a concert in the Great Hall of the People; and at a banquet in his honour told his hosts what they wanted to hear – that the new united Europe was not prepared to see the world run by the Soviet Union and the United States. When he left Peking he was accorded the level of send off normally reserved for a head of state, and then given another rousing reception in Shanghai.[29] He had to abandon a projected visit to Hong Kong in order to fly home for an emergency debate on the collapse of the power-sharing executive in Northern Ireland. But the trip was a personal triumph, very fully reported in the British press and crowned in the public mind with the gift by the Chinese Government of two giant pandas to London Zoo, whose attempts to mate occupied the close attention of the newspapers for the rest of the decade. His unconcealed delight in his reception drew some cynicism: 'Mao was the first person he had seen in months who was actually pleased to see him,' a friend was said to have remarked unkindly.[30]

He returned to Britain with his prestige greatly enhanced: the Tory party had been given a timely reminder of his international stature. Shortly afterwards his morale was further improved by his second venture at conducting a professional symphony orchestra: at André Previn's invitation he conducted the LSO again in Wagner's *Meistersinger* overture in a seventieth birthday gala for the orchestra at the Royal Festival Hall.[31] In addition his period of squatting with Kitson was coming to an end: on 15 July he moved into a new house in Wilton Street which had been made ready for him by Sara Morrison and decorated once again by Jo Pattrick. It was a handsome terraced house in Belgravia, just off Buckingham Palace Road – three floors, with a flat for his housekeeper in the basement – rented on generous terms from the Grosvenor Estate. Wilton Street has remained his London home up to the present, although since he acquired his house in Salisbury in 1986 it has been little more than a metropolitan base.

In mid-June Heath felt ready to move on to the political offensive. In a confident speech to the Welsh Conservative conference at Llandrindod Wells on the 15th he declared that the 'phoney war' was nearly over:

We have had to keep a steady nerve through a time when a wrong move, however well-intentioned, could have given Mr Wilson the excuse he needed to fight an election . . .

While Labour's window-dressing begins to be shown up as the shoddy tinsel it is, as the social contract is exposed for the public relations gimmick which it really is, then we shall be bringing forward a serious and well-thought-out programme.[32]

Two days later, interviewed on ITV's 'World in Action', he repeated the message that the gloves would now be coming off in the House of Commons. The risk of a summer election was all but past: the Government was unlikely to go to the country if defeated on any of the blatantly partisan measures now coming before the House.[33] In the following week the Tories, in combination with the Liberals and the Ulster Unionists, duly mobilised their full voting strength three times: once to strike down (by 308 votes to 299) a new clause added to the Finance Bill to allow trade unions to reclaim some £10 million of tax relief forfeited by their failure to register under the Industrial Relations Act; another time to reject (by 311 to 290) the extension of Government powers to direct private industry.[34] Both issues were grist to Tory charges that the Government was in hock to the unions and dominated by the left. Over the following six weeks, until Parliament rose at the end of July, the Opposition inflicted another eighteen defeats in the chamber, plus more in standing committees. At the same time Labour's lead in the polls fell sharply: Gallup showed the gap down to 3 per cent, and ORC actually put the parties neck and neck.[35]

During June public interest in the idea of a national government quickened. The polls continued to show strong public support, while from various parts of the establishment came apocalyptic warnings that the country was on the verge of hyper-inflation and social collapse: *The Times*, from its editorials through Bernard Levin to the letters page, carried almost daily demands for the politicians to sink their differences and join together before the country became ungovernable. There were suggestions that both Wilson and Heath should stand down in favour of new leaders – perhaps Whitelaw and Roy Jenkins – less tarnished by the failures of the past few years; on 13 June Maurice Macmillan resigned from the Shadow Cabinet in order to argue for a 'Government of all the talents', hinting significantly at 'sacrifices' which might be needed to facilitate this.[36]

But there was no realistic prospect of such a government coming about, short of a complete catastrophe. The memory of 1931 was still too vivid in Labour mythology for any Labour leader to contemplate joining any form of coalition. Wilson predictably rejected the notion absolutely, claiming that his Labour Cabinet, including both Benn and Jenkins, Michael Foot and Shirley Williams, was a coalition in itself and already constituted a national government which he was confident would soon secure a five-year mandate. Likewise the Liberals, though still anxious to be seen as the catalyst for bringing about a national government, insisted that they would take part only if Labour did: they would not join with the Tories alone. In effect, then, Labour's veto covered the Liberals too. Various soundings since February had come to nothing. This situation allowed Heath to play the unity card without risk – for the moment – of anyone calling his bluff. He could claim for the Tories the moral high ground of patriotic responsibility, exploiting the prevailing public mood, while continuing to assail the other parties for their narrow political calculations and sectional self-interest. In practice the language of unity was merely the revival of an old and tested Tory rhetoric – going back at least to Baldwin – with which to beat Labour. It came to Heath quite naturally, without conscious hypocrisy, because he sincerely despised Labour and continued to see himself as the true national leader and the Tory party as his vehicle.

On 26 June he signalled his new strategy in a speech to the Press Club, proposing a five-point (though extraordinarily unspecific) programme of national unity. His most significant concession to the spirit of compromise was an undertaking that the Tories would not after all seek to reintroduce the Industrial Relations Act: in return he challenged Labour to abandon plans for further nationalisation. The economic situation, he asserted, was 'very serious indeed': there was a real danger that 20 per cent inflation would become the accepted norm. He was explicit that he was *not* proposing coalition: 'What we need right now and before all else is a programme for national unity. It must be a programme that the overwhelming majority of people can see is sensible and behind which they can unite.'[37] In a further speech at Oxford ten days later he made it clear that his idea of a 'national' government was a Tory Government, led by himself. Party was still the inescapable fact of British politics. That being so, 'only one party, the Conservatives, can now honestly claim to stand four-square in the centre of British political life'.

In another calculated echo of the Tory past – this time invoking Harold Macmillan – he went on to claim that the result of the February election showed that what the public wanted was a 'middle way'. This time he listed four elements in such a programme. They were a curiously random mixture of hallowed Tory principles with some expedient recent additions. First he put the 'forthright defence of free enterprise'. Second was a 'serious attack' on inflation – in other words a return to statutory prices and incomes policy, with all that that entailed. ('We must have serious and determined economic management.') Third was the need for 'a new spirit in industrial relations'; the Tories' contribution to this, he repeated, was a promise *not* to reintroduce the Industrial Relations Act. Fourth was the protection of small savers suffering under high inflation – in other words subsidies to mortgage payers. Reduced to its bones, what this amounted to was February's central commitment to incomes policy, prudently softened by the dropping of the Industrial Relations Act, titivated with shiny new promises to home owners and beefed up with an old-fashioned attack on public ownership. He was not proposing a genuinely national programme, but merely dressing up the emerging Tory manifesto in national disguise.[38]

In several other speeches during July – he was speaking intensively around the country now, concentrating on marginal constituencies – he continued to couch an Opposition leader's conventional attacks on the Government in the language of co-operation and humility. Repeatedly he spoke of the public's 'great desire . . . for an end to the kind of politics which people describe to me as the politics of the slanging match',[39] and piously suggested that 'perhaps there ought to be a little more modesty and humility all round'.[40] When he preached humility, however, it was usually clear which party he thought had need of it.

There was not much humility in his claim – on the Isle of Wight on 27 July – that the Tories uniquely 'put the people first';[41] nor, arguably, much realism in his promises to shield rate-payers, farmers, home owners, housewives – indeed practically everybody – from the effects of inflation. Detailed proposals remained conspicuously scarce. Nevertheless he was campaigning with confidence, aggression – and perhaps more cynicism than in the past. It has been suggested that he was influenced by the example of the Canadian Prime Minister, Pierre Trudeau, who was reported to have vowed, after a disappointingly narrow victory in 1972, when he had campaigned 'in a highbrow, non-materialistic style', that in future he would 'take the politics out of politics and give the people anything they want'. According to David Butler and Dennis Kavanagh, Heath 'frequently' recalled this remark, with what friends called 'a mixture of puritanical disapproval and wistfulness'.[42]

Meanwhile Gilmour and Patten, with Nigel Lawson and other bright young men in Central Office, were putting together the manifesto. Subtitled 'A national policy from the Conservatives', *Putting Britain First* was an exceptionally well-written and coherent document, a vast improvement on February's hastily written and contradictory effort. Drafts went back and forth through July and August, as first the Steering Committee and then the Shadow Cabinet were brought to endorse the national unity strategy. With each redrafting the unity theme became more pronounced, the tone more conciliatory. The message as it finally emerged was essentially the same as February's, but the tone, though sombre, was much less strident. There were no villains this time: the unions were barely mentioned. The whole nation faced a crisis together and together must find its way through.

The one way catastrophe could be averted was by 'the Government and the people of this country uniting on a national policy'. Yet only after the sixth and final draft had gone to the printers on 30 August was Heath persuaded to include, at the proof stage, a specific undertaking to broaden the base of the next Tory Government beyond the ranks of the Conservative party. Even then he still baulked at the word 'coalition'. The final version made it clear that the party's primary purpose was, as ever, to form a Tory Government:

The Conservative Party, free from dogma and free from dependence upon any single interest, is broadly based throughout the nation. It is our objective to win a clear majority in the House of Commons in this election. But we will use that majority above all to unite the nation. We will not govern in a narrow partisan spirit. After the election we will consult and confer with the leaders of other parties, and with the leaders of the great interests in the nation, in order to secure for the Government's policies the consent and support of all men and women of good will. We will invite people from outside the ranks of our party to join with us in overcoming Britain's difficulties. The nation's crisis should transcend party differences.[43]

The election campaign would test what reality lay behind these easy words. For the moment, however, with the manifesto at the printers, Heath faced the election, whenever it was called, with confidence. On the substantive issue of economic policy he believed he had achieved a formula sufficiently all embracing to unite the whole party, Joseph included. On 5 September, at Preston, Joseph made his most outspoken assault yet on Keynesian orthodoxy. In a speech largely written for him by Alfred Sherman, with contributions from Alan Walters, Samuel Brittan and Peter Jay, he declared unequivocally that 'Inflation is caused by Governments' and questioned the priority traditionally given to preventing unemployment.

639

Unemployment in modern conditions, he argued, was not comparable with the images of misery and destitution which had seared the nation's conscience since the 1930s. By believing that they must overheat the economy to try to prevent unemployment at any cost governments simply fuelled inflation, which in the long run only created more unemployment. The only cure for inflation was to control the money supply – by governments ceasing to print money.[44] Such a speech, by a senior member of the Shadow Cabinet – Joseph had taken over the Home Affairs portfolio in June, when Whitelaw became party chairman and Prior took over shadowing Employment – threatened to blow the Tory party's unity to pieces just days before Wilson was expected to call the election. The suggestion that the Tories would deliberately let unemployment rise was a gift to Labour. Heath tried to stop Joseph delivering it, or at least to tone it down. Jim Prior asked Margaret Thatcher to have a word with him – unaware that Mrs Thatcher was now fully in Joseph's camp.[45] But Joseph refused to be deterred. Heath was understandably annoyed; yet he was able to contain the political damage remarkably successfully by denying that there was any serious difference between them. He was on a tour of Scotland when Joseph detonated his bombshell. At Elgin the same day he tried to defuse it in advance by agreeing that of course control of the money supply was one element – alongside incomes policy – in a comprehensive policy to fight inflation: he promised that a Tory Government would maintain *both* a strong prices and incomes policy *and* 'a firm and consistent control over the money supply'.[46] At Renfrew the next day he denied being in any way embarrassed by Joseph's speech. Nobody had ever imagined that incomes policy by itself was the whole answer: it was 'preposterous' to suggest that Joseph should be dismissed from the Shadow Cabinet – there was no comparison with Powell in 1968. He even claimed to have discussed Joseph's speech with him beforehand.[47]

A few days later the publication of the manifesto gave formal expression to this dual policy: 'To restore confidence in our currency we propose a comprehensive price stabilisation programme. This will use every tolerable means available to fight inflation. We will rigorously control public spending and the money supply and there must be restraint in prices and incomes.'[48] The key word of course was 'tolerable' – meaning no acceptance of unemployment. The manifesto's careful wording was in fact a long way from Joseph's uncompromising monetarist vision. Much greater emphasis was placed on excessive wage settlements as the cause of both inflation and unemployment, and on the continuing need for an incomes policy, voluntary if possible but statutory if necessary. ('No government could honestly say that it will never be necessary to use the law in the national interest to support an effective policy for fighting inflation.') Nevertheless, politically it did the trick. *The Times* had nothing but praise for the document as a whole, and judged the economic section in particular a skilful synthesis, accommodating the different emphases of both Joseph and Robert Carr, an achievement for which credit was due to both men, but also to Heath, to whom the paper paid extravagant tribute:

> Credit should also be given to Mr Heath: he is written off once a month in good times and once a week in bad: indeed he lacks to a phenomenal degree the communicative qualities natural to political leadership: but he does not hesitate to stake his political career on what he thinks right for his country. He has, if anything, too much political courage. It is not a universal attribute.[49]

Heath needed all his courage in these days to carry on in the face of the personal loss he sustained on the night of Monday 2 September, when *Morning Cloud* III sank in a force 9 gale off Shoreham. Despite the imminence of the election he had enjoyed some good sailing in August. *Morning Cloud* practically swept the board in the second half of Cowes Week and then won the 'Round the Goodwins' race from Ramsgate up the Thames estuary, finishing up with an enjoyable week at Burnham-on-Crouch. She was being sailed round, as usual between races, from Burnham to Cowes by an experienced 'movement crew' skippered by Donald Blewett, including for the first time Heath's 23-year-old godson, Christopher Chadd, son of his old battalion commander thirty years before, George Chadd. The wind got up as they came round the North Foreland then seemed to ease, so they pressed on into the Channel. Then conditions worsened again; several other boats put back to Dover, but *Morning Cloud* had been built specifically to withstand the heavy seas of the Fastnet race: Blewett was confident that she would be all right. They had very nearly reached the protection of the Isle of Wight when she was struck by two enormous, possibly freak, waves which knocked her over on her side. Two crewmen, Nigel Cumming and Christopher Chadd, were swept overboard. The other five – two of them injured – managed to get into the life raft but were themselves lucky to survive; after eight hours in the water the raft was eventually washed ashore early next morning near Brighton. Heath was having breakfast in Wilton Street when he was telephoned by the police. He went down immediately to Brighton, but there was no hope of recovering the lost men. The wreck was salvaged a few days later. '*Morning Cloud* was not built to sink like that, or to break up,' Owen Parker told *The Times*. 'She was one of the strongest ships afloat.'[50] Her loss, and the loss of his godson, hit Heath hard, and undoubtedly affected his performance going into the election campaign a fortnight later. If winning the Sydney–Hobart race in January 1970 was the symbolic precursor of his electoral triumph in June, the sinking of *Morning Cloud* III was a bad omen for October 1974. By a curious coincidence, the original *Morning Cloud* – renamed by her new owner *Nuage du Matin* – was torn from her moorings in Jersey and also wrecked the same night. 'The same sea and wind', Heath wrote, 'destroyed both.'[51]

On 8 September Heath left for a three-day visit to New York and Washington, where he met both President Ford (just installed in the White House following Nixon's disgrace) and UN Secretary-General Kurt Waldheim. While he was away the Conservative manifesto was prematurely leaked to three newspapers. This was an embarrassing opening to the Tory campaign – publication had to be brought forward to 12 September, six days before the election was even announced, and Heath had to launch it with a press conference as soon as he got back – but it did little harm: rather the manifesto attracted more attention than normal, most of it favourable. The national unity gambit in particular chimed with the concerns of a large part of the press and was generally applauded. *The Times, Financial Times, Daily Mail, Sunday Times, Observer* and *Economist* all hoped for some form of Conservative-Liberal coalition. The *Sun* and *News of the World* wanted a grand coalition of all three parties, while the *Guardian* frankly supported the Liberals.

The other feature of the manifesto that drew headlines – almost the only specific promise in it – was the pledge to hold mortgage interest rates down to 9·5 per cent. This patent electoral bribe divided the press. Some commentators judged it a reasonable measure of protection for a hard-pressed section of the population and thought it would be a winner; others thought it a cynical contradiction of the party's warnings of the need to cut public expenditure. From the monetarist camp Samuel Brittan gave it 'the prize for economic illiteracy': the only effect would be to fuel inflation. Bernard Levin – a keen supporter of a national government – believed it fatally undercut the Tories' claim to economic responsibility;[52] George Gale in the *Spectator* condemned Mrs Thatcher's 'grotesque bribery'; while Paul Johnson in the *New Statesman* saw in the gulf between Mrs Thatcher's 'lavish promises' and Joseph's 'austere Powellism' evidence of 'a party in disarray'.[53] It was piquant that it was Mrs Thatcher who

took public responsibility for the mortgage promise. The figure of
9·5 per cent was a compromise between Heath's initial desire to go
for 8 per cent and Mrs Thatcher's unwillingness to do more than peg
the rate at 11 per cent. Once persuaded, however, she identified herself unreservedly with the pledge, making herself the star of the Tory
campaign in the process. 'Our plans', she declared on 27 September,
'are absolutely unshakeable, and will be introduced by Christmas.'[54]
(At the same time she promised to abolish domestic rates, an idea it
took her fifteen years to realise – though when she did she forgot that
the 1974 promise was to replace them with 'taxes more broadly based
and related to people's ability to pay'.) More than anything else in the
campaign, the mortgage pledge had Labour rattled: Tony Crosland
furiously dismissed it as 'a pack of lies'.[55] In fact polls suggested that
the public was sceptical and the pledge was, if anything, probably
counterproductive.

Wilson eventually announced on 18 September that the election
would be held on 10 October. Right up to the last minute the
Government continued to publish a stream of White Papers – on sex
equality, consumer protection, pensions and devolution – which
were widely seen as a clever way of publicising the more attractive
parts of the Labour manifesto at public expense. The manifesto itself
retained extensive commitments to further public ownership – of
ports, shipbuilding, the aircraft industry and development land – and
closer public control of industry. But the main weight of Labour's
appeal was on the experience of the team that had 'got Britain back to
work' in March and on the 'Social Contract' between Government
and the unions which had replaced Tory 'confrontation'. It was a
new variant on the slogan 'You Know Labour Government Works'
which had been so successful in 1966. Explicitly rejecting the case for
a coalition, the manifesto declared bluntly that 'there is no meeting
point between us and those with quite different philosophies'.
Labour's idea of a national government was a majority Labour
Government.[56]

The campaign was exceptionally lacklustre. It was not only the
second election in seven months. It was the fourth time that the same
two leaders had faced each other in nine years. Both were now tarnished figures, held equally responsible by much of the public for the
mess the country found itself in; yet each strove to present himself as
the moderate embodiment of national unity, the other as a divisive
ideologue. The country was tired of both of them. Jeremy Thorpe
was fighting his third election as Liberal leader too; while by squabbling in public about whether or not it would join a coalition, and if
so with whom, his party had lost since February much of the gloss

which had made it an attractive third option. The sense of crisis on which all parties harped had become dulled by repetition. The weather was cold and wet. There were few incidents to bring the campaign to life: Enoch Powell was largely preoccupied in Northern Ireland, fighting to return to the House of Commons as an Ulster Unionist. Such own goals as were scored were this time scored by Labour: Denis Healey drew ridicule by trying to pretend that the true level of inflation was only 8·4 per cent, and Shirley Williams embarrassed Wilson (and Roy Jenkins) by declaring that she would not remain in a Government which decided to withdraw from the EEC. It was fairly clear, however, that Wilson and Callaghan were now once again set on staying in the Community, so Europe was not a live issue. The polls showed a steady Labour lead of between 5 per cent and 10 per cent throughout. Given their fallibility both in 1970 and again in February, nothing could be taken for granted; but this time there was no Liberal surge. Realistically the only question seemed to be how large a majority Labour could secure.

Heath led into battle a party still demoralised by its February defeat, with little expectation of victory this time and confused by the self-denying platform on which it was being asked to fight. A programme that enthused the leader writers did nothing for the party faithful. At a rally for Tory candidates at the Europa Hotel on 12 September Heath set out his proposed campaigning style. 'It will be necessary', he conceded almost apologetically, 'to point out the weaknesses and omissions of other parties'; but there would be no 'personalities', no slanging – in short, no 'confrontation'. Edward Du Cann did his best to raise the atmosphere with an ostensible endorsement of his leadership, every word of which everyone in the room knew to be subtly backhanded:

> You do not only lead but command our party. [*This was scarcely a compliment: rather it was the party's principal complaint against him.*] You command more than men and women. It is an army which is fighting with unshakable confidence and purpose. We are a wholly loyal and united party . . . There is no one here who does not fully reflect your own devotion to our cause and above all your integrity. If you attack you need never look behind. We follow closely in support at your right hand. We are most grateful to you for having so clearly and cogently explained the theme on which you will fight the election. [*'You', not 'we'*] . . . We know we can count abundantly on you and you equally know that you can rely on us.[57]

In reality, Heath knew very well that in this election – even more than in June 1970 – he was on his own. He had been given a second chance to retrieve the advantage he had thrown away in February. He had chosen the style, the tone and the agenda on which the party would fight. They would follow him so long as he won. But he was a leader on probation. If he lost again he would surely be finished.

Partly in deliberate pursuit of his new strategy, but possibly also because he was still affected by the loss of *Morning Cloud*, Heath opened his campaign on an extraordinarily muted note. 'In the rather small room in Central Office where he had stood and almost hectored the journalists and television cameras eight months ago,' *The Economist* noted at his first morning press conference on 23 September, 'he now sat and spoke so quietly that it was difficult to hear him at the back.'[58] Sitting instead of standing; saying 'we' instead of 'I'; adopting a more humble and altogether less combative style – this was all part of the attempt to project a new conciliatory image in which he had been carefully coached by Sara Morrison. The press were baffled, as Butler and Kavanagh described:

Mr Heath . . . was unnaturally subdued and so consciously exploiting a low-key, unabrasive approach that he seemed to say nothing. Asked what his first action against inflation would be, he said, 'To see precisely what the situation is.' What would be his next move? 'To take the appropriate action.' When challenged about his new style . . . Mr Heath replied: 'I am adopting the technique you have so often urged upon me of quiet, reasonable conversation.'[59]

'It was a soggy performance in the flesh', *The Economist* commented, 'but . . . came over much better in the excerpts on the television news' – which, of course, was the intention.[60]

The rest of that day typified Heath's campaigning at its best and worst. For some reason he chose to open his campaign in Wales. First he held a question-and-answer session with farmers at Barry. They were hostile to begin with, but 'he answered every question and argument with a mastery of agricultural detail which brought him a deserved cheer at the end'. Then he returned to Cardiff for another 'dismal' press conference before his first evening rally of the campaign, an all-ticket occasion for the party faithful. He was warmly received as he entered the hall. But then he spoke, in his new low-key style, for forty minutes without provoking a single burst of applause.

He livened up a bit in the second week, becoming 'far more forceful' at his morning press conferences (though this time he took only about half of them himself) and in his evening speeches reverting to 'a more traditional campaigning style', mixing up the national unity theme with conventional attacks on Labour.[61] (In the afternoons, however, he experimented with a novel tactic known as 'Talk-Ins with Ted' – informal sessions with small groups of voters at which he was often seen at his best, but by far too few people: they made poor television, so that on some days he barely made the news bulletins at all.) As he got into his stride he repeatedly accused Labour of deliberately misleading the public on economic realities and attacked the Social Contract as a sham: he claimed that wage increases were running at 40 per cent in 1974 and forecast inflation of 30 per cent in 1975. Increasingly the urgency of his language recalled his warnings of 1966 and 1970. At Plymouth he made effective play with the image of Drake's Drum: 'It beats out the truth to wake up a nation fed for months on a diet of tranquillisers and half-truths.'[62] He took to comparing Labour's complacency in the face of the impending crisis with the appeasement of Hitler in the 1930s, and spoke grimly of the country being 'at war' with inflation and unemployment. Yet he remained scrupulously emollient – even abject – towards the trade unions. He regularly deleted from the draft speeches prepared for him any passages that could be construed as anti-union.[63] Asked at his press conference on 30 September what he would do if a union were again to defy a Tory Government's statutory incomes policy, he first retorted that Labour could do nothing at all if a union broke the Social Contract, then gave an answer which spoke eloquently of how far he would go to avoid being forced into another confrontation:

> What does an elected government do in a democracy if the law is defied by any determined group? The answer is this. It conciliates. It arbitrates. It persuades. It cajoles. It seeks ways round. It gathers public support in order to protect the interests of everyone in the country. But in the end it must stand by the law or cease to be a democratic government.[64]

This touched delicately on the key issue of the election: which party could best 'live with' the trade unions. Labour paraded its Social Contract as the guarantee of industrial harmony and lost no opportunity to remind the electorate of the misery and chaos of the three-day week: another Tory Government, ministers alleged, would thrust the country back into industrial conflict, lost production and power cuts. On the other side, Heath's unity gambit was really just another form of social contract which he hoped would arm the next Tory Government with a stronger popular mandate to face down irresponsible unions than the last had commanded. Eventually, however, Heath was forced to tackle head on the charge that the Tories could not work with the unions. In Glasgow on 2 October and again in Bolton two days later he denounced the attempt to blackmail the electorate into voting Labour out of fear:

> If people in Britain were to vote in a socialist government because they were afraid of political strikes, democracy in our country would be dead.
>
> Luckily for our children, intimidating the British people tends to be a policy which boomerangs, because for all our faults we are a proud people, and a people who value our freedom. We do not put up with political protection rackets. So let us debunk that threat once and for all. Union leaders do not appoint governments; the people elect them, and the people will not be intimidated.

'At the end of his speech', *The Times* reported, 'Mr Heath received the greatest reception of this campaign.'[65]

The hole at the heart of Heath's campaign, however, was his national unity appeal. It was the centrepiece of the Tory platform, a bold attempt to seize the high ground, potentially a trump card: there was little enough positive public support for either main party, and a good deal of admittedly somewhat inchoate support for the idea of coalition if Heath could only give it real shape and substance. Yet this he singularly failed to do. It was not a last-minute gimmick, but a calculated strategy which he and his advisers had been working on since the early summer. Yet he still had not thought it through in sufficient detail to carry conviction. As a result the campaign was curiously like February in reverse, with the ideal of national cooperation substituted for the challenge of 'Who Governs?' For the second time in seven months the party committed itself to a risky but potentially popular strategy, then threw away the dividend by pressing its case weakly.

Repeatedly at his press conferences Heath was asked for the names of some of those 'from outside the ranks of our party' who – the manifesto promised – would be invited 'to join us in overcoming Britain's difficulties'. A number of possible candidates were floated in the press – the usual mixture of superannuated politicians and prominent industrialists who always cropped up in discussions of a 'businessmen's government', none of them very inspiring. For once George Gale's acid comment was pretty near the mark: 'I cannot but think', he wrote in the *New Statesman*, 'that if our crisis can be solved by Marks & Spencer [Sir Marcus Sieff] and Toby Low [Lord Aldington], it cannot be half as bad as it is usually made out to be.'[66] In theory the idea that there was a reservoir of non-political expertise available to be tapped for the national good sounded fine: in practice it lacked credibility.

Virtually Heath's only effort to put flesh on his vision of consultation and co-operation was the suggestion that the NEDC should be given an enlarged role, including greater access to Government information than it enjoyed at present, and that its proceedings should be televised. This was supposed to create greater public understanding of the dimensions of the crisis; the intention was worthy, but the effect was merely bathetic. By this point, halfway through the campaign, it had become clear that Heath had to offer something more dramatic. One option was to take a further step down the unity road than he had so far been prepared to take and propose not just a Tory Government mysteriously enhanced by un-named outsiders, but a coalition. The trouble with this was that it takes at least two to have a coalition and both the other parties insisted that they would not join. On the other hand there was political capital to be made from Labour's flat refusal – 55 per cent of voters thought Labour wrong to rule it out[67] – and from the Liberals' tamely tagging along in Labour's wake. At the same time ORC found that considerably more voters (26 per cent) favoured an all-party coalition than wanted a straight Tory Government (15 per cent). Most ordinary people probably assumed that coalition was what Heath was talking about anyway, so there was little to lose.

Another way of showing that he was serious about unity would have been to embrace electoral reform. The result of the February election, giving the Liberals just fourteen seats for six million votes, had created a significant swell of support for a fairer voting system voiced by, among others, *The Times*, the *Guardian*, the *Daily Mail*, the *Daily Express* and the *Sun*. It was not just a question of being nice to the Liberals: on the contrary, a commitment to reform would have been a good ploy – at least in the short term – to help the Tories win back some of the votes lost to them. Despite a lot of urging, however, Heath refused to go beyond the offer of a Speaker's Conference originally made to Thorpe in March and repeated in the manifesto. His failure to grasp that PR was the only guarantee of the new style of politics he was proposing suggested that the party was not really serious, but was still as much as ever in the business of winning on its own.

There was a third option by which, it was increasingly suggested, Heath might lend credibility to his proposal and seize the initiative for his party. This was that he himself should set the example of un-selfish sacrifice by announcing that – in the interest of national unity – he would be willing to step down from the Tory leadership and serve under another more widely acceptable leader. Such an offer would demonstrate to the sceptics that he was serious and not merely exploiting the cheap appeal of unity as a party cry to get himself back into office. It would greatly increase the electoral attraction of the coalition strategy. For all the polls showed that Heath him-self was still a liability to his party. As a potential party Prime Minister he still trailed well behind Wilson, while his personal rating was significantly below his party's.[68] For all his efforts to present himself as a national unifier he was still seen by the elec-torate as a divisive force and an *obstacle* to unity. More than any-thing else, this stubborn perception torpedoed the Tories' attempt to portray themselves as the vehicle of national reconciliation. As a result, not only the press but his own closest advisers began to urge him to make the 'supreme sacrifice'. Michael Wolff, Sara Morrison, Timothy Kitson, Tony Barber and Lord Carrington all tried to persuade him that he had in fact nothing to lose by making a selfless gesture. If he lost the election he would be finished, whether he had offered to stand down or not; if, on the other hand, he were to make the offer and the Tories then won, his posi-tion would in practice be unassailable.

Heath, however, would have none of it. He was too proud. He was perhaps too tired after two weeks of whirlwind electioneering. He was already too embattled to listen to advice even from his closest friends: by this stage he was not sure who his true friends were. It was in any case not in his character to shirk responsibility, to be seen to give up or run away. So long as he was the leader he reckoned it was his job to lead. In this he was supported by at least two of his colleagues, Whitelaw and Peter Walker, and by Toby Aldington, who all argued that it would be fatal to party morale to raise a question mark over the leadership a week before the election. Such defeatism, they believed, would merely invite defeat: Wilson would have a field day with a party which faced the electorate without a leader. Moreover to stand down would be to hand over the right to choose the leader of the Tory party to Jeremy Thorpe. For all these reasons Heath must go on. There was force in these arguments, particularly coming from his party chairman: had he listened to Whitelaw rather than Carrington earlier in the year he might still have been Prime Minister. So at his press conference on 3 October, when pressed about rumours that he was about to step down, he dismissed the idea with asperity: 'I am the leader', he declared, 'and we are going all out to win the election . . . Having won the election I shall ask the other leaders to come along.'[69]

In other words he was now proposing coalition – though not for two more days did he bring himself to use the word. Over the last weekend he released his final message to Conservative candidates in which he stated: 'I have no doubt that the real hope of the British people . . . is that a National Coalition government, involving all the parties, should be formed, and the party differences could be put aside until the crisis is mastered.' Hitherto, the word 'coalition' had been 'a great sticking point'. According to Butler and Kavanagh, 'those around him commented how much the saying of the word seemed to liberate him in the last few days of the campaign'.[70] Yet the word was still only a stick with which to beat Labour and the Liberals. The rest of his message made it clear that the national government he hoped to form was still basically a Tory government: 'When the Conservatives attain a majority . . . I will immediately set out with this majority to establish a government that can transcend party divisions, a government representing men and women of good will of all parties and of none.' He repeated that he would 'consult' the other party leaders, but spoke of bringing into government only 'people of talent and patriotism from all walks of life'.[71] 'Patriotism' in this context was longstanding Tory code – redolent of 1931 – for Labour politicians prepared to break with their party to serve the country. The truth was that behind his public condemnation, Heath was quite happy with Labour's veto on a coalition of parties. After a decade of abominating Wilson, the last thing he wanted was to have to form a coalition with him.

And yet he was serious about wanting to form a non-party government. He had never, after all, had much love for the Tory party either, except as a necessary instrument for realising his vision of Britain. The idea of going beyond it to form a truly 'national' administration had a strong appeal for him; and he was still convinced that he was the man to do it. He did not recognise himself as an obstacle to unity. Jeremy Thorpe likened him to Neville Chamberlain: Heath's mind too was running on 1940, but he rather saw himself as Churchill. He expounded his thinking in an important interview with his sympathetic biographer, George Hutchinson, published in *The Times* on 5 October.

The country, he told Hutchinson, faced a crisis unprecedented since 1945, or even 1931. It was vital to get the public to understand, in order to mobilise the majority to prevent a minority using their strength unfairly. It was important to secure the widest possible agreement.

This is the way my thought processes run: Those of us who have experienced politics over the last 10 to 15 years in high office know that we cannot go on in this country in a situation where every change of government means a reversal of policy. No country can survive on that basis.

Heath himself had of course contributed his share to this process of knee-jerk reversal in 1970, though naturally he did not choose to re-call the fact. Instead he blamed Labour for the fact that there was no 'common ground' left between the parties, even in respect of areas like defence, Europe and pensions, where once the two Front Benches had agreed: Labour in opposition had reversed the policies which it had pursued in government, and had failed to support the Tory Government's efforts to preserve industrial peace. In this polar-ised situation, he argued, the government machine needed a 'blood transfusion' of practical people with experience of the real world. He had attempted this to a limited extent in 1970, with some success. There was now 'a desperate need' for people from outside govern-ment to come in to help overcome the nation's inertia. It was clear to Hutchinson, however, that he meant to invite these still unnamed outsiders as advisers, not as ministers.[72]

Labour was more worried than it admitted by Heath's 'unity' appeal. It feared that the voters might punish it for seeming to go against the prevailing mood – as indeed, to an extent, they probably did. But so long as Heath refused to name names, refused to embrace PR, and refused to put his own position on the line, it was easy to deride his appeal as a cynical last throw by a divided party facing certain defeat. Why had Heath never proposed coalition before 1 March that year? At his press conference on 5 October Wilson was superbly contemptuous:

The fact is that this last-minute offer of a coalition has one purpose and one purpose only. It is a desperate attempt by desperate men to get back into power by any means . . . Beneath the soft, the pleasant and the adjustable face of today's coalition lies the old and, if I may borrow a phrase from the Conservative leader, 'unpleasant and unacceptable face of capitalism'. Coalition would mean Con policies, Con leadership by a Con party for a Con trick. And how long would it last? About as long as it would take to get the country back to last February, back to the other 'cons' – confrontation and conflict.[73]

In the last days of the campaign, with the polls still steadily against him, Heath's confidence never publicly wavered. To those journalists travelling with him, his faith was remarkable, even infectious. 'Throughout', *The Times*'s John Winder summed up, 'he has appeared cheerful, relaxed and confident. Most of all the last, for he is certain that next week he will be called upon to unite the nation and to take upon himself what he has himself called the awesome task of leading Britain in the war against inflation and unemployment.'[74] 'If he really does believe he is fighting for his political life,' *The Economist* agreed, 'he is a far more consummate actor than anyone has suspected.'[75] His optimism was sustained by the response he met wherever he went. On the last Tuesday, 8 October, he had just enjoyed 'a tremendous reception from a crowded meeting in Sowerby in Yorkshire after delivering, extempore, one of his best speeches of the campaign' when he was handed the latest NOP poll to be published in the next day's *Daily Mail*, giving Labour a 14·5 per cent lead. With impressive resilience he carried on with his programme as intended, sinking a pint of bitter in a club in Bradford without betraying a hint of the blow he had just received.[76] He may have remembered NOP's poll in 1970 showing the Tories almost as far behind, less than a week before they won. But this time there were only thirty-six hours to go.

The Tories' private polls did suggest some narrowing of the gap. At his last press conference on 9 October Heath claimed that the party was making headway, only for a journalist to ask, cruelly, if that meant it would peak in fourteen days' time![77] It is likely that once again there was something of a late swing. Going into polling day, senior Tories hoped for no more than to limit Labour's majority to 20 or 30. In the event they did very much better than that. On a poll nearly two million down on February, their share of the vote was within 4 per cent of Labour's – 35.8 per cent compared with 39.2 per cent. (The Liberals slipped back to 18.3 per cent.) They lost another 17 seats to Labour; one to the Liberals (but took 2 back); and another 4 in Scotland to the SNP. The final state of the parties was Labour 319, Conservative 277, Liberals 13, SNP 11, Plaid Cymru 3, Ulster Unionists and others 14 – giving Labour an overall majority of just 3.* In practice, with a majority of 42 over the Conservatives (43 allowing for the Speaker) the Government was a good deal more secure than that implied. There was no need for any sort of coalition or parliamentary arrangement – at least for a couple of years – to keep Labour in office. The Tories could only look forward to a further indefinite period of opposition. Nevertheless the immediate judgment of much of Fleet Street was that Heath had once again confounded the polls and the pundits. For instance, David Wood in *The Times*:

> Plenty of Conservatives are to be found . . . who will say that by the manner and the matter of his campaign, Mr Heath has shrewdly prepared a position from which the Conservative party can make its next challenge for power when the economic crisis has shattered the unity of the Labour Government and demonstrated to the country the urgent need for national unity.[79]

He had indeed done surprisingly well; but the harsh fact was that he had not done well enough. He had now fought four General Elections and lost three of them. With the best will in the world it was hard to see how the party could contemplate a fifth under his leadership.

---

* Heath's own majority in Bexley, Sidcup fell by 2,000:

E. R. G. Heath (Conservative)	18,991
W. J. Jennings (Labour)	11,448
I. R. P. Josephs (Liberal)	6,954
D. H. Jones (Independent)	174
M. J. Norton (Independent)	61
Conservative majority	7,543[78]

34

'The Peasants' Revolt'

FROM the moment the October election was lost it was clear to almost all observers – friends and critics alike – that Heath could not expect to retain the Tory leadership much longer. His critics, most of whom had stayed their hand until the election was out of the way, now felt free to call openly for his departure. Many who had hitherto supported him, and personally still admired him, now reluctantly accepted that he simply did not have enough voter appeal to win elections. It was tough, but there it was: he was an electoral liability. 'For all practical purposes', *The Times* declared on the Monday morning, 'this view is unanimous . . . The popular verdict has to be accepted.'[1]

One man, however, still adamantly refused to read the writing on the wall; or if he did, he refused to heed it. So far as Heath was concerned he was still leader and he would remain leader until a rival appeared who could defeat him; since there was no such rival in sight he saw no need to stand aside. Unlike in 1966, Labour had only succeeded in scraping back into office with a wafer-thin majority. The country was plunging ever deeper into economic crisis; moreover the Government had committed itself to a referendum on continued EEC membership which seemed certain to split the Cabinet apart. British membership of the Community and, latterly, the cure of inflation were the two causes above all on which he had staked his career: he was not going to give up just when both were coming to their resolution. He still confidently expected his warnings of economic catastrophe to be fulfilled sooner rather than later: the need for some sort of crisis government would then become irresistible, and his belief was unshaken that he – by statesmanship, vision and experience – was the only national leader qualified to head it.

It was an honourable ambition, as patriotic as it was egotistical; but he deceived himself. As a result of his egotism, he actually passed up the one option by which he might have been able to hang on. Up to 10 October it was possible to see his refusal to admit defeat as admirable courage in adversity, his belief in eventual victory against all odds as an expression of the sheer willpower which had taken him from Broadstairs to Downing Street in the first place. He was right to carry on after February: indeed he had little alternative. But now the position was different. He had made a valiant attempt to bounce back, but he had failed. With the best will in the world – criticism of his policies and his personality aside – there were powerful and legitimate grounds for arguing that the party needed a change of leader. Both in his own interest and for the sake of safeguarding the sort of Tory politics he believed in, Heath would have been wiser to have recognised the fact. Had he only had the humility, or the political shrewdness, to offer himself immediately for re-election at the beginning of the new parliamentary session against any challenger who might come forward, he would most probably have been confirmed in office: not overwhelmingly, not very enthusiastically, but nevertheless confirmed in such a way that the loyalist mass of the party would have rallied around him again as the elected leader. At worst, had he failed to poll sufficiently well against a token opponent to enable him to carry on, he would almost certainly have been succeeded by a colleague – probably Willie Whitelaw, perhaps Robert Carr – close to his own way of thinking with whom he could have continued to serve, as Alec Douglas-Home had served under him. By refusing to so submit himself, however, he not only further weakened his own position by appearing stubborn, arrogant and impervious to criticism; he also allowed time for his opponents to come up with a previously unconsidered champion who quickly acquired the necessary head of steam to beat him, and went on to overturn everything he had stood for and fought for. The bitter irony of the phenomenon of Thatcherism is that it was Heath himself, by his purblind conduct following the October election, who brought it about. It was Heath who gave Margaret Thatcher the opportunity which she grasped with both hands.

He spent the weekend after the election with Lord Aldington in Kent. In adversity Toby Aldington had become his closest political confidant and foul-weather friend. Every political leader, particularly one with no wife or husband to buoy him up, needs such a support. Nevertheless most of those who consider themselves Heath's friends believe that Aldington was a bad influence who encouraged him, in 1974 and over the next decade, in his attitude of doggedly self-righteous isolation. In the days after the October defeat it was Aldington, more than anyone else, who reinforced his instinct to stand firm and defy his enemies to overthrow him. There were others, admittedly, giving the same advice: Peter Walker, for one, and Willie Whitelaw; Lord Hailsham publicly urged him to sit tight, and so did his old mentor Harold Macmillan. The Establishment was behind him. Other loyal supporters, however, were counselling him the other way. Peter Carrington had already got his word in: just as he had in 1970, he spent polling day with Heath in Sidcup telling him frankly that if he lost the election he should resign at once. But Heath no longer listened to Carrington; nor to Jim Prior. Prior had a long talk with him on Friday afternoon, when Heath emerged from Wilton Street to thank the party workers at Central Office. He told him that his only chance of survival lay in a quick election, though even that was doubtful:

> He replied that he didn't intend to submit himself to a leadership election because he was determined to fight the right wing. I told him that if he refused to go he would probably end up giving them exactly what they wanted . . .
>
> My impression was that Ted by then was only hearing the advice he wished to hear, including some from sources to which previously he had paid scant attention.[2]

Most of those who had been closest to him over the past year gave the same advice: Sara Morrison; Ian Gilmour; both his PPSs, Timothy Kitson and Kenneth Baker; also his Chief Whip until just ten months before, Francis Pym. But this was not the advice he wished to hear.

Meanwhile moves were under way to force the issue. The initiative lay with the Executive of the 1922 Committee. Before the election, the Executive had agreed to meet on the Monday morning after the election at Edward Du Cann's house in Lord North Street – not, they later protested, to discuss the leadership but in order to be on hand for consultation in the event of another inconclusive result, as in February. That had not transpired; but over the weekend every member of the Executive received a stream of 'messages, telephone calls and letters' from Tory MPs demanding early consideration of the leadership. When they met, they were unanimous that there should be a leadership contest 'not necessarily at once, but in the foreseeable future'.[3] Wasting no time, they instructed Du Cann to seek an interview with Heath the same afternoon to inform him of the Executive's view, and arranged to meet again the next day to hear his response. Since Lord North Street had been besieged by reporters and television cameras they agreed to gather at the offices of Du Cann's merchant bank, Keyser Ullman, in Milk Street in the City.

The interview was brief. Du Cann delivered his message, but Heath did not wish to discuss the matter. He regarded Du Cann not as the elected spokesman of the backbenchers but as a longstanding enemy abusing his position to pursue a personal vendetta. Indeed he regarded the whole Executive as a body packed with his opponents: in so far as it included Angus Maude, Neil Marten, Airey Neave and John Biffen – to name only the most prominent – there was now some truth in his complaint. Since by definition it is composed of senior MPs who for one reason or another have not won promotion the Executive is always likely to be coolly disposed towards a long-serving leader. It was not true, however, that they were all right-wingers: Sir Nigel Fisher, for instance, the friend and biographer of Iain Macleod, was a 'One Nation' liberal who believed that the co-alition idea should have been pushed harder at the election; it was a measure of the trouble Heath was in that someone like Fisher was now persuaded, for purely electoral reasons, that he must go. 'On nearly every doorstep,' Fisher wrote three years later, 'if a conversation developed, one's constituent – whether man or woman, Conservative, Liberal or Labour – would say, "I'd vote for you except for Heath," or "You'll never win with Heath," or, quite simply, "I don't like Heath."'[4] This was the common experience that had convinced the whole Executive that the leadership issue should at least be aired. Fisher insists that Du Cann, placed in a deli-cate position by his known antagonism towards Heath, conducted the whole procedure over the next four months with scrupulous rectitude. As an outside contender for the crown himself, it could be said that he was protecting his own interest precisely by *not* being seen to harry Heath out. But Heath had no sustainable complaint against either Du Cann's or the Executive's exercise of their respon-sibility.

The members of the Executive made their separate ways to Milk Street on Tuesday morning and met undetected; when the first of them emerged, however, it was to a barrage of popping flashbulbs. Within hours the *Evening Standard* was on the streets with a sensa-tional story that the 'Milk Street Mafia' was meeting secretly to plot Heath's downfall, illustrated with pictures of senior Tories looking conspiratorial. Plainly someone had leaked the rendezvous, and the Du Cann camp was convinced it was someone in Heath's office. The

immediate effect was deeply embarrassing to Du Cann and his colleagues, who were made to look as if they were acting improperly.
The deeper effect, however, was more damaging to Heath; the impression was planted that he would use all the resources at his
command to discredit his critics. A stream of damaging stories in the
press over the next few weeks about his possible rivals – first Du
Cann, later Mrs Thatcher – seemed to be further evidence of 'dirty
tricks'. The impression that a cornered leader was fighting dirty did
him no good.

The Executive was already displeased by Heath's curt reception of
Du Cann and decided to spell out its view in the form of a letter inviting him to address the first meeting of the full 1922 Committee on
30 October. He declined, publishing his reply but not the Executive's letter. 'This', wrote Nigel Fisher, 'seemed a strange way to
behave to colleagues.'[5] He agreed to meet the Executive, but only
after its own re-election, implying that it had no authority till then.
But this, as the Secretary, Sir Philip Goodhart, wrote to *The Times* a
few days later, was constitutionally incorrect.[6] Once again Heath's
ungracious nit-picking did his cause no good. He could so easily
have defused the situation and won himself some credit by telling the
1922 that he understood the Executive's views and would certainly
hold an election as soon as practicable: he could probably have got
away with postponing it for as much as a year on the argument that
an immediate contest would not be appropriate in view of the economic situation and the impending referendum, if he had only
accepted the principle with a good grace. As it was he gave the impression that he considered it impertinence for the Executive even to
raise the matter. On television on Tuesday evening – in the course of
what *The Times* called 'a sturdy and proud performance in what
could not be other than harrowing circumstances' – he did briefly
appear to recognise that he owed a responsibility to the party. Sceptically welcoming Harold Wilson's new-found enthusiasm for
national unity, he acknowledged that 'The unity of the Conservative
Party is my particular responsibility as its leader.' David Wood took
this as a hint that he was considering his position.[7] But the key phrase
was 'as its leader'. 'I am the leader of the Conservative Party', he
declared bluntly a few days later, 'and my job now is to organise
the Opposition. I am getting on with that job and that is what the
party has got to get on with.'[8] So far as he was concerned the
question of the leadership did not arise.

There are two mitigating excuses for Heath's insensitivity. First,
there was his health. During this fraught period when he was fighting for his political life the thyroid deficiency which had already

begun to affect him while he was still Prime Minister was getting worse. 'The principal characteristics of his condition', Patrick Cosgrave has written, 'were an extraordinary, though intermittent, physical lassitude and an acerbity of temper marked even in a man not hitherto noted for the benevolence of his manner.'[9] This is a hostile account, but it is confirmed with more or less emphasis by colleagues and staff who worked with him in these months. His political judgment was plainly affected throughout this period; the psychological effect of his mysterious illness can only have been to reinforce his sense of being under siege and fighting – perhaps literally – for his life.

The second excuse that can be made for Heath is that Willie Whitelaw – famed for his acute sensitivity to party feeling – did not take the threat to his position seriously either. Whitelaw has written in his memoirs that as party chairman after the October election he observed 'the bitterness, dissension and general bad feeling in the Parliamentary Party'.

> It was only then for the first time that I appreciated the strong feeling against Ted Heath. I thought it most unfair. But even at that time I did not realise how widespread it was. I tended to regard it as the usual grumbling of malcontents who, for one reason or another, had a grudge against the Leader . . . I did not believe that the executive of the 1922 Committee accurately reflected the feelings of the Parliamentary Party.

Whitelaw, like Heath, thought Du Cann was motivated by a personal grievance. As a result, he confesses, he did not maintain as close a relationship with him as should exist between the party chairman and the chairman of the 1922.[10] If Heath was deceived about the true state of feeling in the party he was misled partly by one of those whose job it was to keep him informed.

Whitelaw's first responsibility, however, was to reflect the views of the party in the country; and the fact was that the constituencies remained astonishingly loyal. An opinion poll in late October found that a majority of constituency chairmen wanted Heath to stay;[11] another in early November found that 54 per cent of Tory voters still supported him.[12] This was paradoxical, since his weakness was supposed to be his lack of public appeal. But it was the same in 1990 when the MPs turned against Mrs Thatcher: the Tory faithful do not like it when the parliamentary party exercises its prerogative to change the leader.

So long as he was determined to stay put his strength remained the

lack of any plausible successor. Whitelaw was the most likely in-
heritor if the party wanted to stick with Heath's policies. But what
would be the point of that? No one could really imagine that Whitelaw would expound them more effectively. Keith Joseph, with his
radical advocacy of sound money even at the expense of high unemployment, appeared the likeliest standard bearer if there was to be
a challenge. But *The Times* could still detect little support for what it
called 'the Powellite fringe'; while even before he destroyed all confidence in his political judgment with a foolish speech on 19 October
which appeared to propose compulsory contraception for the lower
classes, Joseph seemed 'too much of an intellectual invert' to make a
successful party leader.[13] 'My dear Nigel,' one Shadow Minister told
Fisher, 'if you chose Keith instead of Heath, it would be like going
straight from the fridge into the freezer.'[14]

Robert Carr was too mild and anyway unwilling to be considered;
Jim Prior was too young and too closely identified with Heath; Mrs
Thatcher was widely seen as promising, but too inexperienced and
too narrow. (*The Economist* described her as 'a lady Joseph, but without the intellectual drive and with a more restricted suburban
appeal'.)[15] Casting the net wider, Du Cann seemed attractive to some
as a substantial figure with some following in the party, untainted by
the failures of the past four years; on the other hand he had never sat
in a Cabinet and his City reputation was dubious. In the *Sunday Telegraph* Peregrine Worsthorne pressed the claim of Lord Hailsham.[16]
Another name canvassed was Christopher Soames, out of Parliament
since 1966, currently one of Britain's EEC commissioners in Brussels
but anxious to return to domestic politics. Soames was a Tory grandee of the old school, married to Churchill's daughter, a former
Cabinet Minister under Macmillan and Home, but still only fifty-
four; the trouble was that the younger MPs who had entered the
house since 1966 did not know him. The fact that he could seriously
be considered showed the difficulty the party was in.

It was part of his critics' case against Heath that nine years after
taking over a party bursting with potential leaders he seemed to have
left it with none at all. It was not his fault that Macleod was dead and
Maudling under a cloud. But one way or another he had also contrived to 'lose' Enoch Powell, Edward Boyle and Soames, while
failing to promote in their places anyone of comparable weight. The
party was ready for a change, *The Economist* concluded, but all the
possible challengers were 'blatantly nervous of stubbing their toes on
Mr Heath's iron frame'.[17] Surveying the field on 8 November *The
Times* judged that no candidate capable of beating him would stand
against him.[18]

Yet without a contest that would either confirm or reject him Heath was a crippled leader. In the debate on the Queen's Speech opening the new Parliament he made 'a strong speech' condemning the irrelevance of Labour's nationalisation programme; which was 'rewarded with virtual silence from the massed backbenchers behind him'.[19] At the packed meeting of the 1922 Committee next day practically every speaker was critical of his leadership: Heath's supporters put it about that the chairman had called only Members known to be hostile to him, but Fisher insists that Du Cann was punctilious in calling everyone who wished to speak. The most telling speech came from the Member for Rutland and Stamford, Kenneth Lewis, who warned pointedly that the Conservative leadership was 'a leasehold not a freehold'.[20] In this atmosphere Heath had difficulty reshaping his Shadow Cabinet. 'His dilemma now', wrote *The Economist*, 'is that, at a time when the Tories should be encouraging new faces and formulating new policies, [he] will have to put more of a premium than ever on the loyalty of trusted colleagues. That is not a re-generating formula.'[21] In a first batch of appointments Heath managed to bring in one new name – John Peyton – to be Shadow Leader of the House. Peyton (Minister of Transport 1970–4) was a somewhat maverick right-winger – indeed a member of the Monday Club – so his promotion was seen as an obvious gesture to the right; but it was the only one. Carrington resumed the leadership in the Lords (in place of Lord Windlesham, another who had announced that he was leaving politics); and Whitelaw would combine shadowing devolution with his role as party chairman. Otherwise there was an embarrassing delay before the full list was complete, while the press speculated about an offer to Du Cann or the possible recall of Maudling. (The delay, it was lamely stated, was due to difficulty in contacting people!) Heath did make an offer to Du Cann, but after seven years in the cold Du Cann was not to be bought off now. Maudling agreed in principle to rejoin, but not immediately. So the reshuffled team contained few surprises. Geoffrey Rippon took over foreign affairs from the retiring Alec Douglas-Home. A number of younger faces – all from the left – were promoted from supporting roles: Paul Channon, Nicholas Scott, Timothy Raison. The appointment of most interest – particularly in retrospect – was that of Margaret Thatcher to assist Carr in shadowing the Treasury.

With hindsight this appears an extraordinarily ill-judged move on Heath's part. It gave Mrs Thatcher precisely the opportunity to make a name for herself by fighting Labour's Finance Bill that Heath himself had used ten years before to steal a march on Maudling. It was an opportunity she exploited brilliantly to demonstrate previously un-suspected leadership potential. No commentator, however, foresaw this at the time. Her promotion was seen as a well-earned reward for her spirited performance during the election. As 'a full-rank specialist in finance and taxation' she would bring much-needed technical re-inforcement as well as a dash of aggression to Carr's unequal duel with Denis Healey; she was 'a rising Conservative star', a possible future Chancellor.[22] But Heath saw no risk to himself in appointing her. She was not at that stage reckoned a serious contender for the leadership, nor had she yet come out as a fully paid-up monetarist. 'Ted knew she had been interested in the economic side,' Peter Walker reflected some years later. 'She was a good performer at the dispatch box and he wanted to recognise her talent.'[23] By making her deputy to Carr he thought only that he was making a shrewd but essentially superficial gesture to the idea of a balanced team. ('They seem unlikely to get on,' *The Economist* commented drily.)[24]

Much more obviously threatening was the re-election *en bloc* of the entire Executive of the 1922. Following the Milk Street episode there had been dark hints emanating from the Heath camp that some of them at least would be unseated. Instead, in an unprecedented vote of confidence, they were all returned: Du Cann himself was unop-posed, the two vice-chairmen and the treasurer were easily re-elected and all Heath's candidates for the other places, in the words of the *Annual Register*, were 'sharply trounced'[25] The parliamentary party evidently did not think it had been misrepresented. 'The loud and prolonged applause which greeted Edward Du Cann's unopposed re-election', wrote Fisher, 'should have been a warning to Heath that his own position was, to say the least, precarious.'[26] No wonder Du Cann was not tempted to join the Shadow Cabinet. This unmis-takable rebuff, however, did have the effect of persuading Heath to offer a more conciliatory face to the Committee. He now realised that he would have to submit himself to re-election. Since he had no intention of resigning, however, the old rules drawn up in 1965 under which he had originally been elected would have to be revised. That procedure was applicable only when there was a vacancy. As Nigel Fisher put it waspishly in his subsequent account: 'It had not occurred to anyone when the rules were first devised in 1965 that a leader who had lost the confidence of a substantial section of the party would wish to continue in office.'[27]

On 14 November Heath deigned to attend another packed meeting of the 1922 Committee and announced that he had invited Alec Home to chair a committee to propose new rules. Though he still did not commit himself, the implication was that he would submit himself for re-election as soon as the new rules were in place. 'I am the servant of the party,' he assured Members; there was 'no question' of his regarding the leadership as a freehold. Simply by appearing, he was given a much warmer reception in person than his name had received in his absence the previous week: a number of MPs spoke up strongly in his support.[28] The composition of Home's committee was agreed next day; it was to submit its recommendations to the leader by the end of the year.

By setting the wheels in motion for a contest Heath had recovered the initiative; he was seen to be preparing to give the party a chance to have its say, but meanwhile he controlled the timetable. Moreover he still had no obvious challenger. New names like Julian Amery, or Francis Pym, were canvassed, only to be shot down. Norman Tebbit recalls that right-wingers of the 1970 intake like himself 'hesitated between Keith Joseph and Edward Du Cann or Geoffrey Howe, but gradually Margaret Thatcher's name came more and more into play'.[29] Tebbit confesses that he barely knew Mrs Thatcher at this stage. But on 21 November Joseph finally told her that he was not going to stand; she immediately took up the challenge and announced that in that case she would. She rang Heath's office and made an appointment to tell him to his face. They had a two-minute interview in the Leader of the Opposition's room at the Commons. He did not stand up, nor invite her to sit down. She announced her intention and he told her bluntly: 'You'll lose.'[30] He thought she was only the first of many hopefuls who would now throw their hats into the ring.

She was certainly not yet one to be taken seriously. She took no steps to organise a serious campaign. For several weeks yet Fisher and her eventual campaign manager, Airey Neave, still hoped that Du Cann would be persuaded to stand; not until January did he finally decline. Up until then Mrs Thatcher herself would have been happy to withdraw in his favour. She was really proposing to stand only because she thought someone ought to: no more than anyone else did she expect to win. An article in *The Economist* on 30 November saw her candidacy – patronisingly, as it seems in retrospect – as an admirable means of allowing the party to choose between Heath and Willie Whitelaw:

If Mr Edward Heath is capable, under whatever election procedure is devised . . . of being beaten . . . by Mrs Margaret Thatcher, then he is well out of a job . . . Mrs Thatcher is precisely the sort of candidate . . . who ought to be able to stand, and lose, harmlessly.

So long as it was quite certain that she could not win, the writer continued, 'she ought . . . to be able to stand against him with profit, giving her party the cathartic feeling of choice and advancing her position within it, arousing little bitterness, in a way that no other candidate . . . probably could'. If there was any possibility that she might win, however, she would put Whitelaw in an impossible position. In that case it would be up to Heath to withdraw immediately in Whitelaw's favour, since a serious contest would tear the party apart.[31]

Home's committee produced its report as promised a week before Christmas. They recommended four significant changes from the 1965 procedure. First, they proposed that when the party was in opposition the leader should be subject to re-election at the beginning of every parliamentary year, with a prospective challenger requiring just two nominations. (This was the provision under which Mrs Thatcher was subsequently challenged, first in 1989 by Sir Anthony Meyer and again in 1990 by Michael Heseltine.) Second, while recommending that the franchise should still be restricted to MPs, they proposed formalising the arrangements for consulting the party in the country. Third, if the contest went to a third ballot they proposed that it be decided by the single transferable vote. The change that mattered, however, was the fourth. The 1965 rules had required that in order to win on the first ballot a candidate must obtain both an absolute majority and a 15 per cent margin over his nearest rival. Home and his colleagues now proposed that this margin be altered to 15 per cent *of all those eligible to vote*. This small change made a big difference, since it meant that a significant number of abstentions could deny the leading candidate victory. In the specific contest now in prospect, in which a lot of Members were thought to be anxious to be rid of Heath but reluctant to instal an inexperienced woman in his place, its application was obvious. It raised the hurdle of approval which Heath had to clear: he had to win well enough on the first ballot to beat not only his one declared challenger but a shadowy host of undeclared rivals as well. It made it more likely that the contest would go to a second or third ballot. With some reason Heath thought the change was aimed deliberately at him, and he resented it. The new provision was immediately dubbed 'Alec's Revenge'.

Heath now knew, however, that he could not postpone an election much longer; once the new rules were approved by the 1922 Committee there was no way that he could reject them or even try to alter what he found objectionable. He was bound to hold an election early in the New Year. But the day after the report was published he gave clear notice that he would still be hard to beat. Against a background of deepening economic gloom – the largest ever monthly trade deficit (£534 million), the pound at its lowest level ever, inflation officially up to 18 per cent, British Leyland on the verge of financial collapse, restrictions on the use of energy closely reminiscent of the three-day week – he laid into the Government with rediscovered vigour. 'Mr Heath opened the debate with a spirited condemnation of the Government's economic strategy,' *The Economist* reported, 'and his dire warnings of impending economic doom . . . earned him loud and enthusiastic cheers from the packed Tory benches.' He even dealt crushingly with Labour interruptions. 'It was the Tory leader's best parliamentary performance in recent memory . . . If Mr Heath can come up with a few more speeches like Wednesday's in the months ahead he will undoubtedly be leader of the Tory party this time next year.'[32] Against this, however, Margaret Thatcher also displayed her growing confidence with an equally impressive performance on the third day of the same debate.

Three days before Christmas Heath narrowly missed being blown up by the IRA. If they had done their homework the terrorists would have known that he was conducting his annual carol concert in Broadstairs that day. Perhaps they did know, since they only missed him by five minutes. He had stayed on longer than planned after the concert, having tea with friends, and was just driving over Vauxhall Bridge when the attack occurred in Wilton Street. A bomb was thrown out of a car on to the first-floor balcony, just outside the window at which he would normally have been working. It was only a small bomb, 2 lb, but the explosion was big enough to cause substantial damage. His housekeeper was fortunately in the basement at the time, and his piano was in a room at the back of the house; but one of his precious Churchill paintings was damaged by flying fragments.[33] Heath was characteristically unmoved by the attack. Once again he had to move out to stay with the faithful Kitson; but the next day he carried on as planned with a visit to Ulster. The attack may have won him some temporary sympathy; but the only lasting result was that like other obvious potential targets he had henceforth to be more closely guarded.

After Christmas the coming contest vied with the economic crisis for attention. For Heath it was inconceivable that at such a moment, with the economic situation daily vindicating his warnings, the Tory party could seriously consider replacing his vast experience with an untried woman. On 14 January his office let it be known that though the new *Morning Cloud*, currently being built at Gosport, was due to be completed in April, Heath did not expect to be able to do much sailing this year 'because the country is in such a state'.[34] As it turned out he had more time for sailing that summer than any previous year since he took it up.

It was only in the New Year that the various strands of discontent in the party, hitherto inchoate, began to come together in a single determined campaign. The critical moment, somewhere around 5 January, was the switch into Mrs Thatcher's camp of Airey Neave. After the event Heath's supporters played up Neave's role as the cunning master of undercover operations, who single-handedly schemed his downfall from motives of personal revenge: at the time they underestimated him, just as they did Mrs Thatcher herself. Famous for having escaped from Colditz during the war, MP for Abingdon since 1953, Neave had loathed Heath ever since Heath, as Chief Whip, had grossly snubbed him when he had reported a heart condition that would oblige him to leave the Government at the 1959 election. (He had been Under-Secretary for Transport.) 'You're finished,' Heath is said to have told him, without a word of sympathy. He subsequently recovered, but he received no further advancement from Heath after 1965; nor did he receive the compensatory knighthood which an MP of twenty years' standing could have expected from any other Conservative Prime Minister. By 1974 Neave was determined that Heath must go, but he did not mind who replaced him; he was by no means a right-winger and first offered his services to Willie Whitelaw. When Whitelaw declined he joined those trying to persuade Du Cann to run; only when Du Cann too finally refused did he switch his efforts to the only candidate prepared to come forward. 'We reckoned without the persistence and almost obsessive scheming of Airey Neave,' Jim Prior wrote in his memoirs. 'Someone who had been determined enough to escape from Colditz was unlikely to be put off by losing a couple of potential candidates, so the next in line was pushed forward. This was Margaret Thatcher.'[35]

Before Neave took over, Mrs Thatcher had only a token campaign. Once Du Cann had ruled himself out and it was clear that there was only going to be one serious challenger on the first ballot, Neave set about transforming her from a stalking horse who might, if she did well enough, clear the way for Whitelaw into a candidate who might actually win the leadership herself. But still he had to play a double game: as well as the support of those who were rapidly coming to realise her positive qualities, he needed the votes on the first ballot of those who emphatically did not want her to win, but only wished to use her as a means to open up the contest to others. Of Du Cann's 25 pledged supporters, for instance, only about 15 were willing unconditionally to switch their allegiance. Many of these became the nucleus of Neave's team, which eventually numbered as many as 50. But Nigel Fisher was prepared to commit himself only for the first ballot, preferring to keep his options open for the second; and there were others who took the same position.[36]

The skill of Neave's operation was that he managed to maximise support for his candidate by encouraging different individuals to back her for all sorts of different reasons, but primarily because she was not Ted Heath. The overwhelming reason for her victory was that backbench Tory MPs were sick of Heath and ready to vote for almost anybody except him. For the most part this reaction was not ideological but personal. Few seriously quarrelled with his policies, though they were confused and bewildered by his failure adequately to explain them; many more simply felt that he had become an electoral liability under whom the party would never win. Some doubtless were aggrieved at his failure over the years to promote or honour them as they thought they deserved: one senior Member allegedly voted against him because he had refused to revive hereditary peerages.[37] But most younger MPs just felt taken for granted. As Fisher put it: 'They would simply like to have been recognised by sight, known by name and occasionally spoken to.'[38] Every MP had his own story of how he had been snubbed by the leader. Julian Critchley, the MP for Aldershot who was to become a persistent critic of Mrs Thatcher, recalled being at dinner in the Members' Dining Room with Jim Prior and two other backbenchers soon after the October 1974 election when Heath came up to their table. He spoke for several minutes to Prior and then walked away again without so much as a nod to Critchley or his companions. 'What can I do with him?' Prior asked apologetically.[39] Tory MPs who had been willing to put up with Heath's remoteness and rudeness so long as he was Prime Minister felt no obligation of personal loyalty to such a graceless boor when he began to look like a loser. This reaction cut across all wings of the party, alienating his natural supporters on the left as much as his habitual critics on the right. The secret ballot offered slighted backbenchers a chance to get their own back.

Mrs Thatcher, guided by Neave, played skilfully on this personal resentment. Fifteen years later she in her turn was seen by her backbenchers as just as remote and overbearing as Heath had ever been; but in 1975 she presented herself as the backbenchers' friend. Initially barely known to many of them, she made herself available to small groups of Members who wanted to meet her and listened sympathetically to their worries, while keeping her own views largely to herself. By deliberate contrast with Heath's presidential grandeur she was modest, courteous and charming, promising a return to collective leadership which would reunite the party and reflect its anxieties. She even promised, if elected, to include Heath in her Shadow Cabinet.[40] But she drew the line at Enoch Powell. She was at pains not to be seen as the candidate of the right.

At the same time she balanced the reassuring private face which she presented to the Tory party in the tea room by a series of brilliant, destructive performances both in the chamber and in committee upstairs, mounting a powerful attack on Denis Healey's Finance Bill and unafraid to take on the bullying Chancellor himself, who unwisely tried to patronise her. ('Some chancellors are microeconomic. Some chancellors are fiscal. This one is just plain cheap,' she retorted to delighted Tory cheers on 22 January.)[41] Exposing the socialist iniquities of capital gains tax she was in her element, giving her demoralised party its first taste of blood in eleven months and showing herself a more formidable parliamentary fighter than Carr, Whitelaw, Geoffrey Howe or anyone else on the Front Bench besides Heath himself. As a result of her unexpectedly strong showing, *The Times* acknowledged, 'far fewer members . . . are speaking dismissively of a woman's candidature . . . than they did a fortnight ago when she announced her challenge'.[42] Uncannily like Heath himself ten years before, she was able to use the platform he had unwittingly given her to demonstrate the combative qualities the party was crying out for.

By comparison Heath's campaign was complacent and inept. It fatally lacked clear direction. Even today it is not certain who was supposed to have been in charge. Peter Walker had masterminded Heath's highly professional campaign against Maudling in 1965 and it was widely assumed by the press – and is still believed by most of Heath's senior colleagues – that he was in charge again. But Walker insists that as a senior ex-minister this time around he kept in the background, while the campaign was run by Heath's two PPSs, Timothy Kitson and Kenneth Baker, with help from one or two others like Nick Scott.[43] But they failed to carry out a sufficiently thorough canvass. Instead of arranging for each Member to be spoken to by a friend who would know the best way to approach him, they made the mistake of trying to sound the whole parliamentary party themselves. But they were known as Heath's creatures. Many Members who had no intention of voting for Heath were understandably – or even just tactfully – less than frank with them. As a result they formed far too optimistic a picture of his support. (This is always a problem for an incumbent leader: Mrs Thatcher's camp was deceived in exactly the same way in 1990.) Not only were Kitson and Baker – and Walker – privately optimistic: they were publicly over-confident, too, giving out that Heath was well ahead and likely to win comfortably on the first ballot, which had the opposite effect to what they intended. It encouraged the substantial number of Members who did not like Mrs Thatcher but wanted Heath out to think they had better vote for her on the first ballot if they were to get a chance to vote for someone else on the second. In this way Heath's managers played into Neave's hands. George Hutchinson believed that they 'succeeded in losing the leadership for him by the manner of their campaign ... With their loud, aggressive, pushing behaviour, they were insensitive to the feelings of many Conservative MPs.' He was particularly critical of their 'astounding decision' to place a newspaper advertisement – signed 'Friends of Ted Heath' – inviting the public to send telegrams of support to their MP. 'If it was not improper, it was certainly injudicious and cannot conceivably have helped Mr Heath.'[44]

His minders also encouraged Heath to undertake an intensive round of entertaining which was embarrassingly out of character. It was true that his frequent failure to recognise his own MPs was a major cause of his unpopularity; but it was not remedied by a belated and obviously phoney interest in them two weeks before the election. Suddenly he was to be found buying drinks for total strangers in the Members' Bar.[45] A grisly series of dinners for small groups of younger MPs which he gave in Kitson's flat (where he was still squatting after the Wilton Street bomb) came later to be christened the 'Last Suppers': he still barely acknowledged some of them, he had no small talk, yet he refused to be drawn into discussing politics. After one dinner, one of those invited told Kitson: 'A marvellous meal, and thank you so much. But perhaps it would be better if you just let us get on with it, without actually producing the leader.'[46] Mrs Thatcher, wisely, did no entertaining.

Heath's one strength, and the second reason his managers overrated his support, remained the all but unanimous backing of the Shadow Cabinet and the party establishment. With the exception of Joseph, practically all the leading figures in the party expressed their strong support for Heath: Carr, Carrington, Whitelaw, Prior, Hailsham, Maudling and last of all – his endorsement held back for maximum effect until the eve of polling – Alec Home. They all praised Heath's vision, experience and great service to the party: conversely they emphasised, more or less explicitly, Mrs Thatcher's inexperience and narrow suburban image. Ian Gilmour warned the party against 'digging our trenches further to the right' and retiring 'behind a privet hedge'.[47] Heath's own contribution, beyond his embarrassing dinner parties, was to go on repeating that he was the leader and intended to remain the leader. Formally announcing his candidacy on 23 January – the day the poll was fixed for Tuesday 4 February – he declared on television: 'I offer myself to the party. I offer myself in the first ballot, and if there are further ballots after that I offer myself in those as well.'[48] He stamped firmly on suggestions that he might withdraw in favour of Whitelaw or Prior if he did not do win outright on the first. 'I am determined to see the procedure through. I have been a fighter all my life.'[49] The tactic, if there was one beyond sheer stubbornness, was to impress on waverers that since he was not going to give up they might as well vote for him on the first ballot to get the thing over quickly. But once again the effect was probably to convince those who wanted a change that their only course was to vote for the challenger.

When nominations closed on 30 January there was a third candidate: Hugh Fraser, a self-consciously old-fashioned right-winger who stood more explicitly than Mrs Thatcher for 'a return to identifiable Tory leadership, and to Tory themes based upon Tory principles'. His platform was a far franker repudiation of the record of 1970–4 than any of Mrs Thatcher's still coded expressions of dissent. But no one could accuse the younger son of the 16th Baron Lovat of speaking from behind a privet hedge. There was another unspoken element in Fraser's appeal: he offered a haven for traditionalists who could not stomach the idea of a woman leader. Nevertheless he was not a serious challenger; the main effect of his intervention was simply to make it harder for Heath to win on the first ballot.

All three candidates were given the opportunity to make their case in a series of articles in the *Daily Telegraph* entitled 'My Kind of Tory Party'. Heath's article was extraordinarily woolly, a familiar vague appeal to moderation, harmony ('a fundamental Conservative word'), balance and national unity. In so far as it had a theme it was the need to correct the 'imbalance . . . between the individual and those who exercise authority over him'. Of how this was to be done in practice there was not a word; while his conclusion was quite fatuously complacent: 'Let us continue the intellectual and moral renaissance which we have started in the new chapter of British politics which lies ahead. Government will then come to us again; and Government will have been deservedly achieved.'[50]

Mrs Thatcher was not very much more specific, but she started from a challenging admission that the last Conservative Government had failed: 'To deny that we failed the people is futile, as well as arrogant. Successful Governments win elections. So do parties with broadly acceptable policies. We lost.' 'One of the reasons for our electoral failure', she added, 'is that people believe that too many Conservatives have become socialists already.' This was the strongest hint she ever let slip that her election would signal the abandonment of the whole tradition of postwar Toryism, rejecting not merely Heath, but Macmillan and Churchill, 'One Nation' and the 'Middle Way' as well. For the most part she hid behind carefully coded Tory buzz words little different from the sort of language Heath and all his predecessors had used before her: 'individual freedom . . . individual prosperity . . . law and order . . . private property . . . rewards for energy, skill and thrift . . . diversity of choice'. What the implementation of these values might involve in practice was left studiously vague.[51] All that mattered was her evident ability to infuse the old values with a new fervour. As Francis Pym later admitted: 'Amidst the shambles and doubts of that time, here was one person who could articulate a point of view with conviction.'[52]

With hindsight the gathering momentum of the Thatcher campaign, coming on top of deep underlying dissatisfaction with Heath, seems unmistakable. Yet it was not obvious at the time. Most of the press – misled both by the overconfidence of the Heath camp on the one hand and Airey Neave's deliberate underplaying of the challenger's support on the other – still expected him to win. 'The fact is', *The Times* reported on 31 January, 'that Conservative Associations in all parts of the country are making known to their MPs that Mr Heath is the preferred leader . . . This . . . has become a general trend and augurs well for Mr Heath.' Since most Members were thought to be anxious above all to avoid a long-drawn-out battle, it was increasingly likely that he would win on first ballot.[53] Supposing he did not, several papers, including *The Times* itself, the *Sunday Times* and the *Observer* came out for Whitelaw. But not a single paper either supported Mrs Thatcher or tipped her to win. Even though they knew she was doing well and would probably poll around a hundred votes, the idea of a woman leader of a major party was still too outlandish to imagine.

The inability of the press – and the Tory establishment – to believe that Mrs Thatcher could win was strikingly exemplified by *The Times*, which abruptly abandoned Heath for reasons which should have led it to support Mrs Thatcher, but instead came out for Whitelaw. The overwhelming issue facing the country, it declared on 1 February, was still inflation. Hitherto Rees-Mogg had enthusiastically applauded Heath's inflation policy. Now, suddenly, he had seen the light:

In this essential respect, Mr Heath is the least suitable of the three candidates on the first ballot; he alone remains committed to his own wrong policies. He was wrong, and he will not admit he was wrong . . . Mr Heath . . . cannot offer a future to the Conservative Party so long as he is the prisoner of his own past.[54]

It seems extraordinary, after such an endorsement of the challenger's central case, that the paper could go on to conclude that the man to offer the party a new beginning was Willie Whitelaw, who had never indicated the least quarrel with Heath's policies. But Whitelaw, it believed, could unite the party, and that was what mattered. To most of Fleet Street, as the poll approached, a Whitelaw victory seemed the most likely outcome. Mrs Thatcher would probably do well enough on the first ballot to oblige Heath to stand down, whatever he might say in advance about fighting on. Then the party would rally around the emollient figure of Willie, who would somehow – by exercising the fabled skills which had brought Unionists and Nationalists together in Ulster – be able to weld his rejected predecessor, Keith Joseph and Mrs Thatcher back into a united team. This benign scenario failed to take account of the momentum that Mrs Thatcher would build up before Whitelaw even got into the ring.

On Monday there was more reassuring news for Heath. A Harris poll in the *Daily Express* found that 70 per cent of Tory voters still preferred him to any rival. (If there had to be a change a similar proportion preferred Whitelaw to Mrs Thatcher.) Then the results of the constituency soundings provided for under the election rules revealed overwhelming support for Heath over Thatcher (though with indications that some of the faithful would have liked a wider choice). For what it was worth the peers' canvass also reported a large majority for Heath.[55] The effect of this rallying of support fed the Heath camp's confidence. It was assumed too readily that MPs, returning to Westminster after spending the weekend in their constituencies, would not go against the views of their local members, so decisively expressed. In the secrecy of the ballot, however, MPs made their own judgment.

To win on the first ballot, Heath would have had to get 139 votes (the parliamentary party numbered 277), *but also* 42 votes more than Mrs Thatcher (to satisfy the 15 per cent rule). If she got 100, he would need 142. Kitson and Baker's over-optimistic head count told them that he would come quite close. Kitson reckoned on 129 'certainties' and another 17 'hopefuls'; realistically he expected something between 125 and 130.[56] Walker is said to have assured Heath he would do considerably better, between 138 and 144.[57] Even this, however, would have meant that the leader had the support of only half the party. It is difficult to see how he could have continued for long after this, even supposing he had scraped together enough extra votes – with additional challengers possibly entering the fray – to squeeze an overall majority on the second ballot. It is hard, therefore, to see on what the confidence of Heath and his supporters was based. The impression is unavoidable that they did not really analyse the figures: they simply could not imagine that he could lose. On the other side the Thatcher camp had formed a much more accurate estimate of how the votes would go. William Shelton's returns gave Heath 122 pledged votes; but he reckoned about the same number for his own candidate. That would certainly be enough to carry her into the second ballot, against Heath if he insisted on going on, or Whitelaw or whoever else came forward. She would then be in a strong position, no longer a stalking horse but a powerful contender in her own right. But this was an unwelcome prospect to many whose votes she needed on the first ballot. Neave therefore quite deliberately played down how well she was doing. To all enquirers he replied: 'Margaret is doing very well, but not quite well enough' – the implication being that she just needed a few more votes to be sure of blocking Heath, but was nowhere near winning herself. Instead of the 120-plus she really had, he let it be known that she had only about 70 pledges.[58]

There are numerous stories of how this devious tactic swung into her lap the votes of middle-of-the-road Members who did not in the least want her to win. Norman Tebbit, for instance, has claimed that he and John Nott persuaded Michael Heseltine that unless he voted for Thatcher on the first ballot he would not get a chance to vote for his preferred candidate, Whitelaw, on the second.[59] (If true, this qualifies the assertion that the whole Shadow Cabinet, with the single exception of Joseph, supported Heath.) More seriously, there was a group possibly numbering as many as 30 centre-left Members led by Sir John Rodgers and Sir Paul Bryan who had originally intended to abstain but decided at the last minute to vote for Mrs Thatcher in order to deny Heath the 15 per cent margin necessary to win.★[60] Neave's stratagem may have conned as many as 40 Tory MPs into voting for a result they did not want.

★ This was the same John Rodgers with whom, twenty-five years before when they were both newly elected Members of the 'Class of '50', Heath used to go on holiday. Paul Bryan had been one of Heath's team in the Whips' office in the late 1950s: but in later years found that Heath barely acknowledged him.[61] He was made a Minister of State at the Department of Employment in 1970, but was replaced (with the compensation of a knighthood, unusually) in 1972. Both men are good examples of Heath's failure to retain the loyalty of once close associates.

The voting took place in Committee Room 14, between 12 noon and 3.30 pm, under the eye of the officers of the 1922 Committee. Heath himself voted just before the end. As the polls closed Kitson bet Shelton £1 that Heath would get more than 130 votes; Shelton in return bet that his candidate would get more than 110.[62] Heath then made what turned out to be his last appearance as Leader at Prime Minister's questions, making his last intervention on the risk of war in the Middle East. 'He was pretty confident,' noted Tony Benn.[63] Then he went back upstairs to his room to await the result. Willie Whitelaw, Peter Walker, John Peyton and Kenneth Baker were with him when Kitson returned, grim faced, with the figures. Against all public expectations, Mrs Thatcher was actually ahead on the first ballot, with 130 votes to his 119. (Hugh Fraser secured 16; 6 Members abstained or were absent, and there were 5 spoiled ballots.)* He had lost outright, to a woman he had never considered a serious rival. There was no possibility of fighting on: he had no option but to re-sign immediately. He took the blow with his customary resilience: 'So,' he said quietly, 'we got it all wrong.'[65] Others were much more emotional than he was – not least Whitelaw, who was now placed in a most invidious position. Senior colleagues, recognising the end of an era, trooped in – some allegedly in tears – to offer sympathy. Toby Aldington was summoned from the City to help draft his letter of resignation, to take effect at once: having announced that he would not be a candidate in the second ballot he appointed Robert Carr as caretaker until the outcome was decided. Then he went home to Wilton Street.

Heath played no part in the unedifying scramble over the next few days as his former supporters, released from their loyalty to him, fell over one another in an attempt to stop the Thatcher bandwagon roll-ing on to victory. Whitelaw, as expected, was the first to come forward within hours of the first ballot, offering himself as the healer who could bind the party's self-inflicted wound. 'Today's result and Ted losing, against the wishes of the party in the country, will un-doubtedly be a traumatic experience for the party,' he declared. 'I can only hope that it might be possible for me to unite the party again.'[66] But he stood little chance unless all the others stood back to give him a free run. Instead Prior, Geoffrey Howe and John Peyton all threw

---

* One of the 'abstainers', extraordinarily, was Jim Prior, who had chosen this of all days to visit the East Midlands; his train was 1½ hours late and he reached West-minster only just in time to hear the result. 'Thank goodness', he wrote in his memoirs, 'my vote would not have made any difference. It was one of the most miserable days of my life.'[64]

their hats into the ring. Comparing notes, Prior and Howe later discovered that they were both urged to stand by Humphrey Atkins.[67] Heath made no effort to restrain them. He owed a particular debt of loyalty to Whitelaw, who could have had the leadership for the asking if he had only been prepared to stand against him; but he preferred to nurse his wounded dignity above the fray. It is doubtful whether he considered any of the rival candidates up to the job: if he had any view about who should succeed him he would probably have favoured Francis Pym.

Whoever the party chose, he did not for a moment believe that he was finished. 'They are absolutely mad to get rid of me, absolutely mad,' he expostulated to the chairman of the Parliamentary Labour Party, Cledwyn Hughes. 'I'm in reserve.' Recording this conversation in his diary, Tony Benn added hopefully: 'We may be witnessing the break-up of the Tory party.'[68] Another Labour diarist, Barbara Castle, too, still did not accept that she had necessarily lost her bet (with her husband) that Heath would still be Tory leader at the next election: 'If the Tories choose Willie Whitelaw and Heath stays in parliamentary life, I have a hunch the Tories may yet call him back.'[69] Heath certainly intended to stay in parliamentary life. He issued a statement the day after the first ballot declaring that he would not be going to the House of Lords, nor take a European job in Brussels, but would remain in the Commons to look after the interests of his constituents; after sixteen years on the Front Bench he would take a rest, enjoy the freedom from routine, and continue to contribute to national debate 'on the great issues facing Britain at home and overseas'.[70] He intended to be, as he put it, 'in reserve' when the party came to its senses.

Meanwhile there was no stopping Margaret Thatcher. With 133 votes on the first ballot she was only 6 short of the simple majority needed to win on the second. In theory, if all those who had voted for her merely to see off Heath now transferred their votes to Whitelaw she could yet have been overtaken. But in practice, by the scale and the manner of her first ballot victory she had built up an unassailable position, attracting new support from many who saw that she could not now be denied her due. By standing and winning on the first ballot she had showed the courage of a true leader: Whitelaw and the others belatedly emerging from under the defeated leader's skirts looked cowardly opportunists by comparison. Whitelaw got a respectable vote; Prior and Howe put down their markers for the future; but the result was never in doubt. The issue was settled on the second ballot: Thatcher 146; Whitelaw 79; Howe 19; Prior 19; Peyton 11. Heath cast no vote, but immediately published a message of 'warm congratulations' in which he formally wished her 'every success' in her new job.[71] He let it be clearly understood that he intended to go to the back benches.

The next day Mrs Thatcher called on him in Wilton Street. This meeting was very brief, but it quickly became the subject of bitter dispute between their rival supporters: what passed between them will probably never be known, but it set their new relationship off on a footing from which it never recovered. Mrs Thatcher's office portrayed her visit as an act of simple courtesy to her predecessor: it was announced that she had pressed him to join the Shadow Cabinet, but that he had declined. Thatcherite sources soon improved on this with stories that he had behaved like a petulant child, retorting rudely 'Won't' and 'Shan't' to her gracious approaches. Kitson, who was in the house but not in the room, utterly denies this. According to his version, Mrs Thatcher asked Heath what he was going to do now. 'Stay on as a Member of the House.' What was he going to do about the imminent referendum? 'I shall play my full part in the campaign.' Did he not think that would be better done from the Front Bench? 'No,' he replied. 'I don't want to get bogged down in organisation. I want to be out front as a campaigner.'[72] Though an accurate précis of his intentions, this may well be an elaboration of his actual words. In fact it is immaterial precisely what was said. Mrs Thatcher knew quite well before she invited herself to Wilton Street that Heath had made it clear that he would not join; and she certainly did not go to persuade him to change his mind. He was still shocked by his defeat and bitter at what he considered her – and Keith Joseph's – treachery after sitting for four years in his Cabinet. He was scarcely likely to receive her with great warmth. What infuriated Heath's supporters was that by calling on him in person she cleverly manipulated the press so that she appeared to have gone out of her way to offer an olive branch while he was seen to have snubbed her: the visit was a skilful public relations exercise designed to put him in the wrong. Kitson tried to limit the damage by keeping her talking for a few minutes himself before she emerged to the waiting cameras.[73] But with the help of some inspired briefing over the following weeks her ploy succeeded. As several other of her colleagues were to discover in the years ahead, her office too could play at 'dirty tricks'.

A few days later Heath flew off to Malaga, with Timothy and Sally Kitson, to lick his wounds in the sun.

PART SIX

Spectre at the Feast

35

Unreconciled

HEATH was just fifty-eight when he was ejected from the Tory leadership in February 1975. His rejection was the beginning of a long period of internal exile unparalleled in British political history. For fifteen – nearly sixteen – years, during the long leadership and record-breaking premiership of his successor, he remained adamantly unreconciled either to her personally or to the economic and social policies which she embraced and pursued with an evangelical vigour. He remained studiously loyal to the Conservative party, easily retained his own seat and campaigned hard at successive General Elections for the return of a Conservative Government; but he rarely had a good word for his successor. He normally contrived never even to mention her name, but regularly denounced her leadership in the strongest terms as a grotesque aberration from the true Conservative tradition represented by his predecessors and himself. For a former Prime Minister and elder statesman thus to cast himself in open and outright opposition to the leadership of his own party over a period of a decade and a half was a phenomenon unprecedented since the eighteenth century, and bitterly resented by party loyalists. Loyalty has traditionally been the Tory party's secret weapon.

Time and again over the century, each new leader has represented a sharp departure from the personality and policies of his predecessor. Bonar Law in 1911, Baldwin in 1923, Churchill in 1940, Macmillan in 1957, Home in 1963 and Heath himself in 1965 had all been in one way or another unexpected leaders who either supplanted a predecessor or came to office over the ambitions of a number of disappointed rivals. But each time the whole party swung quickly behind the new leader. Two leaders before Heath were replaced not as a result of age or ill health but because the party had lost confidence in them. Admittedly neither Arthur Balfour in 1911 nor Alec Douglas-Home in 1965 was defeated in an open challenge; but both would have been happy to carry on if mounting criticism had not persuaded them that it was time to step down. Yet both remained in politics and served with distinction under their successors. Both – but particularly Home, the more recent example and still revered in the party – were repeatedly held up to Heath as models of correct behaviour which he would do well to emulate. His stubborn refusal to do so was widely condemned – even by many who were personally sympathetic to his situation and his views – as childish, arrogant, ill-mannered and simply bad form: he was popularly labelled a 'bad loser', though as Margaret Thatcher became increasingly dominant and increasingly unpopular the lonely single-mindedness of his opposition to her acquired a sort of heroic grandeur which won him some surprising new admirers. For fifteen years he remained a lonely, glowering presence on the political scene, ever present in the House of Commons in his front-row seat below the gangway, a smouldering volcano always liable to erupt at any moment; a powerful critic yet one whose criticism could always be put down to personal pique and brushed aside. It was a sadly wasteful evening to what had been a career of extraordinary dynamism and purpose.

Yet it need not have been like this. Though rejected by Tory MPs, he retained a strong following in the country, both among Conservatives who had never wanted to see him overthrown and among the electorate at large. His popularity strikingly increased as soon as he was no longer leader. There was considerable support for the message he continued to preach. It was humanly very understandable that he should feel bruised by his dismissal, very right and proper that he should wish to withdraw for a while to the back benches. By doing so he actually did the honourable thing, giving Mrs Thatcher breathing space to establish her own authority. She should have been grateful to him for that. By the same token, however, by maintaining his attitude of frozen disdain over the next four years he made it possible for her to marginalise him and ultimately to exclude him from office in 1979. Had he played his cards differently she would have found it hard to resist the powerful instinct for unity in the party which from February 1975 onwards deplored the split between the two leaders and yearned for them to get back together in the interest of defeating Labour. Had he, after a decent interval, been more magnanimous, the odium would have fallen on her if she declined to bring him back. As so often, however, Heath was his own worst enemy. It was partly that magnanimity was not in his character. But it was also an aspect of his honesty: dissembling was not in his character either. He could not feign, like many politicians, a generosity he did not feel, nor loyalty to policies he did not approve.

It was not only injured pride that prevented him embracing Mrs Thatcher with any conviction, though it played a part. He also fundamentally disagreed with her on central areas of policy; as a result, he persuaded himself that she would be a short-term leader, a lightweight stop-gap whose inadequacy would soon be exposed by events. He continued to believe right up to 1990 that the party would eventually come to its senses. If this was a misjudgment, it was one widely shared by his former colleagues who up to 1979 and well into her first term still provided most of Mrs Thatcher's Front Bench. Even if Mrs Thatcher had failed, however, as most of them privately expected, few if any of his former colleagues shared his delusion that the party would ever return to him. It had only voted for her in the first place because she was not him. Since, on the contrary, she proved as lucky and electorally successful as he had been unlucky and unsuccessful it was a massive misjudgment to cast himself as her unforgiving foe. But the truth was that either way, whether Mrs Thatcher crashed or triumphed, he would have retained greater influence with the party – either to moderate her policies or to dispose of her and help determine her successor – had he been seen to support her loyally, as Home had supported him. He was never going to regain the leadership, but he still held a strong position in the party in 1975. But he threw it away.

On winning the leadership Mrs Thatcher moved quickly to establish her authority. Simply by being a woman and projecting a fresher and younger image she signalled a new beginning for the Tory party after the traumatic events of the previous fifteen months. Yet both in terms of policy and personnel she had to go cautiously. She had no mandate to lead the party rapidly to the right; she inherited a Shadow Cabinet almost all of whom had voted for her predecessor and remained broadly loyal to his convictions. However much she might feel privately that Willie Whitelaw, Jim Prior, Francis Pym and others were tarred with the policies which she and Keith Joseph had repudiated, she was in no position to undertake a purge. Whatever her own instincts and long-term intentions, so long as she remained in opposition – right up to 1979 – she was obliged to curb them and conduct herself like any other party leader concerned in the first instance with keeping her party united. Accordingly she made only minor changes in the Shadow Cabinet. She dropped Peter Walker,

Robert Carr and Geoffrey Rippon, plus two of Heath's younger promotions, Paul Channon and Nick Scott. In their places she brought in her own campaign manager, Airey Neave; Angus Maude (whom Heath had sacked in 1965); and most symbolically, as party chairman in place of Whitelaw, the 65-year-old Lord Thorneycroft (who had famously resigned from the Treasury in 1957 in what was now seen as the first stirring of monetarist protest against Macmillan's inflation); but also Norman Fowler, Michael Heseltine, Sally Oppenheim and George Younger (none of them notably 'Thatcherite'). To compensate for the loss of Heath she resurrected Reggie Maudling to be Shadow Foreign Secretary.* Keith Joseph took overall charge of policy development, with Geoffrey Howe as Shadow Chancellor. For the rest she was still surrounded by Heath's old guard of Whitelaw, Carrington, Pym, Prior, Gilmour – and even Hailsham.

She made more sweeping changes at Central Office. Thorneycroft replaced Whitelaw and William Clark replaced Sara Morrison. Angus Maude took over from Ian Gilmour as Chairman of the Research Department. Chris Patten remained as Director of the CRD, but its role was seriously usurped by Joseph's Centre for Policy Studies, headed by the ideologically extreme Alfred Sherman. These new dispositions were all to be expected of a new leader. But Mrs Thatcher also abruptly sacked Michael Wolff from his newly created position as Director-General of the party organisation; this, as it seemed to them, unnecessary vengeance so infuriated Prior and Carr that they withheld their votes for a time in protest. (Heath was still out of the country.) It was a foretaste of things to come, but for the moment an isolated exercise of the new leader's style.

Heath returned from Spain on 18 March and wasted no time in signalling that he did not intend to fade discreetly out of sight. First he gave a television interview in which he repeated his intention of remaining for the present on the back benches, concentrating primarily on foreign affairs, but made it clear that he did not expect to remain on the back benches for ever. (Nor would he accept a peerage.)[2] Then he spoke to the Greater London Young Conservatives, meeting in Hastings on 5 April. (The YCs – then a markedly left-of-centre and pro-European pressure group within the party – were to be a favourite audience in the next few years. He flattered them by

---

* Maudling did not last long. No one could have been less sympathetic to the Thatcher style. Jim Prior thought his days were numbered when he recalled in Shadow Cabinet – ostensibly of Jimmy Carter – Churchill's remark that 'If you feed a grub on royal jelly it may grow into a Queen bee.'[1]

addressing them as 'the future', while they flattered his belief that he had a special *rapport* with 'youth'.)

Disdaining even to mention Mrs Thatcher, let alone to pledge his loyalty, he set out his stall for the next few years: he would not admit that he could have done anything differently between 1970 and 1974: 'I believed then, and I still believe, that I was absolutely right.' But there was a new quality visible in this first speech. 'His forthright delivery . . . showed a new public style and ability to put his case effectively. He also showed a new knock-about humour.' (He even offered an impersonation of Harold Wilson.)[3] After years of reading woodenly from Civil Service or Research Department scripts, Heath could now – for the first time in his life – speak to the electorate unmuzzled.

By a curious quirk of timing, he was presented almost immediately with a matchless platform from which to proclaim his undiminished stature and centrality in British politics. Following Jim Callaghan's successful 'renegotiation' of the 'Tory terms' on which Britain had entered the EEC in 1973, the divided Labour Cabinet had accepted the device of a referendum to let the people decide whether or not the country should stay in the Community. Despite the change in the Tory leadership, Europe was pre-eminently Heath's issue, and Mrs Thatcher – a loyal but never more than lukewarm European – had no practical choice but to stand back and let him, as President of the Conservative Campaign for Europe, lead the party's campaign. (He was also, with Reggie Maudling and Willie Whitelaw, one of eight vice-presidents, under Roy Jenkins, of the all-party pro-EEC umbrella organisation, Britain in Europe.) Their still unequal relationship, at least where Europe was concerned, was dramatically underlined when she formally launched the Tory campaign at a rally at the St Ermin's Hotel on 16 April. Heath, in the chair, listened 'with obvious approval and admiration' as his successor paid fulsome tribute to his achievement in taking Britain into the Community. 'You have done more than anyone else', she told him, 'to ensure Britain's place in Europe.' And she went on, in terms which she would never again be heard to use of him or anyone else, except perhaps Ronald Reagan: 'It is naturally with some temerity that the pupil speaks before the master, because you know more about it than the rest of us.'[4] No wonder Heath listened approvingly. This was in his view the correct and proper way for her to refer to him. If she had only continued to defer to him in this manner he might in time have come round to a fatherly tolerance of her efforts to fill his shoes.

Europe was *his* issue, and he let no one forget it. He had been

against the referendum and scornful of Labour's cosmetic 'renegotiation', which he insisted had achieved nothing that could not have
been secured 'within the natural pattern of the Community's development'.[5] But now he welcomed the chance to settle the issue
once and for all. Though of course he strenuously denied it, he had
always been vulnerable to the charge that he had dragooned the
country into Europe without the 'full-hearted consent of the British
people' which he had declared in 1970 to be necessary. Now the referendum offered the chance to secure that consent unequivocally;
and the polls, after years of reflecting hostility or indifference to
Europe, suggested that with the leaders of all three parties now once
again in favour of staying in, the public was likely to agree. The prize
for Heath was to secure finally the one historic achievement of his
Government, and he threw himself into the campaign with rediscovered vigour, as though the humiliations of the past twelve
months had never been. 'In the eyes of the public', David Butler and
Uwe Kitzinger wrote in their Nuffield volume on the referendum,
'there is no doubt that Ted Heath, indefatigably stumping the
country, was still the leading Conservative pro-Marketeer.'[6] He
appeared on television twice as many times during the campaign as
Mrs Thatcher – 23 times against 11 – and the victory when it was
won was very widely credited to him.

He pitched his appeal at two levels. On one hand was the lofty
positive case he had always made for Britain to regain her lost influence in the world by taking her proper place as part of Europe; on
the other he did not shrink from a strong and often highly personal-
ised attack on the left – above all Tony Benn – who wanted for their
own political ends to take Britain out of the Community. For most
of the campaign it was notable that he largely ignored the dissident
Tory case against Europe, most prominently expounded by Enoch
Powell; but he did specifically answer Powell's apocalyptic warnings
about loss of sovereignty before the campaign began, in the Commons debate on 9 April approving the Government's renegotiated
terms. This was his first speech in the House since February, and
here too it was immediately noticeable how much more freely he
spoke now that he was, for virtually the first time in his career, released from Front Bench responsibility. His speech and Powell's
were the high points of a dull debate. He insisted that all along the
'first purpose' of the Community had been political: initially to foster
Franco–German *rapprochement* and contain Germany within a European framework, now to build Europe's independent strength
vis-à-vis the United States and the Soviet Union. This, he accepted,
did indeed involve some sacrifice of sovereignty:

To me, sovereignty is not something to be hoarded, sterile and barren, carefully protected by the right hon. Member for Down South [Powell] in a great coat with its collar turned up. Nor is sovereignty something which has to be kept in the crypt to be inspected by my right hon. Friend the Member for Banbury [Neil Marten] on the eve of the opening of Parliament.

Sovereignty is something for us as custodians to use in the interests of our own country . . . It is a judgement which we have to make, and I answer without hesitation that the sacrifice of sovereignty, if it be put in that extreme form, or the sharing of sovereignty, the transfer of sovereignty or the offering of sovereignty is fully justified. Indeed, were we not to do so in the modern world, I believe that as a Parliament, as a party and as a Government we should be culpable in the eyes of history. I believe therefore that sovereignty is for this House to use as it thinks best.[7]

The Government won approval for the renegotiated terms by a majority of 226; but more than half the parliamentary Labour party, including 38 ministers, voted against.

Heath's main argument for staying in the Community was, as always, that Britain would be left behind by history if it chose to come out. But he expounded this case with more eloquence and historical perspective in this campaign than ever before. It was 'a tragedy', he argued in an unusually well-written article in *The Times* on 2 June, that Britain had 'allowed herself to succumb to the delusion that the "splendid isolation" of the Victorian age was the norm rather than the exception', and that some should still be 'proffering the myth that in the modern world Britain can survive alone . . . The gulf that separates the pro- and anti-Europeans', he asserted, was 'less about sovereignty or economics and much more about the capacity of Britain to face reality'.

The anti-Europeans want to freeze the past. Their talk of sovereignty would only make sense if the Royal Navy ruled the waves and gunboats could be dispatched anywhere in the world. Their talk of trade only makes sense in terms of colonial territories buying goods at prices which suit the British exporter. And their talk about food only makes sense with an empire supplying food to the mother country at prices that suit the British importer.

Those days, he insisted, had gone for good. By pretending otherwise the anti-Marketeers were creating expectations which could no longer be fulfilled. By contrast Europe offered a positive role for the future:

> The European Community presents us with the opportunity to channel our experience and skill towards great and constructive causes: the security of the western democracies, the renewal of a prosperity for the benefit of all our people and new sources of help for the developing nations of the world. These are noble objectives. They can only be achieved by Britain inside the European Community. It is this which gives us the opportunity in the modern world to fulfil ourselves as a nation.[8]

This was perhaps Heath's best exposition of his European vision in all his years of advocacy; it formed the basis of his appeal throughout the referendum campaign. Yet it must be admitted that it was still a cloudy vision. When he spoke of sharing sovereignty he was careful not to spell out what this might mean in practice. There was not a word about the future development of the Community, the powers of the Commission or the Parliament, of economic and monetary union – even though this had been agreed in principle in 1972 – let alone political union. From the perspective of the arguments of the 1990s – about a common currency, common defence policy and federalism – it is fair to say that Heath and the 'Yes' campaigners kept very quiet about these ultimate objectives, assuming they had fully formulated them. Perhaps they had not. While employing a lofty political rhetoric which admittedly implied something bigger than a mere free trade area, it was characteristic of the pro-Europeans at this period that they invariably seemed to follow the precept of Cardinal Newman's hymn: 'I do not ask to see the distant scene: one step enough for me.' This was unquestionably good politics, from the point of view of inducing an insular British electorate to take the plunge, and not necessarily consciously dishonest. Yet there is undeniably a case for saying that Parliament in 1971 and the country in 1975 was hoodwinked into signing up for more than it was ever told. Ultimate political union may have been implicit in 1975, as Heath would afterwards strenuously claim; but it was certainly not explicit. Later problems might have been less if it had been. On the other hand, as the pro-Europeans undoubtedly feared, Britain might have elected to stay shivering on Dover beach.

In the campaign proper, Heath concentrated on nailing what he called the 'accumulated myths' of the 'No' campaign and painting a grim picture of the consequences of withdrawal. Everywhere he spoke on joint all-party platforms with Labour and Liberal pro-Marketeers – particularly Roy Jenkins and Reg Prentice, Jeremy Thorpe and David Steel. This was a real campaign for Europe such as had never been possible within the straitjacket of party politics. Most of those who took part found it an enormously refreshing experience: in the minds of Labour pro-Europeans like Jenkins and Shirley Williams in particular it sowed a seed which was later to bear fruit in the foundation of the SDP and the Alliance. For Heath the referendum campaign was a tantalising realisation of the sort of national coalition he had been advocating the previous October – with himself the *de facto* leader of all the constructive, forward-looking forces in the country against the reactionary extremists of right and left. For three weeks Mrs Thatcher was marginalised. Wherever he went he was rapturously received – for instance at Leeds Town Hall on 31 May: 'There was no doubting Mr Heath's new-found, or rediscovered, popularity when he appeared looking aggressively bronzed . . . The 2,000-strong crowd rose cheering and clapping as he came in, followed by the uncrowned king of the moderates, Mr Prentice . . . and by the huge form of Mr Cyril Smith.'[9]

On 22 May he was involved in a heated televised debate with Michael Foot, whom he successfully needled with the taunt that the left's vaunted belief in the brotherhood of man did not 'extend beyond Margate'.[10] But the most memorable occasion of the campaign was a debate at the Oxford Union, broadcast live by the BBC, in which Heath and Thorpe faced Barbara Castle and Peter Shore. Mrs Castle was taken aback by the 'adulation' Heath received from the undergraduates before dinner: 'The catcalls of delight were uncontainable. It was a near pandemonium of enthusiasm . . . Heath was the hero of the hour, as he never had been as PM.' When it came to the debate itself, she recorded, 'the most remarkable phenomenon of the evening was Heath'.

> The audience was all his, and he responded to it with a genuineness which was the most impressive thing I have ever seen from him. He stood there, speaking simply, strongly and without a note. They gave him a standing ovation at the end, and he deserved it for the best example I have ever seen of The Man Who Came Back . . .

Afterwards, following a resounding vote for staying in the community, 'Everyone was congratulating Heath and I did too . . . Heath was at his warmest and most natural and thanked me genuinely for the nice things I said to him.' 'The only wry satisfaction' Mrs Castle drew from the evening was 'the realisation of what Mrs Thatcher was up against too'.[11]

Throughout the campaign the polls had pointed to a solid endorsement for staying in, and so it proved: on a good turn out, 67 per cent voted 'Yes', 32 per cent 'No'. The anti-Marketeers who had schemed so persistently for a referendum in the belief that a popular vote would repudiate the mandate to lead Britain into the Community which Heath had claimed in 1971 were hoist with their own petard. During all-day celebrations at the Waldorf Hotel next day, the two leaders of the 'Yes' campaign, Heath and Jenkins, were given heroes' receptions. *The Times* gave due credit to Jenkins, but pride of place to Heath:

> The Achilles of the European cause was Mr Heath. He throughout used the simple, central arguments which go to the heart of political discussion. He spoke with a freedom which he did not show when he had the responsibilities of a Prime Minister or a Party Leader, as a man can speak who has nothing on his mind except to express his own convictions about important matters. The quality, particularly the simplicity and seriousness of Mr Heath's contribution to the referendum debate showed him to be his country's leading statesman, more clearly now than in the height of his power.[12]

The principal loser of the referendum campaign, Tony Benn, was swiftly removed by Harold Wilson from the Department of Industry and politically emasculated within the Labour Cabinet. But the principal winner gained no corresponding reward – partly at least because he did not claim it. This was the moment when, with his pride restored, from a position of renewed public and party approbation, Heath could have gracefully endorsed his successor, even smothered her – however patronisingly – with promises of his support. She was in no position to spurn him. In the House of Commons, on the Monday after the referendum, she paid generous tribute to his performance in the campaign. 'Head in hand, stony-faced,' George Hutchinson reported in *The Times*, 'he made no acknowledgement.'[13] Many Tory MPs were very angry at this gross snub. It would have been so easy just to incline his head: it must have taken extraordinary self-control to stop himself. In a way this tiny episode, spoiling the general atmosphere of mutual congratulation, was a declaration of war: or at least a clear refusal to make peace. A few days later Mrs Thatcher responded by leaking her version of what happened at Wilton Street in February. She insisted that she had invited him to join the Shadow Cabinet, and allowed herself to be quoted graphically and verbatim: 'His reply was instantaneous. I remember it vividly. He turned his head away until it was in profile and said, "No. I've made my position perfectly clear in my statement last week. I'm going to spend a period on the back benches."' She confirmed that the conversation had been very brief and that she had stayed talking to Kitson for several minutes before leaving the house.[14]

Heath was visiting Canada when this interview appeared. On his return he issued a statement of his own angrily denying the 'mischievous reports' circulating about his behaviour that day and particularly the 'monstrous allegations made about a lack of courtesy shown in my own home'. 'I must state categorically', he wrote, 'that there was no discourtesy of any kind at any time, as Mrs Thatcher and Sir Timothy Kitson can confirm ... I was grateful to Mrs Thatcher for coming to see me.' (This was polite but untrue.) 'We spent the time during her visit together.' (This was simply untrue.) Then he unequivocally restated his position:

As she knows, I have consistently maintained my decision ... publicly announced on February 5, not to remain on the front bench but to concentrate on the great issues facing Britain and overseas. That I have been able to do during the referendum campaign at home and on visits abroad. That I shall continue to do in the future.[15]

In the same statement he offered a small olive branch by congratulating the party, Mrs Thatcher and the successful candidate on the result of a recent by-election in West Woolwich – the party's first victory under the new leadership. But this gesture was overshadowed by the extraordinary spectacle of the two leaders publicly squabbling over who had said what to whom. Some Thatcher loyalists condemned Heath's statement for still falling short of a full endorsement. But Norman Tebbit was quick to pronounce it 'satisfactory', since it confirmed authoritatively that he had stayed out of the Shadow Cabinet at his own request.[16] That suited Mrs Thatcher.

For the moment it suited Heath too. He had supreme confidence that the party and the country would in due course realise that he had been, as he invariably put it, 'telling the truth' about the country's situation. He saw no possibility of his inexperienced successor growing into the job which she had so inappropriately snatched, and every likelihood that a government of national unity would soon be required to rescue the country from the crisis into which Labour was plunging it ever deeper. He was not worried that by so conspicuously standing aloof he was cutting himself off from his friends and natural allies who had felt obliged to follow the new leader. Whitelaw above all, having stood against her himself and lost, felt bound in honour to give Mrs Thatcher his total loyalty. The other unrepentant 'Heathites', as they were beginning to be called – Carrington, Prior, Gilmour and the rest – were distressed by his conduct, which seemed to cast them as turncoats for having taken Mrs Thatcher's shilling. As a result they had no choice but to emphasise repeatedly their fealty to the new régime. Carrington in particular made several efforts over the next few years to effect a reconciliation. But Heath, like Greta Garbo, preferred to be alone. He not only maintained little contact with his former colleagues inside the Shadow Cabinet; he made no attempt to link up with Peter Walker, the other principal dissident whom she had dropped from the Front Bench. He scorned to run any sort of cabal. He simply bided his time, speaking his mind to the Young Conservatives, the Tory Reform Group and any other party grouping that would invite him, waiting to be recalled.

Once he had got over the shock, in fact, he began positively to enjoy the new freedom his unattached position gave him. Except for a few months in 1950 he had never been a backbencher before, at liberty to speak on any subject he wished. He had been a Whip, a Minister, a Shadow Minister, Leader of the Opposition and Prime Minister. Now for the first time he was responsible to no one, yet as an ex-Prime Minister he commanded a national – and international – audience. Not only that. He was free to travel the world – usually at someone else's expense; free to sail all summer if he wanted; and free to exploit his celebrity to conduct choirs and orchestras – especially abroad – as he had never been able to do before. Finally, he was able to celebrate all three of these activities in a series of best-selling books which brought him an entirely new audience and a new popularity – as well as a lot of money. His ejection from the cares of leadership was in some ways a rebirth.

He travelled extensively, but without the singleness of purpose of Mrs Thatcher's compulsive globe-trotting after her dismissal in 1990–1. During 1975 he visited Spain, Italy, France, Germany, Ireland, Switzerland, the United States and Canada (twice), China, Hong Kong, Japan and Singapore, and Jordan. Sometimes it was to address an International Chamber of Commerce, the Confederation of German Industries, or French wine growers; sometimes it was to speak at an American university, an international conference or some institution of international good will like the European Youth Centre in Strasbourg; following his successful visit the year before, he returned to China at the invitation of the Chinese Government, and met Mao again; and at the turn of the year he went to Jordan as the personal guest of King Hussein. In subsequent years the pattern was much the same, with frequent short trips to Western Europe and America and longer tours of the Middle East and the Far East. He went back almost every year to Peking, where he was an established favourite of the elderly leadership; but never to Moscow nor – except for one trip in 1977 to Yugoslavia and Romania – anywhere in Eastern Europe. In addition, in 1978 he became a member of the 'North-South Commission' chaired by Willy Brandt: this opened up a whole new area of global travel to examine at first hand the problems of the undeveloped world.

Unlike his successor, Heath generally observed the convention that British politicians abroad do not indulge in domestic politics. In America he spoke in broad terms of the 'crisis of confidence' that he believed Britain was going through – but always optimistically, expressing confidence that the country would come through. In Europe, at international colloquia on the future of capitalism, he did somewhat pointedly condemn those who too 'stridently' lauded the miracle of the free market.[17] Naturally he propagated his belief in balanced economic management, international co-operation and progress towards European unity. Undoubtedly his *amour propre* was massaged by being treated – especially in China – as a senior world statesman. But he did not tour the world making calculated mischief either for the Labour Government or for Mrs Thatcher by overtly promoting himself at their expense. When he wanted to speak about domestic politics he came back to the House of Commons.

Sometimes it was music that took him abroad. In April 1975 André Previn invited him to conduct the LSO in Elgar's *Cockaigne* (very much his signature piece) at two concerts in Cologne and Bonn; the next year he conducted the Chicago Symphony Orchestra; and from 1978 he developed a continuing association with the European Community Youth Orchestra (thereby combining two of his political interests in a musical context). At home he undertook an increasingly busy programme: in October 1975, for instance – just after returning from the Far East – he conducted the English Chamber Orchestra in an all-Mozart programme at the Windsor Festival, and a few days later the Bournemouth Symphony Orchestra in the first half of a gala evening to raise funds for a new concert hall. (On this occasion he conducted Beethoven's Eighth and his old friend Moura Lympany in Franck's *Symphonic Variations*.) Now that he was out of office, his conducting seemed less of a gimmick; the phenomenon of a politician who could do such things began to win him more appreciation than it had done before. He began to appear on television in a musical role, showing the public a side of himself which he had previously kept hidden: the first time in July 1975 as the guest of the American jazz pianist Oscar Peterson, then a few months later on the Michael Parkinson Show, when he played his clavier while Dame Edith Evans recited Shakespeare.[18] The ex-Prime Minister was making a supplementary career in show business.

Then there was sailing. As a result of the loss of the third *Morning Cloud* the previous September Heath had to move quickly if he was to have another boat in time to compete in the trials for the 1975 Admiral's Cup. He did: *Morning Cloud* IV was designed and built in four months flat, of aluminium alloy rather than wood, and launched on 10 May 1975. (The successive *Morning Clouds* were never in fact numbered, but it is the only way to distinguish them.) Time was too short, however, to master the new boat before the trials and for the first time since he had taken up serious sailing in 1969 Heath and his crew were not selected; in fact 1975 was their least successful season overall. 1976 was not much better: that year the press got more copy from *Morning Cloud*'s embarrassments – colliding with a buoy in the Solent, running aground near Ramsgate – than from any famous victories. So *Morning Cloud* V – 44ft, aluminium again, said to have cost £65,000 – was launched in good time for the 1977 Admiral's Cup. This time Heath regained his place in the British team, though not as captain; but Britain did not win. That autumn *Morning Cloud* was a member of the EEC team in the Southern Cross races off Australia; but still Heath could not recover his winning ways of the early 1970s. The professionalism which he had then brought to a still amateurish sport was now matched by other crews; boat design was improving all the time and Heath could no longer command the best. The last time he competed in the Admiral's Cup was 1979. That was the year of the great storm which wreaked havoc on the Fastnet Race: many boats and seventeen crew were lost. *Morning Cloud* almost capsized in the massive seas; two men were nearly washed overboard, and Heath himself was thrown across the cabin and badly bruised. 'It was the worst experience I ever had,' he confessed later. 'It was very frightening – the sort of thing you would never want to experience again.' From that time he began to withdraw from ocean racing.[19]

It was the story of his earlier achievements in sailing, however, which provided the subject of his first book. There was no question yet of Heath, like other ex-prime ministers, writing his memoirs. So far as he was concerned he was still in mid-career: he regarded the party's vote in February 1975 as no more than a temporary interruption. Lord Longford, however, then chairman of the publishers Sidgwick & Jackson, shrewdly suggested that there would be a market for his sailing experiences, a lavishly illustrated account, aimed at the general reader, of how he had come in the space of a few years from messing around in small dinghies at Broadstairs to winning the Sydney–Hobart race and the Admiral's Cup. Heath dictated the book very quickly that summer – the text is only around 40,000 words – and provided most of the pictures (including 32 pages in colour). Simply entitled *Sailing: A Course of My Life*, it was published in time for Christmas at the beginning of December. Helped by four weeks' serialisation in the *Sunday Times* and an intensive programme of signing sessions in bookshops all round the country, it sold phenomenally: 90,000 copies in the first year, over 100,000 in all. American, Japanese and French editions followed. Heath was delighted.

Music offered an obvious follow up for 1976, and Heath duly obliged. The format was the same: basically autobiographical, slightly didactic, aimed at a non-specialist audience, copiously illustrated with pictures of the author playing and conducting and of other great musicians and performers mentioned in the text. Once again Sidgwick had judged the market perfectly. *Music: A Joy for Life* sold 42,000 in advance orders before it even appeared, 60,000 by the end of the year. Touring the country by special train, Heath made 37 radio and 11 television broadcasts and attended 33 signing sessions in 22 days. He claimed that he enjoyed meeting people. At his reported rate of 300 signatures an hour the chance of extensive conversation was limited; but he certainly enjoyed the sensation of the public flocking to see him. So assiduous was he that it was soon said that the rare copies of his books were the unsigned ones.

In January 1977 Jean Rook interviewed him for the *Daily Express*, wondering at the phenomenon of 'the "stuffy" ex-Premier who's suddenly a huge favourite. Today he's a roaring success as an author, but why didn't it happen when he was trying to save the country?' A longstanding fan herself, she believed that his books had allowed the public for the first time to see the real man. 'Now, if you mention he is friendly, amusing, has a beautiful cosy home, drinks, swears, is very good with women . . . people who have read his books don't look at you as if you are mad.'[20]

After *Sailing* and *Music* it was difficult to see how he could keep the golden goose laying; but he managed one more title for 1977. This was *Travels: People and Places in My Life*, frankly a pot-boiler, composed of conventional holiday snaps with a banal commentary recalling his foreign journeys from his first schoolboy trip to Paris to later visits to foreign leaders. Though in a sense the most auto-biographical of the three it was also the most impersonal, lacking the passion which even Heath's wooden prose had been unable to suppress entirely in the other two. *Travels* sold very respectably (around 40,000 copies), but it was the last of the lucrative line – except that in 1977 Heath also produced, as a spin-off from his now nationally known Broadstairs carol concert, *Carols: The Joy of Christmas*. An attractively illustrated collection of forty favourite carols, with words and music, each prefaced with a short personal introduction, *Carols* was a simple idea which usefully filled a real need; it sold 10,000 in hardback and paperback and is still one of the best collections of its kind.

These four books, published in the space of three years, netted Heath something like £300,000. He needed the money, since in his years of power he had acquired some expensive tastes. An element of mystery has always surrounded Heath's personal finances, which have given rise to persistent speculation. Every time he ordered a new *Morning Cloud*, the press and Labour MPs would wonder how he was able to afford it. In fact there is not much to explain. In addition to his MP's salary since 1950, Heath had enjoyed a Cabinet Minister's salary (£5,000) for nine years from 1955, before becoming Leader of the Opposition (£4,500) and then Prime Minister (£14,000 rising to £20,000 in 1972). His outgoings, on the other hand, particularly up to 1965 were relatively low. He had no wife or children to support, no school fees, and he had never owned a house. His flat in Petty France was no more than a cupboard; Albany was smart but inexpensive; Wilton Street he rented on favourable terms from the Grosvenor Estate; when he went to Broadstairs he stayed with his father and stepmother. His piano he was able to buy in 1963 with the proceeds of his Charlemagne Prize: his first stereo system was given him by his grateful constituency to mark his tenth year in Parliament in 1960. Apart from a partiality for champagne, sailing was the one major expense his income had to bear.

Clearly he had no cushion of inherited capital like most previous Conservative leaders. But partly for this reason, by 1965 far more of the expenses of his office were met either by the party or by the tax-payer than had been the case with previous leaders. It was revealed in 1975 that between 1968 and 1970 his assets had been managed – without his detailed knowledge – by Slater Walker (advising Brown, Shipley) who invested on his behalf in 'special situations' not open to the general public, securing a 60 per cent return on £30,000 in two years.[21] This must have helped with the first *Morning Cloud*. In

November 1975 Heath tried to get an injunction to prevent the *Sunday Times* publishing these matters; when Sir Peter Rawlinson's efforts were unavailing, he issued a writ against the paper (which at that very moment was serialising *Sailing*), but later dropped it. There was in fact no suggestion of impropriety. It was Slater Walker the *Sunday Times* was investigating: it only used Heath as an example of Jim Slater's methods.

On becoming Prime Minister in 1970 Heath sold all his shares. ('It cost me a great deal of money,' he told the *Sunday Telegraph* ruefully.)[22] When he left Downing Street he lost first his prime ministerial salary and then the Leader of the Opposition's salary too. But he had a prime ministerial pension (then £10,000) to supplement his basic MP's pay; and a group of businessmen organised by Lord Aldington helped with the cost of the substantial private office he has continued to maintain to this day. While outstandingly generous in many respects and lavish with presents for those who have served him, Heath is distinctly good at getting other people to pay for his major expenses – particularly his travelling and associated hospitality. He is an expensive guest nowadays, since he has come to expect the best wherever he goes.

Yet still he has no 'serious' money. Since 1975 he has needed to earn it to keep up the style of living to which he has become accustomed. The huge success of *Sailing* and *Music* was a great help just when he needed it, and certainly helped pay for the fourth and fifth *Morning Cloud*s. In addition as a roving elder statesman he has been able to command large fees on the international lecture circuit, particularly in Europe and America, plus appearance money for television programmes, even in the late 1980s for a series of advertisements for English cheese. Apart from a few months after the 1964 election, however, when he briefly rejoined Brown, Shipley, he has never sat in a British boardroom or lent his name to a City letterhead. His one well-chosen commercial involvement was to join, in January 1978, the public review board of the international accountancy firm, Arthur Andersen. Heath was the first non-American to be invited, joining such senior figures as former US Treasury Secretary William Simon: the function of the review board is essentially to lend prestige to the firm's worldwide operations. In addition to the undisclosed salary, Heath has been able to do much of his globe-trotting in recent years – particularly to China – on Arthur Andersen business. He told the *Sunday Times*:

My job is to ensure that they maintain a high standard of ethics, integrity and performance. They have more than 200 offices throughout the world, and I can go into any one of them, talk to the partners, staff and clients and form a judgement as to whether they are performing properly. I've probably visited more of their offices than anyone else in the firm.[23]

With all these varied interests, then, Heath was not depressed for long after his relegation to the back benches in 1975. He remained confident that one way or another he would soon be recalled to the country's, if not necessarily the party's, colours. ('You never know what might happen in politics,' he told Jean Rook.)[24] Meanwhile he intended to make the most of his new-found freedom. Thus while politically he gave the appearance of bitterness, privately he was soon more relaxed and happy than he had been for years. In truth he rather enjoyed his public feud with Mrs Thatcher since – at least until 1982 – he continued to regard her as an insignificant lightweight whom the party would soon cast off. Eleven months after his dismissal, Lord Lambton paid tribute to his multi-faceted resurrection.

In the last year he has given a dazzling display of virtuosity: solemn in defeat, indefatigable in the EEC campaign, brave at sea, humorous on television, senatorial on radio, oratorical in the House and musical in Broadstairs. He has presented myriad faces to the public and has seldom been off the front page. Whatever 'that woman' can do, he has seemed to say, 'I can do better'. And in some ways he has proved his point.[25]

One sadness marred this astonishing year. On 15 October his father died, aged eighty-seven. He had grown quite close to the old man in recent years, though he went to Broadstairs less often than he might have done because he could not stand his second stepmother, Mary, whom William Heath had married in 1964 after the death of Doris. But he made a point of involving his father in his own plea-sure at being Prime Minister, inviting him frequently to Downing Street and Chequers. Colleagues and staff were always touched by how considerate Heath was to the old man, and struck by how nice, simple and quietly proud William was of his boy. Heath was a more than dutiful son, and was on occasion sharply critical of others who in his view failed to care properly for their aged parents. He was also devoted to his brother John, still working as a borough surveyor in Harrow; but in 1982 John too died, leaving Heath with no close rela-tives at all.

In the summer of 1976 he celebrated his sixtieth birthday with a splendid party on a boat on the Thames, the first of many such events over the next fifteen years which he held to mark not only successive birthdays but the anniversaries of all the major milestones of his life: his first election to Parliament, the General Election victory that made him Prime Minister, Britain's entry into the EEC. It is perhaps the fact of having no remaining family that leads Heath to make such public events of his private celebrations, inviting former colleagues and associates from every period of his life to relive the memory of his triumphs. The hospitality is lavish, but the blatant purpose of these occasions is the glorification of the host. There is in Ted Heath a strong element of Mr Toad. With the passing years and the diminishing likelihood of a comeback, the emphasis has become increasingly retrospective. But at his sixtieth birthday party he was still looking confidently forward.

The Tory party which gathered in Blackpool in October 1975 for its first conference since the change of leader – and the first since losing power – was a deeply worried and distracted party, still uncertain how its leap in the dark in February would turn out. After a brief surge of support in the spring, the party's poll rating had fallen back by September to where it was a year before, level pegging with Labour in the low-to-middle thirties. Mrs Thatcher had by no means yet established her authority, while Heath – with the referendum campaign and a couple of revelatory speeches in the House – had had a triumphant summer. An opinion poll found that 33 per cent of Tory voters wished he was still leader.[26] Loyal Conservatives had been embarrassed by the two leaders' public conflict of evidence over what had occurred in Wilton Street; they were disturbed and increasingly angry at Heath's apparent inability to accept his dismissal. Already Bernard Levin in *The Times* could write that 'Mr Heath's prolonged fit of the sulks' was doing great damage to the party.[27] Levin was not alone in urging Mrs Thatcher to make him a renewed unambiguous offer of a job worthy of him, and urging him to accept it. Most delegates were desperate to see Heath take the opportunity at Blackpool to affirm publicly and unequivocally his acceptance of the verdict of February and his willingness to serve his successor in any appropriate capacity. But if that were to happen, the new leader and the old had somehow to be stage-managed on and off the platform without an awkward confrontation. The same delicate quadrille was to be re-enacted every October for the next sixteen years. It was announced in advance that Heath did not intend to speak, but on the Wednesday morning he took his place in the front row on the platform. His appearance in the hall was the signal for a standing ovation of astonishing warmth and duration. Mrs Thatcher applauded with the rest. But he did not have to pass her to get to his seat, so they had no chance to meet until the end of the session. Then it was Mrs Thatcher who took the initiative: 'As they both rose to leave the platform, Mrs Thatcher extended her hand to Mr Heath, rather tentatively, some observers thought, and Mr Heath unhesitatingly clasped it. There was almost a sigh of relief in the hall that they had got it over.'[28] The next day's papers carried pictures of the two of them together smiling fixedly for the cameras, Heath looking for all the world like the father of the blushing young bride.

But Heath still failed to offer the unequivocal endorsement the party was looking for. The next day he issued a statement denying reports that he regarded Mrs Thatcher and Keith Joseph as traitors, declaring that he was 'sick and tired, as no doubt Mrs Thatcher is, of those who are peddling such malicious allegations in an attempt to create dissension in the Tory party'.[29] But that was all. In her closing speech to the conference on Friday, Mrs Thatcher held out another subtly barbed olive branch as she spoke of her pride in following in the footsteps of Churchill, Eden, Macmillan, Home and Heath, praising each of them in turn. (Heath's contribution was that he 'successfully led the party to victory in 1970 and brilliantly led the nation into Europe in 1973'.) As *The Times* noted, 'It sounded like a generous tribute to Mr Heath, but at the same time a reminder that he now belongs with the other listed men of destiny to the party's past.'[30] Over the weekend there were suggestions from the Heath camp that he would after all like to 'play a new role, possibly as shadow Foreign Secretary'. But the consensus was that Mrs Thatcher had done all that could be expected of her: it was up to him to make the next move. 'There is no possibility of Mrs Thatcher making a proposition until Mr Heath has demonstrated more clearly his support for her and her new team.'[31]

That he pointedly declined to do. On the contrary he continued to flaunt his independence. 'It has never been a part of our Conservative tradition', he told the Greater London Young Conservatives on 3 November, 'that what was said on the Front Bench was what went. It is vital that there should be full discussion and that differences of view should be given publicity.'[32] This was not, as was widely remarked, a view which he had encouraged over the previous decade when he was leader. Speaking to the Folkestone Young Conservatives a few days later he announced his intention to lead a public debate on 'a wide range of fundamental questions which cover different aspects of our national life'. 'In this way,' he explained, 'I can put to constructive use the freedom I at present enjoy for the benefit . . . of my party and my country.'[33] Asked in a television interview if he was awaiting a recall to the leadership, he did not deny it. 'Oh, I don't discuss that. I'm just getting on with the job which I think I can best do at the moment.' He once again ruled out joining the Shadow Cabinet and brushed aside the idea of taking a job in Brussels, still less a nationalised industry.[34]

But what were the 'big issues' and 'fundamental questions' to which Heath now addressed himself? One, naturally, was Britain's place in Europe now that the threat of withdrawal had been comprehensively banished. Over the next four years Heath consistently urged a more positive British commitment to the Community's development. This was something he could do without disloyalty, since the Tories were the pro-Europe party. It was the Labour Government which was still dragging its feet. By choosing not to join the European Monetary System, Heath warned in July 1978, the Callaghan Government was repeating Britain's fatal error of self-exclusion from 1955 to 1973, betraying future generations for short-term party interest.[35] He also wanted to see the EEC itself develop a greater international role – concerning itself with the 'big issues' instead of getting bogged down in regulating the size of beer glasses – and to see Britain take a leading role in developing a specifically European voice in world affairs.

This was consistent but predictable. More interesting was his continuing preoccupation with the lessons to be learned from the wreck of his Government on the twin rocks of inflation and trade union power, and the problem of how a future Government – Labour or Conservative – could steer around them to reach the promised land of sustained growth and national prosperity. For the whole five years between the three-day week in 1974 and the 'winter of discontent' in 1979 – years of increasing polarisation, fragmentation and mounting political violence – Heath brooded aloud over the complex of problems which had brought him down, the breakdown of consensus and social cohesion, the spectre of ungovernability.

Characteristically Heath believed that Britain's problem was at bottom not a matter of economic policy at all, but a failure of political will and institutions. As he told an audience in Toronto in the summer of 1975:

> Britain is currently having to wrestle with a crisis of authority and a crisis of leadership that arises when the democratic system, reflecting an earlier balance of social and political power, has to accommodate itself to a change of strength within the community. When that occurs, great strains are imposed on the social and democratic fabric.[36]

It was that shift in the balance of social and political power which had wrecked his Government in February 1974. Accordingly, it was not surprising that the problem of accommodating union power figured prominently in the examples he offered the Folkestone Young Conservatives of the sort of 'fundamental questions' which concerned him. For instance, he asked, 'Does Parliament any longer reflect the balance of power and of the interests in the country at large?' Or again: 'Are we really to do no more than shrug our shoulders and accept the state of our industrial relations?'[37] While he asked the questions, however, he never offered clear answers. As Tory leader his last contribution to the union problem in October 1974 had been to promise *not* to reintroduce the 1971 Industrial Relations Act. Over the next five years, while the question of trade union legislation was a hotly contested issue between 'doves' like Jim Prior and backbench 'hawks' like Norman Tebbit, Heath never set out what he would do, beyond tacitly indicating his sympathy with Prior. On the question of accommodating union power within the political system he sometimes hinted at some sort of 'industrial parliament' (an old Liberal idea from the 1920s) – a constitutionally established 'Neddy'. He spoke boldly of institutional reform – even though, he warned, 'in acting imaginatively, we may perhaps offend the prevailing orthodoxy'.[38] But he never spelled out what he meant. The *Times*'s comment on a 1977 lecture on the future of Europe was disappointingly applicable to all the 'big issues' he addressed: 'He describes . . . well, but when it comes to prescription he retreats to extreme generality, even platitude.'[39]

When he came to practical problems of economic management he was more specific, since he was concerned to vindicate his own record. In a series of powerfully argued speeches from his seat below the gangway in the House of Commons in 1975–6 he insisted that his drive for growth had only been thwarted by the devastating rise in world commodity prices – 182 per cent between 1972 and 1974 – culminating in the quadrupling of oil prices.[40] He denied allowing an explosion of money supply, quoting figures to show that the expansion of M1 was below the rate of growth of GDP between 1970 and 1974. 'There is no justification for the argument that M1 . . . was the cause of inflation.' (He simply rejected the monetarists' adoption of M3 as the more accurate measure.)[41] Finally he took pleasure in quoting *Times* editorials from 1971 to 1973 strongly supporting his policies – urging faster growth, the social and moral imperative of cutting unemployment and the vital importance of statutory incomes policy.[42] The point of all this was to argue that the policies which were right then were still right now. The absolute priority, he still passionately believed, was to restore *growth*. 'People must have hope', he insisted in March 1976, 'if they are to live through a dark period. In many circles growth is now . . . a dirty word. But unless we have growth in the economy we can never achieve anything we want in any sphere – social, cultural or otherwise.'[43] He was worried that other countries were moving out of the oil-led recession faster than Britain, and that Britain would only get moving again just in time to be hit by the next world downturn. 'What we must bring home to this country', he urged in one of his very first backbench speeches in April 1975, 'is that priority has got to be given to investment as against claims on consumption and excessive wages.'[44]

In July 1975 Wilson and Healey achieved an agreement with the unions to a new incomes policy limiting pay rises to a flat-rate increase of £6 a week. Heath gave it his qualified support, while believing that it was not yet tough enough. Unlike the monetarists who drew the lesson from 1972–4 that incomes policies were both irrelevant in principle and unworkable in practice, he still believed statutory wage restraint to be 'essential' – though at the same time he still insisted that he would rather it was not:

Anyone who has been in Government thinks of the hours spent by officials, Cabinet committees and the Cabinet itself on settling the whole approach to a statutory pay and prices policy and all that arises from it. Some may want such a policy, but I would never want it for a moment, if it could possibly be avoided.

But the key to incomes policy was public consent. Stages Two and Three of his Government's policy had been accepted by ten million trade unionists, but Stage Three was challenged by one powerful union. Following two years of recession the nation had now to be brought to accept not just smaller rises, but a *reduced* standard of living for the next few years. 'In part', he declared, 'it is a matter of communication' – then added, with a self-mockery that exemplified his rediscovered mastery of the House: 'But who am I to talk about communication?' A moment later he was sombre again. 'Till the nation is asked to recognise these facts in all their stark horror we shall not get a response.' He drew encouragement, however, from the referendum campaign, which had tapped a new level of public support, which must now be mobilised again for the battle against inflation.[45]

There was no need for him to remind the House who had led the referendum campaign. Later that evening, Barbara Castle found the corridors 'buzzing with excitement about Ted Heath's speech – by common agreement the best he has ever made. Apparently it made Margaret look like a tinny amateur and speculation began to circulate as to whether she could survive.'[46] This was just the effect he was seeking to achieve. By adopting the stance of an elder statesman, patriotically placing the lessons of his own hard-won experience at the disposal of the Labour Government while voicing views that were still tacitly shared by a large section – perhaps still the majority – of the Conservative party, he sought to portray Mrs Thatcher as a naïve ideologue seduced by a theoretical chimera while he was grappling responsibly with the problems of the real world. Twelve months later, when the Government achieved a further accord with the unions – Callaghan having in the meantime replaced Wilson as Prime Minister – he once again offered his support with an explicit vindication of government by tripartite discussion, now despised as 'corporatism'.*

'In an impressive plea in the Commons last night', *The Times* reported, 'Mr Heath urged his party's Front Bench not to be so grudging in its attitude to the Government's agreement with the trade unions.'[48] There was, he insisted, 'nothing dishonourable' in his supporting it. Consultation with the TUC and the CBI was no different from what successive Governments had always done with other groups – for instance, sitting down every year with the National Farmers' Union to fix prices and quotas. 'It is a formalisation of what has been going on for many years in the Chancellor of the Exchequer's office in the Treasury before every Budget.'

> It seems to me that we are moving quite deliberately, with industry and trade unions, into the sphere which we have long occupied with other interests . . . If there is anyone who today thinks that Government can move out of this sphere of intense consultation with industry and the trade unions he could not in my view be more mistaken . . . Those countries which have had the greatest success in dealing with their industrial situation are those which . . . have the closest form of consultation with both sides of industry.[49]

---

* The news of Wilson's unexpected resignation found Heath signing copies of *Sailing* in a London bookshop. Pressed by a radio interviewer for his reaction, he was initially non-plussed ('It certainly is extraordinary') but rallied sufficiently to pay tribute to his old adversary's skill in holding his party together, although it was too soon to judge 'the solidity of his achievements'.[47]

This speech made crystal clear the philosophic gulf that divided Heath from Mrs Thatcher. The previous month there had been another flurry of speculation that he might be ready to make his peace with her. In what looked like a co-ordinated series of kites, supporters like Geoffrey Rippon called for his return to the Front Bench; Timothy Kitson publicly suggested that the whole party wanted to see him back in the Shadow Cabinet so as to field 'the best available team' for the next election.[50] But Kitson was no longer Heath's PPS and was not speaking with his approval. Pressed by Robin Day on television to say whether he was 'available', Heath replied as before: 'I am available to play the part I can best do, and at the moment that is in the corner seat below the gangway.'[51] In *The Times* George Hutchinson – the journalist consistently closest to him in these years, and his most sympathetic interpreter – defended his intransigence. It was *policy*, not personal considerations which divided him from Mrs Thatcher.

> It would be a gross mistake to think that he stands off because he is consumed with pique or petulance. The hurt inflicted by his defeat in the leadership ballot has passed, anointed as it has been by the international and national audiences he still commands, by the all-party respect his speeches are given in the House, by the personal loyalty of a considerable section of the Conservative party in the country (80 per cent he has been known to say) and by his altogether unexpected success as an author.[52]

This was fair enough. The trouble was that he *seemed* to be consumed by pique and petulance: it was legitimate to differ from his successor, but he did so with such an ill grace. Interviewed on ITV's 'Face the Press' on 25 July he indignantly denied being a 'bad loser'. But when pressed to say something nice about Mrs Thatcher, he bluntly refused. 'When she became leader of the party, I wished her well and I wished her every success. I don't think anybody can do more than that.' Would she make a good Prime Minister? Again, he was not prepared to say so. It was very difficult to know, he said, until someone actually became Prime Minister. Asked if he was not behaving exactly as Enoch Powell had done in the 1960s, he denied it on the ground that he believed his policies appealed to a majority – 'and probably a great majority' – of people.[53] But then so had Powell.

Heath's refusal to pay the most minimal courtesies due to his successor now prompted even the faithful Hutchinson to write him a blunt open letter in *The Times*, warning that his 'friends and well-wishers are increasingly troubled' by his attitude. He seemed to be going out of his way to widen the rift.

> In all candour I must tell you that you are damaging your own reputation as well as the Conservative interest. You are already estranged from a number of old friends, and others are deeply disturbed . . . You are in danger of losing . . . the good will and respect of the party . . .
>
> Nobody is asking you . . . to join the Shadow Cabinet, but simply to speak up for its leader and her chosen colleagues, most of whom were your own. This is not asking too much . . .
>
> The party is dismayed, disconcerted and rather shocked by your conduct. You must take account of this before it is too late.
>
> With all good wishes,
> Yours ever,
> George[54]

Maybe this got through. Two months later at the party conference, that year in Brighton, Heath made another attempt to mend his fences. He was given an opening by the publication of the party's first general policy document since the change of leader. *The Right Approach* was carefully designed as a unifying document, embracing both monetarism and incomes policy, which Keith Joseph, Geoffrey Howe and Jim Prior could all accept. The drafts were also shown to Heath in a deliberate attempt to square him; the document even made a point of defending the record of his Government – particularly Barber's Chancellorship. If not quite an olive branch, *The Times* judged, 'it certainly goes a long way to vindicate the Conservative years 1970–4 and thereby satisfy Mr Heath's *amour propre*.'[55] Accordingly Heath announced that he would not merely attend the conference this year, but would speak in the policy debate. He was reported, unusually, to be 'acutely nervous'. So was much of the audience: he received only polite cheers and only half a standing ovation as he came down from the platform to speak from the body of the hall. His speech was in truth a highly ambivalent performance. He chose to welcome *The Right Approach* as bringing the party back into 'the mainstream of the Conservative Party's policies over many years'; in other words, he was suggesting, after its flirtation with Powellite fallacies, the party was coming back to him.

> You would not expect me to say that I agree with every word or sentence of it. I did not even agree with every word or sentence in

the documents I signed myself. [Laughter] But it is there as the continued development of policies which we worked out over many years and which we have pursued. I do not find myself in many disagreements with it at all. So I find it encouraging that we are going along this road.

What the representatives wanted to hear, however, was an explicit endorsement of the Leader; and, in his fashion, he gave it to them. It came in a typical passage in which – speaking 'very carefully and slowly so as to raise the maximum number of goose pimples on the flesh of his audience' – he warned that with that summer's financial crisis which had finally driven the Government cap in hand to the IMF, Britain had come to the end of the road. The crunch so long predicted had now arrived. 'I hope', he added. 'that this country will realise that once again I am telling the truth.' The Tory party was well equipped to tackle the situation, because it had never flinched from tough decisions in the past. 'I have no doubt that we would not flinch in future in taking difficult decisions in the national interest. I have complete confidence that they would be taken by Margaret Thatcher and her colleagues on the platform.' This was his only reference to Mrs Thatcher; and in context it was transparently self-serving. But it was 'sufficient to surge the conference forward into prolonged applause'.

While he had the audience eating out of his hand he took the chance to add a barely coded defence of U-turns. No Government facing a crisis could know in advance what tough decisions it might have to take. 'I want to say that any Government in that situation might have to take measures that at the time ran counter to their long-term aspirations and policies. In such a time of crisis, in my experience in politics, this is inevitable. Let us be realistic about this.'

He ended with a rousing call to restore to British politics and British life those 'standards of which we were once intensely proud. [Applause] When are we as a country going to get up and go?' he demanded – just as he had done in 1966, as though 1970–4 had never been. 'That is what the rest of the world is asking. These are the objectives to which I have devoted my political life . . . These are the things I have been fighting for, and these are the things for which I shall go on fighting.'[56]

'When he ended his speech', *The Times* reported, 'Mrs Thatcher was the first to rise on the platform to applaud him and the whole hall stood in a sustained round of cheers and welcoming back.' The next speaker was equally loudly applauded for hoping that Heath would soon resume his place 'in the highest counsels of our party'.

'Today', he exulted, 'we have witnessed the unification of the Conservative Party.' Most commentators agreed. Ronald Butt wrote that 'it would be hard to overrate [the] political significance' of Heath's 'brilliant performance', which unlike Powell's bitter diatribes 'was wholly inside and not outside the Tory tradition . . . It can reasonably be reckoned as one of the greatest services that Mr Heath has done his party.'[57] But as the euphoria cleared, doubts returned. Sceptics noted the 'subtle reservations' and note of self-justification in his endorsement. The *Guardian* interpreted his 'electrifying' speech as 'a scarcely veiled call for a government of national unity', to which his 'ritual gesture to Mrs Thatcher as party leader . . . was added almost in parenthesis. The bald fact . . . was that Mr Heath was speaking to the country as a whole over the heads of the Conservative Conference.'[58]

Whatever reservations might be made, however, it was generally agreed that Heath had finally come down on the side of loyalty and unity. With an election seemingly possible at any moment – the loss of by-elections in such solid Labour strongholds as Workington and Walsall North during November reduced the Government's majority to a single vote – that was what mattered. What is striking about the 'reconciliation' of October 1976 is how far the party leadership had moved to make it possible. It is important to remember that Mrs Thatcher was at this stage a studiously cautious leader, as concerned as any other party leader to keep her party together by appeasing both wings. Despite his graceless conduct, Heath was still a powerful presence in the party; moreover while he stood apart, she still had Willie Whitelaw, Lord Carrington, Jim Prior, Francis Pym, John Davies, Ian Gilmour and Lord Hailsham in her Shadow Cabinet. *The Right Approach* and its more detailed 1977 successor *The Right Approach to the Economy* – signed by Joseph, Howe, Prior and David Howell – represented a careful balancing act. 'Mrs Thatcher', *The Times* declared following her closing speech to the 1976 conference, 'has moved with characteristic caution on to the middle ground of politics and every one of her closest lieutenants knows it . . . The party has rallied on a set of policies and approaches that are markedly closer to Mr Heath than to Sir Keith Joseph.'[59] In the circumstances it was difficult for Heath to withhold his grudging blessing.

In March 1977, however, anticipating the loss of another two by-elections, the Government contrived to extend its survival by means of a parliamentary pact with the Liberals. With the rest of the Tory party, Heath attacked the deal as a cynical manœuvre to postpone a General Election. When Jeremy Thorpe claimed that it was no different from the sort of deal he himself had offered the Liberals in

1974, he retorted that it was quite different: first, he had offered a co-alition and had declined to consider a mere pact; and second, his proposal had started from an acceptance of the verdict of the February election, whereas Callaghan was trying to avoid an election.[60] The upshot, anyway, was that the prospect of an early election faded: in the further two years before Callaghan finally went to the country Mrs Thatcher had time to fasten her authority more firmly and confidently on the Tory party.

Meanwhile, with the incomes policy question fudged, the only major issue on which Heath directly opposed the new party orthodoxy – indeed almost the only issue on which Mrs Thatcher explicitly repudiated his approach – was devolution. Like many people in both parties Heath had been thoroughly alarmed by the advance of the nationalist parties in 1974 – particularly the SNP, which had captured seven seats in February and a further four in October. (Plaid Cymru had advanced from two seats to three.) Back in 1967 he had become convinced that the preservation of the union required some devolution of power to Scotland and Wales, though he had not got around to it when in office. He now believed that Scottish aspirations could only be appeased by a directly elected assembly with its own revenue-raising powers. (He raised some eye-brows by claiming to have 'seen more of Scotland over the past seventeen years than any other national political figure'.)[61] In November 1975 the Labour Government, facing a serious threat to its hegemony in Scotland, proposed to establish assemblies in both Edinburgh and Cardiff. In a powerful speech in January 1976 Heath reaffirmed his support. He made a rare gesture to Mrs Thatcher by endorsing her determination to maintain the union ('as my right hon. Friend the Leader of the Opposition very rightly and eloquently said last Tuesday'), but he went well beyond her in the means he was pre-pared to contemplate to do so. The Scottish demand for devolution was 'a settled conviction' which would not go away. The two parties must drop petty point-scoring and reach agreement on the way for-ward before legislation was brought to the House.

As usual Heath portrayed finding an agreed solution as simply a matter of political will. The will was lacking, however. On the contrary, despite the devolutionist views of her Shadow Scottish Secretary, Alick Buchanan-Smith, and other Scottish Tory MPs, Mrs Thatcher reversed her party's policy; and when Labour's Bill was finally published the Shadow Cabinet decided to oppose it. In the Second Reading debate in December 1976, therefore, Heath re-peated his support for the principle of the Bill and for the first time in his life abstained on a three-line whip. Through the Government's further tribulations with the Scotland Bill in 1977 and 1978 he continued to abstain on the crucial votes.

During 1977 the guarded truce – it was not exactly a *rapprochement* – between Heath and Mrs Thatcher held. Though he continued to insist on his right and duty to express his views, his support of the Devolution Bill was uncontentious in broad policy terms while his continued (but not outspoken) support for pay restraint still fell within the ambit of the party's studiously catch-all programme. As the economy remained stagnant and unemployment rose to 1·5 million he had no difficulty in directing most of his fire against the Government. At that autumn's conference he was invited to give a lecture to the Conservative Political Centre – an invitation that would not have been given without the leader's approval. During the conference proper he ostentatiously moved to the front of the platform during a heated debate on industrial relations to support Jim Prior's refusal to promise to abolish the closed shop. He was warmly received, and the question of his taking office when the Tories eventually returned to power began to be canvassed yet again. 'Mr Heath will not even privately discuss with his closest friends the precise circumstances in which he would be prepared to join a government formed by Mrs Thatcher,' *The Times* reported. 'But one way and another he seems to be responding to the overtures that Mrs Thatcher and the managers of the Conservative Party are making to him . . . It really does begin to look as though he is on the way back.'[62]

At the end of the year Heath's restless travels took him to the Middle East: Egypt, Jordan and Saudi Arabia. On his return, exceptionally, Mrs Thatcher invited him to Flood Street, to brief her on his talks with President Sadat and King Hussein. The conversation lasted forty-five minutes, a good deal longer than their famous encounter in Wilton Street three years before; but the outcome was no better for their relationship. At least this time they had something to talk about; but Heath understood that he had gone there to brief her, and was not amused when she scarcely let him get a word in. Hopes that this initiative might signal a reconciliation were dashed over the next few days. First, Mrs Thatcher's office stamped firmly on speculation that Heath might be asked to play a leading role in the election. Then she herself, in a television interview, made it clear that she had no plans to ask him to join the Shadow Cabinet – while putting the onus of refusal skilfully on to him. 'My guess is that until a general election comes he will obviously want to keep his options open.' As for his possible inclusion in a Tory Government: 'When we know what the election results are, we will have to sit down and think what is going to happen then.'[63] The implication was that so long as she won she would not need him; while if she lost the question would not arise.

In the course of the same interview Mrs Thatcher put further distance between herself and Heath by stirring the race relations pot, raising echoes of Enoch Powell in 1968 by speaking sympathetically of the indigenous population's fears of being 'swamped' by immigrants. Heath did not hesitate to join the chorus of condemnation of her remarks, asserting that the 1971 Immigration Act already gave all the powers needed to prevent further large-scale entry. He charged her with causing 'an unnecessary national row' and expressed his 'utter distaste' for her approach.[64] Willie Whitelaw as shadow Home Secretary was seriously embarrassed, but Mrs Thatcher was unabashed: this was one issue on which she knew she could afford to let her gut convictions show, and indeed the Tory lead in the opinion polls, which had been dwindling, immediately shot up again. Following this latest row Ronald Butt wrote that he now felt sure for the first time that there would be no place for Heath in a Thatcher Government.[65]

Yet still as the election approached it remained important to keep him on-side. It is an axiom of politics that the electorate always punishes a divided party, and Heath was still by far the biggest personality on the Tory side, more popular now than he ever was as Prime Minister. With inflation falling at last, the balance of payments back in surplus and the pound strong, 'Smiling Jim' Callaghan was beginning to look as if he might be hard to beat when he picked his moment – as was universally expected – in the autumn of 1978. Handicapped by her sex, Mrs Thatcher still looked gauche and inexperienced by comparison. Many commentators still felt that the Tory party, deprived by death, scandal and desertion of the other three giants of the Class of 1950, simply could not do without Heath, difficult though he was. 'It is impossible to listen to him', wrote David Wood, 'without recognising that here we have the strongest and best-equipped political mind of his generation . . . Everything he said came from a copious political mind that drew its strength not from shibboleths or fads that live for a day and die, but from experience.'[66] Behind the scenes Whitelaw, Carrington and other old colleagues were continually pressing him to come to the aid of the party. On 5 July, visiting the Penistone by-election, he made yet another effort to oblige. Yet though he brought himself to mention Mrs Thatcher by name, he still contrived to imply that her leadership of the party was somehow incidental: 'During the General Election campaign I shall fight just as hard as I have ever done for the return of a Conservative Government.' He thanked the voters who had supported him in 1970 and 1974, and added:

> They can be assured that I shall continue to play my part and that the change of leadership makes no difference to my determination to instal a Conservative Government once again in office.
>
> I wish Mrs Thatcher and her colleagues every success. Together we must fight hard to gain the victory we all want.[67]

Heath's assurance that he would campaign for the party was what the leadership wanted. At least it removed the lingering fear that he might 'do an Enoch' and withhold his support. Mrs Thatcher was said to be delighted with the 'warm terms' of his endorsement. ('Warm', it was explained, meant 'warm by his normally cool standards'.)[68] At the same time, *The Times* suggested, since he was now widely seen as a figure almost above party, his endorsement should also bring Mrs Thatcher support among 'that section of the electorate where her appeal is weakest and his is strongest'.[69] Typically, however, this latest *rapprochement*, like every other, was immediately soured when Mrs Thatcher unwisely gushed that she always thought of Heath as 'Mr Europe' and claimed that he was always consulted on EEC appointments. He promptly denied it; it was eventually clarified that the Chief Whip, Humphrey Atkins, did not actually consult Heath personally, but someone close to him.[70]

Then, to universal astonishment, Callaghan postponed the expected autumn election and opted to carry on until the spring; and this year the freshly patched-up truce between Heath and Mrs Thatcher did not survive the Tory conference. The issue was once again incomes policy. Over the summer the Government had set a tough 'guideline' for pay rises of 5 per cent. Two years earlier, in deference to the anxieties of Prior and Whitelaw, Mrs Thatcher had felt obliged to fudge her opposition to pay policy. Now she felt strong enough to follow her own instinct. Supported by Keith Joseph and Geoffrey Howe, she condemned the whole paraphernalia of pay restraint and unambiguously promised the unions a return to what they too wanted, free collective bargaining. Heath, remembering his own unwise repudiation of incomes policy in 1970, considered this either naïve or cynically opportunist. In his speech to the conference he stopped just short of open disagreement. But he made 'a stuffy and charmless speech, devoid of all the courtesies and graces which the occasion required. He took a hectoring and regimental tone, not only with the conference, but to his leaders on the platform.'[71] From the height of his great experience he rebuked Mrs

Thatcher for claiming on television that the Government's guideline had broken down already. If that were so, he warned, 'there is nothing for gloating, nothing for joy. We should grieve for our country.'[72]

His speech met with a mixed reception. By contrast Geoffrey Howe won a standing ovation for an outright rejection of incomes policy. Then Heath discovered that his own speech had not been carried on television but had been scheduled to coincide with the twenty-minute 'Playschool' slot. His angry response was to give interviews to both the BBC and 'News at Ten' that evening in which he openly supported Callaghan's 5 per cent limit as being the most the country could afford: 'Free collective bargaining produces massive inflation . . . We cannot have another free for all.' He wanted Government and Opposition to agree a bipartisan policy towards inflation, as they used to do towards defence. 'Both major parties have been confronted: both major parties recognise the national interest has to come first.' Asked if the Opposition should learn from his enforced U-turn in 1972, he replied: 'Yes. Why should I go on making the same mistake?'[73] The implication was that Mrs Thatcher was sadly inexperienced but would quickly bump up against reality if ever she were to find herself in government.

These two outspoken interviews blew the party concordat wide open. Not only was Heath explicitly contradicting Mrs Thatcher and her Shadow Chancellor; he was giving comfort to the enemy by endorsing the central plank of the Government's economic strategy, the issue on which the result of the election probably depended. Heath was unrepentant: next day he quoted from *The Right Approach to the Economy* to show that it was he who was sticking to the party line, Mrs Thatcher who was departing from it.[74] Worse, from the leadership's point of view, was clear poll evidence that Heath enjoyed strong public support. NOP in the *Daily Mail* found that more people (71 per cent) were impressed by his speech (or reports of it) than by Mrs Thatcher's closing speech to the conference (56 per cent).[75] More dramatically, when voters were asked by NOP in early November how they would vote at the General Election if Heath were still Tory leader, a narrow Conservative lead of 3 per cent under Mrs Thatcher was transformed into a massive margin of 14 per cent. Asked in the same poll which would make the better Prime Minister, 55 per cent said Heath, only 33 per cent Mrs Thatcher.[76]

Until Callaghan's pay policy collapsed in a welter of public service strikes over the winter, this was a highly dangerous situation for Mrs Thatcher. Heath was seen to have re-established himself in the public mind as a more popular leader than herself, promoting a policy of

national consensus and co-operation which the public clearly preferred to her more combative instincts. She could not afford to
disown him because she needed his support and because she knew
that most of her senior colleagues in the Shadow Cabinet were still
closer to his thinking than to hers. The polls indicated that the election was likely to be very close: if Callaghan had gone to the country
in October he would probably have won. On 26 October Labour
held Berwick and East Lothian with an increased majority – the first
pro-Government swing at a by-election since 1966. Thatcherite
backbenchers blamed Heath – he had visited the constituency the day
before polling day, still emphasising the importance of the Tories
supporting the Government's policy – but Mrs Thatcher herself had
no choice but to exonerate him and defend his right to express his
views.[77] Trailing both Callaghan and Heath in personal popularity,
she was still in a very weak position.

She was saved by the 'Winter of Discontent'. The public service
unions' refusal to be bound by the guidelines of a Labour Government any more than they had been by Heath's pay policy, their
willingness instead to plunge the country into another period of industrial chaos and misery in many ways more squalid than the
three-day week, served both to discredit Labour's 'special relationship' with the unions and to vindicate those who asserted that pay
policy could never work. With Callaghan brought down by confrontation with the unions just as Heath had been, the way was open
for Mrs Thatcher to try a different approach. Heath's way was finally
discredited not by his own failure but by Callaghan's. The fact was,
as Callaghan sensed, that a 'sea-change' had come over politics between November 1978 and March 1979.[78] Suddenly the Opposition
was far ahead in the polls. The overriding issue in politics was the
unions, and Mrs Thatcher was widely seen as the leader most determined to tackle them: the 'softly-softly' approach hitherto advocated
by Prior was hastily toughened up. By the time the Government lost
(by a single vote) a confidence motion in the House of Commons on
28 March, obliging Callaghan to go to the country on 3 May, the
overwhelming likelihood was that Mrs Thatcher would be elected
with a handsome majority – and owing nothing to Heath.

As a result, he played only a minor role in the election. Central
Office now had no need, as had seemed likely during most of the
previous four years, to involve him conspicuously in the campaign in
order to emphasise party unity. They expected to win anyway. This
is not to say that he did not, as he had promised, campaign
vigorously up and down the country. He did, drawing large and
sympathetic crowds, but it no longer mattered that he never mentioned Mrs Thatcher by name. In fact he said nothing controversial

at all, even on incomes policy: the manifesto – entitled simply *The Conservative Manifesto, 1979* – papered over that dispute by paying lip service to the need for even a Tory Government, 'in framing its monetary and other policies [to] come to some conclusions about the likely scope for pay increases'.[79] Altogether the manifesto gave little warning of the determined break with postwar economic management on which the Government would embark once elected. At most it was seen as a return to some of the aspirations of Heath's 1970 programme: nothing could have been more traditional than the famous poster showing a winding dole queue with the caption 'Labour Isn't Working'. Heath had no difficulty campaigning on such a manifesto. At the same time it was noted that he was almost alone in speaking of foreign policy, and widely suggested that he was announcing his availability for the Foreign Office. At Stirling on 10 April he recalled that he had been a member of every previous Conservative Government since 1945: 'Whenever I have been asked to serve my country I have done so.'[80] Plainly he had come to terms with the unwelcome fact that Mrs Thatcher was going to be Prime Minister and was now ready to swallow his pride sufficiently to accept office from his former Education Secretary.

During the campaign the Conservative lead narrowed: one NOP poll actually put Labour ahead.[81] Callaghan's personal popularity remained high, while Mrs Thatcher – like Heath in 1970 – was a liability to her party. A MORI poll in the last week once again suggested that a Tory lead of 5 per cent would more than triple if she were to be replaced by Heath.[82] But she stuck to her strategy, furiously rejecting suggestions that she should invite him to share a press conference. (At the very idea, it was reported, she 'went white and stormed out of the room. Denis Thatcher . . . subsequently said he had never seen her so upset.')[83] Had she done so, she would have been almost obliged to give him office, which was the last thing she wished to have to do. While the press gave credit to his loyal campaigning and canvassed the possibility of his return, she firmly deflected questions about whether she might bring him back.[84] Had she won very narrowly she might perhaps have had no option; but in the event she won with a comfortable majority of forty-three – bigger than Heath's in 1970. By contrast with his situation then, she was still stuck with a Shadow Cabinet not at all of her own choosing; but at least she had escaped any need to saddle herself with him as well.

In reality it would plainly have been unworkable for Heath to have sat in a Thatcher Cabinet: their political and personal differences were just too deep. She was unquestionably right to recognise the fact – as he too had appeared to recognise it since 1975. Yet the lure of power was strong. In May 1979 Heath did entertain the hope of being recalled to office. Instead of going home to Wilton Street following the declaration of the result in Sidcup – his majority nearly doubled to 13,000* – he drove to Wiltshire to stay with Sara Morrison. There a letter was delivered to him by dispatch rider at five o'clock next morning, informing him that Lord Carrington was to be Foreign Secretary. It was coolly signed 'Margaret Thatcher'.† When Mrs Morrison took the letter up to him he was desperately disappointed. She felt that in his heart he knew quite well that Mrs Thatcher could not possibly have appointed him; yet still he had hoped. They spent the day together looking at a house he was thinking of buying on the Isle of Wight. Heath remained sunk in silence all morning, until cheered by the reception he got from people on the ferry who recognised him. He was encouraged, too, by news of the Cabinet appointments – including the recall of Peter Walker as Minister of Agriculture. That evening he and Mrs Morrison had dinner with Sir Arnold Weinstock of GEC – one of his favourite industrialists – who cleared the air immediately by saying that Keith Joseph at the Department of Industry was a dreadful appointment, at which Heath was delighted. A long day ended in the small hours with Heath happily playing Weinstock's collection of rare harpsichords, politics forgotten.[87] Next day he moved on to stay with Toby Aldington in Kent.

If Heath was foolish to imagine that Mrs Thatcher might have made him Foreign Secretary, he was entitled to be furious at her alternative offer. Two weeks after the election her office let it be known that he had been offered, but had refused, the job of British Ambassador in Washington. There is a long history in British politics of the Washington Embassy being used by prime ministers as a dumping ground for senior politicians whom it is inconvenient to have at home. Austen Chamberlain was insulted when offered it by Baldwin in 1923; Lloyd George likewise rejected it from Churchill in

---

* E. Heath (Conservative)	23,692
F. Keohane (Labour)	10,236
P. Vickers (Liberal)	4,908
A. Webb (National Front)	774
Conservative majority	13,456[85]

† She had actually tried to avoid having to communicate with him directly. Shortly after midnight, as soon as the result was clear, Humphrey Atkins rang Tim Kitson to ask him to tell Heath that he would not be in the Government. Kitson, not relishing the message, told him to do his own dirty work.[86]

1940, but in 1941 Lord Halifax did not feel able to refuse. To offer it *publicly* to Heath, when he had already refused it privately, was an open announcement that she wanted him out of domestic politics. His reply was icy:

Dear Margaret,
    Thank you for your note. As I have said, I do wish to stay in the Commons. I am sure you will be able to find somebody to do the job well.

Yours,
Ted[88]

After five years of mutual suspicion, this 'incredibly foolish offer' (Roy Jenkins's description) was probably the moment when relations between Heath and Mrs Thatcher were irrevocably damaged.[89] Heath never forgot nor forgave. Nearly ten years later in a radio interview he told Robert Carvel that he was 'not cut out to be a postman', which was all that the job of a modern Ambassador was.[90] The *Daily Telegraph*, however, warmly welcomed his decision to remain in the Commons: 'We do not always agree with Mr Heath's pronouncements,' it declared generously. 'But long may he continue to annoy, inspire and goad his countrymen from below the gangway in the House of Commons.'[91] That was precisely what he set himself to do over the next eleven years.

36

Internal Exile

Mrs Thatcher's election as Prime Minister in May 1979 left Heath in a difficult position. There was no precedent for a former Conservative Prime Minister still in the Commons being excluded from a subsequent Conservative Government. Balfour and Home both served loyally under their successors; Baldwin, Churchill, Eden and Macmillan quickly withdrew from active politics. The only recent example, in fact, of an ex-Prime Minister retiring in good health to the back benches was Harold Wilson; but he had stepped down voluntarily and was succeeded by his chosen heir whom he had no disposition to criticise. Heath's situation was very different. He had given such minimal and grudging support over the past four years that no one except Heath himself had seriously expected Mrs Thatcher to include him in her Government. So long as she was only Leader of the Opposition she had been bound to treat him with a degree of public deference. But now she was Prime Minister and he was a back number. As a newly re-elected Tory MP the only course open to him was to give the new Government his blessing and keep his reservations to himself. For the first year and more of the Government's life this was pretty well what he did; but he still could not bring himself to offer a word of positive endorsement.

Interviewed by Jean Rook – again – for the *Daily Express* on 11 May, he was at pains to deny that he had expected office despite his substantial contribution to getting the Government elected. 'I think I did a lot to win the marginals over to us,' he claimed. 'Look how we got rid of John Pardoe.' Altogether over the previous four years he had addressed some 400 party meetings. 'If that's supposed to be "sulking", I just don't know what they're talking about.' It was true that he had never mentioned Mrs Thatcher by name, but he professed to see no reason why he should, since it was the party he was

716

17 With Education Secretary, Margaret Thatcher, at the Conservative
party conference in 1972

18 Into Europe: Heath signs the Accession Treaty with (*left*) Sir Alec
Douglas-Home and (*right*) Geoffrey Rippon

19 *Left* 'Heath out': students demonstrate at Birmingham University, 1973

20 *Below* The battle of Saltley gate: police arrest a picket during the 1972 miners' strike

Opposite

21 *Above left* Canvassing in Bexley in the February 1974 General Election

22 *Above right* Enoch Powell addresses the 1973 party conference in Blackpool, listened to by Heath and Anthony Barber

23 *Below* The three party leaders: with Jeremy Thorpe and Harold Wilson

24   The new leader carries off the old

speaking for, not the leader. 'I want her to succeed', he insisted, 'for the party's sake and the country's.' But asked whether he liked her, he could only reply: 'No comment.' As for himself, he would carry on as before: 'I shall sit on the back benches, look after my constituency and make major speeches. You ask me if I'm still ambitious. I am for my dream of a country that isn't torn apart, one that will catch up with the world instead of lagging behind it as we have been doing.' 'People will only work reasonably together', he added, 'if they can see we're making progress.'[1]

He made no public criticism of Geoffrey Howe's first, boldly monetarist Budget, which lost no time in signalling the Government's radical intentions by cutting public expenditure while also cutting income tax and doubling VAT. Instead he threw himself with his usual vigour into the campaign for the first direct elections to the European Parliament, helping to secure an overwhelmingly one-sided result whereby the Tories – for 51 per cent of the vote on a turnout of only 32 per cent – won 60 of the 81 seats. As though to underline that he was still leader of the party where Europe was concerned he held a reception for the new MEPs (who included his old friend Madron Seligman, elected for West Sussex). Two weeks later he attended a party for Tory MPs at Number 10, which must have cost him an effort. Over the summer he conducted the European Community Youth Orchestra at the Avignon Festival and sailed a lot. In September he left for another extended visit to China and south-east Asia, breaking it briefly to fly home for the funeral of Lord Mountbatten.

He was diplomatically absent from Mrs Thatcher's victory conference that autumn; nor did he speak in the House of Commons. In December he did criticise the Government's proposed new immigration proposals, as foreshadowed by Mrs Thatcher before the election.[2] But for the rest he confined his interventions exclusively to Britain's conduct within the EEC. He renewed his repeated pleas to the Government to join the EMS; but Mrs Thatcher was as deaf to his urgings as Callaghan had been. Her concern was with reducing Britain's contribution to the Community budget, which had grown out of proportion to the strength of Britain's stagnant economy since 1974. Heath initially admitted the justice of her claim. In Frankfurt in November he declared that there was indeed 'a major inequity' in the size of the UK contribution which no member could be expected to accept;[3] but he insisted there was nothing to cause a mature Community a major crisis, and increasingly condemned the Government's approach to the budget issue as too negative. Following the celebrated summit in Dublin at which Mrs Thatcher adamantly refused to be satisfied with less than a full rebate, Heath warned that the Community partners were once again beginning to doubt Britain's commitment to Europe. As the dispute grew more heated in the New Year he condemned Mrs Thatcher's threat to withhold payments to the Community altogether: her provocative tactics, he charged, demonstrated a total misunderstanding of how the Community worked.[4]

At the same time he was more concerned than ever that the Community itself was failing to pull its weight on the world stage. He was alarmed by the Soviet invasion of Afghanistan, but considered the Western (American-led) response – consisting mainly of trade sanctions, the cancelling of cultural exchanges and a boycott of the Moscow Olympics – both feeble and irrelevant. As one who had 'captained two national teams in international sport', he reminded the House in January, he believed in keeping politics out of sport. 'The debate is really about world strategy,' he insisted. 'If it is not, it should be.'[5] As so often, he gave the impression that it was just a question of international will. In a number of speeches and articles during 1980 he spoke in sweeping terms of the need for a 'world strategy', but he rarely descended to detail or the practical difficulty of reconciling differing national interests. He was always inclined to broad global perspectives. In 1980 this tendency was powerfully re-inforced by his work on the Brandt Report.

Heath was invited to serve on the Brandt Commission in 1977. It was established on the initiative of Robert Macnamara, President of the World Bank, as an independent commission of distinguished individuals, deliberately not under the aegis of the United Nations and not financed by the World Bank, to look into the widening gap between the rich developed world ('the North') and the poor developing and undeveloped world ('the South'). The former West German Chancellor Willy Brandt agreed to serve as chairman: like Heath he was under-employed since his loss of office in 1974. Of the other seventeen members, seven – including Heath; the former Swedish Prime Minister, Olof Palme; the former French Minister and EEC Commissioner, Edgard Pisani; and the proprietor of the *Washington Post*, Kay Graham – came from the 'North'; ten – including 'Sonny' Ramphal, Secretary-General of the British Commonwealth, and representatives from such varied countries as India, Malaysia, Tanzania, Kuwait, Colombia and Upper Volta – from the 'South', carefully giving the 'South' a majority. In practice the Commission was dominated over the five years of its existence by the triumvirate of Brandt, Heath and Ramphal. The British journalist Anthony Sampson acted as editorial consultant for the first

(1980) report; much of the second (1983) was written by Heath's then assistant Simon May.

Beyond repeated assertions that a united Europe would be able to do more for undeveloped countries, Heath had hitherto shown little positive interest in the Third World. (Neither, for that matter, had Willy Brandt.) But when the invitation came in 1977 it chimed closely with the lessons he was struggling to draw from the experience of seeing the domestic ambitions of his premiership wrecked by international factors outside his control: the breakdown of the world currency system, soaring commodity prices and, above all, the power of the oil weapon. The international order which had prevailed for a quarter of a century after 1945 had collapsed in the early 1970s, bringing inflation, unemployment and social instability to the industrialised 'North' and famine to the 'South'. The task of statesmanship, he now believed, was to build a new world economic order founded on the interdependence of north and south, a projection on to the global scale of the need for consensus and co-operation which he had embraced at home. It was a task whose urgency was clearest to those like Brandt and himself who had learned from bitter experience that no single Government could achieve very much on its own. It was typical – indeed it was very like his response to Macmillan's invitation to become the Conservative Government's 'Mr Europe' in 1960 – that once the plight of the Third World was placed on his agenda he identified himself with it totally and made it fiercely his own, travelling the world exhaustively, speaking and lobbying for the cause.* Brandt called it 'the biggest challenge to mankind for the remainder of the century'.[7] This was an international challenge on a scale Heath felt was worthy of him.

During 1978–9 the Commission met ten times in nine countries, with a great deal of travelling to specific countries in between to see conditions at first hand. The tenth meeting was hosted by Heath at Leeds Castle in Kent in December 1979. Two months later the completed report – *North-South: A Programme for Survival* – was presented by Brandt to UN Secretary-General Kurt Waldheim in New York and simultaneously launched by Heath at a press conference in London. The headline emphasis of the report was on the crisis facing the 'South': the 800 million men, women and children already destitute; the 17 million children every year dying below the age of 5; blindness affecting 30–40 million; illiteracy rates of over 80 per cent

---

* In June 1980 Heath lunched with Roy Jenkins at his house near Oxford. 'He talked without ceasing: sailing for the first course; music for the second; and the Brandt report for the third. But, particularly on the last, he talked very well.'[6]

in 34 countries; the prospect of cities of 30 million people by the year 2000. The Commission proposed a long-term programme of economic restructuring, plus a four-point emergency programme of increased aid. The essential message of the report, however, was not simply the urgent need for humanitarian aid, but the self-interest of the rich in raising the living standards of the world's poor. Unemployment in the 'North' could only be alleviated by enabling the 'South' to buy the goods which they desperately needed but which at present they could not afford. The world economy was a single mechanism: the 'North' would not regain its prosperity unless the 'South' was helped to prosper too.[8]

What appealed to Heath about the Brandt report was that, first, it was a call to *action* to tackle a looming crisis; second, it was a call for concerted *international* action; and third, it was a call for action by *governments*, recognising that market forces by themselves were not enough. In these ways it reflected both his naturally interventionist temperament and his deepest political beliefs, and also offered a new stick with which to beat the neo-liberals now in power in both Britain and America. For the rest of 1980 Heath traversed Britain and the world preaching the gospel, speaking two or three times a week in parish halls and university unions up and down the country. Of course he was not alone: several Labour veterans of the aid lobby were scarcely less active, but Heath drew more attention both as a former Prime Minister and as a Conservative. Frank Judd said he had never seen such crowded meetings; and Frank McElhone that wherever he went he invariably found that Heath had been before him.[9] It was thus largely due to his efforts that the Brandt Report made more impact in Britain than in any other country: by the end of the year the cheap paperback edition (published by Pan) had sold 68,000 copies, compared with a mere 26,000 in Brandt's own Germany, 31,000 in the United States and 20,000 in France. 10,000 people attended a mass lobby of Parliament to demand 'action on Brandt'. Heath was pleased with the British public's response which, he said in December, was 'greater than he dared hope for'.[10] The Government's response, however, was a different matter.

On 16 June the House of Commons debated the Report. Heath was the unquestioned star, speaking impressively and movingly for thirty-five minutes without a note, urging the Government to accept the Brandt challenge and adopt a form of Marshall Plan for the Third World. Practically every other speaker paid tribute to him: even Enoch Powell, who inevitably dissented fundamentally from the Brandt proposals, acknowledged the 'breath-taking comprehensiveness and competence' of Heath's speech. For the Foreign Office, however, Ian Gilmour played a dead bat and committed the Government to nothing at all.[11] The Government's response was, as the Labour MP Austin Mitchell put it in a later debate, 'just a blank negative, with the Prime Minister criticising aid as hand-outs . . . It was as if . . . they wanted to pretend that the Brandt Report did not exist, like the right hon. Member for Sidcup.'[12] Mrs Thatcher was unsympathetic to the Brandt approach anyway; but Heath's advocacy was all that was needed to ensure that her Government would have nothing to do with it.

At first Heath hoped that other governments might be more positive. He peppered successive summits of Western leaders with pleas for concerted action. In October 1981 a special summit was specifically convened at Cancun in Mexico, attended by leaders from twenty-two countries under the joint chairmanship of the Mexican President and Pierre Trudeau. Some were sympathetic – notably Canada, Australia and the Netherlands. But nothing came of it. President Reagan attended reluctantly, on condition that there was no agenda and no communiqué. Chancellor Schmidt was ill. For Britain Lord Carrington mouthed the usual hollow platitudes. Heath called Cancun 'a terrible disappointment' and condemned the leaders' 'lack of imagination and willpower'.[13] Speaking in Lagos a year later, he pinned the failure unambiguously on Governments 'on both sides of the Atlantic' which did not believe in international co-operation in principle.[14] In truth Brandt was out of step with the temper of the early 1980s. Not only did its proposal for a massive transfer of resources from north to south run counter to the self-help ideology of Ronald Reagan and Mrs Thatcher; it appeared at a time of mounting international tension following the Iranian revolution and the Soviet invasion of Afghanistan. In February 1983 the Commission published an updated report, entitled *Common Crisis: North-South: Co-operation for World Recovery*, which warned that the crisis of the poorest countries had got worse, not better, since 1980 and focused particularly on the mounting problem of Third World indebtedness. But with no international will to do anything about it, Brandt II made even less real impact than Brandt I, and the commission disbanded.

Heath retained a typically possessive interest in the subject. For the rest of the decade he was to be found supporting projects to develop water supplies and sanitation in Africa, or launching campaigns for Oxfam. In November 1984 he joined a Tory backbench revolt against a cut in the Government's aid budget; and the following year he vehemently denounced Britain's 'nasty, narrow-minded' decision to withdraw from UNESCO.[15] Gradually, however, Brandt faded from the front of his concerns and fell into place as just one plank in his wholesale indictment of the failure of statesmanship and short-sighted moral bankruptcy of Thatcherism. His favourite theme was the contrast between the constructive vision of the postwar gener-ation which had built NATO, the IMF and the EEC from the wreckage of 1945 and the feebleness of their present-day successors. The Bretton Woods conference of 1944, he wrote in *The Times* in 1983, lasted twenty-two days and established a financial system that lasted for thirty years. The Marshall Plan was agreed in three weeks and implemented in less than a year. From the Messina conference in 1955 to the creation of the EEC took just two years:

> These remarkable creative political acts, in which wholly new in-stitutions and systems of international order were launched by a mere handful of meetings, starkly highlight the irrelevance of the plethora of ministerial conferences and summits which litter today's international agenda but achieve next to nothing. What is needed are binding agreements, not empty promises: adequate time to reach agreements, rather than two-day media festivals; and the willingness to face up to collective responsibility, rather than to pass the buck.[16]

Creating 'new systems of international order': this was what Heath thought politics at the highest level was about. He had cut his politi-cal teeth in the 1930s and all his formative experiences told him that international disorder led inexorably to war. As the Prime Minister who had taken Britain into Europe, and now as an international elder statesman, he saw himself in the great tradition of George Marshall, Dean Acheson, Konrad Adenauer and Jean Monnet. It was this in-heritance which he believed Ronald Reagan and Margaret Thatcher were betraying and which he yearned, more than anything else in these years, to see restored and built upon.

During most of 1979–80, however, Heath's preoccupation with Brandt had the benefit – certainly from the Government's point of view, and perhaps also from his own – of diverting him from dom-estic politics. Though he regarded Geoffrey Howe's monetarist experiment with a baleful eye, for the first year of the Thatcher Government – indeed for nearly eighteen months – as both inflation (temporarily) and unemployment (enduringly) soared, Heath held his peace. By the autumn of 1980, however, Tory disquiet was beginning to find its voice. On 14 October the aged Harold Mac-millan surfaced on television with a lurid condemnation of the Government's policies; two weeks later Geoffrey Rippon warned of the 'danger of creating a society in which moneylending is the only profitable venture'.[17] Heath was still circumspect, but on 31 October he told a meeting of Birmingham businessmen: 'It cannot be right that we see small businesses built up by hard work over the generations now being forced into bankruptcy.'[18] (He knew what he was talking about: he was thinking specifically of his father's former building firm in Broadstairs.) When he broke cover, however, it was as a result of an unpremeditated explosion.

The occasion was an American election night radio broadcast on 5 November.* He was sitting in the studio, half asleep at 3.30 am, when suddenly the great guru of monetarism himself, Milton Friedman, came on the line from Chicago. At once Heath woke up and let fly, casting restraint to the winds. Ronald Reagan, he declared optimistically, was 'too intelligent' to be persuaded by Friedman's 'ruinous monetarism': 'You want to abolish the industrial base in the same way as is happening in Britain in which smaller firms are going bankrupt more rapidly than ever before.' Unemployment in Britain was now nearing three million, compared with a mere 600,000 in 1973. 'People realise now what the merits of the last government, the last Conservative government, were, compared with the catastrophic things which they see happening to themselves today.'[20]

'Ruinous' and 'catastrophic': this was the first time Heath had spoken out in such terms. A number of Labour MPs, delighted at this distraction from the Opposition's own chronic disarray, promptly put down a motion congratulating him on his frankness. (Norman St John Stevas, then Leader of the House, dutifully characterised this unusual cross-party alliance as 'the blind leading the blind'. Only three months later, however, Stevas was abruptly sacked, after which he began to say very similar things himself.) Next day at Prime Minister's Question Time Mrs Thatcher was goaded by Michael Foot to hit back with 'a withering broadside' at her predecessor. Quoting Heath's resolute foreword to the 1970 manifesto ('Nothing has done Britain more harm . . . than the endless backing and filling we have seen in recent years') she said she was sure Heath would agree that the Government should have the courage to stick to its policy. The first objective, now as in 1970, was to curb inflation. *The Times* recalled Kipling's dictum that 'the female of the species is deadlier than the male'. Below the gangway, Heath 'looked decidedly uneasy'.[21]

---

* Privately he had no use for either candidate, President Carter or Ronald Reagan, dismissing the US election – off the air – as 'a choice between an incompetent and a cowboy actor'.[19]

But Hugo Young in the *Sunday Times* thought that Heath had only blurted out what most Tories privately believed. Beneath the protestations of loyalty, he wrote, 'the party is pullulating with a dissent which does not speak its name in public'. The former zealots had become agnostics and the agnostics sceptics. Even ministers were worried. Heath had cut through the conspiracy of silence. 'Many MPs don't like it, but he says what many of them think . . . about the present government. It seems to me he's done the party a service.'[22] When Parliament reassembled, he intervened on the last day of the debate on the Queen's Speech to expound his critique at greater length. 'Our generation', he affirmed, echoing Jim Callaghan on the other side, 'came into politics to prevent unemployment.' Yet after twenty-five years of rising living standards, unemployment was now back to the levels of the 1930s; and contrary to the Government's official optimism it was getting worse. The economy was heading for disaster unless the Government changed course, lowered interest rates and let the pound fall. By destroying small businesses and endangering large firms, strict adherence to monetarism was defeating its own ends.

> Can it be right to have rates of interest under which those who have spent 20 or 30 years of their lives – as my father did – building up their own family business have found it destroyed in this past year? . . . The cost of unemployment produced by the present interest rates is greater than the interest rate benefit itself.[23]

The Tory benches sat silent through this indictment. Jock Bruce-Gardyne heckled at one point: 'How many elections did you lose?' But Heath told him to go back to writing editorials for the *Daily Telegraph* and he received little support. Trailing Labour by 24 points (32 per cent to 56 per cent) in the latest poll, the Tory party – including half the Cabinet – was deeply worried by where Mrs Thatcher was leading it. Yet she was unbending, adamant that there would be no U-turn. ('You turn if you want to; the lady's not for turning.') Next day in a radio interview she asserted quite specifically that the inflation of the 1970s had been caused by Government spending between 1970 and 1974, and damned Heath and Callaghan equally for advocating once again the old discredited remedies of higher spending and higher borrowing. There was, she repeatedly insisted, 'no alternative' to sound money.[24] The party gritted its teeth, swallowed its doubts and backed her.

At the beginning of 1981 Heath suffered a recurrence of the thyroid trouble that had affected him in the mid-1970s. By March it was serious enough for him to cancel all his engagements for the next two months. It was announced that he would rest at home and stay with friends. In fact he went to stay in a hotel in Torquay, which he left only twice a day for windy walks along the seafront, well wrapped up and flanked by bodyguards.[25] He came up to London only to attend the Budget debate on 16 March. This was the traumatic Budget, piling further deflation on an already deep recession, which drove the leading 'wets' in the Cabinet – Jim Prior, Peter Walker and Ian Gilmour – to the brink of resignation. Curiously, however, Heath did not damn it; rather he detected in it signs that the Chancellor was abandoning strict monetarism and voted *with* the Government to help defeat a backbench revolt against higher petrol tax.[26] Then he went back to Torquay.

At just this moment, when Heath was *hors de combat*, the SDP was founded. Though the new party was a reaction primarily against the leftward trend of Labour, it quickly attracted at least as much public support from former Tory voters alienated by the rightward trend of Thatcherism. Since the issue above all others that had driven Roy Jenkins and his colleagues out of the Labour party was Europe, and their principal economic policy was a call for reflation indistinguishable from that being made inside and outside the Cabinet by Tory 'wets', there was immediate speculation that a number of Tory MPs, and even Heath himself, might join. The SDP was in many ways the embodiment of that aspiration to 'national unity' to which Heath had tried to appeal in 1974. Much of its impetus derived from the liberating experience of the 1975 referendum in which Heath and Jenkins had come together as joint leaders of the European campaign. As early as April 1980, Ian Gilmour – still in the Cabinet – had told Jenkins: 'You and Ted would be a formidable combination.'[27] A year later, when the new party became a reality there seemed a serious possibility that he would join. An apparently well-informed article by Charles Douglas-Home in *The Times* ('Will Ted Heath be the Gang's Biggest Catch?') considered it less a question of whether but when. He clearly had no future in the Tory party. He was said to have indicated that he would not expect to be leader, but he could bring over a group of perhaps twenty MPs (including Walker and Gilmour) who could be a crucial factor in a hung Parliament. Meanwhile, 'Mr Heath's friends . . . think that his enforced idleness gives him useful time to consider his own position.'[28]

In fact this was nonsense. Certainly as the SDP bandwagon rolled that summer with opinion polls, backed by a string of sensational by-elections, suggesting that they might (in alliance with the Liberals) sweep the country at the next election, Heath took a close interest. Half a dozen Tory MPs – in addition to the one who took the plunge – indicated to Roy Jenkins that they were very close to coming over.[29] But Heath held no such conversations with Jenkins or anyone else. Had he been younger he might have been tempted. But there was no way he was going to give Mrs Thatcher the satisfaction of driving him out of the Tory party. His boast was and always remained that he represented the true Tory tradition, the generous 'one nation' Toryism of Churchill, Eden, Macmillan and Home from which Mrs Thatcher and her mean-spirited acolytes were the aberration. He was convinced that sooner or later – and the way things were going in 1981, it would probably be sooner – the party would come back to its true character. The SDP might well have a role to play in bringing that about. He did not in the least blame those of his friends who indicated in 1983 that they intended to vote for the Alliance.[30] Secretly he might even have done so himself. But his public stance depended absolutely on remaining loyal to the Tory party.

'What I want to see', he told the *Guardian*'s interviewer Terry Coleman in November, 'is the Conservative Party reoccupying the middle ground.' It was the Government's abandonment of the centre ground that was allowing the Alliance to usurp it.[31] He still regretted the Liberals' rejection of his offer of coalition in 1974. Now Shirley Williams's stunning capture of the safe Tory seat of Crosby opened up new possibilities. 'If you go on with Crosby after Crosby until the General Election,' he told the *Yorkshire Post*, 'you will have another sort of Government.' He would never change his party, but he did not rule out service – as a Tory – in a coalition with the SDP. In a hung Parliament, 'there might be one or two acceptable invitations'. He was prepared to serve his country wherever he could.[32]

This was pretty unambiguous, but was perhaps insufficiently reported outside Yorkshire. Roy Jenkins for one seems to have failed to grasp the logic of Heath's position:

Heath himself, who must have greatly welcomed our success, nevertheless put the telescope to his blind eye, affected not to see us and behaved in form although not in substance as though it was business as usual in party politics. Three months later he came unnecessarily to Glasgow [where Jenkins was fighting the Hillhead by-election] nominally to support my Conservative opponent, proceeded to deliver a slashing attack on Mrs Thatcher's whole policy at a large public meeting, made some amiable remarks about me at a press conference, and departed. It was a mystifying performance.[33]

The truth was that Heath did welcome the SDP's success and had everything to hope for from an election result that would topple Mrs Thatcher and pull the Tory party back to the middle ground. He would have been happy to go into coalition with Jenkins to reflate the economy and regain the momentum of European integration. But he could not be expected to destroy his standing in the Tory party by saying so. Unlike Jenkins and Shirley Williams, who had given Labour up for lost, he was still in his own mind fighting Mrs Thatcher for the soul of the Tory party. In later years he took the line that the 'Gang of Four' too should have stayed in the Labour party and fought their corner, blaming the SDP for having made Mrs Thatcher's hegemony possible.[34] But this was not his view in 1982. When he returned to the political fray after his illness, he resumed his critique of the Government with renewed vigour; but always from within, as the true guardian of the Conservative faith.

Once again he broke his silence almost by accident. On 1 July 1981 he stood in at short notice for the American economist, J. K. Galbraith, who had been booked to speak to a London business conference on 'The British Economy: Strategies for Renewal'. The recession was now at its worst, with unemployment over three million. A few days earlier riots had erupted in Bristol and Brixton. (In the following weeks they spread to Toxteth and a dozen other English towns and cities.) While ministers insisted that unemployment was no excuse for lawlessness, Heath had no hesitation in blaming crime and racial violence on the Government's 'incomprehensible policies'.

> If you have half a million young people hanging around on the streets all day you will have a massive increase in juvenile crime. Of course you will get racial tension when you have young blacks with less chance of getting jobs . . .
>
> Whether you talk to businessmen or workers they do not understand the *raison d'être* of what is going on. It is extremely dangerous in any democracy not to understand why policies are being pursued, even if they are monetarist.

He repeated his plea for partnership between Government, management and trade unions, not just a 'simple doctrine'.[35]

His speech drew the usual backbench outcry. Two days later Heath appeared on the 'Jimmy Young Programme' and bluntly asserted his right to speak out:

> I am not going to be intimidated by anybody, whether it be from

the press or the battling brigadiers who send me stinking letters. I do not mind. There is no need to write. I am going to tell the country plain home truths which the great majority of people recognise.

I am not going to stop. I shall not be stopped in the House. I shall not be stopped by anyone at No. 10. I shall go on doing it.

His cadence was becoming quite Churchillian. He might almost have added 'I shall fight them on the beaches'. He went on to say that he had never known such intolerance in the party before:

Either you agree with everything and you just become a lackey, in which case you will be described as loyal and 'dry', or you have contrary views and express them, without in any way indulging in personalities, in which case you are disloyal and 'wet' and ought to be chucked out.

I object to the whole level of political discussion at the moment, that there must never be a U-turn, that people are 'wet' or 'dry' and so on. This is childish. Why cannot we discuss the merits of these things, instead of trying to encapsulate them in words like 'wet' or 'dry' or 'U-turn'?

If a Government finds that circumstances change when it is in operation is it not stupid to say we must not change anything we have been doing or which we planned four years ago?[36]

The possibility of a Government 'U-turn' dominated political discussion in the autumn of 1981. It was just over two years since Mrs Thatcher had come to power – just about the point in the Government's life at which Heath, in the simple Thatcherite view of history, had turned tail and run away in 1972. Most of the political world was convinced that Mrs Thatcher would likewise be forced eventually to bow to the intolerable pressure of high unemployment, social unrest and plummeting opinion polls: one MP warned of 'the sharpest and most involuntary U-turn in history' unless the Government acted soon.[37] But she, with Heath's experience explicitly before her as the precedent she must at all costs avoid, was absolutely determined not to be seen to bend. In September she sacked three more 'wets' – Christopher Soames, Mark Carlisle and Ian Gilmour, who came out of Downing Street asserting that the Government was 'heading for the rocks' – and replaced them with younger men of her own stamp – Nigel Lawson, Cecil Parkinson and Norman Tebbit; at the same time she exiled Jim Prior unwillingly to Northern Ireland.

The party conference met against a background of rumbling discontent. Gilmour, Stevas and Rippon led a growing chorus of former ministers calling for a change of course; Peter Walker echoed them discreetly from inside the Cabinet. Fourteen young MPs of the class of 1979 led by William Waldegrave and Chris Patten (dubbed the 'Blue Chip' group) published a pamphlet entitled *Changing Gear*. Another group of four wrote to *The Times*.[38] There was talk of a candidate – perhaps Rippon – standing against Mrs Thatcher for the leadership. Rippon did not rule this out, but said that he would do so only 'in very exceptional circumstances', if there was no other way to force a change.[39]

Heath was generally seen as heading this gathering revolt, but he did not try to lead it. He operated entirely alone, making no attempt to garner support or construct a Heath faction within the party. That he would have thought improper conduct in an ex-Prime Minister. It was beneath his dignity to plot and scheme. He only once attended a backbench committee: then he sat at the back and said nothing.[40] His practice – arrogant or honourable according to taste – was simply to go on saying what he believed, in speeches and interviews, and leave it to others to respond or not as they saw fit. His only organisation was his private office, which consisted of two young research assistants plus three secretaries, all working from his MP's room in the Norman Shaw building. He had also a PPS – appointed by the Tory Whips – to help with his parliamentary work and liaise discreetly with the 'usual channels'. This doubtful honour was held successively by Robert Key, Mark Robinson, Andrew Rowe and, from 1989, by Robert Hughes. Rowe denied that the job was a poisoned chalice: the kiss of death was being the sort of person the Whips thought of appointing in the first place.[41]

On 6 October, the week before the conference, Heath spoke to the Federation of Conservative Students at Manchester and launched 'his fiercest attack so far' on Government policies, claiming that businessmen, workers and ordinary people had all reached the point of saying that the price of monetarism was unacceptable: 'If more than three million unemployed are needed to get inflation down to a level higher than it was 2½ years ago, how many more millions of unemployed will be required to bring it down to . . . to what level? – to a level that has never been revealed?'

'Many of us', he declared, 'have remained silent for a long time on these matters, perhaps for too long, in order that the dire consequences of the present dogmatic policies could be more widely recognised.' But the situation was getting worse, and the policy more dogmatic. 'The time has come to speak out.' It was time, he suggested, for 'a completely fresh assessment of Conservative economic policy', in the interest, he added significantly, not only of the country but also of the party 'for which some of us have worked throughout our political lives'. Was this, the press wondered, a hint that he might himself challenge Mrs Thatcher for the leadership? Rather it was just another assurance that he had no intention of defecting to the SDP.

He proposed his own package of policies, based on European co-operation, 'to break away from the killing treadmill of spiralling interest rates'. As well as membership of the EMS he proposed the reintroduction of exchange controls to 'build a ring fence around European money and capital markets' which were being unnaturally forced up by high US rates; plus a selective programme of capital investment and a 'massive' retraining programme. 'The only alternative is to drag on down the dreary path of ever-deepening recession.' To the charge that such expenditure would fuel inflation, he retorted angrily – still fighting the battles of 1972–4 – 'How dare those who run the biggest budget deficit in history reproach others with the heinous crime of printing money?'[42]

This time Mrs Thatcher got her retaliation in first. Heath's advance text calling for 'a return to consensus politics' reached her on a visit to Australia. She pre-empted him with a 'blistering retort':

> Consensus seems to be the process of abandoning all beliefs, principles, values and policies . . . It is something in which no one believes and to which no one objects . . . It is the process of avoiding the very issues that have to be solved . . . What great causes have ever been fought and won under the banner of 'I stand for consensus'?[43]

Heath's latest blast was immediately condemned by the loyalists, among them Edward Du Cann – 'We want no Teddy Benns in the Tory party' – who just a few months before had himself been urging a national recovery programme. Yet *The Times* warned that his arguments could not so easily be ignored. His 'devastating speech to Conservative students at Manchester yesterday' showed that he remained the Government's 'weightiest critic . . . This time the Conservative reflex which brands him as disloyal will be struggling with a growing suspicion . . . that he is saying exactly what needs to be said.'[44]

Another editorial a few days later judged that Heath's critique scored 'several bulls and a few magpies'. The Government needed to get away from crude monetary targets and find a more balanced policy, without abandoning fiscal rectitude. 'A change of substance is desirable: a change of style is essential . . . She should not in her economic strategy any longer pursue a foolish consistency; she should tack a little.'[45]

Interviewed on 'Panorama' the day before the Tory conference opened, Heath drew encouragement from the sense of growing support: 'You cannot avoid the fact that valid criticisms are being made by our supporters.'[46] Likewise he told Terry Coleman of the *Guardian*: 'I'm in no need of consolation. I think the evidence is growing, very fast, that people do believe that what I'm saying is right.'[47] A Marplan poll found Tory voters divided: 39 per cent were loyal to Mrs Thatcher, but a substantial minority (18 per cent) still wished Heath was leader (while 16 per cent would have preferred Lord Carrington). (NOP found a very similar split: 44 per cent for Thatcher, 24 per cent for Heath.)[48]

At Blackpool, however, the party – although deeply worried – rallied to Mrs Thatcher and Geoffrey Howe. Heath spoke on the first morning, and was listened to politely as he repeated, in more moderate language, his plea for reflation and consensus. 'As he reached the rostrum, the cheering almost drowned the booing.' He relieved the tension with a nervous joke ('Please don't applaud, it may irritate your neighbour'), but ran into some heckling when he warned that the party faced its most critical moment for sixty years. He made it plain that he and his supporters had absolutely no intention of going over to the SDP. 'This is still our party, all of us, all over the country.' But he warned that if the Government did not change course the Alliance might attract enough disillusioned Tory voters to let Labour back in. It was not only the young who were revolting. The plight of the middle-aged unemployed with no prospect of getting another job was even worse. At the end he received 'a respectful but cautious ovation'.[49] Winding up the debate Howe was uncompromising. He too quoted Heath's 1970 pledge not to run away from policies once embarked on; he also quoted tellingly from the same manifesto the promise that 'in implementing all our policies the need to curb inflation will come first, for only then can our broader strategy succeed'. 'If it was true then', he argued, 'when inflation was half as high, it is twice as true today.' He received a standing ovation 'in which Mr Heath had no choice but to join'.[50] Two days later Mrs Thatcher's speech included a conciliatory olive twig – she welcomed the fact that Heath had spoken, acknowledged the right of dissent ('The diversity of our party . . . is part of our strength') and explicitly welcomed his intention to campaign in the imminent Croydon by-election. But she still ruled out a U-turn: 'I will not change just to court popularity.'[51]

Nor did she, in essentials. Yet the Government did acknowledge that its simple faith in controlling the money supply had been un-realistic: inflation was coming down even though the monetary targets had been exceeded. In December the Treasury adopted a broader definition of money supply and Howe's 1982 Budget revised the targets, at the same time raising personal tax allowances and announcing some inducements to industry and small businesses. This was enough to allow Heath to declare, first, that monetarism had lost 'any intellectual justification' it ever had[52] and then jubilantly to pronounce 'the death of monetarism':

> As the money supply has obstinately refused to comply with his brackets, he has moved his brackets to meet the money supply . . . His action is pragmatic . . . and I congratulate him on it . . . We have won the intellectual battle against monetarism and dogma . . . The alien doctrines of Friedman and Hayek remain only to be buried.[53]

His transparent purpose was to proclaim that the lady too had per-formed her U-turn. Strict monetarism, however, turned out to be only the top dressing of Thatcherism. Its abandonment did not im-ply any change in the Government's fundamental character or purpose.

Meanwhile within three weeks of Howe's Budget the political landscape was transformed by Argentina's invasion of the Falkland Islands. Though the invasion raised serious questions about her Government's responsibility for sending the wrong signals to Buenos Aires – Carrington resigned from the Foreign Office in ex-piation – the war that followed was the saving of Mrs Thatcher. Her unflinching determination to recover the islands by military force – and the heroism, professionalism and good luck of the Task Force in actually doing so – rescued her from the pit of unprecedented personal unpopularity and invested her with an aura of invincibility which sustained her until 1990. The resolution which she showed in the South Atlantic reflected back on her economic performance at home: standing up to General Galtieri became equated with her re-fusal to heed the siren voices calling for a U-turn on unemployment. At the end of 1981, with the SDP-Liberal Alliance far ahead in the polls, the survival of her Government looked precarious at best; six months later her triumphant re-election appeared inevitable, as in-deed it proved. The Falklands crowned Mrs Thatcher with the laurels of a successful war leader. For the next seven years she was able to dominate British politics to an extent unprecedented in modern times. The Tory party loves a winner. Heath, the three-times loser, by contrast found himself suddenly more isolated than ever, all but excommunicated and reduced to sniping sourly from the wings. Just when things had seemed to be moving back his way, the 'Falklands Factor' finally extinguished Heath's prospects of rehabilitation.

About the war itself he said remarkably little.* He was just leaving for another visit to China when the invasion occurred, so he took no part in the early, emotional debates on the sending of the Task Force. Not until the fifth debate on 13 May did he intervene, by which time the *Belgrano* and the *Sheffield* had been sunk and British troops were poised to reinvade the islands, while the UN Secretary-General and US Secretary of State Alexander Haig strove for a negotiated settlement. He began by declaring his 'whole-hearted support' for the Government's conduct of the crisis up to now. But as he went on it became clear that he was much more in sympathy with the more conciliatory line being pursued by Francis Pym (the new Foreign Secretary) than with Mrs Thatcher's evident impatience to be at the enemy. He urged the Government to ignore charges of a sell-out and keep on seeking a negotiated settlement, insisting that the wishes of the islanders could not be – as Mrs Thatcher had proclaimed – 'paramount': the interests of 1,600 Falklanders could not be allowed to determine British defence policy. In this respect, he argued, General Galtieri's alleged 'fascism' was irrelevant: Britain had gone to war with Hitler and Mussolini not over their internal policies, but because they threatened British interests.[55] This somewhat surprising *realpolitik* anticipated his attitude to Saddam Hussein and the Gulf War nine years later; in 1982 it evoked the same furious anathemas from the loyalist Tory benches – Bernard Braine, Ivor Stanbrook and Nicholas Winterton to the fore – accusing him of appeasement and lack of patriotism.

Certainly he ended up very close to opposing the use of force to recover the islands. Partly this may have been an instinctive reaction against Mrs Thatcher's bellicosity; partly it reflected a widely remarked pattern that those with personal experience of war were least keen on a resort to arms. (Older colleagues like Willie Whitelaw felt

---

* No more than anyone else did he anticipate the Argentine invasion. Arguing in a defence debate the previous July that the critical area outside NATO was the Gulf, he stated it as an obvious platitude that 'The Falkland Islands are unlikely to cause a major explosion.' No one dissented.[54]

that Mrs Thatcher found it easier to take military decisions precisely because she had never fought herself.) Partly too it reflected his deeply held belief that disputes – political or industrial – could always be resolved by diplomacy and compromise rather than by conflict. The precedent he liked to recall was Kennedy's skilful handling of the Cuba crisis in 1962. Galtieri, he believed, like Khrushchev, had misjudged the likely response to his aggression. But as Kennedy had deliberately left Khrushchev a way to back down without losing face, so Heath argued that the mature course was to leave Galtieri a face-saving way to withdraw.

Once the Battle of Port Stanley was joined he could only applaud the outcome and congratulate the British forces. Nevertheless he still maintained that the policy of 'Fortress Falklands' was an absurd distortion of defence priorities. He was sickened by the victory celebrations which hailed the war as the apotheosis of Thatcherism and the rediscovery of British greatness. He was, frankly, jealous of the laurels now heaped upon Mrs Thatcher; and his bad temper boiled over when she proposed to defuse the tricky question of the origins of the crisis by means of an enquiry that would reach back beyond 1979 to take in the stewardship of previous governments. In the House he angrily demanded to know by what right the Prime Minister 'presumes to institute an enquiry into the policies and management of previous administrations'. He had nothing to hide, he insisted: his sole concern was to preserve the important constitutional principle that 'no Prime Minister, however powerful, has the right to direct an enquiry to go into another Prime Minister's administration'. But the personal animus behind his objection was obvious:

> It is so open to abuse. One administration can go rummaging through the papers of another administration and then use them for its own perverse purposes . . .
>
> Those of us who have experienced the treatment of a previous Administration by herself and her advisers can have no confidence whatever in an enquiry set up without consultation or consideration with the previous Heads of Administration.[56]

Mrs Thatcher replied firmly that she did not need the permission of previous prime ministers, but that she would in fact seek it as a courtesy. 'I shall be astonished if there is any difficulty.'[57] In a radio interview Heath still maintained that she had been wrongly advised, but then wisely changed tack to endorse Jim Callaghan's more telling criticism that she was simply trying to divert attention from her own

Government's responsibility for the war.[58] In the end, once duly consulted, Heath pronounced himself satisfied with the composition and terms of reference of the Franks Committee. When its report was debated by the House he did not speak; and he has scarcely said a word on the subject since.

Mrs Thatcher resisted the temptation to take immediate advantage of the 'Falklands Factor' by going to the country in 1982, but chose to carry on until June 1983. Though unemployment remained appallingly high, there were signs that parts of the economy, at least in the south, were beginning to recover from the harsh medicine of 1979–81: inflation was down to 4 per cent. It began to look as though the conventional wisdom that no Government could possibly be re-elected with a million – let alone three million – people unemployed could after all be defied. This was the spectre which had compelled Heath to take alarm in 1972 and of which he and the other 'wets' had been warning since 1979. Despite the 1981 riots, it now seemed that 'politically intolerable' levels of unemployment could be tolerated by a Government – now facing a divided Opposition – which was prepared to calculate that money in the pockets of the employed majority outweighed the protest votes of the jobless, who were largely concentrated in Labour seats anyway. Heath continued to warn that the Government should not underestimate the difficulty of winning with unemployment so high, pinning his unspoken hopes on the possibility that the Alliance might yet hold the balance. ('One should not assume', he suggested in February, 'that it will not.')[59] He still wanted more done to reflate not just the British but the world economy. But with the relaxation of strict monetary targets the heat had gone out of his attacks on the Government's economic management: in March he was quite benign about Howe's pre-election Budget. From now on the focus of his criticism began to switch from economic policy to the social philosophy of Thatcherism.

In common with most of the party he roundly condemned a leaked 'Think Tank' report – it was leaked by the 'wets' in the Cabinet – proposing the virtual abolition of the National Health Service in favour of private health insurance: such was the outcry that Mrs Thatcher backed down and disowned all knowledge of a report she had in fact strongly favoured.[60] He also repeated his total opposition to education vouchers, and with Gilmour and others abstained in protest at the Government's failure to uprate unemployment benefit in line with inflation. Earlier in the year the death of 'Rab' Butler had given him the chance to point the contrast between the Toryism of Butler's day and the present: 'His was the true moderate Conservatism which did so much to create the stability and prosperity of

post-war Britain.'[61] In a radio interview in October he explicitly rejected what he held to be a betrayal of the Tory tradition of social
obligation:

> It is extraordinary how far the party has been swept by a group
> who . . . do not believe in Toryism at its best.
>
> They do not believe in the responsibility we have to each other,
> recognition that there are some people who are never going to be
> victors in competition, some people who are always going to have
> disadvantages, difficulties, about health and education. It is to
> them we have responsibilities.[62]

Willie Whitelaw did his best to rebut the Government's increasingly uncaring image. But the suspicion was now firmly planted that
the Government had a 'hidden agenda' to dismantle the Welfare State
as soon as it dared.

During the election, however, Heath once again played a loyal and
uncontroversial hand. As in 1979 he campaigned energetically up and
down the country, but he said nothing to rock the boat. He made
headlines only once by suggesting that the Government's initial
policies had made the recession deeper than it need have been;
generally he stuck to his line that monetarism was a folly which was
now dead and buried. He appeared to signal that he was ready to return to office if invited ('That is entirely a matter for the Prime
Minister'), but he cannot seriously have expected a call.[63] Though
the Alliance performed well – winning 25 per cent of the vote to
Labour's 27 per cent – it won only 23 MPs. There was no hung Parliament. On the contrary, Mrs Thatcher secured a crushing overall
majority of 144. This result ended what lingering hopes Heath entertained that she would prove to be a short-lived aberration. She had
come triumphantly through the pit of 1981–2 and was now confirmed as an historic winner, assured of at least two terms in
Downing Street. The Tory party would follow adoringly wherever
she chose to lead it. The 1980s would be the Thatcher decade – with
Heath cast finally into outer darkness.*

---

* 1983 saw another redistribution of constituencies. Heath's seat was only marginally reorganised but splendidly renamed Old Bexley and Sidcup. Under whatever
name, his majority was now unassailable, with the Alliance easily beating Labour
for second place:

E. Heath (Conservative)	22,422
P. Vickers (Liberal Alliance)	9,704
C. Kiff (Labour)	5,116
Conservative majority	12,718[64]

With Mrs Thatcher's hegemony now established for the foresee-able future, Heath settled into a form of internal exile. For the next seven years she swept all before her – not only domestically but in-creasingly on the international stage as well. The 'wets' who since 1975 had kept their heads down or bent with the wind, hoping it would soon blow itself out, were themselves blown away one by one, and dropped from sight. Francis Pym, abruptly sacked from the Foreign Office the moment the election was over, tried to set up a sort of anti-Thatcherite pressure group called Centre Forward; but it lacked any conviction and came to nothing. No one of weight in the party was willing to be associated with it. Dissidence there certainly was within the parliamentary party, as Mrs Thatcher's style became increasingly arbitrary and autocratic; but despite some tricky moments like the Westland affair and her willingness to allow the Americans to use British bases to bomb Libya (both 1986), her force of personality and electoral success – still facing a fractured and dem-oralised opposition – maintained an unstoppable momentum. Military victory in the South Atlantic was soon matched by the defeat at home of Arthur Scargill's NUM: the Tories' sweet revenge for 1972 and 1974, which further underlined the contrast between Mrs Thatcher and her hapless predecessor. Trade union power, left-wing local authorities, and nationalised industries all crumbled before her as she took on the citadels of the Opposition and subdued them in turn.

Almost alone now, Heath still stood out stubbornly against the tide. Pym, Prior, Gilmour and other dismissed ministers now formed a complete alternative Tory Cabinet-in-exile, but none of them conducted a sustained or co-ordinated resistance. Peter Walker voiced occasional carefully coded reservations, but stayed in the Cabinet. Even Michael Heseltine, who dramatically walked out of the Cabinet in 1986, bided his time and took care to say nothing that could be construed as disloyal. Heath alone remained resolutely un-reconciled, outspokenly dismissive of the whole phenomenon and philosophy of Thatcherism. Far more than Neil Kinnock's distracted Labour Party or the stumbling Alliance, he was the embodiment of anti-Thatcherism. To the zealots of the New Right, of course, he had always represented everything that Mrs Thatcher was dedicated to sweeping away: 'consensus', 'corporatism', incomes policy and the mixed economy. But up until 1982–3 these ideas had retained sub-stantial legitimacy and respect, and Heath himself still commanded some residual support. Now it seemed the argument had been won. Practically the whole party – including many who had supported him eagerly at the time – looked back to 1970–4 with embarrassment as a nightmare period never to be repeated. Like Trotsky in the

Soviet Union, Heath became an 'unperson' in Tory history, barely to be distinguished from Wilson and Callaghan: the bright young men who had cut their teeth in his private office – Douglas Hurd, John MacGregor, Kenneth Baker, William Waldegrave – were at pains to cover their tracks and jump aboard the Thatcherite bandwagon. Heath was enthroned as the anti-Christ of the Thatcher Revolution with whom no one hoping for advancement could afford to acknowledge any sympathy or association, past or present.

In a typically perverse way, Heath rather relished his isolation: it proved to him that he was right. He just plugged on, impervious: solitary, thick-skinned, elephantine, often publicly silent for weeks or months at a time, then weighing in with a flurry of angry pronouncements denouncing the whole basis and direction of Government policy. Few of them had any effect: if anything they were counterproductive. His arguments were routinely dismissed as mere jealousy and bile – just Ted blowing off steam again – and the job of other opponents of particular policies was made that much harder. If Heath was against something, it must be all right. Just as his unpopularity and stubbornness had paved the way for her *coup* in 1975, so his unswerving opposition continued paradoxically to legitimise and bolster Mrs Thatcher right through the 1980s.

Yet he had two particular themes which continue to resonate in the 1990s with more prescience than they were given at the time. One, as ever, was Europe; the other was the need for industrial investment, partly to reduce unemployment in the short term but also to rebuild the national infrastructure as the basis of future prosperity in the long term. Both were his old themes reaching right back to the early 1960s: they go deeper than technical questions of economic management – money supply, incomes policy and the like. Leaving aside both ideology and personal considerations, both go to the heart of Heath's deeply felt and serious opposition to what seemed to him the narrow-minded and short-sighted policies of the Thatcher Government.

The question of Britain's place in Europe – at the heart or on the fringe of the Community as it developed – did not catch fire again until the very end of the decade. When it did it was the issue that precipitated Mrs Thatcher's eventual fall; but for most of these years she won more applause than criticism for her continued intransigence over the British budget contribution and the cost of the Common Agricultural Policy. Heath repeatedly charged that her uncompromising attitude merely antagonised Britain's partners and called on the Government to demonstrate its commitment to Europe by joining the Exchange Rate Mechanism (ERM) of the EMS. This Mrs Thatcher resolutely refused to do, despite the well-leaked desire of both her new Chancellor (Nigel Lawson) and her new Foreign Secretary (Geoffrey Howe) to do so. In 1986, however, she consented, apparently without fully grasping its implications, to sign the Single European Act which committed Britain not only to the achievement of a unified internal market (of which she approved) by the end of 1992 but also to accelerated progress towards a European union with common policies on social, industrial and environmental matters. She even breathed new life into the Channel Tunnel project, aborted when Heath fell from office in 1974. Heath welcomed these advances, but remained sceptical of the sincerity of her commitment, until his suspicions were dramatically confirmed by her celebrated Bruges speech in 1988. In the meantime he could only deplore her tendency, on a succession of foreign policy issues from withdrawal from UNESCO through the bombing of Libya to sanctions against South Africa, to side instinctively with her soulmate Ronald Reagan in Washington rather than with the rest of the Community. By so doing she reversed the priority he had tried to establish a decade before, blocked progress towards the development of a single European foreign policy and confirmed all the old doubts among Britain's Community partners about Britain's willingness to throw off the American yoke. More than anything else it was galling for him to see her failing to consolidate, if not positively undoing, his one unquestionable historic achievement.

It was on the Government's handling of the economy, however, that he was most comprehensively scathing. At one level he still focused simply on the 'shameful' level of unemployment, still running at over three million until it began to fall at last in the middle of 1986. Even though it had not, after all, prevented the Tories being re-elected it was still a moral outrage, a human tragedy and a continuing threat to the fabric of society. In a speech to the Peel Society at Tamworth in November 1984 he attacked 'the fatalistic belief that nothing can be done to deal with the problem of massive unemployment'. 'It leads', he warned, 'to a rapid increase in crimes of violence and descent into social conflict.' Inflation was a scourge, but he believed unemployment was worse and did not accept that curing one led necessarily to a reduction of the other. He blamed the depth of the recession on the reversal of postwar economic priorities, and argued for old-fashioned Keynesian public spending to reflate the economy and put people back to work.[65] Mocked by Lawson, he told the House of Commons unabashed, 'I am an avowed advocate of what the Chancellor called voodoo witchcraft.'[66]

But he was also concerned at the permanent loss of manufacturing capacity in the economy. He scorned the idea that Britain could become a service economy, devoted solely to making money on ever-higher rates of interest. 'We cannot live permanently by taking in each other's washing,' became his favourite refrain. Somebody had to make the goods to be washed. It was vital for strategic as well as social reasons to preserve key industries. He condemned the Government's preoccupation with cutting public spending as short-sighted and doctrinaire, and repeatedly drew a critical distinction between current and capital expenditure. Every business in the country financed investment by borrowing: this was quite different from what he termed – in another favourite and unmistakably pointed phrase – 'the kitchen sink economics of the housewife'. 'People are not motivated by being hectored and lectured, nor are they inspired by the refrain of "cut, cut, cut". They want to see the highest quality maintained in public services and are willing to contribute their fair share to the cost.'[67]

In January 1985 he made a strongly worded speech in Sunderland, alleging that the north of England had been reduced, almost to the level of the south of Italy. Britain's manufacturing base was being systematically destroyed. 'How much longer can we let unemployment rage unchecked?' he demanded. 'How much longer can we afford to gamble with our social stability?'

> Unfettered market forces lead to the rich and strong growing richer and stronger and the poor and weak, poorer and weaker, until some conflagration in society acts to restore the balance . . . In Britain we have largely avoided this because as one nation we have always regulated our affairs to ensure that we have all benefited from the economic progress arising from the dynamics of capitalism.

The most successful economies in the modern world, he never tired of pointing out, did not leave their key industries to the mercy of the market but supported them on a basis of consultation and consensus.[68]

On this argument he naturally damned the Government's privatisation programme, the symbolic centrepiece of Mrs Thatcher's drive to dismantle 'socialism'. Though his Government had 'hived off' a few anomalies at the fringes of the public sector, Heath had never questioned that the major national utilities must be owned and managed by the state: the existence of a large public sector was a fact of life, regrettable perhaps but unavoidable, which made it impossible for the Government to keep out of wage determination. Privatisation he regarded as a Powellite fantasy. When the Thatcher Government, encouraged by the unexpected public success of its disposal of British Telecom in 1984, moved on to sell British Aerospace and Britoil in 1985, with British Gas, British Airways and the Trustee Savings Bank in the pipeline for 1986, Heath unleashed, in a lecture to the London Business School in November 1985, 'one of the most outspoken denunciations of Government economic policies that even he has delivered'.[69] He dismissed privatisation as 'an apology for a supply-side policy' which resulted in no increase in competitiveness but merely transferred vital public services from public to private monopoly. The proceeds, he complained, were not being spent on new investment but wasted on consumption – first unemployment benefit, and now tax cuts: 'I can predict with great confidence what the result of tax cuts will be – a new surge in imports of consumer durables from abroad. Not a lasting boost to British capital stock and British industry.' Tax cuts were 'an insult to the intelligence of the British people and an affront to their integrity'.[70]

Such lectures cut no ice at all with a Government which was convinced that it had found the holy grail. ('We are told we are in the middle of an economic miracle,' Heath commented sourly. 'I sometimes wonder whether Government ministers live in the same world as the rest of us.')[71] A few weeks later, however, in February 1986, he played some part in forcing the Government to scrap an agreement to sell off parts of British Leyland (the Land Rover and truck divisions) to the American company General Motors. Coming immediately after the controversial merger of Westland helicopters with the American Sikorski company, which had precipitated Michael Heseltine's resignation, this proposal outraged Heath's patriotism and stirred his anti-Americanism at the same time: 'What is this fatalism, this despair about British industry?' he demanded in the House of Commons. 'How do we restore faith in British industry by selling out to the Americans?'[72]

Pym, Gilmour and Heseltine joined 'ostentatiously' in what *The Times* described as 'a mass Commons revolt led by Mr Edward Heath'.[73] Next day the Government backed down. In reality the swift retreat owed more to Mrs Thatcher's temporary weakness following the Westland affair than to Heath's intervention. But the episode was one issue on which his instincts were in step with those of a majority of the party.

On most other issues the Government, with its huge majority, effortlessly overrode his protests. In January 1984 he led – or at any rate headed – a substantial revolt on the ratecapping Bill. He was joined in the lobby by twenty-three rebels including Rippon, Gilmour, and Maurice Macmillan, while eleven more, including Pym, abstained. This was Heath's first vote against a three-line whip since

1979; it was also thought to be the first time a Government had ever been defied by two former Chief Whips. Heath objected that the Bill raised an issue of principle of the deepest importance for him: the centralisation of power in Whitehall, he claimed, giving unprecedented powers to ministers to control local government, was contrary to Tory philosophy. This was not what he had stood for at every General Election since 1950. Churchill's promise then, he recalled, had been to 'Set the People Free' – not to 'Set the people free to do what we tell them'.[74]

The Times was satirical about Heath as a village Hampden: 'Mr Edward Heath, the arch-apostle of Tory corporatism, author of prices and incomes policies, does not exactly compel admiration as a champion of local authorities.'[75] This did not stop him, however, going on to oppose the abolition of the Greater London Council and the other metropolitan councils, and the similarly high-handed lack of consultation which characterised the abrupt withdrawal of the right of employees at GCHQ (the Government's top-security listening-post) to belong to trade unions.[76] Heath, who had been accused of stubbornness, intolerance and confrontation in his time, was now the apostle of consensus, condemning the divisive policies of his successor. His strictures were widely shared. They formed the staple of the opposition parties' criticism of Mrs Thatcher's style; but they also found an echo within the Tory party, even in the Cabinet. Heath, however, was stuck with his own reputation. It was now universally believed that he had been the most disciplinarian Chief Whip in the party's history. As Prime Minister he had certainly not appeared to welcome criticism any more than she did. He too had been called autocratic, authoritarian and the rest. But above all he had failed where she appeared to be brilliantly successful: she had tamed the unions, beaten inflation, rolled back the public sector and come through recession to at least some form of economic recovery. What did it matter if unemployment remained uncomfortably high and the real basis of the recovery was dangerously shallow? She had won two General Elections and looked a good bet to pull off the hat trick. Few Tories were going to listen to Heath until she began to look like losing: and probably not even then.

Though politically out of favour, Heath was not unhappy in his internal exile. In some respects the role of outcast suited him rather well. He had always been a loner, never a good member of a team unless he was leading it. If he could not be Prime Minister, the role of ex-Prime Minister or anti-Prime Minister accorded better with his egotism than any other. Simply as a politician, concerned to vindicate his own record, he was certainly angry at what he saw as the malicious denial and distortion of his achievements and the reversal or neglect of the causes and values that he had tried to advance. This anger was what the public saw, so that the impression gained ground that he was altogether consumed with bitterness and jealousy. In fact this was very far from the case. Heath had always had that saving grace for a politician, other interests and passions outside politics. He had admittedly no close family – no wife or children – to support and console him. After 1979 he did very much less sailing. But he still had his music, a busy schedule of conducting and concert going. And in 1985 he found a new outlet for his creative energy: a new house which became the centre of his life.

He had been looking for a country house for some time. Since his father's death he had had no great pleasure in going to Broadstairs. He had never cared for his second stepmother, Mary, described by one friend as 'exactly the sort of trivial, gushing woman he most loathed'.[77] She had looked after William well in his last years, but when he died – and Heath lost the Tory leadership – her world fell apart. She became a virtual alcoholic and a severe trial to her famous stepson. In August 1984 she was found dead at her flat, leaving a suicide note. This effectively ended Heath's connection with his home town. He still had an aunt there, and his brother's widow; and his old friends Joy and Teddy Denman lived near by. But that year he gave up the annual carol concert which he had been conducting for nearly fifty years, ever since he was a student. The ostensible reason was that the hall he had always used was demolished, but he could surely have found another. The abandonment of this annual event so long fixed in his calendar symbolised a major shift in the focus of his life.

Within six months of Mary's death he had acquired Arundells, an exceptionally beautiful old house in the Cathedral Close at Salisbury. (The house is basically Queen Anne, though the oldest part dates from 1280 and a good deal is Victorian.) It was found for him by Robert Key, his PPS at the time, who had himself grown up in the Close and was now the local MP. As soon as Heath heard of it he knew it was the house for him. He soon claimed to have fallen in love with Salisbury when he had visited it with the Balliol Players in 1936. More to the point it was a convenient distance down the M3 from London and equally handy for the Solent; and it was just the right sort of town for him. 'It is extraordinarily quiet and peaceful,' he told the *Sunday Times* magazine. 'You wouldn't know you were in a town, let alone a city. It has Britain's best rural cathedral, giving one a sense of continuity which appeals to me as a Tory.'[78] His first musical education had come from church music, so the proximity of the cathedral – and its organ – were a return to his roots. He became a strong supporter of the cathedral and particularly its Spire Appeal, conducting fund-raising concerts and helping to bring down other musicians and celebrities to help the cause. He relishes the Trollopian world of the Close and was quickly accepted into its exclusive society.* As with every other association in his life, Heath has identified himself fiercely with his adopted city.

His house is comfortably large but not enormous – three reception rooms, four bedrooms, three bathrooms plus an annexe/office. The rivers Avon and Nadder join at the bottom of the large garden. There have been conflicting press reports of what he paid for it. In fact he does not own the freehold, but has contrived to lease it for his lifetime on favourable terms from the Church Commissioners. It was in a poor state when he took it over, however, and he was allowed to make a number of structural alterations, mainly restoring it to its original plan. He did not use Jo Pattrick on the interior – Salisbury was too far from London for her – but another designer whom she recommended, Derek Frost, who had to work closely to his instructions. The result is much less sparse and modernist than her style as displayed in Albany in the 1960s and Downing Street in 1970, more lavish and traditional as befits Heath's age and status.[80] But it is still light, airy and colourful, with a lot of apricot and salmon pink. There are pictures everywhere, including his precious Churchills, some by 'my old friend Augustus John', and around the dining room eight John Pipers, including two views of the house commissioned by Heath himself. There are glass and china in display cabinets, oriental rugs on the floor and a specially commissioned Indian fabric on the sofa. To some, the house is a *folie de grandeur*, more a museum than a home. It is indeed full of sailing trophies, pictures and models of the various *Morning Cloud*s, gifts and signed photographs of world leaders – a sort of shrine to Heath's achievements. There are even monogrammed towels and matches. It is a bachelor's love poem to himself. Yet at the same time he is so boyishly proud of it all that few visitors can resist his enthusiasm.

It is the first real home of his own that Heath has ever had. Friends say that he is 'married' to his house, 'besotted' with it.[81] Surrounded by his trophies and mementoes, with his piano and his clavichord and a CD player in every room, looked after by a full-time housekeeper and a gardener, plus his Government-provided driver, fully

* There is another distinguished bachelor in the Close, Sir Philip Shelburne, the former head of privatised Britoil, described as 'a terrific Thatcherite'. He and Heath cannot be asked to dinner together; but it is usually Shelburne who loses out.[79]

guarded night and day, he lives exceedingly well. Sara Morrison has the job of hiring – and firing – his housekeepers: advertising in *The Lady* and sifting through several hundred replies. She once told him it would be easier if he had a wife. 'Easier for you,' he replied. 'Not easier for me. You can fire a housekeeper. You can't fire a wife.'[82]

He very rarely has people to stay, but he entertains a lot, making a particular speciality of Sunday lunch, to which he will invite a dozen assorted guests from all walks of public life – politicians, musicians, journalists, ambassadors, visiting statesmen. The hospitality is lavish, though the atmosphere can be sticky: he can make an embarrassing scene if everything is not served exactly as he wants it. He loves to boast that all the fruit and vegetables are home-grown. (He particularly likes to amaze Americans with his home-grown pumpkin pie.) Whatever the weather, he will show visitors round the garden first. 'Gardening gives me a lot of satisfaction,' he told the *Mail on Sunday* in 1988. 'I don't get actively involved with the clippers and trowel, you understand. I am, however, an extraordinarily gifted supervisor!'

> In the two years since I've been here, I've put in a rose garden and a vegetable garden that provides enough to feed ourselves and fill the deep freeze. It was a protection against Reagan's Third World War . . . I have loganberries, asparagus and pumpkins. I've also created a dell and put in a pond for the carp.[83]

Characteristically, he expects results: he is impatient when the asparagus does not grow as fast as he thinks it should. He also cultivates orchids, collected from all round the world – from Tokyo, Singapore, Hong Kong, Jersey: 'The Governor of Canton gave me a lot.' Another is a present from Fidel Castro. Orchids are another of the trophies of international statesmanship.

Heath's house has been the subject of innumerable newspaper and magazine articles over the last seven years. One of the first appeared in *Woman's Realm* in the summer of 1986:

> Mr Edward Heath lives in one of the most beautiful places in Britain. The striking of Salisbury Cathedral's clock filters down through his garden full of honeysuckle, forget-me-nots, lily-of-the-valley.
>
> Sometimes Mr Heath, in weekend sweater, hands in pockets, ambles down from the honey-coloured house to the stream at the bottom of the garden to see his favourite swan.

At the water's edge, by the sun-dappled ripples, this senior politician – MP for 36 years, PM for four, incredibly approaching his seventieth birthday – takes on the look of a sage old pike. Waiting and watching, outliving all those small fry.

'A garden is very good for patience and taking the long term view,' he muses, and somehow you know he's not just talking about rose-pruning.[84]

Though he always insists to interviewers that he has a lot of friends, and it is true that he can always fill the house with company when he wants, it is also true that his life is fundamentally solitary. But that suits him. He has a need verging on a compulsion to fill his days with meetings, speaking engagements, lunches, dinners, concerts and overseas trips, to keep himself always occupied and on the move; but at the beginning and end of the day he likes to be alone. He described a 'typical' day to the *Sunday Times* in 1989, starting with a pot of tea brought by his housekeeper about 8.30, followed by 'my shower and a light breakfast of toast and a grapefruit', 'some early phone calls' and 'all the papers' ('I read one or two, skim most, and occasionally draft letters to them on matters of fact or policy'); and ending around midnight with a malt whisky, the radio news and 'perhaps some music'. 'Then I go to sleep. I sleep well, and I never dream.' There is something chilling about this last assertion: it suggests either lack of imagination or a deliberate suppression of it – a refusal to admit the possibility of the irrational. Even at moments of crisis Heath has always slept well – he is not a worrier; but at the same time he needs his sleep. 'Some people', he scoffed privately, 'say they can exist on four hours' sleep. If they try and do it, they must be stupid – but in most cases they can't.'[85]

When not abroad, Heath divides his time between Salisbury and London. He still retains Wilton Street and sleeps there when necessary during the week. He has his office in the Norman Shaw building across the road from the House of Commons; and of course he still has his constituency in Bexley and Sidcup. In the *Sunday Times* interview he claimed to visit Bexley 'at least twice a week'.[86] His then agent confirms that this was no exaggeration: he attends around 150 constituency engagements a year.[87] He holds surgeries every two to three weeks, normally in the evening, and is assiduous in pursuing constituents' problems. 'I don't hesitate to use my influence and contacts at the highest level,' he boasts, and ministers in domestic departments over the past thirteen years know it to be true. He is tireless in support of the local hospital, schools and colleges, road schemes and other constituency causes.

The impact of Government policy on Bexley and Sidcup has provided the starting point for many of his most powerful indictments. After forty years in the same seat – give or take a few boundary changes – his constituency is enormously important to him as a sort of extended family. He has known many of his constituents over several generations; he is at ease with them and they are proud of him. Through the Thatcher years, when he was denouncing the Government practically every week, his local Conservative Association remained almost wholly loyal to him. There was no attempt to censure him in all that time. A dinner to mark his seventieth birthday in 1986 was several times oversubscribed. His majority in 1992 was over 15,000. When he is attacked in other quarters of the party he draws strength from the solid support he enjoys in Bexley. Bexley is his political tap root, the main reason why he will not go to the House of Lords.

Throughout the 1980s Heath took on more and more conducting engagements – so much so that he complained he had no time to listen to music. He takes his conducting seriously and is careful not to accept more than he can do well. (It is important to him that he is invited as a musician, not as a celebrity.) In 1980 he met with some criticism when he conducted the European Community Youth Orchestra at Lucerne (*France-Soir* complained that he 'massacred' Mozart);[88] but for the most part critics seem to agree that he conducts at least competently, if without flair. He constantly performs with different orchestras, and his rehearsal time is necessarily limited. For whatever reason, his most conspicuous performances still tend to be abroad rather than at home. In 1984 he took the London Concert Orchestra on a six-concert tour of England (conducting Beethoven, Mozart and Tchaikovsky); and in March 1985 he conducted the *Messiah* at Chatham House. But earlier that year he had conducted a series of concerts in Israel; in 1988 he conducted at the Prague Festival; in 1989 in Salt Lake City (marking the fiftieth anniversary of the Utah Symphony Orchestra) and at the Schleswig-Holstein Festival, where he conducted the Berlin Philharmonic in *Cockaigne*. The undoubted highlight was a gala charity concert which he gave with the Chinese Central Philharmonic Orchestra in the Great Hall of the People in Peking in January 1987 (conducting Tchaikovsky, Dvorak and Elgar). There was an audience of 8,000 in the hall and supposedly 400 million watching on television. The concert was said to have raised $1.25 million for the Chinese handicapped. But to Heath's chagrin: 'The papers here ignored the occasion.'[89]

In 1984–5 Heath helped to promote Andrew Lloyd Webber's *Requiem*. He premièred parts of it (with Sarah Brightman) at his last

Broadstairs carol concert; he then attended the première of the completed work in Manhattan, led the standing ovation and wrote (at his own request) a glowing review in the *Financial Times*. Another work which he set out to champion was Beethoven's Triple Concerto, which he believes to be underrated. On his seventy-third birthday in July 1989 he conducted it with the Trio Zingara at a fund-raising concert for the Salisbury Spire Appeal. He subsequently recorded it with the English Chamber Orchestra (his only recording still in the catalogue, with a Boccherini cello concerto on the other side) and continued to perform it regularly at concerts both in Britain and abroad, usually preceded by a short lecture about its neglected virtues. Heath has said that he would love, more than anything, to conduct *Fidelio* but knows he never will.[90] He remains in demand, however, for gala and other charity concerts at which he regularly proves a considerable draw.

In December 1988 he appeared on 'Desert Island Discs'. The eight records he chose were Vaughan Williams's Sea Symphony and Schubert's Piano Trio in B flat, both of which he had got to know at Oxford; Strauss's *Der Rosenkavalier* ('Very romantic. I adore it'); *Fidelio* ('The greatest of all operas', all about freedom – 'what I've always stood for in my political life'); his own LSO recording of Elgar's *Cockaigne*; Dvorak's New World Symphony (which he had conducted in Peking); his own Broadstairs recording of 'Hark! The Herald Angels Sing'; and, most oddly, the song 'If I Were a Rich Man' from *Fiddler on the Roof*, which he said reminded him of the plight of refugees, but which some might think reflected his own yearning for financial security. For his book he asked for bound volumes of *Hansard* going back to the eighteenth century, but settled for a book of French impressionists. For his luxury he wanted fishing tackle, but made do with a supply of suntan lotion.[91]

Advancing age has gradually obliged him to give up sailing. Following his bad experience in the Fastnet race in 1979 he put *Morning Cloud* V on the market (for £100,000). Then the recurrence of his thyroid problem in 1981 forced him to take a year off serious racing. He missed the Admiral's Cup in both 1981 and 1983. By 1983 he was talking of building a new boat to compete in 1985, even though *Morning Cloud* V was still unsold, the asking price now down to £50,000.[92] She was finally sold in February 1984, but Heath did not buy another. He still sometimes went out in other people's boats but, as he told the *Mail on Sunday*: 'I miss not having my own boat and crew. Lots of people ask me to sail with them, but it's not the same.'[93] In sailing as in politics, Heath had been used to his own command and did not take easily to a subordinate role: he sailed to

25–6 *Above* Heath and William Whitelaw on the platform at the 1976 party conference; *below* Heath speaking from the floor in 1978

27 The 1975 referendum: leading the 'Yes' campaign with Roy Jenkins

28 With Deng Xiaoping in Peking, 1987

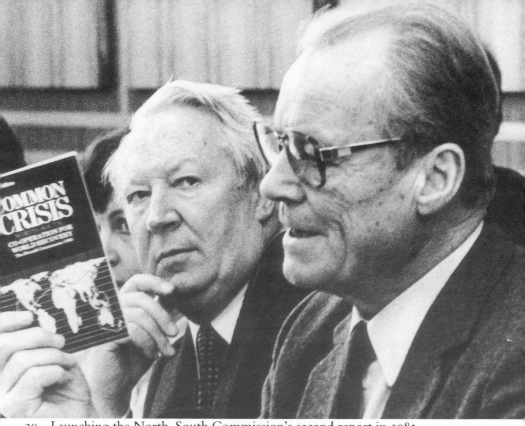

29 Launching the North–South Commission's second report in 1983 with Willy Brandt

30 Negotiating with Saddam Hussein for British hostages in Baghdad, 1990

31 The Tory tradition: Margaret Thatcher and her three predecessors

32 At home in Salisbury

win and had no interest in pottering about. 'I don't sail all that much now,' he told the *Sunday Times* in 1988, 'but I'm always happy to pop down to the Solent and run a new boat through its paces in order to express my opinion for a national newspaper.'[94] By the end of the decade he was doing all sorts of odd things for money, from cheese advertisements to televised humiliation at the hands of Dame Edna Everage.

One reason he needed money was that he was failing to get on with his memoirs. For a long time he refused all inducements to write memoirs: to do so would be to appear to accept that his career was finished, something he did not admit for a moment. (Likewise he steadfastly refused to allow 'his' stained glass window to be put in at Chequers: all past prime ministers are traditionally commemorated in this way, but only when it is certain that they will not be back.) Heath had always intended to write his memoirs, however, and to this end had accumulated an immense archive which was stored for a long time in the basement of the Piccadilly Hotel, until he was required to move it in 1984. It was probably the outcome of the 1983 election which persuaded him that the time had come to seek a publisher. Anticipation quickened as he tried to beat up the price. In March 1985 he promised the *Times* Diary that he would 'spill every uncensored detail'.[95] Shortly afterwards he agreed terms with Lord Weidenfeld and accepted a large advance, plus serialisation money from the *Sunday Times*. He hired a journalist with a suitably discreet pedigree – Michael Trend, son of his former Cabinet Secretary Sir Burke Trend – to help him. He repeatedly assured interviewers that he was working on the book. But nothing appeared, and rumours emerged that he was making minimal progress. He told the *Sunday Times* in 1988 that he would finish in 1989; but he did not. The truth was that he had barely started. Michael Trend departed to assist Norman Tebbit instead. Five years later, in mid-1993, the book has still not appeared.

Why is this? Why does Heath seem unable to write his memoirs, when he can see his contemporaries (Roy Jenkins, Denis Healey) making enviable financial killings out of theirs and when he, more than any of them, is so eager to vindicate his record against what he regards as a systematic campaign of vilification? One reason is that, despite his success as a best-selling author in the 1970s, he is no writer. As a politician he has been characterised by the most bare and functional use of words: a long book is an intimidating enterprise for one who in fifty years has scarcely written anything longer than speeches and newspaper articles. Moreover, unlike most politicians, Heath rarely reads others' memoirs: self-absorbed and self-sufficient, he takes no interest in other men's careers, which only detract from his own. So he has no familiarity with the genre.

More seriously, he simply will not set aside the time to write. He is too busy in the present: he will not make space in his relentless schedule to sit down with his researcher for long periods of concentrated retrospection. When he does, the process is uncongenial to him, first because psychologically he is not an introspective or self-analytic man – he is intensely shy of self-exposure and suspicious of self-indulgence; and second because, if he is honest, much of what he is required to relive sits uneasily with his view of the past as he has refashioned it in his mind since 1974. Much of his language between 1965 and 1972 *was* proto-Thatcherite: there are honourable reasons for his change of rhetoric, but they take some explaining, and it is disconcerting to be faced by his assistants with speeches he would prefer to believe he had never made. It is easier to justify himself in general than in detail. There have been many triumphs in his life: but there have also been bitter failures, and the latter have tended to cancel out the former. It is difficult enough for the biographer to strike a consistent balance between vindication and regret: it must be very much harder for the autobiographer.

Finally, the very act of writing memoirs would be a recognition that his career was over, which he will not admit: he may have accepted eventually that he will never be Prime Minister again, but he is determined to remain in Parliament and he is still looking to the future – particularly the future of Europe, the overriding national debate in which he still believes he has a leading role to play. In 1990 – unknown to Weidenfeld – he signed another contract with Sidgwick & Jackson for a book to be entitled *Our Europe*; this too, however, he has now abandoned. Few of his friends believe that his memoirs will ever be written. In 1991, as a sort of interim substitute, he published four weeks' instalments of memories, billed as 'memoirs', in the glossy picture magazine *Hello!* Apart from some good photographs, however, they are desperately unrevealing: brief, banal and superficial.[96] It is unlikely that the book, if ever finished, will be very different: revelation is not in his nature.

In July 1986 Heath reached his seventieth birthday. As always he celebrated the landmark in style – this time with a party at Leeds Castle in Kent, organised by Toby Aldington. About sixty guests were invited from his three worlds of politics, music and sailing, including all those with whom he had been closely associated over the years, excluding only those who were openly hostile. (Mrs Thatcher was not invited.) Alec Home made a speech of tribute which most of those present thought quite 'perfect'; Heath's reply was equally well judged, not in the least egotistical but humorously self-deprecating and modest. His PPS at the time, Andrew Rowe, thought the whole occasion 'magical'.[97] The warmth and loyalty of Heath's assembled friends was quite extraordinary, and very moving. It is indeed one of the most remarkable things about Heath, which his detractors and the wider public find hard to believe: with all his prickliness and self-absorption, his friends do love him.

Next day, his assistants Peter Luff and Wilf Weeks organised a similar party for all his former secretaries and private office staff. This was a repeat – with a lot of new faces – of the party which Heath himself had held for all his former staff in the redecorated Downing Street in 1971. For this occasion, Luff and Weeks went to immense trouble to secure permission to hold their party at Chiswick House: they had discovered that it was one of the few great houses to which he had never been.[98]

1987 brought him another disappointment, however. The death of Harold Macmillan at the very end of 1986 left a vacancy for the Chancellorship of Oxford University. The Chancellorship is an honorific post, elected by the past and present members of the University. It is traditionally contested on party lines, which normally assures victory to the most distinguished living Conservative, preferably with a continuing connection with Oxford. On paper Heath was entitled to feel that as a Tory ex-Prime Minister who had been President of the Union, was still a Trustee and had returned there regularly to speak, the job should be his almost by right. There was no chance, following the controversy surrounding the university's refusal to grant her an honorary degree in 1985, that Mrs Thatcher would put her name forward. Home was not interested. So on 30 January Heath announced his candidacy. If he expected to be elected by acclamation, however, he was swiftly disabused. His name was a red rag to loyal Oxford Tories still smarting at the insult to Mrs Thatcher: if they could not have her, they would find an alternative candidate to carry the Thatcherite standard. There was no other suitably eminent politician, so they came up with an academic candidate, the Conservative party historian, biographer of Disraeli and Provost of Queen's College, Lord Blake. The result was fatally to split the Tory vote.

The beneficiary of the Tory split was Roy Jenkins, who observed the boost to his own prospects with quiet amusement. 'Heath made it clear from the beginning that he had an immovable determination to stand while commanding neither the enthusiasm of the Prime Minister and the Government nor the confidence of the Oxford right-wing establishment that he could win.'[99] With extraordinary arrogance, he seemed to think that he only needed the support of Balliol – forgetting both the existence of 33 other colleges and the fact that Jenkins too was a Balliol man. His campaign was run by Ashley Raeburn, a Balliol contemporary who had made his career in Shell. The running was made by publishing lists of supporters. 'Almost unbelievably', Jenkins has written. 'Heath's first list' – of only 20 names – 'contained no one from any college other than Balliol.'[100] (Jenkins had 120 names from 30 colleges.) By the end of February Heath had secured 160 endorsements – including Lord Goodman, Lord Beloff, Burke Trend and Robin Day; but Jenkins was way ahead with 410 – led by such heavyweight intellectuals as Sir Freddie Ayer and Sir Isaiah Berlin and including several prominent women (Iris Murdoch, Antonia Fraser). Blake trailed with a mere 67 nominations.

By now the contest – though intrinsically unimportant – had become highly political. With a General Election coming up, Conservative Central Office was not keen to hand a propaganda victory to the Alliance. The Tory camp was riven with recrimination as the Heath and Blake camps each blamed the other for refusing to stand down. On the one hand Heath strove to deny that voting for him was a way to snub Mrs Thatcher – though in fact much of his support came from the left, from people like Michael Foot who loathed Mrs Thatcher and the SDP equally. He stressed his worldwide contacts and his energy as a fund-raiser. On the other Blake denied that he was the Thatcherite candidate and stressed his academic credentials. Jenkins was frankly political, roundly condemning the Government's underfunding of the universities. As a result Mrs Thatcher decided reluctantly to throw the party's weight behind Heath: as soon as she had indicated her (tacit) sanction, all the Oxford-educated loyalists and place seekers declared their support: Hailsham, Whitelaw, Lady Young, William Waldegrave, Norman St John Stevas, Michael Heseltine, Kenneth Baker and Douglas Hurd. Blake felt himself betrayed, and subsequently blamed Norman Tebbit and John Wakeham (Tory chairman and Chief Whip respectively) for backing the wrong horse and letting the non-Conservative Jenkins win.[101]

Polling was on 12 and 14 March, with all-day parties in all the colleges for their alumni, who descended on Oxford to vote. Heath pulled rank to set up his headquarters in Balliol; Jenkins had to use Wadham. The Master of Balliol, Anthony Kenny, remained publicly neutral: privately, however, he supported Jenkins. The result was unpredictable: weight of nominations might count for nothing. In the event the three-way split was pretty close, but Jenkins came through with a clear majority, while Heath finished last (apart from an obscure fourth candidate who won 38 votes). The figures were Jenkins 3,249, Blake 2,674, Heath 2,348. Jenkins in his memoirs denies that he won only as a result of the Tory split, arguing that much of Heath's vote, if he had stood down, would have come to him; and probably the same would have been true if Blake had stood down.[102] Be that as it may, it was an unprecedented rebuff for a Conservative ex-Prime Minister to be denied the Oxford Chancellorship. Heath would unquestionably have been an energetic Chancellor, tireless in travelling the world to drum up money for the university from the Americans and the Japanese. His defeat can be put down partly to politics – his political unpopularity among Oxford Tories who regarded his behaviour since 1975 as disloyal – but partly also to personal reasons. Politics apart, what Oxford was looking for after Macmillan was another urbane and witty raconteur, at ease among dons at a college High Table. Heath was not such a man, as the *Sunday Telegraph* reported during the campaign: 'The mere mention of Heath is greeted by an almost universal volley of distaste. "He'll never get it", said one Conservative college head, "because he's such a blinding bore. When you're put next to him at dinner, he just sits there staring at his food."'[103]

Heath was hurt to lose, but took it impassively as just another of life's disappointments. He was glad at least to have lost to Jenkins, an old friend, a good European and an adequately eminent figure to be Chancellor. He would have bitterly resented losing the job to Blake.

37

The Nemesis of Thatcherism

THERE was never much doubt that Mrs Thatcher would win a
third term when she went to the country in June 1987. Despite
an inexplicable attack of nerves on 'Wobbly Thursday' a week before
polling day, neither Neil Kinnock's 'new look' Labour Party – still
only halfway to rehabilitation – nor the increasingly strained Alliance
ever posed a serious threat. In the event the only significant change
since 1983 was that Labour decisively beat off the Alliance challenge
for second place, sending it into a suicidal nosedive: it made no impact whatever on the Tories. The Government was returned with a
still-massive majority of 102 and a mandate for a further programme
of radical reform of some of the last un-Thatcherised structures of
the Welfare State: the NHS, the education system and local government finance.

This was Heath's twelfth General Election. Unlike 1979 and 1983
he can have nursed no hopes of the outcome. Once again he cam-
paigned unstintingly, speaking all round the country for selected
MPs and candidates whom he regarded as respectable – Robin Squire
('an old friend') in Hornchurch, his former PPS Mark Robinson in
Newport, his former research assistant Simon Burns in Chelmsford.
He campaigned as a detached party elder, still never mentioning the
Prime Minister by name, making no pretence of enthusiasm for her
Government but equally never uttering a word that could be head-
lined as disloyal. Cameras trailed him wherever he went – Butler and
Kavanagh reckoned that Heath, Michael Heseltine and Jeffrey
Archer received more coverage than most members of the Cabinet[1] –
but they were disappointed: in three weeks his only controversial
remarks were directed at the press for running 'the filthiest campaign
I have ever known' – concerned only with personalities and private
scandal rather than the issues.[2] In Hornchurch, the *Guardian*'s Terry

Coleman watched him do his stuff – 'the old pro, showing that he could work a crowd, and press the flesh, as well as any man. He was in and out of a Wimpy bar in a minute flat, having received the promise of two votes for the candidate.' He was closely attended by two detectives, and Coleman counted eleven uniformed police at a discreet distance. But there were no incidents. He was generally warmly received. 'To ninety-five per cent of people he's still a recognizable figure in the streets . . . He's a father figure.'[3]

In Bexley he stood on his record as a constituency MP: his election address stressed his support for local schools and hospitals, and only secondarily the importance of returning a Conservative Government to provide 'sound financial management of the economy' and strong defence. The only coded criticism that could possibly be read between the lines concerned the need for Britain to continue to play a leading role in Europe 'as we have done in the past'.[4] He canvassed the neat, owner-occupied estates like the lord of the manor calling on his tenants: an old man now, short and overweight, waddling up garden paths to have a word whenever the well-drilled team of party workers going ahead found someone at home for him to talk to. At four evening meetings at local schools – each attended by respectable (and respectful) audiences of about sixty, he gave a masterly, quick *tour d'horizon* of world problems, somewhat *de haut en bas* but paying his constituents the compliment of speaking of serious matters seriously; then he answered questions. Here some differences from the Government inevitably emerged, but only obliquely, as differences of detail. Deflecting questions about why he was not in the present Government or why his constituents should vote for a Government which he so frequently and strenuously attacked, he only asked them to vote for him and for the party – he was responsible for no one else. He deplored Labour's continuing unfitness to govern, dismissed the Alliance and promised that 'one-nation' Toryism would come again. Then on to the next meeting.★

As soon as the new Parliament met, however, he intervened to set out, much more critically, the agenda by which he would judge the Government's third term. He congratulated 'the Prime Minister, her colleagues and our party' on the election result – but also paid ironic tribute to the 'remarkable contribution' of the Opposition parties.

★ His majority rose to over 16,000, with 62 per cent of the vote:

E. Heath (Conservative)	24,350
T. Pearce (Liberal/Alliance)	8,076
H. Stoate (Labour)	6,762
Conservative majority	16,274[5]

Then, turning to the Queen's Speech, he pretended to draw comfort from the fact that so far all the items in the programme were still only tentatively formulated, and begged ministers to think again before they pressed ahead. On all the major issues, he warned – jobs, housing, health, education and the poll tax – the Government had less support than it imagined: 'I went over most of the country, from Scotland to Cornwall and across to East Kent, and I was able to talk to people unhindered. They told me what they thought. Our people are worried about all of those things, and they supported us despite them.'

Now – as he had not done during the election – he roundly condemned the poll tax, on the ground that – 'quite apart from the administrative problems' – it took no account of people's ability to pay. 'That is not a radical proposal,' he declared. 'It is a reactionary, regressive proposal.' He recalled that the promise to abolish the rates had originated in the October 1974 party manifesto; but the commitment then had been to replace them with 'taxes more broadly based and related to people's ability to pay'. At that time, he explained, it was assumed that the whole tax system would soon be computerised, enabling national and local taxation to be run together. Thirteen years on, he believed, computerisation must surely now be close at hand: it still offered the best way of dealing with the problem. Presumably he was advocating some form of local income tax, as proposed by the Alliance.

But he reserved his strongest criticism for the proposed education reforms. He condemned both the proposals themselves and the unilateral way they had been brought forward: by contrast he recalled the wide consultation with the teaching unions and the churches which had preceded the 1944 Act – the product of a Coalition Government. He conceded that there was a case for a national curriculum, but warned against the increased powers being loaded on the Secretary of State to determine it. He was delighted that the Government had dropped the fantasy of vouchers. 'That was impractical nonsense from beginning to end,' he mocked. 'Indeed, Sir Keith admitted it in a kind letter to me, saying how it was impracticable, but how nice it would have been if it had been practical.' The real purpose, he alleged, was to help middle-class parents who were already sending their children to private schools. But he strongly attacked the whole principle of introducing competition into education: 'the comparison now being made in so many right-wing quarters that education can be sold like goods in a supermarket is absolutely farcical'. He feared that allowing schools to 'opt out' of local authority control was just 'a side door to vouchers'. Opted-out schools would soon start charging fees. 'With that, fee-paying education will be extended, and that is what I am strongly opposed to.'[6] Rab Butler would be turning in his grave.

Heath had always been intensely grateful for the educational opportunities he had enjoyed: it was a persistent purpose of his political career to try to extend them to others. He knew very well the sacrifices his parents had made for him, but he also knew he could not have gone to Oxford without the help of Kent County Council. He was proud of having been to a local authority grammar school and from Oxford onwards had resented the assumed superiority of private schools. As Tory leader he had been obliged to defend the right to private education; but he never lost an opportunity to remind questioners that Mrs Thatcher in 1970–4 had created more comprehensive schools than any other Education Secretary. Quite simply, he believed in state education: the barely disguised Government policy of encouraging private education at the expense of the state system struck at his deepest personal values. This was Ted Heath speaking from the heart.

The philosophic gulf which divided him from the Government now went much deeper than a dispute over monetarism and economic management – though he continued to deride Lawson for his exclusive reliance on interest rates. ('In golfing terms', he told the House of Commons in what became a favourite metaphor in November 1988, 'the Chancellor could be described as a one-club man, and that club is interest rates. But if one wishes to take on Sandy Lyle and the rest of the world one needs a complete bag of clubs.')[7] His real quarrel was with the fundamental social attitudes which he felt the Government enshrined – the calculated abandonment of the sense of social obligation which had been the hallmark and achievement of his generation, the generation that had come through the war with a desire to build a better world of dignity and opportunity for all. That was the vision which he believed Mrs Thatcher and her hard-faced supporters had betrayed. The Government could still get 'the right results' from the coming session, he concluded, if only ministers would 'listen to the views of those who care deeply about these affairs and want to see progress being made. But many of us are not prepared to go into a reactionary regressive policy of any kind.'[8]

Of course the Government took no notice but pressed on with both the education reforms (brought in by Kenneth Baker) and the poll tax (Nicholas Ridley), not to mention water privatisation, the withdrawal of many social security benefits and the introduction of market mechanisms into the NHS, the attempted reform of the legal profession and an abortive football supporters' membership scheme. Heath steadily opposed every item in the programme; but he did not oppose each Bill persistently in the House of Commons. He limited his interventions and his votes to specific occasions when their impact would be greatest. In December 1987 he spoke against both the Education Bill and the poll tax on Second Reading; on the first he only abstained, but on the second he joined Ian Gilmour, Sir George Young, Barney Hayhoe and a dozen more in voting against the Bill. (Michael Heseltine merely abstained.) He damned the poll tax as wrong in principle and warned that it would do the party damage: 'This measure will always be held against us.' Again he saw the solution in a single computerised tax and benefit system: Ridley intervened satirically to declare himself 'interested and excited' to learn that the party had favoured local income tax back in 1974.[9] Four months later, in April 1988, the Government faced a major revolt on a proposal (the 'Mates amendment') to recognise the principle of ability to pay by introducing a 'banded' system of differential rates. Ridley was forced to dilute the original principle that everyone should pay the same by offering more generous exemptions and rebates; but still 38 Tories voted against the Government. Heath was one of them, but wisely did not speak: it was frequently observed that his speeches had the effect of sending potential rebels scurrying back to the Government lobby. On this occasion the Government's majority fell to just 25. It was back to 63, however, on Third Reading a week later; and the poll tax proceeded on its fateful way.

Heath's mere presence on these major occasions, however, was a gift to the parliamentary sketch writers. He sat, or rather slumped, white-haired and often pale-suited, like a great beached whale, massively immobile in his corner seat below the gangway, exuding rays of silent disapproval towards the Government Front Bench just a few feet to his left – a Front Bench dominated when she was present by the Prime Minister, but more often peopled by his own former aides and assistants: Kenneth Baker, Douglas Hurd, John MacGregor, William Waldegrave, Chris Patten. They could none of them fail to be aware of his disconcerting presence. The atmosphere of this last vertiginous period of Thatcherism, with ministers – few of them now convinced Thatcherites – borne along by a heady sense of invincibility, falling over themselves to do the Prime Minister's bidding, regardless of their private reservations and the mounting disquiet of many of their backbenchers, was well caught by *The Times*'s sketch writer, Craig Brown, in December 1987, describing first Prime Minister's Question Time and then the Second Reading of the Education Bill:

When Members on one side or another are hooting with laughter or shaking with anger, Mr Edward Heath never smiles. But nor does he show disapproval. He simply stares straight ahead, an island inaccessible to others.

As Mrs Margaret Thatcher speaks he stares straight ahead, as if wishing to avert his eyes while this temporary fault is adjusted. Even when she blunders, and the Opposition howl, he remains impassive, giving nothing away . . .

As the Education Reform debate was launched his hand was rather more active than usual, jotting things down on loose sheets of paper, though his face remained devoid of any expression beyond a kind of lonely superiority.

At the Despatch Box Mr Kenneth Baker smarmed and enunciated his way through a long written speech . . . Occasionally Mr Heath's head would turn leftwards towards him, the corners of his eyes bestowing on the Secretary of State for Education a look of something approaching, or even surpassing contempt . . .

Eventually Mr Straw's speech came to an end and Mr Heath loomed slowly to his feet.

Though the feet remained firmly pointed to the front, his body was more often stretching backwards, for it was his own side whom he wished to chastise.

Like a history lesson delivered by a senior teacher who has never quite learned to silence the nuisances, his speech was a compelling mixture of the high ('the great tradition of Disraeli, Balfour and Butler') and the low ('there is no point in the hon. Member chanting like that and then grinning') . . .

Convinced that the limited time allowed for debate was 'a caricature of parliamentary government', Mr Heath refused to give way to interventions. 'There's no time, there's no time,' he kept stressing. He addressed his most damning remarks towards Mr Baker in person. 'I believe that this is very largely a confidence trick,' he said, staring straight at the man he had been ignoring all day.

Mr Baker never exchanged his glance, preferring to sit back and let a patient smirk say it all. After all this strange, sincere, awkward figure, busily making the Opposition so happy and his own side so uncomfortable, could no longer change anything. And Mr Baker could.[10]

In November 1988, amazingly, the *Spectator* named him its 'Parliamentarian of the Year'. 'One of the best tests of a Parliamentarian', the five judges declared, 'is whether the chamber fills when his name appears on the screen. Mr Heath comes top in this test . . . He is one of the very few speakers who can empty the bars of the House of Commons: Members rush in to the Chamber to hear what "the Grocer" has to say.' Not only that. His speeches themselves were 'the eloquent performances of a Statesman'.[11] They were also invariably delivered without a note. It had taken him nearly forty years to master the House of Commons. Up until 1975, reading from prepared scripts, he had bored it nearly to tears. It needed another decade's freedom from responsibility to liberate him fully. But now, in his own clumsy, contrary but oddly compelling way, he was recognised as a parliamentarian. He was immensely proud of the *Spectator* accolade. In September 1991, stung by an editorial in the *Daily Telegraph* listing Mrs Thatcher, Enoch Powell and David Owen as the only speakers who could regularly fill the chamber during the 1980s, he wrote to the paper immodestly reminding the writer of his 1988 award.[12]

Another parliamentary revolt in which Heath joined was over the Government's reform of the Official Secrets Act. When Douglas Hurd, now Home Secretary, introduced a Bill in December 1988, Heath was at first inclined to give him the benefit of the doubt. Admitting that 'It may be said that I have changed since 1972–3', he now argued strongly for an official *information* Act, and specifically for the inclusion of a 'public interest' defence for revealing secret information. He condemned the Government's unduly restrictive use of the 1911 Act in recent cases, and particularly mocked the absurd and futile attempt to prosecute Peter Wright's *Spycatcher* when it was already freely on sale all round the world. (He himself had been offered a copy in Hong Kong: it was in Chinese, and no use to him – but this meant it was available to a billion Chinese while it remained banned in Britain.)[13] He condemned the Prime Minister's humiliating and 'improper' use of the Cabinet Secretary (his own former private secretary Robert Armstrong) to put the Government's case against *Spycatcher* in the Australian courts.[14]

Mrs Thatcher's imperious conduct of government was increasingly in his sights now. He objected strenuously to the lack of time allowed for debating major Bills before they were forced through the Commons. He regularly objected to the Prime Minister's intolerant attitude to criticism. And the Official Secrets debate gave him the opening to denounce the unblushing use of her press secretary, Bernard Ingham, to undermine Cabinet colleagues by means of un-attributable briefings behind their backs. (Francis Pym, John Biffen and Geoffrey Howe were only the most prominent victims of this technique before they were demoted or sacked.) In February 1989 he spoke and voted with a number of other Tories (Richard Shepherd, Jonathan Aitken) in support of the 'public interest' defence, which the Government adamantly resisted. In the course of his speech he denounced the Government's use of 'their press office at no. 10' – he was still careful never to refer to the Prime Minister personally – 'in a way which can be described as corrupt', going 'far beyond not only the achievements but even the aspirations of any previous Government'. (Hurd, he said, knew from his own experience in Number 10 that this was true.) Then, while he was at it, he went on to loose some equally strong language at Mrs Thatcher's friend, Ronald Reagan. The test of the new Secrets Act, he declared, was whether it would allow the public to learn about a British equivalent of the 'Irangate' scandal. The answer was that it would not. Without the American Freedom of Information Act 'we would not have known about the evil policies, the hypocrisy, the corruption and the lies of President Reagan's regime'.*[15] Such strong language could only alienate potential supporters on the Tory benches. The Government secured a comfortable majority of 88.

Mrs Thatcher's attitude to *Spycatcher* and official secrets, Heath believed, was symptomatic of her whole combative approach to politics, which seemed to consist of seeking out one enemy after another to defeat. In May 1988 he delivered another of his solemn warnings attached to the name of a dead statesman, in this case a Harold Macmillan Lecture at the University of Nottingham, entitled 'A Return to One Nation'.

> The current cry . . . is 'Never, never compromise.' We have a Conservative Government in its tenth year of office which has chosen not to use its electoral success to build a truly national policy, but instead to press ahead with a series of divisive and unpopular measures which are causing alarm even among its own supporters.

He conceded – unusually – that the Government had 'several achievements' to its credit. 'But it will crown these achievements with disaster if it persists in the application of policies or in behaviour which are widely seen by the public as authoritarian, unfair or beneficial only to a narrow sector of the population.'[17]

The same evening he went on television and repeated his warning

---

* Heath deplored Mrs Thatcher's personal resuscitation of the 'special relationship': 'I have never been in favour of heads of government kissing each other on both cheeks – even if they are of different sex.'[16]

in much less guarded language, characterising the Prime Minister directly as 'divisive, authoritarian and intolerant'. 'In the light of his own record as Prime Minister', retorted *The Times* next day, 'he is the last Conservative politician entitled to do so.'[18] This was the standard Thatcherite answer to Heath's strictures: not only had his Government failed abjectly in all the areas where she – in the teeth of his opposition – had succeeded, but he had been in his day far *more* authoritarian, socially divisive and intolerant of criticism. This was unquestioningly believed by many Tories who had not been in the House in 1974. It was damaging, because it was true up to a point and in certain respects. It was true that there was a good deal of arm-twisting and some attempts to apply constituency pressure to per-suade doubters to toe the Government line on the Common Market in 1971–2. But that was just about the only policy which the Heath Government pursued with the missionary zeal which Mrs Thatcher applied right across the board; and even on that there was a well-known core of dissidents whose opposition was respected and tolerated. On narrower economic questions the neo-liberals in 1972–4 were such a tiny band that their views could be largely derided and their rebellions ignored. Heath was open to the charge of authoritarianism on account of his brusque manner: he neglected to take his backbenchers into his confidence, but he rammed nothing down their throats that most of them were not more than happy to support. He was certainly not authoritarian with his Cabinet col-leagues, whom he held together as a united team far more successfully than Mrs Thatcher ever did; nor with his political oppo-nents – most obviously the trade unions – whom he went to enormous lengths to persuade and carry with him.

This goes to the heart of the difference between his style of government and hers. He was often remote and personally abrasive, but he was punctiliously correct in his observance of constitutional conventions and established procedures. Donald Maitland's conduct of his press relations was utterly different to Bernard Ingham's bully-ing style. Heath was criticised for holding grand press conferences at Lancaster House instead of speaking to Parliament; but he spoke in the House far more often than Mrs Thatcher. He used regularly to open and close debates with major speeches, while she scarcely attended at all except for Prime Minister's Questions; she also took to holding *ad hoc* press conferences on the street outside Number 10. He conducted Cabinet government, generally speaking, according to the textbook, leaving his ministers to run their own departments very largely without interference; she interfered openly or covertly in everything, driving her senior colleagues to distraction and (in three cases) resignation by her underhand methods and determination to get her way. She politicised the public service by her policy of appointments, from permanent secretaries and heads of nationalised industries to the House of Lords; where he was scrupulously even-handed and culpably niggardly, she lavished honours on friendly newspaper proprietors and editors, and knighthoods and peerages on Tory MPs on an unprecedented scale. Ultimately she regarded the whole machinery of power and patronage as a weapon to be used to impose her political will. Perhaps the difference was just that Heath faced a Labour Opposition which he had to take seriously, whereas Mrs Thatcher was corrupted by having things too much her own way for too long: she learned to cut corners because she got away with it. But the fact is that temperamentally and by conviction she was far more autocratic than he ever was. He genuinely aspired to the ideal of consensus and national unity, even when the unintended consequences of his policies proved divisive: she despised consensus and gloried in trampling on her enemies, without and within.

Six months after his Macmillan Lecture, Heath returned to the question of Mrs Thatcher's 'achievements' in an interview with Hugo Young for the magazine *Marxism Today*. He now denied that, for all the Government's boasted success, the economy was in reality any stronger than it had been in 1979. First, he repeated that by letting sterling rise to $2.22 in 1981, 20 per cent of manufacturing industry had been destroyed. ('That's not coming back. Not at all. That's a permanent loss.') Second, Mrs Thatcher's apparent economic miracle had been achieved only by being prepared to tolerate three million unemployed. ('This is entirely due to the incompetence and powerlessness of the Labour party over this decade.') In truth, with unemployment still over 10 per cent, the current account deficit at £13 billion and the highest interest rates in Europe, much higher than in America or Japan, the economy was *not* stronger. ('How can you say that this is a strong economy with these facts?') He then launched into a familiar call for investment in the public services:

> Look at all the work that needs to be done, for example, on the roads. We are rapidly getting into the position of having the worst road system in the world. Our train system is out of date, we shan't even have a system able to deal with the Channel Tunnel when it is completed. All these aspects of national life need to be dealt with.

It was the same with the social services – particularly the NHS. Queen Mary's hospital in Bexley, for example, just ten years old, was having to close wards for lack of money. 'We have now reached the stage where they are making patients who arrive for treatment pay for parking in the hospital car park.' It was 'a fundamental fallacy', he insisted, that a hospital's efficiency could be measured by savings: on the contrary, the more efficient a hospital was, the more patients it treated and therefore the more it cost. He denied that the NHS was a bottomless pit; but with modern treatments available 'you've got to spend more on people's health and people expect you to spend more'. By starving the NHS the Government was trying to force people into private medicine. Sooner or later, he predicted, the public would revolt:

> What will happen . . . is there will be a rebound and we shall go back to parties which believe in looking after the less fortunate and the social services, as well as the more fortunate. This is an argument which the government is going to lose . . . The point will come when people will just revolt against it. They're not interested in having 20 per cent taxation if they can't get their lives looked after . . . You can't have private medicine for 53 million people.

He was confident that the 'one-nation' tradition within the party would eventually revive, pulling the Government back towards the centre: 'They will have to react to public opinion.'[19] Or as he put it to Sue Lawley on 'Desert Island Discs' the next month: 'Toryism will come back to its rightful philosophy. I have no doubt about that at all.'[20]

But the real issue building up once again within the Tory party was Europe. More than her antagonistic style of government, more even than the poll tax, it was Mrs Thatcher's resistance to the further integration of Europe which cumulatively – to Heath's immense satisfaction – imposed the critical strains on the party which eventually toppled her. Of course she had never been an enthusiastic European. She had gone along with entry in 1971–2 and campaigned for a 'Yes' vote in the referendum in 1975 because it was the party's established policy; but her true feelings about the Community were better revealed by her long battle between 1979 and 1984 to secure a refund on Britain's budget contribution. With the signing of the Single European Act in 1986 and agreement on the completion of the single market by the end of 1992 she appeared to have reconciled herself to a further major advance towards European unity. In the summer of 1988, however – provoked by the reappointment of the

French Socialist Jacques Delors as President of the European Commission – she suddenly dug in her heels. Setting an ambitious agenda for his new term, Delors spoke of creating an 'embryo European Government' within six years, which would make 80 per cent of the laws relating to economic management and social policy over the heads of national parliaments. Mrs Thatcher first denounced him as a fantasist and then, a few weeks later, delivered at Bruges an outspoken and uncompromising repudiation of his ambitions for a federal Europe. She was particularly incensed by Delors's warm reception at the TUC Congress in September. 'We have not', she declared, 'successfully rolled back the frontiers of the state in Britain, only to see them reimposed at a European level, with a European super-state exercising a new dominance from Brussels.'[21]

In the meantime she refused to reappoint Lord Cockfield as one of Britain's two commissioners in Brussels. As Trade Commissioner since 1984, Cockfield had been the driving force behind the momentum to create the single market: he had hoped to continue for a second term to complete the process. His sacking almost sent Heath into a televised apoplexy. On 'Newsnight' he condemned the Prime Minister's action as 'sheer spite', 'a disgrace' and 'a public scandal'. 'The Europeans will deduce', he charged, 'that all the fine words about 1992 really mean nothing and . . . that Mrs Thatcher does not really want it.' Insult was added to injury by her appointment in Cockfield's place of Leon Brittan, the former Trade and Industry Secretary who had been obliged to carry the can for the Prime Minister by resigning at the time of the Westland affair in 1986. This looked like his reward. Heath angrily complained that by appointing 'a discredited Minister' Mrs Thatcher was degrading the idea that commissioners were the servants of the whole Community, not just stooges of their national governments.[22] In due course Heath had to eat his words, as Brittan quickly 'went native' in Brussels and became more federalist than Mrs Thatcher had anticipated. At the time, however, Heath's outburst drew loyalist demands that the party whip be withdrawn from him. 'He is so encrusted with bitterness', alleged a Scottish MP, 'that his judgement is warped. Ted Heath is not an embarrassment to the Prime Minister. He is an embarrassment to British politics. The sooner he follows Lord Cockfield into retirement the better.'[23]

Within weeks of Mrs Thatcher's Bruges speech, there was a debate on Europe at the Tory party conference at Brighton. Heath braved some determined booing and placards reading 'Judas Heath' and 'No to Ted!' to speak for his allotted four minutes from the floor. He rehearsed again the history of the party's European tradition going back to Churchill, commended Mrs Thatcher and Geoffrey Howe by name for signing the Single European Act but insisted that the goal of the Community had never been '*just* a single market'. The Delors plan proposed nothing that had not been agreed, without fuss, by himself, Pompidou and Brandt in 1972: then the single market, a common currency, a European central bank and a common defence and foreign policy were all to be achieved by 1980. Since 1974, as a consequence of the world recession, the momentum had been lost; but the community was now ready to move forward again. He ridiculed the idea that Britain would lose its identity in an integrated Europe: Teddy Taylor representing Southend was just as Scottish as when he sat for Cathcart. He dismissed suggestions that a united Europe would be 'corporatist', held up the United States as an example and warned that the other eleven Governments would press ahead anyway if Britain stood aside.[24]

For the rest of the debate he sat impassively at the far end of the platform looking very isolated as other speakers queued up to denounce him. Jonathan Aitken – MP for Heath's native Thanet, but a passionate anti-European – was loudly clapped for asserting that he had 'misjudged the mood of the conference'; he won a cheap laugh by calling Heath 'a peddler of dreams from Broadstairs-les-deux-Eglises'.[25] There was a hint of division within the Government, however, when Geoffrey Howe on television distanced himself from Mrs Thatcher by defending Heath, saying that he merely wanted to go faster than the Government; he denied that the Government was dragging its feet. On Heath, however, the atmosphere of a television studio had its usual stimulating effect; interviewed the same evening, he was much less diplomatic than in the conference hall, bluntly condemning the Prime Minister as a determined opponent of European unity who was bent on repeating the disastrous mistake of Labour in 1950, while he represented the true Tory tradition. In taking Britain into Europe in 1973, he boasted, 'I was able to do what no one else was able to do or could have done.'[26] As the European debate hotted up over the next three years Heath repeatedly damaged his case by personalising it, as though British membership of the Community was uniquely *his* achievement and *his* concern.

Yet the fact remained that he was still the leading British advocate of the European idea. In his interview with *Marxism Today* the next month he repeated his insistence that nothing was being proposed now that he had not already signed up to as Prime Minister sixteen years before. He welcomed the fact that the trade unions and the Labour party were belatedly coming to see the benefits of European unity; and asserted that there were 'a lot of members of the government who strongly desire European unity to come about as quickly as possible . . . I think you have got to separate the government from the Prime Minister.'[27] This now became a realistic objective. After thirteen years of carrying the Tory party triumphantly with her, Mrs Thatcher had now put herself on a collision course with a significant section of the party – including both her Foreign Secretary and her Chancellor – over the one question on which Heath was entitled to oppose her without being accused of mere personal jealousy and spite. As the question of Britain's role in an evolving Europe returned to the centre of politics as the historic crossroads of the 1990s, so Heath's exile ended and he too returned to the centre of the national debate. Geoffrey Howe, Nigel Lawson, Michael Heseltine notwithstanding, Europe was still *his* issue, and history appeared to be on his side. By setting herself against the tide of history, Heath was confident that Mrs Thatcher had ensured her own defeat – and his vindication. The next two years would bring the revenge he had been anticipating for so long.

But not immediately. In May 1989 – just three weeks before the latest elections to the European Parliament, which the Tories were approaching in some disarray – he made a speech which brought down on his head perhaps more abuse and obloquy than any other in all the years of his internal exile. His offence lay only partly in what he said – a detailed and explicit rebuttal of Mrs Thatcher's Bruges speech – but more in the fact that he chose to say it in Brussels on a day when Mrs Thatcher was in the same city attending a NATO summit. The speech was, as Robert Harris wrote in the *Sunday Times*, 'a stunning onslaught, breaking just about every political convention, not least that politicians do not fight their domestic battles abroad'.[28] 'I have come here today', Heath proclaimed, 'to wipe away the stain . . . left behind last September by what is now known as the Bruges Speech by the British Prime Minister.' He wanted to assure his audience that there were other British Conservatives who believed in a more positive approach to Europe; and that they, not Mrs Thatcher, had the public's support. He then proceeded to set out his positive vision in direct contradiction of her negative one.

Going back to the founding principles of the Community he insisted that the Treaty of Rome 'was never intended solely as a Charter for Economic Liberty. The aim was, and is . . . ever closer political union. The means . . . were and are economic.' The Single European Act, which Mrs Thatcher had signed, did no more than renew the obligations of the Rome Treaty. The specific undertaking which the twelve leaders had agreed was (he quoted the text) 'to transform relations . . . among their states into a European Union'. Mrs Thatcher now invoked the concept of sovereignty to justify opposition to further integration. But this Heath dismissed as 'the doctrine of a period that has passed', meaningless in the modern world of financial and military interdependence. (Britain had surrendered military sovereignty forty years ago by joining NATO.)

> We should beware of politicians who start to complain about the loss of sovereignty. What do they really mean? All too often by 'sovereignty' they mean their own power.
> And they will frequently play this 'sovereignty' card at a time of domestic political difficulty to divert attention.

He argued, on the contrary, as he had always argued, that sovereignty was an asset to be pooled for the benefit of all.

> I do not say this because I am not proud to be British, which of course I am. I do not say this because I wish to see Britain subsumed in a European conglomerate, which of course it never will be. I say this because I believe that in the world today this is the only way in which we can maintain and increase our influence and bring peace and prosperity to our people.

Unlike Mrs Thatcher, he believed that there was 'little in the [Delors] Report with which an intelligent Conservative cannot agree'. A single currency and a central bank, a single economic and monetary policy and free movement of capital were all essential components of the single market. All were based on 'sound Conservative principles' – specifically free enterprise – while reserving to national governments the main elements of public policy: security, justice, education, public spending and revenue.

Repeatedly he struck at Mrs Thatcher by name as never before. First, he strongly condemned the Prime Minister for rejecting the draft 'social chapter' as 'Marxist' before it was even agreed: 'It deserves more than snide comments. It warrants our constructive input.' Then he ridiculed the Prime Minister's repeated formula that Britain would join the EMS 'when the time is ripe'.

> Why does Mrs Thatcher not declare that she has absolutely no intention of becoming a full member ... despite the fact that membership is supported by her Chancellor of the Exchequer, her Foreign Secretary and the Governor of the Bank of England, to name but a few?
> We in the European Community will then know where we stand.

It really is both preposterous and insulting to all concerned for the Prime Minister to pretend otherwise.

Finally he insisted that there was no plan to impose 'some sort of identikit European personality', as Mrs Thatcher had alleged. National characteristics would be no more submerged than regional ones were now. 'There is no Dr Frankenstein in Brussels.'

Of course, if you go to a member of the British public and say: 'Do you want your British way of life taken away, do you want your British pound and your British pint of beer taken away by a lot of nasty foreign Marxists?' of course he will indignantly reply that 'No', he does not.

But I believe the British public, and the whole European public, know that this is not what is on offer.

And I believe they reject such false popularism and such distortions of the truth for the patronising, self-serving hypocrisy that they are.

What people – especially young people – did want to see was peace and prosperity, with fewer border controls and higher standards throughout the Community. He finished as usual by invoking Churchill as the pathfinder for the new Europe which was now coming to fruition.[29]

The outcry was terrific. Not just the usual backbenchers, but Cabinet ministers rushed to dissociate themselves. Kenneth Baker led the loyalist pack, more in mock sorrow than in anger, claiming: 'Ted Heath has gone too far. How sad that personal bitterness and frustrated ambition should blind him to the Government's achievements over the last ten years in Europe.'[30] The *Daily Telegraph* delivered the most magisterial rebuke:

Mr Heath's speech in Brussels on Monday was disgraceful. He chose an overseas capital, where the Prime Minister was attending a Nato summit, to vent his feelings against her. It was an ill-bred performance . . .

In other circumstances, his crushing loneliness and political disappointment would command sympathy. As it is, his behaviour yearly diminishes the dignity of the place he can expect in the history of the Conservative party, and of post-war British politics. The best service Mr Heath can now offer to the state is his silence.[31]

Heath was undeterred. On television, as usual, he went even further than in Brussels, defending his outspokenness:

> One can only reach one conclusion: that she would like to see the break-up of the community. One cannot understand such language in any other way. We have reached the stage where there is no point in going on talking in coded terms. Ex-ministers have been doing that for ten years. One has to speak out because the situation is so serious.[32]

Such an open row was an embarrassment to the Tory party on the eve of the European elections. One MEP, Sir Fred Catherwood, wrote to *The Times* that party workers wished Heath would keep quiet: 'He is doing great damage to those he wants to help.'[33] But Heath strongly denied that he was losing the party votes. On the contrary, he was urging the voters to support Tory candidates who need 'to be backed up in carrying us forward to European unity'.[34] It was Conservative Central Office, with its crassly negative poster campaign ('Say No to a Diet of Brussels') which was letting them down. (The former party chairman Norman Tebbit thought the Tory campaign 'the worst in living memory'.)[35] In fact, as at every European election since 1979, Heath was the effective leader of the Tory cause. On top of the initial furore over his Brussels speech, however, he started a second by alleging that Central Office had tried to prevent him speaking during the election, and then accusing the chairman Peter Brooke of 'lying' when he denied it. This was going too far. Willie Whitelaw and other senior party figures hastened to repudiate the slur. Heath conceded that Brooke was an honourable man, but still insisted that he was lying because he did not know what was going on in his office.[36] (His own office, however, admitted to the *Observer* that they had 'no evidence that the two over-zealous regional agents concerned were acting on instructions from Smith Square'.)[37] Once again there were furious demands from those Heath called 'the usual gang' (William Clark, John Carlisle) for the whip to be removed from him. But the *Independent* still found only strong support for him in Bexley.[38]

Even before polling day on 15 June it was clear that the Government's negative stance was going to backfire on the Conservatives, and that Mrs Thatcher, not Heath, was going to get the blame. 'On the European issue', wrote the *Independent*, 'it is she who is out of touch.' Tory Euro-candidates were embarrassed by the anti-Brussels line of the official campaign; her boasted loyalty to the United States was out of date. 'By drawing attention to the nationalism at the heart of Thatcherism, Mr Heath has raised the temperature of the campaign and made people think. With luck he may even have persuaded more of them to vote.'[39]

On 8 June Mrs Thatcher felt it prudent to utter a word of praise in the House of Commons for Heath's 'vision' in taking Britain into the Community, though she added: 'It has been a successor Conservative Government which has made a success of Britain's membership.'[40] 'Mr Heath', the *Independent* reported, 'slowly nodded twice.'[41] (He later said on television that her words 'astonished everybody in the House, coming from her'.) He ended his campaign 'on his best behaviour', canvassing in Sheffield and then delivering an impeccably uncontentious speech distributed by Central Office. (In fact it was substantially the same text that he had used in Brussels, but stripped of its contentious language.)[42] When the votes were counted Labour won 45 seats to the Tories 32 (40 per cent to 32 per cent, with the Green party taking a flash-in-the-pan 15 per cent and the Liberal Democrats 6 per cent). In terms of percentage share of the vote it was the Conservatives' worst result ever in a national election; and it was widely seen as Mrs Thatcher's first defeat. Conversely the

Garland, *Independent* (20 June 1989)

electorate's rejection of crude anti-Europeanism could be interpreted as a significant victory for Heath.

But there was another Europe, beyond the narrow Community of the Twelve, which suddenly forced itself into the argument during 1989. In a few astonishing months, as President Gorbachev's *perestroika* in the Soviet Union signalled that Moscow would no longer seek to prevent them, the former satellite countries of central and eastern Europe threw off the Communist yoke, tore down the Iron Curtain that had divided the continent for forty years and began to look westward. At first, these events seemed to suit Mrs Thatcher's book. In her Bruges speech in 1988 she had presciently included Warsaw, Prague and Budapest as great European cities which would not always be cut off from European civilisation: she immediately seized on the collapse of the Soviet empire as a clinching argument for calling a halt to the closer integration of the Twelve, in favour of creating a wider, looser Community of Fifteen, Twenty or Twenty-Five. Heath, along with most other long-time supporters of the EC, took the opposite view that it was now more important than ever to complete the single market with all its financial and social ramifications as quickly as possible, to provide a core of stability in the new Europe and act as a model and a magnet for the countries of the east, which would not be ready to join the Community for many years. From a relatively simple question of faster or slower integration, the argument redefined itself between the competing claims of 'deepening' the Community or 'widening' it first.

Heath had not foreseen the collapse of Communism. In a speech in Frankfurt in May to mark the fortieth anniversary of the Federal Republic he had dismissed the possibility of Germany being tempted to look east. If East Germany were ever to become a free democracy, he conceded, it could apply to join the EC. 'But that day appears to be some time away.' 'If perestroika is for real', he challenged, 'then let them tear down the wall.'[43] He clearly had no expectation that five months later they would do exactly that. Likewise in the course of a bad-tempered late-night television discussion during the European election campaign in June he contemptuously rejected the possibility (posed by the former American Defence Secretary, Richard Perle) that the political map of Europe was about to be transformed:

> Does anybody seriously believe that these satellite countries are going to become free democracies and does anyone really believe that Moscow is going to see the disintegration of the Soviet empire?
>
> You talk about Europe as far as the Urals. Now who's going to

divide up the Russian Empire into the Urals [sic] and say this is the European Community and beyond that is something different? It's entirely unrealistic. It's not practical politics, it's not practical economics, it's not practical in any way. It's just part of the general mirage of Gorbachev.[44]

Heath had always been sceptical of Gorbachev (perhaps because Mrs Thatcher so publicly lauded him). Between Moscow and Peking he was a committed partisan of his friends in Peking, who had continued to roll out the red carpet for him practically every year since 1974. He believed that Deng Xiaoping was steadily opening up China to Western economic development and that this was the right way to proceed: he thought that Gorbachev was inviting disaster by imposing political reform without economic liberalisation first. He was thus shocked and wrongfooted by the brutal suppression of the Chinese democracy movement in Tiananmen Square on 4 June. He had identified so closely with Deng and his elderly colleagues that his initial response to the slaughter came across as an apologia for them. In the House of Commons on 13 July he tried to set the record straight, yet still seemed unwilling to condemn the régime out of hand:

> Many of us . . . are still stunned by the trauma in Peking . . . No one believed that it could possibly happen. How could it happen when the people at the top had themselves suffered during the cultural revolution? . . . How could those in authority have allowed the massacre to happen, or indeed authorised it? We still need to know the whole story.

He bitterly denied the allegation of the journalist, Edward Pearce, that he had condoned the killing. 'I could not condone for one moment the massacre in Peking and the executions and shootings in the other cities that followed.' Yet even now he still trusted the Chinese to honour their obligations in Hong Kong.[45] All those conversations with Deng, and before him with Mao, had flattered Heath into believing that he had a special *rapport* with the Peking gerontocracy.

The next day, just before the Commons rose for the summer – that is, just weeks before the breaking of the Berlin Wall – he repeated his disbelief in the possibility of a wider Europe. 'For all Mr Gorbachev's policies, is he prepared to see the break-up of the Soviet Empire? I do not think so for one moment.'[46] Yet when it happened he came to terms with the new situation more quickly than Mrs

Thatcher. She tried for several months to resist the unification of the two parts of Germany. He used its inevitability to reinforce his argument against widening the Community any further. 'The only answer to the fears of those in Europe and elsewhere about a united Germany', he argued when the House reassembled in November, 'is to have a stronger, more tightly bound community.' German unity, he believed, created no problems for Britain: the former occupying powers had no right to stand in the way. But only rapid progress towards a single European currency and a European central bank would bind Germany irrevocably within the EC.[47]

In the course of a wide-ranging speech on the Queen's Speech he was heckled continuously by the right. Yet opposition to the Prime Minister was beginning to grow. That month, for the first time since 1975, she had been challenged for the leadership. Sir Anthony Meyer, a maverick, stoutly pro-European Tory MP of the old school, was not a serious challenger; yet sixty Members took the opportunity either to vote for him or to withhold their support from her. Meyer was widely described as a 'stalking-horse' to encourage a serious candidate – Michael Heseltine, perhaps – to come forward next year. 'I assure the hon. Member', Heath told one heckler, 'that I am not a stalking horse in any way.'[48] But he was enjoying the sense that Mrs Thatcher's hold on the party was slipping.

In February 1990 Heath celebrated another landmark – the fortieth anniversary of his first election to the House. The occasion was marked by a rash of profiles and interviews in the papers, almost all of which were extraordinarily generous. In part, no doubt, the generosity merely reflected a polite instinct not to spoil the party; but at the same time it also indicated a real shift of perception over the previous six or eight months. Suddenly there was a sense that the Thatcher era was ending, that the Tory party might be preparing to move back towards the political centre and that in some respects – notably Europe – Heath might after all turn out to be vindicated. 'Ted Heath is a happy man', wrote Anthony Bevins in the *Independent*, 'full of beans and mischief. After 40 years in the House of Commons he is well respected on the world stage, he remains popular in his constituency . . . and has no intention of retiring from the Commons at the next election.' After eleven years, he told Bevins, Thatcherism was now recognised as a failure: the economy was in a worse state than it had been in at the beginning. Why then was he so determined to stay on? 'I want to see us playing our full part in Europe.'[49]

Again, in a more reflective interview with Michael White in the *Guardian*, Heath looked forward to the opportunities opening up at last in Europe. His only regret was that it had taken so long to win the argument. 'At last we have got the different parties, management and trade unions agreed that our future lies in Europe. If that had happened in 1950, how different the story would have been.' Looking back on his life he recalled some of the great men he had known: Churchill, de Gaulle, Adenauer, Mao and Tito. All were outstanding, but all were different. 'They had nothing to do with all the trivialities of day-to-day politics. They were there to see the world as a whole and what they were going to do about their country's position in it.'[50]

This, of course, was how he saw himself. In his private view of his place in history, this was the company he kept. Significantly, what his five heroes had in common was that they all retained, or regained, power at a great age. Churchill formed his last Government at the age of 77; de Gaulle returned to power in France at the age of 68 and ruled for 11 years; Adenauer became Chancellor of West Germany at the age of 73 and ruled for 14 years; Mao and Tito retained power in China and Yugoslavia well into their eighties. At 73, Heath was a stripling among world statesmen, seasoned like them by years of exile and preparation and now entering his prime. He had no intention of retiring just when the political ice age that had frozen him out of influence was beginning to thaw.

To mark his anniversary he held a lunch for 500 guests at the Savoy. Those invited paid £40 a head, for which they ate smoked fish, beef fillet in a brandy and cream sauce, and chocolate mousse with passion fruit sauce. Even more titillating than the food, however, was the fact that Mrs Thatcher came. (It was a return match, since the previous May Heath had attended a dinner for her tenth anniversary in Downing Street.) Some 130 Tory MPs attended (though fewer than half the Cabinet), but no Labour Members. The only senior political opponent invited was Roy Jenkins, though an impressive turn out of the great and the good was led by both archbishops. Heath was presented with a silver bowl engraved with landmarks of his life – political, nautical and musical – to add to his collection in Salisbury; and appropriate speeches were made by Alec Home (carefully placed between Heath and Mrs Thatcher), Jim Prior, Robin Day and Heath himself, 'who talked about appointing Mrs Thatcher to his Cabinet, welcomed her presence at lunch, and then reminded his guests that the European Community was the only centre of stability after the changes in the East'.[51] (The *Daily Telegraph* thought his speech 'generous', but his sense of humour 'macabre'.)[52] Mrs Thatcher wisely did not respond. But she was photographed looking up at him speaking, laughing gaily, and afterwards they chatted politely for the benefit of the cameras while she admired his bowl. As the Thatcherite MP Nicholas Budgen told the *Telegraph*: 'The Tory party does behave well on these occasions.'[53]

The truce was short-lived, however. 'Barely had the last mouthful of chocolate mousse been digested', *The Times* reported, 'than hostilities resumed with a vengeance.' No sooner had Mrs Thatcher departed than Heath, speaking to the press outside the Savoy, launched 'stinging attacks' on her economic policies, the poll tax and her attitude to South Africa, the EC and Germany. He specifically rejected the fear of German unification which she had voiced most pointedly in a speech to the Board of Deputies of British Jews a few days earlier. 'They are not evil people,' he rebuked her. 'We got rid of the evil people. We defeated them in war and then we tried them at Nuremberg.'[54] He spoke as if he had done it himself while she was still at school.

For Peter Jenkins, writing in the *Independent*, the Savoy lunch marked a significant reversal of political fortune. For the past fifteen years, he wrote, Conservative Central Office and the Thatcher press had put the boot into Heath at every opportunity. 'Today the boot is on the other foot and, as he surveys the plight of the Government, Mr Heath is entitled to a shoulder-heaving laugh' – though Jenkins thought he might prefer to weep 'at the sight of Britain in such unsplendid isolation'. It was to Heath's credit that he saw Britain's European future early and consistently and he was right. In his domestic policies he had been as unlucky as she was lucky. ('Each, perhaps, was possessed of more determination than political sensitivity and skill.') In the 1980s she had provided a necessary corrective to what had gone before; yet – Jenkins judged – he might better represent the future. He was never simply a paternalist or a 'wet', but he understood that 'in a predominantly market economy the state too has its part to play in the promotion of industry and social well-being'.

> Now the spectre of decline is hovering once more and Britain's standing in the world again in question. The pendulum may be beginning to swing. When Mrs Thatcher came to power the state was in disrepute, accused of interfering too much in people's lives. Now the complaint is of the state's neglect, its failure to undertake the tasks which are properly its. Today may mark the beginning also of the rehabilitation of Edward Heath.[55]

Even Tory commentators were changing their tune. 'Lone Tory voice comes in from the cold' ran the headline of Michael Jones's column in the *Sunday Times*;[56] while Alexander Chancellor, in the *Independent on Sunday*, headlined a generally hostile article: 'Sulker Ted, the boy who got it right on Europe'.

> In all the 15 long, frustrating years since he was forced to surrender the Conservative leadership to Mrs Thatcher, that bloated old curmudgeon Ted Heath can have spent few such enjoyable weeks as the one which has just ended . . .
>
> With events in Europe, and particularly in Germany, occupying the centre of the political debate, Mr Heath is the one who speaks with seeming authority and vision, while Mrs Thatcher appears petulant and fearful. Even people who have mocked and denigrated him in the past now seem finally disposed to crown him . . . with the laurels of elder statesmanship.[57]

When Heath spoke in the Commons the day after his celebration, Michael Jones noted, 'the well-attended Tory benches listened attentively. It was not always so. In the dog years for One Nation Toryism after Mrs Thatcher came to power, he was more or less a lone and allegedly bitter voice, although I never found him so. Today . . . he is isolated no longer.'

Michael Heseltine, Nigel Lawson, Geoffrey Howe and Douglas Hurd were all now saying more or less similar things. As a result of this growing split, the Tory party might soon be offered its first choice of alternative strategies since 1975. With Labour at last offering serious opposition and consistently ahead in the polls – the latest gave Labour its biggest lead since October 1980, no less than seventeen points – the Government faced a real prospect of defeat unless the economy recovered quickly. 'If there is no relief in sight by the party conference,' Jones predicted, 'Mrs Thatcher could face a fresh leadership challenge this autumn.'[58]

Before that, however, there occurred another of those sudden international convulsions which wrench British politics from their accustomed parochial concerns. On the night of 2 August Iraq invaded and occupied the neighbouring oil-rich emirate of Kuwait, in pursuit of a longstanding territorial claim. Within days a massive international operation had been mobilised, led by the United States but under the aegis of the United Nations (no longer hamstrung by the Soviet veto), to condemn the aggressor and force him to withdraw. Mrs Thatcher immediately committed British forces to support the American effort; indeed there were carefully leaked suggestions that – happening to be on a visit to the United States at the time – she played a key role in stiffening President Bush's resolve. The rest of the year was overhung by the shadow of war in the Gulf, as Saddam Hussein refused to withdraw and the UN coalition – comprising in the end some twenty-nine countries, but primarily the United States, Britain, France, Saudi Arabia and Egypt – slowly assembled a sufficient force to overwhelm what was thought to be Saddam's powerful military machine. British public opinion, fanned by the tabloid press, was bellicose; the Labour leadership agreed scarcely less strongly that Saddam must be forced to disgorge what he had grabbed. Practically the whole political spectrum, excluding only the Labour left and the Greens, was united in support of the United Nations. With the possible exception of Tony Benn, however, the most prominent and outspoken dissenter from the general war fever was Ted Heath. Only months after basking in the new-found glow of his fortieth anniversary in February, he was back in the doghouse in September, drawing down on himself another load of obloquy and near-universal condemnation.

Heath took a far stronger line against war in the Gulf than he had over the Falklands, though some of his opposition stemmed from the same reasons. In part, the very idea of Britain going to war, even under the authority of the United Nations, offended against his faith in increasing international co-operation and his conviction in principle that disputes must be able somehow to be settled by negotiation. But this internationalist idealism co-existed with a growing sense of *realpolitik* – an elder statesman's weary acceptance that the world was full of unpleasant régimes which could not always be confronted but had to be lived with. The resort to war, he believed – particularly in the Middle East – rarely solved anything but only heightened tension, increased intransigence on all sides and piled up greater problems for the future. In addition Heath's hostility to military action in the Gulf was unquestionably sharpened by Mrs Thatcher's enthusiasm for it – the strong impression she gave of welcoming another military adventure to restore her failing popularity as the Falklands had done in 1982 – and by his dislike of seeing the Americans acting as the world's policeman, with Britain tagging along in support instead of acting with Europe. Back in 1968 he had strongly opposed the Wilson Government's withdrawal of British forces from the Gulf and promised to reverse it; once in office, however, he had found it effectively irreversible, since when he had believed that the defence of the Gulf states must be a matter for the Arabs themselves. He certainly did not want to see the Americans establish a presence in the region. All these attitudes were reinforced by a longstanding specific interest in Kuwait.

Back in 1961, when he was Lord Privy Seal at the Foreign Office under Alec Home, primarily responsible for the EEC negotiations but also dealing with lesser matters in much of the rest of the world, it had fallen to Heath to negotiate the independence of Kuwait. For nearly seventy years the emirate had been essentially (though not formally) a British protectorate: Britain guaranteed Kuwait's integrity initially against Turkey and subsequently – when Iraq was created out of the British mandate at the end of the First World War – against Iraq. In 1961 Kuwait – now thanks to oil immensely wealthy, but still politically the private fiefdom of the al-Sabah family – had become formally independent. Within weeks, however, Iraq had massed troops on the border and asserted a claim to sovereignty. On 28 June 1961 Heath told the House of Commons that British forces were being sent to defend Kuwait. For Labour, Denis Healey asked about the possibility of UN troops taking part. Heath did not rule it out; but in the event UN participation was vetoed by the Soviet Union. The British forces stayed in the region for three months, until they were replaced by forces of the Arab League.[59] As in 1990, Iraq's claim on Kuwait aroused the opposition of practically the entire Arab world; on this occasion Iraq backed down without war. Twenty-nine years on, few people in Britain remembered anything of this history. But Heath and Healey had been here before.

It might be imagined that his involvement in negotiating and then securing the independence of Kuwait all those years ago would have given Heath a personal commitment to defending its integrity. In fact it had the opposite effect. He was well aware that the borders of Kuwait were a subject of longstanding dispute and much less clear on the ground than they looked on the map; in addition, his experience in 1961 had left him with a deep personal dislike and even contempt for Kuwait – a prejudice not dispelled by the excellent Kuwaiti banker who served on the Brandt Commission. Saddam Hussein's attack on Kuwait, therefore – though he could not publicly condone it – had his sympathy: he believed that Iraq's claim against Kuwait had some foundation, and off the record he was inclined to think the Kuwaitis had got what they deserved.

There was one further factor influencing Heath's attitude to the crisis: his dislike of having Western policy dictated by Israel. Part of Saddam's strategy was to neutralise Arab hostility to his ambitions by posing as the heir to Nasser, the leader of the Arab world's determination to wipe Israel off the map. His massive build up of military power was a threat aimed ultimately at Israel. The Israelis were naturally eager for an excuse to strike pre-emptively against Iraq to destroy this threat before Saddam acquired nuclear weapons; and the Israeli lobby was disproportionately powerful in Washington. Ever since 1967 Heath had taken the clear view that Israel should withdraw from the territories occupied in that year, in accordance with UN Resolution 242. He had always believed that there could be no lasting settlement in the Middle East without a solution of the Palestinian problem – which required flexibility by Israel. He was strongly opposed to a war against Iraq which was calculated to reinforce Israeli intransigence.

Finally, Heath almost certainly saw in the crisis a chance to put his long experience, tireless globe-trotting and wide international contacts to good use to promote a settlement which should not only save the world from war but also redound to the glory of Ted Heath. This is not to say that he was not perfectly sincere in his arguments; but at the same time his high-profile efforts gave off a strong sense of an old man's last throw on the international stage, a gambler staking his reputation on pulling off a freelance diplomatic *coup* in the teeth of his own Government and most of the international community, operating under the American-led auspices of the UN. As both sides dug in and war threatened Heath would have dearly loved to achieve a solution off his own bat.

His first public response to the invasion was given in the emergency debate of the recalled House of Commons on 6 September. Speaking immediately after Mrs Thatcher and Neil Kinnock, he supported the sending of troops to the Gulf; but he specified that they should be used only under the authority of the UN – Mrs Thatcher refused to be so constrained – and he hoped they would not have to be used at all. He believed that Saddam, like General Galtieri, had misjudged the international response to his aggression and would now be looking for an excuse to back down. So far, in stressing the necessity of taking no action without the authority of the UN, he was in line with Labour, Liberal Democrat and a good deal of Conservative opinion. (The Liberal Democrats' leader, Paddy Ashdown, speaking next, revealed that he had been one of the British troops whom Heath had dispatched to Kuwait in 1961.)[60] Ten days later, however, he went out on a limb in a Sunday lunchtime interview with Brian Walden by proposing that Saddam should be offered concessions to avert a 'ghastly' war in the Middle East. Dusting off once again his favourite historical analogy, he cited President Kennedy's skilful handling of the 1962 Cuba crisis as the model of how to make it possible for an opponent to withdraw without losing face. He proposed a whole raft of inducements which his Arab neighbours might offer to Saddam as part of a negotiated settlement: concessions over oil rights, the writing off of debts, transfer of the disputed islands of Bubiyan and Warbah, even a plebiscite in Kuwait. He insisted that contrary to much of the jingoistic reporting in the British press Saddam was *not* another Hitler. 'We were told Nasser was a Hitler,' he recalled. 'We were told Castro was a Hitler.'[61]

'Ted the Traitor' screamed the *Daily Star* next morning. 'Heath: Appease Saddam' was the *Daily Express*'s paraphrase of his remarks.[62] The charge of appeasement was widely echoed, not least by Mrs Thatcher, who happened to be visiting Prague and took the opportunity to apologise publicly for Britain's shame in the 1930s, with obvious reference to current events. Churchill's grandson wrote to *The Times* asserting that Saddam Hussein was indeed another Hitler and 'appeasement' was the only word for Heath's proposals:

> In spite of a record of butchery which far surpasses anything that Hitler had notched up by the time of Munich, Mr Heath calls for Kuwait to hand over certain Kuwaiti islands and oil fields to the Iraqi dictator. If that does not amount to appeasement and a rewarding of aggression, what does?[63]

Heath was lucidly defended in the following weekend's *Sunday Times* by Robert Harris, who pointed out that Heath had made it quite clear that there could be no deal without Saddam first withdrawing from Kuwait, and had said nothing more than the Deputy Secretary of the American State Department had also suggested on television. The same edition of the *Sunday Times*, however, also contained a vicious article by Norman Stone, Professor of Modern History at Oxford, alleging that Saddam Hussein, faced with the condemnation of the entire world, had found just one friend: Ted Heath. Stone repeated the charge of appeasement and went on to link it with Heath's apologia on behalf of the Chinese leadership after Tiananmen Square and some remarks he had made expressing alarm at the breakdown of order in East Germany. He explained all these performances by diagnosing Heath as a power-worshipper; this also accounted for his love of Brussels, as well as his jealousy of Mrs Thatcher. (Stone was a leading light of the Bruges group; he is now a Trustee of the Thatcher Foundation.) Heath's role in British politics, Stone concluded, would be seen in the future as 'malign': 'He espoused power-worship, all concrete blocks and paper money. He gave comfort to Messrs Deng, Honecker and Saddam. He held back the recovery of Britain by a decade: he will hold a position in the history books as the most inept British Prime Minister since Lord North.'[64]

Heath was understandably furious at this sweeping attack and, unusually, was stung into a reply which appeared in the same space two weeks later. He was 'astonished' at Stone's article, he wrote, 'not simply because it was an irresponsible and hostile personal attack on myself, but more because it was a poorly argued piece, full of massive inaccuracies and wild exaggerations'. It was provoked by his suggestion that 'diplomatic as well as military solutions should be sought . . . to avoid a terrible conflict which, some say, has the potential of being worse than Vietnam'. He specifically denied appeasement, arguing that 'the current situation is completely different from that faced by Neville Chamberlain. One simply cannot compare Saddam's position today with that of Hitler in 1938.'

There was 'a fundamental distinction', he argued, 'between appeasement and negotiation'. The former involved the sacrifice of a moral principle, the latter merely some change in the *status quo* in order to make progress. 'I have always been clear that the Iraqis must completely withdraw from Kuwait, and all of my suggestions have carried that as a condition.'

> On the other hand I have been willing to accept . . . the holding of a plebiscite among Kuwaiti nationals in order to determine support for the emir. This is in keeping with democratic principles . . . It is an adjustment made in order to avoid a much worse outcome: the bloody war that no responsible expert denies will result.

The same proposal, he noted, had been made by President Mitterrand and even 'to some extent' by President Bush in his recent address to the UN. 'I fail to see how any of this makes me "a friend of Saddam".'

He went on to refute the suggestion that he had 'given comfort' to Deng and Honecker, while standing by his statement that 'there is nothing to be gained from constantly dwelling on the tragedy of Tiananmen Square' and his worry that periods of 'rapid and uncontrollable change . . . can be dangerous'. A professor of history, he thought, should understand that better than anyone. Professor Stone's remarks, on the contrary, were shockingly 'misplaced and ill-informed'.

> Most of all it was the tone of his remarks which showed an aggressiveness and a lack of objectivity which is scarcely tolerable in a politician and is, surely, intolerable in a professor of history. After

reading his article in the *Sunday Times* many parents of Oxford students must be both horrified and disgusted that the higher education of our children should rest in the hands of such a man.[65]

Yet unquestionably Heath had laid himself open to the charge of appeasement. He seemed inexplicably reluctant to condemn Saddam and, as Winston Churchill pointed out, determined to ignore not only his already bloodstained record – his oppression of his own people, his long and futile war against Iran and the gratuitous brutality of his conquest of Kuwait – but also the future threat to the region represented by his development of chemical and nuclear weapons. For all his insistence that Saddam must withdraw from Kuwait as part of any settlement, he seemed willing to reward his withdrawal with substantial concessions. His repeated comparison with the Cuba crisis did not really apply, since Kennedy had given Khrushchev nothing: he was firm that all the Soviet missiles on Cuba must be withdrawn, and they were. (Only much later were some obsolete American missiles withdrawn from Turkey.) He claimed that no 'moral principle' was involved, but many would say that not being seen to reward aggression *was* a moral principle, clearly enunciated by Mrs Thatcher at that month's Tory party conference: 'You don't negotiate with someone who marches into another country, devastates it, killing whoever stands in his way. You get him out, make him pay and see that he is never in a position to do these things again.'[66]

Unattractive and irresponsible though much of the tabloid jingoism was, this was a principle which people understood. Heath claimed that he was motivated not by sympathy with Saddam but by the desire to avert a 'ghastly' war, 'worse than Vietnam'. But he could not have it both ways. If Iraq did not pose a serious military threat comparable with Hitler's Germany, then why should defeating him be so bloody? *Realpolitik* might regrettably dictate appeasing China, but why a tinpot dictator like Saddam whose army did not in the end detain the American-led coalition more than a few hours? Heath's gloomy prognostications did not add up.

Within days of his reply to Stone, however, Heath invited further criticism by announcing – in the middle of the Tory conference – that he was flying to Baghdad to meet Saddam in person. Ostensibly he was going on a purely humanitarian mission to try to free some of the several hundred British hostages being held by Saddam as a 'human shield' against an Allied attack. Again he was furiously condemned for giving comfort to the enemy. He was following a path

already trodden by the discredited Austrian President, Kurt Waldheim; the black American presidential candidate, Jesse Jackson; and
the British Muslim leader, Yusuf Islam, all of whom had come back
with some hostages. But Heath was by far the biggest figure so far to
visit Baghdad since the beginning of the crisis. Though he insisted
that he was going at the request of the hostages' families – 'I felt . . .
that I could not go on living with myself if I refused to go' – and
would not be talking about anything else, it was inevitable after the
position he had already taken up that he would be suspected of hoping to act as an intermediary in peace negotiations, thus undercutting
the American and British Government's insistence on unconditional
withdrawal. He had in fact secured the approval of the Foreign
Office – Douglas Hurd felt unable to veto a humanitarian mission;
but other ministers and Tory backbenchers thought Hurd should
have done so. 'It's a disaster. He's a meddler. The Foreign Office
should have blocked him,' one minister was quoted as saying.[67] 'It's
totally improper . . . It will send all the wrong signals to Saddam,'
said another.[68] The Defence Secretary, Tom King, openly warned
that Heath would be used by Saddam: 'The Iraqis wouldn't agree to
him coming unless they saw some advantage for themselves.'[69] Heath
replied that he could take care of himself: 'He [Saddam] will not be able
to photograph *me* carrying babies down the steps of the aircraft.'[70]

He was obviously enjoying the furore he had caused, especially
since the public appeared to support him. Even as they excoriated
Saddam, the newspapers were full of human stories of the plight of
the hostages – particularly one little boy cynically paraded by the
dictator on television – and there was much criticism of the
Government's failure to secure their release; a poll in the *Sunday Correspondent* found that a majority thought Heath was right to go.[71]
Garland's cartoon in the *Independent*, titled 'Comeback Bid By Ex-
Champion' showed Heath as a jockey (riding 'Gulf Mission') gaining
fast on Mrs Thatcher. (The reference was to the emergence from retirement of Lester Piggott.)[72] An article in the same paper the
previous day had no doubt that Heath's real purpose was more ambitious than he admitted: 'It would be naïve to suppose that the arrival
of a former Tory prime minister – even one as detached from
government as Mr Heath – will not have wider implications in
Baghdad. And Mr Heath is not naïve.' The suspicion was that Heath
would encourage Saddam to withdraw from Kuwait behind his own
secure border, leaving the international force 'stranded in the desert'.
In that case, 'Arab opinion could quickly turn against the continued
Anglo–US presence in the Gulf.'[73]

Heath was obliged to postpone his visit by a week, but he eventually left London on 19 October, seen off by some of the anxious

families and accompanied by his personal doctor, Jeffrey Easton.* He flew first to Amman to see his old friend King Hussein, who was reported to feel that President Bush and Mrs Thatcher had taken insufficient account of Jordan's position. Next day he went on to Baghdad, where he met the Iraqi Foreign Minister, Tariq Aziz, and handed over a list of seventy hostages whom he hoped to be allowed to bring out; and the following day he had a three-hour meeting with Saddam Hussein. The British Ambassador was not in attendance. Until Heath writes his memoirs there is no way of knowing what passed between him and Saddam. What is clear is that Saddam impressed him as calm, well informed, lucid and not in the least mad; although Heath was in no position to negotiate, he must have told Saddam his view of the situation and his understanding of the American-British position. On the question of the hostages, however, Saddam was less accommodating than Heath must have hoped. In addition to the 70 most urgent cases, he also raised the plight of other Britons stranded in Iraq and Kuwait at the time of the invasion; some reports suggested that he hoped to come away with as many as 200. A Boeing 747 of Richard Branson's Virgin Airways, equipped with life-support machines, an intensive care unit and a team of doctors and nurses, was standing by to fly them out. But Heath had to cancel a press conference planned for him to make a triumphant announcement of his success. Haggling over numbers went on all the next day, before he finally secured the release of just 33 of the most seriously sick, with a promise that another 30 would be allowed to go soon. Heath – dubbed 'the Pied Piper of Baghdad' – touched down at Gatwick in the early hours of 24 October, basking in the gratitude of his happy flock and their families ('He's a great, great Englishman; a humanitarian.' 'He's a saint') and claiming a significant success.[74] But a 'ministerial source' whispered sourly to the *Independent*: 'To come back with only 33 must be disappointing for Ted.'[75]

In the Commons next day Heath was greeted with 'a tremendous ovation' from the Labour benches, eager to exploit the Government's embarrassment. Neil Kinnock mischievously invited Mrs Thatcher to congratulate Heath on the result of his mission. She was careful to do no such thing. 'We welcome the return of the hostages whose release was secured by my Right Hon. Friend,' she conceded, but went on to point out that there were still some 1,400 Britons still held in Iraq and Kuwait.[76] Government spokesmen rubbed in the

---

* Dr Easton had taken over from Sir Brian Warren in 1986, when Heath moved to Salisbury.

point that Heath had achieved only a very marginal success, irrelevant to the real issue of the continuing occupation of Kuwait. Indeed it was true that Heath's success was limited, compared with the tally of hostages brought home both by those who had preceded him and those who followed in what now became a busy traffic of elder statesmen to Baghdad. Soon afterwards Saddam decided that he had milked the hostages for all the propaganda value they were going to yield and allowed them all to go home. What effect Heath's mission had, therefore, it is hard to say: probably fairly little, either for good or bad. The hostage issue faded away: the American/British/French/ Egyptian/Saudi military build up on the borders of Iraq and Kuwait continued, with no sign of Saddam withdrawing either genuinely or tactically. Meanwhile domestic politics dramatically reasserted themselves.

Heath played no part in the fall of Mrs Thatcher. He had the sense, when the accumulated resentments of her slighted ministers finally caught up with her, to hold his tongue: a word from him at the wrong moment would have been more likely to save her skin than hasten her departure. Instead he watched and waited and enjoyed the spectacle: only afterwards did he crow over his successor's belated nemesis and bestow his blessing on the new Prime Minister. It was not the Gulf crisis which toppled Mrs Thatcher, but – to Heath's immense satisfaction – Europe. The poll tax, Labour's persistent lead in the opinion polls and the loss of the Eastbourne by-election to the Liberal Democrats all played their part in creating the climate of disaffection which led Tory MPs to vote against her; but it was fundamental disagreement with her negative attitude to Europe which drove first Nigel Lawson (in October 1989) and then Geoffrey Howe (in November 1990) to resign and – most lethally – drove Howe to explain frankly to the House of Commons his reasons for doing so. Howe's *démarche* was the signal for Michael Heseltine (whose own resignation four years earlier had also been provoked by a difference over Europe) to come out openly at last to stand against her. He did not win, but by securing 152 votes to her 204 he forced her to withdraw. Ironically, Mrs Thatcher was only 4 votes short of the number needed to satisfy the condition to which Heath had so objected in 1975, requiring the leading candidate to win by a margin of 15 per cent of the total eligible to vote. Without that condition she might have been able to brazen it out and rally the party behind her at least for a little longer. Without the 1975 innovation of annual contests, even when the party was in power, she might not have faced another challenge in 1990 at all. But it was under the 1975 rules that she had snatched the leadership fifteen years before; and 'Alec's Revenge' did for her in the end too. Heath was entitled to a quiet gloat.

When the news of her resignation came through he rang his office with a gleeful admonition to 'Rejoice! Rejoice!' and celebrated by buying his staff champagne.

It was not only her passionate resistance to a single currency and the spectre of a federal Europe that had made Mrs Thatcher seem out of touch by 1990. During the short campaign she attempted to brand Heseltine's support for a more active industrial policy as 'more akin to some of the Labour party's policies: intervention, corporatism, everything that dragged us down'.[77] The smear backfired: the fact that 152 Tories nevertheless voted for Heseltine showed that the old bogey words had lost much of their force. The fact that Heseltine did not go on to win was due more to suspicion of his personality than to doubts about his Toryism: faced with mounting public concern about inadequate national investment and poor public services the Tory party was ready to dump the free market certainties of Thatcherism and return – as Heath had always said it would – to more pragmatic and voter-friendly policies. John Major was the beneficiary of this change of mood. Promoted as Mrs Thatcher's favoured son – in opposition to the 'corporatist' Heseltine and an old Etonian 'wet', Douglas Hurd – he was at pains to show, in his attitude both to Europe and to domestic policy, that he was no Thatcherite. He was 'post-Thatcherite', perhaps, pressing on with the reform of education and the National Health Service and privatisation of the remaining public utilities, but he moved quickly to abolish the poll tax, raise child allowances and in other respects present a gentler face to the electorate. Almost his first public statement as Prime Minister was to express the ideal of creating a 'classless society'. He was at heart a 'one nation' Tory. Heath probably voted for Hurd in the second ballot (having voted for Heseltine in the first). But he was happy to see Major as an overdue return to the tradition from which Mrs Thatcher had been a ghastly aberration. He looked forward to the post-Thatcher era.

So far as the Gulf was concerned, however, the change of Prime Minister made little difference. Mrs Thatcher was cheated of her war, but Major slipped smoothly into the role of Bush's loyal ally. As the military build up continued into 1991 – the UN had set a deadline of 15 January for Iraq to leave Kuwait – Heath became ever more critical of the apparent lack of international will to find a diplomatic solution. He claimed that the UN Secretary-General, Pérez de Cuéllar, was being prevented from pursuing a settlement, and accused Bush of playing politics with the crisis for domestic reasons, talking tough to show the American public that he was not a 'wimp'. Just before Christmas – the same day, coincidentally, that Major was also in Washington to visit Bush – Heath was invited to give evidence before the Senate Armed Services Committee: the only European to be so invited. Before leaving he set out his views at length to the *Independent*. The talk at the time was of a so-called 'nightmare scenario' by which Saddam would withdraw partially from Kuwait, putting Bush's fragile coalition under strain. Heath maintained, on the contrary, that the real nightmare would be a military victory over Iraq. The Americans and British would be left occupying a devastated and hostile country, while the whole Arab world would turn against them. As well as a political nightmare there would be an ecological nightmare. It was authoritatively reported that Iraq had already deep-mined the Kuwaiti oil wells and, if forced to leave, would fire them. 'It will be the biggest fire the world has ever known.' The prevailing winds would make the Saudi oil fields too hot to operate, if Saddam had not already destroyed them with long-range weapons. 'The world will lose between 40 and 50 per cent of its oil supplies and . . . the industry of the Western world would grind to a halt.' War with Iraq, he predicted, would quickly turn into 'the third world war, because of the number of countries involved . . . You can't limit a war today.'

This global catastrophe, Heath believed, could be averted simply by taking seriously the issues in dispute between Iraq and Kuwait – for instance over the borders which he had negotiated in 1961.

The argument from the Iraqi side is that during the war with Iran the Kuwaitis moved the border forward some 30 to 40 miles nearer to Iraq. I don't know if that is correct or not but it ought to be settled by discussions, if necessary with an intermediary. It doesn't justify a war.

The same applied to the arguments over oil and the islands covering Iraq's entrance to the Gulf. The wording of UN Resolution 660, Heath maintained, actually provided the basis for a settlement, if Bush and Major wanted one: while the much-quoted Paragraph Two called for Iraq to withdraw from Kuwait immediately, Paragraph Three called for the two countries to settle their differences immediately. 'The word "immediately" in both clauses meant they were to be simultaneous, but this has been forgotten. In speeches, the British prime ministers have never mentioned that these differences have to be resolved. We hear that Saddam Hussein has to get out and that's that.'

This was all very well; but what Heath never acknowledged was that it was Saddam who had resorted to force to try to resolve his 'differences' with Kuwait: he seemed wilfully to ignore the fact that Saddam had already gone to war on 2 August. He still insisted that Saddam was not another Hitler, and was keen to underline at every opportunity that he had met him:

> If the Armed Services Committee ask for my opinion of Saddam Hussein I shall endeavour to give it. I notice people have stopped calling him mad. This was all part of the build up at the beginning. He is not mad in the least. He's a very astute person, a clever person. He made a misjudgment about Kuwait and I am sure that he recognises now that it was a misjudgment. He was very calm during the three hours I talked to him, never once raised his voice . . .
>
> I don't believe that he is trying to conquer the whole of the Middle East . . . We had similar accusations that Nasser was a Hitler and he was so stupid he could never operate the canal. We were wrong on that. It is the same when we try to discredit Saddam Hussein. It is very wrong. It is unjustifiable.★[78]

He spoke as though invading Kuwait was a mistake that anyone might make. Now he did sound very like Neville Chamberlain believing he could make a reasonable bargain with Hitler. His dire predictions of military and ecological disaster were honourable, legitimate and to some extent well founded: but they would have carried more weight if his wish to avert an attack on Saddam had not appeared to be motivated by sympathy – even admiration – for the dictator. 'Funny', the *Independent* had headlined a profile of Heath back in September, ' – he doesn't look like an appeaser.'[80] But more and more he was talking like one.

He was on stronger ground in the House of Commons debate on 15 January – the day the UN deadline expired – pleading for economic sanctions to be given longer to work before the coalition committed itself to war. It had been accepted back in August, he argued, that sanctions would not begin to work for four or five months. 'But all the indications are that they are bound to be effective.' 'Why?' someone interjected. 'Because it is the one case in the modern world', Heath replied, 'where a country is cut off from revenue and supplies.' It would be 'unforgivable to go to war because of impatience'.[81]

★ At one of Heath's Salisbury dinner parties one of his guests asked: 'But isn't Saddam Hussein a truly evil man?' Heath replied: 'The world is full of evil men – and women.'[79]

In a heavyweight contest of rival doom-mongers, however, Heath was now being outgunned from the Labour benches by Denis Healey. Healey was arguing much the same case – for continued sanctions and exploring President Mitterrand's last-minute peace proposals, warning of the incalculable consequences of going to war – but he was able to deploy it with much greater conviction because he was not suspected of sympathy for Saddam. (Did either of them, one wonders, recall their exchanges of thirty years earlier, when Heath had been the Minister responding to Healey's warnings against committing British troops?) While Healey's grim prognostications compelled respect even from those who disagreed with him, Heath's speech in this debate was woolly and diffuse and he lost the attention of the House. There was an unintentionally revealing moment when he asserted that Iraq should leave Kuwait. A Labour Member asked whether he had told Saddam that. 'Ah,' said Heath, 'that really requires a fee.' He quickly realised what he had said and tried to make a joke of it, looking around the House with shoulders heaving. But the damage was done. 'That's all you're interested in,' Dennis Skinner called out. The implication that Heath was holding back for the lucrative lecture circuit information which he would not share with the House of Commons was too near the bone to be laughed off.[82]

Once the Allied bombardment of Iraq had begun Heath accepted that there could be no ceasefire until victory was achieved; but he still predicted a long war with devastating economic and ecological consequences, and – war or no war – he continued to attack the Government at every opportunity. Appearing on 'Question Time' on 31 January, he condemned what he saw as the escalation of Allied war aims from the defence of Saudi Arabia and the liberation of Kuwait to the overthrow of Saddam and the dismantling of Iraq's nuclear capacity; he accused the Government of making 'mercenaries' of British soldiers by going 'cap in hand' to the Germans to help pay for the Allied effort;[83] and three days later he was attacking Douglas Hurd for proposing that an Allied peace-keeping force might remain in the Middle East after the war was over. This, he maintained, was a job for the Arab League – as in 1961 – not for the West. 'This is the new imperialism, and I am against the new imperialism. It is not our job to go throwing our forces around the world and saying "This is an evil man" and so on.'[84]

If the Americans were going to start enforcing UN resolutions against Iraq, he demanded, they should do the same with Israel. Instead he feared that Israel's restraint in not retaliating against Iraqi missile attacks would turn out to have been dearly bought in terms of continuing American support for Israel's intransigence over Palestine. Reverting once again to his doubtful parallel with the Cuba crisis, he still maintained that the way to save Saddam's face was to link the Iraq–Kuwait problem with the wider Arab-Israeli dispute by means of a comprehensive regional peace conference.[85]

In the event the swift and sweeping Allied victory seemed to mock the Cassandras. Following six weeks of bombing Iraqi defences, the coalition forces rolled over Saddam's vaunted army in a few days, virtually unopposed. Saddam did not unleash chemical weapons: the heaviest British casualties came from misdirected American 'friendly fire'. When it was all over the *Sunday Times* ran a gloating feature exposing the 'Jeremiahs' who must now 'eat their words', highlighting selected quotations from Heath and Healey alongside others from Tony Benn, Tam Dalyell, Vanessa Redgrave and Bruce Kent.[86] Heath kept his own counsel. But gradually, as the fruits of victory turned sour, the doom-mongers began to look not quite so wrong after all. First of all, the Iraqi army did fire the Kuwaiti oil wells as it withdrew, and if the ecological damage was not so catastrophic as had been feared, it was still pretty serious. It took more than a year to put out all the fires. Second, Heath's jaundiced view of the Kuwaitis – 'I negotiated Kuwait's independence, I know the Kuwaitis all too well'[87] – was fully borne out by the aftermath of the war, when the ruling al-Sabah family, once restored, negated all promises of greater democracy and carried on exactly as before. Was this what the West had been fighting for? Above all, the war did end messily, leaving arguably a more unstable position in the region than had existed before, with Saddam partially disarmed but still in power, still able to oppress his own people and resume his extermination of the Kurds in defiance of the world. To many in Britain and America this did not feel like victory.

But then the fact that the Americans had failed to finish the job was due partly to the warnings of people like Heath that they had no mandate from the UN to overthrow Saddam. General Schwarzkopf had wanted to drive on to Baghdad, but Bush heeded advice that this would put the unity of the coalition under too much strain. In effect he recoiled from Heath's 'nightmare scenario', the total defeat of Iraq followed by the necessity for an extended occupation; he abjured Heath's 'new imperialism' and brought American troops home as soon as possible. A year later, however, Heath appeared to criticise him for this too. On 'Question Time' again in February 1992 he compared the abortive rebellions against Saddam by the Kurds in the north and Muslim rebels in southern Iraq with the Hungarian uprising in 1956 and the 'Prague Spring' of 1968: the West encouraged oppressed peoples to revolt, then stood aside and let them be wiped out. His argument was not that the West should have helped the rebels, but rather that it should not have encouraged them in the first place. He was still reluctant to hear a word against Saddam: he insisted that the Kurds were a problem equally in Turkey and Iran, and that a solution would have to involve all three countries; he rejected any case for renewed war against Iraq; and he asserted that Saddam was still strong because his people believed he had done well. When Gerald Kaufman riposted that no one knew what the Iraqi people believed, Heath changed the subject to demand whether Kaufman would enforce UN resolutions against Israel. He concluded by suggesting that the real problem facing the world in 1992 was that so many more countries would soon have nuclear weapons; yet he never acknowledged that there were grounds for alarm at Iraq's nuclear ambitions.[88]

The verdict on Heath's attitude to the Gulf war must be that it was courageous but wrong-headed and inconsistent. He finished up half-vindicated by the messy outcome, which bore out his warnings that the use of force rarely produced clean solutions; but not really so, since the military prosecution of the war was strikingly successful, and the postwar disillusion stemmed from political failure to follow up the military success. Meanwhile a brutal dictator bidding to become an expansionist regional superpower was effectively pinned back; and the authority of the UN was usefully enhanced. Within a year Israel was induced to attend a peace conference on the Palestinian problem, though the prospects of progress did not look bright. These were significant achievements, none of which Heath recognised because he gave the impression of being determined to damn the whole British-American enterprise from the start – partly from loathing of Mrs Thatcher, partly from dislike of the Americans, partly from inexplicable sympathy with Saddam and partly from a desire, after fifteen years of frustration, to reclaim a role for himself on the world stage as peacemaker. Overall it was an inglorious performance in which his motives appeared both mixed and morally flawed.

38

Grandfather of the House

As Mrs Thatcher passed reluctantly into history, Heath refused to do the same. Those who had imagined that he was kept going only by determination to outlast her, and might now be content to retire gracefully, were disabused. On the contrary, the passing of the Thatcher era merely opened a new chapter in which Heath saw a fresh role for himself as a sort of crusty but kindly old bachelor uncle to the new Prime Minister and his predominantly young Cabinet, encouraging and supporting them in their bid to free themselves from the lingering curse of the wicked stepmother. Mrs Thatcher's removal allowed him to criticise her more freely than he could when she was Prime Minister. He could no longer be denounced as disloyal: instead, by heaping warm approval on John Major he was able to cast himself as the loyalist and Mrs Thatcher and her disinherited allies as the troublemakers. He could not fail to derive ironic satisfaction from the sight of Mrs Thatcher being blamed for behaving at least as badly towards her successor as he had done towards her, swanning around the world making unrepentant speeches to American and Japanese audiences calculated to cause the maximum embarrassment to Major's struggling Government back home. There was admittedly an element of wishful thinking in Heath's belief that the party, in repudiating Mrs Thatcher, had returned to him; but it was lent credence by the clear determination of Major and his new party chairman, Chris Patten, to be seen to be making a fresh start. With the return of Michael Heseltine to the Department of the Environment, charged specifically with replacing the poll tax, and the retention of no more than one or two Thatcherite true believers in the new Cabinet, the new Government was anxious to portray itself as reuniting all tendencies in the Tory party around a post-Thatcherite consensus. Heath was entitled to feel that after fifteen years of Thatcherite winter, the spring had come at last.

He made no secret of his delight. The new Prime Minister, he declared in March 1991, was 'sending a refreshing breeze through the Conservative party. At last we are beginning to shed the albatrosses that have weighed us down over the last few years.'[1] During a Commons debate on the replacement of the poll tax he pledged his full support to Major in the 'enormous task' he had undertaken, apologising ironically to those Labour Members who had 'strongly and loudly supported me over the last fifteen difficult years'. He urged the Government to take its time before deciding what to put in place of the poll tax, emphasising that undue haste and lack of consultation had led to the poll tax débâcle, just as 'sheer bile against an authority which at that moment did not happen to be Conservative' had led to the ill-considered abolition of the GLC and the other metropolitan authorities set up in 1972.[2] The next month he warmly welcomed Major's imprecise but positive statement that he wanted Britain to be 'at the heart of Europe'. Addressing an Anglo-American Conference at Lancaster House, he praised Major's 'formidable' impact on Britain's attitude to the EC. First, as Chancellor, he had succeeded where Nigel Lawson had failed by taking Britain belatedly into the ERM. 'Now, as Prime Minister, he is taking dramatic steps to re-establish Britain at the forefront of the development of the Community. His speech in Bonn earlier this year was music to my ears. To hear John Major say that he wants Britain to be at the heart of Europe was truly welcome.'

He specifically praised the fact that Major had unveiled his 'safe haven' plan for protecting the Kurds to the Community rather than to the Americans, thus 'ensuring that the European Community is at the forefront of international affairs'.[3] This, he believed, was how a common foreign policy should work; no previous Prime Minister except himself had ever been willing to put Europe first in this way. He went well beyond Major, however, in claiming that the disappearance of sterling and the emergence of a single currency issued by a European central bank was now 'inevitable'. Heath was plainly trying to force the pace by hailing Major as a good European and sweeping him along in a momentum of congratulation and flattery.

He might exaggerate the new Prime Minister's enthusiasm for European integration; yet there were plenty more signs of a post-Thatcher spring in the air, not least in the unfamiliar language now coming out of Downing Street and Central Office. Not only did Major speak with conviction of his desire to create a 'classless society', placing the improvement of public services – particularly state education, the National Health Service and public transport – high on his personal agenda. In the course of a speech to the Tory

Women's Conference in June his speechwriters allowed him to refer to a 'quiet revolution':[4] a phrase pregnant with echoes of 1970 which could not possibly have been put into Mrs Thatcher's mouth at any time in the previous seventeen years. Then there was the document which was supposed to embody the essential spirit of 'Majorism': the 'Citizen's Charter'. The use of the word 'Charter' was a throwback to a previous period of Tory adjustment to a changed political climate, the seminal period of 'Rab' Butler's 'charters' after the war; it might also have recalled, to those who could remember it, Heath's abortive 'Charter for the People' in the summer of 1974. Chris Patten, Director of the Conservative Research Department at that time, could not possibly have forgotten it; nor, one would have thought, could it fail to ring a distant bell with Kenneth Baker, William Waldegrave or Tony Newton. Patten's resurrection of the idea across the gap of seventeen years was a signal that the Thatcher era was over.

There was more balm to Heath's soul at the party conference in October. For the first time since 1973, Heath attended the whole conference and sat on the platform every day, while Mrs Thatcher stayed away – except on the Wednesday morning, when she made a regal appearance with her successor and received a tumultuous reception, composed equally of idolatry and guilt, gratitude for eleven glorious years and a desperate hope that she would now keep quiet. That morning it was Heath who stayed away. After lunch, however, she unexpectedly returned to keep the new Home Secretary Kenneth Baker up to the mark in the law and order debate, so the two ex-leaders shared the platform, Heath muttering audibly throughout Baker's speech while she ostentatiously applauded.[5] Then on the final day, with Heath but not Mrs Thatcher sitting behind him, Major twice went out of his way to mention his name equally with hers. First he placed his own humble origins in succession to those of his two predecessors – 'the builder's son from Broadstairs' and 'the grocer's daughter from Grantham' – in order to boast that the Tories were 'the party of opportunity'; then, endeavouring to hold the party together on Europe, he traced the Tories' longstanding commitment back through Macmillan who had first applied to join the Community, Heath who had succeeded and Mrs Thatcher who had signed the Single European Act (and joined the ERM).[6] This was of course a way of distancing himself from Mrs Thatcher by putting her on a level with Heath – just as in 1975 she had pointedly relegated Heath to the pantheon of leaders past. The difference was that this time Major's words equally had the effect of restoring Heath to a level with Mrs Thatcher and readmitting 1965–75 as a legitimate chapter of the Tory past alongside 1975–90. Major was not by any means declaring himself a Heathite: like any new leader he was simply trying to unite his party. Yet it was clear that in many of his essential attitudes he was closer to Heath than to Mrs Thatcher.

Over the summer, however, he had been embarrassed by both of them. Heath's satisfaction with the outcome of the previous autumn's putsch did not still his animus against Mrs Thatcher: on the contrary, it gave it freer rein. In the middle of June he erupted in the most violent and unmuzzled explosion of anger and contempt for the former Prime Minister that he had let off in the whole of the previous sixteen years, going beyond the strongest language he had ever directed at her – at least in public – at the height of her power. As so often, this outburst was unpremeditated, the trigger the text of a speech by Mrs Thatcher handed to him just before he went on television. It was the second of a brace of speeches which she had delivered in Chicago and New York – reportedly for £25,000 a time – vehemently affirming her opposition to European monetary union or any further progress towards a supranational Europe ('half-baked European schemes') and advocating instead 'an Atlantic Economic Community' – a much wider and looser free trade area comprising the EC, EFTA and the new democracies of eastern Europe on the one hand, and North America on the other. This latest offensive was unashamedly designed to wreck Major's carefully constructed unity platform of open-minded scepticism towards further European integration. 'I have been very quiet at home,' she confessed, 'which has taken a very great effort . . . I think a little less silence might be called for on my part.'[7] How often Heath had said the same thing since 1979! Yet except for his Brussels reply to her Bruges speech in 1989 he had never attacked her Government so brazenly abroad.

He had already spent most of the day in radio and television studios recording interviews in connection with his latest success in securing the release of a British engineer held in Iraq on a spying charge. He was on his way to be interviewed on Channel Four News when he received a faxed text from New York of Mrs Thatcher's speech. 'His temperature rose sharply as he turned its pages in his car,' Heath's private secretary, Robert Vaudry, told the *Daily Telegraph*: 'He found the speech quite abhorrent. He'd just had enough.'[8] By the time he got to the studio he was ready to explode; and he did. 'His fury was transmitted, unfiltered, as the programme went on the air.'[9] He accused Mrs Thatcher bluntly of telling 'falsehoods – in ordinary English, lies' in an attempt to discredit the EEC.

She says that the European Commission is autocratic in its decision-making. It is nothing of the sort. It can only take decisions if ministers agree on those decisions.

These are blatant falsehoods, and the history which she purports to put forward is again entirely false. She is also so ignorant that she does not realise we have a European culture as well as individual national aspects. Beethoven is European; Goethe is European; Michelangelo is European. These are all part of European culture and she has no realisation of that at all.

'At times,' the *Daily Mail* reported, 'his rage was so intense that he was almost spluttering. Several times he refused to allow presenter Jon Snow to interrupt him as he blasted the woman who ousted him from the Tory leadership.'[10] When Snow asked him what the Tory row over Europe was doing to John Major's election chances, Heath replied furiously:

What it is doing is showing that Mrs Thatcher is entirely out of touch with events in this country. She does not realise the situation John Major is having to deal with; she doesn't realise she was the cause of it; and she doesn't realise that in Europe she is regarded not just as irresponsible but entirely not be considered at all in any way . . .

Once launched there was no stopping him. It all poured out, as he widened the indictment from her views on Europe to cover the entire record of her Government:

She goes on talking about the results of freedom in this country; she shows no appreciation of the ghastly legacy she has left her successor . . .

She talks about the glories of the poll tax. Well, this country repudiated the poll tax because it was unfair, unmanageable and expensive . . .

She doesn't realise she was pushed so unceremoniously out of No. 10 because of what she said about Europe – and the party wouldn't stand for it . . .

She talks about the great partnership with Reagan. She doesn't seem to realise Reagan is completely discredited in the US.[11]

'It was wonderful,' gloated a Labour MP. 'He seemed to flip. He was almost incoherent with rage.'[12] Aware that he had gone too far to draw back, Heath renewed his onslaught a few hours later on 'Newsnight'. The three-hour interval had done nothing to cool his temper: on the contrary, he repeated everything he had said before, if anything more strongly. He denied that his outspokenness would astonish people:

A lot of people won't be astonished because they are sick and tired
of hearing this from Mrs Thatcher . . . If Mrs Thatcher is going
round the world making speeches of this kind, then she must expect to be answered by us in our own country . . . Why doesn't
she come and make these speeches in the House of Commons, and
then we can challenge every single sentence which she produces?
Why doesn't she come and do them on a platform? I'll go on a
platform and challenge every single sentence.

She was out to 'smear and damage' the Community, but her claims
were all 'quite ridiculous'. As for her slighting reference to 'little
European minds', he retorted contemptuously: 'The little mind is her
own – minute, that's what it is.'[13]

It was, as the *Daily Mail* put it, 'the most extraordinary attack ever
by one former Prime Minister on another'.[14] The press struggled to
find sufficiently colourful imagery to do justice to it: Heath and Mrs
Thatcher were likened to 'dinosaurs wrestling in mud', 'ferrets in a
sack', Punch and Judy, Darby and Joan.[15] It was striking, however,
that the row was not reported simply as another exhibition of bad
sportsmanship by Heath: the papers generally blamed Mrs Thatcher
for her wantonly unhelpful ego trip in New York as much as Heath
for responding to her. Indeed while there was initial sympathy for
Major being so comprehensively upstaged by the brawling of his
two predecessors, suggestions quickly began to emerge that Heath's
eruption had served the Government's interest. 'Maggie's repudiation of the ERM, which she signed the Government up to, would
have stolen all the headlines and caused Major a lot of anguish,' a
Central Office official told the *Sunday Times*. 'Ted's bombshell relegated that to the small print. He did it deliberately.' Addressing a
press gallery lunch the day after the rumpus, Patten significantly rebuked Mrs Thatcher for endangering the achievements of her
Government by disrupting party unity, but did not mention Heath.
There was much editorial condemnation of both of them. ('With
friends like these two,' the *Sunday Times* commiserated, 'Mr Major
does not need enemies.')[16] But the practical effect of 'the battle of the
dinosaurs' was to rally the party to close ranks around John Major,
thus confirming and hastening the marginalisation of Mrs Thatcher:
which was just what Heath wanted.

Heath undoubtedly felt that he had helped to lance the Thatcher
boil once and for all. In a confident (and perfectly coherent) article
for the *Daily Mail* ('Why I had to speak out at last') he repeated that
she was 'clearly out of touch with both the party and the country'

over Europe, which was why she had been 'unceremoniously evicted from Number 10'; and challenged her to face him in open argument:

Mrs Thatcher's utterances have come as no surprise to me, for I have come to expect them, but I have been incensed by the way she has chosen to run away to America, where sympathetic and ill-informed audiences will flatter her vanity, rather than face up to the reality in Britain.

On Tuesday night I had no option but to counter her falsehoods on Europe . . .

I will offer her a challenge. I propose a televised debate between us . . . in which the question of Europe could be fully aired, as she has demanded.

The rest of the article was devoted to demolishing her portrayal of the Community as bureaucratic, centralist, unaccountable, inward-looking and protectionist. But he finished by repeating his belief that he was at one with Major over Europe, while she was isolated:

I am proud to support John Major. What this country needs is for John Major to continue to show his commitment to a united Europe.

By far the best way for him to do this is to attack Mrs Thatcher's speeches head on. That is the quickest way to rid ourselves of the spectre of an isolated Britain on the fringes of Europe – a spectre that she alone has created.[17]

The European Movement – now run by Heath's former assistant, Peter Luff – actually tried to set up a televised debate; but Mrs Thatcher let it be known that she was treating Heath's attack 'with the contempt it deserves'.[18] A few days later she reinforced the impression that she preferred to keep away from Britain by giving an hour-long interview to David Frost for American television – it was subsequently shown in Britain on a satellite channel – and intimating that she would not take part in a Commons debate on 26 June. In the event she changed her mind and did both attend and speak. In a bravura performance she pledged her full support for Major, even as she destroyed his negotiating position at the forthcoming Luxemburg summit by reaffirming her total rejection of monetary union: 'It would be the greatest abdication of . . . sovereignty in our history.'[19] Heath spoke in the same debate, but refrained from answering Mrs Thatcher directly. Nevertheless his speech was one of his most explicit arguments for pressing on towards a fully federal Europe as fast as possible. Why was there such fear of federalism, he demanded, when Britain had given federal systems to Australia, Canada and Nigeria? (Never had he spelled out so clearly that he envisaged Britain reduced to the status of New South Wales or Manitoba.) A single currency, he insisted, was not only inevitable but would be good for British industry, forcing it to become as efficient as German industry.

For the Government Douglas Hurd steered an elegant middle course between the contending titans, stressing that a single currency was not a practical option at present but declining to rule it out for all time: 'In years to come [it] might become feasible and even attractive.'[20] This was good enough for Heath, who was confident that so long as the Government did not close the door on British participation in advance, a future Government would be bound to join in when the single currency became a reality. All attention now focused on the Maastricht summit at the end of the year, when a new treaty was due to be signed laying down the next steps in the integration of the Community. The Government's principal objective was to avert an open split in the party just before the General Election by avoiding being trapped into making a binding commitment either way. Major would really have liked to get the Election out of the way before the summit; but the worsening state of the economy – and the opinion polls – ruled that out. The approaching Election exerted a powerful pressure for unity. Nevertheless Mrs Thatcher and her supporters – inadequately dubbed 'Euro-sceptics' by the press – with Norman Tebbit and Nicholas Ridley to the fore, prepared to die in the last ditch in defence of British sovereignty, the Bank of England and the pound. Fearing that the argument was going against them, they seized – like Tony Benn in 1972 – on the idea of a referendum to test public support before any further surrender of sovereignty. This finally brought the first direct confrontation between Heath and Mrs Thatcher in the House of Commons (or anywhere else) since 1975.

It was on 20 November, the first day of a two-day debate on the Government's negotiating stance at Maastricht, that Mrs Thatcher lent her support to the call for a referendum, arguing that since all three parties supported monetary union there was no other way for opposition to make itself felt. Overnight there was a momentary wobble, as Downing Street appeared to suggest that the Government was willing to accede to this demand. Opening the second day's debate, however, Hurd firmly rejected the idea as contrary to parliamentary democracy, recalling that Mrs Thatcher herself had led the Tory party into the lobby against the 1975 referendum. Then, following the Shadow Foreign Secretary, Gerald Kaufman, Heath rose in his usual corner place below the gangway. Mrs Thatcher sat two rows behind on the other side of the aisle. He began by welcoming the fact that all three parties now spoke with broadly the same voice on Europe. He repeated his support for a single currency and the pooling of sovereignty, which was in accordance with the objective laid down in 1972.

Then he turned to the referendum proposal and, like Hurd, quoted Mrs Thatcher's own words against the 1975 referendum: 'It would bind and fetter parliamentary sovereignty in practice,' she had declared. Amid laughter, he went on: 'I agree with her entirely. I see no reason to change that view, or her view, at this moment or in future. I do not believe in referendums as a means of government.'

The House held its breath as Mrs Thatcher rose to intervene. 'I know that I inherited that position from him', she conceded, 'and I loyally upheld it.' She struck the word 'loyally' with an icy emphasis. 'May I ask him now: it looks to me as if the three parties are going to be for a single currency and for sacrificing a great deal of work which has previously been the right of Parliament. How are the people to make their views known?'

Heath dismissed the difficulty: 'This constantly occurs in parliamentary history,' he declared loftily. 'Rubbish,' interjected Nicholas Budgen. 'Such a limited vocabulary,' Heath retorted. The voters could make their views known 'in a variety of ways', and judge candidates 'on a variety of questions'. But he did not answer her question. He merely reached for another well-worn quotation, from Attlee this time, which Mrs Thatcher had cited in 1975 – that referenda were 'a device for demagogues and dictators'. Then he repeated his strong support for the Prime Minister and sat down. The moment had passed.[21]

Though some 30 Tories had put their names to amendments rejecting monetary union and demanding a referendum, these were not called; at the same time the Government had framed the substantive motion so broadly that practically all shades of opinion, including the two diametrically opposed ex-prime ministers, were able to support it. Only six intransigents (including John Biffen and Richard Body) voted against it, while Tebbit, Teddy Taylor and a handful more abstained. The Government obtained a majority of 101 for its 'constructive negotiating approach'.[22] Next day, however, Mrs Thatcher returned to the attack, declaring on ITV that it was 'arrogant and wrong' for the Government to refuse a referendum. The spectacle of Margaret Thatcher calling John Major 'arrogant' took the nation's breath away. Major himself, *The Times* reported, was 'said to be furious at the stream of disparaging remarks from his predecessor . . . He shares the view of senior Tory figures that Edward

Heath's criticism of her leadership pales into insignificance when compared with the damage she is causing to the party's re-election prospects.'[23] The pleasure with which such comments were read in Salisbury can be imagined.

Yet Heath was not so pleased with the result of Maastricht. With a small but noisy section of his party watching him closely for any hint of weakness, Major went to the summit requiring to secure 'concessions' from the other eleven Community partners to accommodate Britain's reservations. He came back claiming 'game, set and match for Britain'. After protracted negotiations which came close to breakdown he came away with a treaty which appeased the 'Euro-sceptics' in two crucial respects. First, Britain was allowed to opt out of progress towards monetary union, postponing to a later date the decision whether or not to join in a single currency. Second, he secured the removal from the treaty of the proposed 'social chapter', involving the harmonisation of such matters as working hours, trade union rights and maternity leave, which the Government maintained – echoing Mrs Thatcher in her Bruges speech – would reverse the most distinctive achievements of the Tory Government in the 1980s and raise labour costs in Britain. Major returned to a 'hero's welcome from Tory MPs', relieved more than anything that he had secured an agreement which would avert a party split. Even Tebbit called it 'a skilful rearguard action', while Mrs Thatcher declared herself 'absolutely thrilled'.[24] Heath said little. He could be happy that the Government had not ruled out joining a single currency in the future, and he hoped that the next Government would have second thoughts about the 'social chapter' after the election; but he bitterly regretted that Britain was yet again dragging its feet, standing aloof from the early stages of Community developments while the other eleven pressed on with arrangements to suit themselves. This was not what he had hoped for when Major spoke of putting Britain 'at the heart of Europe'. He did not speak in the debate approving the treaty just before Christmas, when the Government secured a somewhat reduced majority of eighty-six.

He consoled himself that all the most prominent 'Euro-sceptics' would be leaving the House at the forthcoming election. Mrs Thatcher had announced her intention of standing down, and so too had most of her former ministers: Tebbit, Ridley, Cecil Parkinson, John Wakeham, Nigel Lawson, Geoffrey Howe. Heath took great delight in dismissing Tebbit and the rest as being of no further consequence, since they would not be in the next House. He spoke grandly of 'those of us who will be fighting the election', as though he – at seventy-five – represented the future, when all the superannuated Thatcherites would have retired. He, of course, had no intention of retiring. Apart from anything else he was determined to become Father of the House. Since 1987 that purely honorary title had been held by Sir Bernard Braine by the accident that back in 1950, when they were both newly elected Members, Braine had happened to sign the register before Heath. There is no good reason why Heath should be so keen to be Father of the House, except that he likes to collect any rewards for longevity that are going. He has no need of the guaranteed platform it offers, since as an ex-Prime Minister he can always speak immediately after the party leaders anyway; nor can one see him as a source of fatherly advice to new Members.

Nevertheless he went into the 1992 election not merely dismissing suggestions that he should retire but insisting that he would stand at the following election as well. 'I have a contribution to make,' he told Alexander Chancellor of the *Independent*. 'But what sort of contribution?' Chancellor wondered. 'Making speeches,' he replied. He had only scorn for those who, having reached their ministerial peak, were now going off to cash in their experience in the City. 'You can't blame me if the Tebbits of the world pack it in because they haven't got the guts to carry on.'[25] His serious attitude to Parliament as the forum of real national debate, not merely a playpen for careerists, won praise from the *Guardian* columnist Edward Pearce, whom Heath had once denounced as 'poisonous and pernicious', but who now paid him generous tribute:

> He has . . . fought all his corners. A steadily integrating Europe, socially responsive Conservatism, empirical judgement over privatisation, each has been argued with wit, the odd flash of irk, but steadily growing good humour. Consequently, most of us onlookers have a better appreciation of what he stands for and a vastly greater liking for the man.

In the age of the 'bio-degradable legislature', Pearce argued, too few elder statesmen now stayed on after leaving office to lend their experience to the national debate.[26] It is a good point. With Michael Foot, Denis Healey and Merlyn Rees standing down on the Labour side of the House, as well as the whole Thatcher–Ridley–Tebbit–Howe generation on the Tory side (former 'wets' like Walker and Gilmour were going too), virtually the only backbench voices left in the House with any senior ministerial experience are Tony Benn and Peter Shore. The greyest head in John Major's Government is Douglas Hurd. Thus at the age of seventy-seven Heath is not so much the Father as the Grandfather of the House. So long as his health holds up he brings to bear a perspective which no one else can match.

By contrast with the three previous General Elections, Heath fought the 1992 election as an explicit supporter not just of the Conservative Party but of the Government. His return to the fold was symbolised by the fact that he even spoke – by invitation – in John Major's Huntingdon constituency. In Bexley the schools and church halls where he spoke to his faithful constituents were decorated with posters of Major as well as himself. Whereas he could never bring himself to mention Mrs Thatcher, his speeches this time were built around a 'ringing endorsement' of the Prime Minister. In his adoption speech he spoke of the high esteem in which, on his travels, he found that Major was held around the world. He praised him as 'his own man' who had 'killed the poll tax stone dead'; as 'the sort of leader we want for this country, and have got'; and as 'a former banker who *likes* to say YES!' (by contrast with Mrs Thatcher's characteristic refrain of 'No, no, no').[27] At other meetings he made a point of emphasising that on local issues of concern to Bexley he had been able to make personal representations direct to Major. He lost no opportunity to contrast Major's reasonableness and accessibility with his predecessor's dogma and spite, and welcomed the party's return to classlessness, balance and 'one nation' Conservatism.

Yet at the same time he still made clear his differences from the party line on several key policies. On Europe he continued to treat Major's hard-won reservations at Maastricht as purely tactical, and repeated his confidence that Major would sign up for the single currency and the social chapter as soon as he had won his own mandate. He did not believe it would prove feasible in practice for Britain to stand aside from the developments agreed by the other eleven members: he persisted in declaring that the European argument was essentially won.[28]

On all the 'big issues' of the 1992 election – taxation, the need for investment in public services, devolution, even Europe – Heath was still closer to Labour's line than to the Government. Yet such was his faith in Major that he still warned in the strongest terms against a Labour Government:

> You show me a Labour Government that has not damaged the economy, broken its promises, changed its mind, mismanaged, bungled and borrowed blindly.
> Believe me, I have seen them come and go over the years and I have witnessed one Labour leader after another promise you everything and serve up nothing.[29]

At this election, however, unlike 1983 and 1987, a Labour victory appeared to be a serious possibility. The polls were pointing consistently to the probability of a hung Parliament, with Labour expected to be the largest party and the Liberal Democrats likely to hold the balance of power. There was intense speculation about possible pacts and coalitions, the chance of Paddy Ashdown being able to secure a commitment to proportional representation as the price of Liberal Democrat support and the possibility of a second election before the end of the year: several papers ran articles recalling February 1974 and Heath's abortive attempt to patch up a coalition with Jeremy Thorpe. At Bexley, asked about his attitude to proportional representation, Heath too remembered those traumatic days. His difficulty, he recalled, was that whatever the Cabinet might have agreed, he could not commit the Tory party in Parliament to support a change in the voting system: he could do no more than offer a Speaker's Conference. John Major would find himself in the same position. Nevertheless he strongly implied that he himself would now favour PR: he talked about the different systems – the German, the Irish, the Israeli – and clearly suggested that it was a matter not of principle but of choosing the right system. Though he called on the country to give Major the fourth successive Conservative victory which 'I believe he personally deserves', he appeared to believe that in a hung Parliament the Government should be willing to embrace PR and form a coalition with the Liberal Democrats itself rather than let Labour in.[30]

In the event, of course, the 1992 election was not a replay of February 1974 but of June 1970. Like Heath twenty-two years before, Major confounded the pundits who had written him off as a loser by coming from behind in the final days to secure a small but workable Tory majority of 21.[*]

Just as in 1970, Europe was the dog that never barked in the campaign. Just four months before, political debate had been dominated by the speed and direction of the development of the Community and Britain's part in it. But Major's diplomatic balancing act at Maastricht had succeeded in taking the issue out of politics for the

---

[*] On a high turn out (81 per cent), Heath's vote actually went up by 100, though his majority fell by 500, while the Labour candidate overtook the Liberal Democrat for second place. Heath still won over 60 per cent of the vote:

E. R. G. Heath (Conservative)	24,450
Ms D. Brierly (Labour)	8,751
D. J. Nicolle (Liberal Democrat)	6,438
B. Rose (Alternative Conservative)	733
R. Stephens (NLP)	148
Conservative majority	15,699[31]

duration, allowing the Tory party to unite gratefully around a face-saving compromise which left all options open. Heath was exceptional in that he still placed Europe at the centre of his campaign. He remained confident that whatever tactical ground Major had been obliged to give in December, he would 'come out completely for Europe' after the election and take Britain, as he had promised, back to 'the heart of Europe, where we belong'. He hymned the history of the Community since 1945 as 'the greatest success story of the twentieth century', the one element of stability in a dangerous world, and looked forward to further and faster development, while warning against trying to bring in the new ex-Communist democracies of eastern Europe too quickly.[32] In April 1992 the Community appeared to be in the middle of one of its periodic leaps forward, exuding a confidence and an inevitability which was once again – as in the late 1950s – carrying Britain doubtfully along, if only from fear of being left behind. For the first time since 1970 both main parties were more or less fully committed to Britain's place in a steadily integrating Europe. Heath believed that his life's argument was finally won.

Two weeks after the election he finally accepted an honour. As an ex-Prime Minister he could have accepted an earldom at any time in the previous eighteen years: since he had no heir there could be no objection to his taking an hereditary title. But not only had he no wish to leave the Commons: he could never have accepted an honour from Mrs Thatcher. The Order of the Garter, however, was a different matter: it allowed him to stay in the Commons, and it was in the personal gift of the Queen. Previous former prime ministers – Churchill, Attlee, Eden, Wilson and Callaghan – had accepted the Garter. It was an appropriate honour, and it sounded well. With practically every 'senior' backbencher on the Tory side, no matter how obscure, now boasting a knighthood, it was time for the most senior of all to pull rank. So plain unvarnished Mr Heath finally metamorphosed into Sir Edward. At the same time he finally allowed his stained glass window with his new coat of arms to be installed at Chequers.

When the new House met he showed that he had lost none of his capacity to annoy his own party. As Father of the House he had to preside over the election of a new Speaker. Labour was backing the first woman to stand for the post, Betty Boothroyd; but the Tories could not agree on a single candidate to put up against her. Heath did not feel constrained by his office to be impartial. Along with some other senior Conservatives like John Biffen, he made it clear that he thought it was Labour's turn to supply a Speaker. When it came to the vote he moved only two names, Miss Boothroyd and the former

Northern Ireland Secretary, Peter Brooke. Miss Boothroyd was elected. Tories who believed that the majority party should naturally get its way in the election of the Speaker as in everything else complained that Heath had fixed the result by not offering the House a wider choice. But Heath thoroughly enjoyed his moment of ceremony. *The Times*'s columnist Matthew Parris memorably captured the scene of his formal entry, in morning dress, bowing three times before the vacant Chair:

> Sir Edward looked as if he had been practising all morning: the bows were just so: not too deep, not too perfunctory, each impeccably timed, each undertaken with slow dignity and gruff expression. He resembled Edward Bear doing his stoutness exercises in front of the mirror.

He seemed to take a special delight in presiding over a House of which Mrs Thatcher was no longer a member.

> Few of us in our lifetimes will see again an expression of more profound pleasure spread across an old gentleman's face. If there had been any way, within parliamentary rules, for Sir Edward to climb on to the table and . . . chant in the general direction of Finchley, 'I'm the king of the castle . . .' then he would have done so.[33]

If Heath imagined, however, that the ghost of Mrs Thatcher was finally exorcised from the Tory party, or her influence on the European debate ended, he was to be rudely disillusioned in the months ahead.

Epilogue

A T the time of the 1992 General Election, Heath believed that the European argument was 'now won'. With the Maastricht Treaty signed – albeit with some British reservations – the Labour party fully in support and all the leading Tory sceptics having left the Commons, he expected John Major to use Britain's presidency of the Council of Ministers to put Britain 'at the heart of Europe' as never before, as the Community pressed on towards closer integration. The reality was very different. Even before the British election – within weeks of the treaty being signed – there were signs all over the continent that the mood of confidence had died and the forward momentum represented by the Maastricht process was stalled. Under the threat of recession all countries were once more, as in 1973, tending to look inward. There was growing resentment in Britain, Spain, Italy and elsewhere that cripplingly high interest rates – necessitated by the cost of German unification – were being imposed via the ERM on the whole of Europe. Political paralysis in France, with three years yet to run of Mitterrand's exhausted presidency; a historic defeat for the Christian Democrat-led coalition in Italy, followed by a welter of corruption scandals which threatened the very survival of the state; an alarming resurgence of neo-Nazi parties in Germany, accompanied by a spate of racial violence; bloody civil war in what was formerly Yugoslavia, exposing the helplessness of the Community to intervene on its own doorstep; the fear of total civic collapse in the former Soviet Union; stalemate in the GATT talks threatening a trade war with the United States: suddenly debate about deepening or widening the European Community seemed a remote irrelevance.

The first blow to the Maastricht process was dealt by the Danish referendum in July 1992, which returned a narrow majority against ratification. This upset greatly encouraged the opponents of the treaty in every member country, and focused attention on the French referendum in September. If France rejected the treaty that would be the end of it. Six months earlier French ratification had been assumed to be a formality; but Mitterrand's Government was now so unpopular that there was a serious risk of a 'No' vote simply as a protest. In theory the mounting evidence that public opinion right across the Community was coming to share British doubts about the pace of integration should have placed a re-elected British Government in a strong position to use the presidency to put a British interpretation on the Maastricht process, hard-headed but positive. In practice, however, Major's authority was all but destroyed on 'Black Wednesday' – 16 September – when intense speculation forced Britain, along with Italy, to leave the ERM and float the pound. The humiliating collapse of what had been claimed to be the central pillar of the Government's economic policy left Major's European credentials in ruins, and enormously encouraged the Tory 'Euro-sceptics', vigorously led by the ennobled but by no means retired Lady Thatcher and Lord Tebbit. Four days later the French returned a 'Yes' vote as narrow as the Danish 'No'. This left Major still committed to ratifying the treaty through Parliament, but with his party more openly and bitterly split on the subject of Europe than it had ever been in the previous thirty years.

All this was deeply disappointing to Heath. Though he was reluctant to criticise a Prime Minister whom he had endorsed so glowingly at the election, he became increasingly exasperated with Major's failure to press on quickly with ratification. On television on 21 September he complained of 'a vacuum of leadership'. He refused to blame the Germans for the pound's problems in the ERM, but rather blamed 'Lady Thatcher' for having joined too late and at the wrong level. More fundamentally he condemned the speculators for cynically picking off one currency after another, and argued that the débâcle actually demonstrated the need for a single currency to defeat them.[1] But his principal demand was that Major should not hide behind the Danes, waiting to see how they would resolve their difficulties, but accept the obligation of the presidency to give a positive lead. If the Danes elected to stay outside, he insisted at the time of the Edinburgh summit in December, that was their affair. On Channel Four News he drew an explicit comparison between Major's hesitancy and his own resolution in 1972: 'I would have driven on after the election. But that's my approach. That's how we got into the Community.'[2]

As the Tory rebels stepped up their campaign to force the Government to allow the British people – like the French and the Danes – a referendum on the treaty, Heath maintained his vehement opposition to the idea. In the *Observer* in March 1993 he recalled, correctly, that he had always been against referenda and declared that for Major to attempt to buy off the rebels by means of a 'squalid deal' would denote 'incredible weakness'.[3] By this stage that was probably true, yet it still looked the most likely outcome, as the Government – despite an exertion of arm-twisting and constituency pressure far beyond Pym's efforts in 1972 – struggled to retain control of its majority. But Heath had failed to learn the lesson of the 1975 referendum. That too originated as a squalid deal forced on Wilson as a device to keep his party together; yet the result disappointed Benn and the anti-Marketeers, who had expected it to lead to withdrawal from the Community. Instead it had provided the opportunity for an open and serious debate on the merits of membership – the only such debate in thirty years – as a result of which the pro-Marketeers were able to secure a resounding victory which set the seal of 'full-hearted consent' on British entry which Heath's parliamentary victory alone had failed to confer. Heath's achievement in 1971–2 needed the popular endorsement which the referendum gave it. The same applies to the Maastricht Treaty. Despite twenty years in the Community – an anniversary which he characteristically marked with a lavish ball in Bexley on New Year's Eve – Heath and his allies have signally failed to create enthusiasm for the European idea. There is no serious alternative. A referendum campaign would expose the same unconvincing alliance of sentimental little Englanders of left and right which was so decisively routed in 1975. It is the only way Heath's European argument can finally be won. But he cannot see it.

On the domestic front the mounting troubles of Major's Government increasingly vindicated Heath's persistent warnings over the previous fifteen years. As the Thatcherite 'miracle' of the 1960s dissolved into the harsh reality of renewed recession and an accelerating sense of national decay, the two themes he had sounded most strenuously – the importance of the manufacturing base and the social consequences of long-term mass unemployment – began to be acknowledged even within the Government. In a candid interview with the *Independent* in March 1993 John Major explicitly admitted that the rundown of manufacturing had been economically damaging and spoke critically of the legacy he had inherited from his predecessor.[4] A few days later Michael Heseltine published a report which estimated that the damage would take decades to repair.[5] At the same time a frightening rise in juvenile crime belatedly focused national attention on the alienated underclass of unemployed, under-educated youngsters with no prospect of a decent life in a society which rejected them. Of course the old Tory aspiration to forge 'One

Nation', to which Heath constantly harked back through the 1980s, was always a bit of a piety. But by 1993 the country was suddenly shocked to discover the extent to which, more starkly than at any point since 1940, it had become two nations again. In the face of mounting national alarm the Tory party is now fumbling desperately, as Heath always said it would, to rediscover its pre-Thatcher tradition of social responsibility.

Sir Edward is emphatically not retiring. He is still an active constituency MP and still in the thick of the national debate. But the Government's small majority and his own passionate concern to see the Maastricht Treaty ratified and the Euro-rebels beaten require that he attend the House more regularly than has been his habit for the past twenty years. At his age that is a burden: more than once he has had to re-arrange overseas trips in order to vote. If the present Parliament runs its course he will be eighty by the time of the next election. Though he has not said so, the likelihood is that he will choose that moment to bow out – perhaps finally to concentrate on his long-neglected memoirs. A further factor is a possible threat to his seat from the Boundary Commissioners. He would not want to submit to the business of reselection, with the risk of possible rejection: he has had enough disappointments in his life without finishing with another. He will be sorry not to make fifty years' unbroken service in the House; but it will have been a remarkable career even so. He has outlasted all his contemporaries; and his reputation is beginning to be restored.

Notes and References

1 Broadstairs

1 *Conservative Party Conference Report* (1953), p. 116.
2 Andrew Roth, *Heath and the Heathmen* (Routledge & Kegan Paul, 1972), p. 22.
3 Ibid., p. 20.
4 Interview with Kenneth Harris, *Observer* (23 Jan 1966).
5 'Panorama', BBC TV (30 July 1962).
6 Marian Evans, *Ted Heath: A Family Portrait* (William Kimber, 1970), p. 48.
7 Margaret Laing, *Edward Heath, Prime Minister* (Sidgwick & Jackson, 1972), p. 28.
8 Edward Heath, *Music: A Joy for Life* (Sidgwick & Jackson, 1976), p. 7.
9 Evans, *Ted Heath*, p. 49.
10 Roth, *Heath and the Heathmen*, p. 21.
11 Heath, *Music*, p. 14.
12 Laing, *Edward Heath*, p. 23.
13 Roth, *Heath and the Heathmen*, p. 26.
14 Laing, *Edward Heath*, p. 29.
15 Ibid., p. 32.
16 Ibid., p. 34.
17 Roth, *Heath and the Heathmen*, p. 25.
18 Interview with Kenneth Harris, *Observer* (23 Jan 1966).
19 Roth, *Heath and the Heathmen*, p. 27.
20 Laing, *Edward Heath*, p. 38.
21 Ibid., pp. 38–9.
22 Roth, *Heath and the Heathmen*, p. 27.
23 *Evening Standard* (28 July 1965).

2 Balliol and the Union

1 George Hutchinson, *Edward Heath: A Personal and Political Biography* (Longman, 1970), p. 18.
2 Interview with Kenneth Harris, *Observer* (23 Jan 1966).
3 Edward Heath, *Music: A Joy for Life* (Sidgwick & Jackson, 1976), p. 27.
4 Margaret Laing, *Edward Heath, Prime Minister* (Sidgwick & Jackson, 1972), p. 49.

5 Andrew Roth, *Heath and the Heathmen* (Routledge & Kegan Paul, 1972), p. 29.
6 Interview with Lord Goodman.
7 Laing, *Edward Heath*, p. 49.
8 E. R. G. Heath, 'A Secondary Schoolboy's View', *Spectator* (19 April 1940), re-printed *Spectator* (12 July 1975).
9 Hutchinson, *Edward Heath*, p. 35.
10 Laing, *Edward Heath*, p. 49.
11 'This Week', ITV (20 March 1969).
12 'Panorama', BBC TV (30 July 1962).
13 Hutchinson, *Edward Heath*, pp. 33–4.
14 Ibid., p. 35.
15 Laing, *Edward Heath*, p. 48.
16 Hutchinson, *Edward Heath*, p. 34.
17 Ibid., p. 18.
18 Interview with Kenneth Harris, *Observer* (23 Jan 1966).
19 Drusilla Scott, *A. D. Lindsay: A Biography* (Blackwell, 1971).
20 Hutchinson, *Edward Heath*, p. 19.
21 Ibid., pp. 19–20.
22 Heath, *Music*, p. 16.
23 Christopher Hollis, *The Oxford Union* (Evans Bros, 1965), p. 197.
24 Laing, *Edward Heath*, p. 49.
25 David Walter, *The Oxford Union: Playground of Power* (Macdonald, 1984), p. 211.
26 *Isis* (19 Feb 1936).
27 Ibid. (11 March 1936).
28 Ibid. (13 May 1936).
29 Ibid. (3 June 1936).
30 Laing, *Edward Heath*, p. 57.
31 *Isis* (4 Nov 1936).
32 Ibid. (20 Jan 1937).
33 Ibid. (10 Nov 1937).
34 Ibid. (25 Jan 1939).
35 Ibid. (24 April 1938).
36 Ibid. (25 May 1938); Walter, *Oxford Union*, p. 110.
37 *Isis* (8 June 1938).
38 Walter, *Oxford Union*, p. 98.
39 *Isis* (4 Nov 1936); Walter, *Oxford Union*, p. 98.
40 Edward Heath, *Travels: People and Places in My Life* (Sidgwick & Jackson, 1977), pp. 11–31.
41 Hutchinson, *Edward Heath*, p. 25.
42 *Isis* (8 June 1938).
43 Heath, *Travels*, pp. 36–43.
44 *Isis* (19 Oct 1938).
45 Hutchinson, *Edward Heath*, p. 30.
46 *Isis* (19 Oct 1938).
47 Hutchinson, *Edward Heath*, p. 29.
48 *Isis* (23 Nov 1938).
49 Ibid. (25 Jan 1939).
50 Ibid. (1 Feb 1939).
51 John Barnes and David Nicholson (ed.), *The Empire at Bay: The Leo Amery Diaries, 1929–45* (Hutchinson, 1988), p. 544.
52 Walter, *Oxford Union*, p. 111.
53 *Isis* (8 March 1939).

54 Ibid. (18 Jan 1939).
55 *Daily Telegraph* (6 Jan 1939).
56 *Isis* (8 Feb 1939).
57 Hutchinson, *Edward Heath*, p. 36.
58 Heath, *Music*, pp. 50–1.
59 Heath, *Travels*, pp. 49–58.

3 'A Good War'

1 'The World Goes By', BBC radio talk (14 Feb 1940).
2 *Evening News* (18 Nov 1966).
3 Margaret Laing, *Edward Heath, Prime Minister* (Sidgwick & Jackson, 1972), p. 72.
4 Ibid.
5 Ibid., pp. 72–3.
6 *History of 107 HAA Regiment RA, 1940–5*, p. 8.
7 Andrew Roth, *Heath and the Heathmen* (Routledge & Kegan Paul, 1972), p. 46.
8 Ibid.
9 Laing, *Edward Heath*, p. 74.
10 Roth, *Heath and the Heathmen*, p. 46.
11 Laing, *Edward Heath*, p. 74.
12 Roth, *Heath and the Heathmen*, p. 46.
13 George Hutchinson, *Edward Heath: A Personal and Political Biography* (Longman, 1970), p. 41.
14 Laing, *Edward Heath*, p. 73.
15 Roth, *Heath and the Heathmen*, p. 47.
16 Lieutenant Stephen Wilde on 'Panorama', BBC TV (30 July 1962).
17 Roth, *Heath and the Heathmen*, pp. 48–9.
18 *History of 107 HAA Regiment*, p. 26.
19 Ibid., p. 34.
20 Hutchinson, *Edward Heath*, p. 43.
21 Ibid., p. 44.
22 *History of 107 HAA Regiment*, p. 55.
23 Edward Heath, *Travels: People and Places in My Life* (Sidgwick & Jackson, 1977), p. 12.
24 Ibid., p. 113.
25 Ibid., p. 115.

4 Some False Starts

1 Marian Evans, *Ted Heath: A Family Portrait* (William Kimber, 1970), esp. pp. 9–32.
2 Andrew Roth, *Heath and the Heathmen* (Routledge & Kegan Paul, 1972), p. 11.
3 *Bexleyheath Observer* (14 Nov 1947).
4 Margaret Laing, *Edward Heath, Prime Minister* (Sidgwick & Jackson, 1972), p. 98.
5 Ibid., p. 100.
6 Ibid.
7 Peter Hennessy, *Cabinet* (Blackwell, 1986), p. 74.
8 George Hutchinson, *Edward Heath: A Personal and Political Biography* (Longman, 1970), p. 47.
9 Ibid., p. 50.

10 Ibid., p. 51.
11 Ibid.
12 Ibid., p. 52.
13 *Bexleyheath Observer* (14 Nov 1947).
14 Ibid. (22 Aug 1947).
15 Hutchinson, *Edward Heath*, pp. 54–5.
16 Ibid., p. 56.
17 Roth, *Heath and the Heathmen*, p. 60.
18 *Bexleyheath Observer, Kentish Independent* (14 Nov 1947).
19 Hutchinson, *Edward Heath*, p. 61.
20 Laing, *Edward Heath*, p. 85.
21 House of Commons, 8 Feb 1967 (740/1672–87).
22 Roth, *Heath and the Heathmen*, p. 62.
23 Evans, *Ted Heath*, p. 19.
24 Ibid., p. 37.
25 *Bexleyheath Observer* (10 Feb 1950).
26 Ibid.
27 Ibid. (12 March 1948).
28 Ibid. (30 Sept 1949).
29 *Erith Observer* (30 Jan 1948).
30 *Bexley Citizen* (Jan 1950).
31 *Bexleyheath Observer* (16 Sept 1948).
32 Ibid.
33 Ibid. (27 Jan 1950).
34 Ibid. (24 Sept 1948).
35 Ibid. (24 Feb 1950).
36 Ibid. (17 Feb 1950).
37 Ibid. (3 March 1950).

5 The Class of 1950

1 Marian Evans, *Ted Heath: A Family Portrait* (William Kimber, 1970), p. 91.
2 Ibid., p. 80.
3 *Bexleyheath Observer* (24 March 1950).
4 House of Commons, 2 May 1950 (474/1576–7).
5 Ibid., 4, 10, 11 May 1950 (474/233–4; 475/70, 548).
6 Ibid., 26 June 1950 (476/1959–64).
7 *Bexleyheath Observer* (23 June 1950).
8 George Hutchinson, *Edward Heath: A Personal and Political Biography* (Longman, 1970), p. 71.
9 Edward Heath, *Parliament and People* (Conservative Political Centre, 1960).
10 Andrew Roth, *Heath and the Heathmen* (Routledge & Kegan Paul, 1972), p. 77.
11 Interview with Lord Carr.
12 I. Macleod and A. Maude (ed.), *One Nation: A Tory Approach to Social Problems* (Conservative Political Centre, 1950).
13 Interview with James Margach, *Sunday Times* (3 Oct 1965).
14 House of Commons, 8 March 1951 (485/779–87); 16 June 1951 (489/91–3).
15 Hutchinson, *Edward Heath*, p. 78.
16 Evans, *Ted Heath*, p. 74.
17 Ibid., p. 85.
18 *Bexleyheath Observer* (19 Oct 1951).
19 Ibid. (2 Nov 1951).

20 Roth, *Heath and the Heathmen*, p. 88.
21 Margaret Laing, *Edward Heath, Prime Minister* (Sidgwick & Jackson, 1972), p. 112.
22 Evans, *Ted Heath*, p. 90.
23 Heath, *Parliament and People*.
24 Evans, *Ted Heath*, p. 90.
25 *Sunday Express* (17 May 1970).
26 *Bexleyheath Observer* (16 Feb 1951).
27 Ibid. (9 Jan, 25 Dec 1953).
28 Ibid. (26 March 1954).
29 *Conservative Party Conference Report* (1953), p. 116 (10 Oct 1953).
30 Roth, *Heath and the Heathmen*, p. 92.
31 Ian Trethowan, *Split Screen* (Hamish Hamilton, 1984), p. 57.
32 *Bexleyheath Observer* (15 Oct 1954).
33 Edward Heath, *Travels: People and Places in My Life* (Sidgwick & Jackson, 1977), p. 120.
34 *Bexleyheath Observer* (15 Oct 1954).
35 Ibid. (13 May 1955).
36 Ibid. (3 June 1955).
37 Hutchinson, *Edward Heath*, pp. 82–3.

6 Chief Whip

1 Interview with Robert Carvel, BBC Radio Four (28 Jan 1988).
2 Anthony Eden, *Full Circle* (Cassell, 1960), p. 549.
3 George Hutchinson, *Edward Heath: A Personal and Political Biography* (Longman, 1970), p. 83.
4 Eden, *Full Circle*, p. 549.
5 *The Economist* (7 July 1956).
6 Margaret Laing, *Edward Heath, Prime Minister* (Sidgwick & Jackson, 1972), p. 113.
7 *Evening Standard* (29 Feb 1956).
8 CAB CM(56)53 (26 July 1956).
9 *Bexleyheath Observer* (5 Oct 1956).
10 Henry Fairlie, *Daily Mail* (20 May 1959).
11 *Sunday Times* (8 April 1962).
12 *Star* (23 Nov 1956).
13 Andrew Roth, *Heath and the Heathmen* (Routledge & Kegan Paul, 1972), p. 107.
14 Earl of Kilmuir, *Political Adventure: The Memoirs of the Earl of Kilmuir* (Weidenfeld & Nicolson, 1964), p. 281.
15 Laing, *Edward Heath*, p. 115.
16 Hugh Thomas, *The Suez Affair* (Weidenfeld & Nicolson, 1967), p. 168.
17 Roth, *Heath and the Heathmen*, p. 107.
18 *Daily Express* (7 Dec 1956).
19 *Observer* (9 Dec 1956).
20 *The Economist* (1 Dec 1956).
21 Hutchinson, *Edward Heath*, p. 85.
22 *Sunday Times* (n.d.); Roth, *Heath and the Heathmen*, p. 110.
23 *The Economist* (8 Dec 1956).
24 Andrew Roth, *Enoch Powell: Tory Tribune* (Macdonald, 1970), p. 159.
25 Hutchinson, *Edward Heath*, p. 86.
26 *Evening Standard* (24 April 1959).

27 *Sunday Express* (10 Jan 1971).
28 Harold Macmillan, *Riding the Storm* (Macmillan, 1971), p. 373.
29 *Daily Express* (2 Dec 1962).
30 George Hutchinson, *Evening Standard* (17 Feb 1958); see also Henry Fairlie, *Daily Mail* (20 May 1959).
31 Hutchinson, *Edward Heath*, p. 87.
32 Roth, *Heath and the Heathmen*, p. 118.
33 *Independent* (2 Jan 1989).
34 Lucille Iremonger, 'Edward Heath', in John P. Mackintosh (ed.), *British Prime Ministers in the Twentieth Century*, vol.II (Weidenfeld & Nicolson, 1978), p. 150.
35 John Vincent, *The Times* (n.d., 1983).
36 Laing, *Edward Heath*, p. 114.
37 Interview with Kenneth Harris, *Observer* (23 Jan 1966).
38 *Observer* (18 Oct 1959).
39 Interview with James Margach, *Sunday Times* (30 Oct 1965).
40 Hutchinson, *Edward Heath*, p. 83.
41 Edward Heath, *Parliament and People* (Conservative Political Centre, 1960), p. 20.
42 Edward Heath, *Travels: People and Places in My life* (Sidgwick & Jackson, 1977), p. 133.
43 *Bexleyheath Observer* (26 Sept 1958).
44 Ibid. (8 March 1957).
45 Ibid. (14 March 1958).
46 Ibid. (9 Oct 1959).

7 'Mr Europe'

1   *Observer* (18 Oct 1959).
2   *The Economist* (17 Oct 1959).
3   *The Times* (13 Feb 1960).
4   *Sunday Times* (14 Feb 1960).
5   *The Economist* (20 Feb 1960).
6   Ibid. (12 March 1960).
7   Ibid. (17 April 1960).
8   *Daily Express* (16 Nov 1959).
9   Edward Heath, *Parliament and People* (Conservative Political Centre, 1960), p. 25.
10 Eric Wigham, *Strikes and the Government, 1893–1974* (Macmillan, 1976), p. 125.
11 *The Times* (28 July 1960).
12 *Financial Times* (28 July 1960).
13 Nora Beloff, *The General Says No* (Penguin, 1963), p. 97.
14 Conservative party conference (Scarborough), 13 Oct 1960.
15 *The Times* (28 Sept 1960).
16 Conservative party conference, 13 Oct 1960.
17 *The Economist* (13 Dec 1960).
18 *Manchester Guardian* (5 Nov 1960).
19 Janet Morgan (ed.), *The Backbench Diaries of Richard Crossman* (Hamish Hamilton and Jonathan Cape, 1981), p. 908 (14 Feb 1960).
20 *Sunday Telegraph* (12 Feb 1961).
21 *The Times* (28 Feb 1961).
22 House of Commons, 17 May 1961 (640/1379–1400).
23 *The Economist* (20 May 1961).
24 Edward Heath, *Travels: People and Places in My Life* (Sidgwick & Jackson, 1977), p. 131.

25 *The Times* (18 Aug 1961).
26 *The Economist* (20 Aug 1961).
27 *The Times* (31 July 1961).
28 Eric Roll, *Crowded Hours* (Faber, 1985), pp. 113–15.
29 Ibid.
30 Cmnd 1565, *Annual Register, 1961*, pp. 518–28.
31 Roll, *Crowded Hours*, p. 121.
32 Beloff, *The General Says No*, p. 114.
33 *The Economist* (22 July 1961).
34 See Heath's review of Monnet's *Memoirs* in *The Times* (19 March 1978).
35 Conservative party conference (Brighton), 10 Dec 1961.
36 House of Commons, 3 Aug 1961 (645/1670–89).
37 Beloff, *The General Says No*, p. 115.
38 Harold Macmillan, *At the End of the Day* (Macmillan, 1973), p. 118.
39 Piers Dixon, *Double Diploma: The Life of Sir Pierson Dixon* (Hutchinson, 1968), pp. 288–9.
40 *The Economist* (15 Sept 1962).
41 Ibid. (13 Oct 1962).
42 'Conference Report', BBC TV (11 Oct 1962).
43 *Conservative Party Conference Report* (1962), pp. 61–6 (11 Oct 1962).
44 *Sunday Times* (30 Oct 1962).
45 Dixon, *Double Diploma*, p. 301.
46 Macmillan, *At the End of the Day*, p. 363.
47 Roll, *Crowded Hours*, p. 127; Beloff, *The General Says No*, p. 162.
48 George Ball, *The Discipline of Power* (Bodley Head, 1968), p. 162.
49 Beloff, *The General Says No*, pp. 162–4.
50 Roll, *Crowded Hours*, p. 117.
51 Anthony Sampson, *Observer* (2 May 1971).
52 Miriam Camps, *Britain and the European Community, 1955–63* (Princeton University Press and Oxford University Press, 1964), p. 491.
53 Ibid., p. 492; Beloff, *The General Says No*, p. 16; *The Times* (30 Jan 1963).
54 Beloff, *The General Says No*, p. 16.
55 Camps, *Britain and the European Community*, p. 493.
56 *The Times* (24 May 1963).
57 *Sunday Times* (29 Aug 1965).
58 Macmillan, *At the End of the Day*, p. 354.
59 *The Economist* (23 Dec 1961).
60 *Sunday Times* (8 April 1962).
61 T. F. Lindsay, *Parliament from the Press Gallery* (Macmillan, 1967), p. 99.
62 *Evening Standard* (18 Feb 1963).
63 *Sunday Express* (29 Sept 1963).
64 *Evening Standard* (18 Feb 1963).
65 Ibid. (7 March 1963).
66 House of Commons, 20 March 1963 (674/361–3).
67 Ibid., 1, 8 July 1963 (680/33–5, 863–70)
68 Crossman, *Backbench Diaries*, pp. 1015–16 (17 July 1963).
69 Anthony Sampson, *Observer* (2 May 1971).
70 *Daily Telegraph* (21 June 1963); Philip Goodhart, *The 1922: The Story of the Conservative Backbenchers' Parliamentary Committee* (Macmillan, 1973), p. 191.
71 Interview with Mrs Jo Pattrick.
72 Margaret Laing, *Edward Heath: Prime Minister* (Sidgwick & Jackson, 1972), p. 151.
73 *Sunday Times* (1 Aug 1965); *Observer* (16 Jan 1966).

8 After Blackpool

1 'Conference Report', BBC TV (8 Oct 1963).
2 *Daily Telegraph* (9 Oct 1963).
3 'Conference Report', BBC TV (8 Oct 1963).
4 *The Times* (10 Oct 1963).
5 *The Economist* (12 Oct 1963).
6 *Daily Telegraph* (10 Oct 1963).
7 e.g. Vicky in *Evening Standard* (16 Oct 1963) and Cummings in *Sunday Express*, reprinted in Alistair Horne, *Macmillan, 1957–86* (Macmillan, 1989).
8 *Spectator* (11 and 18 Oct 1963).
9 James Prior, *A Balance of Power* (Hamish Hamilton, 1986), p. 33.
10 Alan Thompson, *The Day Before Yesterday* (Panther/Sidgwick & Jackson, 1971), p. 219.
11 Andrew Roth, *Heath and the Heathmen* (Routledge & Kegan Paul, 1972), p. 174.
12 'Panorama', BBC TV (18 Oct 1963).
13 'Gallery', BBC TV (24 Oct 1963).
14 *The Economist* (26 Oct 1963).
15 Interview with James Margach, *Sunday Times* (3 Oct 1965).
16 House of Commons, 14 Nov 1963 (684/323–49).
17 Ibid., 18 June 1964 (696/1538–47).
18 Ibid., 14 Nov 1963 (684/323–49).
19 Ibid.
20 Ibid.
21 See Ronald Butt, *The Power of Parliament* (Constable, 1967), ch. 9, pp. 251–74.
22 Lord Home of the Hirsel, *The Way the Wind Blows* (Collins, 1976), p. 189.
23 Jock Bruce-Gardyne and Nigel Lawson, *The Power Game* (Macmillan, 1976), p. 100.
24 Peter Hennessy, *Cabinet* (Blackwell, 1986), p. 66.
25 House of Commons, 15 Jan 1964 (687/224–30).
26 Ibid., 10 March 1964 (691/255–76).
27 Ibid. (691/276–87).
28 Ibid. (691/354–8).
29 George Hutchinson, *Edward Heath: A Personal and Political Biography* (Longman, 1970), p. 129.
30 *Daily Sketch* (27 Feb 1964); Douglas Jay in House of Commons, 10 March 1964 (691/276–87).
31 House of Commons, 24 March 1964 (693/367–422).
32 Ibid. (693/416–20).
33 BBC TV (20 Jan 1967), quoted in Butt, *Power of Parliament*, p. 269.
34 Butt, *Power of Parliament*, p. 269.
35 House of Commons, 13 May 1964 (695/846).
36 Ibid. (695/530–4).
37 Ibid.
38 Hennessy, *Cabinet*, p. 66.
39 *New Statesman* (9 Oct 1970).
40 House of Commons, 14 Nov 1963 (684/323–49).
41 Ibid.
42 Ibid., 3 Dec 1963 (685/1003).
43 Ibid., 14 Nov 1963 (684/323–49).
44 'Gallery', BBC TV (24 Oct 1963).
45 *The Times* (2 Nov 1963).

46 e.g. House of Commons, 18 June 1964 (696/1538–47).
47 *Sunday Telegraph* (7 June 1964).
48 *The Economist* (12 Sept 1964).
49 David Butler and Anthony King, *The British General Election of 1964* (Macmillan, 1965), pp. 172–3.
50 *Sunday Times* (19 April 1964).
51 *Daily Mirror* (9 Oct 1964).
52 Unidentified cutting.
53 Butler and King, *General Election of 1964*, pp. 123–4.
54 *The Times* (14 Oct 1964).
55 See Richard Rose in *The Times* (17 Oct 1964).
56 *The Times* (16 Oct 1964).

9 'A New Kind of Tory Leader'

1   *The Times* (24 Oct 1964).
2   Ibid. (9 Nov 1964).
3   House of Commons, 10 Nov 1964 (701/952–3).
4   *Guardian* (10 Nov 1964).
5   House of Commons, 1 Mar 1965 (707/1037).
6   *The Times* (28 Nov 1964).
7   'Panorama', BBC TV (22 Feb 1965); *The Times* (8 Dec 1964).
8   *The Times* (24 Jan 1965).
9   *Yorkshire Post* (13 March 1965).
10 *Birmingham Post* (2 Jan 1965).
11 'Gallery', BBC TV (29 Oct 1964); *The Times* (8 Dec 1964).
12 *Spectator* (11 Dec 1964).
13 Heath to Lady Davidson, in John Ramsden, *The Making of Conservative Party Policy: The Conservative Research Department since 1929* (Longman, 1980), p. 241.
14 James Douglas to Sir Michael Fraser, March 1965, ibid., p. 242.
15 *Birmingham Post* (2 Jan 1965).
16 *Daily Telegraph* (5 Feb 1965).
17 *Spectator* (2 April 1965).
18 Private information.
19 House of Commons, 7 April 1965 (710/490–519).
20 Edward Heath in *Spectator* (23 July 1965).
21 *The Times* (25 June 1965).
22 Margaret Laing, *Edward Heath, Prime Minister* (Sidgwick & Jackson, 1972), p. 165.
23 Interview with Lord Walker; Peter Walker, *The Ascent of Britain* (Sidgwick & Jackson, 1977), p. 58.
24 *Daily Mail* (30 Oct 1964).
25 *Sunday Times* (7 Feb 1965).
26 *Daily Telegraph* (26 March 1965).
27 *Sunday Express* (3 Jan 1965).
28 *Guardian* (21 Jan 1965).
29 Ibid. (22 April 1965).
30 *The Times* (25 May 1965).
31 *Sunday Express* (27 June 1965).
32 *Sunday Telegraph* (18 July 1965).
33 *Guardian* (28 June 1965).
34 *Sunday Telegraph* (18 July 1965).

35 *Sunday Times* (18 July 1965).
36 *Observer* (25 July 1965); Anthony Sampson, *Anatomy of Britain Today* (Hodder & Stoughton, 1965), p. 81.
37 *The Economist* (24 July 1965).
38 Sampson, *Anatomy of Britain Today*, p. 78.
39 *Daily Mail* (26 July 1965).
40 'Panorama', BBC TV (26 July 1975).
41 *The Economist* (10 July 1965).
42 Interview with Lord Walker.
43 Ibid.
44 *New Statesman* (30 July 1965).
45 Lord Boyle's entry on Maudling in the *Dictionary of National Biography, 1971–80* ed. Lord Blake and C. S. Nicholls (Oxford University Press, 1986), pp. 557–9.
46 *Daily Telegraph*, quoted in *Evening News* (26 July 1965).
47 *Guardian*, quoted in ibid.
48 Ibid. (28 July 1965).
49 *Observer* (6 June 1965).
50 *The Times* (31 May 1965); *The Economist* (17 June 1965).
51 Nigel Fisher, *The Tory Leaders: Their Struggle for Power* (Weidenfeld & Nicolson, 1977), p. 126.
52 Interview with Lord Walker.
53 *Sunday Times* (1 Aug 1965).
54 Press summarised in *Evening News* (26 July 1965).
55 *New Statesman* (30 July 1965).
56 Interview with Lord Walker.
57 Reginald Maudling, *Memoirs* (Sidgwick & Jackson, 1978), p. 134.
58 *Guardian* (28 July 1965).
59 *Sunday Times* (1 Aug 1965).
60 *Daily Mirror* (28 July 1965).
61 *Sunday Times* (1 Aug 1965).
62 *Daily Worker* (28 July 1965).
63 *Daily Sketch* (28 July 1965).
64 *Guardian* (28 July 1965).
65 *Spectator* (30 July 1965).
66 *The Economist* (31 July 1965).
67 *Guardian* (28 July 1965).
68 *The Economist* (31 July 1965).

10 Establishing Authority

1 Christopher Booker, *The Neophiliacs* (Collins, 1969; Fontana edn, 1970), pp. 27–30.
2 *Weekend Telegraph* (24 Sept 1965).
3 *Observer* (10 Oct 1965).
4 Ibid. (10 Oct 1965).
5 *Daily Mail* (n.d.).
6 House of Commons, 2 Aug 1965 (717/1070–87).
7 Richard Crossman, *Diaries of a Cabinet Minister*, vol. 1 (Hamish Hamilton & Jonathan Cape, 1975), p. 299 (2 Aug 1965).
8 House of Commons, 2 Aug 1965 (717/1186).
9 *The Times* (3 Aug 1965).
10 House of Commons, 2 Aug 1965 (717/1196–81).

11 *The Times* (3 Aug 1965).
12 House of Commons, 1 March 1966 (725/1225).
13 Ibid., 14 Dec 1965 (722/1088).
14 Ibid., 21 April 1966 (727/84).
15 James Prior, *A Balance of Power* (Hamish Hamilton, 1986), p. 40.
16 Crossman, *Diaries of a Cabinet Minister*, vol.1, p. 293 (28 July 1965).
17 *The Economist* (9 Oct 1965).
18 *Sunday Times* (3 Oct 1965).
19 *Weekend Telegraph* (24 Sept 1965).
20 *Observer* (23 Jan 1966).
21 Unidentified cutting.
22 *The Economist* (15 Sept 1965).
23 Crossman, *Diaries of a Cabinet Minister*, vol.1, p. 348 (13 Oct 1965).
24 Prior, *A Balance of Power*, p. 39.
25 *The Times* (14 Oct 1965).
26 *The Economist* (16 Oct 1965).
27 Ibid.
28 *Conservative Party Conference Report* (1965), pp. 23–5 (13 Oct 1965).
29 *Daily Telegraph* (14 Oct 1965).
30 *Conservative Party Conference Report* (1965), pp. 140–4 (16 Oct 1965).
31 *Evening Standard* (16 Oct 1965).
32 *Spectator* (15 Oct 1965).
33 Tony Benn, *Out of the Wilderness* (Hutchinson, 1987), p. 337 (19 Oct 1965).
34 Crossman, *Diaries of a Cabinet Minister*, vol.1, p. 351 (17 Oct 1965).
35 *The Times* (14 Oct 1965).
36 Prior, *A Balance of Power*, p. 39.
37 Margaret Laing, *Edward Heath, Prime Minister* (Sidgwick & Jackson, 1972), p. 214.
38 Prior, *A Balance of Power*, p. 39.
39 Enoch Powell, obituary of Lord Duncan-Sandys, *Independent* (27 Nov 1992).
40 John Ramsden, *The Making of Conservative Party Policy* (Longman, 1980), p. 249.
41 *Conservative Party Conference Report* (1965), p. 26 (13 Oct 1965).
42 Ibid., p. 25.
43 *The Economist* (15 Sept 1965).
44 *The Times* (22 July 1968).
45 House of Commons, 12 Nov 1965 (720/532–41).
46 Ibid., 21 Dec 1965 (722/1882–98).
47 Benn, *Out of the Wilderness*, p. 354 (23 Nov 1965).
48 House of Commons, 9 Nov 1965 (720/55).
49 *The Times* (22 July 1968).
50 *Spectator* (14 Jan 1966).
51 Ibid. (21 Jan 1966).
52 Crossman, *Diaries of a Cabinet Minister*, vol.1, p. 451 (9, 10 Feb 1966).
53 House of Commons, 23 Feb 1965 (725/435–55).
54 T. F. Lindsay, *Parliament from the Press Gallery* (Macmillan, 1967), p. 39.
55 Ramsden, *Making of Conservative Party Policy*, p. 252.
56 Crossman, *Diaries of a Cabinet Minister*, vol.1, p. 483 (27 March 1966).
57 *Sunday Telegraph* (27 March 1966).
58 *The Times* (22 March 1966).
59 Crossman, *Diaries of a Cabinet Minister*, vol.1, p. 489 (1 April 1966).
60 *The Times Guide to the House of Commons* (1966), p. 16.
61 *The Times* (2 March 1966).

62 Cecil King, *The Cecil King Diary, 1965–70* (Jonathan Cape, 1972), p. 64 (30 March 1966).
63 *The Times* (22 July 1968).
64 Robert Rhodes James, *Ambitions and Realities, 1964–70* (Weidenfeld & Nicolson, 1972), pp. 98–9.

11   Pressures of Opposition

1   *Conservative Party Conference Report* (1966), p. 34 (12 Oct 1966).
2   ICBH witness seminar, 4 Oct 1989 (*Contemporary Record* [Feb 1990]).
3   R. M. Punnett, *Front Bench Opposition* (Heinemann, 1973), pp. 137–75).
4   James Prior, *A Balance of Power* (Hamish Hamilton, 1986), p. 42.
5   Peter Rawlinson, *A Price Too High* (Weidenfeld & Nicolson, 1989), p. 247.
6   Prior, *A Balance of Power*, p. 53.
7   Ibid., p. 43.
8   *Evening Post* (9 Sept 1967).
9   Interview with Sir Edward Du Cann.
10 Nigel Fisher, *Iain Macleod* (Deutsch, 1973), p. 286.
11 Prior, *A Balance of Power*, p. 55.
12 'Panorama', BBC TV (16 Oct 1967).
13 David Butler and Michael Pinto-Duchinsky, *The British General Election of 1970* (Macmillan, 1971), p. 89.
14 *Weekend Telegraph* (24 Sept 1965).
15 John Ramsden, *The Making of Conservative Party Policy* (Longman, 1980), p. 248.
16 House of Commons, 1 Dec 1966 (737/642–64).
17 *Daily Mail* (3 Nov 1965).
18 *The Times* (7 Feb 1966).
19 Ibid.
20 *Conservative Party Conference Report* (1968), p. 128 (12 Oct 1968).
21 *Sunday Times* (3 Oct 1965).
22 Peter Hennessy, *Whitehall* (Secker & Warburg, 1989), p. 211.
23 *Sunday Times* (3 Oct 1965).
24 Richard Crossman, *The Diaries of a Cabinet Minister* vol.III (Hamish Hamilton and Jonathan Cape, 1977), p. 716 (4 Nov 1969).
25 House of Commons, 11 Aug 1966 (733/1891–1902).
26 Ibid., 12 Nov 1969 (791/452–6).
27 *Conservative Party Conference Report* (1968), p. 125 (12 Oct 1968).
28 Samuel Brittan, *Left or Right? The Bogus Dilemma* (Secker & Warburg, 1968), p. 115.
29 Brittan, *Left or Right?*, p. 22.
30 Richard Crossman, *The Diaries of a Cabinet Minister*, vol.II (Hamish Hamilton and Jonathan Cape, 1976), p. 582 (20 Nov 1967).
31 *The Times* (21 Nov 1967).
32 Ibid.
33 Robert Skidelsky to Edward Boyle, 9 Dec 1967 (Boyle papers, MS 660/7194).
34 House of Commons, 28 April 1966 (727/1071–85).
35 *The Economist* (7 Aug 1965).
36 Ibid. (18 Sept 1965).
37 House of Commons, 31 Oct 1967 (753/15–24).
38 *Conservative Party Conference Report* (1968), p. 127 (12 Oct 1968).
39 'This Week' (20 March 1969).

40 House of Commons, 8 Feb, 21 and 29 June, 7 July 1966 (724/224–40; 730/286–7, 1798–9; 731/696–713).
41 Prior, *A Balance of Power*, p. 48.
42 *The Times* (12 March, 7 June 1969).
43 House of Commons, 19 June 1969 (785/701–2).
44 *Conservative Party Conference Report* (1969), p. 140 (11 Oct 1969).
45 'Panorama', BBC TV (2 Feb 1970).
46 Cecil King, *The Cecil King Diary* (Jonathan Cape, 1972), p. 263 (25 June 1969).
47 ICBH witness seminar, 4 Oct 1989.
48 *Action Not Words*, p. 4.
49 *The Times* (21 Feb 1966).
50 House of Commons, 3 June 1966 (733/492–503).
51 Ibid., 19 March 1968 (761/303–9).
52 Crossman, *Diaries of a Cabinet Minister*, vol.II, p. 107 (3 Nov 1966).
53 *The Times* (9 July 1967).
54 Ibid. (24 July 1968).
55 *A Better Tomorrow*, p. 6.
56 ICBH witness seminar, 4 Oct 1989.
57 Douglas Hurd, *An End to Promises* (Collins, 1979), p. 13.
58 *Weekend Telegraph* (24 Sept 1965).
59 House of Commons, 22 Nov 1967 (754/1315–30).
60 *A Better Tomorrow*, pp. 14–15.
61 *Weekend Telegraph* (24 Sept 1965).
62 *The Times* (2 Feb 1970).
63 *Action Not Words*.
64 *The Times* (18 June 1967).
65 *Conservative Party Conference Report* (1969), p. 140 (11 Oct 1968).
66 Lord Blake and C. S. Nicholls, *Dictionary of National Biography, 1981–5* (Oxford University Press, 1990), p. 50.
67 *The Times* (29 March 1990).
68 *Action Not Words*, p. 6.

12 'Selsdon Man'

1   ICBH witness seminar, 4 Oct 1989 (*Contemporary Record* [Feb 1990]).
2   *Spectator* (22 Oct 1965).
3   *Sunday Telegraph* (7 Nov 1965).
4   *The Times* (4 Feb 1967).
5   Ibid. (24 April 1967).
6   Patrick Cosgrave, *The Lives of Enoch Powell* (Bodley Head, 1989), p. 228.
7   Phillip Whitehead, *The Writing on the Wall; Britain in the Seventies* (Michael Joseph/Channel Four, 1985), pp. 32–3.
8   Cosgrave, *Lives of Enoch Powell*, p. 220.
9   *The Times* (22 Feb 1968).
10 Terry Coleman, *Movers and Shakers* (Deutsch, 1987), p. 106.
11 William Whitelaw, *The Whitelaw Memoirs* (Aurum, 1989), p. 64.
12 *Financial Times* (June 1969).
13 Cecil King, *The Cecil King Diary, 1965–70* (Jonathan Cape, 1972) p. 264 (3 July 1969).
14 *The Times* (24 July 1968).
15 Speech at York, 2 Sept 1968.
16 *Conservative Party Conference Report* (1968), p. 126 (12 Oct 1968).

17 *The Times* (27 Jan 1969).
18 Cosgrave, *Lives of Enoch Powell*, p. 270.
19 *The Economist* (7 Feb 1970).
20 *Financial Times* (June 1969).
21 House of Commons, 17 Nov 1966 (736/651–8).
22 Ibid., 9 May 1967 (746/1282–1300).
23 James Prior, *A Balance of Power* (Hamish Hamilton, 1986), p. 53.
24 *A Better Tomorrow*, p. 28.
25 John Ramsden, *The Making of Conservative Party Policy* (Longman, 1980), p. 276.
26 Samuel Brittan, *Left or Right? The Bogus Dilemma* (Secker & Warburg, 1968), p. 134.
27 Edward Heath, *Sailing: A Course of My Life* (Sidgwick & Jackson, 1975) p. 16.
28 Ibid., p. 24.
29 Ibid., p. 25.
30 Interview with Owen Parker and Robin Aisher.
31 Heath, *Sailing*, p. 54.
32 Ibid., pp. 58–69.
33 Ibid., p. 8.
34 Ibid., p. 69.
35 *The Times* (15 Jan 1970).
36 Ibid. (31 Dec 1966).
37 *Sunday Express* (17 April 1970).
38 *Observer* (16 Jan 1966).
39 Interview with Moura Lympany.
40 Cecil King, *The Cecil King Diary, 1965–70* (Jonathan Cape, 1972), p. 145 (26 Sept 1967).
41 *Sunday Times* (3 Oct 1965); see also *Observer* (16 Jan 1966).
42 *Evening Standard* (12 Oct 1970).
43 *The Economist* (30 May 1970).
44 *Sunday Times* (17 May 1970).
45 House of Commons, 28 April 1966 (727/1071–85).
46 Richard Crossman, *The Diaries of a Cabinet Minister*, vol.II (Hamish Hamilton and Jonathan Cape, 1976), p. 545 (31 Oct 1967).
47 House of Commons, 3 Aug 1966 (733/610).
48 Ibid., 31 Oct 1966 (735/41).
49 Prior, *A Balance of Power*, p. 55.
50 *Conservative Party Conference Report* (1968), p. 129 (12 Oct 1968).
51 *The Times* (30 Dec 1967).
52 *Financial Times* (June 1969).
53 *The Times* (4 July 1969).
54 *The Economist* (24 Jan 1970).
55 Richard Crossman, *The Diaries of a Cabinet Minister*, vol.III (Hamish Hamilton and Jonathan Cape, 1977), p. 788 (25 Jan 1970).
56 ICBH witness seminar, 4 Oct 1989.
57 *The Times* (2 Feb 1970).
58 *The Economist* (7 Feb 1970).
59 Whitehead, *The Writing on the Wall*, p. 40.
60 *Spectator* (7 Feb 1970).
61 Crossman, *Diaries*, vol.III, p. 801 (2 Feb 1970).
62 *New Statesman* (7 Feb 1970).

13 Victory from the Jaws of Defeat

1 *Sunday Times* (17 May 1970).
2 James Prior, *A Balance of Power* (Hamish Hamilton, 1986), p. 56.
3 ICBH witness seminar, 4 Oct 1989 (*Contemporary Record* [Feb 1990]); Nigel Fisher, *Iain Macleod* (Deutsch, 1973), p. 303).
4 Lord Carrington, *Reflect on Things Past* (Collins, 1988), p. 214.
5 *The Economist* (16 June 1970).
6 *A Better Tomorrow*, pp. 1–2.
7 Douglas Hurd, *An End to Promises: Sketch of a Government, 1970–4* (Collins, 1979), p. 14.
8 *A Better Tomorrow*, pp. 6, 11.
9 Ibid., p. 6.
10 Ibid., pp. 13–25.
11 Ibid., p. 24.
12 Ibid., pp. 28–9.
13 *Conservative Party Conference Report* (1969), p. 140 (11 Oct 1969).
14 *Spectator* (23 May 1970).
15 Tony Benn, *Office Without Power: Diaries 1968–72* (Hutchinson, 1988), p. 194 (11 Aug 1969).
16 *The Times* (9 June 1970).
17 *The Economist* (6 June 1970).
18 *Spectator* (13 June 1970).
19 Ibid.
20 David Butler and Michael Pinto-Duchinsky, *The British General Election of 1970* (Macmillan, 1971), p. 152.
21 Ibid., p. 155.
22 Prior, *A Balance of Power*, p. 59.
23 Hurd, *An End to Promises*, p. 18.
24 Ibid., p. 22.
25 Prior, *A Balance of Power*, p. 59.
26 *The Times* (15 June 1970).
27 Butler and Pinto-Duchinsky, *General Election of 1970*, pp. 160–1.
28 Ibid., pp. 161–2.
29 *The Times* (18 June 1970).
30 Butler and Pinto-Duchinsky, *General Election of 1970*, pp. 168, 223.
31 Ibid., p. 167.
32 *The Times* (16 June 1970).
33 *The Economist* (20 June 1970).
34 *Spectator* (20 June 1970).
35 Marcia Falkender, *Downing Street in Perspective* (Weidenfeld & Nicolson, 1983), p. 51.
36 Barbara Castle, *The Castle Diaries, 1964–70* (Weidenfeld & Nicolson, 1984), p. 805 (13 June 1970).
37 Prior, *A Balance of Power*, p. 59.
38 Hurd, *An End to Promises*, p. 16.
39 Butler and Pinto-Duchinsky, *General Election of 1970*, p. 179.
40 Richard Crossman, *The Diaries of a Cabinet Minister*, vol.III (Hamish Hamilton and Jonathan Cape, 1977), p. 949 (19 June 1970).
41 *The Times* (17 June 1970).
42 ICBH witness seminar, 4 Oct 1989.
43 Ibid.

44 *The Times* (26 June, 1 July 1969).
45 Carrington, *Reflect on Things Past*, p. 214.
46 Terry Coleman, *Thatcher's Britain: A Journey Through the Promised Lands* (Bantam, 1987), p. 77.
47 *The Times* (20 June 1970).
48 Hurd, *An End to Promises*, p. 25.
49 *Evening Standard* (12 Oct 1970).
50 Butler and Pinto-Duchinsky, *General Election of 1970*, p. 341; Douglas Schoen, *Enoch Powell and the Powellites* (Macmillan, 1977); Patrick Cosgrave, *The Lives of Enoch Powell* (Bodley Head, 1989), pp. 284–90.
51 *Daily Express* (19 June 1970).
52 *The Times* (19 June 1970).
53 Hurd, *An End to Promises*, p. 26.
54 *Daily Mail* (19 June 1970).

14 'A New Style of Government'

1 Margaret Laing, *Edward Heath, Prime Minister* (Sidgwick & Jackson, 1972).
2 *The Times* (20 June 1970).
3 *Observer* (21 June 1970).
4 See Harold Wilson, *The Governance of Britain* (Weidenfeld & Nicolson, 1976; Sphere, 1977), p. 104.
5 Interview with Barbara Hosking.
6 Ibid.
7 Marcia Falkender, *Downing Street in Perspective* (Weidenfeld & Nicolson, 1983), pp. 104–5.
8 Barbara Castle, *The Castle Diaries, 1974–6* (Weidenfeld & Nicolson, 1980), p. 35.
9 Wilson, *Governance of Britain*, pp. 81, 105–6.
10 Castle, *Diaries, 1974–6*, pp. 219–20.
11 Falkender, *Downing Street*, p. 122.
12 Castle, *Diaries, 1974–6*, p. 220.
13 *Observer* (25 April 1971).
14 Leo Abse, *Private Member* (Macdonald, 1973), p. 49.
15 Edward Heath, *Music: A Joy for Life* (Sidgwick & Jackson, 1976), pp. 130–2.
16 *Observer* (21 June 1970).
17 Lord Hailsham, *The Door Wherein I Went* (Collins, 1975), p. 287.
18 Interview with Sir Edward Du Cann.
19 Terry Coleman, *Movers and Shakers* (Deutsch, 1987), pp. 12–13.
20 R. M. Punnett, *Front Bench Opposition* (Heinemann, 1973), p. 374.
21 *The Times* (3 July 1970).
22 House of Commons, 2 July 1970 (803/58).
23 Ibid. (803/95–6).
24 *The Economist* (11 July 1970).
25 e.g. Jock Bruce-Gardyne, *Whatever Happened to the Quiet Revolution?* (Charles Knight, 1974).
26 *The Economist* (1 Aug 1970).
27 Interview with Lady Macleod.
28 Phillip Whitehead, *The Writing on the Wall: Britain in the Seventies* (Michael Joseph/Channel Four, 1985), p. 55.
29 *The Times* (22, 24 July 1970); *The Economist* (25 July, 1 Aug 1970).
30 *The Times* (27 July 1970).
31 *New Statesman* (31 July 1970).

32 House of Commons, 7 July 1970 (803/490).
33 *Observer* (21 June 1970).
34 *Conservative Party Conference Report* (1970), p. 130 (10 Oct 1970).
35 *The Economist* (5 Sept 1970).

15 'The Quiet Revolution'

1   Peter Rawlinson, *A Price Too High* (Weidenfeld & Nicolson, 1989), pp. 157–60.
2   See Edward Heath, *Travels: People and Places in My Life* (Sidgwick & Jackson, 1977), pp. 120–1.
3   *The Times* (1 Oct 1970).
4   Norman Tebbit, *Upwardly Mobile* (Weidenfeld & Nicolson, 1988), p. 100.
5   *Liverpool Daily Post* (31 July 1971).
6   *The Times* (25 Sept 1970).
7   Ibid. (10 Oct 1970).
8   Ibid. (9 Oct 1970).
9   *Conservative Party Conference Report* (1970), pp. 128–32 (10 Oct 1970).
10 *Evening Standard* (12 Oct 1970).
11 *New Statesman* (8 Dec 1970).
12 *Fortune* (April 1971).
13 Douglas Hurd, *An End to Promises: Sketch of a Government, 1970–4* (Collins, 1979), p. 138.
14 *Fortune* (April 1971).
15 *Conservative Party Conference Report* (1970), p. 131.
16 *Evening Standard* (1–2 June 1972).
17 Peter Hennessy, *Whitehall* (Secker & Warburg, 1989), pp. 235–6.
18 Ibid., p. 221.
19 *Evening Standard* (1–2 June 1972).
20 Hennessy, *Whitehall*, pp. 221–2.
21 Lord Rothschild, *Random Variables* (Collins, 1984), pp. 75–6.
22 Hurd, *An End to Promises*, p. 39.
23 Barbara Castle, *The Castle Diaries, 1974–6* (Weidenfeld & Nicolson, 1980), pp. 219–24.
24 Tessa Blackstone and William Plowden, *Inside the Think Tank: Advising the Cabinet, 1971–83* (Heinemann, 1988), p. 39.
25 Hennessy, *Whitehall*, p. 227.
26 Lord Rothschild, *Meditations of a Broomstick* (Collins, 1977), pp. 114–15.
27 Hennessy, *Whitehall*, pp. 229–30.
28 Blackstone and Plowden, *Inside the Think Tank*, pp. 76–7.
29 Ibid., pp. 134–5, 149–50.
30 Hennessy, *Whitehall*, p. 231.
31 Rothschild, *Meditations of a Broomstick*, pp. 92–5.
32 *The Times* (25 Sept 1973).
33 Hennessy, *Whitehall*, p. 235.
34 Rothschild, *Meditations of a Broomstick*, pp. 121–3; *The Times* (13 Oct 1973).
35 *The Times* (19 Dec 1973).
36 Blackstone and Plowden, *Inside the Think Tank*, pp. 94–5.
37 Hurd, *An End to Promises*, p. 38.
38 Rothschild, *Meditations of a Broomstick*, p. 169.
39 Ibid., p. 170.
40 Peter Hennessy, *Cabinet* (Blackwell, 1986), p. 20.
41 Hurd, *An End to Promises*, pp. 35–6.

42   Hennessy, *Whitehall*, pp. 242–3.
43   Hugo Young, *One of Us* (Macmillan, 1989), pp. 73–4.
44   *The Times* (12 Aug 1970).
45   Ibid. (10 Nov 1970).
46   Ibid. (12 Nov 1970).
47   Richard Clutterbuck, *Britain in Agony: The Growth of Political Violence* (Faber, 1978; Penguin edn, 1980), p. 43.
48   e.g. Barbara Castle in House of Commons, 22 Feb 1971 (812/32).
49   *New Statesman* (25 Nov 1970).
50   House of Commons, 8 Feb 1971 (811/80–3); Norman Tebbit, *Upwardly Mobile* (Weidenfeld & Nicolson, 1988), p. 103.
51   *The Times* (8 Feb 1971).
52   Ibid.
53   *Evening Standard* (7 Jan 1971).
54   *Sunday Times* (28 Feb 1971).

16   Special Relationships

1   Tony Benn, *Office Without Power: Diaries 1968–72* (Hutchinson, 1988), p. 437 (29 June 1972).
2   Lord Carrington, *Reflect on Things Past* (Collins, 1988), p. 254.
3   *Annual Register 1970*, p. 39.
4   *Conservative Party Conference Report* (1970), p. 129 (10 Oct 1970).
5   *The Times* (25 Oct 1970).
6   Douglas Hurd, *An End to Promises: Sketch of a Government, 1970–4* (Collins, 1979), p. 53.
7   Andrew Roth, *Heath and the Heathmen* (Routledge & Kegan Paul, 1972), p. 220.
8   *The Times* (22 Jan 1971).
9   Hurd, *An End to Promises*, p. 53.
10   House of Lords, 1 Dec 1971 (326/326–9).
11   *The Times* (11 Dec 1971).
12   *Conservative Party Conference Report* (1973), p. 132 (13 Oct 1973).
13   *Conservative Party Conference Report* (1970), p. 129 (10 Oct 1970).
14   Hurd, *An End to Promises*, p. 42.
15   Edward Heath, *Old World, New Horizons: Britain, Europe and the Atlantic Alliance* (Harvard, 1970), pp. 72–3.
16   Ibid., p. 4.
17   Peter Hennessy and Caroline Anstey, *Moneybags and Brains: The Anglo-American 'Special Relationship' since 1945* (Strathclyde/BBC, 1990), p. 25.
18   Carrington, *Reflect on Things Past*, pp. 221–2.
19   Peter Hennessy, *Cabinet* (Blackwell, 1986), p. 150.
20   Henry Kissinger, *Years of Upheaval* (Weidenfeld & Nicolson/Michael Joseph, 1982), p. 140.
21   Ibid., pp. 140–1.
22   Henry Kissinger, *The White House Years* (Weidenfeld & Nicolson/Michael Joseph, 1979), p. 934.
23   Kissinger, *Years of Upheaval*, p. 141.
24   Kissinger, *The White House Years*, p. 937.
25   Ibid., p. 425.
26   Roth, *Heath and the Heathmen*, p. 224.
27   *The Times* (4 Jan 1973).
28   Stephen Ambrose, *Nixon: The Triumph of a Politician, 1962–72* (Simon & Schuster, New York, 1989), p. 486.

29 Hennessy and Anstey, *Moneybags and Brains*, p. 17.
30 Willy Brandt, *People and Politics: The Years 1960–75* (Collins, 1978), p. 310.
31 Hennessy and Anstey, *Moneybags and Brains*, p. 17.
32 Kissinger, *Years of Upheaval*, p. 142.
33 Ibid., p. 189.
34 Ibid., p. 192.
35 Ibid.
36 Ibid., p. 137.
37 Home, *Where the Wind Blows*, pp. 250–1.
38 Peter Wright, *Spycatcher: The Candid Autobiography of a Senior Intelligence Officer* (Viking, 1987), p. 345.
39 Home, *Where the Wind Blows*, p. 250.
40 Carrington, *Reflect on Things Past*, pp. 242–5.
41 Ibid., p. 245.
42 *The Times* (1 Nov 1970).
43 Ibid. (5 Nov 1970).
44 House of Commons, 30 Oct 1973 (863/37–8); Kissinger, *Years of Upheaval*, p. 712.
45 Kissinger, *Years of Upheaval*, p. 720.
46 *The Times* (13 Nov 1973).

17 Reversing the Veto

1 Douglas Hurd, *An End to Promises: Sketch of a Government, 1970–4* (Collins, 1979), pp. 58–9.
2 Uwe Kitzinger, *Diplomacy and Persuasion: How Britain Joined the Common Market* (Thames & Hudson, 1973), pp. 77–88.
3 *The Times* (22 Jan 1971).
4 Ibid. (13 Feb 1971).
5 *Observer* (21 March 1971).
6 Tony Benn, *Office Without Power: Diaries, 1968–72* (Hutchinson, 1988), p. 318 (7 Dec 1970).
7 Kitzinger, *Diplomacy and Persuasion*, pp. 115–16.
8 *The Times* (6 April 1971).
9 Willy Brandt, *People and Politics: The Years 1960–75* (Collins, 1978), p. 249.
10 Hurd, *An End to Promises*, p. 62.
11 *The Times* (18 May 1971).
12 Kitzinger, *Diplomacy and Persuasion*, p. 119.
13 Ibid.
14 Phillip Whitehead, *The Writing on the Wall: Britain in the Seventies* (Michael Joseph/Channel Four, 1985), p. 61.
15 *The Times* (21 May 1971); Kitzinger, *Diplomacy and Persuasion*, p. 120.
16 Edward Heath, *Sailing: A Course of My Life* (Sidgwick & Jackson, 1975), p. 181.
17 Ibid.
18 *The Times* (22 May 1971).
19 Ibid. (25 May 1971).
20 Ibid.; *Spectator* (12 June 1971).
21 House of Commons, 24 May 1971 (818/31–47).
22 *The Economist* (12 June 1971).
23 e.g. Martin Holmes in *Contemporary Record* (Nov 1989).
24 Christopher Lord, 'Heath Defended', *Contemporary Record* (April 1990).
25 Kitzinger, *Diplomacy and Persuasion*, p. 291.
26 Hurd, *An End to Promises*, p. 64.

18 'Kill the Bill'

1 *The Economist* (20 June 1970).
2 Eric Silver, *Victor Feather, TUC* (Gollancz, 1973), p. 188.
3 *The Economist* (4 July 1970).
4 Jack Jones, *Union Man* (Collins, 1986), p. 227.
5 House of Commons, 26 Nov 1970 (807/651–6).
6 Ibid., 15 Dec 1970 (808/1129–43).
7 *The Times* (3 July 1970).
8 Interview with Lord Carr.
9 *Guardian* (16 Nov 1970).
10 Jones, *Union Man*, p. 228.
11 *The Times* (24 Feb 1971).
12 Phillip Whitehead, *The Writing on the Wall: Britain in the Seventies* (Michael Joseph/Channel Four, 1985), p. 73.
13 *The Times* (26 April 1971).
14 'Analysis', BBC TV (18 June 1971); *The Times* (19 June 1971).
15 *The Times* (25 Jan 1972).
16 Ibid. (5 July 1971).
17 Ibid. (15 July 1971).
18 *Daily Telegraph* (18 June 1971).
19 *Conservative Party Conference Report* (1971), pp. 126–30 (16 Oct 1971).
20 *Spectator* (16 Oct 1971).
21 e.g. Barber in House of Commons, 18 Feb 1971 (811/2157), Heath in House of Commons, 18 March 1971 (813/1642–5).
22 House of Commons, 30 July 1971 (814/1397).
23 *The Times* (3 Nov 1971).
24 Ibid. (18 Nov 1971).
25 Ibid. (16 Oct 1971).
26 Ibid. (22 Nov 1971).
27 Ibid. (4 Dec 1971).

19 Heathmen on the Home Front

1 Andrew Roth, *Heath and the Heathmen* (Routledge & Kegan Paul, 1972).
2 Interview with Lord Walker.
3 Ibid.
4 David Butler and Anne Sloman, *British Political Facts, 1900–79* (Macmillan, 1980), p. 303.
5 Ibid., p. 397; *Annual Register, 1971*, pp. 7–9.
6 Philip Norton, *Conservative Dissidents: Dissent Within the Parliamentary Conservative Party, 1970–4* (Temple Smith, 1978), pp. 130–5.
7 *The Times* (20 July 1973).
8 *Conservative Party Conference Report* (1971), pp. 127–8.
9 Timothy Raison, *Tories and the Welfare State: A History of Conservative Social Policy since the Second World War* (Macmillan, 1990), p. 74.
10 *Evening Standard* (7 June 1971).
11 Raison, *Tories and the Welfare State*, p. 84; Morrison Halcrow, *Keith Joseph: A Single Mind* (Macmillan, 1989), pp. 45–56.
12 Raison, *Tories and the Welfare State*, p. 83.
13 Ibid., p. 84; Barbara Castle, *The Castle Diaries, 1974–6* (Weidenfeld & Nicolson,

1980), pp. 53n, 100n; Harold Wilson, *Final Term: The Labour Government, 1974–6* (Weidenfeld & Nicolson/Michael Joseph, 1979), pp. 126–8.

14 Roger Hadley and Stephen Hatch, *Social Welfare and the Failure of the State* (Allen & Unwin, 1981), p. 77.

15 David Widgery, *Health in Danger: The Crisis in the National Health Service* (Macmillan, 1979), p. 144.

16 *Royal Commission on the National Health Service*, Cmnd 7615 (HMSO, 1979), pp. 22, 165.

17 *Mail on Sunday* (5 Jan 1986).

18 Nicholas Wapshott and George Brock, *Thatcher* (Futura, 1983), pp. 97–8.

19 Peter Rawlinson, *A Price Too High: An Autobiography* (Weidenfeld & Nicolson, 1989), pp. 245–6.

20 Ibid., p. 248.

21 Interview with Lord Walker; Peter Walker, *The Ascent of Britain* (Sidgwick & Jackson, 1977), p. 198.

22 Interview with Lord Pym.

23 Hugo Young, *One of Us: A Biography of Margaret Thatcher* (Macmillan, 1989), p. 67.

24 Susan Crosland, *Tony Crosland* (Jonathan Cape, 1982), p. 148.

25 Young, *One of Us*, p. 68.

26 House of Commons, 14 June 1971 (819/42–56).

27 *Sun* (25 Nov 1971).

28 *Conservative Party Conference Report* (1971), p. 128.

29 Young, *One of Us*, p. 69.

30 *The Times* (26 June 1971).

31 House of Commons, 19 Feb 1973 (851/41–57).

32 Raison, *Tories and the Welfare State*, p. 79.

33 *Annual Register, 1972*, p. 36.

34 *The Times* (2 Dec 1970).

35 Norton, *Conservative Dissidents*, p. 113.

36 *The Times* (19 Nov 1973).

37 Norton, *Conservative Dissidents*, pp. 154–6.

38 *The Times* (12 Dec 1973).

39 Ibid. (5 March 1974).

40 Rawlinson, *A Price Too High*, pp. 202–4; Patrick Cosgrave, *The Lives of Enoch Powell* (Bodley Head, 1989), p. 301.

41 Cosgrave, *The Lives of Enoch Powell*, p. 303.

42 *The Times* (21 Sept 1972).

43 Ibid.

44 Ibid. (11 Oct 1972).

45 Ibid. (1 Dec 1972).

46 Butler and Sloman, *British Political Facts*, pp. 299–300.

47 *The Times* (19 Dec 1972).

48 Ibid.

49 Reginald Maudling, *Memoirs* (Sidgwick & Jackson, 1978), p. 193.

50 *The Times* (23 July 1977); Maudling, *Memoirs*, p. 204.

20 The Vote for Europe

1 Uwe Kitzinger, *Diplomacy and Persuasion: How Britain Joined the Common Market* (Thames & Hudson, 1973), pp. 352–63.

2 Willy Brandt, *People and Politics: The Years 1960–75* (Collins, 1978), p. 250.

3   Kitzinger, *Diplomacy and Persuasion*, pp. 357–64.
4   *The Times* (8 July 1971).
5   Ibid. (9 July 1971).
6   Ibid. (15 July 1971).
7   House of Commons, 21 July 1971 (821/1452–69); *The Times* (22 July 1971).
8   Kitzinger, *Diplomacy and Persuasion*, p. 177.
9   *The Times* (14 Oct 1971).
10 Kitzinger, *Diplomacy and Persuasion*, p. 168.
11 Phillip Whitehead, *The Writing on the Wall: Britain in the Seventies* (Michael Joseph/Channel Four, 1985), p. 67.
12 *The Times* (13 July 1971).
13 Ibid. (15 July 1971).
14 Ibid. (6 May 1970).
15 Ibid. (12 Oct 1971).
16 Interview with Lord Pym.
17 Tony Benn, *Office Without Power, 1968–72* (Hutchinson, 1988), p. 379.
18 House of Commons, 16 Dec 1976 (922/1787–8).
19 Interview with Lord Pym.
20 House of Commons, 21 Oct 1971 (823/912).
21 Douglas Hurd, *An End to Promises: Sketch of a Government, 1970–4* (Collins, 1979), p. 69.
22 House of Commons, 28 Oct 1971 (823/2104).
23 Ibid. (823/2202–12).
24 David Spanier, *Europe, Our Europe* (Secker & Warburg, 1972), p. 184.
25 Ibid., p. 179.
26 *The Times* (28 Oct 1971).
27 Spanier, *Europe, Our Europe*, p. 181.
28 Andrew Roth, *Heath and the Heathmen* (Routledge & Kegan Paul, 1972), p. 226; Spanier, *Europe, Our Europe*, p. 184.
29 Edward Heath, *Music: A Joy for Life* (Sidgwick & Jackson, 1976), p. 130.

21   First Blood to the Miners

1   Martin Holmes, *Political Pressure and Economic Policy: British Government, 1970–4* (Butterworth, 1982), p. 63.
2   *The Times* (19 Nov 1971).
3   Ibid. (24 Nov 1971).
4   *The Economist* (27 Nov 1971).
5   *The Times* (21 Jan 1972).
6   House of Commons, 24 Jan 1972 (829/997–1024).
7   Ibid. (829/1024–42).
8   *The Times* (26 Jan 1972).
9   Douglas Hurd, *An End to Promises: Sketch of a Government, 1970–4* (Collins, 1979), p. 89.
10 *The Times* (24 Jan 1972).
11 Phillip Whitehead, *The Writing on the Wall: Britain in the Seventies* (Michael Joseph/Channel Four, 1985), p. 82.
12 Interview with Lord Rothschild.
13 *The Times* (26 Jan 1972).
14 James Prior, *A Balance of Power* (Hamish Hamilton, 1986), p. 74.
15 House of Commons, 30 Jan 1978 (943/70–83).
16 Holmes, *Political Pressure and Economic Policy*, p. 48.

17 *The Times* (11 Jan 1972).
18 *New Statesman* (19 Jan 1972).
19 Whitehead, *The Writing on the Wall*, p. 74.
20 Richard Clutterbuck, *Britain in Agony: The Growth of Political Violence* (Faber, 1978; Penguin edn, 1980), pp. 61–3.
21 Ibid., p. 60.
22 Whitehead, *The Writing on the Wall*, p. 74.
23 Holmes, *Political Pressure and Economic Policy*, p. 69.
24 House of Commons, 18 Jan 1972 (829/300).
25 *The Times* (9 Feb 1972).
26 Clutterbuck, *Britain in Agony*, pp. 65–72.
27 Whitehead, *The Writing on the Wall*, p. 75.
28 Ibid., p. 76.
29 Prior, *A Balance of Power*, p. 73.
30 Robert Taylor, *The Fifth Estate: Britain's Unions in the Seventies* (Routledge & Kegan Paul, 1978), p. 265.
31 Clutterbuck, *Britain in Agony*, p. 75.
32 Hurd, *An End to Promises*, p. 103.
33 Whitehead, *The Writing on the Wall*, p. 76.
34 *The Times* (11 Feb 1972).
35 Ibid. (15 Feb 1972).
36 Ibid. (12 Feb 1972).
37 Ibid. (15 Feb 1972).
38 Ibid. (29 Feb 1972).
39 Wilberforce Report, Cmnd 4903 (HMSO, 1972).
40 Interview with Mick McGahey.
41 Joe Gormley, *Battered Cherub* (Hamish Hamilton, 1982), p. 113.
42 *Sunday Times* (20 Feb 1972).
43 Hurd, *An End to Promises*, p. 103.
44 *Sunday Times* (20 Feb 1972).
45 *The Times* (21 Feb 1972).
46 Holmes, *Political Pressure*, p. 70.
47 *The Times* (21 Feb 1972).
48 Ibid. (28 Feb 1972).
49 Ibid. (11 March 1972).
50 Ibid. (10 March 1972).
51 Ibid. (8 March 1972).

22 The Abolition of Stormont

1 Paul Arthur and Keith Jeffery, *Northern Ireland since 1968* (Blackwell, 1988), p. 98.
2 Douglas Hurd, *An End to Promises: Sketch of a Government, 1970–4* (Collins, 1979), p. 102.
3 *Conservative Party Conference Report* (1972) (14 Oct 1972).
4 *A Better Tomorrow*, p. 25.
5 J. J. Lee, *Ireland, 1912–85* (Cambridge University Press, 1989), p. 434.
6 Ibid.
7 William Whitelaw, *The Whitelaw Memoirs* (Aurum Press, 1989), p. 78.
8 Brian Faulkner, *Memoirs of a Statesman* (Weidenfeld & Nicolson, 1978), pp. 92–4.
9 *Sunday Times* (26 March 1972).

10 House of Commons, 22 March 1971 (814/34–44).
11 Faulkner, *Memoirs*, p. 120.
12 Patrick Bishop and Eamonn Mallie, *The Provisional IRA* (Heinemann, 1987), pp. 144–5.
13 Lee, *Ireland*, p. 437.
14 *Annual Register, 1971*, p. 50.
15 Lee, *Ireland*, p. 437.
16 *Daily Telegraph* (27 Aug 1971); reprinted in Charles Moore and Simon Heffer (ed.), *A Tory Seer: The Selected Journalism of T. E. Utley* (Hamish Hamilton, 1989), pp. 231–5.
17 Ibid.
18 *The Times* (3 March 1972).
19 Faulkner, *Memoirs*, p. 127.
20 *The Times* (20 Aug 1971).
21 *Annual Register, 1971*, p. 26.
22 *Conservative Party Conference Report* (1971), pp. 128–9.
23 *Annual Register, 1972*, pp. 36–7.
24 *Sunday Times* (26 March 1972).
25 Ibid.
26 Reginald Maudling, *Memoirs* (Sidgwick & Jackson, 1978), p. 191.
27 Heath/Burke Trend interview with Robert Mackenzie, *Listener* (22 April 1976).
28 Hurd, *An End to Promises*, p. 102.
29 Whitelaw, *Memoirs*, p. 81.
30 David Bleakley, *Faulkner* (Mowbrays, 1974), p. 108.
31 Interview with Sir Robin Chichester-Clark.
32 *Sunday Times* (26 March 1972).
33 Bleakley, *Faulkner*, p. 105.
34 *Sunday Times* (26 March 1972).
35 Bleakley, *Faulkner*, p. 108; Faulkner, *Memoirs*, p. 149,.
36 Whitelaw, *Memoirs*, p. 80.
37 Faulkner, *Memoirs*, pp. 151–2.
38 Phillip Whitehead, *The Writing on the Wall: Britain in the Seventies* (Michael Joseph/Channel Four, 1985), p. 165.
39 *The Times* (23 March 1972).
40 Faulkner, *Memoirs*, p. 153.
41 Whitelaw, *Memoirs*, p. 80.
42 Faulkner, *Memoirs*, p. 153.
43 Maudling, *Memoirs*, p. 188.
44 Whitelaw, *Memoirs*, p. 82.
45 *Financial Times*, (25 March 1972).
46 House of Commons, 24 March 1972 (833/1859–63).
47 *Financial Times* (25 March 1972).
48 Ibid.
49 Philip Norton, *Conservative Dissidents: Dissent Within the Parliamentary Conservative Party, 1970–4* (Temple Smith, 1978), p. 87.

23 U-Turn: Industry

1 *The Times* (24 Jan 1972).
2 Phillip Whitehead, *The Writing on the Wall: Britain in the Seventies* (Michael Joseph/Channel Four, 1985), p. 69.
3 *The Times* (25 Jan 1972).

4   Ibid.
5   Ibid. (27 Jan 1972).
6   Ibid.
7   Whitehead, *The Writing on the Wall*, p. 68.
8   *The Times* (17 Feb 1972).
9   Douglas Hurd, *An End to Promises: Sketch of a Government, 1970–4*, (Collins, 1979), p. 102.
10   House of Commons, 17 Feb 1972 (831/752).
11   Philip Norton, *Conservative Dissidents: Dissent Within the Parliamentary Conservative Party, 1970–4* (Temple Smith, 1978), p. 74.
12   *The Times* (18 Feb 1972).
13   Ibid.
14   Christopher Mayhew, *Time to Explain* (Hutchinson, 1987), pp. 190–1.
15   Norton, *Conservative Dissidents*, pp. 74–82.
16   Kenneth Harris, *David Owen, Personally Speaking* (Weidenfeld & Nicolson, 1987), p. 102.
17   Uwe Kitzinger, *Diplomacy and Persuasion: How Britain Joined the Common Market* (Thames & Hudson, 1973), pp. 352–66.
18   *The Times* (15 June 1972).
19   Ibid. (14 July 1972).
20   *Conservative Party Conference Report* (1972), pp. 125–9 (14 Oct 1972).
21   *The Times* (29 Feb 1972).
22   Martin Holmes, *Political Pressure and Economic Policy: British Government, 1970–4* (Butterworth, 1982), p. 44.
23   *The Times* (9 Feb 1972).
24   Ibid. (29 Feb 1972).
25   Ibid.
26   *The Economist* (4 April 1972).
27   *Evening Standard* (1–2 June 1972).
28   *The Times* (6 March 1972).
29   House of Commons, 21 March 1972 (833/1343–90).
30   *The Times* (22 March 1972).
31   Whitehead, *The Writing on the Wall*, p. 82.
32   Interview with Sir Leo Pliatzky.
33   Leo Pliatzky, *Getting and Spending: Public Expenditure, Employment and Inflation* (Blackwell, 1982), p. 109.
34   Whitehead, *The Writing on the Wall*, p. 83.
35   *The Times* (17 May 1972).
36   Ibid. (18 May 1972).
37   Interviews with Lord Joseph, Lord Pym, Lord Carr, Lord Prior and Lord Walker.
38   *Observer* (Dec 1985), quoted in Hugo Young, *One of Us: A Biography of Margaret Thatcher* (Macmillan, 1989), p. 77; Nicholas Ridley, *'My Style of Government': The Thatcher Years* (Hutchinson, 1991), p. 4.
39   *The Times* (23 May 1972).
40   Tony Benn, *Office Without Power: Diaries 1968–72* (Hutchinson, 1988), p. 41 (22 March 1972).
41   House of Commons, 22 May 1972 (837/1083–91, 1103–8).
42   Ibid., 28 July 1972 (841/2399–402).
43   Norton, *Conservative Dissidents*, pp. 90–8.
44   *Evening Standard* (1–2 June 1972).
45   Lord Carrington, *Reflect on Things Past* (Collins, 1988), p. 256.
46   *Evening Standard* (1–2 June 1972).

47 *Observer* (14 July 1977).
48 Interview with Lord Ezra.
49 Hurd, *An End to Promises*, pp. 92–3.
50 Norman Tebbit, *Upwardly Mobile* (Weidenfeld & Nicolson, 1988), p. 106.
51 House of Commons, 22 May 1972 (837/1023–37).
52 Ibid., 11 Dec 1972 (848/31–40).
53 Ibid., 20 Feb 1973 (851/243–58).
54 Interview with Lord Walker; Peter Walker, *The Ascent of Britain* (Sidgwick & Jackson, 1977), pp. 61–2.
55 Holmes, *Political Pressure and Economic Policy*, p. 51.
56 *The Times* (24 June 1972).
57 Ibid.

24 The Collapse of the Industrial Relations Act

1   *The Times* (14 April 1972).
2   Phillip Whitehead, *The Writing on the Wall: Britain in the Seventies* (Michael Joseph/Channel Four, 1985), p. 77.
3   Jock Bruce-Gardyne, *Whatever Happened to the Quiet Revolution?* (Charles Knight, 1974), p. 85.
4   *The Times* (16 June 1972).
5   Martin Holmes, *Political Pressure and Economic Policy: British Government, 1970–4* (Butterworth, 1982), p. 35.
6   Whitehead, *The Writing on the Wall*, p. 78.
7   *The Times* (15 June 1972).
8   Cecil King, *The Cecil King Diary, 1970–4* (Jonathan Cape, 1975), p. 210 (15 June 1972).
9   John Mortimer, *In Character* (Penguin, 1984), p. 13.
10 House of Commons, 25 July 1972 (743/1563).
11 J. A. G. Griffith, *The Politics of the Judiciary* (Fontana, 1977), p. 72.
12 Ibid., p. 73.
13 Jack Jones, *Union Man* (Collins, 1986), p. 254.
14 *The Times* (21 June 1972).
15 Griffith, *The Politics of the Judiciary*, p. 45.
16 Sir John Donaldson, 'Lessons from the Industrial Court', *Law Quarterly Review* (1975), cited in Griffith, *The Politics of the Judiciary*, p. 76.
17 Griffith, *The Politics of the Judiciary*, pp. 76–7.
18 Michael Moran, *The Politics of Industrial Relations* (Macmillan, 1977), pp. 147–8.
19 *The Economist* (12 Aug 1972).
20 King, *Diary*, p. 223 (10 Aug 1972).

25 U-Turn: Inflation

1   Samuel Brittan and Peter Lilley, *The Delusion of Incomes Policy* (Temple Smith, 1977), p. 165.
2   Martin Holmes, *Political Pressure and Economic Policy: British Government, 1970–4* (Butterworth, 1982), p. 82.
3   *Sunday Times* (14 May 1972); *The Times* (15 May 1972).
4   *The Times* (15 June 1972).
5   Ibid.
6   *Sunday Times* (14 May 1972).

7   Jack Jones, *Union Man* (Collins, 1986), p. 255.
8   House of Commons, 3 July 1972 (840/59–87).
9   *The Times* (12 Sept 1972).
10 Ibid. (15 June 1972).
11 *The Economist* (8 July 1972).
12 Brittan and Lilley, *The Delusion of Incomes Policy*, p. 165.
13 Eric Silver, *Victor Feather, TUC* (Gollancz, 1973), p. 210.
14 *The Times* (29 Sept 1972).
15 Ibid.
16 *The Economist* (30 Sept 1992).
17 *The Times* (27 Sept 1972).
18 Ibid. (28 Sept 1972).
19 *The Economist* (30 Sept 1972).
20 *Conservative Party Conference Report* (1972), pp. 125–9 (14 Oct 1972).
21 Phillip Whitehead, *The Writing on the Wall: Britain in the Seventies* (Michael Joseph/Channel Four, 1985), p. 87.
22 Ibid. p. 88.
23 Silver, *Victor Feather*, pp. 210–11.
24 Eric Wigham, *Strikes and the Government, 1893–1974* (Macmillan, 1976), p. 172.
25 Jones, *Union Man*, p. 257.
26 Wigham, *Strikes and the Government*, p. 172.
27 *The Times* (17 Oct 1972).
28 Ibid. (3 Nov 1972).
29 Holmes, *Political Pressure and Economic Policy*, p. 84.
30 Jones, *Union Man*, p. 257.
31 Whitehead, *The Writing on the Wall*, p. 88.
32 Douglas Hurd, *An End to Promises: Sketch of a Government, 1970–4* (Collins, 1979), p. 104.
33 Cecil King, *The Cecil King Diary, 1970–4* (Jonathan Cape, 1975), p. 228 (6 Oct 1972).
34 Ibid., p. 234 (28 Oct 1972).
35 House of Commons, 31 Oct 1972 (845/35–59).
36 Whitehead, *The Writing on the Wall*, p. 87.
37 *Spectator* (4 Nov 1972).
38 *The Economist* (28 Oct 1972).
39 *The Times* (31 Oct 1972).
40 Ibid. (3 Nov 1972).
41 House of Commons, 6 Nov 1972 (845/622–7).
42 Hurd, *An End to Promises*, p. 105.
43 House of Commons, 6 Nov 1972 (845/631).
44 *The Times* (7 Nov 1972).
45 *Spectator* (11 Nov 1972).
46 *The Times* (7 Nov 1972).
47 *Independent* (26 Oct 1989).
48 *The Times* (21 Oct 1972).
49 Philip Norton, *Conservative Dissidents: Dissent Within the Parliamentary Conservative Party, 1970–4* (Temple Smith, 1978), p. 119.
50 Interview with Lord Croham.
51 *The Economist* (14 Oct 1972).
52 Ibid.
53 Ibid.
54 *The Times* (12 Oct 1972).
55 *Conservative Party Conference Report* (1972), pp. 125–9 (14 Oct 1972).

56 Nicholas Ridley, *'My Style of Government': The Thatcher Years* (Hutchinson, 1991), pp. 5–6.
57 Holmes, *Political Pressure and Economic Policy*, p. 100; David Butler and Anne Sloman, *British Political Facts, 1900–79* (Macmillan, 1980), p. 240.

26   The Prime Minister and His Office

1 Martin Holmes, *Political Pressure and Economic Policy: British Government, 1970–4* (Butterworth, 1982), pp. 130–2; see also Geoffrey Rippon to *The Times* (12 Oct 1981).
2 Interviews with Lord Pym, Lord Prior, Lord Walker.
3 *Evening Standard* (1–2 June 1972).
4 Interview with Lord Home.
5 Interview with Lord Walker.
6 Interview with Lord Joseph.
7 Peter Walker, *The Ascent of Britain* (Sidgwick & Jackson, 1977), p. 58.
8 Interview with Lord Whitelaw.
9 *Observer* (17 April 1977).
10 Edward Heath interviewed by David Dilks, on 'Politics Now', BBC Radio Four (24 Feb 1977).
11 Peter Hennessy, *Cabinet* (Blackwell, 1986), p. 77.
12 Interview with Dilks, 'Politics Now'.
13 Interview with Lord Carr.
14 Interview with Lord Hunt of Tanworth.
15 Interview with Lord Carr.
16 Interview with Dilks, 'Politics Now'.
17 Lord Carrington, *Reflect on Things Past* (Collins, 1988).
18 Interview with Lord Pym.
19 *Evening Standard* (12 Oct 1970).
20 Robert Harris, *Good and Faithful Servant: A Biography of Bernard Ingham* (Faber, 1991), p. 92.
21 Douglas Hurd, *An End to Promises: Sketch of a Government, 1970–4* (Collins, 1979), pp. 137–8.
22 *New Statesman* (26 Nov 1976).
23 Interview with Barbara Hosking.
24 Hennessy, *Cabinet*, p. 73.
25 Interview with Lord Hunt of Tanworth.
26 Hennessy, *Cabinet*, pp. 20, 79.
27 Holmes, *Political Pressure and Economic Policy*, pp. 130–1; Peter Hennessy, *Whitehall* (Secker & Warburg, 1989), pp. 237–9.
28 Interview with Lord Roll.
29 Hurd, *An End to Promises*, p. 36.
30 Interview with Lord Whitelaw.
31 House of Commons, 21 Nov 1979 (974/460–9).
32 Peter Wright, *Spycatcher: The Candid Autobiography of a Senior Intelligence Officer* (Viking, 1987), p. 372; David Leigh, *The Wilson Plot: The Intelligence Services and the Discrediting of a Prime Minister, 1945–76* (Heinemann, 1988), p. 206.
33 Wright, *Spycatcher*, p. 359.
34 Leigh, *The Wilson Plot*, p. 97.
35 Ibid., pp. 204–5.
36 House of Commons, 15 Jan 1988 (125/607–12).
37 Anthony Sampson: *The Changing Anatomy of Britain* (Hodder & Stoughton, 1982), p. 7.

38 *The Times* (30 Nov 1972).
39 Interview with Barbara Hosking.
40 Edward Heath, *Music: A Joy for Life* (Sidgwick & Jackson, 1976), pp. 168–71.
41 Interview with Barbara Hosking.
42 Heath, *Music*, pp. 176–9.
43 *The Times* (26 Nov 1971).
44 Edward Heath, *Sailing: A Course of My Life* (Sidgwick & Jackson, 1975), p. 111.
45 Interview with Charles Wintour and Robert Carvel, *Evening Standard* (1–2 June 1972).
46 Heath, *Sailing*, p. 113.
47 Ibid.
48 Ibid., pp. 126–7.
49 Ibid., p. 115.
50 Ibid., p. 134.
51 Ibid., p. 142.
52 *The Times* (19 Aug 1971).
53 Ibid. (16 July 1971).
54 Ibid. (20 July 1971).
55 *Private Eye* (30 July 1971).
56 *New Statesman* (18 Feb 1972).
57 *Guardian* (27 April 1972).
58 James Margach, *The Abuse of Power: The War Between Downing Street and the Media* (W. H. Allen, 1978; Star edn, 1979), p. 157.
59 Interview with Sir Donald Maitland.
60 Ibid.; Margach, *The Abuse of Power*, p. 171; *Private Eye* (19 Nov, 31 Dec 1971); Harris, *Good and Faithful Servant*, p. 78.
61 *Observer* (22 Feb 1972).
62 Private information.
63 *Evening Standard* (1–2 June 1972).
64 Michael Cockerell, *Live from Number Ten: The Inside Story of Prime Ministers and Television* (Faber, 1988), p. 169; Hurd, *An End to Promises*, p. 73.
65 Cockerell, *Live from Number Ten*, p. 173.
66 Hurd, *An End to Promises*, pp. 81, 73.
67 Cockerell, *Live from Number Ten*, p. 193.
68 *Evening Standard* (7–10 June 1971).
69 Ibid. (1–2 June 1972).
70 *New Statesman* (5 Oct 1973).
71 Cockerell, *Live from Number Ten*, pp. 180–3, 188–9.
72 Margach, *The Abuse of Power*, p. 166.
73 Hurd, *An End to Promises*, p. 76.

27 The Prime Minister and His Party

1 James Prior, *A Balance of Power* (Hamish Hamilton, 1986), p. 101.
2 Philip Norton and Arthur Aughey, *Conservatives and Conservatism* (Temple Smith, 1981), p. 255.
3 Ibid., p. 221.
4 Martin Holmes, *Political Pressure and Economic Policy: British Government, 1970–4* (Butterworth, 1982), p. 130.
5 Lord Carrington, *Reflect on Things Past* (Collins, 1988), pp. 260–1.
6 Norman Tebbit, *Upwardly Mobile* (Weidenfeld & Nicolson, 1988), p. 123.
7 John Ramsden, *The Making of Conservative Party Policy: The Conservative Research Department since 1929* (Longman, 1980), p. 295.

8 Ibid.
9 Interview with Lord Pym.
10 Philip Norton, *Conservative Dissidents: Dissent Within the Parliamentary Conservative Party, 1970–4* (Temple Smith, 1978), p. 208.
11 Julian Critchley, 'The Unknown Whip', *Illustrated London News* (Oct 1971), in Norton, *Conservative Dissidents*, p. 169.
12 Tebbit, *Upwardly Mobile*, p. 128.
13 Interview with Lord Pym.
14 *The Times* (24 Jan 1972).
15 *Spectator* (2 Dec 1972).
16 Prior, *A Balance of Power*, p. 101.
17 Norton, *Conservative Dissidents*, p. 229.
18 *Financial Times* (24 Nov 1972).
19 Nigel Fisher, *The Tory Leaders: Their Struggle for Power* (Weidenfeld & Nicolson, 1977), p. 141.
20 Norton, *Conservative Dissidents*, p. 230.
21 *The Times* (1 March 1973).
22 Ibid. (24 Nov 1972).
23 *Financial Times* (24 Nov 1972).
24 Interview with Sir Timothy Kitson.
25 Humphrey Berkeley, *Crossing the Floor* (Allen & Unwin, 1972), p. 109; Norton, *Conservative Dissidents*, p. 243.
26 Norton, *Conservative Dissidents*, p. 234.
27 Interview with Dr Thomas Stuttaford.
28 Norton, *Conservative Dissidents*, p. 174.
29 *The Times*, (25 May 1972).

28   The Barber Boom

1 *Director* (June 1973).
2 Brendon Sewill, 'In Place of Strikes', in Ralph Harris and Brendon Sewill, *British Economic Policy, 1970–4: Two Views* (IEA, 1975), p. 45.
3 Samuel Brittan, *The Economic Consequences of Democracy* (Temple Smith, 1977), p. 9.
4 Martin Holmes, *Political Pressure and Economic Policy: British Government, 1970–4* (Butterworth, 1982), p. 129.
5 *The Times* (7 March 1973).
6 *The Economist* (24 Feb 1973).
7 *The Times* (7 March 1973).
8 *Spectator* (10 March 1973).
9 *The Economist* (10 March 1973).
10 *The Times* (2 May 1973).
11 Ibid. (16 May 1973).
12 Ibid. (15 May 1973).
13 Ibid. (22 May 1973).
14 *Daily Telegraph* (22 May 1973).
15 House of Commons, 21 May 1973 (857/52).
16 Roger Bacon and Walter Eltis, *Britain's Economic Problem: Too Few Producers* (Macmillan, 1976).
17 *The Times* (5 Feb 1973).
18 Interview with Lord Roll.
19 Peter Walker, *The Ascent of Britain* (Sidgwick & Jackson, 1977), p. 61.
20 Cecil King, *The Cecil King Diary, 1970–4* (Jonathan Cape, 1975), p. 267 (28 Feb 1973).

21 Phillip Whitehead, *The Writing on the Wall: Britain in the Seventies* (Michael Joseph/Channel Four, 1985), p. 93.
22 Ibid., pp. 92–5.
23 House of Commons, 15 May 1973, (856/1243).
24 Lucille Iremonger, 'Edward Heath', in *British Prime Ministers in the Twentieth Century*, ed. John P. Mackintosh, vol. II (Weidenfeld & Nicolson, 1978), p. 165.
25 Whitehead, *The Writing on the Wall*, p. 95.
26 Sewill, 'In Place of Strikes', p. 37.
27 House of Commons, 18 July 1973 (860/498–515).
28 Sewill, 'In Place of Strikes', p. 45; Edmund Dell, *A Hard Pounding: Politics and Economic Crisis, 1974–6* (Oxford University Press, 1991), p. 10.
29 Alan Sked and Chris Cook, *Post-War Britain: A Political History* (Penguin, 1979), p. 258.
30 *The Economist* (1 Sept 1973).
31 *The Times* (28 July 1973).
32 *The Economist* (1 Sept 1973).
33 Interview with Lord Walker.
34 *The Times* (18 Jan 1973).
35 *The Economist* (20 Jan 1973).
36 *The Times* (20 Jan 1973).
37 Philip Norton, *Conservative Dissidents: Dissent Within the Parliamentary Conservative Party, 1970–4* (Temple Smith, 1978), pp. 120–2.
38 *The Economist* (27 Jan 1973).
39 *The Times* (6, 15 Feb 1973).
40 Ibid. (8 March 1973).
41 Ibid. (6 Feb 1973).
42 Ibid.
43 Ibid. (27 March 1973).
44 *The Economist* (31 March 1973).
45 Douglas Hurd, *An End to Promises: Sketch of a Government, 1970–4* (Collins, 1979), p. 108.
46 *The Times* (16 Feb 1973).
47 Brittan, *Economic Consequences of Democracy*, p. 59.
48 *The Times* (25 Sept 1973).
49 Interview with Lord Whitelaw.
50 *The Economist* (1 Sept 1973).
51 Ibid. (8 Sept 1973).
52 Hurd, *An End to Promises*, p. 112.
53 *The Times* (9 Oct 1973).
54 *New Statesman* (12 Oct 1973).
55 *The Economist* (13 Oct 1973).
56 *New Statesman* (12 Oct 1973).
57 *The Times* (9 Oct 1973).
58 *Conservative Party Conference Report* (1973), p. 67.
59 *The Economist* (13 Oct 1973).
60 *The Times* (15 Oct 1973).
61 *Conservative Party Conference Report* (1973), pp. 131–7.
62 *Daily Telegraph* (15 Oct 1973).
63 *The Economist* (8 Sept 1973).

29 Whitelaw in Ulster

1 William Whitelaw, *The Whitelaw Memoirs* (Aurum Press, 1989), p. 92.
2 Brian Faulkner, *Memoirs of a Statesman* (Weidenfeld & Nicolson, 1978), p. 157.

3   *Sunday Times* (30 April 1989).
4   House of Commons, 22 June 1972 (839/722).
5   Whitelaw, *Memoirs*, p. 98.
6   Ibid., p. 100.
7   Ibid.
8   Patrick Bishop and Eamonn Mallie, *The Provisional IRA* (Heinemann, 1987), p. 178.
9   Ibid., p. 179.
10 *The Times* (19 July 1972).
11 Whitelaw, *Memoirs*, pp. 101–2.
12 *The Times* (20 July 1972).
13 Faulkner, *Memoirs*, p. 160.
14 *The Times* (17 Nov 1972).
15 Ibid. (5 Sept 1973).
16 Ibid. (30 Aug 1973).
17 Whitelaw, *Memoirs*, pp. 117–18.
18 Faulkner, *Memoirs*, p. 223.
19 Whitelaw, *Memoirs*, p. 119.
20 *Annual Register, 1973*, p. 31.
21 Faulkner, *Memoirs*, p. 228.
22 Ibid., p. 232.
23 Ibid., p. 229.
24 Ibid., p. 235.
25 Ibid., p. 236.
26 Ibid.
27 See J. J. Lee, *Ireland 1912–85* (Cambridge University Press, 1989), pp. 447–8.
28 House of Commons, 10 Dec 1973 (866/28–41).
29 Phillip Whitehead, *The Writing on the Wall: Britain in the Seventies* (Michael Joseph/Channel Four, 1985), p. 171.

30   Oil and Coal

1   *The Times* (2 Jan 1973).
2   Ibid. (5 Jan 1973).
3   Edward Heath, *Music: A Joy for Life* (Sidgwick & Jackson, 1976), p. 134.
4   *The Times* (3 Oct 1973).
5   Ibid. (1 Jan 1973).
6   Ibid. (2 Jan 1973).
7   *Conservative Party Conference Report* (1973), p. 133 (13 Oct 1973).
8   *Annual Register, 1973*, p. 26.
9   *The Times* (4 Dec 1973).
10 Ibid. (15 Oct 1973).
11 *Conservative Party Conference Report* (1973), p. 133 (13 Oct 1973).
12 *The Times* (17 Dec 1973).
13 Willy Brandt, *People and Politics* (Collins, 1978), pp. 276–7.
14 Interview with Lord Hunt of Tanworth.
15 *The Times* (19 Dec 1973).
16 Douglas Hurd, *An End to Promises: Sketch of a Government, 1970–4* (Collins, 1979), pp. 114–15.
17 *The Times* (17 March 1973).
18 Ibid. (3 July 1973).
19 Joe Gormley, *Battered Cherub* (Hamish Hamilton, 1982), p. 124.
20 Ibid., pp. 124–5.

21 Ibid.
22 Lord Boardman, ICBH witness seminar, 9 Feb 1988 (*Contemporary Record* [Spring 1988]), p. 42.
23 Interview with Lord Walker.
24 Hurd, *An End to Promises*, p. 114.
25 Tessa Blackstone and William Plowden, *Inside the Think Tank: Advising the Cabinet, 1971–83* (Heinemann, 1988), pp. 76–7; interview with Lord Rothschild.
26 *The Times* (11 Oct 1973).
27 *The Economist* (13 Oct 1973).
28 Hurd, *An End to Promises*, p. 115.
29 Stephen Fay and Hugo Young, *The Fall of Heath* (Sunday Times, 1976), p. 14.
30 Phillip Whitehead, *The Writing on the Wall: Britain in the Seventies* (Michael Joseph/Channel Four, 1985), p. 104.
31 Gormley, *Battered Cherub*, p. 128.
32 *The Times* (24 Oct 1973).
33 Ibid. (16 Nov 1973).
34 *The Economist* (23 Nov 1973).
35 *The Times* (23 Nov 1973).
36 Whitehead, *The Writing on the Wall*, p. 104.
37 Gormley, *Battered Cherub*, p. 131.
38 Fay and Young, *The Fall of Heath*, p. 6.
39 *The Times* (29 Jan 1974).
40 Martin Holmes, *Political Pressure and Economic Policy: British Government, 1970–4* (Butterworth, 1982), p. 107, quoting Thames Television transcript, 'Miners: State of Emergency' (15 March 1978).
41 *The Times* (29 Nov 1973).
42 Ibid. (30 Nov 1973).
43 Hurd, *An End to Promises*, pp. 117–18.
44 Ibid., p. 119.
45 *The Economist* (8 Dec 1973).
46 *The Times* (3 Dec 1973).
47 Fay and Young, *The Fall of Heath*, p. 18.
48 William Whitelaw, *The Whitelaw Memoirs* (Aurum Press, 1989), p. 128.
49 Gormley, *Battered Cherub*, p. 135.
50 Interview with Brendon Sewill.
51 Hurd, *An End to Promises*, p. 117.
52 Brendon Sewill, 'In Place of Strikes', in Ralph Harris and Brendon Sewill, *British Economic Policy, 1970–4: Two Views* (IEA, 1975), pp. 63–4.
53 *The Times* (21 Nov 1973).
54 Hurd, *An End to Promises*, p. 120; James Prior, *A Balance of Power* (Hamish Hamilton, 1986), pp. 88–9; Peter Walker, *Staying Power* (Sidgwick & Jackson, 1977), pp. 114–15.
55 Prior, *A Balance of Power*, p. 89.
56 *The Economist* (22 Dec 1973).
57 Hurd, *An End to Promises*, pp. 121–2.
58 Michael Cockerell, *Live from Number 10: The Inside Story of Prime Ministers and Television* (Faber, 1988), pp. 193–4.
59 *The Times* (14 Dec 1973).

31 The Three-Day Week

1 *The Times* (14 Dec 1973).
2 Ibid. (2, 5 Jan 1974).

3   David Butler and Dennis Kavanagh, *The British General Election of February 1974* (Macmillan, 1974), p. 34.
4   Douglas Hurd, *An End to Promises: Sketch of a Government, 1970–4* (Collins, 1979), pp. 123–4.
5   Interview with Brendon Sewill.
6   Interview with Lord Rothschild.
7   Interview with Lord Walker.
8   ICBH witness seminar, 9 Feb 1988 (*Contemporary Record* [Spring 1988]), p. 44.
9   Stephen Fay and Hugo Young, *The Fall of Heath* (Sunday Times, 1976), p. 25.
10 Hurd, *An End to Promises*, p. 127.
11 James Prior, *A Balance of Power* (Hamish Hamilton, 1986), p. 91.
12 Butler and Kavanagh, *General Election of 1974*, p. 35.
13 Hurd memo for Heath, 15 Jan 1974, printed in Hurd, *An End to Promises*, p. 129.
14 Lord Boardman, in ICBH witness seminar, p. 45.
15 Fay and Young, *The Fall of Heath*, p. 27.
16 Hurd, *An End to Promises*, p. 130.
17 Fay and Young, *The Fall of Heath*, p 23.
18 Prior, *A Balance of Power*, pp. 90–1.
19 Interviews with Lord Pym and Lord Carr.
20 Peter Walker, *Staying Power* (Bloomsbury, 1991), pp. 116–17.
21 *The Economist* (12 Jan 1974).
22 *The Times* (9 Jan 1974).
23 Lord Carrington, *Reflect on Things Past* (Collins, 1988), p. 262.
24 Fay and Young, *The Fall of Heath*, p. 20; see also Keith Middlemas, *Industry, Unions and the Government: Twenty-One Years of NEDC* (Macmillan, 1983), pp. 85–6.
25 Ibid., p. 21.
26 Interview with Lord Murray of Epping Forest.
27 Phillip Whitehead, *The Writing on the Wall: Britain in the Seventies* (Michael Joseph/Channel Four, 1985), p. 107.
28 Martin Holmes, *Political Pressure and Economic Policy: British Government, 1970–4* (Butterworth, 1982), p. 110.
29 ICBH witness seminar, p. 43.
30 Whitehead, *The Writing on the Wall*, p. 107.
31 Holmes, *Political Pressure and Economic Policy*, p. 110.
32 *The Times* (10 Jan 1974).
33 ICBH witness seminar, p. 43.
34 Ibid.
35 Ibid., p. 44.
36 *The Times* (10 Jan 1974).
37 Lord Boardman in ICBH witness seminar, p. 43; Prior, *A Balance of Power*, p. 92.
38 *The Times* (12 Jan 1974).
39 'Miners, State of Emergency', Thames Television, (15 March 1978), quoted in Holmes, *Political Pressure and Economic Policy*, p. 110.
40 Fay and Young, *The Fall of Heath*, p 22; interview with Mick McGahey.
41 House of Commons, 10 Jan 1974 (867/65–73).
42 *Listener* (25 Oct 1979).
43 Fay and Young, *The Fall of Heath*, p. 22.
44 Prior, *A Balance of Power*, p. 92.
45 ICBH witness seminar, p. 44.
46 Ibid.

47 Interview with Mick McGahey.
48 Fay and Young, *The Fall of Heath*, pp. 21–2.
49 ICBH witness seminar, p. 43.
50 *The Times* (14 Jan 1974).
51 Fay and Young, *The Fall of Heath*, p. 26.
52 *The Times* (14 Jan 1974).
53 Ibid.
54 Ibid. (16 Jan 1974).
55 Whitehead, *The Writing on the Wall*, p. 109.
56 Prior, *A Balance of Power*, p. 92.
57 *The Times* (19, 24 Jan 1974).
58 *Sunday Times* (7 May 1989).
59 *The Times* (19 Jan 1974).
60 *The Economist* (26 Jan 1974).
61 *The Times* (23 Jan 1974).
62 Ibid.
63 Joe Gormley, *Battered Cherub* (Hamish Hamilton, 1982), p. 139.
64 Hurd, *An End to Promises*, p. 131.
65 *The Times* (25 Jan 1974).
66 Ibid.
67 Gormley, *Battered Cherub*, p. 139.
68 *The Times* (28 Jan 1974).
69 House of Commons, 24 Jan 1974 (867/1898–1903).
70 Fay and Young, *The Fall of Heath*, p. 29.
71 Hurd, *An End to Promises*, p. 131.
72 Whitehead, *The Writing on the Wall*, p. 110.
73 *The Times* (29 Jan 1974).
74 *The Economist* (2 Feb 1974).
75 *The Times* (1 Feb 1974).
76 Ibid. (2 Feb 1974).
77 Ibid. (31 Jan, 4 Feb 1974).
78 *The Economist* (2 Feb 1974).
79 *The Times* (4 Feb 1974).
80 Ibid. (5 Feb 1974).
81 House of Commons, 5 Feb 1974 (868/1037–40).
82 Hurd, *An End to Promises*, p. 132.
83 *The Times* (7 Feb 1974).
84 House of Commons, 6 Feb 1974 (868/1242).
85 *The Times* (25 Jan, 7 Feb 1974).
86 Hurd, *An End to Promises*, p. 134.
87 Ibid., pp. 135–6.
88 *Daily Express* (8 Feb 1974).
89 *The Times* (8 Feb 1974).
90 Ibid.
91 Ibid. (9 Feb 1974).

32 'Who Governs?'

1 e.g. David Butler, quoted in Tony Benn, *Against the Tide: Diaries 1973–6* (Hutchinson, 1989), p. 106 (10 Feb 1974).
2 *The Times* (15 Feb 1974).
3 *Guardian* (9 Feb 1974).

4   *The Times* (13 Feb 1974).
5   Ibid. (8 Feb 1974).
6   Ibid. (18 Feb 1974).
7   Ibid. (12 Feb 1974).
8   Ibid. (13 Feb 1974).
9   Ibid. (9 Feb 1974).
10   Cecil King, *The Cecil King Diary, 1970–4* (Jonathan Cape, 1975), p. 345 (16 Feb 1974).
11   David Butler and Dennis Kavanagh, *The British General Election of February 1974* (Macmillan, 1974), p. 266.
12   *The Economist* (16 Feb 1974).
13   Ibid.
14   *Firm Action for a Fair Britain: The Conservative Manifesto* (1974).
15   *The Economist* (2 March 1974).
16   Butler and Kavanagh, *General Election of February 1974*, p. 83.
17   Ibid.
18   George Hutchinson in *The Times* (16 Feb 1974).
19   *The Times* (16 Feb 1974).
20   Benn, *Against the Tide*, p. 166.
21   *The Economist* (16 Feb 1974).
22   *The Times* (23 Feb 1974).
23   Butler and Kavanagh, *General Election of February 1974*, p. 121.
24   *The Times* (15 Feb 1974).
25   Ibid. (21 Feb 1974).
26   Ibid. (8 Feb 1974).
27   Ibid (27 Feb 1974); Butler and Kavanagh, *General Election of February 1974*, p. 139.
28   *The Times* (16 Feb 1974).
29   Butler and Kavanagh, *General Election of February 1974*, p. 87.
30   *The Times* (26 Feb 1974).
31   Ibid. (27 Feb 1974).
32   Ibid. (8 Feb 1974).
33   Ibid.
34   Ibid. (27 Feb 1974).
35   Ibid. (23 Feb 1974).
36   Ibid. (27 Feb 1974).
37   Ibid. (28 Feb 1974).
38   Ibid. (20, 21 Feb 1974).
39   Ibid. (8 Feb 1974).
40   Ibid. (25 Feb 1974).
41   Ibid.
42   Butler and Kavanagh, *General Election of February 1974*, p. 193.
43   *The Times* (21 Feb 1974).
44   Ibid. (23 Feb 1974).
45   Ibid. (26 Feb 1974).
46   Michael Cockerell, *Live from Number 10: The Inside Story of Prime Ministers and Television* (Faber, 1988), p. 200.
47   Butler and Kavanagh, *General Election of February 1974*, p. 160.
48   *The Times* (23 Feb 1974).
49   Ibid. (25 Feb 1974).
50   Ibid.
51   Ibid. (25, 26 Feb 1974).
52   Ibid. (27 Feb 1974).

53 Ibid.
54 Butler and Kavanagh, *General Election of February 1974*, p. 110.
55 *The Times* (27 Feb 1974).
56 Ibid.
57 Cockerell, *Live from Number 10*, p. 203.
58 *The Times* (28 Feb 1974).
59 *Daily Mail* (28 Feb 1974).
60 *The Times* (1 March 1974).
61 Ibid. (2 March 1974).
62 *The Economist* (20 July 1974).
63 Butler and Kavanagh, *General Election of February 1974*, p. 313.
64 Ibid., p. 253.
65 James Prior, *A Balance of Power* (Hamish Hamilton, 1986), p. 95.
66 Interview with Rosemary Wolff.
67 Interview with Jeremy Thorpe.
68 David Steel, *Against Goliath* (Weidenfeld & Nicolson, 1989), p. 80.
69 Peter Walker, *Staying Power* (Bloomsbury, 1991), p. 125.
70 King, *Diary*, p. 349 (4 March 1974).
71 Phillip Whitehead, *The Writing on the Wall: Britain in the Seventies* (Michael Joseph/Channel Four, 1985), p. 114.
72 *The Times* (4 March 1974).
73 Ibid.
74 William Whitelaw, *The Whitelaw Memoirs* (Aurum Press, 1989), p. 134; Lord Carrington, *Reflect on Things Past* (Collins, 1988), p. 266.
75 *Spectator* (9 March 1974).
76 *The Times* (5 March 1974).
77 Ibid. (9 March 1974).
78 Ibid. (5 March 1974).

33 'National Unity'

1   Interview with Sir Timothy Kitson.
2   *The Times* (6 March 1974).
3   Ibid. (20 March 1974).
4   *The Economist* (16 March 1974).
5   House of Commons, 12 March 1974 (870/54–67).
6   Phillip Whitehead, *The Writing on the Wall: Britain in the Seventies* (Michael Joseph/Channel Four, 1985), p. 132.
7   Morrison Halcrow, *Keith Joseph: A Single Mind* (Macmillan, 1989), p. 58.
8   *The Economist* (16 March 1974).
9   James Prior, *A Balance of Power* (Hamish Hamilton, 1986), p. 97; Halcrow, *Keith Joseph*, p. 65.
10 *The Economist* (16 March 1974).
11 David Butler and Dennis Kavanagh, *The British General Election of October 1974* (Macmillan, 1975), p. 41.
12 *The Economist* (16 March 1974).
13 John Ramsden, *The Making of Conservative Party Policy: The Conservative Research Department since 1929* (Longman, 1980), p. 304.
14 *The Times* (5 April 1974).
15 Butler and Kavanagh, *General Election of October 1974*, p. 42; Ramsden, *The Making of Conservative Party Policy*, p. 306.
16 Hugo Young, *One of Us: A Biography of Margaret Thatcher* (Macmillan, 1989), pp. 82–3.

17 *Contemporary Record* (Spring 1987); Halcrow, *Keith Joseph*, p. 71.
18 Peter Walker, *Staying Power* (Bloomsbury, 1991), p. 126; interview with Lord Walker.
19 Whitehead, *The Writing on the Wall*, p. 324.
20 Walker, *Staying Power*, p. 126.
21 *The Times* (1 April 1974).
22 Ibid. (10 May 1974).
23 *The Economist* (27 April 1974).
24 Butler and Kavanagh, *General Election of October 1974*, pp. 42–3; Ramsden, *The Making of Conservative Party Policy*, pp. 306–7.
25 Interview with Lord Gilmour.
26 *The Times* (2, 3, 4 May 1974).
27 Ibid. (10 May 1974).
28 Ibid. (27 May 1974).
29 Ibid. (26, 28 May, 3 June 1974); interview with Clare Hollingworth; Edward Heath, *Travels: People and Places in My Life* (Sidgwick & Jackson, 1977), pp. 202–21.
30 Robert Behrens, *The Conservative Party from Heath to Thatcher* (Saxon House, 1980), p. 24.
31 *The Times* (9 June 1974).
32 Ibid. (17 June 1974).
33 Ibid. (18 June 1974).
34 Ibid. (22 June 1974).
35 Butler and Kavanagh, *General Election of October 1974*, p. 52.
36 Ibid., p. 44.
37 *The Times* (27 June 1974).
38 Ibid. (6 July 1974).
39 Ibid. (23 July 1974).
40 Ibid. (20 Sept 1974).
41 Ibid. (29 July 1974).
42 Butler and Kavanagh, *General Election of October 1974*, p. 45.
43 *Putting Britain First*, pp. 3–4.
44 *The Times* (6 Sept 1974); Halcrow, *Keith Joseph*, p. 71.
45 Prior, *A Balance of Power*, p. 97.
46 *The Times* (6 Sept 1974).
47 Ibid. (7 Sept 1974).
48 *Putting Britain First*, p. 3.
49 *The Times* (10 Sept 1974).
50 Ibid. (4 Sept 1974).
51 Edward Heath, *Sailing: A Course of My Life* (Sidgwick & Jackson, 1975), p. 155.
52 *The Times* (3 Oct 1974).
53 Halcrow, *Keith Joseph*, p. 75; *Spectator* (11 Oct 1974).
54 *The Times* (28 Sept 1974).
55 Ibid. (25 Sept 1974).
56 Butler and Kavanagh, *General Election of October 1974*, p. 60.
57 *The Times* (13 Sept 1974).
58 *The Economist* (28 Sept 1974).
59 Butler and Kavanagh, *General Election of October 1974*, pp. 106–7.
60 *The Economist* (28 Sept 1974).
61 Ibid. (5 Oct 1974).
62 *The Times* (28 Sept 1974).
63 Butler and Kavanagh, *General Election of October 1974*, p. 131.
64 *The Times* (1 Oct 1974).

65 Ibid. (5 Oct 1974).
66 *New Statesman* (11 Oct 1974).
67 Butler and Kavanagh, *General Election of October 1974*, p. 124.
68 *The Times* (21 Sept 1974).
69 Ibid. (4 Oct 1974).
70 Butler and Kavanagh, *General Election of October 1974*, p. 129.
71 *The Times* (7 Oct 1974).
72 Ibid. (5 Oct 1974).
73 Ibid. (6 Oct 1974).
74 Ibid. (5 Oct 1974).
75 *The Economist* (5 Oct 1974).
76 Ibid. (12 Oct 1974).
77 Butler and Kavanagh, *General Election of October 1974*, p. 135n.
78 *The Times* (12 Oct 1974).
79 Ibid.

34 'The Peasants' Revolt'

1 *The Times* (14 Oct 1974).
2 James Prior, *A Balance of Power* (Hamish Hamilton, 1986), p. 98.
3 Nigel Fisher, *The Tory Leaders: Their Struggle for Power* (Weidenfeld & Nicolson, 1977), pp. 147–8.
4 Ibid., p. 147.
5 Fisher, *Tory Leaders*, p. 151.
6 *The Times* (22 Oct 1974).
7 Ibid. (16 Oct 1974).
8 *The Economist* (2 Nov 1974).
9 Patrick Cosgrave, *Margaret Thatcher: The First Term* (Bodley Head, 1985), p. 16.
10 William Whitelaw, *The Whitelaw Memoirs* (Aurum Press, 1989), p. 142.
11 Morrison Halcrow, *Keith Joseph: A Single Mind* (Macmillan, 1989), p. 91.
12 *The Times* (11 Nov 1974).
13 Ibid. (14 Oct 1974).
14 Fisher, *Tory Leaders*, p. 159.
15 *The Economist* (19 Oct 1974).
16 *Sunday Telegraph* (19 Jan 1975).
17 *The Economist* (9 Nov 1974).
18 *The Times* (8 Nov 1974).
19 Ibid. (30 Oct 1974).
20 Fisher, *Tory Leaders*, p. 155.
21 *The Economist* (2 Nov 1974).
22 *The Times* (7 Nov 1974).
23 Peter Walker, *Staying Power* (Bloomsbury, 1991), p. 127.
24 *The Economist* (9 Nov 1974).
25 *Annual Register, 1974*, p. 39.
26 Fisher, *Tory Leaders*, p. 155.
27 Ibid., p. 156.
28 *The Times* (15 Nov 1974).
29 Norman Tebbit, *Upwardly Mobile* (Weidenfeld & Nicolson, 1988), p. 140.
30 Phillip Whitehead, *The Writing on the Wall: Britain in the Seventies* (Michael Joseph/Channel Four, 1985), p. 327; Nicholas Wapshott and George Brock, *Thatcher* (Futura, 1983), p. 122.
31 *The Economist* (30 Nov 1974).

32 Ibid. (21 Dec 1974).
33 *The Times* (23 Dec 1974).
34 Ibid. (15 Jan 1975).
35 Prior, *A Balance of Power*, p. 99.
36 Fisher, *Tory Leaders*, p. 163.
37 Philip Norton, *Conservative Dissidents: Dissent Within the Parliamentary Conservative Party, 1970–4* (Temple Smith, 1978), p. 237.
38 Fisher, *Tory Leaders*, p. 165.
39 Whitehead, *The Writing on the Wall*, p. 325.
40 *The Times* (4 Feb 1975).
41 House of Commons, 22 Jan 1975 (884/1554).
42 *The Times* (23 Jan 1975).
43 Walker, *Staying Power*, p. 128.
44 *The Times* (8 Feb 1975).
45 Fisher, *Tory Leaders*, pp. 166–7.
46 *Guardian* (11 April 1978).
47 *The Times* (31 Jan 1975).
48 Ibid. (24 Jan 1975).
49 Ibid. (31 Jan 1975).
50 *Daily Telegraph* (3 Feb 1975).
51 Ibid. (30 Jan 1975).
52 Francis Pym, *The Politics of Consent* (Hamish Hamilton, 1984), p. 5.
53 *The Times* (31 Jan 1975).
54 Ibid. (1 Feb 1975).
55 Fisher, *Tory Leaders*, pp. 170–1.
56 Ibid., p. 167.
57 Patrick Cosgrave, *Margaret Thatcher: A Tory and Her Party* (Hutchinson, 1978), p. 71.
58 Fisher, *Tory Leaders*, pp. 168–9; Cosgrave, *Margaret Thatcher*, p. 70.
59 Tebbit, *Upwardly Mobile*, p. 141.
60 Wapshott and Brock, *Thatcher*, p. 131; interview with Lord Gilmour.
61 Interview with Sir Paul Bryan.
62 Wapshott and Brock, *Thatcher*, p. 135.
63 Tony Benn, *Against the Tide: Diaries 1973–6* (Hutchinson, 1989), p. 311 (4 Feb 1975).
64 Prior, *A Balance of Power*, p. 100.
65 Cosgrave, *Margaret Thatcher*, p. 72; Wapshott and Brock, *Thatcher*, p. 135.
66 *Financial Times* (5 Feb 1975).
67 Prior, *A Balance of Power*, p. 100.
68 Benn, *Against the Tide*, p. 319 (18 Feb 1975).
69 Castle, *Diaries*, p. 303 (5 Feb 1975).
70 *The Times* (6 Feb 1975).
71 Ibid. (12 Feb 1975).
72 Wapshott and Brock, *Thatcher*, p. 144.
73 Interview with Sir Timothy Kitson.

35   Unreconciled

1 James Prior, *A Balance of Power* (Hamish Hamilton, 1986), p. 108.
2 *The Times* (27 March 1975).
3 *Sunday Times* (6 April 1975).
4 *The Times* (17 April 1975).

5   Ibid. (20 March 1975).
6   David Butler and Uwe Kitzinger, *The 1975 Referendum* (Macmillan, 1976), p. 77.
7   House of Commons, 9 April 1975 (889/1274–86).
8   *The Times* (2 June 1975).
9   Ibid. (1 June 1975).
10 Ibid. (22 May 1975).
11 Barbara Castle, *The Castle Diaries, 1974–6* (Weidenfeld & Nicolson, 1980), pp. 405–6.
12 *The Times* (4 June 1975).
13 Ibid. (14 June 1975).
14 Ibid. (21 June 1975).
15 Ibid. (28 June 1975).
16 Ibid. (30 June 1975).
17 Ibid. (22 Nov 1975).
18 Edward Heath, *Music: A Joy for Life* (Sidgwick & Jackson, 1976), pp. 128–9, 147–8, 160–3.
19 Edward Heath, *Sailing: A Course of My Life* (Sidgwick & Jackson, 1975), pp. 157–8, 183–4; interviews with Robin Aisher, Owen Parker; John Rousmaniere, *Fastnet Force 10* (Nautical Books, 1980), pp. 239–43.
20 *Daily Express* (14 Jan 1977).
21 *Sunday Times* (9 Nov 1975); see also Charles Raw, *Slater Walker: An Investigation of a Financial Phenomenon* (Deutsch, 1977), pp. 256, 266.
22 *Sunday Telegraph* (16 Oct 1977).
23 *Sunday Times Magazine* (8 Jan 1989).
24 *Daily Express* (14 Jan 1977).
25 *The Times* (12 Jan 1976).
26 Ibid. (7 Oct 1975).
27 Ibid. (23 Sept 1975).
28 Ibid. (9 Oct 1975).
29 Ibid.
30 Ibid. (11 Oct 1975).
31 Ibid. (13 Oct 1975).
32 Ibid. (6 Nov 1975).
33 Ibid. (17 Nov 1975).
34 Ibid.
35 Ibid. (11 July 1978).
36 Ibid. (30 June 1975).
37 Ibid. (17 Nov 1975).
38 Ibid. (6 May 1976).
39 Ibid. (13 Oct 1977).
40 House of Commons, 10 March 1976 (907/459–74).
41 Ibid., 7 July 1976 (914/1408–28).
42 Ibid.
43 Ibid., 10 March 1976 (907/459–74).
44 Ibid., 24 April 1975 (890/1760–1).
45 Ibid., 22 July 1975 (896/339–49).
46 Castle, *Diaries*, p. 473.
47 *The Times* (17 March 1976).
48 Ibid. (8 July 1976).
49 House of Commons, 7 July 1976 (914/1408–28).
50 *The Times* (12, 14 June 1976).
51 Ibid. (26 June 1976).

52 Ibid. (21 June 1976).
53 Ibid. (26 July 1976).
54 Ibid. (31 July 1976).
55 Ibid. (5 Oct 1976).
56 *Conservative Party Conference Report* (1976), pp. 62–4 (6 Oct 1976).
57 *The Times* (7 Oct 1976).
58 *Guardian* (7 Oct 1976).
59 *The Times* (9 Oct 1976).
60 Ibid. (5 April 1977).
61 Ibid. (7 Dec 1976).
62 Ibid. (12 Oct 1977).
63 Ibid. (31 Jan 1978).
64 Ibid. (14 Feb 1978).
65 Ibid. (16 Feb 1978).
66 Ibid. (8 May 1978).
67 Ibid. (6 July 1978).
68 Ibid. (7 July 1978).
69 Ibid. (6 July 1978).
70 Ibid. (8, 12 July 1977).
71 Ibid. (23 Oct 1978).
72 *Conservative Party Conference Report* (1978) (11 Oct 1978).
73 *The Times* (12 Oct 1978).
74 Ibid. (13 Oct 1978).
75 *Daily Mail* (18 Oct 1978).
76 *The Times* (10 Nov 1978).
77 Ibid. (4 Nov 1978).
78 Bernard Donoughue, *Prime Minister: The Conduct of Policy Under Harold Wilson and James Callaghan* (Jonathan Cape, 1987), p. 191.
79 David Butler and Dennis Kavanagh, *The British General Election of 1979* (Macmillan, 1980), p. 154.
80 *Daily Telegraph* (11 April 1979).
81 Butler and Kavanagh, *General Election of 1979*, p. 192.
82 Ibid., p. 323.
83 *Sunday Times* (4 June 1979).
84 *Daily Telegraph* (3 May 1979).
85 *The Times* (5 May 1979).
86 Interview with Sir Timothy Kitson.
87 Interview with Sara Morrison.
88 *Daily Telegraph* (19 May 1979).
89 Interview with Sir Timothy Kitson; Roy Jenkins, *European Diary, 1977–81* (Collins, 1989), p. 449 (20 May 1979).
90 BBC Radio Four (28 Jan 1988).
91 *Daily Telegraph* (19 May 1979).

36 Internal Exile

1 *Daily Express* (11 May 1979).
2 *The Times* (10 Dec 1979).
3 Ibid. (10 Nov 1979).
4 Ibid. (31 March 1980).
5 House of Commons, 28 Jan 1980 (977/959–74).
6 Roy Jenkins, *European Diary, 1977–81* (Collins, 1989), p. 613 (27 June 1980).

7   *The Times* (13 Feb 1980).
8   *North-South: A Programme for Survival*, reprinted in *Annual Register, 1980*, pp. 492–9.
9   House of Commons, 24 July 1981 (9/761–8).
10 *The Times* (4 Dec 1980).
11 House of Commons, 16 June 1980 (986/1175–9).
12 Ibid., 24 July 1981 (9/761–8).
13 *The Times* (27 Oct 1981).
14 Ibid. (19 Oct 1982).
15 House of Commons, 22 Nov 1984 (68/438–42).
16 *The Times* (5 April 1983).
17 Ibid. (3 Nov 1980).
18 Ibid. (1 Nov 1980).
19 *Now!* (5 Dec 1980).
20 *The Times* (6 Nov 1980).
21 Ibid.
22 *Sunday Times* (9 Nov 1980).
23 House of Commons, 27 Nov 1980 (994/602–6).
24 *The Times* (29 Nov 1980).
25 Ibid. (19 March 1981).
26 Ibid. (17 March 1981).
27 Jenkins, *European Diary*, p. 587 (7 April 1980).
28 *The Times* (24 April 1981).
29 Roy Jenkins, *A Life at the Centre* (Macmillan, 1991), pp. 553–4.
30 Interview with Sara Morrison.
31 *Guardian* (Nov 1981), reprinted in Terry Coleman, *Movers and Shakers: Conversations with Uncommon Men* (Deutsch, 1987), pp. 119–24.
32 *Yorkshire Post* (28 Nov 1981).
33 Jenkins, *A Life at the Centre*, p. 554.
34 e.g. interview with Hugo Young, *Marxism Today* (Nov 1988).
35 *The Times* (2 July 1981).
36 Ibid. (4 July 1981).
37 Ibid. (5 Oct 1981).
38 Ibid. (13 Oct 1981).
39 Ibid. (20 Oct 1981).
40 Private information.
41 Interview with Andrew Rowe.
42 *The Times* (7 Oct 1981).
43 Ibid.
44 Ibid.
45 Ibid. (13 Oct 1981).
46 Ibid.
47 Coleman, *Movers and Shakers*, p. 124.
48 *The Times* (9 Oct 1981).
49 Ibid. (15 Oct 1981).
50 Ibid.
51 Ibid. (17 Oct 1981).
52 Ibid. (3 Dec 1981).
53 Ibid. (15 March 1982); House of Commons, 15 March 1982 (20/36–43).
54 House of Commons, 7 July 1981 (8/293–8).
55 Ibid., 13 May 1982 (23/964–9).
56 Ibid., 1 July 1982 (26/1038–9).
57 Ibid. (26/1039–40).

58   *The Times* (3 July 1982).
59   Ibid. (7 Feb 1983).
60   Hugo Young, *One of Us: A Biography of Margaret Thatcher* (Macmillan, 1989), pp. 300–1.
61   *The Times* (10 March 1982).
62   Ibid. (7 Oct 1982).
63   Ibid. (18 May 1983).
64   Ibid. (11 June 1983).
65   Ibid. (1 Dec 1984).
66   House of Commons, 15 Jan 1985 (71/227–32).
67   *The Times* (1 Dec 1984).
68   Ibid. (15 Jan 1985).
69   Ibid. (28 Nov 1985).
70   Ibid.
71   Ibid.
72   House of Commons, 5 Feb 1986 (91/324–8).
73   *The Times* (6 Feb 1986).
74   House of Commons, 17 Jan 1984 (52/184–8).
75   *The Times* (19 Jan 1984).
76   Ibid. (20 Feb 1984).
77   Private information.
78   *Sunday Times* magazine (8 Jan 1989).
79   Private information.
80   Interview with Mrs Jo Pattrick; *The Times* (4 Jan 1992).
81   Interviews with Moura Lympany, Andrew Rowe.
82   Interview with Sara Morrison.
83   'You', *Mail on Sunday* magazine (13 Nov 1988).
84   *Woman's Realm* (Summer 1986).
85   *Sunday Times* magazine (8 Jan 1989).
86   Ibid.
87   Interview with Tom Jolly.
88   *The Times* (18 Aug 1980).
89   *Sunday Times* magazine (8 Jan 1989).
90   'Comparing Notes', BBC Radio Four (22 May 1990).
91   'Desert Island Discs', BBC Radio Four (18 Dec 1988).
92   *Evening Standard* (2 Aug 1983).
93   'You', *Mail on Sunday* (13 Nov 1988).
94   *Sunday Times* magazine (8 Jan 1989).
95   *The Times* (18 March 1985).
96   *Hello!* (June 1991).
97   Interview with Andrew Rowe.
98   Interview with Rosemary Wolff.
99   Jenkins, *A Life at the Centre*, p. 607.
100 Ibid. p. 608.
101 *Daily Telegraph* (31 March 1987).
102 Jenkins, *A Life at the Centre*, p. 610.
103 *Sunday Telegraph* (8 Feb 1987).

37   The Nemesis of Thatcherism

1   David Butler and Dennis Kavanagh, *The British General Election of 1987* (Macmillan, 1988), p. 95.

2   *The Times* (30 May 1987).
3   Terry Coleman, *Thatcher's Britain: A Journey Through the Promised Lands* (Bantam, 1987), pp. 67–8.
4   Heath's Election Address, Old Bexley and Sidcup, May 1987.
5   *The Times* (13 June 1987).
6   House of Commons, 2 July 1987 (118/665–71).
7   Ibid., 29 Nov 1988 (142/598–604).
8   Ibid., 22 July 1987 (118/665–71).
9   Ibid., 17 Dec 1987 (124/1261–3).
10 *The Times* (2 Dec 1987).
11 *Spectator* (26 Nov 1988).
12 *Daily Telegraph* (5 Sept 1991).
13 House of Commons, 21 Dec 1988 (144/478–82).
14 *The Times* (5 Jan 1988).
15 House of Commons, 2 Feb 1989 (146/487–9).
16 *The Times* (4 Sept 1990).
17 Ibid. (14 May 1988).
18 Ibid. (16 May 1988).
19 *Marxism Today* (Nov 1988).
20 'Desert Island Discs', BBC Radio Four (18 Dec 1988).
21 *The Times* (20 Sept 1988).
22 Ibid. (23 July 1988).
23 *Sunday Times* (24 July 1988).
24 *The Times* (14 Oct 1988).
25 Ibid.
26 Ibid.
27 *Marxism Today* (Nov 1988).
28 *Sunday Times* (4 June 1989).
29 *The Times* (30 May 1989).
30 *Independent* (30 May 1989).
31 *Daily Telegraph* (31 May 1989).
32 *Independent* (30 May 1989).
33 *The Times* (11 June 1989).
34 *Independent* (30 May 1989).
35 *Annual Register, 1989*, p. 23.
36 *Independent* (31 May 1989).
37 *Observer* (4 June 1989).
38 *Independent* (31 May 1989).
39 Ibid. (12 June 1989).
40 House of Commons, 8 June 1989 (154/366).
41 *Independent* (9 June 1989).
42 *The Times* (14 June 1989).
43 Speech in Frankfurt, 9 May 1989. (Text by courtesy of Mr Heath's private office.)
44 'After Dark', Channel Four (10 June 1989).
45 House of Commons, 13 July 1989 (156/1176–9).
46 Ibid., 14 July 1989 (156/1265–7).
47 Ibid., 28 Nov 1989 (162/610–16).
48 Ibid.
49 *Independent* (19 Feb 1990).
50 *Guardian* (21 Feb 1990).
51 *The Times* (22 Feb 1990).
52 *Daily Telegraph* (22 Feb 1990).

53 Ibid.
54 *The Times* (22 Feb 1990).
55 *Independent* (21 Feb 1990).
56 *Sunday Times* (25 Feb 1990).
57 *Independent on Sunday* (25 Feb 1990).
58 *Sunday Times* (25 Feb 1990).
59 House of Commons, 28 June, 5 July 1961 (643/448–9, 1445–50).
60 Ibid., 6 Sept 1990 (177/751–3).
61 *The Times* (17 Sept 1990).
62 *Daily Star, Daily Express* (17 Sept 1990).
63 *The Times* (18 Sept 1990).
64 *Sunday Times* (23 Sept 1990).
65 Ibid. (7 Oct 1990).
66 *The Times* (13 Oct 1990).
67 *Independent* (12 Oct 1990).
68 *Daily Mail* (12 Oct 1990).
69 *Independent* (16 Oct 1990).
70 Ibid. (12 Oct 1990).
71 *Sunday Correspondent* (14 Oct 1990).
72 *Independent* (17 Oct 1990).
73 Ibid. (16 Oct 1990).
74 *Sunday Correspondent* (28 Oct 1990).
75 *Independent* (24 Oct 1990).
76 House of Commons, 25 Oct 1990 (178/498–9).
77 *The Times* (15 Nov 1990).
78 *Independent* (20 Dec 1990).
79 *Sunday Times* (23 June 1991).
80 *Independent* (22 Sept 1990).
81 House of Commons, 15 Jan 1991 (183/751–5).
82 Ibid.
83 'Question Time', BBC TV (31 Jan 1991); *The Times* (1 Feb 1991).
84 'On the Record', ITV (3 Feb 1991); *The Times* (4 Feb 1991).
85 'Question Time' (31 Jan 1991).
86 *Sunday Times* (3 March 1991).
87 'Question Time' (31 Jan 1991).
88 Ibid. (13 Feb 1992).

38 Grandfather of the House

1   *The Times* (15 March 1991).
2   House of Commons, 27 March 1991 (188/985–8).
3   *The Times* (26 Feb 1991).
4   Ibid. (28 June 1991).
5   *Independent on Sunday* (13 Oct 1991).
6   *The Times* (12 Oct 1991).
7   Ibid. (19 Oct 1991).
8   *Daily Telegraph* (20 Oct 1991).
9   *Sunday Times* (23 Oct 1991).
10 *Daily Mail* (19 Oct 1991).
11 *The Times* (19 Oct 1991).
12 *Sunday Times* (23 Oct 1991).
13 *Daily Mail* (19 Oct 1991).

14 Ibid.
15 *Sunday Times* (23 Oct 1991).
16 Ibid.
17 *Daily Mail* (20 June 1991).
18 *The Times* (21 June 1991).
19 House of Commons, 26 June 1991 (193/1026–31).
20 Ibid. (193/1007–17).
21 Ibid., 21 Nov 1991 (199/457–65).
22 *The Times* (22 Nov 1991).
23 Ibid. (25 Nov 1991).
24 Ibid. (8 Feb 1992).
25 *Independent* (25 March 1992).
26 *Guardian* (18 March 1992).
27 Adoption speech, Old Bexley and Sidcup, 19 March 1992. (Text by courtesy of Mr Heath's private office.)
28 *Independent* (25 March 1992).
29 Adoption speech, 19 March 1992.
30 Bexley, 30 March 1992.
31 *The Times* (11 April 1992).
32 Bexley, 30 March 1992.
33 *The Times* (28 April 1992).

Epilogue

1 Channel Four News (21 Sept 1992).
2 Ibid. (8 Dec 1992).
3 *Observer* (14 March 1993).
4 *Independent* (4 March 1993).
5 Ibid. (15 March 1993).

Bibliography

Leo Abse, *Private Member* (Macdonald, 1973).

Andrew Alexander and Alan Watkins, *The Making of the Prime Minister, 1970* (Jonathan Cape, 1970).

Stephen Ambrose, *Nixon: The Triumph of a Politician, 1962–72* (Simon & Schuster, New York, 1990).

Paul Arthur and Keith Jeffery, *Northern Ireland since 1968* (Blackwell, 1988).

Roger Bacon and Walter Eltis, *Britain's Economic Problem: Too Few Producers* (Macmillan, 1976).

George Ball, *The Discipline of Power* (Bodley Head, 1968).

John Barnes and David Nicholson (ed.), *The Empire at Bay: The Leo Amery Diaries, 1929–45* (Hutchinson, 1988).

Robert Behrens, *The Conservative Party from Heath to Thatcher* (Saxon House, 1980).

Nora Beloff, *The General Says No* (Penguin, 1963).

Tony Benn, *Out of the Wilderness: Diaries, 1963–7* (Hutchinson, 1987).

—, *Office Without Power: Diaries, 1968–72* (Hutchinson, 1988).

—, *Against the Tide: Diaries, 1973–6* (Hutchinson, 1989).

—, *Conflicts of Interest: Diaries, 1977–80* (Hutchinson, 1990).

Humphrey Berkeley, *Crossing the Floor* (Allen & Unwin, 1972).

Patrick Bishop and Eamonn Mallie, *The Provisional IRA* (Heinemann, 1987).

Tessa Blackstone and William Plowden, *Inside the Think Tank: Advising the Cabinet, 1971–83* (Heinemann, 1988).

Robert Blake, *A History of Rhodesia* (Eyre Methuen, 1977).

—, *The Conservative Party from Peel to Thatcher* (Methuen, 1985).

Robert Blake and John Patten (ed.), *The Conservative Opportunity* (Macmillan, 1976).

David Bleakley, *Faulkner* (Mowbrays, 1974).

Christopher Booker, *The Neophiliacs* (Collins, 1969).

Willy Brandt, *People and Politics: The Years 1960–75* (Collins, 1978).

—, *The Economic Consequences of Democracy* (Temple Smith, 1977).

Samuel Brittan, *Left or Right? The Bogus Dilemma* (Secker & Warburg, 1968).

Samuel Brittan and Peter Lilley, *The Delusion of Incomes Policy* (Temple Smith, 1977).

Jock Bruce-Gardyne, *Whatever Happened to the Quiet Revolution?* (Charles Knight, 1974).

Jock Bruce-Gardyne and Nigel Lawson, *The Power Game* (Macmillan, 1976).

David Butler and Anthony King, *The British General Election of 1964* (Macmillan, 1965).

—, *The British General Election of 1966* (Macmillan, 1966).

David Butler and Michael Pinto-Duchinsky, *The British General Election of 1970* (Macmillan, 1971).

· Bibliography ·

David Butler and Dennis Kavanagh, *The British General Election of February 1974* (Macmillan, 1974).
—, *The British General Election of October 1974* (Macmillan, 1975).
—, *The British General Election of 1979* (Macmillan, 1980).
—, *The British General Election of 1983* (Macmillan, 1984).
—, *The British General Election of 1987* (Macmillan, 1988).
David Butler and Uwe Kitzinger, *The 1975 Referendum* (Macmillan, 1976).
David Butler and Anne Sloman, *British Political Facts, 1900–79* (Macmillan, 1980).
Ronald Butt, *The Power of Parliament* (Constable, 1967).
Miriam Camps, *Britain and the European Community, 1955–63* (Princeton and Oxford University Press, 1964).
Lord Carrington, *Reflect on Things Past* (Collins, 1988).
Barbara Castle, *The Castle Diaries, 1964–70* (Weidenfeld & Nicolson, 1984).
—, *The Castle Diaries, 1974–6* (Weidenfeld & Nicolson, 1980).
Randolph S. Churchill, *The Fight for the Tory Leadership* (Mayflower, 1964).
Richard Clutterbuck, *Britain in Agony: The Growth of Political Violence* (Faber, 1978).
Michael Cockerell, *Live from Number Ten: The Inside Story of Prime Ministers and Television* (Faber, 1988).
Terry Coleman, *Movers and Shakers: Conversations with Uncommon Men* (Deutsch, 1987).
—, *Thatcher's Britain: A Journey Through the Promised Lands* (Bantam, 1987).
Patrick Cosgrave, *Margaret Thatcher: A Tory and Her Party* (Hutchinson, 1978).
—, *Margaret Thatcher: The First Term* (Bodley Head, 1985).
—, *Carrington: A Life and a Policy* (Dent, 1985).
—, *The Lives of Enoch Powell* (Bodley Head, 1989).
Julian Critchley, *Heseltine: The Unauthorised Biography* (Deutsch, 1987).
Susan Crosland, *Tony Crosland* (Jonathan Cape, 1982).
Richard Crossman, *The Diaries of a Cabinet Minister*, vols I–III, (Hamish Hamilton and Jonathan Cape, 1975–7).
Edmund Dell, *A Hard Pounding: Politics and Economic Crisis, 1974–6* (Allen & Unwin, 1981).
Piers Dixon, *Double Diploma: The Life of Sir Pierson Dixon* (Hutchinson, 1968).
Bernard Donoughue, *Prime Minister: The Conduct of Policy Under Harold Wilson and James Callaghan* (Jonathan Cape, 1987).
Anthony Eden, *Full Circle* (Cassell, 1960).
Marian Evans, *Ted Heath: A Family Portrait* (William Kimber, 1970).
Marcia Falkender, *Downing Street in Perspective* (Weidenfeld & Nicolson, 1983).
Brian Faulkner, *Memoirs of a Statesman* (Weidenfeld & Nicolson, 1978).
Stephen Fay and Hugo Young, *The Fall of Heath* (Sunday Times, 1976).
Nigel Fisher, *Iain Macleod* (Deutsch, 1973).
—, *The Tory Leaders: Their Struggle for Power* (Weidenfeld & Nicolson, 1977).
Andrew Gamble, *The Conservative Nation* (Routledge, 1974).
Ian Gilmour, *Inside-Right: A Study of Conservatism* (Hutchinson, 1977).
Robert C. Good, *UDI: The International Politics of the Rhodesian Rebellion* (Faber, 1973).
Philip Goodhart, *The 1922: The Story of the Conservative Backbenchers' Parliamentary Committee* (Macmillan, 1973).
Joe Gormley, *Battered Cherub* (Hamish Hamilton, 1982).
J. A. G. Griffith, *The Politics of the Judiciary* (Fontana, 1977).
Lord Hailsham, *The Door Wherein I Went* (Collins, 1975).
Roger Hadley and Stephen Hatch, *Social Welfare and the Failure of the State* (Allen & Unwin, 1981).
Morrison Halcrow, *Keith Joseph: A Single Mind* (Macmillan, 1989).
Kenneth Harris, *David Owen, Personally Speaking* (Weidenfeld & Nicolson, 1987).
—, *Margaret Thatcher* (Weidenfeld & Nicolson, 1988).
Ralph Harris and Brendon Sewill, *British Economic Policy, 1970–4: Two Views* (Institute of Economic Affairs, 1975).

Robert Harris, *Good and Faithful Servant: A Biography of Bernard Ingham* (Faber, 1991).
Ian Harvey, *To Fall Like Lucifer* (Sidgwick & Jackson, 1971).
Denis Healey, *The Time of My Life* (Michael Joseph, 1989).
Edward Heath, *Parliament and People* (Conservative Political Centre, 1960).
—, *Old World, New Horizons: Britain, Europe and the Atlantic Alliance* (Harvard, 1970).
—, *Sailing: A Course of My Life* (Sidgwick & Jackson, 1975).
—, *Music: A Joy for Life* (Sidgwick & Jackson, 1976).
—, *Travels: People and Places in My Life* (Sidgwick & Jackson, 1977).
—, *Carols: The Joy of Christmas* (Sidgwick & Jackson, 1977).
Peter Hennessy, *Cabinet* (Blackwell, 1986).
—, *Whitehall* (Secker & Warburg, 1989).
Peter Hennessy and Caroline Anstey, *Moneybags and Brains: The Anglo-American 'Special Relationship' since 1945* (Strathclyde/BBC, 1990).
Peter Hennessy and Anthony Seldon (ed.), *Ruling Performance: British Governments from Attlee to Thatcher* (Blackwell, 1985).
Judy Hillman and Peter Clarke, *Geoffrey Howe: A Quiet Revolutionary* (Weidenfeld & Nicolson, 1988).
History of 107 HAA Regiment RA, 1940–5.
Christopher Hollis, *The Oxford Union* (Evans Bros, 1965).
Martin Holmes, *Political Pressure and Economic Policy: British Government 1970–4* (Butterworth, 1982).
Lord Home of the Hirsel, *The Way the Wind Blows* (Collins, 1976).
Alistair Horne, *Macmillan: 1957–86* (Macmillan, 1989).
Douglas Hurd, *An End to Promises: Sketch of a Government, 1970–4* (Collins, 1979).
—, *Vote to Kill* (Collins, 1975).
George Hutchinson, *Edward Heath: A Personal and Political Biography* (Longman, 1970).
Robert Jackson, *Rebels and Whips* (Macmillan, 1968).
Keith Jeffery and Peter Hennessy, *States of Emergency: British Governments and Strike-breaking since 1919* (Routledge & Kegan Paul, 1983).
Roy Jenkins, *European Diary, 1977–81* (Collins, 1989).
—, *A Life at the Centre* (Macmillan, 1991).
Aubrey Jones, *The New Inflation: The Politics of Prices and Incomes* (Penguin, 1973).
Jack Jones, *Union Man* (Collins, 1986).
Keith Joseph, *Reversing the Trend: A Critical Reappraisal of Conservative Economic and Social Policies* (Barry Rose, 1975).
—, *Stranded in the Middle Ground* (Conservative Political Centre, 1976).
William Keegan, *Mrs Thatcher's Economic Experiment* (Allen Lane, 1984).
The Earl of Kilmuir, *Political Adventure: The Memoirs of the Earl of Kilmuir* (Weidenfeld & Nicolson, 1964).
Cecil King, *The Cecil King Diary, 1965–70* (Jonathan Cape, 1972).
—, *1970–4* (Jonathan Cape, 1975).
Henry Kissinger, *The White House Years* (Weidenfeld & Nicolson/Michael Joseph, 1979).
—, *Years of Upheaval* (Weidenfeld & Nicolson/M. Joseph, 1982).
Uwe Kitzinger, *Diplomacy and Persuasion: How Britain Joined the Common Market* (Thames & Hudson, 1973).
Margaret Laing, *Edward Heath, Prime Minister* (Sidgwick & Jackson, 1972).
Zig Layton-Henry (ed.), *Conservative Party Politics* (Macmillan, 1980).
J. J. Lee, *Ireland, 1912–85* (Cambridge University Press, 1989).
David Leigh, *The Wilson Plot: The Intelligence Services and the Discrediting of a Prime Minister, 1945–76* (Heinemann, 1988).
Russell Lewis, *Margaret Thatcher: A Personal and Political Biography* (Routledge, 1975).
T. F. Lindsay, *Parliament from the Press Gallery* (Macmillan, 1967).
John P. Mackintosh (ed.), *British Prime Ministers in the Twentieth Century*, vol. II (Weidenfeld & Nicolson, 1978).

Iain Macleod and Angus Maude (ed.), *One Nation: A Tory Approach to Social Problems* (Conservative Political Centre, 1950).
Harold Macmillan, *Riding the Storm, 1956–9* (Macmillan, 1971).
—, *At the End of the Day, 1961–3* (Macmillan, 1973).
James Margach, *The Abuse of Power: The War Between Downing Street and the Media* (W.H. Allen, 1978; Star, 1979).
David Marquand, *The Unprincipled Society: New Demands and Old Politics* (Jonathan Cape, 1987).
Barbara Marshall, *Willy Brandt* (Cardinal, 1990).
Reginald Maudling, *Memoirs* (Sidgwick & Jackson, 1978).
Christopher Mayhew, *Time to Explain* (Hutchinson, 1987).
Keith Middlemas, *Politics in Industrial Society: The Experience of the British System since 1911* (Deutsch, 1979).
—, *Industry, Unions and the Government: Twenty-One Years of NEDC* (Macmillan, 1983).
—, *Power, Competition and the State*, vol. II, *Threats to the Post-War Settlement: Britain 1961–74* (Macmillan, 1990).
—, *Power, Competition and the State*, vol. III, *The End of the Post-War Era: Britain since 1974* (Macmillan, 1991).
Charles Moore and Simon Heffer (ed.), *A Tory Seer: The Selected Journalism of T. E. Utley* (Hamish Hamilton, 1989).
Michael Moran, *The Politics of Industrial Relations* (Macmillan, 1977).
Janet Morgan (ed.), *The Backbench Diaries of Richard Crossman* (Hamish Hamilton and Jonathan Cape, 1981).
John Mortimer, *In Character* (Penguin, 1984).
H. G. Nicholas, *The British General Election of 1950* (Macmillan, 1951).
Joshua Nkomo, *The Story of My Life* (Methuen, 1984).
Philip Norton, *Conservative Dissidents: Dissent Within The Parliamentary Conservative Party, 1970–4* (Temple Smith, 1978).
Philip Norton and Arthur Aughey, *Conservatives and Conservatism* (Temple Smith, 1981).
Anthony Part, *The Making of a Mandarin* (Deutsch, 1990).
Ben Pimlott, *Harold Wilson* (HarperCollins, 1992).
Leo Pliatzky, *Getting and Spending: Public Expenditure, Employment and Inflation* (Blackwell, 1982).
Clive Ponting, *Breach of Promise: Labour in Power, 1964–70* (Hamish Hamilton, 1989).
Enoch Powell, *Reflections of a Statesman* (Bellew, 1991).
James Prior, *A Balance of Power* (Hamish Hamilton, 1986).
R. M. Punnett, *Front Bench Opposition* (Heinemann, 1973).
Francis Pym, *The Politics of Consent* (Hamish Hamilton, 1984).
Timothy Raison, *Tories and the Welfare State: A History of Conservative Social Policy since the Second World War* (Macmillan, 1990).
John Ramsden, *The Making of Conservative Party Policy: The Conservative Research Department since 1929* (Longman, 1980).
Charles Raw, *Slater Walker: An Investigation of a Financial Phenomenon* (Deutsch, 1977).
Peter Rawlinson, *A Price Too High: An Autobiography* (Weidenfeld & Nicolson, 1989).
John Redcliffe-Maud, *Experiences of an Optimist* (Hamish Hamilton, 1981).
Merlyn Rees, *Northern Ireland: A Personal Perspective* (Methuen, 1985).
Robert Rhodes James, *Ambitions and Realities, 1964–70* (Weidenfeld & Nicolson, 1972).
Nicholas Ridley, *'My Style of Government': The Thatcher Years* (Hutchinson, 1991).
Eric Roll, *Crowded Hours* (Faber, 1985).
Andrew Roth, *Heath and the Heathmen* (Routledge & Kegan Paul, 1972).
—, *Enoch Powell: Tory Tribune* (Macdonald, 1970).
Lord Rothschild, *Meditations of a Broomstick* (Collins, 1977).
—, *Random Variables* (Collins, 1984).

John Rousmaniere, *Fastnet Force 10* (Nautical Books, 1980).
Anthony Sampson, *Anatomy of Britain* (Hodder & Stoughton, 1962).
—, *Anatomy of Britain Today* (Hodder & Stoughton, 1965).
—, *The New Anatomy of Britain* (Hodder & Stoughton, 1971).
—, *The Changing Anatomy of Britain* (Hodder & Stoughton, 1982).
Drusilla Scott, *A. D. Lindsay: A Biography* (Blackwell, 1971).
Douglas Schoen, *Enoch Powell and the Powellites* (Macmillan, 1977).
Eric Silver, *Victor Feather, TUC* (Gollancz, 1973).
Alan Sked and Chris Cook, *Post-War Britain:A Political History* (Penguin, 1979).
David Spanier, *Europe, Our Europe* (Secker & Warburg, 1972).
David Steel, *Against Goliath* (Weidenfeld & Nicolson, 1989).
Michael Stewart, *The Jekyll and Hyde Years: Politics and Economic Policy since 1964* (Dent, 1977).
Robert Taylor, *The Fifth Estate: Britain's Unions in the Seventies* (Routledge, 1978).
Norman Tebbit, *Upwardly Mobile* (Weidenfeld & Nicolson, 1988).
Hugh Thomas, *The Suez Affair* (Weidenfeld & Nicolson, 1967).
Alan Thompson, *The Day Before Yesterday* (Panther/Sidgwick & Jackson, 1971).
The Times Guide to the House of Commons, 1966 (Times Books, 1966).
The Times Guide to the House of Commons, October 1974 (Times Books, 1974).
Ian Trethowan, *Split Screen* (Hamish Hamilton, 1984).
William Waldegrave, *The Binding of Leviathan: Conservatism and the Future* (Hamish Hamilton, 1978).
Peter Walker, *The Ascent of Britain* (Sidgwick & Jackson, 1977).
—, *Staying Power* (Bloomsbury, 1991).
David Walter, *The Oxford Union: Playground of Power* (Macdonald, 1984).
Nicholas Wapshott and George Brock, *Thatcher* (Futura, 1983).
Phillip Whitehead, *The Writing on the Wall: Britain in the Seventies* (Michael Joseph/Channel Four, 1985).
William Whitelaw, *The Whitelaw Memoirs* (Aurum Press, 1989).
David Widgery, *Health in Danger: The Crisis in the National Health Service* (Macmillan, 1979).
Eric Wigham, *Strikes and the Government, 1893–1974* (Macmillan, 1976).
Harold Wilson, *The Labour Government, 1964–70* (Weidenfeld & Nicolson/Michael Joseph, 1971).
—, *Final Term: The Labour Government, 1974–6* (Weidenfeld & Nicolson/Michael Joseph, 1979).
—, *The Governance of Britain* (Weidenfeld & Nicolson, 1976).
Elaine Windrich, *Britain and the Politics of Rhodesian Independence* (Croom Helm, 1978).
Peter Wright, *Spycatcher: The Candid Autobiography of a Senior Intelligence Officer* (Viking, 1987).
Hugo Young, *One of Us: A Biography of Margaret Thatcher* (Macmillan, 1989).

Official publications

Annual Register
Conservative Party Conference Reports
Hansard
Conservative Party Manifestos (1965–79)

Index

(*Note:* Individuals are normally listed under the name by which they are best known, or by which they were known at the time of their first significant appearance in the text.)

Abse, Leo, 295n
Acheson, Dean, 722
Adams, Gerry, 548
Adams, Vyvyan, 60
Adamson, Campbell, 419, 470, 474–5, 581; and Industrial Relations Act, 464, 608–9
Adenauer, Konrad, 116, 131, 313, 722, 775
Admiral's Cup, 250, 499, 500, 692, 693, 748
Aisher, Owen, 255
Aitken, Jonathan, 383, 506, 761, 766
Aitken, Sir Max, 254, 255, 339
Albany, 72, 136–8, 190–1, 248–9, 253, 256, 257, 275–6, 284, 292, 623, 694
Aldington, Lord, 105, 146, 182, 462, 648, 649, 674, 695, 714, 750; foul-weather friend of EH, 655–6
Alexander, Andrew, 195, 234, 235, 280n
Allen, Alf, 474
Allen, Sir Douglas (Lord Croham), 446, 470, 474, 476, 480–1, 581
Allen, Sir Hugh, 24, 38, 53
Alliance Party (Northern Ireland), 548
Alport, Cuthbert, 71, 76–7
Amadeus Quartet, 295
Amery, Julian, 22, 34, 36, 71, 663
Amery, Leo, 36
Amin, Idi, 338, 340, 393, 512
Andersen, Arthur, 695–6
Andrews, Jack, 432
Angry Brigade, 392, 411
Annenberg, Walter, 294
Annual Register, 427, 662

Arab–Israeli war (1973), 348–50, 557–8, 561, 563
Archer, Jeffrey, 390, 754
Armstrong, Robert, 24, 290, 295, 356, 433, 491, 493, 495, 616, 630, 760; relationship with EH, 488–9
Armstrong, Dr Thomas, 24, 290
Armstrong, Sir William, 58, 318, 323, 448, 462, 470, 572, 589; relationship with EH, 326, 446, 452, 490–2, 536; and incomes policy, 470, 471–2, 474, 531, 536; and miners' strike, 562, 566–7, 579; collapse, 589
Ashdown, Paddy, 780
ASLEF, 458, 571, 599
Asquith, H. H., 15, 16, 542
Astor, Lady, 36
Atkins, Humphrey, 103, 675, 710, 714n
Attlee, Clement, 50, 80, 273, 282, 362, 490, 801, 806
AUEW, 368, 464
Ayer, Sir Freddie, 752
Aziz, Tariq, 785

Bacon, Roger, 526
Baker, Kenneth, 630, 656, 668, 672, 674, 738, 752, 757, 758–9, 769, 795
Baldwin, Stanley, 206, 637, 679, 714, 716
Balfour, Arthur, 680, 716, 759
Ball, George, 129
Balliol College, 15–24, 28, 29, 34, 38, 752–3
Balniel, Lord, 213, 298
Barber, Anthony, 102, 148, 174, 213, 216, 225, 297, 299, 302, 353, 377, 402, 512, 519, 538, 611, 627, 649; Tory party chairman (1967–70), 215, 248, 269, 510; Chancellor of the Exchequer (1970–4), 218, 303–4, 309, 327–9, 369–71,

372, 374, 383–4, 387, 389, 407, 409, 419, 421, 445–6, 447, 448, 454–5, 458, 463, 474, 481, 485, 523–6, 529–31, 533, 539, 559, 566, 570, 571, 704; relationship with EH, 303–4, 523; and miners' strike, 580–4, 585, 593, 594
Barbirolli, Sir John, 41, 497
Barnes, Sir Denis, 475, 490
Bartlett, Vernon, 35, 36
Bax, Arnold, 137
BBC, 507, 607, 608
Beamish, Sir Tufton, 181
Beaverbrook, Lord, 57, 124
Beecham, Sir Thomas, 24
Beloff, Max, 27, 752
Beloff, Nora, 114, 123, 131, 181, 356
Bell, Ronald, 27, 31, 236
Beneš, Edouard, 42
Benn, Tony, 143, 449, 461, 575, 611, 637, 675, 688, 778, 791, 803; on EH, 199, 205, 337, 604, 674; and EEC, 247, 402, 403, 684, 800, 809; at DTI (1974–6), 371, 381, 453
Berger, Jean, 252, 254
Berkeley, Humphrey, 181, 518
Berlin, Sir Isaiah, 752
Bernstein, Leonard, 496
Berrill, Sir Kenneth, 324
Betjeman, Sir John, 390
Bevan, Aneurin, 67n, 76–7, 207, 328, 384
Bevin, Ernest, 67, 74
Bevins, Anthony, 774
Bevins, Reginald, 71
Bexley, 60–2, 64–8, 73, 75, 80–2, 85–6, 88–9, 93, 105–6, 161–2, 164–5, 209, 282–4, 520–1, 613–14, 653, 714, 736, 746–7, 755, 770, 804–6, 809, 811
Bexleyheath Observer, 66, 77, 82, 88
Biffen, John, 214, 247, 298, 440, 449–50, 482–3, 516, 519, 525, 532, 631, 657, 760, 806
Biggs-Davison, John, 23, 36, 95, 545

865

Birch, Nigel, 98
Birmingham Post, 170, 172
Blake, George, 135
Blake, Lord, 751-3
Blakenham, Lord, 116, 152, 160
Bleakley, David, 431
Blewett, Donald, 641
Bligh, Timothy, 64
Blunt, Anthony, 492-3
Boardman, Tom, 449, 566
Body, Richard, 480, 482, 517, 801
Bond, Alan, 254
Bonham Carter, Mark, 18-19
Booker, Christopher, 190
Boothroyd, Betty, 806-7
Boxer, Mark ('Marc'), 610
Boyd-Carpenter, John, 15, 213, 426
Boyle, Sir Edward, 93, 148, 161, 164, 180, 213; relationship with EH, 105, 237; and education, 236-7; and race relations, 242-3
Boyne, Harry, 180
Braddock, Bessie, 72
Brandt Commission, 691, 718-21, 779
Brandt, Willy, 342, 344, 345, 346, 397, 404, 442, 445, 559-60, 561, 571, 766; on EH, 357; and North-South Commission, 718-19
Braine, Bernard, 71, 733, 803
Bramall, Ashley, 20, 27, 29, 49, 60, 62, 65-8, 81-2, 106
Branson, Richard, 785
Brezhnev, Leonid, 346
Brightman, Sarah, 747
Brittan, Leon, 765
Brittan, Samuel, 224, 225, 523, 535, 639, 642
Broadstairs, 3-6, 9, 13, 21, 41, 51-2, 61, 64, 72, 80, 83, 182, 250-1, 255, 655, 665, 693, 694, 696, 743, 766; carol concerts, 24, 53, 249, 496, 694, 743, 748
Broakes, Nigel, 527
Bromley-Davenport, Sir Walter, 181
Brook, Sir Norman, 491
Brooke, Peter, 770, 806-7
Brookeborough, Lord, 542
Brown, Craig, 758-9
Brown, George, 160, 169, 224, 291, 353, 436; and Department of Economic Affairs, 149, 159, 230, 234, 314
Brown, Shipley, 63, 64, 67, 80, 167, 695
Bruce-Gardyne, Jock, 449-50, 482, 524, 724
Bryan, Sir Paul, 102, 673n
Buchanan-Smith, Alick, 707
Buchan-Hepburn, Patrick, 79, 82-3, 85, 89, 91
Budgen, Nicholas, 776, 801
Burgess, Guy, 135

Burnet, Alastair, 184, 308, 503, 505
Burns, Simon, 754
Bush, George, 778, 782, 785, 787, 788, 791
Bushe, Rosemary, 201, 630
Butler, David, 289, 612, 628, 638, 645, 650, 684, 754
Butler, R. A., 59, 76, 89, 91, 96, 97, 98, 119, 148, 151-2, 164, 167, 183, 294, 312, 634, 735, 757, 759, 795; and Tory leadership, 136, 139-41, 143-4, 146-7
Butt, Ronald, 517, 533, 706, 709

Cahill, Joe, 544
Callaghan, James, 603, 611, 628, 724, 734, 806; as Chancellor of the Exchequer (1964-7), 169, 173, 223, 224, 230; and Northern Ireland, 299, 425, 426; as Prime Minister (1976-9), 316, 320, 351, 493, 561, 574, 577, 709, 710, 711-13, 724, 738; and EEC, 362, 403, 561, 644, 683, 699, 702, 717
Campbell, Gordon, 213, 297, 379
Campbell, Jean, 312
Camps, Miriam, 131
Carlisle, John, 770
Carlisle, Mark, 728
Carr, Robert, 71, 182, 213, 242, 264, 302, 377, 392, 411, 474, 477, 485, 487, 489, 564, 570, 579, 585, 611, 655, 660, 669, 674, 682; and 'One Nation', 77-8; and industrial relations reform, 78, 220, 229-30; as Employment Secretary (1970-2), 297, 301, 328-9, 364-9, 370, 371, 408, 410, 413-14, 417-19, 421, 449, 457-60, 464-6, 539; as Home Secretary (1972-4), 340, 393, 395, 539; as Shadow Chancellor, 627, 628, 631, 641, 661-2, 668
Carrington, Lord, 213, 215, 216, 270, 283, 302, 339, 377, 401, 402, 408, 410, 485, 519, 632, 656, 661, 669; on EH, 283, 451, 487; as Defence Secretary (1970-4), 297, 332, 336, 338, 340-1, 347; and unemployment, 408, 410, 451; and Northern Ireland, 428, 430, 432; as Tory party chairman (1972-4), 482, 511, 520, 569, 571, 573, 577, 580, 585-6, 593, 603, 607, 611, 616, 617, 629, 649, 650; as Energy Secretary (1974), 579-80, 587, 588; under Mrs Thatcher, 682, 690, 706, 709, 714, 721, 731, 732
Carson, Ned, 83-4
Carter, Jimmy, 682n, 723n
Carvel, Robert, 87, 94, 443, 451, 715

Castle, Barbara, 293-4, 320, 384, 589, 603, 628; and industrial relations reform, 112, 228-9, 365, 367, 466; and EEC, 247, 687; on EH, 279, 294, 675, 687-8, 701-2
Castro, Fidel, 745, 781
Catherwood, Sir Fred, 770
CBI, 304, 309, 419, 463-4, 468-9, 470, 472-8, 483, 523, 525, 527, 532, 575, 581, 582, 591, 601, 608, 702
Centre for Policy Studies, 627, 682
Chadd, Christopher, 641
Chadd, George, 43, 44, 45, 54, 55, 641
Chamberlain, Austen, 714
Chamberlain, Neville, xv, 32, 33, 34, 35, 37, 42, 334, 407, 411, 447, 491; compared to EH, 312, 650, 782, 789
Chancellor, Alexander, 777, 803
Channel Tunnel, 380-1, 495, 739, 763
Channon, Paul, 202, 298, 434, 544, 661, 682
Chappell, Frank, 473, 582
Charlton, Michael, 436, 505
Chataway, Christopher, 275, 278, 331, 449-50, 453, 528
Chatham House school, 11-14
Chequers, 99, 126, 293-6, 338, 342, 428, 462, 472, 475, 487, 490, 494, 534, 585, 611, 623, 696, 749; redecoration of, 293-4
Chichester-Clark, James, 425, 426
Chichester-Clark, Robin, 182, 431
China, 257, 344, 347, 634-5, 691, 695, 733, 747, 773, 781-2
Chissell, Joan, 497
Chou Enlai, 634
Church of England, 9-10, 62, 258, 492
Church Times, 62-3, 65
Churchill, Anthony, 252, 254
Churchill, Randolph, 140
Churchill, Sir Winston, xvi, 30, 32, 65, 66, 67, 73, 79, 82, 85, 86, 88, 105, 131, 137, 235, 293, 411, 438, 474, 519, 612, 650, 679, 682n, 716, 775, 781, 806; and Europe, 74, 76, 362, 766, 769; and the Tory tradition, 100, 166, 199, 206, 267, 593, 671, 698, 726
Churchill, Winston, 162, 781, 783
Clapham, Sir Michael, 474, 582
Clark, George, 604
Clark, William, 174, 179, 682, 770
Clegg, Professor Hugh, 470
Clement, Dick, 505
Clutterbuck, Richard, 416
coal industry, 453, 483, 737; 1972 strike, 406, 412-20, 421-2; 1973-4 dispute, 561-3, 564-73, 574-5, 579-80, 582-97, 599-601, 607-8, 626

· *Index* ·

Cockerell, Michael, 613
Cockfield, Lord, 532, 765
Cole, G. D. H., 26
Coleman, Terry, 299, 726, 731;
  on EH, 283, 754–5
Common Agricultural Policy
  (CAP), 123, 125, 352, 355, 398,
  556, 559, 738
Commonwealth, British, 149,
  163, 336–40, 494; and EEC
  entry, 117–19, 122, 124–5,
  126–7, 134, 354, 360, 398; and
  immigration, 237–8, 241–4,
  273, 340, 392–3, 481, 512, 709;
  conferences: (1962), 126; (1971),
  338–9, 494; (1973), 339, 494,
  500
Compton, Sir Edmund, 426
Concorde, 318, 321–2, 380–1
Connally, John, 343 and n
Conservative party, xvi–xx,
  37–8, 59, 60, 71; conferences:
  (1953), 3, 86; (1960), 117;
  (1961), 124, 126; (1962), 124,
  126–7; (1963), 139–43; (1965),
  196–8, 199, 206; (1966), 212;
  (1967), 215; (1968), 224, 227,
  245, 261–2; (1969), 248, 273;
  (1970), 305, 309–12, 315, 338;
  (1971), 372–4, 379, 399–400,
  429; (1972), 393, 423, 448,
  473–4, 481; (1973), 512, 538–40,
  558–9; (1975), 697–8; (1976),
  704–6; (1978), 710–11; (1979),
  717; (1981), 729, 731–2; (1988),
  765–6; (1990), 783; (1991), 795;
  leadership contests: (1957), 97;
  (1963), 139–47; (1965), 175–85;
  (1975), 63–76; (1990), 786–7;
  Research Department, 59, 167,
  171–3, 218–19, 233, 264, 325,
  513, 629, 682; organisation,
  214–15, 509–12, 628–9; 1922
  Committee, 132, 216, 482–3,
  515–17, 656–8, 661–3, 664; and
  EEC, 75–6, 124, 126–7, 247–8,
  356, 396–7, 399–400, 405,
  437–41, 514, 684, 764–72;
  794–82; manifestos: *Putting
  Britain Right Ahead* (1965), 197,
  202–3, 204, 206, 208; *Action
  Not Words* (1966), 208, 220,
  231, 238, 243, 270; *Fair Deal at
  Work* (1968), 220, 228, 229; *A
  Better Tomorrow* (1970), 232,
  235, 267, 270–3, 310, 371, 539;
  Firm Action for a Fair Britain
  (Feb 1974), 600–3; *Putting
  Britain First* (Oct 1974), 638–9,
  640–2; *The Right Approach*
  (1976), 704–5, 706; *The Right
  Approach to the Economy* (1977),
  706, 711; *The Conservative
  Manifesto, 1979*, 713
Constantine, Sir Learie, 246
Cooper, Sir Frank, 550
Cooper, Jack, 474
Corfield, Frederick, 331–2, 449

Cosgrave, Liam, 550, 553
Cosgrave, Patrick, 240, 373, 480;
  on EH, 373, 515, 659
counter-inflation policy (1972–4):
  Stage One, 479–83; Stage
  Two, 483, 522, 531–4, 535–6;
  Stage Three, 535–9, 561–2,
  564–73, 580–6, 588–9, 590–2,
  596–7, 599–600, 601, 612, 626
Cousins, Frank, 110, 191, 304
Couve de Murville, Maurice,
  126, 128, 130
CPRS (Central Policy Review
  Staff), 222, 317–25, 447, 485,
  489, 493, 513, 568, 735
Craig, William, 430, 431, 542,
  546–7, 553–4, 615
Cripps, Stafford, 73
Critchley, Julian, 514, 667
Cromer, Lord, 275
Crosland, Anthony, 36, 236,
  379, 387, 609, 628, 643
Crossman, Richard, 26, 34, 207,
  223, 225, 232, 378, 381, 384;
  on EH, 118, 136, 192, 193, 199,
  209, 260, 263–4, 265–6, 281
Crouch, David, 415
Crowther-Hunt, Lord, 617
Cuba crisis (1962), 734, 780, 783,
  791
Cumming, Nigel, 641
Cummings (cartoonist), 148

Daily Express, 87, 96, 111, 124,
  164, 285, 593, 648, 672, 693,
  716, 781
Daily Mail, 178, 182, 190, 276,
  286, 607–8, 610, 613, 642, 648,
  711, 798
Daily Mirror, 81, 162, 183, 210,
  291, 595, 600
Daily Sketch, 182, 184
Daily Star, 781
Daily Telegraph, 136, 145, 175,
  427, 540, 593, 670–1, 724, 760,
  776, 796; on EH, 133, 180, 198,
  208, 371, 715, 769, 775; EH in,
  670
Daily Worker, 183
Dalton, Hugh, 28, 29, 31, 466
Daly, Lawrence, 414, 570
Dalyell, Tam, 791
Davies, John, 354, 377, 706; at
  DTI (1970–2), 149, 303–5,
  309–10, 314, 331, 371, 415,
  417–18, 421, 442–3, 447–9, 453
Day, Robin, 142, 217, 266, 505,
  590, 703, 752, 775
Deedes, William, 60, 71, 504
de Gaulle, General: and British
  application to join EEC, xvii,
  120, 123–34, 151, 154, 246–7,
  335, 341, 352, 354, 358–9, 362,
  363, 396–7; role model, 313,
  454, 495, 504, 775
de Havilland, Olivia, 295
Delors, Jacques, 764–5, 768
Democratic Unionist Party (DUP),

  425n, 546, 548, 554, 615
Deng Xiaoping, 634, 773, 781–2
Denman, Joy, 182, 743
Denman, Teddy, 182, 743
Denning, Lord, 459–61
'Desert Island Discs', 748, 764
devaluation (1967), 224–6
Devlin, Bernadette, 425n, 429–30
devolution, 631, 707–8, 804
Dilhorne, Lord, 213
Dilks, David, 486
Dines, Edward, 60–1
Disraeli, Benjamin, 77, 79, 151,
  271, 300, 494, 751, 759
Dixon, Sir Pierson, 119–20, 125,
  126, 128, 137
Donaldson, Sir John, 457,
  459–60, 461–2, 465
Donoughue, Bernard, 324
Donovan, Lord, 220
Douglas, James, 172, 279
Douglas-Home, Sir Alec: *see*
  Home, Lord
Douglas-Home, Charles, 725
Downing Street: redecoration,
  290, 292–3; entertaining,
  294–6, 494–5
Drumalbyn, Lord, 149
Du Cann, Edward, 149, 161, 298,
  303, 450, 519, 528, 624, 730; re-
  lationship with EH, 149, 162, 483,
  516; Tory party chairman, 175,
  190, 201, 214–15, 510, 629; chairman of 1922 Committee, 482–3,
  515, 516, 524, 644, 656–8, 659,
  661, 662–3, 666; leadership
  contender, 658, 660, 663, 666–7
Dutschke, Rudi, 392

Easton, Dr Jeffrey, 785 and n
Easton, Marian: *see* Heath,
  Marian
Eccles, Lord, 388–91
Economist, The, 91, 96, 110, 116,
  118, 119, 123, 148, 270, 280,
  301, 305, 361, 364, 407, 443,
  473, 503, 530, 564, 569, 572,
  592, 600, 604, 615, 627, 628,
  632–3, 642, 660, 661, 662; on
  EH, 109, 126, 133, 144–5, 160,
  178, 184–5, 194, 197, 204, 226,
  246, 260, 263, 265, 274, 279,
  309, 466–7, 481, 566, 587, 591,
  645, 652, 663, 665; on incomes
  policy, 309, 470–2, 478, 532,
  534, 536–7, 538; on growth,
  523–5
Eden, Anthony, 32, 34, 49, 61,
  100, 103, 113, 267, 294, 503,
  609, 698, 716, 726, 806; and
  EEC, 74, 76, 124, 362; as
  Prime Minister (1955–7), 88–9,
  90–3, 96–7, 334, 447, 519; on
  EH, 89, 91
Eden, Sir John, 304–5, 331, 374,
  448–9
education, 18–19, 66, 235–7,
  387–9, 736, 756–7, 758–9

EETPU, 473, 483, 582
Elizabeth II, 90, 138, 146, 284, 415, 556, 617, 618, 625, 806; and EH, 492, 493–4
Elliot, Walter, 77
Eltis, Walter, 526
Emery, Peter, 174, 449, 579
Erhard, Ludwig, 132, 313
European Community Youth Orchestra, 691, 717, 747
European Economic Community (EEC), 74–6; British application: (1962–3), 112, 113, 116–33; (1967), 246–7; (1970–2), 299–300, 334, 336, 352–63, 396–405; British entry (1973), 436–42, 555–6; British membership, 345, 348–51, 555–61, 578, 654, 699, 717–18, 738–9, 764–92, 794–802; referendum (1975), 654, 683–8, 764; economic and monetary union, 557, 766, 767–8; summits: Paris (1972), 442, 557, 766; Copenhagen (1973), 559–60; Dublin (1979), 717–18; Maastricht (1991), 800–2; Edinburgh (1992), 809
European Free Trade Association (EFTA), 113, 116, 117–19, 122, 124, 134, 149, 162, 169, 191, 335, 446, 796
European Monetary System (EMS), 699, 717, 730, 738–9, 768–9, 794, 795, 798, 808–9
European Parliament, 556, 557, 686; elections: (1979), 717; (1989), 767, 770–2
Evans, Dame Edith, 692
Evening Standard (London), 87, 135n, 196, 198, 259, 280, 312, 383–4, 443–4, 485, 487–8, 504, 506, 657
Exchange Rate Mechanism (ERM): *see* European Monetary System
Ezra, Derek, 412–13, 457, 564–5

Falkender, Lady: *see* Williams, Marcia
Falklands war (1982), 732–5, 778
Fastnet race, 252–3, 499, 500; (1979), 692, 748
Faulds, Andrew, 521
Faulkner, Brian, 426–33, 542, 546, 548–52, 553, 615; on EH, 426, 428, 431–2
Feather, Victor, 367, 368, 414, 419, 461, 463, 470, 471–2, 474–5, 477, 491, 581, 583; and tripartite talks, 470–2, 474–5, 477; relationship with EH, 111, 474–5, 582
Figgures, Sir Frank, 470, 531
Financial Times, 114, 116, 244–5, 262–3, 433, 516, 748
Fisher, Nigel, 71, 181, 216, 270, 516–17, 657–8, 660, 662–3, 667;

on EH, 517, 658
Fitt, Gerry, 425n, 427, 546, 549, 553–4
Fitzgerald, Garret, 550
Foot, Dingle, 15
Foot, John, 15
Foot, Michael, 438, 465–6, 478, 611, 626, 628, 637, 687, 723, 752, 803; on EH, 154
Forbes, Bryan, 505
Ford, Gerald, 642
Fort, Richard, 77
Fortune, 312, 313
Fowler, Norman, 682
Fox, Uffa, 499
Franco, General, 36
Franks Committee, 734–5
Fraser, Lady Antonia, 752
Fraser, Hugh, 15, 20, 40, 524, 670, 674
Fraser, Sir Michael, 59, 172, 211, 215, 218, 248, 513, 573, 593, 629
Friedman, Milton, 723, 732
Frost, David, 799
Frost, Derek, 744
Fulton, Lord, 18, 22, 38
Fyfe, Alan, 29

Gaitskell, Hugh, 124, 126–7, 180, 209, 266, 335
Galbraith, J. K., 727
Gale, George, 274–5, 279, 477, 648
Galtieri, General, 732–4, 780
Gandhi, Indira, 344
Gardiner, Lord, 426
Garland, Nicholas, 771, 784
General Elections: (1950), 65–8; (1951), 80–2; (1955), 88–9; (1959), 106–7; (1964), 160–5; (1966), 208–11; (1970), 269–86; (Feb 1974), 593–615; (Oct 1974), 643–53; (1979), 712–14; (1983), 736; (1987), 754–5; (1992), 803–6
Giles, Rear-Admiral Morgan, 251
Gilmour, Sir Ian, 181, 656, 721, 803; in 1970–4 Government, 298, 336, 579; and Conservative Research Department, 629, 633–4, 638; and Mrs Thatcher, 669, 682, 728–9, 737, 741, 758
Giscard d'Estaing, Valéry, 360, 561
Gladstone, W. E., 15, 138, 255, 271, 273, 424, 494, 542
Goad, James, 464
Godber, Joseph, 148, 213, 298, 336, 386
Goebbels, Josef, 31
Goering, Hermann, 48
Goodhart, Sir Philip, 658
Goodman, Arnold, 18, 339, 752
Gorbachev, Mikhail, 772–3
Gordon Walker, Patrick, 26, 33–4, 169–70, 236

Gormley, Joe, 412–14, 418–19, 562–3, 564–70, 582–3, 588, 590, 592, 593, 596, 599
Gorton, John, 254, 255
Graham, Kay, 718
Greater London Council (GLC), 159, 217, 495; abolition, 742, 794
Green party, 771, 778
Greene, Sir Sidney, 474, 580–1, 584
Greenhill, Sir Denis, 338
Greenwood, Anthony, 15
Griffith, J. A. G., 461, 465
Griffiths, James, 87
Grigg, John, 180, 237n
Grimond, Jo, 617
Gromyko, Andrei, 346
Grosvenor, Peter, 278
Guardian, 118, 184, 356, 521, 598, 642, 648, 726, 731, 774–5; on EH, 168–9, 180, 366, 502, 706, 754–5, 803
Guinness, Jonathan, 393
Gulf crisis (1990–1), 777–92
Gunter, Ray, 366

Haig, Alexander, 733
Hailsham, Lord (Quintin Hogg), 34, 135, 148, 157–9, 213, 220, 237, 243, 264, 309, 511, 656, 669, 682, 706, 752; and Tory leadership, 136, 139–40, 143, 177, 660; Lord Chancellor (1970–4), 297, 302, 354, 377, 485
Haines, Joe, 290–1, 488, 490
Haley, Sir William, 144
Halifax, Lord, 32, 715
Hall, John, 174
Hall, Lord, 331
Hall, Sir Robert, 222
Hallstein, Professor, 118
Harcourt, Sir William, 171
Hare, John: *see* Blakenham, Lord
Harlech, Lord, 213
Harman, Nicholas, 505
Harrington, Major William, 44–5
Harris, Kenneth, 12, 101, 195, 290, 296, 305
Harris, Robert, 767, 781
Harvey, Ian, 27, 31, 35, 55, 71
Haydon, Robin, 489
Hayek, Friedrich von, 732
Hayhoe, Barney, 758
Healey, Denis, 34, 299, 575, 603, 609, 749, 779, 790–1, 803; as Chancellor (1974–9), 627, 628, 644, 662, 668, 701
Heath, Doris (stepmother), 81, 251
Heath, Edith (née Pantony – mother), 5–10, 12–14, 23, 40, 51–4, 72, 259; death, 80–1
Heath, Edward
family and childhood: 3–14; influence of mother, 5, 6–8, 12, 80–1; influence of father, 5–6, 12; early awareness of Europe, 3–4; schooldays, 6,

Heath, Edward – *cont.*
9, 11–14; early political ideas,
12–13
at Oxford (1935–9): Balliol,
15–16, 18, 22–3; influence of
A. D. Lindsay, 22–3;
Oxford Union, 25–30, 31–2,
33; President of the Union,
35–7; visits Nazi Germany,
30–1; visits Spain, 32–3; opposition to fascism, 31–2, 33–4, 37;
Conservatism, 37–8
war service (1939–45): visits
USA, 40–2; in Royal
Artillery, 42–9; Adjutant,
43–6; in liberation of
Europe, 45–7; in occupied
Germany, 47–9; European
vision, 48–9
early career (1945–50): in Civil
Service, 56–9; adopted for
Bexley, 60–1; prospective
candidate, 61–2, 64–8; on
Church Times, 62–3; with
Brown, Shipley, 63, 80; on
Conservatism, 61–2, 66–7;
wins Bexley, 67–8
*rising through the ranks (1950–
65)*: nurses Bexley, 73, 85–6,
105–6, 162; re-elected, 81–2,
88–9, 106, 164–5; maiden
speech, 73–6; European
vision, 74–6; member of
'One Nation', 76–9; Whip
(1951–5), 79, 82–5; Chief
Whip (1955–9), 89, 90–104;
mother's death, 80–1;
travels, 87–8; and Suez
crisis, 90, 92–7; and Eden,
91, 93; influence of
Macmillan, 97–100, 141,
146–7; Minister of Labour
(1959–60), 108–12; averts rail
strike, 109–10; and trade
union reform, 110–12; Lord
Privy Seal (1960–3), 112–36;
appointed, 112–15; European
vision, 113–15; leads EEC
negotiations, 116–33;
nicknamed 'Grocer', 125n;
and security scandals, 135–6;
leadership contender, 136,
139–42, 144–5, 164; apostle
of 'modernisation', 134–5,
147, 150–1, 158–60, 162–4,
170–1; and 1963 leadership
contest, 139–47; and Home,
143–4, 146–7, 148–9;
President of the Board of
Trade (1963–4), 147–59;
abolition of retail price
maintenance, 150–7; regional
policy, 157–9; and Wilson,
149–50, 160, 162–4, 169–70,
180; in 1964 election, 160–4;
in opposition (1964–5),
167–74; leads policy review,
167, 170–3; 1965 leadership

contest, 175–82; compared
with Maudling, 177–80, 182;
wins Tory leadership, 182–5
*Leader of the Opposition (1965–
70)*: 189–288; aides, 190,
201–2, 233, 248–9; in
Parliament, 191–3, 260–1,
263; duel with Wilson,
191–3, 204–5, 209, 223–4,
260–1, 274–5; and party
conferences, 196–200, 261–3;
political vision, 194–5, 259,
263, 283; lack of political
philosophy, 193–5, 233–5,
239, 266–7; inability to
communicate, 198, 206,
262–3; low popularity
rating, 198–9, 206, 217,
258–9, 268–9, 276;
relationship with Tory
party, 196–201, 206, 216,
244–6; Shadow Cabinet,
202, 213–14, 215–16; and
Macleod, 216, 231–2;
relations with other
colleagues, 216, 258–9;
policy making, 202–3,
212–13, 218–23, 228–38; and
Rhodesia, 204–5; in 1966
election, 208–11; and party
organisation, 214–15; and
devaluation, 224–5; defence,
226–8; machinery of
government, 221–2; trade
union reform, 218–21,
228–30; incomes policy,
230–4, 272; industrial policy,
234–5, 272; health, 235;
education, 235–7; immig-
ration, 237–8, 241–6, 273; and
Powell, 239–48, 264, 277;
sacks Powell, 243–4; com-
mitment to EEC, 246–8, 273;
Selsdon Park conference,
264–6, 268; in 1970 election,
269–86; prices, 281–2; wins
election, 283–6, 289–90
Prime Minister (1970–4): 289–
619; enjoyment of office,
289–90, 294–6, 484;
redecorates Downing Street
and Chequers, 292–6, 494;
official entertaining, 294–5,
494–5; staff, 290–1, 488–90;
style of government,
484–95; appoints Cabinet,
296–8; loss of Macleod,
302–3; in Parliament, 300,
360, 403–4, 433, 439,
479–80, 502–3, 587, 591; on
television, 308–9, 420–1,
436–7, 459, 467, 472–3,
505–6, 572–3, 587, 595–6,
612–13; declares 'quiet
revolution', 310–12, 313–14;
hijacking incident, 307–8,
484; relations with Barber,
303–4, 523; Home, 335–6;

Mrs Thatcher, 385–7;
Maudling, 391, 394–5; other
colleagues, 376–8, 484–8;
party conferences, 309–12,
315, 338, 372–3, 473–4, 512,
539–40, 558–9; and Civil
Service, 490–2; and William
Armstrong, 490–1, 589;
reform of Whitehall, 314–27;
'Think Tank', 317–23;
security services, 492–3;
relations with the Queen,
493–4; press relations, 290–1,
503–8; press conferences,
504–5; and BBC, 506;
inability to communicate,
501–8; relations with Tory
party, 509–21; party
organisation, 519–20; use of
honours, 519–20; opinion
polls, 332–3, 466, 483, 512,
534, 537, 575, 578, 586, 593,
598, 605–6, 610–12, 613; *and
Northern Ireland*: 299, 406,
423–35, 542–54; abolition of
Stormont, 430–5;
Sunningdale conference,
550–3; *and EEC entry*: 299–
300, 334–5, 336, 352–63;
persuades Pompidou to lift
veto, 358–60; wins House of
Commons vote, 396–405;
signs Accession Treaty, 436;
carries legislation, 437–41;
'Fanfare for Europe', 555–6;
Copenhagen summit,
557–60; *foreign policy*: 334–51;
Commonwealth relations,
337–40; sale of arms to
South Africa, 299, 337–8;
Rhodesia, 339–40; 'East of
Suez', 340–1; Ugandan
Asians, 340, 393–4; nuclear
weapons, 341; Anglo-
American relations, 341–6,
348–51; USSR, 346–7;
China, 347; Malta, 347;
Middle East War, 348–50,
557–8; *and Industrial Relations
Act*: 301–2, 308–9, 311,
329–31, 364–9, 457–67,
601–2; *and inflation*: 311,
328–30, 369–70, 468–82;
rejects incomes policy,
329–30, 469–74; counter-
inflation policy, 479–80,
531–9, 562–9, 580–6, 589–91,
596–602, 606, 616; and
Rolls-Royce nationalisation:
331–2; Upper Clyde
shipbuilders, 371, 442–4; and
unemployment, 374, 407–12,
443–5, 455, 483; 1972
miners' strike, 412–22;
Industry Act (1972), 446–54;
floats sterling, 454–5;
growth policy, 522–31;
criticises industry, 526–7,

Heath, Edward – *cont.*
528; *and TUC*: 369, 421,
444–5, 457, 533, 580–5,
590–1; and CBI, 370;
tripartite talks, 468, 470,
472–9, 483; *social policy*:
housing, 300, 378–9; local
government reorganisation,
379–80; NHS, 381–5;
education, 387–9; museum
charges, 389–91; *and 1973–4
miners' dispute*: 561–73,
574–6, 579–97; and oil crisis,
563, 572–6, 594–7;
reluctance to hold General
Election, 575–9, 585–7, 595;
calls General Election,
593–7; in Feb 1974 election,
598–9, 603–16; appeals for
national unity, 602–3, 605;
holds coalition talks with
Liberals, 616–18; resigns, 618
*Leader of the Opposition
(1974–5)*: 623–76; loss of
office, 623–4; leadership
criticised, 624–6, 654–66;
and Shadow Cabinet, 627–8,
661–2; and party
organisation, 628–9; staff,
628–9; resignation honours,
629; policy review, 630–4,
637–8; 'national unity'
campaign, 633–4, 636–41,
645, 647–51; visits China,
634–5; boat lost, 641–2; in
Oct 1974 election, 643–53;
refuses to resign leadership,
649, 654–9; promotes Mrs
Thatcher, 661–2; house
bombed, 665; leadership
challenged, 663–4, 666–74;
inept campaign, 668–9,
672–3; defeated, 674;
1975–93: 679–811; declines to
endorse Mrs Thatcher,
675–6, 679–81, 683, 688–90,
697–8, 702–5, 708–15,
716–17; loyal to
Conservative party, 679–80,
697–8, 703–6, 709, 736;
defends his record, 683, 700,
705; in EEC referendum
(1975), 683–8; travels, 690–1,
708, 717; and China, 690–1,
717, 733, 773; relations with
former colleagues, 690, 706,
729, 737–8, 741–2; on
Britain's problems, 699–701;
urges full participation in
EEC, 699, 717–18, 738–9,
764–72, 794, 796–802,
808–9; support Labour
Government's incomes
policy, 701–2, 710–11;
supports devolution, 707–8;
in 1979 election, 712–13;
hopes for office, 713–14;
refuses Washington

Embassy, 714–15; and EEC
elections 717, 770–2; and
Brandt Commission,
718–22; criticises Mrs
Thatcher, 718, 761–2, 765–9,
770, 796–8, 799, 800–1;
denounced by Thatcherites,
723, 727–8, 730–1, 737–8,
769, 781–2; and SDP, 725–7,
730–1; condemns
unemployment, 708, 713,
723–4, 727, 735, 739, 763;
condemns monetarism,
723–4, 727, 732, 736, 739,
757; condemns Thatcher
Government, 723–4, 727–30,
735–6, 738–42, 755–64; and
Falklands war (1982), 732–5;
upholds 'One Nation'
Toryism, 735–6, 740, 761,
764; in 1983 election, 736;
criticises loss of
manufacturing, 739–40;
condemns privatisation,
740–1; and Bexley, 746–7,
754–5, 803–6, 809, 811;
contests Oxford
Chancellorship, 751–3; in
1987 election, 754–5;
condemns poll tax, 756, 758;
condemns education reforms,
756–7, 759; compared
with Mrs Thatcher,
762–3, 770–1, 776; and collapse
of Soviet empire, 772–4;
celebrates forty years in
Parliament, 774–7; and Gulf
crisis (1991–2), 777–86,
787–92; defends Saddam
Hussein, 780–2, 787–8;
brings out British hos-
tages, 783–6; opposes war,
787–92; welcomes fall
of Mrs Thatcher, 786–7,
793–4; supports Major,
793–5, 802, 804, 808–9;
opposes EEC referendum,
800–1, 809–10; supports Maastricht Treaty, 802, 808–10;
in 1992 election, 803–6;
Father of the House, 803,
806–7; accepts Garter, 806
character: self-sufficiency, 7–9,
10–11, 20–2, 44, 52, 55–6,
80–1, 83–4, 101–2, 172,
200–1, 217, 249, 258–60, 269,
285–6, 290, 342, 490, 576–7,
690, 742, 745–6, 750; self-
control, 45, 130, 276, 467,
570, 652; selfishness, 7,
10–11, 52, 654–5; ambition,
13, 16, 51, 58, 138, 141, 143,
146, 176, 492, 495; 'charm',
21, 29, 35–6, 94, 191, 487;
friendliness, 21, 29, 58, 61,
83, 94, 101, 121, 190, 487;
coldness, 189, 201, 216, 258,
502, 510, 513, 515–16, 667,

669; rudeness, 7, 83, 101,
102, 184, 502, 516, 667, 762;
determination, 11, 35, 64,
114, 130, 151–4, 155–6, 178,
180, 184–5; aggression,
168–9, 178, 184, 265–6;
stubbornness, 153–4, 155–6,
259, 612–13, 623, 654–6, 670,
680–1, 742; patience, 108,
109, 121, 476–8, 566, 579,
586; pride, 649, 655, 680–1,
697, 703–4, 715, 742;
courage, 269, 283, 433, 467,
570, 623, 641; patriotism,
225–6, 334–6, 381, 478, 497,
499, 654; stamina, 43, 123,
476; arrogance, 153, 155–6,
216, 286, 289–90, 510, 655;
autocracy, 487, 502, 515,
517, 742, 762–3; insecurity,
201, 286, 294; *organisational
ability*: 21, 36, 43–4, 47,
57–8, 83–4, 91, 120, 159,
184–5; leadership qualities,
14, 45, 47, 120–1, 173–4, 259,
485–7; mastery of detail, 44,
99, 120–1, 132–3, 161, 167,
173–4, 184–5, 190, 194, 485;
working methods, 63, 83,
102, 120–1, 149, 171–2, 173–4,
185, 201–2, 215–16, 217,
248–9, 261, 248–9, 290–1,
357–8, 484–9, 490, 507–8,
746; political skill, 83, 90–1,
92, 94–7, 101, 109, 114, 120,
131; loss of political skill,
103–4, 259, 260, 484, 491–2,
503, 513, 517–20;
bureaucratic mentality, 57,
155, 326, 452, 490–2, 502;
wishful thinking, 154,
222–3, 313, 464–5, 713–14;
sense of humour, 29, 52, 54,
58, 101, 185, 257–8, 275, 285,
305, 487, 488, 570, 775;
inability to communicate,
115, 185, 198, 200, 260,
262–3, 274, 373–4, 484,
501–9, 512, 540, 701;
speaking style, 27–8, 30, 35,
103, 118, 126, 133, 168–9,
191–3, 194, 197–8, 260–1; on
television, 160–2, 209, 278,
505–7; image, 178, 180,
183–5, 189–91, 260, 266–7,
274, 279, 501–2, 609;
classlessness, 18–19, 41–2, 60,
72, 144, 160, 171, 177–8, 180,
183–4, 190, 199–200, 377;
relations with family: 52, 696;
friends, 21, 44, 102, 105, 136,
236, 249, 256–8, 746, 750–1;
girlfriends, 53–5; attitude to
women, 53–6, 256–6, 385–6,
489–90; relations with
colleagues, 258–9, 487;
relations with journalists,
87, 503–4, 507; religion, 7,

Heath, Edward – *cont.*
10, 258–9; health, 104, 576–7, 658–9, 724–5; money, 255–6, 694–5, 749; homes: Artillery Mansions, Petty France, 72; Albany, 136–8; Wilton Street, 635; Salisbury, 743–6; collection of paintings, 137, 190, 744; bestselling books, 692–4; failure to write memoirs, 749–50; birthdays and anniversaries, 696–7, 750–1, 774–6, 809
music: early experiences, 9–10; at school, 14; at Oxford, 16–18, 23–5; record collection, 17; musical taste, 24–5, 191; considers musical career, 38; Broadstairs carol concerts, 24, 53, 249, 496, 743; in USA, 41; in the war, 44–5; principal relaxation, 249, 496; at Downing Street and Chequers, 294–6, 405, 495–6; conducts LSO, 496–8, 635, 691; other conducting, 691–2, 717, 747–8; 'Desert Island Discs', 748
sailing: takes up, 250–1; buys first *Morning Cloud*, 251; crew, 252; wins Sydney–Hobart race (1969), 253–5, 263; cost, 255, 500–1; as Prime Minister, 498–501; loss of *Morning Cloud*, 641–2; in 1979 Fastnet race, 692, 748; gives up, 748–9
Heath, John, (brother), 6, 9, 42, 51, 53; death, 696
Heath, Marian (sister-in-law), 51–4, 81; on EH, 52–4, 64, 72
Heath, Mary (stepmother), 696, 743
Heath, William (father), 5–6, 8, 10, 11, 12–14, 23, 40, 51, 72, 81, 743; death, 696
Heathcote Amory, Derek, 85, 87, 112, 303
Heffer, Eric, 500
Hello!, 750
Hennessy, Peter, 315–16, 322, 326–7, 486, 490
Heron, Conrad, 584–5
Heseltine, Michael, 36, 202, 314, 316, 379, 673, 682, 737, 741, 752, 754, 758, 767, 774, 777, 793, 810; in 1970–4 Government, 298, 449; challenges Mrs Thatcher, 664, 786–7
Hess, Rudolf, 48
Higgins, Terence, 298
Hill, Lord, 507
Himmler, Heinrich, 31
Hitler, Adolf, 31, 33, 34, 324, 733, 781, 782, 783, 789
Hoare, Samuel, 21, 113
Hoffman, Abe, 394

Hogg, Quintin: *see* Hailsham, Lord
Hollingworth, Clare, 257
Home, Lady, 175, 292
Home, Lord (Sir Alec Douglas-Home), xvi, 190, 205, 208, 212, 213, 257, 377, 385, 485, 487, 609, 628, 629, 655, 660, 661, 662–3, 664, 669, 716, 751, 775, 786; as Foreign Secretary (1960–3), 112–13, 116, 118, 135, 779; (1970–4), 296–7, 299, 335–6, 337–40, 347, 348, 351, 354, 399–400, 401, 402, 428, 432, 436, 439, 492, 512, 550, 558, 560; and Tory leadership, 139–47, 166–8, 170, 172–3, 174–7, 179, 181, 199–200, 201, 210, 239, 269, 679; Prime Minister (1963–4), 148–9, 152, 156, 159–61, 163–4, 204, 334, 451, 519
Honecker, Erich, 781–2
Hordern, Peter, 524
Hornsby-Smith, Dame Patricia, 521
Horsbrugh, Florence, 385
Hosking, Barbara, 290, 489–90
Hoskyns, John, 222
housing, 66, 208, 378–9, 631, 634, 638; sale of council houses, 300, 379, 631; mortage subsidies, 631, 642–3
Howard, John, 141
Howe, Sir Geoffrey, 627, 663, 668, 674–5, 682, 704, 706, 710–11, 760, 777, 802; in 1970–4 Government, 298, 299, 438, 459–60, 536; as Chancellor (1979–83), 717, 722, 731–2, 735; as Foreign Secretary (1983–9), 739, 766–8; topples Mrs Thatcher, 786
Howell, David, 190, 195, 248, 270, 283, 706; and reform of Whitehall, 298, 315–16, 325; in 1970–4 Government, 434, 489, 550, 579
Huggins, Sir Godfrey, 88
Hughes, Cledwyn, 675
Hughes, Robert, 729
Hughes-Young, Michael, 102
Hume, John, 427, 546
Hunt, Sir John, 320–1, 487, 490, 491, 577, 581
Hurd, Douglas, xvi, 629–30, 633, 738, 752, 758, 760–1, 777, 784, 787, 790, 800–1, 803; in EH's private office, 216, 233, 248, 259, 280, 285, 291–2, 361, 399, 488–9, 492, 513, 568, 579, 585, 586; on EH, xvi, 271, 276, 284, 299, 357–8, 363, 419, 439, 452, 488, 505–6, 508, 534–5, 537, 570, 576, 577, 578, 593–4; on 1970–4 Government, 312–13, 319–20, 325, 326, 340–1, 353, 403, 408, 417, 431, 476, 479, 561, 563, 564, 587–8, 589

Hussein, King, 691, 785
Hutchinson, George, 153, 610, 650–1, 669; on EH, 688, 703–4
Hyde, James, 47

Ibbs, Sir Robin, 316, 324
immigration, 237–8, 241–4, 273, 340, 392–3, 481, 512, 709
In Place of Strife (1968), 228–9, 230, 263, 365, 583
Independent, 770, 778, 803, 810; on EH, 771, 774, 776, 784, 785, 789
Independent on Sunday, 777
industrial relations, 108–12, 203, 219–21, 228–30, 301–2, 329–30, 369–70, 412–22, 442–3, 457–66, 468–83, 531–4, 535–41, 561–73, 574–97, 599–602, 699–700, 708, 711–12
Industrial Relations Act (1971), 155, 297, 300, 306, 331, 364–9, 411, 414, 456, 457–67, 469, 471–2, 476, 601–2, 608, 631–2, 636, 637–8; reasons for failure, 464–6
Industry Act (1972), 446–54, 487, 491, 539
inflation, 100, 230–4, 281–2, 311, 328–30, 369–70, 468–82, 531–9, 562–9, 580–6, 589–91, 596–7, 599–602, 606, 616, 625, 637, 638, 640–1, 644, 699–702, 711, 713
Ingham, Bernard, 488n, 760, 762
IRA, 411, 425–8, 430, 493, 543–5, 547–8, 553, 665
Iremonger, Lucille, 100–1, 528
Isis, 18, 26, 62; on EH, 21, 27, 28, 29, 30, 35, 36–7
Islam, Yussuf, 784
Israel, 92–3, 348–50, 557–8, 563, 779–80, 790–1, 792
Isserlis, 'Sandy', 290

Jackson, Jesse, 784
Jackson, Tom, 330, 367
Jarratt, Alex, 458
Jay, Douglas, 153, 157
Jay, Peter, 410, 524, 525, 639
Jellicoe, Lord, 298, 315, 377, 571
Jenkin, Patrick, 298, 574, 579
Jenkins, Hugh, 391
Jenkins, Peter, 366, 776
Jenkins, Roy, 169, 479, 603, 628, 636, 637, 644, 715, 725–7, 749, 775; as Chancellor (1967–70), 230, 268, 408–9, 470; and EEC, 400–5, 438, 683, 687, 688; and Oxford Chancellorship, 751–3; on EH, 21, 33, 606, 719n, 726
Job, Charles, 68
Jobert, Michel, 356, 358
John, Augustus, 137, 744
Johnson, Lyndon, 335, 342
Johnson, Paul, 156, 642; on EH, 312, 501–2, 506–7
Johnson-Smith, Geoffrey, 275
Jones, Aubrey, 71, 470

Jones, Jack, 329, 367, 458, 460, 462, 470, 472, 493, 541, 581, 584, 609; in tripartite talks, 421, 474–7, 479; on EH, 462, 476
Jones, Michael, 777
Joseph, Sir Keith, 95, 103, 148, 161, 164, 181, 303; in Shadow Cabinet (1965–70), 204, 213, 231, 234, 242; Social Services Secretary, 297, 331, 377–8, 381–5, 388, 389, 448, 485, 486, 526, 539; repudiates 1970–4 Government, 627, 631–2, 639–41, 642, 676, 681; and Tory leadership, 660, 663; and Mrs Thatcher, 669, 672, 673, 682, 698, 704, 706, 710, 714, 757
Jowett, Benjamin 15–16, 23
Judd, Frank, 720
Junor, John, 487

Kaiser, Philip, 22, 32
Kane, Jock, 414, 418
Karajan, Herbert von, 236, 556
Kaufman, Gerald, 180, 490, 792, 800
Kaunda, Kenneth, 338
Kavanagh, Dennis, 612, 628, 638, 645, 650, 754
Kay, Duncan, 252
Kennedy, John F., 128, 144, 190, 193n, 296, 341–2, 343n, 344; and Cuba crisis, 734, 780, 783
Kenny, Anthony, 752
Kent, Bruce, 791
Kent, John, 303–4, 426
Kerr, Russell, 366
Kerruish, J. R. J., 30, 33, 35
Kershaw, Anthony, 201, 216, 248
Key, Robert, 729, 743
Khaled, Leila, 307–8, 484
Khrushchev, Nikita, 138, 734, 783
Kilmuir, Lord, 85, 92, 94, 97
King, Cecil, 230, 460, 477, 527; on EH, 210, 258, 467, 600
King, Tom, 466, 784
Kinnock, Neil, 737, 754, 780, 785
Kirk, Peter, 95, 298, 556
Kisch, Royalton, 18
Kissinger, Henry, 342–6, 349, 558, 603; on EH, 342, 345
Kitson, Sally, 490, 676
Kitson, Timothy, 703, 714n; EH's PPS, 291, 436n, 489, 515, 518, 593, 618, 623–4, 630, 635, 649, 656, 665, 668–9, 672–4, 676, 689
Kitzinger, Uwe, 356, 358, 400, 684
Kosygin, Alexei, 346
Kuwait, 777–85, 787–92

Labour party, xvii, 160, 163, 208, 268–9, 603, 605, 609, 636–7, 754, 763, 804–5; and EEC, 124, 126–7, 223, 246–7, 352–3, 356,

361–2, 396–8, 400–5, 437–41, 556, 684–8, 766, 770–1, 804, 808; EH on, 61, 66, 163, 169–70, 198, 223–4, 273–4, 276–7, 602–3, 636, 646–7, 651, 763, 804
Laing, Margaret, 202
Laing, Sir Maurice, 251
Lambton, Anthony, 179, 696
Lancaster, Osbert, 191, 390
Law, Andrew Bonar, 679
Lawley, Sue, 748, 764
Lawson, Nigel, 207, 573, 600, 633, 638, 728, 802; as Chancellor (1983–9), 739, 757, 767, 768, 777, 786, 794
Leather, Ted, 280
Le Marchant, Spencer, 624
Lee, J. J., 425
Lee, Sir Frank, 116, 119
Lee Kuan Yew, 227
Legge-Bourke, Sir Harry, 85, 360, 450, 515
Lever, Harold, 403
Levin, Bernard, 413, 636, 642; on EH, 500, 697
Lewis, Doris: *see* Heath, Doris
Lewis, Kenneth, 661
Liberal Democrats, 780, 805
Liberal party, 161–2, 164, 209, 284, 379, 439, 483, 512, 537, 578, 586, 630–1, 633, 643–4, 648, 652, 725; in Feb 1974 election, 598, 609–12, 613–15; coalition talks with EH, 616–18, 648; Lib-Lab pact, 706–7
Lindemann, 'Prof' Frederick, 30
Lindsay, A. D., 15–17, 22–3, 34, 97
Lindsay, T. F., 113
Lloyd, Selwyn, 98, 113, 145, 152, 167, 195, 202, 205, 213, 230, 293, 303, 470; Speaker (1971–6), 404, 407, 503
Lloyd George, David, 271, 542, 553, 714
Lloyd Webber, Andrew, 747–8
local government, 78, 741–2, 794; 1973 reorganisation, 379–80
Longden, Gilbert, 77
Longford, Lord, 34, 693
Lonrho, 528–9
Lord, Christopher, 362
Lothian, Lord, 41
Low, Toby: *see* Aldington, Lord
LSO (London Symphony Orchestra), 489, 496–7, 635, 691
Luff, Peter, 751, 799
Luns, Josef, 347
Lympany, Moura, 249, 256, 258, 691
Lynch, Jack, 428–9, 550

Maastricht Treaty, 800–2, 804–5, 808–10, 811
McElhone, Frank, 720
McGahey, Michael, 566–7, 569–70, 584, 590–1, 593
MacGregor, John, 633, 738, 758;

in EH's private office, 190, 195, 201, 202, 216, 233, 248
McGuinness, Martin, 544
Macintosh, Ronald, 581, 583–4
Mackeson, Sir Harry, 82
Maclean, Donald, 135
Macleod, Eve, 302
Macleod, Iain, 59, 71, 84, 87, 88, 99, 108–9, 136, 152, 161, 167–8, 171, 174, 193n, 195, 309, 377, 516, 519, 624, 634, 657, 660; and 'One Nation', 77–9; Minister of Labour (1955–9), 108–9, 110; and Tory leadership, 139–40, 142–7, 148, 181, 184; Shadow Chancellor (1965–70), 212, 213, 216, 218, 228, 231–3, 240, 242–3, 264, 269–70, 281, 327, 328n, 523, 631; as Chancellor (1970), 296, 297, 301, 408–9; death, 302–3, 485
Macmillan, Lady Dorothy, 98, 292
Macmillan, Harold, 34, 49, 64, 86, 88, 89, 96, 410, 503, 511, 630, 656, 660, 682, 716, 719, 722, 751, 761; and EEC, xvii, 76, 112, 113–15, 116, 118–19, 120, 124, 125–8, 132, 335, 341, 353, 396, 404, 436, 795; Prime Minister (1957–63), 90, 97–100, 103–4, 106, 109, 112, 113, 135–6, 137, 151, 157, 158, 196n, 239, 266, 292–3, 294, 334, 341–2, 343, 377, 385, 485, 491, 504, 509, 517, 519, 679; EH's relationship with, 91, 98–100, 107, 146–7, 514; on EH, 106; resignation, 139–47; and the Tory tradition, xix, 147, 166, 203, 206, 267, 593, 637, 671, 698, 726
Macmillan, Maurice, 628, 636, 741; Employment Secretary (1972–3), 449, 458, 474, 564, 566
Macnamara, Robert, 718
Macnee, Sir David, 443
Macstiofan, Sean, 545
Mail on Sunday, 745, 748
Maitland, Donald, 290–1, 488n, 489, 503, 762
Maitland, Patrick, 95–6
Major, John, xvi: Prime Minister (1990–), 505n, 634n, 787, 788, 793–805, 808–10; and EEC, 794–5, 798–9, 802, 804–6, 808–10
Malcolm, George, 23
Mansholt, Dr Sicco, 128–9
Mao Zedong, 634–5, 691, 773, 775
Maplin airport project, 380–1, 495, 517
Margach, James, 194–5, 222, 258, 269; on EH, 96–7, 183
Margaret, Princess, 415
Markham, Sir Frank, 153

Marks, Derek, 87
Marples, Ernest, 71, 213
Marshall, George, 722
Marten, Neil, 440, 482, 657, 685
Marxism Today, 763, 766–7
Masefield, Peter, 57–8
Matthews, Very Rev. W. R., 36
Maud, Sir John (Lord Redcliffe-Maud), 300, 379
Maude, Angus, 71, 85, 206, 657, 682; and 'One Nation', 76–9
Maudling, Reginald, 59, 71, 80, 87, 99, 116, 118, 119, 161, 164, 167, 172, 302, 303, 470, 519, 525, 660, 661, 669, 682 and n, 683; as Chancellor (1962–4), 136, 148–9, 152, 160, 166, 169, 444, 522; and Tory leadership, 139–47, 168, 170, 175–83, 192, 202, 214; in opposition (1964–70), 192, 202, 204, 213, 215–16, 225, 230–2, 240, 253, 631; Home Secretary (1970–2), 296, 297, 309, 377, 391–5, 401, 414–16, 418, 485, 539; and Northern Ireland, 299, 392, 424–6, 428–30, 432–3, 507; resignation, 394–5, 466, 624
Maxwell Fyfe, Sir David: *see* Kilmuir, Lord
Maxwell-Hyslop, Robin, 482
May, Lewis, 60
May, Simon, 719
Mayhew, Christopher, 27, 28, 33, 59, 439–41
Meir, Golda, 348
Melchett, Lord, 331
Mellish, Robert, 439
Menuhin, Yehudi, 294
Meyer, Sir Anthony, 664, 774
Meyjes, Richard, 316
MI5, MI6, 492–3
Mikoyan, Anastas, 150n
Millar, Ronald, 489
Milne, Eddie, 614
miners' strike (1972), 412–22, 468, 561
miners' strike (1974), 561–73, 574–97, 599–605, 626
Minney, R. J., 89
Mintoff, Dom, 347, 348 and n
Mitchell, Austin, 721
Mitterrand, François, 495, 782, 790, 808–9
Monckton, Walter, 86, 108
Monday Club, 246, 340, 393, 661
money supply, 455–6, 471, 480–1, 529, 639–40, 700–1, 732, 757
Monnet, Jean, 124, 131, 403, 405, 722
Moran, Michael, 466
Morning Cloud, 251–6, 261, 305, 359 and n, 498–501, 623, 641–2, 645, 665, 692, 694, 744, 748
Morris, Charles, 16
Morrison, Charles, 145n, 257
Morrison, Herbert, 80, 81

Morrison, John (Lord Margadale), 145, 195–6
Morrison, Sara, 145n, 635, 645, 649, 656, 714, 745; at Conservative Central Office, 257, 510, 629, 682
Mortimer, John, 460n
Mountbatten, Lord, 717
Moussadeq, Dr, 81
Murdoch, Iris, 752
Murray, Len, 580–4, 609
museum charges, 389–91
Mussolini, Benito, 32, 477, 733

Nabarro, Gerald, 71, 576
Nasser, Colonel, 87–8, 90, 308, 779, 781, 789
National Coal Board (NCB), 412–13, 417, 419, 562, 564–5, 566, 568, 580, 601, 607–8
National Economic Development Council (NEDC), 463, 470, 580–3, 648
National Front, 394
National Health Service (NHS), 67, 78, 207, 235, 381–5, 735–6, 763–4, 787; 1973 reorganisation, 384–5
National Industrial Relations Court (NIRC), 457–62, 464–6
National Institute of Economic and Social Research (NIESR), 523, 525, 530
National Union of Mineworkers (NUM), 324, 369, 406, 438–9, 468, 531; 1972 strike, 412–22; 1973–4 dispute, 561–73, 579, 582, 584, 587–8, 590, 591–2, 595–7, 599–601, 607–8, 626; 1984–5 strike, 737
National Union of Public Employees (NUPE), 329, 712
National Union of Railwaymen (NUR), 109–10, 458, 580
NATO (North Atlantic Treaty Organisation), 336, 347, 349
Neave, Airey, 101, 657, 663, 666–7, 671, 673, 682
Negrin, Juan, 32
New Statesman, 180, 331, 413, 470, 538, 642, 648; on EH, 266, 312, 501–2
'News at Ten', 265, 275, 711
News of the World, 182, 642
'Newsnight', 765, 797–8
Newton, Tony, 633, 795
Nicholls, Harmar, 172
Nicholson, Sir Godfrey, 181
Nicolson, Nigel, 95
Nield, Sir William, 354, 446
Nixon, Richard, 284, 294, 332, 347, 404, 454, 480, 516, 635, 642; and EH, 342–6
Noble, Michael, 158, 213, 298
Norman, Dr H. C., 11, 14, 17, 18, 20
Normanton, Tom, 450
North Sea oil, 526, 558–9, 561, 596

Northern Ireland, xix, 299, 385, 392, 422, 423–35, 439, 449, 487, 507, 517, 542–54, 578–9, 615, 617, 644; casualty figures, 423, 427, 429–30, 545; elections, 425n, 548, 554; internment, 426–8, 543; abolition of Stormont, 430–5, 542–3; 'Operation Motorman', 545–6; power-sharing Executive, 548–50, 553–4; Sunningdale conference, 550–3
Norton, Philip, 514, 518–19, 520
Nott, John, 298, 673
Nutting, Anthony, 93, 95
Nyerere, Julius, 338

Obote, Milton, 338–9
O'Brien, Conor Cruise, 550
Observer, 108, 135, 195, 504, 671, 770; on EH, 101, 181, 190, 356; EH in, 810
O'Connell, David, 544
Official Secrets Act, 760–1
oil crisis (1973), xix, 320–1, 348–50, 531, 547, 557–60, 561, 563–4, 566–8, 570–1, 574–5, 594, 596, 606, 630, 700
Onassis, Aristotle, 105
'One Nation', xviii, 76–9, 85, 110, 158, 203, 239, 266, 605, 671, 726, 761, 764, 777, 787, 804, 810–11
O'Neill, Sir Con, 354, 359
OPEC, 558, 563
Open University, 328n, 388
opinion polls, 174, 459, 602n, 606, 636; on EEC, 127, 333, 356, 396–7, 684, 688; on EH, 145, 182, 217, 245, 649, 659, 672, 697, 711, 713, 731, 784; on the parties, 159–60, 164, 198–9, 208, 215, 217, 245, 262, 268, 276, 279–81, 332–3, 466, 483, 512, 534, 537, 575, 578, 586, 593, 598, 605–6, 610–12, 613, 619, 630, 633, 643, 644, 648, 652, 711–12, 713, 724, 732, 777, 786, 805; on Enoch Powell, 244–5; on the miners, 415, 420; on Northern Ireland, 429
Oppenheim, Sally, 682
Owen, David, 440, 760
Oxford Union, 15, 20, 25–38, 687–8, 751
Oxford University, 13–14, 15–38; Chancellorship, 751–3

Paisley, Dr Ian, 425n, 431, 434, 542–3, 546–9, 615, 617
Pakenham, Frank: *see* Longford, Lord
Palme, Olof, 718
'Panorama', 21, 178, 217, 230, 265, 275, 358n, 429, 437, 467, 505, 538, 590, 607, 731
PAR (Programme Analysis and Review), 315–16, 447

Pardoe, John, 421, 450, 716
Parker, John, 36
Parker, Lord, 428
Parker, Owen, 251–2, 498
Parkinson, Cecil, 511, 728, 802
Parkinson, Michael, 692
Parris, Matthew, 807
Part, Sir Anthony, 448
Paterson, Peter, 273–4
Patten, Chris, 629, 633, 634n,
    638, 682, 729, 758, 793–5
Pattrick, Jo, 137, 257, 292, 293,
    635, 744
Pay Board, 531–2, 536, 570,
    589–91, 596, 599, 607–8, 626
Pearce, Edward, 733; on EH, 803
Pearce, Lord, 339
Pearson, Lord Justice, 301–2
Peel, Jack, 367
Pérez de Cuéllar, Javier, 733, 787
Perle, Richard, 772
Perón, Juan, 477
Peters, Mary, 490
Peterson, Oscar, 692
Peyton, John, 331, 661, 674, 675
Philby, Kim, 135
Pike, Mervyn, 161, 213
Piper, John, 744
Pisani, Edgard, 718
Plaid Cymru, 614, 652, 707
Pliatzky, Sir Leo, 446–7
Plowden, Lord, 222, 527
Plummer, Desmond, 495
poll tax, 756, 757, 786, 793–4,
    804
Pompidou, Georges, 247, 341,
    342, 351, 397, 404, 442, 498,
    504, 560–1, 571, 766; and
    British EEC entry, 352–63
Poulson, John, 297
Powell, Enoch, 59, 71, 85, 87,
    97, 98, 100, 136, 148, 167, 168,
    202, 298, 302, 309, 519, 624,
    640, 660, 668, 703, 706, 710,
    720, 760; and 'One Nation',
    77–9; and Tory leadership,
    139–40, 144, 146–7, 177, 179,
    180–1, 182; free market ideas,
    158, 170–1, 180, 204, 206–7,
    212, 220, 225–6, 231–2, 239,
    331, 410, 454, 480, 538–9, 596;
    and defence, 226, 239–40; and
    immigration, 238, 239, 241–6,
    264, 284, 340, 392–3, 481, 709;
    and EEC, 247, 399, 403, 438,
    440, 684–5; challenge to EH,
    239, 244–8, 270, 277, 279, 281,
    284; and 1970–4 Government,
    308, 332, 374, 450, 455, 479,
    482, 512, 516, 517, 532, 538–9;
    and Northern Ireland, 434,
    543, 545, 644; in Feb 1974
    election, 599, 607, 613, 614
Powell, Sir Richard, 149
Prentice, Reg, 461, 590, 687
Previn, André, 496–7, 635, 691
Price, David, 95, 149
Price Commission, 532, 535,
    536, 606

Prior, James, xx, 247, 309, 377,
    627, 640, 660, 666, 669, 674,
    675, 682n, 775; EH's PPS,
    196n, 201, 207, 216, 248, 259,
    276, 292; on EH, 146, 193, 201,
    214, 228, 261, 269, 408, 509,
    515–16, 577, 656, 667; in
    1970–4 Government, 298, 354,
    395, 416, 485, 489, 519, 571,
    572; under Mrs Thatcher, 466,
    681, 690, 700, 706, 708, 710,
    712, 725, 728, 737; and Feb
    1974 election, 571, 577, 583,
    585–6, 593, 603, 616
Prior, Jane, 207, 261, 490
Private Eye, 125n, 303–4, 373n,
    385, 426, 501
Profumo affair, 135, 141, 493
Promenade concerts, 24, 197
proportional representation,
    616–17, 648–9, 651, 805
Pye, Reginald, 64–7, 73, 85,
    88–9, 106, 162, 282
Pym, Francis, 309, 593, 656, 663,
    671, 675; Chief Whip (1970–3),
    103, 104, 361, 386, 399, 400–2,
    405, 434, 438–41, 458, 482,
    487, 503, 513–15, 518, 520, 532,
    809; Northern Ireland
    Secretary (1973–4), 550, 554,
    579, 615; under Mrs Thatcher,
    681, 706, 733, 737, 741, 760

'Question Time', 790, 791

Race, Tony, 43
Raeburn, Ashley, 752
Raison, Timothy, 661
Ramphal, 'Sonny', 718
Ramsden, John, 629
Raven, Kay, 53–6
Rawlinson, Peter, 213, 264, 386,
    695; Attorney-General
    (1970–4), 299, 308, 332, 550
Rayner, Sir Derek, 316
Reading, Brian, 216, 248
Reagan, Ronald, 683, 721–2,
    723n, 739, 745, 761
Redgrave, Vanessa, 791
Redmayne, Martin, 152, 213
Rees, Merlyn, 543, 544, 803
Rees-Mogg, William, 148, 410,
    503, 504, 524, 532, 538, 585,
    671–2
Reid, Jimmy, 371, 442
Resale Price Maintenance,
    abolition of, 150–7, 438, 515
Rhodesia, 204–5, 335, 337–9,
    512, 517
Rhys-Williams, Sir Brandon, 383
Ridley, Adam, 568
Ridley, Nicholas, 182, 214, 235,
    450, 482–3, 516, 525, 532, 631,
    757, 802–3; at DTI (1970–2),
    298, 304–5, 331, 374, 448–9
Rippon, Geoffrey, 92, 213, 628,
    661, 682, 703, 722–3, 729, 741;

in 1970–4 Government, 297–8,
    303, 331, 377, 380; and EEC
    negotiations, 303–4, 336,
    354–6, 360–2, 396, 398, 402,
    405, 436
Robens, Lord, 331, 412, 561
Roberts, Margaret: *see* Thatcher,
    Margaret
Robinson, John, 354
Robinson, Mark, 729, 754
Rodgers, John, 60, 673 and n
Rodgers, William, 400
Roll, Sir Eric, 119–22, 128, 129,
    137, 491
Rolls-Royce, 331–2, 442
Rook, Jean, 696, 716; on EH, 693
Rose, Richard, 610
Ross, Dick, 568
Ross, William, 157
Rostow, W. W., 23
Roth, Andrew, 87, 355
Rothschild, Victor, 408, 490, 563,
    570, 577, 589; and CPRS, 317–
    25, 489, 513; and MI5, 492–3
Rowe, Andrew, 729, 751
Rowland, 'Tiny', 528
Royle, Anthony, 347
Ryder, Don, 467

Saddam Hussein, 733, 778–86,
    788–92
Sainsbury, Sir Robert, 390
Salisbury, Lord, 97, 98, 113
Sampson, Anthony, 6, 718–19;
    on EH, 294
Sampson, Sammy, 252, 254
Sandys, Duncan, 98, 181, 202,
    213, 440, 528; and EEC, 76,
    114–15, 124, 126, 130
Scamp, Sir Jack, 329
Scanlon, Hugh, 329, 367, 421,
    472, 474–7, 584, 609
Scargill, Arthur, 414–17, 569, 737
Scheel, Walter, 560
Schmidt, Helmut, 561, 721
Schreiber, Mark, 317, 325
Schuman, Robert, 74, 131–2
Schuman Plan (1950), 74–5, 114
Schwarzkopf, Norman, 791
Scott, Nicholas, 661, 668, 682
Scott-James, Anne, 190–1
SDLP, 425n, 426–7, 431–2, 543,
    545–51, 554, 569, 672
SDP, 687, 725–7, 731, 732, 752
SDP–Liberal Alliance, 687, 725–
    6, 732, 735, 736, 737, 754–6
Seligman, Madron, 21, 38–9, 53,
    55, 105, 119, 167, 195, 250, 256,
    283, 737
Seligman, Nancy-Joan, 105, 119,
    136, 167, 195, 250
Selsdon Park conference (1970),
    233, 235, 264–5, 268, 539;
    'Selsdon Man', xviii, 265–7,
    391, 539
Sewill, Brendon, 161, 213, 233,
    282, 417, 523, 529, 530, 576,
    581, 630

Sharples, Richard, 251
Shelton, William, 673, 674
Shepherd, Richard, 761
Sherman, Alfred, 627, 639, 682
Shinwell, Emanuel, 80
Shore, Peter, 247, 687, 803
Short, Edward, 236, 387–8
Shrapnel, Norman: on EH, 168–9, 502
Siddall, Norman, 564
Sidgwick & Jackson, 693–4
Sieff, Sir Marcus, 648
Silver, Robert, 37n
Silverman, Sidney, 92
Simon, Sir John, 27, 32
Simon, William, 695
Single European Act, 739, 764, 766–9, 795
Skeet, Trevor, 450
Skidelsky, Robert, 226
Skinner, Dennis, 407, 500, 790
Slater, Arthur, 254
Slater, Colonel F., 45
Slater Walker, 694–5
Smith, Cyril, 483, 687
Smith, Ian, 204–5, 335, 339
Snow, Jon, 797
SNP, 614, 652, 707
Soames, Christopher, 71, 240, 660, 728; and EEC, 76, 114–15, 121, 130, 356, 358, 556
'Social Contract', 478, 609, 643, 646–7
Solti, Sir Georg, 236
South Africa, 299, 337–8, 739, 776
Spaak, Paul-Henri, 126
Spanier, David, 404
Sparrow, John, 324
Spearman, Alexander, 95
Spectator, 140, 171, 184, 206–7, 240, 274–5, 477, 480, 524; EH in, 18–19; on EH, 145, 198, 265, 273, 373, 515, 618, 759–60
Spycatcher, 347, 760–1
Squire, Robin, 754
Stanbrook, Ivor, 733
Steel, David, 174–5, 617, 687
steel industry, 235, 453, 483, 485
Stephens, Olin, 251, 499
sterling: devaluation (1967), 224–6; sterling balances, 355–6, 357, 360–1; floated (1972), 454–5, 484, 530, 557; floated (1992), 809
Stern, Isaac, 295
Stevas, Norman St John, 181, 391, 400, 723, 729, 752
Stevenson, Dennis, 453
Stewart, Michael, 236, 291, 441
Stokes, John, 31
Stone, Norman, 781–3
Stonehouse, John, 151, 155, 528
Stormont, abolition, 430–5, 484, 505, 555–6, 615
Straw, Jack, 759
Street, Peter, 40
Stuart, James, 92

Suez crisis (1956), 90, 91, 92–7
Summerskill, Edith, 67
Sun, 388, 595, 648
Sunday Citizen, 192
Sunday Correspondent, 784
Sunday Express, 124, 134, 487
Sunday Telegraph, 182, 209, 695; on EH, 753
Sunday Times, 127, 149, 183, 194–5, 222, 269, 582, 587, 671, 693, 695–6, 746, 749; on EH, 94, 97, 109, 133, 260, 724, 767, 776–7, 781–3, 791, 798
Sunningdale conference (1973), 550–3, 570, 579, 615, 617
Swain, Tom, 407
Swann, Sir Michael, 507
Sydney–Hobart race (1969), 253–5, 256, 263, 278, 340, 499, 642, 693

Taverne, Dick, 441, 534, 614
Taylor, Humphrey, 633
Taylor, Teddy, 399, 443, 449, 766, 801
Tebbit, Norman, 266, 749, 770, 802–3; on 1970–4 Government, 308, 332, 452, 514; and election of Mrs Thatcher, 663, 673; under Mrs Thatcher, 466, 511, 689, 700, 728, 752; and EEC, 802, 809
TGWU, 109–11, 302, 457–60, 462, 493
'That Was The Week That Was', 161
Thatcher, Denis, 713
Thatcher, Margaret, xiv, xvi, 68, 82, 166, 181, 222, 267, 297, 377, 395, 507, 618, 751–2, 795; compared with EH, xv, xvii–xix, 12, 16, 255, 313, 334, 385, 492, 762–3; in opposition (1965–70), 105, 213–14, 237; in 1970–4 Government, 448, 485; Education Secretary (1970–4), 297, 300, 328 and n, 381, 385–91, 486, 526, 757; in opposition (1974–5), 627, 628, 631–2, 640, 642–3, 661–2; wins Tory leadership, 655, 658, 660, 663–76; and EH, 214, 385–6, 487–8, 676, 679–81, 688–9, 696, 697–8, 703–5, 708–9, 710, 713–15, 716–17, 731–2, 750, 771, 775–6, 807; as Tory leader, 509, 510, 519, 520, 629, 679–80, 681–2, 687, 690, 697–9, 702, 705–6, 708, 709–12, 726, 729, 774, 777; as Prime Minister (1979–90), 316, 320, 324–5, 339, 351, 378, 379, 384, 423, 466, 486, 489, 494, 505 and n, 680, 717–18, 721, 722, 723–4, 728, 730, 732–6, 737–42, 754, 758, 760–1, 762–3, 764–5, 770–2, 773; and EEC, xvii, 248, 362, 717–18, 738–9, 764–9, 770–2, 776–7, 795, 796–801, 802, 809;

EH condemns, 78, 723, 729–30, 736, 740–2, 756–7, 760–2, 763–4, 765, 767–9, 796–9, 800–1; and Falklands war (1982), 732–5; and Gulf crisis (1990), 777–8, 780–1, 783–6, 787, 792; loses Tory leadership, 659, 786–7, 793; out of office, 690, 793, 795, 802
'Think-Tank': see CPRS
Thomas, Peter, 298, 482, 510–11
Thomson, George, 353, 403, 441, 556
Thorneycroft, Peter, 98, 100, 114, 161, 202, 239, 682
Thorpe, Jeremy, 436, 439, 528, 592–3, 610–11, 643, 649, 650, 687; coalition talks with EH, 616–18, 648, 706–7
three-day week (1974), 771–2, 574–5, 584, 599
Times, The, 120–1, 164, 181, 200, 221, 235, 264, 278, 393, 503, 504, 506, 521, 610, 641, 650–1, 658, 660, 668, 671–2, 698, 700, 705, 706, 723, 729, 741, 749, 770, 776, 781, 801–2; on EH: 109, 113, 119, 144, 174, 182, 192, 197, 206, 209, 225, 232, 263, 274, 285, 329, 332, 339, 404, 422, 436, 455, 479, 497, 515, 532, 592, 604, 612, 625, 633, 647, 652, 654, 672, 688, 697, 702, 703–4, 708, 710, 725, 730, 742, 758–9, 762, 807; on 1970–4 Government: 366, 371, 391, 394, 408, 410, 413, 419–20, 421, 422, 432, 437–8, 439, 441, 443, 448, 472, 475, 517, 518, 523, 524–5, 530, 533, 558, 560; on Barber, 303, 329, 446, 481, 523, 524, 581; on unemployment, 407, 410; on inflation, 470–1, 480, 534, 595; on 1974 miners' strike, 564, 569, 579, 585, 588, 590; supports coalition, 617, 636, 642, 648; EH in: 685–6, 722
Tito, Marshal, 775
Tovey, Sir Donald, 24
Toynbee, Philip, 20–1, 27
trade figures, 149, 164, 169, 268, 408, 522–5, 530–1, 606
Trend, Sir Burke, 317–18, 320, 323, 326, 345, 487, 490–1, 749, 752
Trend, Michael, 749
Trethowan, Ian, 87, 503; on EH, 204, 206, 210, 232
Trollope, Anthony, 99
Trudeau, Pierre, 338, 638, 721
TUC, 110–11, 229, 309, 329, 411, 457, 593, 601, 608, 702, 765; and Industrial Relations Act, 330, 364–5, 367–9, 458–9, 463, 465–7; and counter-inflation policy, 421, 444–5, 468, 470–9, 481, 483, 532–4, 536; and 1974 miners' strike, 572, 580–6, 587, 590–2

Tucker, Geoffrey, 248, 489, 505, 506, 633
Tuzo, Sir Harry, 430
Twomey, Seamus, 548

Ugandan Asians, 340, 393–4, 512, 517
Ulster Defence Association, 543–4, 546
Ulster Unionists, 400, 424–6, 428–9, 430–5, 542–3, 546–54, 569, 615, 617, 636, 644, 652, 672
unemployment, 13, 66, 272, 369–71, 373–4, 406–12, 442–6, 455, 466, 529, 713, 723–4, 728–9, 735, 740, 810–11
United Nations (UN), 93, 95, 338, 557, 733, 777–80, 782, 787–92; UNESCO, 721, 739
Upper Clyde Shipbuilders (UCS), 322, 371–2, 442–5, 498
USA, 721–2, 733, 808; EH visits, 40–2, 80, 338, 342, 642, 788; relations with, 336, 341–6, 348–51; and Gulf war (1991), 777–8, 787–8, 790–2
USSR, 346–7, 718, 721, 772–4, 808
Utley, T. E., 427–8; on EH, 371–2

Vassall, William, 135
Vaudry, Robert, 796
Vaughan-Morgan, Sir John, 154
Vere-Harvey, Sir Arthur, 181
Vicky (cartoonist), 135n, 196
Victoria, Queen, 494
Vietnam War, 228, 241, 335, 344, 782–3
Vincent, John, 101

Wakeham, John, 752, 802
Waldegrave, William, 318, 568, 613, 629, 729, 738, 752, 758, 795
Walden, Brian, 780
Waldheim, Kurt, 642, 719, 784
Walker, Ernest, 24
Walker, Peter, 174, 195, 202, 210, 213, 218, 386, 413, 530, 631, 803; runs EH's leadership campaign (1965), 178–9, 181–2, 190, 668; on EH, 174, 452, 453, 485–6, 527, 577, 617, 662; Environment Secretary (1970–2), 297, 300, 314, 370–1, 377–81, 384, 486; at DTI, 314, 453, 483, 485, 562–3, 565, 572, 579 and n; and 1975 leadership contest, 649, 656, 668–9, 672–3, 674; under Mrs Thatcher, 681–2, 690, 714, 725, 729, 737
Walker-Smith, Sir Derek, 67, 72, 124, 126
Walters, Alan, 480, 627, 639
Walton, Raymond, 29

Walton, Sir William, 294, 495
Warren, Sir Brian, 104, 630, 785n
Watkins, Alan, 171, 240, 280n, 305, 312, 331, 538; on EH, 198, 266
Watkinson, Harold, 71, 119
Watt, David, 244–5, 246, 516, 518; on EH, 262
Waugh, Auberon, 501
Webster, Sir Richard, 629
Wedderburn, Bill, 768
Weekend Telegraph, 190, 234
Weeks, Wilf, 751
Weidenfeld, Lord, 749–50
Weinstock, Arnold, 714
West, Harry, 554
Westland affair (1986), 737, 741, 765
White, Michael, 774–5
Whitehead, Phillip, 447, 460, 474, 581, 631
Whitelaw, William, xx, 102, 626, 683, 752; Chief Whip (1964–70), 104, 172–3, 190, 201, 213, 214, 243, 246, 248, 264, 269, 282; on EH, 259, 284, 492; in 1970–4 Government, 297, 302, 309, 320, 366, 367, 377, 391, 402, 408, 410, 418, 449, 458, 485–6, 489, 511, 519, 520, 536, 609; Northern Ireland Secretary (1972–3), 424, 425–6, 427, 432–4, 542–50, 552–4, 615; Employment Secretary (1973–4), 569–71, 578–9, 582, 588, 589–90, 592, 596; and Feb 1974 election, 585, 586, 587, 603, 605, 618; and Tory leadership, 617, 636, 655, 660, 664, 666, 669–70, 671–5; in opposition (1974–9), 626, 627–8, 629, 640, 649, 650, 659, 668; under Mrs Thatcher, 681, 690, 706, 709, 710, 733–4, 736, 770
Widgery, Lord, 429
Wigg, George, 223
Wigham, Eric, 475
Wilberforce, Lord, 330, 417–19, 461, 561, 564, 592
Wilkinson, Ellen, 385
Williams, Marcia (Lady Falkender), 279, 291, 292–4, 488, 490
Williams, Shirley, 387, 582, 637, 644, 687, 726, 727
Wilson, Harold, xv, xviii, 716, 738, 806; compared with EH, xv, 13, 59, 193–4, 225, 233, 258–9, 274, 290–4, 296, 312, 334, 377, 488, 490, 493–5, 507, 562; as Labour leader, 134, 149, 160, 162–3, 180, 184, 190, 217, 266, 300, 333, 409–10, 411, 439, 479, 529, 541, 587, 643, 649; Prime Minister (1964–70), 149, 165, 166, 196n, 206, 210, 217,

223–6, 228–9, 241, 290, 293, 296, 407, 489, 520, 778; EHon, 162, 163, 169, 223–4, 225, 271, 305, 596, 683, 702n; on EH, 192, 265, 312, 407, 500, 651–2; duel with EH, 191–4, 200, 204–5, 208–9, 224, 260–1, 263, 501; in 1966 election, 206–7, 208–9; in 1970 election 269–70, 273–5, 277–8, 280–2; and EEC, 246–8, 335, 352, 353, 354, 356, 361–2, 398–9, 402, 403, 436; and Northern Ireland, 299, 425, 429, 544, 554; and machinery of government, 314, 316, 319–20, 324–5, 326–7; and Rhodesia, 204–5, 335; and USA, 335, 342, 351; and trade union reform, 228–9, 263, 367, 466, 583; and 1973–4 miners' dispute, 570, 590–1, 592, 596; in Feb 1974 election, 599, 604, 608–9, 610–11, 614, 617–19; Prime Minister (1974–6), 478, 623–5, 628, 632, 634, 636–7, 643, 658, 688, 702; in Oct 1974 election, 643–4, 649–50, 651–2
Wilson, Sir Horace, 491
Winckler, Professor, 31, 39
Winder, John, 652
Windlesham, Lord, 434, 661
'winter of discontent' (1978–9), 574, 712
Winterton, Nicholas, 399 and n, 733
Wintour, Charles, 443, 451
Wolff, Michael: EH's aide, 216, 248, 261, 269, 291–2, 489, 505, 513, 572, 579, 613, 616, 649; in Tory Central Office, 629, 682
Wolff, Rosemary, 616
Woman's Realm, 745
Wood, Alan, 30, 32, 33
Wood, David: on EH, 145, 285, 332, 515, 585–6, 587, 592, 653, 658, 709
Wood, Sir Henry, 24
Woodcock, George, 110–11
Woolton, Lord, 59, 60
Wormser, Olivier, 128, 129–30
Worsthorne, Peregrine, 118, 660
Wright, Peter, 346–7, 493, 760
Wyndham, John, 99

Yorkshire Post, 87, 726
Young, Sir George, 758
Young, Hugo, 763; on EH, 260, 724
Young, Jimmy, 727
Young, Lady, 752
Young Conservatives, 103, 134, 231, 393, 526, 533, 682–3
Younger, George, 682

Zuckerman, Pinchas, 295
Zuckerman, Sir Solly, 168